PHILIP'S

STREET ATLAS
North
Yorkshire

GW00672163

www.philips-maps.co.uk
First published in 2002 by
Philip's, a division of
Octopus Publishing Group Ltd
www.octopusbooks.co.uk
2-4 Heron Quays, London E14 4JP
An Hachette UK Company
www.hachettelivre.co.uk

Third edition 2009
First impression 2009
NYOCA

978-1-84907-002-7 (spiral)

© Philip's 2009

o¦s Ordnance Survey®

This product includes mapping data licensed
from Ordnance Survey® with the permission
of the Controller of Her Majesty's Stationery
Office. © Crown copyright 2009. All rights
reserved. Licence number 100011710.

Speed camera data provided by
PocketGPSWorld.com Ltd

Post Office is a trade mark of Post Office Ltd in
the UK and other countries.

Printed by Toppan, China

Contents

II Mobile safety cameras

III **Key to map symbols**

IV **Key to map pages**

VI **Route planning**

X **Administrative and Postcode boundaries**

1 **Street maps** at 1¾ inches to 1 mile

208 **Street maps** at 3½ inches to 1 mile

233 **Street map** of York at 7 inches to 1 mile

234 **Index** of towns, villages, streets, hospitals, industrial
estates, railway stations, schools, shopping centres,
universities and places of interest

Digital Data

The exceptionally high-quality mapping found in this atlas is available as digital data in TIFF format,
which is easily convertible to other bitmapped (raster) image formats.

The index is also available in digital form as a standard database table. It contains all the details
found in the printed index together with the National Grid reference for the map square in which each
entry is named.

For further information and to discuss your requirements, please contact
victoria.dawbarn@philips-maps.co.uk

Mobile safety cameras

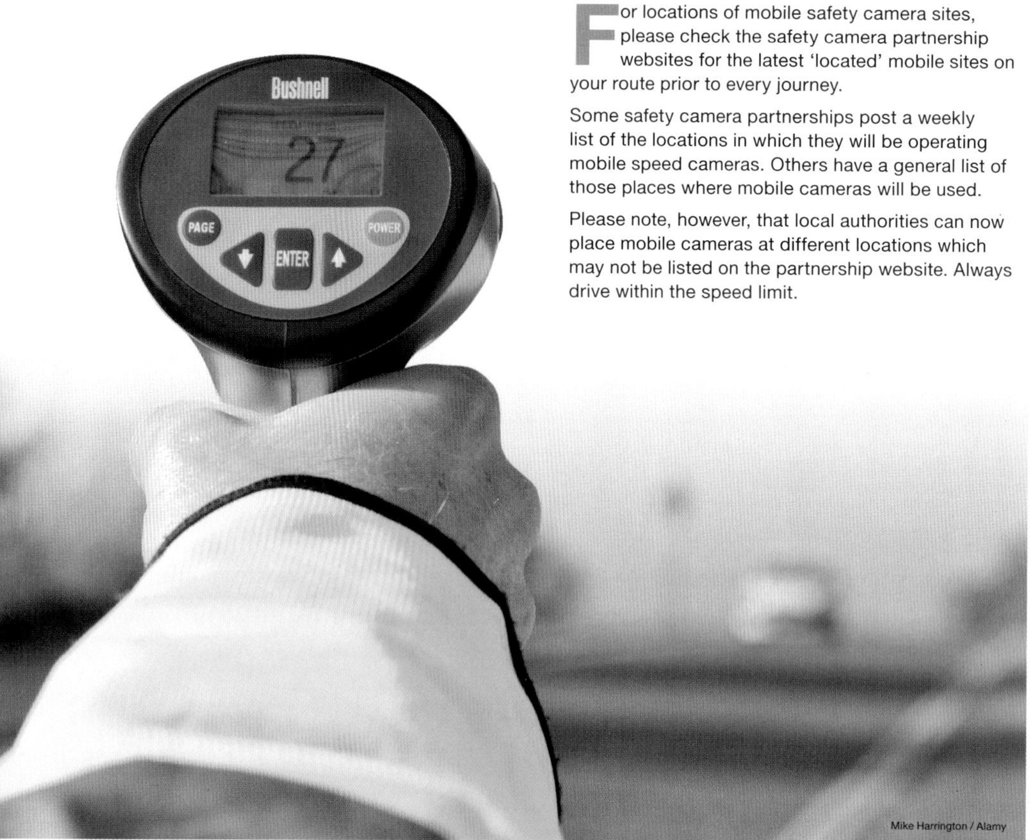

Mike Harrington / Alamy

For locations of mobile safety camera sites, please check the safety camera partnership websites for the latest 'located' mobile sites on your route prior to every journey.

Some safety camera partnerships post a weekly list of the locations in which they will be operating mobile speed cameras. Others have a general list of those places where mobile cameras will be used.

Please note, however, that local authorities can now place mobile cameras at different locations which may not be listed on the partnership website. Always drive within the speed limit.

Useful websites

Cumbria safety Cameras
www.cumbriasafetycameras.org

Durham Constabulary
www.durham.police.uk/durhamc/central_deps/operations/scu.php

East Riding safety camera partnership
www.eastriding.gov.uk/safetycamerapartnership

Lancashire Partnership for Road Safety
www.safe2travel.co.uk

South Yorkshire safety camera partnership
www.safetycamera.org/home

West Yorkshire safety camera partnership
www.safetycameraswestyorkshire.co.uk

Further information
www.dvla.gov.uk
www.thinkroadsafety.gov.uk
www.dft.gov.uk
www.road-safe.org

Key to map symbols

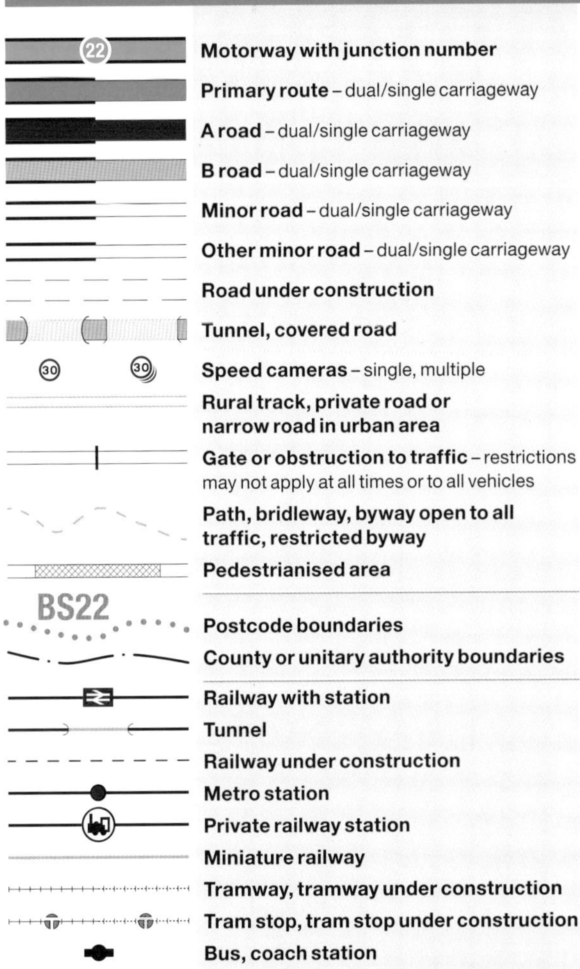

Motorway with junction number	
Primary route – dual/single carriageway	
A road – dual/single carriageway	
B road – dual/single carriageway	
Minor road – dual/single carriageway	
Other minor road – dual/single carriageway	
Road under construction	
Tunnel, covered road	
Speed cameras – single, multiple	
Rural track, private road or narrow road in urban area	
Gate or obstruction to traffic – restrictions may not apply at all times or to all vehicles	
Path, bridleway, byway open to all traffic, restricted byway	
Pedestrianised area	
BS22 Postcode boundaries	
County or unitary authority boundaries	
Railway with station	
Tunnel	
Railway under construction	
Metro station	
Private railway station	
Miniature railway	
Tramway, tramway under construction	
Tram stop, tram stop under construction	
Bus, coach station	

Ambulance station
Coastguard station
Fire station
Police station
Accident and Emergency entrance to hospital
H Hospital
+ Place of worship
i Information centre – open all year
P Shopping centre, parking
PO Park and Ride, Post Office
Camping site, caravan site
Golf course, picnic site
Church · ROMAN FORT · Non-Roman antiquity, Roman antiquity
Univ · Important buildings, schools, colleges, universities and hospitals
Woods, built-up area
River Medway · Water name
River, weir
Stream
Canal, lock, tunnel
Water
Tidal water
58 ◀ 87 · Adjoining page indicators and overlap bands – the colour of the arrow and band indicates the scale of the adjoining or overlapping page (see scales below)
246
The dark grey border on the inside edge of some pages indicates that the mapping does not continue onto the adjacent page
The small numbers around the edges of the maps identify the 1-kilometre National Grid lines

Abbreviations

Acad	Academy	Meml	Memorial
Allot Gdns	Allotments	Mon	Monument
Cemy	Cemetery	Mus	Museum
C Ctr	Civic centre	Obsy	Observatory
CH	Club house	Pal	Royal palace
Coll	College	PH	Public house
Crem	Crematorium	Recn Gd	Recreation ground
Ent	Enterprise		
Ex H	Exhibition hall	Resr	Reservoir
Ind Est	Industrial Estate	Ret Pk	Retail park
IRB Sta	Inshore rescue boat station	Sch	School
		Sh Ctr	Shopping centre
Inst	Institute	TH	Town hall / house
Ct	Law court	Trad Est	Trading estate
L Ctr	Leisure centre	Univ	University
LC	Level crossing	W Twr	Water tower
Liby	Library	Wks	Works
Mkt	Market	YH	Youth hostel

Enlarged maps only

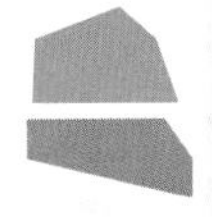

Railway or bus station building
Place of interest
Parkland

The map scale on the pages numbered in green is 1¾ inches to 1 mile
2.76 cm to 1 km • 1:36206

| 0 | ½ mile | 1 mile | 1½ miles | 2 miles |
| 0 | 500m | 1 km | 1½ km | 2km |

The map scale on the pages numbered in blue is 3½ inches to 1 mile
5.52 cm to 1 km • 1:18103

| 0 | ¼ mile | ½ mile | ¾ mile | 1 mile |
| 0 | 250m | 500m | 750m | 1km |

The map scale on the pages numbered in red is 7 inches to 1 mile
11.04 cm to 1 km • 1:9051

| 0 | 220yds | 440yds | 660yds | ½ mile |
| 0 | 125m | 250m | 375m | 500m |

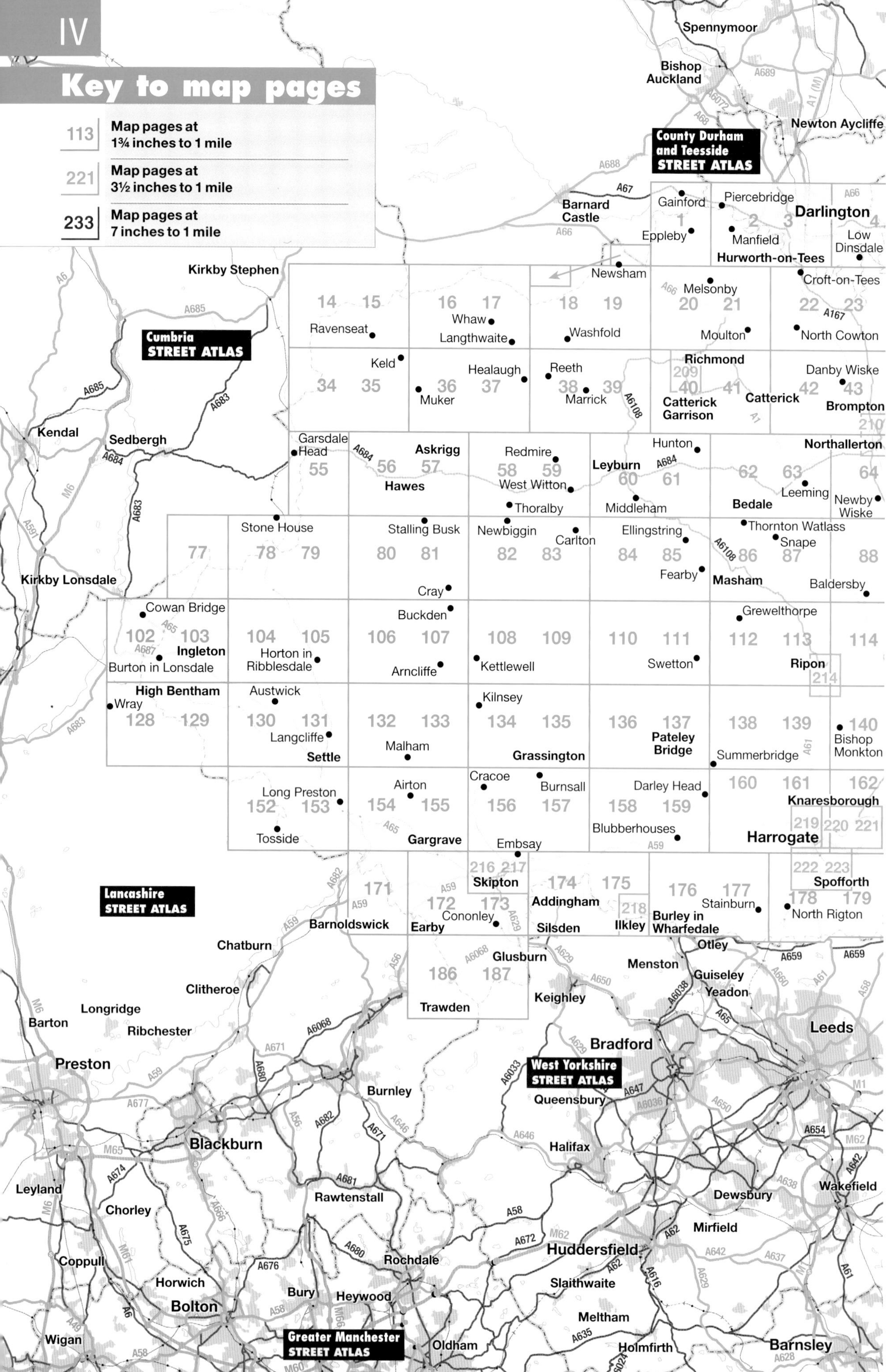

IV

113	Map pages at 1¾ inches to 1 mile
221	Map pages at 3½ inches to 1 mile
233	Map pages at 7 inches to 1 mile

County Durham and Teesside STREET ATLAS

Cumbria STREET ATLAS

Lancashire STREET ATLAS

West Yorkshire STREET ATLAS

Greater Manchester STREET ATLAS

Spennymoor

Bishop Auckland

Newton Aycliffe

Barnard Castle

Gainford   Piercebridge   Darlington
Eppleby   Manfield   Low Dinsdale
Newsham   Hurworth-on-Tees
1 2 3

Kirkby Stephen

Melsonby   Croft-on-Tees
Washfold   20 21   22 23   North Cowton
14 15   16 17   18 19   Moulton
Ravenseat   Whaw   Richmond   Danby Wiske
Langthwaite   209
Keld   Healaugh   Reeth   40 41   42 43
34 35   36 37   38 39   Catterick   Brompton
Muker   Marrick   Garrison   Catterick

Kendal
Sedbergh

Garsdale Head   Redmire   Hunton   Northallerton
55   56 57   58 59   Leyburn   62 63   64
Hawes   West Witton   60 61   Leeming   Newby Wiske
Thoralby   Middleham   Bedale
Stone House   Stalling Busk   Newbiggin   Ellingstring   Thornton Watlass
77   78 79   80 81   82 83   84 85   86 87   88
Carlton   Fearby   Snape
Cray   Masham   Baldersby

Kirkby Lonsdale

Cowan Bridge   Buckden   Grewelthorpe
102 103   104 105   106 107   108 109   110 111   112 113   114
Ingleton   Horton in   Arncliffe   Kettlewell   Swetton   Ripon
Burton in Lonsdale   Ribblesdale   214

High Bentham   Austwick   Kilnsey   Pateley   Bishop Monkton
Wray   128 129   130 131   132 133   134 135   136 137   138 139   140
Langcliffe   Malham   Grassington   Bridge   Summerbridge
Settle

Cracoe   Darley Head   160 161 162
Long Preston   Airton   Burnsall   Knaresborough
152 153   154 155   156 157   158 159   219 220 221
Tosside   Gargrave   Embsay   Blubberhouses   Harrogate
222 223   Spofforth
216 217   174 175   176 177   178 179
171   Skipton   Addingham   Stainburn   North Rigton
172 173   Silsden   Burley in   Otley
Barnoldswick   Earby   Cononley   Ilkley   Wharfedale
Chatburn   218   Menston   Guiseley
Glusburn   Yeadon
Clitheroe   186 187   Keighley
Longridge   Trawden
Ribchester   Bradford   Leeds
Barton
Preston   Queensbury
Burnley   Halifax
Blackburn
Dewsbury   Wakefield
Leyland   Rawtenstall   Mirfield
Chorley   Huddersfield
Coppull   Rochdale   Slaithwaite
Horwich   Bury   Heywood   Meltham
Bolton   Oldham   Holmfirth   Barnsley
Wigan

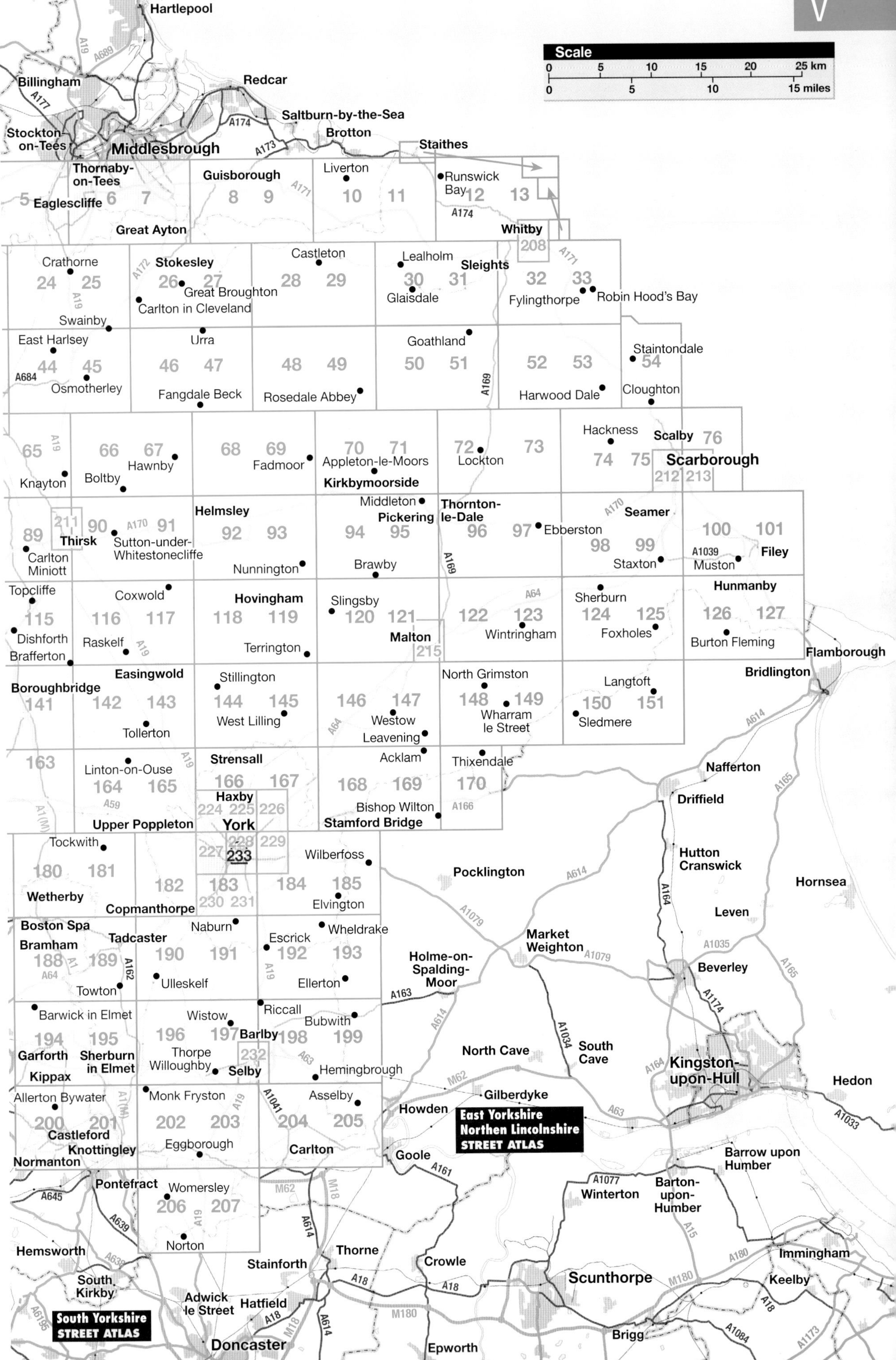
Scale
0 5 10 15 20 25 km
0 5 10 15 miles
Hartlepool
A19
A689
Billingham
A177
Redcar
Saltburn-by-the-Sea
A174
Stockton-on-Tees
Middlesbrough
A173
Brotton
Staithes
Thornaby-on-Tees
Guisborough
Liverton
Runswick Bay
5 Eaglescliffe 6 7
8 9
A171
10 11
12 13
A174
Great Ayton
Whitby
208
Crathorne
24 25
A19
A172
Stokesley
26 27
Great Broughton
Carlton in Cleveland
Swainby
Castleton
28 29
Lealholm
30 31
Sleights
Glaisdale
32 33
Fylingthorpe
Robin Hood's Bay
A171
East Harlsey
44 45
A684
Osmotherley
Urra
46 47
Fangdale Beck
48 49
Rosedale Abbey
Goathland
50 51
A169
52 53
Harwood Dale
Staintondale
54
Cloughton
65
A19
Knayton
66 67
Hawnby
Boltby
68 69
Fadmoor
70 71
Appleton-le-Moors
Kirkbymoorside
72 73
Lockton
Hackness
74 75
Scalby 76
Scarborough
212 213
89
211
Thirsk
90 91
A170
Sutton-under-Whitestonecliffe
Carlton Miniott
Helmsley
92 93
Nunnington
Middleton
Pickering
94 95
Brawby
Thornton-le-Dale
96 97
Ebberston
A169
A170
Seamer
98 99
Staxton
100 101
A1039
Muston
Filey
Topcliffe
115
Dishforth
Brafferton
Coxwold
116 117
Raskelf
A19
Hovingham
118 119
Terrington
Slingsby
120 121
Malton
215
122 123
A64
Wintringham
Sherburn
124 125
Foxholes
Hunmanby
126 127
Burton Fleming
Flamborough
Bridlington
Boroughbridge
141
Easingwold
142 143
Tollerton
Stillington
144 145
West Lilling
146 147
A64
Westow
Leavening
North Grimston
148 149
Wharram le Street
Langtoft
150 151
Sledmere
A614
163
A1(M)
Linton-on-Ouse
164 165
A59
A19
Upper Poppleton
Strensall
166 167
Haxby
224 225 226
York
227 228 229
233
Acklam
168 169
Bishop Wilton
Stamford Bridge
Thixendale
170
A166
Nafferton
A165
Driffield
Hutton Cranswick
Hornsea
Tockwith
180 181
Wetherby
182
Copmanthorpe
183
230 231
184 185
Wilberfoss
Elvington
Pocklington
A614
A1079
A164
Leven
Boston Spa
Bramham
188 189
A1
A64
A162
Tadcaster
Towton
Naburn
190 191
Ulleskelf
Escrick
192 193
A19
Wheldrake
Ellerton
Market Weighton
A1079
Holme-on-Spalding-Moor
A163
A1035
Beverley
A165
A1174
Barwick in Elmet
194 195
Garforth
Sherburn in Elmet
Kippax
Wistow
196 197
Thorpe Willoughby
Riccall
Barlby
232
Selby
198 199
Bubwith
A63
Hemingbrough
A614
North Cave
A1034
South Cave
A164
Kingston-upon-Hull
Hedon
A1033
Allerton Bywater
200 201
A1(M)
Castleford
Knottingley
Normanton
Monk Fryston
202 203
A19
Eggborough
A1041
204 205
Asselby
Carlton
Howden
M62
Gilberdyke
East Yorkshire Northern Lincolnshire STREET ATLAS
A63
Goole
A161
Barrow upon Humber
A645
Pontefract
Womersley
206 207
A19
Norton
A639
M62
M18
A614
A1077
Winterton
Barton-upon-Humber
A15
Hemsworth
A638
South Kirkby
Stainforth
Thorne
A18
Crowle
A18
Scunthorpe
M180
A180
Immingham
Keelby
A18
Adwick le Street
Hatfield
A18
M18
A614
M180
A6195
South Yorkshire STREET ATLAS
Doncaster
Epworth
Brigg
A1084
A1173

Route Planning

Scale

0	5	10	15 km

0	5	10 miles

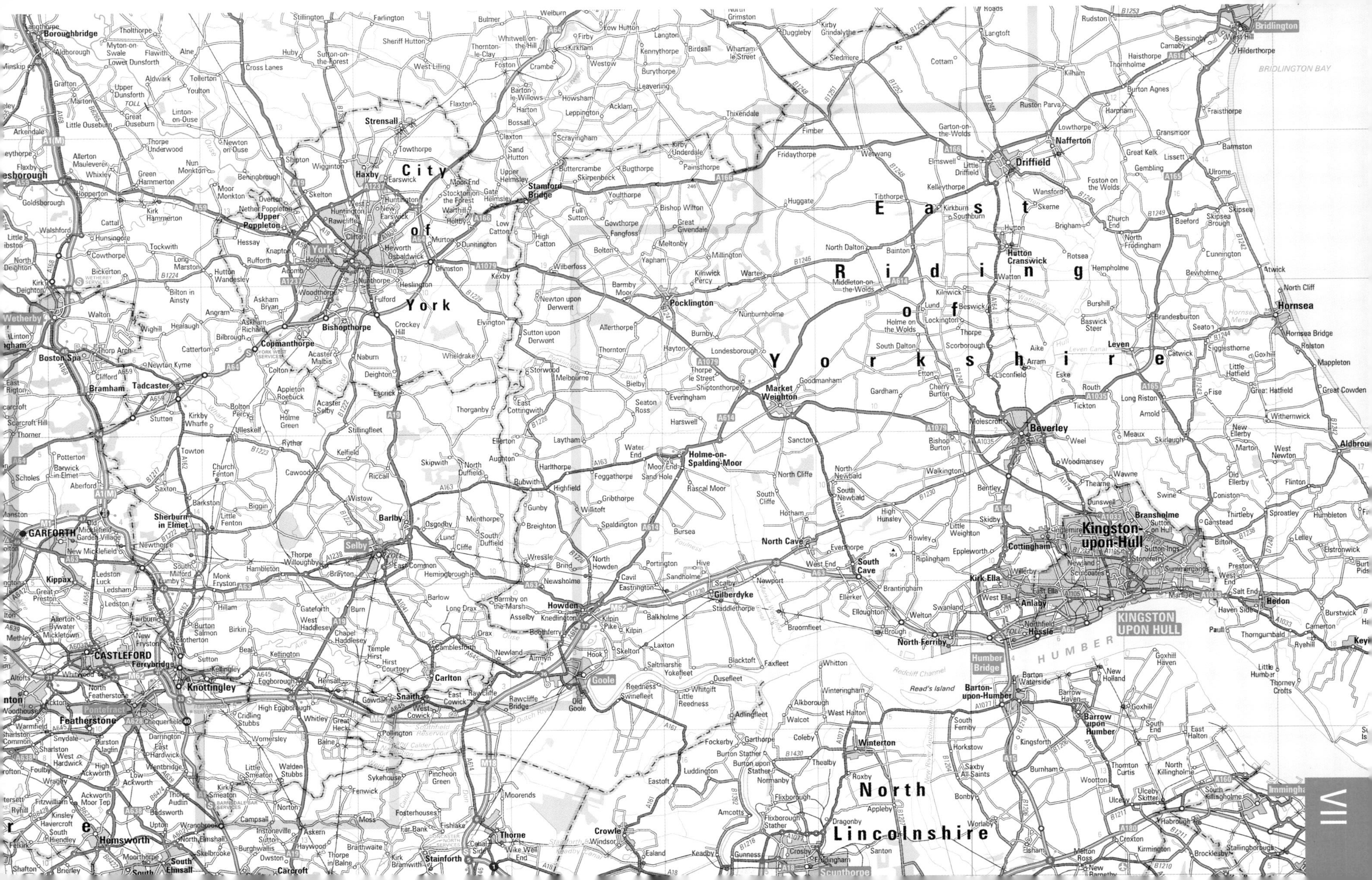

VII
East Riding of Yorkshire
City of York
North Lincolnshire
HUMBER
KINGSTON UPON HULL
Kingston-upon-Hull
Bridlington
BRIDLINGTON BAY
Hornsea
Driffield
Nafferton
Beverley
Market Weighton
Pocklington
Howden
Goole
Selby
York
Tadcaster
Castleford
Knottingley
Ferrybridge
Barton-upon-Humber
Humber Bridge
Barrow upon Humber
Winterton
Hedon
Leven
North Cave
South Cave
Holme-on-Spalding-Moor
Gilberdyke
Snaith
Thorne
Stainforth
Hemsworth
Featherstone
Sherburn in Elmet
Garforth
Kippax
Boroughbridge
Upper Poppleton
Haxby
Strensall
Stamford Bridge
Copmanthorpe
Bishopthorpe
Barlby
Carlton
Crowle
Scunthorpe
Cottingham
Hessle
Anlaby
Kirk Ella
North Ferriby
Wetherby
Boston Spa
Bramham

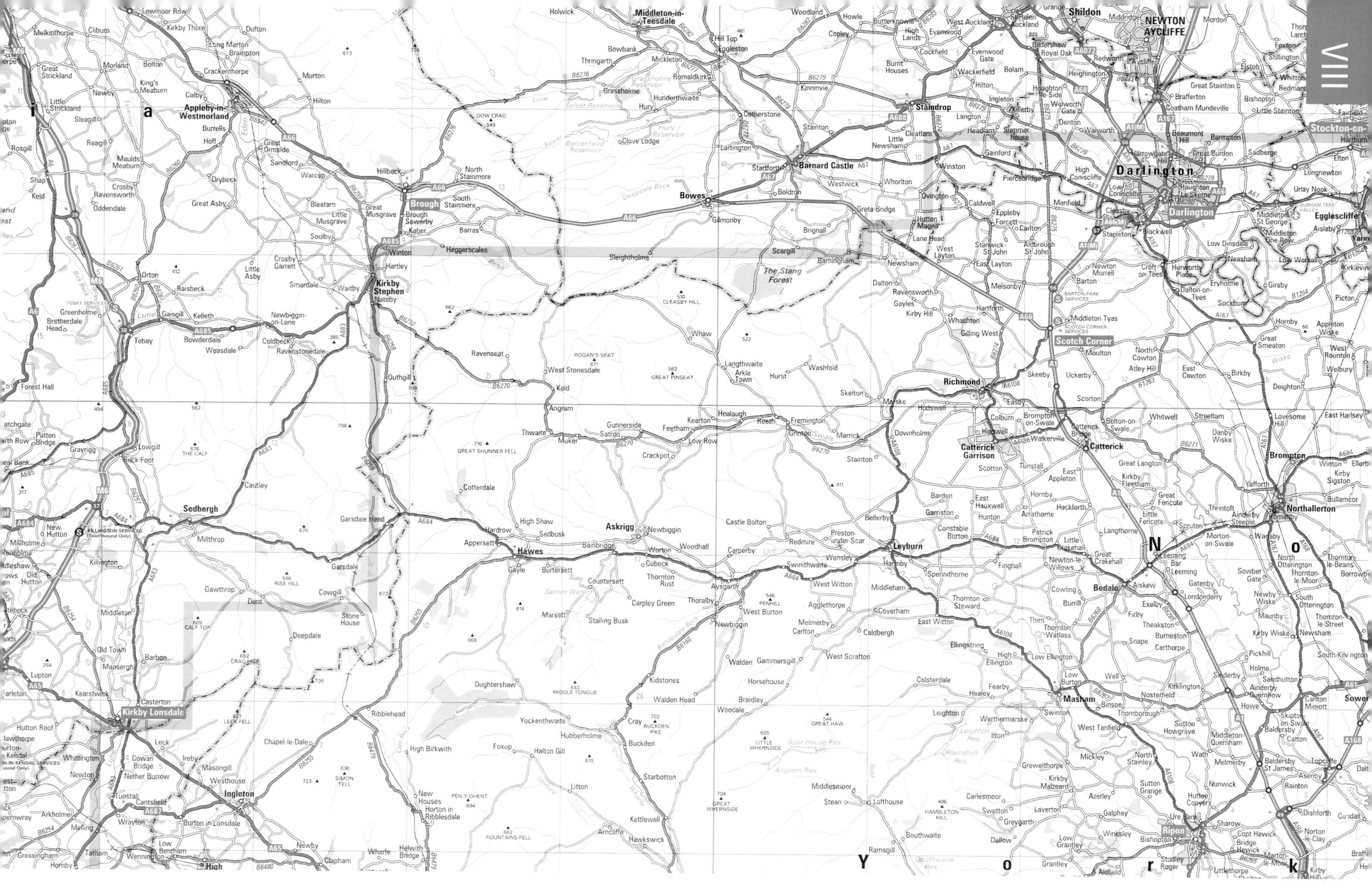
VIII
Darlington
Northallerton
Richmond
Catterick
Catterick Garrison
Scotch Corner
Leyburn
Bedale
Masham
Ripon
Barnard Castle
Bowes
Staindrop
Shildon
NEWTON AYCLIFFE
Middleton-in-Teesdale
Appleby-in-Westmorland
Kirkby Stephen
Brough
Hawes
Askrigg
Sedbergh
Kirkby Lonsdale
Ingleton
Tebay
Orton
Eaglescliffe
Stockton-on-
Brompton
The Stang Forest
GREAT SHUNNER FELL
ROGAN'S SEAT
GREAT PINSEAT
BUCKDEN PIKE
GREAT WHERNSIDE
PEN-Y-GHENT
CALF TOP
THE CALF
DOW CRAG
Y
o
r
k

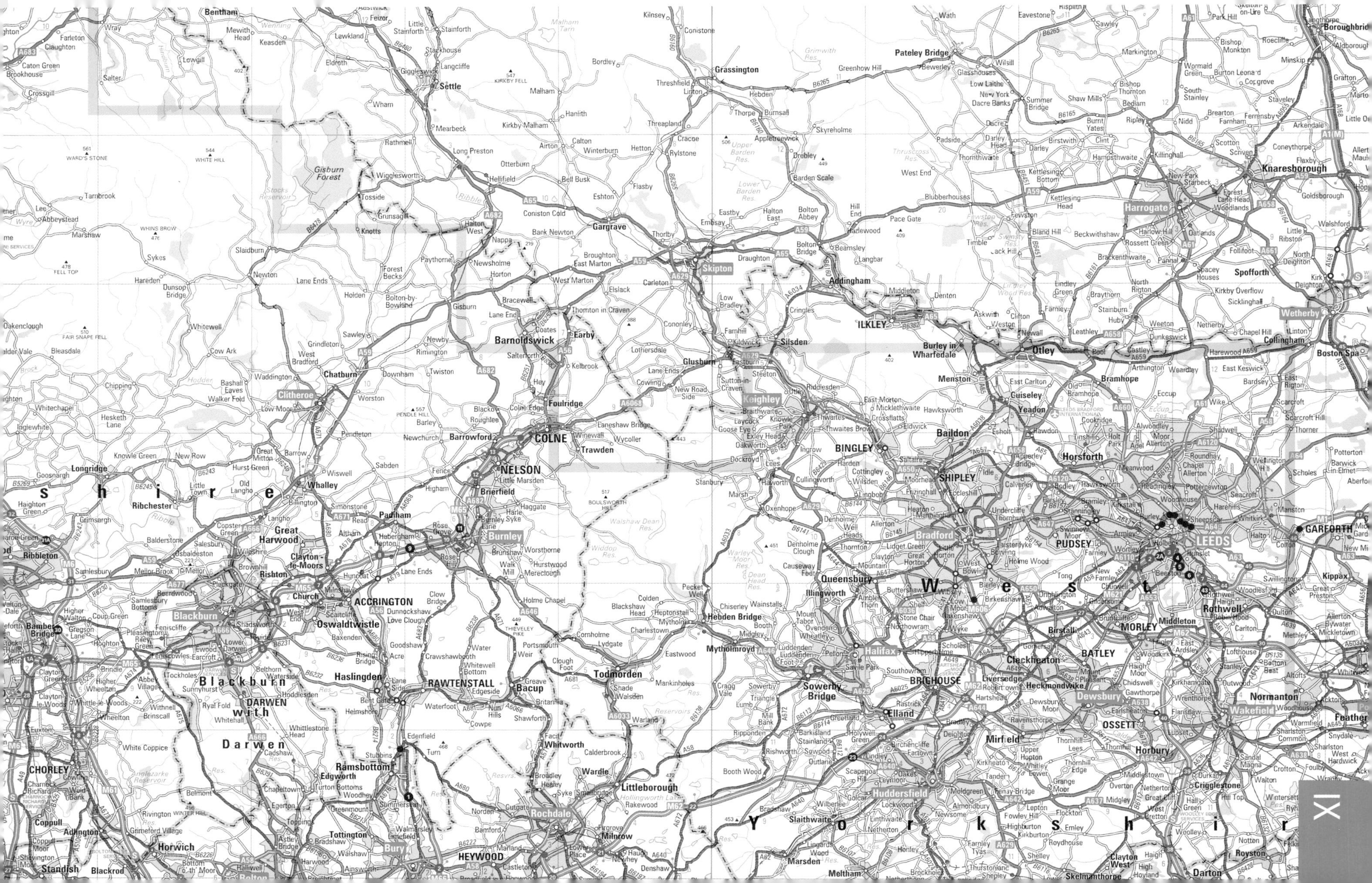

Bentham
Settle
Grassington
Pateley Bridge
Boroughbridge
Knaresborough
Harrogate
Spofforth
Wetherby
Collingham
Boston Spa
Skipton
Gargrave
Addingham
Ilkley
Burley in Wharfedale
Otley
Silsden
Keighley
Bingley
Baildon
Menston
Guiseley
Yeadon
Bramhope
Horsforth
Shipley
Bradford
Pudsey
LEEDS
GARFORTH
Kippax
Rothwell
Middleton
MORLEY
BATLEY
Cleckheaton
Heckmondwike
Dewsbury
OSSETT
Wakefield
Normanton
Featherstone
Horbury
Mirfield
Huddersfield
BRIGHOUSE
Elland
Halifax
Queensbury
Illingworth
Sowerby Bridge
Hebden Bridge
Mytholmroyd
Todmorden
Littleborough
Rochdale
Milnrow
HEYWOOD
Bury
Ramsbottom
Edgworth
RAWTENSTALL
Bacup
Haslingden
ACCRINGTON
Oswaldtwistle
Burnley
Padiham
NELSON
Brierfield
COLNE
Trawden
Foulridge
Barnoldswick
Earby
Glusburn
Clitheroe
Chatburn
Whalley
Great Harwood
Clayton-le-Moors
Rishton
Blackburn
DARWEN
Blackburn with Darwen
Longridge
Ribchester
Ribbleton
CHORLEY
Horwich
Adlington
Coppull
Standish
Blackrod
Gisburn Forest
Slithwaite
Marsden
Meltham
Skelmanthorpe
Clayton West
Darton
Royston
Crigglestone
s h i r e
W e s t
Y o r k s h i r e

Administrative and Postcode boundaries

Legend

- County and unitary authority boundaries
- District boundaries
- Postcode boundaries
- Area covered by this atlas

Scale

0 5 10 15 20 25 30 35 40 km
0 5 10 15 20 25 miles

County labels: County Durham · Cumbria · Lancashire · Bradford · Leeds · Wakefield · Selby · York · East Riding of Yorkshire · Kingston-upon-Hull · North Yorkshire · Ryedale · Scarborough · Hambleton · Richmondshire · Harrogate · Darlington · Redcar and Cleveland

Grid reference letters: NZ · OV · TA · SE · SD · NY

Selected postcode districts and places: TS21, TS18, TS4, TS6, TS3, TS5, TS7, TS17, TS16, TS8, TS9, TS14, TS12, TS13, TS15, DL12, CA17, DL11, DL8, DL10, DL9, DL2, DL3, DL1, DL7, DL6, LA10, LA6, LA2, BD24, BD23, BD20, BB18, BB8, BB22, BB7, HG3, HG4, HG1, HG2, HG5, LS29, LS21, LS22, LS23, LS17, LS14, LS15, LS24, LS25, LS26, WF6, WF7, WF8, WF10, WF11, DN6, DN14, YO7, YO51, YO61, YO62, YO60, YO30, YO26, YO32, YO19, YO23, YO24, YO10, YO41, YO42, YO1, YO31, YO8, YO13, YO12, YO11, YO14, YO16, YO25, YO17, YO18, YO21, YO22

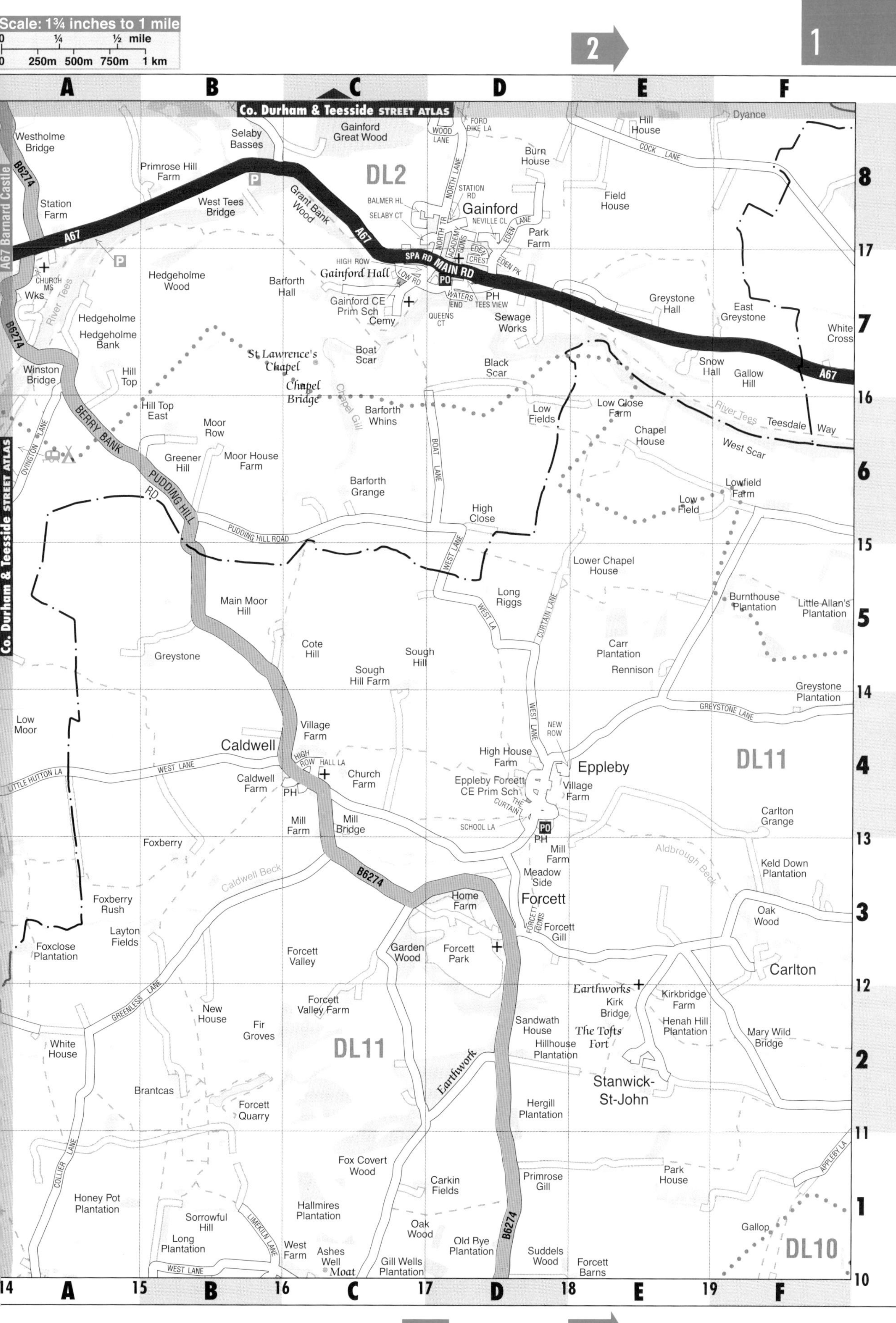
Co. Durham & Teesside STREET ATLAS
Westholme Bridge
Selaby Basses
Gainford Great Wood
Primrose Hill Farm
DL2
Station Farm
West Tees Bridge
Grant Bank Wood
Gainford
Burn House
Hill House
Dyance
Field House
Park Farm
A67
Hedgeholme Wood
Barforth Hall
Gainford Hall
MAIN RD
Gainford CE Prim Sch
Cemy
Sewage Works
Greystone Hall
East Greystone
White Cross
Hedgeholme
Hedgeholme Bank
St Lawrence's Chapel
Boat Scar
Black Scar
Snow Hall
Gallow Hill
Winston Bridge
Hill Top
Chapel Bridge
Barforth Whins
Low Fields
Low Close Farm
Chapel House
Teesdale Way
West Scar
Hill Top East
Moor Row
Greener Hill
Moor House Farm
Barforth Grange
High Close
Low Field
Lowfield Farm
BERRY BANK
PUDDING HILL RD
PUDDING HILL ROAD
Lower Chapel House
Long Riggs
Main Moor Hill
Burnthouse Plantation
Little Allan's Plantation
Greystone
Cote Hill
Sough Hill
Sough Hill Farm
Carr Plantation
Rennison
Greystone Plantation
Low Moor
Village Farm
Caldwell
High House Farm
Eppleby
DL11
Caldwell Farm
Church Farm
Eppleby Forcett CE Prim Sch
Village Farm
Mill Farm
Mill Bridge
Carlton Grange
Foxberry
Mill Farm
Meadow Side
Keld Down Plantation
Foxberry Rush
Home Farm
Forcett
Oak Wood
Layton Fields
Foxclose Plantation
Forcett Valley
Garden Wood
Forcett Park
Forcett Gill
Carlton
Earthworks
Kirk Bridge
Kirkbridge Farm
Forcett Valley Farm
New House
Fir Groves
DL11
Sandwath House
The Tofts Fort
Henah Hill Plantation
Mary Wild Bridge
White House
Hillhouse Plantation
Earthwork
Stanwick-St-John
Brantcas
Forcett Quarry
Hergill Plantation
Fox Covert Wood
Carkin Fields
Primrose Gill
Park House
Honey Pot Plantation
Hallmires Plantation
Sorrowful Hill
Gallop
Long Plantation
Oak Wood
Old Rye Plantation
DL10
West Farm
Ashes Well
Moat
Gill Wells Plantation
Suddels Wood
Forcett Barns
B6274
A67 Barnard Castle

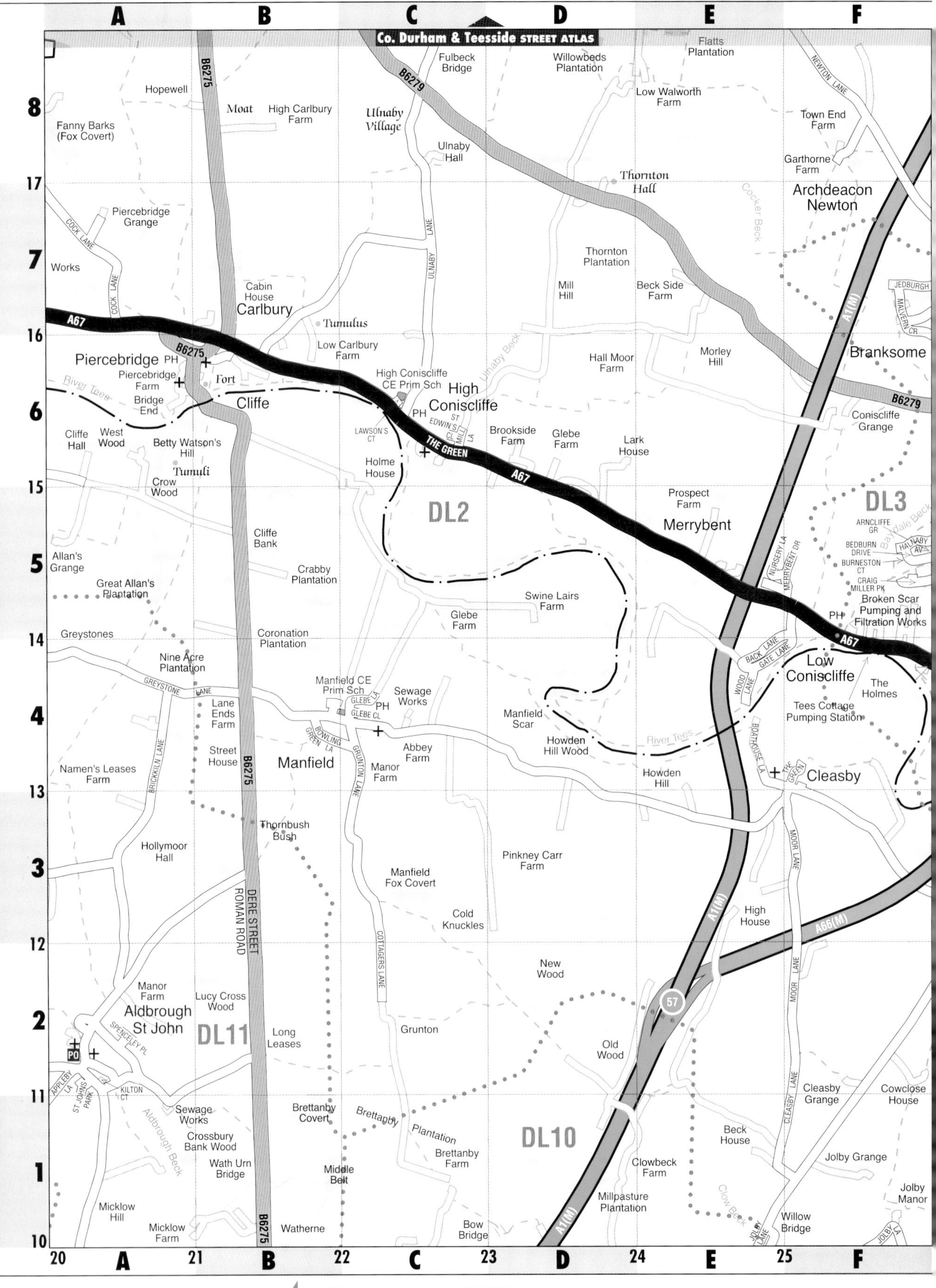

Co. Durham & Teesside STREET ATLAS

A **B** **C** **D** **E** **F**

Hopewell

Fanny Barks
(Fox Covert)

B6275

Moat

High Carlbury
Farm

Ulnaby
Village

Ulnaby
Hall

Fulbeck
Bridge

B6279

Willowbeds
Plantation

Flatts
Plantation

Low Walworth
Farm

Town End
Farm

Garthorne
Farm

Thornton
Hall

Archdeacon
Newton

Piercebridge
Grange

Works

COCK LANE

Cabin
House

Carlbury

Tumulus

Low Carlbury
Farm

ULNABY LANE

Thornton
Plantation

Mill
Hill

Beck Side
Farm

Branksome

JEDBURGH

MALVERN CR

A1(M)

B6279

A67

Piercebridge PH
B6275

Piercebridge
Farm

Bridge
End

Cliffe

Fort

Cliffe
Hall

West
Wood

Betty Watson's
Hill

Tumuli

Crow
Wood

Allan's
Grange

River Tees

High Coniscliffe
CE Prim Sch

PH

LAWSON'S
CT

Holme
House

THE GREEN

ST
EDWIN'S
CL
MILL
LA

High
Coniscliffe

Brookside
Farm

Ulnaby Beck

Glebe
Farm

Hall Moor
Farm

Lark
House

Morley
Hill

A67

Coniscliffe
Grange

DL2

DL3

Prospect
Farm

Merrybent

NURSERY LA

MERRYBENT DR

ARNCLIFFE
GR
BEDBURN
DRIVE
BURNESTON
CT
CRAIG
MILLER PK

HANABY AV

Bay Dale Beck

Broken Scar
Pumping and
Filtration Works

Great Allan's
Plantation

Greystones

Nine Acre
Plantation

GREYSTONE LANE

Cliffe
Bank

Crabby
Plantation

Coronation
Plantation

Glebe
Farm

Swine Lairs
Farm

Manfield
Scar

PH
A67

BACK LANE
GATE LANE
WOOD LANE

Low
Coniscliffe

The
Holmes

Namen's Leases
Farm

BRICKKILN LANE

Lane Ends
Farm

Street
House

DERE STREET

Manfield CE
Prim Sch

GLEBE
ST
GLEBE CL

PH

GREEN LA

BOWLING LA

Manfield

GRUNTON LANE

Abbey
Farm

Manor
Farm

Howden
Hill Wood

River Tees

Howden
Hill

BOATHOUSE LA

Tees Cottage
Pumping Station

Tees Cottage
Pumping Station

THE
GREEN

Cleasby

Hollymoor
Hall

B6275

Thornbush
Bush

Manfield
Fox Covert

Cold
Knuckles

Pinkney Carr
Farm

A1(M)

High
House

A66(M)

MOOR LANE

Manor
Farm

Aldbrough
St John

DL11

SPENCELEY PL

Lucy Cross
Wood

ROMAN ROAD

Long
Leases

COTTAGERS LANE

Grunton

New
Wood

57

Old
Wood

Cleasby
Grange

CLEASBY LANE

Cowclose
House

PO

KILTON
CT

ST JOHN'S
PARK

APPLEBY

Aldbrough Beck

Sewage
Works

Crossbury
Bank Wood

Wath Urn
Bridge

B6275

Brettanby
Covert

Middle
Belt

Watherne

Brettanby

Plantation

Brettanby
Farm

DL10

Bow
Bridge

Clowbeck
Farm

Millpasture
Plantation

A1(M)

Clow Beck

Beck
House

Willow
Bridge

Jolby Grange

JOLBY
LANE

Jolby
Manor

Micklow
Hill

Micklow
Farm

20 **A** **21** **B** **22** **C** **23** **D** **24** **E** **25** **F**

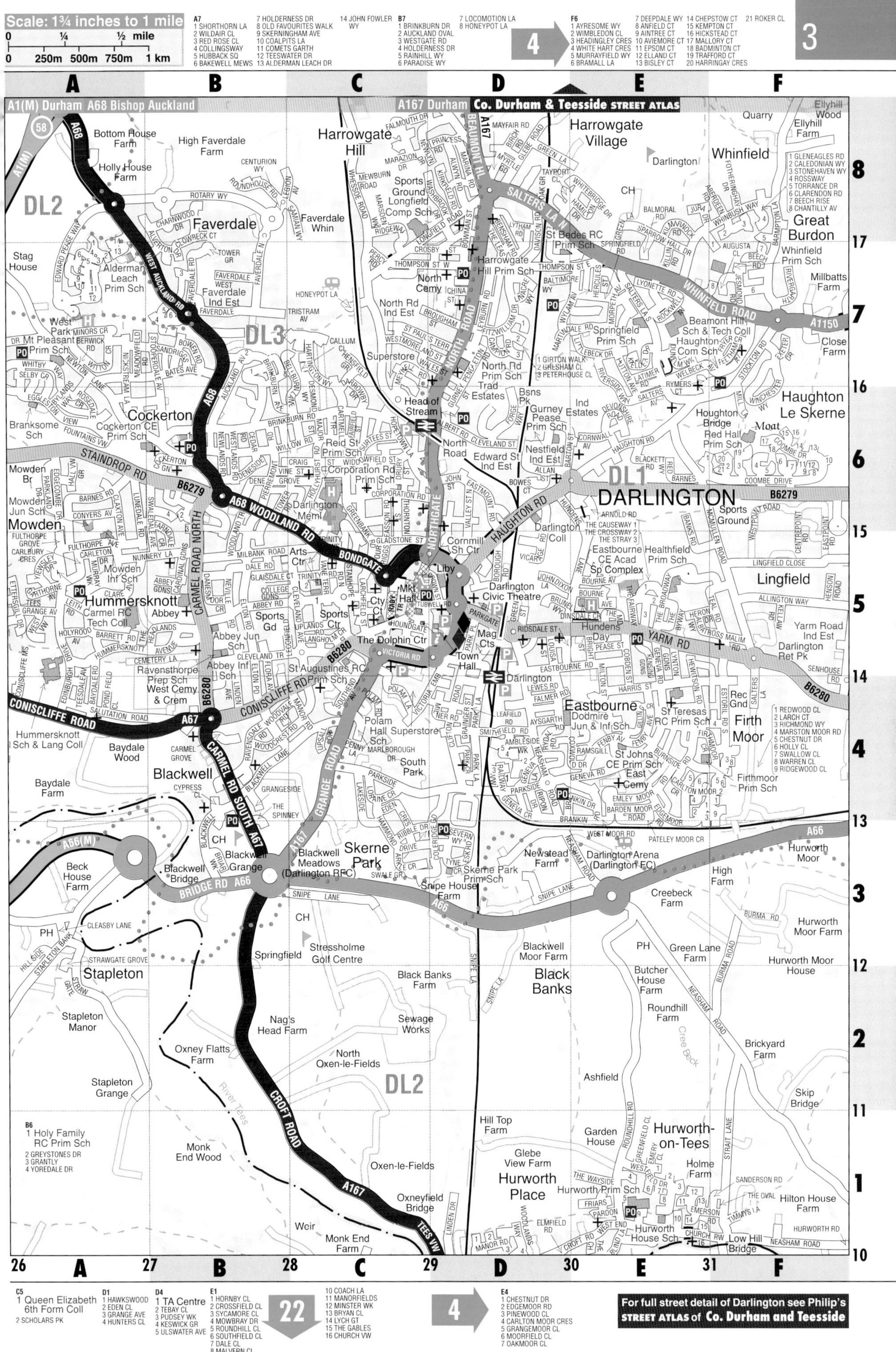

Scale: 1¾ inches to 1 mile
0 ¼ ½ mile
0 250m 500m 750m 1 km
A7
1 SHORTHORN LA
2 WILDAIR CL
3 RED ROSE CL
4 COLLINGSWAY
5 HUBBACK SQ
6 BAKEWELL MEWS
7 HOLDERNESS DR
8 OLD FAVOURITES WALK
9 SKERNINGHAM AVE
10 COALPITS LA
11 COMETS GARTH
12 TEESWATER DR
13 ALDERMAN LEACH DR
14 JOHN FOWLER WY
B7
1 BRINKBURN DR
2 AUCKLAND OVAL
3 WESTGATE RD
4 HOLDERNESS DR
5 RAINHILL WY
6 PARADISE WY
7 LOCOMOTION LA
8 HONEYPOT LA
4
F6
1 AYRESOME WY
2 WIMBLEDON CL
3 HEADINGLEY CRES
4 WHITE HART CRES
5 MURRAYFIELD WY
6 BRAMALL LA
7 DEEPDALE WY
8 ANFIELD CT
9 AINTREE CT
10 AVIEMORE CT
11 EPSOM CT
12 ELLAND CT
13 BISLEY CT
14 CHEPSTOW CT
15 KEMPTON CT
16 HICKSTEAD CT
17 MALLORY CT
18 BADMINTON CT
19 TRAFFORD CT
20 HARRINGAY CRES
21 ROKER CL
3
A B C D E F
A1(M) Durham A68 Bishop Auckland
A167 Durham
Co. Durham & Teesside STREET ATLAS
DL2
Bottom House Farm
High Faverdale Farm
Holly House Farm
Harrowgate Hill
Harrowgate Village
Whinfield
Quarry
Ellyhill Wood
Ellyhill Farm
Darlington
1 GLENEAGLES RD
2 CALEDONIAN WY
3 STONEHAVEN WY
4 ROSSWAY
5 TORRANCE DR
6 CLARENDON RD
7 BEECH RISE
8 CHANTILLY AV
Faverdale
Faverdale Whin
Sports Ground Longfield Comp Sch
Stag House
Alderman Leach Prim Sch
Faverdale Ind Est
St Bedes RC Prim Sch
Harrowgate Hill Prim Sch
Great Burdon
Whinfield Prim Sch
Millbatts Farm
WHINFIELD ROAD
SALTERS LA N
NORTH ROAD
WEST AUCKLAND RD
North Cemy
North Rd Ind Est
DL3
West Park
Mt Pleasant Prim Sch
Springfield Prim Sch
Beamont Hill Sch & Tech Coll
Haughton Com Sch
Close Farm
Superstore
1 GIRTON WALK
2 GILSHAM CL
3 PETERHOUSE CL
North Rd Prim Sch
Trad Estates
Bsns Pk
Ind Estates
Cockerton
Cockerton CE Prim Sch
Branksome Sch
Head of Stream
Gurney Pease Prim Sch
Haughton Le Skerne
Haughton Bridge
Red Hall Prim Sch
Moat
North Road
Edward St Ind Est
Nestfield Ind Est
DL1
DARLINGTON
STAINDROP RD
B6279
Mowden Br
Mowden Jun Sch
Mowden
Reid St Prim Sch
Corporation Rd Prim Sch
Darlington Meml
A68 WOODLAND RD
BONDGATE
NORTHGATE
HAUGHTON RD
Darlington Coll
Cornmill Sh Ctr
Sports Ground
Eastbourne Healthfield Prim Sch
Sp Complex
Lingfield
Mowden Inf Sch
Arts Ctr
Liby
Mkt Hall
Cty Ct
Darlington Civic Theatre
Hummersknott
Carmel RC Tech Coll
Abbey
CARMEL ROAD NORTH
Sports Gd
Sports Ctr
The Dolphin Ctr
Mag Cts
Town Hall
Hundens Day
YARM RD
Yarm Road Ind Est
Darlington Ret Pk
Abbey Jun Sch
Abbey Inf Sch
Ravensthorpe Prep Sch
West Cemy & Crem
St Augustines RC Prim Sch
VICTORIA RD
Darlington
Eastbourne
Dodmire Jun & Inf Sch
St Teresas RC Prim Sch
Rec Gnd
Firth Moor
B6280
CONISCLIFFE ROAD
CONISCLIFFE RD
A67
Hummersknott Sch & Lang Coll
Baydale Wood
Blackwell
Polam Hall Sch
Superstore
South Park
St Johns CE Prim Sch
East Cemy
1 REDWOOD CL
2 LARCH CT
3 RICHMOND WY
4 MARSTON MOOR RD
5 CHESTNUT DR
6 HOLLY CL
7 SWALLOW CL
8 WARREN CL
9 RIDGEWOOD CL
Firthmoor Prim Sch
Baydale Farm
CARMEL RD SOUTH
GRANGE ROAD
A66
A66(M)
Beck House Farm
Blackwell Bridge
Blackwell Grange
Blackwell Meadows (Darlington RFC)
Skerne Park
Skerne Park Prim Sch
Snipe House Farm
Newstead Farm
Darlington Arena (Darlington FC)
Hurworth Moor
High Farm
Creebeck Farm
BRIDGE RD A66
SNIPE LANE
Hurworth Moor Farm
CLEASBY LANE
STRAWGATE GROVE
Stapleton
Springfield
Stressholme Golf Centre
Blackwell Moor Farm
Black Banks Farm
Black Banks
Butcher House Farm
Green Lane Farm
Hurworth Moor House
Stapleton Manor
Nag's Head Farm
Sewage Works
Roundhill Farm
Brickyard Farm
Oxney Flatts Farm
North Oxen-le-Fields
DL2
Ashfield
Cree Beck
Stapleton Grange
River Tees
Skip Bridge
CROFT ROAD
Hill Top Farm
Garden House
Hurworth-on-Tees
B6
1 Holy Family RC Prim Sch
2 GREYSTONES DR
3 GRANTLY
4 YOREDALE DR
Monk End Wood
Oxen-le-Fields
Glebe View Farm
Hurworth Place
Hurworth Prim Sch
Holme Farm
Oxneyfield Bridge
A167
Weir
Monk End Farm
Hurworth House Sch
Low Hill Bridge
Hilton House Farm
8 17 7 16 6 15 5 14 4 13 3 12 2 11 1 10
26 A 27 B 28 C 29 D 30 E 31 F
C5
1 Queen Elizabeth 6th Form Coll
2 SCHOLARS PK
D1
1 HAWKSWOOD
2 EDEN CL
3 GRANGE AV
4 HUNTERS CL
D4
1 TA Centre
2 TEBAY CL
3 PUDSEY WK
4 KESWICK GR
5 ULSWATER AVE
E1
1 HORNBY CL
2 CROSSFIELD CL
3 SYCAMORE CL
4 MOWBRAY DR
5 ROUNDHILL CL
6 SOUTHFIELD CL
7 DALE CL
8 MALVERN CL
9 GREENSIDE CT
10 COACH LA
11 MANORFIELDS
12 MINSTER WK
13 BRYAN CL
14 LYCH GT
15 THE GABLES
16 CHURCH VW
22
4
E4
1 CHESTNUT DR
2 EDGEMOOR RD
3 PINEWOOD CL
4 CARLTON MOOR CRES
5 GRANGEMOOR CL
6 MOORFIELD CL
7 OAKMOOR CL
For full street detail of Darlington see Philip's STREET ATLAS of Co. Durham and Teesside

Scale: 1¾ inches to 1 mile

0   ¼   ½ mile
0   250m 500m 750m 1 km

A   B   C   D   E   F

Co. Durham & Teesside STREET ATLAS

8

Burdon Hall
Burdon Grange Farm
Carcut Beck
Sewage Works
Sadberge
St Andrews Ct
DARLINGTON BACK LA
TS21
Bewley Hill
Salter Carr Farm
NORTON BACK LANE

17

Carcut Bridge
BISHOPTON LA
PH
EAST CL
NORTON
NORTON DALE RD
ABBEY RD
STOCKTON RD
Sadberge Reservoir
DARLINGTON ROAD
BEACON HILL
PH
Newton Grange Farm
Rectory Farm
Eddlethorpe Farm
Longnewton Reservoir
Farfields Farm
THE WILLOW CHASE 1
VANE CT 2
THE CL 3
WOODLAND WY 4
THE YEW WK 5
Hang Thorn Farm

7

DL1
A1150   A66
A66
A66
West End Farm
PH
Middle Town Farm

16

Little Burdon
BUESS LANE
A66
Toft Hill
1 WEST ROW
2 THE ORCHARD
3 BEACON GRANGE PK
4 CHURCH LANE
5 HILLHOUSE LA
6 GOODWOOS CL
Bumper Hall
Spring House Farm
Hardstones Farm
MILL LANE
Mill Hill Farm

B6279
South Burdon
Sadberge Hall Farm
Street House Farm
Sadberge Hall
SADBERGE ROAD
White House Farm
West Moor
West Gate Fox Covert

15

LINGFIELD CL
DUDLEY RD
ALLINGTON WAY
LINGFIELD WAY
Morton Palms Farm
Midway Farm
CHELTENHAM CT
St George's Gate
Highfield
High Goosepool Farm
MILL LANE
Long Plantation
Low Goosepool Farm
Westgate Farm
Sewage Works

5

MORTON CT
PALMS CT
Woodlands
WILD CL
Palm Bridge
SADBERGE RD
HAMBY RD
HEATHER CL
Maxgate Farm
HARPERS TR
PH
West Hartburn Village
DL2

14

B6280
A67
PH
Morton Grange
STATION ROAD
WOODLANDS GN
STANSTED GR
SHANNON LEA
OAKTREE JUNC
Foster House
A67
Tees-side Airport

4

ALDERMAN BEST RD
PIONEER CT
A66
Maidendale Farm
Stodhoe Farm
Middleton St George
St Georges CE Prim Sch
PO
Dinsdale
YARM ROAD
SWAIN CT
2 ALEXANDRA 1
FAIRFAX RD
WASHINGTON AVE
YARM ROAD
THE OAKS
ASHDALE CL
OAK TREE CL
H
Middleton St George
Durham Tees Valley Airport

13

Morton Farm
Thorntree Farm
THORNTREE GD
CHAPEL CL
PINE CL
High Scrog Farm
THE BEECHES
THE SPINNEY 1
DENVER DR 2
Middleton Hall
THE CRES
Oak Tree

3

East Flat Plantation
Hunger Hill Farm
NEASHAM ROAD
HUNTERS GN
1 ST MARGARETS CL
2 ST ANNES GDNS
COATHAM AV
DESMOND
CEDAR GR
ROPNER GDNS
1 THE OAKLANDS
2 EAST VIEW
Sewage Works
Middleton One Row
ARCHER
THE FRONT
Robinson's Plantation
Featherstone House

12

Low Maidendale Farm
Brass Castle Farm
CH
Woodhead Farm
Dinsdale Park
YHE PADDOCK
CASTLE CL
CHURCH LA
CHURCH CL
Motte
Dinsdale Wood
Sewage Works
West Middleton Farm
East Middleton Farm
Church House Farm
TS16

2

Birch Carr Plantation
Neasham Springs
Over Dinsdale Grange
Over Dinsdale Hall
Over Dinsdale Wood
River Tees

11

Cold Comfort Farm
Stonybank Plantation
Dibdale Plantation
THE CLOSE
DIBRAT ROAD
Manor House
Earthworks
Low Dinsdale
Howe Hill Cottages
Crosshill Wood
Low Middleton
Trafford Hill

1

Low Neasham Springs
Neasham
NEASHAM RD
FERN LA
TEESWAY
Hill Top House
NEASHAM HILL
Neasham Hill Farm
Rose Hill
Low Moor Farm
The Gill
Fatten Hill
Newsham Grange

10

HURWORTH RD
Paddock Wood
SOCKBURN LA
Black Wood
Teesside Way
Spa Wells (Sulphur)
Scarhill Plantation
Hill House
Howe Hill Cottages

32   A   33   B   34   C   35   D   36   E   37   F

C4
1 GRENDON GDNS
2 THE GREENWAY
3 CEDARWOOD
4 POUNTEYS CL
5 WESTACRES
6 DINSDALE CT
7 DINSDALE CL
8 THE MEADOWS
9 MT PLEASANT CL
10 FARNBOROUGH CT
11 RINGWAY GR
12 YEADON WALK
13 HEATHROW CL
14 MANSTON CT
15 PRESTWICK CT

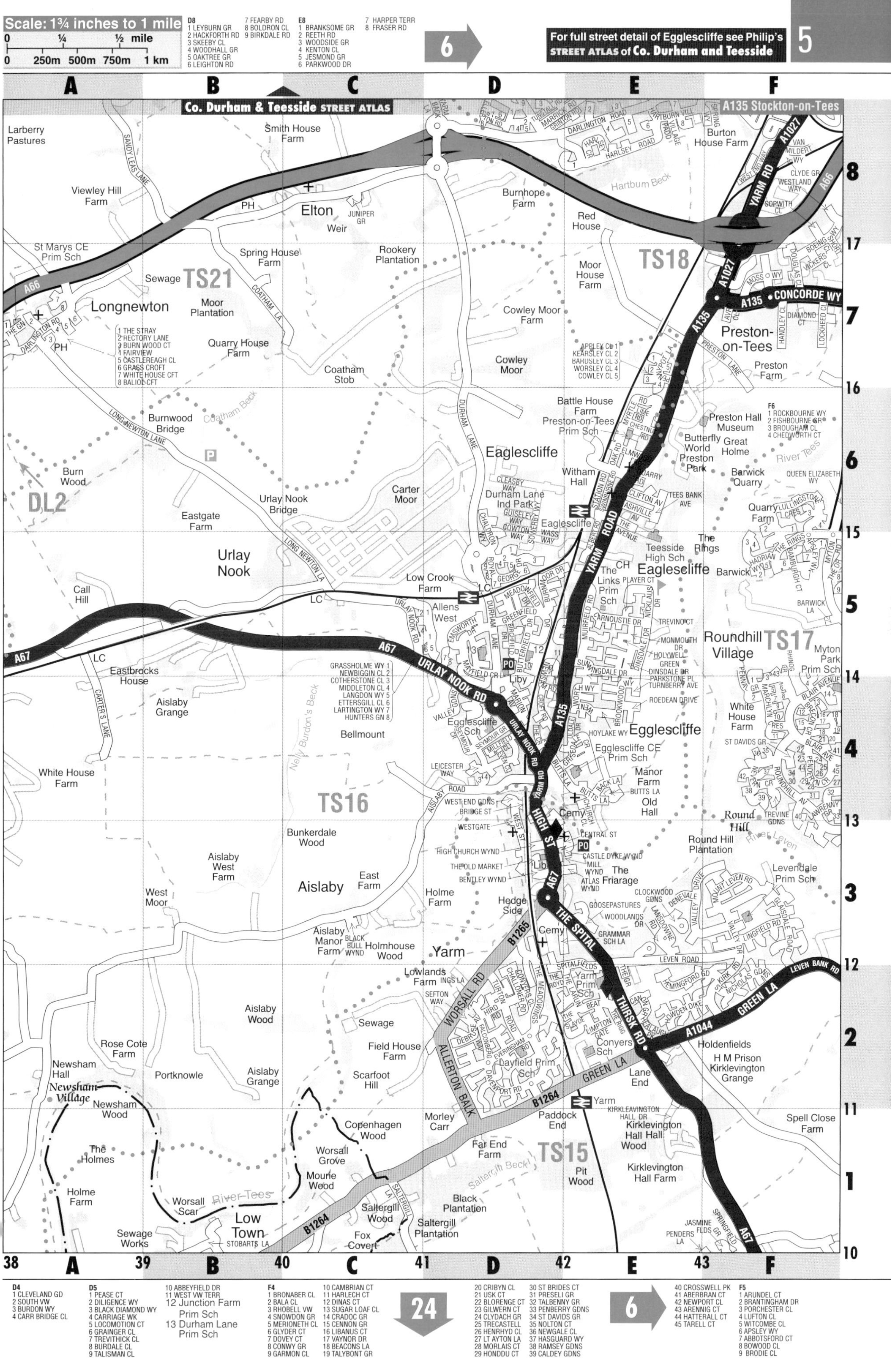

Scale: 1¾ inches to 1 mile
0 ¼ ½ mile
0 250m 500m 750m 1 km
D8
1 LEYBURN GR
2 HACKFORTH RD
3 SKEEBY CL
4 WOODHALL GR
5 OAKTREE GR
6 LEIGHTON RD
7 FEARBY RD
8 BOLDRON CL
9 BIRKDALE RD
E8
1 BRANKSOME GR
2 REETH RD
3 WOODSIDE GR
4 KENTON CL
5 JESMOND GR
6 PARKWOOD DR
7 HARPER TERR
8 FRASER RD
6
For full street detail of Egglescliffe see Philip's STREET ATLAS of Co. Durham and Teesside
5
A B C D E F
Co. Durham & Teesside STREET ATLAS
A135 Stockton-on-Tees
Larberry Pastures
Smith House Farm
Viewley Hill Farm
Elton
Weir
JUNIPER GR
Burnhope Farm
Red House
Hartburn Beck
Burton House Farm
St Marys CE Prim Sch
Spring House Farm
Rookery Plantation
TS18
TS21
Sewage
Longnewton
Moor Plantation
Moor House Farm
Cowley Moor Farm
Preston-on-Tees
Quarry House Farm
Coatham Stob
Cowley Moor
Preston Farm
1 THE STRAY
2 RECTORY LANE
3 BURN WOOD CT
4 FAIRVIEW
5 CASTLEREAGH CL
6 GRASS CROFT
7 WHITE HOUSE CFT
8 BALIOL CFT
APPLEY CL 1
KEARSLEY CL 2
BARDSLEY CL 3
WORSLEY CL 4
COWLEY CL 5
Battle House Farm
Preston-on-Tees Prim Sch
F6
1 ROCKBOURNE WY
2 FISHBOURNE GR
3 BROUGHAM CL
4 CHEDWORTH CT
Preston Hall Museum
Butterfly World
Preston Park
Great Holme
River Tees
Burnwood Bridge
Coatham Beck
Burn Wood
DL2
Eaglescliffe
Witham Hall
Barwick Quarry
Carter Moor
Durham Lane Ind Park
Urlay Nook Bridge
Eastgate Farm
Quarry Farm
Urlay Nook
Teesside High Sch
The Rings
Low Crook Farm
The Links
Eaglescliffe
Barwick
Call Hill
Allens West
Roundhill Village
TS17
Myton Park Prim Sch
A67
Eastbrocks House
URLAY NOOK RD
GRASSHOLME WY 1
NEWBIGGIN CL 2
COTHERSTONE CL 3
MIDDLETON CL 4
LANGDON WY 5
ETTERSGILL CL 6
LARTINGTON WY 7
HUNTERS GN 8
Aislaby Grange
Egglescliffe Sch
White House Farm
Bellmount
Egglescliffe
Egglescliffe CE Prim Sch
White House Farm
Manor Farm
TS16
Old Hall
Bunkerdale Wood
Round Hill Plantation
Aislaby West Farm
East Farm
The Friarage
Levendale Prim Sch
West Moor
Aislaby
Holme Farm
Hedge Side
Aislaby Manor Farm
Holmhouse Wood
Yarm
Lowlands Farm
Yarm Prim Sch
Aislaby Wood
Sewage
Field House Farm
Holdenfields
H M Prison Kirklevington Grange
Rose Cote Farm
Conyers Sch
Layfield Prim Sch
Newsham Hall
Newsham Village
Portknowle
Aislaby Grange
Scarfoot Hill
Lane End
Newsham Wood
Copenhagen Wood
Morley Carr
Paddock End
Kirklevington Hall Hall Wood
Spell Close Farm
The Holmes
Worsall Grove
Far End Farm
TS15
Kirklevington Hall Farm
Holme Farm
Mourie Wood
Pit Wood
Worsall Scar
River Tees
Low Town
Black Plantation
Saltergill Wood
Saltergill Plantation
Sewage Works
Fox Covert
38 39 40 41 42 43
8 17 7 16 6 15 5 14 4 13 3 12 2 11 1 10
D4
1 CLEVELAND GD
2 SOUTH VW
3 BURDON WY
4 CARR BRIDGE CL
D5
1 PEASE CT
2 DILIGENCE WY
3 BLACK DIAMOND WY
4 CARRIAGE WK
5 LOCOMOTION CT
6 GRAINGER CL
7 TREVITHICK CL
8 BURDALE CL
9 TALISMAN CL
10 ABBEYFIELD DR
11 WEST VW TERR
12 Junction Farm Prim Sch
13 Durham Lane Prim Sch
F4
1 BRONABER CL
2 BALA CL
3 RHOBELL VW
4 SNOWDON GR
5 MERIONETH CL
6 GLYDER CT
7 DOVEY CT
8 CONWY GR
9 GARMON CL
10 CAMBRIAN CT
11 HARLECH CT
12 DINAS CT
13 SUGAR LOAF CL
14 CRADOC GR
15 CENNON GR
16 LIBANUS CT
17 VAYNOR DR
18 BEACONS LA
19 TALYBONT GR
24
20 CRIBYN CL
21 USK CT
22 BLORENGE CT
23 GILWERN CT
24 CLYDACH GR
25 TRECASTELL
26 HENRHYD CL
27 LT AYTON LA
28 MORLAIS CT
29 HONDDU CT
30 ST BRIDES CT
31 PRESELI GR
32 TALBENNY GR
33 PENBERRY GDNS
34 ST DAVIDS GR
35 NOLTON CT
36 NEWGALE CL
37 HASGUARD WY
38 RAMSEY GDNS
39 CALDEY GDNS
6
40 CROSSWELL PK
41 ABERBRAN CT
42 NEWPORT CL
43 ARENNIG CT
44 HATTERALL CT
45 TARELL CT
F5
1 ARUNDEL CT
2 BRANTINGHAM DR
3 PORCHESTER CL
4 LUFTON CL
5 WITCOMBE CL
6 APSLEY WY
7 ABBOTSFORD CT
8 BOWOOD CL
9 BRODIE CL

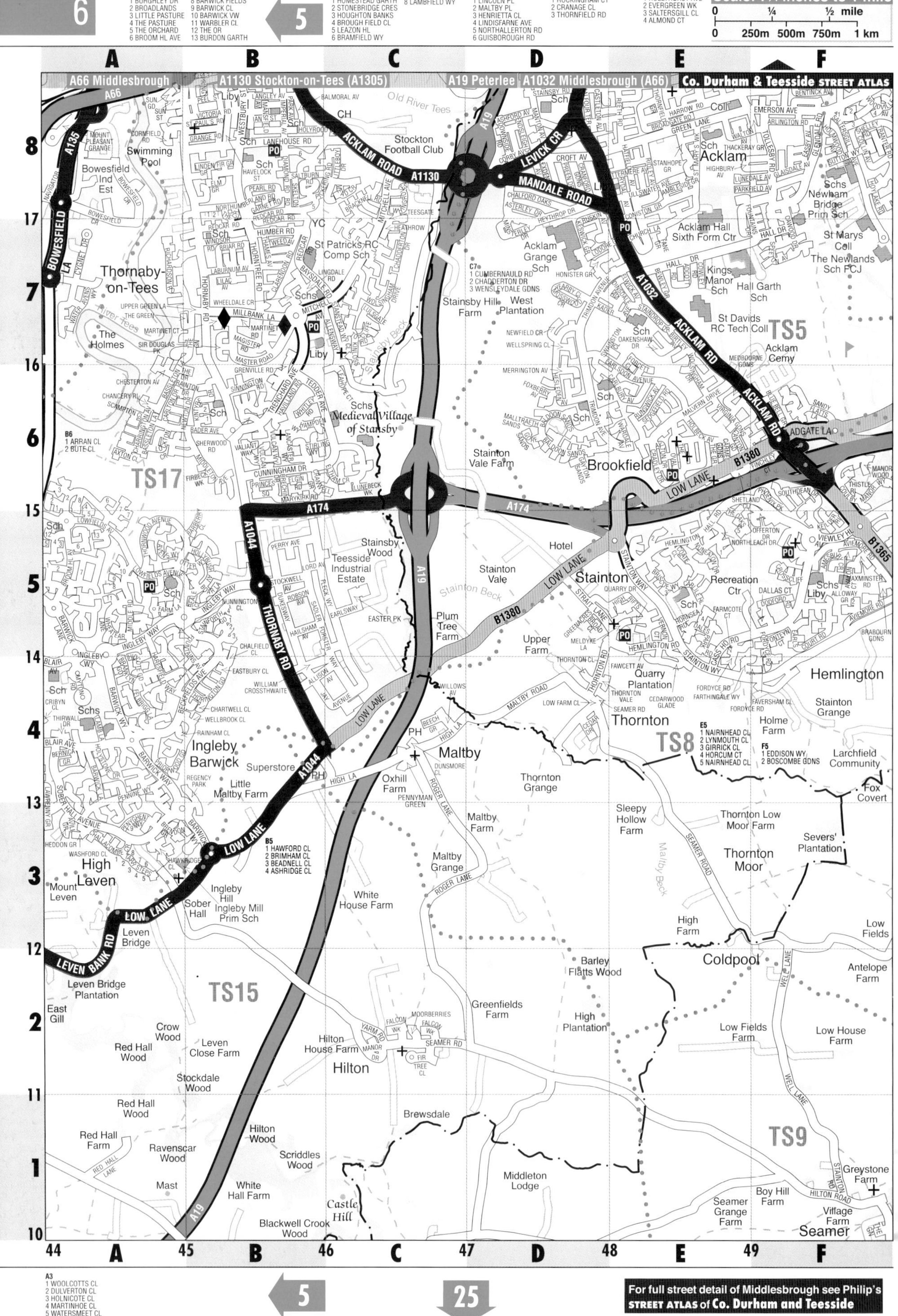

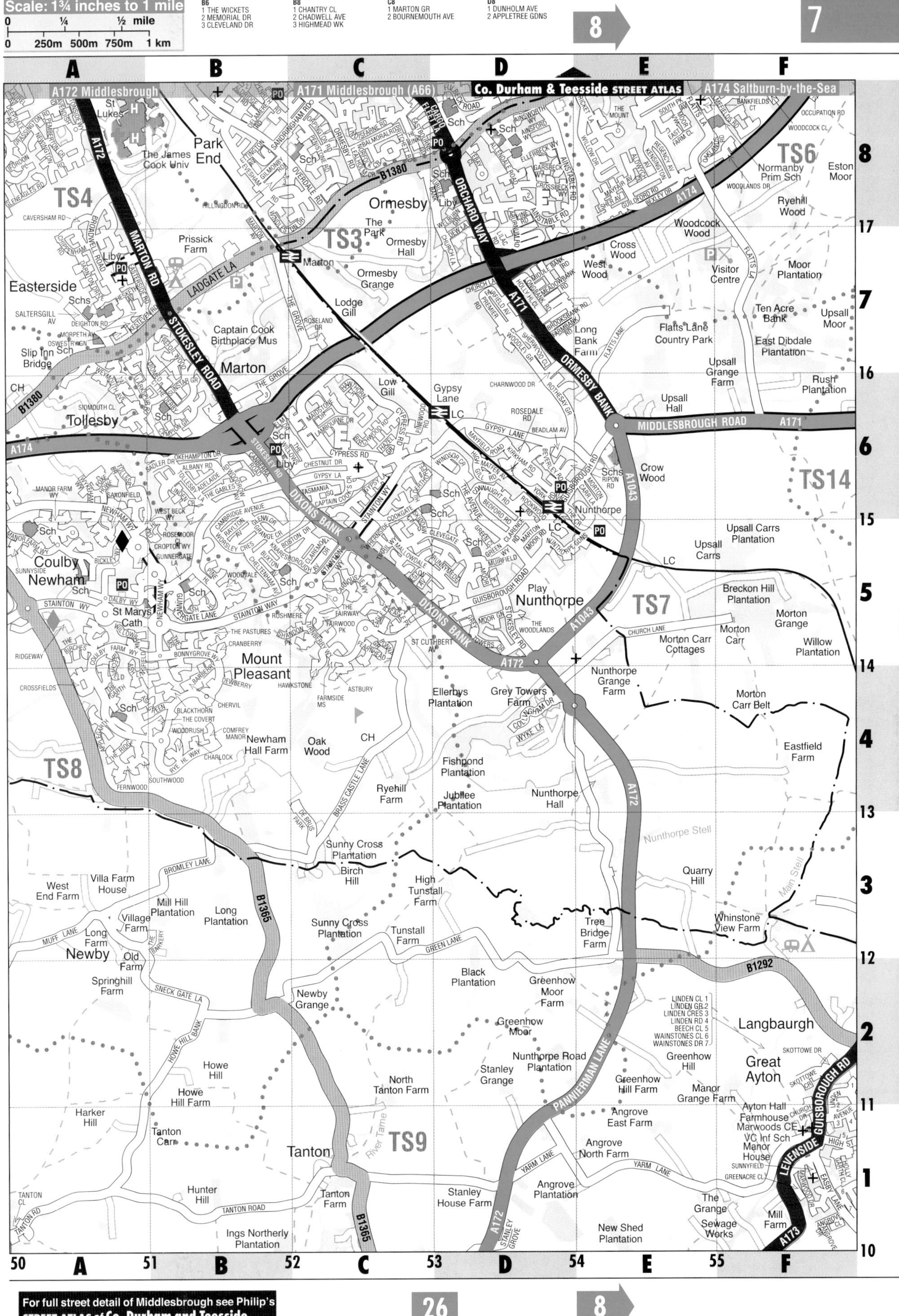

7

D6
1 REDWING RISING
2 PEREGRINE CT
3 Galley Hill Prim Sch

F7
1 WHELDRAKE CL
2 HESLINGTON GDNS
3 HUBY CT
4 BROMPTON AVE
5 ALLERSTON WY
6 HOVINGHAM DR

7 MONKTON RISE
8 THIRLBY WY
9 EDSTON DR
10 SKELTON CT
11 CARLTON CL
12 MINISKIP CL
13 APPLETON CL

14 WOODALE CL
15 SLEIGHTS CT
16 Prior Pursglove Coll
17 Askham Bryan Coll
18 Chaloner Prim Sch

Scale: 1¾ inches to 1 mile

0   ¼   ½ mile
0   250m   500m   750m   1 km

Co. Durham & Teesside STREET ATLAS

A   B   C   D   E   F

TS6

Guide Post Wood
Far Moor Plantation
Wilton Moor
Moordale Wood

Harrison's Plantation
Low Park Wood

Eston Moor
High Barnaby Farm
Bank Pasture Wood

Carlin Howe Farm
REDCAR ROAD
Tocketts Bridge Farm
B1269

17

Barnaby Moor
Bank Field
Poplar Farm
Crow Well Corner Plantation
North Cote Farm
Howlbeck Farm
Howlbeck Mill Farm
Laurence Jackson Sch
BROCKRIGG CT
A171

7

Claphams Wood
Barnaby Side
Park Wood
GUISBOROUGH
AYTON CT
BORROWBY
Mill Farm
Barnaby Side Farm
Scugdale Farm
Woodhouse
The Triangle
Pool
Priory (rems of)

16

Cross Keys Plantation
Barnaby Grange
MIDDLESBROUGH ROAD
Roseberry MT
MIDDLESBROUGH ROAD
W END
Libv
Mus
PO
RUFC

A171 MIDDLESBROUGH ROAD
TS14
STUMP CROSS

6

Hemble Hill Farm
BLIND LA
Lowcross Farm
STOKESLEY ROAD
Montagu's Harrier
Kingfisher Dr
Fulmar Head
Osprey Cl
St Paulinus RC Prim Sch
Visitor Centre
Forest & Walkway Country Park
Hutton Gate
Hutton Prim Sch
Highcliffe Prim Sch
Lowcross Av
Scholars Gate
Enfield Sh Ctr

East Upsall Farm
Cleveland Way
Low Farm
Pinchinthorpe House
Thomas's Wood
Home Farm
Hutton Hall
Lowcross Woods
Wykeham Av

15

TS7
Boundary Plantation
Spite Hall
Little Acre Farm
Bousdale Woods
Bousdale Farm
Hutton Lowcross Woods
Reed's Wood
Kemplah Wood
Kemplah Top
Holme Wood
Highcliff Wood
1 BUCCLEUCH CL
2 BLACKMORE CL

5

The Flats
Pinchinthorpe Hall
Lee's Wood
Hall Heads
Hutton Village
Hutton Wood
Highcliff Wood

14

Snow Hall
A173
Mount House Farm
Hall Heads Wood
Blue Lake Wood
Highcliff Nab
F6
1 FOUNTAINS CL
2 BELMANGATE
3 BAYSDALE CL
4 CHALONER CT
5 DULVERTON WY
6 WHEATLANDS CL
7 Belmont Prim Sch

4

Newton under Roseberry
PH
Bridlegill Wood
Hanging Stone Wood
Hutton Lowcross Woods
Blue Lake Wood
Highcliffe Farm

13

Whitegate Farm
ROSEBERRY LA
Cockle Scar
Roseberry Topping
Pinchinthorpe Moor
Newton Moor
Hutton Moor
Gisborough Moor
Codhill Heights

3

Newton Wood
Roseberry Common
Howden Gill
Sleddale Farm

NEWTON ROAD
Quarry House
LANGBAURGH CL
Cliff Rigg Quarry
TS9
Slacks Wood
Great Ayton Moor

12

A173
Cliff Ridge Wood
Airyholme Farm
Ayton Banks Farm
Lonsdale Plantation
Kildale Moor

2

ROSEBERRY AV
ROSEBERRY RD
Roseberry Prim Sch
FARM GARTH
Ryehill Farm
Slacks Wood
AIRYHOLME LANE
DIKES LANE
High Intake Plantation
Oak Tree Farm

ARTHUR ST
CLEVELAND ST
FRANKFIELD MS
CAPTAIN COOK'S WY
Cleveland Lodge
Gribdale Terrace
Lonsdale Slack Wood
Lonsdale Farm

11

ROSEHILL
ADDISON RD
School Farm
STATION ROAD
Great Ayton
Ayton Banks Wood
Hunter's Scar
Coate Moor
Bankside Farm
YO21
Pale End Plantation

Libv
Mus
PO
High St

1

BYEMOOR AV
OLD MILL WYND
Neatstead Farm
Woodhouse Farm
Little Ayton Moor
Easby Moor
Captain Cooks Monument
Mill Bank Wood
Coate Moor
Pale End
New Row
Woodend Farm

BYEMOOR CL
WAINSTONES DR
EASBY LA
CROSS LA
Grange Farm
Brookside Farm
Little Ayton
Low Plantation

10

56   A   57   B   58   C   59   D   60   E   61   F

A2
1 ORCHARD CL
2 BRADLEYS TERR
3 CHURCHILL CL
4 SPENCE CT
5 ROWAN DR
6 CENTRAL WY
7 CALIFORNIA GR

8 ROSEBERRY DR
9 OAKLANDS
10 THE HAWTHORNS
11 ROMANY RD
12 WOODBINE CL
13 WHINSTONE VW
14 EDWARD KITCHING TERR

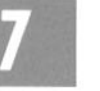

7   27

For full street detail of Guisborough see Philip's **STREET ATLAS of Co. Durham and Teesside**

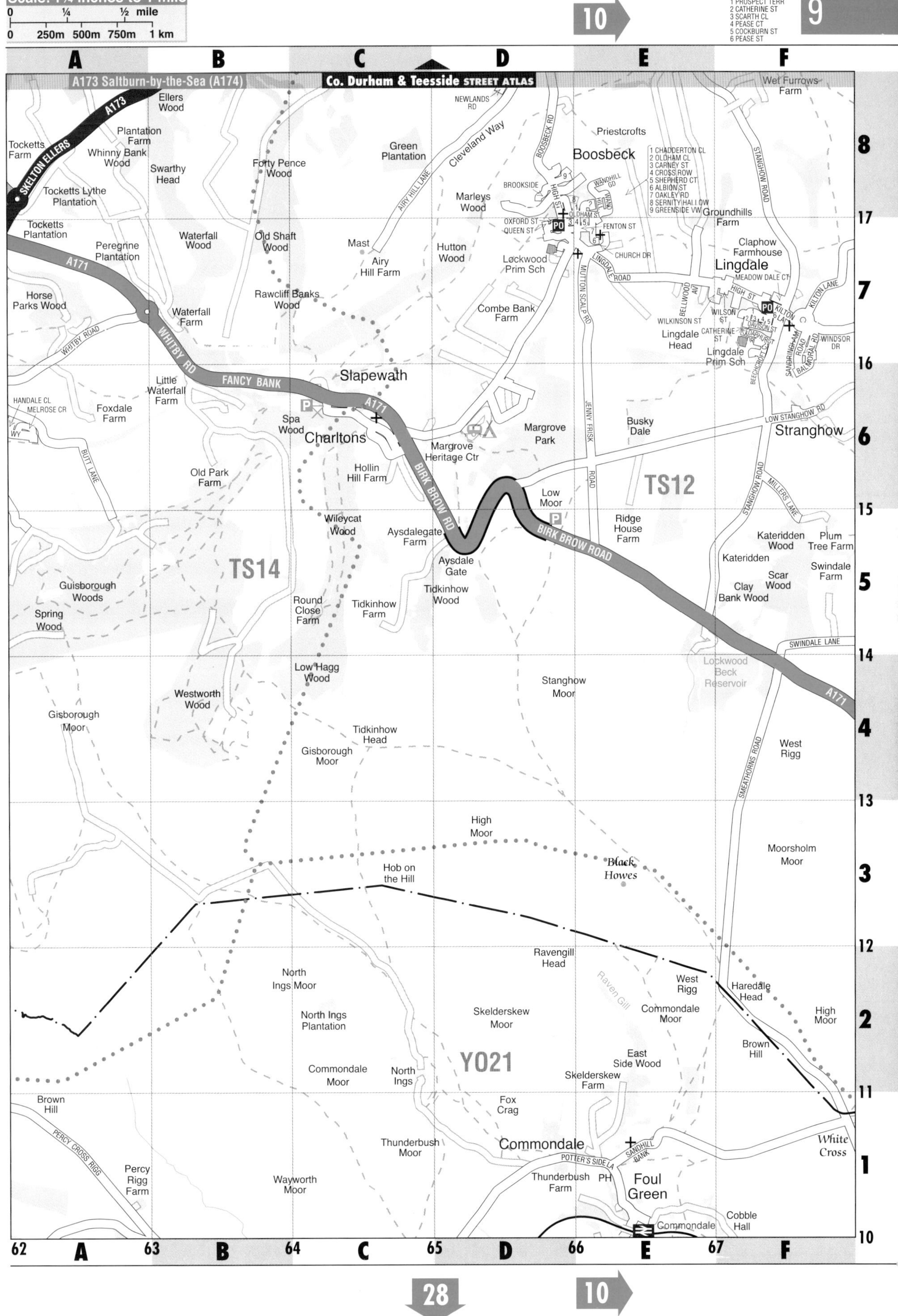
A173 Saltburn-by-the-Sea (A174)
Co. Durham & Teesside STREET ATLAS
Boosbeck
1 CHADDERTON CL
2 OLDHAM CL
3 CARNEY ST
4 CROSS ROW
5 SHEPHERD CT
6 ALBION ST
7 OAKLEY RD
8 SERNITY HALLOW
9 GREENSIDE VW
Lingdale
Stranghow
Slapewath
Charltons
Commondale
Foul Green
TS14
TS12
YO21
Margrove Heritage Ctr
Lockwood Beck Reservoir
Black Howes
White Cross

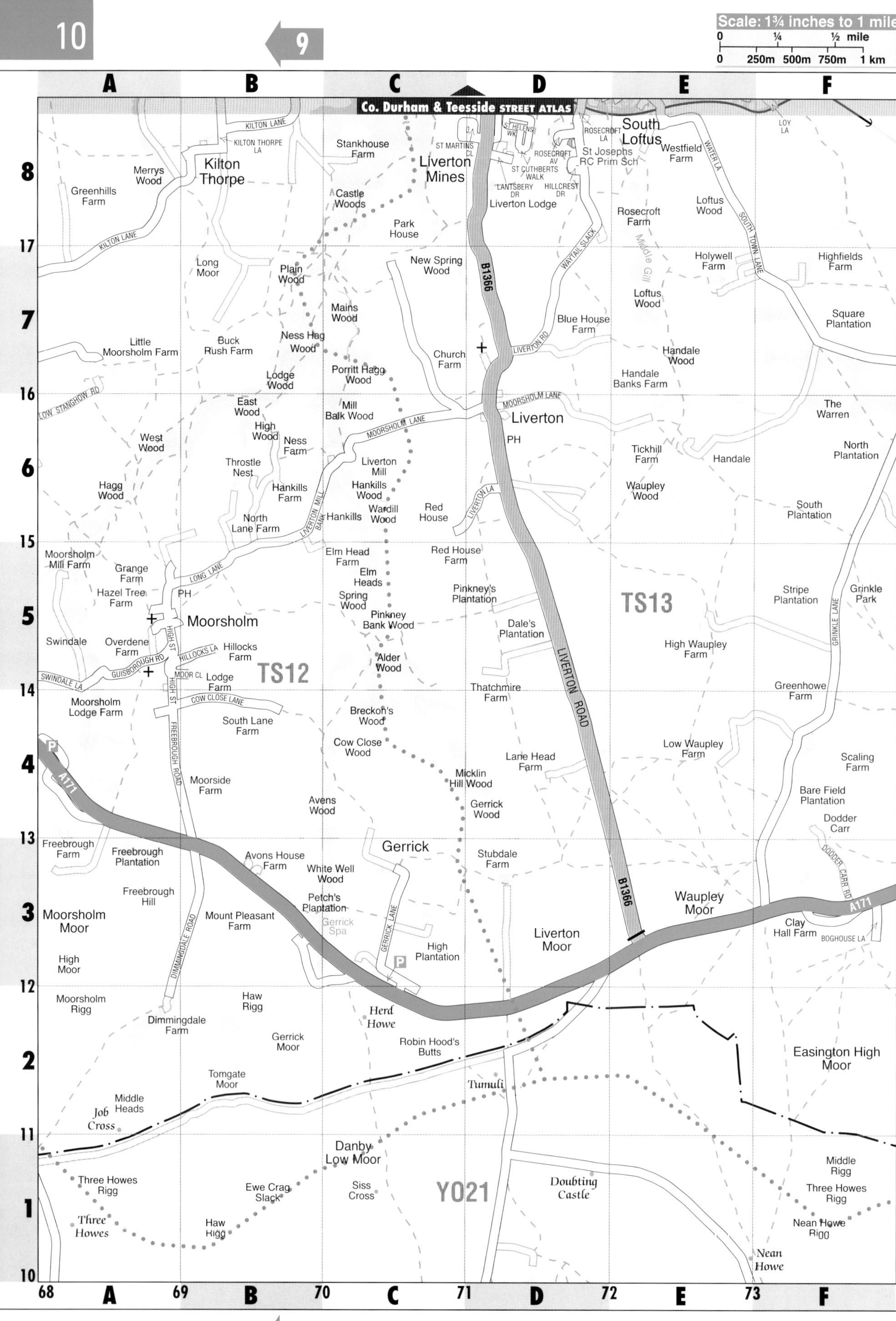

Co. Durham & Teesside STREET ATLAS

A   B   C   D   E   F

8

Greenhills Farm

Merrys Wood

KILTON LANE

KILTON THORPE LA

Kilton Thorpe

Stankhouse Farm

ST MARTINS

St Helens Wk

Liverton Mines

ROSECROFT AV

ST CUTHBERTS WALK

South Loftus

ROSECROFT CL

St Josephs RC Prim Sch

Westfield Farm

LOY LA

17

KILTON LANE

Long Moor

Plain Wood

Castle Woods

Park House

LANTSBERY DR

HILLCREST DR

Liverton Lodge

B1366

WAYTAIL SLACK

Rosecroft Farm

Loftus Wood

WATER LA

SOUTH TOWN LANE

Highfields Farm

7

Little Moorsholm Farm

Buck Rush Farm

Ness Hag Wood

Mains Wood

New Spring Wood

Church Farm

Blue House Farm

LIVERTON RD

Loftus Wood

Holywell Farm

Square Plantation

16

LOW STANGHOW RD

Lodge Wood

East Wood

Porritt Hagg Wood

Mill Balk Wood

MOORSHOLM LANE

Moorsholm Lane

Liverton

Handale Wood

Handale Banks Farm

The Warren

6

West Wood

High Wood

Ness Farm

Liverton Mill

PH

Tickhill Farm

Handale

North Plantation

Hagg Wood

Throstle Nest

Hankills Farm

Hankills Wood

Wardill Wood

Red House

LIVERTON LA

Waupley Wood

South Plantation

15

Moorsholm Mill Farm

Grange Farm

North Lane Farm

LIVERTON MILL BANK

Hankills

LONG LANE

Elm Head Farm

Red House Farm

Red House Farm

Stripe Plantation

Grinkle Park

Hazel Tree Farm

PH

Elm Heads

Spring Wood

Pinkney's Plantation

Dale's Plantation

High Waupley Farm

GRINKLE LANE

5

Swindale

Overdene Farm

Moorsholm

HILLOCKS LA

Hillocks Farm

TS12

Pinkney Bank Wood

Thatchmire Farm

LIVERTON ROAD

Greenhowe Farm

SWINDALE LA

GUISBOROUGH RD

HIGH ST

MOOR CL

Lodge Farm

Alder Wood

TS13

14

Moorsholm Lodge Farm

HIGH ST

FREEBROUGH ROAD

COW CLOSE LANE

South Lane Farm

Breckoh's Wood

Cow Close Wood

Lane Head Farm

Low Waupley Farm

Scaling Farm

4

P

A171

Freebrough Farm

Freebrough Plantation

Moorside Farm

Avens Wood

Micklin Hill Wood

Gerrick Wood

Bare Field Plantation

Dodder Carr

13

Freebrough Hill

Avons House Farm

White Well Wood

DODDER CARR RD

Moorsholm Moor

Mount Pleasant Farm

Petch's Plantation

GERRICK LANE

Stubdale Farm

Waupley Moor

A171

3

DIMMINGDALE ROAD

Gerrick Spa

P

High Plantation

Liverton Moor

B1366

Clay Hall Farm

BOGHOUSE LA

High Moor

Haw Rigg

Herd Howe

12

Moorsholm Rigg

Dimmingdale Farm

Gerrick Moor

Robin Hood's Butts

Easington High Moor

2

Tomgate Moor

Middle Heads

Tumuli

Job Cross

Danby Low Moor

Middle Rigg

11

Three Howes Rigg

Ewe Crag Slack

Siss Cross

YO21

Doubting Castle

Three Howes Rigg

Nean Howe Rigg

Three Howes

Haw Rigg

Nean Howe

10

68   A   69   B   70   C   71   D   72   E   73   F

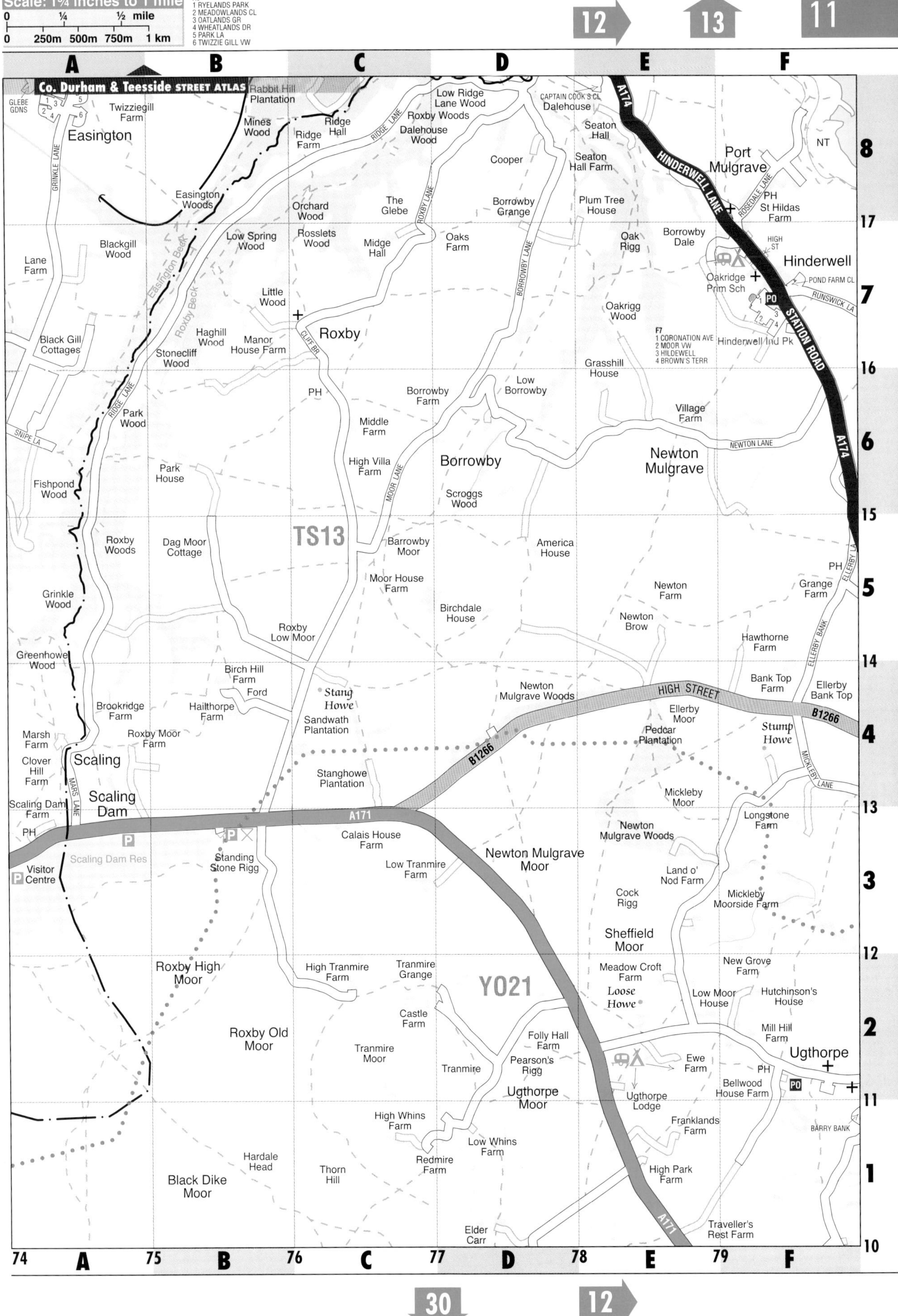

Scale: 1¾ inches to 1 mile

0   ¼   ½ mile
0 250m 500m 750m 1 km

A8
1 RYELANDS PARK
2 MEADOWLANDS CL
3 OATLANDS GR
4 WHEATLANDS DR
5 PARK LA
6 TWIZZIE GILL VW

12

13

11

Co. Durham & Teesside STREET ATLAS

GLEBE GDNS
1
2 3
4   5 6

Twizziegill Farm

Easington

Rabbit Hill Plantation

Mines Wood

Ridge Hall

Ridge Farm

Low Ridge Lane Wood

Roxby Woods

Dalehouse Wood

Dalehouse

CAPTAIN COOK'S CL

A174

Seaton Hall

Port Mulgrave

NT

8

Easington Woods

Orchard Wood

The Glebe

Cooper

Seaton Hall Farm

Plum Tree House

HINDERWELL LANE

ROSEDALE LANE

PH
St Hildas CH

17

Blackgill Wood

Lane Farm

Low Spring Wood

Rosslets Wood

Midge Hall

Oaks Farm

Borrowby Grange

Oak Rigg

Borrowby Dale

HIGH ST

Hinderwell

POND FARM CL

Haghill Wood

Little Wood

Manor House Farm

CLIF BR

Roxby

BORROWBY LANE

ROXBY LANE

Oakrigg Wood

Oakridge Prim Sch

PO

RUNSWICK LA

STATION ROAD

7

Black Gill Cottages

Stonecliff Wood

Park Wood

PH

Middle Farm

Borrowby Farm

Low Borrowby

Grasshill House

Hinderwell Ind Pk

F7
1 CORONATION AVE
2 MOOR VW
3 HILDEWELL
4 BROWN'S TERR

16

SNIPE LA

RIDGE LANE

Roxby Beck

Park House

High Villa Farm

MOOR LANE

Borrowby

Newton Mulgrave

Village Farm

NEWTON LANE

6

A174

Fishpond Wood

Roxby Woods

Dag Moor Cottage

Scroggs Wood

15

ELLERBY LA

Grinkle Wood

Barrowby Moor

America House

Newton Farm

PH

Grange Farm

5

RIDGE LANE

Greenhowe Wood

Moor House Farm

Birchdale House

Newton Brow

Hawthorne Farm

ELLERBY BANK

14

Roxby Low Moor

Stang Howe

Newton Mulgrave Woods

HIGH STREET

Bank Top Farm

Ellerby Bank Top

Brookridge Farm

Birch Hill Farm

Hailthorpe Farm

Ford

Sandwath Plantation

Ellerby Moor

Pedcar Plantation

Stump Howe

B1266

4

Marsh Farm

Roxby Moor Farm

B1266

Mickleby Moor

MICKLEBY LANE

Clover Hill Farm

Scaling

Stanghowe Plantation

Newton Mulgrave Woods

Longstone Farm

13

Scaling Dam Farm

MARS LANE

Scaling Dam

A171

Calais House Farm

Land o' Nod Farm

Mickleby Moorside Farm

PH

Visitor Centre

P
Standing Stone Rigg

P

Low Tranmire Farm

Newton Mulgrave Moor

Cock Rigg

3

Scaling Dam Res

Roxby High Moor

Sheffield Moor

12

High Tranmire Farm

Tranmire Grange

YO21

Meadow Croft Farm

New Grove Farm

Hutchinson's House

Roxby Old Moor

Castle Farm

Loose Howe

Low Moor House

Mill Hill Farm

Ugthorpe

2

Tranmire Moor

Tranmire

Folly Hall Farm

Pearson's Rigg

Ewe Farm

PH

PO

Bellwood House Farm

High Whins Farm

Ugthorpe Moor

Ugthorpe Lodge

Franklands Farm

BARRY BANK

11

Hardale Head

Low Whins Farm

Redmire Farm

Thorn Hill

High Park Farm

1

Black Dike Moor

Elder Carr

A171

Traveller's Rest Farm

10

Scale: 1¾ inches to 1 mile

0   ¼   ½ mile
0 250m 500m 750m 1 km

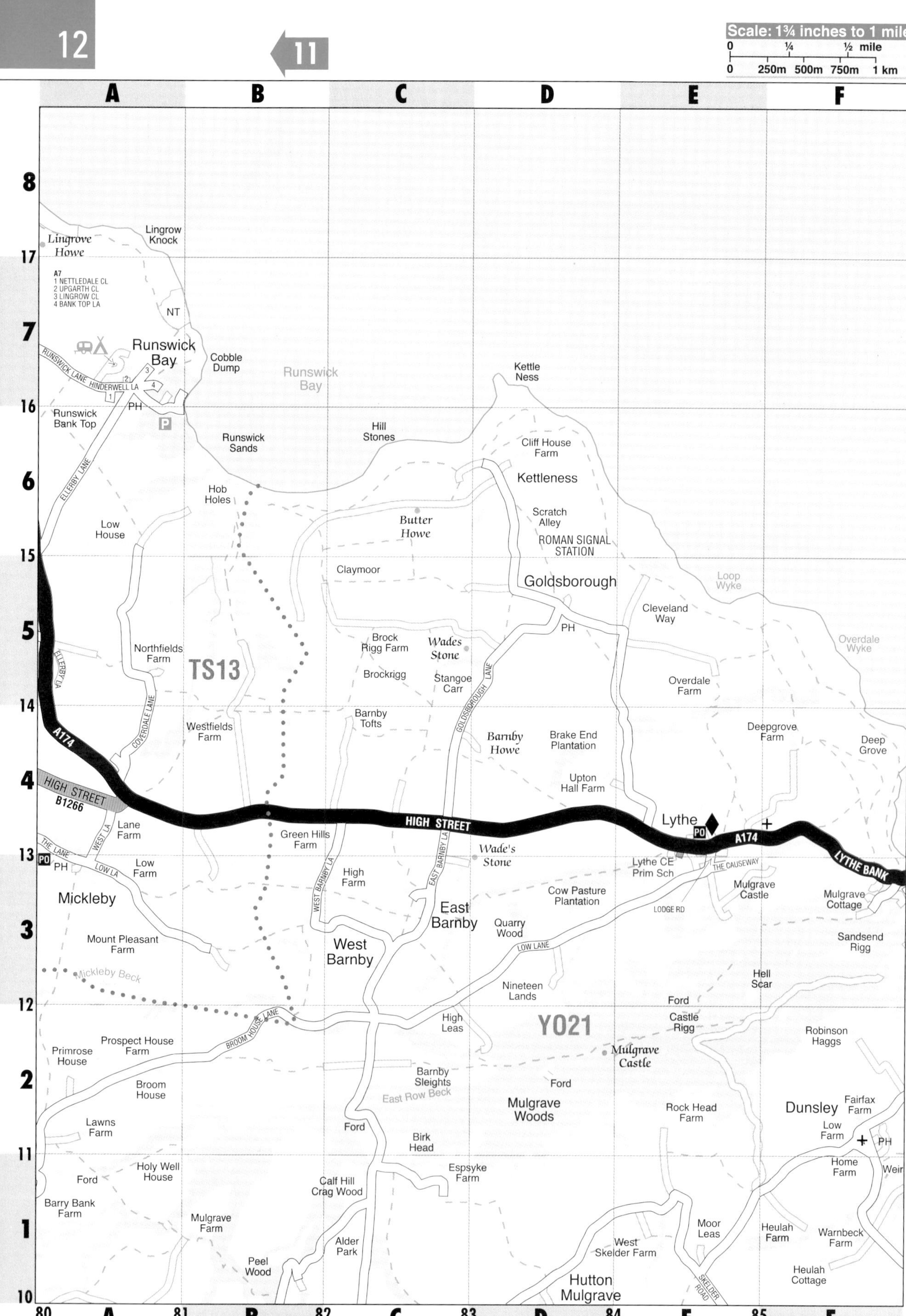

A B C D E F

8

17

Lingrove Howe
Lingrow Knock

A7
1 NETTLEDALE CL
2 UPGARTH CL
3 LINGROW CL
4 BANK TOP LA

NT

7

Runswick Bay

Cobble Dump

Runswick Bay

Kettle Ness

16

Runswick Bank Top

PH
P

Runswick Sands

Hill Stones

Cliff House Farm

Kettleness

6

Hob Holes

Butter Howe

Scratch Alley

ROMAN SIGNAL STATION

15

Low House

Claymoor

Goldsborough

Loop Wyke

5

Northfields Farm

TS13

Brock Rigg Farm

Wades Stone

PH

Cleveland Way

Overdale Wyke

Brockrigg

Stangoe Carr

Overdale Farm

Deepgrove Farm

Deep Grove

14

Westfields Farm

Barnby Tofts

Barnby Howe

Brake End Plantation

4

HIGH STREET
B1266

A174

Lane Farm

Green Hills Farm

Upton Hall Farm

Lythe
PO

A174

LYTHE BANK

13

THE LANE
PO
PH

Low Farm

High Farm

Wade's Stone

Lythe CE Prim Sch

THE CAUSEWAY

Mulgrave Castle

Mulgrave Cottage

WEST LA
LOW LA

Mickleby

Cow Pasture Plantation

LODGE RD

Sandsend Rigg

3

Mount Pleasant Farm

West Barnby

East Barnby

Quarry Wood

LOW LANE

Hell Scar

Mickleby Beck

Nineteen Lands

YO21

Castle Rigg

12

Primrose House

Prospect House Farm

BROOM HOUSE LANE

High Leas

Mulgrave Castle

Robinson Haggs

2

Broom House

Barnby Sleights

East Row Beck

Ford

Mulgrave Woods

Rock Head Farm

Dunsley

Fairfax Farm

Low Farm

PH

Lawns Farm

Ford

Birk Head

Espsyke Farm

Home Farm

Weir

11

Ford

Holy Well House

Calf Hill Crag Wood

West Skelder Farm

Moor Leas

Heulah Farm

Warnbeck Farm

1

Barry Bank Farm

Mulgrave Farm

Alder Park

SKELDER ROAD

Heulah Cottage

Peel Wood

Hutton Mulgrave

10

80 A 81 B 82 C 83 D 84 E 85 F

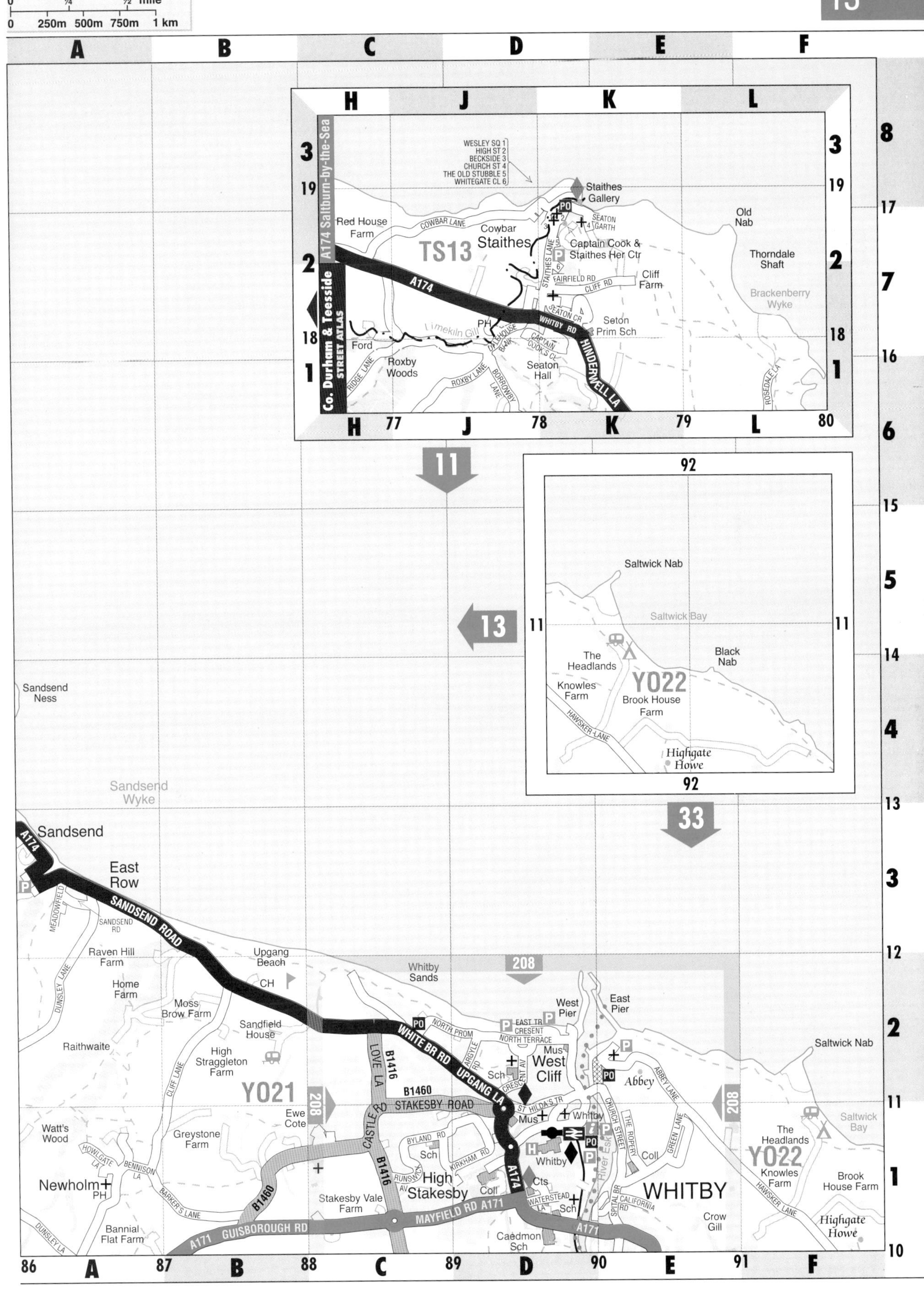

Scale: 1¾ inches to 1 mile

For full street detail of the highlighted area see page 208.

Scale: 1¾ inches to 1 mile

0   ¼   ½ mile
0   250m   500m   750m   1 km

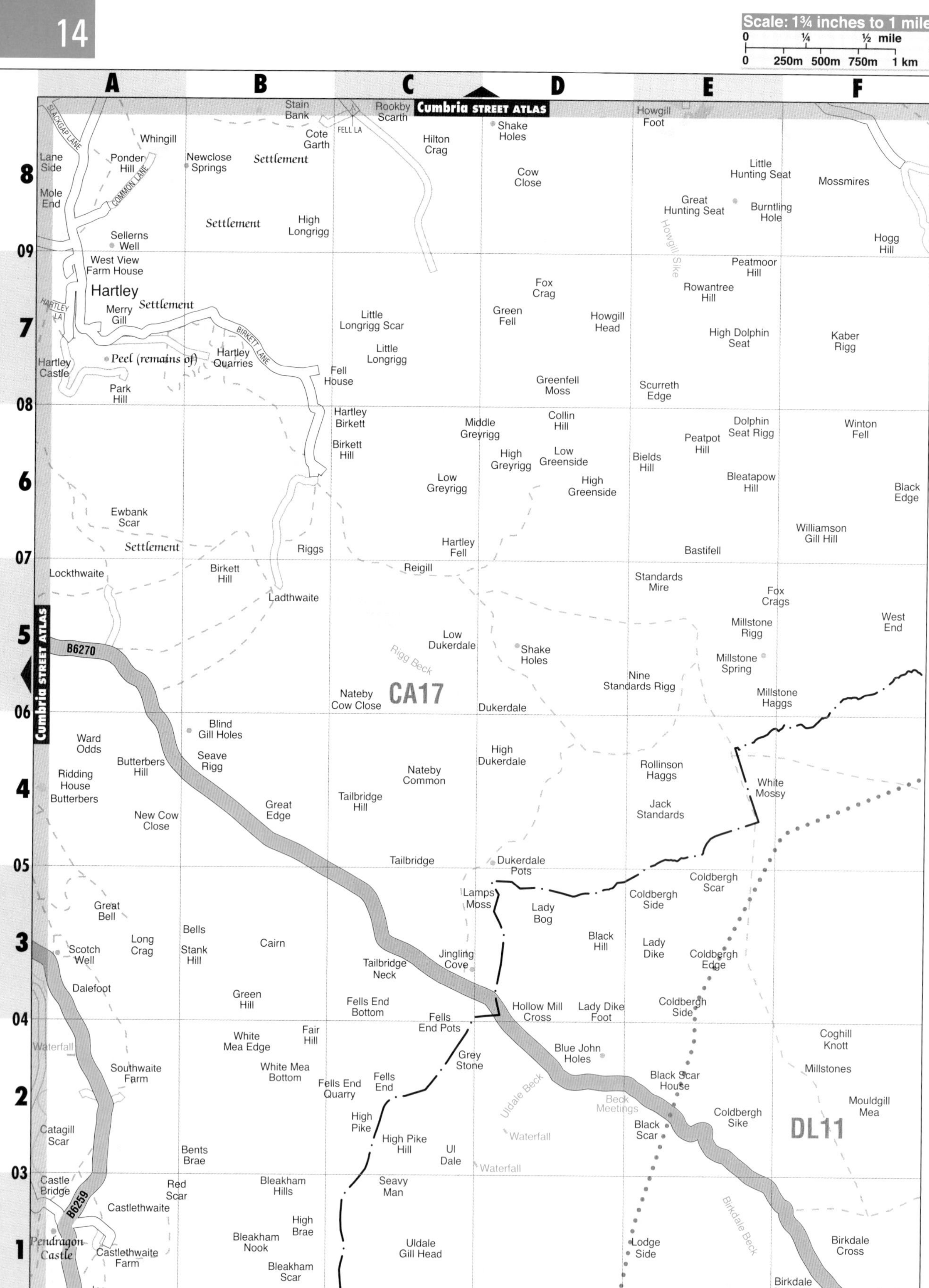

Cumbria STREET ATLAS

CA17

DL11

Cumbria STREET ATLAS

B6270

B6259

B6270

Labels (A8–F8):
Lane Side, Mole End, Whingill, Ponder Hill, Newclose Springs, Cote Garth, Stain Bank, Settlement, FELL LA, Rookby Scarth, Hilton Crag, Shake Holes, Cow Close, Howgill Foot, Little Hunting Seat, Mossmires, Great Hunting Seat, Burntling Hole, Hogg Hill

Labels (09 row):
Sellerns Well, West View Farm House, Settlement, High Longrigg, Howgill Sike, Peatmoor Hill

Labels (7 row):
Hartley, Merry Gill, Settlement, HARTLEY LA, BIRKETT LANE, Hartley Quarries, Little Longrigg Scar, Little Longrigg, Fell House, Green Fell, Fox Crag, Howgill Head, Greenfell Moss, High Dolphin Seat, Rowantree Hill, Kaber Rigg

Labels (08 row):
Hartley Castle, Peel (remains of), Park Hill, Hartley Birkett, Birkett Hill, Middle Greyrigg, Collin Hill, High Greyrigg, Low Greenside, High Greenside, Scurreth Edge, Bields Hill, Peatpot Hill, Dolphin Seat Rigg, Winton Fell

Labels (6 row):
Ewbank Scar, Settlement, Low Greyrigg, Hartley Fell, Bastifell, Bleatapow Hill, Williamson Gill Hill, Black Edge

Labels (07 row):
Lockthwaite, Birkett Hill, Riggs, Ladthwaite, Reigill, Standards Mire, Fox Crags, West End, Millstone Rigg

Labels (5 row):
B6270, Rigg Beck, Low Dukerdale, Shake Holes, Nine Standards Rigg, Millstone Spring, Millstone Haggs

Labels (06 row):
Nateby Cow Close, Dukerdale

Labels (4 row):
Ward Odds, Ridding House Butterbers, Butterbers Hill, Blind Gill Holes, Seave Rigg, Great Edge, Tailbridge Hill, Nateby Common, High Dukerdale, Rollinson Haggs, Jack Standards, White Mossy

Labels (05 row):
New Cow Close, Tailbridge, Dukerdale Pots, Coldbergh Scar

Labels (3 row):
Great Bell, Scotch Well, Long Crag, Bells Stank Hill, Cairn, Tailbridge Neck, Lamps Moss, Lady Bog, Jingling Cove, Black Hill, Lady Dike, Coldbergh Side, Coldbergh Edge

Labels (04 row):
Dalefoot, Green Hill, Fells End Bottom, Fells End Pots, Hollow Mill Cross, Lady Dike Foot, Coldbergh Side

Labels (2 row):
Waterfall, Southwaite Farm, White Mea Edge, Fair Hill, White Mea Bottom, Fells End Quarry, Fells End, Grey Stone, Blue John Holes, Beck Meetings, Black Scar House, Coghill Knott, Millstones, Mouldgill Mea, Uldale Beck

Labels (03 row):
Catagill Scar, Bents Brae, Red Scar, Bleakham Hills, High Pike, High Pike Hill, Ul Dale, Waterfall, Black Scar, Coldbergh Sike

Labels (1 row):
Castle Bridge, Pendragon Castle, Castlethwaite, Castlethwaite Farm, Bleakham Nook, High Brae, Seavy Man, Uldale Gill Head, Lodge Side, Birkdale Beck, Birkdale Cross

Labels (02 row):
Ing Hill, Goodwife Stones, Lindrigg Scars, Bleakham Scar, Lodge Hags, Low Birkdale Bog, Birkdale Common, Crook Seal

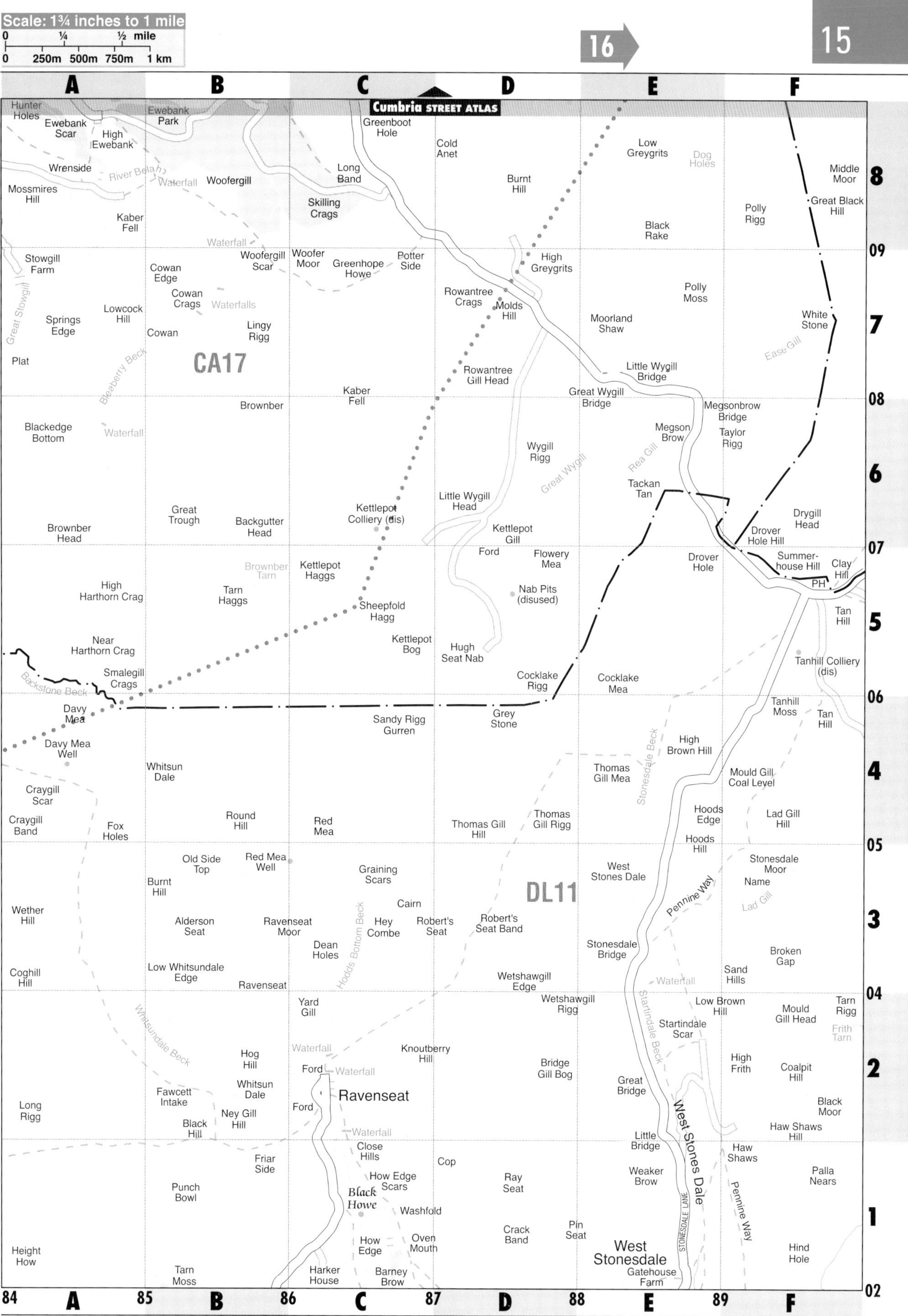

Cumbria STREET ATLAS

A B C D E F

8
09
7
08
6
07
5
06
4
05
3
04
2
1
02

Hunter Holes
Ewebank Scar
High Ewebank
Ewebank Park
Greenboot Hole
Cold Anet
Low Greygrits
Dog Holes
Middle Moor
Wrenside
River Bela?
Woofergill
Burnt Hill
Great Black Hill
Mossmires Hill
Waterfall
Black Rake
Polly Rigg
Kaber Fell
Skilling Crags
Long Band
High Greygrits
Stowgill Farm
Waterfall
Woofergill Scar
Woofer Moor
Greenhope Howe
Potter Side
Moorland Shaw
Polly Moss
White Stone
Cowan Edge
Rowantree Crags
Molds Hill
Cowan Crags
Waterfalls
Little Wygill Bridge
Great Stowgill
Springs Edge
Lowcock Hill
Cowan
Lingy Rigg
Rowantree Gill Head
Great Wygill Bridge
Plat
CA17
Kaber Fell
Little Wygill Head
Wygill Rigg
Great Wygill
Megsonbrow Bridge
Ease Gill
Blackedge Bottom
Brownber
Rea Gill
Megson Brow
Taylor Rigg
Bleaberry Beck
Waterfall
Great Wygill
Drygill Head
Great Trough
Backgutter Head
Kettlepot Colliery (dis)
Little Wygill Head
Tackan Tan
Drover Hole Hill
Summer-house Hill
Clay Hill
Brownber Head
Kettlepot Gill
Ford
Flowery Mea
Drover Hole
PH
Tan Hill
Brownber Tarn
Kettlepot Haggs
Nab Pits (disused)
High Harthorn Crag
Tarn Haggs
Sheepfold Hagg
Kettlepot Bog
Hugh Seat Nab
Tanhill Colliery (dis)
Near Harthorn Crag
Cocklake Rigg
Cocklake Mea
Tan Hill
Backstone Beck
Smalegill Crags
Davy Mea
Tanhill Moss
Davy Mea Well
Sandy Rigg Gurren
Grey Stone
High Brown Hill
Stonesdale Beck
Craygill Scar
Whitsun Dale
Thomas Gill Mea
Mould Gill Coal Level
Craygill Band
Fox Holes
Round Hill
Red Mea
Thomas Gill Hill
Thomas Gill Rigg
Hoods Edge
Lad Gill Hill
Hoods Hill
Wether Hill
Old Side Top
Red Mea Well
Graining Scars
DL11
West Stones Dale
Stonesdale Moor
Name
Burnt Hill
Cairn
Lad Gill
Coghill Hill
Alderson Seat
Ravenseat Moor
Hey Combe
Robert's Seat
Robert's Seat Band
Stonesdale Bridge
Sand Hills
Broken Gap
Low Whitsundale Edge
Dean Holes
Wetshawgill Edge
Waterfall
Hoods Bottom Beck
Ravenseat
Whitsundale Beck
Yard Gill
Wetshawgill Rigg
Low Brown Hill
Mould Gill Head
Tarn Rigg
Startindale Scar
Frith Tarn
Hog Hill
Knoutberry Hill
High Frith
Coalpit Hill
Waterfall
Whitsun Dale
Ford
Waterfall
Bridge Gill Bog
Startindale Beck
Great Bridge
Black Moor
Fawcett Intake
Ford
Ney Gill Hill
Ravenseat
Haw Shaws Hill
Long Rigg
Black Hill
Little Bridge
West Stones Dale
STONESDALE LANE
Haw Shaws
Palla Nears
Friar Side
Close Hills
Cop
Weaker Brow
How Edge Scars
Ray Seat
Punch Bowl
Black Howe
Washfold
Pin Seat
Hind Hole
Height How
How Edge
Oven Mouth
Crack Band
West Stonesdale
Pennine Way
Tarn Moss
Harker House
Barney Brow
Gatehouse Farm

Scale: 1¾ inches to 1 mile

0   ¼   ½ mile
0 250m 500m 750m 1 km

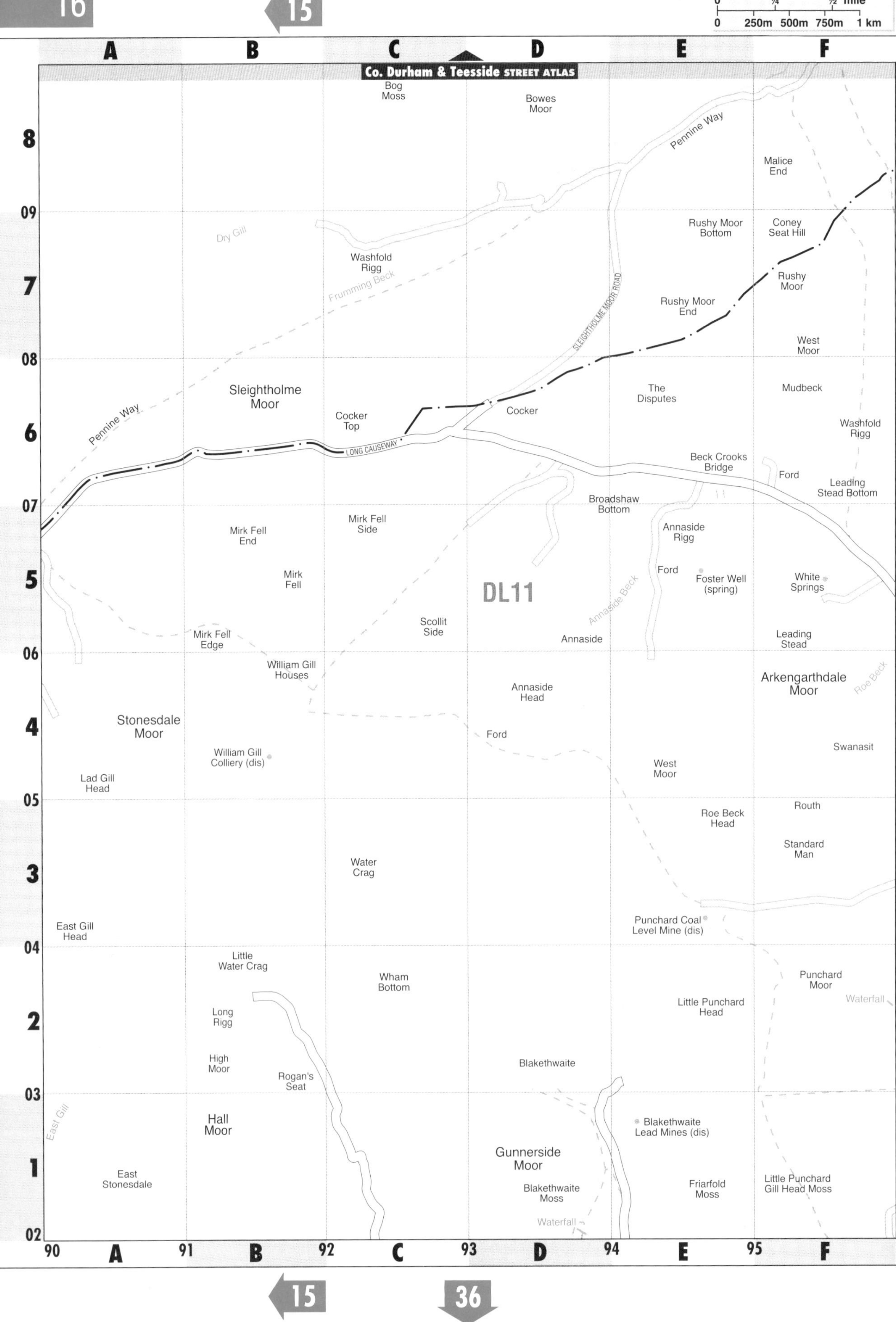

Co. Durham & Teesside STREET ATLAS

A   B   C   D   E   F

Bog Moss

Bowes Moor

Pennine Way

Malice End

Dry Gill

Washfold Rigg

Frumming Beck

SLEIGHTHOLME MOOR ROAD

Rushy Moor Bottom

Coney Seat Hill

Rushy Moor

Sleightholme Moor

Rushy Moor End

West Moor

Pennine Way

Cocker Top

Cocker

The Disputes

Mudbeck

Washfold Rigg

LONG CAUSEWAY

Beck Crooks Bridge

Ford

Leading Stead Bottom

Broadshaw Bottom

Mirk Fell Side

Mirk Fell End

Annaside Rigg

Annaside Beck

Ford

Foster Well (spring)

White Springs

Mirk Fell

DL11

Scollit Side

Annaside

Leading Stead

Mirk Fell Edge

William Gill Houses

Annaside Head

Arkengarthdale Moor

Roe Beck

Stonesdale Moor

Ford

West Moor

Swanasit

William Gill Colliery (dis)

Lad Gill Head

Roe Beck Head

Routh

Standard Man

East Gill Head

Water Crag

Punchard Coal Level Mine (dis)

Little Water Crag

Wham Bottom

Punchard Moor

Waterfall

Long Rigg

Little Punchard Head

High Moor

Rogan's Seat

Blakethwaite

East Gill

Hall Moor

Blakethwaite Lead Mines (dis)

Gunnerside Moor

Little Punchard Gill Head Moss

East Stonesdale

Blakethwaite Moss

Friarfold Moss

Waterfall

90   A   91   B   92   C   93   D   94   E   95   F

Scale: 1¾ inches to 1 mile
0 ¼ ½ mile
0 250m 500m 750m 1 km

18

A B C D E F

Bow Hills Head
Bleakhow Moss
Spanham Scar
Waterfall
Bow Hills
Bow Hills Moss
Tom Bog Rigg
High Seavy Rigg
Middle Bent
Scargill High Moor
Scargill Mine (dis)
8
09
Tarnhow Hill
White Crag Moss
White Crag
White Crag
Robin Dub (spring)
Jinglepot Hole
Long Rigg
White Crag End
7
Faggergill Moss
08
Dale Head Common
Elsey Crag
Doorgill Head
Mud Beck
West Moor
Faggergill Scar
Hoove Tarn
Cleasby Hill
6
Peat Moor
Shivery Scar
Hurrgill Head
Stang
Faggergill Moor
Hurrgill Rigg
Faggergill Lead Mine (dis)
Hoove
07
Ravens Park
DL11
5
New Bridge
Dale Head
Peat Moor Rigg
Hart Holes
Arndale Head
Smithson Holes Green
Hill Top Farm
Shaw Side
Gale Head Moor
STANG TOP
06
High Faggergill
The Rigg
Park Head
Stang Side
Roe Beck Bridge
Shepherd's Lodge
4
Seal Houses Moor
Punchard Gate House
Routh Top
Low Faggergill
Shaw Farm
Dry Gill Bottom
Kitley Hill House
05
Punchard House
Punchard Gill Bridge
Dry Gill Edge
Alcock Hush Mine (dis)
Seal Houses
Low Moor
Peat Moor Hill
Routh Level Mine (dis)
Tongue End
Whaw Bridge
3
Whaw
Float Lead Shafts (dis)
Ford
Whaw Gill Bridge
Wood House
STANG LANE
Windegg Ings
Little Punchard Gill
Stone's Lead Level Mine (dis)
Arkengarthdale
High Eskeleth Farm
Whaw Gill
04
Waterfall
Hill Side
Windegg Scar
Danby Lead Level Mine (dis)
Whaw Moor
Eskeleth Bridge
Stang Bridge
Low Moor
2
Whaw Edge
Scar House
Crag End
Peat Moor Green
Rowantree Head
Low Rake
West House
North Rake Hush
Hotel
03
Arkengarthdale CE Prim Sch
Flincher Bottom Moss
Moulds Top
Langthwaite Scar
Great Pinseat
Langthwaite
Booze Moor
BOULDERSHAW LANE
High Green
1
Forefield Rake
Wetshaw Head
Surrender Ground
Ford
Booze
Sewage Works
Whetshaw Bottom
Turf Moor Hush
02

96 A 97 B 98 C 99 D 00 E 01 F

37
18

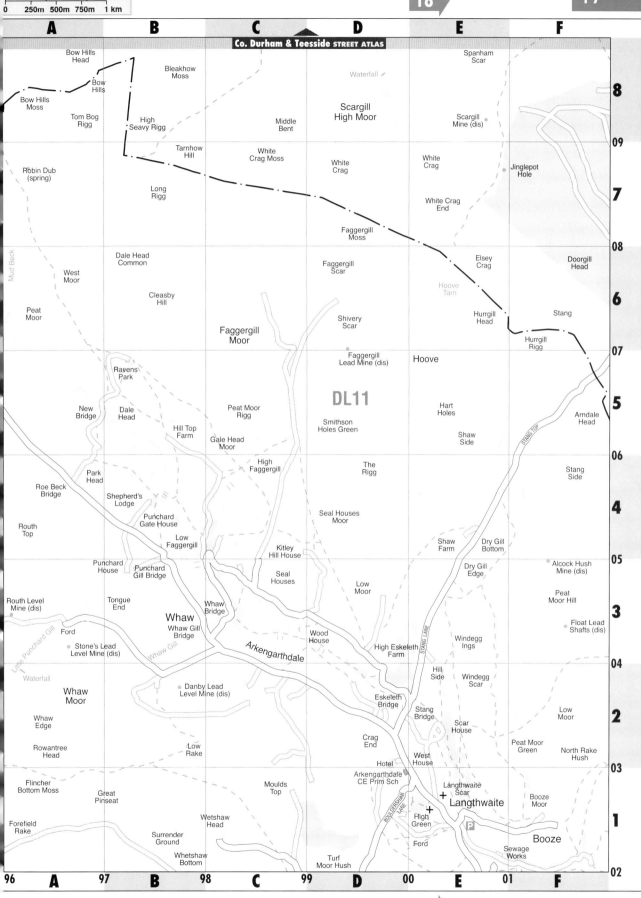

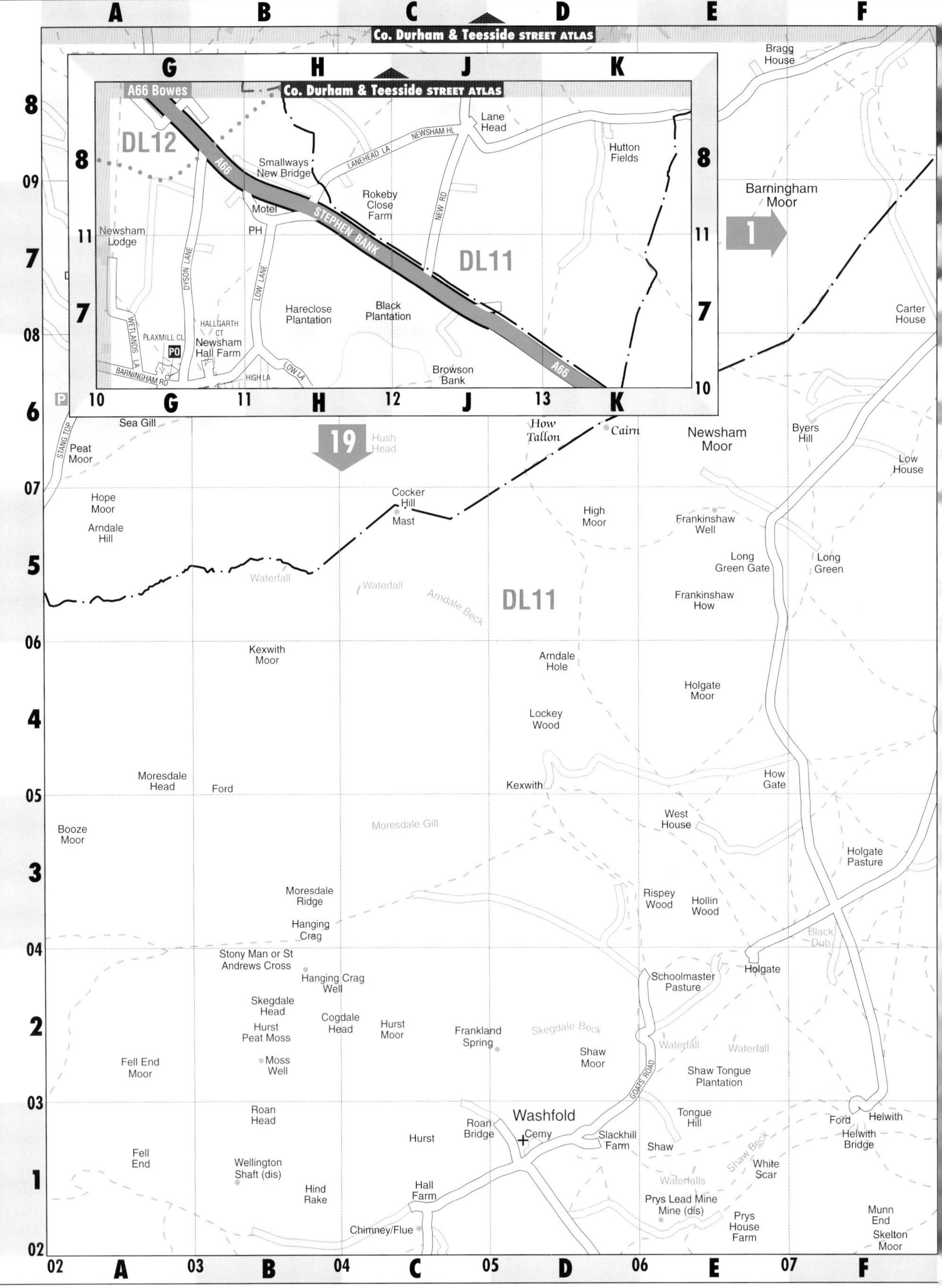

A B C D E F

G H J K

Co. Durham & Teesside STREET ATLAS

A66 Bowes

DL12

Smallways
New Bridge

Newsham
Lodge

Motel

PH

Rokeby
Close
Farm

STEPHEN BANK

NEWSHAM HL

LANEHEAD LA

Lane
Head

Hutton
Fields

Barningham
Moor

DL11

Carter
House

DYSON LANE

LOW LANE

Hareclose
Plantation

Black
Plantation

Newsham
Hall Farm

HALLGARTH
CT

PLAXMILL CL

WETLANDS LA

BARNINGHAM RD

PO

Browson
Bank

A66

Sea Gill

Peat
Moor

STANG TOP

P

Hush
Head

How
Tallon

Cairn

Newsham
Moor

Byers
Hill

Low
House

Hope
Moor

Arndale
Hill

Cocker
Hill

Mast

High
Moor

Frankinshaw
Well

Long
Green Gate

Long
Green

Bragg
House

Waterfall

Waterfall

Arndale Beck

DL11

Frankinshaw
How

Kexwith
Moor

Arndale
Hole

Holgate
Moor

Lockey
Wood

How
Gate

Moresdale
Head

Ford

Kexwith

West
House

Holgate
Pasture

Booze
Moor

Moresdale Gill

Black
Dub

Moresdale
Ridge

Hanging
Crag

Rispey
Wood

Hollin
Wood

Holgate

Stony Man or St
Andrews Cross

Hanging Crag
Well

Schoolmaster
Pasture

Skegdale
Head

Cogdale
Head

Hurst
Moor

Frankland
Spring

Skegdale Beck

Shaw
Moor

Waterfall

Waterfall

Hurst
Peat Moss

Moss
Well

Shaw Tongue
Plantation

Fell End
Moor

GOATS ROAD

Roan
Head

Roan
Bridge

Washfold

Cemy

Slackhill
Farm

Tongue
Hill

Shaw

Ford

Helwith

Helwith
Bridge

Fell
End

Hurst

White
Scar

Wellington
Shaft (dis)

Hind
Rake

Hall
Farm

Waterfalls

Shaw Beck

Chimney/Flue

Prys Lead Mine
Mine (dis)

Prys
House
Farm

Munn
End

Skelton
Moor

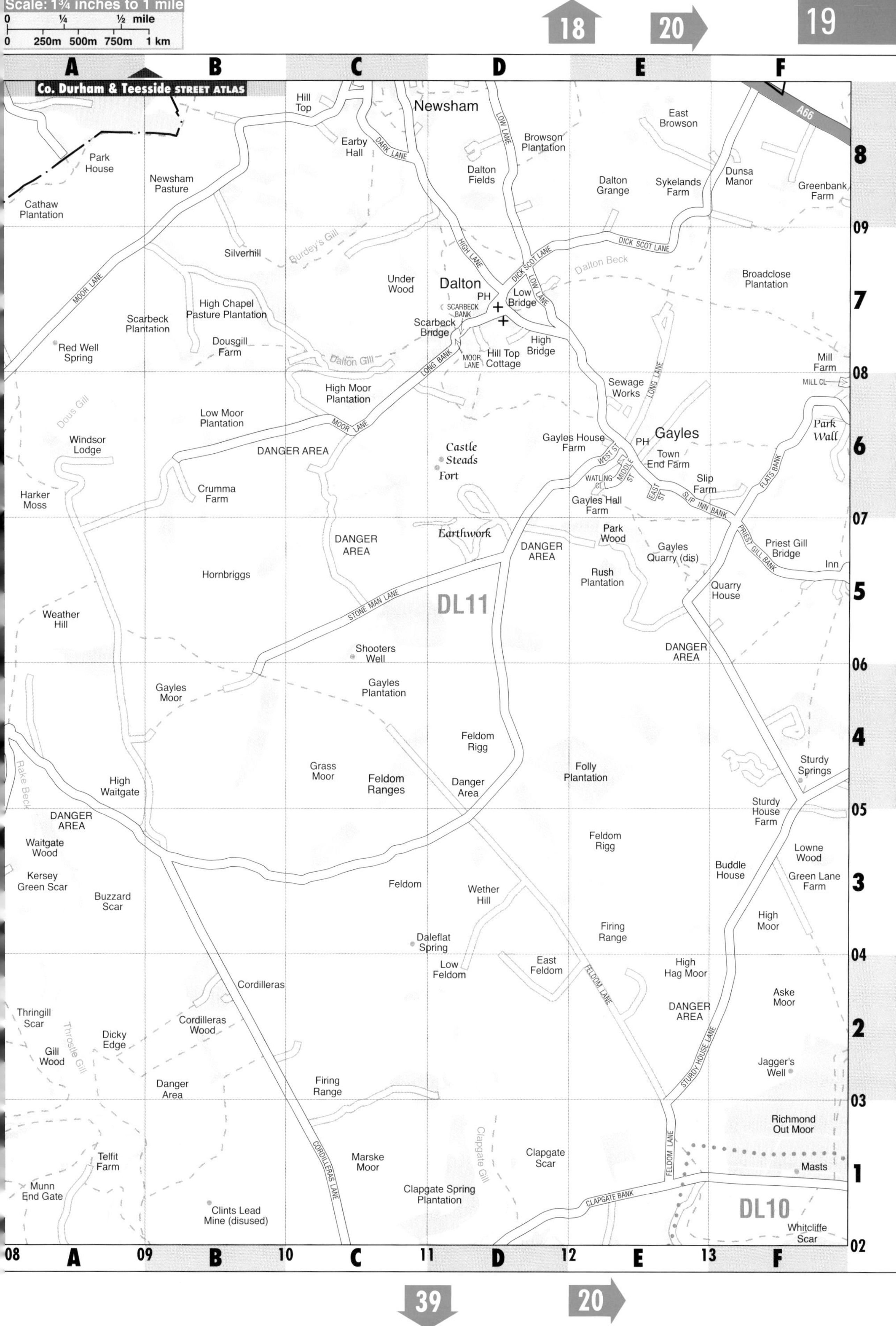
Co. Durham & Teesside STREET ATLAS
Hill Top
Newsham
Earby Hall
DARK LANE
LOW LANE
Browson Plantation
East Browson
A66
Park House
Newsham Pasture
Dalton Fields
Dalton Grange
Sykelands Farm
Dunsa Manor
Greenbank Farm
Cathaw Plantation
Burdey's Gill
Silverhill
HIGH LANE
DICK SCOT LANE
Dalton Beck
Broadclose Plantation
MOOR LANE
Under Wood
Dalton
PH
Low Bridge
SCARBECK BANK
Scarbeck Bridge
High Chapel Pasture Plantation
Scarbeck Plantation
Dousgill Farm
Red Well Spring
Dalton Gill
LONG BANK
MOOR LANE
Hill Top Cottage
High Bridge
Mill Farm
MILL CL
Dous Gill
High Moor Plantation
Sewage Works
LONG LANE
Low Moor Plantation
Windsor Lodge
DANGER AREA
Castle Steads Fort
Gayles House Farm
Gayles
Town End Farm
Park Wall
FLATS BANK
WEST ST
MIDDLE ST
WATLING CL
EAST ST
Slip Farm
SLIP INN BANK
Harker Moss
Crumma Farm
Gayles Hall Farm
Earthwork
Park Wood
Gayles Quarry (dis)
PRIEST GILL BANK
Priest Gill Bridge
Inn
Hornbriggs
Rush Plantation
Quarry House
Weather Hill
STONE MAN LANE
DL11
Shooters Well
Gayles Moor
Gayles Plantation
Feldom Rigg
Sturdy Springs
Rake Beck
Grass Moor
Feldom Ranges
Danger Area
Folly Plantation
High Waitgate
Sturdy House Farm
Waitgate Wood
Lowne Wood
Kersey Green Scar
Buddle House
Green Lane Farm
Buzzard Scar
Feldom
Wether Hill
High Moor
Daleflat Spring
Firing Range
Low Feldom
East Feldom
High Hag Moor
FELDOM LANE
Cordilleras
Aske Moor
Thringill Scar
Cordilleras Wood
Dicky Edge
Throstle Gill
Gill Wood
Jagger's Well
STURDY HOUSE LANE
Danger Area
Richmond Out Moor
CORDILLERAS LANE
Clapgate Gill
Telfit Farm
Marske Moor
Clapgate Scar
FELDOM LANE
Masts
Munn End Gate
Clapgate Spring Plantation
CLAPGATE BANK
DL10
Clints Lead Mine (disused)
Whitcliffe Scar
A B C D E F
08 09 10 11 12 13
8 7 6 5 4 3 2 1
09 08 07 06 05 04 03 02

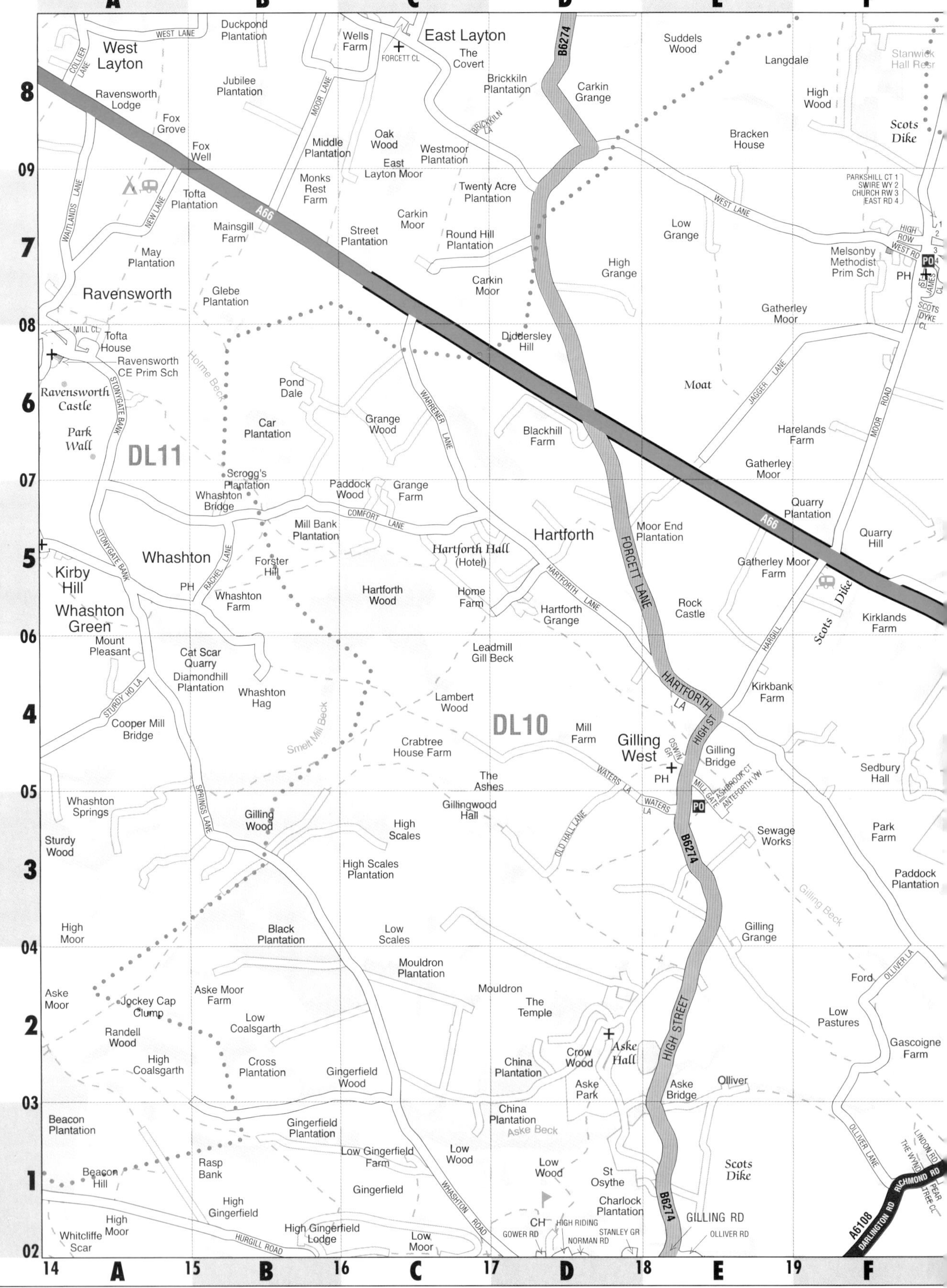

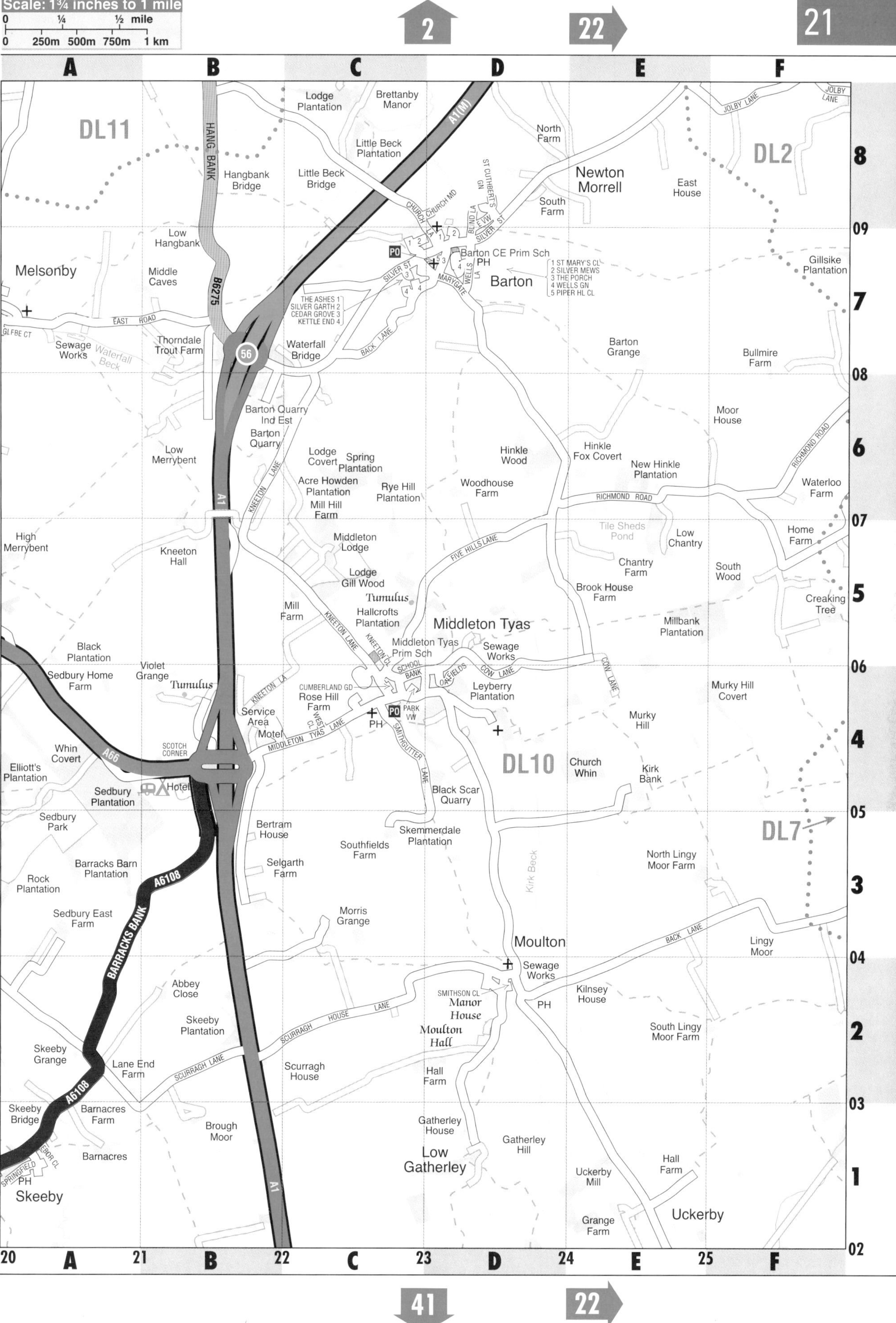

21
3

C8
1 LEWIS CL
2 CARROLL PL
3 RECTORY LA
4 THE MILL RACE

D8
1 LINDEN DRIVE
2 BAXBY TERRACE
3 BELGRAVE TERR
4 CEDAR MEWS
5 GRANGE AVE
6 FOX CL

7 WOODLANDS WAY
8 AVON ROAD
9 ASHVILLE DRIVE

Jolby Farm
Croft Grange
Monk End
Croft Prim Sch
South PD
Hurworth Comp Sch
Sewage Works
Newbus Grange
Crow Wood
Crow Wood
Castle Wood
Clervaux Castle
Sweet Well Wood
Old Spa Farm
Cemy
Croft-on-Tees
Low Hail Farm
Eryholme Wood
Dobbs Hall Farm
West Wood
Pheasant Covert
New Spa
Tees Bridge
High Rockliffe
Eryholme Scar
Paradise Farm
Little Stranbrough Plantation
Canny Well Wood
Richmond Road
River Tees
Low Rockliffe
Rockliffe Scar
Brickyard Farm
Eryholme Lane
Black Wood
Stand Alone
Bay Horse Farm
Dalton Wood
Bullmire Whin
Willow Garth
Stranbrough Plantation
DL2
RUSKIN CL 1
BYRON CT 2
ORCHARD CL 3
Moat
PH
Dalton-on-Tees
Holmes Plantation
Burn Sike
Pepperfield Farm
Burn Sike Bridge
Tewit Castle
Westfields
Lodge Farm
Wilson Hill Plantation
Walmire Plantations
West Vince Moor
Vince Moor
Dalton Bridge
West Lane
Northallerton Road
Rear Wood
Thorntree House
Halnaby Hall
Croft Motor Racing Circuit
White House
Steadfield House Farm
Birch Carr
Moorhouse Farm
Cowper House Farm
A167
DL10
Birch Springs
Portobello
Bagley Farm
B1263
Haswell Grange
Forty Acre Wood
Barf House
Cowton Moor
Cowton Fields Farm
Halnaby Grange
Dalton Gates Farm
Paddock Farm Water Gardens
Markstone House
Dalton Gates
DL6
Cowton Grange
Moulton Lane
Cockleberry Farm
Bowlturner House
Tender Heads Plantations
Back Lane
Holywell Lane
Cramble Cross
North Cowton
Corn Hill
Raby Lane
West View Farm
North & South Cowton Prim Sch
HILL TOP CT
Lancaster Rd
SILVER HL
Springfield Farm
Cemy
Raby Cottages
Station Farm
Uckerby Fox Covert
HOLYWELL LA
GREEN LANE
ST IVES CL
PH
ANVIL WAY
BLACKSMITH CT
Redmire Hall Farm
Black Wood
Temple House Farm
ST MARY'S CL
East Cowton
CONYERS RD
PO
White Head Farm
Cross Rein Farm
Manor House
Sewage Works
DL7
PH
GOLDEN ACRES
DAKYN CL
BOYNTON RD
WYCLIFFE RD
Bungalow Farm
Howl Beck
High Greenbury
East Cowton CE Prim Sch
Green Lane Farm
DL10
Westfield House
PH
Atley Fields
Church Farm
Castle Hill
Manor House
Thistle Wood
Sewage Works
Greenbury Grange
Scorton Road Farm
B1263
Atley Hill
Cowton Castle
Old Hall Farm

21
42

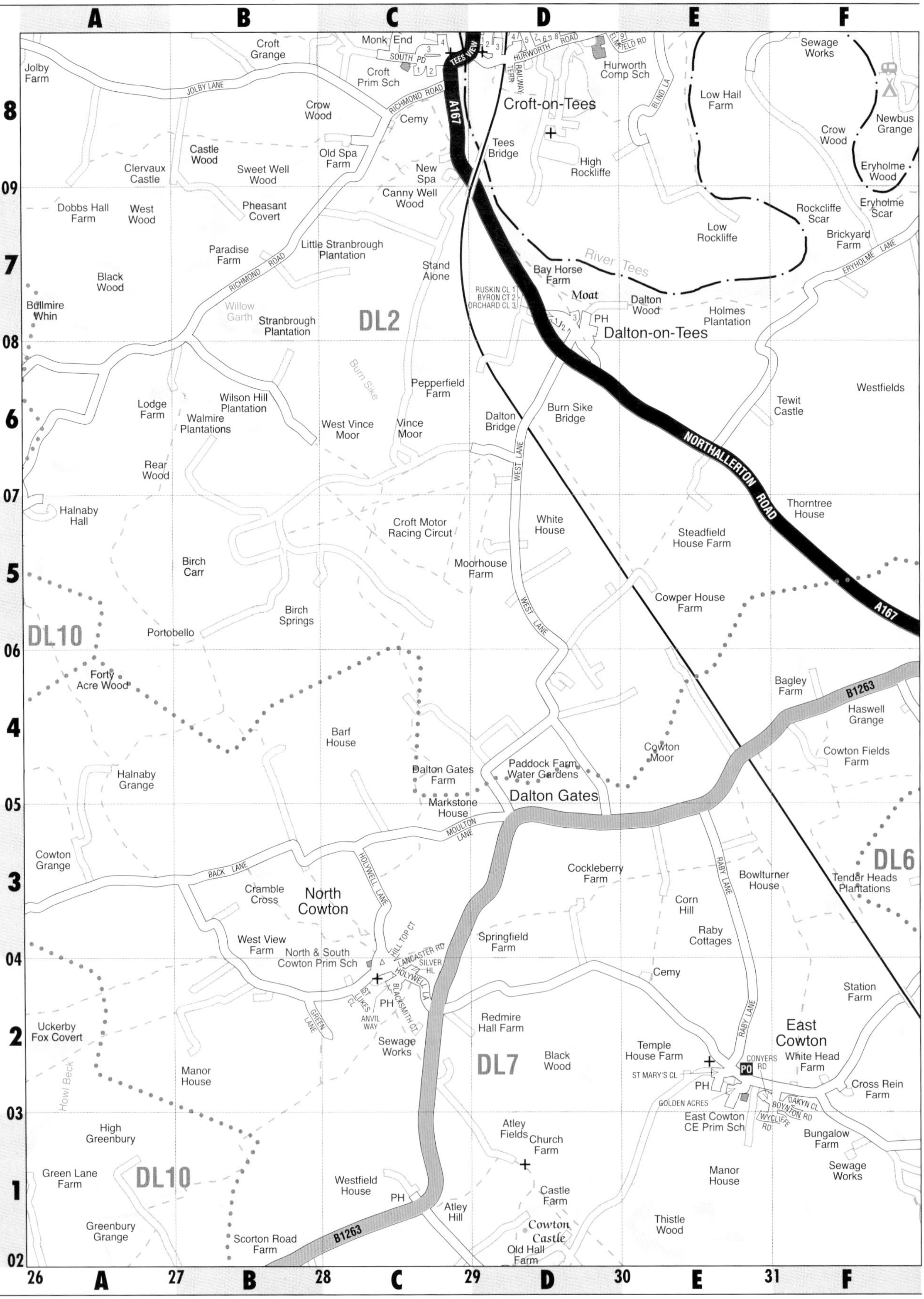

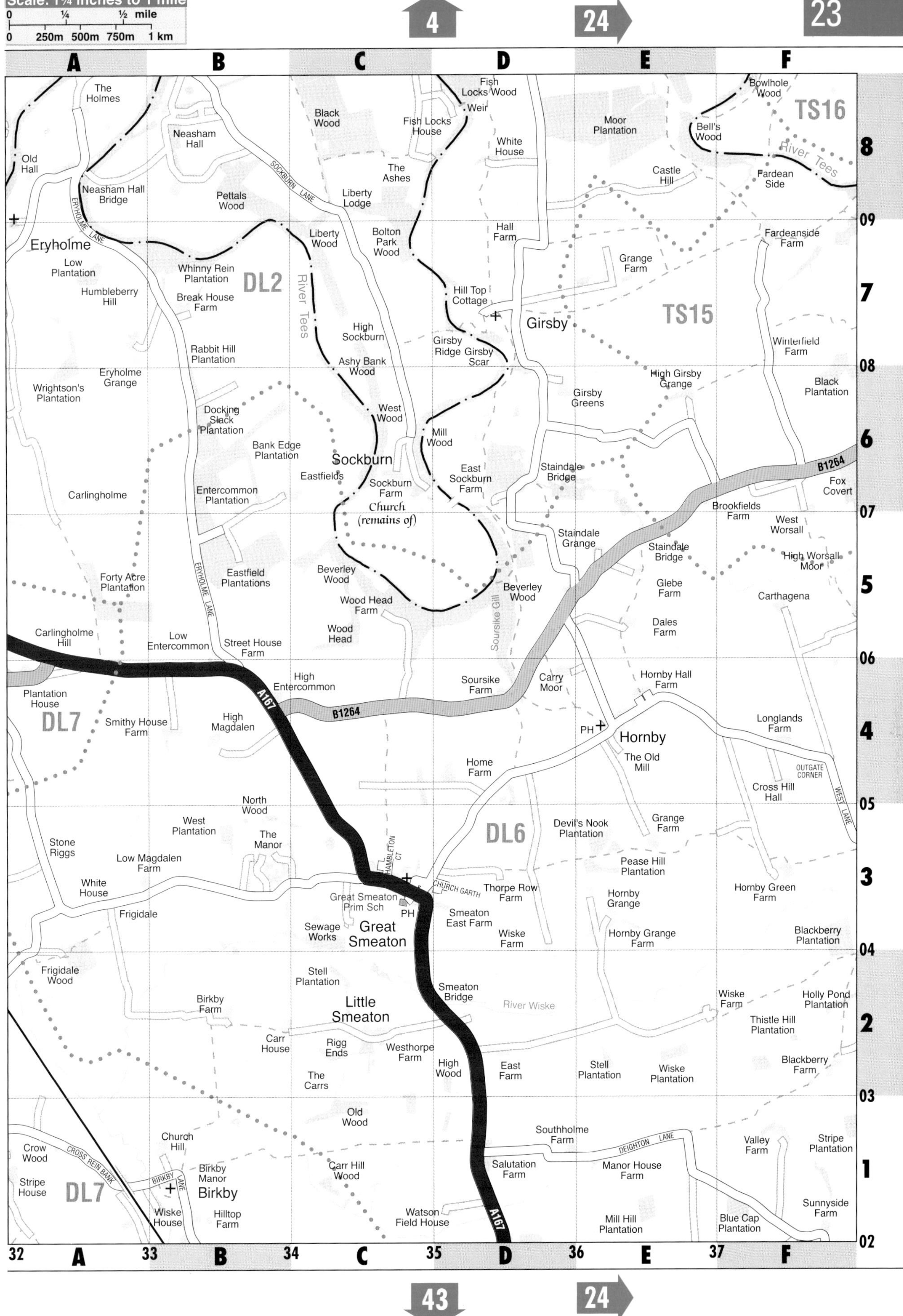

Scale: 1¾ inches to 1 mile
0
¼
½ mile
0
250m 500m 750m 1 km
4
24
A
B
C
D
E
F
The Holmes
Neasham Hall
Black Wood
Fish Locks Wood
Weir
Fish Locks House
White House
Moor Plantation
Bowlhole Wood
TS16
Bell's Wood
River Tees
Old Hall
Sockburn Lane
The Ashes
Castle Hill
Fardean Side
Neasham Hall Bridge
Pettals Wood
Liberty Lodge
Eryholme Lane
Eryholme
Liberty Wood
Bolton Park Wood
Hall Farm
Fardeanside Farm
Low Plantation
Whinny Rein Plantation
DL2
River Tees
Grange Farm
Humbleberry Hill
Break House Farm
Hill Top Cottage
Girsby
TS15
High Sockburn
Girsby Ridge
Girsby Scar
Winterfield Farm
Rabbit Hill Plantation
Ashy Bank Wood
Eryholme Grange
High Girsby Grange
Black Plantation
Wrightson's Plantation
Docking Slack Plantation
West Wood
Girsby Greens
Mill Wood
Bank Edge Plantation
Sockburn
Staindale Bridge
B1264
Eastfields
East Sockburn Farm
Carlingholme
Entercommon Plantation
Sockburn Farm
Church (remains of)
Fox Covert
Brookfields Farm
West Worsall
Staindale Grange
Staindale Bridge
High Worsall Moor
Eastfield Plantations
Beverley Wood
Forty Acre Plantation
Beverley Wood
Glebe Farm
Carthagena
Wood Head Farm
Soursike Gill
Dales Farm
Carlingholme Hill
Low Entercommon
Street House Farm
Wood Head
Plantation House
High Entercommon
Soursike Farm
Carry Moor
Hornby Hall Farm
DL7
Smithy House Farm
A167
High Magdalen
B1264
PH
Hornby
Longlands Farm
The Old Mill
Home Farm
Outgate Corner
Cross Hill Hall
West Lane
North Wood
West Plantation
The Manor
DL6
Devil's Nook Plantation
Grange Farm
Stone Riggs
Low Magdalen Farm
Hambleton Ct
Pease Hill Plantation
White House
Church Garth
Thorpe Row Farm
Hornby Grange
Hornby Green Farm
Frigidale
Great Smeaton Prim Sch
PH
Smeaton East Farm
Sewage Works
Great Smeaton
Wiske Farm
Hornby Grange Farm
Blackberry Plantation
Frigidale Wood
Stell Plantation
Smeaton Bridge
Little Smeaton
Wiske Farm
Holly Pond Plantation
Birkby Farm
River Wiske
Thistle Hill Plantation
Carr House
Rigg Ends
Westhorpe Farm
High Wood
East Farm
Stell Plantation
Wiske Plantation
Blackberry Farm
The Carrs
Old Wood
Southholme Farm
Church Hill
Deighton Lane
Valley Farm
Stripe Plantation
Crow Wood
Cross Rein Bank
Birkby Manor
Carr Hill Wood
Salutation Farm
Manor House Farm
Stripe House
DL7
Birkby Lane
Birkby
Wiske House
Hilltop Farm
Watson Field House
A167
Mill Hill Plantation
Blue Cap Plantation
Sunnyside Farm
8
09
7
08
6
07
5
06
4
05
3
04
2
03
1
02
32
33
34
35
36
37
43
24

E8
1 ASH GR
2 BIRCH CL
3 BRAESIDE
4 GROVE BANK
5 KNOWLES CL
6 WESTLANDS
7 HALL MOOR CL
8 THE GREEN
9 STRATHMORE DR
10 MOOR CL
11 ST MARTINS WY
12 MANOR GARTH

F8
1 JASMINE FIELDS
2 TOWN END CL
3 LEVINGTON CT
4 LEVINGTON MS
5 PENDERS CL

Scale: 1¾ inches to 1 mile
0   ¼   ½ mile
0 250m 500m 750m 1 km

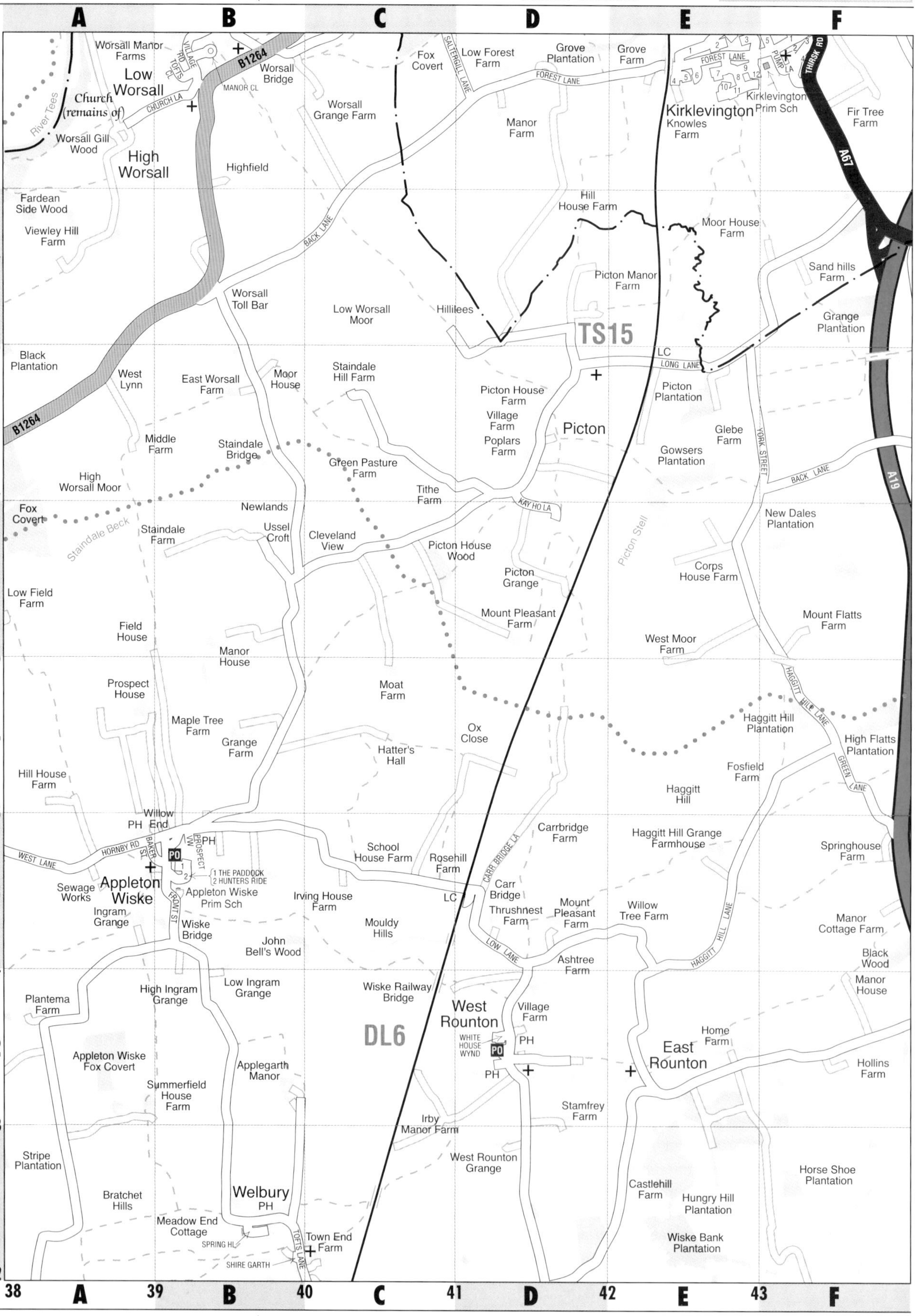

Grid columns: A B C D E F (top), A B C D E F (bottom)
Grid rows: 8, 09, 7, 08, 6, 07, 5, 06, 4, 05, 3, 04, 2, 03, 1, 02
Bottom easting: 38 39 40 41 42 43

Place labels (reading across the map):

Worsall Manor Farms · Low Worsall · Worsall Bridge · B1264 · MANOR CL · Fox Covert · Low Forest Farm · Grove Plantation · Grove Farm · FOREST LANE · Kirklevington · FOREST LANE · Kirklevington Prim Sch · THIRSK RD · Fir Tree Farm · A67

River Tees · Church (remains of) · Worsall Gill Wood · High Worsall · CHURCH LA · VILLAGE TOFTS · Highfield · Worsall Grange Farm · Manor Farm · Knowles · PUMP LA

Fardean Side Wood · Viewley Hill Farm · BACK LANE · Hill House Farm · Moor House Farm · Sand hills Farm

Worsall Toll Bar · Low Worsall Moor · Hillilees · Picton Manor Farm · TS15 · Grange Plantation

Black Plantation · West Lynn · East Worsall Farm · Moor House · Staindale Hill Farm · Picton House Farm · Village Farm · Poplars Farm · Picton · LC · LONG LANE · Picton Plantation · Glebe Farm · YORK STREET

B1264 · Middle Farm · Staindale Bridge · Green Pasture Farm · Gowsers Plantation · BACK LANE

High Worsall Moor · Newlands · Tithe Farm · KAY HO LA · Picton Stell · New Dales Plantation

Fox Covert · Staindale Beck · Staindale Farm · Ussel Croft · Cleveland View · Picton House Wood · Picton Grange · Corps House Farm · Mount Flatts Farm

Low Field Farm · Field House · Mount Pleasant Farm · West Moor Farm · Mount Flatts Farm

Manor House · Moat Farm · HAGGITT HILL LANE

Prospect House · Maple Tree Farm · Grange Farm · Hatter's Hall · Ox Close · Haggitt Hill Plantation · High Flatts Plantation · GREEN LANE

Hill House Farm · Fosfield Farm · Haggitt Hill

Willow End · PH · HORNBY RD · BAKER ST · PROSPECT VW · PH · PO · Carrbridge Farm · Haggitt Hill Grange Farmhouse · Springhouse Farm

WEST LANE · 1 THE PADDOCK · 2 HUNTERS RIDE · School House Farm · Rosehill Farm · CARR BRIDGE LA · Carr Bridge · Mount Pleasant Farm · Willow Tree Farm · Manor Cottage Farm

Sewage Works · Appleton Wiske · Appleton Wiske Prim Sch · Irving House Farm · LC · Threshnest · Ashtree Farm · HAGGITT HILL LANE · Black Wood

Ingram Grange · FRONT ST · Wiske Bridge · John Bell's Wood · Mouldy Hills · LOW LANE · Manor House

Plantema Farm · High Ingram Grange · Low Ingram Grange · Wiske Railway Bridge · West Rounton · Village Farm · East Rounton · Home Farm · Hollins Farm

Appleton Wiske Fox Covert · Summerfield House Farm · Applegarth Manor · WHITE HOUSE WYND · PO · PH · DL6 · Stamfrey Farm

Stripe Plantation · Bratchet Hills · Welbury · PH · Meadow End Cottage · SPRING HL · TOFTS LANE · Town End Farm · Irby Manor Farm · West Rounton Grange · Castlehill Farm · Hungry Hill Plantation · Horse Shoe Plantation · SHIRE GARTH · Wiske Bank Plantation

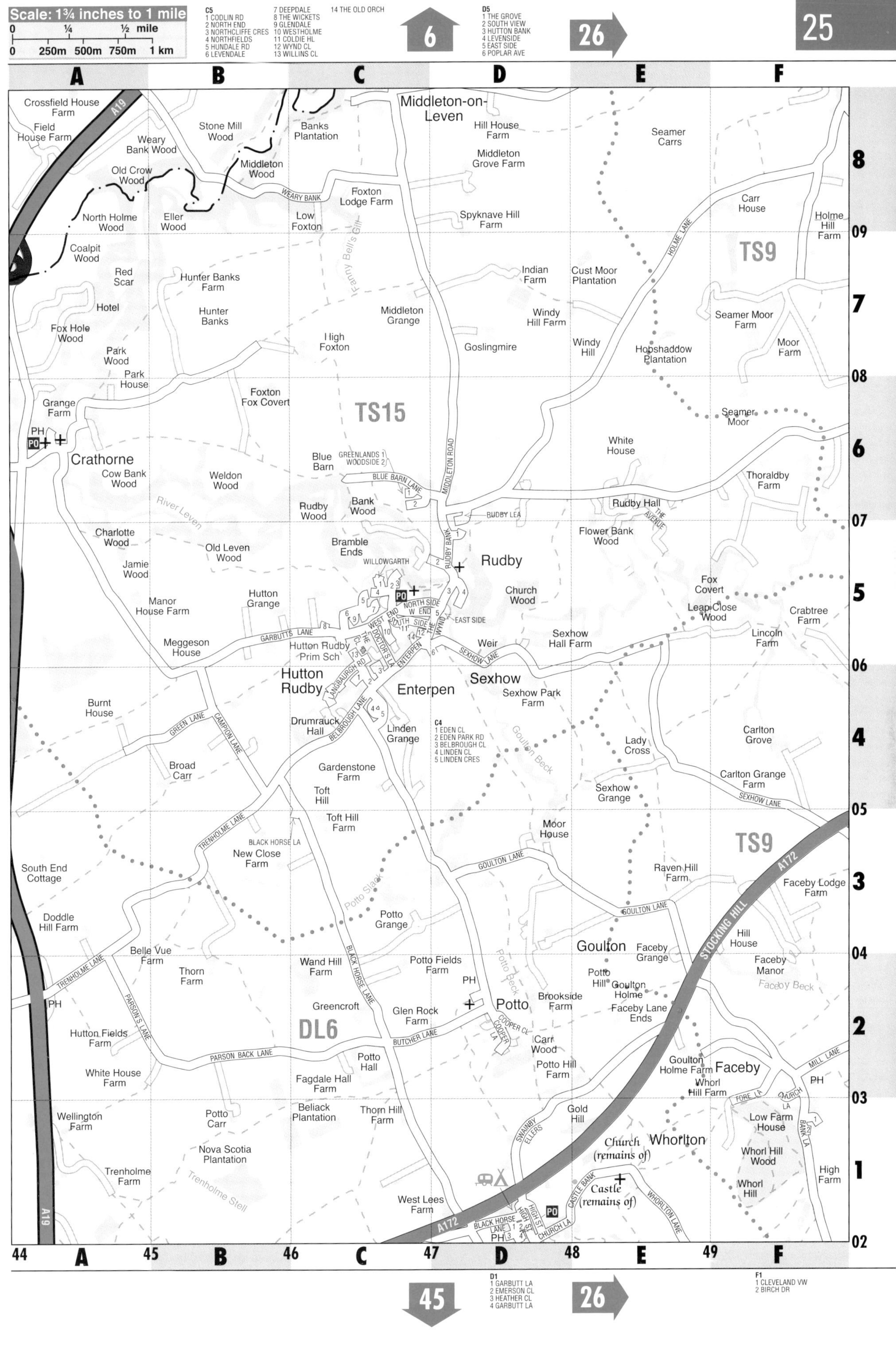

Scale: 1¾ inches to 1 mile
0 ¼ ½ mile
0 250m 500m 750m 1 km
C5
1 CODLIN RD
2 NORTH END
3 NORTHCLIFFE CRES
4 NORTHFIELDS
5 HUNDALE RD
6 LEVENDALE
7 DEEPDALE
8 THE WICKETS
9 GLENDALE
10 WESTHOLME
11 COLDIE HL
12 WYND CL
13 WILLINS CL
14 THE OLD ORCH
6
D5
1 THE GROVE
2 SOUTH VIEW
3 HUTTON BANK
4 LEVENSIDE
5 EAST SIDE
6 POPLAR AVE
26
25
A
B
C
D
E
F
Crossfield House Farm
Field House Farm
A19
Weary Bank Wood
Stone Mill Wood
Banks Plantation
Middleton-on-Leven
Hill House Farm
Seamer Carrs
Old Crow Wood
Middleton Wood
Middleton Grove Farm
8
WEARY BANK
Foxton Lodge Farm
Carr House
North Holme Wood
Eller Wood
Low Foxton
Spyknave Hill Farm
Holme Hill Farm
09
Coalpit Wood
Fanny Bell's Gill
HOLME LANE
TS9
Red Scar
Hunter Banks Farm
Indian Farm
Cust Moor Plantation
Hotel
Hunter Banks
Middleton Grange
Windy Hill Farm
Seamer Moor Farm
7
Fox Hole Wood
High Foxton
Goslingmire
Windy Hill
Hobshaddow Plantation
Moor Farm
Park Wood
Park House
08
Grange Farm
Foxton Fox Covert
TS15
Seamer Moor
PH
PO
Crathorne
Blue Barn
GREENLANDS 1
WOODSIDE 2
MIDDLETON ROAD
White House
6
Cow Bank Wood
Weldon Wood
BLUE BARN LANE
Thoraldby Farm
River Leven
Rudby Wood
Bank Wood
RUDBY LEA
Rudby Hall
THE AVENUE
07
Charlotte Wood
Old Leven Wood
Bramble Ends
Flower Bank Wood
Jamie Wood
WILLOWGARTH
RUDBY BANK
Rudby
Fox Covert
5
Manor House Farm
Hutton Grange
PO
NORTH SIDE
W END
Church Wood
Leap Close Wood
Crabtree Farm
WEST END
SOUTH SIDE
EAST SIDE
THE WYND
Meggeson House
GARBUTTS LANE
THE CL
DOCTOR'S LA
Weir
Sexhow Hall Farm
Lincoln Farm
Hutton Rudby Prim Sch
ENTERPEN
SEXHOW LANE
06
Hutton Rudby
LANGBAURGH RD
Enterpen
Sexhow
Sexhow Park Farm
Burnt House
BELBROUGH LANE
Drumrauck Hall
Linden Grange
C4
1 EDEN CL
2 EDEN PARK RD
3 BELBROUGH CL
4 LINDEN CL
5 LINDEN CRES
Goulton Beck
Carlton Grove
GREEN LANE
CAMPION LANE
Lady Cross
4
Broad Carr
Gardenstone Farm
Carlton Grange Farm
Toft Hill
Sexhow Grange
SEXHOW LANE
05
Toft Hill Farm
TRENHOLME LANE
Moor House
BLACK HORSE LA
TS9
New Close Farm
South End Cottage
GOULTON LANE
Raven Hill Farm
A172
Potto Slack
Faceby Lodge Farm
3
Doddle Hill Farm
GOULTON LANE
Potto Grange
STOCKING HILL
Hill House
Belle Vue Farm
Goulton
Faceby Grange
04
Thorn Farm
Wand Hill Farm
BLACK HORSE LANE
Potto Fields Farm
Faceby Manor
TRENHOLME LANE
Potto Beck
Potto Hill
Goulton Holme
Faceby Beck
PH
PH
Greencroft
Glen Rock Farm
Potto
Brookside Farm
PARSON'S LANE
Faceby Lane Ends
2
Hutton Fields Farm
DL6
COOPER CL
COOPER LA
BUTCHER LANE
Carr Wood
MILL LANE
PARSON BACK LANE
Potto Hall
Goulton Holme Farm
Faceby
White House Farm
Potto Hill Farm
PH
Fagdale Hall Farm
Whorl Hill Farm
FORE LA
CHURCH LA
03
Wellington Farm
Beliack Plantation
Thorn Hill Farm
Gold Hill
Low Farm House
Potto Carr
SWAINBY ELLERS
BANK LA
Church (remains of)
Whorlton
Nova Scotia Plantation
Whorl Hill Wood
1
Trenholme Farm
Trenholme Stell
CASTLE BANK
Castle (remains of)
High Farm
Whorl Hill
West Lees Farm
A19
A172
BLACK HORSE LANE
HIGH ST
PO
WHORLTON LANE
PH
CHURCH LA
02
44
A
45
B
46
C
47
D
48
E
49
F
D1
1 GARBUTT LA
2 EMERSON CL
3 HEATHER CL
4 GARBUTT LA
F1
1 CLEVELAND VW
2 BIRCH DR
45
26

25
7

C8
1 CEDARWOOD AVE
2 BEECHWOOD AVE
3 DALEWOOD WK
4 CHERRYWOOD AVE
5 COPSEWOOD WK
6 ELMWOOD CL
7 PINEWOOD WK
8 MEADOWFIELD
9 QUEENS DR

C7
1 SPRINGFIELD GDNS
2 WESTFIELD RD
3 WEAVERS CT
4 THE GARTH
5 MANOR CL
6 THE STRIPE
7 THREE TUNS WYND
8 ANGEL CT
9 LEVEN WYND
10 BRIDGE RD
11 THE BEECHES
12 LADY HULLOCKS CT
13 ROSE HL DR
14 ST MARYS CL
15 WEST GN

Scale: 1¾ inches to 1 mile
0 ¼ ½ mile
0 250m 500m 750m 1 km

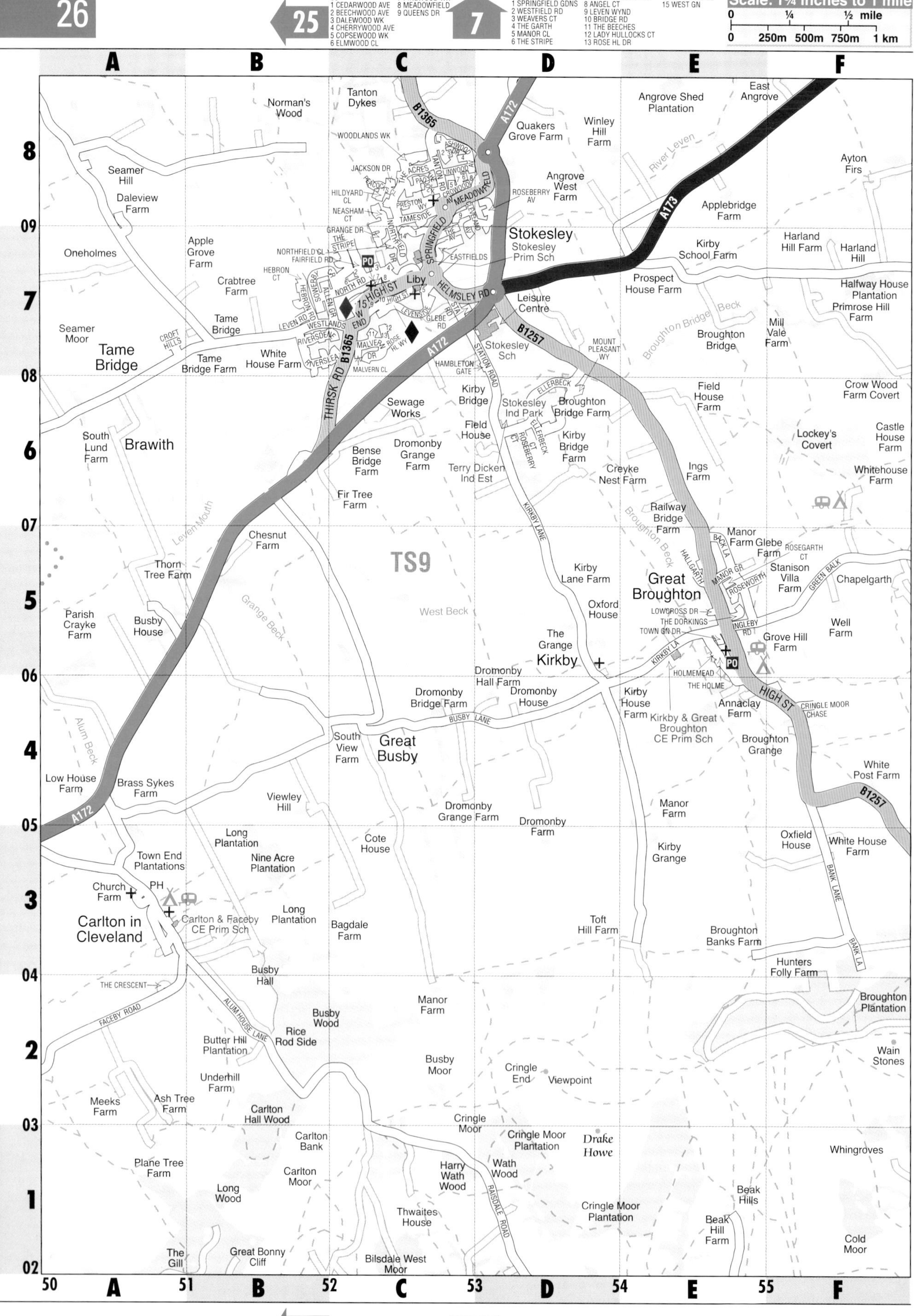

25
46

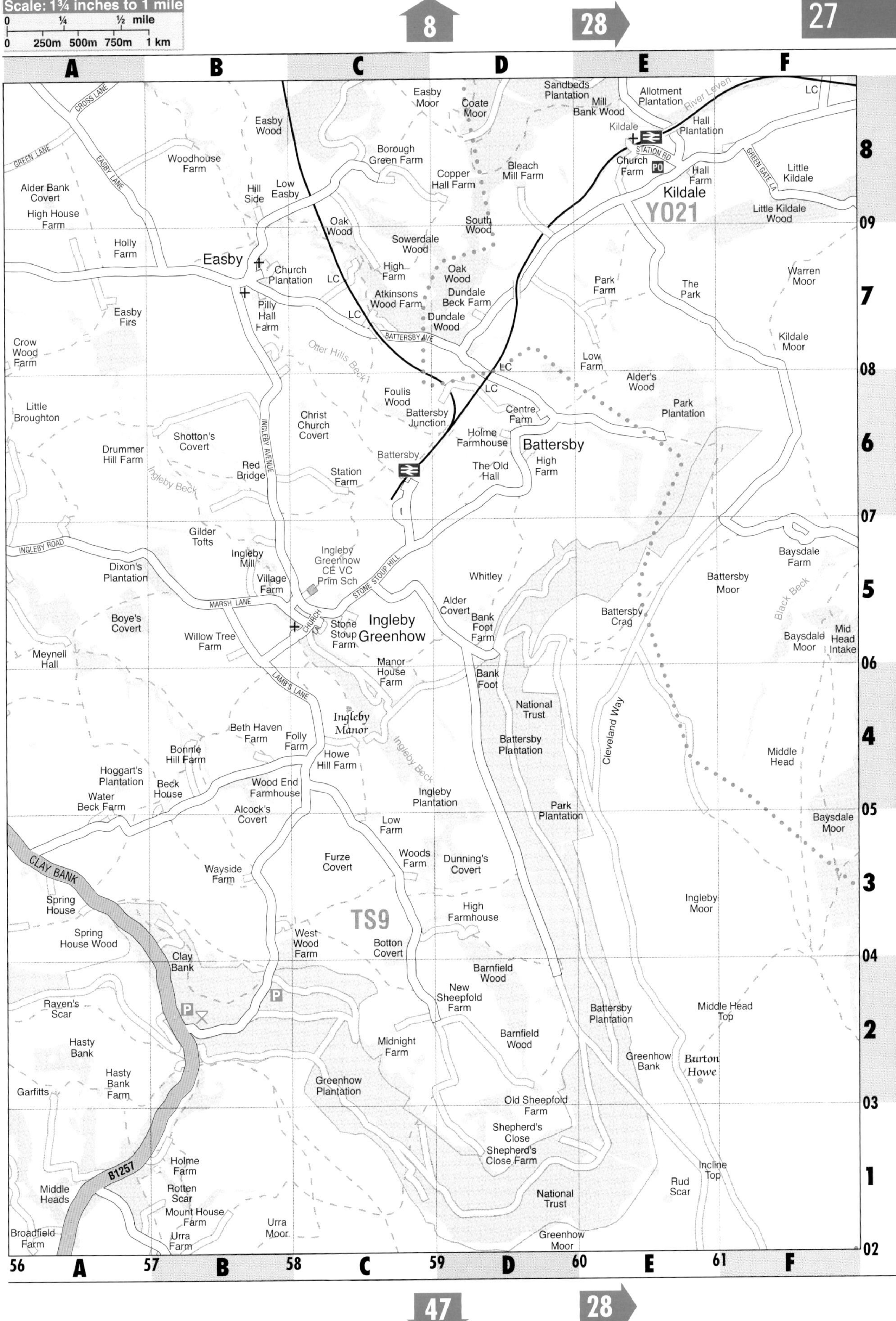
Scale: 1¾ inches to 1 mile
0 ¼ ½ mile
0 250m 500m 750m 1 km
8
28
A B C D E F
Easby Moor
Coate Moor
Sandbeds Plantation
Mill Bank Wood
Allotment Plantation
River Leven
LC
Kildale
Hall Plantation
Easby Wood
Borough Green Farm
Woodhouse Farm
Station Rd
Church Farm
PO
Green Gate La
Little Kildale
Cross Lane
Green Lane
Easby Lane
Alder Bank Covert
High House Farm
Hill Side
Low Easby
Copper Hall Farm
Bleach Mill Farm
Hall Farm
Kildale
YO21
Little Kildale Wood
Holly Farm
Oak Wood
Sowerdale Wood
South Wood
Easby
Church Plantation
High Farm
Oak Wood
Park Farm
The Park
Warren Moor
Easby Firs
Pilly Hall Farm
Atkinsons Wood Farm
Dundale Beck Farm
Dundale Wood
Battersby Ave
Crow Wood Farm
Otter Hills Beck
Low Farm
Kildale Moor
Little Broughton
Foulis Wood
Alder's Wood
Christ Church Covert
Battersby Junction
Centre Farm
Park Plantation
Drummer Hill Farm
Shotton's Covert
Holme Farmhouse
Battersby
Ingleby Avenue
Battersby
Red Bridge
Station Farm
The Old Hall
High Farm
Ingleby Beck
Ingleby Road
Gilder Tofts
Ingleby Greenhow CE VC Prim Sch
Baysdale Farm
Dixon's Plantation
Ingleby Mill
Whitley
Battersby Moor
Village Farm
Stone Stoup Hill
Marsh Lane
Alder Covert
Black Beck
Boye's Covert
Church La
Stone Stoup Farm
Ingleby Greenhow
Bank Foot Farm
Battersby Crag
Mid Head Intake
Willow Tree Farm
Baysdale Moor
Meynell Hall
Manor House Farm
Bank Foot
Lamb's Lane
National Trust
Ingleby Manor
Cleveland Way
Beth Haven Farm
Folly Farm
Battersby Plantation
Middle Head
Bonnie Hill Farm
Howe Hill Farm
Ingleby Beck
Hoggart's Plantation
Beck House
Wood End Farmhouse
Ingleby Plantation
Water Beck Farm
Alcock's Covert
Park Plantation
Baysdale Moor
Low Farm
Clay Bank
Wayside Farm
Furze Covert
Woods Farm
Dunning's Covert
Spring House
Ingleby Moor
High Farmhouse
TS9
Spring House Wood
West Wood Farm
Botton Covert
Clay Bank
Barnfield Wood
New Sheepfold Farm
Raven's Scar
P
Battersby Plantation
Middle Head Top
Hasty Bank
Midnight Farm
Barnfield Wood
Greenhow Bank
Burton Howe
Hasty Bank Farm
Garfitts
Greenhow Plantation
Old Sheepfold Farm
Shepherd's Close
Shepherd's Close Farm
Holme Farm
Incline Top
B1257
Middle Heads
Rotten Scar
Rud Scar
National Trust
Mount House Farm
Broadfield Farm
Urra Farm
Urra Moor
Greenhow Moor
8
09
7
08
6
07
5
06
4
05
3
04
2
03
1
02
56 57 58 59 60 61
47
28

Scale: 1¾ inches to 1 mile

0   ¼   ½ mile
0   250m 500m 750m 1 km

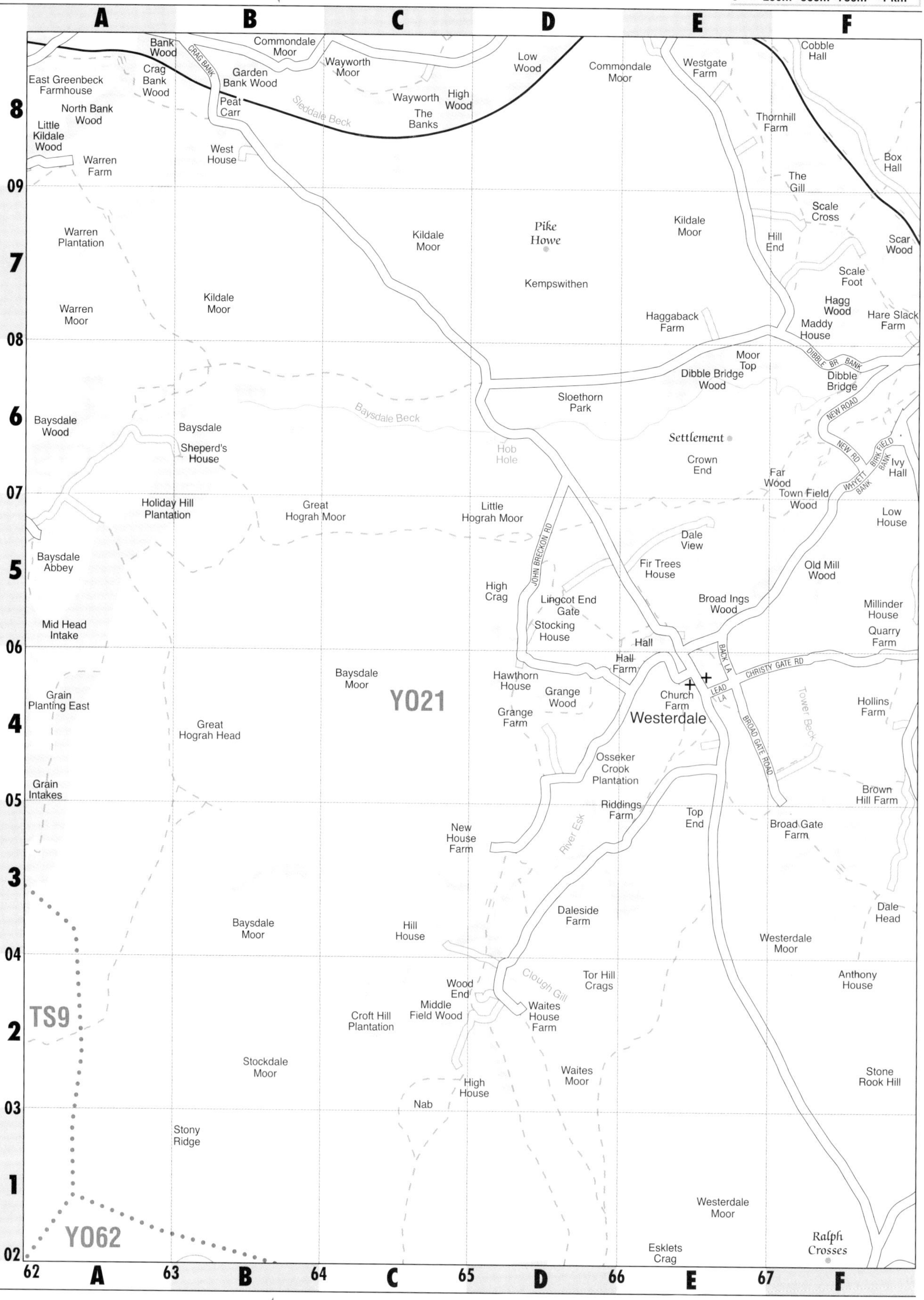

A   B   C   D   E   F

8

East Greenbeck Farmhouse
North Bank Wood
Little Kildale Wood
Warren Farm

Bank Wood
Crag Bank Bank Wood
Garden Bank Wood
Peat Carr
West House

Commondale Moor
Wayworth Moor
Wayworth The Banks
High Wood

Low Wood
Commondale Moor

Westgate Farm
Cobble Hall
Thornhill Farm
Box Hall

CRAG BANK
Sleddale Beck

09

The Gill
Scale Cross
Scar Wood

7

Warren Plantation
Kildale Moor
Pike Howe
Kildale Moor
Hill End
Scale Foot

08

Warren Moor
Kildale Moor
Kempswithen
Haggaback Farm
Moor Top
Dibble Bridge Wood
Hagg Wood
Maddy House
Hare Slack Farm
DIBBLE BR BANK
Dibble Bridge

6

Baysdale Wood
Baysdale
Sheperd's House
Baysdale Beck
Sloethorn Park
Settlement
Crown End
Far Wood
Town Field Wood
NEW ROAD
BIRK FIELD BANK
Ivy Hall

07

Holiday Hill Plantation
Great Hograh Moor
Little Hograh Moor
Hob Hole
Dale View
Old Mill Wood
Low House
NEW RD
WHITT BANK

5

Baysdale Abbey
High Crag
Lingcot End Gate
Fir Trees House
Broad Ings Wood
Millinder House

JOHN BRECKON RD

06

Mid Head Intake
Stocking House
Hall
Quarry Farm
Baysdale Moor
Hall Farm
BACK LA
LEAD LA

4

Grain Planting East
Great Hograh Head
YO21
Hawthorn House
Grange Wood
Church Farm
Westerdale
CHRISTY GATE RD
Hollins Farm
Grange Farm
Tower Beck

05

Grain Intakes
Riddings Farm
Top End
Broad Gate Farm
Brown Hill Farm
New House Farm
Osseker Crook Plantation
River Esk
BROAD GATE ROAD

3

TS9

Daleside Farm
Dale Head

04

Baysdale Moor
Hill House
Tor Hill Crags
Westerdale Moor
Anthony House

2

Croft Hill Plantation
Wood End
Middle Field Wood
Waites House Farm
Clough Gill
Stockdale Moor

03

Stony Ridge
High House
Nab
Waites Moor
Stone Rook Hill

1

Westerdale Moor

02

YO62
Esklets Crag
Ralph Crosses

62 A 63 B 64 C 65 D 66 E 67 F

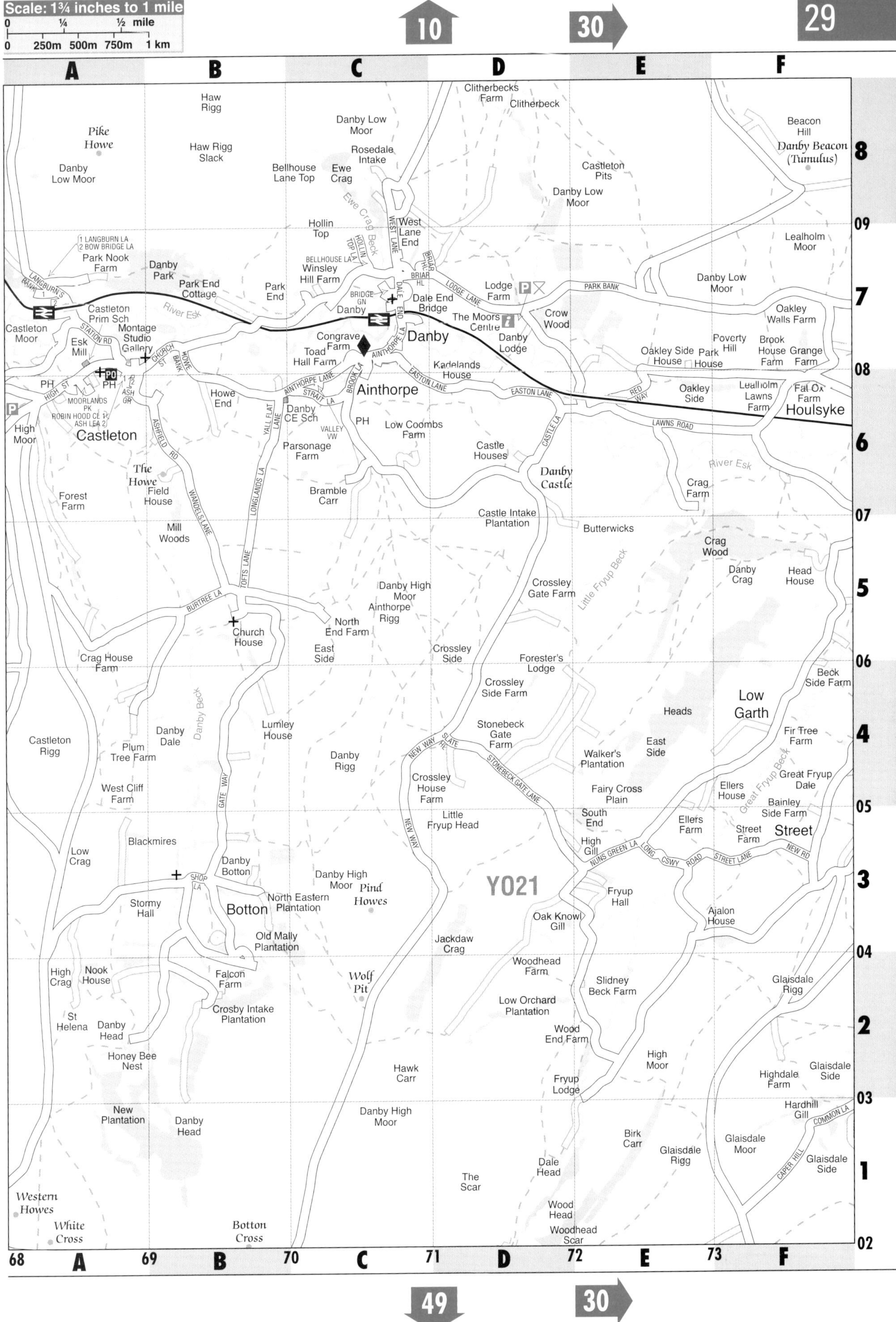
A
B
C
D
E
F
Haw Rigg
Clitherbecks Farm
Clitherbeck
Pike Howe
Danby Low Moor
Haw Rigg Slack
Danby Low Moor
Rosedale Intake
Beacon Hill
Danby Beacon (Tumulus)
Bellhouse Lane Top
Ewe Crag
Castleton Pits
Danby Low Moor
Ewe Crag Beck
Hollin Top
West Lane End
WEST LANE
1 LANGBURN LA
2 BOW BRIDGE LA
Lealholm Moor
Park Nook Farm
Danby Park
BELLHOUSE LA
HOLLIN TOP LA
Winsley Hill Farm
BRIAR HL
LODGE LANE
Danby Low Moor
LANGBURN'S BANK
Park End Cottage
Park End
BRIDGE GN
DALE END
Dale End Bridge
Lodge Farm
PARK BANK
Castleton Prim Sch
River Esk
Danby
The Moors Centre
Crow Wood
Oakley Walls Farm
Castleton Moor
STATION RD
Montage Studio Gallery
Congrave Farm
Danby
Danby Lodge
Esk Mill
CHURCH ST
HOWE BANK
Toad Hall Farm
AINTHORPE LA
Poverty Hill
Brook House Farm
Grange Farm
Oakley Side House
Park House
Kadelands House
PH
HIGH ST
PO
PH
ASH GR
Howe End
AINTHORPE LANE
STRAIT LA
BROOK LA
Ainthorpe
EASTON LANE
EASTON LANE
RED WAY
Oakley Side
Lealholm Lawns Farm
Fat Ox Farm
Houlsyke
MOORLANDS PK
ROBIN HOOD CL
ASH LEA
Danby CE Sch
YALL FLAT LANE
PH
Low Coombs Farm
LAWNS ROAD
High Moor
Castleton
VALLEY VW
Parsonage Farm
CASTLE LA
Castle Houses
Danby Castle
River Esk
ASHFIELD RD
The Howe
Field House
Crag Farm
Forest Farm
LONGLANDS LA
Bramble Carr
WANDELS LANE
Castle Intake Plantation
Butterwicks
Mill Woods
Crag Wood
Little Fryup Beck
TOFTS LANE
Danby Crag
Head House
Danby High Moor
Crossley Gate Farm
BURTREE LA
Ainthorpe Rigg
North End Farm
Church House
East Side
Crossley Side
Forester's Lodge
Crag House Farm
Beck Side Farm
Crossley Side Farm
Low Garth
Heads
Danby Beck
Lumley House
Stonebeck Gate Farm
Castleton Rigg
Danby Dale
Fir Tree Farm
Danby Rigg
NEW WAY
SLATE HL
East Side
Walker's Plantation
Plum Tree Farm
STONEBECK GATE LANE
Great Fryup Beck
Great Fryup Dale
Crossley House Farm
Fairy Cross Plain
Ellers House
West Cliff Farm
GATE WAY
Bainley Side Farm
Little Fryup Head
South End
Ellers Farm
Street Farm
Street
NEW WAY
Blackmires
High Gill
NUNS GREEN LA
LONG CSWY ROAD
STREET LANE
NEW RD
Low Crag
Danby Botton
Danby High Moor
Pind Howes
SHOP LA
YO21
Fryup Hall
North Eastern Plantation
Stormy Hall
Botton
Ajalon House
Oak Knowl Gill
Old Mally Plantation
Jackdaw Crag
Woodhead Farm
High Crag
Nook House
Falcon Farm
Wolf Pit
Slidney Beck Farm
Glaisdale Rigg
Low Orchard Plantation
Crosby Intake Plantation
St Helena
Danby Head
Wood End Farm
High Moor
Honey Bee Nest
Hawk Carr
Highdale Farm
Glaisdale Side
Fryup Lodge
Hardhill Gill
New Plantation
Danby Head
Danby High Moor
COMMON LA
Birk Carr
Glaisdale Moor
Glaisdale Rigg
Glaisdale Side
CAPER HILL
Dale Head
The Scar
Western Howes
White Cross
Botton Cross
Wood Head
Woodhead Scar
8
09
7
08
6
07
5
06
4
05
3
04
2
03
1
02
68
69
70
71
72
73

29
11

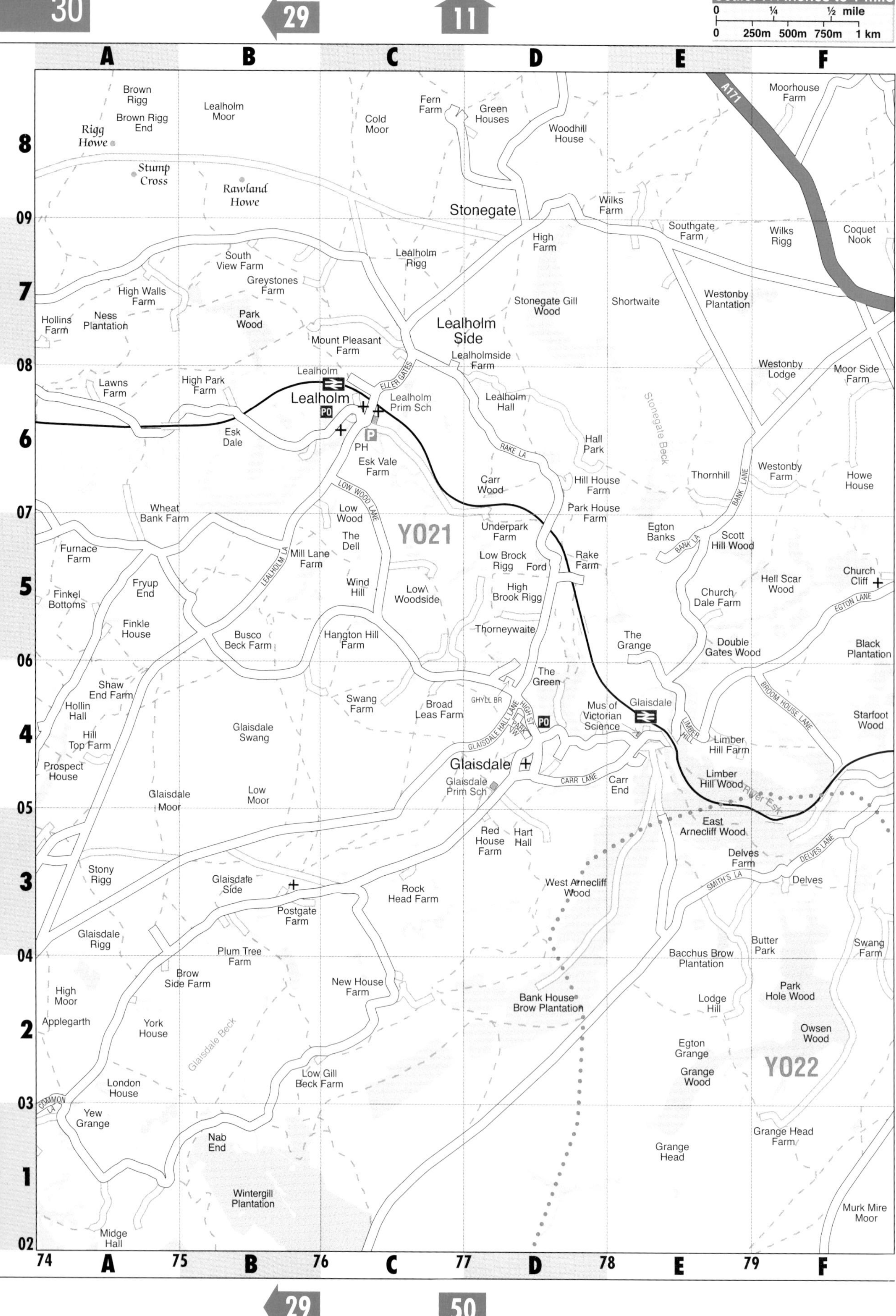
Scale: 1¾ inches to 1 mile
0 ¼ ½ mile
0 250m 500m 750m 1 km
A B C D E F
8
09
7
08
6
07
5
06
4
05
3
04
2
03
1
02
74 75 76 77 78 79
Brown Rigg
Brown Rigg End
Rigg Howe
Stump Cross
Lealholm Moor
Rawland Howe
Cold Moor
Fern Farm
Green Houses
Woodhill House
Moorhouse Farm
A171
Stonegate
Wilks Farm
Southgate Farm
Wilks Rigg
Coquet Nook
High Farm
Lealholm Rigg
South View Farm
Greystones Farm
High Walls Farm
Hollins Farm
Ness Plantation
Park Wood
Mount Pleasant Farm
Lealholm Side
Stonegate Gill Wood
Shortwaite
Westonby Plantation
Lealholmside Farm
Westonby Lodge
Moor Side Farm
Lawns Farm
High Park Farm
Lealholm
Lealholm
ELLER GATES
Lealholm Prim Sch
Lealholm Hall
Stonegate Beck
PO
Esk Dale
PH
Esk Vale Farm
RAKE LA
Hall Park
Carr Wood
Hill House Farm
Thornhill
BANK LANE
Westonby Farm
Howe House
LOW WOOD LANE
Low Wood
Wheat Bank Farm
YO21
Underpark Farm
Park House Farm
Egton Banks
BANK LA
Scott Hill Wood
Furnace Farm
The Dell
Mill Lane Farm
LEALHOLM LA
Low Brock Rigg
Ford
Rake Farm
Hell Scar Wood
Church Cliff
Fryup End
Finkel Bottoms
Wind Hill
Low Woodside
High Brook Rigg
Church Dale Farm
EGTON LANE
Finkle House
Busco Beck Farm
Hangton Hill Farm
Thorneywaite
The Grange
Double Gates Wood
Black Plantation
The Green
Shaw End Farm
Hollin Hall
Swang Farm
Broad Leas Farm
GHYLL BR
Mus of Victorian Science
Glaisdale
BROOM HOUSE LANE
Starfoot Wood
Glaisdale Swang
HIGH ST
GLAISDALE HALL LANE
PARK VW
PO
LIMBER HILL
Limber Hill Farm
Hill Top Farm
Prospect House
Glaisdale
Glaisdale Prim Sch
CARR LANE
Carr End
Limber Hill Wood
River Esk
Glaisdale Moor
Low Moor
East Arnecliff Wood
Red House Farm
Hart Hall
Delves Farm
DELVES LANE
Stony Rigg
Glaisdale Side
Rock Head Farm
West Arnecliff Wood
SMITH'S LA
Delves
Postgate Farm
Glaisdale Rigg
Butter Park
Swang Farm
Plum Tree Farm
Bacchus Brow Plantation
Brow Side Farm
New House Farm
High Moor
Bank House Brow Plantation
Lodge Hill
Park Hole Wood
Applegarth
York House
Glaisdale Beck
Owsen Wood
Egton Grange
Grange Wood
YO22
London House
Low Gill Beck Farm
COMMON LA
Yew Grange
Nab End
Grange Head Farm
Grange Head
Wintergill Plantation
Murk Mire Moor
Midge Hall

29
50

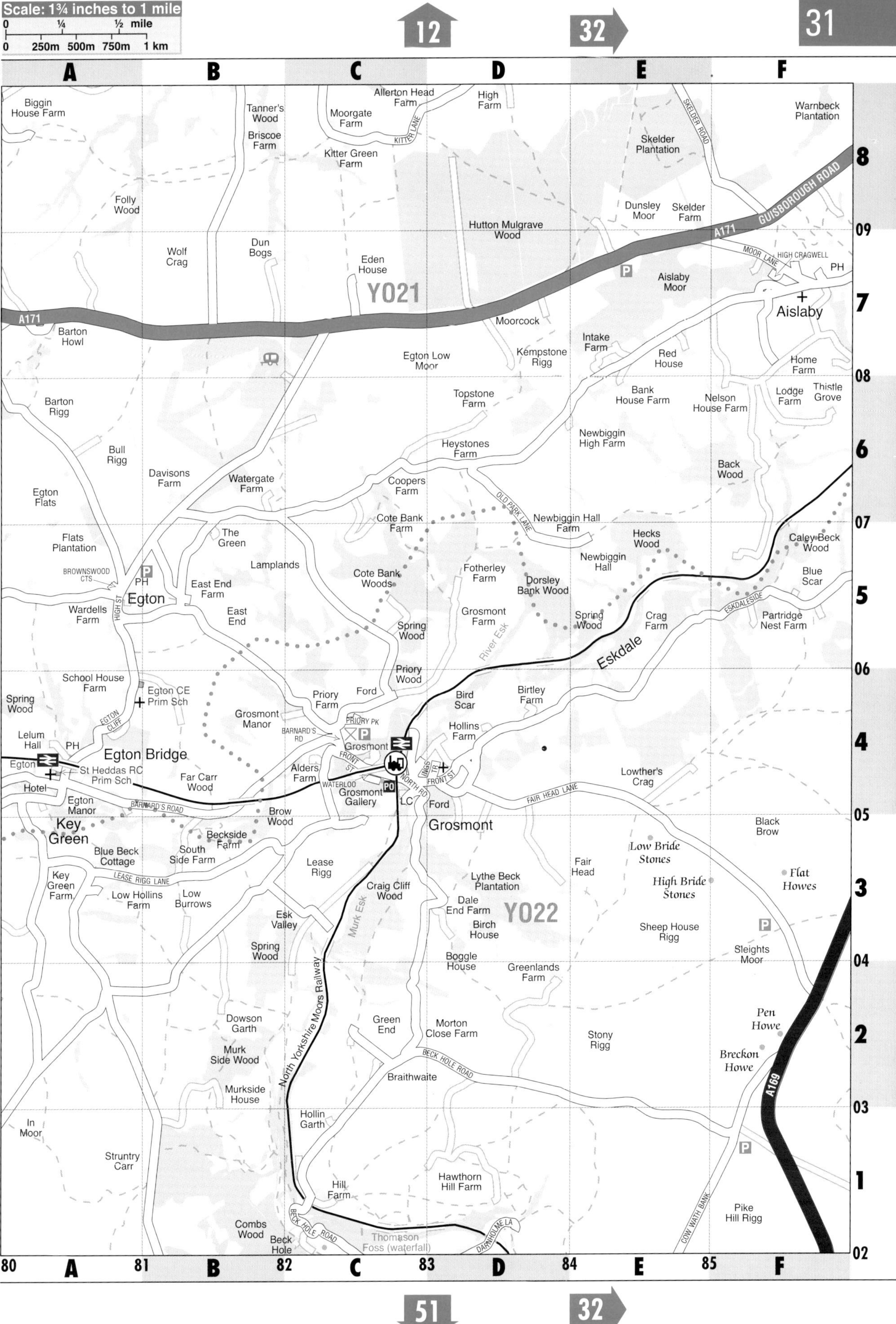

Scale: 1¾ inches to 1 mile
0 ¼ ½ mile
0 250m 500m 750m 1 km
12
32
A
B
C
D
E
F
Biggin House Farm
Tanner's Wood
Allerton Head Farm
Moorgate Farm
KITTER LANE
High Farm
SKELDER ROAD
Warnbeck Plantation
Briscoe Farm
Kitter Green Farm
Skelder Plantation
8
GUISBOROUGH ROAD
Folly Wood
Hutton Mulgrave Wood
Dunsley Moor
Skelder Farm
09
A171
Wolf Crag
Dun Bogs
Eden House
MOOR LANE
HIGH CRAGWELL
PH
YO21
Aislaby Moor
7
Aislaby
A171
Barton Howl
Moorcock
Intake Farm
Kempstone Rigg
Red House
Egton Low Moor
Home Farm
08
Barton Rigg
Topstone Farm
Bank House Farm
Nelson House Farm
Lodge Farm
Thistle Grove
Newbiggin High Farm
Bull Rigg
Heystones Farm
6
Davisons Farm
Back Wood
Watergate Farm
Coopers Farm
Egton Flats
OLD PARK LANE
Cote Bank Farm
Newbiggin Hall Farm
07
The Green
Hecks Wood
Flats Plantation
Caley Beck Wood
Lamplands
Newbiggin Hall
BROWNSWOOD CTS
Cote Bank Woods
Fotherley Farm
Blue Scar
PH
East End Farm
Dorsley Bank Wood
5
Egton
HIGH ST
ESKDALESIDE
Wardells Farm
East End
Grosmont Farm
Spring Wood
Crag Farm
Partridge Nest Farm
Spring Wood
River Esk
Eskdale
Priory Wood
06
School House Farm
Egton CE Prim Sch
Priory Farm
Ford
Bird Scar
Birtley Farm
Spring Wood
EGTON CLIFF
Grosmont Manor
PRIORY PK
Hollins Farm
Lelum Hall
PH
BARNARD'S RD
Grosmont
4
Egton Bridge
FRONT ST
INGS TR
FRONT ST
Lowther's Crag
Egton
St Heddas RC Prim Sch
Far Carr Wood
Alders Farm
WATERLOO
NORTH RD
FAIR HEAD LANE
Hotel
Grosmont Gallery
PO
LC
Ford
Egton Manor
BARNARD'S ROAD
Brow Wood
05
Black Brow
Key Green
Grosmont
Beckside Farm
Low Bride Stones
South Side Farm
Blue Beck Cottage
Lease Rigg
Fair Head
Flat Howes
High Bride Stones
3
Key Green Farm
LEASE RIGG LANE
Craig Cliff Wood
Lythe Beck Plantation
Low Hollins Farm
Low Burrows
Dale End Farm
YO22
Murk Esk
Esk Valley
Birch House
Sheep House Rigg
Spring Wood
Boggle House
Sleights Moor
Greenlands Farm
04
North Yorkshire Moors Railway
Pen Howe
Dowson Garth
Green End
Morton Close Farm
Stony Rigg
2
Murk Side Wood
Breckon Howe
BECK HOLE ROAD
Braithwaite
A169
Murkside House
03
In Moor
Hollin Garth
Struntry Carr
Hill Farm
Hawthorn Hill Farm
1
COW WATH BANK
Pike Hill Rigg
Combs Wood
BECK HOLE ROAD
Beck Hole
Thomason Foss (waterfall)
DARNHOLME LA
02
80
81
82
83
84
85
51
32

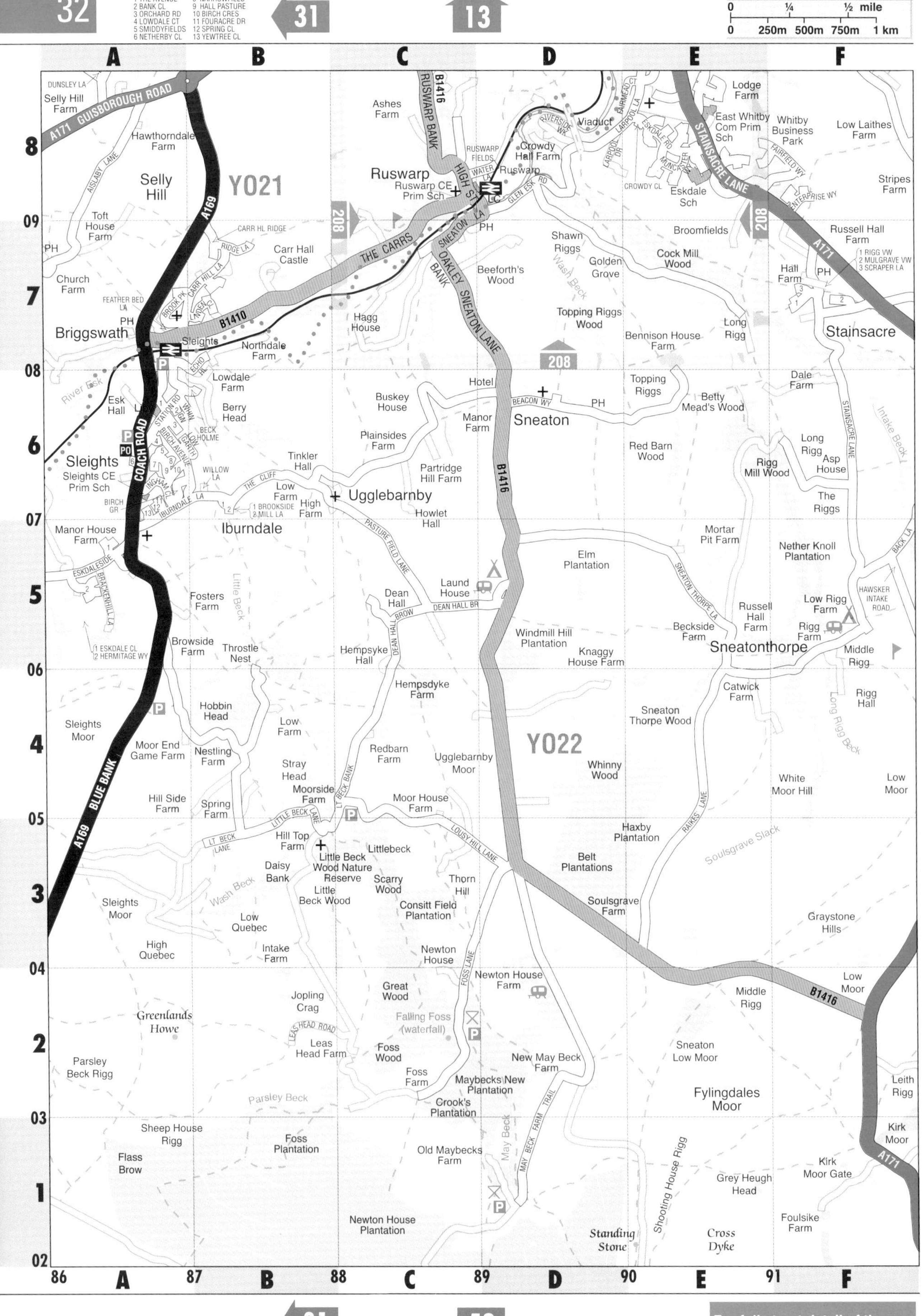

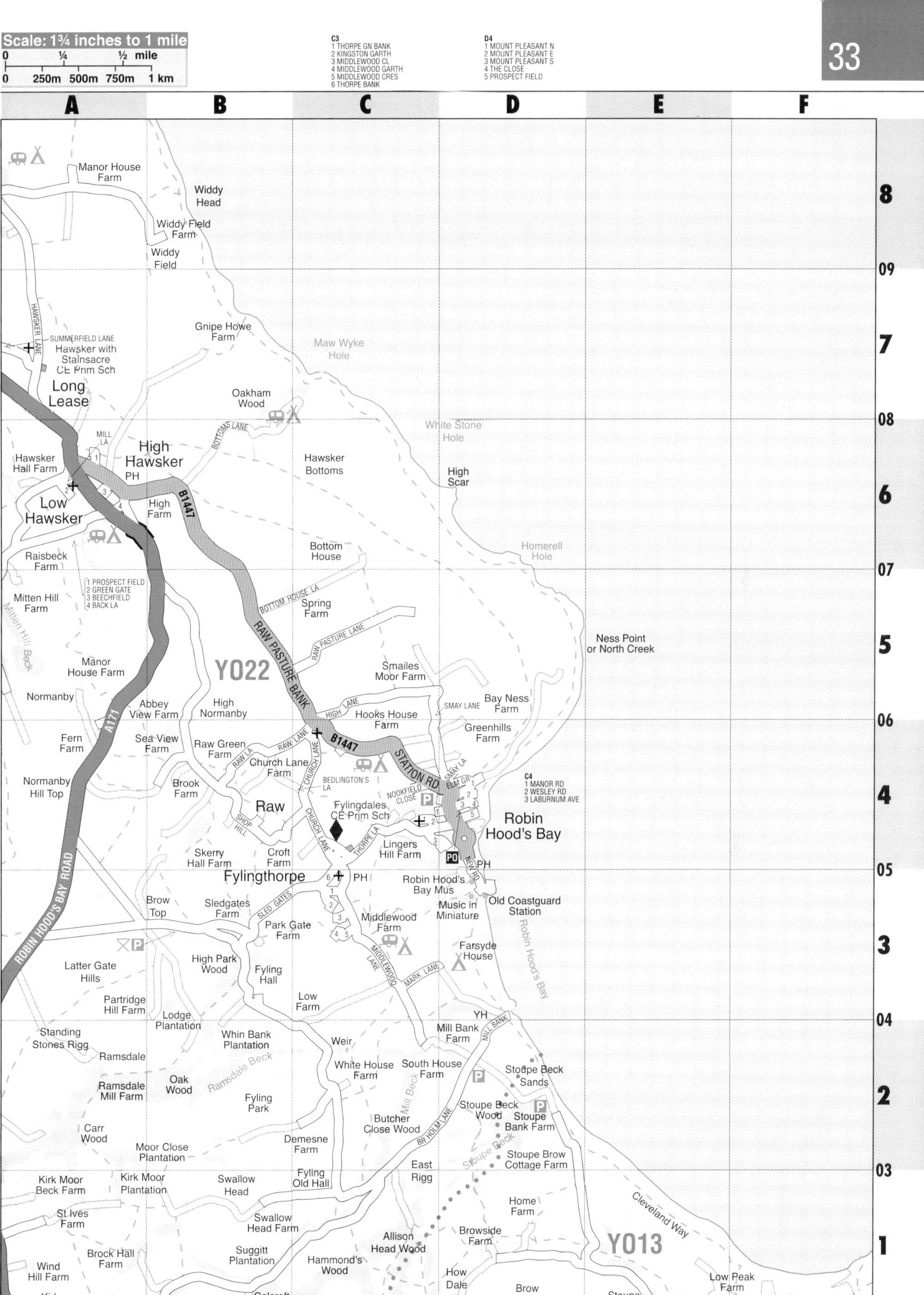

C3
1 THORPE GN BANK
2 KINGSTON GARTH
3 MIDDLEWOOD CL
4 MIDDLEWOOD GARTH
5 MIDDLEWOOD CRES
6 THORPE BANK

D4
1 MOUNT PLEASANT N
2 MOUNT PLEASANT E
3 MOUNT PLEASANT S
4 THE CLOSE
5 PROSPECT FIELD

A **B** **C** **D** **E** **F**

Manor House Farm

Widdy Head

Widdy Field Farm

Widdy Field

Gnipe Howe Farm

Maw Wyke Hole

Summerfield Lane
Hawsker with Stainsacre CE Prim Sch

Long Lease

Oakham Wood

White Stone Hole

MILL LA

High Hawsker PH

Hawsker Bottoms

High Scar

Hawsker Hall Farm

Low Hawsker

High Farm

B1447

BOTTOMS LANE

Homerell Hole

Raisbeck Farm

Bottom House

1 PROSPECT FIELD
2 GREEN GATE
3 BEECHFIELD
4 BACK LA

BOTTOM HOUSE LA

Spring Farm

Mitten Hill Farm

RAW PASTURE BANK

RAW PASTURE LANE

Ness Point or North Creek

YO22

Manor House Farm

Smailes Moor Farm

Normanby

Abbey View Farm

High Normanby

HIGH LANE

Hooks House Farm

SMAY LANE

Bay Ness Farm

A171

Sea View Farm

Raw Green Farm

B1447

Greenhills Farm

Fern Farm

RAW LA

Church Lane Farm

CHURCH LANE

STATION RD

ELM GR

SMAY LA

C4
1 MANOR RD
2 WESLEY RD
3 LABURNUM AVE

Normanby Hill Top

Brook Farm

Raw

BEDLINGTON'S LA

NOOKFIELD CLOSE

P

Robin Hood's Bay

SHOP HILL

Fylingdales CE Prim Sch

THORPE LA

PO

PH

Skerry Hall Farm

Croft Farm

Lingers Hill Farm

Fylingthorpe

PH

Robin Hood's Bay Mus

Old Coastguard Station

Brow Top

Sledgates Farm

SLED GATES

Park Gate Farm

Middlewood Farm

Music in Miniature

MIDDLEWOOD LANE

Latter Gate Hills

High Park Wood

Fyling Hall

Low Farm

MARK LANE

Farsyde House

Robin Hood's Bay

Partridge Hill Farm

Lodge Plantation

Whin Bank Plantation

YH

Mill Bank Farm

MILL BANK

Standing Stones Rigg

Ramsdale

Weir

White House Farm

South House Farm

P

Stoupe Beck Sands

Ramsdale Mill Farm

Oak Wood

Ramsdale Beck

Fyling Park

Butcher Close Wood

Mill Beck

Stoupe Beck Wood

P

Stoupe Bank Farm

Carr Wood

Moor Close Plantation

Demesne Farm

BR HOLM LANE

Stoupe Brow Cottage Farm

Kirk Moor Beck Farm

Kirk Moor Plantation

Swallow Head

Fyling Old Hall

East Rigg

Stoupe Beck

Cleveland Way

St Ives Farm

Swallow Head Farm

Allison Head Wood

Home Farm

Browside Farm

YO13

Low Peak Farm

Wind Hill Farm

Brock Hall Farm

Suggitt Plantation

Hammond's Wood

How Dale

Brow Moor

Stoupe Brow

Stoupe Brow Farm

Kirk Moor

Colcroft Farm

Skelton Bank Wood

ROBIN HOOD'S BAY ROAD

Mitten Hill Beck

Scale: 1¾ inches to 1 mile

0   ¼   ½ mile

0   250m 500m 750m 1 km

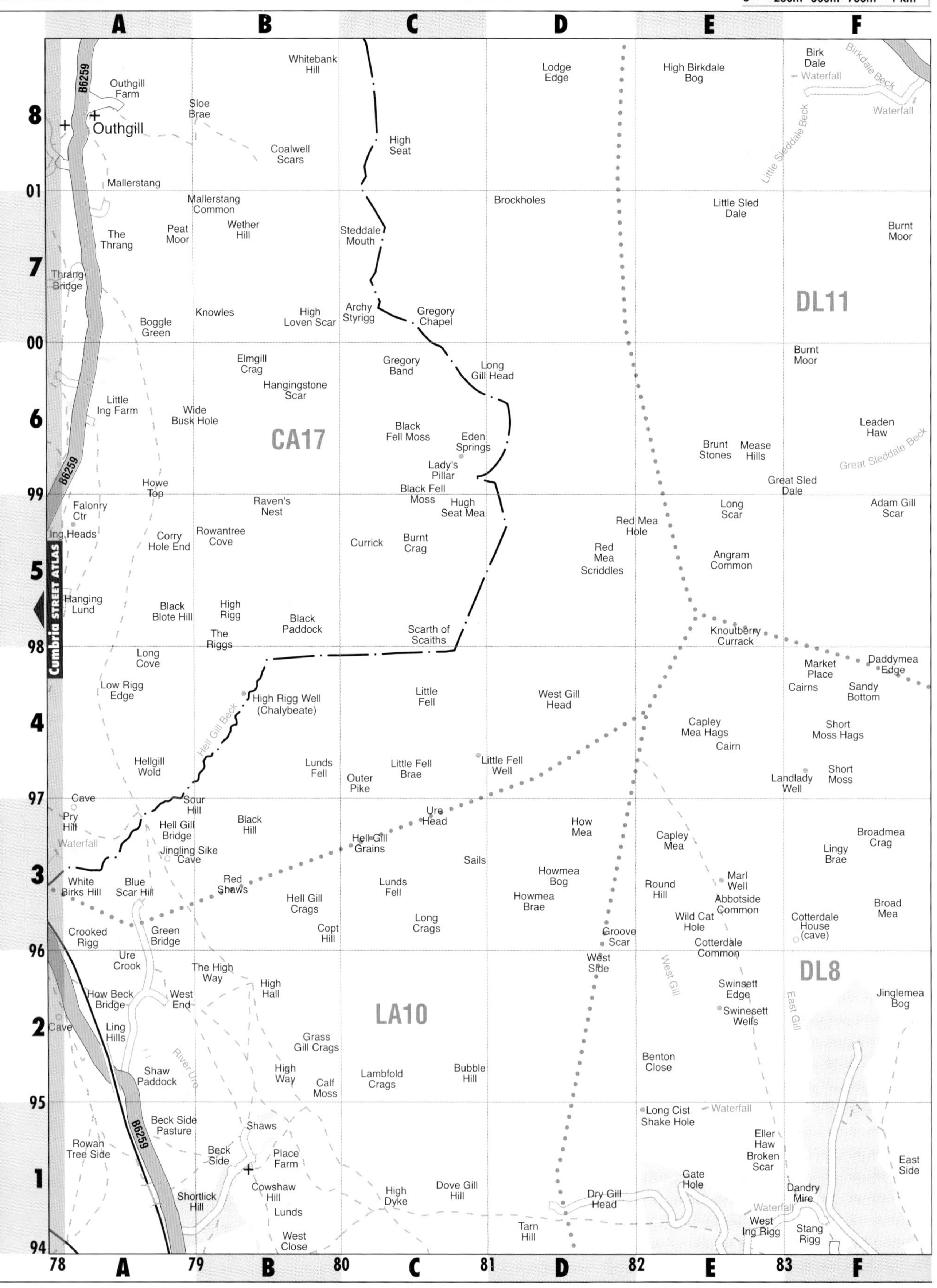

A   B   C   D   E   F

8

B6259

Outhgill
Farm
Sloe
Brae
+ + Outhgill
Mallerstang

Whitebank
Hill
Coalwell
Scars
High
Seat

Lodge
Edge

High Birkdale
Bog

Birk
Dale
Waterfall
Waterfall

Little Sleddale Beck

01

Mallerstang
Common
Peat
Moor
The
Thrang
Wether
Hill

Steddale
Mouth

Brockholes

Little Sled
Dale

Burnt
Moor

7

Thrang
Bridge

Boggle
Green
Knowles
High
Loven Scar
Archy
Styrigg
Gregory
Chapel

DL11

00

B6259

Elmgill
Crag
Hangingstone
Scar
Gregory
Band
Long
Gill Head

Burnt
Moor

6

Little
Ing Farm
Wide
Busk Hole

CA17

Black
Fell Moss
Eden
Springs
Leaden
Haw

Great Sleddale Beck

99

Falonry
Ctr
Ing
Heads
Howe
Top
Raven's
Nest
Rowantree
Cove
Lady's
Pillar
Black Fell
Moss
Hugh
Seat Mea
Brunt
Stones
Mease
Hills
Great Sled
Dale
Adam Gill
Scar

Currick
Burnt
Crag
Red Mea
Hole
Long
Scar

5

Hanging
Lund
Corry
Hole End
Black
Blote Hill
High
Rigg
Black
Paddock
Red
Mea
Scriddles
Angram
Common

98

Long
Cove
The
Riggs
Scarth of
Scaiths
Knoutberry
Currack

Low Rigg
Edge
High Rigg Well
(Chalybeate)
Little
Fell
West Gill
Head
Market
Place
Cairns
Daddymea
Edge
Sandy
Bottom

4

Hell Gill Beck

Hellgill
Wold
Lunds
Fell
Little Fell
Brae
Little Fell
Well
Capley
Mea Hags
Cairn
Short
Moss Hags
Short
Moss

97

Cave
Pry
Hill
Sour
Hill
Outer
Pike
Ure
Head
How
Mea
Landlady
Well

Waterfall
Hell Gill
Bridge
Black
Hill
Hell Gill
Grains
Capley
Mea
Broadmea
Crag

3

White
Birks Hill
Blue
Scar Hill
Jingling Sike
Cave
Red
Shaws
Lunds
Fell
Sails
Howmea
Bog
Round
Hill
Marl
Well
Abbotside
Common
Lingy
Brae
Broad
Mea

Crooked
Rigg
Green
Bridge
Hell Gill
Crags
Copt
Hill
Long
Crags
Howmea
Brae
Groove
Scar
Wild Cat
Hole
Cotterdale
House
(cave)

96

How Beck
Bridge
West
End
The High
Way
High
Hall
West
Side
Cotterdale
Common
Swinsett
Edge
DL8

Ure
Crook
Ling
Hills

LA10

Swinesett
Wells
Jinglemea
Bog

2

Cave
Shaw
Paddock
Grass
Gill Crags
Benton
Close

East Gill

West Gill

River Ure

95

Beck Side
Pasture
High
Way
Calf
Moss
Lambfold
Crags
Bubble
Hill
Long Cist
Shake Hole
Waterfall

Shaws
Place
Farm
Eller
Haw
Broken
Scar
East
Side

1

Rowan
Tree Side
Beck
Side
+ Cowshaw
Hill
High
Dyke
Dove Gill
Hill
Dry Gill
Head
Gate
Hole
Waterfall
Dandry
Mire

B6259

Shortlick
Hill
Lunds
Tarn
Hill
West
Ing Rigg
Stang
Rigg

94

West
Close

78   A   79   B   80   C   81   D   82   E   83   F

Scale: 1¾ inches to 1 mile

15
36

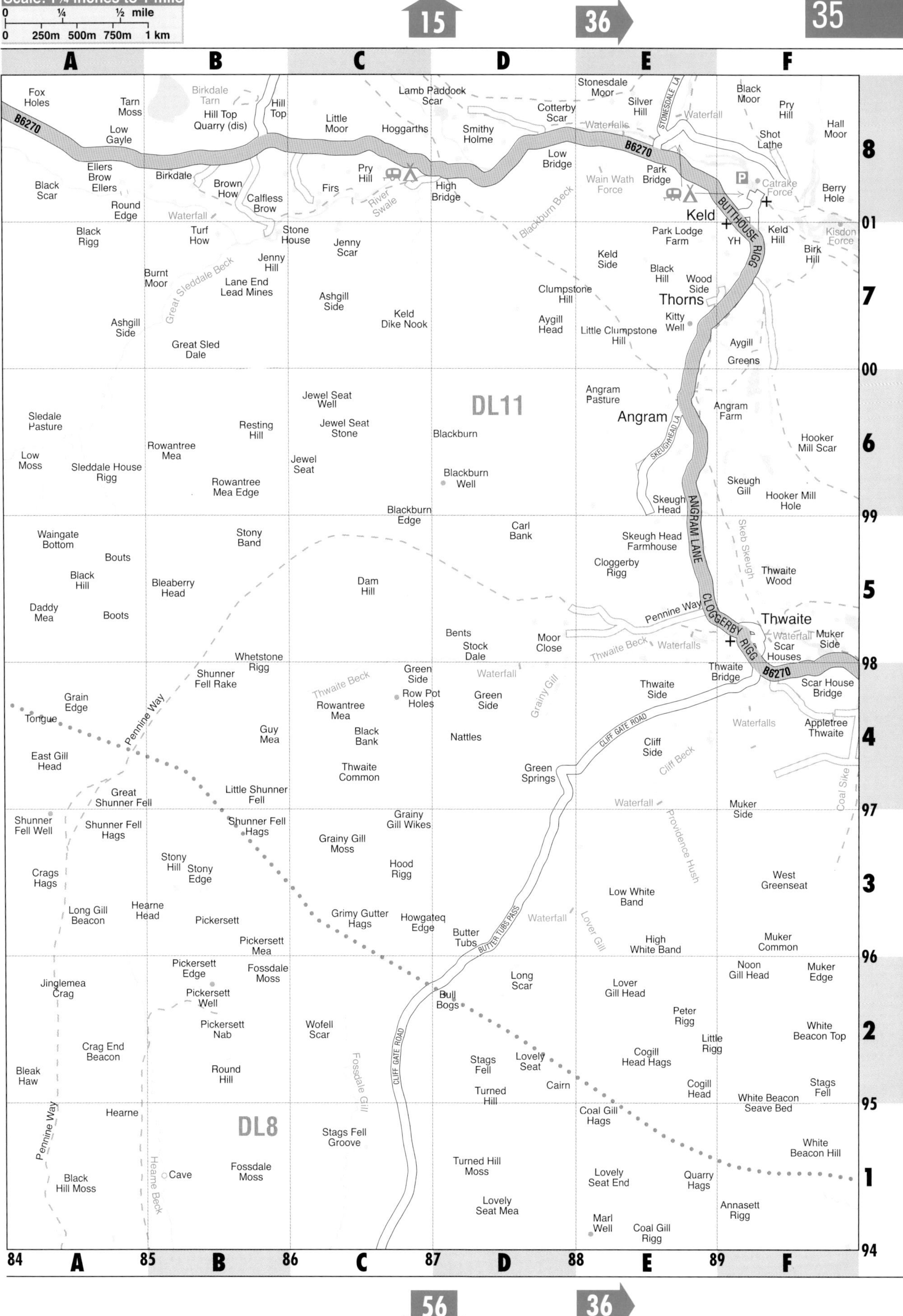
0 ¼ ½ mile
0 250m 500m 750m 1 km
A B C D E F
8 01 7 00 6 99 5 98 4 97 3 96 2 95 1 94
84 85 86 87 88 89
Fox Holes
Tarn Moss
Low Gayle
Birkdale Tarn
Hill Top Quarry (dis)
Hill Top
Little Moor
Lamb Paddock Scar
Hoggarths
Smithy Holme
Cotterby Scar
Stonesdale Moor
Silver Hill
STONESDALE LA
Waterfall
Waterfalls
Black Moor
Pry Hill
Shot Lathe
Hall Moor
B6270
Ellers Brow Ellers
Black Scar
Birkdale
Brown How
Calfless Brow
Round Edge
Waterfall
Firs
Pry Hill
River Swale
High Bridge
Low Bridge
Wain Wath Force
Park Bridge
Catrake Force
Berry Hole
Keld
BUTTHOUSE RIGG
Keld Hill
Kisdon Force
YH
Park Lodge Farm
Black Rigg
Turf How
Stone House
Jenny Hill
Jenny Scar
Blackburn Beck
Keld Side
Birk Hill
Black Hill
Wood Side
Burnt Moor
Great Sleddale Beck
Lane End Lead Mines
Ashgill Side
Keld Dike Nook
Clumpstone Hill
Thorns
Kitty Well
Aygill Head
Little Clumpstone Hill
Ashgill Side
Great Sled Dale
Aygill Greens
Jewel Seat Well
DL11
Angram Pasture
Angram
Angram Farm
Sledale Pasture
Resting Hill
Jewel Seat Stone
Blackburn
SKEUGHHEAD LA
Hooker Mill Scar
Low Moss
Rowantree Mea
Sleddale House Rigg
Jewel Seat
Blackburn Well
Rowantree Mea Edge
Skeugh Head
Skeugh Gill
Hooker Mill Hole
Blackburn Edge
ANGRAM LANE
Carl Bank
Waingate Bottom
Stony Band
Skeugh Head Farmhouse
Skeb Skeugh
Bouts
Cloggerby Rigg
Thwaite Wood
Black Hill
Bleaberry Head
Dam Hill
Daddy Mea
Boots
Pennine Way
CLOGGERBY RIGG
Thwaite
Bents
Stock Dale
Moor Close
Thwaite Beck
Waterfalls
Waterfall
Muker Side
Scar Houses
Whetstone Rigg
Shunner Fell Rake
Green Side
Waterfall
Thwaite Bridge
B6270
Grain Edge
Thwaite Beck
Rowantree Mea
Row Pot Holes
Green Side
Grainy Gill
Thwaite Side
Scar House Bridge
Tongue
Pennine Way
Guy Mea
Black Bank
Nattles
CLIFF GATE ROAD
Waterfalls
Appletree Thwaite
East Gill Head
Cliff Side
Cliff Beck
Thwaite Common
Green Springs
Great Shunner Fell
Little Shunner Fell
Waterfall
Coal Sike
Shunner Fell Well
Shunner Fell Hags
Shunner Fell Hags
Grainy Gill Wikes
Providence Hush
Muker Side
Grainy Gill Moss
Stony Hill
Crags Hags
Stony Edge
Hood Rigg
West Greenseat
Low White Band
Long Gill Beacon
Hearne Head
Pickersett
Grimy Gutter Hags
Howgateq Edge
Butter Tubs
BUTTER TUBS PASS
Waterfall
Lover Gill
Pickersett Mea
High White Band
Muker Common
Pickersett Edge
Fossdale Moss
Long Scar
Jinglemea Crag
Pickersett Well
Bull Bogs
Lover Gill Head
Noon Gill Head
Muker Edge
Pickersett Nab
Wofell Scar
Peter Rigg
White Beacon Top
Crag End Beacon
Fossdale Gill
CLIFF GATE ROAD
Stags Fell
Lovely Seat
Cogill Head Hags
Little Rigg
Bleak Haw
Round Hill
Turned Hill
Cairn
Cogill Head
Stags Fell
White Beacon Seave Bed
Pennine Way
Hearne
DL8
Stags Fell Groove
Coal Gill Hags
White Beacon Hill
Hearne Beck
Cave
Fossdale Moss
Turned Hill Moss
Lovely Seat End
Quarry Hags
Black Hill Moss
Annasett Rigg
Lovely Seat Mea
Marl Well
Coal Gill Rigg

56
36

35
16
Scale: 1¾ inches to 1 mile

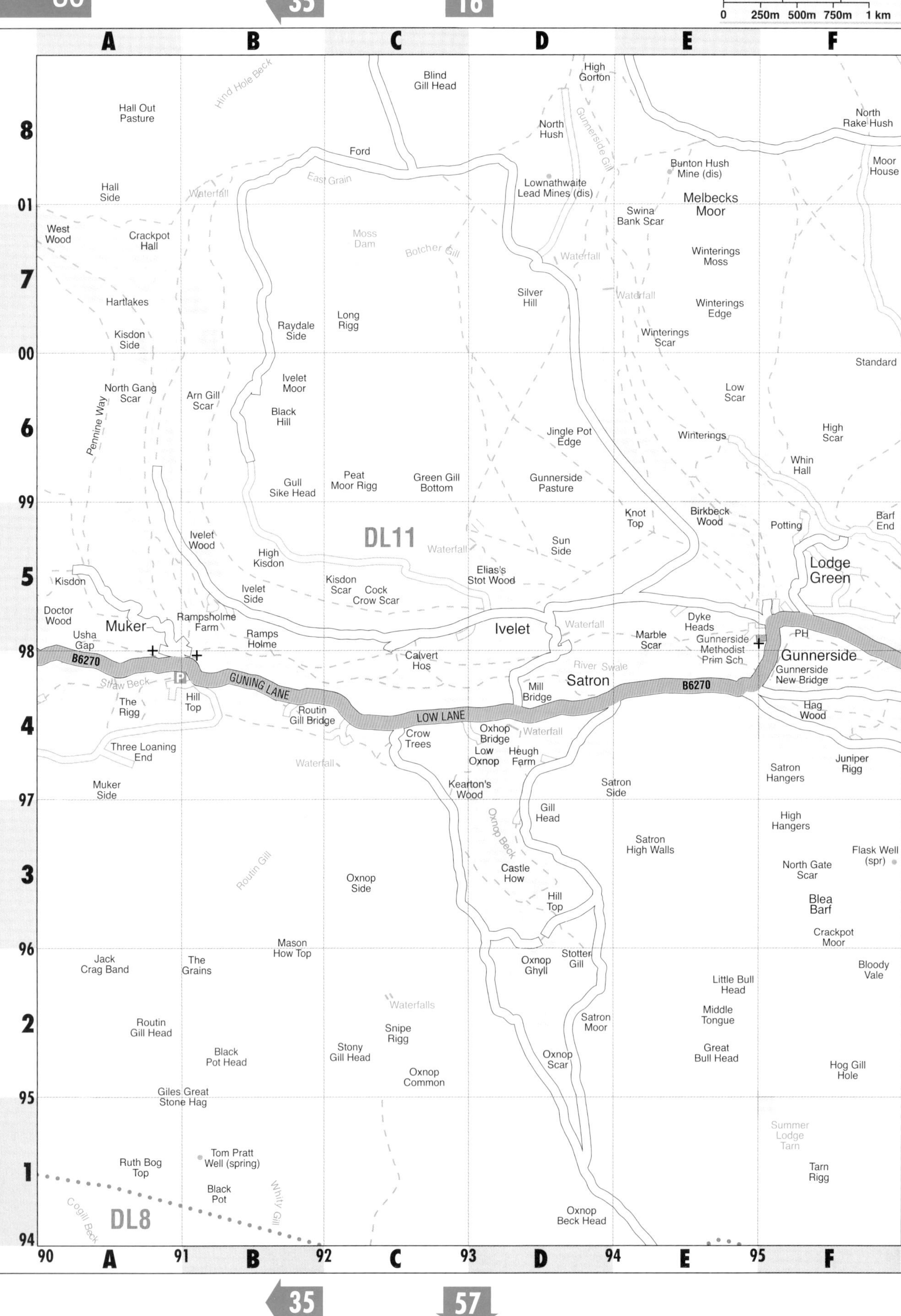
A
B
C
D
E
F
Hall Out Pasture
Hind Hole Beck
Blind Gill Head
High Gorton
North Hush
Gunnerside Gill
North Rake Hush
Ford
East Grain
Moor House
Bunton Hush Mine (dis)
Hall Side
Waterfall
Lownathwaite Lead Mines (dis)
Melbecks Moor
Swina Bank Scar
West Wood
Crackpot Hall
Moss Dam
Botcher Gill
Winterings Moss
Hartlakes
Silver Hill
Winterings Edge
Kisdon Side
Raydale Side
Long Rigg
Winterings Scar
Standard
North Gang Scar
Arn Gill Scar
Ivelet Moor
Low Scar
Pennine Way
Black Hill
Jingle Pot Edge
Winterings
High Scar
Whin Hall
Gull Sike Head
Peat Moor Rigg
Green Gill Bottom
Gunnerside Pasture
Knot Top
Birkbeck Wood
Barf End
Potting
DL11
Ivelet Wood
High Kisdon
Sun Side
Lodge Green
Kisdon
Kisdon Scar
Cock Crow Scar
Elias's Stot Wood
Ivelet Side
Doctor Wood
Muker
Rampsholme Farm
Ramps Holme
Ivelet
Dyke Heads
Marble Scar
PH
Usha Gap
Gunnerside Methodist Prim Sch
B6270
Calvert Hos
Gunnerside
River Swale
Straw Beck
GUNING LANE
Mill Bridge
Satron
Gunnerside New Bridge
The Rigg
Hill Top
Routin Gill Bridge
LOW LANE
Hag Wood
Crow Trees
Oxnop Bridge
Low Oxnop
Heugh Farm
Three Loaning End
Juniper Rigg
Satron Hangers
Muker Side
Kearton's Wood
Satron Side
Gill Head
High Hangers
Oxnop Beck
Satron High Walls
Flask Well (spr)
Routin Gill
North Gate Scar
Castle How
Oxnop Side
Hill Top
Blea Barf
Crackpot Moor
Mason How Top
Jack Crag Band
The Grains
Oxnop Ghyll
Stotter Gill
Bloody Vale
Little Bull Head
Waterfalls
Middle Tongue
Routin Gill Head
Satron Moor
Snipe Rigg
Black Pot Head
Stony Gill Head
Oxnop Scar
Great Bull Head
Hog Gill Hole
Oxnop Common
Giles Great Stone Hag
Summer Lodge Tarn
Tom Pratt Well (spring)
Ruth Bog Top
Tarn Rigg
Black Pot
Whity Gill
Cogill Beck
DL8
Oxnop Beck Head
90
91
92
93
94
95

35
57

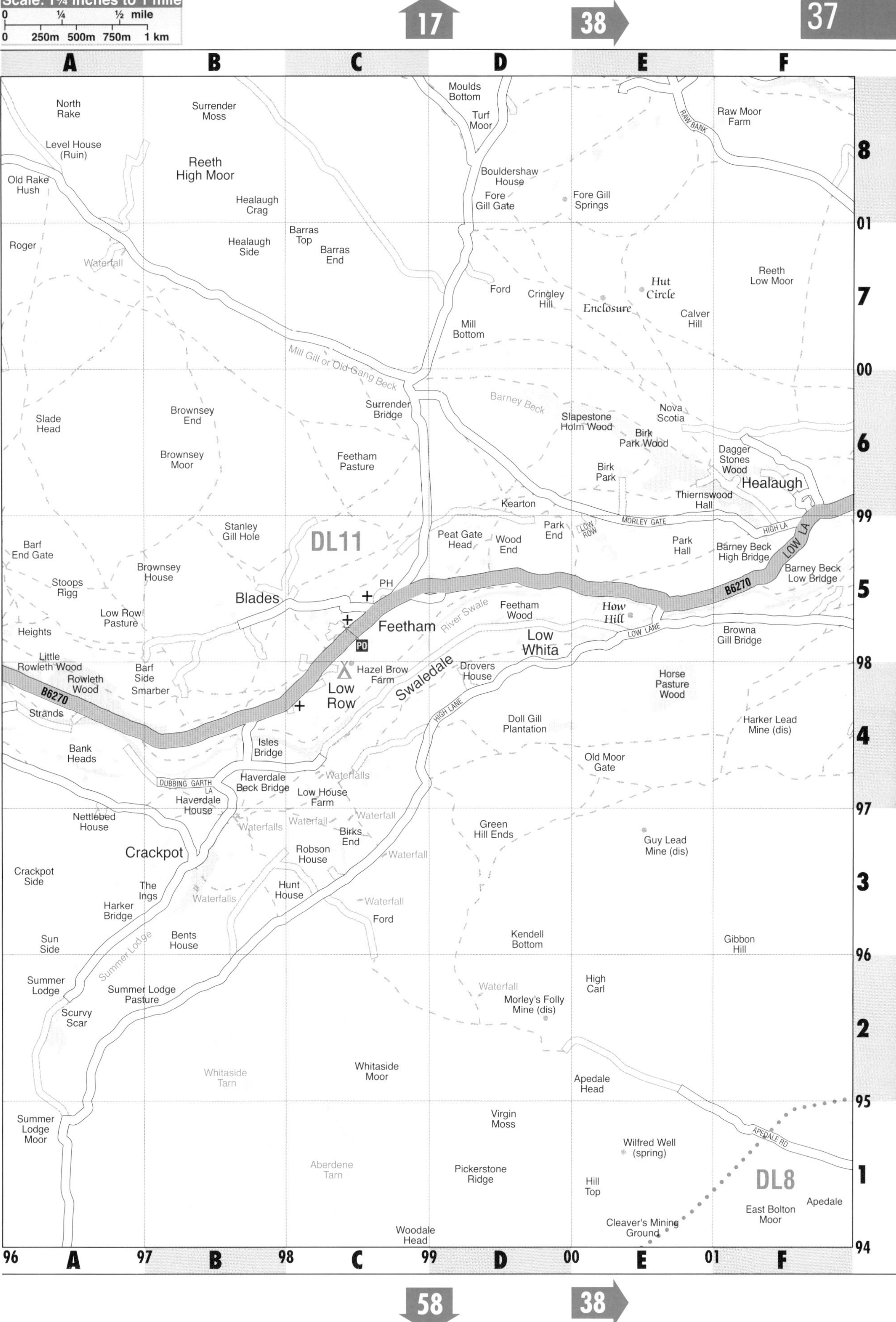

A   B   C   D   E   F

North Rake

Surrender Moss

Raw Moor Farm

RAW BANK

Level House (Ruin)

Reeth High Moor

8

Old Rake Hush

Healaugh Crag

Bouldershaw House

Fore Gill Springs

01

Roger

Healaugh Side

Barras Top

Barras End

Ford

Fore Gill Gate

Hut Circle

Reeth Low Moor

7

Waterfall

Cringley Hill

Enclosure

Calver Hill

Mill Bottom

00

Mill Gill or Old Gang Beck

Barney Beck

Slade Head

Brownsey End

Surrender Bridge

Slapestone Holm Wood

Nova Scotia

6

Brownsey Moor

Feetham Pasture

Birk Park Wood

Dagger Stones Wood

Healaugh

Birk Park

Thiernswood Hall

Kearton

MORLEY GATE

HIGH LA

LOW LA

99

Stanley Gill Hole

Peat Gate Head

Wood End

Park End

LOW ROW

Park Hall

Barney Beck High Bridge

Barf End Gate

DL11

PH

Barney Beck Low Bridge

Stoops Rigg

Brownsey House

Blades

Feetham

River Swale

Feetham Wood

How Hill

B6270

5

Low Row Pasture

PO

Low Whita

LOW LANE

Browna Gill Bridge

Heights

Hazel Brow Farm

Swaledale

Drovers House

98

Little Rowleth Wood

Barf Side Smarber

Low Row

Horse Pasture Wood

B6270

Rowleth Wood

Doll Gill Plantation

HIGH LANE

Harker Lead Mine (dis)

4

Strands

Isles Bridge

Old Moor Gate

Bank Heads

Haverdale Beck Bridge

Waterfalls

DUBBING GARTH LA

Low House Farm

97

Nettlebed House

Haverdale House

Waterfalls

Waterfall

Green Hill Ends

Guy Lead Mine (dis)

Crackpot

Birks End

3

Crackpot Side

The Ings

Robson House

Sun Side

Harker Bridge

Waterfalls

Hunt House

Kendell Bottom

Gibbon Hill

Bents House

Ford

96

Summer Lodge

Summer Lodge Pasture

Waterfall

High Carl

Scurvy Scar

Summer Lodge

Morley's Folly Mine (dis)

2

Whitaside Tarn

Whitaside Moor

Apedale Head

95

Summer Lodge Moor

Virgin Moss

Wilfred Well (spring)

APEDALE RD

DL8

1

Aberdene Tarn

Pickerstone Ridge

Hill Top

East Bolton Moor

Apedale

Woodale Head

Cleaver's Mining Ground

94

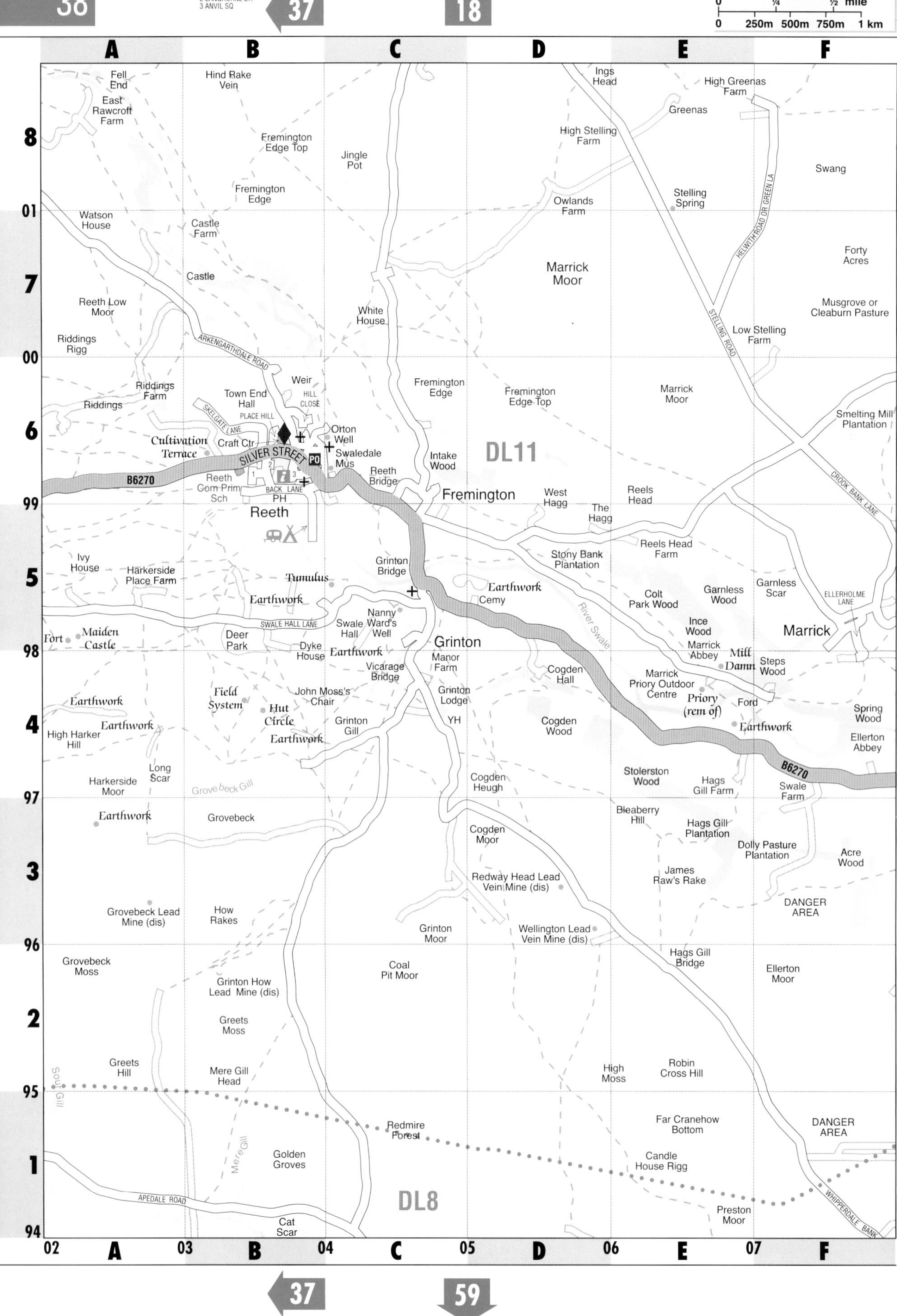

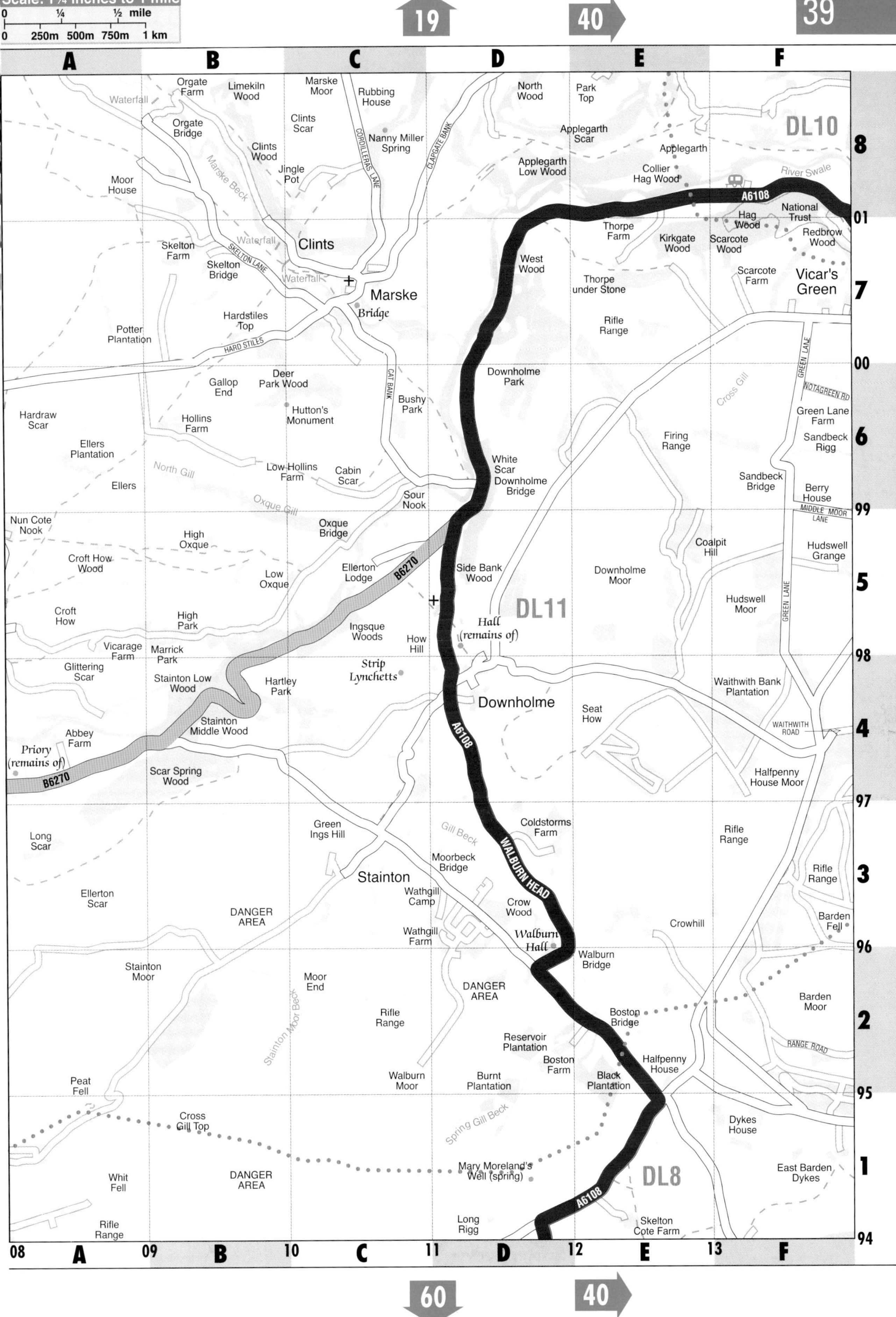

Scale: 1¾ inches to 1 mile
0 ¼ ½ mile
0 250m 500m 750m 1 km
19
40
A B C D E F
Waterfall
Orgate Farm
Limekiln Wood
Marske Moor
Rubbing House
North Wood
Park Top
Orgate Bridge
Clints Scar
Nanny Miller Spring
CORDILLERAS LANE
CLAPGATE BANK
Applegarth Scar
DL10
Clints Wood
Marske Beck
Applegarth
Moor House
Jingle Pot
Applegarth Low Wood
Collier Hag Wood
River Swale
A6108
National Trust
Skelton Farm
Waterfall
Clints
SKELTON LANE
Thorpe Farm
Hag Wood
Kirkgate Wood
Scarcote Wood
Redbrow Wood
Skelton Bridge
Waterfall
West Wood
Marske
Bridge
Thorpe under Stone
Scarcote Farm
Vicar's Green
Hardstiles Top
HARD STILES
Potter Plantation
Rifle Range
Downholme Park
GREEN LANE
NOTAGREEN RD
Deer Park Wood
Gallop End
CAT BANK
Hutton's Monument
Bushy Park
Cross Gill
Hardraw Scar
Hollins Farm
Green Lane Farm
Firing Range
Sandbeck Rigg
Ellers Plantation
North Gill
Low Hollins Farm
Cabin Scar
White Scar
Downholme Bridge
Ellers
Sandbeck Bridge
Berry House
Sour Nook
Oxque Gill
MIDDLE MOOR LANE
Nun Cote Nook
Oxque Bridge
High Oxque
Coalpit Hill
Hudswell Grange
Croft How Wood
Ellerton Lodge
B6270
Side Bank Wood
Downholme Moor
Low Oxque
DL11
Hudswell Moor
GREEN LANE
Croft How
High Park
Ingsque Woods
Hall (remains of)
How Hill
Vicarage Farm
Marrick Park
Glittering Scar
Strip Lynchetts
Waithwith Bank Plantation
Stainton Low Wood
Hartley Park
Downholme
Seat How
WAITHWITH ROAD
Abbey Farm
Stainton Middle Wood
A6108
Priory (remains of)
Scar Spring Wood
Halfpenny House Moor
B6270
Long Scar
Green Ings Hill
Gill Beck
Coldstorms Farm
Rifle Range
Moorbeck Bridge
WALBURN HEAD
Rifle Range
Stainton
Ellerton Scar
Wathgill Camp
Crow Wood
DANGER AREA
Barden Fell
Crowhill
Wathgill Farm
Walburn Hall
Walburn Bridge
Stainton Moor
Moor End
DANGER AREA
Stainton Moor Beck
Barden Moor
Rifle Range
Boston Bridge
Reservoir Plantation
RANGE ROAD
Boston Farm
Halfpenny House
Peat Fell
Walburn Moor
Burnt Plantation
Black Plantation
Cross Gill Top
Spring Gill Beck
Dykes House
Mary Moreland's Well (spring)
Whit Fell
DANGER AREA
DL8
East Barden Dykes
A6108
Rifle Range
Long Rigg
Skelton Cote Farm
8 01 7 00 6 99 5 98 4 97 3 96 2 95 1 94
08 A 09 B 10 C 11 D 12 E 13 F
60
40

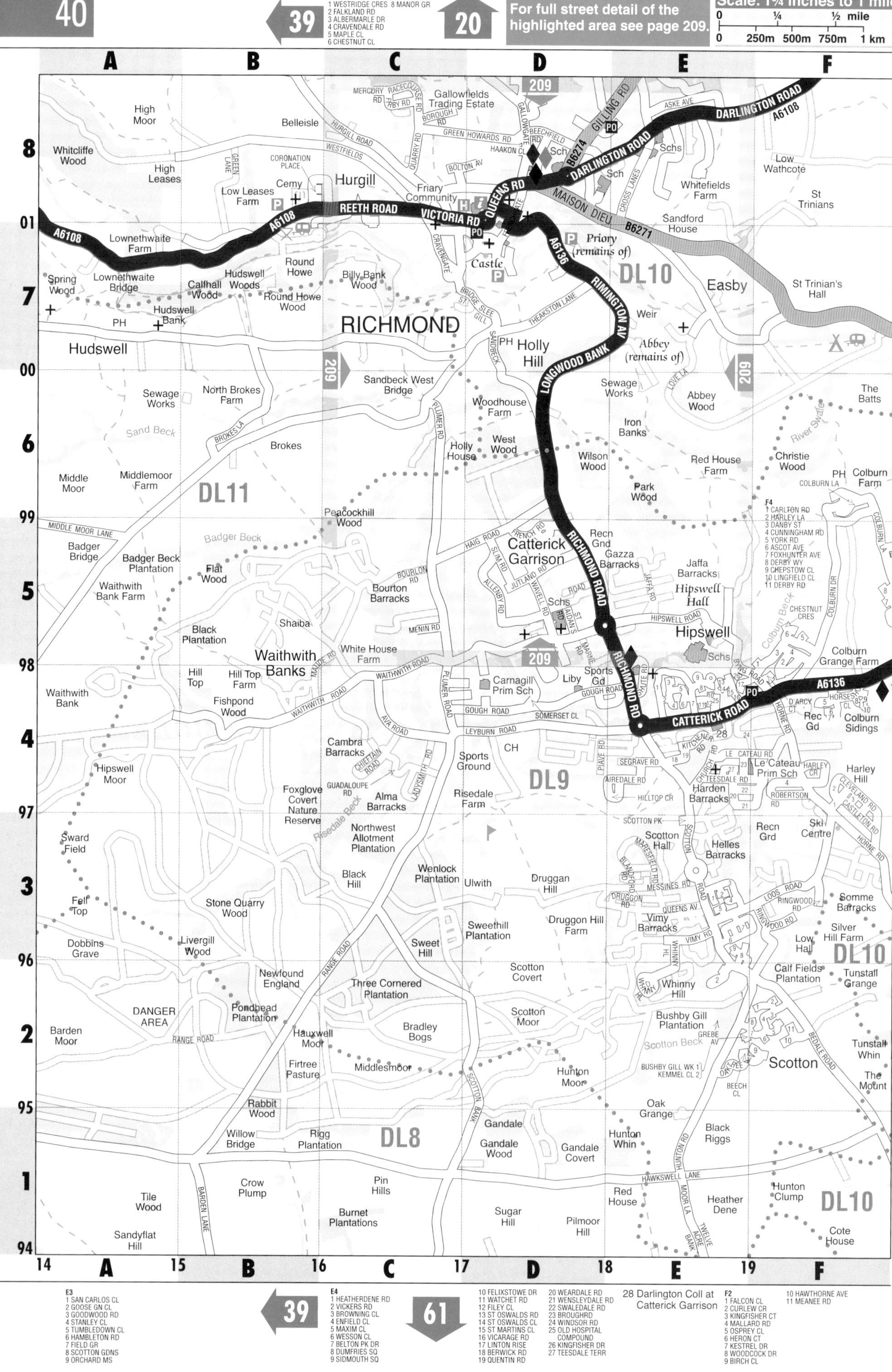
F5
1 WESTRIDGE CRES
2 FALKLAND RD
3 ALBERMARLE DR
4 CRAVENDALE RD
5 MAPLE CL
6 CHESTNUT CL
7 GRANGE RD
8 MANOR GR
39
20
For full street detail of the highlighted area see page 209.
Scale: 1¾ inches to 1 mile
0 ¼ ½ mile
0 250m 500m 750m 1 km
A B C D E F
8
01
7
00
6
99
5
98
4
97
3
96
2
95
1
94
14 15 16 17 18 19
High Moor
Whitcliffe Wood
High Leases
Belleisle
Low Leases Farm
Cemy
Hurgill
Coronation Place
Westfields
Hurgill Road
Quarry Rd
Mercury Rd
Racecourse Rd
Frby Rd
Borough Rd
Gallowfields Trading Estate
Green Howards Rd
Gallowgate
Beechfield
Haakon Cl
Bolton Av
Friary Community
Gilling Rd
B6274
Aske Ave
Darlington Road
A6108
Sch
Schs
Low Wathcote
Whitefields Farm
Cross Lanes
Maison Dieu
B6271
St Trinians
Sandford House
Queens Rd
Reeth Road
Victoria Rd
Cravengate
PO
A6108
Lownethwaite Farm
Lownethwaite Bridge
Spring Wood
Calfhall Wood
Hudswell Woods
Round Howe
Round Howe Wood
Billy Bank Wood
Castle
Priory (remains of)
A6136
DL10
Easby
St Trinian's Hall
Bridge St
Slee Gill
Theakston Lane
Rimington Av
Hudswell Bank
PH
Hudswell
RICHMOND
Weir
Abbey (remains of)
Sandbeck
Holly Hill
Longwood Bank
209
Sandbeck West Bridge
Sewage Works
North Brokes Farm
Brokes La
Sand Beck
Abbey Wood
Love La
Iron Banks
The Batts
Woodhouse Farm
Plumer Rd
Brokes
Holly House
West Wood
Wilson Wood
Red House Farm
River Swale
Christie Wood
Middle Moor
Middlemoor Farm
DL11
Park Wood
PH Colburn Farm
Colburn La
F4
1 CARLTON RD
2 HARLEY LA
3 DANBY ST
4 CUNNINGHAM RD
5 YORK RD
6 ASCOT AVE
7 FOXHUNTER AVE
8 DERBY WY
9 CHEPSTOW CL
10 LINGFIELD CL
11 DERBY RD
Middle Moor Lane
Peacockhill Wood
Badger Beck
Haig Road
French Rd
Catterick Garrison
Richmond Road
Recn Gnd
Gazza Barracks
Jaffa Rd
Jaffa Barracks
Hipswell Hall
Badger Bridge
Badger Beck Plantation
Flat Wood
Waithwith Bank Farm
Bourlon Rd
Bourton Barracks
Slim Rd
Jutland Rd
Allenby Rd
Wavell Rd
Schs
St Aidans Rd
Colburn Dr
Chestnut Cres
Colburn Beck
Shaiba
Black Plantation
Menin Rd
Hipswell Road
Hipswell
White House Farm
Waithwith Banks
Maude Rd
Waithwith Road
Marne Rd
Colburn Grange Farm
Hill Top
Hill Top Farm
Carnagill Prim Sch
Liby
Sports Gd
Gough Road
Cote Rd
Byng Road
A6136
D'Arcy Ct
Horsés Cl
Rec Gd
Colburn Sidings
Waithwith Bank
Fishpond Wood
Ava Road
Gough Road
Somerset Cl
Catterick Road
Horne Rd
Leyburn Road
Kitchener Rd
28
Cambra Barracks
Chieftain Road
Ladysmith Rd
Sports Ground
CH
Piave Rd
Segrave Rd
Le Cateau Rd
Church Rd
Le Cateau Prim Sch
Harley Cr
Harley Hill
Hipswell Moor
Guadaloupe Rd
Foxglove Covert Nature Reserve
Alma Barracks
Risedale Farm
DL9
Airedale Rd
Teesdale Rd
Harden Barracks
Hilltop Cr
Robertson Rd
Cleveland Rd
Castleton Rd
Risedale Beck
Scotton Pk
Northwest Allotment Plantation
Scotton Hall
Marsfield Rd
Scotton Rd
Helles Barracks
Recn Grd
Ski Centre
Horne Rd
Sward Field
Black Hill
Wenlock Plantation
Ulwith
Druggan Hill
Blandford Rd
Messines Rd
Druggon Rd
Queens Av
Loos Road
Ringwood Rd
Somme Barracks
Fell Top
Stone Quarry Wood
Sweethill Plantation
Druggon Hill Farm
Vimy Barracks
Vimy Rd
Silver Hill Farm
Low Hall
Dobbins Grave
Livergill Wood
Sweet Hill
Whinny
DL10
Newfound England
Range Road
Three Cornered Plantation
Scotton Covert
Whinny Hill
Calf Fields Plantation
Tunstall Grange
DANGER AREA
Pondhead Plantation
Scotton Moor
Bushby Gill Plantation
Barden Moor
Range Road
Hauxwell Moor
Bradley Bogs
Scotton Beck
Grebe Av
Tunstall Whin
Firtree Pasture
Middlesmoor
Hunton Moor
Bushby Gill Wk
Kemmel Cl
Scotton
Bedale Road
Beech Cl
The Mount
Scotton Bank
Rabbit Wood
Oak Grange
Willow Bridge
Rigg Plantation
DL8
Gandale
Gandale Wood
Gandale Covert
Hunton Whin
Black Riggs
Hunton Rd
Hawkswell Lane
Crow Plump
Pin Hills
Tile Wood
Barden Lane
Burnet Plantations
Sugar Hill
Pilmoor Hill
Red House
Moor La
Heather Dene
Hunton Clump
DL10
Cote House
Sandyflat Hill
Bank
Twelve Acre
E3
1 SAN CARLOS CL
2 GOOSE GN CL
3 GOODWOOD RD
4 STANLEY CL
5 TUMBLEDOWN CL
6 HAMBLETON RD
7 FIELD GR
8 SCOTTON GDNS
9 ORCHARD MS
39
E4
1 HEATHERDENE RD
2 VICKERS RD
3 BROWNING CL
4 ENFIELD CL
5 MAXIM CL
6 WESSON CL
7 BELTON PK DR
8 DUMFRIES SQ
9 SIDMOUTH SQ
61
10 FELIXSTOWE DR
11 WATCHET RD
12 FILEY CL
13 ST OSWALDS RD
14 ST OSWALDS CL
15 ST MARTINS CL
16 VICARAGE RD
17 LINTON RISE
18 BERWICK RD
19 QUENTIN RD
20 WEARDALE RD
21 WENSLEYDALE RD
22 SWALEDALE RD
23 BROUGHRD
24 WINDSOR RD
25 OLD HOSPITAL COMPOUND
26 KINGFISHER DR
27 TEESDALE TERR
28 Darlington Coll at Catterick Garrison
F2
1 FALCON CL
2 CURLEW CR
3 KINGFISHER CT
4 MALLARD RD
5 OSPREY CL
6 HERON CT
7 KESTREL DR
8 WOODCOCK DR
9 BIRCH CL
10 HAWTHORNE AVE
11 MEANEE RD

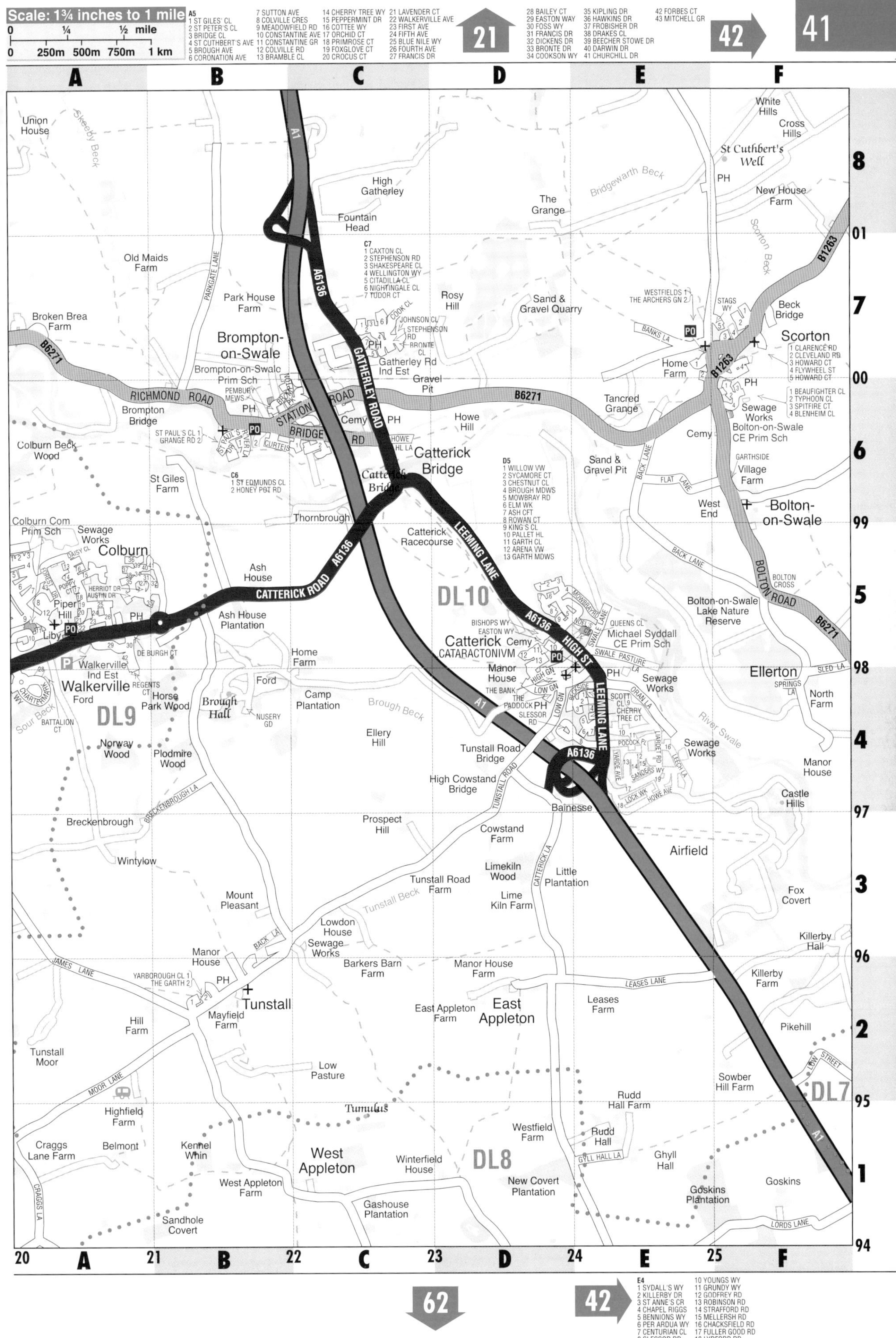
Scale: 1¾ inches to 1 mile
0 ¼ ½ mile
0 250m 500m 750m 1 km
A5
1 ST GILES' CL
2 ST PETER'S CL
3 BRIDGE CL
4 ST CUTHBERT'S AVE
5 BROUGH AVE
6 CORONATION AVE
7 SUTTON AVE
8 COLVILLE CRES
9 MEADOWFIELD RD
10 CONSTANTINE AVE
11 CONSTANTINE GR
12 COLVILLE RD
13 BRAMBLE CL
14 CHERRY TREE WY
15 PEPPERMINT DR
16 COTTEE WY
17 ORCHID CT
18 PRIMROSE CT
19 FOXGLOVE CT
20 CROCUS CT
21 LAVENDER CT
22 WALKERVILLE AVE
23 FIRST AVE
24 FIFTH AVE
25 BLUE NILE WY
26 FOURTH AVE
27 FRANCIS DR
21
28 BAILEY CT
29 EASTON WAY
30 FOSS WY
31 FRANCIS DR
32 DICKENS DR
33 BRONTE DR
34 COOKSON WY
35 KIPLING DR
36 HAWKINS DR
37 FROBISHER DR
38 DRAKES CL
39 BEECHER STOWE DR
40 DARWIN DR
41 CHURCHILL DR
42 FORBES CT
43 MITCHELL GR
42
A B C D E F
Union House
Skeeby Beck
White Hills
Cross Hills
St Cuthbert's Well
PH
Bridgewarth Beck
New House Farm
High Gatherley
Fountain Head
The Grange
Scorton Beck
B1263
Old Maids Farm
PARKGATE LANE
A6136
A1
C7
1 CAXTON CL
2 STEPHENSON RD
3 SHAKESPEARE CL
4 WELLINGTON WY
5 CITADILLA CL
6 NIGHTINGALE CL
7 TUDOR CT
Rosy Hill
Sand & Gravel Quarry
WESTFIELDS 1
THE ARCHERS GN 2
STAGS WY
Beck Bridge
Broken Brea Farm
Park House Farm
Brompton-on-Swale
GATHERLEY ROAD
Gatherley Rd Ind Est
BANKS LA
PO
Scorton
1 CLARENCE RD
2 CLEVELAND RD
3 HOWARD CT
4 FLYWHEEL ST
5 HOWARD CT
B6271
Brompton-on-Swale Prim Sch
Gravel Pit
Home Farm
Tancred Grange
1 BEAUFIGHTER CL
2 TYPHOON CL
3 SPITFIRE CT
4 BLENHEIM CL
RICHMOND ROAD
PEMBURY MEWS
STATION ROAD
BRIDGE RD
Cemy
HOWE HL LA
Howe Hill
Sewage Works
Bolton-on-Swale CE Prim Sch
Brompton Bridge
ST PAUL'S CL 1
GRANGE RD 2
CURTEIS
Colburn Beck Wood
Catterick Bridge
D5
1 WILLOW VW
2 SYCAMORE CT
3 CHESTNUT CL
4 BROUGH MDWS
5 MOWBRAY RD
6 ELM WK
7 ASH CFT
8 ROWAN CT
9 KING'S CL
10 PALLET HL
11 GARTH CL
12 ARENA VW
13 GARTH MDWS
Sand & Gravel Pit
BACK LANE
FLAT LANE
GARTHSIDE
Village Farm
St Giles Farm
C6
1 ST EDMUNDS CL
2 HONEY POT RD
West End
Bolton-on-Swale
Colburn Com Prim Sch
Sewage Works
Thornbrough
Catterick Racecourse
LEEMING LANE
BACK LANE
Colburn
DAISY CL
POPPY CT
HERRIOT DR
AUSTIN DR
Ash House
CATTERICK ROAD
DL10
BOLTON CROSS
BOLTON ROAD
Piper Hill
Ash House Plantation
MOWBRAY RD
BISHOPS WY
EASTON WY
NOEL CT
SWALE LANE
QUEENS CL
Michael Syddall CE Prim Sch
Bolton-on-Swale Lake Nature Reserve
Liby
Catterick
CATARACTONIVM
HIGH ST
SWALE PASTURE LA
Walkerville Ind Est
DE BURGH CT
Home Farm
Manor House
Ellerton
SLED LA
SPRINGS LA
North Farm
Walkerville
REGENTS CT
Ford
Camp Plantation
THE BANK
HIGH GN
LOW GN
BECKSIDE
SCOTT CL
CHERRY TREE CT
ORAN LA
Sewage Works
Ford
Horse Park Wood
Brough Hall
THE PADDOCK
SLESSOR RD
Brough Beck
CHARTERMAN WY
BATTALION CT
Sour Beck
DL9
NUSERY GD
Ellery Hill
River Swale
Norway Wood
Plodmire Wood
Tunstall Road Bridge
A6136
POCOCK PL
LIARDET RD
Sewage Works
High Cowstand Bridge
TUNSTALL ROAD
YARDE AVE
LEECH LA
SANDERS WY
LOCK WK
HOWE AVE
Manor House
BRECKENBROUGH LA
Castle Hills
Breckenbrough
Bainesse
Prospect Hill
Cowstand Farm
Airfield
Wintylow
Limekiln Wood
CATTERICK LA
Little Plantation
Tunstall Road Farm
Lime Kiln Farm
Mount Pleasant
Tunstall Beck
Fox Covert
Lowdon House
BACK LA
Sewage Works
Killerby Hall
JAMES LANE
Manor House
Barkers Barn Farm
Manor House Farm
YARBOROUGH CL 1
THE GARTH 2
PH
LEASES LANE
Killerby Farm
Leases Farm
Tunstall
Mayfield Farm
East Appleton Farm
East Appleton
Hill Farm
Pikehill
Tunstall Moor
LOW STREET
Low Pasture
MOOR LANE
Sowber Hill Farm
Rudd Hall Farm
DL7
Tumulus
Highfield Farm
Westfield Farm
Rudd Hall
Craggs Lane Farm
Belmont
Kennel Whin
West Appleton
Winterfield House
DL8
GYLL HALL LA
Ghyll Hall
West Appleton Farm
New Covert Plantation
Goskins Plantation
Goskins
CRAGGS LA
Sandhole Covert
Gashouse Plantation
LORDS LANE
8 01 7 00 6 99 5 98 4 97 3 96 2 95 1 94
20 21 22 23 24 25
62
42
E4
1 SYDALL'S WY
2 KILLERBY DR
3 ST ANNE'S CR
4 CHAPEL RIGGS
5 BENNIONS WY
6 PER ARDUA WY
7 CENTURIAN CL
8 SLESSOR RD
9 HARRIS DR
10 YOUNGS WY
11 GRUNDY WY
12 GODFREY RD
13 ROBINSON RD
14 STRAFFORD RD
15 MELLERSH RD
16 CHACKSFIELD RD
17 FULLER GOOD RD
18 LYDFORD RD
19 LIARDET RD

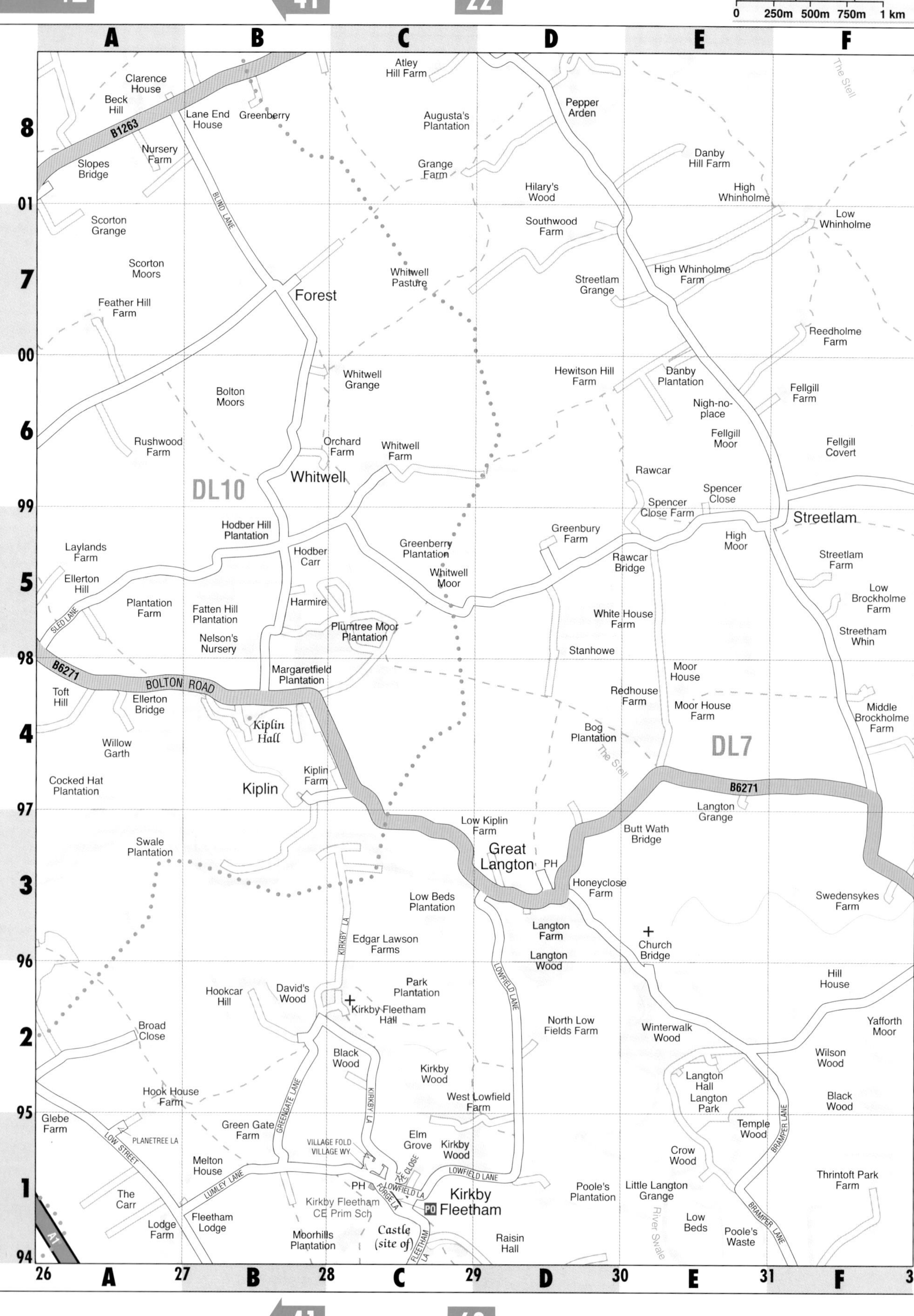

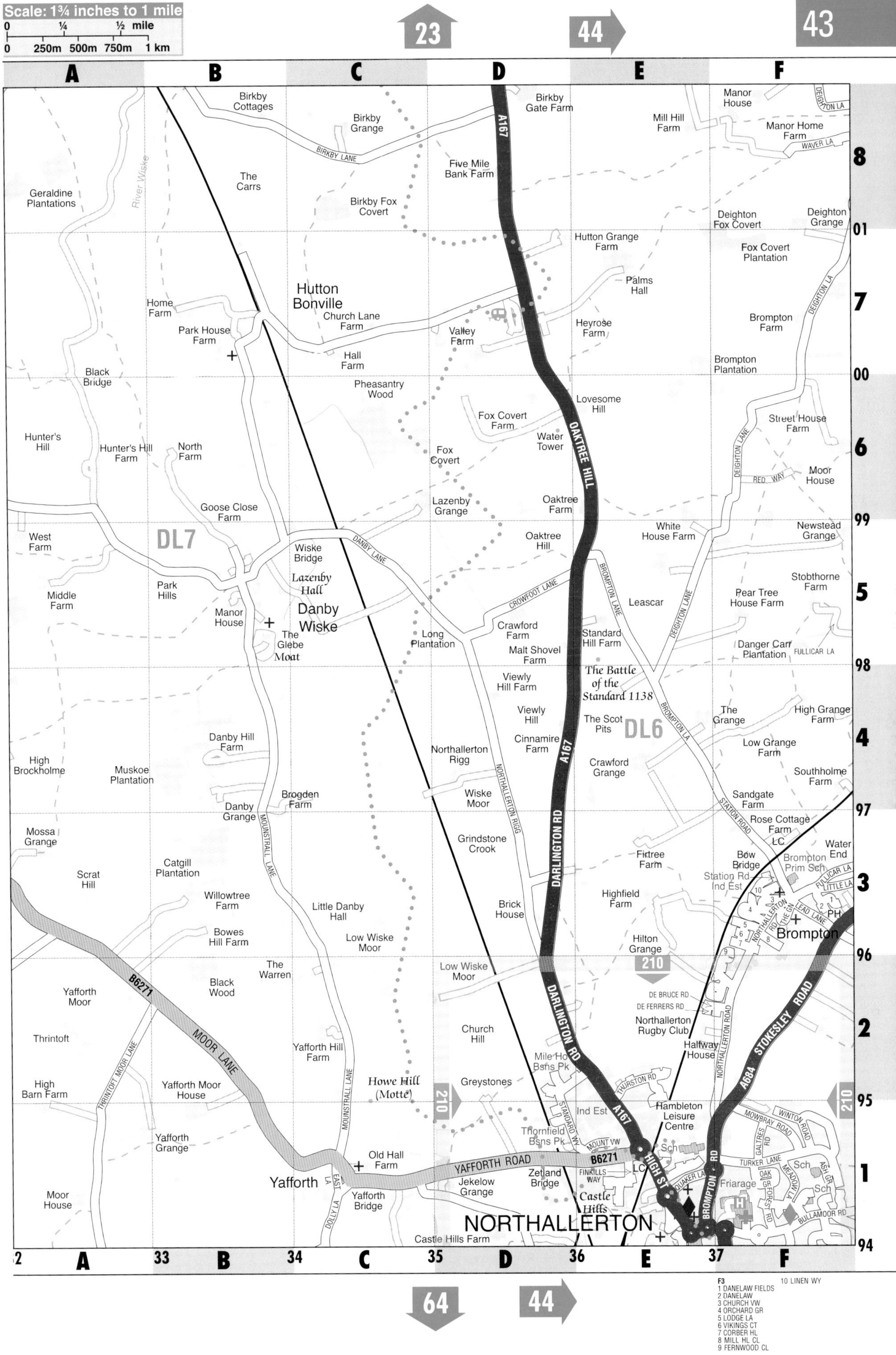
Birkby Cottages
Birkby Grange
Birkby Gate Farm
Mill Hill Farm
Manor House
Manor Home Farm
Birkby Lane
Five Mile Bank Farm
The Carrs
Birkby Fox Covert
Geraldine Plantations
River Wiske
Deighton Fox Covert
Deighton Grange
Hutton Grange Farm
Fox Covert Plantation
Palms Hall
Hutton Bonville
Church Lane Farm
Home Farm
Park House Farm
Valley Farm
Heyrose Farm
Brompton Farm
Hall Farm
Brompton Plantation
Black Bridge
Pheasantry Wood
Lovesome Hill
Fox Covert Farm
Street House Farm
Hunter's Hill
Hunter's Hill Farm
North Farm
Water Tower
Oaktree Hill
Fox Covert
Moor House
Red Way
Goose Close Farm
Lazenby Grange
Oaktree Farm
West Farm
DL7
Wiske Bridge
Danby Lane
Oaktree Hill
White House Farm
Newstead Grange
Lazenby Hall
Brompton Lane
Stobthorne Farm
Middle Farm
Park Hills
Manor House
Danby Wiske
Crowfoot Lane
Leascar
Pear Tree House Farm
The Glebe
Moat
Long Plantation
Crawford Farm
Standard Hill Farm
Deighton Lane
Danger Carr Plantation
Fullicar La
Malt Shovel Farm
Viewly Hill Farm
The Battle of the Standard 1138
Viewly Hill
The Scot Pits
DL6
The Grange
High Grange Farm
Danby Hill Farm
Cinnamire Farm
Low Grange Farm
High Brockholme
Muskoe Plantation
Northallerton Rigg
Crawford Grange
Southholme Farm
Brogden Farm
Wiske Moor
Sandgate Farm
Danby Grange
Rose Cottage Farm
Mossa Grange
Grindstone Crook
Mounstrall Lane
Darlington Rd
Station Road
Fitree Farm
Bow Bridge
Water End
Scrat Hill
Catgill Plantation
Brompton Prim Sch
Station Rd Ind Est
Willowtree Farm
Little Danby Hall
Brick House
Highfield Farm
Bowes Hill Farm
Low Wiske Moor
Hilton Grange
Brompton
PH
Lead Lane
Little La
The Warren
Low Wiske Moor
Black Wood
Yafforth Moor
B6271
De Bruce Rd
De Ferrers Rd
Northallerton Rugby Club
Moor Lane
Stokesley Road
Church Hill
Halfway House
Thrintoft
Yafforth Hill Farm
Mile Ho Bsns Pk
Northallerton Road
A684
Thrintoft Moor Lane
High Barn Farm
Yafforth Moor House
Howe Hill (Motte)
Greystones
Thurston Rd
Ind Est
Hambleton Leisure Centre
Mowbray Road
Winton Road
Yafforth Grange
Mounstrall Lane
Thornfield Bsns Pk
Standard Wy
Mount Vw
Old Hall Farm
Yafforth Road
Galtres Rd
Turker Lane
Ash Gr
Yafforth
Zetland Bridge
Finkills Way
High St
Quaker La
Friarage
Meadow La
Oak Rd
Forest Rd
Jekelow Grange
Castle Hills
Moor House
Yafforth Bridge
Dolly La
East La
Northallerton
Brompton Rd
Bullamoor Rd
Castle Hills Farm
Sch
LC
A167
Oaktree Hill
Waver La
Deighton La
F3
1 Danelaw Fields
2 Danelaw
3 Church Vw
4 Orchard Gr
5 Lodge La
6 Vikings Ct
7 Corber Hl
8 Mill Hl Cl
9 Fernwood Cl
10 Linen Wy

43 24

Scale: 1¾ inches to 1 mile
0 ¼ ½ mile
0 250m 500m 750m 1 km

A B C D E F

Moat Side
Deighton
Town Farm
WAVER LA
Greenhills
Glebe Farm
TOFTS LANE
LC
South View Farm
GREEN LANE
Siddle Grange
8
DEIGHTON LANE
Lingfield Farm
Broomfield Farm
Thorntree Farm
Brecken Hill
Grinklecarr Farm
Town End
Tile Shed Farm
Brick Pond Plantation
Sydal Lodge
Longlands Farm
01
Welbury Fox Covert
Pity Me Wood
Larch Plantation
Welbury Grange
Renny Farm
Winchatt
7
Long Lane Plantation
Deepdale
Baulk Bridge
LOW MOOR LANE
QUAKER'S LANE
Nova Scotia Wood
Thornflatt Farm
Moat
Harsley Grove Farm
Bankside Farm
Wye Carrs
00
Northfield House
Wray House
Wye Carr
Wyecarr Plantation
GOOSECROFT LA
Deepdale Farm
PH
Hawksnest
6
Northfield Farm
LONG LANE
East Harlsey
Morton Grange Farm
Reepool Bridge
Fingay Hill
Harlsey Beck
Pond Plantation
99
LC
DL6
Jubilee Plantation
Stobthorne Farm
Low Moor Farm
Harlsey Grange
STONY LANE
5
West Harlsey
High House Farm
Low Moor
Bruntcliffe Farm
Kettlewell Farm
98
Harlsey Castle
Moat
Lowfield Farm
Brompton Beck
Little Beech Hill
Bruntcliffe Plantation
4
Fir Tree Farm
Winton Plantation
Mount Pleasant Farm
Fox Covert
Mount House
Fullicar House
Winton Beck
FEATHERBED LA
Hallikeld Bridge
97
Ashbridge Farm
FULLICAR LANE
Winton Grange
Rabbit Hill
Tumulus
Beech Hill
Little Bridge Farm
Hallikeld Farm
Winton
A684
STOKESLEY ROAD
A684
High Park House
Dun Close Hill
LITTLE LA
3
Lenthor Farm
Winton Manor Farm
Village Farm
Ellerbeck
Ford
Cemy
Hill House
Foxton Wood
Ford
Foxton Mill Farm
How Beck
Field Head
Foxton
96
Foxton Farm
Flance Acres
BANKS ROAD
The Banks
Stank Hall
Sigston Castle Plantation
Flance Acres Farm
Thorntree Farm
Bulla Moor
2
Old Thompson's Plantation
Ashton House Farm
Sigston Castle
Sigston Castle
Stank Farm
Close Farm
Fox Covert
West Farm
Newsham Grange
BANKS ROAD
FOXTON LANE
Sigston Bridge
Ashton Plantation
95
Harrogate House Farm
Turker Beck
Lodge Farm
Smithy Farm
Jeater Houses
The Hollows
Harrowgate Gill
Manor Farm
1
Pasture House Farm
Kirby Sigston
North Farm
Fox Covert
Bullamoor
Bullamoor Farm
HIGH LANE
BULLAMOOR ROAD
Oaktree Farm
Sigston Grange
Potters Close
PH
Sowerby House Farm
CHESTER LANE
Sigston Wood
A19
SCHOLLA LANE
94

38 A 39 B 40 C 41 D 42 E 43 F

43 65

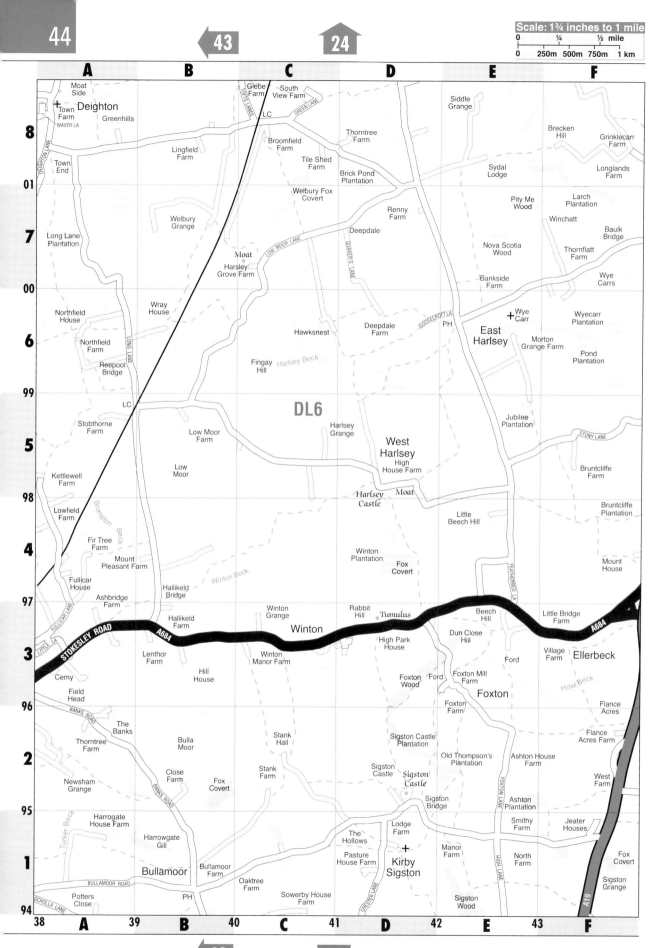

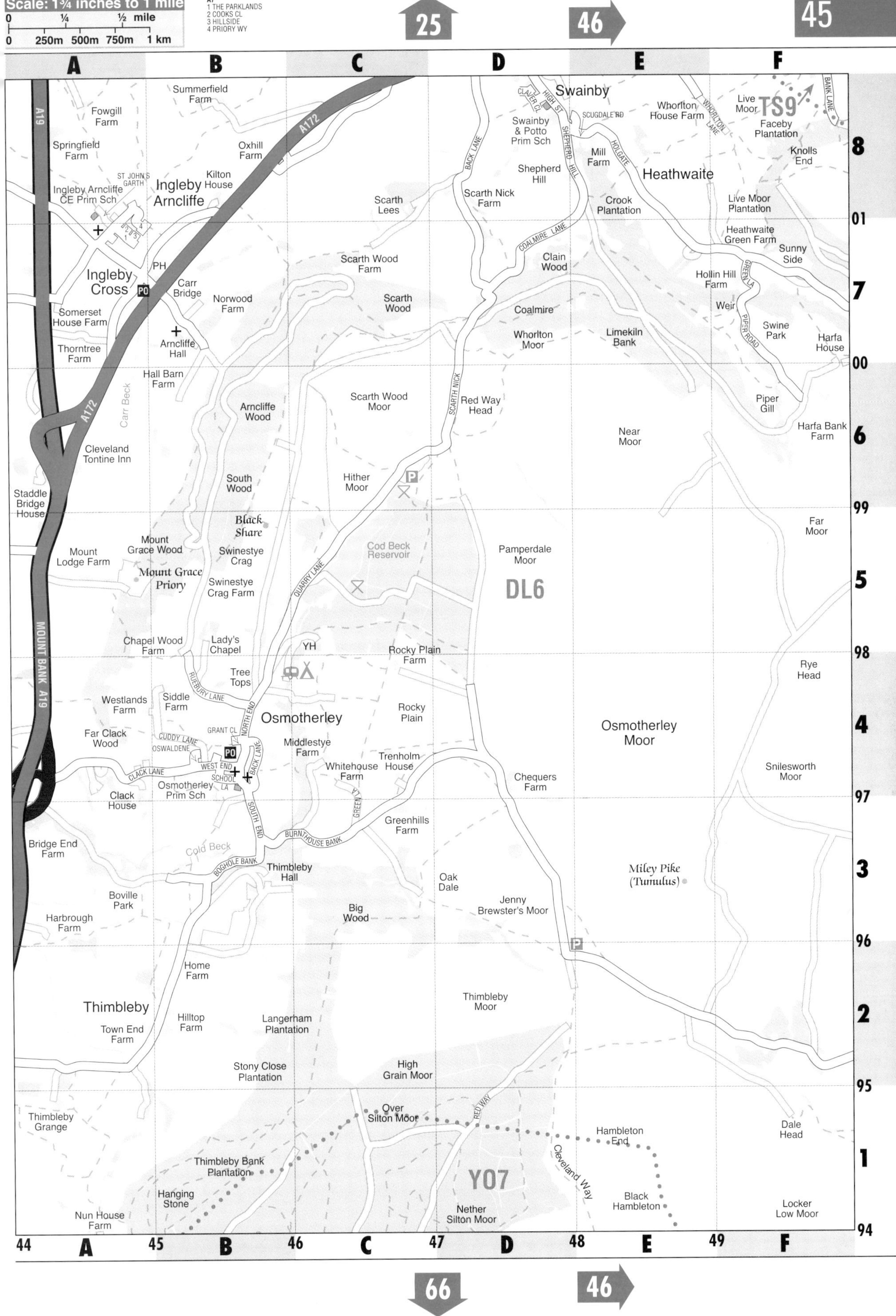

Scale: 1¾ inches to 1 mile
0 ¼ ½ mile
0 250m 500m 750m 1 km
A7
1 THE PARKLANDS
2 COOKS CL
3 HILLSIDE
4 PRIORY WY
25
46
A B C D E F
Summerfield Farm
Fowgill Farm
Springfield Farm
Oxhill Farm
Kilton House
Ingleby Arncliffe
ST JOHN'S GARTH
Ingleby Arncliffe CE Prim Sch
Ingleby Cross
PH
PO
Carr Bridge
Norwood Farm
Somerset House Farm
Thorntree Farm
Arncliffe Hall
Hall Barn Farm
Carr Beck
A172
A19
Swainby
Swainby & Potto Prim Sch
CLAVER CL
HIGH ST
SCUGDALE RD
SHEPHERD HILL
HOLGATE
Whorlton House Farm
WHORLTON LANE
Live Moor
TS9
BANK LANE
Faceby Plantation
Knolls End
Mill Farm
Heathwaite
Shepherd Hill
BACK LANE
Scarth Nick Farm
Scarth Lees
Crook Plantation
Live Moor Plantation
Heathwaite Green Farm
Sunny Side
COALMIRE LANE
Clain Wood
Scarth Wood Farm
Scarth Wood
Hollin Hill Farm
GREEN LA
Weir
PIPER ROAD
Coalmire
Whorlton Moor
Limekiln Bank
Swine Park
Harfa House
Piper Gill
Harfa Bank Farm
Scarth Wood Moor
SCARTH NICK
Red Way Head
Arncliffe Wood
Cleveland Tontine Inn
Near Moor
Staddle Bridge House
South Wood
Hither Moor
P
Black Share
Mount Grace Wood
Mount Lodge Farm
Swinestye Crag
Cod Beck Reservoir
Pamperdale Moor
Far Moor
Mount Grace Priory
Swinestye Crag Farm
QUARRY LANE
DL6
Chapel Wood Farm
Lady's Chapel
YH
Rocky Plain Farm
Rye Head
MOUNT BANK A19
Tree Tops
RUEBURY LANE
Westlands Farm
Siddle Farm
NORTH END
Osmotherley
Rocky Plain
Osmotherley Moor
GRANT CL
Far Clack Wood
CUDDY LANE
OSWALDENE
Middlestye Farm
Trenholm House
Whitehouse Farm
Snilesworth Moor
WEST END
CLACK LANE
SCHOOL LA
BACK LANE
Chequers Farm
Osmotherley Prim Sch
Clack House
SOUTH END
GREEN LA
Greenhills Farm
BURNTHOUSE BANK
Bridge End Farm
Cold Beck
BOGHOLE BANK
Thimbleby Hall
Oak Dale
Miley Pike (Tumulus)
Boville Park
Jenny Brewster's Moor
Harbrough Farm
Big Wood
Home Farm
Thimbleby
Hilltop Farm
Langerham Plantation
Thimbleby Moor
Town End Farm
Stony Close Plantation
High Grain Moor
Thimbleby Grange
Over Silton Moor
RED WAY
Hambleton End
Dale Head
Thimbleby Bank Plantation
Cleveland Way
Hanging Stone
YO7
Black Hambleton
Locker Low Moor
Nun House Farm
Nether Silton Moor
8
01
7
00
6
99
5
98
4
97
3
96
2
95
1
94
44 A 45 B 46 C 47 D 48 E 49 F
66
46

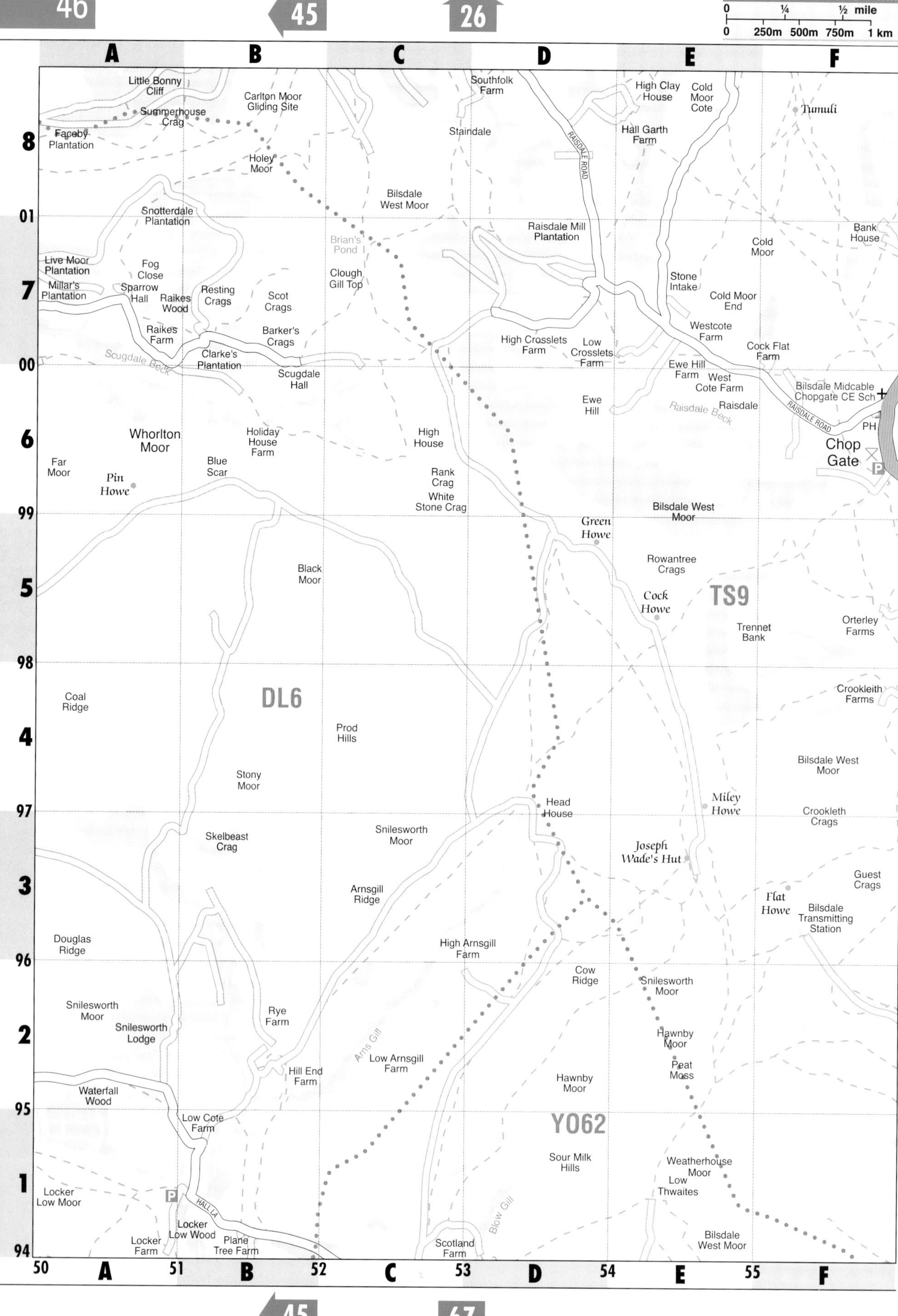

Little Bonny Cliff
Summerhouse Crag
Faceby Plantation
Carlton Moor Gliding Site
Southfolk Farm
Staindale
High Clay House
Cold Moor Cote
RAISDALE ROAD
Hall Garth Farm
Tumuli

Holey Moor
Snotterdale Plantation
Bilsdale West Moor
Raisdale Mill Plantation
Cold Moor
Bank House

Live Moor Plantation
Millar's Plantation
Fog Close
Sparrow Hall
Raikes Wood
Resting Crags
Scot Crags
Clough Gill Top
Brian's Pond
Stone Intake
Cold Moor End
Westcote Farm

Raikes Farm
Clarke's Plantation
Barker's Crags
Scugdale Hall
High Crosslets Farm
Low Crosslets Farm
Ewe Hill Farm
West Cote Farm
Cock Flat Farm
Bilsdale Midcable Chopgate CE Sch

Scugdale Beck
Raisdale Beck
Ewe Hill
Raisdale
RAISDALE ROAD
PH
Chop Gate
P

Whorlton Moor
Holiday House Farm
High House
Rank Crag
White Stone Crag
Green Howe
Bilsdale West Moor

Far Moor
Pin Howe
Blue Scar
Rowantree Crags
Cock Howe
TS9

Black Moor
Orterley Farms
Trennet Bank

Coal Ridge
DL6
Crookleith Farms

Prod Hills
Bilsdale West Moor

Stony Moor
Head House
Miley Howe
Crookleth Crags

Skelbeast Crag
Snilesworth Moor
Joseph Wade's Hut
Guest Crags

Douglas Ridge
Arnsgill Ridge
Flat Howe
Bilsdale Transmitting Station

High Arnsgill Farm
Cow Ridge
Snilesworth Moor

Snilesworth Moor
Snilesworth Lodge
Rye Farm
Ams Gill
Low Arnsgill Farm
Hawnby Moor
Peat Moss

Waterfall Wood
Hill End Farm
YO62

Low Cote Farm
Sour Milk Hills
Hawnby Moor
Weatherhouse Moor
Low Thwaites

Locker Low Moor
P
HALL LA
Locker Low Wood
Plane Tree Farm
Blow Gill
Scotland Farm
Bilsdale West Moor

Locker Farm

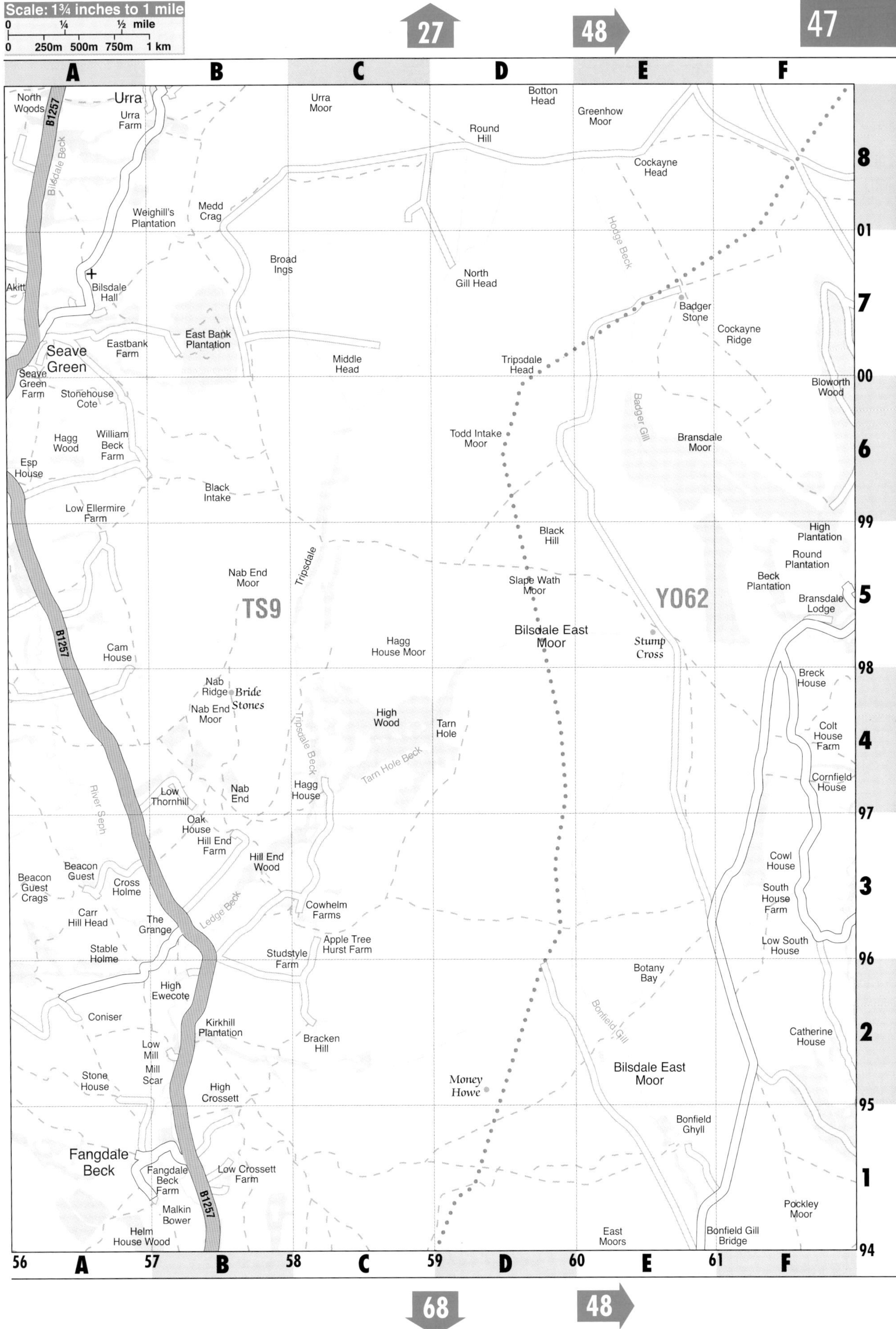

Scale: 1¾ inches to 1 mile
0 ¼ ½ mile
0 250m 500m 750m 1 km
27
48
A B C D E F
North Woods
Urra
Urra Farm
Urra Moor
Botton Head
Greenhow Moor
Round Hill
Cockayne Head
B1257
Bilsdale Beck
Weighill's Plantation
Medd Crag
Broad Ings
North Gill Head
Hodge Beck
Akitt
Bilsdale Hall
Badger Stone
Cockayne Ridge
Seave Green
Eastbank Farm
East Bank Plantation
Middle Head
Tripsdale Head
Seave Green Farm
Stonehouse Cote
Blowarth Wood
Badger Gill
Hagg Wood
William Beck Farm
Todd Intake Moor
Bransdale Moor
Esp House
Black Intake
Low Ellermire Farm
Black Hill
High Plantation
Round Plantation
Nab End Moor
Tripsdale
Slape Wath Moor
Beck Plantation
TS9
YO62
Bransdale Lodge
Cam House
Hagg House Moor
Bilsdale East Moor
Stump Cross
Nab Ridge
Bride Stones
Breck House
Nab End Moor
High Wood
Tarn Hole
Colt House Farm
Tripsdale Beck
Tarn Hole Beck
River Seph
Low Thornhill
Nab End
Hagg House
Cornfield House
Oak House
Hill End Farm
Hill End Wood
Cowl House
Beacon Guest Crags
Beacon Guest
Cross Holme
South House Farm
Carr Hill Head
Ledge Beck
Cowhelm Farms
The Grange
Apple Tree Hurst Farm
Low South House
Stable Holme
Studstyle Farm
Botany Bay
High Ewecote
Coniser
Kirkhill Plantation
Bonfield Gill
Catherine House
Low Mill
Bracken Hill
Mill Scar
Stone House
High Crossett
Money Howe
Bilsdale East Moor
Bonfield Ghyll
Fangdale Beck
Fangdale Beck Farm
Low Crossett Farm
Malkin Bower
Pockley Moor
Helm House Wood
East Moors
Bonfield Gill Bridge
8
01
7
00
6
99
5
98
4
97
3
96
2
95
1
94
56 A 57 B 58 C 59 D 60 E 61 F
68
48

47
28

Scale: 1¾ inches to 1 mile

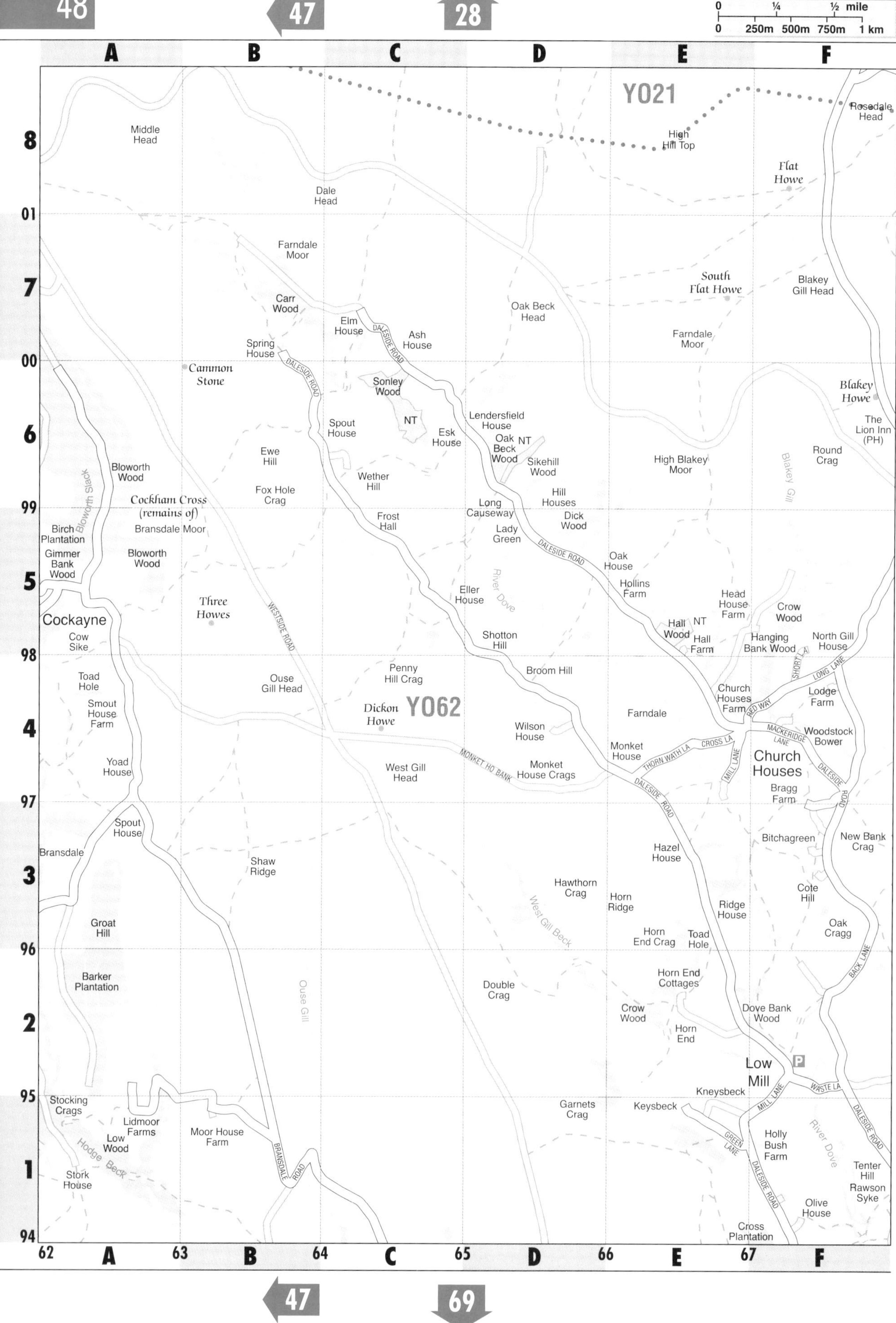

A B C D E F
Y021
Rosedale Head
Middle Head
High Hill Top
Flat Howe
Dale Head
Farndale Moor
South Flat Howe
Blakey Gill Head
Carr Wood
Oak Beck Head
Elm House
Ash House
Farndale Moor
Spring House
Cammon Stone
Sonley Wood
Blakey Howe
NT
Lendersfield House
The Lion Inn (PH)
Spout House
Esk House
Oak Beck Wood
Round Crag
Ewe Hill
Sikehill Wood
High Blakey Moor
Blakey Gill
Bloworth Slack
Bloworth Wood
Wether Hill
Fox Hole Crag
Hill Houses
Cockham Cross (remains of)
Long Causeway
Dick Wood
Frost Hall
Birch Plantation
Bransdale Moor
Lady Green
Gimmer Bank Wood
Bloworth Wood
Oak House
Hollins Farm
River Dove
Eller House
Three Howes
Head House Farm
Crow Wood
Cockayne
Hall Wood
Hall Farm
Hanging Bank Wood
North Gill House
Cow Sike
Shotton Hill
Broom Hill
Toad Hole
Penny Hill Crag
Ouse Gill Head
Church Houses Farm
Lodge Farm
Smout House Farm
Dickon Howe
Y062
Farndale
Wilson House
Woodstock Bower
Monket House
Church Houses
Yoad House
West Gill Head
Monket House Crags
Bragg Farm
Spout House
Bitchagreen
New Bank Crag
Bransdale
Hazel House
Shaw Ridge
Hawthorn Crag
Horn Ridge
Cote Hill
Ridge House
Oak Cragg
Groat Hill
West Gill Beck
Horn End Crag
Toad Hole
Barker Plantation
Ouse Gill
Double Crag
Horn End Cottages
Crow Wood
Dove Bank Wood
Horn End
Low Mill
Stocking Crags
Garnets Crag
Keysbeck
Kneysbeck
Lidmoor Farms
Moor House Farm
Holly Bush Farm
Low Wood
Hodge Beck
River Dove
Tenter Hill
Stork House
Rawson Syke
Olive House
Cross Plantation
WESTSIDE ROAD
DALESIDE ROAD
MONKET HO BANK
THORN WATH LA
CROSS LA
MILL LANE
RED WAY
SHORT LA
LONG LANE
MACKERIDGE LANE
BACK LANE
WASTE LA
GREEN LANE
BRANSDALE ROAD
P
8 01 7 00 6 99 5 98 4 97 3 96 2 95 1 94
62 63 64 65 66 67

47
69

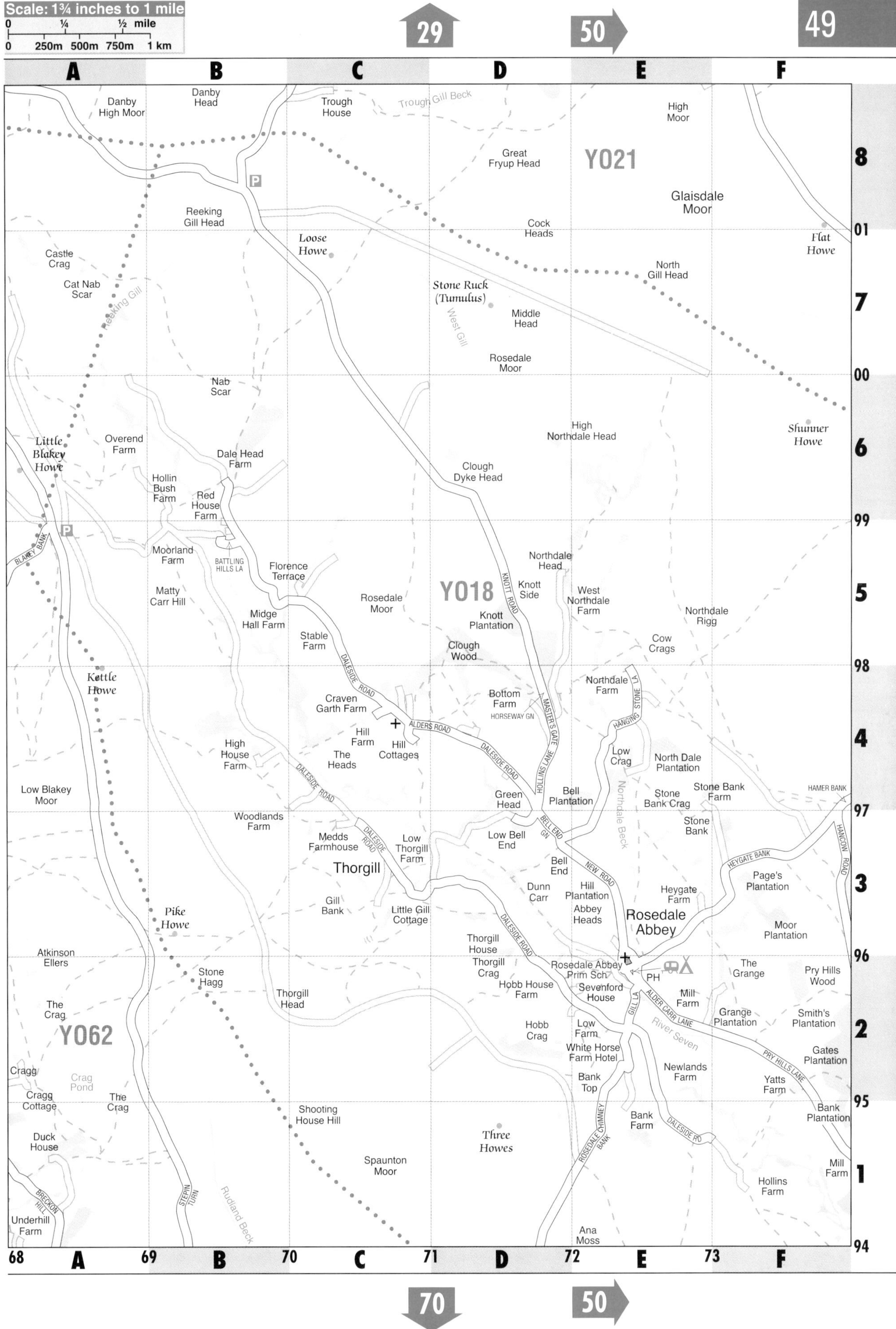

Scale: 1¾ inches to 1 mile
0 ¼ ½ mile
0 250m 500m 750m 1 km
29
50
49
A B C D E F
Danby High Moor
Danby Head
Trough House
Trough Gill Beck
High Moor
Great Fryup Head
YO21
Glaisdale Moor
Reeking Gill Head
Cock Heads
Flat Howe
Castle Crag
Loose Howe
North Gill Head
Cat Nab Scar
Reeking Gill
Stone Ruck (Tumulus)
West Gill
Middle Head
Rosedale Moor
Nab Scar
High Northdale Head
Shunner Howe
Little Blakey Howe
Overend Farm
Dale Head Farm
Clough Dyke Head
Hollin Bush Farm
Red House Farm
BLAKEY BANK
Moorland Farm
BATTLING HILLS LA
Florence Terrace
Northdale Head
Matty Carr Hill
Rosedale Moor
YO18
KNOTT ROAD
Knott Side
West Northdale Farm
Northdale Rigg
Midge Hall Farm
Knott Plantation
Stable Farm
Clough Wood
Cow Crags
Kettle Howe
DALESIDE ROAD
Bottom Farm
HORSEWAY GN
Northdale Farm
STONE LA
Craven Garth Farm
HANGING
MASTER'S GATE
ALDERS ROAD
Hill Farm
Hill Cottages
High House Farm
The Heads
DALESIDE ROAD
HOLLINS LANE
Low Crag
North Dale Plantation
Low Blakey Moor
DALESIDE ROAD
Green Head
Bell Plantation
Stone Bank Crag
Stone Bank Farm
HAMER BANK
Northdale Beck
Woodlands Farm
BELL END GN
Stone Bank
Medds Farmhouse
DALESIDE ROAD
Low Thorgill Farm
Low Bell End
HANCOW ROAD
HEYGATE BANK
Thorgill
Bell End
NEW ROAD
Page's Plantation
Gill Bank
Little Gill Cottage
Dunn Carr
Hill Plantation
Heygate Farm
Pike Howe
Abbey Heads
Rosedale Abbey
Moor Plantation
Thorgill House
DALESIDE ROAD
Atkinson Ellers
Thorgill Crag
Rosedale Abbey Prim Sch
The Grange
Pry Hills Wood
Stone Hagg
Hobb House Farm
Sevenford House
PH
Thorgill Head
Mill Farm
The Crag
GILL LA
ALDER CARR LANE
Grange Plantation
Smith's Plantation
YO62
Hobb Crag
Low Farm
River Seven
White Horse Farm Hotel
Gates Plantation
Cragg
Crag Pond
PRY HILLS LANE
Newlands Farm
Bank Top
Yatts Farm
Cragg Cottage
The Crag
Shooting House Hill
Bank Plantation
ROSEDALE CHIMNEY BANK
Bank Farm
DALESIDE RD
Duck House
Three Howes
Spaunton Moor
Mill Farm
BRECKON HILL
STEPIN TURN
Rudland Beck
Hollins Farm
Underhill Farm
Ana Moss
8 01 7 00 6 99 5 98 4 97 3 96 2 95 1 94
68 69 70 71 72 73
70
50

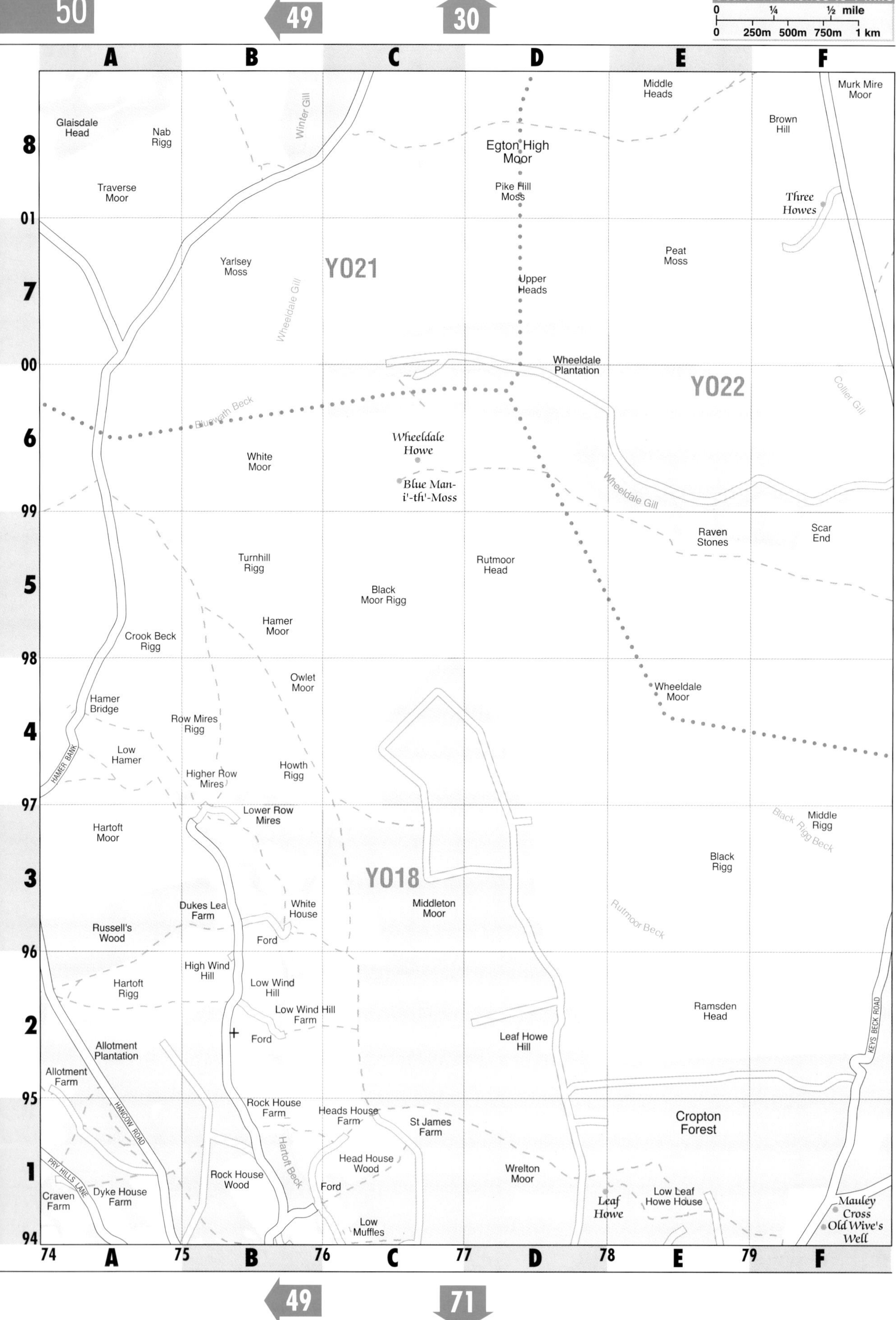

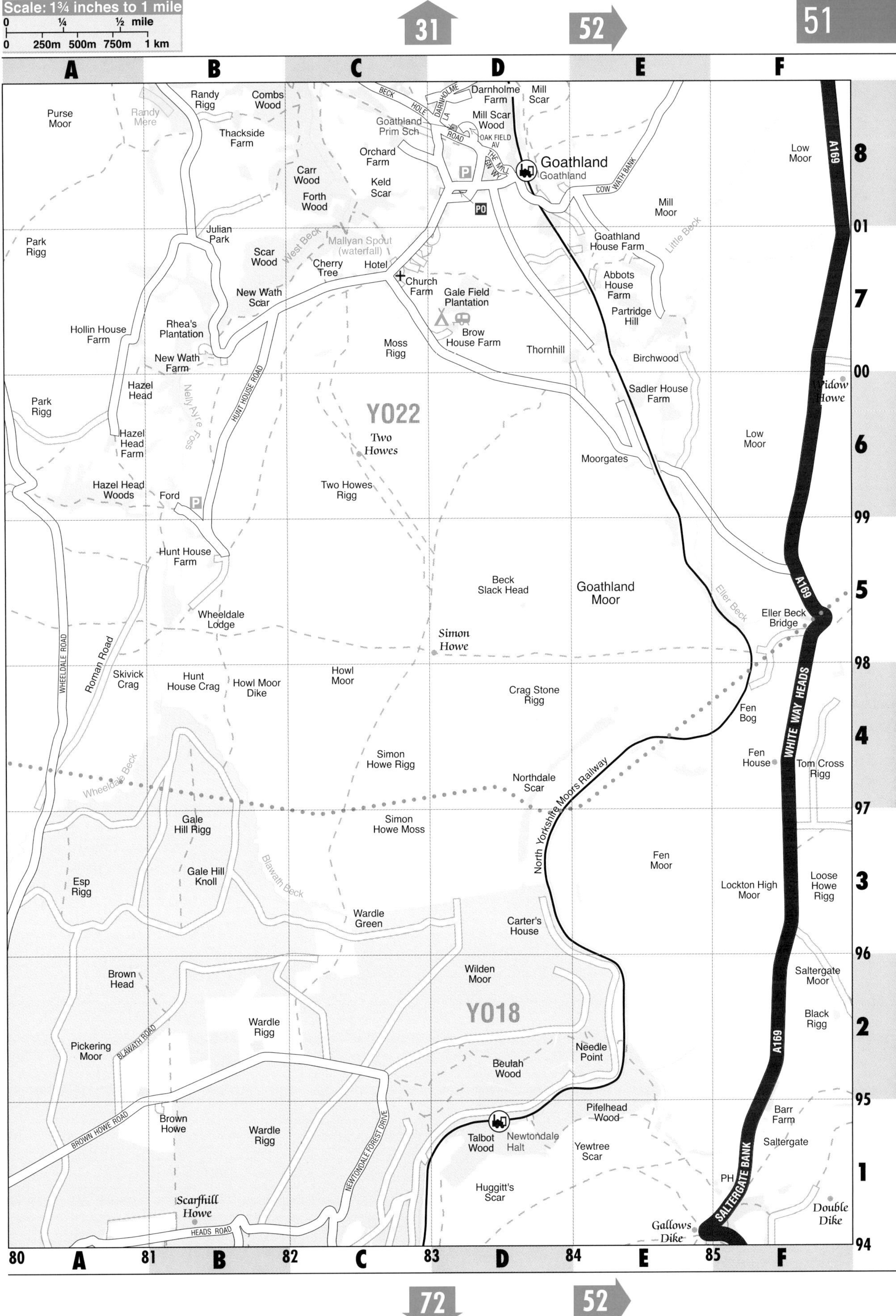
Scale: 1¾ inches to 1 mile
0 ¼ ½ mile
0 250m 500m 750m 1 km
31
52
A
B
C
D
E
F
Purse Moor
Randy Mere
Randy Rigg
Combs Wood
Thackside Farm
Beck Hole
Darnholme La
Darnholme Farm
Mill Scar
Goathland Prim Sch
Mill Scar Wood
Road
Oak Field Av
The Will Gn Wy
Orchard Farm
Goathland
Goathland
Cow Wath Bank
Low Moor
Carr Wood
Keld Scar
Forth Wood
PO
Mill Moor
Julian Park
Park Rigg
Scar Wood
West Beck
Mallyan Spout (waterfall)
Cherry Tree
Hotel
Goathland House Farm
Little Beck
Church Farm
Abbots House Farm
New Wath Scar
Gale Field Plantation
Partridge Hill
Hollin House Farm
Rhea's Plantation
Brow House Farm
Moss Rigg
Thornhill
New Wath Farm
Birchwood
Hazel Head
Hunt House Road
Sadler House Farm
Widow Howe
Park Rigg
YO22
Nelly Ayre Foss
Hazel Head Farm
Two Howes
Low Moor
Moorgates
Hazel Head Woods
Ford
Two Howes Rigg
Hunt House Farm
Beck Slack Head
Goathland Moor
A169
Eller Beck
Wheeldale Lodge
Eller Beck Bridge
Simon Howe
Wheeldale Road
Roman Road
Skivick Crag
Hunt House Crag
Howl Moor Dike
Howl Moor
Crag Stone Rigg
White Way Heads
Fen Bog
Simon Howe Rigg
Fen House
Tom Cross Rigg
Wheeldale Beck
Northdale Scar
North Yorkshire Moors Railway
Gale Hill Rigg
Simon Howe Moss
Fen Moor
Gale Hill Knoll
Blawath Beck
Esp Rigg
Lockton High Moor
Loose Howe Rigg
Wardle Green
Carter's House
Brown Head
Wilden Moor
Saltergate Moor
YO18
Wardle Rigg
Black Rigg
Blawath Road
Pickering Moor
Needle Point
A169
Beulah Wood
Brown Howe Road
Brown Howe
Wardle Rigg
Newtondale Forest Drive
Pifelhead Wood
Barr Farm
Talbot Wood
Newtondale Halt
Yewtree Scar
Saltergate
PH
Saltergate Bank
Huggitt's Scar
Scarfhill Howe
Heads Road
Gallows Dike
Double Dike
8
01
7
00
6
99
5
98
4
97
3
96
2
95
1
94
80
81
82
83
84
85
72
52

51
32

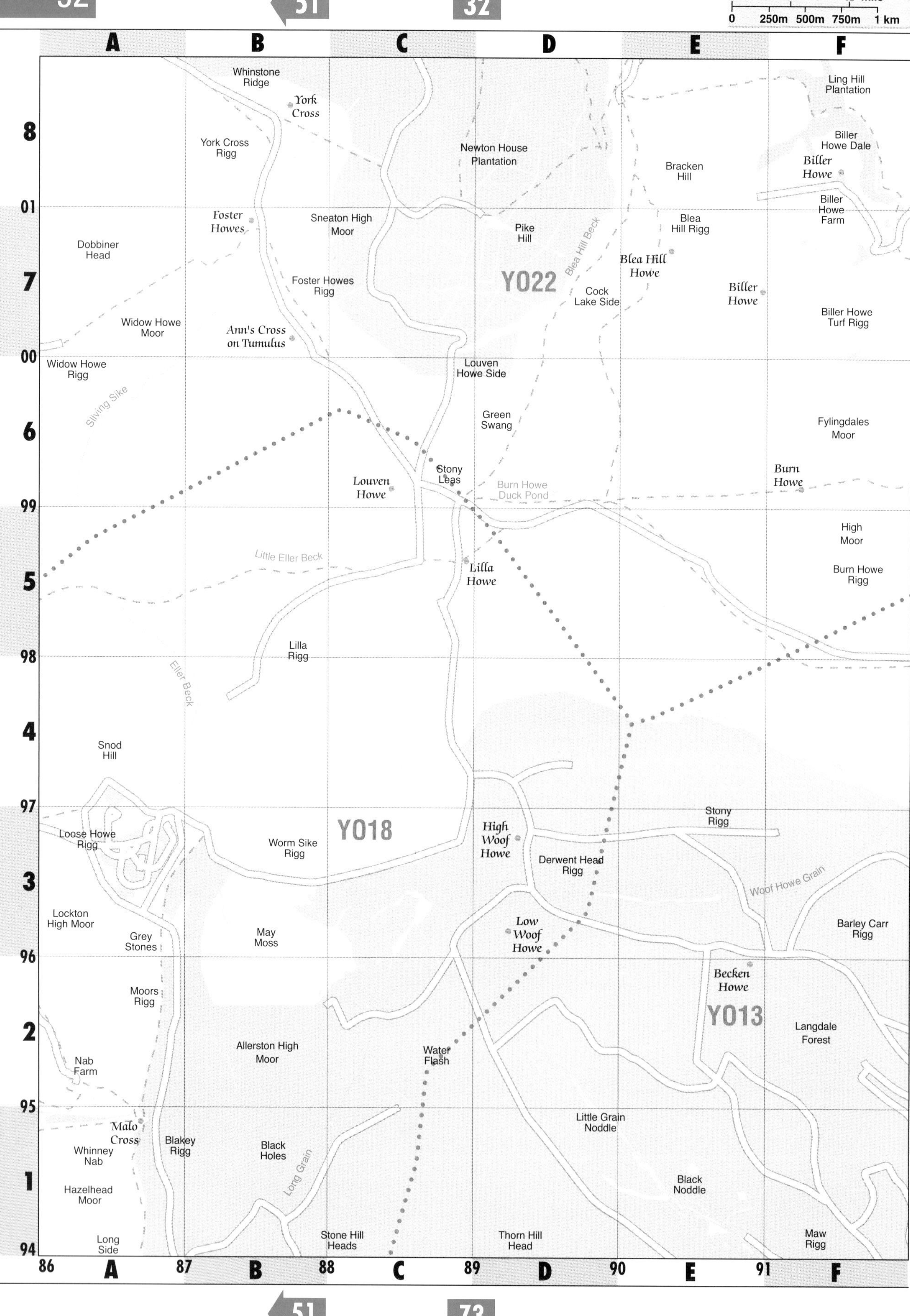
Scale: 1¾ inches to 1 mile
0 ¼ ½ mile
0 250m 500m 750m 1 km
A B C D E F
8
01
7
00
6
99
5
98
4
97
3
96
2
95
1
94
86 87 88 89 90 91
Whinstone Ridge
York Cross
York Cross Rigg
Newton House Plantation
Ling Hill Plantation
Biller Howe Dale
Biller Howe
Bracken Hill
Biller Howe Farm
Foster Howes
Sneaton High Moor
Pike Hill
Blea Hill Beck
Blea Hill Rigg
Dobbiner Head
Blea Hill Howe
YO22
Foster Howes Rigg
Cock Lake Side
Biller Howe
Biller Howe Turf Rigg
Widow Howe Moor
Ann's Cross on Tumulus
Widow Howe Rigg
Louven Howe Side
Sliving Sike
Green Swang
Fylingdales Moor
Stony Leas
Louven Howe
Burn Howe
Burn Howe Duck Pond
High Moor
Little Eller Beck
Lilla Howe
Burn Howe Rigg
Lilla Rigg
Eller Beck
Snod Hill
Stony Rigg
Loose Howe Rigg
Worm Sike Rigg
YO18
High Woof Howe
Derwent Head Rigg
Woof Howe Grain
Lockton High Moor
Barley Carr Rigg
Grey Stones
May Moss
Low Woof Howe
Becken Howe
Moors Rigg
YO13
Langdale Forest
Allerston High Moor
Water Flash
Nab Farm
Malo Cross
Little Grain Noddle
Whinney Nab
Blakey Rigg
Black Holes
Long Grain
Black Noddle
Hazelhead Moor
Long Side
Stone Hill Heads
Thorn Hill Head
Maw Rigg

51
73

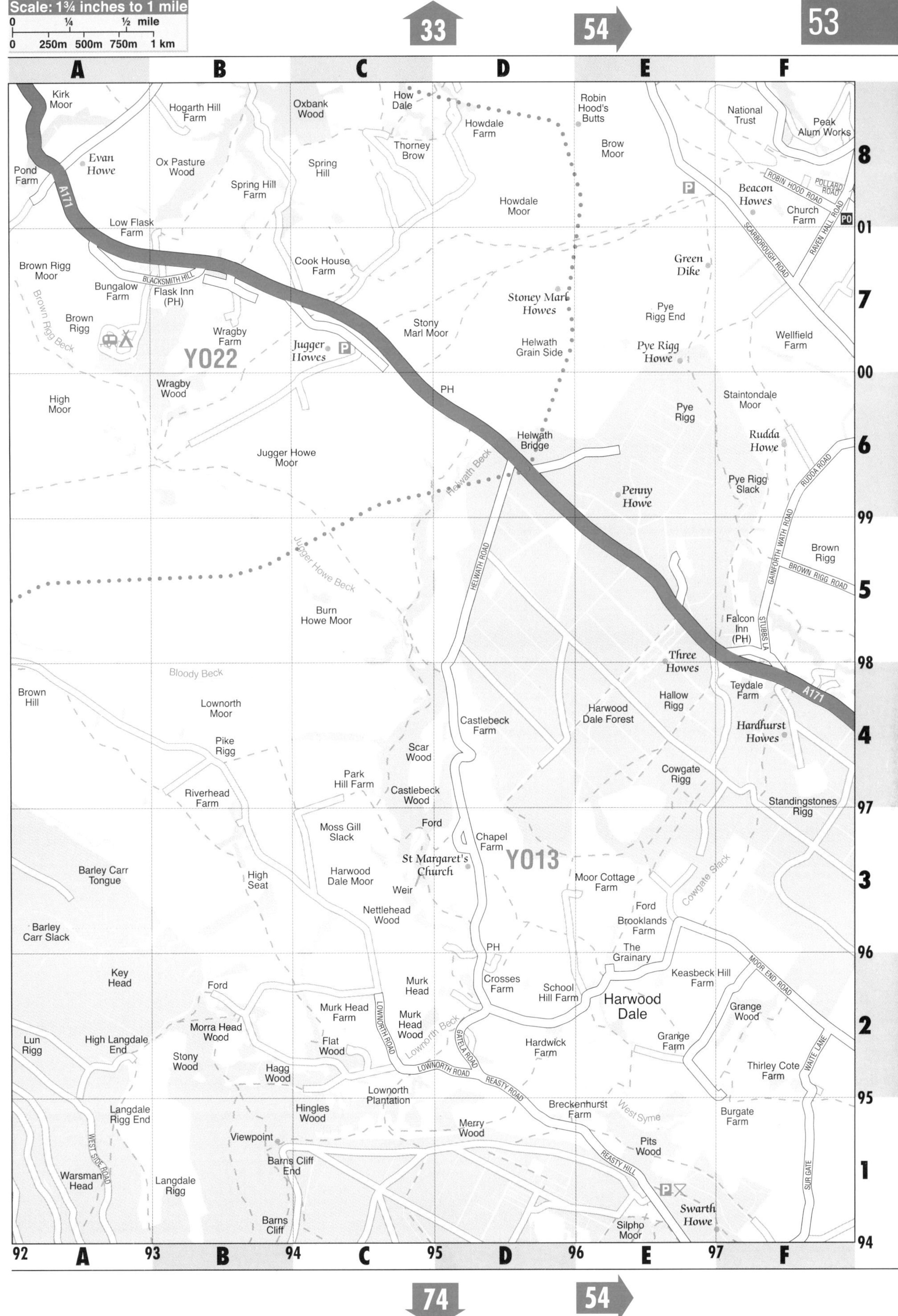
Scale: 1¾ inches to 1 mile
33
54
A
B
C
D
E
F
Kirk Moor
Hogarth Hill Farm
Oxbank Wood
How Dale
Robin Hood's Butts
National Trust
Peak Alum Works
Howdale Farm
Thorney Brow
Brow Moor
Evan Howe
Ox Pasture Wood
Spring Hill
Pond Farm
Spring Hill Farm
Howdale Moor
Beacon Howes
Church Farm
Low Flask Farm
Brown Rigg Moor
Cook House Farm
Green Dike
Bungalow Farm
Flask Inn (PH)
Stoney Marl Howes
Brown Rigg
Wragby Farm
Stony Marl Moor
Pye Rigg End
Wellfield Farm
Jugger Howes
Helwath Grain Side
Pye Rigg Howe
YO22
High Moor
Wragby Wood
PH
Staintondale Moor
Pye Rigg
Rudda Howe
Helwath Bridge
Jugger Howe Moor
Pye Rigg Slack
Penny Howe
Brown Rigg
Burn Howe Moor
Falcon Inn (PH)
Three Howes
Bloody Beck
Brown Hill
Lownorth Moor
Teydale Farm
Hallow Rigg
Harwood Dale Forest
Castlebeck Farm
Hardhurst Howes
Pike Rigg
Scar Wood
Cowgate Rigg
Park Hill Farm
Castlebeck Wood
Riverhead Farm
Standingstones Rigg
Ford
Moss Gill Slack
Chapel Farm
YO13
St Margaret's Church
Barley Carr Tongue
High Seat
Harwood Dale Moor
Moor Cottage Farm
Weir
Ford
Nettlehead Wood
Brooklands Farm
Barley Carr Slack
PH
The Grainary
Key Head
Ford
Murk Head
Crosses Farm
School Hill Farm
Keasbeck Hill Farm
Murk Head Farm
Harwood Dale
Grange Wood
Morra Head Wood
Murk Head Wood
Lun Rigg
High Langdale End
Flat Wood
Grange Farm
Hardwick Farm
Stony Wood
Hagg Wood
Thirley Cote Farm
Lownorth Plantation
Langdale Rigg End
Hingles Wood
Breckenhurst Farm
West Syme
Burgate Farm
Merry Wood
Viewpoint
Pits Wood
Barns Cliff End
Warsman Head
Langdale Rigg
Swarth Howe
Barns Cliff
Silpho Moor
A171
BLACKSMITH HILL
ROBIN HOOD ROAD
POLLARD ROAD
SCARBOROUGH ROAD
RAVEN HALL ROAD
RUDDA ROAD
GAINFORTH WATH ROAD
BROWN RIGG ROAD
STUBBS LA
HELWATH ROAD
LOWNORTH ROAD
GATELA ROAD
REASTY ROAD
REASTY HILL
MOOR END ROAD
WAITE LANE
SUR GATE
WEST SIDE ROAD
Brown Rigg Beck
Jugger Howe Beck
Helwath Beck
Lownorth Beck
Cowgate Slack
8
01
7
00
6
99
5
98
4
97
3
96
2
95
1
94
92
93
94
95
96
97
74
54

53

Scale: 1¾ inches to 1 mile

0   ¼   ½   mile
0 250m 500m 750m 1 km

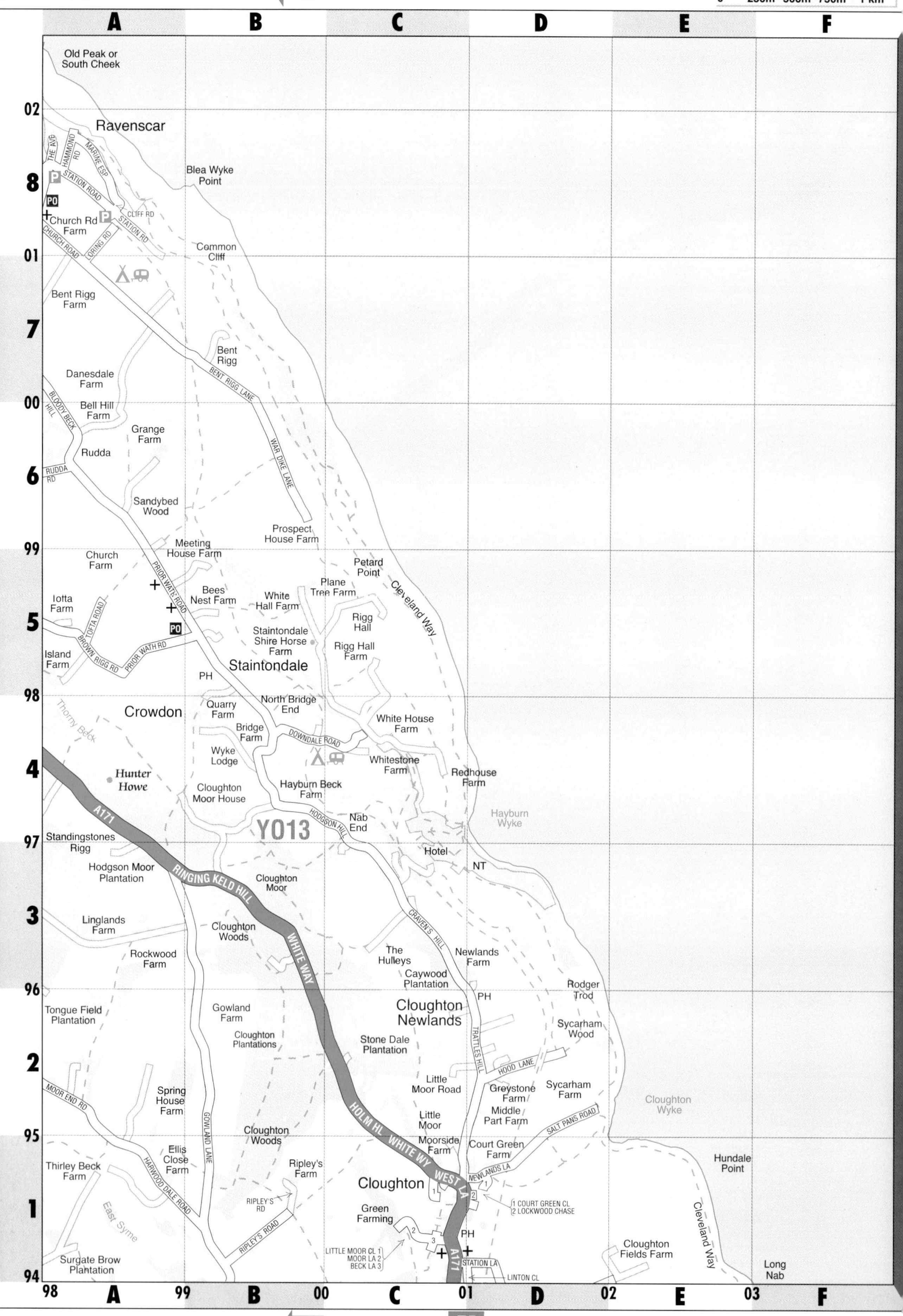

A   B   C   D   E   F

Old Peak or South Cheek

02

Ravenscar

8   Blea Wyke Point

THE AVG
HAMMOND RD
MARINE ESP
STATION ROAD
PO
P
CLIFF RD
Church Rd Farm
STATION RD
SPRING RD
P

01

CHURCH ROAD
Common Cliff

Bent Rigg Farm

7

Bent Rigg

Danesdale Farm
BENT RIGG LANE

00

BLOODY HILL
Bell Hill Farm
Grange Farm
WAR DIKE LANE

6

RUDDA RD
Rudda

Sandybed Wood

Prospect House Farm

99

Church Farm
Meeting House Farm
Petard Point
Cleveland Way

Iotta Farm
Bees Nest Farm
White Hall Farm
Plane Tree Farm

5

PRIOR WATH ROAD
PO
Staintondale Shire Horse Farm
Rigg Hall

IOTTA ROAD
BROWN RIGG RD
PRIOR WATH RD
Rigg Hall Farm

Island Farm
Staintondale

98

PH
North Bridge End

Crowdon
Quarry Farm
DOWNDALE ROAD
White House Farm

Thorny Beck
Bridge Farm
Whitestone Farm
Redhouse Farm

4

Hunter Howe
Wyke Lodge
Hayburn Beck Farm
Hayburn Wyke

A171
Cloughton Moor House
HODGSON HILL
Nab End

97

Standingstones Rigg
YO13
Hotel

Hodgson Moor Plantation
RINGING KELD HILL
Cloughton Moor
NT

3

Linglands Farm
Cloughton Woods
CRAVEN'S HILL

Rockwood Farm
WHITE WAY
The Hulleys
Newlands Farm

96

Tongue Field Plantation
Gowland Farm
Caywood Plantation
Rodger Trod

MOOR END RD
Cloughton Plantations
PH
Sycarham Wood

2

GOWLAND LANE
Stone Dale Plantation
TRATTLES HILL
HOOD LANE

Spring House Farm
Little Moor Road
Greystone Farm
Sycarham Farm

Cloughton Woods
Little Moor
Middle Part Farm
SALT PANS ROAD
Cloughton Wyke

95

HARWOOD DALE ROAD
Moorside Farm
Court Green Farm
Hundale Point

Thirley Beck Farm
Ellis Close Farm
HOLM HL
WHITE WY
WEST LA
NEWLANDS LA

Ripley's Farm
Cloughton
1 Court Green Cl
2 Lockwood Chase
Cleveland Way

1

EAST SYME
RIPLEY'S RD
Green Farming
2

RIPLEY'S ROAD
LITTLE MOOR CL 1
MOOR LA 2
BECK LA 3
3
PH
A171
STATION LA
Cloughton Fields Farm
Long Nab

Surgate Brow Plantation
LINTON CL

94

98   A   99   B   00   C   01   D   02   E   03   F

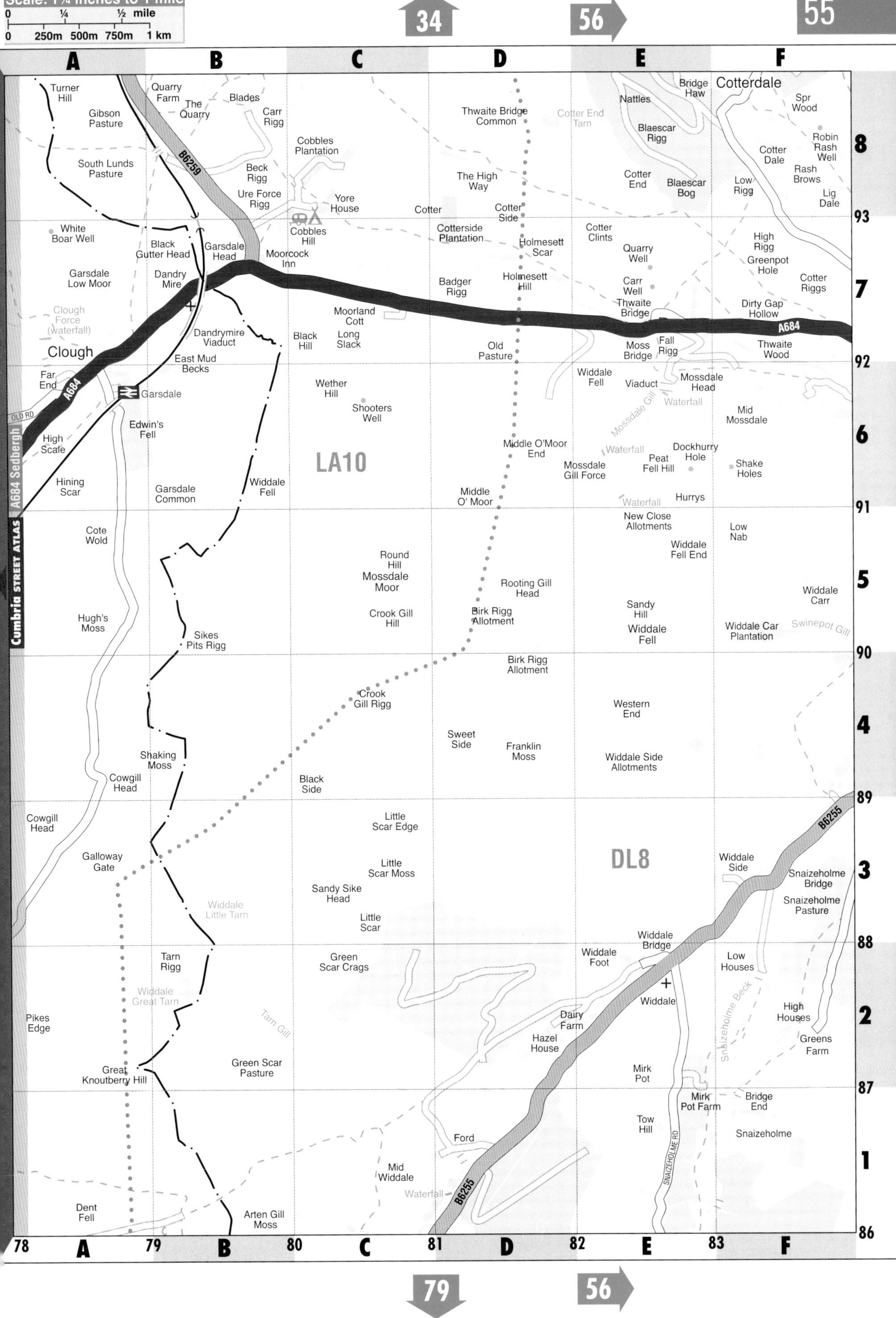
Scale: 1¾ inches to 1 mile
0 ¼ ½ mile
0 250m 500m 750m 1 km
34
56
A B C D E F
Turner Hill
Gibson Pasture
Quarry Farm
The Quarry
Blades
Carr Rigg
Cobbles Plantation
Thwaite Bridge Common
Cotter End Tarn
Nattles
Bridge Haw
Cotterdale
Spr Wood
Blaescar Rigg
Robin Rash Well
South Lunds Pasture
B6259
Beck Rigg
Ure Force Rigg
Yore House
The High Way
Cotter
Cotter Side
Cotter End
Blaescar Bog
Low Rigg
Cotter Dale
Rash Brows
Lig Dale
White Boar Well
Black Gutter Head
Garsdale Head
Cobbles Hill
Moorcock Inn
Cotterside Plantation
Holmesett Scar
Cotter Clints
Quarry Well
High Rigg
Greenpot Hole
Garsdale Low Moor
Dandry Mire
Badger Rigg
Holmesett Hill
Carr Well
Cotter Riggs
Clough Force (waterfall)
Moorland Cott
Thwaite Bridge
Dirty Gap Hollow
A684
Dandrymire Viaduct
Black Hill
Long Slack
Old Pasture
Moss Bridge
Fall Rigg
Thwaite Wood
Clough
East Mud Becks
Far End
A684
Garsdale
Wether Hill
Widdale Fell
Viaduct
Mossdale Head
OLD RD
Waterfall
Mid Mossdale
Shooters Well
Mossdale Gill
High Scale
Edwin's Fell
Middle O'Moor End
Waterfall
Dockhurry Hole
LA10
Peat Fell Hill
Mossdale Gill Force
Shake Holes
Hining Scar
Garsdale Common
Widdale Fell
Middle O' Moor
Waterfall
Hurrys
A684 Sedbergh
Cumbria STREET ATLAS
Cote Wold
New Close Allotments
Low Nab
Widdale Fell End
Round Hill
Mossdale Moor
Rooting Gill Head
Widdale Carr
Hugh's Moss
Crook Gill Hill
Birk Rigg Allotment
Sandy Hill
Widdale Fell
Widdale Car Plantation
Swinepot Gill
Sikes Pits Rigg
Birk Rigg Allotment
Crook Gill Rigg
Western End
Sweet Side
Franklin Moss
Widdale Side Allotments
Shaking Moss
Cowgill Head
Black Side
Cowgill Head
Little Scar Edge
B6255
Galloway Gate
Little Scar Moss
DL8
Widdale Side
Snaizeholme Bridge
Sandy Sike Head
Snaizeholme Pasture
Widdale Little Tarn
Little Scar
Widdale Bridge
Tarn Rigg
Green Scar Crags
Widdale Foot
Low Houses
Widdale Great Tarn
Widdale
Pikes Edge
Tarn Gill
Dairy Farm
Snaizeholme Beck
High Houses
Hazel House
Greens Farm
Great Knoutberry Hill
Green Scar Pasture
Mirk Pot
Mirk Pot Farm
Bridge End
Tow Hill
Snaizeholme
Ford
SNAIZEHOLME RD
Mid Widdale
B6255
Dent Fell
Waterfall
Arten Gill Moss
93 8 7 92 6 91 5 90 4 89 3 88 2 87 1 86
78 A 79 B 80 C 81 D 82 E 83 F
79
56

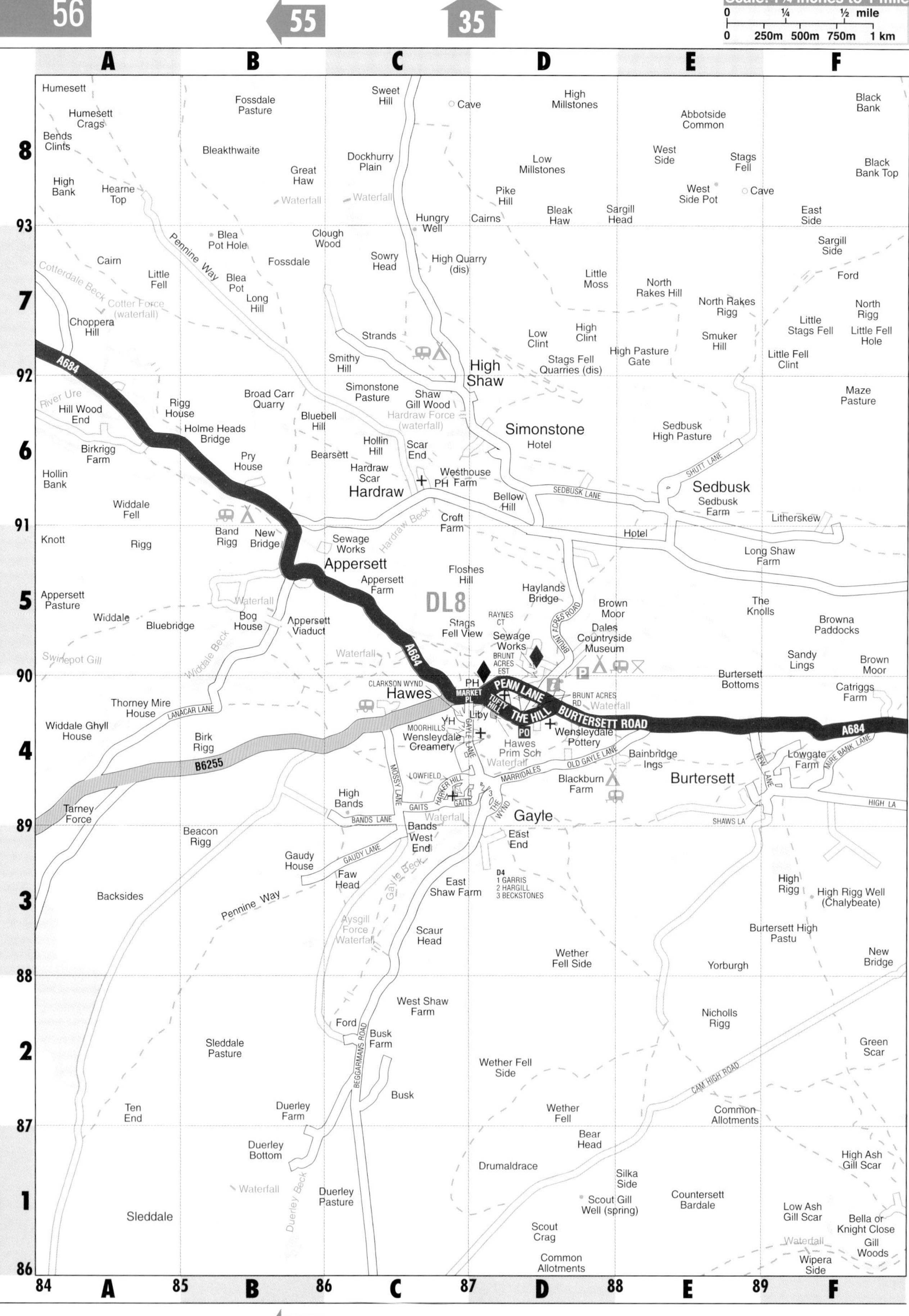

A   B   C   D   E   F

8
Humesett
Humesett Crags
Bends Clints
High Bank
Hearne Top

Fossdale Pasture
Bleakthwaite
Great Haw
Waterfall

Sweet Hill
Dockhurry Plain
Waterfall

Cave
High Millstones

Abbotside Common
West Side
Stags Fell
West Side Pot
Cave

Black Bank
Black Bank Top
East Side

93

7
Cairn
Little Fell
Choppera Hill

Pennine Way
Cotterdale Beck
Cotter Force (waterfall)

Blea Pot Hole
Blea Pot
Long Hill
Fossdale

Clough Wood
Sowry Head
Hungry Well
High Quarry (dis)

Cairns
Low Millstones
Pike Hill
Bleak Haw

Little Moss
North Rakes Hill
North Rakes Rigg
Sargill Head
High Pasture Gate

Sargill Side
Ford
North Rigg
Smuker Hill
Little Stags Fell
Little Fell Clint
Little Fell Hole

92

6
A684
River Ure
Hill Wood End
Birkrigg Farm
Hollin Bank
Knott

Rigg House
Broad Carr Quarry
Holme Heads Bridge
Pry House
Bluebell Hill
Bearsett

Smithy Hill
Simonstone Pasture
Hollin Hill
Hardraw Scar
Scar End
Hardraw
Shaw Gill Wood
Hardraw Force (waterfall)
Westhouse Farm
PH

Strands
High Shaw
High Clint
Low Clint
Stags Fell Quarries (dis)
High Pasture Gate

Simonstone
Hotel
Sedbusk High Pasture

Maze Pasture

91
Widdale Fell
Rigg

Band Rigg
New Bridge
Sewage Works
Appersett
Appersett Farm

Croft Farm
Bellow Hill

SHUTT LANE
Sedbusk
Sedbusk Farm
Hotel
SEDBUSK LANE
Litherskew

Long Shaw Farm

5
Appersett Pasture
Widdale
Bluebridge

Waterfall
Bog House
Appersett Viaduct
Widdale Beck
Swinepot Gill

Floshes Hill
DL8
Stags Fell View
Waterfall

Haylands Bridge
RAYNES CT
Sewage Works
BRUNT ACRES EST

BRUNT ACRES ROAD
Brown Moor
Dales Countryside Museum

The Knolls
Browna Paddocks
Sandy Lings
Brown Moor

90
Thorney Mire House
Widdale Ghyll House
Birk Rigg

LANACAR LANE
Clarkson Wynd
Hawes
MARKET PL
PH
YH
Wensleydale Creamery
MOORHILLS
PO
THE HILL
PENN LANE
Liby
Hawes Prim Sch
Wensleydale Pottery
BURTERSETT ROAD
BRUNT ACRES RD
Waterfall
OLD GAYLE LANE
Bainbridge Ings
Blackburn Farm

Burtersett Bottoms
Catriggs Farm
A684
Lowgate Farm
Burtersett
NEW LANE
URE BANK LANE
HIGH LA

4
B6255
Birk Rigg
MOSSY LANE
HARKER HILL
GAITS
Lowfield
Gayle
GAITS
THE WYND
MARRIDALES
SHAWS LA

89
Tarney Force
Beacon Rigg
High Bands
BANDS LANE
Waterfall
Bands West End
East End
GAUDY LANE
D4
1 GARRIS
2 HARGILL
3 BECKSTONES
High Rigg
High Rigg Well (Chalybeate)

3
Backsides
Gaudy House
Faw Head
Pennine Way
Gayle Beck
East Shaw Farm
Aysgill Force Waterfall
Scaur Head

Wether Fell Side
Yorburgh
Burtersett High Pastu
New Bridge

88
West Shaw Farm
Busk Farm
Ford
BEGGARMANS ROAD
Nicholls Rigg
Green Scar

2
Sleddale Pasture
Busk
Wether Fell Side
Wether Fell
CAM HIGH ROAD
Common Allotments

87
Ten End
Duerley Farm
Duerley Bottom
Bear Head
Silka Side
Countersett Bardale
High Ash Gill Scar

1
Sleddale
Waterfall
Duerley Beck
Duerley Pasture
Drumaldrace
Scout Gill Well (spring)
Scout Crag
Common Allotments
Low Ash Gill Scar
Waterfall
Bella or Knight Close
Gill Woods
Wipera Side

86
84   A   85   B   86   C   87   D   88   E   89   F

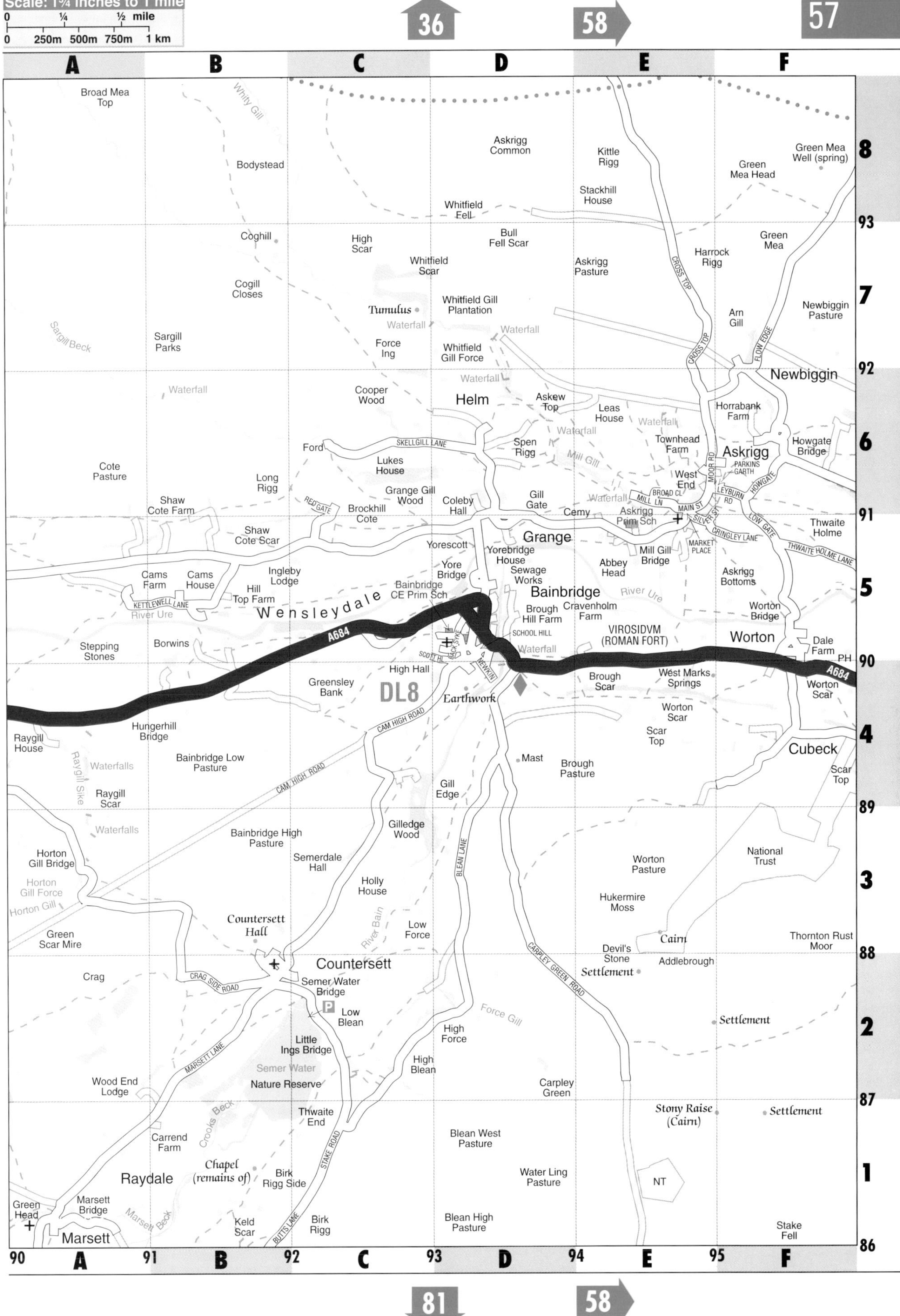
Scale: 1¾ inches to 1 mile
0 ¼ ½ mile
0 250m 500m 750m 1 km
36
58
A B C D E F
Broad Mea Top
Whity Gill
Askrigg Common
Kittle Rigg
Green Mea Well (spring)
Green Mea Head
Bodystead
Stackhill House
Whitfield Fell
Coghill
High Scar
Bull Fell Scar
Askrigg Pasture
Harrock Rigg
Green Mea
Whitfield Scar
Cogill Closes
Whitfield Gill Plantation
Tumulus
Waterfall
Newbiggin Pasture
Arn Gill
Sargill Beck
Sargill Parks
Force Ing
Whitfield Gill Force
CROSS TOP
FLOW EDGE
Newbiggin
Cooper Wood
Helm
Askew Top
Leas House
Horrabank Farm
SKELLGILL LANE
Ford
Spen Rigg
Mill Gill
Townhead Farm
Askrigg
Howgate Bridge
PARKINS GARTH
MOOR RD
Lukes House
Cote Pasture
Long Rigg
Grange Gill Wood
West End
BROAD CL
MILL LN
LEYBURN RD
HOWGATE
Shaw Cote Farm
RED GATE
Brockhill Cote
Coleby Hall
Gill Gate
Cemy
Askrigg Prim Sch
MAIN ST
SILVER ST
LOW GATE
Thwaite Holme
Shaw Cote Scar
Yorescott
Grange
Mill Gill Bridge
MARKET PLACE
CRINGLEY LANE
THWAITE HOLME LANE
Cams Farm
Cams House
Ingleby Lodge
Yore Bridge
Yorebridge House
Sewage Works
Abbey Head
Askrigg Bottoms
Hill Top Farm
Bainbridge CE Prim Sch
Bainbridge
River Ure
KETTLEWELL LANE
Wensleydale
Brough Hill Farm
Cravenholm Farm
Worton Bridge
SCHOOL HILL
VIROSIDVM (ROMAN FORT)
Worton
Dale Farm
PH
A684
Stepping Stones
Borwins
BACK SKYE
SCOTT HL
NEWKIN
High Hall
Brough Scar
West Marks Springs
Worton Scar
Greensley Bank
DL8
Earthwork
Worton Scar
CAM HIGH ROAD
Scar Top
Raygill House
Hungerhill Bridge
Cubeck
Waterfalls
Raygill Sike
Bainbridge Low Pasture
Mast
Brough Pasture
Scar Top
Raygill Scar
Gill Edge
Gilledge Wood
Bainbridge High Pasture
National Trust
Horton Gill Bridge
Semerdale Hall
BLEAN LANE
Worton Pasture
Horton Gill Force
Horton Gill
Holly House
Hukermire Moss
River Bain
Countersett Hall
Low Force
Cairn
Thornton Rust Moor
Green Scar Mire
Devil's Stone
Countersett
Addlebrough
CARPLEY GREEN ROAD
Crag
CRAG SIDE ROAD
Semer Water Bridge
Settlement
P
Low Blean
Force Gill
Little Ings Bridge
High Force
High Blean
MARSETT LANE
Semer Water Nature Reserve
Wood End Lodge
Carpley Green
Stony Raise (Cairn)
Crooks Beck
Thwaite End
STAKE ROAD
Carrend Farm
Blean West Pasture
Chapel (remains of)
Raydale
Birk Rigg Side
Water Ling Pasture
NT
Green Head
Marsett Bridge
Marsett Beck
Keld Scar
BUTTS LANE
Birk Rigg
Blean High Pasture
Stake Fell
Marsett
8 93 7 92 6 91 5 90 4 89 3 88 2 87 1 86
90 91 92 93 94 95
81
58

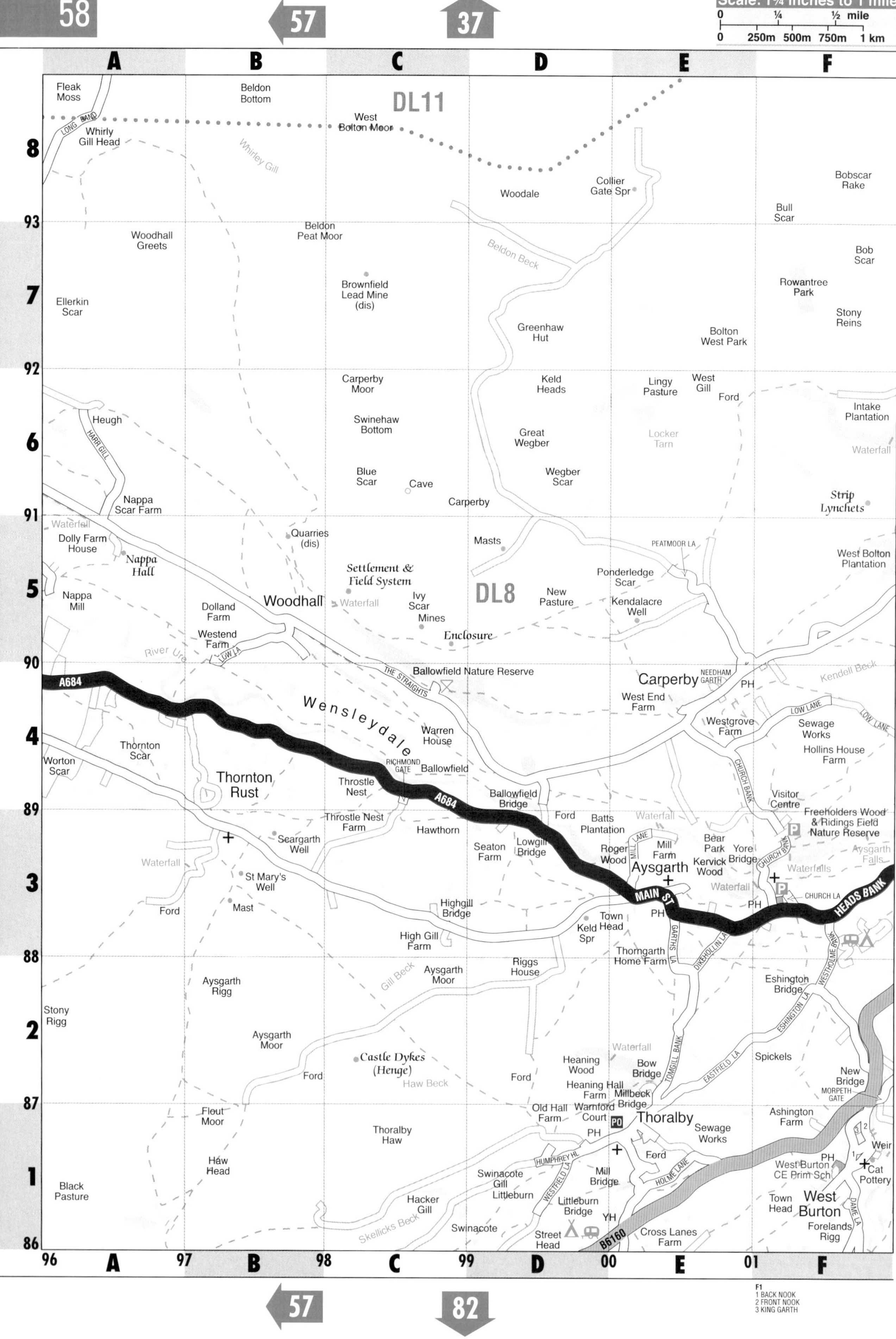

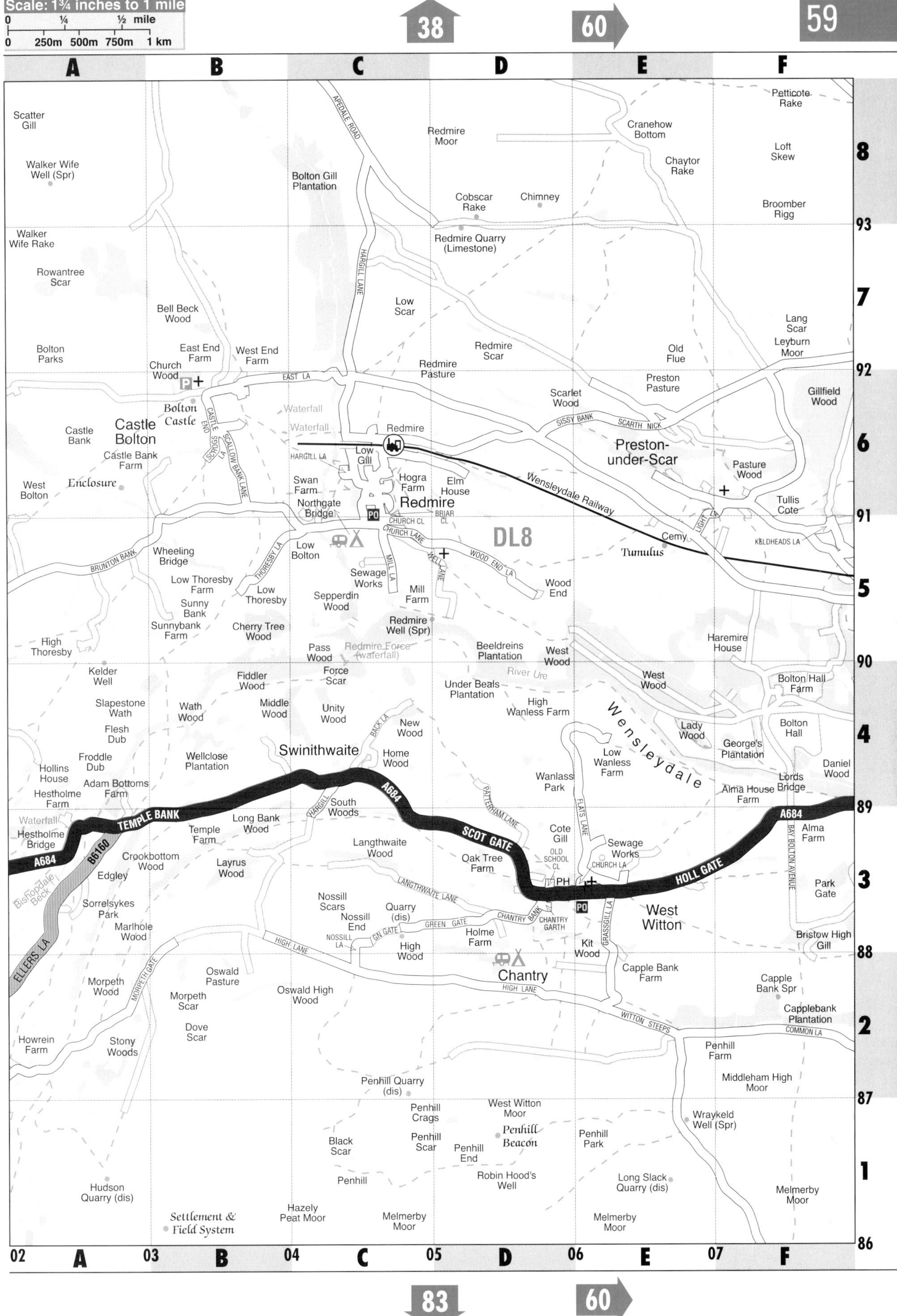

Scale: 1¾ inches to 1 mile
0 ¼ ½ mile
0 250m 500m 750m 1 km
38
60
A B C D E F
8 93 7 92 6 91 5 90 4 89 3 88 2 87 1 86
02 03 04 05 06 07
Scatter Gill
Walker Wife Well (Spr)
Walker Wife Rake
Rowantree Scar
Bell Beck Wood
Bolton Parks
Church Wood
East End Farm
West End Farm
Bolton Castle
Castle Bolton
Castle Bank
Castle Bank Farm
Enclosure
West Bolton
Bolton Gill Plantation
Redmire Moor
Cobscar Rake
Chimney
Redmire Quarry (Limestone)
Cranehow Bottom
Chaytor Rake
Petticote Rake
Loft Skew
Broomber Rigg
Low Scar
Redmire Scar
Redmire Pasture
Old Flue
Lang Scar
Leyburn Moor
Preston Pasture
Scarlet Wood
Gillfield Wood
Waterfall
Waterfall
Redmire
Low Gill
Hogra Farm
Elm House
Swan Farm
Northgate Bridge
Redmire
Preston-under-Scar
Pasture Wood
Tullis Cote
Wensleydale Railway
DL8
Cemy
Tumulus
Wheeling Bridge
Low Bolton
Low Thoresby Farm
Low Thoresby
Sunny Bank
Sunnybank Farm
Sewage Works
Sepperdin Wood
Mill Farm
Wood End
Redmire Well (Spr)
Cherry Tree Wood
High Thoresby
Pass Wood
Redmire Force (waterfall)
Beeldreins Plantation
West Wood
River Ure
Haremire House
Kelder Well
Fiddler Wood
Force Scar
Under Beals Plantation
High Wanless Farm
West Wood
Bolton Hall Farm
Slapestone Wath
Wath Wood
Middle Wood
Unity Wood
New Wood
Wensleydale
Lady Wood
Bolton Hall
Flesh Dub
Froddle Dub
Wellclose Plantation
Swinithwaite
Home Wood
Low Wanless Farm
George's Plantation
Daniel Wood
Hollins House
Adam Bottoms Farm
Hestholme Farm
Wanlass Park
Lords Bridge
Alma House Farm
Waterfall
Hestholme Bridge
Temple Farm
Long Bank Wood
South Woods
Alma Farm
Crookbottom Wood
Edgley
Layrus Wood
Langthwaite Wood
Cote Gill
Oak Tree Farm
Sewage Works
Bishopdale Beck
Sorrelsykes Park
Nossill Scars
Nossill End
Quarry (dis)
Holme Farm
West Witton
Park Gate
Marlhole Wood
High Wood
Kit Wood
Bristow High Gill
Chantry
Capple Bank Farm
Capple Bank Spr
Morpeth Wood
Oswald Pasture
Oswald High Wood
Morpeth Scar
Capplebank Plantation
Dove Scar
Howrein Farm
Stony Woods
Penhill Farm
Middleham High Moor
Penhill Quarry (dis)
West Witton Moor
Penhill Crags
Wraykeld Well (Spr)
Black Scar
Penhill Scar
Penhill Beacon
Penhill End
Penhill Park
Penhill
Robin Hood's Well
Long Slack Quarry (dis)
Melmerby Moor
Hudson Quarry (dis)
Hazely Peat Moor
Melmerby Moor
Melmerby Moor
Settlement & Field System
APEDALE ROAD
HARGILL LANE
EAST LA
CASTLE END
SCHOOL LA
SCALLOW BANK LANE
SISSY BANK
SCARTH NICK
HARGILL LA
CHURCH CL
BRIAR CL
CHURCH LANE
BRUNTON BANK
THORESBY LA
MILL LA
WELL LANE
WOOD END LA
KELDHEADS LA
LIGHT LA
BACK LA
A684
TEMPLE BANK
B6160
HARGILL
PATTERHAM LANE
FLATS LANE
SCOT GATE
OLD SCHOOL CL
CHURCH LA
HOLL GATE
BAY BOLTON AVENUE
LANGTHWAITE LANE
GREEN GATE
CHANTRY BANK
CHANTRY GARTH
GRASSGILL LA
NOSSILL LA
GN GATE
HIGH LANE
HIGH LANE
WITTON STEEPS
COMMON LA
ELLERS LA
MORPETH GATE
PO
PH
83
60

59
39

D5
1 SPRINGFIELD CL
2 DALE WY
3 WOODBURN DR
4 THORNBOROUGH CRES
5 WOODSIDE
6 MAYTHORNE
7 WENSLEYDALE AVE
8 LOVE LA
9 HIGH ST
10 THE NURSERIES
11 SHAWL TERR
12 HARMBY RD
13 BOLTON WY
14 BOLTON CT
15 WENSLEY RD
16 RAILWAY ST
17 YOREDALE AVE
18 HETTON GARTH
19 SOUTH VW
20 ST MATTHEW'S CL
21 MIDDLEHAM RD
22 PARK VW
23 ELLERCLOSE RD
24 CLIFF DR
25 HAWTHORN CL
26 QUARRY HILLS LA

Scale: 1¾ inches to 1 mile
0 ¼ ½ mile
0 250m 500m 750m 1 km

A B C D E F

Bellerby Moor
High Breary Wood
A6108
8
Leyburn Moor
WHIPPERDALE BANK
Bellerby Moor
Bellerby Moor
Danger Area
RUNS BANK
Gateland Well (spring)
Friar Ings
Westfields Farm
MOOR ROAD
SCHOOL LA
MILL LANE
PO
93
Forty Acre Wood
HERON TREE CL
Sewage Works
DANGER AREA
DANGER AREA
Bellerby
MILL LA
STUDDAH CL
CHURCH ST
Red Bank Farm
Layburn Moor
Sewage Works
7
Manor House
Frog Hole (spring)
South Dyke Farm
Moor Farm
CROSS HEAD BANK
Bellerby Beck
Bellerby Camp
SOUTH MOOR LA
South Moor
Leyburn Moor
92
Fox Covert
Brookside
Cote Pasture
Leyburn Moor
WASHFOLD LANE
Rock Castle
Cow Close
Harmby Moor
Yarker Bank Farm
BELLERBY ROAD
6
Black Quarry (Limestone)
High Side
Harmby Moor House
DALE GR 1
I'ANSON CL 2
RUMFORD WY 3
DALE WY 4
Broats
Settlement & Field System
Warren Wood
YARKER BANK LA
WHIPPERDALE BANK
Moor Quarry
Park Grange
91
MOUNT DR
Givendale Wood
The Scars
GROVE SQ
MOOR RD
Liby
RICHMOND RD
The Wensleydale Sch
Thowker Wood
Leyburn Shawl Plantation
St Peter & St Paul RC Prim Sch
Leyburn Prim Sch
Leyburn
LC
DL8
Sewage Works
Westfield
Brick Garth Plantation
Wensleydale Railway
RISEBER
Maythorne Well
5
Wensley Bridge
P
ROWAN CT
BRENTWOOD
Woodlands
Leyburn
Hell Gill Cottage
Cemy
PO
LC
The Teapottery
ARGILL
i
HARMBY RD
Waterfalls
Wensleydale Rugby Club
A6108
90
White Rose Candles
Flatts Farm
Leyburn Bsns Pk
A684
Wensley Park
Wensley
PH
Cliff Lodge
CURLEW CL
Harmby
MILL LA
The Glebe
Wensleydale
LOW WOOD LANE
MIGHTENS' BANK
Fairy Well (spring)
GILL HAR
COLLIWATH LANE
Craken House Farm
ANNAS GARTH
4
LOW LANE
MIDDLEHAM LA
Cemy
Miller Wood
Wensley Bridge
Leyburn Old Glebe Field Nature Reserve
The Wisings
Howe Hills
Sewage Works
HARGILL CL
Spennithorne CE Prim Sch
Wrang Beck
River Ure
A684
SYCAMORE CL
BROOKSIDE
GREEN LA
89
Wensley Ings
Middleham Bridge
Spennithorne
PH
GALE BANK
Gale Bank Plantation
Hungry Hills
Ford
MILL FLATS LA
Gale Bank
Sewage Works
3
Mount Park Farm
HOLLINS
The Parks
Tower
LEYBURN RD
88
The Mount
PARK LANE
Park Farm
Spigot Lodge Plantation
Millers Gill Plantation
EAST WITTON RD
PARK LA
Middleham Low Moor
Middleham CE Prim Sch
PO
2
Capplebank Plantation
Spigot Lodge
Refuse Tip
Mast
Middleham
Moat
Middleham Castle
A6108
CANAAN LA
COMMON LANE
William's Hill Ring & Bailey
STRAIGHT LA
Manor House Farm
87
P
Ashgill
Cotescue Woods
Cotescue Park
Pinker's Pond
Low Moor
Beckwith Head
Brecongill
The Forbidden Corner
Thorngill
COVERHAM LA
Cover Banks
Tupgill Park
COVERHAM LANE
COTESCUE BANK
Hullo Bridge
River Cover
1
Agglethorpe
Cold Kelds (spring)
Cover Scar
Sewage Works
Coverham Bridge
Coverham Abbey (remains of)
East Witton Lodge
Low Gill Farm
Coverham
HANGHOW LANE
WEST FIELD LANE
BIRD RIDDING LA
Ford
86

08 A 09 B 10 C 11 D 12 E 13 F

59
84

E2
1 ST ALKELDA'S RD
2 KINGSLEY DR
3 NORTH RD
4 THE SPRINGS
5 PARK LA
6 CHURCH ST
7 KIRKGATE
8 BACK LA
9 MARKET PL
10 BACK ST
11 GROVE TERR
12 DOG HILL
13 SHARP HL CL

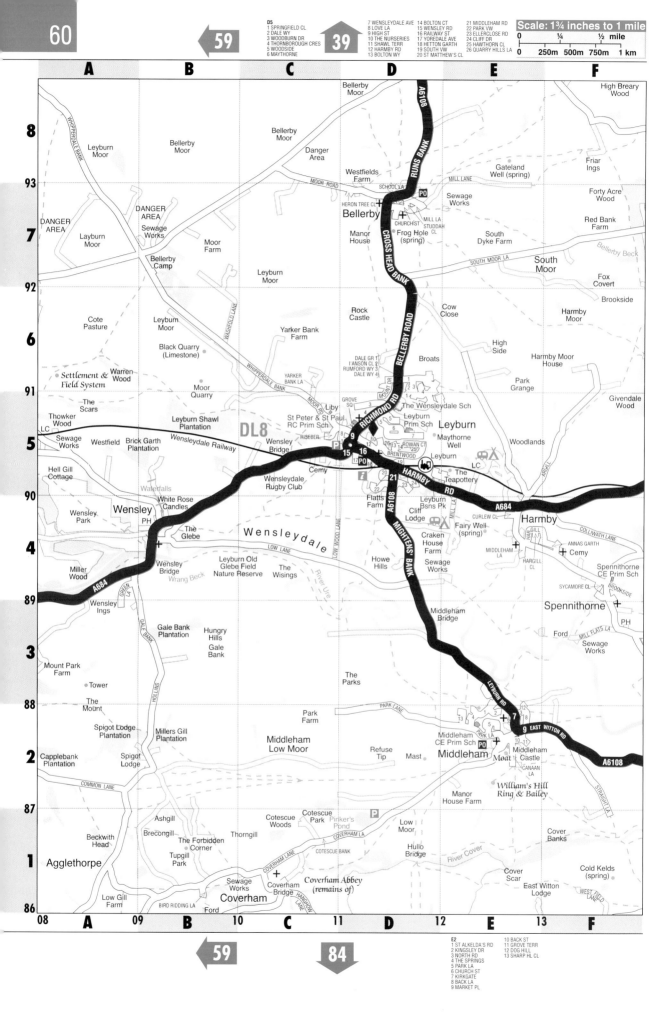

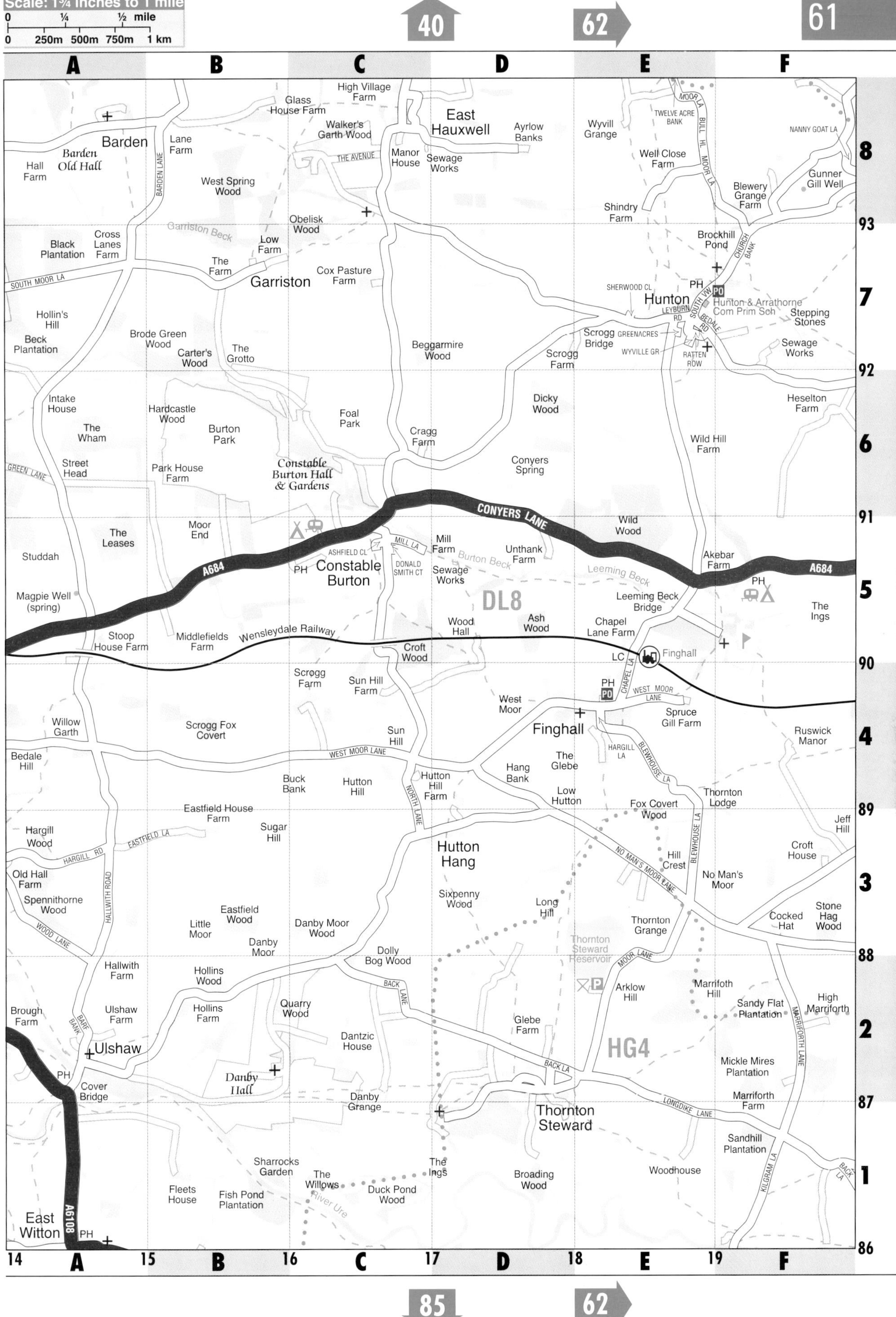

Barden
Hall Farm
Barden Old Hall
Black Plantation
Cross Lanes Farm
Lane Farm
West Spring Wood
BARDEN LANE
High Village Farm
Glass House Farm
Walker's Garth Wood
THE AVENUE
East Hauxwell
Manor House
Sewage Works
Ayrlow Banks
Wyvill Grange
Well Close Farm
MOOR LA
TWELVE ACRE BANK
BULL HL MOOR LA
NANNY GOAT LA
Shindry Farm
Blewery Grange Farm
Gunner Gill Well
SOUTH MOOR LA
Hollin's Hill
Beck Plantation
The Farm
Garriston
Garriston Beck
Obelisk Wood
Low Farm
Cox Pasture Farm
Brockhill Pond
CHURCH BANK
Brode Green Wood
Carter's Wood
The Grotto
Beggarmire Wood
SHERWOOD CL
Hunton
PO
PH
Hunton & Arrathorne Com Prim Sch
Stepping Stones
LEYBURN RD
SOUTH VW
BEDALE RD
Scrogg Bridge
GREENACRES
WYVILLE GR
RATTEN ROW
Sewage Works
Intake House
The Wham
Hardcastle Wood
Burton Park
Scrogg Farm
Dicky Wood
Wild Hill Farm
Heselton Farm
GREEN LANE
Street Head
Park House Farm
Foal Park
Cragg Farm
Conyers Spring
Studdah
The Leases
Moor End
Constable Burton Hall & Gardens
CONYERS LANE
Wild Wood
Akebar Farm
A684
A684
Magpie Well (spring)
A684
PH
ASHFIELD CL
Constable Burton
MILL LA
DONALD SMITH CT
Mill Farm
Burton Beck
Unthank Farm
Sewage Works
Leeming Beck
Leeming Beck Bridge
PH
The Ings
DL8
Stoop House Farm
Middlefields Farm
Wensleydale Railway
Croft Wood
Wood Hall
Ash Wood
Chapel Lane Farm
LC
Finghall
Willow Garth
Scrogg Farm
Sun Hill Farm
West Moor
PH
PO
West Moor Lane
Spruce Gill Farm
Ruswick Manor
Bedale Hill
Scrogg Fox Covert
Sun Hill
WEST MOOR LANE
Buck Bank
Hutton Hill
Hutton Hill Farm
NORTH LANE
Hang Bank
Finghall
The Glebe
Low Hutton
HARGILL LA
BLEWHOUSE LA
Fox Covert Wood
Thornton Lodge
Jeff Hill
Croft House
Hargill Wood
HARGILL RD
EASTFIELD LA
Eastfield House Farm
Sugar Hill
Hutton Hang
Sixpenny Wood
Long Hill
NO MAN'S MOOR LANE
Hill Crest
No Man's Moor
Cocked Hat
Stone Hag Wood
Old Hall Farm
Spennithorne Wood
HALLWITH ROAD
Little Moor
Eastfield Wood
Danby Moor Wood
Danby Moor
Danby Moor Wood
Thornton Grange
Thornton Steward Reservoir
P
Arklow Hill
Marrifoth Hill
Sandy Flat Plantation
High Marriforth
WOOD LANE
Brough Farm
BARR BANK
Hallwith Farm
Hollins Wood
Hollins Farm
Quarry Wood
Dolly Bog Wood
BACK LANE
Glebe Farm
MOOR LANE
MARRIFORTH LANE
Mickle Mires Plantation
Ulshaw
Ulshaw Farm
Dantzic House
HG4
Marriforth Farm
PH
Cover Bridge
Danby Hall
Danby Grange
BACK LA
Thornton Steward
LONGDIKE LANE
Sandhill Plantation
East Witton
A6108
PH
Sharrocks Garden
The Willows
The Ings
Duck Pond Wood
River Ure
Broading Wood
Woodhouse
KILGRAM LA
BACK LA
Fleets House
Fish Pond Plantation

40   62

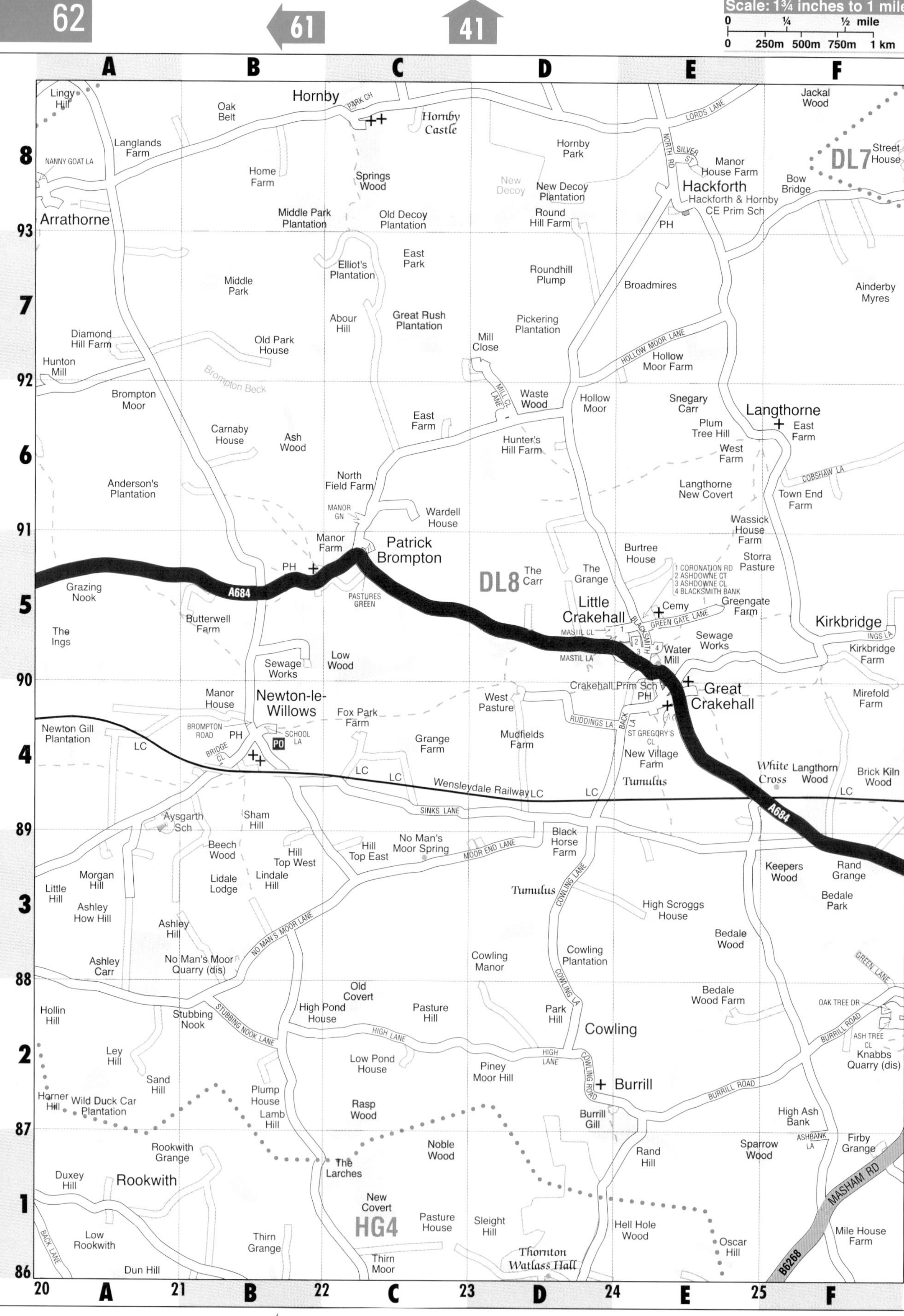

Lingy Hill

NANNY GOAT LA

Langlands Farm

Arrathorne

Hunton Mill

Diamond Hill Farm

Brompton Moor

Anderson's Plantation

Grazing Nook

The Ings

Hornby

Oak Belt

Home Farm

PARK CH

Springs Wood

Hornby Castle

Middle Park Plantation

Old Decoy Plantation

Middle Park

Elliot's Plantation

East Park

Abour Hill

Great Rush Plantation

Old Park House

Carnaby House

Ash Wood

Brompton Beck

North Field Farm

MANOR GN

Wardell House

Manor Farm

PH

Patrick Brompton

PASTURES GREEN

Butterwell Farm

Low Wood

Sewage Works

Manor House

Newton-le-Willows

BROMPTON ROAD

PH

BRIDGE CL

SCHOOL LA

PO

Fox Park Farm

Grange Farm

Newton Gill Plantation

LC

Aysgarth Sch

Sham Hill

Beech Wood

Hill Top West

Lidale Lodge

Lindale Hill

Hill Top East

No Man's Moor Spring

MOOR END LANE

Little Hill

Morgan Hill

Ashley How Hill

Ashley Hill

Ashley Carr

No Man's Moor Quarry (dis)

NO MAN'S MOOR LANE

STUBBING NOOK LANE

Hollin Hill

Ley Hill

Stubbing Nook

Sand Hill

Old Covert

High Pond House

HIGH LANE

Pasture Hill

Horner Hill

Wild Duck Car Plantation

Plump House

Lamb Hill

Low Pond House

Rasp Wood

Piney Moor Hill

HIGH LANE

Rookwith Grange

The Larches

Noble Wood

BACK LANE

Duxey Hill

Rookwith

New Covert

HG4

Pasture House

Sleight Hill

Low Rookwith

Thirn Grange

Thirn Moor

Thornton Watlass Hall

Hornby Park

New Decoy

New Decoy Plantation

Round Hill Farm

LORDS LANE

NORTH RD

SILVER ST

Manor House Farm

Hackforth

Hackforth & Hornby CE Prim Sch

PH

Jackal Wood

DL7

Street House

Bow Bridge

Roundhill Plump

Broadmires

Ainderby Myres

Pickering Plantation

HOLLOW MOOR LANE

Hollow Moor Farm

Mill Close

MILL LANE

Waste Wood

Hollow Moor

Snegary Carr

Plum Tree Hill

West Farm

Langthorne New Covert

Langthorne

East Farm

COBSHAW LA

Town End Farm

East Farm

Hunter's Hill Farm

DL8

Burtree House

The Carr

The Grange

1 CORONATION RD
2 ASHDOWNE CT
3 ASHDOWNE CL
4 BLACKSMITH BANK

Wassick House Farm

Storra Pasture

Greengate Farm

Kirkbridge

Little Crakehall

Cemy

MASTIL CL

BLACKSMITH'S

GREEN GATE LANE

Sewage Works

Water Mill

Kirkbridge Farm

INGS LA

MASTIL LA

West Pasture

Crakehall Prim Sch

PH

Great Crakehall

Mirefold Farm

Sewage Works

Low Wood

Fox Park Farm

Grange Farm

Mudfields Farm

RUDDINGS LA

BACK LANE

St Gregory's Cl

New Village Farm

Tumulus

White Cross

Langthorn Wood

Brick Kiln Wood

LC

A684

LC

Wensleydale Railway

LC

SINKS LANE

LC

Black Horse Farm

Tumulus

COWLING LANE

High Scroggs House

Keepers Wood

Rand Grange

Bedale Park

GREEN LANE

No Man's Moor Spring

Cowling Manor

COWLING LA

Cowling Plantation

Bedale Wood

Bedale Wood Farm

OAK TREE DR

BURRILL ROAD

ASH TREE CL

Knabbs Quarry (dis)

Stubbing Nook

Old Covert

High Pond House

Pasture Hill

Park Hill

Cowling

COWLING RD

HIGH LANE

Low Pond House

Piney Moor Hill

Burrill

Burrill Gill

BURRILL ROAD

High Ash Bank

ASHBANK LA

Firby Grange

Sparrow Wood

Rasp Wood

Noble Wood

Rand Hill

Hell Hole Wood

Oscar Hill

Mile House Farm

MASHAM RD

B6268

New Covert

Pasture House

Sleight Hill

Thornton Watlass Hall

Dun Hill

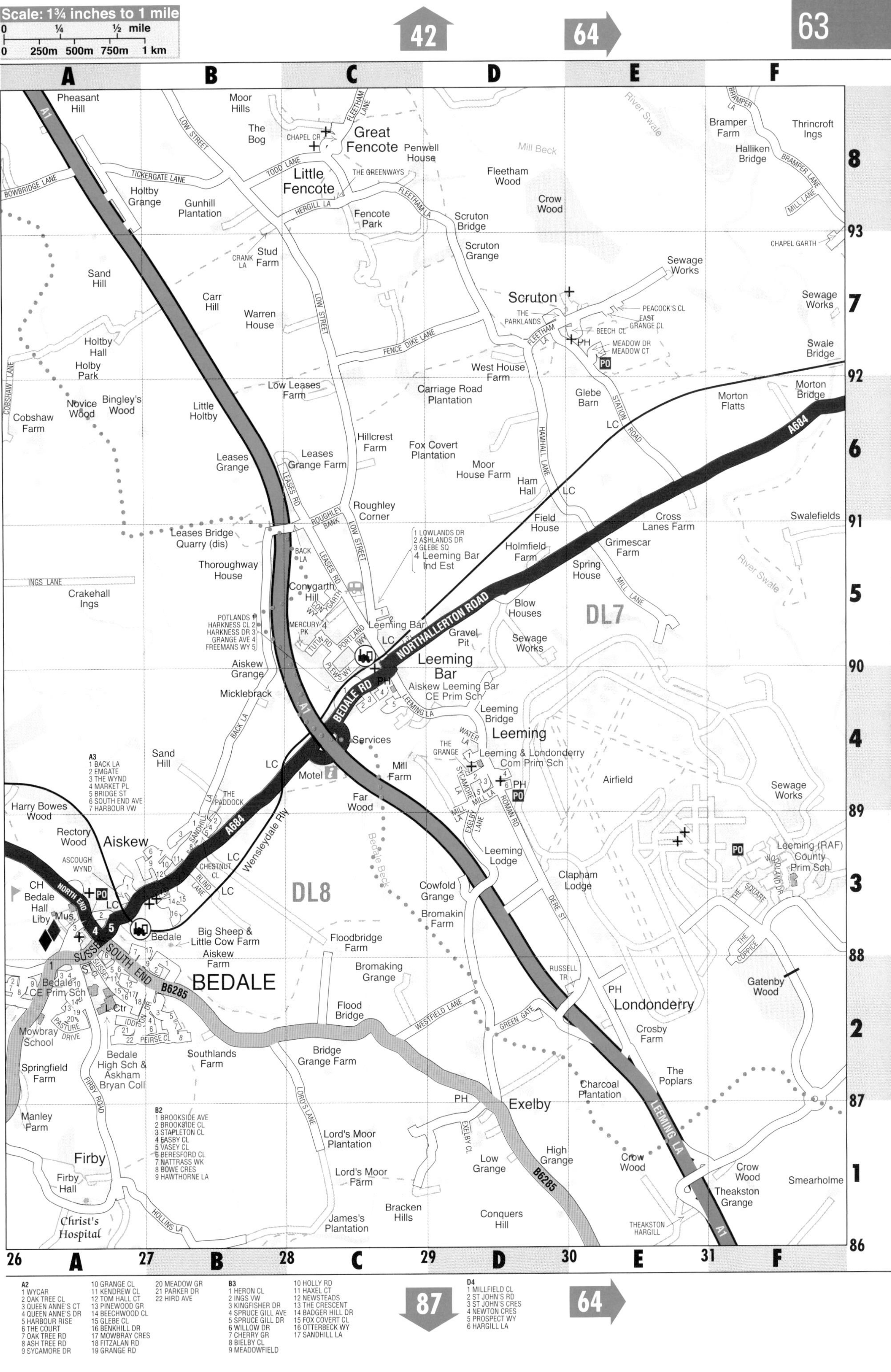
Scale: 1¾ inches to 1 mile
0 ¼ ½ mile
0 250m 500m 750m 1 km
42
64
A
B
C
D
E
F
Pheasant Hill
Moor Hills
The Bog
CHAPEL CR
Great Fencote
Little Fencote
Penwell House
FLEETHAM LANE
LOW STREET
TODD LANE
TICKERGATE LANE
BOWBRIDGE LANE
THE GREENWAYS
HERGILL LA
FLEETHAM LA
Holtby Grange
Gunhill Plantation
Fencote Park
Fleetham Wood
Mill Beck
River Swale
Crow Wood
Scruton Bridge
Scruton Grange
Bramper Farm
BRAMPER LA
Halliken Bridge
BRAMPER LANE
Thrincroft Ings
MILL LANE
CHAPEL GARTH
Sewage Works
Sand Hill
CRANK LA
Stud Farm
Carr Hill
Warren House
Scruton
THE PARKLANDS
PEACOCK'S CL
EAST GRANGE CL
BEECH CL
MEADOW DR
MEADOW CT
PH
PO
Swale Bridge
Holtby Hall
Holby Park
FENCE DIKE LANE
West House Farm
COBSHAW LANE
Cobshaw Farm
Novice Wood
Bingley's Wood
Little Holtby
Low Leases Farm
Carriage Road Plantation
Glebe Barn
STATION ROAD
Morton Flatts
Morton Bridge
A684
LC
Leases Grange
Leases Grange Farm
LEASES RD
Hillcrest Farm
Fox Covert Plantation
Moor House Farm
Ham Hall
HAMHALL LANE
ROUGHLEY BANK
Roughley Corner
Swalefields
Field House
Cross Lanes Farm
Leases Bridge Quarry (dis)
BACK LA
1 LOWLANDS DR
2 ASHLANDS DR
3 GLEBE SQ
4 Leeming Bar Ind Est
Holmfield Farm
Grimescar Farm
INGS LANE
Crakehall Ings
Thoroughway House
Conygarth Hill
Spring House
MILL LANE
NORTHALLERTON ROAD
Blow Houses
DL7
POTLANDS 1
HARKNESS CL 2
HARKNESS DR 3
GRANGE AVE 4
FREEMANS WY 5
MERCURY PK
TUTIN RD
PORTLAND WY
PLEWS WY
Leeming Bar
Gravel Pit
Sewage Works
Aiskew Grange
Leeming Bar
Aiskew Leeming Bar CE Prim Sch
Micklebrack
BEDALE RD
LEEMING LA
Leeming Bridge
Leeming
A1
Services
WATER LA
THE GRANGE
Leeming & Londonderry Com Prim Sch
A3
1 BACK LA
2 EMGATE
3 THE WYND
4 MARKET PL
5 BRIDGE ST
6 SOUTH END AVE
7 HARBOUR VW
Sand Hill
Motel
Mill Farm
SYCAMORE LA
ROMAN RD
Airfield
Sewage Works
THE PADDOCK
Far Wood
Harry Bowes Wood
Rectory Wood
SANDHILL LA
Wensleydale Rly
MILL LA
EXELBY LANE
Leeming Lodge
Aiskew
ASCOUGH WYND
CHESTNUT CL
BLIND LANE
Bedale Beck
DL8
Leeming (RAF)
County Prim Sch
WOODLAND DR
THE SQUARE
CH
Bedale Hall
Liby
Mus
NORTH END
Cowfold Grange
Clapham Lodge
Bromakin Farm
DERE ST
Bedale
Big Sheep & Little Cow Farm
Aiskew Farm
Floodbridge Farm
THE COPPICE
SUSSEX ST
SOUTH END
Bedale CE Prim Sch
BEDALE
B6285
Bromaking Grange
RUSSELL TR
Gatenby Wood
L Ctr
PASTURE DRIVE
PEIRSE CL
Flood Bridge
WESTFIELD LANE
GREEN GATE
Londonderry
Mowbray School
Bedale High Sch & Askham Bryan Coll
Southlands Farm
Bridge Grange Farm
Crosby Farm
Springfield Farm
FIRBY ROAD
The Poplars
Charcoal Plantation
LORD'S LANE
Exelby
Manley Farm
B2
1 BROOKSIDE AVE
2 BROOKSIDE CL
3 STAPLETON CL
4 EASBY CL
5 VASEY CL
6 BERESFORD CL
7 NATTRASS WK
8 BOWE CRES
9 HAWTHORNE LA
Lord's Moor Plantation
EXELBY CL
High Grange
LEEMING LA
Firby
Lord's Moor Farm
Low Grange
Crow Wood
Crow Wood
Smearholme
Firby Hall
Theakston Grange
Christ's Hospital
HOLLINS LA
James's Plantation
Bracken Hills
Conquers Hill
THEAKSTON HARGILL
8
93
7
92
6
91
5
90
4
89
3
88
2
87
1
86
26
27
28
29
30
31
A2
1 WYCAR
2 OAK TREE CL
3 QUEEN ANNE'S CT
4 QUEEN ANNE'S DR
5 HARBOUR RISE
6 THE COURT
7 OAK TREE RD
8 ASH TREE RD
9 SYCAMORE DR
10 GRANGE CL
11 KENDREW CL
12 TOM HALL CT
13 PINEWOOD GR
14 BEECHWOOD CL
15 GLEBE CL
16 BENKHILL DR
17 MOWBRAY CRES
18 FITZALAN RD
19 GRANGE RD
20 MEADOW GR
21 PARKER DR
22 HIRD AVE
B3
1 HERON CL
2 INGS VW
3 KINGFISHER DR
4 SPRUCE GILL AVE
5 SPRUCE GILL DR
6 WILLOW DR
7 CHERRY GR
8 BIELBY CL
9 MEADOWFIELD
10 HOLLY RD
11 HAXEL CT
12 NEWSTEADS
13 THE CRESCENT
14 BADGER HILL DR
15 FOX COVERT CL
16 OTTERBECK WY
17 SANDHILL LA
87
D4
1 MILLFIELD CL
2 ST JOHN'S RD
3 ST JOHN'S CRES
4 NEWTON CRES
5 PROSPECT WY
6 HARGILL LA
64

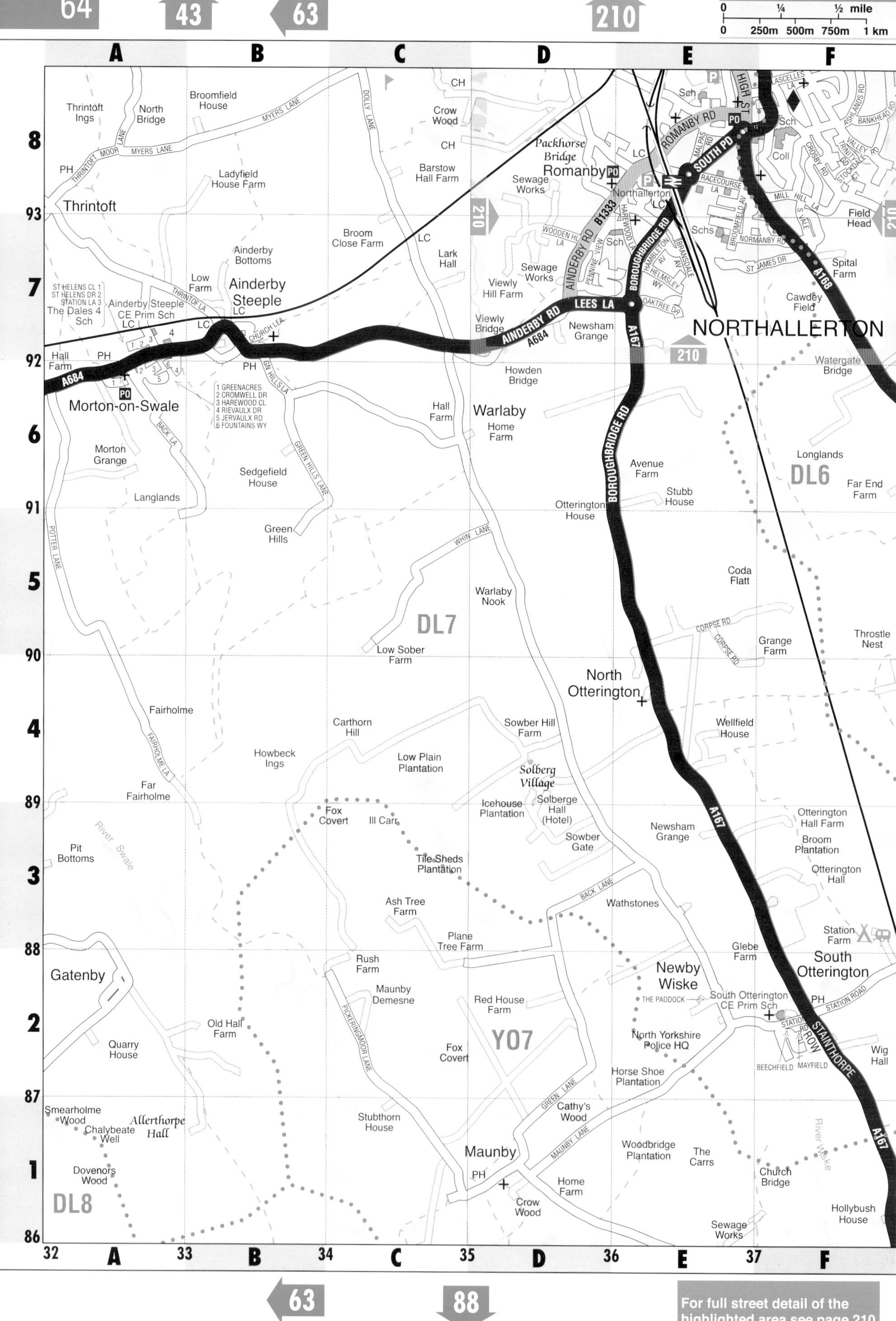

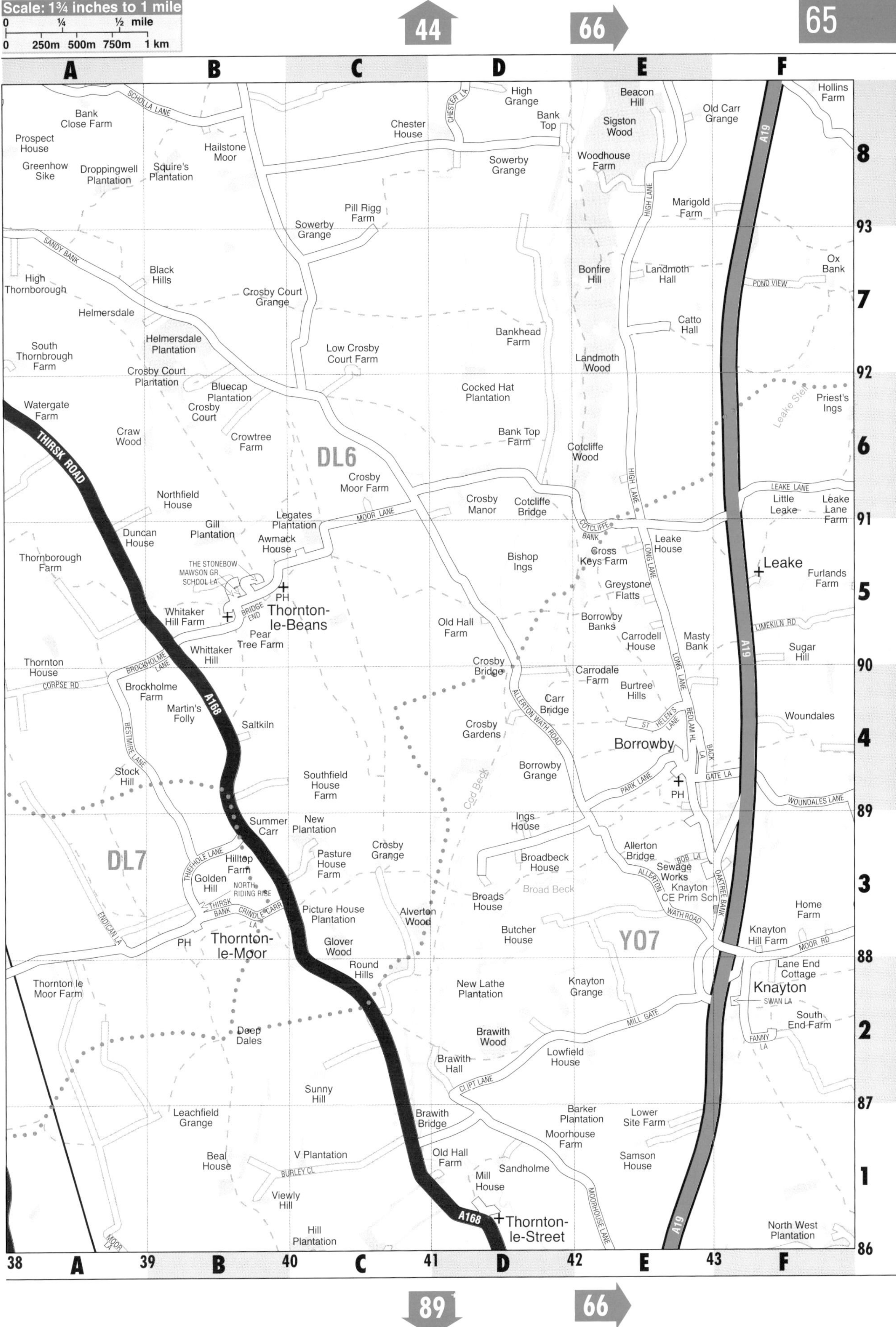
Scale: 1¾ inches to 1 mile
0 ¼ ½ mile
0 250m 500m 750m 1 km
44
66
A B C D E F
Bank Close Farm
Prospect House
Greenhow Sike
Droppingwell Plantation
Squire's Plantation
Hailstone Moor
SCHOLLA LANE
Chester House
CHESTER LA
High Grange
Bank Top
Beacon Hill
Sigston Wood
Old Carr Grange
Hollins Farm
Sowerby Grange
Woodhouse Farm
Marigold Farm
HIGH LANE
Pill Rigg Farm
Sowerby Grange
SANDY BANK
Black Hills
High Thornborough
Helmersdale
Crosby Court Grange
Bonfire Hill
Landmoth Hall
Ox Bank
POND VIEW
Catto Hall
South Thornbrough Farm
Helmersdale Plantation
Low Crosby Court Farm
Bankhead Farm
Landmoth Wood
Crosby Court Plantation
Bluecap Plantation
Crosby Court
Cocked Hat Plantation
Priest's Ings
Leake Stell
Watergate Farm
THIRSK ROAD
Craw Wood
Crowtree Farm
Bank Top Farm
Cotcliffe Wood
DL6
Crosby Moor Farm
Northfield House
Crosby Manor
Cotcliffe Bridge
HIGH LANE
LEAKE LANE
Little Leake
Leake Lane Farm
Legates Plantation
MOOR LANE
Gill Plantation
Duncan House
Awmack House
COTCLIFFE BANK
Leake House
Bishop Ings
Cross Keys Farm
LONG LANE
Thornborough Farm
THE STONEBOW
MAWSON GR
SCHOOL LA
Leake
Furlands Farm
PH
Greystone Flatts
Whitaker Hill Farm
BRIDGE END
Thornton-le-Beans
Old Hall Farm
Borrowby Banks
Pear Tree Farm
LIMEKILN RD
Carrodell House
Masty Bank
Whittaker Hill
A19
Sugar Hill
Thornton House
BROCKHOLME LANE
Crosby Bridge
Carrodale Farm
CORPSE RD
Brockholme Farm
Burtree Hills
Martin's Folly
A168
ALLERTON WATH ROAD
Carr Bridge
Woundales
ST HELEN'S LANE
Saltkiln
Crosby Gardens
BEDLAM HL
Borrowby
BACK LA
BESTMIRE LANE
Stock Hill
Cod Beck
Southfield House Farm
Borrowby Grange
GATE LA
PARK LANE
PH
WOUNDALES LANE
Summer Carr
New Plantation
Ings House
DL7
THIEFHOLE LANE
Hilltop Farm
Pasture House Farm
Crosby Grange
Allerton Bridge
BOB LA
Broadbeck House
Sewage Works
Golden Hill
NORTH RIDING RISE
ALLERTON
Knayton CE Prim Sch
Broad Beck
OAKTREE BANK
THIRSK BANK
CRINDLE CARR LA
Picture House Plantation
Broads House
WATH ROAD
Home Farm
ENDICAN LA
Alverton Wood
Butcher House
Knayton Hill Farm
PH
Thornton-le-Moor
Glover Wood
YO7
MOOR RD
Round Hills
Lane End Cottage
Thornton le Moor Farm
New Lathe Plantation
Knayton Grange
Knayton
SWAN LA
South End Farm
MILL GATE
Deep Dales
Brawith Wood
FANNY LA
Brawith Hall
Lowfield House
CLIPT LANE
Sunny Hill
Leachfield Grange
Brawith Bridge
Barker Plantation
Lower Site Farm
Moorhouse Farm
Beal House
V Plantation
Old Hall Farm
Samson House
BURLEY CL
Sandholme
Mill House
Viewly Hill
MOORHOUSE LANE
Thornton-le-Street
North West Plantation
Hill Plantation
MOOR LA
8 93 7 92 6 91 5 90 4 89 3 88 2 87 1 86
38 A 39 B 40 C 41 D 42 E 43 F
89
66

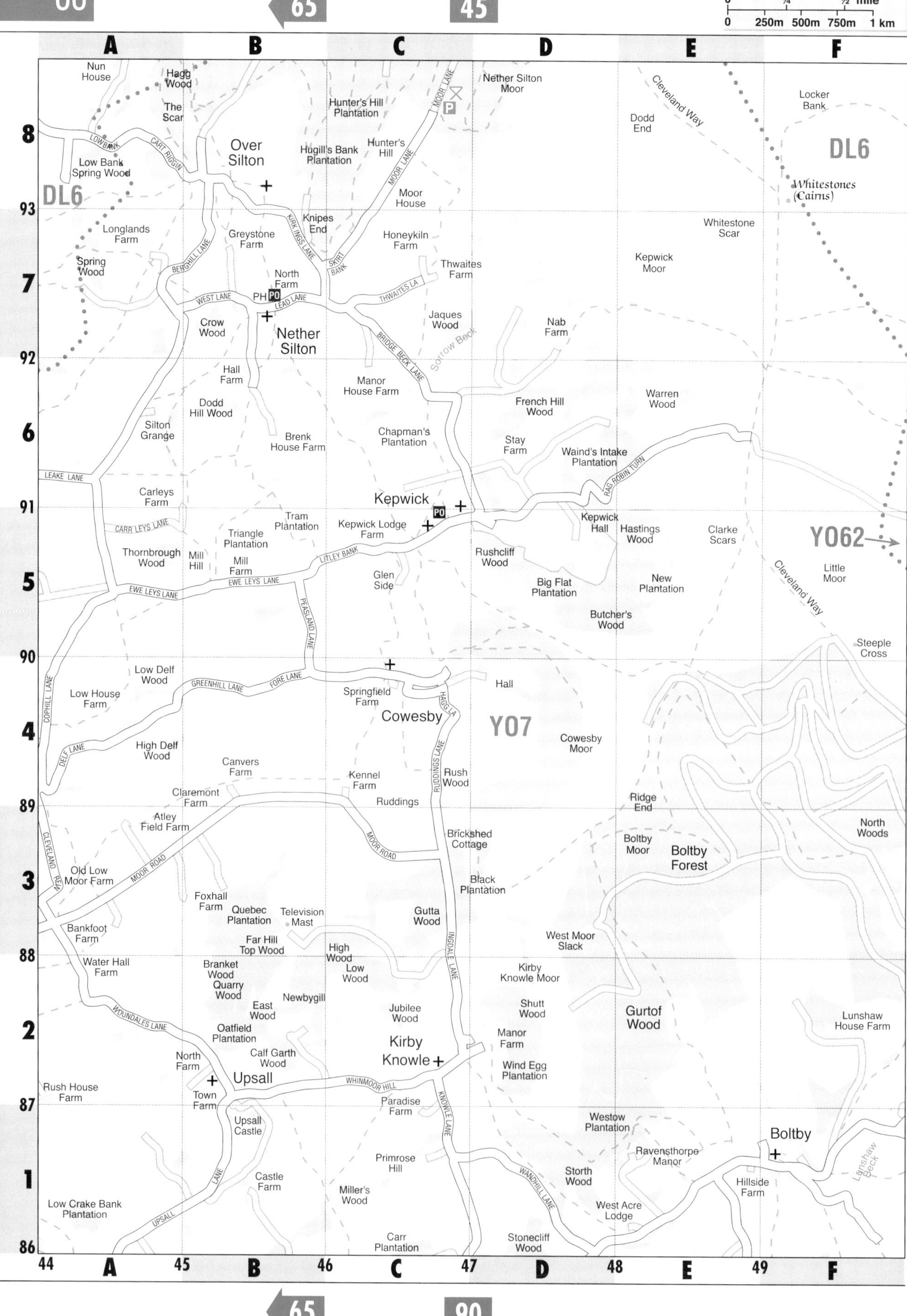
65
45
Scale: 1¾ inches to 1 mile
0 ¼ ½ mile
0 250m 500m 750m 1 km
Nun House
Hagg Wood
The Scar
Over Silton
Hunter's Hill Plantation
Nether Silton Moor
Locker Bank
Dodd End
Cleveland Way
DL6
Low Bank Spring Wood
Hugill's Bank Plantation
Hunter's Hill
Moor House
Whitestones (Cairns)
Knipes End
Greystone Farm
Longlands Farm
Honeykiln Farm
Whitestone Scar
Spring Wood
North Farm
Thwaites Farm
Kepwick Moor
PH
Nether Silton
Crow Wood
Jaques Wood
Nab Farm
Sorrow Beck
Hall Farm
Manor House Farm
French Hill Wood
Warren Wood
Dodd Hill Wood
Silton Grange
Brenk House Farm
Chapman's Plantation
Stay Farm
Waind's Intake Plantation
Carleys Farm
Kepwick
Tram Plantation
Kepwick Lodge Farm
Kepwick Hall
Hastings Wood
Clarke Scars
Triangle Plantation
Thornbrough Wood
Mill Hill
Mill Farm
Rushcliff Wood
YO62
Glen Side
Big Flat Plantation
New Plantation
Little Moor
Butcher's Wood
Steeple Cross
Low Delf Wood
Low House Farm
Hall
Springfield Farm
Cowesby
YO7
Cowesby Moor
High Delf Wood
Canvers Farm
Kennel Farm
Rush Wood
Claremont Farm
Ruddings
Ridge End
Atley Field Farm
Brickshed Cottage
North Woods
Boltby Moor
Boltby Forest
Old Low Moor Farm
Black Plantation
Foxhall Farm
Quebec Plantation
Television Mast
Gutta Wood
Bankfoot Farm
West Moor Slack
Far Hill Top Wood
High Wood
Low Wood
Water Hall Farm
Branket Wood
Quarry Wood
Kirby Knowle Moor
East Wood
Newbygill
Shutt Wood
Jubilee Wood
Gurtof Wood
Lunshaw House Farm
Oatfield Plantation
Manor Farm
North Farm
Calf Garth Wood
Kirby Knowle
Wind Egg Plantation
Upsall
Rush House Farm
Town Farm
Paradise Farm
Westow Plantation
Upsall Castle
Boltby
Ravensthorpe Manor
Primrose Hill
Storth Wood
Lunshaw Beck
Castle Farm
Hillside Farm
Miller's Wood
West Acre Lodge
Low Crake Bank Plantation
Carr Plantation
Stonecliff Wood
LOWBANK
CART RIGGIN
MOOR LANE
KIRK INGS LANE
SKIRT BANK
BERGHILL LANE
WEST LANE
LEAD LANE
THWAITES LA
BRIDGE BECK LANE
LEAKE LANE
RAG ROBIN TURN
CARR LEYS LANE
LITLEY BANK
EWE LEYS LANE
PEASLAND LANE
GREENHILL LANE
FORE LANE
HAGG LA
COPHILL LANE
DELF LANE
RUDDINGS LANE
MOOR ROAD
CLEVELAND WAY
INGDALE LANE
WOUNDALES LANE
WHINMOOR HILL
KNOWLE LANE
WANDHILL LANE
UPSALL LANE
A B C D E F
8 93 7 92 6 91 5 90 4 89 3 88 2 87 1 86
44 45 46 47 48 49
65
90

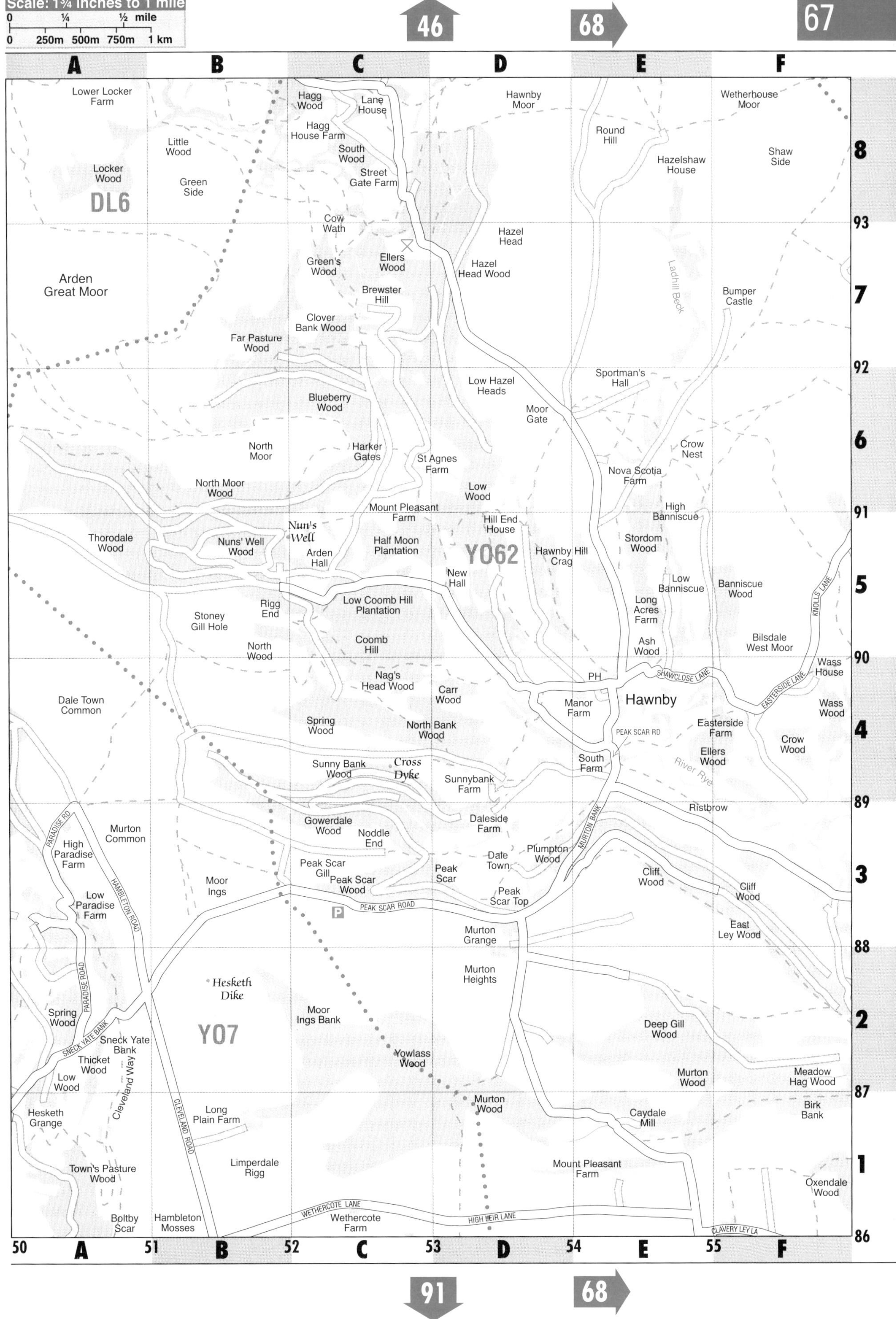
Scale: 1¾ inches to 1 mile
0 ¼ ½ mile
0 250m 500m 750m 1 km
46
68
A B C D E F
Lower Locker Farm
Hagg Wood
Lane House
Hawnby Moor
Wetherhouse Moor
Little Wood
Hagg House Farm
Round Hill
Shaw Side
Locker Wood
Green Side
South Wood
Hazelshaw House
Street Gate Farm
DL6
Cow Wath
Hazel Head
Ellers Wood
Green's Wood
Hazel Head Wood
Arden Great Moor
Ladhill Beck
Brewster Hill
Bumper Castle
Clover Bank Wood
Far Pasture Wood
Sportman's Hall
Low Hazel Heads
Blueberry Wood
Moor Gate
North Moor
Harker Gates
St Agnes Farm
Crow Nest
Nova Scotia Farm
North Moor Wood
Low Wood
Mount Pleasant Farm
High Banniscue
Hill End House
Nun's Well
Thorodale Wood
Nuns' Well Wood
Half Moon Plantation
Stordom Wood
Arden Hall
YO62
Hawnby Hill Crag
Low Banniscue
New Hall
Banniscue Wood
Low Coomb Hill Plantation
KNOLLS LANE
Rigg End
Long Acres Farm
Stoney Gill Hole
Coomb Hill
Bilsdale West Moor
North Wood
Ash Wood
Wass House
PH
SHAWCLOSE LANE
Nag's Head Wood
Carr Wood
Dale Town Common
Manor Farm
Hawnby
EASTERSIDE LANE
Wass Wood
Spring Wood
North Bank Wood
Easterside Farm
PEAK SCAR RD
Crow Wood
Ellers Wood
Sunny Bank Wood
Cross Dyke
South Farm
River Rye
Sunnybank Farm
Ristbrow
PARADISE RD
Murton Common
Gowerdale Wood
Daleside Farm
High Paradise Farm
Noddle End
MURTON BANK
Plumpton Wood
Peak Scar Gill
Dale Town
Moor Ings
Peak Scar
Cliff Wood
Cliff Wood
HAMBLETON ROAD
Peak Scar Wood
Low Paradise Farm
Peak Scar Top
P
PEAK SCAR ROAD
East Ley Wood
Murton Grange
PARADISE ROAD
Murton Heights
Hesketh Dike
Spring Wood
Moor Ings Bank
Deep Gill Wood
SNECK YATE BANK
YO7
Sneck Yate Bank
Yowlass Wood
Thicket Wood
Murton Wood
Meadow Hag Wood
Cleveland Way
Low Wood
Murton Wood
Birk Bank
Hesketh Grange
Long Plain Farm
CLEVELAND ROAD
Caydale Mill
Limperdale Rigg
Mount Pleasant Farm
Town's Pasture Wood
Oxendale Wood
WETHERCOTE LANE
Boltby Scar
Hambleton Mosses
Wethercote Farm
HIGH LEIR LANE
CLAVERY LEY LA
8
93
7
92
6
91
5
90
4
89
3
88
2
87
1
86
50 51 52 53 54 55
91
68

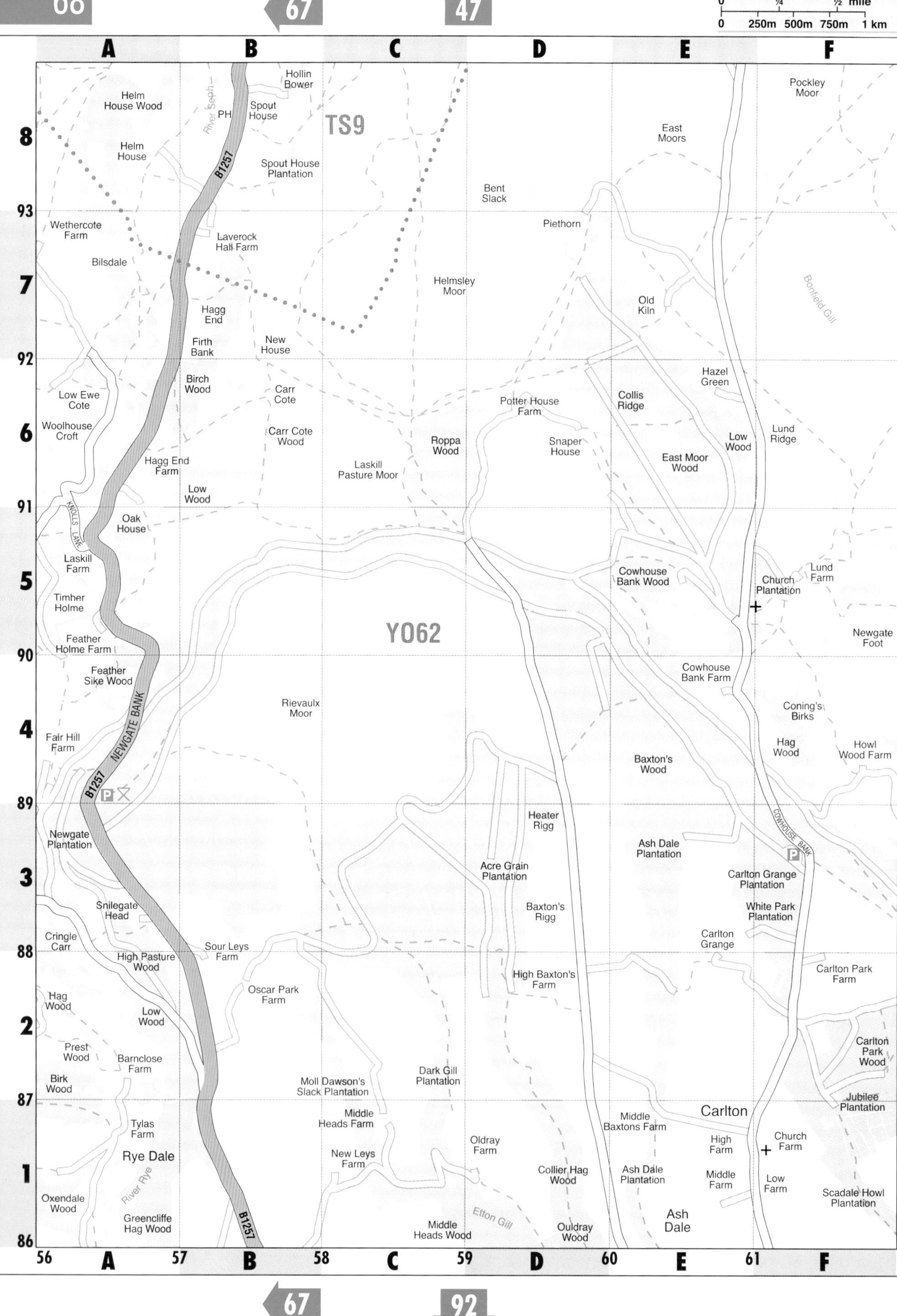

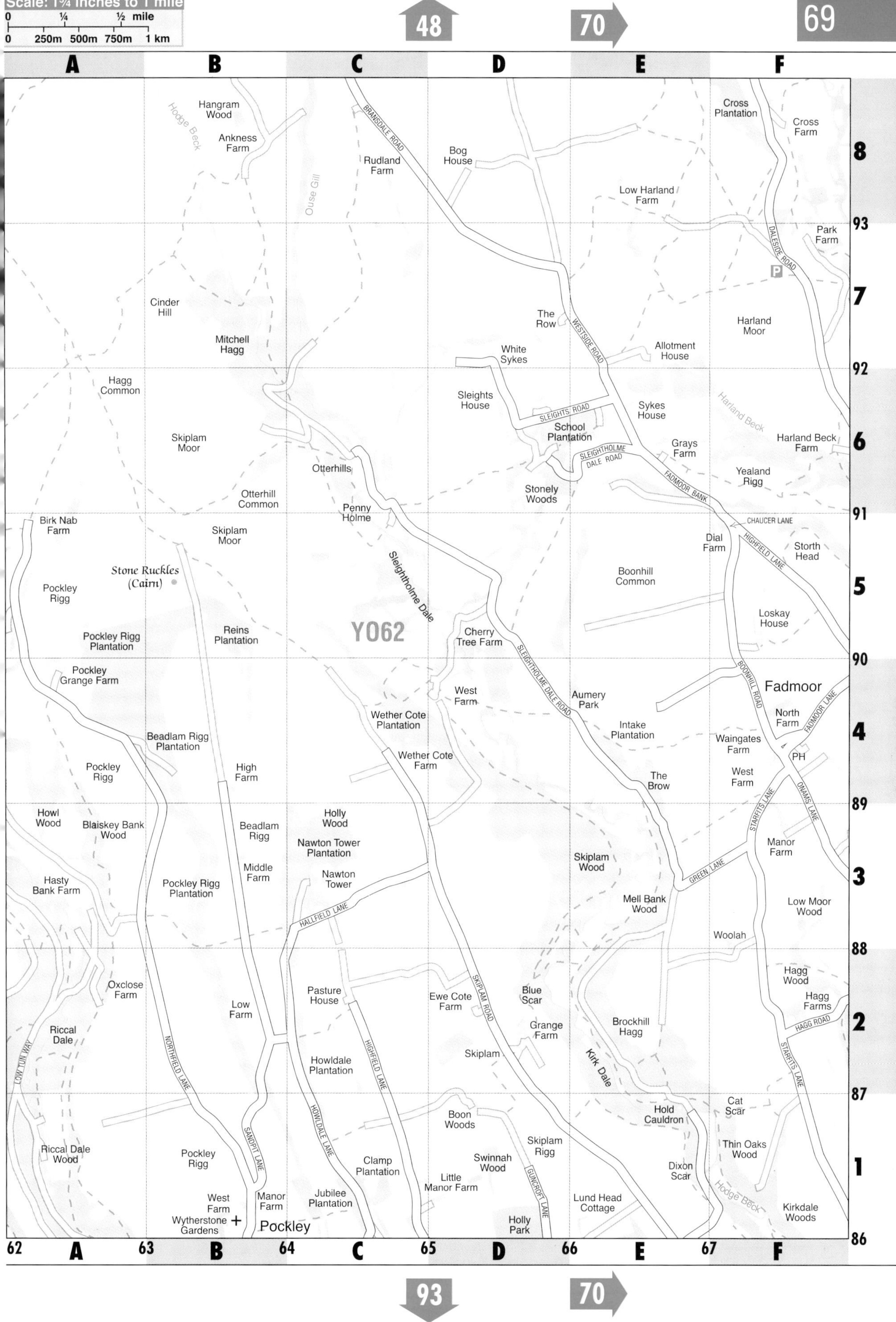

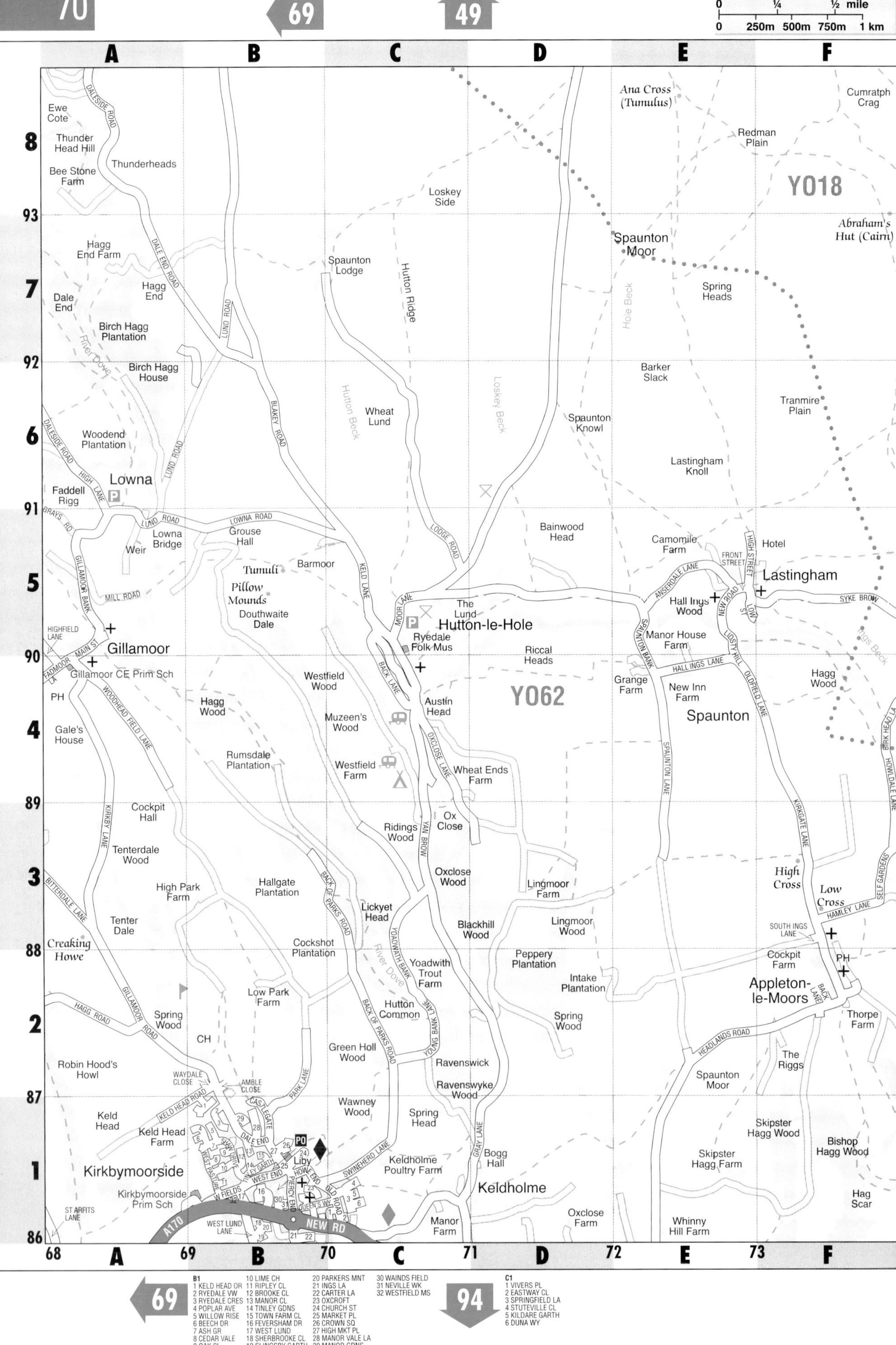

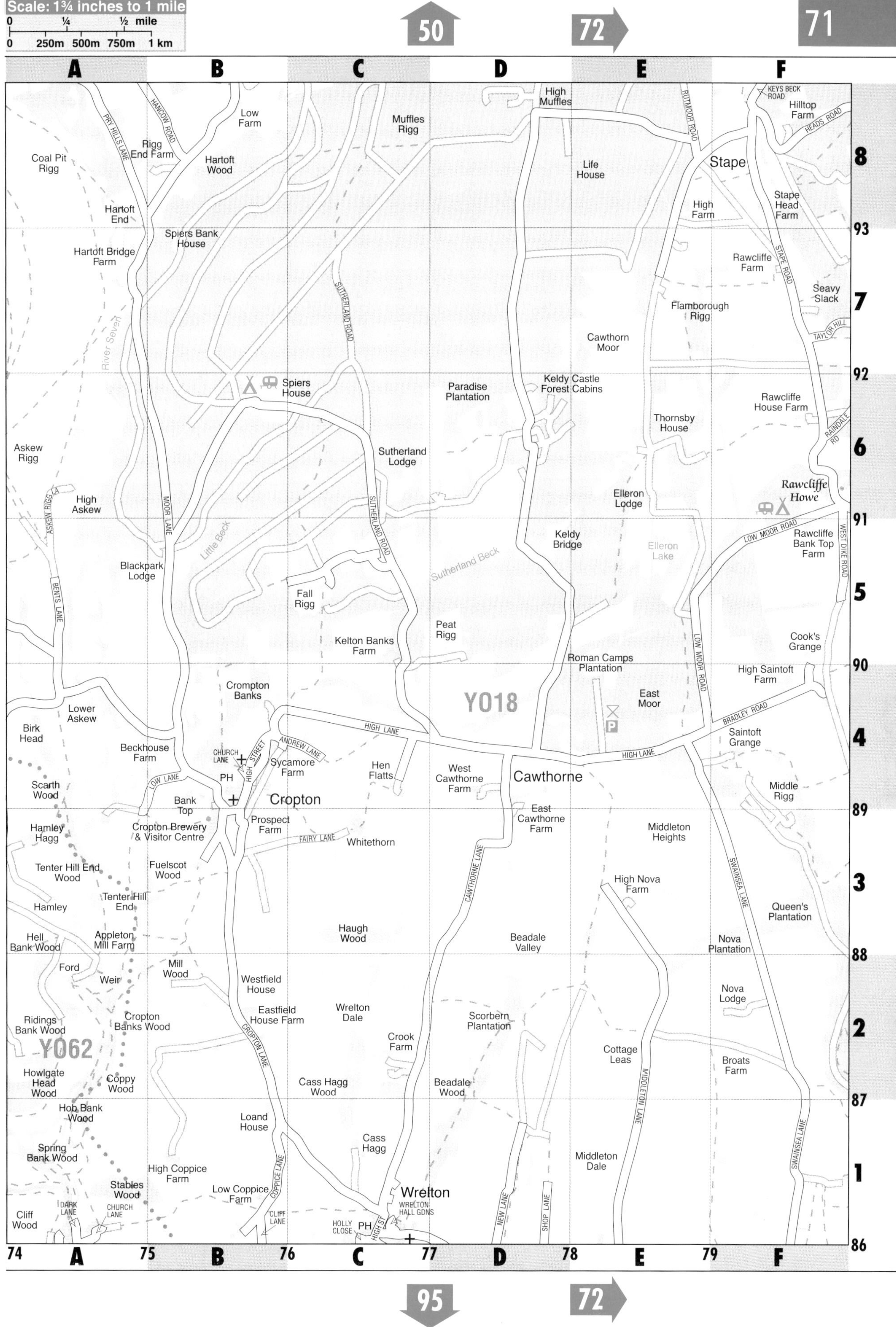

Scale: 1¾ inches to 1 mile
0 ¼ ½ mile
0 250m 500m 750m 1 km
50
72
A B C D E F
8
93
7
92
6
91
5
90
4
89
3
88
2
87
1
86
74 75 76 77 78 79
Coal Pit Rigg
Pry Hills Lane
Hancow Road
Rigg End Farm
Low Farm
Hartoft Wood
Muffles Rigg
High Muffles
Rutmoor Road
Keys Beck Road
Hilltop Farm
Heads Road
Stape
Life House
Hartoft End
High Farm
Stape Head Farm
Spiers Bank House
Hartoft Bridge Farm
Rawcliffe Farm
Stape Road
Seavy Slack
Sutherland Road
Flamborough Rigg
River Seven
Taylor Hill
Cawthorn Moor
Spiers House
Paradise Plantation
Keldy Castle Forest Cabins
Rawcliffe House Farm
Thornsby House
Raindale Rd
Askew Rigg
Sutherland Lodge
High Askew
Askew Rigg La
Moor Lane
Elleron Lodge
Rawcliffe Howe
Little Beck
Keldy Bridge
Low Moor Road
Rawcliffe Bank Top Farm
Blackpark Lodge
Sutherland Beck
Elleron Lake
West Dike Road
Bents Lane
Fall Rigg
Peat Rigg
Kelton Banks Farm
Cook's Grange
Low Moor Road
Roman Camps Plantation
High Saintoft Farm
Crompton Banks
YO18
East Moor
Lower Askew
Bradley Road
Birk Head
High Lane
Saintoft Grange
Beckhouse Farm
Church Lane
High Street
Andrew Lane
Sycamore Farm
Hen Flatts
West Cawthorne Farm
Cawthorne
High Lane
Scarth Wood
PH
Low Lane
Middle Rigg
Bank Top
Cropton
East Cawthorne Farm
Hamley Hagg
Cropton Brewery & Visitor Centre
Prospect Farm
Middleton Heights
Fairy Lane
Whitethorn
Tenter Hill End Wood
Fuelscot Wood
Cawthorne Lane
High Nova Farm
Swainsea Lane
Tenter Hill End
Hamley
Queen's Plantation
Haugh Wood
Appleton Mill Farm
Hell Bank Wood
Beadale Valley
Nova Plantation
Ford
Mill Wood
Weir
Westfield House
Nova Lodge
Cropton Lane
Eastfield House Farm
Wrelton Dale
Cropton Banks Wood
Ridings Bank Wood
Scorbern Plantation
YO62
Crook Farm
Cottage Leas
Broats Farm
Middleton Lane
Howlgate Head Wood
Coppy Wood
Cass Hagg Wood
Beadale Wood
Hob Bank Wood
Loand House
Cass Hagg
Spring Bank Wood
Coppice Lane
Middleton Dale
Swainsea Lane
High Coppice Farm
Stables Wood
Low Coppice Farm
Wrelton
New Lane
Shop Lane
Cliff Wood
Dark Lane
Church Lane
Cliff Lane
Holly Close
High St
Wrelton Hall Gdns
95
72

71
51
Scale: 1¾ inches to 1 mile

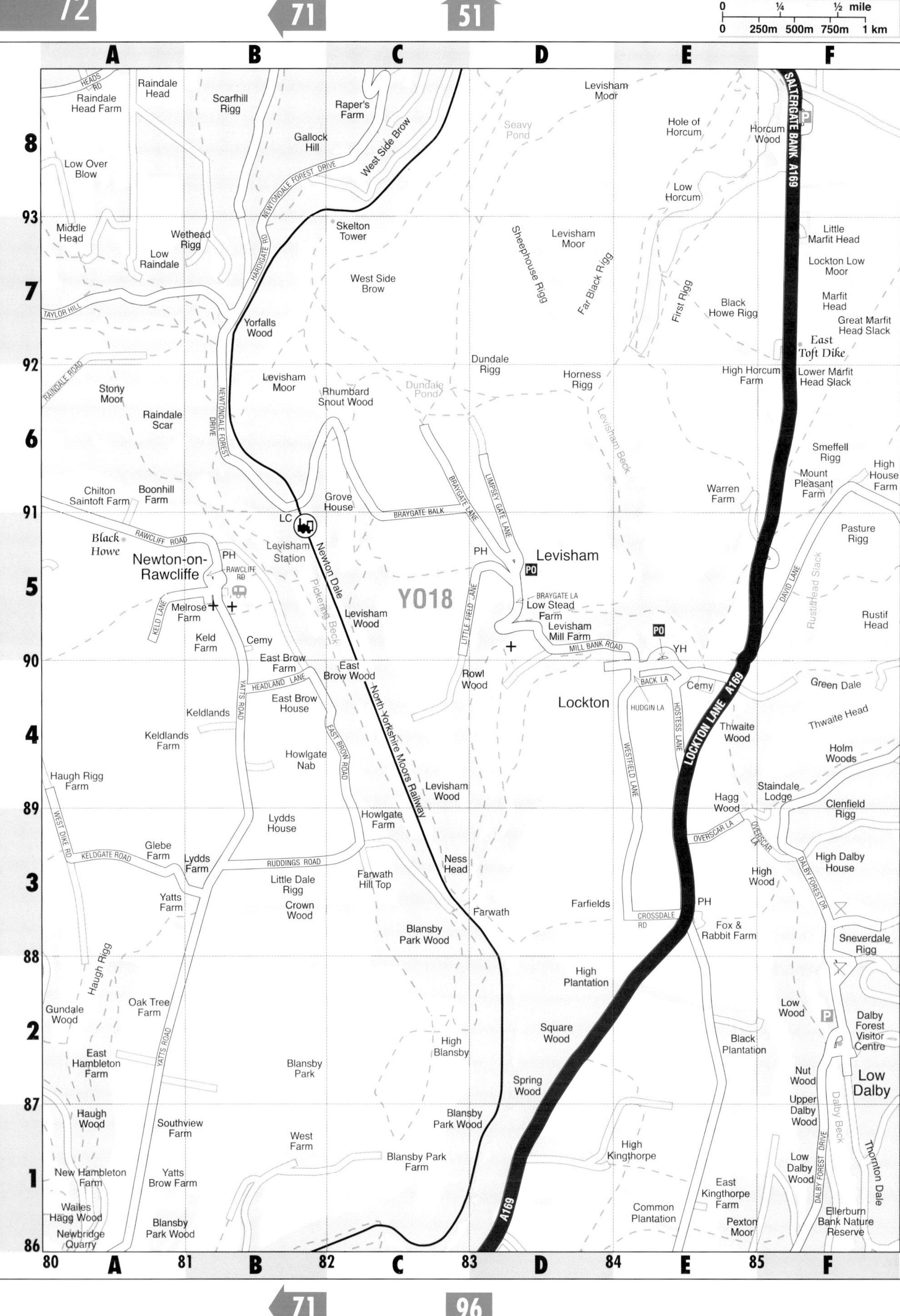
A
B
C
D
E
F
8
93
7
92
6
91
5
90
4
89
3
88
2
87
1
86
80
81
82
83
84
85
Raindale Head Farm
Raindale Head
Scarfhill Rigg
Raper's Farm
Gallock Hill
West Side Brow
NEWTONDALE FOREST DRIVE
Levisham Moor
Seavy Pond
Hole of Horcum
Horcum Wood
SALTERGATE BANK A169
Low Over Blow
Low Horcum
Middle Head
Wethead Rigg
Low Raindale
HARDIGATE RD
Skelton Tower
West Side Brow
Sheephouse Rigg
Far Black Rigg
First Rigg
Black Howe Rigg
Little Marfit Head
Lockton Low Moor
Marfit Head
Great Marfit Head Slack
East Toft Dike
TAYLOR HILL
Yorfalls Wood
RAINDALE ROAD
Stony Moor
Levisham Moor
Rhumbard Snout Wood
Dundale Pond
Dundale Rigg
Horness Rigg
High Horcum Farm
Lower Marfit Head Slack
Raindale Scar
Levisham Beck
Smeffell Rigg
Mount Pleasant Farm
High House Farm
Chilton Saintoft Farm
Boonhill Farm
Grove House
BRAYGATE BALK
BRAYGATE LANE
LIMPSEY GATE LANE
Warren Farm
Black Howe
RAWCLIFF ROAD
LC
Levisham Station
Newton Dale
PH
Levisham
PO
Pasture Rigg
Newton-on-Rawcliffe
RAWCLIFF RD
YO18
Melrose Farm
KELD LANE
Pickering Beck
Levisham Wood
LITTLE FIELD LANE
BRAYGATE LA
Low Stead Farm
Levisham Mill Farm
DAVID LANE
Rustifhead Slack
Rustif Head
Keld Farm
Cemy
East Brow Farm
East Brow Wood
MILL BANK ROAD
YH
HEADLAND LANE
Rowl Wood
BACK LA
Cemy
Green Dale
Lockton
HUDGIN LA
HOSTESS LANE
LOCKTON LANE A169
Thwaite Wood
Thwaite Head
East Brow House
Keldlands
YATTS ROAD
Keldlands Farm
EAST BROW ROAD
North Yorkshire Moors Railway
Howlgate Nab
Holm Woods
Haugh Rigg Farm
WESTFIELD LANE
Staindale Lodge
Levisham Wood
Hagg Wood
Clenfield Rigg
WEST DIKE RD
Lydds House
Howlgate Farm
OVERSCAR LA
Glebe Farm
KELDGATE ROAD
Lydds Farm
RUDDINGS ROAD
Ness Head
High Dalby House
Little Dale Rigg
Farwath Hill Top
High Wood
DALBY FOREST DR
Yatts Farm
Crown Wood
Farwath
Farfields
PH
CROSSDALE RD
Fox & Rabbit Farm
Blansby Park Wood
Sneverdale Rigg
Haugh Rigg
High Plantation
Gundale Wood
Oak Tree Farm
Low Wood
Dalby Forest Visitor Centre
High Blansby
Square Wood
Black Plantation
East Hambleton Farm
YATTS ROAD
Blansby Park
Nut Wood
Low Dalby
Spring Wood
Upper Dalby Wood
Haugh Wood
Southview Farm
Blansby Park Wood
Dalby Beck
West Farm
High Kingthorpe
Thornton Dale
Blansby Park Farm
Low Dalby Wood
New Hambleton Farm
Yatts Brow Farm
DALBY FOREST DRIVE
East Kingthorpe Farm
A169
Common Plantation
Wailes Hagg Wood
Ellerburn Bank Nature Reserve
Blansby Park Wood
Pexton Moor
Newbridge Quarry

71
96

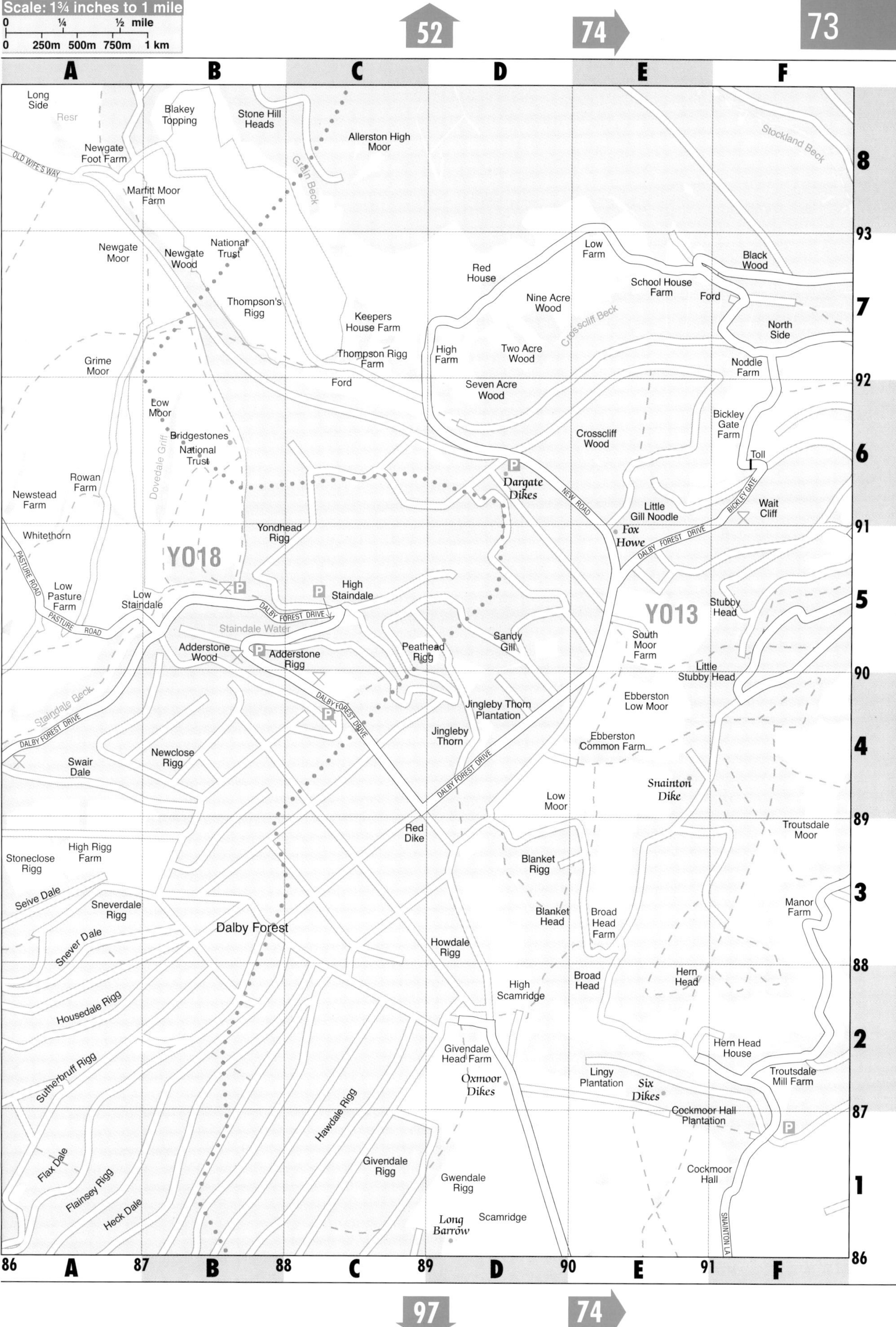
Scale: 1¾ inches to 1 mile
0 ¼ ½ mile
0 250m 500m 750m 1 km
52
74
A B C D E F
Long Side
Resr
Blakey Topping
Stone Hill Heads
Allerston High Moor
Stockland Beck
Newgate Foot Farm
OLD WIFE'S WAY
Grain Beck
Marfitt Moor Farm
Newgate Moor
Newgate Wood
National Trust
Low Farm
Black Wood
Red House
School House Farm
Thompson's Rigg
Nine Acre Wood
Ford
Keepers House Farm
Crosscliff Beck
North Side
Grime Moor
Thompson Rigg Farm
High Farm
Two Acre Wood
Noddle Farm
Ford
Seven Acre Wood
Low Moor
Bickley Gate Farm
Crosscliff Wood
Bridgestones
National Trust
Dovedale Griff
Toll
Rowan Farm
Dargate Dikes
NEW ROAD
Newstead Farm
Little Gill Noodle
BICKLEY GATE
Wait Cliff
Whitethorn
Fox Howe
DALBY FOREST DRIVE
Yondhead Rigg
PASTURE ROAD
YO18
Low Pasture Farm
Low Staindale
High Staindale
YO13
Stubby Head
DALBY FOREST DRIVE
PASTURE ROAD
Staindale Water
South Moor Farm
Adderstone Wood
Adderstone Rigg
Peathead Rigg
Sandy Gill
Little Stubby Head
Staindale Beck
DALBY FOREST DRIVE
Jingleby Thorn Plantation
Ebberston Low Moor
DALBY FOREST DRIVE
Jingleby Thorn
Ebberston Common Farm
Swair Dale
Newclose Rigg
DALBY FOREST DRIVE
Snainton Dike
Low Moor
Red Dike
Troutsdale Moor
Stoneclose Rigg
High Rigg Farm
Blanket Rigg
Seive Dale
Sneverdale Rigg
Manor Farm
Blanket Head
Broad Head Farm
Dalby Forest
Snever Dale
Howdale Rigg
High Scamridge
Broad Head
Hern Head
Housedale Rigg
Hern Head House
Givendale Head Farm
Sutherbruff Rigg
Lingy Plantation
Troutsdale Mill Farm
Oxmoor Dikes
Six Dikes
Cockmoor Hall Plantation
Hawdale Rigg
Flax Dale
Givendale Rigg
Gwendale Rigg
Cockmoor Hall
Flainsey Rigg
SNAINTON LA
Heck Dale
Scamridge
Long Barrow
8 93 7 92 6 91 5 90 4 89 3 88 2 87 1 86
86 87 88 89 90 91
97
74

74   ◀ 73   ▲ 53

Scale: 1¾ inches to 1 mile
0   ¼   ½ mile
0   250m   500m   750m   1 km

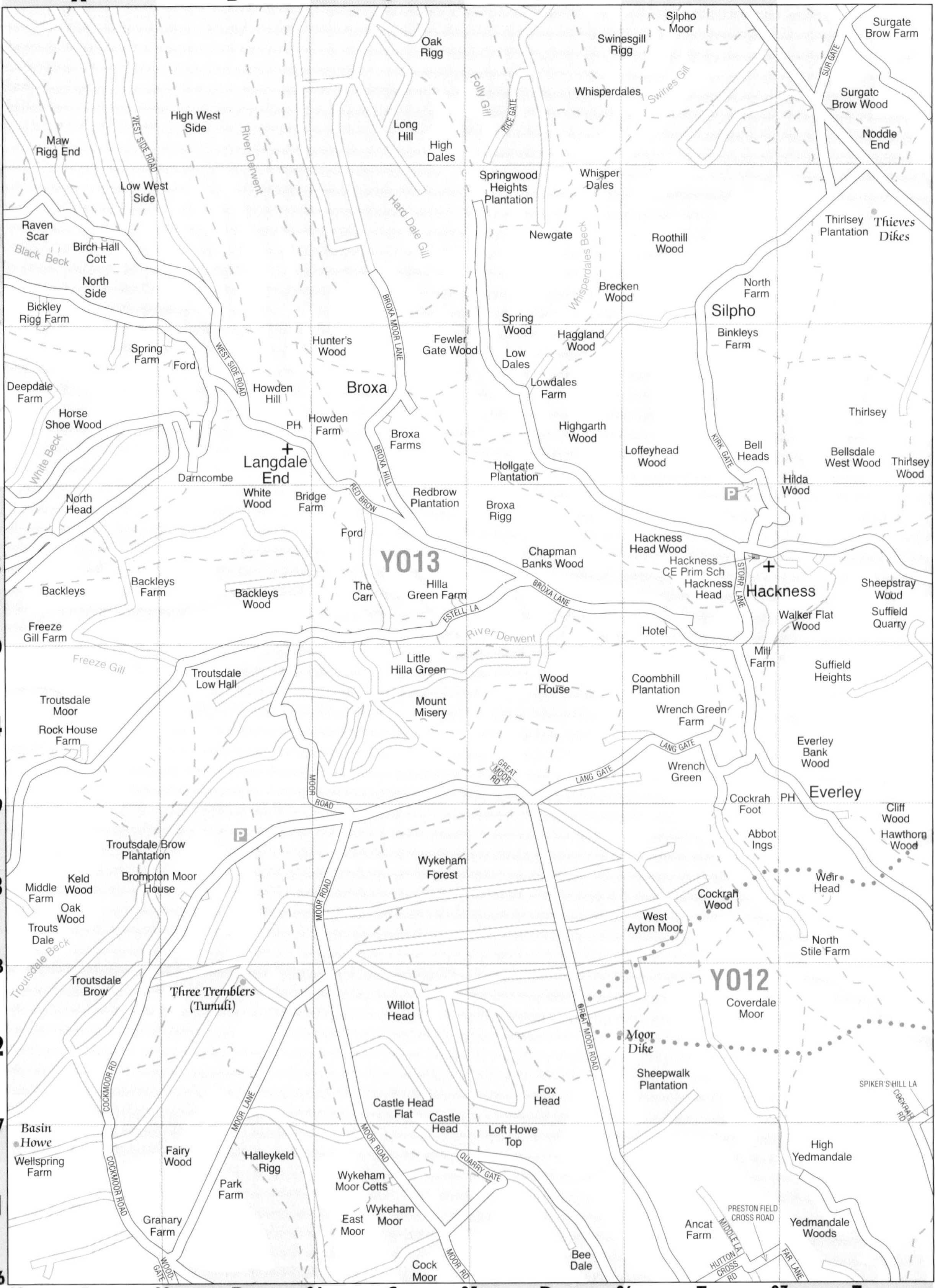

A B C D E F

8

Maw Rigg End
High West Side
Oak Rigg
Silpho Moor
Swinesgill Rigg
Whisperdales
Surgate Brow Farm
Surgate Brow Wood
Long Hill
High Dales
Folly Gill
RICE GATE
SUR GATE
Noddle End

93

Low West Side
Springwood Heights Plantation
Whisper Dales
Thirlsey Plantation
Thieves Dikes

7

Raven Scar
Black Beck
Birch Hall Cott
North Side
Newgate
Roothill Wood
Brecken Wood
North Farm
Silpho

92

Bickley Rigg Farm
Spring Farm
Ford
Hunter's Wood
Fewler Gate Wood
Spring Wood
Low Dales
Haggland Wood
Lowdales Farm
Binkleys Farm

6

Deepdale Farm
Horse Shoe Wood
White Beck
Howden Hill
PH
Howden Farm
Broxa
BROXA MOOR LANE
Broxa Farms
BROXA HILL
Highgarth Wood
Loffeyhead Wood
Bell Heads
KIRK GATE
Thirlsey
Thirlsey Wood
Bellsdale West Wood

91

North Head
Langdale End
Darncombe
White Wood
Bridge Farm
RED BROW
Redbrow Plantation
Broxa Rigg
Hollgate Plantation
P
Hilda Wood

5

Backleys
Backleys Farm
Backleys Wood
Freeze Gill Farm
YO13
The Carr
Ford
Hilla Green Farm
ESTELL LA
Chapman Banks Wood
BROXA LANE
Hackness Head Wood
Hackness CE Prim Sch
Hackness Head
STORR LANE
Hackness
Sheepstray Wood
Suffield Quarry
Walker Flat Wood

90

Freeze Gill
Troutsdale Low Hall
Little Hilla Green
River Derwent
Wood House
Hotel
Mill Farm
Suffield Heights

4

Troutsdale Moor
Rock House Farm
Mount Misery
Coombhill Plantation
Wrench Green Farm
LANG GATE
Everley Bank Wood

89

Troutsdale Brow Plantation
Brompton Moor House
P
MOOR ROAD
Wrench Green
LANG GATE
Cockrah Foot
PH
Everley
Abbot Ings
Cliff Wood
Hawthorn Wood

3

Middle Farm
Keld Wood
Oak Wood
Trouts Dale
Troutsdale Beck
GREAT MOOR RD
Wykeham Forest
West Ayton Moor
Cockrah Wood
Weir Head
North Stile Farm

88

Troutsdale Brow
Three Tremblers (Tumuli)
YO12
Coverdale Moor
SPIKER'S HILL LA

2

COCKMOOR RD
MOOR LANE
Willot Head
MOOR ROAD
Moor Dike
Sheepwalk Plantation

87

Basin Howe
Wellspring Farm
Fairy Wood
Halleykeld Rigg
Castle Head Flat
Castle Head
MOOR ROAD
QUARRY GATE
Loft Howe Top
Fox Head
High Yedmandale
COCKRAH RD

1

COCKMOOR ROAD
Park Farm
Wykeham Moor Cotts
East Moor
Wykeham Moor
Ancat Farm
PRESTON FIELD CROSS ROAD
MIDDLE LA
Yedmandale Woods
TAR LANE

Granary Farm
WOOD GATE
Cock Moor
MOOR RD
Bee Dale
HUTTON CROSS RD

86

92 A 93 B 94 C 95 D 96 E 97 F

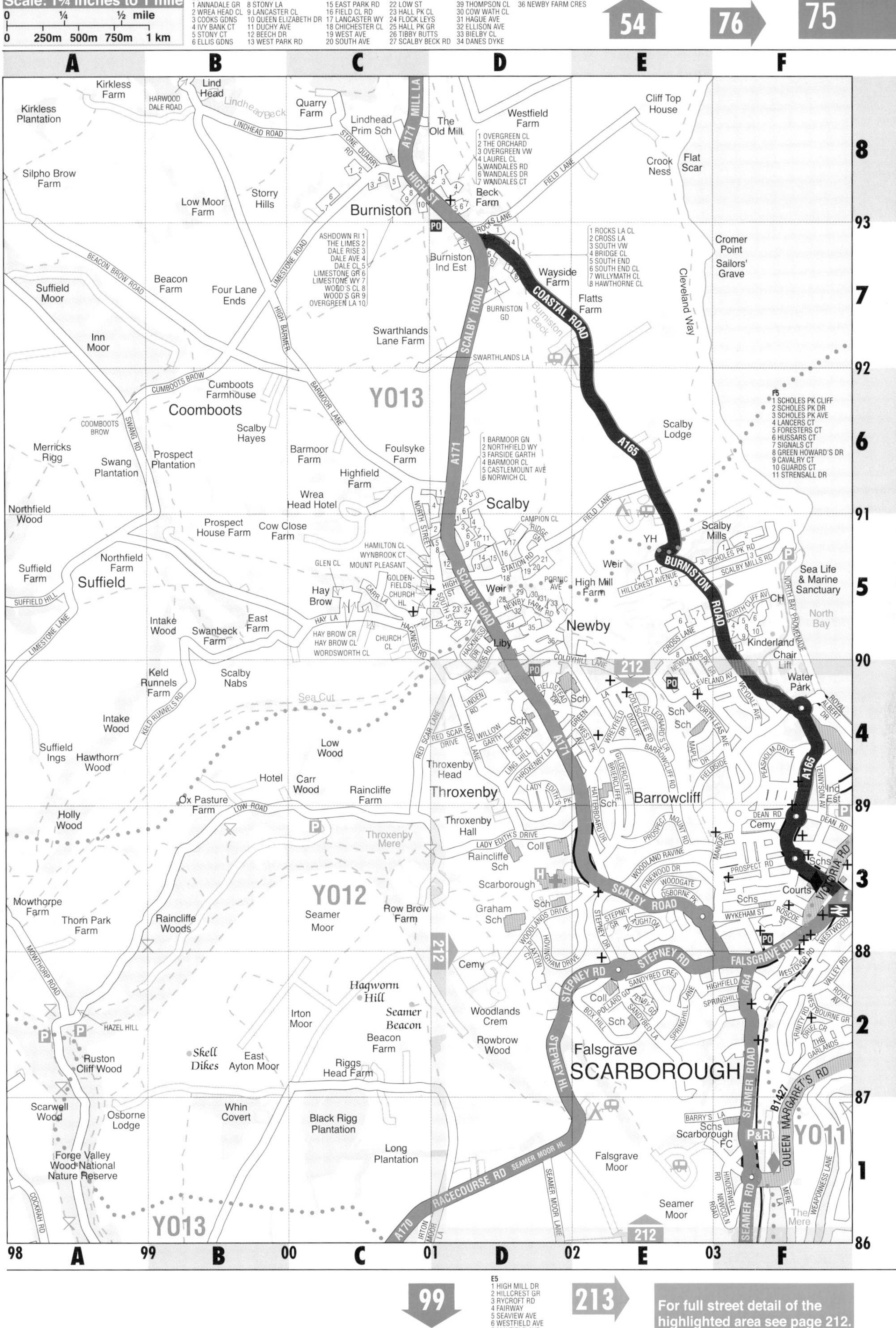

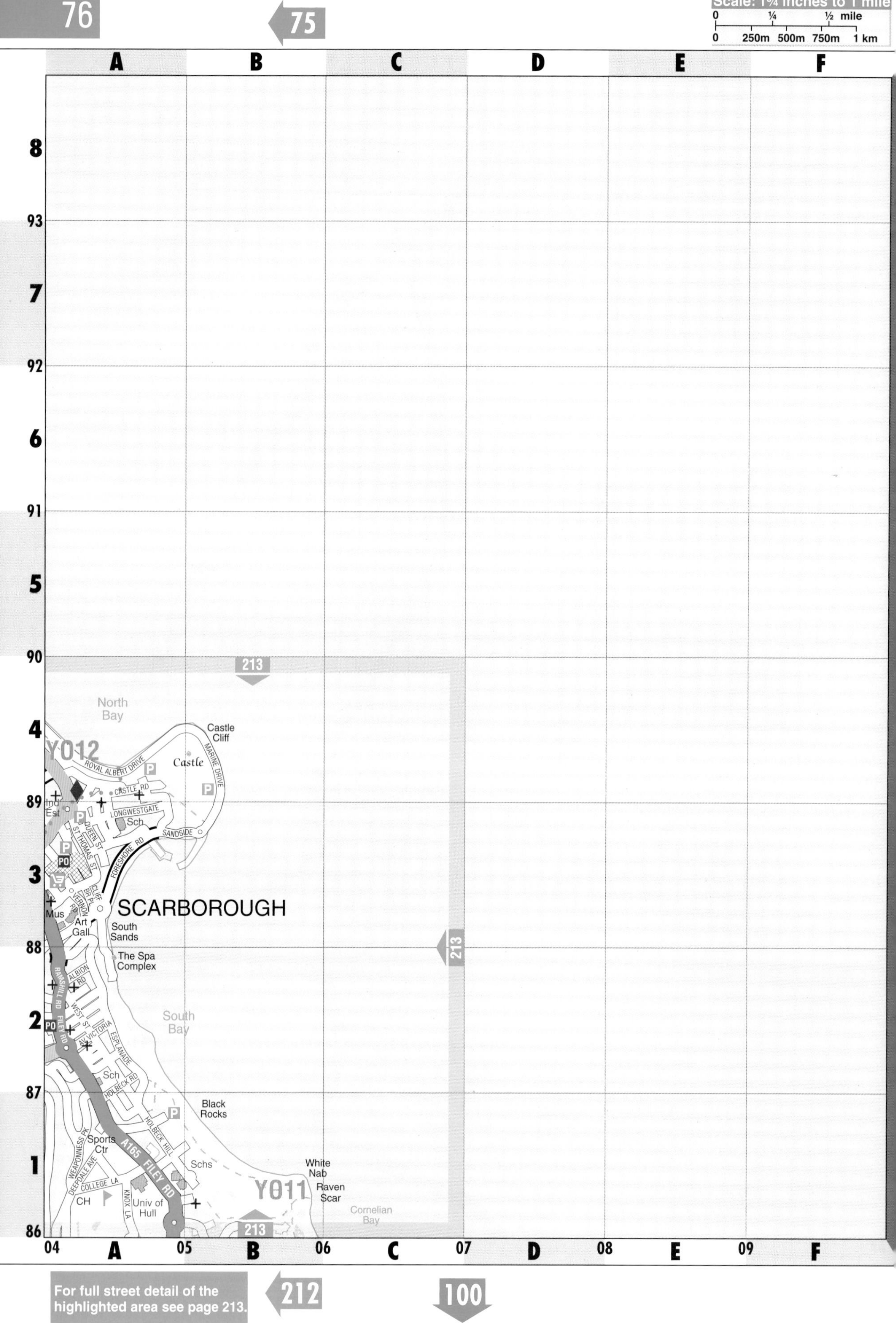

A **B** **C** **D** **E** **F**

8

93

7

92

6

91

5

90

◢ 213 ◣

North
Bay

4

Castle
Cliff

YO12

ROYAL ALBERT DRIVE

Castle

P

MARINE DRIVE

89

Ind
Est

CASTLE RD

P

LONGWESTGATE

Sch

P

SANDSIDE

QUEEN ST

ST THOMAS ST

FORESHORE RD

213

3

Mus

CLIFF

VERNON

SCARBOROUGH

Art
Gall

South
Sands

88

The Spa
Complex

213

ALBION RD

WEST ST

2

PO

HANSOM RD

FLEET RD

VICTORIA

ESPLANADE

South
Bay

Sch

HOLBECK RD

87

P

Black
Rocks

HOLBECK HILL

A165 FILEY RD

1

WEAPONNESS PK

Sports
Ctr

Schs

White
Nab

DEEPDALE AVE

COLLEGE LA

CH

KNOX LA

Univ of
Hull

YO11

Raven
Scar

Cornelian
Bay

86

04   **A**   05   **B**   06   **C**   07   **D**   08   **E**   09   **F**

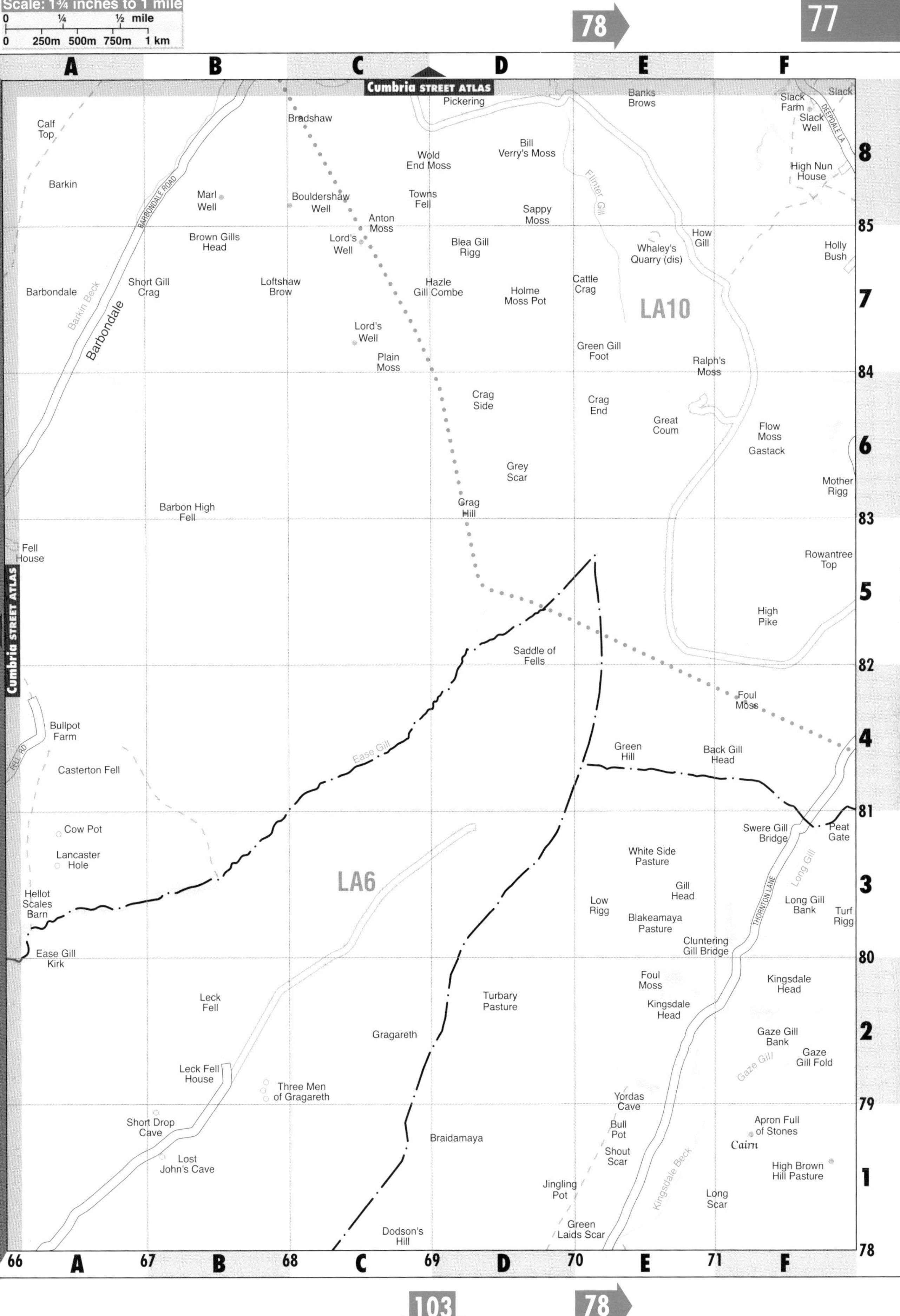

Cumbria STREET ATLAS

A   B   C   D   E   F

Calf
Top

Banks
Brows

Slack
Farm   Slack

Slack
Well

Pickering

Bradshaw

8

Bill
Verry's Moss

Wold
End Moss

High Nun
House

Barkin

Marl
Well

Bouldershaw
Well

Towns
Fell

Sappy
Moss

85

Anton
Moss

Brown Gills
Head

Lord's
Well

Blea Gill
Rigg

Whaley's
Quarry (dis)

How
Gill

Holly
Bush

Barbondale

Short Gill
Crag

Loftshaw
Brow

Hazle
Gill Combe

Holme
Moss Pot

Cattle
Crag

LA10

7

Lord's
Well

Green Gill
Foot

Plain
Moss

Ralph's
Moss

84

Crag
Side

Crag
End

Great
Coum

Flow
Moss

6

Barbon High
Fell

Grey
Scar

Gastack

Mother
Rigg

83

Fell
House

Grag
Hill

Rowantree
Top

5

Saddle of
Fells

High
Pike

82

Foul
Moss

Bullpot
Farm

4

Casterton Fell

Green
Hill

Back Gill
Head

Swere Gill
Bridge

Peat
Gate

81

Cow Pot

White Side
Pasture

Lancaster
Hole

LA6

Gill
Head

Long Gill
Bank

Long Gill

Turf
Rigg

3

Hellot
Scales
Barn

Low
Rigg

Blakeamaya
Pasture

Thornton Lane

Ease Gill
Kirk

Cluntering
Gill Bridge

80

Leck
Fell

Turbary
Pasture

Foul
Moss

Kingsdale
Head

Kingsdale
Head

Gragareth

Gaze Gill
Bank

Gaze
Gill Fold

2

Leck Fell
House

Gaze Gill

Three Men
of Gragareth

Yordas
Cave

79

Short Drop
Cave

Braidamaya

Bull
Pot

Apron Full
of Stones

Cairn

Lost
John's Cave

Shout
Scar

Kingsdale Beck

High Brown
Hill Pasture

1

Jingling
Pot

Long
Scar

Dodson's
Hill

Green
Laids Scar

78

A   66   B   67   68   C   69   D   70   E   71   F   78

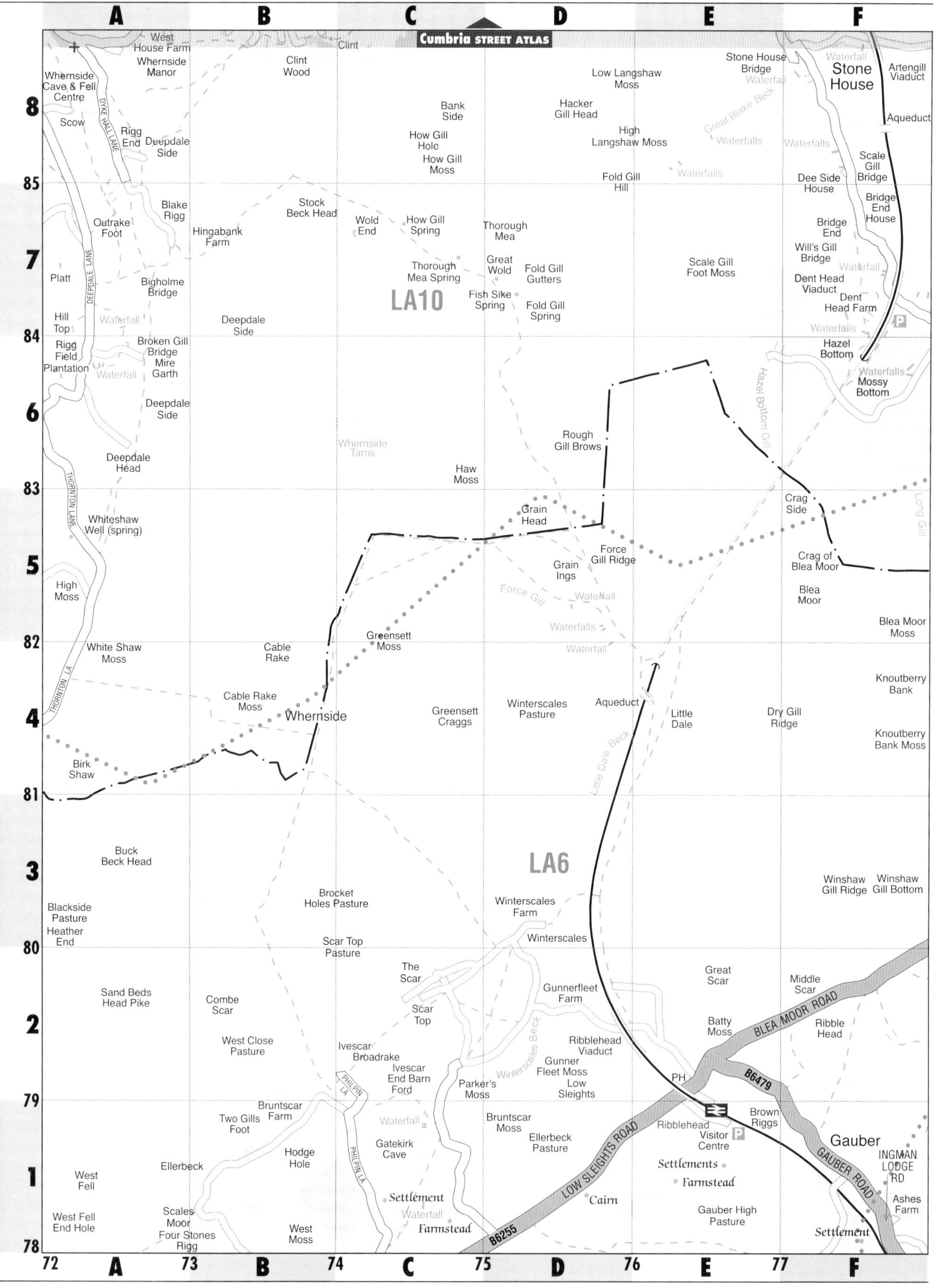

Cumbria STREET ATLAS

West House Farm
Whernside Manor
Clint Wood
Clint
Whernside Cave & Fell Centre
Scow
Rigg End
Deepdale Side
Bank Side
Hacker Gill Head
Low Langshaw Moss
Stone House Bridge
Waterfall
Stone House
Artengill Viaduct
Aqueduct
How Gill Hole
How Gill Moss
High Langshaw Moss
Great Blake Beck
Waterfalls
Waterfall
Scale Gill Bridge
Platt
Outrake Foot
Blake Rigg
Hingabank Farm
Stock Beck Head
Wold End
How Gill Spring
Fold Gill Hill
Waterfalls
Dee Side House
Bridge End House
Thorough Mea
Scale Gill Foot Moss
Will's Gill Bridge
Bridge End
Hill Top
Bigholme Bridge
Deepdale Side
Thorough Mea Spring
Great Wold
Fold Gill Gutters
LA10
Dent Head Viaduct
Dent Head Farm
Waterfall
Fish Sike Spring
Fold Gill Spring
Rigg Field Plantation
Broken Gill Bridge
Mire Garth
Waterfall
Hazel Bottom
Waterfalls
Mossy Bottom
Deepdale Side
Deepdale Head
Rough Gill Brows
Hazel Bottom Gill
Whiteshaw Well (spring)
Whernside Tarns
Haw Moss
Crag Side
Long Gill
Grain Head
Crag of Blea Moor
High Moss
Force Gill Ridge
Blea Moor
White Shaw Moss
Cable Rake
Greensett Moss
Grain Ings
Force Gill
Waterfall
Blea Moor Moss
Cable Rake Moss
Waterfalls
Knoutberry Bank
Whernside
Greensett Craggs
Winterscales Pasture
Aqueduct
Little Dale
Dry Gill Ridge
Knoutberry Bank Moss
Birk Shaw
Little Dale Beck
Buck Beck Head
LA6
Winshaw Gill Ridge
Winshaw Gill Bottom
Blackside Pasture
Heather End
Brocket Holes Pasture
Winterscales Farm
Sand Beds Head Pike
Scar Top Pasture
Combe Scar
The Scar
Winterscales
Gunnerfleet Farm
Great Scar
Middle Scar
West Close Pasture
Scar Top
Ribblehead Viaduct
Batty Moss
BLEA MOOR ROAD
Ribble Head
Ivescar Broadrake
Ivescar End Barn Ford
Parker's Moss
Gunner Fleet Moss Low Sleights
B6479
PH
Bruntscar Farm
Two Gills Foot
Waterfall
Bruntscar Moss
Ellerbeck Pasture
Ribblehead
Visitor Centre
Brown Riggs
Gauber
GAUBER ROAD
INGMAN LODGE RD
West Fell
Ellerbeck
Hodge Hole
Gatekirk Cave
Settlement
Waterfall
Settlements
Farmstead
Cairn
Ashes Farm
West Fell End Hole
Scales Moor
Four Stones Rigg
West Moss
Farmstead
B6255
LOW SLEIGHTS ROAD
Gauber High Pasture
Settlement

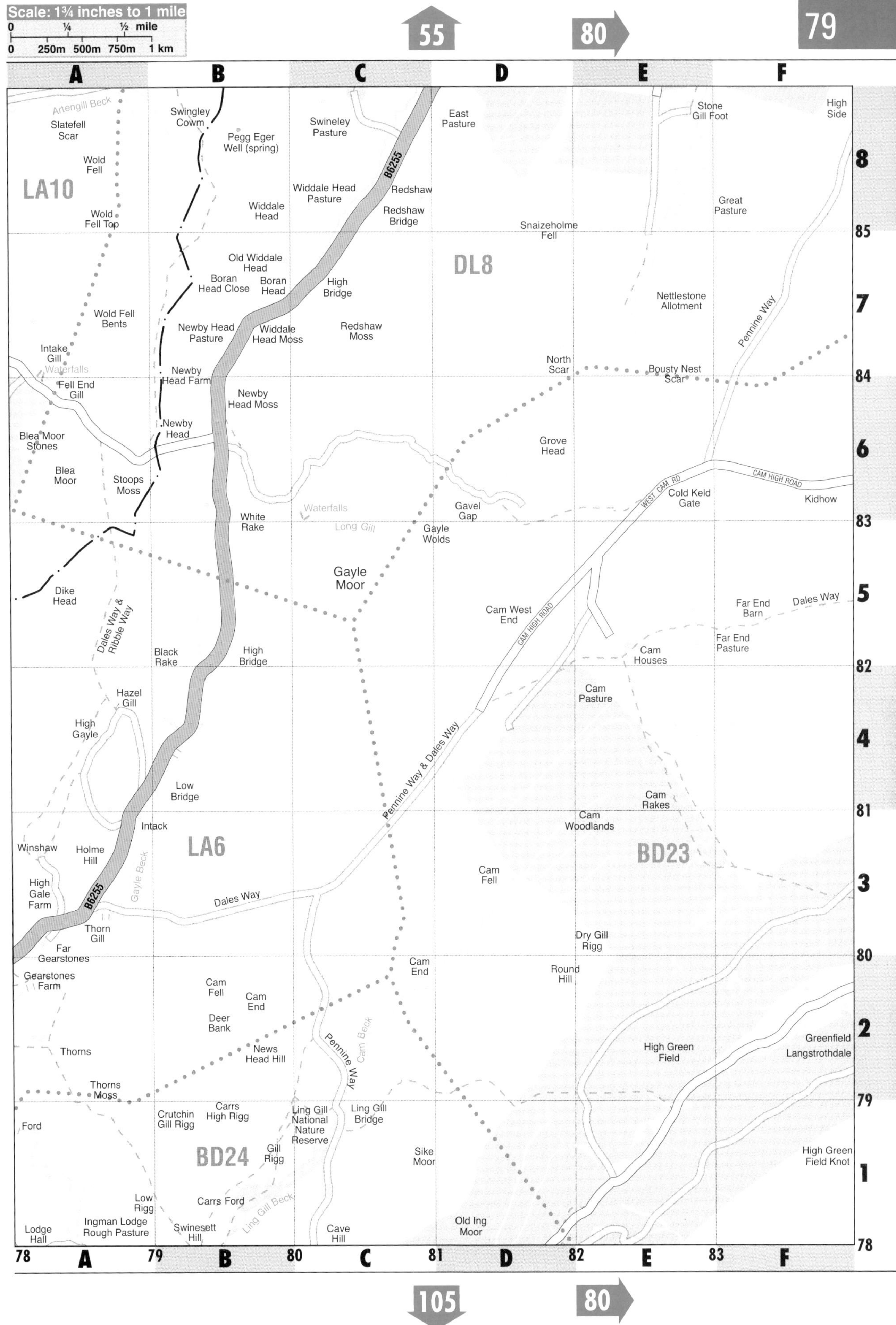

A   **B**   **C**   **D**   **E**   **F**

Artengill Beck

Swingley Cowm

Slatefell Scar

Pegg Eger Well (spring)

Swineley Pasture

East Pasture

Stone Gill Foot

High Side

8

Wold Fell

LA10

Widdale Head

Widdale Head Pasture

Redshaw

Great Pasture

85

Wold Fell Top

Redshaw Bridge

Snaizeholme Fell

B6255

Old Widdale Head

DL8

Nettlestone Allotment

Pennine Way

7

Wold Fell Bents

Boran Head Close

Boran Head

High Bridge

84

Intake Gill

Newby Head Pasture

Widdale Head Moss

Redshaw Moss

North Scar

Bousty Nest Scar

Waterfalls

Fell End Gill

Newby Head Farm

Newby Head Moss

Grove Head

6

Blea Moor Stones

Newby Head

West Cam Rd

Cold Keld Gate

Cam High Road

Kidhow

83

Blea Moor

Stoops Moss

White Rake

Waterfalls

Long Gill

Gayle Wolds

Gavel Gap

Dike Head

Dales Way & Ribble Way

Gayle Moor

Cam West End

Far End Barn

Dales Way

5

Black Rake

High Bridge

Cam Houses

Far End Pasture

82

Hazel Gill

Cam Pasture

High Gayle

4

Low Bridge

Cam Rakes

81

Intack

LA6

Cam Woodlands

BD23

Winshaw

Holme Hill

Gayle Beck

Dales Way

Pennine Way & Dales Way

Cam Fell

3

High Gale Farm

B6255

Thorn Gill

Dry Gill Rigg

80

Far Gearstones

Cam End

Round Hill

Gearstones Farm

Cam Fell

Cam End

High Green Field

Greenfield Langstrothdale

2

Deer Bank

Cam Beck

Thorns

News Head Hill

Pennine Way

Thorns Moss

79

Ford

Crutchin Gill Rigg

Carrs High Rigg

Ling Gill National Nature Reserve

Ling Gill Bridge

High Green Field Knot

Gill Rigg

Sike Moor

1

BD24

Low Rigg

Carrs Ford

Ling Gill Beck

Cave Hill

Old Ing Moor

Lodge Hall

Ingman Lodge Rough Pasture

Swinesett Hill

78

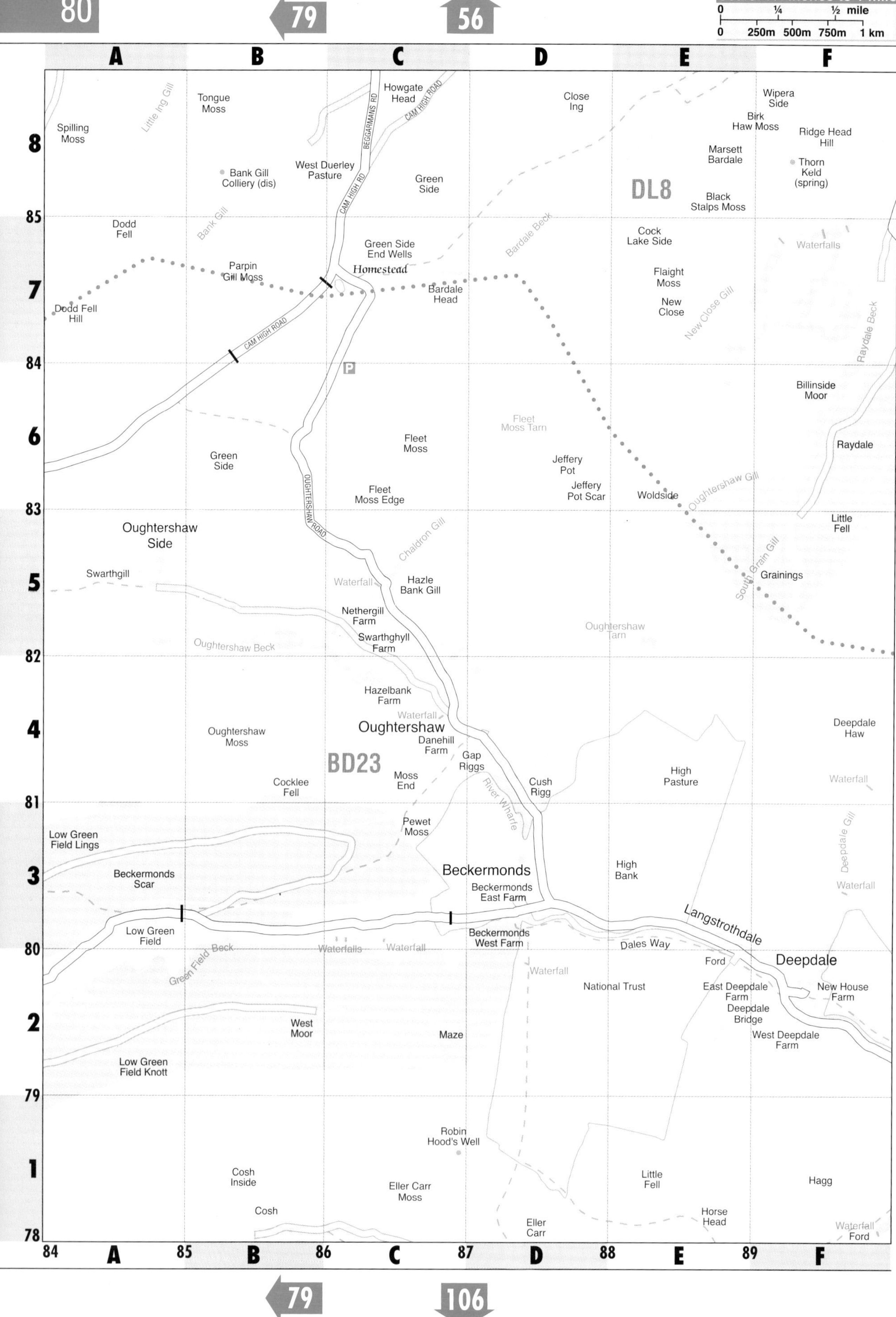
79
56
Scale: 1¾ inches to 1 mile
0 ¼ ½ mile
0 250m 500m 750m 1 km
A B C D E F
8 85 7 84 6 83 5 82 4 81 3 80 2 79 1 78
Spilling Moss
Little Ing Gill
Tongue Moss
Howgate Head
BEGGARMANS RD
CAM HIGH ROAD
Close Ing
Wipera Side
Birk Haw Moss
Ridge Head Hill
Marsett Bardale
Thorn Keld (spring)
Bank Gill Colliery (dis)
West Duerley Pasture
CAM HIGH RD
Green Side
DL8
Black Stalps Moss
Dodd Fell
Bank Gill
Bardale Beck
Cock Lake Side
Waterfalls
Green Side End Wells
Parpin Gill Moss
Homestead
Flaight Moss
Bardale Head
Dodd Fell Hill
New Close
New Close Gill
Raydale Beck
CAM HIGH ROAD
Billinside Moor
Fleet Moss Tarn
Fleet Moss
Raydale
Green Side
Jeffery Pot
Jeffery Pot Scar
Oughtershaw Gill
Fleet Moss Edge
Woldside
OUGHTERSHAW ROAD
Little Fell
Oughtershaw Side
Chaldron Gill
South Grain Gill
Swarthgill
Grainings
Waterfall
Hazle Bank Gill
Nethergill Farm
Oughtershaw Tarn
Swarthghyll Farm
Oughtershaw Beck
Hazelbank Farm
Waterfall
Deepdale Haw
Oughtershaw
Oughtershaw Moss
Danehill Farm
Gap Riggs
BD23
High Pasture
Moss End
Cush Rigg
Cocklee Fell
Waterfall
River Wharfe
Pewet Moss
Low Green Field Lings
Deepdale Gill
High Bank
Beckermonds Scar
Beckermonds
Beckermonds East Farm
Waterfall
Langstrothdale
Low Green Field
Beckermonds West Farm
Beck
Waterfalls
Waterfall
Dales Way
Deepdale
Ford
Green Field
Waterfall
National Trust
East Deepdale Farm
New House Farm
Deepdale Bridge
West Moor
Maze
West Deepdale Farm
Low Green Field Knott
Robin Hood's Well
Cosh Inside
Eller Carr Moss
Little Fell
Hagg
Cosh
Horse Head
Eller Carr
Waterfall Ford
84 85 86 87 88 89

Scale: 1¾ inches to 1 mile

57
82

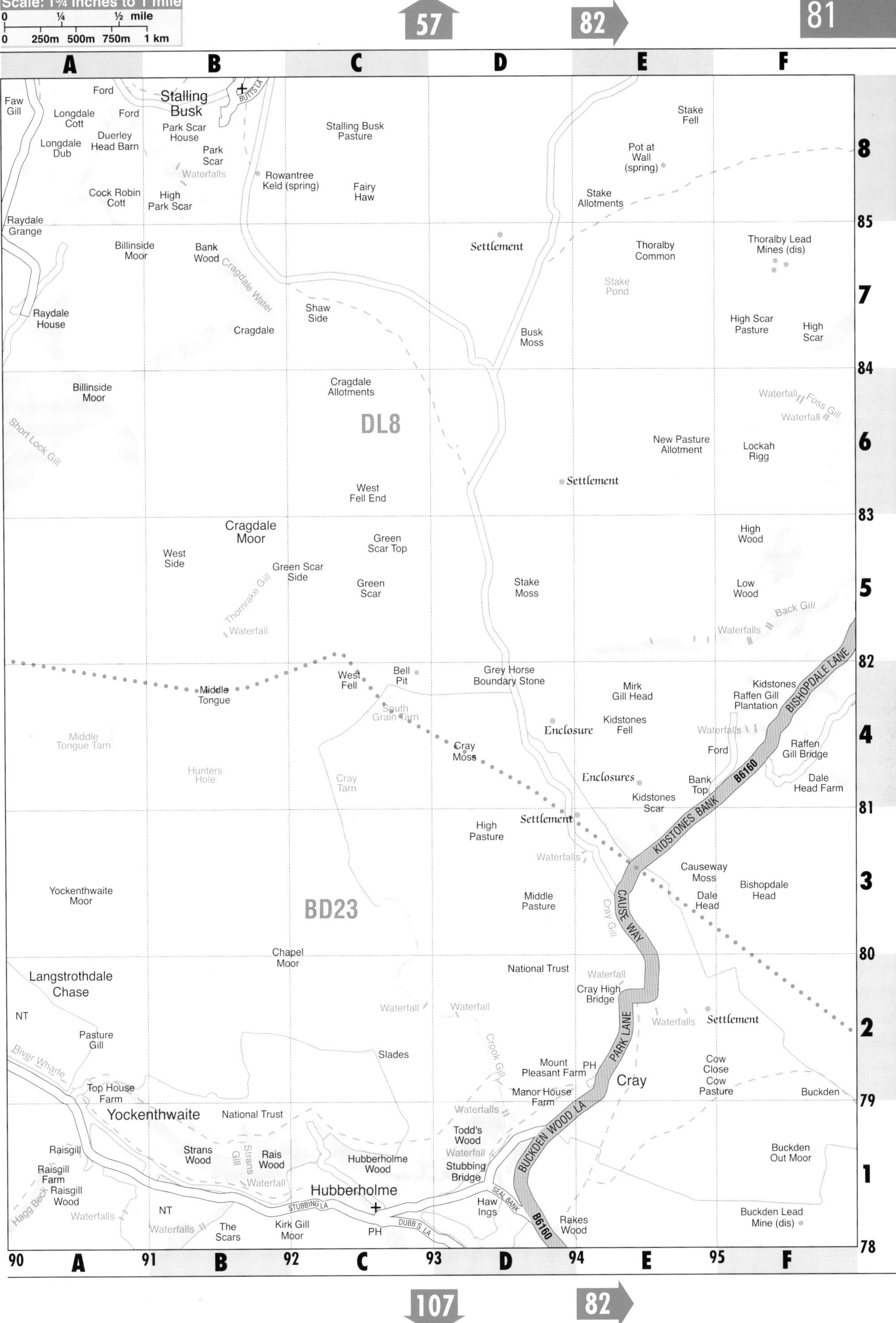
0
¼
½ mile
0
250m
500m
750m
1 km
A
B
C
D
E
F
Faw Gill
Ford
Stalling Busk
Longdale Cott
Ford
Park Scar House
Longdale Dub
Duerley Head Barn
Park Scar
Waterfalls
Stalling Busk Pasture
Stake Fell
Pot at Wall (spring)
Rowantree Keld (spring)
Fairy Haw
Cock Robin Cott
High Park Scar
Stake Allotments
Raydale Grange
Billinside Moor
Bank Wood
Cragdale Water
Settlement
Thoralby Common
Thoralby Lead Mines (dis)
Stake Pond
Raydale House
Cragdale
Shaw Side
Busk Moss
High Scar Pasture
High Scar
Billinside Moor
Cragdale Allotments
Waterfall
Foss Gill
Waterfall
DL8
Short Lock Gill
New Pasture Allotment
Lockah Rigg
Settlement
West Fell End
Cragdale Moor
Green Scar Top
High Wood
West Side
Green Scar Side
Thornrake Gill
Green Scar
Stake Moss
Low Wood
Back Gill
Waterfall
Waterfalls
West Fell
Bell Pit
Grey Horse Boundary Stone
Mirk Gill Head
Kidstones Raffen Gill Plantation
BISHOPDALE LANE
Middle Tongue
South Grain Tarn
Middle Tongue Tarn
Enclosure
Kidstones Fell
Waterfalls
Cray Moss
Ford
Raffen Gill Bridge
Hunters Hole
Cray Tarn
Enclosures
Bank Top
B6160
Dale Head Farm
Kidstones Scar
KIDSTONES BANK
High Pasture
Settlement
Waterfalls
Causeway Moss
Yockenthwaite Moor
BD23
Middle Pasture
CAUSE WAY
Cray Gill
Dale Head
Bishopdale Head
Chapel Moor
National Trust
Langstrothdale Chase
Waterfall
Cray High Bridge
NT
Waterfall
Waterfall
PARK LANE
Waterfalls
Settlement
Pasture Gill
River Wharfe
Slades
Crook Gill
Mount Pleasant Farm
PH
Cray
Cow Close
Cow Pasture
Top House Farm
Manor House Farm
Buckden
Yockenthwaite
National Trust
Waterfalls
BUCKDEN WOOD LA
Todd's Wood
Raisgill
Strans Wood
Strans Gill
Rais Wood
Hubberholme Wood
Waterfall
Buckden Out Moor
Raisgill Farm
Stubbing Bridge
Raisgill Wood
Waterfall
Hubberholme
Hagg Beck
STUBBING LA
SEAL BANK
Haw Ings
Waterfalls
NT
Waterfalls
The Scars
Kirk Gill Moor
DUBB'S LA
PH
B6160
Rakes Wood
Buckden Lead Mine (dis)
8
85
7
84
6
83
5
82
4
81
3
80
2
79
1
78
90
91
92
93
94
95

107
82

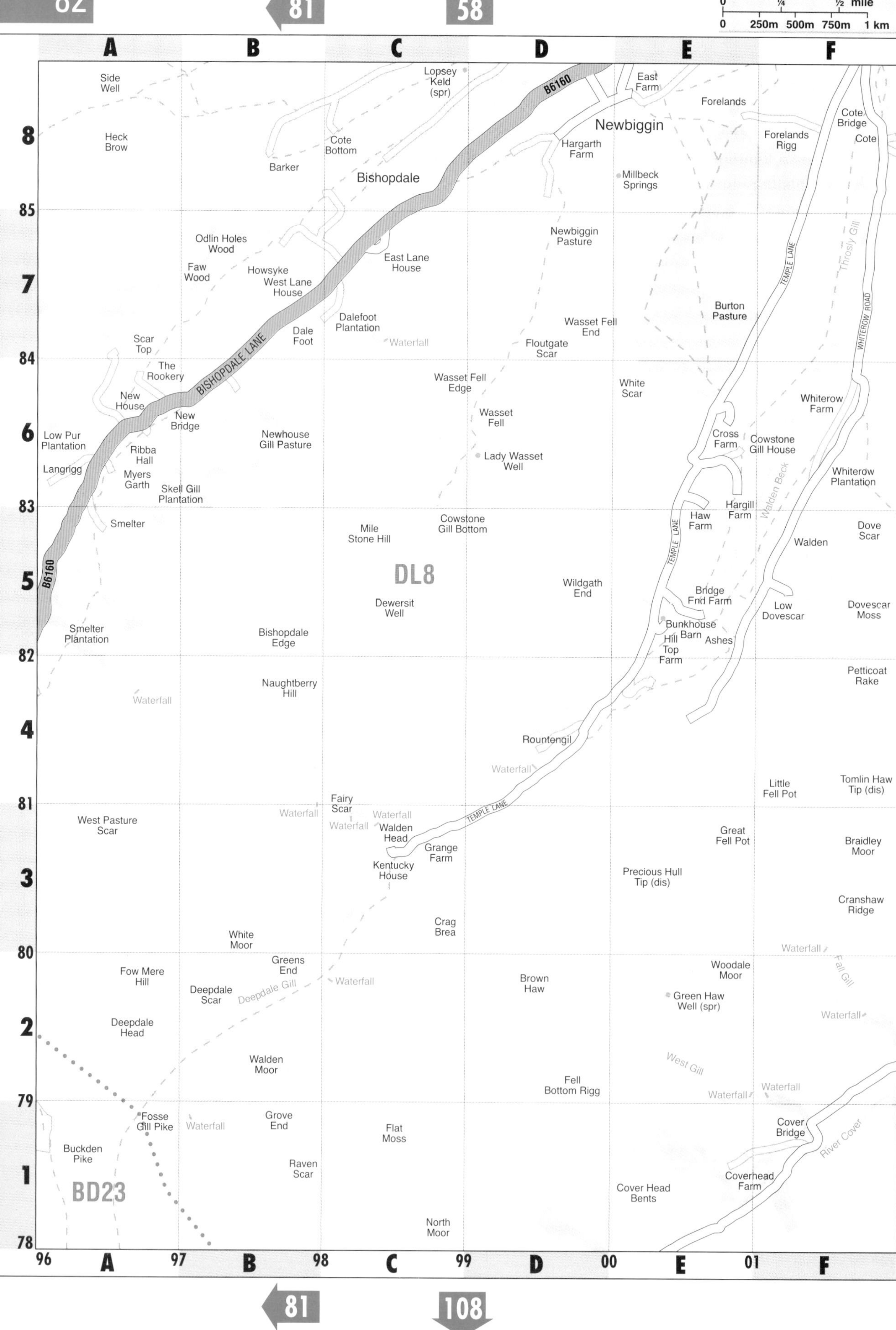
81
58
Scale: 1¾ inches to 1 mile
A
B
C
D
E
F
Side Well
Lopsey Keld (spr)
B6160
East Farm
Forelands
Newbiggin
Cote Bridge
Heck Brow
Cote Bottom
Hargarth Farm
Forelands Rigg
Cote
Barker
Bishopdale
Millbeck Springs
Odlin Holes Wood
Newbiggin Pasture
Throsly Gill
Faw Wood
Howsyke
West Lane House
East Lane House
TEMPLE LANE
Burton Pasture
WHITEROW ROAD
Dale Foot
Dalefoot Plantation
Wasset Fell End
Scar Top
Waterfall
Floutgate Scar
The Rookery
BISHOPDALE LANE
Wasset Fell Edge
White Scar
Whiterow Farm
New House
New Bridge
Wasset Fell
Low Pur Plantation
Newhouse Gill Pasture
Cross Farm
Cowstone Gill House
Ribba Hall
Lady Wasset Well
Walden Beck
Whiterow Plantation
Langrigg
Myers Garth
Skell Gill Plantation
Hargill Farm
Smelter
Cowstone Gill Bottom
Haw Farm
Dove Scar
Mile Stone Hill
Walden
DL8
Wildgath End
Bridge End Farm
Dewersit Well
Low Dovescar
Dovescar Moss
Smelter Plantation
Bishopdale Edge
Bunkhouse Barn
Hill Top Farm
Ashes
Petticoat Rake
Naughtberry Hill
Rountengil
Little Fell Pot
Tomlin Haw Tip (dis)
Fairy Scar
West Pasture Scar
Walden Head
Great Fell Pot
Braidley Moor
Grange Farm
Kentucky House
Precious Hull Tip (dis)
Cranshaw Ridge
Crag Brea
White Moor
Greens End
Fow Mere Hill
Woodale Moor
Fall Gill
Deepdale Scar
Deepdale Gill
Brown Haw
Green Haw Well (spr)
Deepdale Head
West Gill
Walden Moor
Fell Bottom Rigg
Fosse Gill Pike
Grove End
Cover Bridge
Buckden Pike
Flat Moss
River Cover
Raven Scar
Coverhead Farm
BD23
Cover Head Bents
North Moor
8
85
7
84
6
83
5
82
4
81
3
80
2
79
1
78
96
97
98
99
00
01
81
108

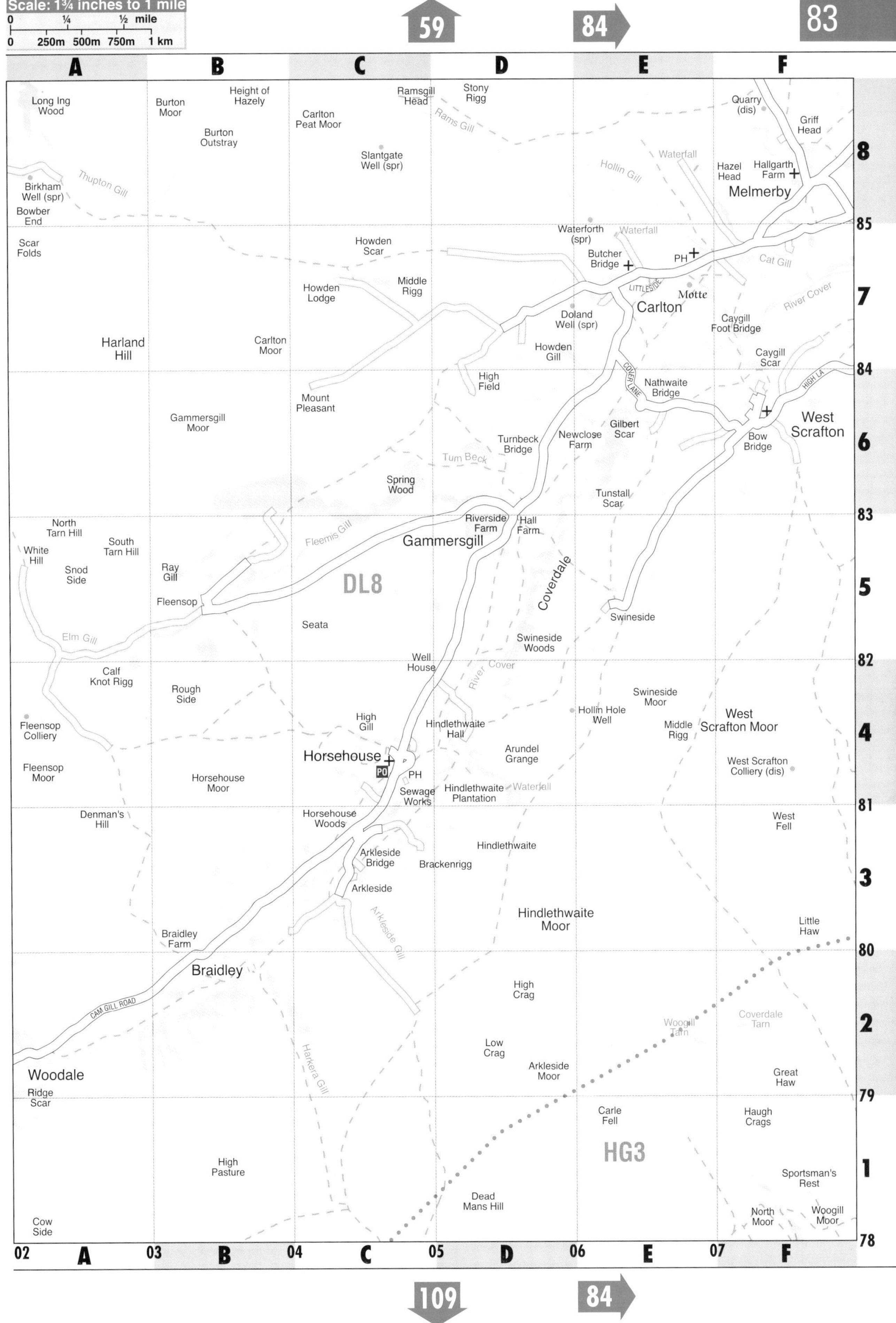
Scale: 1¾ inches to 1 mile
0 ¼ ½ mile
0 250m 500m 750m 1 km
59
84
A B C D E F
Long Ing Wood
Burton Moor
Height of Hazely
Burton Outstray
Carlton Peat Moor
Ramsgill Head
Stony Rigg
Rams Gill
Quarry (dis)
Griff Head
Slantgate Well (spr)
Waterfall
Hollin Gill
Hazel Head
Hallgarth Farm
Melmerby
Birkham Well (spr)
Thupton Gill
Bowber End
Scar Folds
Howden Scar
Waterforth (spr)
Waterfall
Butcher Bridge
PH
Cat Gill
Howden Lodge
Middle Rigg
Littleside
Motte
Carlton
River Cover
Doland Well (spr)
Caygill Foot Bridge
Harland Hill
Carlton Moor
Howden Gill
Caygill Scar
High Field
Cover Lane
Nathwaite Bridge
High La
Mount Pleasant
Gammersgill Moor
Gilbert Scar
West Scrafton
Turnbeck Bridge
Newclose Farm
Bow Bridge
Turn Beck
Spring Wood
Tunstall Scar
North Tarn Hill
Riverside Farm
Hall Farm
White Hill
South Tarn Hill
Fleemis Gill
Gammersgill
Snod Side
Ray Gill
DL8
Coverdale
Fleensop
Swineside
Seata
Elm Gill
Swineside Woods
Well House
River Cover
Calf Knot Rigg
Rough Side
Swineside Moor
High Gill
Hollin Hole Well
West Scrafton Moor
Fleensop Colliery
Hindlethwaite Hall
Middle Rigg
Arundel Grange
Horsehouse
PO
PH
West Scrafton Colliery (dis)
Fleensop Moor
Horsehouse Moor
Sewage Works
Hindlethwaite Plantation
Waterfall
Denman's Hill
Horsehouse Woods
West Fell
Arkleside Bridge
Hindlethwaite
Brackenrigg
Arkleside
Arkleside Gill
Hindlethwaite Moor
Little Haw
Braidley Farm
Braidley
High Crag
Cam Gill Road
Woogill Tarn
Coverdale Tarn
Harkera Gill
Low Crag
Woodale
Arkleside Moor
Great Haw
Ridge Scar
Carle Fell
Haugh Crags
HG3
High Pasture
Sportsman's Rest
Dead Mans Hill
North Moor
Woogill Moor
Cow Side
8 85 7 84 6 83 5 82 4 81 3 80 2 79 1 78
02 03 04 05 06 07

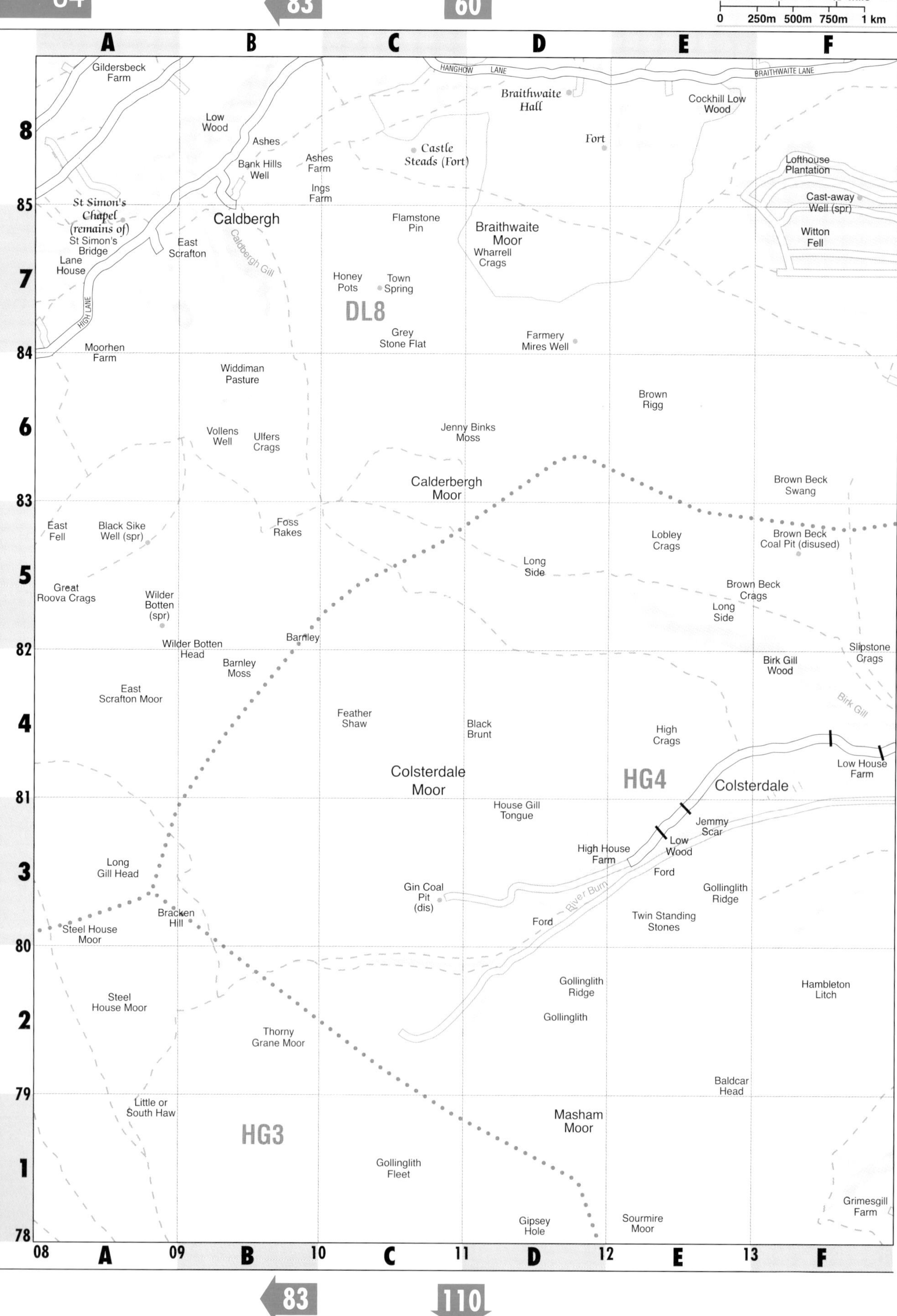

Scale: 1¾ inches to 1 mile

0   ¼   ½ mile
0   250m 500m 750m 1 km

A   **B**   **C**   **D**   **E**   **F**

HANGHOW LANE

BRAITHWAITE LANE

8

Gildersbeck Farm

Low Wood

Braithwaite Hall

Cockhill Low Wood

Ashes

Bank Hills Well

Ashes Farm

Castle Steads (Fort)

Fort

Lofthouse Plantation

Ings Farm

Cast-away Well (spr)

85

St Simon's Chapel (remains of)

Caldbergh

Flamstone Pin

Braithwaite Moor

Witton Fell

St Simon's Bridge

Wharrell Crags

Lane House

East Scrafton

Caldbergh Gill

7

Honey Pots

Town Spring

DL8

Moorhen Farm

Grey Stone Flat

Farmery Mires Well

84

Widdiman Pasture

Brown Rigg

6

Vollens Well

Ulfers Crags

Jenny Binks Moss

Calderbergh Moor

Brown Beck Swang

83

East Fell

Black Sike Well (spr)

Foss Rakes

Lobley Crags

Brown Beck Coal Pit (disused)

Long Side

5

Great Roova Crags

Wilder Botten (spr)

Brown Beck Crags

Long Side

Wilder Botten Head

Barnley

Slipstone Crags

82

Barnley Moss

Birk Gill Wood

Birk Gill

East Scrafton Moor

4

Feather Shaw

Black Brunt

High Crags

Low House Farm

81

Colsterdale Moor

House Gill Tongue

HG4

Colsterdale

Jemmy Scar

3

Long Gill Head

Gin Coal Pit (dis)

High House Farm

Low Wood

Ford

Gollinglith Ridge

Bracken Hill

Ford

Twin Standing Stones

River Burn

Steel House Moor

80

Steel House Moor

Gollinglith Ridge

Hambleton Litch

2

Thorny Grane Moor

Gollinglith

Little or South Haw

Baldcar Head

79

HG3

Masham Moor

1

Gollinglith Fleet

Grimesgill Farm

Gipsey Hole

Sourmire Moor

78

08   **A**   **09**   **B**   **10**   **C**   **11**   **D**   **12**   **E**   **13**   **F**

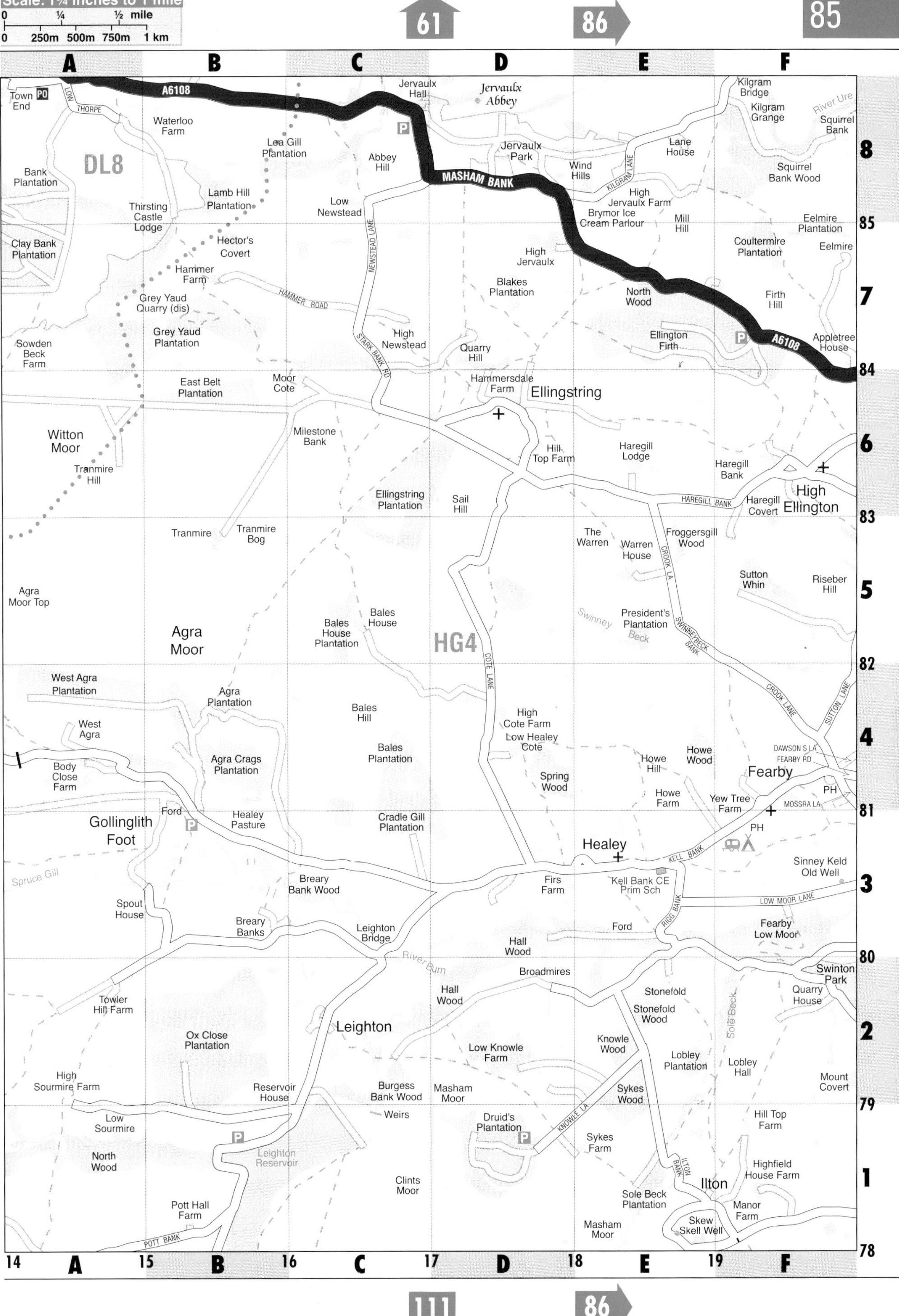

Scale: 1¾ inches to 1 mile
0 ¼ ½ mile
0 250m 500m 750m 1 km
61
86
85
A
B
C
D
E
F
Town End
PO
LOW THORPE
A6108
Waterloo Farm
Lea Gill Plantation
Jervaulx Hall
Jervaulx Abbey
Kilgram Bridge
Kilgram Grange
River Ure
Squirrel Bank
DL8
Bank Plantation
Abbey Hill
Jervaulx Park
Lane House
KILGRAM LANE
Wind Hills
MASHAM BANK
Squirrel Bank Wood
8
Lamb Hill Plantation
Low Newstead
High Jervaulx Farm
Brymor Ice Cream Parlour
Mill Hill
Eelmire Plantation
85
Thirsting Castle Lodge
Clay Bank Plantation
Hector's Covert
NEWSTEAD LANE
High Jervaulx
Coultermire Plantation
Eelmire
Hammer Farm
HAMMER ROAD
Blakes Plantation
North Wood
7
Grey Yaud Quarry (dis)
Firth Hill
Grey Yaud Plantation
High Newstead
STARK BANK RD
Quarry Hill
Ellington Firth
Appletree House
Sowden Beck Farm
84
East Belt Plantation
Moor Cote
Hammersdale Farm
Ellingstring
Witton Moor
Milestone Bank
Hill Top Farm
Haregill Lodge
Haregill Bank
6
Tranmire Hill
High Ellington
Ellingstring Plantation
Sail Hill
HAREGILL BANK
Haregill Covert
83
Tranmire
Tranmire Bog
The Warren
Warren House
Froggersgill Wood
CROOK LA
Sutton Whin
Riseber Hill
Agra Moor Top
5
Bales House
Bales House Plantation
President's Plantation
Swinney Beck
Agra Moor
HG4
SWINNEYBECK BANK
COTE LANE
82
West Agra Plantation
Agra Plantation
Bales Hill
CROOK LANE
SUTTON LANE
West Agra
High Cote Farm
Low Healey Cote
4
Body Close Farm
Agra Crags Plantation
Bales Plantation
Howe Hill
Howe Wood
DAWSON'S LA
FEARBY RD
Fearby
Spring Wood
Howe Farm
Yew Tree Farm
PH
MOSSRA LA
81
Gollinglith Foot
Ford
Healey Pasture
Cradle Gill Plantation
Healey
KELL BANK
PH
Spruce Gill
Breary Bank Wood
Firs Farm
Kell Bank CE Prim Sch
Sinney Keld Old Well
3
Spout House
LOW MOOR LANE
Breary Banks
Leighton Bridge
Ford
RIGG BANK
Fearby Low Moor
River Burn
Hall Wood
80
Broadmires
Swinton Park
Towler Hill Farm
Hall Wood
Stonefold
Quarry House
Stonefold Wood
Sole Beck
Leighton
2
Ox Close Plantation
Low Knowle Farm
Knowle Wood
Lobley Plantation
Lobley Hall
High Sourmire Farm
Reservoir House
Burgess Bank Wood
Masham Moor
Sykes Wood
Mount Covert
79
Low Sourmire
Weirs
Druid's Plantation
KNOWLE LA
Hill Top Farm
North Wood
Leighton Reservoir
Sykes Farm
ILTON BANK
Highfield House Farm
1
Clints Moor
Ilton
Pott Hall Farm
Sole Beck Plantation
Manor Farm
Masham Moor
Skew Skell Well
POTT BANK
78
14
15
16
17
18
19
111
86

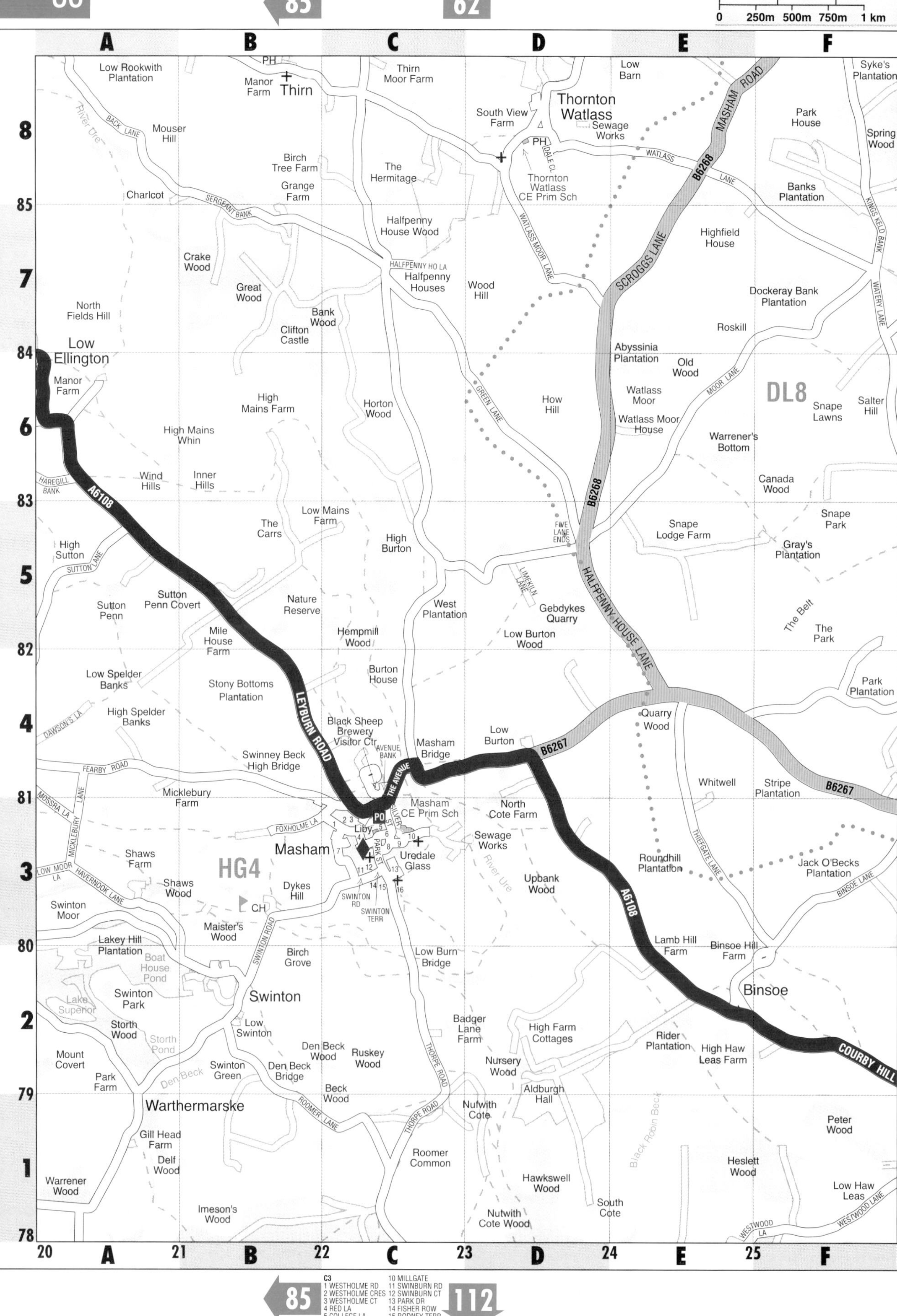

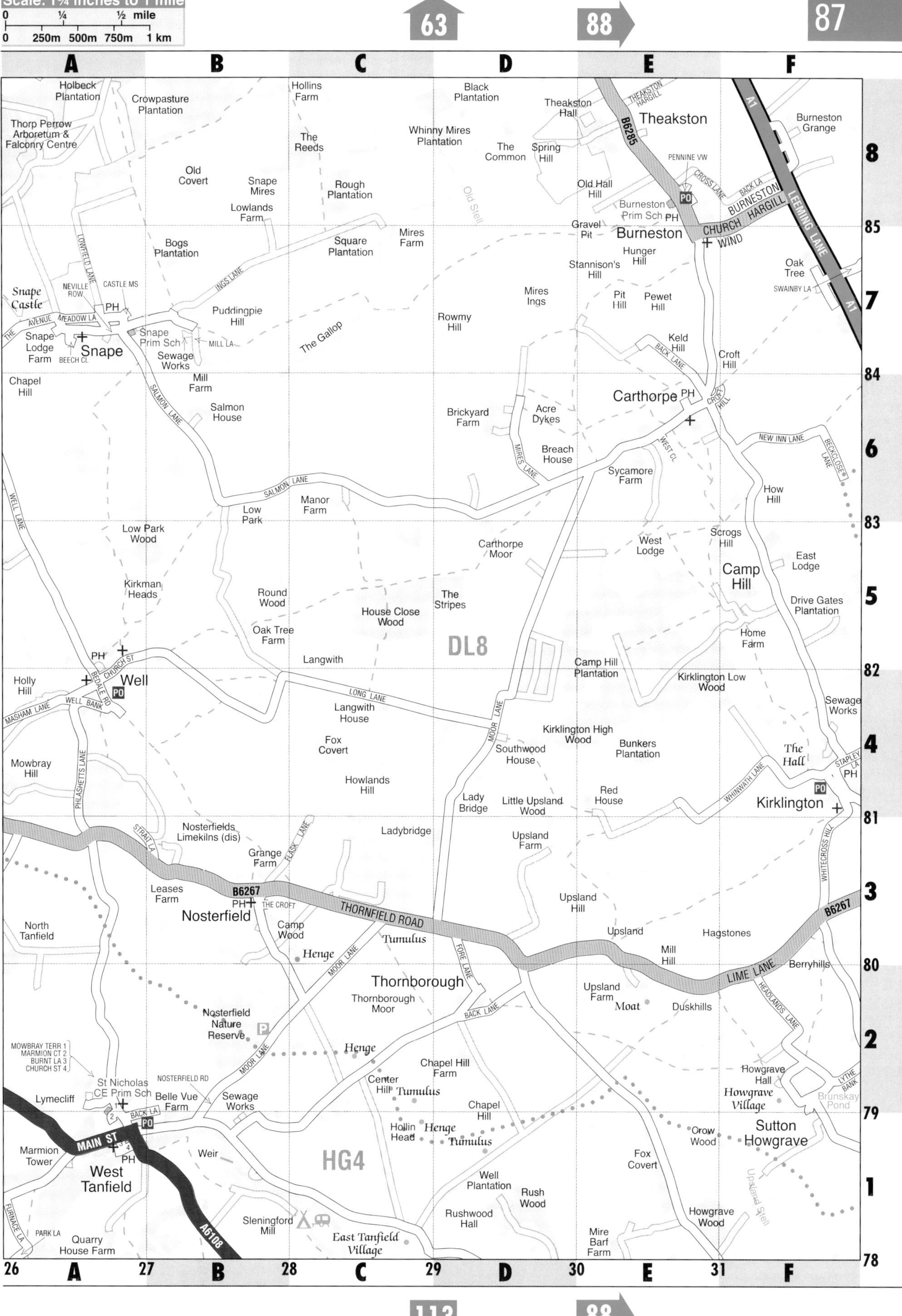

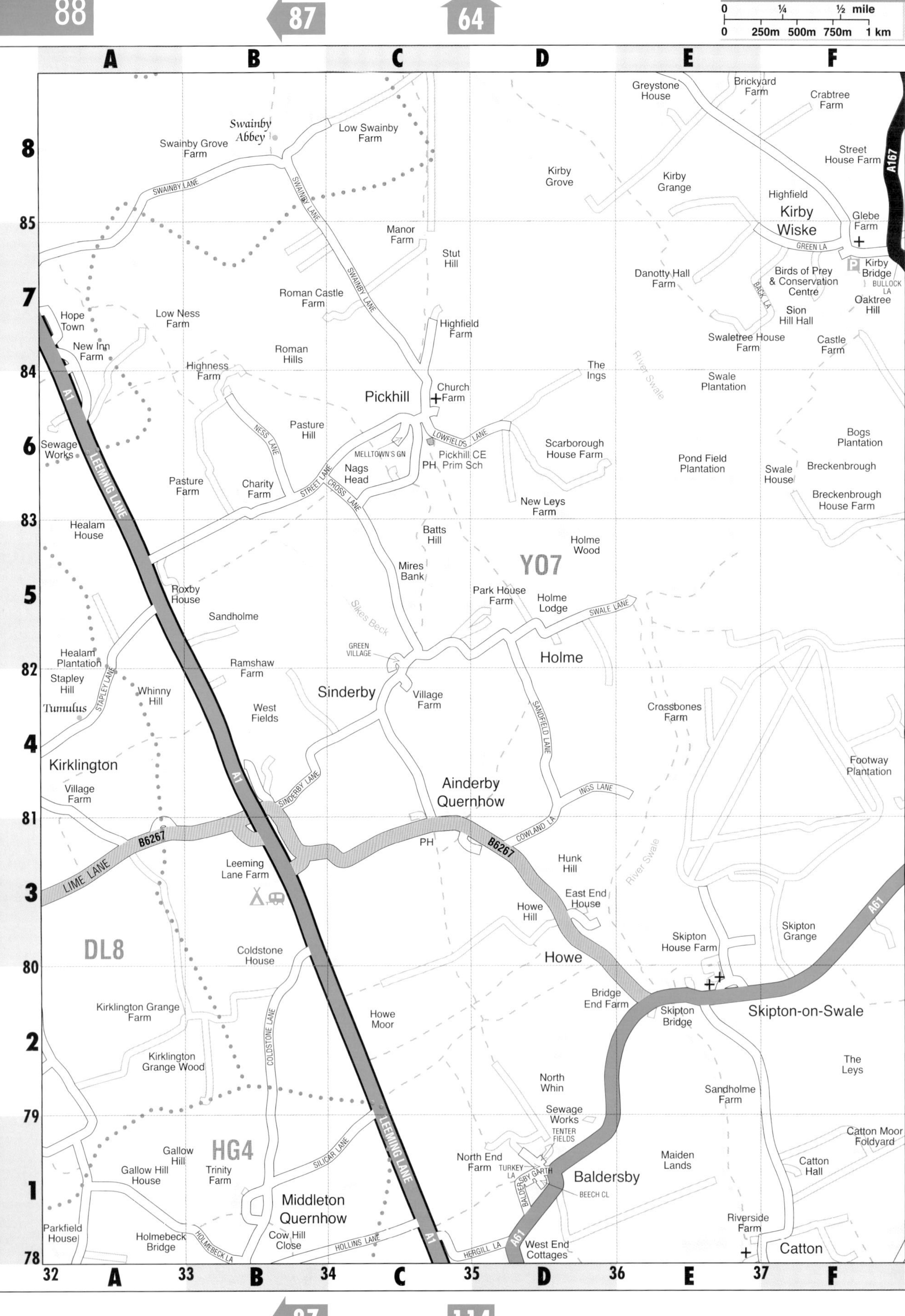

A   B   C   D   E   F

8

Swainby Abbey

Greystone House

Brickyard Farm

Crabtree Farm

Swainby Grove Farm

Low Swainby Farm

Kirby Grove

Kirby Grange

Street House Farm

A167

85

Manor Farm

Highfield

Kirby Wiske

Glebe Farm

GREEN LA

Kirby Bridge

7

SWAINBY LANE

Roman Castle Farm

Stut Hill

Danotty Hall Farm

Birds of Prey & Conservation Centre

BACK LA

P

BULLOCK LA

Oaktree Hill

Hope Town

Low Ness Farm

Highfield Farm

Sion Hill Hall

Castle Farm

New Inn Farm

Highness Farm

Roman Hills

Swaletree House Farm

84

A1

Pickhill

Church Farm

The Ings

River Swale

Swale Plantation

NESS LANE

Pasture Hill

LOWFIELDS LANE

Scarborough House Farm

Pond Field Plantation

Swale House

Bogs Plantation

Breckenbrough

6

Sewage Works

LEEMING LANE

STREET LANE

MELLTOWN'S GN

Nags Head

Pickhill CE Prim Sch

PH

Swale Plantation

Breckenbrough House Farm

Pasture Farm

Charity Farm

CROSS LANE

New Leys Farm

83

Healam House

Batts Hill

Holme Wood

YO7

5

Roxby House

Mires Bank

Park House Farm

Holme Lodge

SWALE LANE

Sandholme

Sikes Beck

Ramshaw Farm

GREEN VILLAGE

Holme

82

STAPLEY LANE

Healam Plantation

Whinny Hill

Sinderby

Village Farm

Crossbones Farm

Stapley Hill

West Fields

Tumulus

SANDFIELD LANE

Footway Plantation

4

Kirklington

SINDERBY LANE

Ainderby Quernhow

INGS LANE

Village Farm

COWLAND LA

81

B6267

B6267

PH

River Swale

LIME LANE

Leeming Lane Farm

Hunk Hill

Skipton House Farm

Skipton Grange

A61

3

East End House

Howe Hill

DL8

Coldstone House

Howe

Skipton-on-Swale

80

COLDSTONE LANE

Bridge End Farm

Skipton Bridge

Kirklington Grange Farm

Howe Moor

North Whin

Sandholme Farm

The Leys

2

Kirklington Grange Wood

Sewage Works

Maiden Lands

Catton Moor Foldyard

TENTER FIELDS

Catton Hall

79

LEEMING LANE

SILICAR LANE

Gallow Hill

North End Farm

TURKEY LA

Baldersby

HG4

Gallow Hill House

Trinity Farm

BEECH CL

BATTERSBY GARTH

Riverside Farm

Catton

1

Parkfield House

Middleton Quernhow

HOLMEBECK LA

Cow Hill Close

HOLLINS LANE

HERGILL LA

A61

West End Cottages

78

Holmebeck Bridge

A1

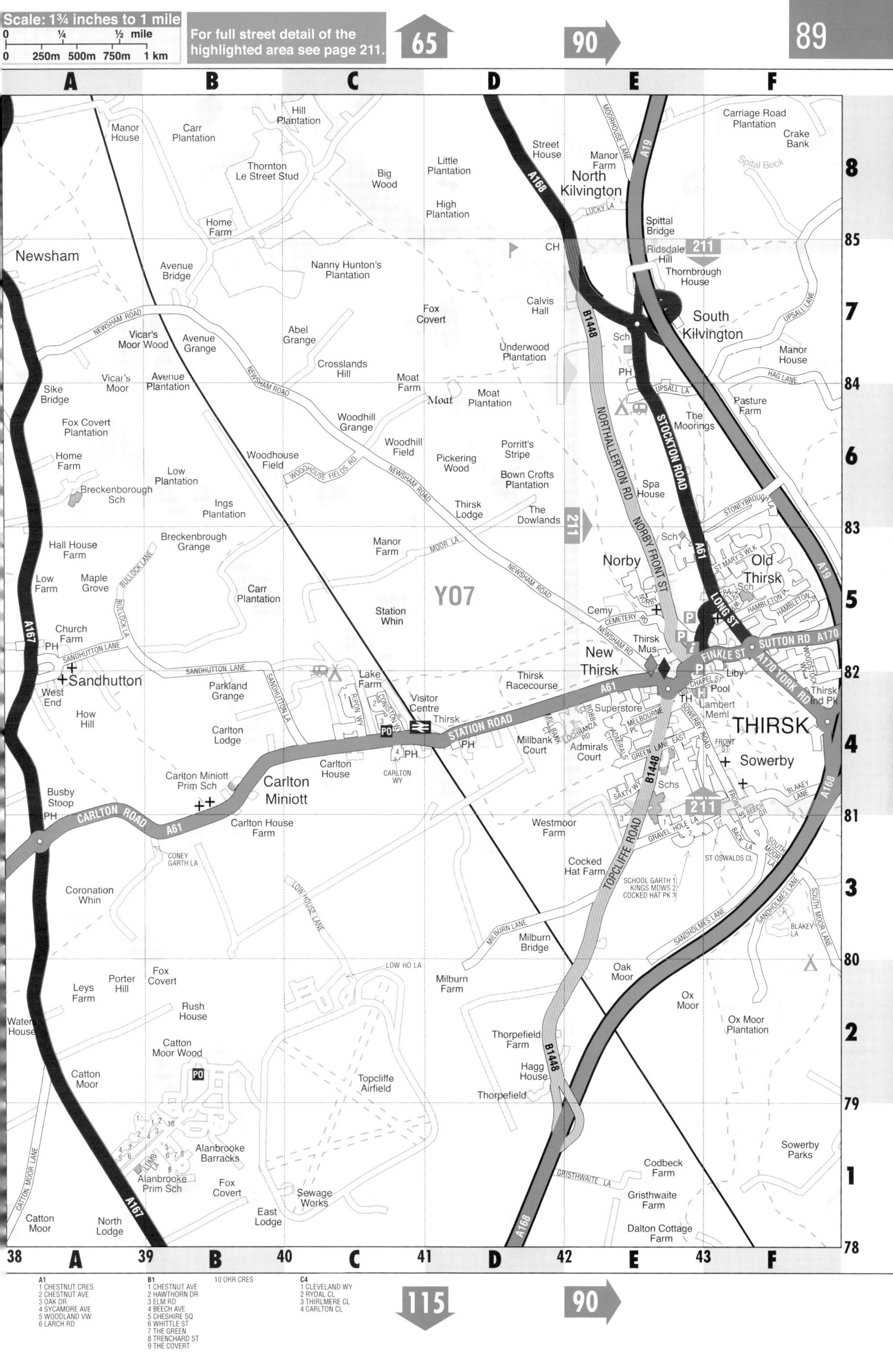

Scale: 1¾ inches to 1 mile
0 ¼ ½ mile
0 250m 500m 750m 1 km
For full street detail of the highlighted area see page 211.
65
90
89
A
B
C
D
E
F
8
85
7
84
6
83
5
82
4
81
3
80
2
79
1
78
38
39
40
41
42
43
Manor House
Carr Plantation
Hill Plantation
Thornton Le Street Stud
Big Wood
Little Plantation
High Plantation
Street House
Manor Farm
North Kilvington
MOORHOUSE LANE
A19
A168
LUCKY LA
Carriage Road Plantation
Crake Bank
Spital Beck
Spittal Bridge
Home Farm
Newsham
Avenue Bridge
Nanny Hunton's Plantation
CH
Ridsdale Hill
211
Thornbrough House
Calvis Hall
South Kilvington
UPSALL LANE
NEWSHAM ROAD
Vicar's Moor Wood
Avenue Grange
Abel Grange
Fox Covert
B1448
Sch
Underwood Plantation
Manor House
Crosslands Hill
PH
Sike Bridge
Vicar's Moor
Avenue Plantation
Moat Farm
Moat
Moat Plantation
UPSALL LA
HAG LANE
Pasture Farm
Fox Covert Plantation
Woodhill Grange
NORTHALLERTON RD
STOCKTON ROAD
The Moorings
Home Farm
Woodhouse Field
Woodhill Field
Pickering Wood
Porritt's Stripe
Low Plantation
WOODHOUSE FIELDS RD
Bown Crofts Plantation
Spa House
Breckenborough Sch
Ings Plantation
Thirsk Lodge
The Dowlands
STONEYBROUGH
Breckenbrough Grange
Sch
Hall House Farm
Manor Farm
MOOR LA
NORBY FRONT ST
A61
ST MARY'S WLK
Old Thirsk
Norby
BULLOCK LANE
Low Farm
Maple Grove
Carr Plantation
Y07
Sch
BULLOCK LA
Station Whin
HAMBLETON PL
NORBY
Cemy
CEMETERY RD
LONG ST
Church Farm
PH
SANDHUTTON LANE
Thirsk Mus
New Thirsk
FINKLE ST
SUTTON RD A170
WOODSTOCK WY
Sandhutton
SANDHUTTON LANE
Lake Farm
Thirsk Racecourse
A61
Liby
West End
Parkland Grange
SANDHUTTON LA
RIPON WY
CONISTON WY
Visitor Centre
Thirsk
CHAPEL ST
Pool
A170 YORK RD
Thirsk Ind Pk
How Hill
PO
STATION ROAD
ROBB CT
TH
Superstore
Lambert Meml
Carlton Lodge
PH
MILLBANK CT
LOCHRANZA RD
MELBOURNE PL
SOWERBY ROAD
THIRSK
Millbank Court
Admirals Court
ADMIRALS CT
GREEN LANE EAST
FRONT ST
PH
Sowerby
CARLTON WY
Carlton Miniott Prim Sch
Carlton House
Carlton Miniott
B1448
Schs
SAXTY WY
BLAKEY LANE
Busby Stoop
PH
CARLTON ROAD
A61
Carlton House Farm
Westmoor Farm
211
BECH GR
GRAVEL HOLE LA
BACK LA
SOUTH MOOR LA
CONEY GARTH LA
ST OSWALDS CL
Cocked Hat Farm
TOPCLIFFE ROAD
SCHOOL GARTH 1
KINGS MDWS 2
COCKED HAT PK 3
Coronation Whin
LOW HOUSE LANE
SANDHOLMES LANE
SANDHOLMES LANE
SOUTH MOOR LANE
BLAKEY LA
Milburn Bridge
MILBURN LANE
A167
LOW HO LA
Oak Moor
Fox Covert
Porter Hill
Leys Farm
Milburn Farm
Ox Moor
Water House
Rush House
Ox Moor Plantation
Thorpefield Farm
Catton Moor Wood
Catton Moor
PO
Topcliffe Airfield
Hagg House
Thorpefield
Alanbrooke Barracks
LUMB LA
Sowerby Parks
Codbeck Farm
Alanbrooke Prim Sch
Fox Covert
GRISTHWAITE LA
CATTON MOOR LANE
Sewage Works
Gristhwaite Farm
Catton Moor
North Lodge
East Lodge
Dalton Cottage Farm
A1
1 CHESTNUT CRES
2 CHESTNUT AVE
3 OAK DR
4 SYCAMORE AVE
5 WOODLAND VW
6 LARCH RD
B1
1 CHESTNUT AVE
2 HAWTHORN DR
3 ELM RD
4 BEECH AVE
5 CHESHIRE SQ
6 WHITTLE ST
7 THE GREEN
8 TRENCHARD ST
9 THE COVERT
10 ORR CRES
C4
1 CLEVELAND WY
2 RYDAL CL
3 THIRLMERE CL
4 CARLTON CL
115
90

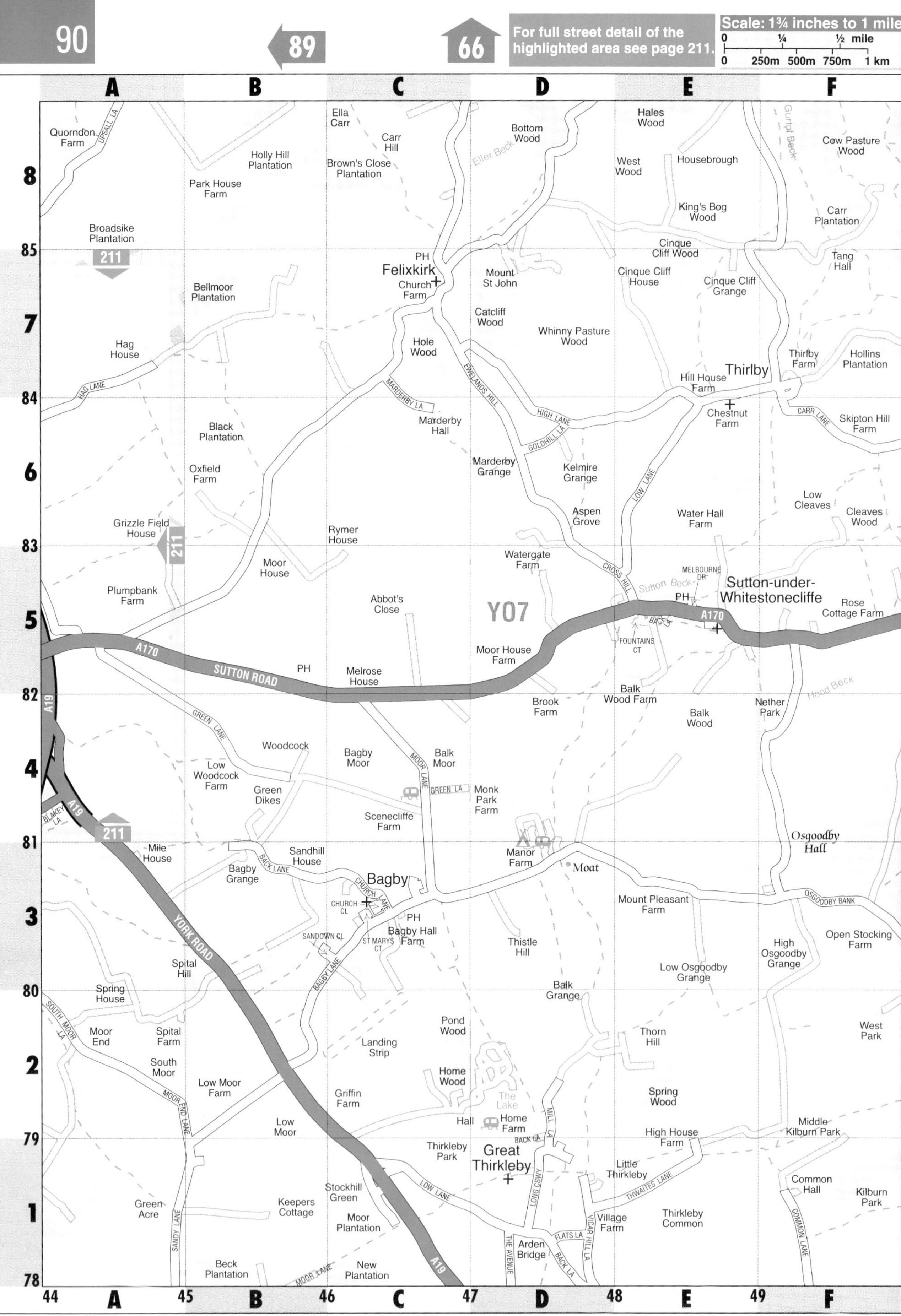

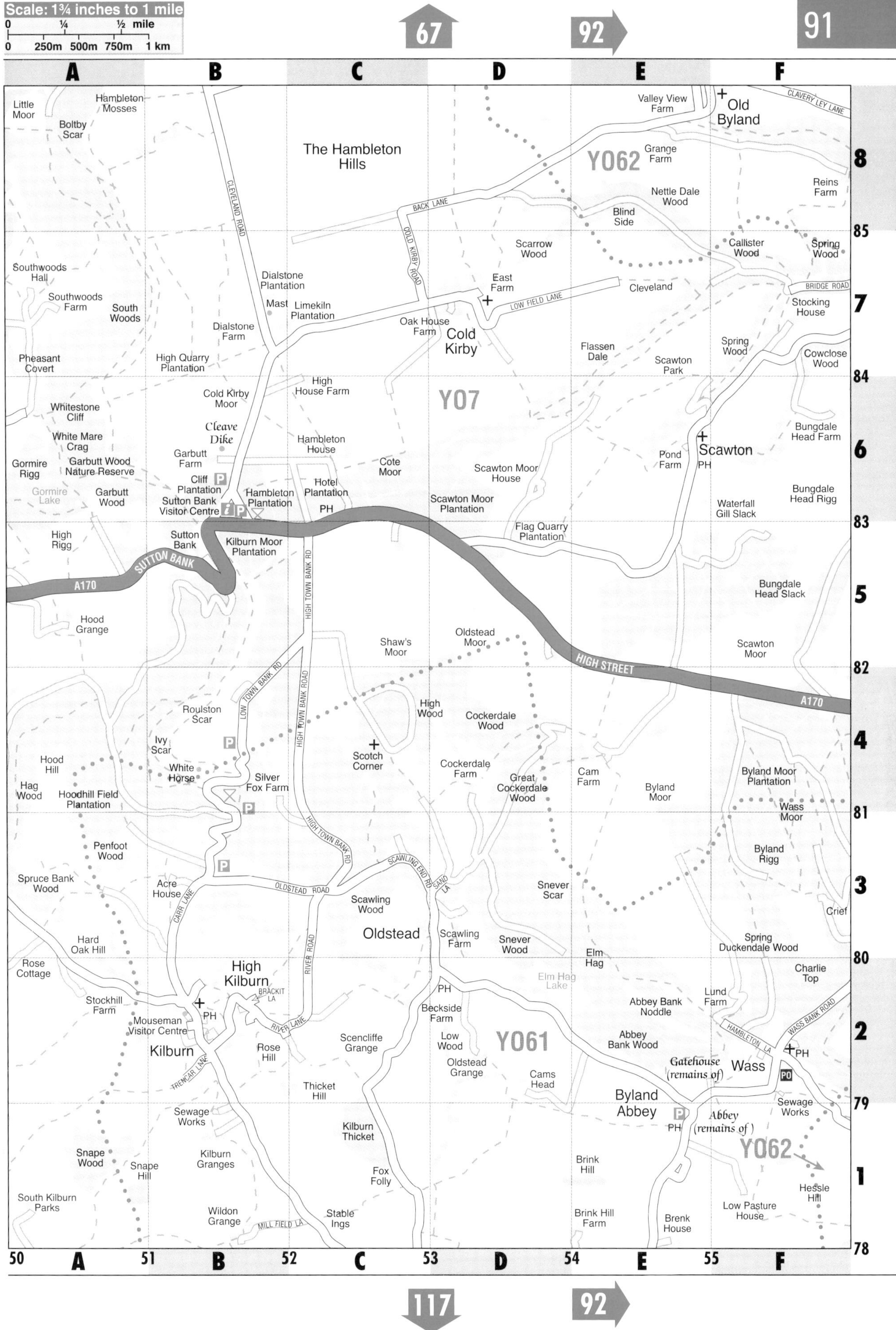
Little Moor
Hambleton Mosses
Boltby Scar
The Hambleton Hills
Valley View Farm
Old Byland
CLAVERY LEY LANE
YO62
Grange Farm
Nettle Dale Wood
Reins Farm
Blind Side
BACK LANE
CLEVELAND ROAD
OLD KIRBY ROAD
Scarrow Wood
Callister Wood
Spring Wood
Southwoods Hall
Southwoods Farm
South Woods
Dialstone Plantation
Mast
Limekiln Plantation
East Farm
LOW FIELD LANE
Cleveland
BRIDGE ROAD
Stocking House
Dialstone Farm
Oak House Farm
Cold Kirby
Flassen Dale
Spring Wood
Cowclose Wood
Pheasant Covert
High Quarry Plantation
Scawton Park
High House Farm
Cold Kirby Moor
YO7
Whitestone Cliff
Cleave Dike
White Mare Crag
Hambleton House
Bungdale Head Farm
Gormire Rigg
Garbutt Farm
Garbutt Wood Nature Reserve
Cote Moor
Scawton Moor House
Pond Farm
Scawton
PH
Cliff Plantation
Gormire Lake
Garbutt Wood
Sutton Bank Visitor Centre
Hambleton Plantation
Hotel Plantation
PH
Scawton Moor Plantation
Waterfall Gill Slack
Bungdale Head Rigg
High Rigg
Sutton Bank
Kilburn Moor Plantation
Flag Quarry Plantation
SUTTON BANK
A170
HIGH TOWN BANK RD
Bungdale Head Slack
Hood Grange
Shaw's Moor
Oldstead Moor
Scawton Moor
HIGH STREET
A170
LOW TOWN BANK RD
Roulston Scar
High Wood
Cockerdale Wood
Ivy Scar
Scotch Corner
Hood Hill
White Horse
Cockerdale Farm
Great Cockerdale Wood
Cam Farm
Byland Moor
Byland Moor Plantation
Hag Wood
Hoodhill Field Plantation
Silver Fox Farm
Wass Moor
Penfoot Wood
HIGH TOWN BANK RD
Byland Rigg
Spruce Bank Wood
Acre House
OLDSTEAD ROAD
SCAWLING END RD
SAND LA
Scawling Wood
Snever Scar
CARR LANE
Crief
Hard Oak Hill
Oldstead
Scawling Farm
Snever Wood
Spring Duckendale Wood
Rose Cottage
RIVER ROAD
Elm Hag
Elm Hag Lake
Charlie Top
High Kilburn
BRACKIT LA
PH
Stockhill Farm
Beckside Farm
Abbey Bank Noddle
Lund Farm
WASS BANK ROAD
HAMBLETON LA
PH
Mouseman Visitor Centre
RIVER LANE
Scencliffe Grange
Low Wood
YO61
Abbey Bank Wood
Kilburn
Rose Hill
Oldstead Grange
Gatehouse (remains of)
Wass
PO
TRENCAR LANE
Thicket Hill
Cams Head
Byland Abbey
Sewage Works
Sewage Works
Abbey (remains of)
PH
Kilburn Thicket
YO62
Snape Wood
Snape Hill
Kilburn Granges
Fox Folly
Brink Hill
Hessle Hill
South Kilburn Parks
Wildon Grange
MILL FIELD LA
Stable Ings
Brink Hill Farm
Brenk House
Low Pasture House
A B C D E F
8 85 7 84 6 83 5 82 4 81 3 80 2 79 1 78
50 51 52 53 54 55

91 68

Scale: 1¾ inches to 1 mile

0   ¼   ½ mile
0   250m 500m 750m 1 km

F6
1 ELMSLAC CL
2 CANONS GARTH LA
3 STONE GARTH
4 HIGH ST
5 CHURCH ST
6 CASTLEGATE
7 BUCKINGHAM SQ
8 BUCKINGHAM SQ
9 BORGATE
10 MARKET PL
11 MARKET PL
12 BRIDGE ST
13 RYEGATE
14 POTTERGATE
15 BELL'S CT
16 EASTGATE
17 THE CRESCENT
18 SOUTH GATE
19 SOUTHLANDS
20 ALLENBY RD
21 CHAPEL CL
22 CROSLAND CL
23 CONOWL CL
24 ACRES CL
25 RICCAL DR
26 STORFY CL
27 BR FARM CL

F7
1 BAXTON'S SPRUNT
2 WARWICK PL
3 ELMSLAC RD
4 RUTLAND PL
5 ASHWOOD CL
6 WITHINGTON RD
7 ELM GN
8 VILLIERS CT
9 ELMSLAC CL

A   B   C   D   E   F

8 Far Hag Wood, Crabtree Hall, Ouldray Wood, Ash Dale Plantation, Lambert Hag Wood, Harriet Air Farm, High Leys Farm, Baxton's Grange, Cliff Stud, Dick Wood, Air Bank Wood, Reins Farm, Rievaulx, High Ash Plantation, Beckdale East Wood

85 Spring Wood, Ashberry Wood, Temple, Rievaulx Abbey, Barton Hag Wood, Helmsley

7 Bridge Road, Cowclose Wood, Ashberry Farm, Abbot Hagg Farm, Abbot Hag Wood, Briery Hill Wood, Stilton House Farm, Helmsley Sports Club, Helmsley Prim Sch, Swanland Road, Hagg Hall, Hags Wood, B1257, Skurvhill Lane, Beckdale Rd, Feversham Rd, Carlton Lane, Ryedale Close, YH

84 Manor House Farm, Quarry Bank Wood, Griff Farm, Monday Howl Plantation, High Street, Bondgate, Library, PO, Station

6 Bungdale Wood, Tongue Rigg, Snip Gill Windypit, Hollins Wood, Griff Village, Whinny Bank Wood, Blackdale Howl Wood, Cleveland Wy, Helmsley Walled Garden, Castle, Paddock Cl, Archaeology Store, Visitor Centre, Duncombe Park National Nature Reserve

83 Spring Wood, Spring Bank Wood, Duncombe Park, Plockwoods Bank Wood, Antofts, Rye Dale

5 Red Deer Park, Scawton Moor, Sword Gill, Castle Gill, Park Plain Wood, Park Hill Wood, Mill Bank Wood, A170, **YO7**, **YO62**, River Rye

82 Sword Rigg Slack, Far Moor Park, Beech Wood, Sproxton Hall Farm

4 High Street, A170, Westwood Rigg Slack, Sproxton Moor, Cote Lane, Waterloo Plantation, Court House Farm, Sproxton, Aspin Farm, Wass Moor, B1257

81 Waterloo Farm, Tom Smith's Cross, Towdale Rigg, Mason Gill Wood, Hag Lane, Holly Bower, Low Street

3 Wass Moor, Shallowdale Gill Slack, Double Dikes, Painter Rigg, Pry Rigg Plantation, Pry Rigg Farm, Oxclose Wood, Golden Square Wood, Grange Wood, **YO61**, College Moor

80 Studford Farm, High Street, Dropping Gill Plantation, Salmon's Wood, Black Firs Plantation, Golden Square Farm

2 High Woods Farm, Low Wood, Priest Barn Farm, West Wood Lane, Studford Ring, Tumulus, Tumuli, Tumulus, Grange Moor Plantation, Stockings Lane, Noddle Hill, Glebe Farm, Beacon House

79 Burtis Wood, Westwood Whins, Trudlock Hill, South View Farm, Manor Farm, The Orchard, Beacon Bank, Ampleforth College, Bath Wood, Oswaldkirk Hag, Carr House, Carr Lane, Back Lane, East Lane, Ault Lane

1 Jerry Carr Bank, Carr Lodge, PH, St. Hildas CE Prim Sch, Station Road, Mill Lane, St Benedicts RC Prim Sch, Lion Wood, Wass Grange, Mill Farm, **Ampleforth**, Lowlands Farm

78

56   A   57   B   58   C   59   D   60   E   61   F

91 118

C1
1 BIRDFORTH WY
2 FAIRFAX CL
3 VALLEY VW
4 OLD STATION RD
5 THE ORCHARD
6 ST HILDA'S WK

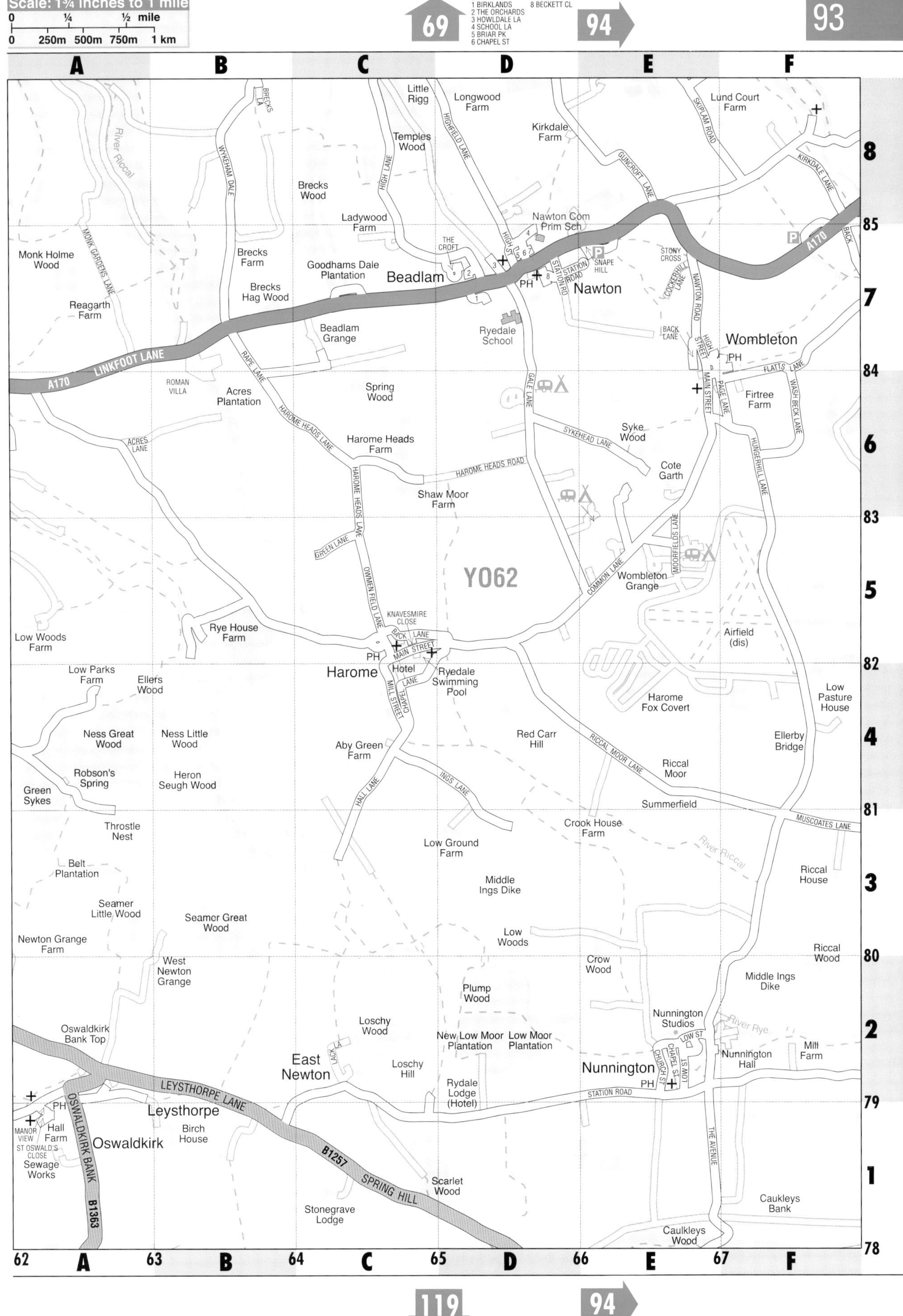

Scale: 1¾ inches to 1 mile

0   ¼   ½   mile

0   250m 500m 750m 1 km

69   94   93

D7
1 BIRKLANDS
2 THE ORCHARDS
3 HOWLDALE LA
4 SCHOOL LA
5 BRIAR PK
6 CHAPEL ST
7 BELLABY PK
8 BECKETT CL

A   B   C   D   E   F

8
85
7
84
6
83
5
82
4
81
3
80
2
79
1
78

62   A   63   B   64   C   65   D   66   E   67   F   78

River Riccal
MONK GARDENS LANE
Monk Holme Wood
Reagarth Farm
Low Woods Farm
Low Parks Farm
Ness Great Wood
Robson's Spring
Green Sykes
Throstle Nest
Belt Plantation
Seamer Little Wood
Newton Grange Farm
Oswaldkirk Bank Top
Leysthorpe
Oswaldkirk
Hall Farm
Manor View
ST OSWALD'S CLOSE
Sewage Works
B1363
PH

WYKEHAM DALE
BRECKS LA
Brecks Wood
Brecks Farm
Brecks Hag Wood
Ladywood Farm
Goodhams Dale Plantation
Beadlam Grange
ROMAN VILLA
Acres Plantation
ACRES LANE
RAPE LANE
LINKFOOT LANE
A170
Ellers Wood
Ness Little Wood
Heron Seugh Wood
Seamor Great Wood
West Newton Grange
LEYSTHORPE LANE
Birch House
B1267
SPRING HILL
Stonegrave Lodge

HIGH LANE
Little Rigg
Temples Wood
HIGHFIELD LANE
Longwood Farm
Kirkdale Farm
THE CROFT
Beadlam
Spring Wood
HAROME HEADS LANE
Harome Heads Farm
HAROME HEADS ROAD
Shaw Moor Farm
GREEN LANE
OMMENFIELD LANE
Rye House Farm
KNAVESMIRE CLOSE
BECK LANE
MAIN STREET
Harome
Hotel
MILL STREET
CHAPEL LANE
Aby Green Farm
HALL LANE
INGS LANE
LACY LA
East Newton
Loschy Wood
Loschy Hill
Rydale Lodge (Hotel)
Scarlet Wood

Nawton Com Prim Sch
HIGH ST
PH
Nawton
STATION ROAD
GALE LANE
Ryedale School
SYKEHEAD LANE
Syke Wood
YO62
Ryedale Swimming Pool
Red Carr Hill
Low Ground Farm
Middle Ings Dike
Low Woods
Plump Wood
New Low Moor Plantation
Low Moor Plantation
Crow Wood
Crook House Farm
STATION ROAD

SHIPLAM ROAD
Lund Court Farm
GUNCROFT LANE
STONY CROSS
Snape Hill
COCKERHILL LANE
NAWTON ROAD
BACK LANE
HIGH STREET
MAIN STREET
PAGE LANE
FLATTS LANE
WASH BECK LANE
HUNGERHILL LANE
KIRKDALE LANE
BACK
A170
P
Wombleton
PH
Firtree Farm
Cote Garth
WOODFIELD LANE
COMMON LANE
Wombleton Grange
Airfield (dis)
Harome Fox Covert
RICCAL MOOR LANE
Riccal Moor
Summerfield
MUSCOATES LANE
River Riccal
Low Pasture House
Ellerby Bridge
Riccal House
Riccal Wood
Middle Ings Dike
River Rye
Nunnington Studios
Nunnington Hall
Mill Farm
LOW ST
CHAPEL ST
CHURCH ST
Nunnington
PH
THE AVENUE
Caukleys Bank
Caukleys Wood

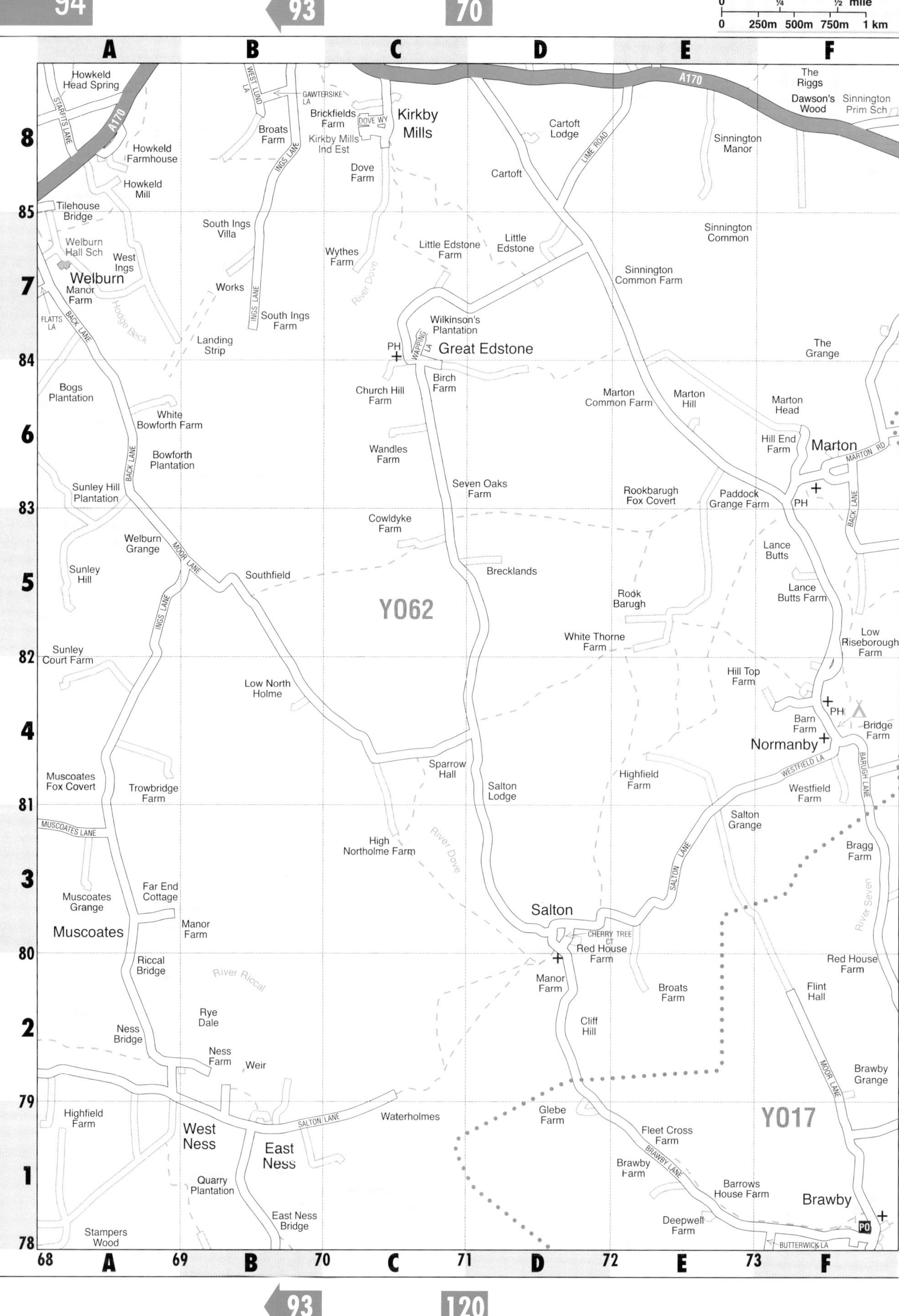

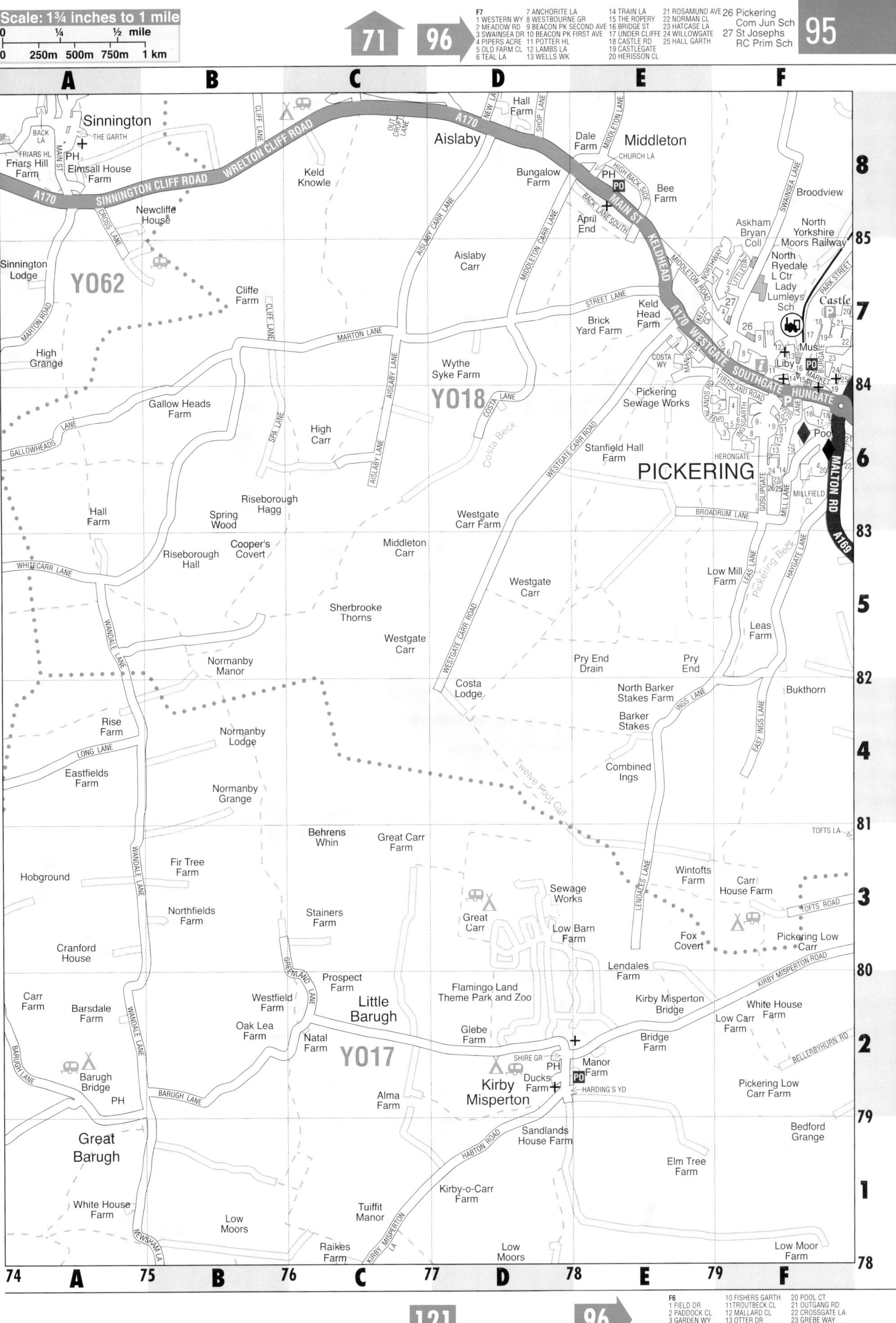

95
72

Scale: 1¾ inches to 1 mile

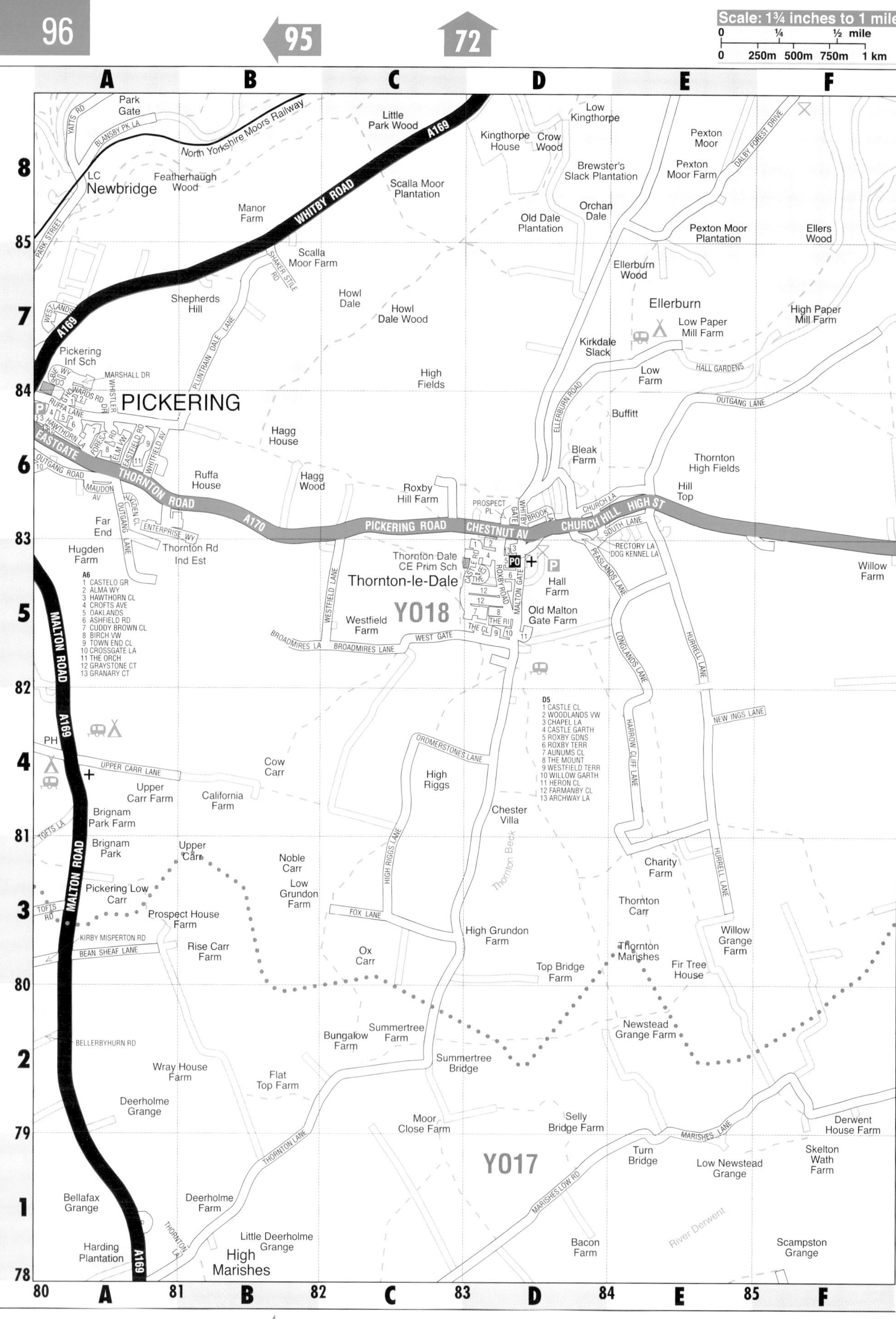
0 ¼ ½ mile
0 250m 500m 750m 1 km
A B C D E F
8
85
7
84
6
83
5
82
4
81
3
80
2
79
1
78
80 A 81 B 82 C 83 D 84 E 85 F
Park Gate
YATTS RD
BLANSBY PK LA
North Yorkshire Moors Railway
Little Park Wood
A169
WHITBY ROAD
Low Kingthorpe
Kingthorpe House
Crow Wood
Pexton Moor
DALBY FOREST DRIVE
LC
Newbridge
Featherhaugh Wood
Brewster's Slack Plantation
Pexton Moor Farm
Scalla Moor Plantation
Manor Farm
Orchan Dale
Old Dale Plantation
Pexton Moor Plantation
Ellers Wood
PARK STREET
Scalla Moor Farm
SHAKER STILE RD
Ellerburn Wood
Howl Dale
Howl Dale Wood
Shepherds Hill
Ellerburn
Low Paper Mill Farm
High Paper Mill Farm
WESTLANDS
PLUNTRAIN DALE LANE
Kirkdale Slack
Pickering Inf Sch
MARSHALL DR
HALL GARDENS
Low Farm
High Fields
PICKERING
WHISTLER DR
RUFFA LANE
EDWARDS RD
OUTGANG LANE
ELLERBURN ROAD
Buffitt
HAWTHORN LA
FOREST RD
ELM VW
EASTFIELD RD
WHITFIELD AV
Hagg House
Bleak Farm
Thornton High Fields
EASTGATE
OUTGANG ROAD
THORNTON ROAD
Ruffa House
Hagg Wood
Roxby Hill Farm
Hill Top
MAUDON AV
HUGDEN CL
PROSPECT PL
WHITBY GATE
BROOK LA
CHURCH LA
CHURCH HILL
HIGH ST
A170
PICKERING ROAD
CHESTNUT AV
Far End
ENTERPRISE WY
SOUTH LANE
Hugden Farm
Thornton Rd Ind Est
RECTORY LA
DOG KENNEL LA
Thornton Dale CE Prim Sch
PO
CASTLE RD
ROXBY ROAD
MALTON GATE
Hall Farm
Willow Farm
A6
1 CASTELO GR
2 ALMA WY
3 HAWTHORN CL
4 CROFTS AVE
5 OAKLANDS
6 ASHFIELD RD
7 CUDDY BROWN CL
8 BIRCH VW
9 TOWN END CL
10 CROSSGATE LA
11 THE ORCH
12 GRAYSTONE CT
13 GRANARY CT
WESTFIELD LANE
Thornton-le-Dale
YO18
PEASLANDS LANE
Westfield Farm
THE RI
Old Malton Gate Farm
THE CL
BROADMIRES LA
BROADMIRES LANE
WEST GATE
LONGLANDS LANE
HURRELL LANE
MALTON ROAD
D5
1 CASTLE CL
2 WOODLANDS VW
3 CHAPEL LA
4 CASTLE GARTH
5 ROXBY GDNS
6 ROXBY TERR
7 AUNUMS CL
8 THE MOUNT
9 WESTFIELD TERR
10 WILLOW GARTH
11 HERON CL
12 FARMANBY CL
13 ARCHWAY LA
NEW INGS LANE
PH
ORDMERSTONES LANE
HARROW CLIFF LANE
UPPER CARR LANE
Cow Carr
High Riggs
Upper Carr Farm
California Farm
Brignam Park Farm
Chester Villa
TOFTS LA
Brignam Park
Upper Carr
Noble Carr
Thornton Beck
Charity Farm
HIGH RIGGS LANE
Low Grundon Farm
Pickering Low Carr
Thornton Carr
TOFTS RD
Prospect House Farm
FOX LANE
High Grundon Farm
Willow Grange Farm
KIRBY MISPERTON RD
Thornton Marishes
BEAN SHEAF LANE
Rise Carr Farm
Ox Carr
Top Bridge Farm
Fir Tree House
Newstead Grange Farm
Summertree Farm
Bungalow Farm
BELLERBYHURN RD
Summertree Bridge
Wray House Farm
Flat Top Farm
Deerholme Grange
Moor Close Farm
Selly Bridge Farm
Derwent House Farm
MARISHES LANE
THORNTON LANE
Turn Bridge
YO17
Low Newstead Grange
Skelton Wath Farm
MARISHES LOW RD
Bellafax Grange
Deerholme Farm
River Derwent
THORNTON LA
Little Deerholme Grange
Bacon Farm
Scampston Grange
Harding Plantation
High Marishes

95
122

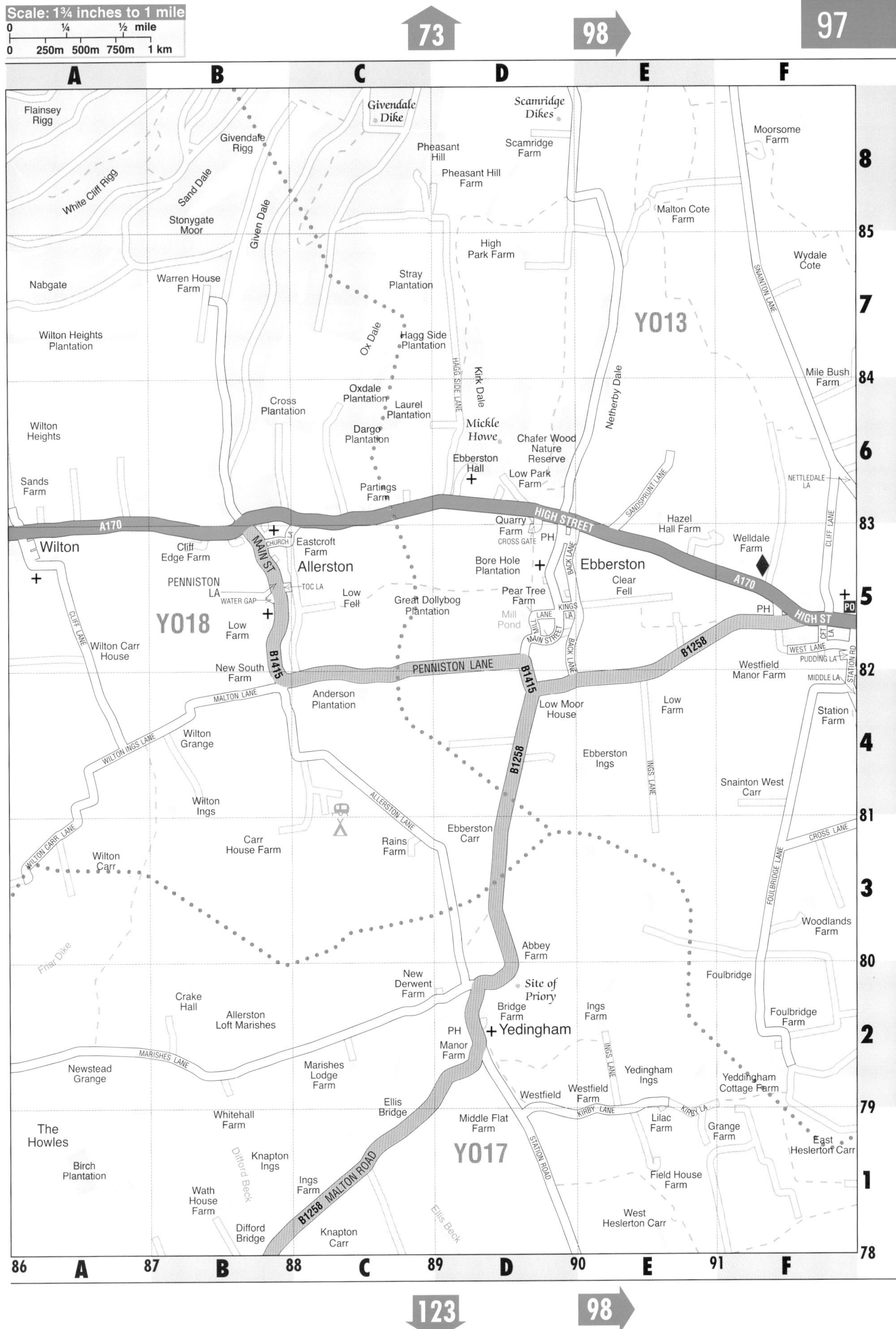
Scale: 1¾ inches to 1 mile
73
98
Flainsey Rigg
Givendale Rigg
Givendale Dike
Scamridge Dikes
Pheasant Hill
Scamridge Farm
Moorsome Farm
Pheasant Hill Farm
White Cliff Rigg
Sand Dale
Stonygate Moor
Given Dale
Malton Cote Farm
High Park Farm
Wydale Cote
Nabgate
Warren House Farm
Stray Plantation
Sainton Lane
Y013
Wilton Heights Plantation
Ox Dale
Hagg Side Plantation
Mile Bush Farm
Hagg Side Lane
Kirk Dale
Netherby Dale
Cross Plantation
Oxdale Plantation
Laurel Plantation
Wilton Heights
Dargo Plantation
Mickle Howe
Chafer Wood Nature Reserve
Sands Farm
Ebberston Hall
Low Park Farm
Nettledale La
Partings Farm
Sandsprunt Lane
A170
High Street
Quarry Farm
Hazel Hall Farm
Cliff Lane
Wilton
Cliff Edge Farm
Church
Eastcroft Farm
Cross Gate
PH
Welldale Farm
Main St
Allerston
Bore Hole Plantation
Back Lane
Ebberston
Penniston La
Toc La
Clear Fell
Water Gap
Low Fell
Great Dollybog Plantation
Pear Tree Farm
PO
Y018
Low Farm
Mill Pond
Lane
Kings La
PH
High St
Wilton Carr House
Main Street
Cft La
West Lane
B1415
Penniston Lane
B1258
Pudding La
New South Farm
Westfield Manor Farm
Middle La
Station Rd
Malton Lane
Anderson Plantation
Low Moor House
Low Farm
Station Farm
Wilton Grange
Wilton Ings Lane
Ebberston Ings
Ings Lane
Snainton West Carr
Wilton Ings
Allerston Lane
Ebberston Carr
Cross Lane
Wilton Carr Lane
Carr House Farm
Rains Farm
Wilton Carr
Foulbridge Lane
Woodlands Farm
Friar Dike
Abbey Farm
Foulbridge
New Derwent Farm
Site of Priory
Crake Hall
Allerston Loft Marishes
Bridge Farm
Ings Farm
Foulbridge Farm
PH
Yedingham
Manor Farm
Newstead Grange
Marishes Lane
Marishes Lodge Farm
Ings Lane
Yedingham Ings
Yeddingham Cottage Farm
Ellis Bridge
Westfield
Westfield Farm
Kirby Lane
Kirby La
Whitehall Farm
Middle Flat Farm
Lilac Farm
Grange Farm
The Howles
Station Road
East Heslerton Carr
Y017
Birch Plantation
Difford Beck
Knapton Ings
Ings Farm
Field House Farm
Wath House Farm
B1258 Malton Road
Ellis Beck
West Heslerton Carr
Difford Bridge
Knapton Carr
A B C D E F
1 2 3 4 5 6 7 8
78 79 80 81 82 83 84 85
86 87 88 89 90 91
123
98

97
74

Scale: 1¾ inches to 1 mile

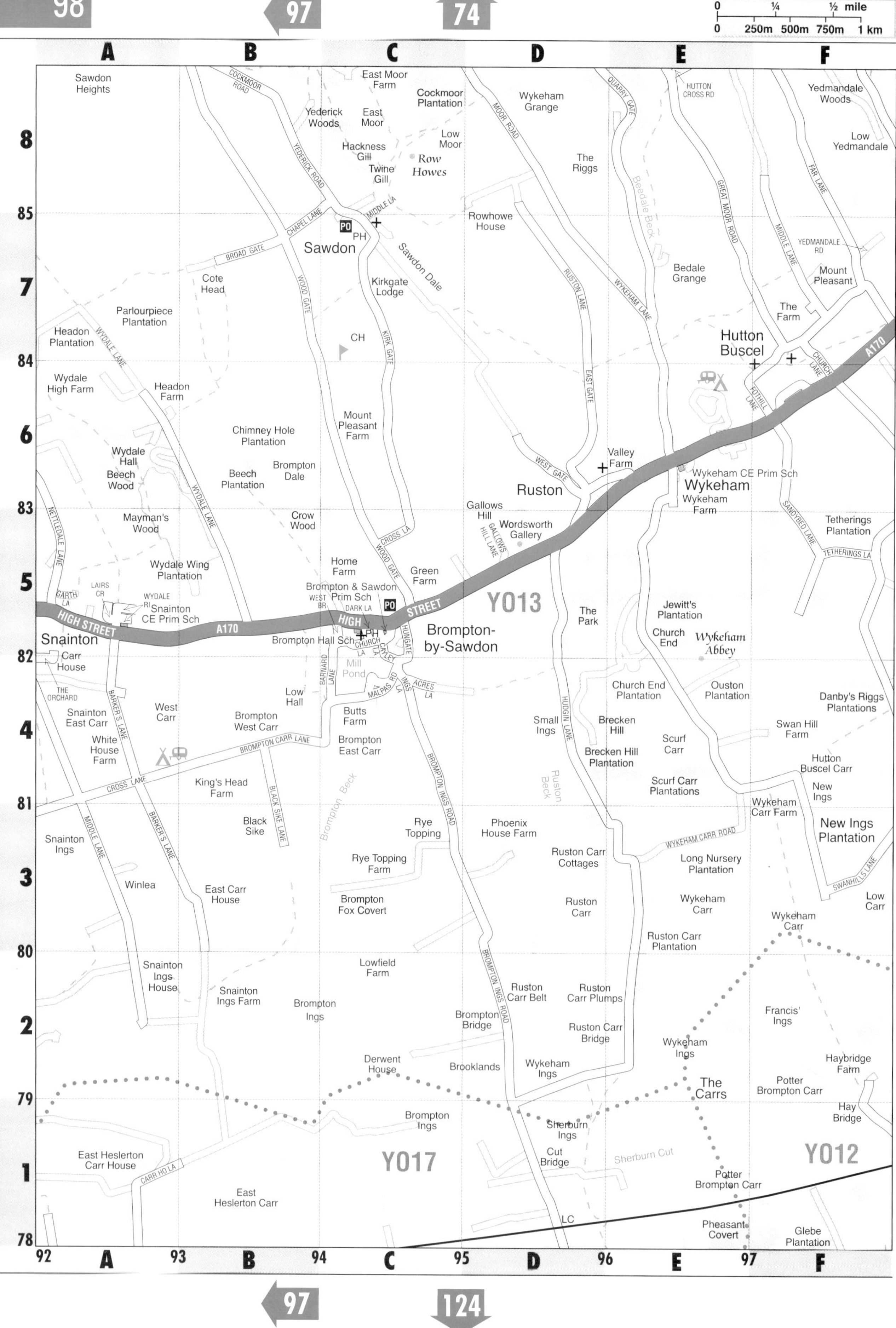
Sawdon Heights
East Moor Farm
Cockmoor Plantation
Yederick Woods
East Moor
Low Moor
Hackness Gill
Row Howes
Twine Gill
Wykeham Grange
The Riggs
Yedmandale Woods
Low Yedmandale
Sawdon
Sawdon Dale
Rowhowe House
Kirkgate Lodge
Cote Head
Parlourpiece Plantation
Headon Plantation
Wydale High Farm
Headon Farm
Bedale Grange
Mount Pleasant
The Farm
Hutton Buscel
Mount Pleasant Farm
Chimney Hole Plantation
Wydale Hall
Beech Wood
Beech Plantation
Brompton Dale
Valley Farm
Ruston
Wykeham CE Prim Sch
Wykeham
Wykeham Farm
Mayman's Wood
Crow Wood
Gallows Hill
Wordsworth Gallery
Tetherings Plantation
Wydale Wing Plantation
Home Farm
Green Farm
Brompton & Sawdon Prim Sch
Snainton CE Prim Sch
YO13
The Park
Jewitt's Plantation
Snainton
Carr House
Brompton Hall Sch
Brompton-by-Sawdon
Church End
Wykeham Abbey
Mill Pond
Low Hall
Church End Plantation
Ouston Plantation
Danby's Riggs Plantations
West Carr
Snainton East Carr
Brompton West Carr
Butts Farm
Small Ings
Brecken Hill
Scurf Carr
Swan Hill Farm
White House Farm
Brompton East Carr
Brecken Hill Plantation
Hutton Buscel Carr
King's Head Farm
Scurf Carr Plantations
New Ings
Black Sike
Rye Topping
Phoenix House Farm
Wykeham Carr Farm
New Ings Plantation
Snainton Ings
Rye Topping Farm
Ruston Carr Cottages
Long Nursery Plantation
Winlea
East Carr House
Brompton Fox Covert
Ruston Carr
Wykeham Carr
Low Carr
Ruston Carr Plantation
Snainton Ings House
Lowfield Farm
Snainton Ings Farm
Brompton Ings
Ruston Carr Belt
Ruston Carr Plumps
Francis' Ings
Brompton Bridge
Ruston Carr Bridge
Wykeham Ings
Derwent House
Brooklands
Haybridge Farm
The Carrs
Potter Brompton Carr
Hay Bridge
Sherburn Ings
East Heslerton Carr House
YO17
Cut Bridge
Sherburn Cut
YO12
Potter Brompton Carr
East Heslerton Carr
LC
Pheasant Covert
Glebe Plantation
COCKMOOR ROAD
YEDERICK ROAD
MOOR ROAD
QUARRY GATE
HUTTON CROSS RD
MIDDLE LA
CHAPEL LANE
BROAD GATE
WOOD GATE
KIRK GATE
RUSTON LANE
WYKEHAM LANE
GREAT MOOR ROAD
FAR LANE
MIDDLE LANE
YEDMANDALE RD
CHURCH LANE
FOTHILL LANE
A170
WYDALE LANE
EAST GATE
WEST GATE
NETTLEDALE LANE
CROSS LA
GALLOWS HILL LANE
SANDYBED LANE
TETHERINGS LA
GARTH LA
LAIRS CR
WYDALE RI
HIGH STREET
DARK LA
WEST BR
HUNGATE
CHURCH LA
CAYLEY LA
BARNARD LANE
MALPAS RD
INGS LA
ACRES LA
HUDGIN LANE
BARKER'S LANE
BROMPTON CARR LANE
CROSS LANE
BLACK SIKE LANE
BROMPTON INGS ROAD
WYKEHAM CARR ROAD
SWANHILLS LANE
Brompton Beck
Ruston Beck
Beedale Beck
CARR HO LA
THE ORCHARD
PO
PH
CH
A B C D E F
8 85 7 84 6 83 5 82 4 81 3 80 2 79 1 78
92 93 94 95 96 97

97
124

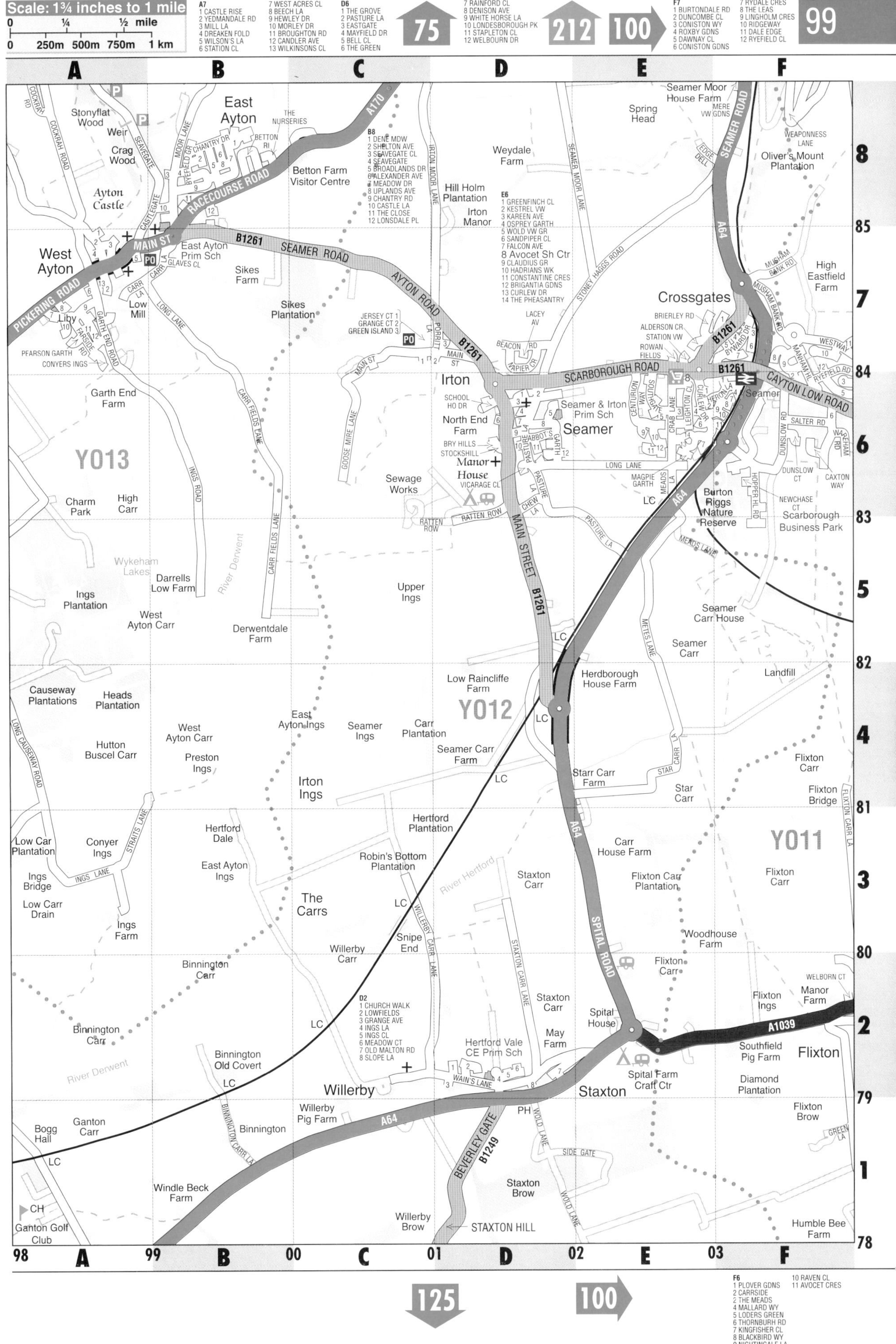

Scale: 1¾ inches to 1 mile
0 ¼ ½ mile
0 250m 500m 750m 1 km
A7
1 CASTLE RISE
2 YEDMANDALE RD
3 MILL LA
4 DREAKEN FOLD
5 WILSON'S LA
6 STATION CL
7 WEST ACRES CL
8 BEECH LA
9 HEWLEY DR
10 MORLEY DR
11 BROUGHTON RD
12 CANDLER AVE
13 WILKINSONS CL
D6
1 THE GROVE
2 PASTURE LA
3 EASTGATE
4 MAYFIELD DR
5 BELL CL
6 THE GREEN
75
7 RAINFORD CL
8 DENISON AVE
9 WHITE HORSE LA
10 LONDESBOROUGH PK
11 STAPLETON CL
12 WELBOURN DR
212
100
F7
1 BURTONDALE RD
2 DUNCOMBE CL
3 CONISTON WY
4 ROXBY GDNS
5 DAWNAY CL
6 CONISTON GDNS
7 RYDALE CRES
8 THE LEAS
9 LINGHOLM CRES
10 RIDGEWAY
11 DALE EDGE
12 RYEFIELD CL
A B C D E F
Stonyflat Wood
Weir
Crag Wood
Ayton Castle
West Ayton
East Ayton
THE NURSERIES
BETTON RI
Betton Farm Visitor Centre
B8
1 DENE MDW
2 SHELTON AVE
3 SEAVEGATE CL
4 SEAVEGATE
5 BROADLANDS DR
6 ALEXANDER AVE
7 MEADOW DR
8 UPLANDS AVE
9 CHANTRY RD
10 CASTLE LA
11 THE CLOSE
12 LONSDALE PL
A170
RACECOURSE ROAD
MAIN ST
B1261
SEAMER ROAD
AYTON ROAD
East Ayton Prim Sch
GLAVES CL
Sikes Farm
Sikes Plantation
Low Mill
PICKERING ROAD
Liby
PEARSON GARTH
CONYERS INGS
GARTH END ROAD
LONG LANE
Hill Holm Plantation
Irton Manor
Weydale Farm
E6
1 GREENFINCH CL
2 KESTREL VW
3 KAREEN AVE
4 OSPREY GARTH
5 WOLD VW GR
6 SANDPIPER CL
7 FALCON AVE
8 Avocet Sh Ctr
9 CLAUDIUS GR
10 HADRIANS WK
11 CONSTANTINE CRES
12 BRIGANTIA GDNS
13 CURLEW DR
14 THE PHEASANTRY
SEAMER MOOR LANE
STONEY HAGGS ROAD
Spring Head
Seamer Moor House Farm
MERE VW GDNS
EDGE DELL
SEAMER ROAD
A64
WEAPONNESS LANE
Oliver's Mount Plantation
High Eastfield Farm
MUSHAM BANK RD
Crossgates
BRIERLEY RD
ALDERSON CR
STATION VW
ROWAN FIELDS
LACEY AV
BEACON RD
NAPIER CR
JERSEY CT 1
GRANGE CT 2
GREEN ISLAND 3
PO
MAIN ST
Irton
SCHOOL HO DR
North End Farm
BRY HILLS
STOCKSHILL
Manor House
VICARAGE CL
SCARBOROUGH ROAD
Seamer & Irton Prim Sch
Seamer
LONG LANE
MAGPIE GARTH
LC
CAYTON LOW ROAD
WESTWAY
RYEFIELD RD
SALTER RD
DUNSLOW CT
CAXTON WAY
Burton Riggs Nature Reserve
NEWCHASE CT
HOPPER HL RD
Scarborough Business Park
Garth End Farm
YO13
Charm Park
High Carr
GOOSE MIRE LANE
Sewage Works
RATTEN ROW
MAIN STREET
PASTURE LA
MEADS LANE
Wykeham Lakes
Darrells Low Farm
Ings Plantation
West Ayton Carr
Derwentdale Farm
River Derwent
CARR FIELDS LANE
INGS ROAD
Upper Ings
Seamer Carr House
Seamer Carr
METES LANE
Landfill
Causeway Plantations
Heads Plantation
Low Raincliffe Farm
YO12
Herdborough House Farm
West Ayton Carr
East Ayton Ings
Seamer Ings
Carr Plantation
Seamer Carr Farm
Hutton Buscel Carr
Preston Ings
Irton Ings
Starr Carr Farm
STAR CARR LA
Star Carr
Flixton Carr
Flixton Bridge
LONG CAUSEWAY ROAD
STRAITS LANE
Hertford Dale
Hertford Plantation
YO11
Low Car Plantation
Conyer Ings
East Ayton Ings
Robin's Bottom Plantation
Carr House Farm
Flixton Carr Plantation
Flixton Carr
FLIXTON CARR LA
Ings Bridge
INGS LANE
Low Carr Drain
The Carrs
Staxton Carr
River Hertford
Ings Farm
Snipe End
WILLERBY CARR LANE
Woodhouse Farm
Binnington Carr
Willerby Carr
STAXTON CARR LANE
SPITAL ROAD
Flixton Carr
Flixton Ings
Manor Farm
WELBORN CT
D2
1 CHURCH WALK
2 LOWFIELDS
3 GRANGE AVE
4 INGS LA
5 INGS CL
6 MEADOW CT
7 OLD MALTON RD
8 SLOPE LA
Staxton Carr
Spital House
May Farm
Binnington Carr
A1039
Southfield Pig Farm
Flixton
Hertford Vale CE Prim Sch
Binnington Old Covert
WAIN'S LANE
Willerby
Staxton
Spital Farm Craft Ctr
Diamond Plantation
Willerby Pig Farm
Bogg Hall
Ganton Carr
Binnington
BINNINGTON CARR LA
A64
BEVERLEY GATE
B1249
PH
WOLD LANE
SIDE GATE
Flixton Brow
GREEN LA
Windle Beck Farm
Staxton Brow
CH
Ganton Golf Club
Willerby Brow
STAXTON HILL
Humble Bee Farm
8 85 7 84 6 83 5 82 4 81 3 80 2 79 1 78
98 A 99 B 00 C 01 D 02 E 03 F
125
100
F6
1 PLOVER GDNS
2 CARRSIDE
3 THE MEADS
4 MALLARD WY
5 LODERS GREEN
6 THORNBURH RD
7 KINGFISHER CL
8 BLACKBIRD WY
9 NIGHTINGALE LA
10 RAVEN CL
11 AVOCET CRES

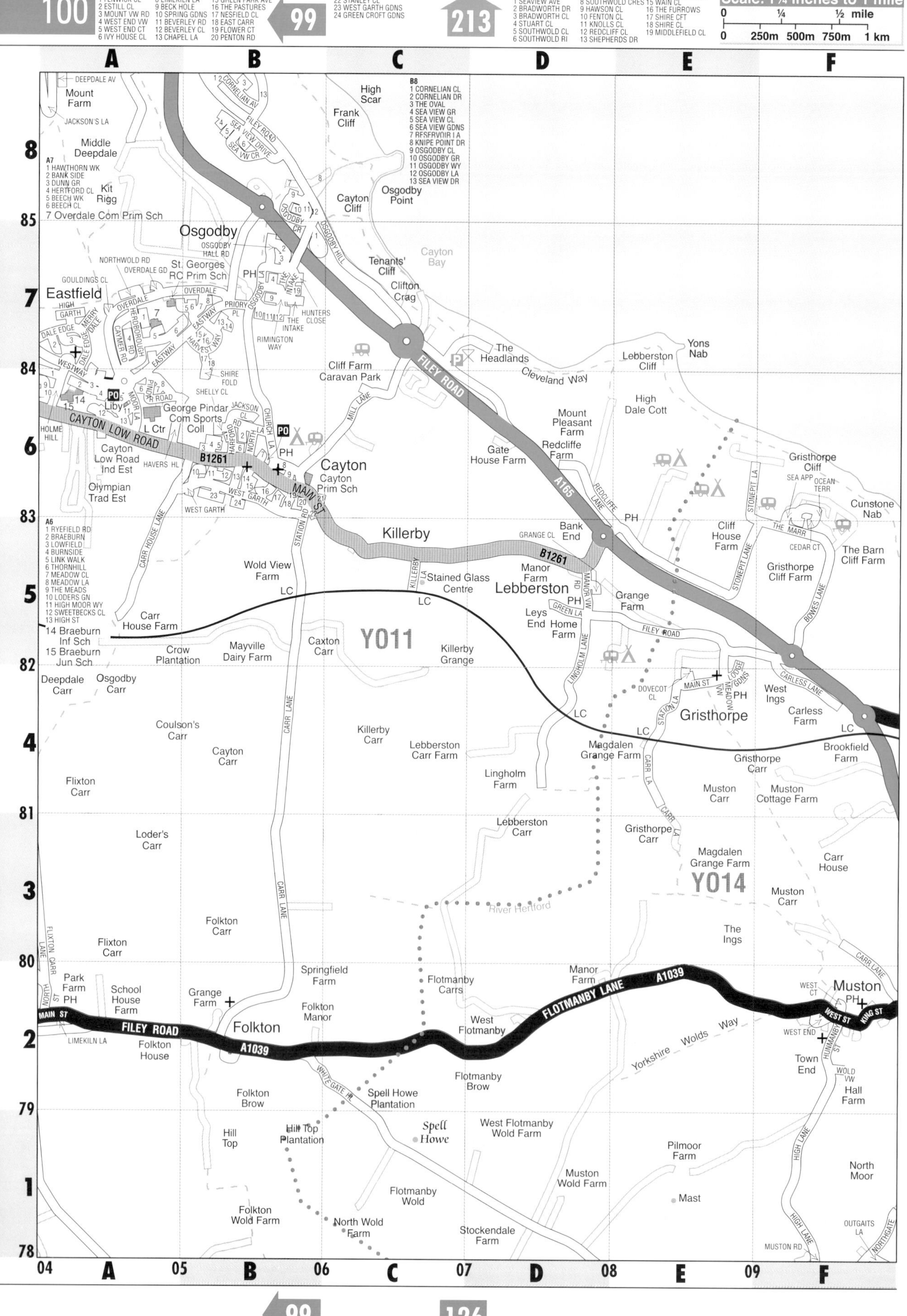
B6
1 FENWICK CL
2 ESTILL CL
3 MOUNT VW RD
4 WEST END VW
5 WEST END CT
6 IVY HOUSE CL
7 LODGE CL
8 LIMEKILN LA
9 BECK HOLE
10 SPRING GDNS
11 BEVERLEY RD
12 BEVERLEY CL
13 CHAPEL LA
14 GREEN PARK RD
15 GREEN PARK AVE
16 THE PASTURES
17 NESFIELD CL
18 EAST CARR
19 FLOWER CT
20 PENTON RD
21 EAST LEA VW
22 STANLEY CL
23 WEST GARTH GDNS
24 GREEN CROFT GDNS
99
213
B7
1 SEAVIEW AVE
2 BRADWORTH DR
3 BRADWORTH CL
4 STUART CL
5 SOUTHWOLD CL
6 SOUTHWOLD RI
7 SOUTHWOLD
8 SOUTHWOLD CRES
9 HAWSON CL
10 FENTON CL
11 KNOLLS CL
12 REDCLIFF CL
13 SHEPHERDS DR
14 PLOUGHMANS CT
15 WAIN CL
16 THE FURROWS
17 SHIRE CFT
18 SHIRE CL
19 MIDDLEFIELD CL
Scale: 1¾ inches to 1 mile
0 ¼ ½ mile
0 250m 500m 750m 1 km
A B C D E F
8
85
7
84
6
83
5
82
4
81
3
80
2
79
1
78
04 05 06 07 08 09
A7
1 HAWTHORN WK
2 BANK SIDE
3 DUNN GR
4 HERTFORD CL
5 BEECH WK
6 BEECH CL
7 Overdale Com Prim Sch
B8
1 CORNELIAN CL
2 CORNELIAN DR
3 THE OVAL
4 SEA VIEW GR
5 SEA VIEW CL
6 SEA VIEW GDNS
7 RESERVOIR LA
8 KNIPE POINT DR
9 OSGODBY CL
10 OSGODBY GR
11 OSGODBY WY
12 OSGODBY LA
13 SEA VIEW DR
A6
1 RYEFIELD RD
2 BRAEBURN
3 LOWFIELD
4 BURNSIDE
5 LINK WALK
6 THORNHILL
7 MEADOW CL
8 MEADOW LA
9 THE MEADS
10 LODERS GN
11 HIGH MOOR WY
12 SWEETBECKS CL
13 HIGH ST
14 Braeburn Inf Sch
15 Braeburn Jun Sch
DEEPDALE AV
Mount Farm
JACKSON'S LA
Middle Deepdale
Kit Rigg
Osgodby
OSGODBY HALL RD
NORTHWOLD RD
OVERDALE GD
St. Georges RC Prim Sch
GOULDINGS CL
Eastfield
HIGH GARTH
DALE EDGE
WESTWAY
OVERDALE
HERDBOROUGH
EASTWAY
PRIORY PL
HUNTERS CLOSE
THE INTAKE
RIMINGTON WAY
SHIRE FOLD
SHELLY CL
Liby
George Pindar Com Sports Coll
L Ctr
HOLME HILL
CAYTON LOW ROAD
B1261
Cayton Low Road Ind Est
HAVERS HL
Olympian Trad Est
WEST GARTH
MAIN ST
CHURCH LA
PO
PH
High Scar
Frank Cliff
Cayton Cliff
Osgodby Point
Cayton Bay
Tenants' Cliff
Clifton Crag
Cliff Farm Caravan Park
MILL LANE
Cayton
Cayton Prim Sch
FILEY ROAD
The Headlands
Cleveland Way
Lebberston Cliff
Yons Nab
High Dale Cott
Mount Pleasant Farm
Redcliffe Farm
Gate House Farm
A165
REDCLIFFE LANE
Gristhorpe Cliff
SEA APP
OCEAN TERR
Cunstone Nab
Cliff House Farm
THE MARR
CEDAR CT
STONEPIT LANE
The Barn Cliff Farm
Gristhorpe Cliff Farm
BOWES LANE
Bank End
GRANGE CL
Killerby
B1261
Manor Farm
Lebberston
Grange Farm
CARR HOUSE LANE
STATION RD
Wold View Farm
KILLERBY LA
Stained Glass Centre
LC
Carr House Farm
Crow Plantation
Mayville Dairy Farm
Caxton Carr
YO11
Killerby Grange
Leys End
Home Farm
GREEN LA
MANOR VW
FILEY ROAD
LINGHOLM LANE
DOVECOT CL
MAIN ST
STATION LA
MEADOW VW
LODGE GDNS
Gristhorpe
West Ings
CARLESS LANE
Carless Farm
Deepdale Carr
Osgodby Carr
Coulson's Carr
Cayton Carr
Killerby Carr
Lebberston Carr Farm
Magdalen Grange Farm
Gristhorpe Carr
Brookfield Farm
Flixton Carr
Lingholm Farm
Muston Carr
Muston Cottage Farm
CARR LA
CARR LANE
Loder's Carr
Lebberston Carr
Gristhorpe Carr
Magdalen Grange Farm
Carr House
YO14
Muston Carr
River Hertford
Folkton Carr
Flixton Carr
The Ings
FLIXTON CARR LANE
HILTON ST
Park Farm
School House Farm
Grange Farm
Springfield Farm
Flotmanby Carrs
Manor Farm
Muston
WEST CT
KING ST
WEST ST
MAIN ST
FILEY ROAD
Folkton
A1039
LIMEKILN LA
Folkton House
Folkton Manor
West Flotmanby
FLOTMANBY LANE
A1039
Yorkshire Wolds Way
WEST END
HUNMANBY ST
Town End
WOLD VW
Hall Farm
WHITE GATE HL
Folkton Brow
Spell Howe Plantation
Flotmanby Brow
Hill Top
Hill Top Plantation
Spell Howe
West Flotmanby Wold Farm
Pilmoor Farm
North Moor
HIGH LANE
Muston Wold Farm
Flotmanby Wold
Mast
Folkton Wold Farm
North Wold Farm
Stockendale Farm
OUTGAITS LA
MUSTON RD
NORTHGATE

Scale: 1¾ inches to 1 mile

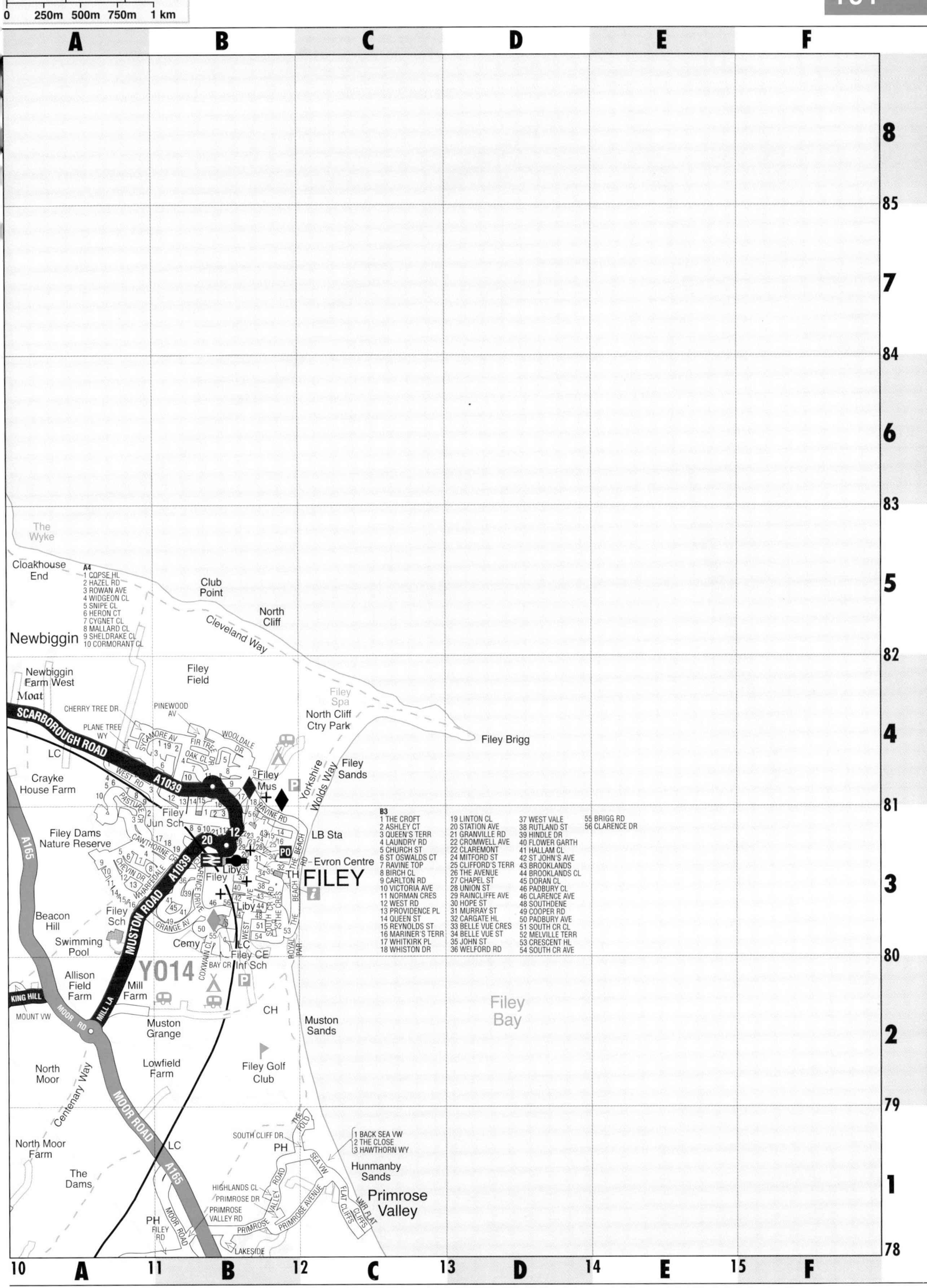

A3
1 SANDPIPER CL
2 TEAL CL
3 CURLEW DR
4 HAREWOOD DR
5 SILVERWOOD AVE
6 BURNSALL CL
7 LANGSETT AVE
8 LEYBURN PL
9 BARDEN PL
10 RIVELIN WY
11 FEWSTON CL
12 COLLINGHAM WY
13 WASHBURN CL
14 WHARNCLIFFE PL
15 MIDHOPE WY
16 EWDEN CL

B4
1 LARCH GR
2 WILLOW CL
3 CEDAR GR
4 GROVE HILL RD
5 HORNDALE RD
6 THORN TREE AVE
7 ALMOND CL
8 ARNDALE WY
9 CHURCH CLIFF DR
10 ELM CL
11 ALMOND GR
12 ASH GR
13 ASH RD
14 GROVE RD
15 THE GARDENS
16 THE CROFT
17 RAVINE HL
18 CHURCH CL
19 SYCAMORE AVE

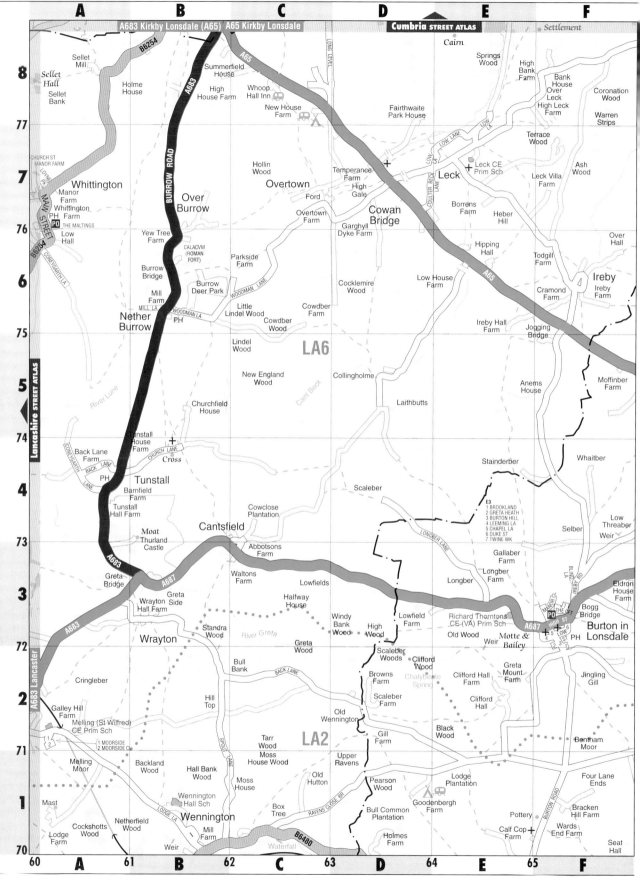

A B C D E F

Settlement

Cairn

8

Sellet Mill
B6254
Sellet Hall
Sellet Bank
Holme House
Summerfield House
High House Farm
Whoop Hall Inn
New House Farm
Springs Wood
High Bank Farm
Bank House Over Leck
Coronation Wood
Warren Strips
High Leck Farm

77

CHURCH ST
MANOR FARM
LOYNE PL
A683
BURROW ROAD
Hollin Wood
Overtown
Fairthwaite Park House
LOW LANE
LOW LA
Terrace Wood
Ash Wood

7

Whittington
Manor Farm
Whittington Farm
PH
PO THE MALTINGS
Over Burrow
Temperance Farm
High Gale
Leck
Leck CE Prim Sch
Leck Villa Farm
Borrens Farm
Heber Hill

76

MAIN STREET
B6254
Low Hall
Yew Tree Farm
CALACVM (ROMAN FORT)
Burrow Bridge
Ford
Overtown Farm
Cowan Bridge
Garghyll Dyke Farm
Hipping Hall
Todgill Farm
Over Hall

6

CONEYGARTH LA
Mill Farm
MILL LA
PH
Burrow Deer Park
Parkside Farm
Little Lindel Wood
Cowdber Wood
Cocklemire Wood
Cowdber Farm
Low House Farm
Cramond Farm
Ireby
Ireby Farm
WOODMAN LANE
WOODMAN LA
Nether Burrow

75

LA6
River Lune
Lindel Wood
Carr Beck
Jogging Bridge
Ireby Hall Farm

5

Churchfield House
New England Wood
Collingholme
Laithbutts
Anems House
Moffinber Farm

74

Back Lane Farm
CONEYGARTH LANE
BACK LANE
Tunstall House Farm
CHURCH LANE
Cross
Stainderber
Whaitber

4

A683
Tunstall
PH
Barnfield Farm
Tunstall Hall Farm
Scaleber
E3
1 BROOKLAND
2 GRETA HEATH
3 BURTON HILL
4 LEEMING LA
5 CHAPEL ST
6 DUKE ST
7 TWINE WK
Selber
Low Threaber Weir

73

Moat Thurland Castle
Cantsfield
Cowclose Plantation
Abbotsons Farm
LONGBER LANE
Gallaber Farm
Longber Farm
Eldron House Farm

3

A683
Greta Bridge
A687
Wrayton Hall Farm
Greta Side
Waltons Farm
Lowfields
Halfway House
Lowfield Farm
Richard Thorntons CE (VA) Prim Sch
Longber
A687
BLIND LA
IREBY RD
THE CFT
HIGH ST
Bogg Bridge
Burton in Lonsdale

72

A683 Lancaster
Wrayton
Standra Wood
River Greta
Greta Wood
Windy Bank Wood
High Wood
Old Wood
Weir
Motte & Bailey
PH
PO
MARSH CL
Greta Mount Farm
Jingling Gill

2

A683 Lancaster
Cringleber
Galley Hill Farm
Melling (St Wilfred) CE Prim Sch
Hill Top
Bull Bank
BACK LANE
Scaleber Woods
Browns Farm
Scaleber Farm
Clifford Wood
Chalybeate Spring
Clifford Hall Farm
Black Wood
Clifford Hall
Bentham Moor

71

1 MOORSIDE
2 MOORSIDE CL
Melling Moor
Backland Wood
Hall Bank Wood
Tarr Wood
Moss House Wood
Moss House
LA2
Old Hutton
Upper Ravens
Gill Farm
Old Wennington
Lodge Plantation
Four Lane Ends

1

Mast
Lodge Farm
Cockshotts Wood
Netherfield Wood
Wennington Hall Sch
Wennington
LODGE LA
SHOTS LANE
Mill Farm
Box Tree
Old Hutton
RAVENS CLOSE BR
Pearson Wood
Bull Common Plantation
Goodenbergh Farm
Holmes Farm
Pottery
Calf Cop Farm
BURTON ROAD
Bracken Hill Farm
Wards End Farm
Seat Hall

70
Weir
B6480
Waterfall

60 A 61 B 62 C 63 D 64 E 65 F

A   **B**   **C**   **D**   **E**   **F**

Parker Plantation

Notts Pot

Ireby Fell Cavern

Marble Steps Pot

Blea Dubs

Deep Moss

Standing Stone Scar

Braida Garth

Moss at Back o'th Rigg

8

Ireby Fell

Low Douk Cave

TURBARY ROAD

North End

Thorney Rig

Keld Head Scar

Kingsdale

George's Scar

North Green

Braida Garth Wood

Lord's Lot Top

Rigg End

Scales Moor

Rantree Moss

Rigg Moss

77

Leck Fell

TURBARY ROAD

North End Scar

Keld Head

Ewes Top Moss

Twisleton Scars

7

TOW SCAR RD

Tow Scar

Ford

Scales Moor

Ewes Top

Twisleton Scars

Rock Side

Dry Gill Cave

76

Masongill Fell Lane

Parr Bank Farm

Masongill

Hall

Lodge Farm

Fell Side

Raven Ray

Thornton Force

River Twiss

Twisleton Scar End

Scar End

Twisleton Hall

Twisleton Dale House

River Doe

Waterfall

B6255

6

Galegreen

Westgate

WESTGATE LANE

Mast

Waterfalls Walk

Waterfalls

Beezleys

Beezley Falls

Waterfall

75

Kirksteads

Fellbeck Farm

Cowgill Farm

LA6

Manor House Wood

Pecca Falls

Thornton Hall

Manor House

Snow Falls

Quarry Wood

Quarry

Skirwith Cave

5

Eccles Farm

Bank House

BANK HO LA

Westhouse

Westhouse Farm

Manor House Farm

Swilla Glen

Lenny Wood

Waterfall

74

Trees Farm

High Threaber Farm

Lower Westhouse

PH

SMITHY LANE

A65 NEW ROAD

THORNTON LANE

PH

Thornton in Lonsdale

CHURCH ST 1
BANK HALL CL 2
THE RAKE 3
BELL HORSE GT 4
THE SQUARE 5
MAIN STREET 6
SEED HILL 7
UPPERGATE 8
THE BROW 9

YH

THACKING LA

B6255

Storrs Cave

Settlement & Field System

4

Gooda

A687

Halsteads

P

Waterfall

Holme Head

Weir

Ingleton Mid Sch

8 HIGH ST

Fell End Farm

Waterfall

73

Lowfields

Lowfield Farm

Lund Farm

Scrogg's Wood

Lund Holme Farm

Lund Holme

New Bridge

BANK BOTTOM

MAIN ST

BRIDGE MEWS

Liby

CROFT RD

BACK GATE

BOWLAND VW

LOW DEMESNE

Ingleton Prim Sch

Ingleton

Cemy

Jenkins's Bridge

Jenkin Beck

Settlement

3

Clarrick House Farm

River Greta

BENTHAM RD

Wilson Wood Farm

Stackstead Farm

WARTH LANE

Ingleton Ind Est

ENTER LA

Moorgarth

CAPLAM OLD RD

Yarlsber Farm

Slatenber

Barnoldswick Lane

Kepp House

Barnoldswick

Park Foot Farmhouse

Warth House

Enter Farm

Hotel

Moorgarth Bridge

Moorgarth Farm

Greenwood Leghe

GREEN LANE

LONKABER LANE

Lowkbers

Duck Dub Farm

OLD RD

72

Stephen's Wood

Faccon Farm

Parkfoot Bridge

Foredale Farm

Foredales House

Newfield Farm

Lane House

Lowkbers

LA2

Cold Cotes

Brackenber Farmhouse

71

BENTHAM MOOR ROAD

Bentham Moor Fourlands Hill

Fourlands House

Raygill House

Broats House

Broats Farm

Langber Farm

Stubb Farm

Nutstile

2

Fourlands House Farm

Black Banks Plantation

LA2

Over Raygill

WINDY HILL

Nookdales House

Nookdales Farm

Langber End Farm

LANGBER END LA

Whinney Mire

WHINNEY MIRE LA

LA2

Goat Gap

Goat Gap Farm

1

Ghyllhead Farm

ROBIN LANE

Thornber

DUMB TOM'S LANE

Tatterthorn

Nutgill Farm

NUTGILL LA

A65

Whinney Mire

Newby Moor

Newby Moor Bridge

70

D3
1 BURNMOOR CRES
2 INGLEBOROUGH PK DR
3 INGLEBOROUGH PK CL
4 LOW DEMESNE CL
5 ELLERINGTON CL
6 MANOR CL
7 BROOKACRE
8 FEATHERBECK CL
9 MALT DUBS CL
10 THE INGLES
11 GREEN MEADOW CL

103
78

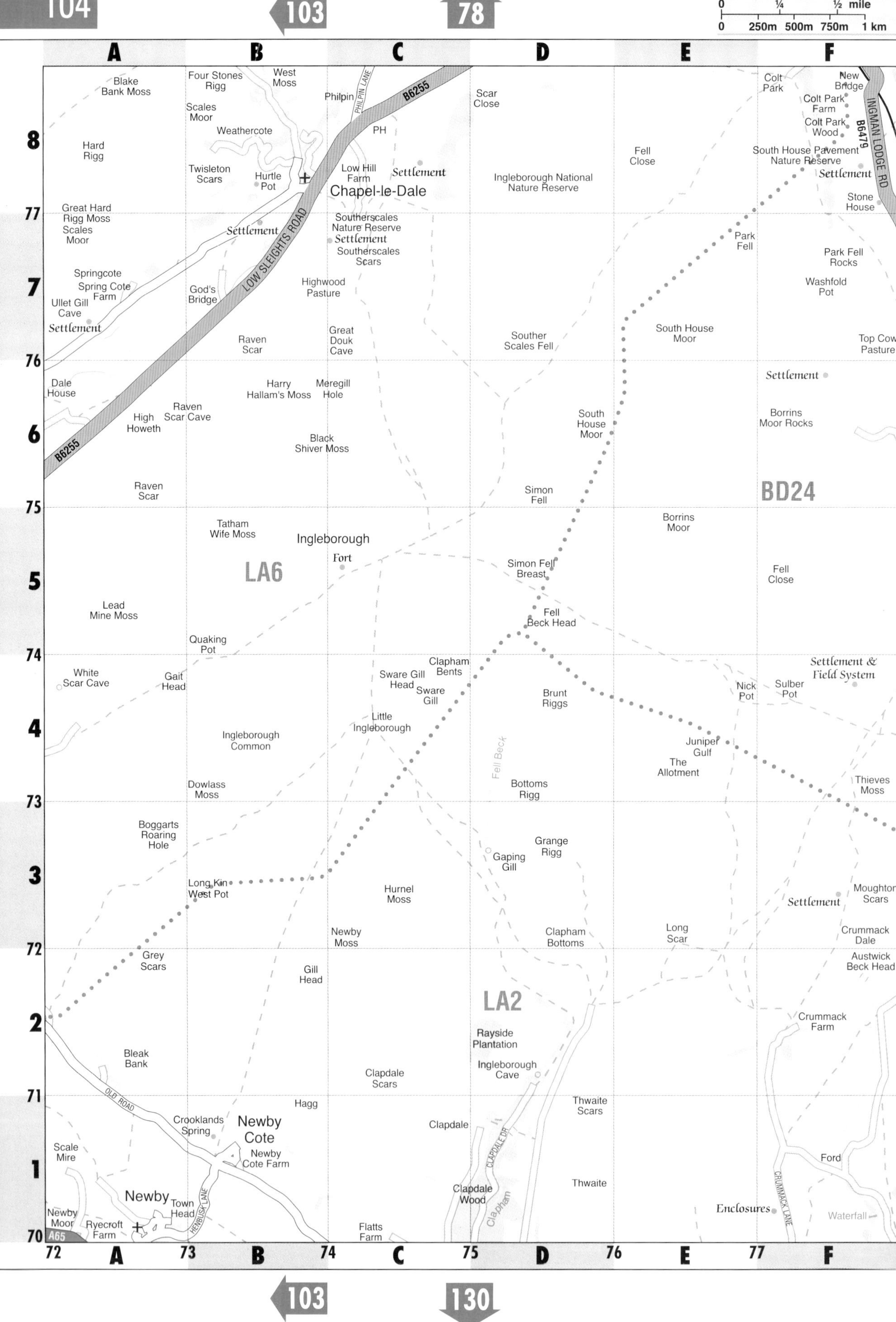
Scale: 1¾ inches to 1 mile
0 ¼ ½ mile
0 250m 500m 750m 1 km
A B C D E F
8
77
7
76
6
75
5
74
4
73
3
72
2
71
1
70
72 A 73 B 74 C 75 D 76 E 77 F
Blake Bank Moss
Four Stones Rigg
West Moss
Philpin
PHILPIN LANE
B6255
Scar Close
Colt Park
New Bridge
Colt Park Farm
Colt Park Wood
B6479
INGMAN LODGE RD
Scales Moor
Weathercote
PH
Hard Rigg
Fell Close
South House Pavement Nature Reserve
Settlement
Twisleton Scars
Hurtle Pot
Low Hill Farm
Settlement
Chapel-le-Dale
Ingleborough National Nature Reserve
Stone House
Great Hard Rigg Moss
Scales Moor
Settlement
LOW SLEIGHTS ROAD
Southerscales Nature Reserve
Settlement
Southerscales Scars
Park Fell
Park Fell Rocks
Springcote
Spring Cote Farm
Ullet Gill Cave
Settlement
God's Bridge
Highwood Pasture
Washfold Pot
Raven Scar
Great Douk Cave
Souther Scales Fell
South House Moor
Top Cow Pasture
Dale House
Harry Hallam's Moss
Meregill Hole
Settlement
Raven Scar Cave
High Howeth
South House Moor
Borrins Moor Rocks
B6255
Black Shiver Moss
Raven Scar
Simon Fell
BD24
Tatham Wife Moss
Ingleborough
Borrins Moor
Fort
LA6
Simon Fell Breast
Fell Close
Lead Mine Moss
Fell Beck Head
Quaking Pot
Clapham Bents
Settlement & Field System
White Scar Cave
Gait Head
Sware Gill Head
Sware Gill
Brunt Riggs
Nick Pot
Sulber Pot
Little Ingleborough
Ingleborough Common
Fell Beck
Juniper Gulf
The Allotment
Dowlass Moss
Bottoms Rigg
Thieves Moss
Boggarts Roaring Hole
Grange Rigg
Gaping Gill
Long Kin West Pot
Hurnel Moss
Moughton Scars
Settlement
Newby Moss
Clapham Bottoms
Long Scar
Crummack Dale
Grey Scars
Gill Head
Austwick Beck Head
LA2
Crummack Farm
Rayside Plantation
Bleak Bank
Ingleborough Cave
Clapdale Scars
OLD ROAD
Thwaite Scars
Hagg
Crooklands Spring
Newby Cote
Clapdale
Scale Mire
Newby Cote Farm
CLAPDALE DR
Ford
Thwaite
Clapdale Wood
Newby
Town Head
HENBUSK LANE
CRUMMACK LANE
Enclosures
Newby Moor
Ryecroft Farm
Clapham
Waterfall
Flatts Farm
A65

103
130

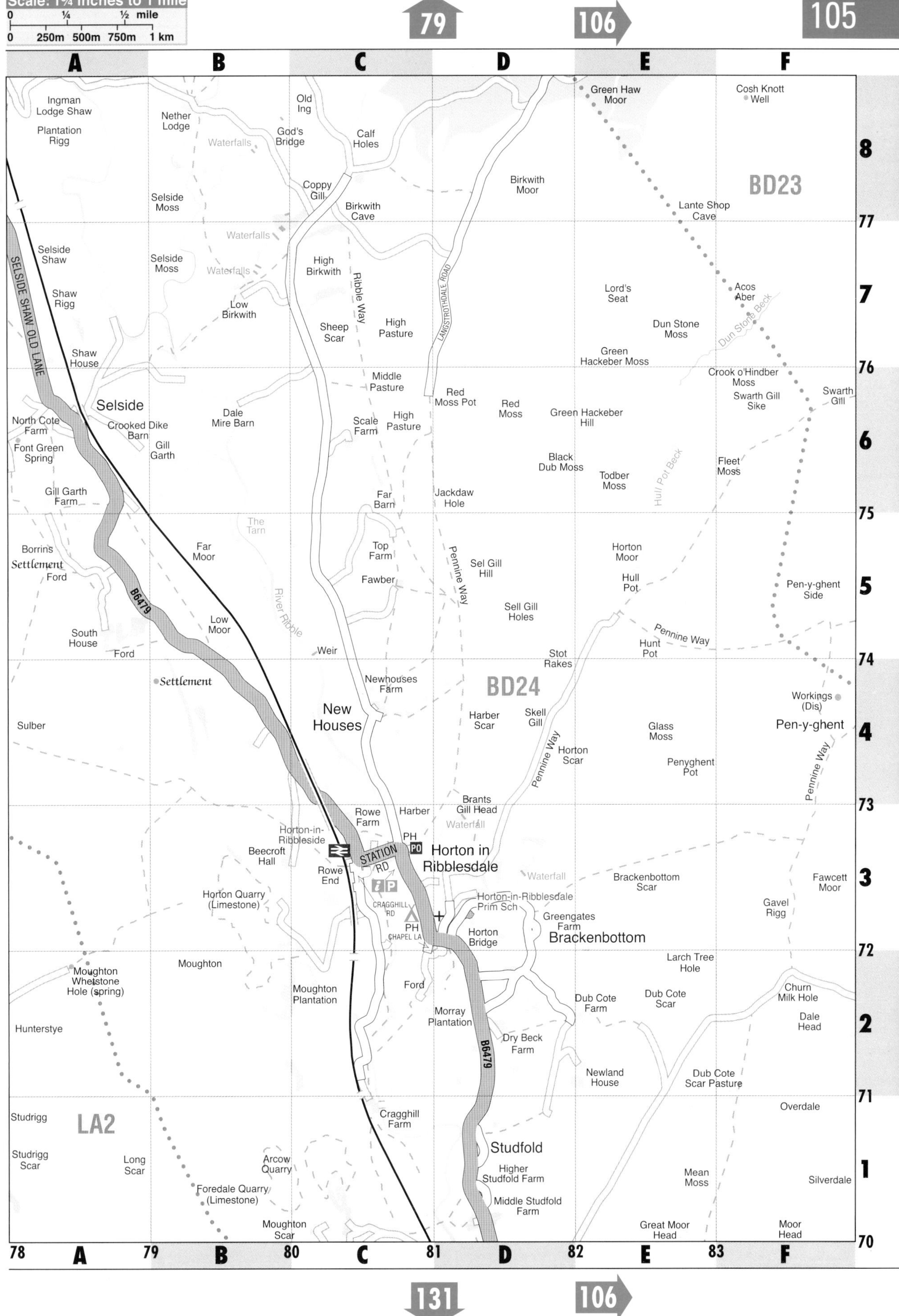
Scale: 1¾ inches to 1 mile
0 ¼ ½ mile
0 250m 500m 750m 1 km
79
106
A B C D E F
Ingman Lodge Shaw
Plantation Rigg
Nether Lodge
Old Ing
God's Bridge
Calf Holes
Green Haw Moor
Cosh Knott Well
Waterfalls
Coppy Gill
Birkwith Cave
Birkwith Moor
BD23
Lante Shop Cave
Selside Moss
Selside Shaw
Shaw Rigg
High Birkwith
Ribble Way
LANGSTROTHDALE ROAD
Lord's Seat
Acos Aber
Dun Stone Beck
Low Birkwith
Sheep Scar
High Pasture
Dun Stone Moss
Green Hackeber Moss
SELSIDE SHAW OLD LANE
Shaw House
Middle Pasture
Crook o'Hindber Moss
Selside
Red Moss Pot
Red Moss
Green Hackeber Hill
Swarth Gill Sike
Swarth Gill
North Cote Farm
Crooked Dike Barn
Dale Mire Barn
Scale Farm
High Pasture
Font Green Spring
Gill Garth
Black Dub Moss
Hull Pot Beck
Fleet Moss
Todber Moss
Gill Garth Farm
Far Barn
Jackdaw Hole
The Tarn
Borrins
Settlement
Ford
Far Moor
Top Farm
Pennine Way
Sel Gill Hill
Horton Moor
Hull Pot
Fawber
Pen-y-ghent Side
B6479
River Ribble
Sell Gill Holes
Low Moor
Pennine Way
Hunt Pot
South House
Ford
Weir
Stot Rakes
Settlement
Newhouses Farm
BD24
Workings (Dis)
New Houses
Harber Scar
Skell Gill
Glass Moss
Pen-y-ghent
Sulber
Horton Scar
Penyghent Pot
Brants Gill Head
Rowe Farm
Harber
Waterfall
Horton-in-Ribbleside
PH
PO
Beecroft Hall
STATION RD
Horton in Ribblesdale
Rowe End
Waterfall
Brackenbottom Scar
Fawcett Moor
Horton Quarry (Limestone)
CRAGGHILL RD
Horton-in-Ribblesdale Prim Sch
Gavel Rigg
Greengates Farm
PH
CHAPEL LA
Horton Bridge
Brackenbottom
Moughton
Larch Tree Hole
Moughton Whetstone Hole (spring)
Moughton Plantation
Ford
Churn Milk Hole
Dub Cote Farm
Dub Cote Scar
Morray Plantation
Dale Head
Hunterstye
Dry Beck Farm
B6479
Newland House
Dub Cote Scar Pasture
Overdale
Studrigg
LA2
Cragghill Farm
Studfold
Studrigg Scar
Long Scar
Arcow Quarry
Higher Studfold Farm
Mean Moss
Silverdale
Foredale Quarry (Limestone)
Middle Studfold Farm
Moughton Scar
Great Moor Head
Moor Head
8
77
7
76
6
75
5
74
4
73
3
72
2
71
1
70
78 79 80 81 82 83
131
106

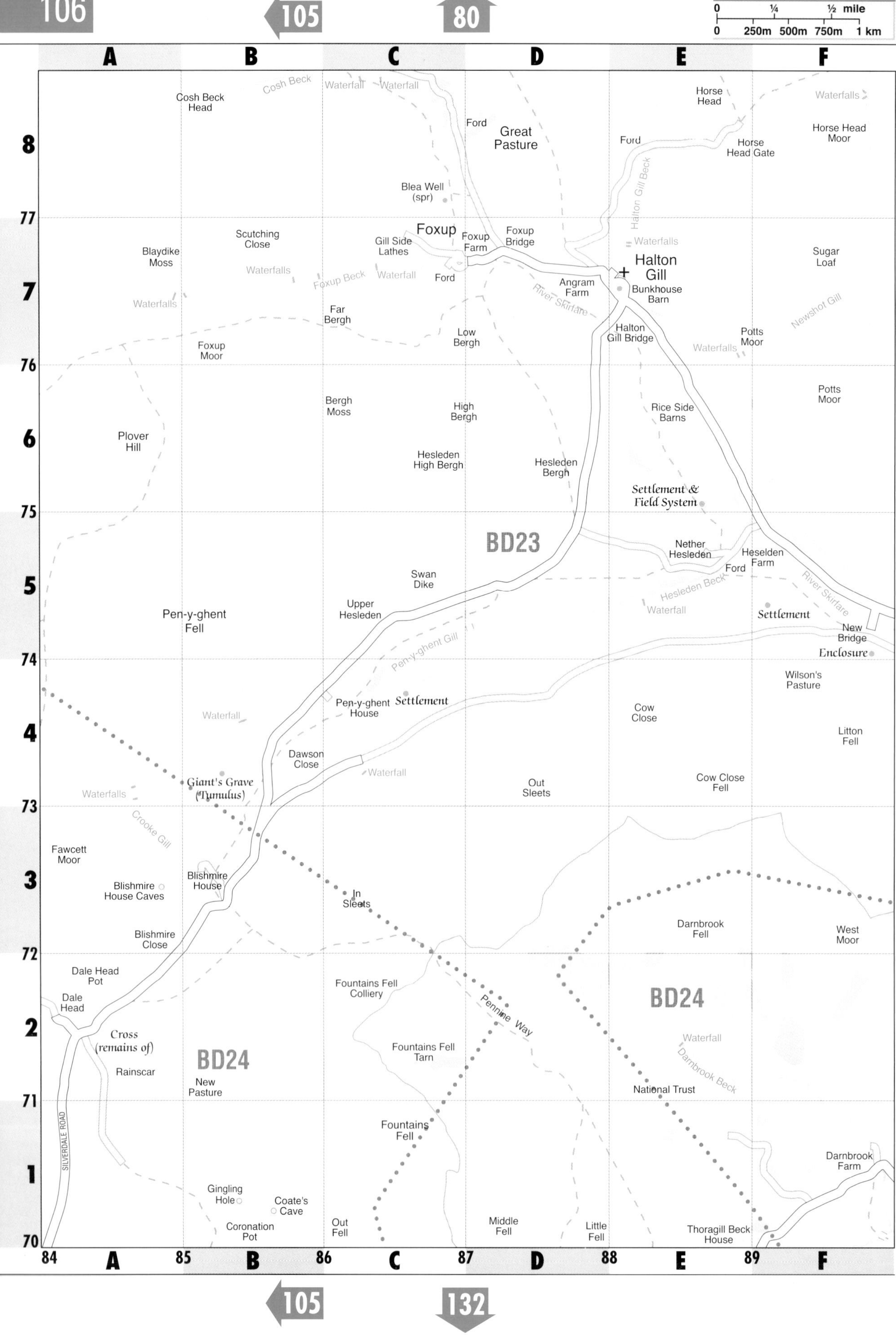

A   **B**   **C**   **D**   **E**   **F**

Cosh Beck

Waterfall Waterfall

Waterfalls

8

Cosh Beck
Head

Ford

Great
Pasture

Horse
Head

Ford

Horse
Head Gate

Horse Head
Moor

Waterfalls

77

Blea Well
(spr)

Foxup

Halton Gill Beck

Sugar
Loaf

Scutching
Close

Gill Side
Lathes

Foxup
Farm

Foxup
Bridge

Waterfalls

Halton
Gill

7

Blaydike
Moss

Waterfalls

Ford

Angram
Farm

Bunkhouse
Barn

Newshot Gill

Waterfalls

Foxup Beck Waterfall

River Skirfare

Halton
Gill Bridge

Potts
Moor

Waterfalls

Far
Bergh

76

Foxup
Moor

Low
Bergh

Rice Side
Barns

Potts
Moor

6

Plover
Hill

Bergh
Moss

High
Bergh

Hesleden
High Bergh

Hesleden
Bergh

75

Settlement &
Field System

BD23

Nether
Hesleden

Heselden
Farm

5

Pen-y-ghent
Fell

Upper
Hesleden

Swan
Dike

Ford

Hesleden Beck

Waterfall

River Skirfare

Settlement

New
Bridge

Enclosure

74

Pen-y-ghent Gill

Wilson's
Pasture

Waterfall

Waterfall

Pen-y-ghent
House

Settlement

Cow
Close

Litton
Fell

4

Dawson
Close

Waterfall

Out
Sleets

Cow Close
Fell

Giant's Grave
(Tumulus)

73

Waterfalls

Crooke Gill

Fawcett
Moor

Blishmire
House

In
Sleets

Darnbrook
Fell

West
Moor

3

Blishmire
House Caves

Blishmire
Close

Dale Head
Pot

72

Fountains Fell
Colliery

Pennine Way

BD24

Dale
Head

BD24

Fountains Fell
Tarn

Waterfall

Darnbrook Beck

2

Cross
(remains of)

Rainscar

New
Pasture

National Trust

71

SILVERDALE ROAD

Fountains
Fell

Darnbrook
Farm

1

Gingling
Hole

Coate's
Cave

Coronation
Pot

Out
Fell

Middle
Fell

Little
Fell

Thoragill Beck
House

70

84   **A**   **85**   **B**   **86**   **C**   **87**   **D**   **88**   **E**   **89**   **F**

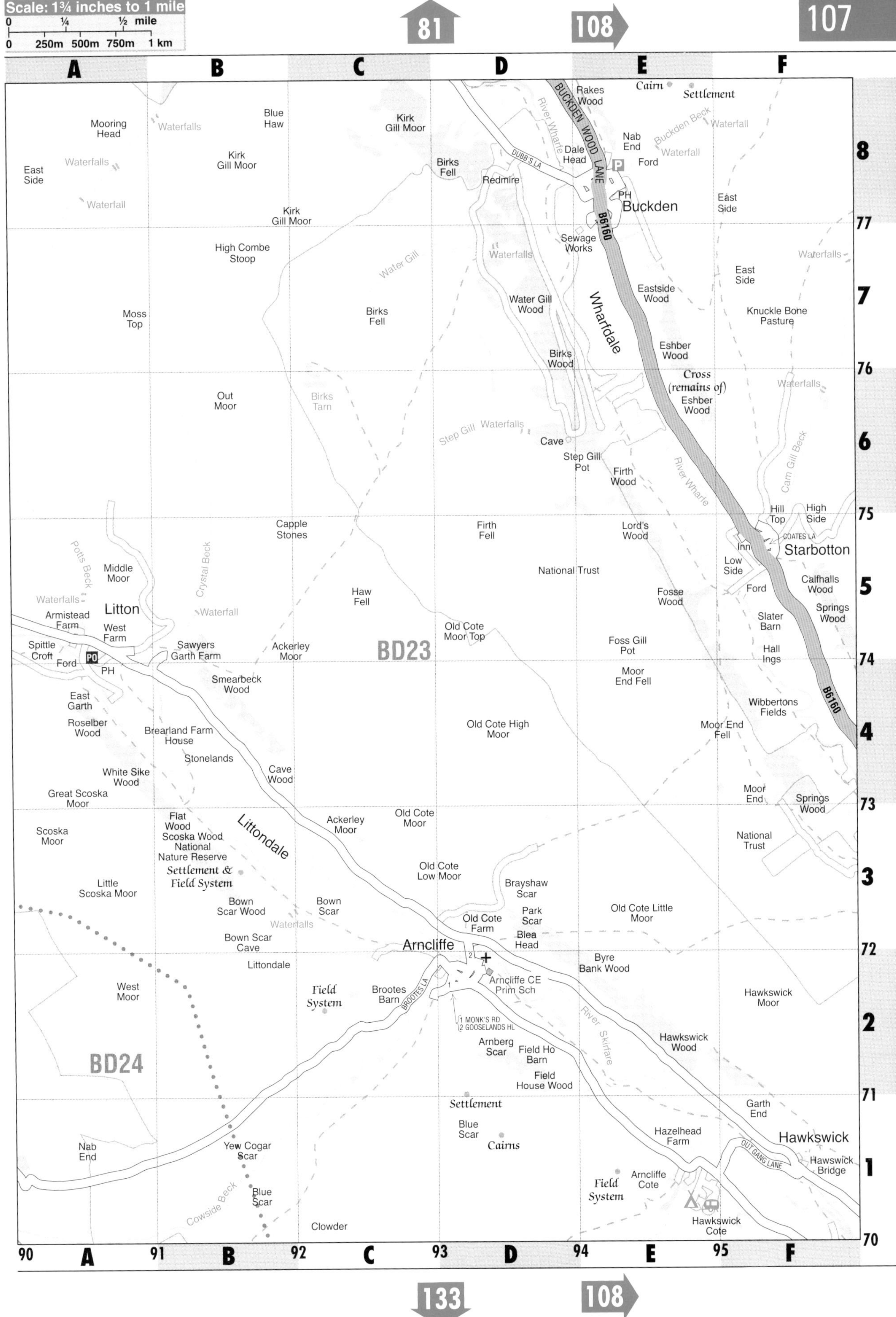

Scale: 1¾ inches to 1 mile

0   ¼   ½ mile
0 250m 500m 750m 1 km

A B C D E F

8

East Side

Mooring Head

Waterfalls

Waterfalls

Waterfall

Blue Haw

Kirk Gill Moor

Kirk Gill Moor

Kirk Gill Moor

High Combe Stoop

Moss Top

Birks Fell

Kirk Gill Moor

Birks Fell

Water Gill

Waterfalls

DUBB'S LA

Birks Fell

Redmire

River Wharfe

BUCKDEN WOOD LANE

Rakes Wood

Dale Head

Nab End
Ford

Cairn

Settlement

Buckden Beck

Waterfall

Waterfall

P

PH
Buckden

B6160

East Side

77

Out Moor

Birks Tarn

Water Gill Wood

Birks Wood

Sewage Works

Waterfalls

Wharfedale

Eastside Wood

Eshber Wood

Cross
(remains of)
Eshber Wood

East Side

Knuckle Bone Pasture

Waterfalls

Waterfalls

7

76

6

Step Gill
Waterfalls

Cave

Step Gill Pot

Firth Wood

River Wharfe

Cam Gill Beck

75

Capple Stones

Firth Fell

Lord's Wood

Hill Top

High Side

COATES LA

Middle Moor

Potts Beck

Crystal Beck

Waterfalls

Litton

Armistead Farm

West Farm

Spittle Croft

Ford
PO
PH

Waterfall

Sawyers Garth Farm

Ackerley Moor

Haw Fell

National Trust

Old Cote Moor Top

Fosse Wood

Foss Gill Pot

Inn
Low Side

Ford

Slater Barn

Hall Ings

Starbotton

Calfhalls Wood

Springs Wood

5

74

BD23

East Garth

Roselber Wood

Great Scoska Moor

Smearbeck Wood

Brearland Farm House

Stonelands

White Sike Wood

Cave Wood

Old Cote High Moor

Moor End Fell

Moor End Fell

Wibbertons Fields

B6160

4

Scoska Moor

Flat Wood
Scoska Wood
National
Nature Reserve
Settlement &
Field System

Littondale

Ackerley Moor

Old Cote Moor

Old Cote Low Moor

Moor End

Springs Wood

National Trust

73

3

Little Scoska Moor

West Moor

BD24

Bown Scar Wood

Bown Scar Cave

Bown Scar

Littondale

Waterfalls

Field System

Brootes Barn

BROOTES LA

Arncliffe

Old Cote Farm

Brayshaw Scar

Park Scar

Blea Head

Arncliffe CE Prim Sch

Byre Bank Wood

Hawkswick Moor

72

2

Nab End

Yew Cogar Scar

Blue Scar

Cowside Beck

1 MONK'S RD
2 GOOSELANDS HL

Arnberg Scar

Field Ho Barn

Field House Wood

River Skirfare

Hawkswick Wood

Settlement

Blue Scar

Cairns

Hazelhead Farm

Garth End

Hawkswick

OUT GANG LANE

71

1

Clowder

Field System

Arncliffe Cote

Hawkswick Cote

Hawkswick Bridge

70

90 A 91 B 92 C 93 D 94 E 95 F

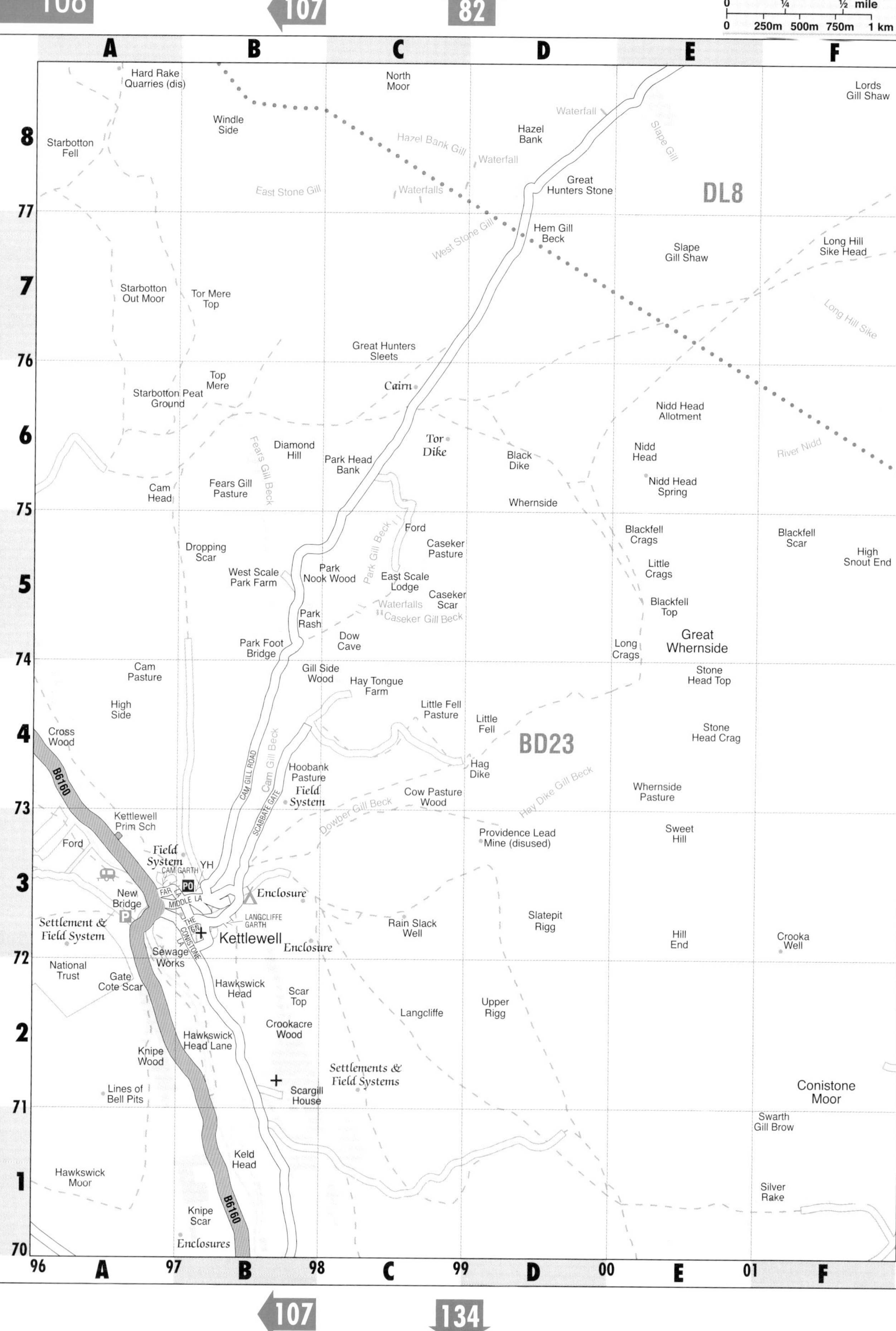

A   B   C   D   E   F

8

Hard Rake
Quarries (dis)

North
Moor

Waterfall

Lords
Gill Shaw

Starbotton
Fell

Windle
Side

Hazel Bank Gill

Hazel
Bank

Slape Gill

DL8

East Stone Gill

Waterfall

77

Waterfalls

Great
Hunters Stone

West Stone Gill

Hem Gill
Beck

Slape
Gill Shaw

Long Hill
Sike Head

7

Starbotton
Out Moor

Tor Mere
Top

Long Hill Sike

76

Great Hunters
Sleets

Nidd Head
Allotment

River Nidd

Top
Mere

Cairn

6

Starbotton Peat
Ground

Diamond
Hill

Tor
Dike

Nidd
Head

Fears Gill Beck

Park Head
Bank

Nidd Head
Spring

Cam
Head

Fears Gill
Pasture

Black
Dike

75

Whernside

Park Gill Beck

Dropping
Scar

Ford

Caseker
Pasture

Blackfell
Crags

Blackfell
Scar

High
Snout End

5

West Scale
Park Farm

Park
Nook Wood

East Scale
Lodge

Caseker
Scar

Little
Crags

Blackfell
Top

Waterfalls

Caseker Gill Beck

Park
Rash

Dow
Cave

Long
Crags

Great
Whernside

Park Foot
Bridge

74

Cam
Pasture

Gill Side
Wood

Hay Tongue
Farm

Stone
Head Top

4

High
Side

Little Fell
Pasture

Little
Fell

BD23

Stone
Head Crag

Cross
Wood

Cam Gill Road

Cam Gill Beck

Hoobank
Pasture
**Field
System**

Hag
Dike

Hay Dike Gill Beck

Whernside
Pasture

73

Kettlewell
Prim Sch

Scargate Gate

Cow Pasture
Wood

Providence Lead
Mine (disused)

Sweet
Hill

Ford

**Field
System**
CAM GARTH
YH
PO

Dowber Gill Beck

3

New
Bridge

Enclosure

FAR
MIDDLE LA

LANGCLIFFE
GARTH

Rain Slack
Well

Slatepit
Rigg

Hill
End

Crooka
Well

**Settlement &
Field System**

THE GRN

CONISTONE

Kettlewell

Enclosure

72

National
Trust

Gate
Cote Scar

Sewage
Works

Hawkswick
Head

Scar
Top

Langcliffe

Upper
Rigg

2

Hawkswick
Head Lane

Crookacre
Wood

Knipe
Wood

**Settlements &
Field Systems**

Conistone
Moor

Lines of
Bell Pits

Scargill
House

71

Swarth
Gill Brow

Keld
Head

1

Hawkswick
Moor

B6160

Silver
Rake

Knipe
Scar

70

Enclosures

96   A   97   B   98   C   99   D   00   E   01   F

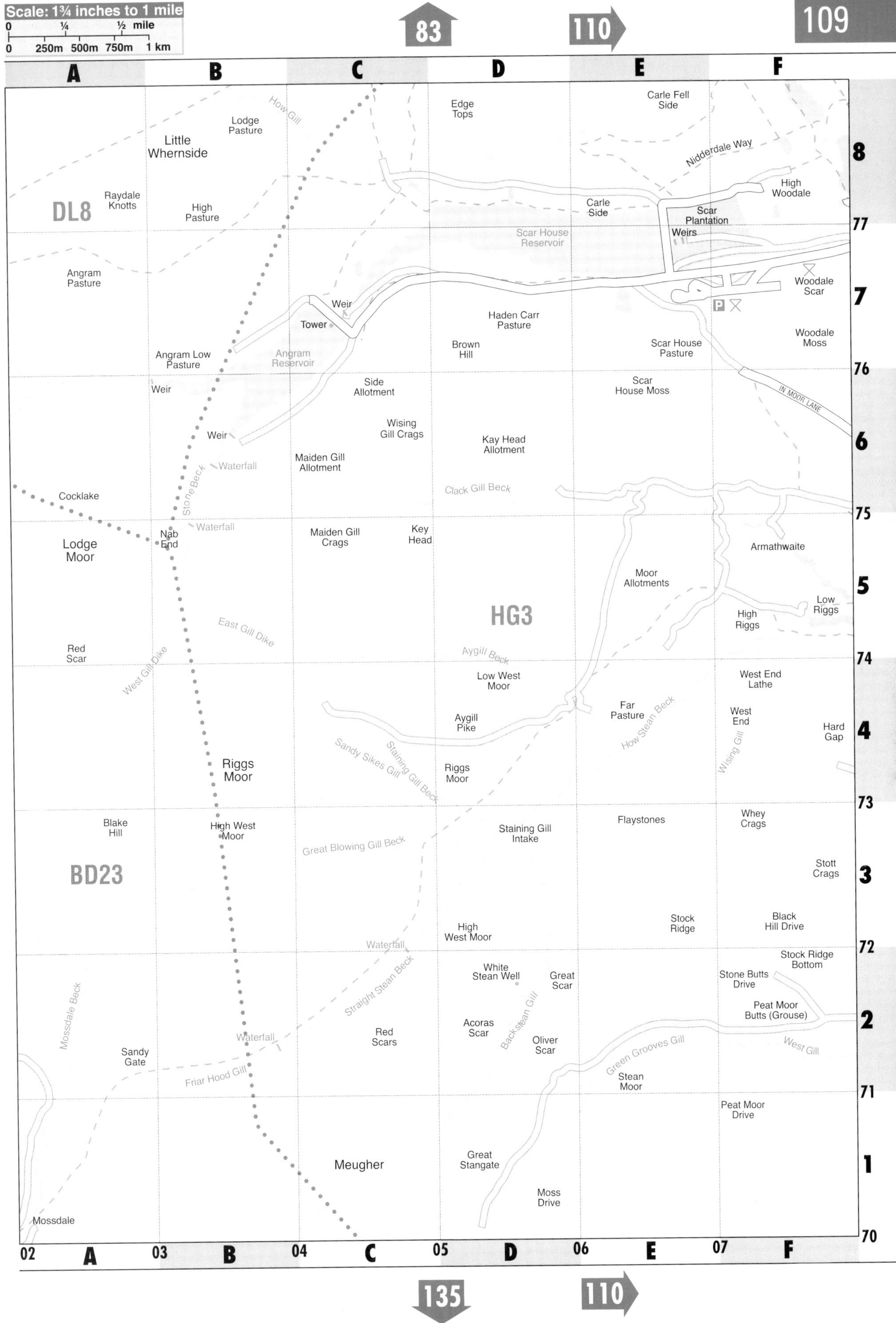
Scale: 1¾ inches to 1 mile
0 ¼ ½ mile
0 250m 500m 750m 1 km
83
110
A B C D E F
How Gill
Edge Tops
Carle Fell Side
Lodge Pasture
Little Whernside
Nidderdale Way
8
High Woodale
Raydale Knotts
DL8
High Pasture
Carle Side
Scar Plantation
77
Scar House Reservoir
Weirs
Angram Pasture
Woodale Scar
7
Weir
Tower
Haden Carr Pasture
P
Woodale Moss
Brown Hill
Scar House Pasture
Angram Low Pasture
Angram Reservoir
76
Side Allotment
Scar House Moss
Weir
In Moor Lane
Wising Gill Crags
Kay Head Allotment
6
Weir
Maiden Gill Allotment
Waterfall
Stone Beck
Clack Gill Beck
Cocklake
75
Waterfall
Nab End
Maiden Gill Crags
Key Head
Lodge Moor
Armathwaite
Moor Allotments
5
HG3
Low Riggs
High Riggs
East Gill Dike
Red Scar
Aygill Beck
74
West Gill Dike
Low West Moor
West End Lathe
Far Pasture
How Stean Beck
West End
Aygill Pike
Hard Gap
4
Sandy Sikes Gill
Staining Gill Beck
Wising Gill
Riggs Moor
Riggs Moor
73
Blake Hill
High West Moor
Flaystones
Whey Crags
Staining Gill Intake
Great Blowing Gill Beck
BD23
Stott Crags
3
Stock Ridge
Black Hill Drive
High West Moor
72
Waterfall
Stock Ridge Bottom
White Stean Well
Great Scar
Stone Butts Drive
Straight Stean Beck
Mossdale Beck
Peat Moor Butts (Grouse)
2
Acoras Scar
Backstean Gill
Red Scars
Waterfall
West Gill
Green Grooves Gill
Oliver Scar
Sandy Gate
Friar Hood Gill
Stean Moor
71
Peat Moor Drive
Meugher
Great Stangate
1
Moss Drive
Mossdale
70
02 A 03 B 04 C 05 D 06 E 07 F
135
110

109
84

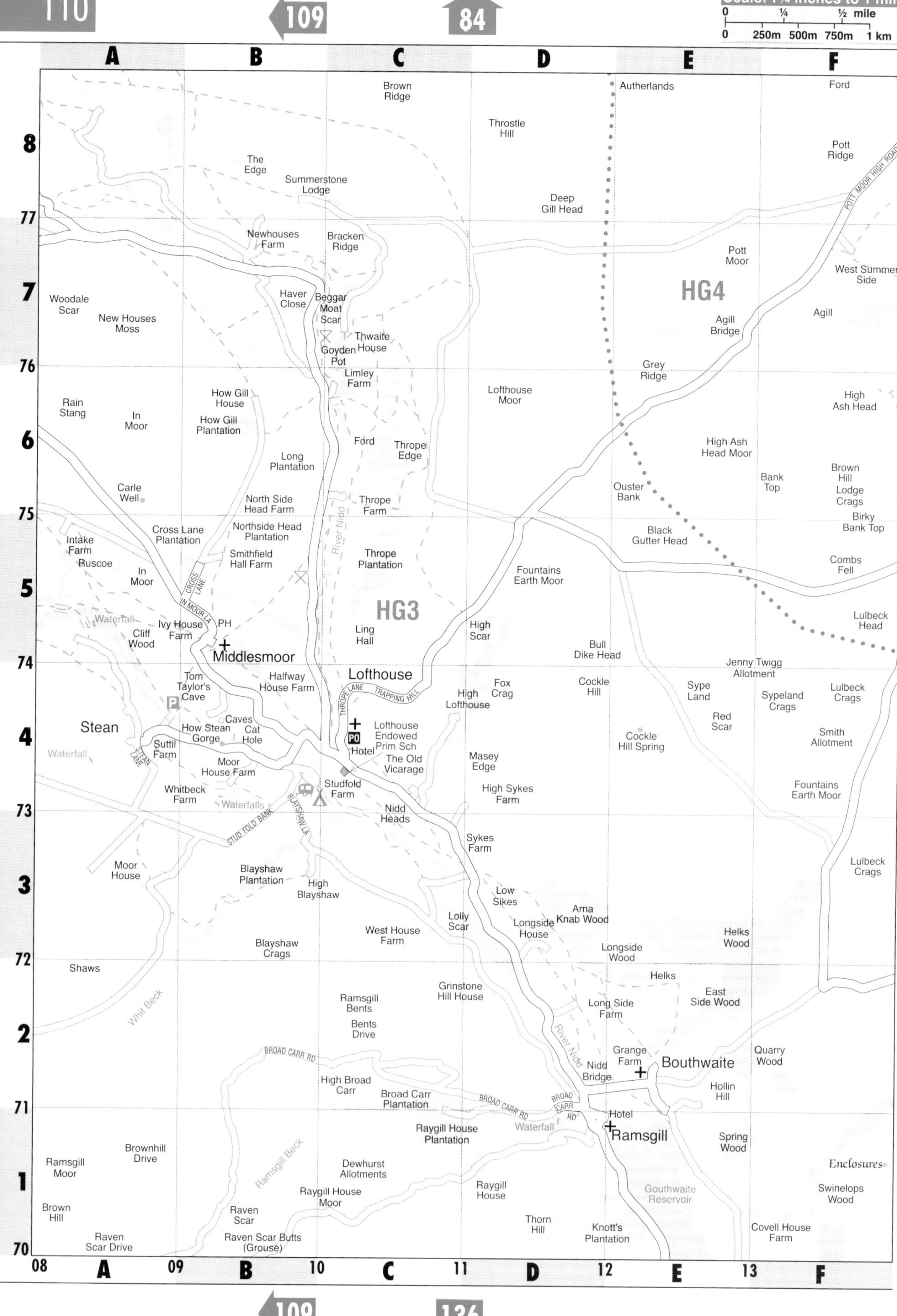
Scale: 1¾ inches to 1 mile
0 ¼ ½ mile
0 250m 500m 750m 1 km
A B C D E F
8
77
7
76
6
75
5
74
4
73
3
72
2
71
1
70
08 09 10 11 12 13
Brown Ridge
Throstle Hill
Authorlands
Ford
Pott Ridge
POTT MOOR HIGH ROAD
The Edge
Summerstone Lodge
Deep Gill Head
Newhouses Farm
Bracken Ridge
Pott Moor
West Summer Side
HG4
Woodale Scar
New Houses Moss
Haver Close
Beggar Moat Scar
Agill Bridge
Agill
Thwaite House
Goyden Pot
Limley Farm
Grey Ridge
Lofthouse Moor
Rain Stang
In Moor
How Gill House
How Gill Plantation
High Ash Head
Ford
Thrope Edge
High Ash Head Moor
Long Plantation
Brown Hill
Bank Top
Carle Well
North Side Head Farm
Thrope Farm
Ouster Bank
Lodge Crags
Birky Bank Top
River Nidd
Cross Lane Plantation
Northside Head Plantation
Black Gutter Head
Intake Farm
Ruscoe
Smithfield Hall Farm
Thrope Plantation
Combs Fell
In Moor
Fountains Earth Moor
CROSS LANE
IN MOOR LA
HG3
Waterfall
Ivy House Farm
PH
Cliff Wood
Ling Hall
High Scar
Lulbeck Head
Middlesmoor
Bull Dike Head
Jenny Twigg Allotment
Lofthouse
Tom Taylor's Cave
Halfway House Farm
THROPE LANE
TRAPPING HILL
Fox Crag
High Lofthouse
Cockle Hill
Sype Land
Sypeland Crags
Lulbeck Crags
Caves
Stean
How Stean Gorge
Cat Hole
Lofthouse Endowed Prim Sch
Hotel
Red Scar
Cockle Hill Spring
Smith Allotment
Waterfall
Suttil Farm
STEAN LANE
Moor House Farm
The Old Vicarage
Masey Edge
Studfold Farm
High Sykes Farm
Fountains Earth Moor
Whitbeck Farm
Waterfalls
STUD FOLD BANK
BLAYSHAW LA
Nidd Heads
Sykes Farm
Moor House
Blayshaw Plantation
High Blayshaw
Lulbeck Crags
Low Sikes
Lolly Scar
Longside House
Arna Knab Wood
West House Farm
Helks Wood
Blayshaw Crags
Longside Wood
Shaws
Helks
Grinstone Hill House
Whit Beck
Ramsgill Bents
Long Side Farm
East Side Wood
Bents Drive
River Nidd
Grange Farm
Quarry Wood
BROAD CARR RD
Nidd Bridge
Bouthwaite
High Broad Carr
Broad Carr Plantation
BROAD CARR RD
BROAD CARR RD
Hollin Hill
Hotel
Raygill House Plantation
Waterfall
Ramsgill
Brownhill Drive
Spring Wood
Ramsgill Moor
Ramsgill Beck
Dewhurst Allotments
Enclosures
Raygill House Moor
Raygill House
Gouthwaite Reservoir
Swinelops Wood
Brown Hill
Raven Scar
Thorn Hill
Knott's Plantation
Covell House Farm
Raven Scar Drive
Raven Scar Butts (Grouse)

109
136

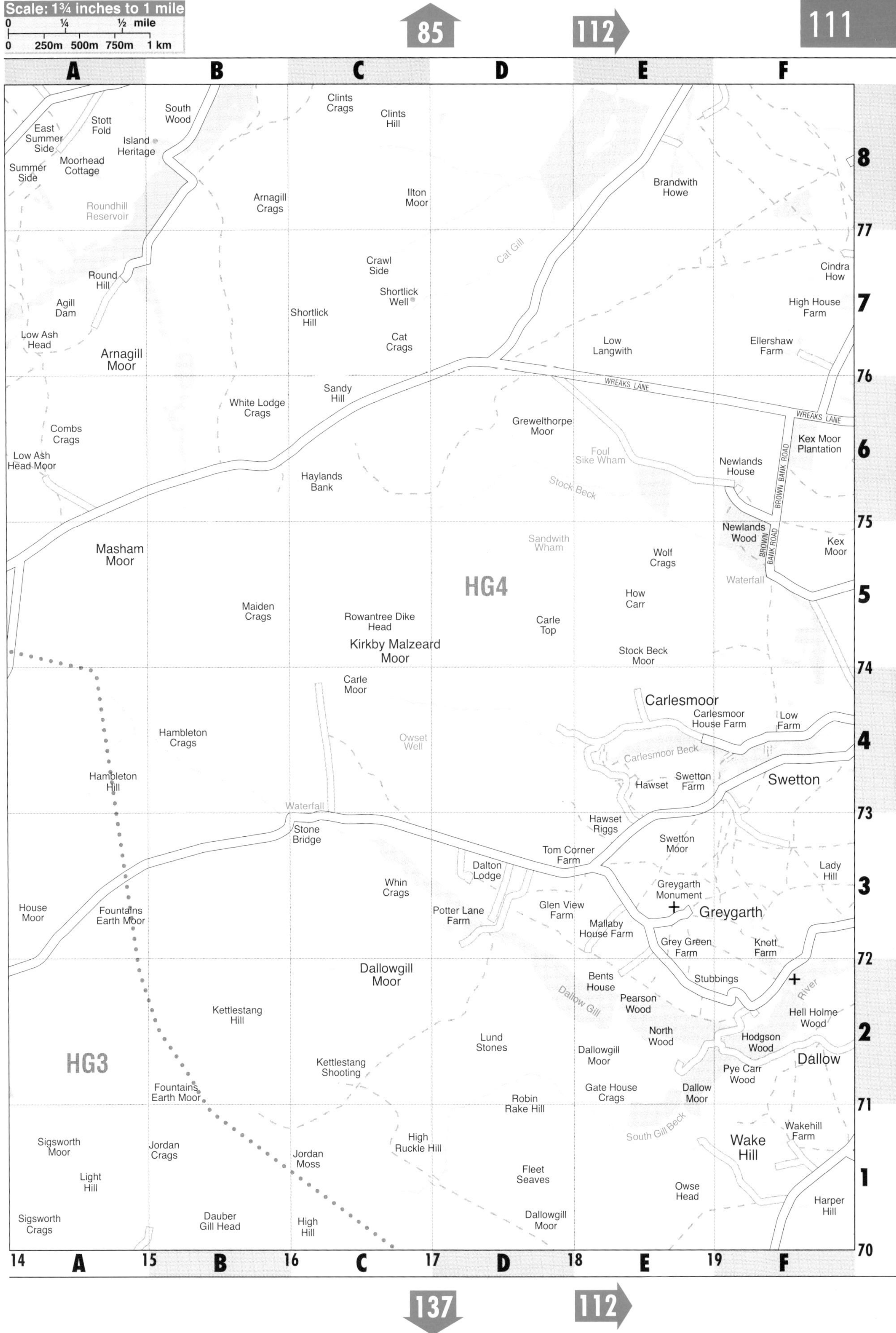

Scale: 1¾ inches to 1 mile

| 0 | ¼ | ½ mile |
| 0 | 250m | 500m | 750m | 1 km |

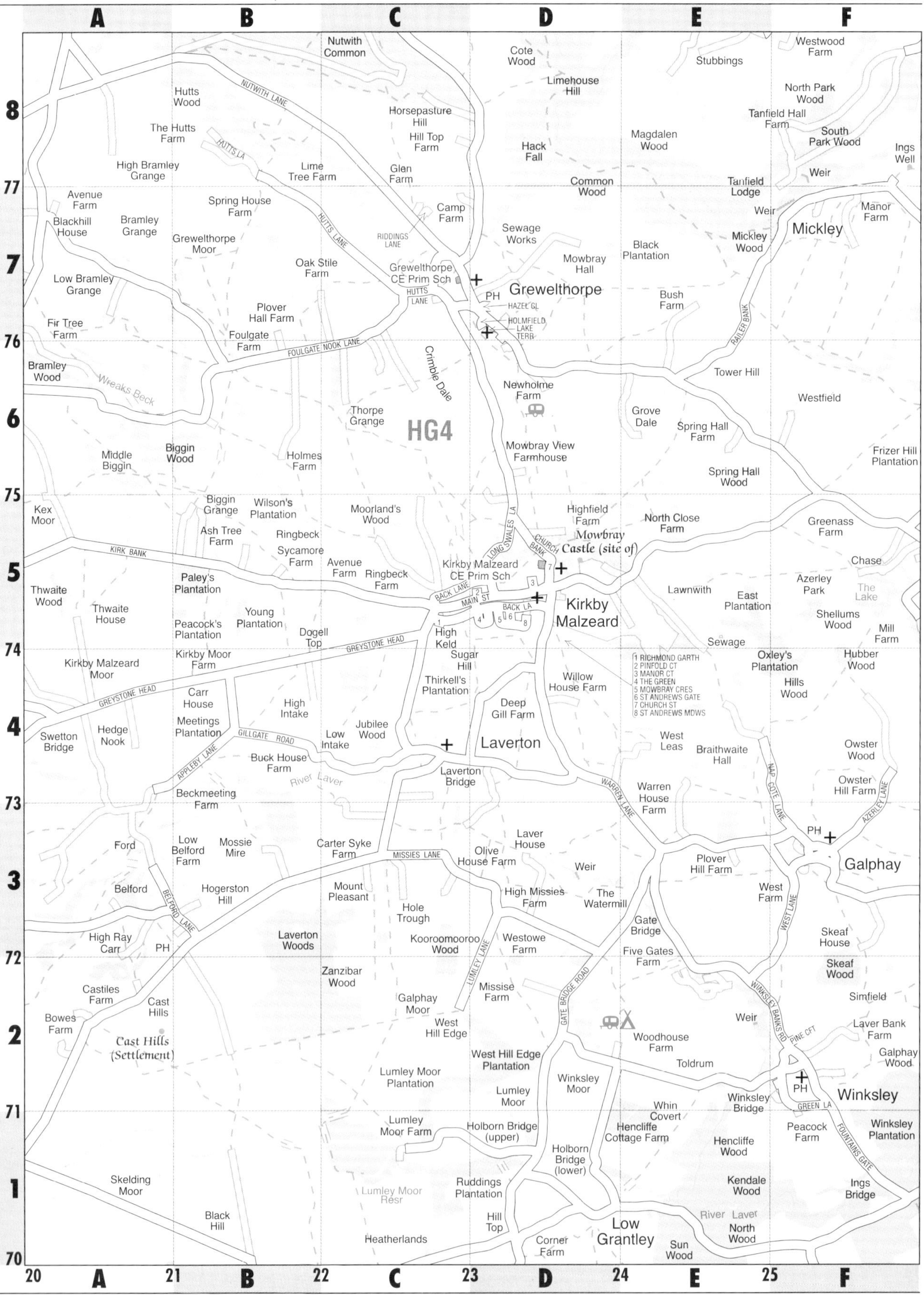

A   B   C   D   E   F

8

Nutwith Common
Cote Wood
Limehouse Hill
Stubbings
Westwood Farm
Hutts Wood
North Park Wood
Tanfield Hall Farm
South Park Wood
Ings Well
NUTWITH LANE
The Hutts Farm
Horsepasture Hill
Hack Fall
Magdalen Wood
HUTTS LA
Hill Top Farm
High Bramley Grange
Lime Tree Farm
Glen Farm
Common Wood
Tanfield Lodge
Weir
Mickley

77

Avenue Farm
Spring House Farm
Camp Farm
Weir
Mickley Wood
Manor Farm
Blackhill House
HUTTS LANE
Grewelthorpe Moor
RIDDINGS LANE
Sewage Works
Mowbray Hall
Black Plantation
Bramley Grange
Oak Stile Farm
Grewelthorpe CE Prim Sch
Grewelthorpe
Bush Farm

7

Low Bramley Grange
PH
HAZEL GL
RAILER BANK
Plover Hall Farm
HUTTS LANE
HOLMFIELD LAKE TERR
Fir Tree Farm
Foulgate Farm
FOULGATE NOOK LANE
Newholme Farm
Tower Hill
Westfield

76

Bramley Wood
Wreaks Beck
Crimble Dale
Grove Dale
Spring Hall Farm
Thorpe Grange
HG4
Mowbray View Farmhouse
Spring Hall Wood
Frizer Hill Plantation

6

Middle Biggin
Biggin Wood
Holmes Farm
Highfield Farm
North Close Farm
Greenass Farm
Kex Moor
Biggin Grange
Wilson's Plantation
Moorland's Wood
LONG SWALES LA
CHURCH BANK
Mowbray Castle (site of)
Chase
The Lake

75

Ash Tree Farm
Ringbeck
Kirkby Malzeard CE Prim Sch
Lawnwith
East Plantation
Azerley Park
Thwaite Wood
Paley's Plantation
Sycamore Farm
Avenue Farm
Ringbeck Farm
BACK LANE
MAIN ST
BACK LA
Kirkby Malzeard
Shellums Wood
Mill Farm

5

Thwaite House
Peacock's Plantation
Young Plantation
High Keld
Sewage
Hubber Wood
Kirkby Moor Farm
Dogell Top
GREYSTONE HEAD
Sugar Hill
Oxley's Plantation
Hills Wood

74

Kirkby Malzeard Moor
Carr House
High Intake
Thirkell's Plantation
Deep Gill Farm
Willow House Farm
1 RICHMOND GARTH
2 PINFOLD CT
3 MANOR CT
4 THE GREEN
5 MOWBRAY CRES
6 ST ANDREWS GATE
7 CHURCH ST
8 ST ANDREWS MDWS
GREYSTONE HEAD
Meetings Plantation
Jubilee Wood
Laverton
West Leas
Braithwaite Hall
Owster Wood

4

Swetton Farm
Hedge Nook
GILLGATE ROAD
Low Intake
Buck House Farm
Laverton Bridge
NAP COTE LANE
Owster Hill Farm
Warren House Farm
AZERLEY LANE

73

Beckmeeting Farm
River Laver
Laver House
Weir
PH
Galphay
APPLEBY LANE

3

Ford
Low Belford Farm
Mossie Mire
Carter Syke Farm
Olive House Farm
The Watermill
Plover Hill Farm
West Farm
Belford
Hogerston Hill
MISSIES LANE
High Missies Farm
WARREN LANE
WEST LANE
High Ray Carr
PH
Mount Pleasant
Hole Trough
Kooroomooroo Wood
Westowe Farm
Gate Bridge
Skeaf House

72

Castiles Farm
BELFORD LANE
Laverton Woods
Zanzibar Wood
Five Gates Farm
Simfield
Bowes Farm
Cast Hills
Missise Farm
GATE BRIDGE ROAD
Galphay Moor
Skeaf Wood
Laver Bank Farm
Cast Hills (Settlement)
West Hill Edge
Weir
WINKSLEY BANKS RD
Galphay Wood

2

Woodhouse Farm
Toldrum
PINE CFT
Lumley Moor Plantation
West Hill Edge Plantation
Winksley Moor
Winksley Bridge
PH
Winksley
LUMLEY LANE

71

Lumley Moor Farm
Lumley Moor
Whin Covert
Hencliffe Cottage Farm
Hencliffe Wood
GREEN LA
Peacock Farm
Winksley Plantation
FOUNTAINS GATE

1

Skelding Moor
Holborn Bridge (upper)
Ruddings Plantation
Holborn Bridge (lower)
Kendale Wood
Ings Bridge
Black Hill
Lumley Moor Resr
Hill Top
Corner Farm
Low Grantley
Sun Wood
North Wood
River Laver
Heatherlands

70

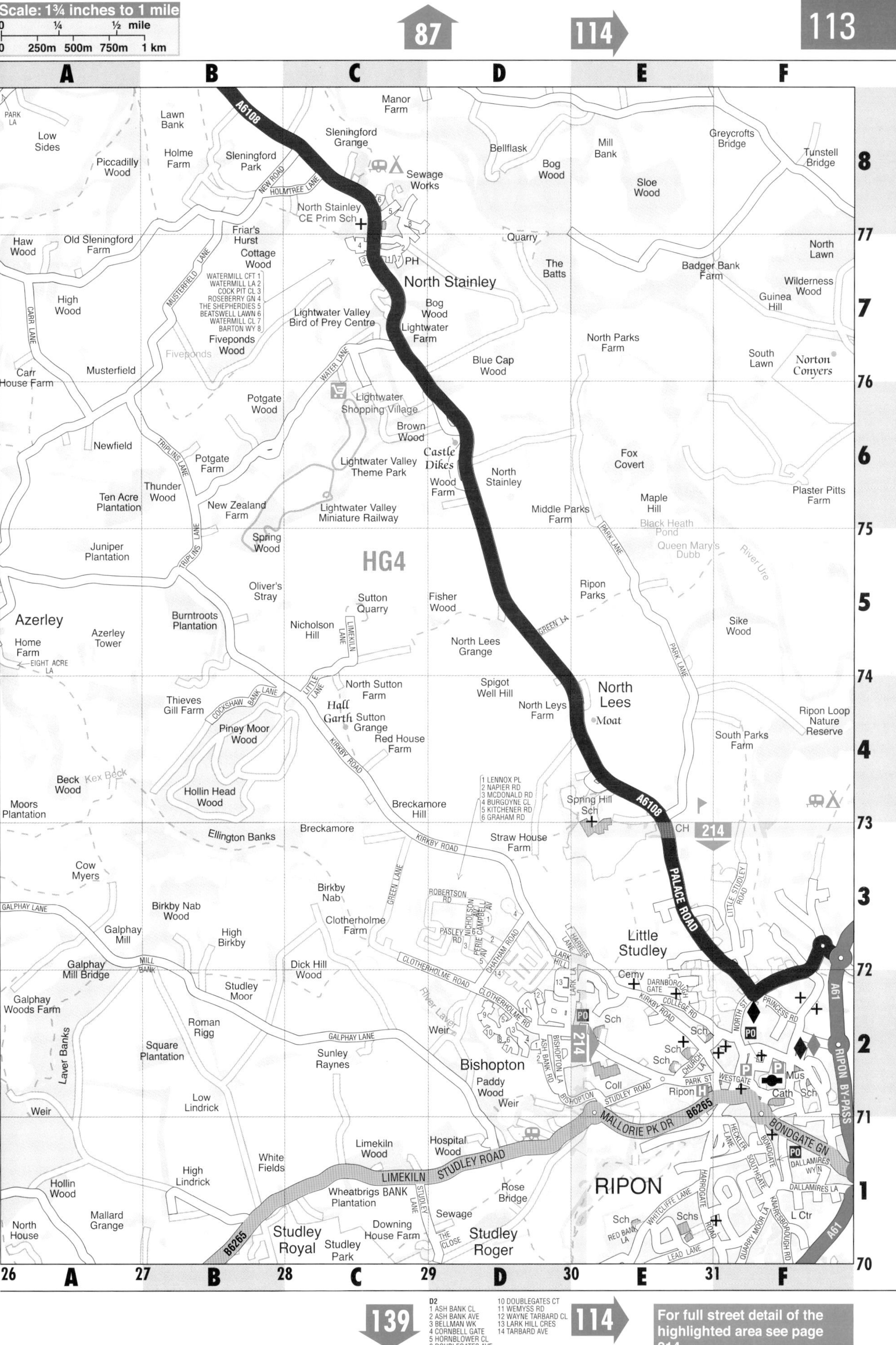

Scale: 1¾ inches to 1 mile

0 ¼ ½ mile
0 250m 500m 750m 1 km

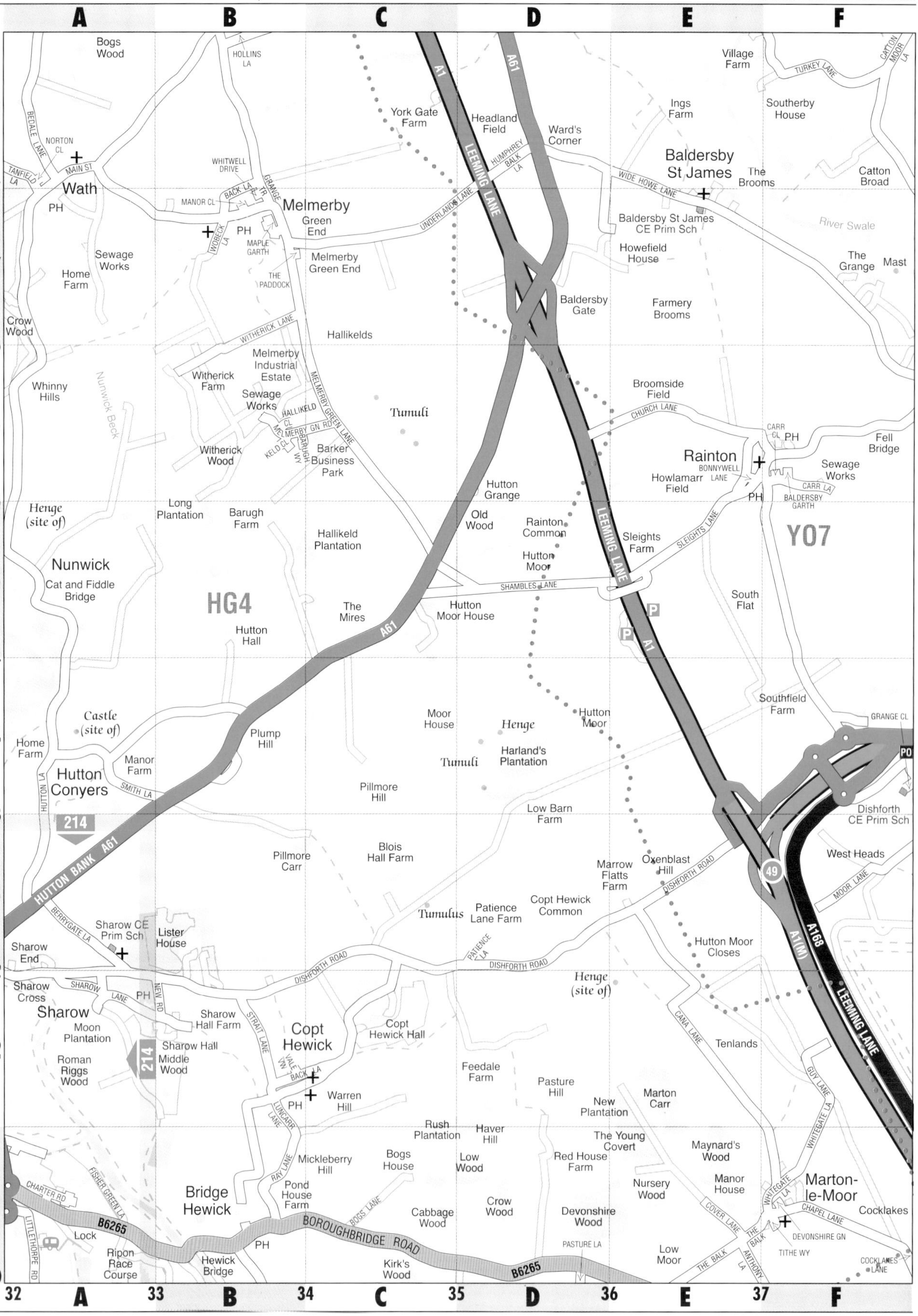

A B C D E F

8

Bogs Wood

HOLLINS LA

York Gate Farm

Headland Field

Ward's Corner

Ings Farm

Village Farm

TURKEY LANE

Southerby House

CATTON MOOR LANE

NORTON CL

BECALE LANE

MAIN ST

TANFIELD LA

77 Wath

PH

WHITWELL DRIVE

MANOR CL

BACK LA

GRANGE LA

Melmerby Green End

HUMPHREY BALK LA

UNDERLANDS LANE

LEEMING LANE

WIDE HOWE LANE

Baldersby St James

The Brooms

Catton Broad

Home Farm

Sewage Works

WITBECK LA

PH

MAPLE GARTH

THE PADDOCK

Melmerby Green End

Baldersby St James CE Prim Sch

Howefield House

River Swale

The Grange

Mast

7

Crow Wood

WITHERICK LANE

Hallikelds

Baldersby Gate

Farmery Brooms

76

Whinny Hills

Nunwick Back

Witherick Farm

Melmerby Industrial Estate

Sewage Works

HALLIKELD CL

MELMERBY GREEN RD

MELMERBY GREEN LANE

Tumuli

Broomside Field

CHURCH LANE

CARR CL

PH

Fell Bridge

6

Witherick Wood

KELD CL

Barker Business Park

Rainton

BONNYWELL LANE

Sewage Works

CARR LA

PH

BALDERSBY GARTH

75

Henge (site of)

Long Plantation

Barugh Farm

Hallikeld Plantation

Hutton Grange

Old Wood

Rainton Common

Howlamarr Field

Sleights Farm

SLEIGHTS LANE

Y07

Nunwick

HG4

Hutton Hall

The Mires

A61

Hutton Moor House

Hutton Moor

SHAMBLES LANE

5

Cat and Fiddle Bridge

South Flat

LEEMING LANE

P

P

74 A1

Castle (site of)

Plump Hill

Moor House

Henge

Hutton Moor

Southfield Farm

GRANGE CL

PO

4

Home Farm

HUTTON LA

Manor Farm

SMITH LA

Tumuli

Harland's Plantation

Hutton Conyers

Pillmore Hill

Low Barn Farm

Dishforth CE Prim Sch

West Heads

73

214

HUTTON BANK A61

Pillmore Carr

Blois Hall Farm

Marrow Flatts Farm

Oxenblast Hill

DISHFORTH ROAD

49

MOOR LANE

A1(M)

3

BERRYGATE LA

Sharow CE Prim Sch

Lister House

Tumulus

Patience Lane Farm

Copt Hewick Common

PATIENCE LA

Hutton Moor Closes

A168

LEEMING LANE

Sharow End

Sharow Cross

SHAROW LANE

PH

NEW RD

DISHFORTH ROAD

DISHFORTH ROAD

Henge (site of)

CANA LANE

GUY LANE

72

2

Sharow

Moon Plantation

214

Sharow Hall Middle Wood

STRAIT LANE

Sharow Hall Farm

Copt Hewick

Copt Hewick Hall

Feedale Farm

Pasture Hill

New Plantation

Marton Carr

Tenlands

Maynard's Wood

Manor House

WHITEGATE LA

Marton-le-Moor

71

Roman Riggs Wood

BACK LANE

PH

Warren Hill

LONGARR LANE

Rush Plantation

Haver Hill

The Young Covert

Nursery Wood

COVER LANE

WHITEGATE LA

Cocklakes

CHAPEL LANE

1

CHARTER RD

FISHER GREEN LA

Bridge Hewick

RAY LANE

Mickleberry Hill

Pond House Farm

Bogs House

Low Wood

Cabbage Wood

Crow Wood

Red House Farm

Devonshire Wood

Low Moor

THE BALK

ANTHON LA

Devonshire GN

TITHE WY

COCKLAKES LANE

70

LITTLEHORPE RD

Lock

B6265

Ripon Race Course

Hewick Bridge

PH

BOGS LANE

BOROUGHBRIDGE ROAD

Kirk's Wood

B6265

PASTURE LA

32 A 33 B 34 C 35 D 36 E 37 F

For full street detail of the highlighted area see page 214.

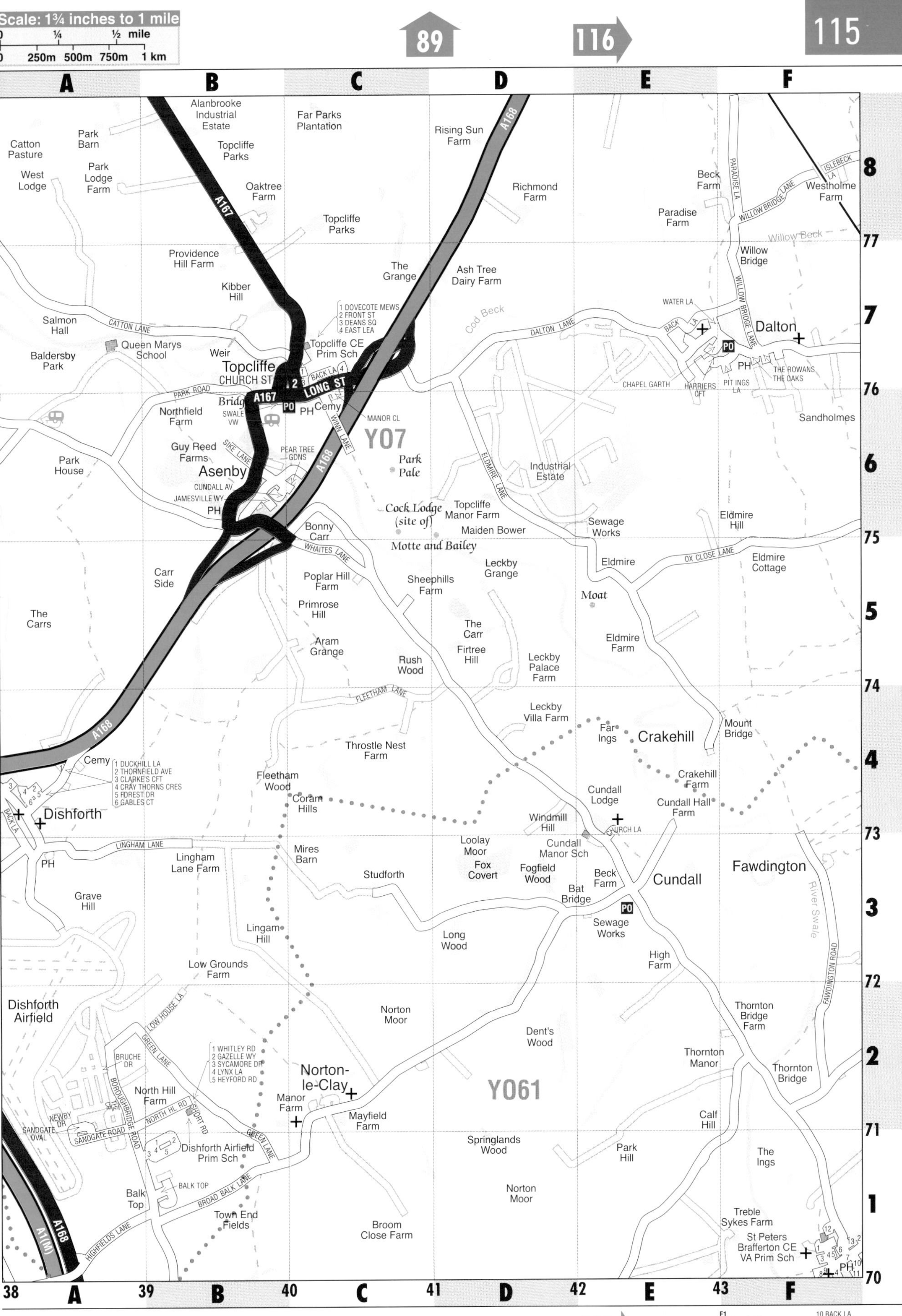

A   B   C   D   E   F

8
77
7
76
6
75
5
74
4
73
3
72
2
71
1
70

Catton Pasture
Park Barn
West Lodge
Park Lodge Farm
Alanbrooke Industrial Estate
Topcliffe Parks
Oaktree Farm
Far Parks Plantation
Topcliffe Parks
Rising Sun Farm
Richmond Farm
Beck Farm
Paradise Farm
Westholme Farm
Willow Beck
Willow Bridge
Dalton

Providence Hill Farm
Kibber Hill
A167
The Grange
Ash Tree Dairy Farm
Cod Beck
DALTON LANE
WATER LA
BACK LA
PH
THE ROWANS THE OAKS

Salmon Hall
Baldersby Park
CATTON LANE
Queen Marys School
Weir
Topcliffe
CHURCH ST
1 DOVECOTE MEWS
2 FRONT ST
3 DEANS SQ
4 EAST LEA
Topcliffe CE Prim Sch
CHAPEL GARTH
HARRIERS CFT
PIT INGS LA

Northfield Farm
PARK ROAD
A167
Bridge
SWALE VW
PO
PH
Cemy
MANOR CL
Y07
Industrial Estate
Sandholmes

Park House
Guy Reed Farms
Asenby
SIKE LANE
PEAR TREE GDNS
WIDM LANE
A168
Park Pale
Cock Lodge (site of)
Topcliffe Manor Farm
Maiden Bower
ELDMIRE LANE
Sewage Works
Eldmire Hill

CUNDALL AV
JAMESVILLE WY
PH
Bonny Carr
WHAITES LANE
Motte and Bailey
Sheephills Farm
Leckby Grange
Moat
Eldmire
OX CLOSE LANE
Eldmire Cottage

Carr Side
Poplar Hill Farm
Primrose Hill
The Carr
Firtree Hill
Leckby Palace Farm
Eldmire Farm

The Carrs
Aram Grange
Rush Wood
Leckby Villa Farm
FLEETHAM LANE
Far Ings
Crakehill
Mount Bridge

Cemy
1 DUCKHILL LA
2 THORNFIELD AVE
3 CLARKE'S CFT
4 CRAY THORNS CRES
5 FOREST DR
6 GABLES CT
Throstle Nest Farm
Fleetham Wood
Crakehill Farm
Cundall Hall Farm

Dishforth
PH
LINGHAM LANE
Lingham Lane Farm
Coram Hills
Mires Barn
Cundall Lodge
Windmill Hill
Cundall Manor Sch
CHURCH LA
Fawdington

Grave Hill
LOW HOUSE LA
Lingham Hill
Studforth
Loolay Moor
Fox Covert
Fogfield Wood
Beck Farm
Cundall
River Swale

Low Grounds Farm
Long Wood
Bat Bridge
PO
Sewage Works
High Farm
FAWDINGTON ROAD

Dishforth Airfield
GREEN LANE
BOROUGHBRIDGE ROAD
Bruche Dr
North Hill Farm
NORTH HL RD
1 WHITLEY RD
2 GAZELLE WY
3 SYCAMORE DR
4 LYNX LA
5 HEYFORD RD
Norton Moor
Dent's Wood
Thornton Bridge Farm
Thornton Manor
Thornton Bridge

Newby Dr
Sandgate Oval
SANDGATE ROAD
Norton-le-Clay
Manor Farm
Mayfield Farm
Y061
Springlands Wood
Park Hill
Calf Hill
The Ings

Balk Top
BALK TOP
BROAD BALK LANE
Town End Fields
Broom Close Farm
Norton Moor
Treble Sykes Farm
St Peters Brafferton CE VA Prim Sch
PH

A1(M)
A168
HIGHFIELDS LANE

38 39 40 41 42 43

F1
1 HOLLY GARTH
2 MANOR DR
3 BAFFERTON HALL GDNS
4 HALL LANE
5 FOX GARTH
6 THE ORCHARDS
7 RASKELF RD
8 THE MALTINGS
9 BRIDGE ST
10 BACK LA
11 THE LEAS
12 ST PETERS CL
13 BIRCHWOOD GDNS

115
90
Scale: 1¾ inches to 1 mile

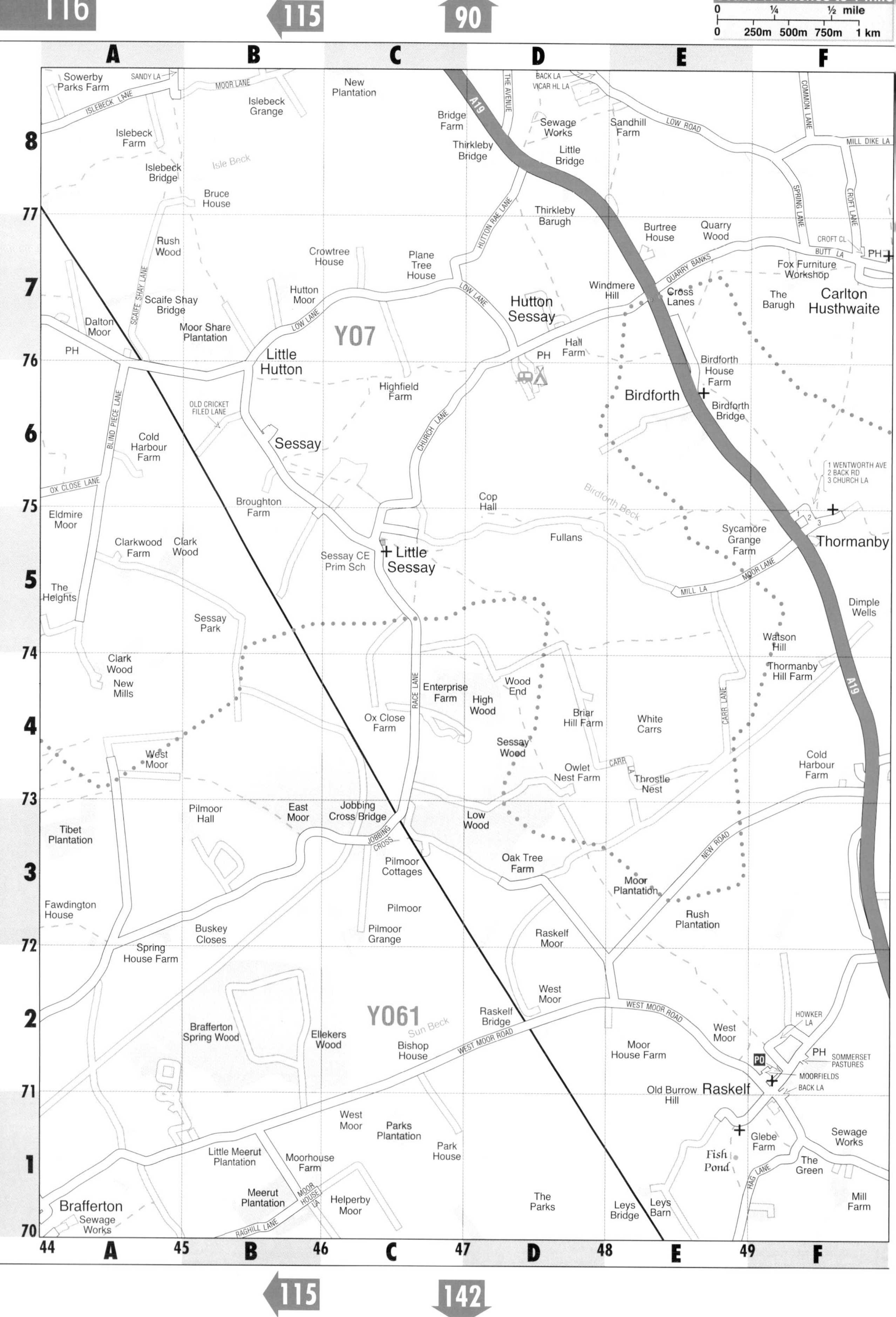
A B C D E F
8
77
7
76
6
75
5
74
4
73
3
72
2
71
1
70
44 45 46 47 48 49
Sowerby Parks Farm
SANDY LA
ISLEBECK LANE
MOOR LANE
New Plantation
Islebeck Grange
Islebeck Farm
Isle Beck
Islebeck Bridge
Bruce House
Rush Wood
SCAIFE SHAY LANE
Scaife Shay Bridge
Dalton Moor
PH
Moor Share Plantation
Hutton Moor
LOW LANE
Crowtree House
Plane Tree House
Y07
Little Hutton
Highfield Farm
BLIND PIECE LANE
OLD CRICKET FILED LANE
Cold Harbour Farm
Sessay
OX CLOSE LANE
Broughton Farm
Eldmire Moor
Clarkwood Farm
Clark Wood
Sessay CE Prim Sch
Little Sessay
The Heights
Sessay Park
Clark Wood
New Mills
West Moor
Tibet Plantation
Pilmoor Hall
East Moor
Jobbing Cross Bridge
JOBBING CROSS
Fawdington House
Buskey Closes
Spring House Farm
Pilmoor Cottages
Pilmoor
Pilmoor Grange
Y061
Brafferton Spring Wood
Ellekers Wood
Sun Beck
Bishop House
WEST MOOR ROAD
West Moor
Parks Plantation
Little Meerut Plantation
Moorhouse Farm
Meerut Plantation
MOOR HOUSE LA
Helperby Moor
RAGHILL LANE
Brafferton
Sewage Works
Park House
A19
Bridge Farm
THE AVENUE
BACK LA
VICAR HL LA
Sewage Works
Thirkleby Bridge
Little Bridge
Sandhill Farm
LOW ROAD
HUTTON RAE LANE
Thirkleby Barugh
LOW LANE
Hutton Sessay
PH
Hall Farm
CHURCH LANE
Cop Hall
Fullans
RACE LANE
Enterprise Farm
Ox Close Farm
High Wood
Wood End
Sessay Wood
Low Wood
Oak Tree Farm
Raskelf Moor
West Moor
Raskelf Bridge
The Parks
Burtree House
Quarry Wood
Windmere Hill
QUARRY BANKS
Cross Lanes
Birdforth
Birdforth House Farm
Birdforth Bridge
Birdforth Beck
Sycamore Grange Farm
MILL LA
MOOR LANE
Briar Hill Farm
White Carrs
Owlet Nest Farm
CARR LA
Throstle Nest
CARR LANE
Moor Plantation
NEW ROAD
Rush Plantation
WEST MOOR ROAD
Moor House Farm
West Moor
Old Burrow Hill
Raskelf
Leys Bridge
Leys Barn
Fish Pond
HAG LANE
COMMON LANE
MILL DIKE LA
SPRING LANE
CROFT LANE
CROFT CL
BUTT LA
PH
Fox Furniture Workshop
The Barugh
Carlton Husthwaite
1 WENTWORTH AVE
2 BACK RD
3 CHURCH LA
Thormanby
Dimple Wells
Watson Hill
Thormanby Hill Farm
Cold Harbour Farm
HOWKER LA
PH
PO
SOMMERSET PASTURES
MOORFIELDS
BACK LA
Glebe Farm
Sewage Works
The Green
Mill Farm

115
142

91
118

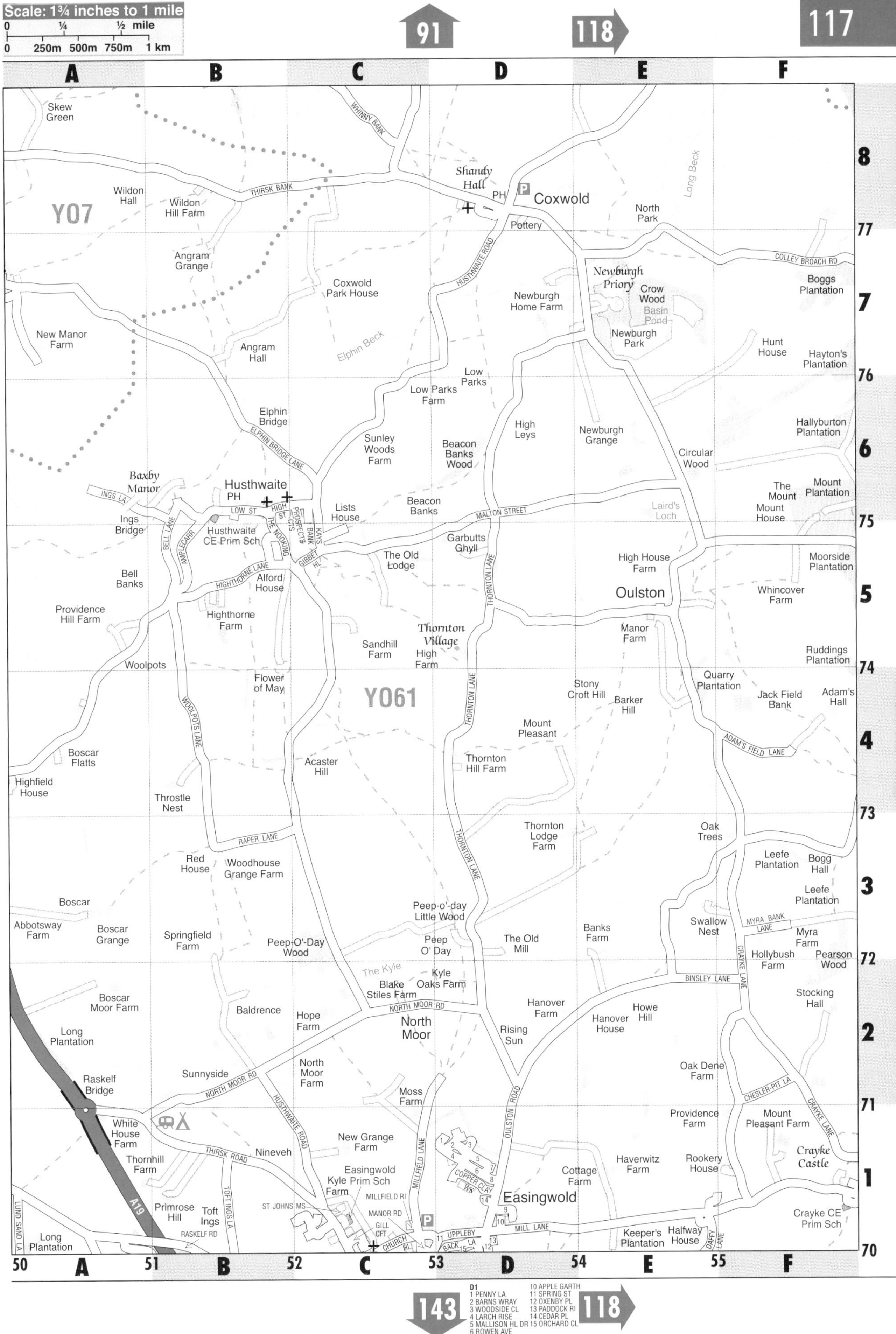
Scale: 1¾ inches to 1 mile
0 ¼ ½ mile
0 250m 500m 750m 1 km
A B C D E F
8 77 7 76 6 75 5 74 4 73 3 72 2 71 1 70
50 51 52 53 54 55
Skew Green
Wildon Hall
Wildon Hill Farm
YO7
THIRSK BANK
WHINNY BANK
Shandy Hall
PH
Coxwold
Pottery
North Park
Long Beck
COLLEY BROACH RD
Boggs Plantation
Angram Grange
HUSTHWAITE ROAD
Newburgh Priory
Crow Wood
Basin Pond
Newburgh Home Farm
Coxwold Park House
New Manor Farm
Angram Hall
Elphin Beck
Newburgh Park
Hunt House
Hayton's Plantation
Low Parks
Low Parks Farm
Elphin Bridge
ELPHIN BRIDGE LANE
High Leys
Newburgh Grange
Hallyburton Plantation
Sunley Woods Farm
Beacon Banks Wood
Circular Wood
Baxby Manor
Husthwaite
PH
INGS LA
Beacon Banks
The Mount
Mount Plantation
Mount House
LOW ST
HIGH ST
CTS
PROSPECTS
KAYS BANK
Lists House
MALTON STREET
Laird's Loch
Ings Bridge
BELL LANE
AMPLECARR
Husthwaite CE Prim Sch
THE NOOKING
GIBBET HL
Garbutts Ghyll
The Old Lodge
High House Farm
Moorside Plantation
HIGHTHORNE LANE
Alford House
THORNTON LANE
Oulston
Whincover Farm
Bell Banks
Providence Hill Farm
Highthorne Farm
Thornton Village
Manor Farm
Sandhill Farm
High Farm
Ruddings Plantation
Woolpots
Flower of May
YO61
Stony Croft Hill
Barker Hill
Quarry Plantation
Jack Field Bank
Adam's Hall
WOOLPOTS LANE
Mount Pleasant
ADAM'S FIELD LANE
Boscar Flatts
Acaster Hill
Thornton Hill Farm
Highfield House
Throstle Nest
Thornton Lodge Farm
Oak Trees
RAPER LANE
Leefe Plantation
Bogg Hall
Red House
Woodhouse Grange Farm
Leefe Plantation
Boscar
Peep-o'-day Little Wood
Swallow Nest
MYRA BANK LANE
Abbotsway Farm
Boscar Grange
Springfield Farm
Peep-O'-Day Wood
Peep O' Day
The Old Mill
Banks Farm
Myra Farm
CRAYKE LANE
Hollybush Farm
Pearson Wood
The Kyle
Kyle Oaks Farm
Blake Stiles Farm
BINSLEY LANE
Stocking Hall
Boscar Moor Farm
Baldrence
NORTH MOOR RD
Hanover Farm
Hope Farm
North Moor
Hanover House
Howe Hill
Rising Sun
Long Plantation
Raskelf Bridge
Sunnyside
North Moor Farm
Oak Dene Farm
NORTH MOOR RD
Moss Farm
CHESLER-PIT LA
HUSTHWAITE ROAD
OULSTON ROAD
Providence Farm
Mount Pleasant Farm
CRAYKE LANE
White House Farm
Thornhill Farm
THIRSK ROAD
Nineveh
New Grange Farm
MILLFIELD LANE
Crayke Castle
Haverwitz Farm
Rookery House
Easingwold Kyle Prim Sch
Cottage Farm
COPPER CLAY WK
A19
Kyle Farm
MILLFIELD RI
Easingwold
Crayke CE Prim Sch
LUND SAND LA
Primrose Hill
Toft Ings
TOFT INGS LA
ST JOHNS MS
MANOR RD
P
GILL CFT
MILL LANE
Keeper's Plantation
Halfway House
DAFFY LANE
Long Plantation
RASKELF RD
CHURCH HL
UPPLEBY
BACK LA
D1
1 PENNY LA
2 BARNS WRAY
3 WOODSIDE CL
4 LARCH RISE
5 MALLISON HL DR
6 ROWEN AVE
7 TOWER CFT
8 LIME TREE AVE
9 THORNLANDS
10 APPLE GARTH
11 SPRING ST
12 OXENBY PL
13 PADDOCK RI
14 CEDAR PL
15 ORCHARD CL

143
118

117
92

Scale: 1¾ inches to 1 mile

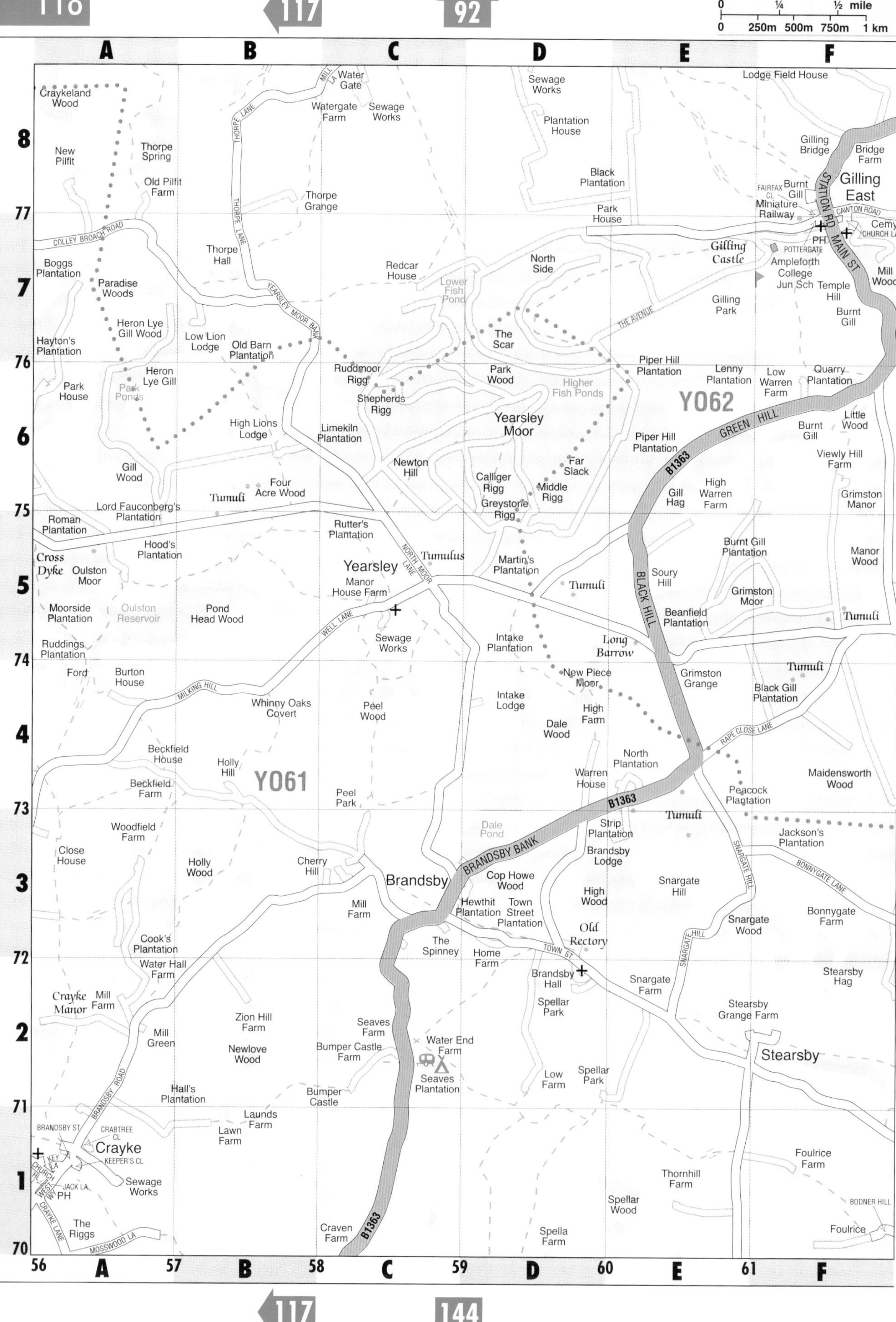

Craykeland Wood
Water Gate
Watergate Farm
Sewage Works
Plantation House
Lodge Field House
Gilling Bridge
Bridge Farm
Gilling East
New Pilfit
Thorpe Spring
Old Pilfit Farm
Thorpe Grange
Black Plantation
Park House
Burnt Gill
Miniature Railway
Cemy
PH
Gilling Castle
Ampleforth College
Jun Sch
Temple Hill
Mill Wood
Boggs Plantation
Paradise Woods
Thorpe Hall
Redcar House
Lower Fish Pond
North Side
Gilling Park
Burnt Gill
Heron Lye Gill Wood
Low Lion Lodge
Old Barn Plantation
The Scar
Hayton's Plantation
Ruddmoor Rigg
Park Wood
Piper Hill Plantation
Lenny Plantation
Low Warren Farm
Quarry Plantation
Park House
Park Ponds
Heron Lye Gill
Shepherds Rigg
Higher Fish Ponds
YO62
High Lions Lodge
Limekiln Plantation
Yearsley Moor
Piper Hill Plantation
Burnt Gill
Little Wood
Viewly Hill Farm
Gill Wood
Newton Hill
Far Slack
Calliger Rigg
Middle Rigg
Gill Hag
High Warren Farm
Grimston Manor
Tumuli
Four Acre Wood
Lord Fauconberg's Plantation
Greystone Rigg
Roman Plantation
Rutter's Plantation
Hood's Plantation
Tumulus
Martin's Plantation
Burnt Gill Plantation
Manor Wood
Cross Dyke
Oulston Moor
Yearsley
Manor House Farm
Tumuli
Soury Hill
Grimston Moor
Moorside Plantation
Oulston Reservoir
Pond Head Wood
Beanfield Plantation
Tumuli
Ruddings Plantation
Sewage Works
Intake Plantation
Long Barrow
Ford
Burton House
New Piece Moor
Grimston Grange
Tumuli
Black Gill Plantation
Whinny Oaks Covert
Peel Wood
Intake Lodge
Dale Wood
High Farm
Beckfield House
Holly Hill
YO61
North Plantation
Warren House
Maidensworth Wood
Beckfield Farm
Peel Park
Peacock Plantation
Tumuli
Woodfield Farm
Dale Pond
Strip Plantation
Jackson's Plantation
Close House
Holly Wood
Cherry Hill
Brandsby
Cop Howe Wood
Brandsby Lodge
Snargate Hill
Mill Farm
Hewthit Plantation
Town Street Plantation
High Wood
Old Rectory
Snargate Wood
Bonnygate Farm
Cook's Plantation
The Spinney
Home Farm
Water Hall Farm
Brandsby Hall
Snargate Farm
Stearsby Hag
Crayke Manor
Mill Farm
Spellar Park
Stearsby Grange Farm
Zion Hill Farm
Seaves Farm
Mill Green
Newlove Wood
Bumper Castle Farm
Water End Farm
Stearsby
Seaves Plantation
Low Farm
Spellar Park
Hall's Plantation
Bumper Castle
Launds Farm
Lawn Farm
Crayke
Sewage Works
PH
Foulrice Farm
Thornhill Farm
Spellar Wood
The Riggs
Craven Farm
Spella Farm
Foulrice
COLLEY BROACH ROAD
THORPE LANE
MILL LA
YEARSLEY MOOR BANK
NORTH MOOR LANE
WELL LANE
MILKING HILL
BRANDSBY BANK
B1363
GREEN HILL
BLACK HILL
THE AVENUE
STATION RD
MAIN ST
CAWTON ROAD
CHURCH LA
POTTERGATE
FAIRFAX CL
RAPE CLOSE LANE
SNARGATE HILL
BONNYGATE LANE
TOWN ST
BRANDSBY ROAD
BRANDSBY ST
CRABTREE CL
KEEPER'S CL
KEY LA
CHURCH HL
WEST WY
JACK LA
CRAYKE LANE
MOSSWOOD LA
BODNER HILL

117
144

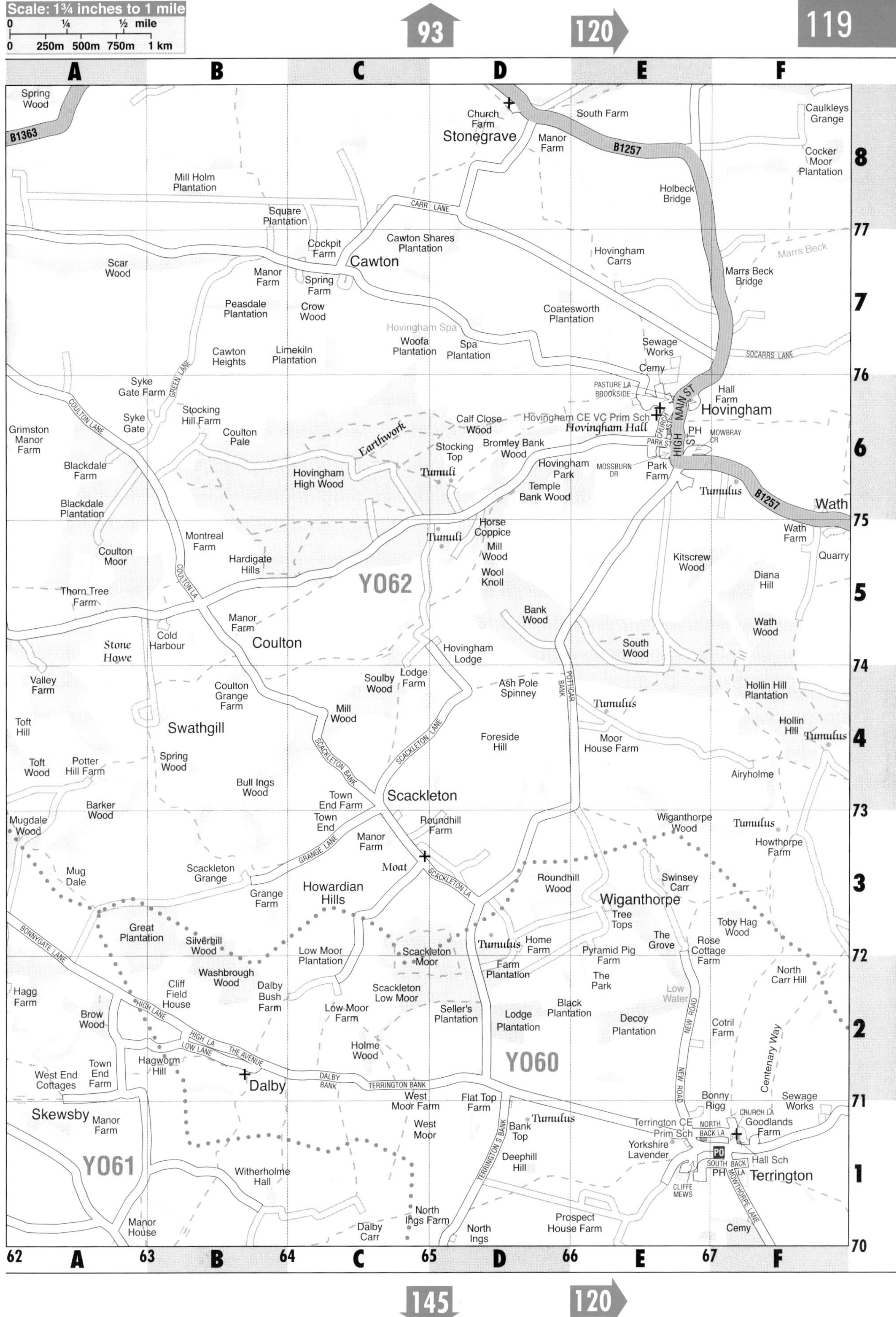
Scale: 1¾ inches to 1 mile
0 ¼ ½ mile
0 250m 500m 750m 1 km
93
120
A B C D E F
8 77 7 76 6 75 5 74 4 73 3 72 2 71 1 70
62 63 64 65 66 67
Spring Wood
B1363
Church Farm
Stonegrave
South Farm
Manor Farm
B1257
Caulkleys Grange
Cocker Moor Plantation
Mill Holm Plantation
Holbeck Bridge
Square Plantation
CARR LANE
Cockpit Farm
Cawton Shares Plantation
Cawton
Hovingham Carrs
Marrs Beck
Marrs Beck Bridge
Scar Wood
Manor Farm
Spring Farm
Peasdale Plantation
Crow Wood
Coatesworth Plantation
Hovingham Spa
Woofa Plantation
Spa Plantation
Sewage Works
SOCARRS LANE
Cawton Heights
Limekiln Plantation
Cemy
GREEN LANE
Syke Gate Farm
PASTURE LA
BROOKSIDE
MAIN ST
Hall Farm
Hovingham
COULTON LANE
Stocking Hill Farm
Calf Close Wood
Hovingham CE VC Prim Sch
Grimston Manor Farm
Syke Gate
Coulton Pale
Earthwork
Hovingham Hall
CHURCH ST
PH
MOWBRAY CR
Stocking Top
Bromley Bank Wood
PARK ST
HIGH ST
Blackdale Farm
Hovingham High Wood
Tumuli
Hovingham Park
MOSSBURN DR
Park Farm
Temple Bank Wood
Tumulus
Blackdale Plantation
Wath
Horse Coppice
Tumuli
Wath Farm
Montreal Farm
Coulton Moor
Mill Wood
Kitscrew Wood
Quarry
Hardigate Hills
Diana Hill
COULTON LA
Wool Knoll
Thorn Tree Farm
YO62
Bank Wood
Manor Farm
Wath Wood
Stone Howe
Cold Harbour
Coulton
Hovingham Lodge
South Wood
Valley Farm
Lodge Farm
Soulby Wood
Ash Pole Spinney
POTTICAR BANK
Hollin Hill Plantation
Coulton Grange Farm
Tumulus
Mill Wood
Toft Hill
Swathgill
Hollin Hill
Tumulus
Foreside Hill
Moor House Farm
SCACKLETON LANE
SCACKLETON BANK
Toft Wood
Potter Hill Farm
Spring Wood
Airyholme
Bull Ings Wood
Town End Farm
Scackleton
Barker Wood
Wiganthorpe Wood
Mugdale Wood
Town End
Roundhill Farm
Tumulus
Howthorpe Farm
GRANGE LANE
Manor Farm
Mug Dale
Moat
Scackleton Grange
Roundhill Wood
Swinsey Carr
Grange Farm
Howardian Hills
SCACKLETON LA
Wiganthorpe
Tree Tops
Toby Hag Wood
Great Plantation
BONNYGATE LANE
Silverbill Wood
The Grove
Tumulus
Home Farm
Rose Cottage Farm
Scackleton Moor
Pyramid Pig Farm
Low Moor Plantation
Farm Plantation
North Carr Hill
Washbrough Wood
The Park
Hagg Farm
Cliff Field House
Dalby Bush Farm
Scackleton Low Moor
Low Water
Black Plantation
Brow Wood
HIGH LANE
Low Moor Farm
Seller's Plantation
Lodge Plantation
Decoy Plantation
NEW ROAD
Cotril Farm
Centenary Way
HIGH LA
LOW LANE
THE AVENUE
Holme Wood
YO60
Town End Farm
Hagworm Hill
West End Cottages
Dalby
DALBY BANK
TERRINGTON BANK
West Moor Farm
Flat Top Farm
Bonny Rigg
Sewage Works
CHURCH LA
Skewsby
Manor Farm
Tumulus
Bank Top
Terrington CE Prim Sch
NORTH BACK LA
Goodlands Farm
West Moor
TERRINGTON S BANK
Yorkshire Lavender
PO
Hall Sch
YO61
Deephill Hill
SOUTH BACK LA
PH
Terrington
Witherholme Hall
CLIFFE MEWS
MOWTHORPE LANE
North Ings Farm
Prospect House Farm
Manor House
Dalby Carr
North Ings
Cemy
145
120

119
94

Scale: 1¾ inches to 1 mile

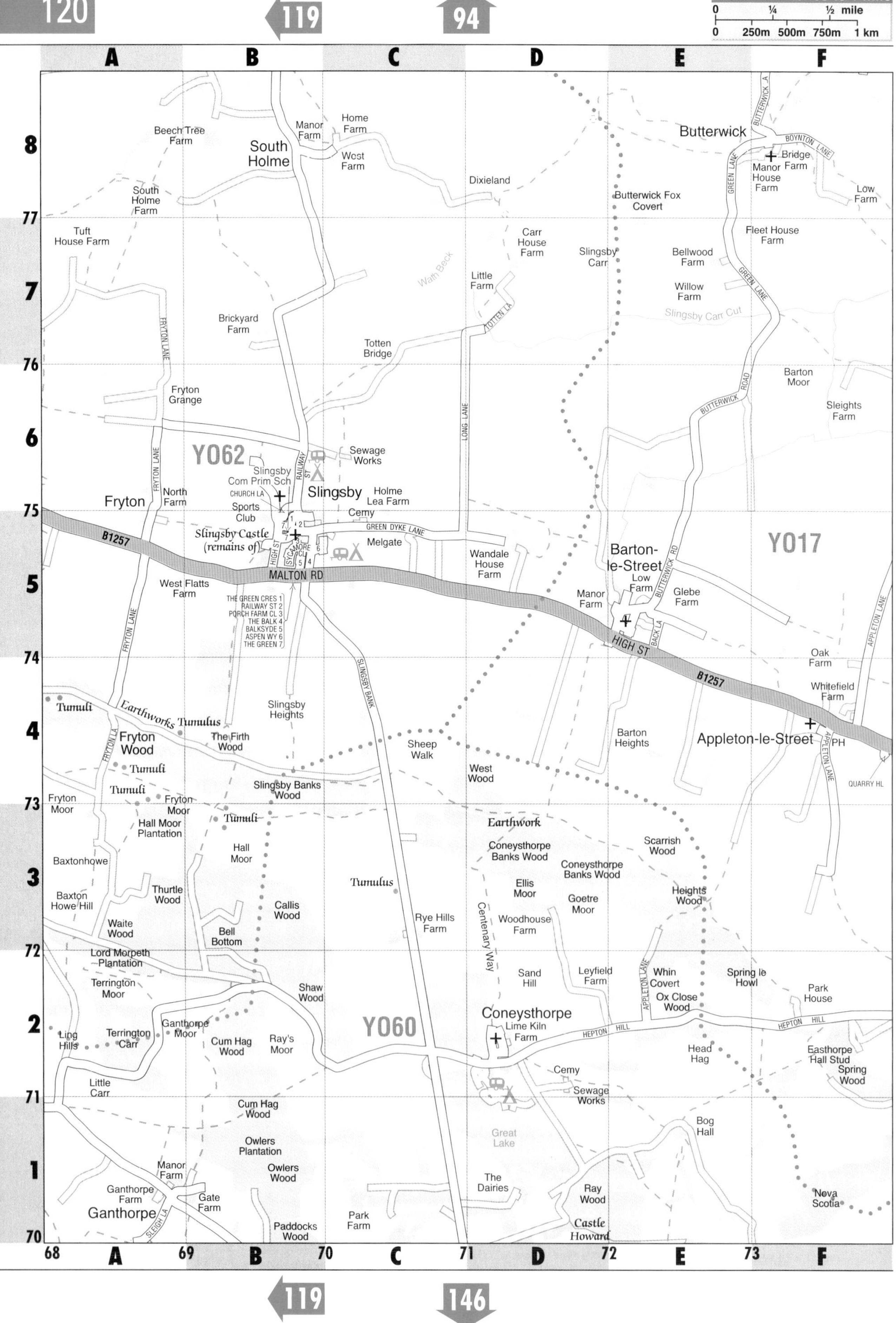
South Holme
Beech Tree Farm
Manor Farm
Home Farm
West Farm
South Holme Farm
Dixieland
Butterwick
Bridge Farm
Manor House Farm
Low Farm
Butterwick Fox Covert
Tuft House Farm
Carr House Farm
Slingsby Carr
Bellwood Farm
Fleet House Farm
Little Farm
Willow Farm
Slingsby Carr Cut
Brickyard Farm
Totten Bridge
Barton Moor
Sleights Farm
Fryton Grange
YO62
Sewage Works
Slingsby Com Prim Sch
Slingsby
Holme Lea Farm
Fryton
North Farm
Sports Club
Cemy
Slingsby Castle (remains of)
Melgate
Wandale House Farm
Barton-le-Street
YO17
Low Farm
Glebe Farm
Manor Farm
MALTON RD
B1257
HIGH ST
West Flatts Farm
THE GREEN CRES 1
RAILWAY ST 2
PORCH FARM CL 3
THE BALK 4
BALKSYDE 5
ASPEN WY 6
THE GREEN 7
Oak Farm
Whitefield Farm
Slingsby Heights
Tumuli
Earthworks
Tumulus
Fryton Wood
The Firth Wood
Sheep Walk
Barton Heights
Appleton-le-Street
PH
QUARRY HL
West Wood
Slingsby Banks Wood
Fryton Moor
Hall Moor Plantation
Earthwork
Coneysthorpe Banks Wood
Scarrish Wood
Hall Moor
Baxtonhowe
Tumulus
Ellis Moor
Goetre Moor
Heights Wood
Baxton Howe Hill
Thurtle Wood
Callis Wood
Waite Wood
Bell Bottom
Rye Hills Farm
Centenary Way
Woodhouse Farm
Lord Morpeth Plantation
Terrington Moor
Shaw Wood
Sand Hill
Leyfield Farm
Whin Covert
Spring le Howl
Park House
Ox Close Wood
Ganthorpe Moor
YO60
Coneysthorpe
Lime Kiln Farm
HEPTON HILL
Ling Hills
Terrington Carr
Cum Hag Wood
Ray's Moor
Head Hag
Easthorpe Hall Stud
Spring Wood
Little Carr
Cemy
Sewage Works
Cum Hag Wood
Great Lake
Bog Hall
Owlers Plantation
Owlers Wood
Manor Farm
The Dairies
Ray Wood
Nova Scotia
Ganthorpe Farm
Gate Farm
Ganthorpe
Paddocks Wood
Park Farm
Castle Howard

119
146

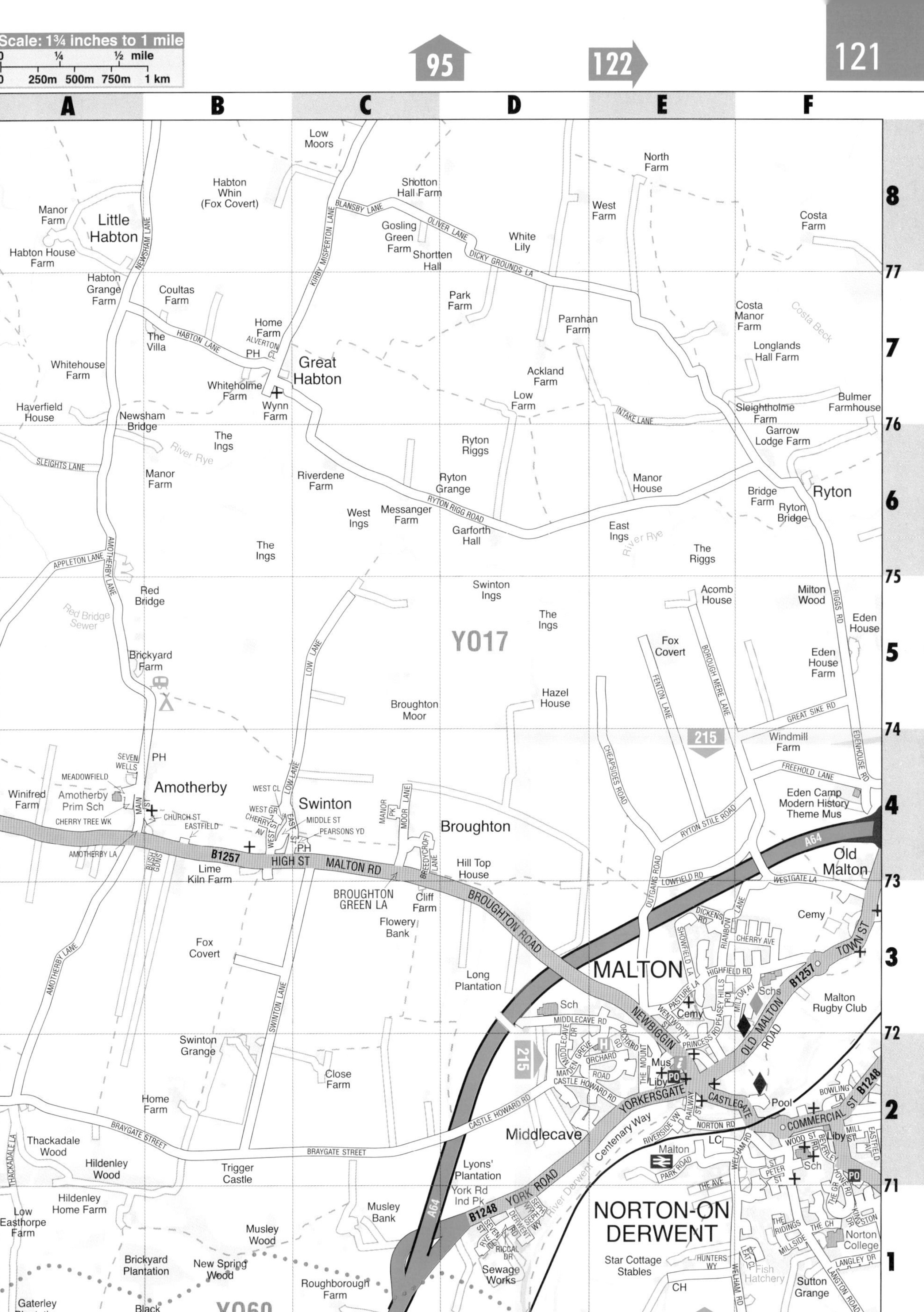

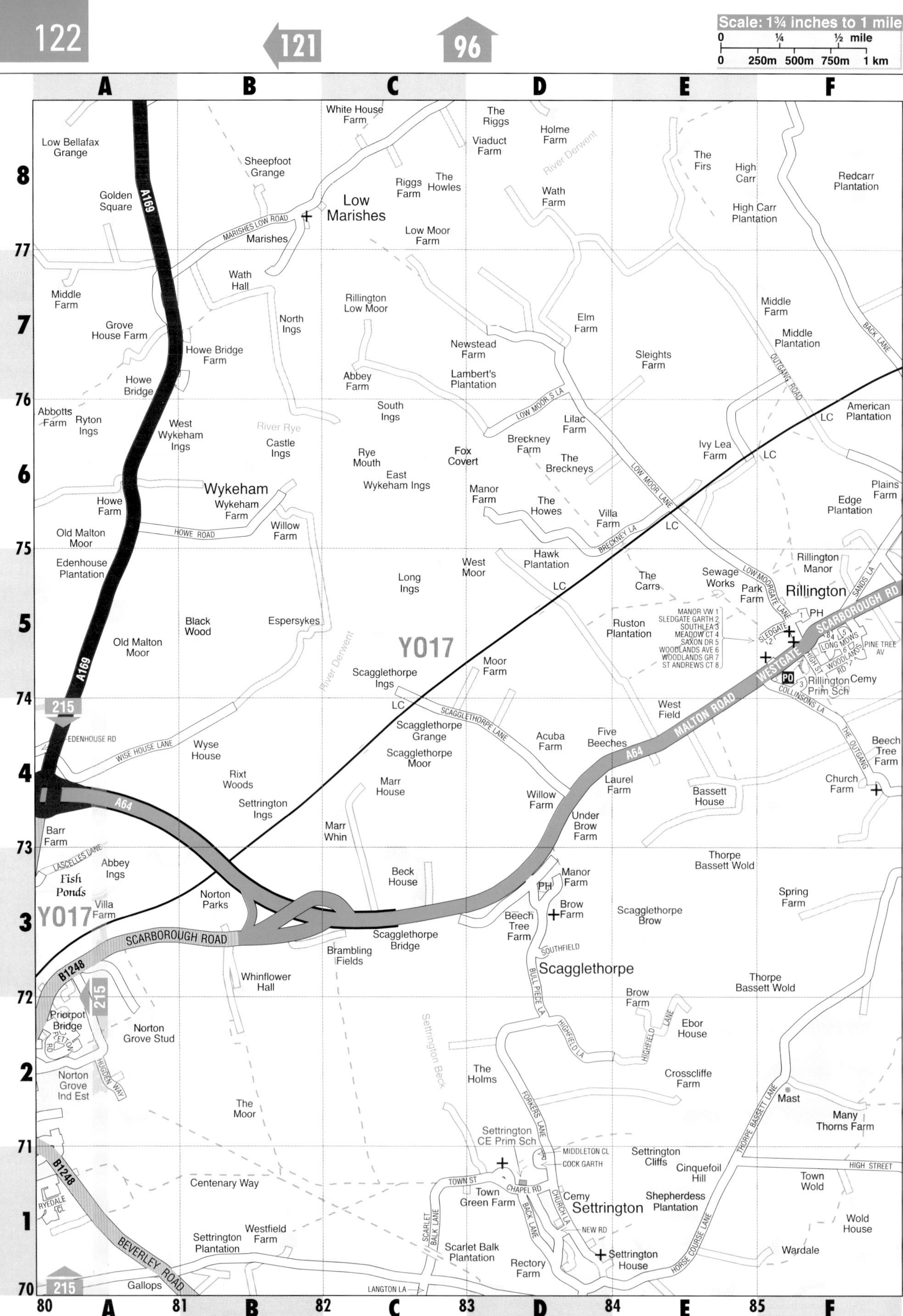

A   B   C   D   E   F

8
Low Bellafax Grange
White House Farm
The Riggs
Viaduct Farm
Holme Farm
River Derwent
The Firs
High Carr
Redcarr Plantation
Golden Square
Sheepfoot Grange
Riggs Farm
The Howles
Wath Farm
High Carr Plantation

77
A169
Marishes Low Road
Marishes
Low Marishes
Low Moor Farm

7
Middle Farm
Wath Hall
Rillington Low Moor
Newstead Farm
Elm Farm
Sleights Farm
Middle Farm
Middle Plantation
Back Lane
Grove House Farm
North Ings
Lambert's Plantation

76
Howe Bridge Farm
Abbey Farm
South Ings
Breckney Farm
Lilac Farm
Outgang Road
American Plantation
Abbotts Farm
Howe Bridge
River Rye
Castle Ings
The Breckneys
Ivy Lea Farm
LC
Ryton Ings

6
West Wykeham Ings
Wykeham
Wykeham Farm
Rye Mouth
East Wykeham Ings
Fox Covert
The Howes
Manor Farm
Villa Farm
Plains Farm
Edge Plantation
Howe Farm
Willow Farm
Low Moor Lane
Breckney La
LC

75
Old Malton Moor
Howe Road
Hawk Plantation
LC
The Carrs
Sewage Works
Rillington Manor
Edenhouse Plantation
West Moor
Park Farm
Rillington
Black Wood
Long Ings
Espersykes

5
A169
Old Malton Moor
Moor Farm
Ruston Plantation
MANOR VW 1
SLEDGATE GARTH 2
SOUTHLEA 3
MEADOW CT 4
SAXON DR 5
WOODLANDS AVE 6
WOODLANDS GR 7
ST ANDREWS CT 8
Sledgate Lane
PH
Scarborough Rd
Long Mdws
Pine Tree Av
Westgate
Rillington Prim Sch
Cemy

74
215
Scagglethorpe Ings
LC
Scagglethorpe Lane
West Field
Malton Road
PO
Collinsons La
Beech Tree Farm
Edenhouse Rd
Wise House Lane
Wyse House
Scagglethorpe Grange
Acuba Farm
Five Beeches
A64

4
A64
Rixt Woods
Scagglethorpe Moor
Marr House
Willow Farm
Laurel Farm
Bassett House
The Outgang
Church Farm
Settrington Ings
Under Brow Farm

73
Barr Farm
Marr Whin
Thorpe Bassett Wold
Spring Farm
Lascelles Lane
Abbey Ings
Beck House
Manor Farm
Scagglethorpe Brow

3
Y017
Fish Ponds
Villa Farm
Norton Parks
Scagglethorpe Bridge
PH
Brow Farm
Scagglethorpe Brow
Thorpe Bassett Wold
Scarborough Road
Brambling Fields
Beech Tree Farm
Southfield
Scagglethorpe

B1248
Whinflower Hall
Bull Piece La
Brow Farm
Thorpe Bassett Wold

72
215
Priorpot Bridge
Highfield Lane
Ebor House

2
Norton Grove Stud
The Moor
The Holms
Forkers Lane
Crosscliffe Farm
Many Thorns Farm
Norton Grove Ind Est
Huggate Way
Mast

71
Centenary Way
Settrington CE Prim Sch
Middleton Cl
Cock Garth
Settrington Cliffs
Cinquefoil Hill
Town Wold
B1248
Ryedale Cl
Town St
Chapel Rd
Church La
Settrington
Shepherdess Plantation
High Street
Wold House

1
Westfield Farm
Town Green Farm
Back Lane
New Rd
Horse Course Lane
Wardale
Settrington Plantation
Scarlet Balk Lane
Scarlet Balk Plantation
Rectory Farm
Cemy
Settrington House
Thorpe Bassett Lane

70
215
Beverley Road
Gallops
Langton La

80   A   81   B   82   C   83   D   84   E   85   F

215

148

For full street detail of the highlighted area see page 215.

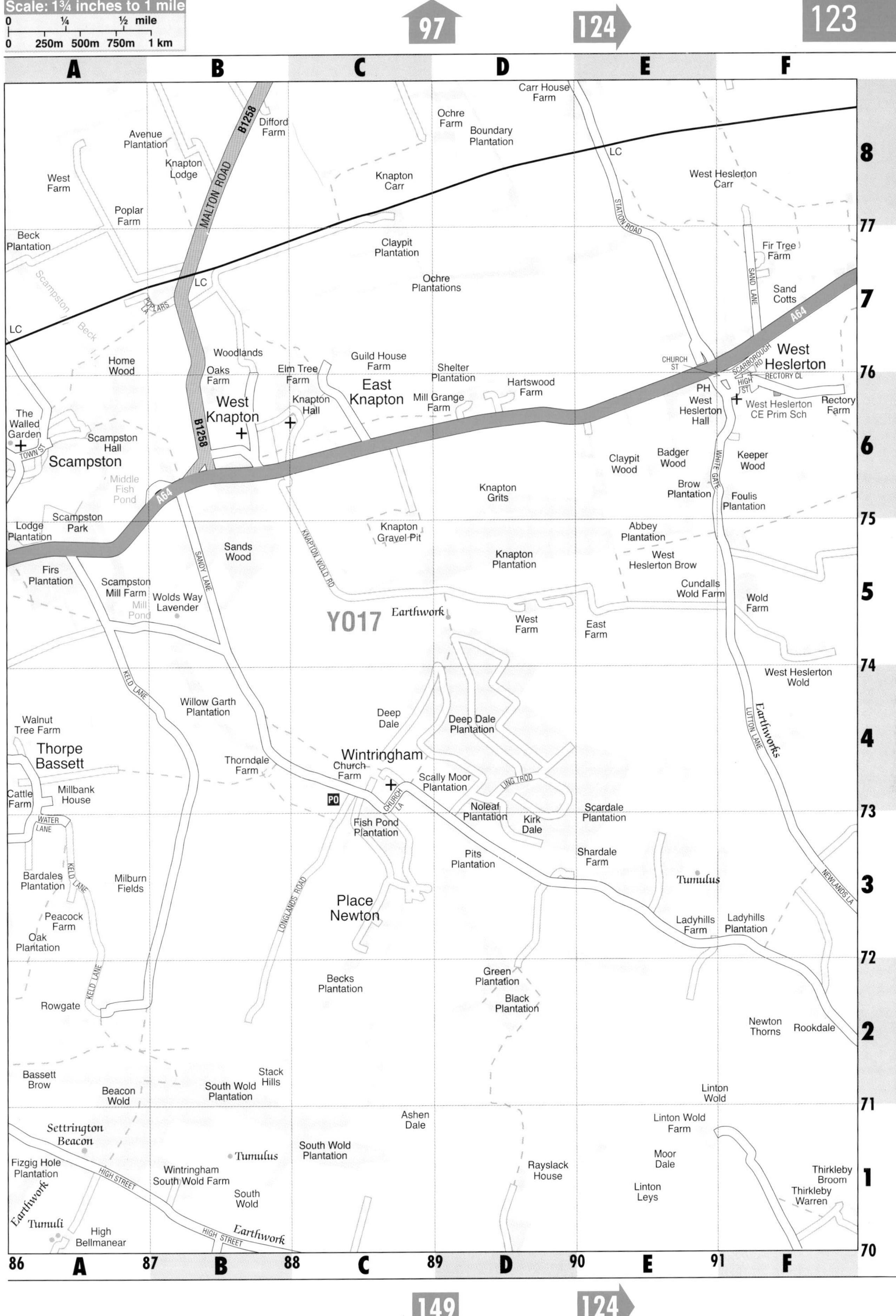

A   B   C   D   E   F

8

West Farm

Avenue Plantation

Knapton Lodge

B1258 MALTON ROAD

Difford Farm

Ochre Farm

Boundary Plantation

Carr House Farm

LC

West Heslerton Carr

STATION ROAD

77

Poplar Farm

Knapton Carr

Beck Plantation

Claypit Plantation

Ochre Plantations

Fir Tree Farm

Sand Cotts

A64

SAND LANE

7

LC

POPLARS

Scampston Beck

LC

Home Wood

Woodlands

Oaks Farm

Elm Tree Farm

Guild House Farm

Shelter Plantation

Hartswood Farm

CHURCH ST

SCARBOROUGH RD

West Heslerton

HIGH ST

Rectory Cl

76

The Walled Garden

Scampston Hall

West Knapton

B1258

Knapton Hall

East Knapton

Mill Grange Farm

PH West Heslerton Hall

West Heslerton CE Prim Sch

Rectory Farm

Scampston

TOWN ST

6

Middle Fish Pond

A64

Claypit Wood

Badger Wood

Brow Plantation

WHITE GATE

Keeper Wood

Foulis Plantation

Lodge Plantation

Scampston Park

Knapton Grits

Knapton Gravel Pit

75

Firs Plantation

Scampston Mill Farm

Mill Pond

Sands Wood

KNAPTON WOLD RD

Knapton Plantation

Abbey Plantation

West Heslerton Brow

Cundalls Wold Farm

Wold Farm

5

Wolds Way Lavender

Y017

Earthwork

West Farm

East Farm

West Heslerton Wold

74

Walnut Tree Farm

KELD LANE

Willow Garth Plantation

Deep Dale

Deep Dale Plantation

LUTTON LANE

Earthworks

4

Thorpe Bassett

Thorndale Farm

Wintringham

LING TROD

Cattle Farm

Millbank House

Church Farm

Scally Moor Plantation

Scardale Plantation

NEWLANDS LA

73

WATER LANE

PO

CHURCH LA

Noleaf Plantation

Kirk Dale

Bardales Plantation

KELD LANE

Milburn Fields

Fish Pond Plantation

Pits Plantation

Shardale Farm

3

Peacock Farm

LONGLANDS ROAD

Place Newton

Tumulus

Oak Plantation

Ladyhills Farm

Ladyhills Plantation

72

Rowgate

Becks Plantation

Green Plantation

Black Plantation

Newton Thorns

Rookdale

2

Bassett Brow

Beacon Wold

South Wold Plantation

Stack Hills

Linton Wold

71

Settrington Beacon

Ashen Dale

Linton Wold Farm

Fizgig Hole Plantation

HIGH STREET

Tumulus

South Wold Plantation

Rayslack House

Moor Dale

Thirkleby Broom

1

Earthwork

Wintringham South Wold Farm

South Wold

Linton Leys

Thirkleby Warren

Tumuli

High Bellmanear

HIGH STREET

Earthwork

123
98

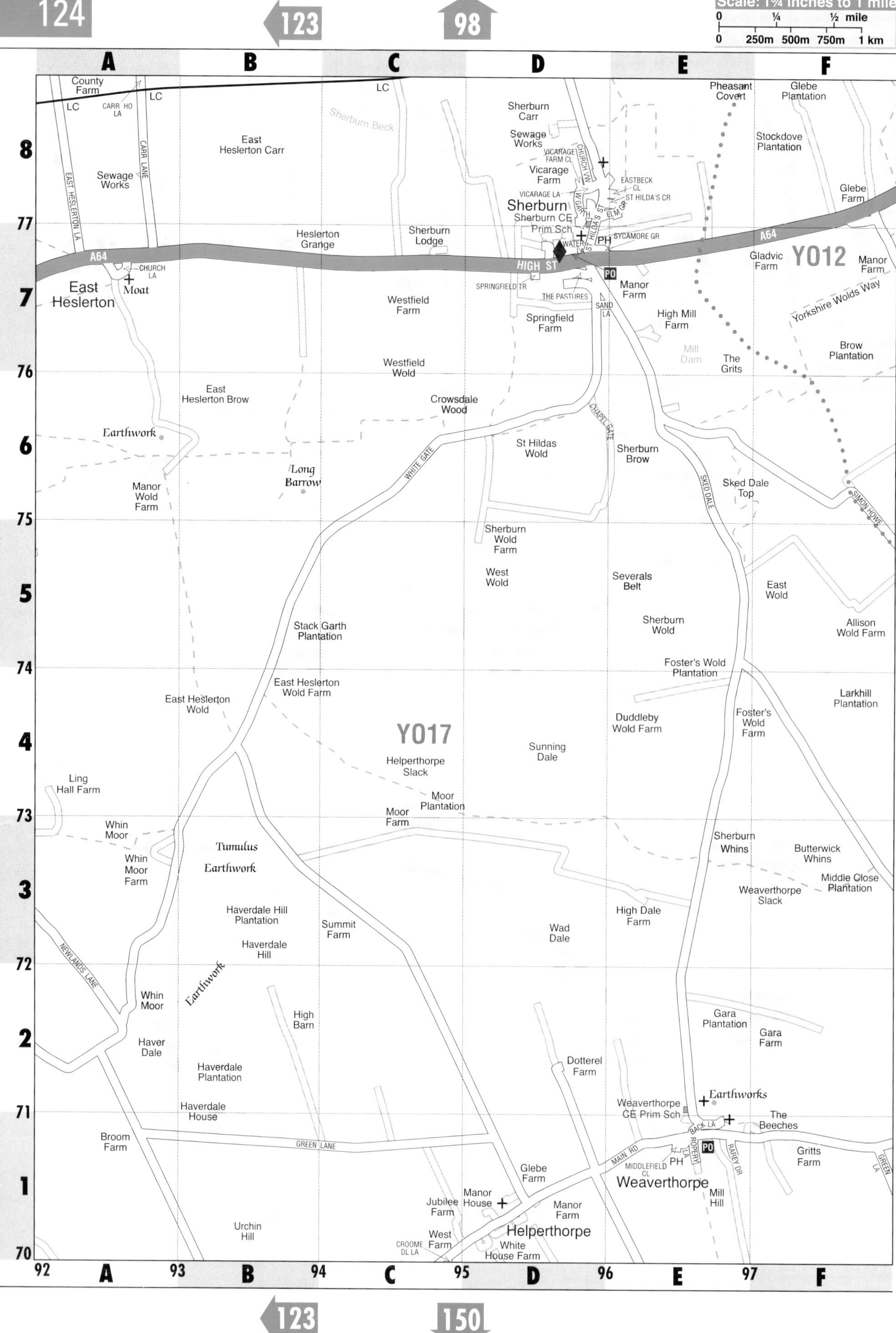
Scale: 1¾ inches to 1 mile
0 ¼ ½ mile
0 250m 500m 750m 1 km
A B C D E F
8 77 7 76 6 75 5 74 4 73 3 72 2 71 1 70
92 93 94 95 96 97
County Farm
LC
CARR HO LA
Sherburn Beck
East Heslerton Carr
Sherburn Carr
Sewage Works
Pheasant Covert
Glebe Plantation
Stockdove Plantation
Sewage Works
CARR LANE
EAST HESLERTON LA
VICARAGE FARM CL
Vicarage Farm
CHURCH VW
EASTBECK CL
ST HILDA'S CR
VICARAGE LA
Sherburn
W GARTH
ELM GR
ST HILDAS ST
Glebe Farm
Sherburn CE Prim Sch
Heslerton Grange
Sherburn Lodge
WATER LA
PH
SYCAMORE GR
A64
CHURCH LA
HIGH ST
PO
Gladvic Farm
YO12
Manor Farm
East Heslerton
Moat
SPRINGFIELD TR
THE PASTURES
Manor Farm
Westfield Farm
SAND LA
High Mill Farm
Yorkshire Wolds Way
Springfield Farm
Mill Dam
The Grits
Brow Plantation
Westfield Wold
East Heslerton Brow
Crowsdale Wood
CHAPEL GATE
Earthwork
WHITE GATE
St Hildas Wold
Sherburn Brow
Long Barrow
SKED DALE
Sked Dale Top
Manor Wold Farm
SIMON HOWE
Sherburn Wold Farm
West Wold
Severals Belt
East Wold
Sherburn Wold
Allison Wold Farm
Stack Garth Plantation
Foster's Wold Plantation
East Heslerton Wold Farm
Larkhill Plantation
East Heslerton Wold
YO17
Duddleby Wold Farm
Foster's Wold Farm
Sunning Dale
Helperthorpe Slack
Ling Hall Farm
Moor Plantation
Moor Farm
Whin Moor
Tumulus
Sherburn Whins
Butterwick Whins
Whin Moor Farm
Earthwork
Middle Close Plantation
Weaverthorpe Slack
Haverdale Hill Plantation
Summit Farm
High Dale Farm
Wad Dale
Haverdale Hill
NEWLANDS LANE
Earthwork
Whin Moor
High Barn
Gara Plantation
Gara Farm
Haver Dale
Dotterel Farm
Haverdale Plantation
Earthworks
Haverdale House
Weaverthorpe CE Prim Sch
The Beeches
BACK LA
Broom Farm
GREEN LANE
ROPERY LA
RAREY DR
Gritts Farm
MAIN RD
PO
MIDDLEFIELD CL
PH
GREEN LA
Glebe Farm
Weaverthorpe
Mill Hill
Manor House
Jubilee Farm
Manor Farm
Urchin Hill
West Farm
Helperthorpe
CROOME DL LA
White House Farm

123
150

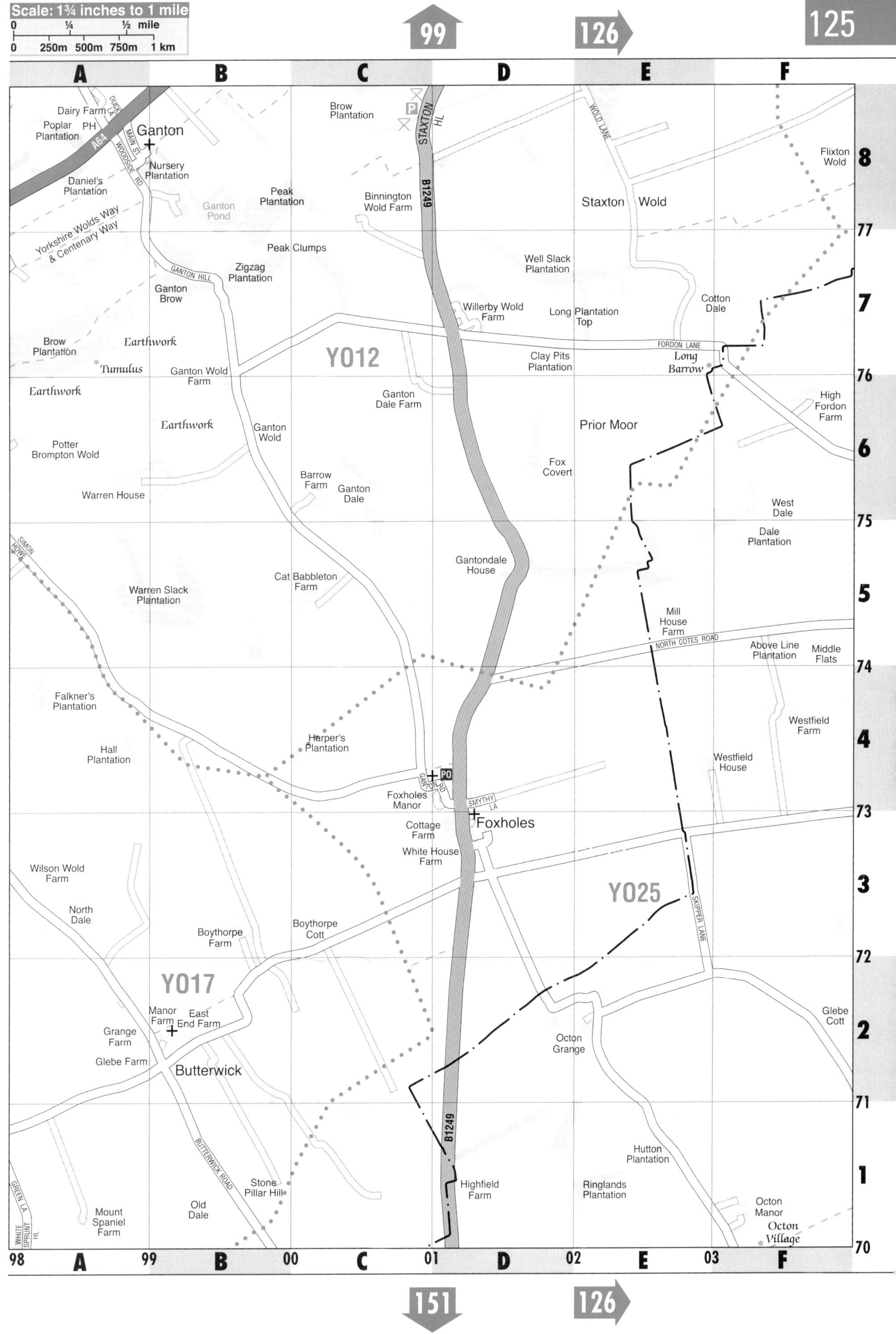
Scale: 1¾ inches to 1 mile
0 ¼ ½ mile
0 250m 500m 750m 1 km
99
126
A B C D E F
Dairy Farm
Poplar Plantation
PH
Ganton
A64
DUCK LA
MAIN ST
WOODSIDE RD
Nursery Plantation
Daniel's Plantation
Ganton Pond
Peak Plantation
Yorkshire Wolds Way & Centenary Way
Peak Clumps
GANTON HILL
Zigzag Plantation
Ganton Brow
Brow Plantation
Earthwork
Tumulus
Ganton Wold Farm
Earthwork
Earthwork
Ganton Wold
Potter Brompton Wold
Warren House
Brow Plantation
STAXTON HL
B1249
Binnington Wold Farm
Willerby Wold Farm
YO12
Ganton Dale Farm
Barrow Farm
Ganton Dale
Gantondale House
Cat Babbleton Farm
Warren Slack Plantation
SIMON HOWE
Falkner's Plantation
Hall Plantation
Harper's Plantation
GANTON RD
PO
Foxholes Manor
SMYTHY LA
Foxholes
Cottage Farm
White House Farm
Wilson Wold Farm
North Dale
Boythorpe Farm
Boythorpe Cott
YO17
Manor Farm
East End Farm
Grange Farm
Glebe Farm
Butterwick
BUTTERWICK ROAD
Stone Pillar Hill
Old Dale
Mount Spaniel Farm
GREEN LA
WHITE SPRUNT HL
B1249
Highfield Farm
WOLD LANE
Staxton Wold
Flixton Wold
Well Slack Plantation
Long Plantation Top
Cotton Dale
FORDON LANE
Long Barrow
Clay Pits Plantation
High Fordon Farm
Prior Moor
Fox Covert
West Dale
Dale Plantation
Mill House Farm
NORTH COTES ROAD
Above Line Plantation
Middle Flats
Westfield Farm
Westfield House
YO25
SKIPPER LANE
Octon Grange
Glebe Cott
Hutton Plantation
Ringlands Plantation
Octon Manor
Octon Village
8 77 7 76 6 75 5 74 4 73 3 72 2 71 1 70
98 99 00 01 02 03
151
126

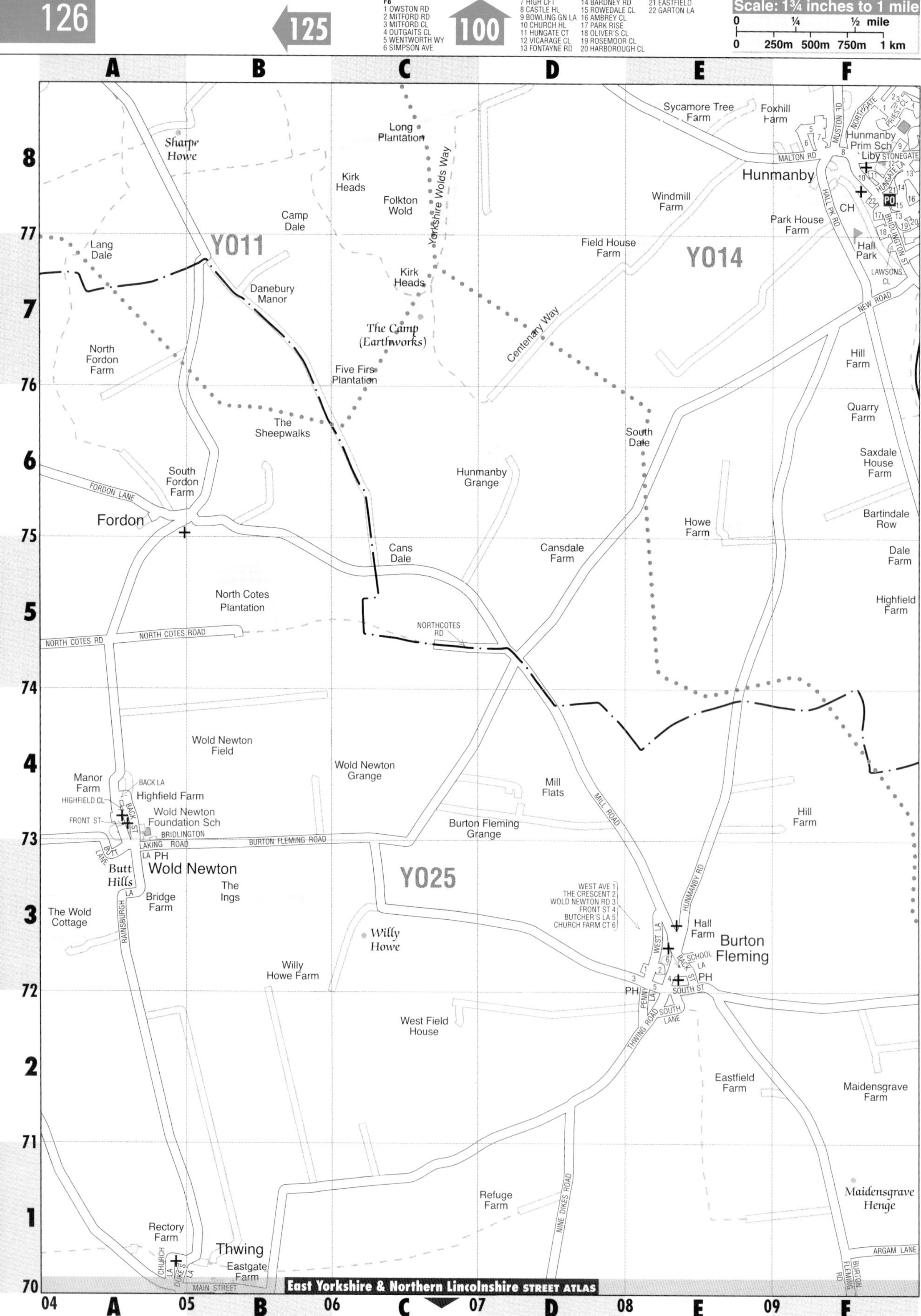

125

100

125

F8
1 OWSTON RD
2 MITFORD RD
3 MITFORD CL
4 OUTGAITS CL
5 WENTWORTH WY
6 SIMPSON AVE

7 HIGH CFT
8 CASTLE HL
9 BOWLING GN LA
10 CHURCH HL
11 HUNGATE CT
12 VICARAGE CL
13 FONTAYNE RD

14 BARDNEY RD
15 ROWEDALE CL
16 AMBREY CL
17 PARK RISE
18 OLIVER'S CL
19 ROSEMOOR CL
20 HARBOROUGH CL

21 EASTFIELD
22 GARTON LA

Scale: 1¾ inches to 1 mile

0   ¼   ½   mile
0 250m 500m 750m 1 km

Sharpe Howe

Long Plantation

Sycamore Tree Farm

Foxhill Farm

Hunmanby Prim Sch

Lib

Stonegate

Hunmanby

PO

CH

8

Kirk Heads

Folkton Wold

Windmill Farm

Malton Rd

YO11

77

Lang Dale

Camp Dale

Yorkshire Wolds Way

Field House Farm

YO14

Park House Farm

Hall Park

CH

Danebury Manor

Kirk Heads

7

North Fordon Farm

The Camp (Earthworks)

Centenary Way

Hill Farm

Five Firs Plantation

South Dale

Quarry Farm

76

The Sheepwalks

Hunmanby Grange

Saxdale House Farm

6

South Fordon Farm

Bartindale Row

FORDON LANE

Dale Farm

Fordon

Cansdale Farm

Howe Farm

75

Cans Dale

Highfield Farm

North Cotes Plantation

NORTHCOTES RD

5

NORTH COTES RD

NORTH COTES ROAD

74

Wold Newton Field

Wold Newton Grange

Mill Flats

Hill Farm

4

Manor Farm

BACK LA

HIGHFIELD CL

Highfield Farm

MILL ROAD

Burton Fleming Grange

FRONT ST

Wold Newton Foundation Sch

BRIDLINGTON

BURTON FLEMING ROAD

LAKING ROAD

73

LA PH

YO25

Wold Newton

WEST AVE 1
THE CRESCENT 2
WOLD NEWTON RD 3
FRONT ST 4
BUTCHER'S LA 5
CHURCH FARM CT 6

Hall Farm

Burton Fleming

Butt Hills

Bridge Farm

The Ings

WEST LA

RAINSBURGH LA

3

The Wold Cottage

Willy Howe

BACK SCHOOL LA

PH

PH

SOUTH ST

Willy Howe Farm

PENNY LA

SOUTH LANE

72

West Field House

THWING ROAD

HUNMANBY RD

Eastfield Farm

Maidensgrave Farm

2

71

NINE DIKES ROAD

Refuge Farm

Maidensgrave Henge

1

Rectory Farm

ARGAM LANE

CHURCH LA

Thwing

Eastgate Farm

BURTON FLEMING RD

70

MAIN STREET

East Yorkshire & Northern Lincolnshire STREET ATLAS

04   A   05   B   06   C   07   D   08   E   09   F

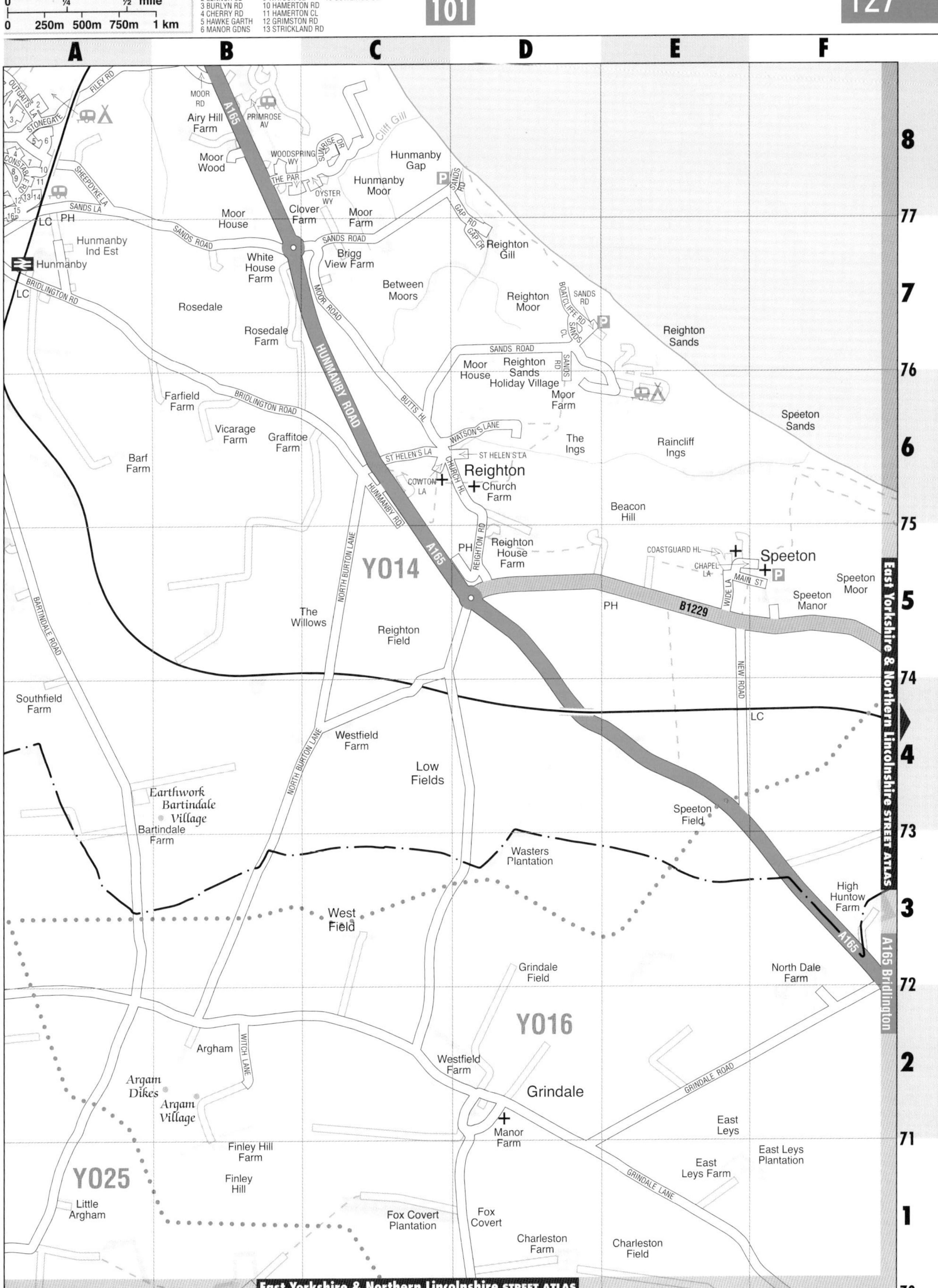

Scale: 1¾ inches to 1 mile

0   ¼   ½   mile
0   250m   500m   750m   1 km

A8
1 WRANGHAM DR
2 LENNOX CL
3 BURLYN RD
4 CHERRY RD
5 HAWKE GARTH
6 MANOR GDNS
7 CECIL RD
8 HOWES RD
9 WATSON CL
10 HAMERTON RD
11 HAMERTON CL
12 GRIMSTON RD
13 STRICKLAND RD
14 PERCY RD
15 HAVERCROFT RD
16 COWLINGS CL

East Yorkshire & Northern Lincolnshire STREET ATLAS

A165 Bridlington

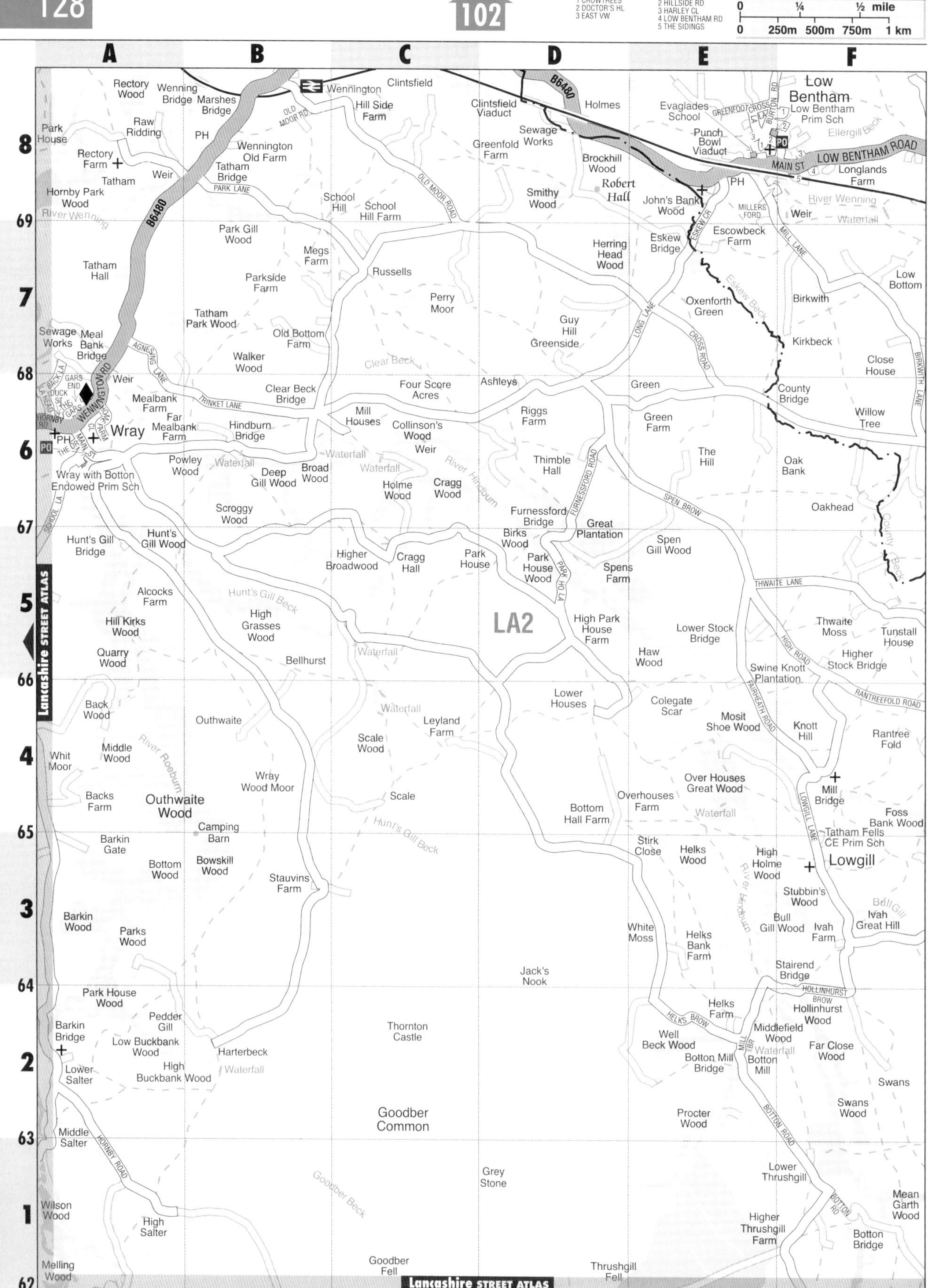

E8
1 CROWTREES
2 DOCTOR'S HL
3 EAST VW

F8
1 YEWTREE DR
2 HILLSIDE RD
3 HARLEY CL
4 LOW BENTHAM RD
5 THE SIDINGS

Scale: 1¾ inches to 1 mile

0   ¼   ½ mile
0   250m   500m   750m   1 km

A   B   C   D   E   F

Rectory Wood
Wenning Bridge
Marshes Bridge
Clintsfield
Wennington
Clintsfield Viaduct
Holmes
B6480
Low Bentham
Low Bentham Prim Sch
Ellergill Beck
Evaglades School
Greenfoot Cross
Park House
Raw Ridding
PH
Hill Side Farm
Clintsfield Farm
Sewage Works
Greenfold Farm
Brockhill Wood
Punch Bowl Viaduct
PO
Main St
Low Bentham Road
Longlands Farm

8

Rectory Farm
Wennington Old Farm
Tatham Bridge
Park Lane
School Hill
School Hill Farm
Old Moor Rd
Smithy Wood
Robert Hall
John's Bank Wood
PH
Millers Ford
Weir
River Wenning
Waterfall

Hornby Park Wood
Tatham
Weir
Herring Head Wood
Eskew Bridge
Escowbeck Farm

69

River Wenning
B6480
Park Gill Wood
Megs Farm
Russells
Perry Moor
Guy Hill Greenside
Green
Eskew Beck
Birkwith

Tatham Hall
Parkside Farm
Oxenforth Green
Kirkbeck

7

Tatham Park Wood
Old Bottom Farm
Clear Beck
Ashleys
Green Farm
Cross Road
Close House

68

Sewage Works
Meal Bank Bridge
Weir
Walker Wood
Clear Beck Bridge
Four Score Acres
Riggs Farm
Green
County Bridge
Willow Tree

Agness Lane
Gars End
Duck St
Wennington Rd
Thinket Lane
Mealbank Farm
Far Mealbank Farm
Hindburn Bridge
Mill Houses
Collinson's Wood
Weir
Thimble Hall
The Hill
Oak Bank

6

Wray
PH
PO
Powley Wood
Waterfall
Deep Gill Wood
Broad Wood
Holme Wood
Cragg Wood
River Hindburn
Furnessford Bridge
Spen Brow
Oakhead

Wray with Botton Endowed Prim Sch
Scroggy Wood
Waterfall
Birks Wood
Great Plantation
Spen Gill Wood

67

Hunt's Gill Bridge
Hunt's Gill Wood
Higher Broadwood
Cragg Hall
Park House
Park House Wood
Spens Farm
Thwaite Lane

Furnessford Rd
Park Ho La
Alcocks Farm
High Grasses Wood
High Park House Farm
Lower Stock Bridge
Thwaite Moss
Tunstall House
Higher Stock Bridge

5

Hill Kirks Wood
LA2
Swine Knott Plantation
Spen Brow

Hunt's Gill Beck
Bellhurst
Waterfall
Haw Wood

Quarry Wood

66

Back Wood
Waterfall
Lower Houses
Colegate Scar
Mosit Shoe Wood
Knott Hill
Rantree Fold

Outhwaite
Leyland Farm
Rantreefold Road

River Roeburn
Scale Wood
Over Houses Great Wood
Waterfall

4

Whit Moor
Middle Wood
Wray Wood Moor
Scale
Overhouses Farm
Mill Bridge
Foss Bank Wood

Backs Farm
Outhwaite Wood
Bottom Hall Farm
Tatham Fells CE Prim Sch

65

Barkin Gate
Camping Barn
Hunt's Gill Beck
Stirk Close
Helks Wood
High Holme Wood
Lowgill

Bottom Wood
Bowskill Wood
Stauvins Farm
White Moss
Helks Bank Farm
Stubbin's Wood
Ivah Farm
Ivah Great Hill

3

Barkin Wood
Parks Wood
Bull Gill Wood
Bull Gill Wood
River Hindburn

Stairend Bridge

64

Park House Wood
Jack's Nook
Helks Farm
Hollinhurst Brow
Hollinhurst Wood

Barkin Bridge
Pedder Gill
Thornton Castle
Helks Brow
Well Beck Wood
Middlefield Wood
Far Close Wood

2

Lower Salter
Low Buckbank Wood
Harterbeck
Waterfall
Botton Mill Bridge
Botton Mill
Swans

High Buckbank Wood
Procter Wood
Swans Wood

63

Middle Salter
Hornby Road
Goodber Common
Botton Road

1

Wilson Wood
High Salter
Grey Stone
Lower Thrushgill
Mean Garth Wood

Higher Thrushgill Farm
Botton Rd
Botton Bridge

Melling Wood
Goodber Fell
Goodber Beck
Thrushgill Fell

62

60   A   61   B   62   C   D   64   E   65   F

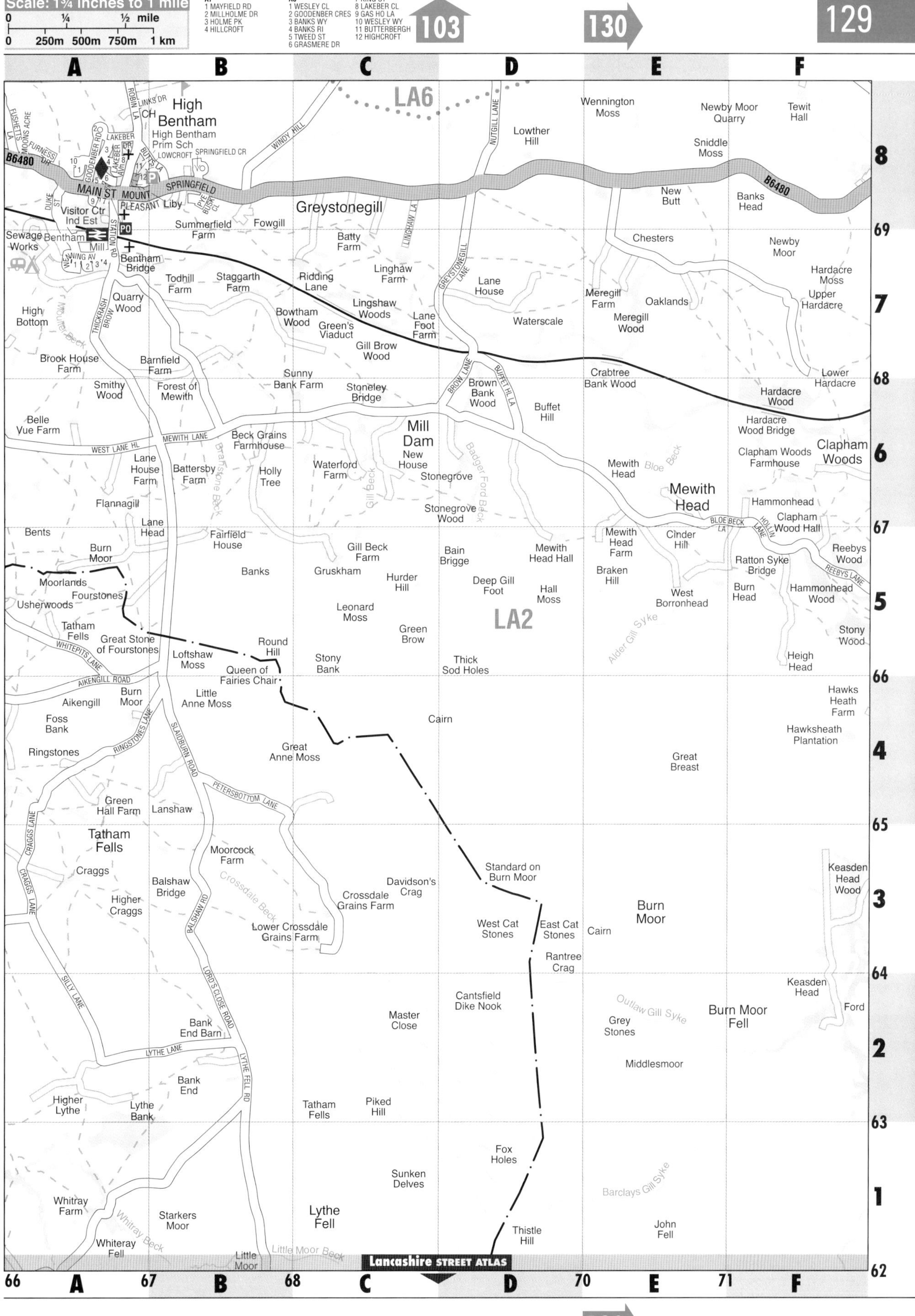
High Bentham
High Bentham Prim Sch
Greystonegill
LA6
LA2
Lowther Hill
Wennington Moss
Newby Moor Quarry
Tewit Hall
Sniddle Moss
New Butt
Banks Head
B6480
Visitor Ctr Ind Est
Sewage Works
Bentham
Summerfield Farm
Fowgill
Batty Farm
Chesters
Newby Moor
Hardacre Moss
Upper Hardacre
Bentham Bridge
Todhill Farm
Staggarth Farm
Ridding Lane
Linghaw Farm
Lane House
Meregill Farm
Oaklands
Meregill Wood
High Bottom
Quarry Wood
Bowtham Wood
Green's Viaduct
Lingshaw Woods
Lane Foot Farm
Waterscale
Gill Brow Wood
Brook House Farm
Barnfield Farm
Sunny Bank Farm
Crabtree Bank Wood
Lower Hardacre
Smithy Wood
Forest of Mewith
Stoneley Bridge
Brown Bank Wood
Hardacre Wood
Buffet Hill
Belle Vue Farm
Mill Dam
Beck Grains Farmhouse
Hardacre Wood Bridge
Clapham Woods Farmhouse
Clapham Woods
New House
Stonegrove
Mewith Head
Lane House Farm
Battersby Farm
Holly Tree
Waterford Farm
Mewith Head
Flannagill
Hammonhead
Clapham Wood Hall
Stonegrove Wood
Lane Head
Bents
Fairfield House
Gill Beck Farm
Bain Brigge
Mewith Head Hall
Mewith Head Farm
Cinder Hill
Reebys Wood
Burn Moor
Banks
Gruskham
Ratton Syke Bridge
Moorlands
Hurder Hill
Deep Gill Foot
Braken Hill
Fourstones
Leonard Moss
Hall Moss
West Borronhead
Burn Head
Hammonhead Wood
Usherwoods
Tatham Fells
Great Stone of Fourstones
Round Hill
Green Brow
Stony Wood
Loftshaw Moss
Queen of Fairies Chair
Stony Bank
Thick Sod Holes
Heigh Head
Aikengill
Burn Moor
Little Anne Moss
Hawks Heath Farm
Foss Bank
Cairn
Hawksheath Plantation
Ringstones
Great Anne Moss
Great Breast
Green Hall Farm
Lanshaw
Tatham Fells
Moorcock Farm
Standard on Burn Moor
Keasden Head Wood
Craggs
Balshaw Bridge
Davidson's Crag
Crossdale Grains Farm
Higher Craggs
Burn Moor
West Cat Stones
East Cat Stones
Cairn
Lower Crossdale Grains Farm
Rantree Crag
Keasden Head
Cantsfield Dike Nook
Master Close
Grey Stones
Burn Moor Fell
Ford
Bank End Barn
Middlesmoor
Bank End
Higher Lythe
Lythe Bank
Tatham Fells
Piked Hill
Fox Holes
Sunken Delves
Whitray Farm
Starkers Moor
Lythe Fell
Thistle Hill
John Fell
Whiteray Fell
Little Moor
Lancashire STREET ATLAS
66 67 68 70 71
62 63 1 2 64 3 65 4 66 5 67 6 68 7 69 8
A B C D E F

129

C8
1 THE GREEN
2 CLAPDALE WY
3 CROSS HAW LA

104

Scale: 1¾ inches to 1 mile

| 0 | ¼ | ½ | mile |

0   250m   500m   750m   1 km

A   B   C   D   E   F

HENBUSK LA
A65
Laithbutts
Bank Plantation
Limekiln Plantation
Norber
Sowerthwaite Farm

8 Green Close
Lodge Bank Plantation
OLD ROAD
EGGSHELL LA
The Lake
Thwaite Plantation

Lodge Bank Farm
RIVERSIDE
Home Plantation
Thwaite Top
Clapham

B6480
Brickkiln Plantation
PO
OLD RD
Clapham CE Prim Sch

69
Newby Moor
THE GREEN
STATION RD

Long Tram Plantation

Austwick CE Prim Sch
HALL CL

7
Nutta Farm
Calterber Bridge
Crina Bottom Farm
Bowsber
B6480
Austwick
PANS LA
MAIN ST
PO
WOOD LANE
Startinghaw End

Hazel Hall Farm
NEW CL LA
Bowsber Plantation

68
River Wenning
Clapham
Conisber
New Close Plantation
Sandaber
Stepping Stones
Earthworks

Wenning Bank Bridge
Conisber Plantation
Harden Bridge
HOLME LANE
GRANSTOBER LANE
A65

Clapham Viaduct
WENNING BANK
Austwick Beck
ORCABER LANE
PH

6
Wenning Side
Meldingscale Farm
Clapham Moor Bridge
Waters
Orcaber Farm
Dalesbridge Outdoor Centre
Sewage Works

Moss Farm
Black Hill
Meldingscale Plantation
LA2
Waters Bridge
Black Plantation
Gayclops
CROW NEST ROAD

67
Clapham Moor
Lawsings
LAWSINGS BROW
Fen Beck
Austwick Moss
Lawkland Moss
Bark Head
Lawkland

Dubgarth
Dubgarth Hill
Jack Beck
Mast
Middlesber
SHEPHERD GATE

5
REEBYS LA
Keasden
Lane Side Bridge
FLUMMERBER LANE
ELDROTH RD
Kettles Beck
Lanshaw Farm
Lawkland Hall Farm
Lawkland Hall

Turnerford Bridge
Watson House
Cragg Lane Bridge
Low Dyke House

66
Hawksheath Wood
Cow Gill
KETTLESBECK BR
ELDROTH RD
Slated Farm

Brockabank Wood
Clapham Moor
Coppy House
Cragg Bank Bridge
School Bridge
Ford
Eldroth
Lawkland Hall Wood

4
Long Bank
Low Birks
Low Kettlesbeck
CRAGG LANE
Eldroth House Farm

Keasden Head
Dub Syke
Middle Birks
Kettles Beck
Black Bank Syke
ELDROTH ROAD
Blaithwaite

65
Rantree
Hobson's Gill Wood
KEASDEN ROAD
Willow Tree
Knott Coppy
FOUR LANE ENDS

3
Moss House
High Birks
Silver Hills Plantation
Lingthwaite
SCHOOL LANE
KING'S GATE
Black Bank
STACKHOUSE LANE

Hill Top
Birks Plantation
New Kettlesbeck Farm
BLACK BANK ROAD

64
Woodgill Farm
Sheephouse Plantation
Kettlesbeck
GARNET BROW LANE
Howith Farm
Accerhill Hall

2
Bracken Garth
Brow Side
Israel Farm
Ravenshaw
Butterfield Gap
Langrigg
Routster Green
BACK LANE
CROSS LANE

Birk Knott
High Grains Plantation
High Grain
Water Garth
Routster Farm
WHAM LANE

63
Ing Close
Waterfalls
BD24

1
Haw Hill
White Syke Hill
Leva Green
Brown Bark
Sandford Beck
Moss Bank
Wham

62
Round Hill Bridge
Reca Bank Moss
Ingleby House Hill
Deep Moss
Sand Holes Hill

72   73   74   75   76   77

A   B   C   D   E   F

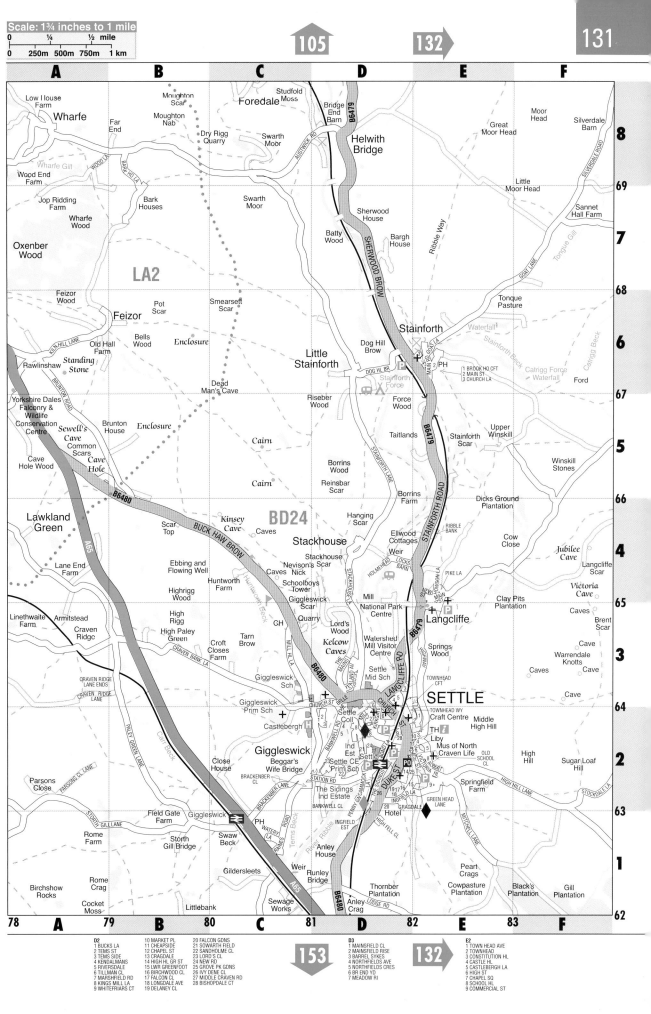

| A | B | C | D | E | F |

8
69
7
68
6
67
5
66
4
65
3
64
2
63
1
62

78   79   80   81   82   83

Wharfe
Low House Farm
Far End
Wood End Farm
Jop Ridding Farm
Wharfe Wood
Oxenber Wood
Wharfe Gill
WOOD LA
BARK HO LA
Bark Houses
Standing Stone
Feizor
Feizor Wood
Pot Scar
Bells Wood
Old Hall Farm
Rawlinshaw
KILN HILL LANE
LA2

Moughton Scar
Moughton Nab
Dry Rigg Quarry
Foredale
Studfold Moss
Swarth Moss
Swarth Moor
AUSTWICK RD
B6479
Bridge End Barn
Helwith Bridge
Batty Wood
Sherwood House
Bargh House
SHERWOOD BROW

Great Moor Head
Moor Head
Silverdale Barn
SILVERDALE ROAD
Little Moor Head
Sannet Hall Farm
GOAT LANE
Tongue Gill

Smearseft Scar
Enclosure
Dead Man's Cave
Little Stainforth
Dog Hill Brow
DOG HL BR
Stainforth Force
Riseber Wood
Force Wood
Stainforth
Stainforth Beck
Waterfall
Tonque Pasture
MAIN RD
GOAT LA
PH
1 BROOK HO CFT
2 MAIN ST
3 CHURCH LA
Catrigg Force Waterfall
Ford

Yorkshire Dales Falconry & Wildlife Conservation Centre
Sewell's Cave
Common Scars
Cave Hole
Brunton House
Enclosure
Cave Hole Wood
BRUNTON ROAD
Cairn
Cairn
Borrins Wood
Reinsbar Scar
Borrins Farm
Taitlands
Stainforth Scar
Upper Winskill
STAINFORTH LANE
STAINFORTH ROAD
B6479
Winskill Stones
Dicks Ground Plantation
Cow Close
Jubilee Cave
Langcliffe Scar
Victoria Cave

B6480
Lawkland Green
A65
Scar Top
Kinsey Cave
Caves
BUCK HAW BROW
BD24
Stackhouse
Hanging Scar
Ellwood Cottages
Weir
RIBBLE BANK
Clay Pits Plantation
Caves
Brent Scar
Cave
Warrendale Knotts
Caves
Cave
Cave

Linethwaite Farm
Armitstead
Craven Ridge
CRAVEN RIDGE LANE ENDS
CRAVEN RIDGE LANE
Ebbing and Flowing Well
Highrigg Wood
Huntworth Farm
High Rigg
High Paley Green
CRAVEN BANK LA
Croft Closes Farm
Tarn Brow
CH
Giggleswick Sch
Giggleswick Prim Sch
Castlebergh
Stackhouse Scar
Nevison's Nick
Caves Nick
Schoolboys Tower
Giggleswick Scar
Quarry
Lord's Wood
Kelcow Caves
National Park Centre
Mill
MILL HL LA
B6480
Settle Mid Sch
Watershed Mill Visitor Centre
LANGCLIFFE RD
HOLMEHEAD
LOCKS BARN
PIKE LA
NEW RD
MAIN
JOHNSON LA
Langcliffe
Springs Wood
HIGHWAY
TOWNHEAD CFT
High Hill
Sugar Loaf Hill
STOCKDALE LA

Parsons Close
PARSONS CL LANE
STORTH GILL LANE
PALEY GREEN LANE
Cell Beck
Field Gate Farm
BRACKENBER LANE
BRACKENBER CL
Close House
Gigglewick
Beggar's Wife Bridge
STATION RD
The Sidings Ind Estate
BANKWELL CL
CHURCH ST
BELLE
BANKWELL RD
Settle Coll
Settle CE Prim Sch
KIRKGATE
THE SHAMBLES
CHURCH
SETTLE
Craft Centre
TOWNHEAD WY
TH
Liby
Mus of North Craven Life
OLD SCHOOL CL
Middle High Hill
High Hill
Springfield Farm
HIGH HILL LANE
MITCHELL LANE

Rome Farm
Storth Gill Bridge
Swaw Beck
Gigglewick
Field Gate Farm
PH
WATERY LA
RAINES ROAD
Tems Beck
PENNY GN
COMMON RD
DUKE ST
INGFIELD EST
INGFIELD LA
GRAGDALE
Hotel
GREEN HEAD LANE
Peart Crags
Cowpasture Plantation
Black's Plantation
Gill Plantation

Birchshow Rocks
Rome Crag
Cocket Moss
Littlebank
Gildersleets
Weir
Runley Bridge
Sewage Works
A65
B6480
Anley House
LODGE RD
Anley Crag
Thornber Plantation

D2
1 BUCKS LA
2 TEMS ST
3 TEMS SIDE
4 KENDALMANS
5 RIVERSDALE
6 TILLMAN CL
7 MARSHFIELD RD
8 KINGS MILL LA
9 WHITEFRIARS CT
10 MARKET PL
11 CHEAPSIDE
12 CHAPEL ST
13 CRAGDALE
14 HIGH HL GR ST
15 LWR GREENFOOT
16 BIRCHWOOD CL
17 FALCON CL
18 LONGDALE AVE
19 DELANEY CL
20 FALCON GDNS
21 SOWARTH FIELD
22 SANDHOLME CL
23 LORD'S CL
24 NEW RD
25 GROVE PK GDNS
26 IVY DENE CL
27 MIDDLE CRAVEN RD
28 BISHOPDALE CT

D3
1 MAINSFIELD CL
2 MAINSFIELD RISE
3 BARREL SYKES
4 NORTHFIELDS AVE
5 NORTHFIELDS CRES
6 BR END YD
7 MEADOW RI

E2
1 TOWN HEAD AVE
2 TOWNHEAD
3 CONSTITUTION HL
4 CASTLE HL
5 CASTLEBERGH LA
6 HIGH ST
7 CHAPEL SQ
8 SCHOOL HL
9 COMMERCIAL ST

131
106

Scale: 1¾ inches to 1 mile

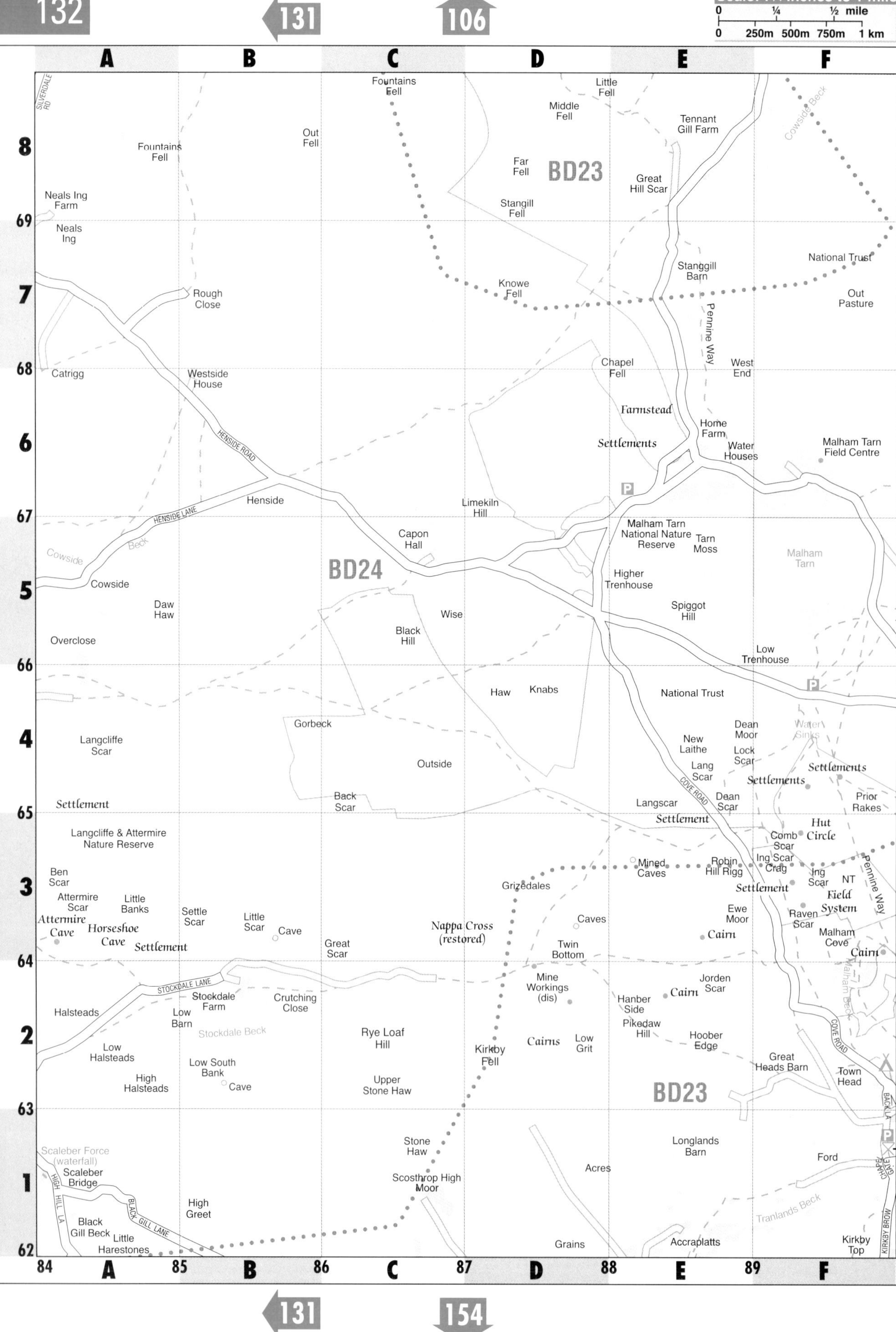
Fountains Fell
Little Fell
Middle Fell
Tennant Gill Farm
Out Fell
Fountains Fell
Far Fell
BD23
Great Hill Scar
Neals Ing Farm
Stangill Fell
Neals Ing
Stanggill Barn
National Trust
Knowe Fell
Rough Close
Out Pasture
Pennine Way
Chapel Fell
West End
Catrigg
Westside House
Farmstead
Home Farm
Settlements
Water Houses
Malham Tarn Field Centre
HENSIDE ROAD
Henside
Limekiln Hill
HENSIDE LANE
Capon Hall
Malham Tarn National Nature Reserve
Tarn Moss
Malham Tarn
Cowside Beck
BD24
Higher Trenhouse
Cowside
Daw Haw
Wise
Spiggot Hill
Black Hill
Overclose
Low Trenhouse
Haw
Knabs
National Trust
Gorbeck
Dean Moor
Langcliffe Scar
New Laithe
Water Sinks
Lock Scar
Outside
Lang Scar
Settlements
Settlements
COVE ROAD
Back Scar
Dean Scar
Prior Rakes
Settlement
Langscar
Settlement
Hut Circle
Langcliffe & Attermire Nature Reserve
Comb Scar
Mined Caves
Robin Hill Rigg
Ing Scar Crag
Ben Scar
Grizedales
Ing Scar
NT
Settlement
Field System
Attermire Scar
Little Banks
Ewe Moor
Settle Scar
Little Scar
Caves
Raven Scar
Attermire Cave
Horseshoe Cave
Cave
Nappa Cross (restored)
Cairn
Malham Cove
Settlement
Great Scar
Twin Bottom
Cairn
Mine Workings (dis)
Jorden Scar
STOCKDALE LANE
Stockdale Farm
Crutching Close
Cairn
Hanber Side
Halsteads
Low Barn
Pikedaw Hill
Stockdale Beck
Rye Loaf Hill
Malham Beck
Hoober Edge
Low Halsteads
Cairns
Low Grit
Kirkby Fell
Low South Bank
Great Heads Barn
Town Head
High Halsteads
Cave
Upper Stone Haw
BD23
BACK LA
Stone Haw
Longlands Barn
Scaleber Force (waterfall)
Ford
Scaleber Bridge
Acres
Scosthrop High Moor
CHAPEL GATE
HIGH HILL LA
BLACK GILL LANE
High Greet
Tranlands Beck
Black Gill Beck
Little Harestones
Grains
Accraplatts
Kirkby Top
KIRKBY BROW
SILVERDALE RD
A
B
C
D
E
F
8
69
7
68
6
67
5
66
4
65
3
64
2
63
1
62
84
85
86
87
88
89

131
154

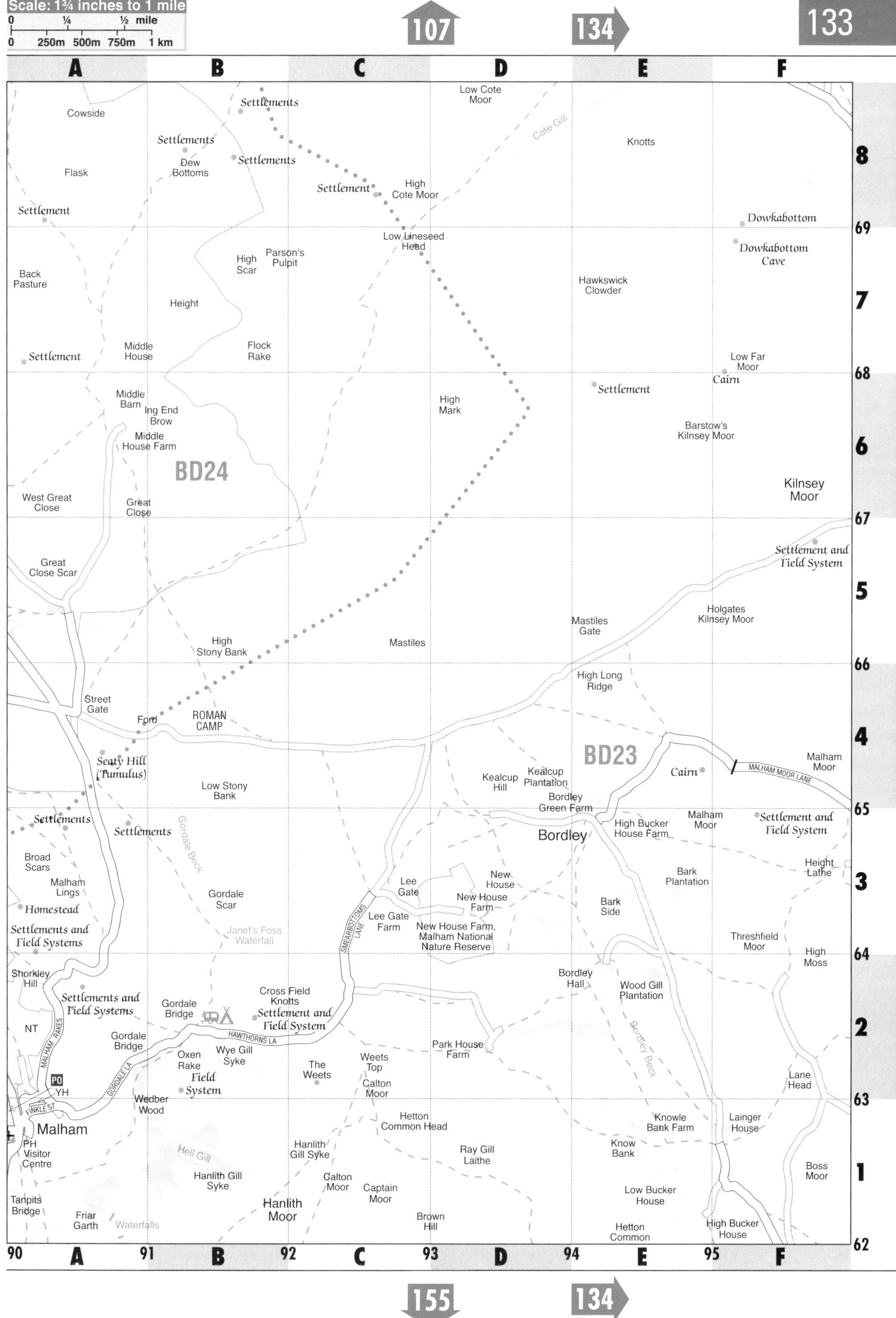

A   B   C   D   E   F

8

Cowside

Settlements

Low Cote Moor

Knotts

Settlements

Flask

Dew Bottoms

Settlements

Cote Gill

Settlement

Settlement

High Cote Moor

Dowkabottom

69

High Scar

Parson's Pulpit

Low Lineseed Head

Dowkabottom Cave

Back Pasture

7

Height

Hawkswick Clowder

Settlement

Middle House

Flock Rake

68

Middle Barn

Ing End Brow

High Mark

Settlement

Low Far Moor

Cairn

6

Middle House Farm

BD24

Barstow's Kilnsey Moor

West Great Close

Great Close

Kilnsey Moor

67

Great Close Scar

Settlement and Field System

5

High Stony Bank

Mastiles

Mastiles Gate

Holgates Kilnsey Moor

66

Street Gate

High Long Ridge

Ford

ROMAN CAMP

BD23

Cairn

Malham Moor

4

MALHAM MOOR LANE

Seaty Hill (Tumulus)

Low Stony Bank

Kealcup Hill

Kealcup Plantation

Bordley Green Farm

Cairn

Malham Moor

Settlement and Field System

65

Settlements

Settlements

Bordley

High Bucker House Farm

Malham Moor

Height Lathe

3

Broad Scars

Gordale Scar

Lee Gate

New House

Bark Side

Bark Plantation

Malham Lings

Gordale Beck

Lee Gate Farm

New House Farm

Homestead

New House Farm, Malham National Nature Reserve

Threshfield Moor

64

Settlements and Field Systems

Janet's Foss Waterfall

Bordley Hall

Wood Gill Plantation

High Moss

Shorkley Hill

Cross Field Knotts Settlement and Field System

2

NT

Settlements and Field Systems

Gordale Bridge

HAWTHORNS LA

Park House Farm

Bordley Beck

Lane Head

Gordale Bridge

Wye Gill Syke

Oxen Rake Field System

The Weets

Weets Top

Calton Moor

63

PO

GORDALE LA

Wedber Wood

Knowle Bank Farm

Lainger House

YH

Malham

Hetton Common Head

Know Bank

1

FINKLE ST

PH

Visitor Centre

Hanlith Gill Syke

Hanlith Gill Syke

Ray Gill Laithe

Low Bucker House

Boss Moor

Tanpits Bridge

Hell Gill

Galton Moor

Captain Moor

High Bucker House

Friar Garth

Waterfalls

Hanlith Moor

Brown Hill

Hetton Common

62

90   A   91   B   92   C   93   D   94   E   95   F

Scale: 1¾ inches to 1 mile

0   ¼   ½ mile
0   250m   500m   750m   1 km

A   B   C   D   E   F

Scar Gill Barn
River Skirfare
High Wind Bank
B6160
Ford
Mossdale Scar
Black Edge

Sleets Gill Wood
Waterfall
Amerdale Dub
Swineber Scar
New Close Allotments
Bycliffe

Weir
Skirfare Bridge
Throstles Nest Farm
River Wharfe
Settlements Field Systems
Kelber
Gill House

Old North Cote
Pinder Stile
Hill Castles Scar
Mast

Kilnsey Crag
Low Ox Pasture
Kilnsey Moor
Hotel
Kilnsey
Conistone
Dib
Bull Scar
Hut Circles and Enclosures
Nook
Burrows Pasture

High Ox Pasture
Cool Scar Quarry
THE GREEN
MASTILES LANE
Kilnsey Park
Home Farm
Conistone Bridge
Cairn
Downs Pasture

Cool
Cool Scar
Bow Bridge
Old Pasture
Dales Way

Howgill
Settlement and Field Systems
Outgang Hill
Chapel House
Sewage Works
Hut Circles and Field System
BD23
Cairn
Settlement and Field System
Bare House

Green Haw Hill
Waterfall
Cairn
Dib Scar
Sweet Side

Chapel House Farm
Cairn
Sweet Side
Field System
Yarnbury

Settlement
Robin Hood's Well
Grass Wood Nature Reserve
Bastow Wood
Field System
Henge

Chapel House Wood
Settlement and Field System
Dewbottom Scar
Gregory Scar
Settlement
Cairn
Kimpergill Hill
Settlements

Cairn
Netherside Hall Sch
BRACKEN FIELD 1
CRAG VW 2
HILLSIDE CL 3
RIVENDELL 4
GORDALE CL 5
BRAZENGATE 6
KILN DR 7
GRASS WOOD LANE
Cove Scar
Medieval Village (site of)
Field System
Spring House
New House Farm

MALHAM MOOR LANE
HARD GATE
Quarry
Long Ashes Leisure Club
WOOD ACRE CLOSE
Ghaistrill's Strid
Mirefield
High Garnshaw House

Cave Scar
Settlement
Hut Circle and Enclosures
Low Field Farm
Wharfedale RUFC
BADGER GATE 1
WHARFE VIEW 2
RAINES LEA 3
WHARFE LA 4
BULL ING
GRASSINGTON
Grassington
Edge Top
Mast

Cow Close Wood
B6160
Upper Wharfedale Sch
PO
Liby
14
WATER ST
Upper Wharfedale Folk Mus & Visitor Ctr
Edge Side
Garnshaw House

WOOD LA
Lower Heights Farm
SKIRETHORNS LANE
PH
10
Grassington CE Prim Sch
HEBDEN ROAD
High Cross

GRYSEDALE LA
Lower Height
Grysedale House
OLD HALL CH
Skirethorns
Threshfield
Threshfield Prim Sch
Weir
Linton Falls
P
Isingdale Halfway Farm
B6265

Threshfield Moor
Grisedale Gate Farm
MOOR LANE
OLD MONKHOLME ST
Threshfield Bridge
Bow Bridge
P
CHURCH ROAD
Sewage Works
Lythe House

TARNS LANE
Tarns Plantation
Manor House Farm
Lythe Plantation
River Wharfe

Boss Moor
Linton Moor
Linton
Farlands Plantation
LAURADALE LANE
B6265
Nook Farm
PH
Grange Farm
Brows Plantation
Waddy Plantation
B6160

B6265
Lauraldale Bridge
THORPE LA

96   A   97   B   98   C   99   D   00   E   01   F

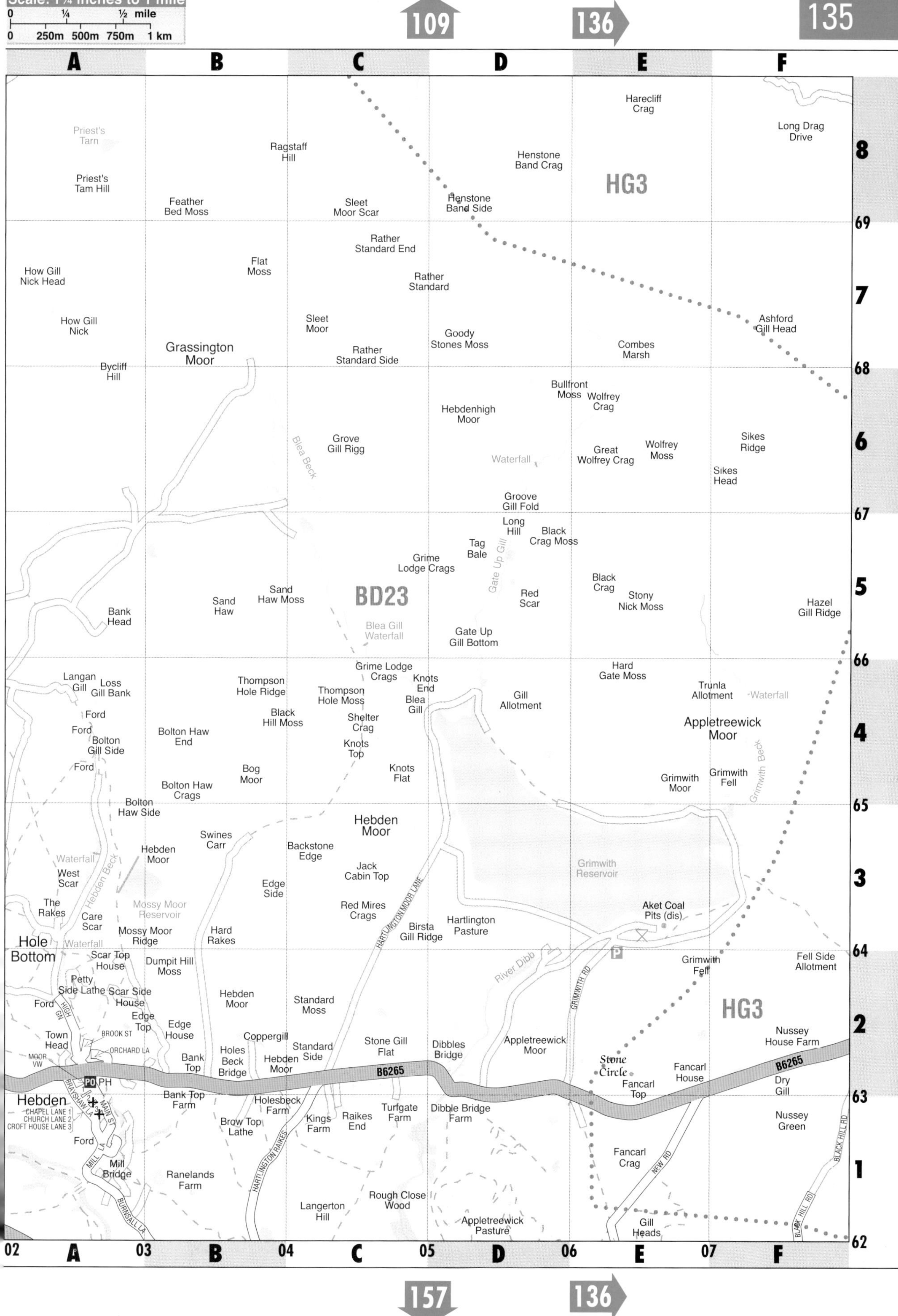

Scale: 1¾ inches to 1 mile

0   ¼   ½ mile

0 250m 500m 750m 1 km

A B C D E F

8

Priest's
Tarn

Priest's
Tarn Hill

Harecliff
Crag

Long Drag
Drive

Ragstaff
Hill

Henstone
Band Crag

HG3

Feather
Bed Moss

Sleet
Moor Scar

Henstone
Band Side

69

Flat
Moss

Rather
Standard End

7

How Gill
Nick Head

Rather
Standard

How Gill
Nick

Sleet
Moor

Goody
Stones Moss

Combes
Marsh

Ashford
Gill Head

Bycliff
Hill

Grassington
Moor

Rather
Standard Side

68

Bullfront
Moss

Wolfrey
Crag

6

Hebdenhigh
Moor

Grove
Gill Rigg

Great
Wolfrey Crag

Wolfrey
Moss

Sikes
Ridge

Blea Beck

Waterfall

Sikes
Head

Groove
Gill Fold

67

Long
Hill

Black
Crag Moss

Tag
Bale

Grime
Lodge Crags

Gate Up Gill

Black
Crag

5

Sand
Haw Moss

BD23

Red
Scar

Stony
Nick Moss

Sand
Haw

Bank
Head

Blea Gill
Waterfall

Gate Up
Gill Bottom

Hazel
Gill Ridge

66

Grime Lodge
Crags

Hard
Gate Moss

Langan
Gill

Loss
Gill Bank

Thompson
Hole Ridge

Knots
End

Trunla
Allotment

Waterfall

4

Ford

Thompson
Hole Moss

Blea
Gill

Gill
Allotment

Appletreewick
Moor

Ford

Black
Hill Moss

Shelter
Crag

Bolton
Gill Side

Bolton Haw
End

Ford

Knots
Top

Bog
Moor

Knots
Flat

Grimwith
Moor

Grimwith
Fell

Grimwith Beck

Bolton Haw
Crags

65

Bolton
Haw Side

Hebden
Moor

Swines
Carr

Backstone
Edge

Waterfall

West
Scar

Hebden
Moor

Grimwith
Reservoir

3

The
Rakes

Edge
Side

Jack
Cabin Top

Care
Scar

Mossy Moor
Reservoir

Red Mires
Crags

Hartlington
Pasture

Aket Coal
Pits (dis)

Waterfall

Hard
Rakes

Birsta
Gill Ridge

River Dibb

Grimwith
Fell

Fell Side
Allotment

64

Hole
Bottom

Scar Top
House

Dumpit Hill
Moss

Mossy Moor
Ridge

HARTLINGTON MOOR LANE

P

Petty
Side Lathe

Scar Side
House

Hebden
Moor

Standard
Moss

GRIMWITH RD

HG3

2

Ford

Edge
Top

Edge
House

Nussey
House Farm

Town
Head

BROOK ST

Coppergill

Standard
Side

Stone Gill
Flat

Dibbles
Bridge

Appletreewick
Moor

Stone
Circle

Fancarl
House

B6265

MOOR
VW

ORCHARD LA

Bank
Top

Holes
Beck
Bridge

Hebden
Moor

Fancarl
Top

Dry
Gill

63

PO PH

Bank Top
Farm

Holesbeck
Farm

Kings
Farm

Raikes
End

Turfgate
Farm

Dibble Bridge
Farm

Nussey
Green

Hebden

CHAPEL LANE 1
CHURCH LANE 2
CROFT HOUSE LANE 3

MILL LA

MAIN ST

Brow Top
Lathe

HARTLINGTON RAKES

Fancarl
Crag

NEW RD

BLACK HILL RD

Ford

Mill
Bridge

Ranelands
Farm

Langerton
Hill

Rough Close
Wood

Appletreewick
Pasture

Gill
Heads

BLACK HILL RD

1

BURNSALL LA

62

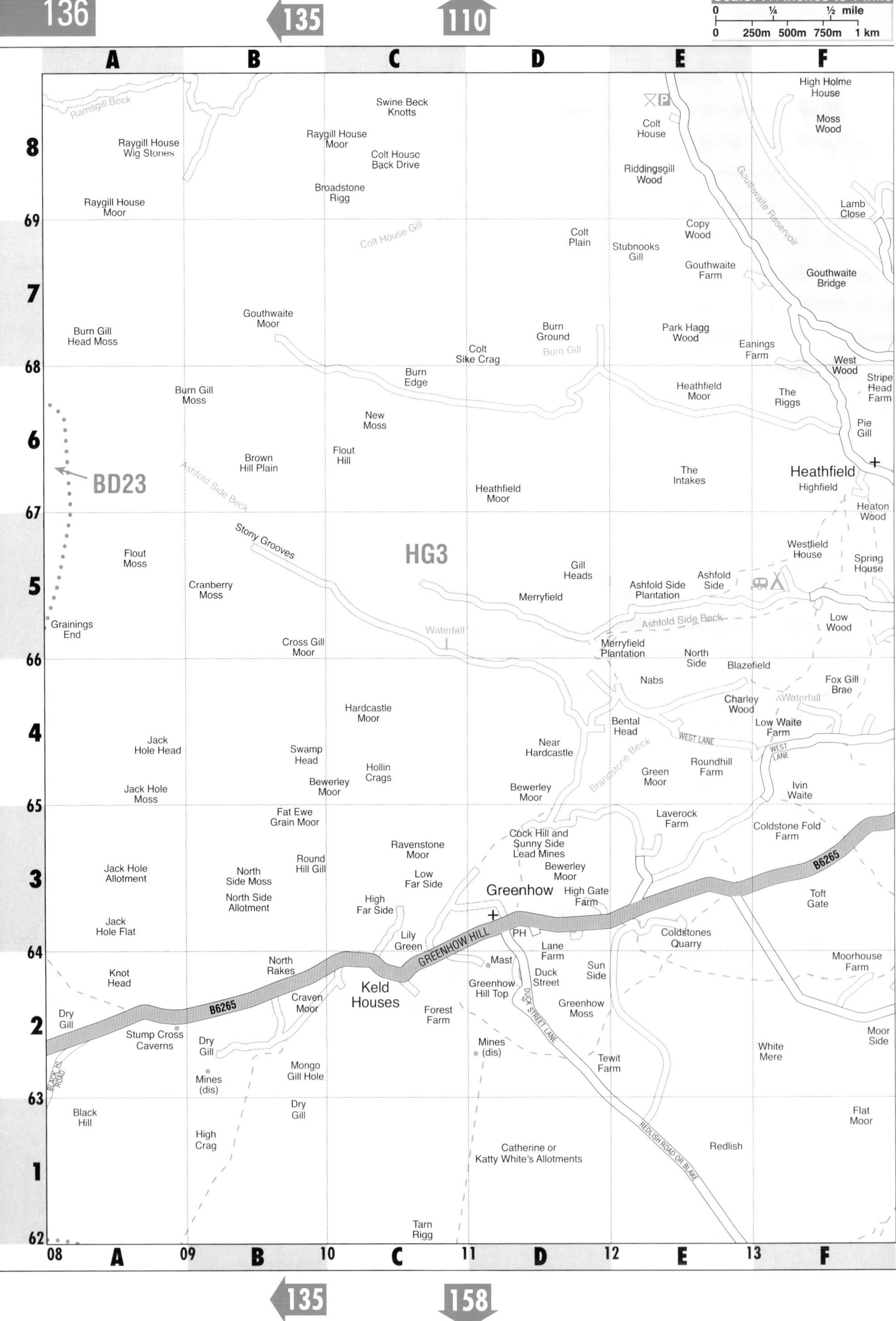

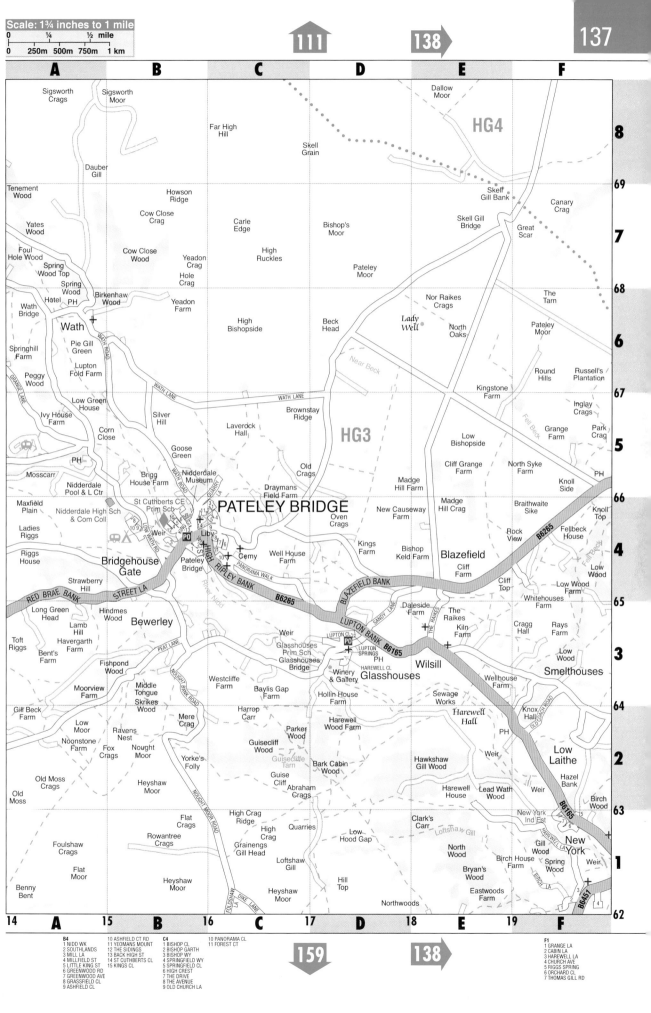

Scale: 1¾ inches to 1 mile

0   ¼   ½   mile
0 250m 500m 750m 1 km

111
138
137

A   B   C   D   E   F

8
Sigsworth Crags
Sigsworth Moor
Far High Hill
Skell Grain
Dallow Moor
HG4

69
Dauber Gill
Howson Ridge
Skell Gill Bank
Canary Crag

7
Tenement Wood
Cow Close Crag
Carle Edge
Bishop's Moor
Skell Gill Bridge
Great Scar
Yates Wood
Cow Close Wood
High Ruckles
Pateley Moor

68
Foul Hole Wood
Yeadon Crag
Hole Crag
Pateley Moor
Nor Raikes Crags
The Tarn
Spring Wood Top
Spring Wood
Birkenhaw Wood
Yeadon Farm
High Bishopside
Beck Head
Lady Well
North Oaks
Pateley Moor

6
Wath Bridge
Hotel PH
Wath
Pie Gill Green
Springhill Farm
Lupton Fold Farm
Peggy Wood
Round Hills
Russell's Plantation

67
Low Green House
Wath Lane
Wath Lane
Kingstone Farm
Inglay Crags

5
Mosscarr
Ivy House Farm
Corn Close
PH
Silver Hill
Goose Green
Laverock Hall
Brownstay Ridge
HG3
Low Bishopside
Grange Farm
Park Crag
Cliff Grange Farm
North Syke Farm
Knoll Side

66
Maxfield Plain
Nidderdale Pool & L Ctr
Nidderdale High Sch & Com Coll
Brigg House Farm
Nidderdale Museum
St Cuthberts CE Prim Sch
Draymans Field Farm
Old Crags
Madge Hill Farm
New Causeway Farm
Madge Hill Crag
Braithwaite Sike
Rock View
Fellbeck House
Knoll Top
PH
B6265

4
Ladies Riggs
Weir
Lib
PO
PATELEY BRIDGE
Oven Crags
Well House Farm
Kings Farm
Bishop Keld Farm
Blazefield
Cliff Farm
Low Wood
Riggs House
Pateley Bridge
Cemy
Cliff Top
Low Wood Farm
Whitehouses Farm

65
Red Brae Bank
Street La
Long Green Head
Hindmes Wood
Strawberry Hill
Bewerley
Panorama Walk
River Nidd
High Ripley Bank
B6265
Blazefield Bank
Daleside Farm
The Raikes
Sandy Lane
Kiln Farm
Cragg Hall
Rays Farm

3
Lamb Hill
Havergarth Farm
Bent's Farm
Toft Riggs
Fishpond Wood
Peat Lane
Weir
Glasshouses Prim Sch
Glasshouses Bridge
Lupton Cl
PO
Lupton Springs PH
Lupton Bank
B6165
Wilsill
Wellhouse Farm
Low Wood
Smelthouses
Winery & Gallery
Harewell Cl
Glasshouses

64
Gill Beck Farm
Moorview Farm
Middle Tongue Skrikes Wood
Westcliffe Farm
Harrop Carr
Harewell Wood Farm
Sewage Works
Harewell Hall
Knox Hall
Old Coach Road
PH
Low Laithe

2
Low Moor
Noonstone Farm
Ravens Nest
Fox Crags
Nought Moor
Mere Crag
Baylis Gap Farm
Hollin House Farm
Parker Wood
Guisecliff Wood
Bark Cabin Wood
Hawkshaw Gill Wood
Weir
Hazel Bank
Nought Bank Road
Yorke's Folly
Guisecliff Tarn
Guise Cliff
Harewell House
Lead Wath Wood
New York Ind Est
Birch Wood
B6165

1
Old Moss Crags
Old Moss
Heyshaw Moor
Flat Crags
Rowantree Crags
High Crag Ridge
High Crag
Quarries
Abraham Crags
Low Hood Gap
Clark's Carr
Loftshaw Gill
North Wood
New York
Gill Wood
Spring Wood
Weir
Foulshaw Crags
Foldshaw La
Dike Lane
Grainengs Gill Head
Loftshaw Gill
Hill Top
Bryan's Wood
Birch House Farm
Birch La
Harewell La
Flat Moor
Benny Bent
Heyshaw Moor
Heyshaw Moor
Northwoods
Eastwoods Farm
B6451

62

B4
1 NIDD WK
2 SOUTHLANDS
3 MILL LA
4 MILLFIELD ST
5 LITTLE KING ST
6 GREENWOOD RD
7 GREENWOOD AVE
8 GRASSFIELD CL
9 ASHFIELD CL
10 ASHFIELD CT RD
11 YEOMANS MOUNT
12 THE SIDINGS
13 BACK HIGH ST
14 ST CUTHBERTS CL
15 KINGS CL

C4
1 BISHOP CL
2 BISHOP GARTH
3 BISHOP WY
4 SPRINGFIELD WY
5 SPRINGFIELD
6 HIGH CREST
7 THE DRIVE
8 THE AVENUE
9 OLD CHURCH LA

10 PANORAMA CL
11 FOREST CT

F1
1 GRANGE LA
2 CABIN LA
3 HAREWELL LA
4 CHURCH AVE
5 RIGGS SPRING
6 ORCHARD CL
7 THOMAS GILL RD

A B C D E F

Skelding Moor
Skell Gill
Skell Gill Wood
Crag House
High Skelding Farm
West Skelding Farm
Ford
DRIFT LANE
BRADFIELD LANE
Low Green Farm
Hollin Farm
Low Skelding Farm
High Grantley
Fountains CE Prim Sch
Ten Acre Plantation
Hungate Wood
Hungate
Sun Wood
Sunny Bank Wood
Grantley Hall
Horsleygate Farm
MOOR LANE
Cat Crag

Low Huller Stones
Brim Bray Pond
River Skell
Miss Wood
Risplith
B6265
Low Kirby Wood
Gill Farm
Aldfield Spa
Spa Gill Wood

West Farm
Grange Farm
Smaden Head
Smaden Head Wood
Eavestone
HG4
Highfield Top
Birka Carr
Hollin Hill Farm
Gowbusk
GREEN LANE
Lee Mires Farm
Grange Farm
Hind House
Low Gate
Low Gate Farm
Low Gate Lane

Eavestone Moor
Brim House Farm
Hill Top Farm
Eavestone Lake
Ravens Crag
Yaudhouse Head Farm
Fishpond Wood
Sunny View Farm
CHURCH CL
St Michael's MD
PH
Sawley
Green Bank Wood
Hall Gates Farm
Sawley Hall

Pateley Moor
CROSSGATES
Middle Rigg Farm
Sawley Moor Lane
Sawley Moor House
Moor Lane Farm
Lacon Hall
MIDDYCAR BANK
GREEN LANE

Quarry House
Springhill Farm
High Moor
Sawley Moor
Booth Wood
Hebden Wood
Hebden Bridge
Wet Car Wood
Ashfield House

Springfield Farm
Trout Beck Farm
Collar Stoop
Collarstoop Moor
B6265
HEBDEN BECK

Great Wood
North Pasture
High North Farm
North Owl
Burnt Plantation
Warsill Hall Farm
Calf Haugh
Hebden Wood Farm
BARKHOUSE BANK

North Pasture Farm
Hare Heads
Warsill
Rabbit Hill Farm
Warren House
South East Farm
Low Farm
Volla Wood Farm
Volla Wood
CARELESS HO LANE
Careless House Farm
Raventofts Hall

Visitor Centre
Brimham Rocks
Summer Wood House
Middle Farm
Whinny Hill
High Gill Moor
Gill Moor
Highfield House

High Wood Farm
P
Brimham Moor
Spring Wood
South Farm
Low Gill Moor
West Wood
Gill Moor Farm

High Wood
Riva Hill Farm
Beckside Farm
East Wood
Park House Farm
Woodfield Farm
Bowes Green Farm
Colber House Farm

Braisty Woods
Kimberley House Farm
Brimham
HG3
Shepherds Lodge Farm
Woodfield House
COLBER LANE
Hatton House Farm
Bishop Thornton CE Prim Sch
Bishop Thornton

Woolwich Farm
Needham's Crag
Moor Side
Fiddler's Green
Broom Hill Wood
Brimham Lodge
BRIMHAM ROCKS RD
Brimham Lodge Farm
Fox Wood
Hardgate Farm
Thornton Grange
CUT THROAT LANE
GRANGE CL

High Pasture Farm
Prospect House
Black House
Cowgate Farm
LOW MILL CT
MILL BANK
Thornton Beck

Old Spring Wood
Summerbridge Prim Sch
Hartwith Crags
HARTWITH BANK
Hill Top Farm
Standing Stone Hill
Brimham Hall Farm
STRIPE LANE
Hartwith Moor
Mansion House Farm
Spa Wood
High Eppage Wood
Trustee Wood
Flask House Farm
Shaw Mills
PH
LAW LANE

PO
B6165
Summerbridge
Highfield Farm
Spring House Wood
Spring House Farm
High Winsley Farm

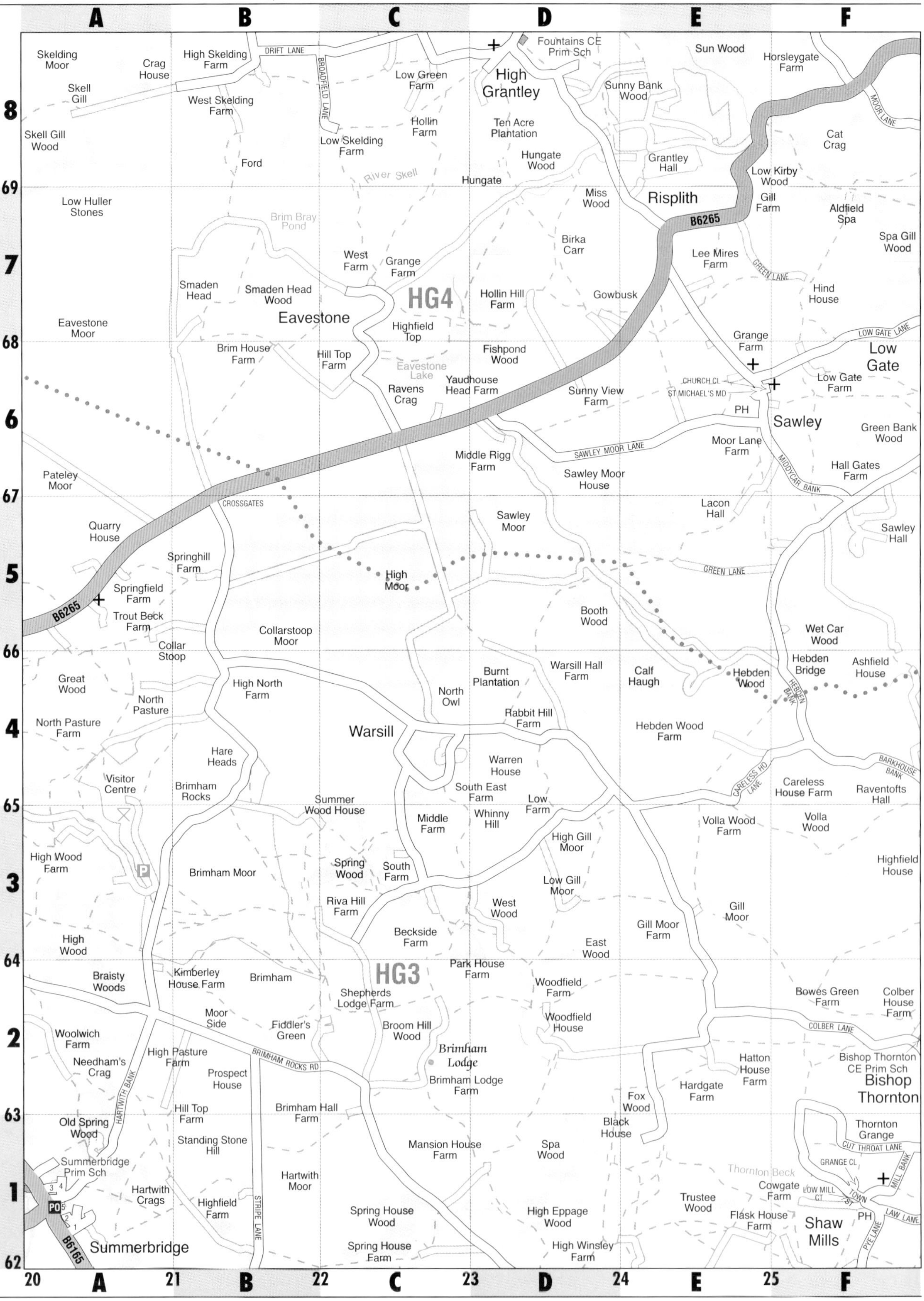

A1
1 WHINBUSH LANE
2 THE CRESCENT
3 HARTWITH AVE
4 HARTWITH GN
5 WHINFIELD BWS

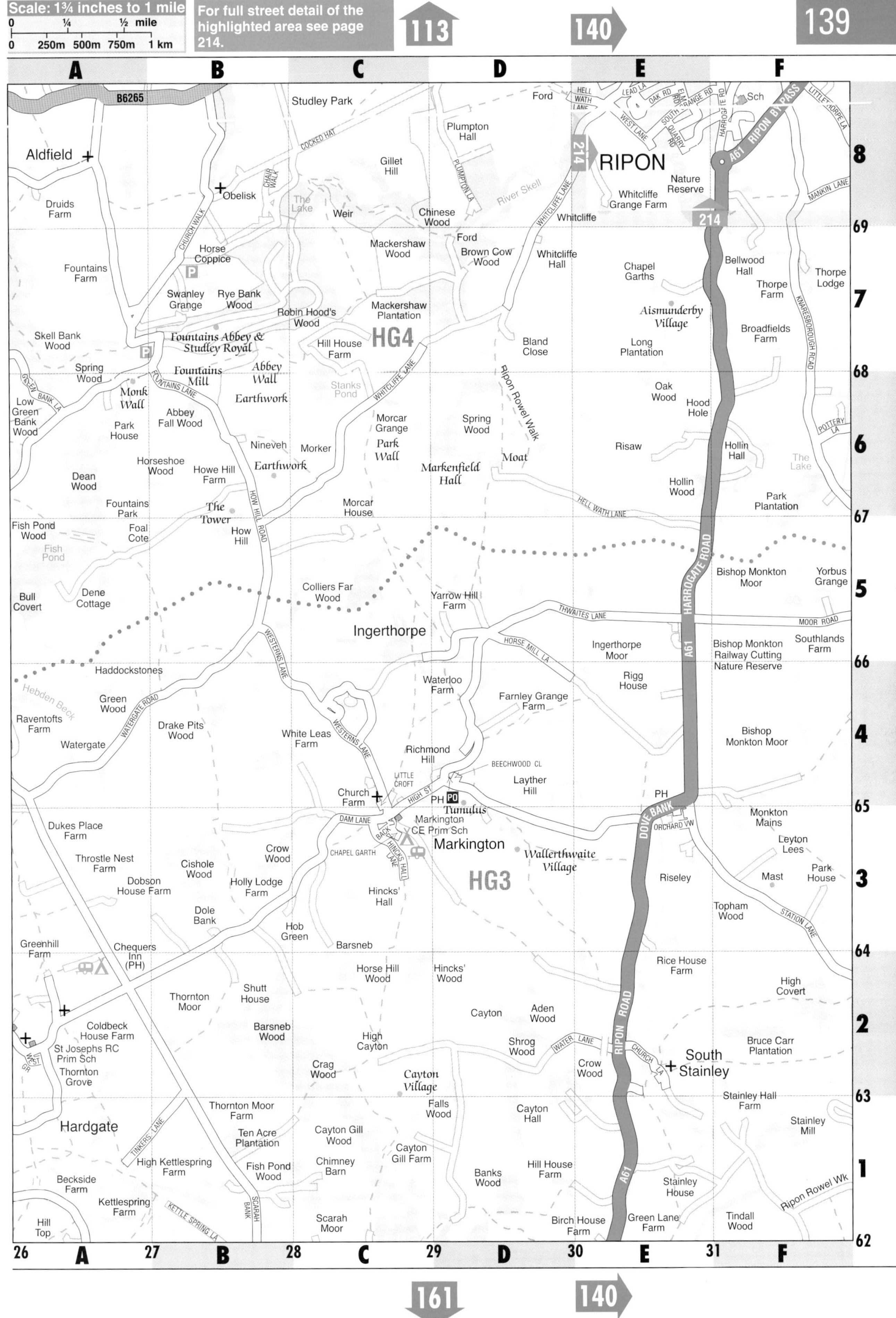

Scale: 1¾ inches to 1 mile

0 ¼ ½ mile
0 250m 500m 750m 1 km

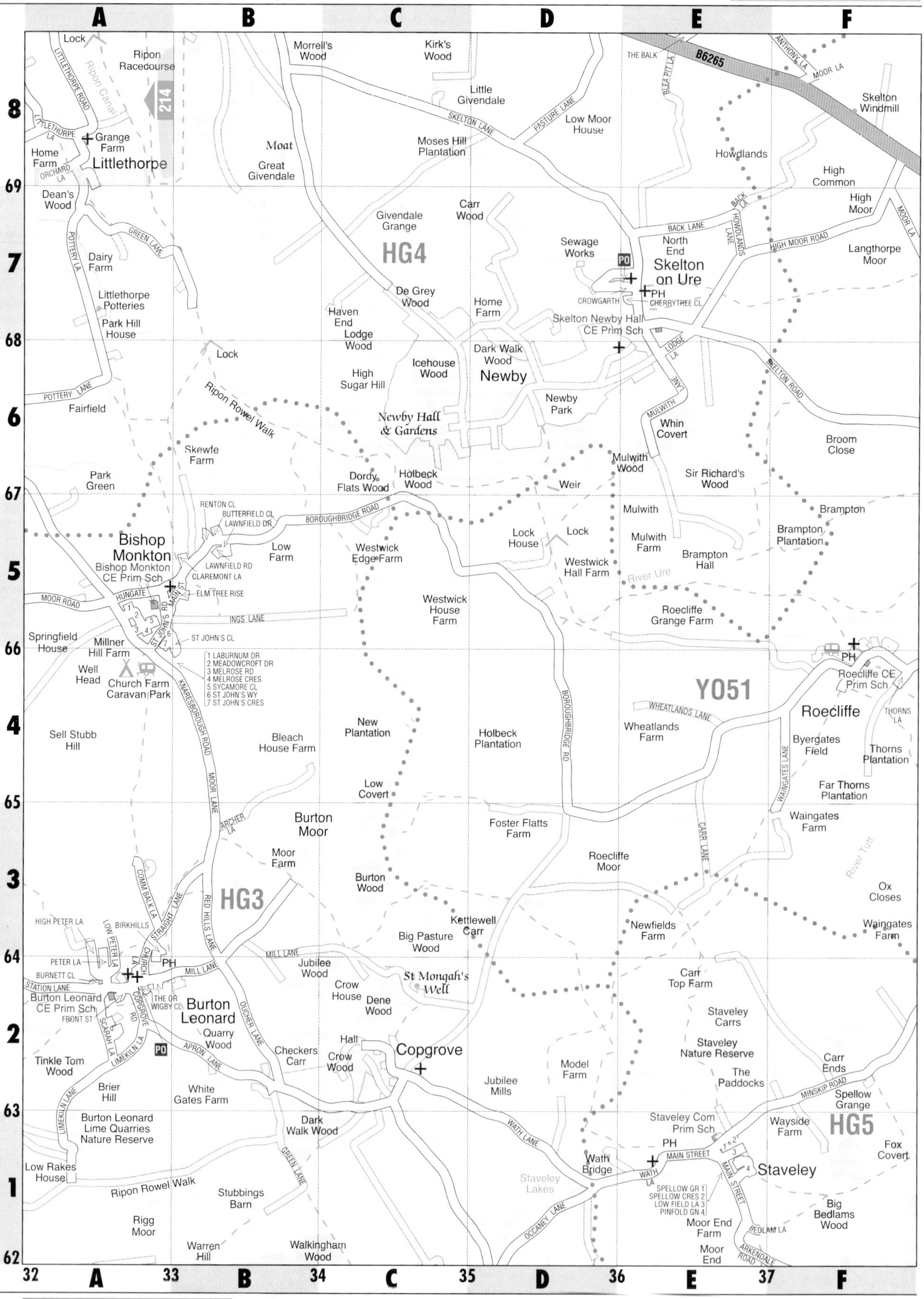

A **B** **C** **D** **E** **F**

Lock
Ripon Racecourse
214

8

Morrell's Wood
Kirk's Wood
Little Givendale
Moses Hill Plantation
Low Moor House
THE BALK
B6265
ANTHONY LA
MOOR LA
Skelton Windmill

Grange Farm
Littlethorpe
Home Farm
ORCHARD LA
Moat
Great Givendale
Howlands
High Common
High Moor
Langthorpe Moor

69

Dean's Wood
Givendale Grange
Carr Wood
BACK LANE
HOWLANDS LANE
High Moor Road
MOOR LA

7

Dairy Farm
POTTERY LA
GREEN LANE
HG4
De Grey Wood
Home Farm
Sewage Works
PO
North End
Skelton on Ure
PH
CROWGARTH
CHERRYTREE CL
BACK LANE
Littlethorpe Potteries
Park Hill House
Haven End Lodge Wood
Icehouse Wood
Dark Walk Wood
Skelton Newby Hall CE Prim Sch
LODGE LA

68

Lock
High Sugar Hill
Newby
Newby Park
MULWITH LANE
Whin Covert
SKELTON ROAD

6

POTTERY LANE
Fairfield
Ripon Rowel Walk
Newby Hall & Gardens
Mulwith Wood
Sir Richard's Wood
Broom Close
Skewfe Farm
Dordy Flats Wood
Holbeck Wood
Weir
Mulwith
Brampton
Brampton Plantation

67

Park Green
RENTON CL
BUTTERFIELD CL
LAWNFIELD DR
BOROUGHBRIDGE ROAD
Westwick Edge Farm
Lock House
Lock
Mulwith Farm
Mulwith
Brampton Hall

5

MOOR ROAD
Bishop Monkton
Bishop Monkton CE Prim Sch
HUNGATE
LAWNFIELD RD
CLAREMONT LA
ELM TREE RISE
Low Farm
Westwick House Farm
Westwick Hall Farm
River Ure
Roecliffe Grange Farm

66

Springfield House
Millner Hill Farm
ST JOHN'S CL
1 LABURNUM DR
2 MEADOWCROFT DR
3 MELROSE RD
4 MELROSE CRES
5 SYCAMORE CL
6 ST JOHN'S WY
7 ST JOHN'S CRES
PH
Roecliffe CE Prim Sch

4

Well Head
Church Farm Caravan Park
KNARESBOROUGH ROAD
MOOR LANE
Sell Stubb Hill
Bleach House Farm
New Plantation
Holbeck Plantation
YO51
Roecliffe
Wheatlands Farm
WHEATLANDS LANE
THORNS LA
Thorns Plantation
Far Thorns Plantation

65

ARCHER LA
Burton Moor
Moor Farm
Low Covert
Foster Flatts Farm
Roecliffe Moor
CARR LANE
WAINGATES LANE
Waingates Farm
River Tutt
Ox Closes

3

COMM BALK LA
RED HILLS LANE
STRAIGHT LANE
HG3
Burton Wood
Kettlewell Carr
Newfields Farm
Waingates Farm

High Peter La
BIRKHILLS
LOW PETER LA
PH
MILL LANE
Jubilee Wood
Big Pasture Wood
St Mongah's Well
Carr Top Farm

64

PETER LA
BURNETT CL
CHURCH LA
COPGROVE RD
MILL LANE
DUCHER LANE
Crow House
Dene Wood
Staveley Carrs
Staveley Nature Reserve
Carr Ends

STATION LANE
Burton Leonard CE Prim Sch
FRONT ST
LIMEKILN LA
SCRAH ST
PO
Burton Leonard
Quarry Wood
APRON LANE
Checkers Carr
Hall
Crow Wood
Copgrove
Model Farm
The Paddocks
Spellow Grange

2

Tinkle Tom Wood
Brier Hill
White Gates Farm
Jubilee Mills
Staveley Com Prim Sch
Wayside Farm
HG5
Fox Covert

63

LIMEKILN LANE
Burton Leonard Lime Quarries Nature Reserve
Dark Walk Wood
GREEN LANE
WATH LANE
Wath Bridge
WATH LA
PH
MAIN STREET
Staveley
MINSKIP ROAD
Bedlams Wood

Low Rakes House
Ripon Rowel Walk
Stubbings Barn
Staveley Lakes
SPELLOW GR 1
SPELLOW CRES 2
LOW FIELD LA 3
PINFOLD GN 4
BEDLAM LA
Big Bedlams Wood

1

Rigg Moor
Warren Hill
Walkingham Wood
OCCANEY LANE
Moor End Farm
Moor End
ARKENDALE ROAD

62

32 **A** **33** **B** **34** **C** **35** **D** **36** **E** **37** **F**

For full street detail of the highlighted area see page 214.

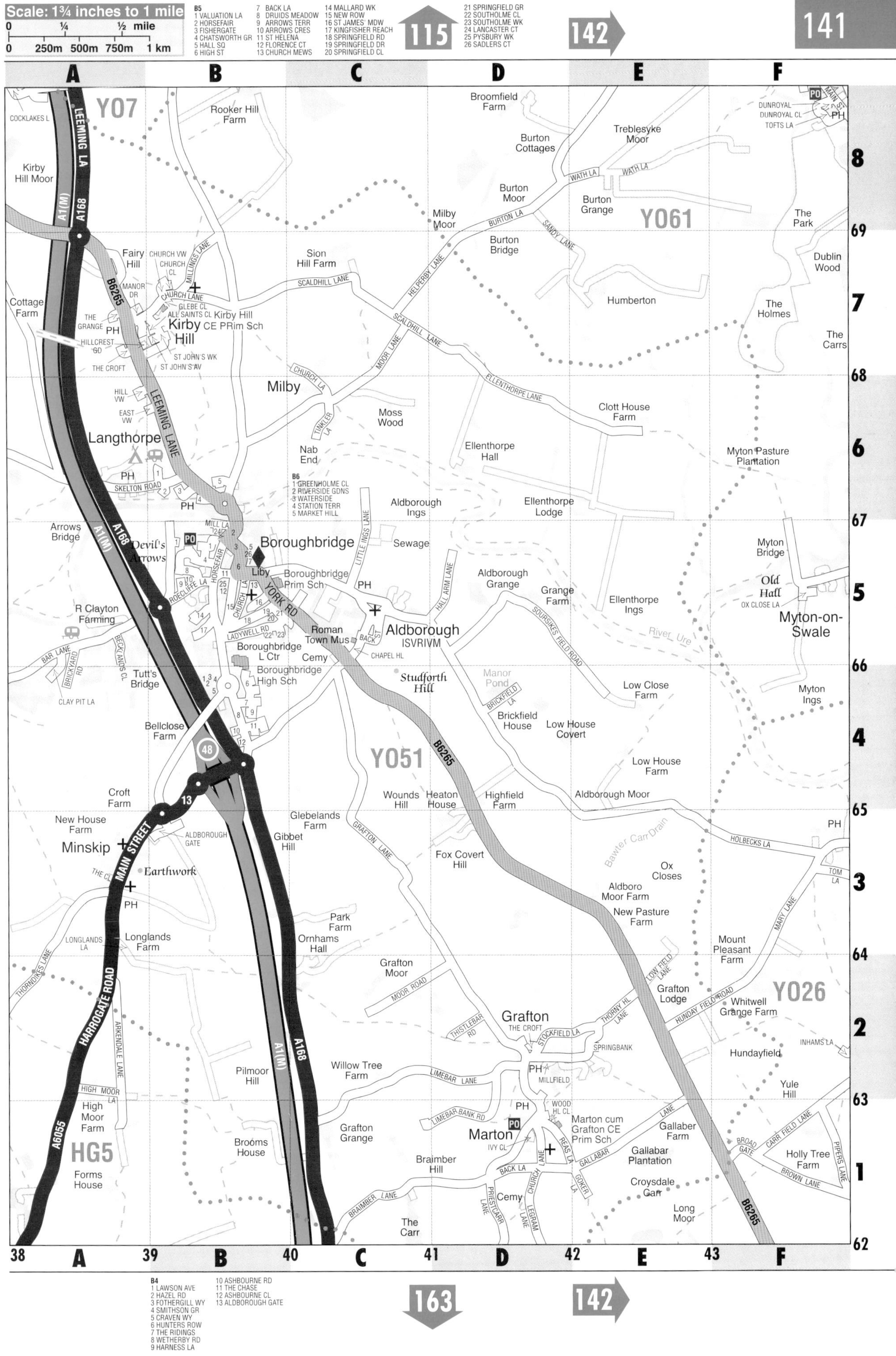
Scale: 1¾ inches to 1 mile
0 ¼ ½ mile
0 250m 500m 750m 1 km
B5
1 VALUATION LA
2 HORSEFAIR
3 FISHERGATE
4 CHATSWORTH GR
5 HALL SQ
6 HIGH ST
7 BACK LA
8 DRUIDS MEADOW
9 ARROWS TERR
10 ARROWS CRES
11 ST HELENA
12 FLORENCE CT
13 CHURCH MEWS
14 MALLARD WK
15 NEW ROW
16 ST JAMES' MDW
17 KINGFISHER REACH
18 SPRINGFIELD RD
19 SPRINGFIELD DR
20 SPRINGFIELD CL
21 SPRINGFIELD GR
22 SOUTHOLME CL
23 SOUTHOLME WK
24 LANCASTER CT
25 PYSBURY WK
26 SADLERS CT
115
142
141
A B C D E F
YO7
COCKLAKES L
LEEMING LA
Rooker Hill Farm
Broomfield Farm
Burton Cottages
Treblesyke Moor
DUNROYAL
DUNROYAL CL
TOFTS LA
MAIN ST
PO
PH
Kirby Hill Moor
A1(M)
A168
WATH LA
Burton Moor
Burton Grange
YO61
Milby Moor
BURTON LA
SANDY LANE
The Park
Burton Bridge
Dublin Wood
Fairy Hill
CHURCH VW
CHURCH CL
MILLINGS LANE
Sion Hill Farm
SCALDHILL LANE
HELPERBY LANE
B6265
MANOR DR
CHURCH LANE
GLEBE CL
ALL SAINTS CL
Kirby Hill CE PRim Sch
Humberton
Cottage Farm
THE GRANGE
Kirby Hill
The Holmes
HILLCREST GD
THE CROFT
ST JOHN'S WK
ST JOHN'S AV
MOOR LANE
The Carrs
Milby
CHURCH LA
ELLENTHORPE LANE
HILL VW
EAST VW
LEEMING LANE
Moss Wood
TINKLER LA
Clott House Farm
Langthorpe
Nab End
Ellenthorpe Hall
Myton Pasture Plantation
SKELTON ROAD
B6
1 GREENHOLME CL
2 RIVERSIDE GDNS
3 WATERSIDE
4 STATION TERR
5 MARKET HILL
Aldborough Ings
Ellenthorpe Lodge
Arrows Bridge
MILL LA
Devil's Arrows
Boroughbridge
LITTLE INGS LANE
Sewage
Myton Bridge
Liby
Boroughbridge Prim Sch
HALL ARM LANE
Aldborough Grange
Grange Farm
Old Hall
OX CLOSE LA
HORSEFAIR
ROECLIFFE LA
YORK RD
Ellenthorpe Ings
Myton-on-Swale
R Clayton Farming
LADYWELL RD
Roman Town Mus
BACK ST
Aldborough
ISVRIVM
SOURSIKES FIELD ROAD
River Ure
BAR LANE
BRICKYARD RD
BECKLANDS CL
Boroughbridge L Ctr
Cemy
CHAPEL HL
Tutt's Bridge
Boroughbridge High Sch
Studforth Hill
Manor Pond
BRICKFIELD LA
Low Close Farm
Myton Ings
CLAY PIT LA
Brickfield House
Low House Covert
Bellclose Farm
48
YO51
Low House Farm
Croft Farm
13
Wounds Hill
Heaton House
Highfield Farm
Aldborough Moor
New House Farm
Glebelands Farm
ALDBOROUGH GATE
Gibbet Hill
GRAFTON LANE
Minskip
MAIN STREET
Bawter Carr Drain
HOLBECKS LA
Fox Covert Hill
THE CL
Earthwork
Ox Closes
TOM LA
Aldboro Moor Farm
New Pasture Farm
MARY LANE
Park Farm
LONGLANDS LA
Longlands Farm
Ornhams Hall
Mount Pleasant Farm
THORNDIKES LANE
Grafton Moor
MOOR ROAD
LOW FIELD LANE
Grafton Lodge
YO26
HARROGATE ROAD
THORNY HL LANE
HUNDAY FIELD ROAD
Whitwell Grange Farm
Grafton
THE CROFT
THISTLEBAR RD
STOCKFIELD LA
ARKENDALE LANE
SPRINGBANK
INHAMS LA
Hundayfield
Willow Tree Farm
LIMEBAR LANE
MILLFIELD
Yule Hill
Pilmoor Hill
HIGH MOOR LA
High Moor Farm
LIMEBAR BANK RD
WOOD HL CL
Marton cum Grafton CE Prim Sch
Gallaber Farm
CARR FIELD LANE
Grafton Grange
Marton
A6055
HG5
Brooms House
IVY CL
REAS LA
BROAD GATE
Holly Tree Farm
PIPERS LANE
Braimber Hill
BACK LA
GALLABAR
Gallabar Plantation
BROWN LANE
Forms House
GOKER LA
Croysdale Carr
PRIESTCARR LANE
LEGRAM LANE
BRAIMBER LANE
Long Moor
The Carr
8 69 7 68 6 67 5 66 4 65 3 64 2 63 1 62
38 39 40 41 42 43
B4
1 LAWSON AVE
2 HAZEL RD
3 FOTHERGILL WY
4 SMITHSON GR
5 CRAVEN WY
6 HUNTERS ROW
7 THE RIDINGS
8 WETHERBY RD
9 HARNESS LA
10 ASHBOURNE RD
11 THE CHASE
12 ASHBOURNE CL
13 ALDBOROUGH GATE
163
142

141
116

Scale: 1¾ inches to 1 mile

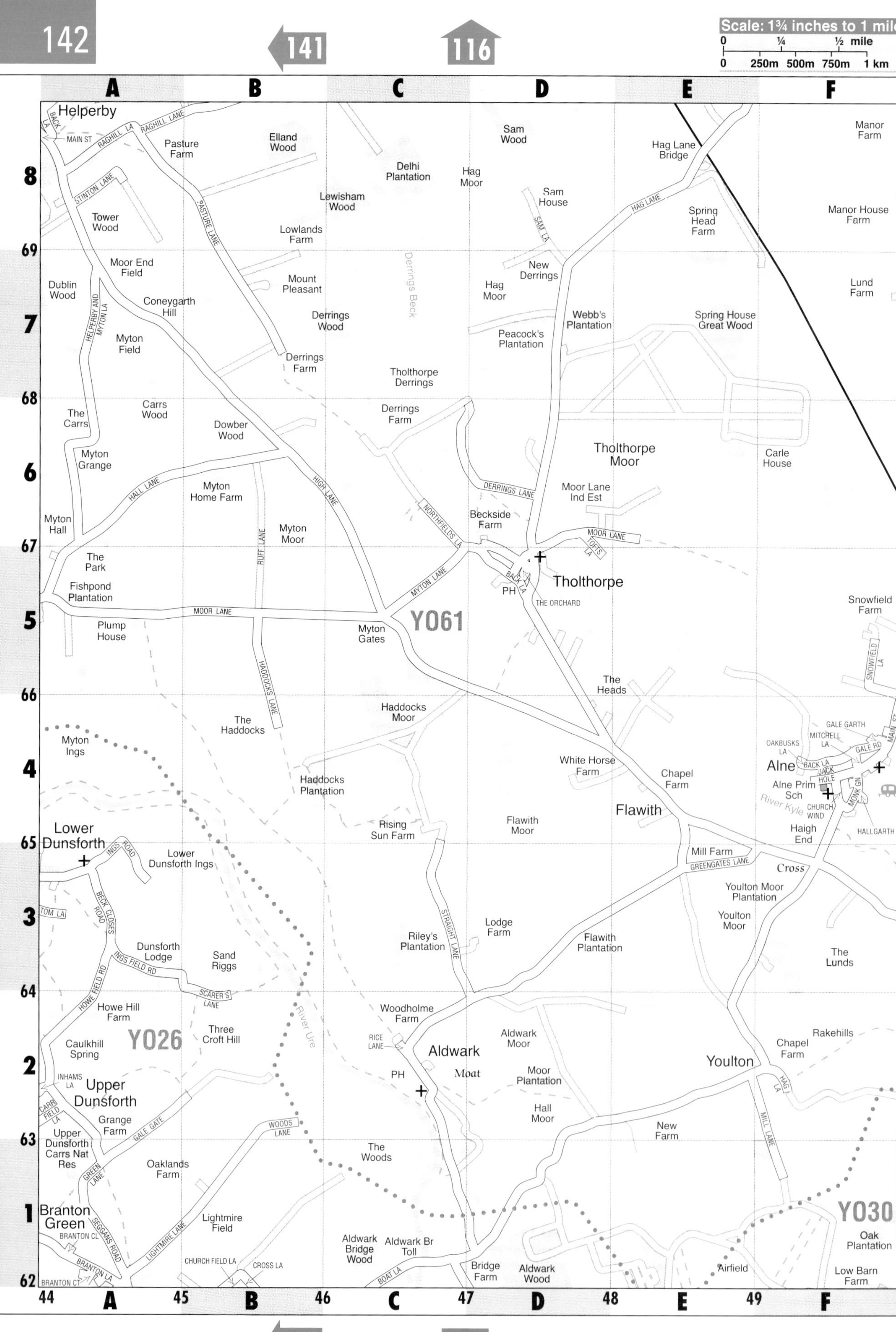
Helperby
Pasture Farm
Elland Wood
Delhi Plantation
Hag Moor
Sam Wood
Sam House
Hag Lane Bridge
Manor Farm
Manor House Farm
Tower Wood
Lewisham Wood
Lowlands Farm
Spring Head Farm
Moor End Field
Dublin Wood
Mount Pleasant
Hag Moor
New Derrings
Lund Farm
Coneygarth Hill
Derrings Wood
Derrings Beck
Webb's Plantation
Spring House Great Wood
Myton Field
Peacock's Plantation
Derrings Farm
Tholthorpe Derrings
The Carrs
Carrs Wood
Dowber Wood
Derrings Farm
Tholthorpe Moor
Carle House
Myton Grange
Myton Home Farm
Moor Lane Ind Est
Myton Hall
Myton Moor
Beckside Farm
The Park
Tholthorpe
Fishpond Plantation
PH
Plump House
Myton Gates
YO61
Snowfield Farm
The Heads
The Haddocks
Haddocks Moor
Myton Ings
White Horse Farm
Chapel Farm
Alne
Alne Prim Sch
Haddocks Plantation
Flawith
River Kyle
Haigh End
Rising Sun Farm
Flawith Moor
Lower Dunsforth
Lower Dunsforth Ings
Mill Farm
Cross
Youlton Moor Plantation
Youlton Moor
Riley's Plantation
Lodge Farm
Flawith Plantation
Dunsforth Lodge
Sand Riggs
The Lunds
Howe Hill Farm
Woodholme Farm
Rakehills
Caulkhill Spring
YO26
Three Croft Hill
River Ure
Aldwark Moor
Aldwark
Moat
Chapel Farm
Youlton
Upper Dunsforth
PH
Moor Plantation
Grange Farm
Hall Moor
Upper Dunsforth Carrs Nat Res
Oaklands Farm
New Farm
The Woods
Branton Green
Lightmire Field
YO30
Oak Plantation
Aldwark Bridge Wood
Aldwark Br Toll
Bridge Farm
Aldwark Wood
Airfield
Low Barn Farm
BACK LA
MAIN ST
RAGHILL LA
RAGHILL LANE
STINTON LANE
PASTURE LANE
HAG LANE
SAM LA
HELPERBY AND MYTON LA
HIGH LANE
HALL LANE
DERRINGS LANE
NORTHFIELDS LA
MOOR LANE
TOFTS LA
RUFF LANE
MYTON LANE
BACK LA
THE ORCHARD
MOOR LANE
HADDOCKS LANE
SNOWFIELD LA
GALE GARTH
MITCHELL LA
OAKBUSKS LA
GALE RD
MAIN ST
BACK LA
JACK HOLE
MONK GN
CHURCH WIND
HALLGARTH
INGS ROAD
GREENGATES LANE
TOM LA
BECK CLOSES ROAD
STRAIGHT LANE
INGS FIELD RD
HOWE FIELD RD
SCARER'S LANE
RICE LANE
INHAMS LA
HAG LA
CARR FIELD LA
GALE GATE
WOODS LANE
MILL LANE
GREEN LANE
SEGGANS ROAD
BRANTON CL
LIGHTMIRE LANE
BRANTON LA
CHURCH FIELD LA
CROSS LA
BOAT LA
BRANTON CT
A B C D E F
8 69 7 68 6 67 5 66 4 65 3 64 2 63 1 62
44 45 46 47 48 49

141
164

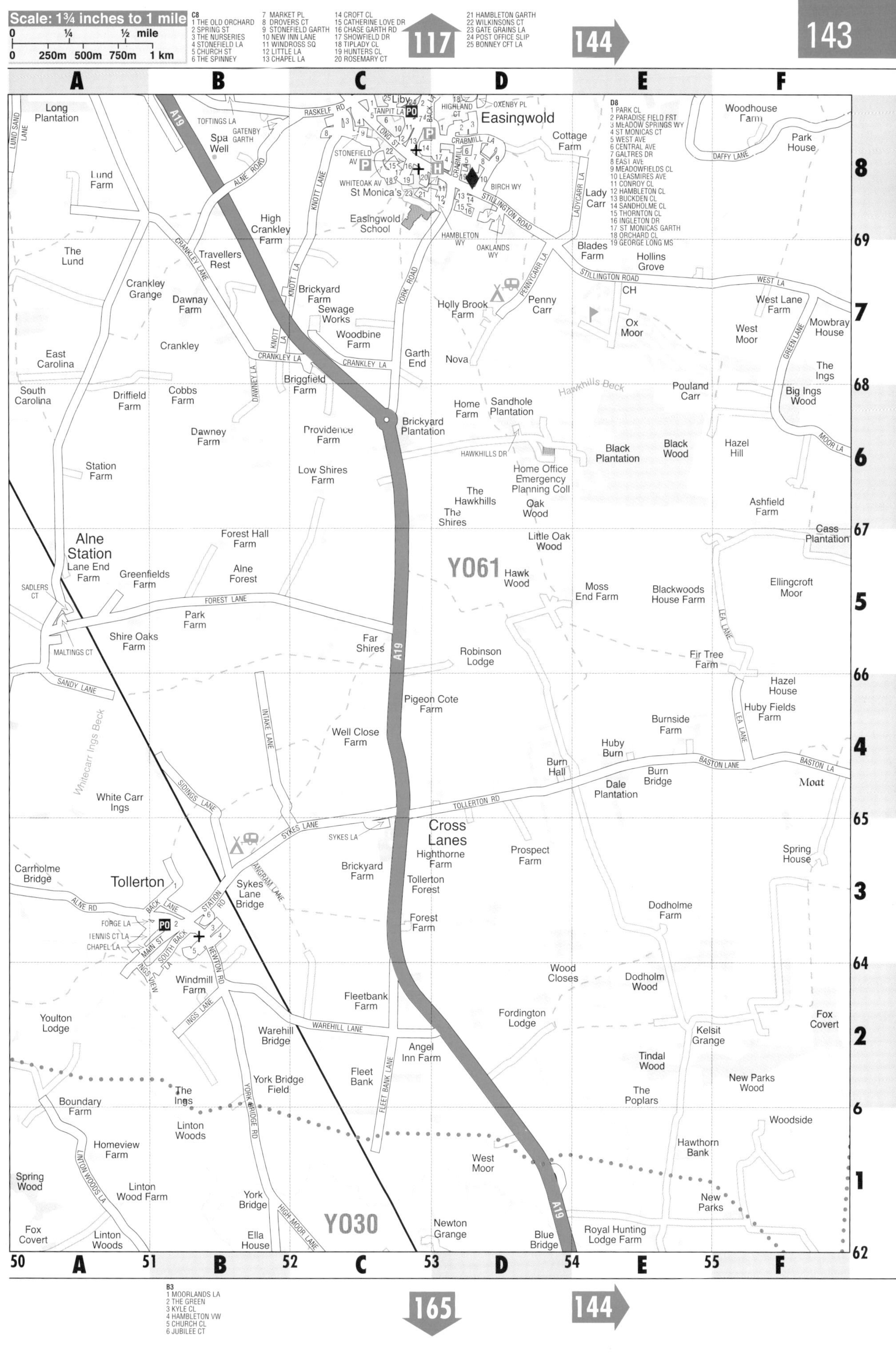
Scale: 1¾ inches to 1 mile
0 ¼ ½ mile
0 250m 500m 750m 1 km
C8
1 THE OLD ORCHARD
2 SPRING ST
3 THE NURSERIES
4 STONEFIELD LA
5 CHURCH ST
6 THE SPINNEY
7 MARKET PL
8 DROVERS CT
9 STONEFIELD GARTH
10 NEW INN LANE
11 WINDROSS SQ
12 LITTLE LA
13 CHAPEL LA
14 CROFT CL
15 CATHERINE LOVE DR
16 CHASE GARTH RD
17 SHOWFIELD DR
18 TIPLADY CL
19 HUNTERS CL
20 ROSEMARY CT
21 HAMBLETON GARTH
22 WILKINSONS CT
23 GATE GRAINS LA
24 POST OFFICE SLIP
25 BONNEY CFT LA
117
144
143
A
B
C
D
E
F
D8
1 PARK CL
2 PARADISE FIELD EST
3 MEADOW SPRINGS WY
4 ST MONICAS CT
5 WEST AVE
6 CENTRAL AVE
7 GALTRES DR
8 EAST AVE
9 MEADOWFIELDS CL
10 LEASMIRES AVE
11 CONROY CL
12 HAMBLETON CL
13 BUCKDEN CL
14 SANDHOLME CL
15 THORNTON CL
16 INGLETON DR
17 ST MONICAS GARTH
18 ORCHARD CL
19 GEORGE LONG MS
Long Plantation
LUND SAND LANE
A19
TOFTINGS LA
GATENBY GARTH
Spa Well
RASKELF RD
Liby
TANPIT LA
BACK LA
HIGHLAND CT
OXENBY PL
Easingwold
Cottage Farm
Woodhouse Farm
Park House
DAFFY LANE
8
Lund Farm
ALNE ROAD
KNOTT LANE
STONEFIELD AV
LONG ST
CRABMILL LA
WHITEOAK AV
St Monica's
BIRCH WY
STILLINGTON ROAD
LADYCARR LA
Lady Carr
High Crankley Farm
Easingwold School
HAMBLETON WY
OAKLANDS WY
69
The Lund
CRANKLEY LANE
Travellers Rest
Blades Farm
Hollins Grove
STILLINGTON ROAD
WEST LA
Crankley Grange
Dawnay Farm
KNOTT LA
Brickyard Farm
Sewage Works
YORK ROAD
Holly Brook Farm
PENNYCARR LA
Penny Carr
CH
West Lane Farm
7
Ox Moor
West Moor
Mowbray House
GREEN LANE
Crankley
Woodbine Farm
East Carolina
CRANKLEY LA
CRANKLEY LA
Garth End
Nova
The Ings
South Carolina
Driffield Farm
Cobbs Farm
DAWNEY LA
Briggfield Farm
Hawkhills Beck
Pouland Carr
68
Big Ings Wood
Brickyard Plantation
Home Farm
Sandhole Plantation
Dawney Farm
Providence Farm
HAWKHILLS DR
Black Plantation
Black Wood
Hazel Hill
MOOR LA
6
Station Farm
Low Shires Farm
Home Office Emergency Planning Coll
The Hawkhills
Oak Wood
The Shires
Ashfield Farm
Cass Plantation
67
Forest Hall Farm
Alne Station
Little Oak Wood
Lane End Farm
Greenfields Farm
Alne Forest
YO61
Hawk Wood
Moss End Farm
Blackwoods House Farm
Ellingcroft Moor
SADLERS CT
FOREST LANE
5
Park Farm
Shire Oaks Farm
Far Shires
MALTINGS CT
Robinson Lodge
LEA LANE
Fir Tree Farm
66
SANDY LANE
Hazel House
Pigeon Cote Farm
Whitecarr Ings Beck
Huby Fields Farm
Burnside Farm
INTAKE LANE
Well Close Farm
Huby Burn
LEA LANE
4
Burn Hall
BASTON LANE
BASTON LA
Burn Bridge
Moat
Dale Plantation
White Carr Ings
SIDINGS LANE
TOLLERTON RD
65
SYKES LANE
Cross Lanes
SYKES LA
Highthorne Farm
Prospect Farm
Spring House
Carrholme Bridge
Brickyard Farm
Tollerton
Sykes Lane Bridge
Tollerton Forest
3
ALNE RD
BACK LANE
STATION RD
ANGRAM LANE
Dodholme Farm
FORGE LA
PO
TENNIS CT LA
CHAPEL LA
MAIN ST
SOUTH BACK LA
INGS VIEW
NEWTON RD
Forest Farm
64
Wood Closes
Dodholm Wood
Windmill Farm
Fleetbank Farm
Youlton Lodge
INGS LANE
Warehill Bridge
WAREHILL LANE
Fordington Lodge
Fox Covert
Kelsit Grange
2
Angel Inn Farm
Tindal Wood
Boundary Farm
The Ings
York Bridge Field
Fleet Bank
FLEET BANK LANE
New Parks Wood
The Poplars
6
Linton Woods
YORK BRIDGE RD
Woodside
Homeview Farm
Hawthorn Bank
West Moor
LINTON WOODS LA
Spring Wood
1
Linton Wood Farm
New Parks
York Bridge
A19
HIGH MOOR LANE
YO30
Newton Grange
Royal Hunting Lodge Farm
Fox Covert
Linton Woods
Ella House
Blue Bridge
62
50
51
52
53
54
55
B3
1 MOORLANDS LA
2 THE GREEN
3 KYLE CL
4 HAMBLETON VW
5 CHURCH CL
6 JUBILEE CT
165
144

143
118

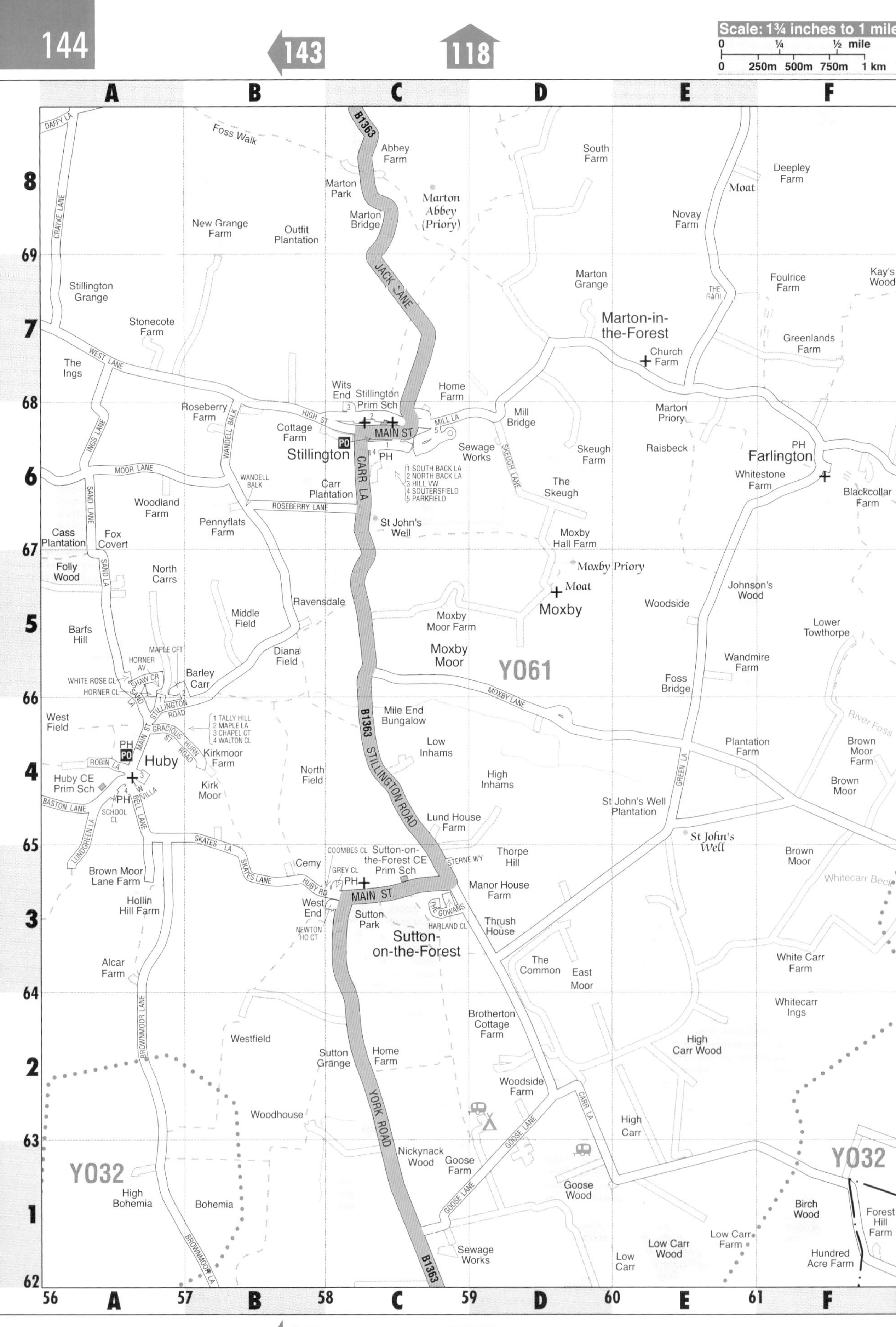
Scale: 1¾ inches to 1 mile
Stillington
Huby
Sutton-on-the-Forest
Marton-in-the-Forest
Farlington
Moxby
YO61
YO32
B1363
Marton Abbey (Priory)
Moxby Priory
Moxby Moor
Abbey Farm
Marton Park
Marton Bridge
New Grange Farm
Outfit Plantation
Stillington Grange
Stonecote Farm
The Ings
Roseberry Farm
Cottage Farm
Stillington Prim Sch
Wits End
Home Farm
Mill Bridge
Sewage Works
Skeugh Farm
The Skeugh
Moxby Hall Farm
South Farm
Marton Grange
Church Farm
Novay Farm
Deepley Farm
Foulrice Farm
Kay's Wood
Greenlands Farm
Marton Priory
Raisbeck
Whitestone Farm
Blackcollar Farm
Woodland Farm
Pennyflats Farm
Carr Plantation
St John's Well
Cass Plantation
Fox Covert
Folly Wood
North Carrs
Middle Field
Ravensdale
Moxby Moor Farm
Woodside
Johnson's Wood
Lower Towthorpe
Barfs Hill
Diana Field
Barley Carr
Wandmire Farm
Foss Bridge
West Field
Mile End Bungalow
Low Inhams
High Inhams
Kirkmoor Farm
Kirk Moor
North Field
Plantation Farm
Brown Moor Farm
Brown Moor
Huby CE Prim Sch
Lund House Farm
St John's Well Plantation
Thorpe Hill
Brown Moor Lane Farm
Cemy
Sutton-on-the-Forest CE Prim Sch
Manor House Farm
Hollin Hill Farm
West End
Sutton Park
Thrush House
The Common
East Moor
White Carr Farm
Alcar Farm
Whitecarr Ings
Westfield
Brotherton Cottage Farm
Sutton Grange
Home Farm
High Carr Wood
Woodside Farm
Woodhouse
High Carr
Nickynack Wood
Goose Farm
Goose Wood
High Bohemia
Bohemia
Birch Wood
Forest Hill Farm
Low Carr Farm
Low Carr Wood
Low Carr
Hundred Acre Farm
Foss Walk
River Foss
Whitecarr Beck
DAFFY LA
CRAYKE LANE
WEST LANE
INGS LANE
MOOR LANE
SAND LANE
WANDELL BALK
HIGH ST
MAIN ST
CARR LA
MILL LA
JACK LANE
SKEUGH LANE
ROSEBERRY LANE
MOXBY LANE
STILLINGTON ROAD
GREEN LA
SKATES LA
HUBY RD
YORK ROAD
GOOSE LANE
BROWNMOOR LANE
BASTON LANE
LUNDGREEN LA
BELL LANE
ROBIN LA
SCHOOL CL
1 SOUTH BACK LA
2 NORTH BACK LA
3 HILL VW
4 SOUTERSFIELD
5 PARKFIELD
1 TALLY HILL
2 MAPLE LA
3 CHAPEL CT
4 WALTON CL
COOMBES CL
GREY CL
NEWTON HO CT
STERNE WY
HARLAND CL
THE GOWANS
THE GAOL
Moat
PO
PH

143
166

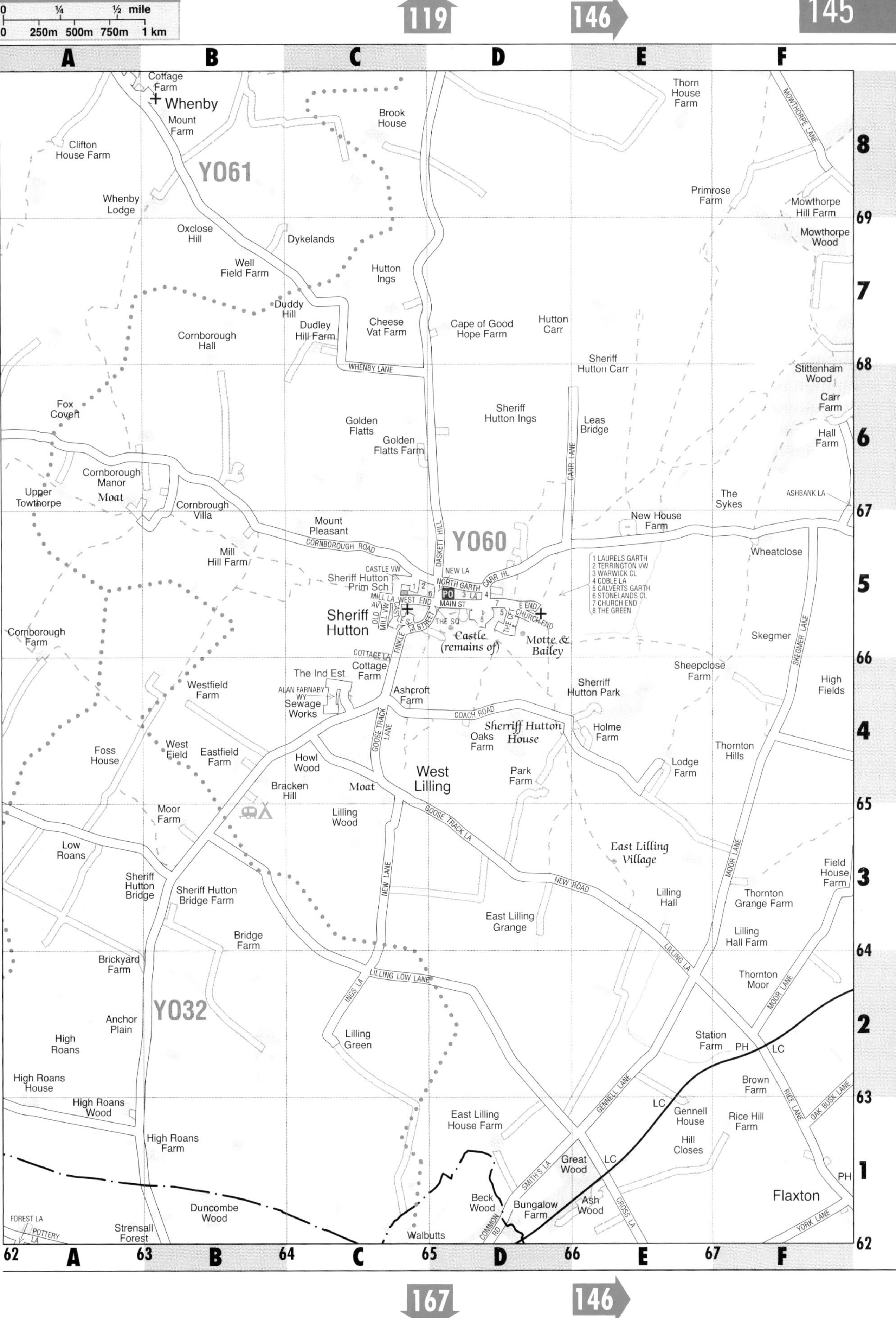
A
B
C
D
E
F
Cottage Farm
Whenby
Mount Farm
Clifton House Farm
YO61
Brook House
Thorn House Farm
MOWTHORPE LANE
8
Whenby Lodge
Primrose Farm
Mowthorpe Hill Farm
69
Oxclose Hill
Dykelands
Mowthorpe Wood
Well Field Farm
Hutton Ings
7
Duddy Hill
Dudley Hill Farm
Cheese Vat Farm
Cape of Good Hope Farm
Hutton Carr
Cornborough Hall
WHENBY LANE
Sheriff Hutton Carr
Stittenham Wood
68
Fox Covert
Sheriff Hutton Ings
Carr Farm
Golden Flatts
Leas Bridge
Hall Farm
6
Golden Flatts Farm
CARR LANE
Cornborough Manor
Moat
Upper Towthorpe
Cornbrough Villa
The Sykes
ASHBANK LA
New House Farm
67
Mount Pleasant
DASKETT HILL
YO60
CORNBOROUGH ROAD
Wheatclose
Mill Hill Farm
CASTLE VW
NEW LA
1 LAURELS GARTH
2 TERRINGTON VW
3 WARWICK CL
4 COBLE LA
5 CALVERTS GARTH
6 STONELANDS CL
7 CHURCH END
8 THE GREEN
Sheriff Hutton Prim Sch
NORTH GARTH
CARR HL
PO
5
MILL LA
WEST END
MAIN ST
E END
OLD MILL VW
Sheriff Hutton
THE SQ
THE CFT
CHURCH END
Castle (remains of)
Motte & Bailey
Cornborough Farm
Skegmer
COTTAGE LA
FINKLE STREET
66
The Ind Est
Cottage Farm
Sheepclose Farm
SKEGMER LANE
Westfield Farm
ALAN FARNABY WY
Sewage Works
Ashcroft Farm
Sheriff Hutton Park
High Fields
COACH ROAD
GOOSE TRACK LANE
Sherriff Hutton House
Holme Farm
4
Foss House
West Field
Eastfield Farm
Oaks Farm
Thornton Hills
Howl Wood
West Lilling
Park Farm
Lodge Farm
Bracken Hill
Moat
65
Moor Farm
Lilling Wood
GOOSE TRACK LA
Low Roans
East Lilling Village
MOOR LANE
Field House Farm
3
Sheriff Hutton Bridge
Sheriff Hutton Bridge Farm
NEW LANE
NEW ROAD
Lilling Hall
Thornton Grange Farm
East Lilling Grange
Bridge Farm
Lilling Hall Farm
LILLING LA
64
Brickyard Farm
LILLING LOW LANE
INGS LA
Thornton Moor
MOOR LANE
YO32
Anchor Plain
2
High Roans
Lilling Green
Station Farm
PH
LC
High Roans House
Brown Farm
High Roans Wood
East Lilling House Farm
GENNELL LANE
LC
Gennell House
RICE LANE
OAK BUSK LANE
63
Rice Hill Farm
High Roans Farm
Hill Closes
SMITH'S LA
Great Wood
LC
PH
1
Beck Wood
Bungalow Farm
Ash Wood
Flaxton
Duncombe Wood
COMMON RD
CROSS LA
FOREST LA
POTTERY LA
Strensall Forest
Walbutts
YORK LANE
62
62
63
64
65
66
67

145
120

Scale: 1¾ inches to 1 mile

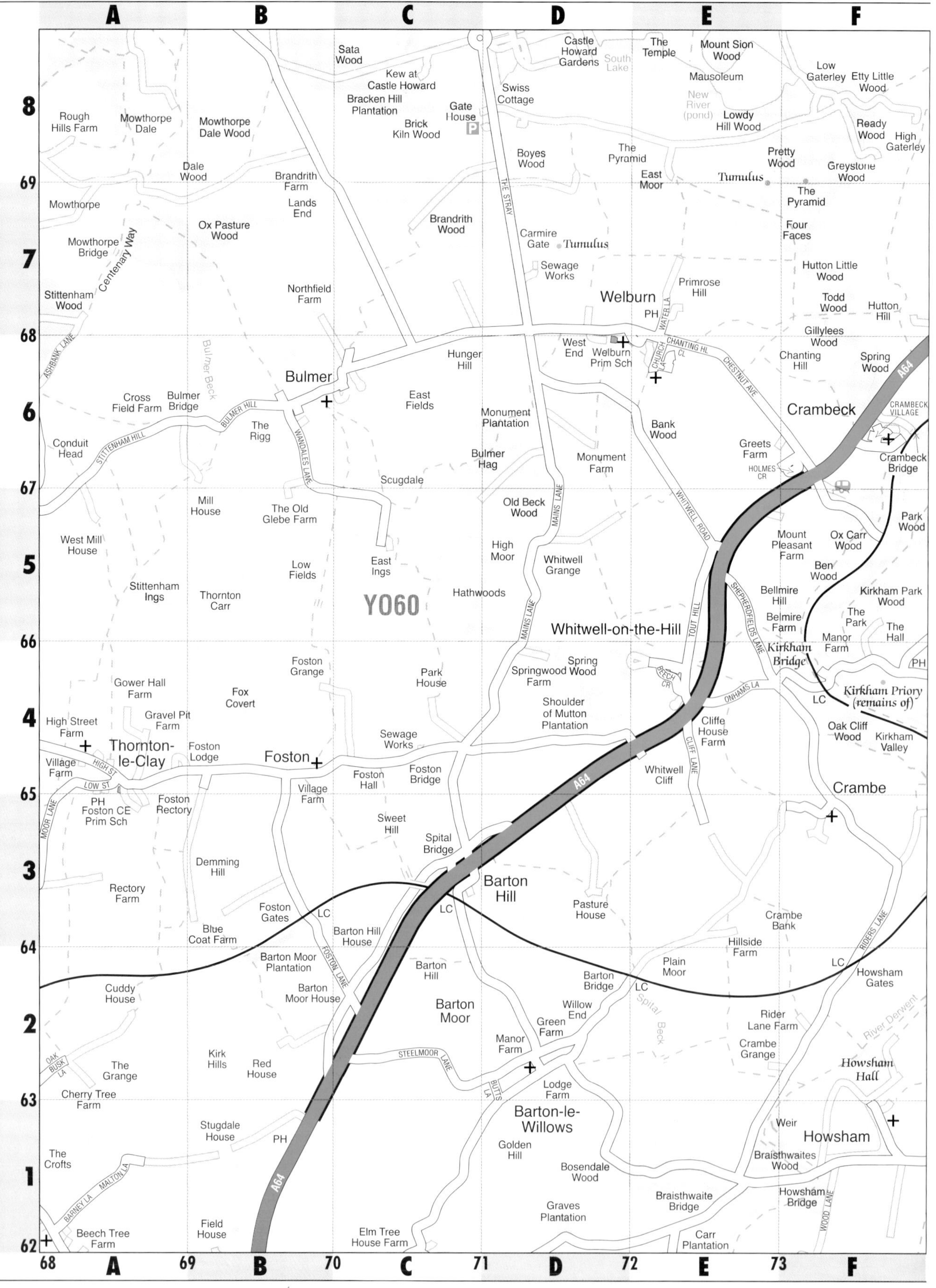

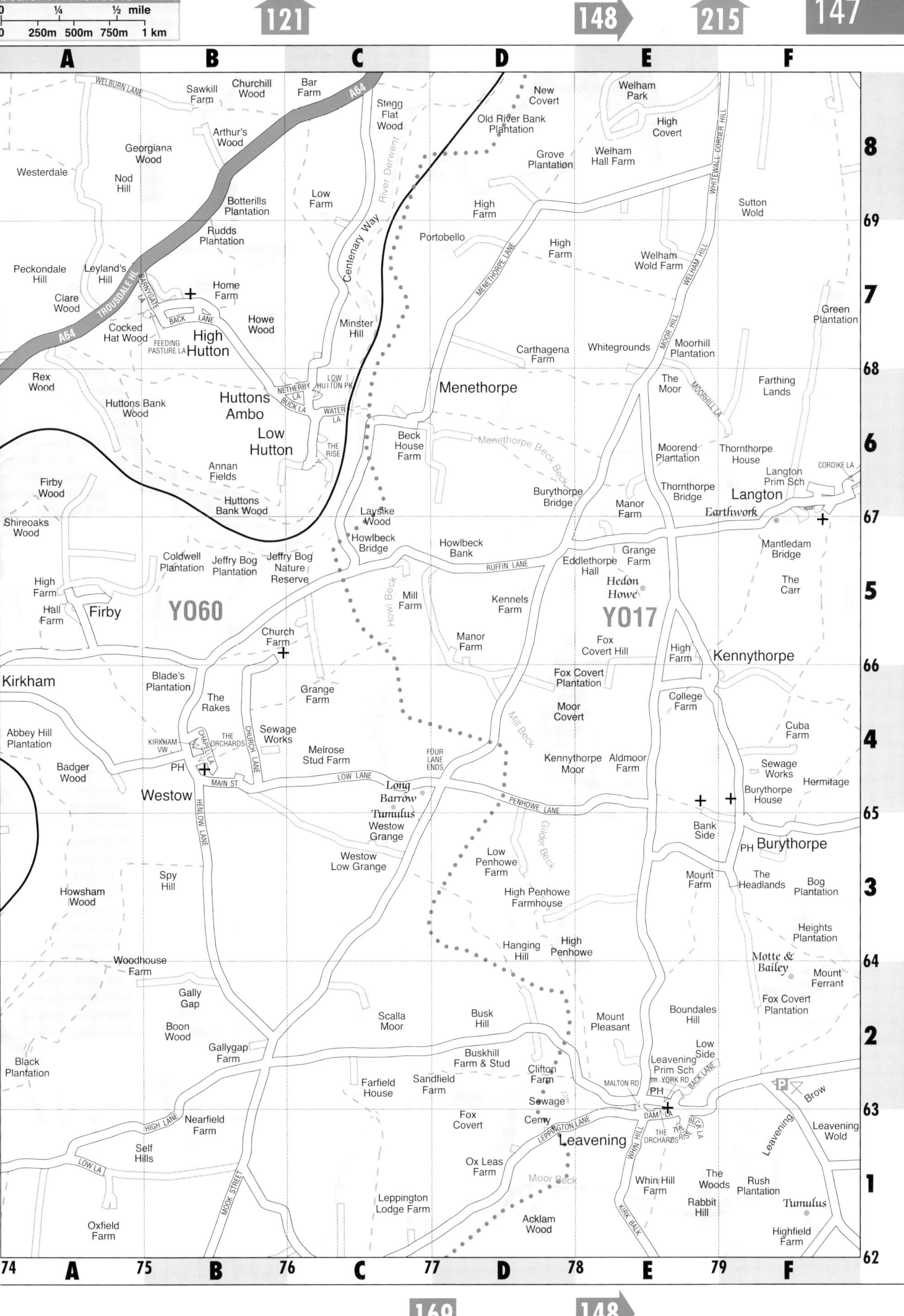

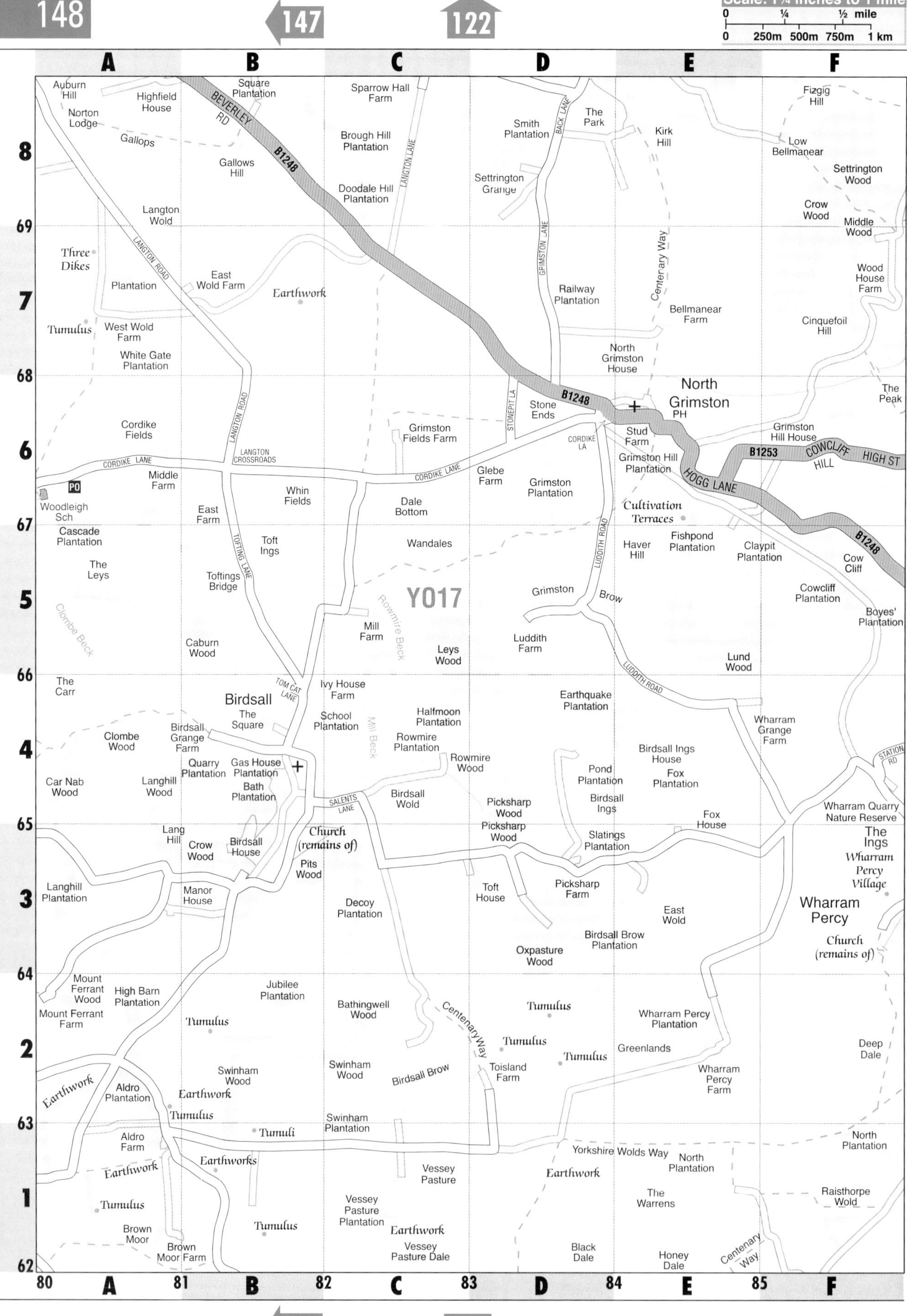

Scale: 1¾ inches to 1 mile
0   ¼   ½ mile
0 250m 500m 750m 1 km

8
Auburn Hill
Highfield House
Square Plantation
Sparrow Hall Farm
BEVERLEY RD
B1248
Smith Plantation
The Park
Kirk Hill
Fizgig Hill
Low Bellmanear
Settrington Wood
Norton Lodge
Gallops
Gallows Hill
Brough Hill Plantation
Settrington Grange
Crow Wood
Middle Wood

69
Three Dikes
Langton Wold
Doodale Hill Plantation
LANGTON LANE
GRIMSTON LANE
Railway Plantation
Centenary Way
Bellmanear Farm
Cinquefoil Hill
Wood House Farm

7
Plantation
East Wold Farm
Earthwork
LANGTON ROAD
North Grimston House

68
West Wold Farm
White Gate Plantation
Tumulus

6
Cordike Fields
LANGTON ROAD
LANGTON CROSSROADS
Grimston Fields Farm
STONEPIT LA
Stone Ends
B1248
North Grimston
PH
The Peak
Grimston Hill House
COWCLIFF HILL
HIGH ST
CORDIKE LANE
Stud Farm
B1253
HOGG LANE
B1248
Cordike Lane
Middle Farm
Whin Fields
Glebe Farm
CORDIKE LA
Grimston Hill Plantation
Cultivation Terraces
Woodleigh Sch
PO
Woodleigh Sch
East Farm
Dale Bottom
Grimston Plantation

67
Cascade Plantation
Toft Ings
Wandales
LUDDITH ROAD
Haver Hill
Fishpond Plantation
Claypit Plantation
Cow Cliff
The Leys
Toftings Bridge
TOFTING LANE
Grimston
Cowcliff Plantation

5
Clombe Beck
Rowmire Beck
YO17
Brow
Luddith Farm
Boyes' Plantation

66
The Carr
Caburn Wood
Mill Farm
Leys Wood
Lund Wood
Wharram Grange Farm
TOM CAT LANE
Ivy House Farm
Halfmoon Plantation
Earthquake Plantation
LUDDITH ROAD
STATION RD

4
Clombe Wood
Birdsall Grange Farm
Birdsall
The Square
School Plantation
Rowmire Plantation
Rowmire Wood
Pond Plantation
Birdsall Ings House
Fox Plantation
Wharram Quarry Nature Reserve
Car Nab Wood
Langhill Wood
Quarry Plantation
Gas House Plantation
Bath Plantation
Mill Beck
Birdsall Wold
Birdsall Ings
Fox House
The Ings

65
Lang Hill
Crow Wood
Birdsall House
SALENTS LANE
Church (remains of)
Pits Wood
Picksharp Wood
Picksharp Wood
Slatings Plantation
Fox House
Wharram Percy Village
Wharram Percy

3
Langhill Plantation
Manor House
Decoy Plantation
Toft House
Picksharp Farm
East Wold
Church (remains of)
Birdsall Brow Plantation

64
Mount Ferrant Wood
High Barn Plantation
Jubilee Plantation
Bathingwell Wood
CentenaryWay
Tumulus
Wharram Percy Plantation
Deep Dale
Mount Ferrant Farm
Tumulus
Tumulus
Greenlands

2
Earthwork
Aldro Plantation
Swinham Wood
Swinham Wood
Birdsall Brow
Oxpasture Wood
Tumulus
Wharram Percy Farm
Earthwork
Tumulus
Toisland Farm

63
Aldro Farm
Tumuli
Swinham Plantation
Yorkshire Wolds Way
North Plantation
North Plantation
Earthwork
Earthworks
Vessey Pasture
Earthwork
The Warrens
Raisthorpe Wold

1
Tumulus
Vessey Pasture Plantation
Earthwork
Black Dale
Honey Dale
Centenary Way
Brown Moor
Brown Moor Farm
Tumulus
Vessey Pasture Dale

62

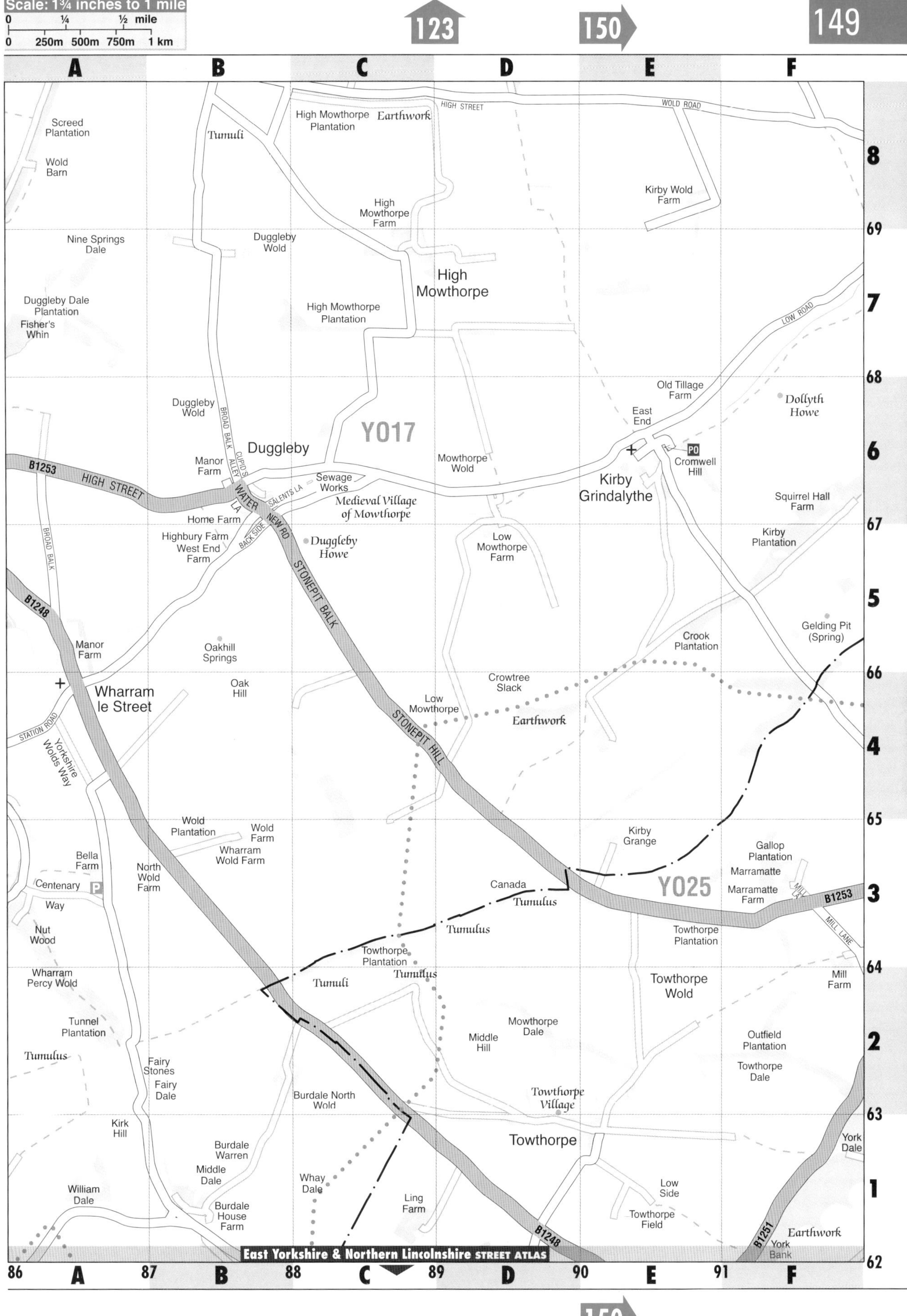

Scale: 1¾ inches to 1 mile

0   ¼   ½ mile
0   250m 500m 750m 1 km

123

150

149

A   B   C   D   E   F

8

Screed
Plantation

Wold
Barn

Tumuli

High Mowthorpe
Plantation   Earthwork

HIGH STREET

WOLD ROAD

Kirby Wold
Farm

69

Nine Springs
Dale

Duggleby
Wold

High
Mowthorpe
Farm

High
Mowthorpe

LOW ROAD

7

Duggleby Dale
Plantation
Fisher's
Whin

High Mowthorpe
Plantation

68

Duggleby
Wold

Old Tillage
Farm

Dollyth
Howe

BROAD BALK

CUPID'S ALLEY

Y017

East
End

6

B1253

HIGH STREET

Duggleby

Manor
Farm

WATER LA

SALENTS LA

Sewage
Works

Mowthorpe
Wold

Kirby
Grindalythe

PO
Cromwell
Hill

Squirrel Hall
Farm

67

BROAD BALK

B1248

Home Farm

Highbury Farm
West End
Farm

NEW RD

BACK SIDE

Medieval Village
of Mowthorpe

Duggleby
Howe

Low
Mowthorpe
Farm

Kirby
Plantation

5

STONEPIT BALK

Manor
Farm

Oakhill
Springs

Crook
Plantation

Gelding Pit
(Spring)

66

STATION ROAD

+

Wharram
le Street

Oak
Hill

Crowtree
Slack

Low
Mowthorpe

Earthwork

4

Yorkshire Wolds Way

STONEPIT HILL

65

Wold
Plantation

Wold
Farm

Wharram
Wold Farm

Kirby
Grange

Gallop
Plantation
Marramatte

Bella
Farm

North
Wold
Farm

Canada

Tumulus

Y025

Marramatte
Farm

B1253

MILL LANE

3

Centenary
Way

Nut
Wood

Tumulus

Towthorpe
Plantation

Towthorpe
Plantation

Wharram
Percy Wold

Towthorpe
Plantation

Tumuli

Tumulus

Towthorpe
Wold

Mill
Farm

64

Tunnel
Plantation

Tumulus

Middle
Hill

Mowthorpe
Dale

Outfield
Plantation

Towthorpe
Dale

2

Fairy
Stones
Fairy
Dale

Burdale North
Wold

Towthorpe
Village

63

Kirk
Hill

Burdale
Warren
Middle
Dale

Whay
Dale

Ling
Farm

Towthorpe

Low
Side

York
Dale

William
Dale

Burdale
House
Farm

B1248

Towthorpe
Field

B1251
York
Bank

Earthwork

1

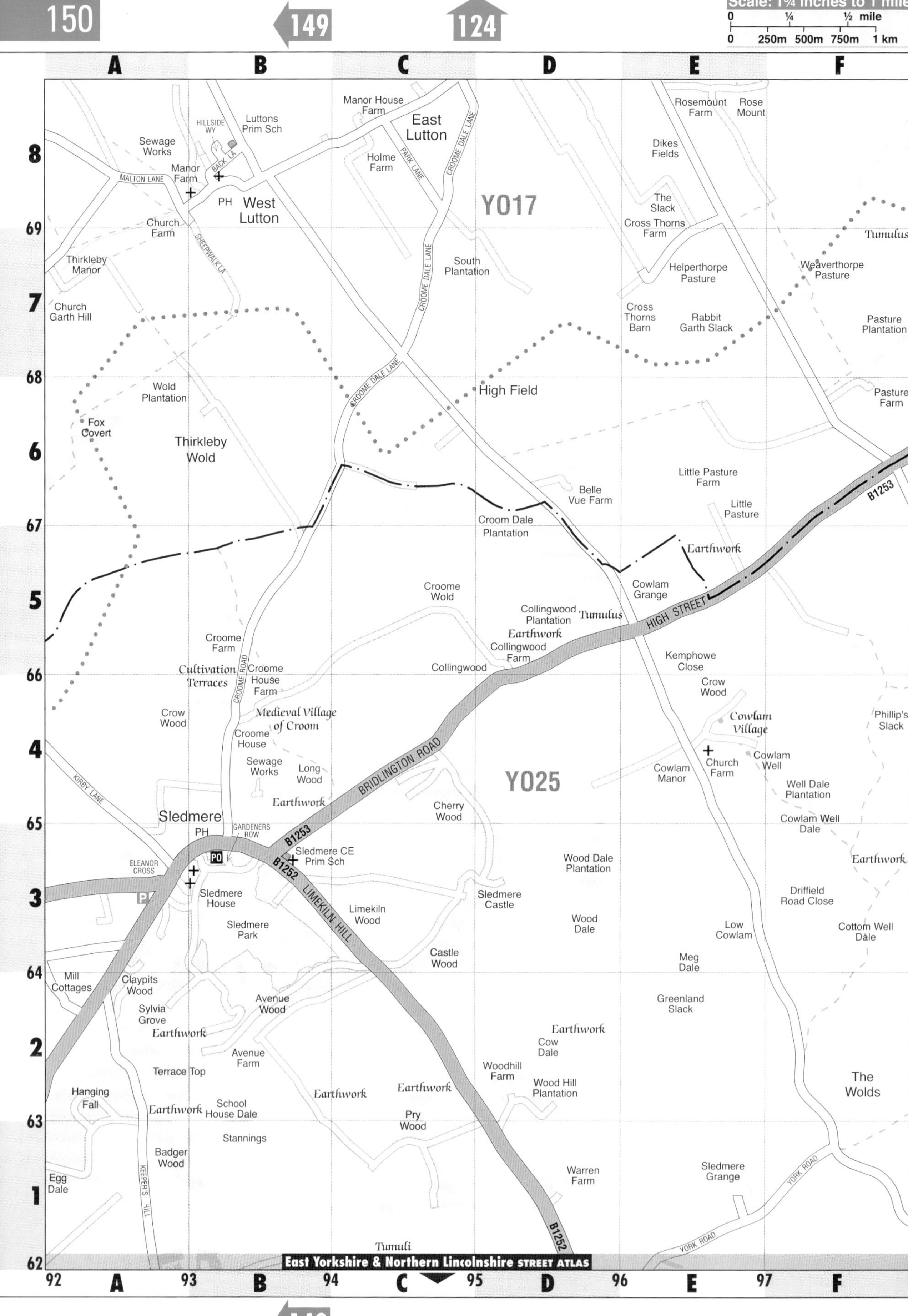

Scale: 1¾ inches to 1 mile

0   ¼   ½ mile
0 250m 500m 750m 1 km

A B C D E F

8

Sewage Works
HILLSIDE WY
Luttons Prim Sch
Manor House Farm
East Lutton
Manor Farm
PH
West Lutton
Holme Farm
PARK LANE
CROOME DALE LANE
Rosemount Farm
Rose Mount
Dikes Fields

69

MALTON LANE
Church Farm
Thirkleby Manor
SHEEPWALK LA
YO17
The Slack
Cross Thorns Farm
Helperthorpe Pasture
Weaverthorpe Pasture
Tumulus

7

Church Garth Hill
South Plantation
CROOME DALE LANE
Cross Thorns Barn
Rabbit Garth Slack
Pasture Plantation

68

Wold Plantation
Fox Covert
Thirkleby Wold
High Field
Pasture Farm

6

CROOME DALE LANE
Belle Vue Farm
Croom Dale Plantation
Little Pasture Farm
Little Pasture
B1253

67

Croome Wold
Earthwork
Collingwood Plantation
Tumulus
Earthwork
Cowlam Grange
HIGH STREET

5

Croome Farm
Cultivation Terraces
CROOME ROAD
Croome House Farm
Collingwood Farm
Collingwood
Tumulus
Kemphowe Close
Crow Wood

66

Crow Wood
Medieval Village of Croom
Croome House
Cowlam Village
Phillip's Slack

4

KIRBY LANE
Sewage Works
Long Wood
BRIDLINGTON ROAD
YO25
Cowlam Manor
Church Farm
Cowlam Well
Well Dale Plantation

65

Sledmere
PH
GARDENERS ROW
Earthwork
B1253
Cherry Wood
Cowlam Well Dale
Earthwork

3

ELEANOR CROSS
P
PO
Sledmere House
Sledmere CE Prim Sch
B1252
Limekiln Wood
Sledmere Castle
Wood Dale Plantation
Driffield Road Close
Cottom Well Dale

Sledmere Park
LIMEKILN HILL
Castle Wood
Wood Dale
Low Cowlam

64

Mill Cottages
Claypits Wood
Sylvia Grove
Avenue Wood
Meg Dale
Greenland Slack

2

Earthwork
Avenue Farm
Earthwork
Cow Dale
The Wolds

Hanging Fall
Terrace Top
Earthwork
Earthwork
Woodhill Farm
Wood Hill Plantation

63

Earthwork
School House Dale
Stannings
KEEPER'S HILL
Pry Wood
Warren Farm
Sledmere Grange
YORK ROAD

1

Egg Dale
Badger Wood
B1252
York Road

62

Tumuli
East Yorkshire & Northern Lincolnshire STREET ATLAS

92 A 93 B 94 C 95 D 96 E 97 F

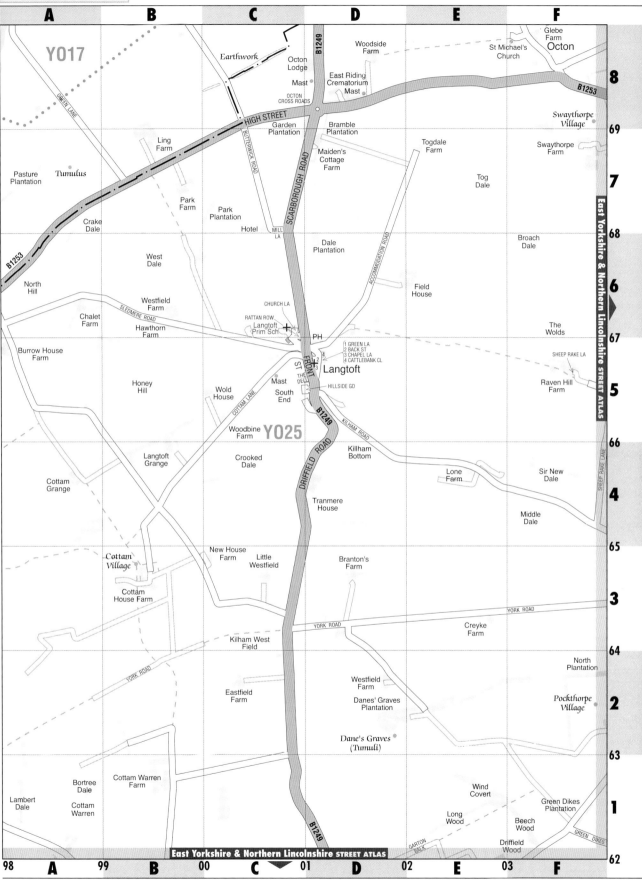

A B C D E F

8
69
7
68
6
67
5
66
4
65
3
64
2
63
1
62

YO17

Green Lane

Earthwork

Octon Lodge

Woodside Farm

St Michael's Church

Glebe Farm

Octon

B1249

Mast

East Riding Crematorium Mast

B1253

Swaythorpe Village

HIGH STREET

OCTON CROSS ROADS

Garden Plantation

Bramble Plantation

Swaythorpe Farm

Ling Farm

BUTTERWICK ROAD

Maiden's Cottage Farm

Togdale Farm

Tog Dale

Pasture Plantation

Tumulus

SCARBOROUGH ROAD

Park Farm

Park Plantation

Hotel

Dale Plantation

Broach Dale

Crake Dale

MILL LA

ACCOMMODATION ROAD

Field House

B1253

North Hill

West Dale

Westfield Farm

SLEDMERE ROAD

CHURCH LA

The Wolds

Chalet Farm

Hawthorn Farm

RATTAN ROW

Langtoft Prim Sch

PH

1 GREEN LA
2 BACK ST
3 CHAPEL LA
4 CATTLEBANK CL

SHEEP RAKE LA

Burrow House Farm

COTTAM LANE

FRONT ST

Langtoft

Raven Hill Farm

Honey Hill

Wold House

Mast

South End

THE DELL

HILLSIDE GD

SHEEP RAKE LANE

Woodbine Farm

YO25

Killham Bottom

Langtoft Grange

Crooked Dale

B1249

KILHAM ROAD

Lone Farm

Sir New Dale

Cottam Grange

DRIFFIELD ROAD

Tranmere House

Middle Dale

Cottam Village

New House Farm

Little Westfield

Branton's Farm

Cottam House Farm

YORK ROAD

YORK ROAD

Creyke Farm

Kilham West Field

North Plantation

YORK ROAD

Eastfield Farm

Westfield Farm

Danes' Graves Plantation

Pockthorpe Village

Dane's Graves (Tumuli)

Lambert Dale

Bortree Dale

Cottam Warren Farm

Cottam Warren

Wind Covert

Long Wood

Green Dikes Plantation

Beech Wood

GARTON BALK

GREEN DIKES

Driffield Wood

B1249

East Yorkshire & Northern Lincolnshire STREET ATLAS

East Yorkshire & Northern Lincolnshire STREET ATLAS

98 A 99 B 00 C 01 D 02 E 03 F

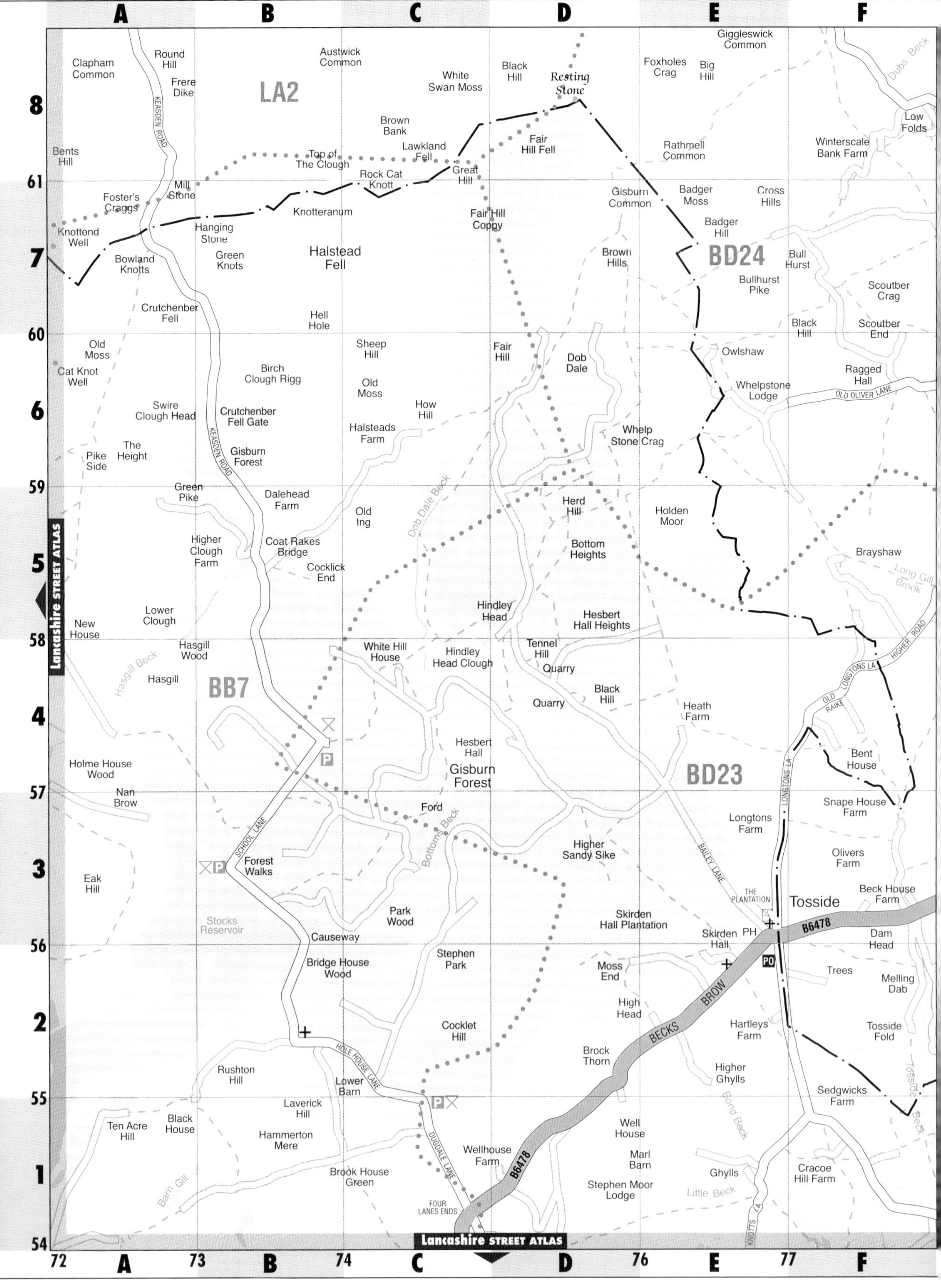

A **B** **C** **D** **E** **F**

Clapham Common
Round Hill
Frere Dike
LA2
Austwick Common
White Swan Moss
Black Hill
Resting Stone
Foxholes Crag
Big Hill
Giggleswick Common
Low Folds

Bents Hill
Brown Bank
Fair Hill Fell
Rathmell Common
Winterscale Bank Farm

Foster's Craggs
Mill Stone
Top of The Clough
Lawkland Fell
Rock Cat Knott
Great Hill
Gisburn Common
Badger Moss
Cross Hills

Knottond Well
Hanging Stone
Knotteranum
Fair Hill Coppy
Badger Hill
BD24
Bull Hurst

Bowland Knotts
Green Knots
Halstead Fell
Brown Hills
Bullhurst Pike
Black Hill
Scoutber Crag

Crutchenber Fell
Hell Hole
Fair Hill
Dob Dale
Owlshaw
Scoutber End

Old Moss
Sheep Hill
Whelpstone Lodge
Old Oliver Lane
Ragged Hall

Cat Knot Well
Birch Clough Rigg
Old Moss
How Hill
Whelp Stone Crag

Swire Clough Head
Crutchenber Fell Gate
Halsteads Farm
Herd Hill
Holden Moor
Brayshaw

Pike Side
The Height
Gisburn Forest
Dalehead Farm
Old Ing
Long Gill Brook

Green Pike
Coat Rakes Bridge
Bottom Heights
Higher Clough Farm
Cocklick End

Lower Clough
Hindley Head
Hesbert Hall Heights

New House
Hasgill Wood
White Hill House
Hindley Head Clough
Tennel Hill
Quarry
BB7
Hasgill

BB7
Quarry
Black Hill
Heath Farm
Higher Road
Old Raike
Longtons La.

Holme House Wood
Hesbert Hall
Gisburn Forest
Longtons Farm
Bent House

Nan Brow
Ford
BD23
Snape House Farm

Forest Walks
Higher Sandy Sike
Olivers Farm

Eak Hill
Stocks Reservoir
Park Wood
Skirden Hall Plantation
The Plantation
Tosside
Beck House Farm

Causeway
Stephen Park
Moss End
Skirden Hall
PH
B6478
Dam Head

Bridge House Wood
High Head
PO
Trees
Melling Dab

Cocklet Hill
Brock Thorn
BECKS BROW
Hartleys Farm
Tosside Fold

Rushton Hill
Lower Barn
Higher Ghylls
Sedgwicks Farm

Ten Acre Hill
Black House
Laverick Hill
Well House
Ghylls
Cracoe Hill Farm

Hammerton Mere
Brook House Green
Wellhouse Farm
B6478
Marl Barn
Stephen Moor Lodge
Little Beck

FOUR LANES ENDS

72 **A** 73 **B** 74 **C** **D** 76 **E** 77 **F**

Scale: 1¾ inches to 1 mile

0 ¼ ½ mile
0 250m 500m 750m 1 km

131
154
153

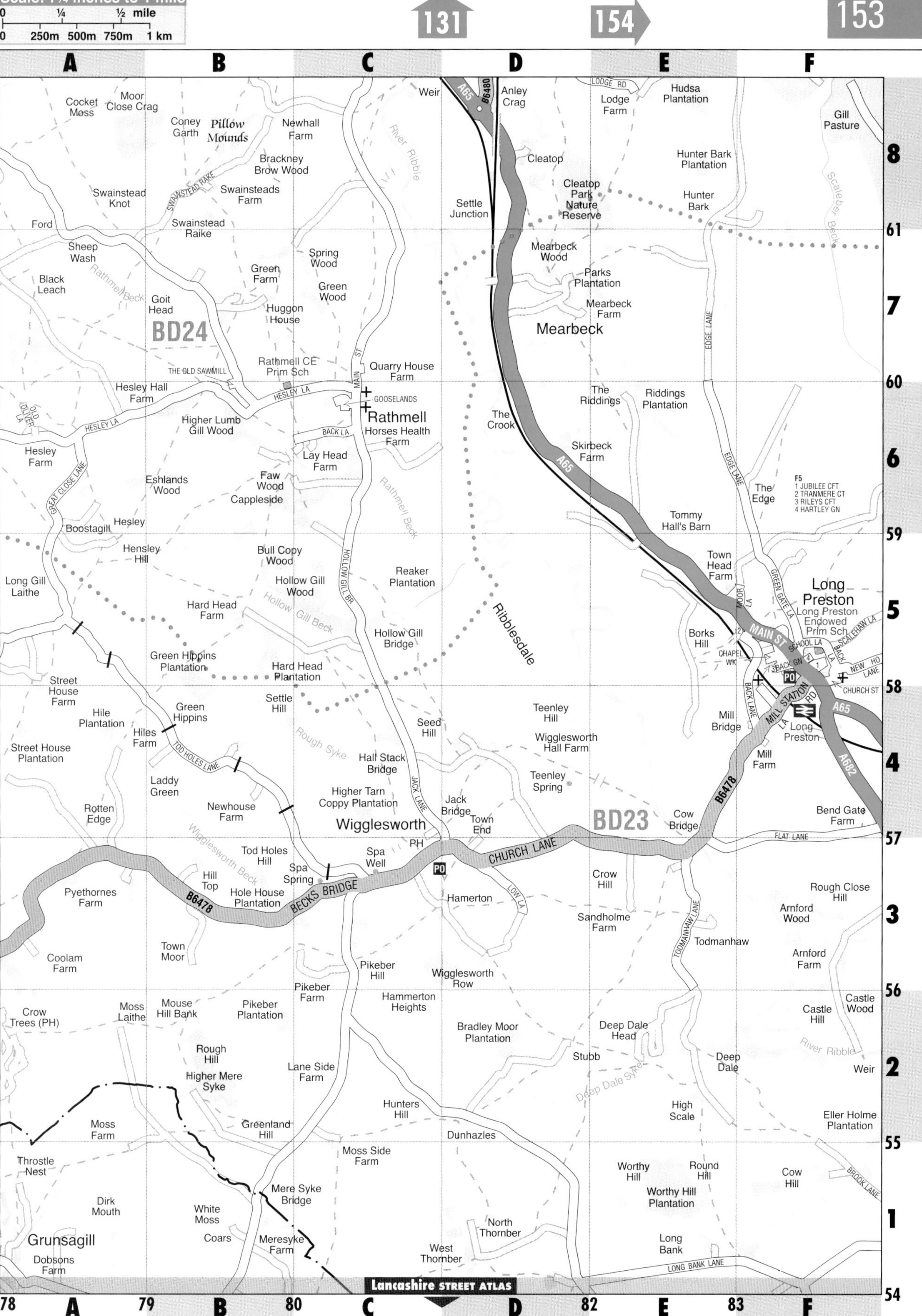

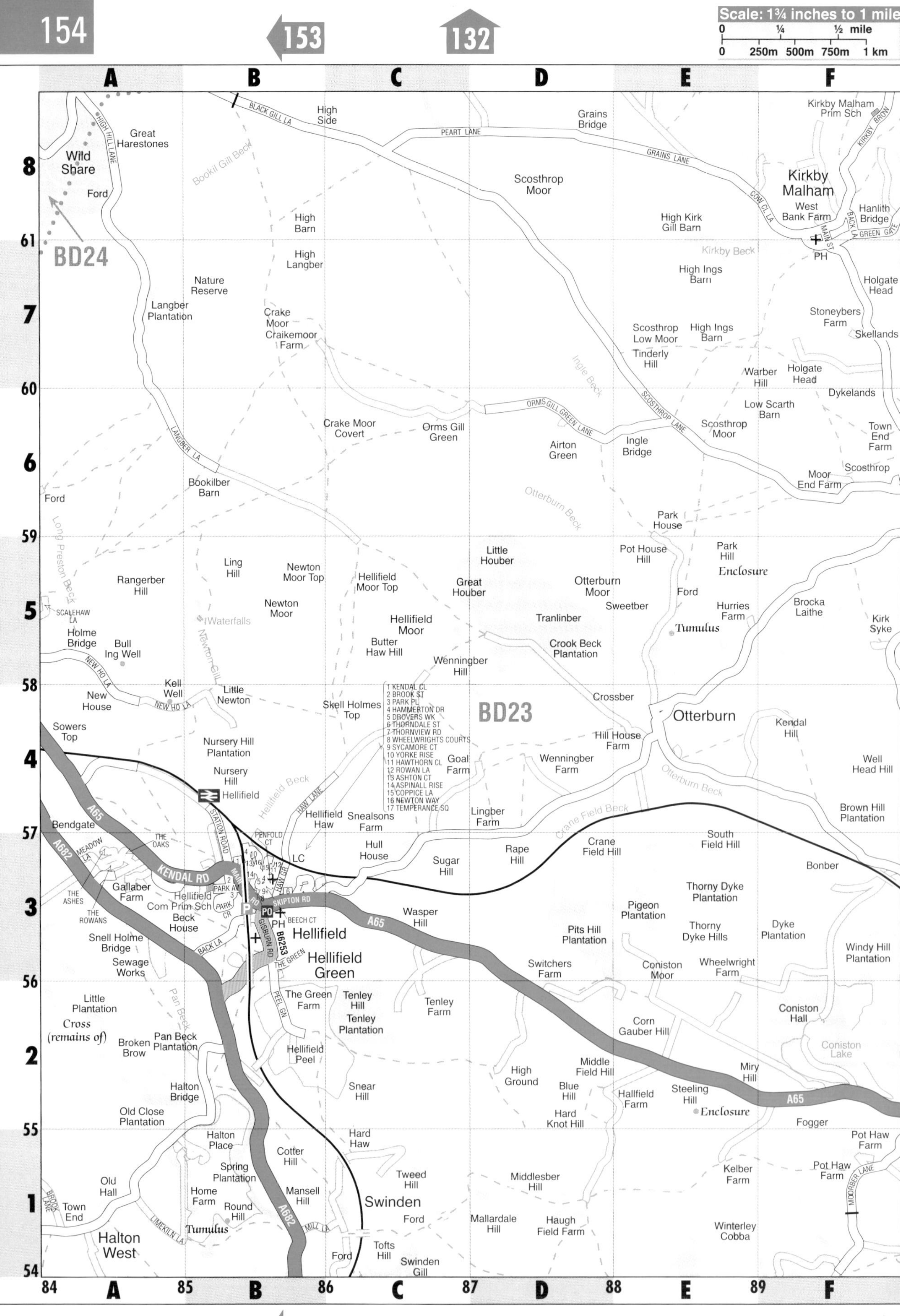

Scale: 1¾ inches to 1 mile

133
156

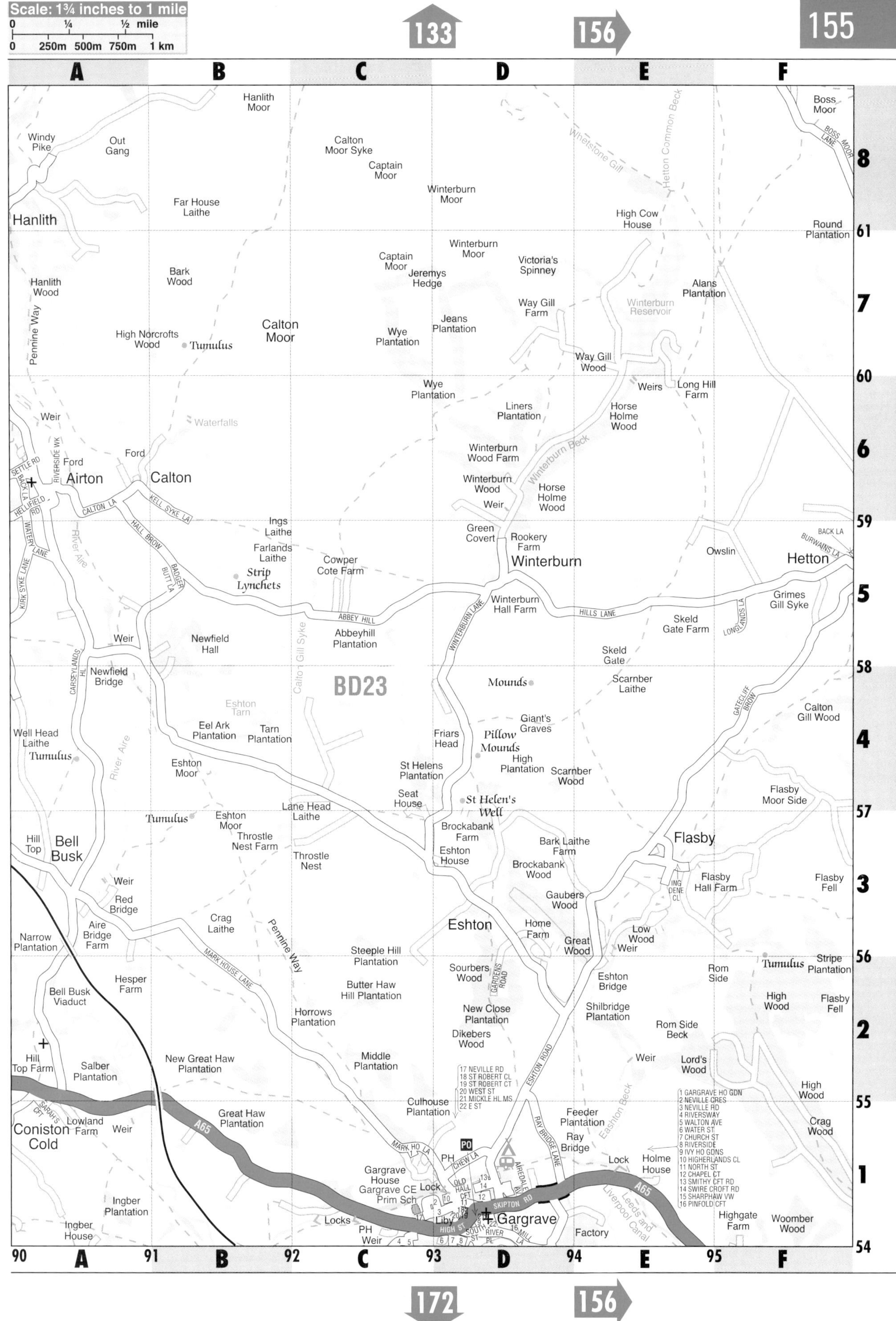

Hanlith Moor
Windy Pike
Out Gang
Calton Moor Syke
Captain Moor
Winterburn Moor
Far House Laithe
Hanlith
High Cow House
Round Plantation
Boss Moor
Winterburn Moor
Captain Moor
Jeremys Hedge
Victoria's Spinney
Hanlith Wood
Bark Wood
Alans Plantation
Way Gill Farm
Winterburn Reservoir
Pennine Way
Jeans Plantation
High Norcrofts Wood
Tumulus
Calton Moor
Wye Plantation
Way Gill Wood
Wye Plantation
Weirs
Long Hill Farm
Liners Plantation
Horse Holme Wood
Weir
Waterfalls
Winterburn Wood Farm
Ford
Airton
Calton
Winterburn Wood
Horse Holme Wood
Weir
Green Covert
Rookery Farm
Ings Laithe
Farlands Laithe
Winterburn
Owslin
Hetton
Cowper Cote Farm
Strip Lynchets
Winterburn Hall Farm
Grimes Gill Syke
Skeld Gate Farm
Abbeyhill Plantation
Weir
Newfield Hall
Skeld Gate
Newfield Bridge
BD23
Mounds
Scarnber Laithe
Eshton Tarn
Giant's Graves
Calton Gill Wood
Eel Ark Plantation
Tarn Plantation
Friars Head
Pillow Mounds
Well Head Laithe
Tumulus
Eshton Moor
St Helens Plantation
High Plantation
Scarnber Wood
Seat House
St Helen's Well
Flasby Moor Side
Lane Head Laithe
Tumulus
Eshton Moor
Brockabank Farm
Bark Laithe Farm
Flasby
Hill Top
Bell Busk
Throstle Nest Farm
Throstle Nest
Eshton House
Brockabank Wood
Flasby Hall Farm
Flasby Fell
Weir
Gaubers Wood
Red Bridge
Crag Laithe
Eshton
Home Farm
Low Wood
Aire Bridge Farm
Great Wood
Weir
Narrow Plantation
Steeple Hill Plantation
Tumulus
Stripe Plantation
Sourbers Wood
Eshton Bridge
Rom Side
Hesper Farm
Butter Haw Hill Plantation
High Wood
Flasby Fell
Bell Busk Viaduct
New Close Plantation
Shilbridge Plantation
Horrows Plantation
Rom Side Beck
Dikebers Wood
Hill Top Farm
Salber Plantation
New Great Haw Plantation
Middle Plantation
Weir
Lord's Wood
High Wood
Culhouse Plantation
Feeder Plantation
Lowland Farm
Weir
Great Haw Plantation
Crag Wood
Coniston Cold
Ray Bridge
Lock
Holme House
PO
PH
Gargrave House
Gargrave CE Prim Sch
Lock
Ingber Plantation
Locks
Liby
Gargrave
Highgate Farm
Woomber Wood
Ingber House
PH
Weir
Factory
Whetstone Gill
Hetton Common Beck
Winterburn Beck
River Aire
Calton Gill Syke
Eshton Beck
Leeds and Liverpool Canal
A65
SETTLE RD
BACK LA
RIVERSIDE WK
HELLIFIELD RD
WATERY LANE
KIRK SYKE LANE
CALTON LA
KELL SYKE LA
HALL BROW
BADGER BUTT LA
ABBEY HILL
WINTERBURN LANE
HILLS LANE
LONGLANDS LA
BACK LA
BURWAINS LA
BOSS MOOR LANE
GATECLIFF BROW
CARSEYLANDS HL
ING DENE CL
MARK HOUSE LANE
GARDENS ROAD
ESHTON ROAD
RAY BRIDGE LANE
AIREDALE AV
MARK HO LA
CHEW LA
OLD HALL CFT
SKIPTON RD
HIGH ST
SOUTH ST
RIVER PL
MILL LA
SARAH'S CFT
17 NEVILLE RD
18 ST ROBERT CL
19 ST ROBERT CT
20 WEST ST
21 MICKLE HL MS
22 E ST
1 GARGRAVE HO GDN
2 NEVILLE CRES
3 NEVILLE RD
4 RIVERSWAY
5 WALTON AVE
6 WATER ST
7 CHURCH ST
8 RIVERSIDE
9 IVY HO GDNS
10 HIGHERLANDS CL
11 NORTH ST
12 CHAPEL CT
13 SMITHY CFT RD
14 SWIRE CROFT RD
15 SHARPHAW VW
16 PINFOLD CFT
0 ¼ ½ mile
0 250m 500m 750m 1 km
A B C D E F
8 61 7 60 6 59 5 58 4 57 3 56 2 55 1 54
90 91 92 93 94 95

172
156

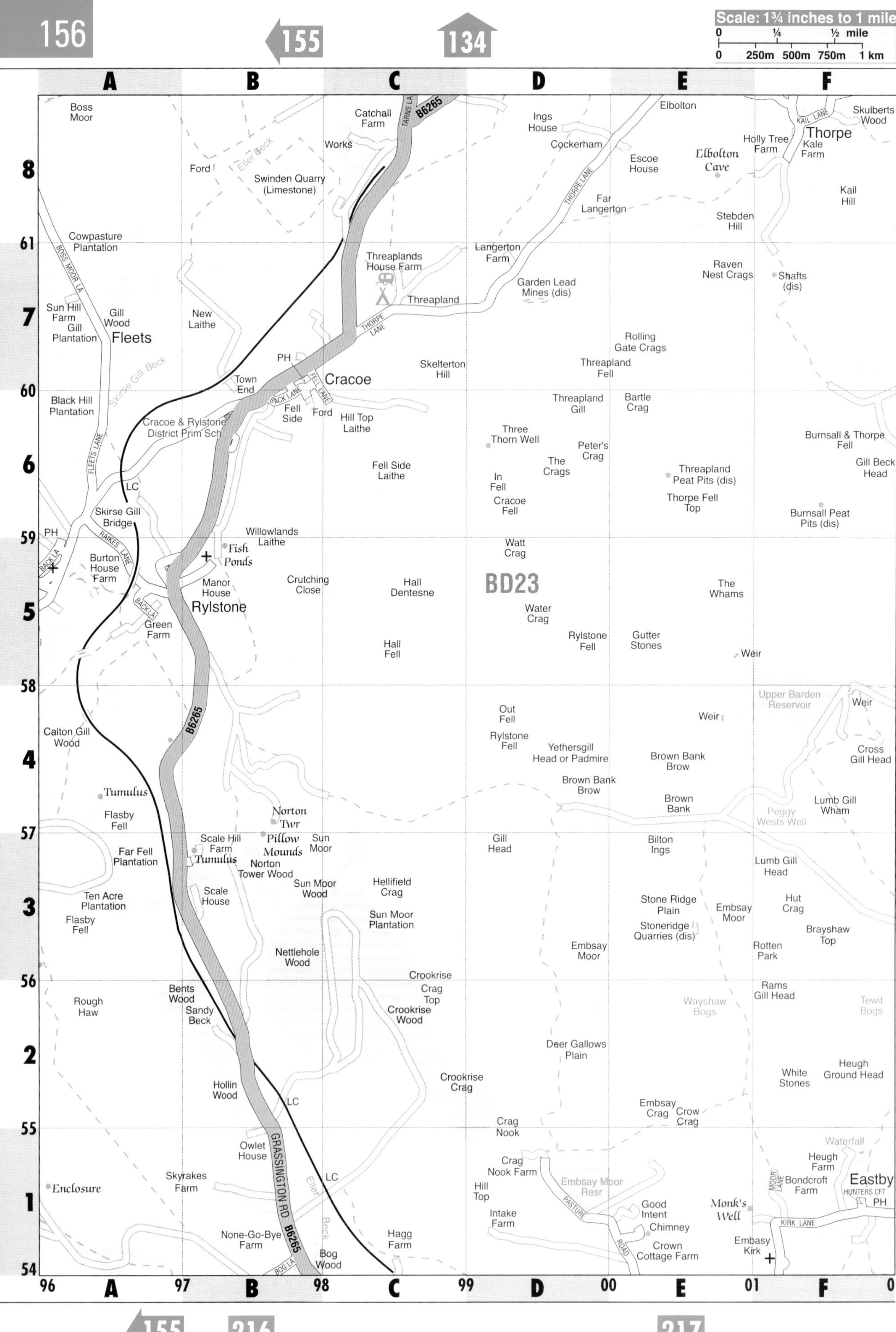

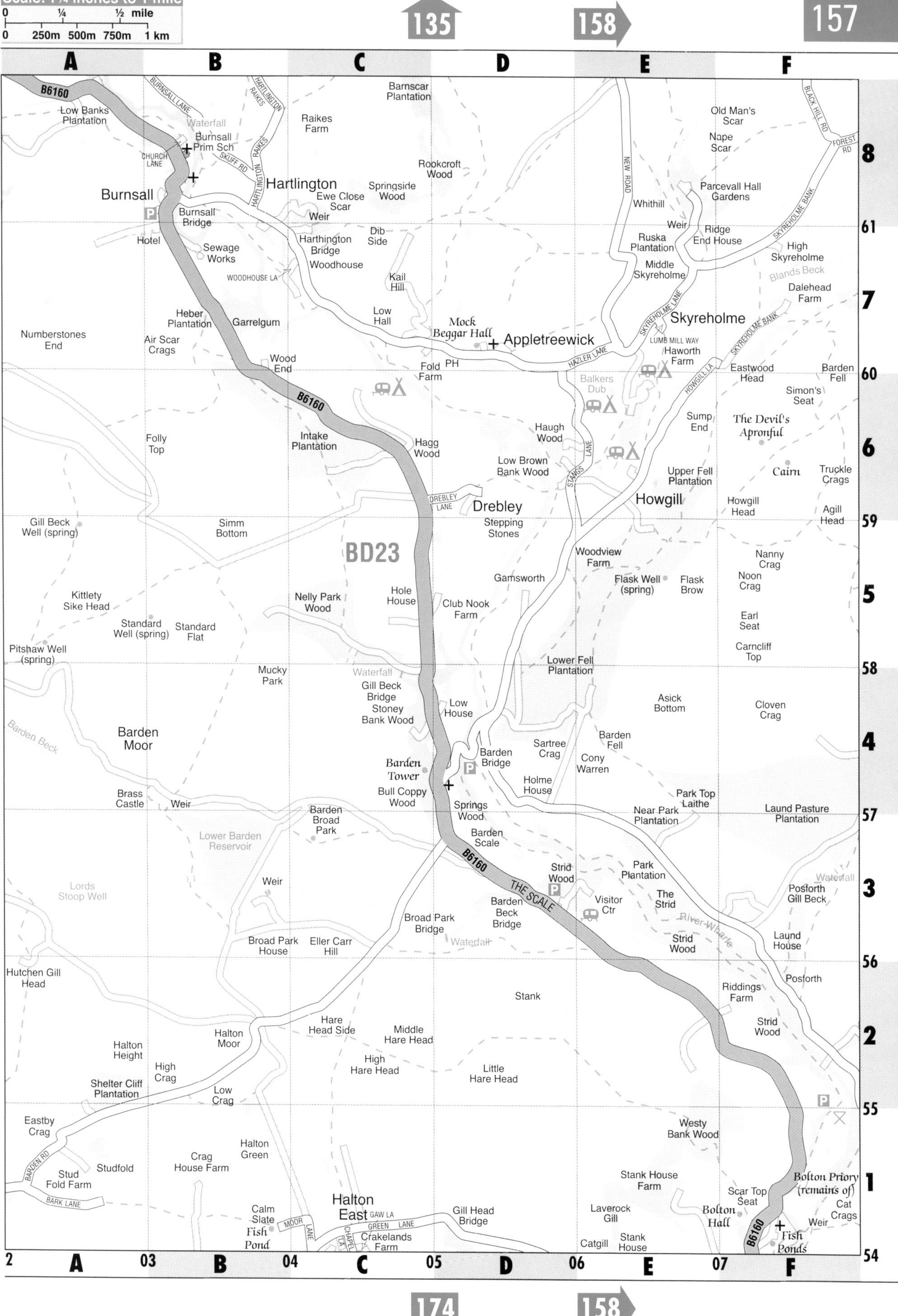
Scale: 1¾ inches to 1 mile
0 ¼ ½ mile
0 250m 500m 750m 1 km
135
158
174
158
A B C D E F
B6160
Low Banks Plantation
Burnsall
Burnsall Prim Sch
Hartlington
Raikes Farm
Barnscar Plantation
Rookcroft Wood
Springside Wood
Ewe Close Scar
Weir
Burnsall Bridge
Hotel
Sewage Works
Harthington Bridge
Woodhouse
Dib Side
Kail Hill
Low Hall
Mock Beggar Hall
Appletreewick
Heber Plantation
Garrelgum
Air Scar Crags
Numberstones End
Wood End
Fold Farm
PH
Old Man's Scar
Nape Scar
Parcevall Hall Gardens
Whithill
Ruska Plantation
Ridge End House
High Skyreholme
Middle Skyreholme
Skyreholme
Dalehead Farm
Haworth Farm
Eastwood Head
Barden Fell
Balkers Dub
Simon's Seat
The Devil's Apronful
Sump End
Haugh Wood
Hagg Wood
Intake Plantation
Folly Top
Low Brown Bank Wood
Upper Fell Plantation
Cairn
Truckle Crags
Drebley
Howgill
Howgill Head
Agill Head
Stepping Stones
Gill Beck Well (spring)
Simm Bottom
BD23
Woodview Farm
Nanny Crag
Gamsworth
Flask Well (spring)
Flask Brow
Noon Crag
Kittlety Sike Head
Nelly Park Wood
Hole House
Club Nook Farm
Standard Well (spring)
Standard Flat
Earl Seat
Pitshaw Well (spring)
Carncliff Top
Mucky Park
Lower Fell Plantation
Gill Beck Bridge
Stoney Bank Wood
Low House
Asick Bottom
Cloven Crag
Barden Moor
Barden Beck
Barden Tower
Barden Bridge
Sartree Crag
Barden Fell
Cony Warren
Holme House
Bull Coppy Wood
Brass Castle
Weir
Springs Wood
Park Top Laithe
Near Park Plantation
Laund Pasture Plantation
Barden Broad Park
Lower Barden Reservoir
Barden Scale
Strid Wood
Park Plantation
Lords Stoop Well
THE SCALE
Visitor Ctr
The Strid
Posforth Gill Beck
Barden Beck Bridge
River Wharfe
Broad Park Bridge
Strid Wood
Laund House
Broad Park House
Eller Carr Hill
Hutchen Gill Head
Stank
Posforth
Riddings Farm
Hare Head Side
Middle Hare Head
Strid Wood
Halton Moor
Halton Height
High Hare Head
Little Hare Head
High Crag
Shelter Cliff Plantation
Low Crag
Eastby Crag
Westy Bank Wood
Halton Green
Crag House Farm
Studfold
Stud Fold Farm
Stank House Farm
Bolton Priory (remains of)
Scar Top Seat
Cat Crags
Halton East
Calm Slate
Gill Head Bridge
Laverock Gill
Bolton Hall
Weir
Fish Pond
Crakelands Farm
Catgill
Stank House
Fish Ponds
BURNSALL LANE
HARTLINGTON RAIKES
HARTLINGTON
CHURCH LANE
SKUFF RD
WOODHOUSE LA
NEW ROAD
BLACK HILL RD
FOREST RD
SKYREHOLME BANK
SKYREHOLME LANE
LUMB MILL WAY
HAZLER LANE
HOWGILL LA
STANGS LANE
DREBLEY LANE
BARDEN RD
BARK LANE
MOOR LANE
GAW LA
GREEN LANE
CHAPEL LA
Waterfall
8 61 7 60 6 59 5 58 4 57 3 56 2 55 1 54
2 03 04 05 06 07

157
136

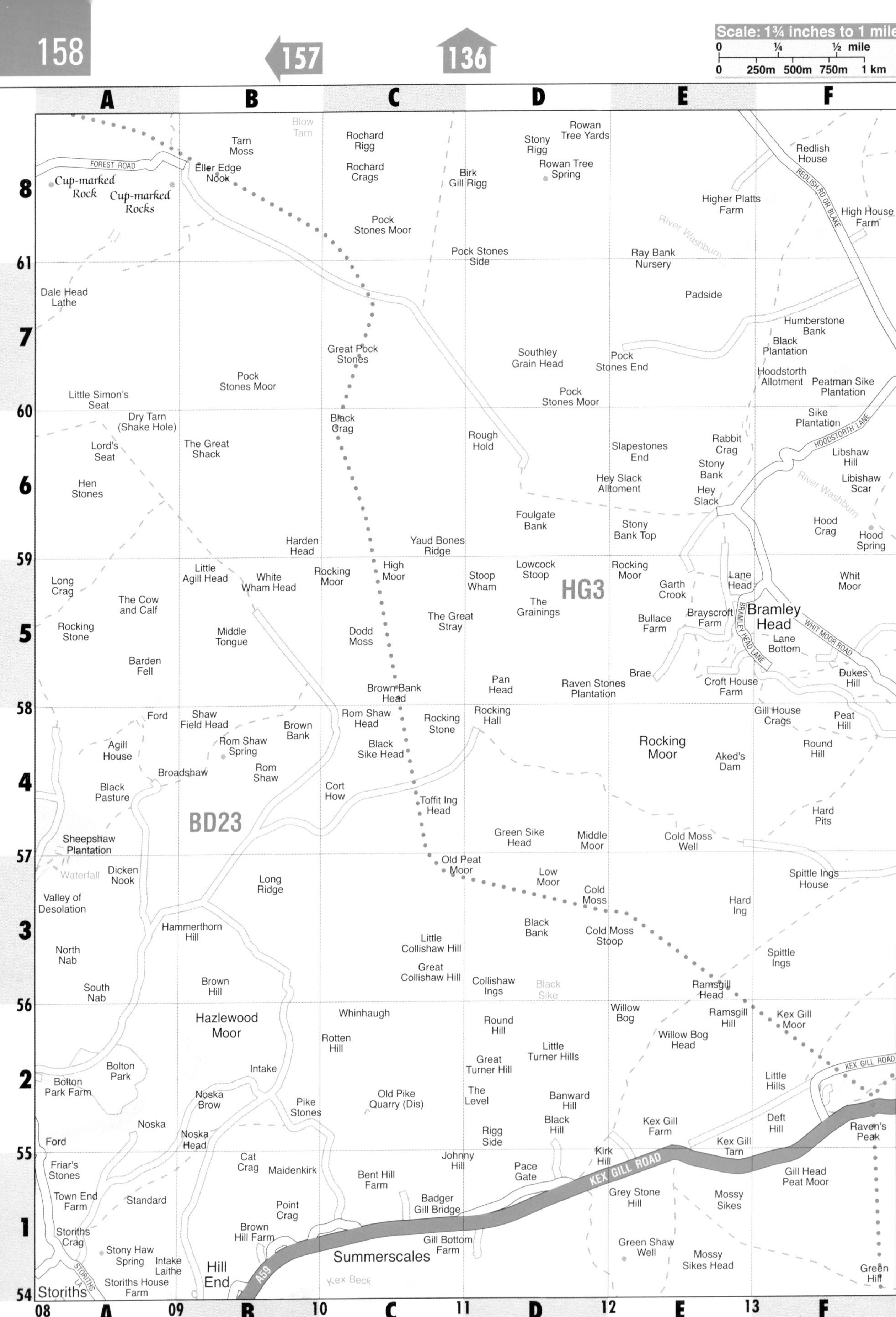
Scale: 1¾ inches to 1 mile
0 ¼ ½ mile
0 250m 500m 750m 1 km
A B C D E F
Tarn Moss
Blow Tarn
Rochard Rigg
Rochard Crags
Stony Rigg
Rowan Tree Yards
Rowan Tree Spring
Birk Gill Rigg
Redlish House
FOREST ROAD
Cup-marked Rock
Cup-marked Rocks
Eller Edge Nook
Pock Stones Moor
Higher Platts Farm
REDLISH RD OR BLAKE
High House Farm
River Washburn
Pock Stones Side
Ray Bank Nursery
Dale Head Lathe
Padside
Humberstone Bank
Black Plantation
Great Pock Stones
Southley Grain Head
Pock Stones End
Pock Stones Moor
Hoodstorth Allotment
Peatman Sike Plantation
Little Simon's Seat
Pock Stones Moor
Sike Plantation
Dry Tarn (Shake Hole)
Black Crag
Rough Hold
HOODSTORTH LANE
Lord's Seat
The Great Shack
Slapestones End
Rabbit Crag
Libshaw Hill
Stony Bank
Hen Stones
Hey Slack Allotment
Hey Slack
Libshaw Scar
Foulgate Bank
Hood Crag
Stony Bank Top
Hood Spring
Harden Head
Yaud Bones Ridge
Little Agill Head
White Wham Head
Rocking Moor
High Moor
Stoop Wham
Lowcock Stoop
Rocking Moor
Long Crag
HG3
Lane Head
Whit Moor
Garth Crook
The Cow and Calf
The Grainings
The Great Stray
Brayscroft Farm
Bramley Head
Rocking Stone
Middle Tongue
Dodd Moss
Bullace Farm
BRAMLEY HEAD LANE
WHIT MOOR ROAD
Lane Bottom
Barden Fell
Pan Head
Raven Stones Plantation
Brae
Croft House Farm
Dukes Hill
Brown Bank Head
Ford
Shaw Field Head
Rom Shaw Head
Rocking Stone
Rocking Hall
Gill House Crags
Peat Hill
Brown Bank
Agill House
Rom Shaw Spring
Black Sike Head
Rocking Moor
Round Hill
Aked's Dam
Rom Shaw
Broadshaw
Black Pasture
Cort How
Toffit Ing Head
BD23
Hard Pits
Sheepshaw Plantation
Green Sike Head
Middle Moor
Cold Moss Well
Old Peat Moor
Waterfall
Dicken Nook
Low Moor
Spittle Ings House
Long Ridge
Valley of Desolation
Cold Moss
Hard Ing
Hammerthorn Hill
Black Bank
Cold Moss Stoop
Little Collishaw Hill
North Nab
Spittle Ings
Great Collishaw Hill
Collishaw Ings
Black Sike
Brown Hill
Ramsgill Head
South Nab
Willow Bog
Hazlewood Moor
Whinhaugh
Round Hill
Ramsgill Hill
Kex Gill Moor
Willow Bog Head
Rotten Hill
Little Turner Hills
Great Turner Hill
Bolton Park
Intake
KEX GILL ROAD
Little Hills
Bolton Park Farm
The Level
Noska Brow
Old Pike Quarry (Dis)
Banward Hill
Pike Stones
Black Hill
Kex Gill Farm
Deft Hill
Noska
Noska Head
Rigg Side
Raven's Peak
Ford
Kirk Hill
Kex Gill Tarn
Cat Crag
Johnny Hill
KEX GILL ROAD
Friar's Stones
Maidenkirk
Bent Hill Farm
Pace Gate
Gill Head Peat Moor
Grey Stone Hill
Town End Farm
Standard
Point Crag
Badger Gill Bridge
Mossy Sikes
Storiths Crag
Brown Hill Farm
Gill Bottom Farm
Green Shaw Well
Stony Haw Spring
Summerscales
Mossy Sikes Head
Intake Laithe
Hill End
Green Hill
STORITHS LA
A59
Storiths House Farm
Kex Beck
Storiths
8 61 7 60 6 59 5 58 4 57 3 56 2 55 1 54
08 09 10 11 12 13

Scale: 1¾ inches to 1 mile

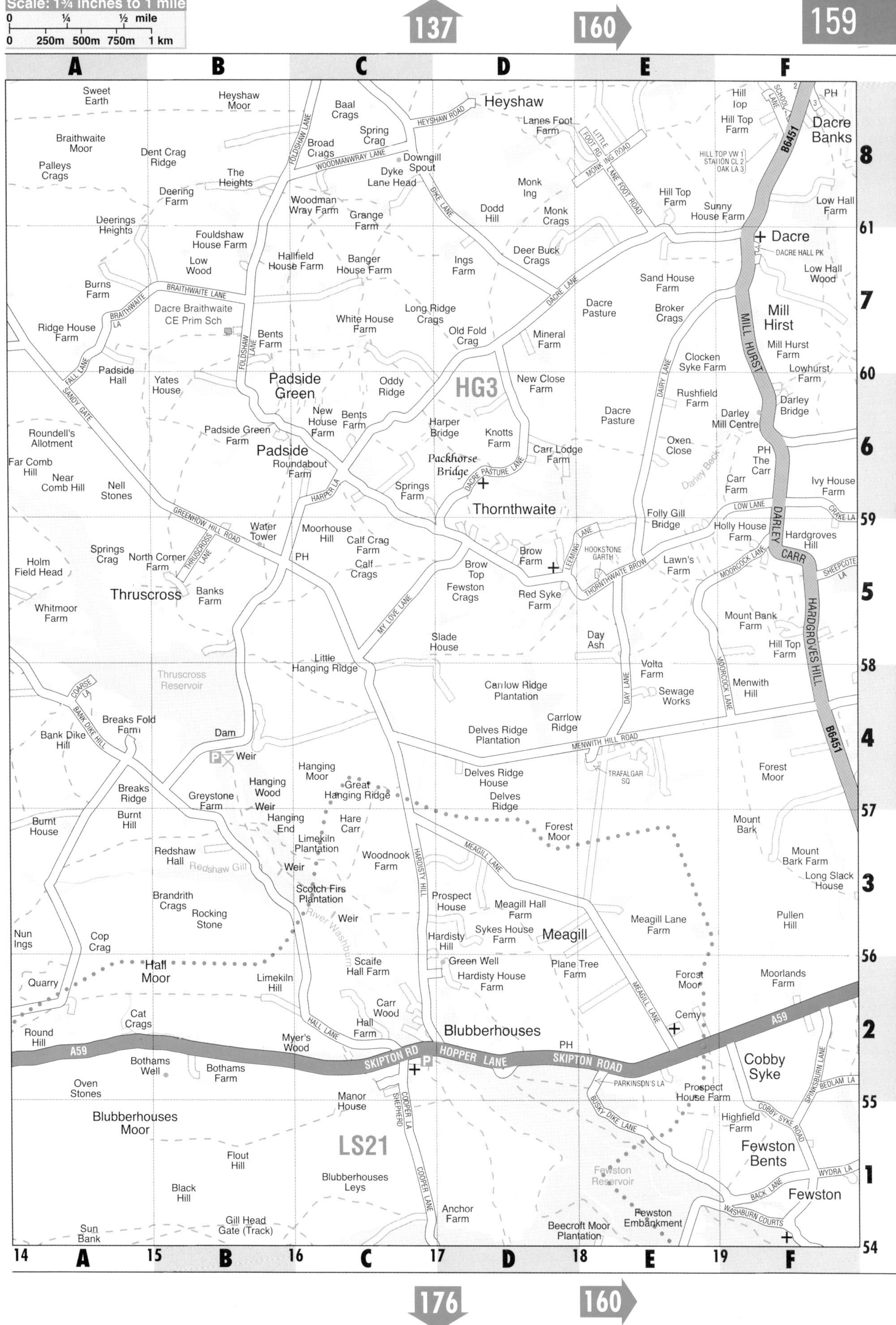
137
160
Sweet Earth
Heyshaw Moor
Baal Crags
Heyshaw
Lanes Foot Farm
Hill Top
Hill Top Farm
Dacre Banks
PH
Braithwaite Moor
Dent Crag Ridge
Palleys Crags
Broad Crags
Spring Crag
Downgill Spout
HILL TOP VW 1
STATION CL 2
OAK LA 3
The Heights
Dyke Lane Head
Monk Ing
Deering Farm
Woodman Wray Farm
Grange Farm
Dodd Hill
Monk Crags
Hill Top Farm
Sunny House Farm
Low Hall Farm
Deerings Heights
Fouldshaw House Farm
Dacre
DACRE HALL PK
Hallfield House Farm
Banger House Farm
Ings Farm
Deer Buck Crags
Low Wood
Sand House Farm
Low Hall Wood
Burns Farm
Broker Crags
Mill Hirst
Dacre Braithwaite CE Prim Sch
Dacre Pasture
Long Ridge Crags
White House Farm
Ridge House Farm
Bents Farm
Old Fold Crag
Mineral Farm
Mill Hurst Farm
Clocken Syke Farm
Lowhurst Farm
Padside Hall
Yates House
Padside Green
Oddy Ridge
HG3
New Close Farm
Rushfield Farm
Darley Bridge
Darley Mill Centre
New House Farm
Bents Farm
Dacre Pasture
Roundell's Allotment
Harper Bridge
Knotts Farm
Oxen Close
Padside Green Farm
Padside
Carr Lodge Farm
PH
The Carr
Packhorse Bridge
Roundabout Farm
Far Comb Hill
Near Comb Hill
Darley Beck
Carr Farm
Ivy House Farm
Nell Stones
Springs Farm
Thornthwaite
Folly Gill Bridge
Holly House Farm
Hardgroves Hill
Water Tower
Moorhouse Hill
Calf Crag Farm
Springs Crag
North Corner Farm
Brow Farm
HOOKSTONE GARTH
Lawn's Farm
Holm Field Head
PH
Calf Crags
Brow Top
Thruscross
Banks Farm
Fewston Crags
Red Syke Farm
Whitmoor Farm
Mount Bank Farm
Slade House
Day Ash
Hill Top Farm
Little Hanging Ridge
Volta Farm
Thruscross Reservoir
Carlow Ridge Plantation
Sewage Works
Menwith Hill
Breaks Fold Farm
Carrlow Ridge
Bank Dike Hill
Dam
Delves Ridge Plantation
Weir
Hanging Moor
Delves Ridge House
TRAFALGAR SQ
Forest Moor
Breaks Ridge
Hanging Wood
Great Hanging Ridge
Greystone Farm
Delves Ridge
Weir
Burnt Hill
Burnt House
Hanging End
Hare Carr
Forest Moor
Mount Bark
Limekiln Plantation
Redshaw Hall
Redshaw Gill
Woodnook Farm
Mount Bark Farm
Weir
Long Slack House
Scotch Firs Plantation
Prospect House
Meagill Hall Farm
Brandrith Crags
Rocking Stone
Weir
Pullen Hill
River Washburn
Sykes House Farm
Meagill
Meagill Lane Farm
Nun Ings
Cop Crag
Hardisty Hill
Green Well
Plane Tree Farm
Hall Moor
Scaife Hall Farm
Hardisty House Farm
Forest Moor
Moorlands Farm
Quarry
Limekiln Hill
Carr Wood
Cat Crags
Hall Farm
Blubberhouses
Cemy
Round Hill
Myer's Wood
PH
Cobby Syke
Bothams Well
Bothams Farm
Oven Stones
Prospect House Farm
Manor House
Highfield Farm
Blubberhouses Moor
LS21
Fewston Bents
Flout Hill
Fewston Reservoir
Blubberhouses Leys
Black Hill
Fewston
Anchor Farm
Fewston Embankment
Sun Bank
Gill Head Gate (Track)
Beecroft Moor Plantation
HEYSHAW ROAD
SCHOOL LANE
B6451
FOLDSHAW LANE
WOODMANWRAY LANE
LITTLE FOOT RD
MONK ING ROAD
LANE FOOT ROAD
DIKE LANE
BRAITHWAITE LANE
BRAITHWAITE LA
DACRE LANE
FOLDSHAW LANE
MILL HURST
FALL LANE
SANDY GATE
DAIRY LANE
DACRE PASTURE LANE
HARPER LA
GREENHOW HILL ROAD
LOW LANE
CRAKE LA
DARLEY CARR
THRUSCROSS LANE
LEEMING LANE
THORNTHWAITE BROW
MOORCOCK LANE
SHEEPCOTE LA
MY LOVE LANE
HARDGROVES HILL
COARSE LA
BANK DIKE HILL
MOORCOCK LANE
DAY LANE
MENWITH HILL ROAD
MEAGILL LANE
HARDISTY HILL
MEAGILL LANE
HALL LANE
A59
SKIPTON RD
HOPPER LANE
SKIPTON ROAD
PARKINSON'S LA
SHEPHERD LA
COOPER LA
RUSKY DIKE LANE
COBBY SYKE ROAD
SPINKSBURN LANE
BEDLAM LA
WYDRA LA
BACK LANE
WASHBURN COURTS
COOPER LANE
A B C D E F
14 15 16 17 18 19
54 55 1 2 56 3 57 4 58 5 59 6 60 7 61 8
176
160

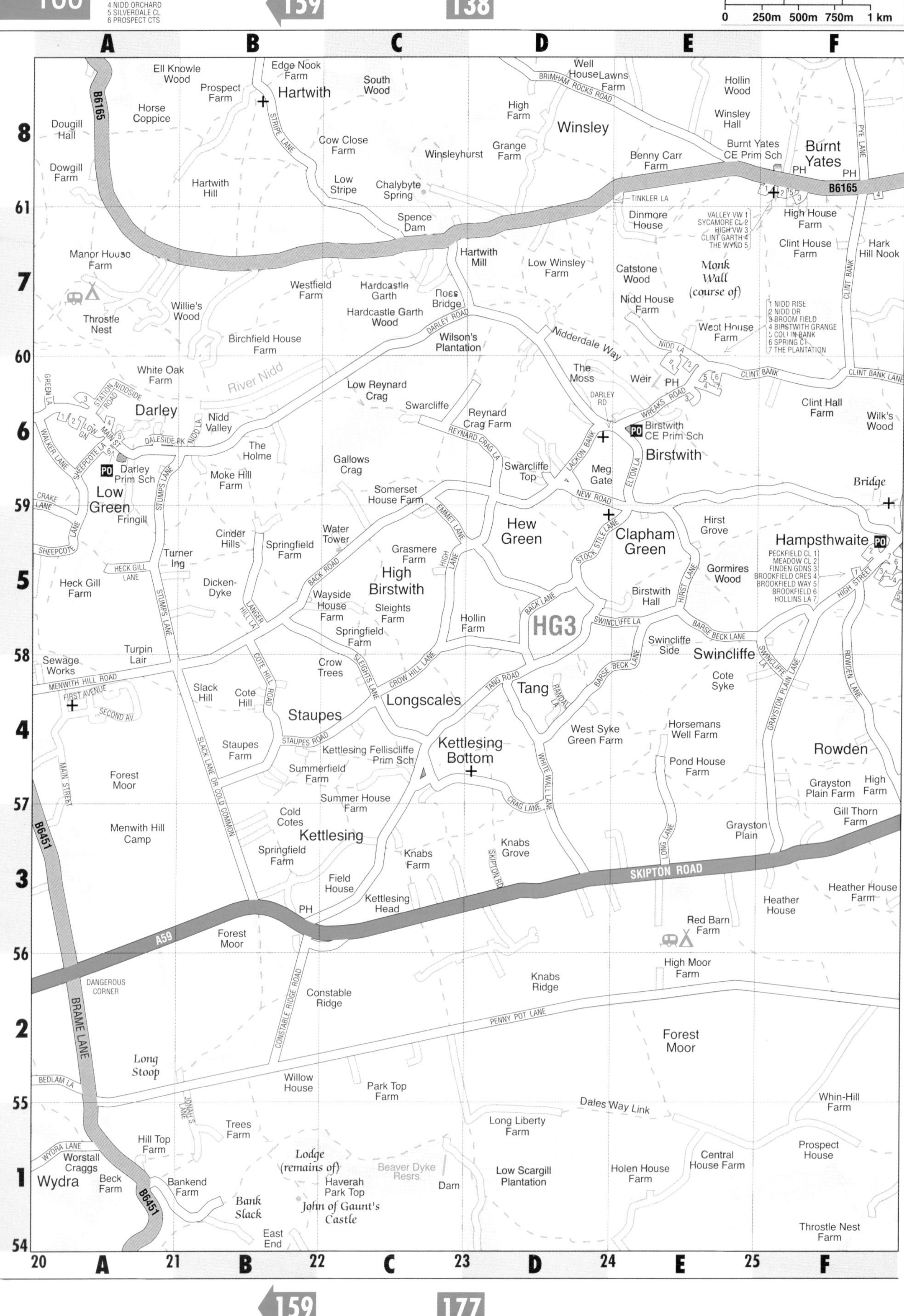

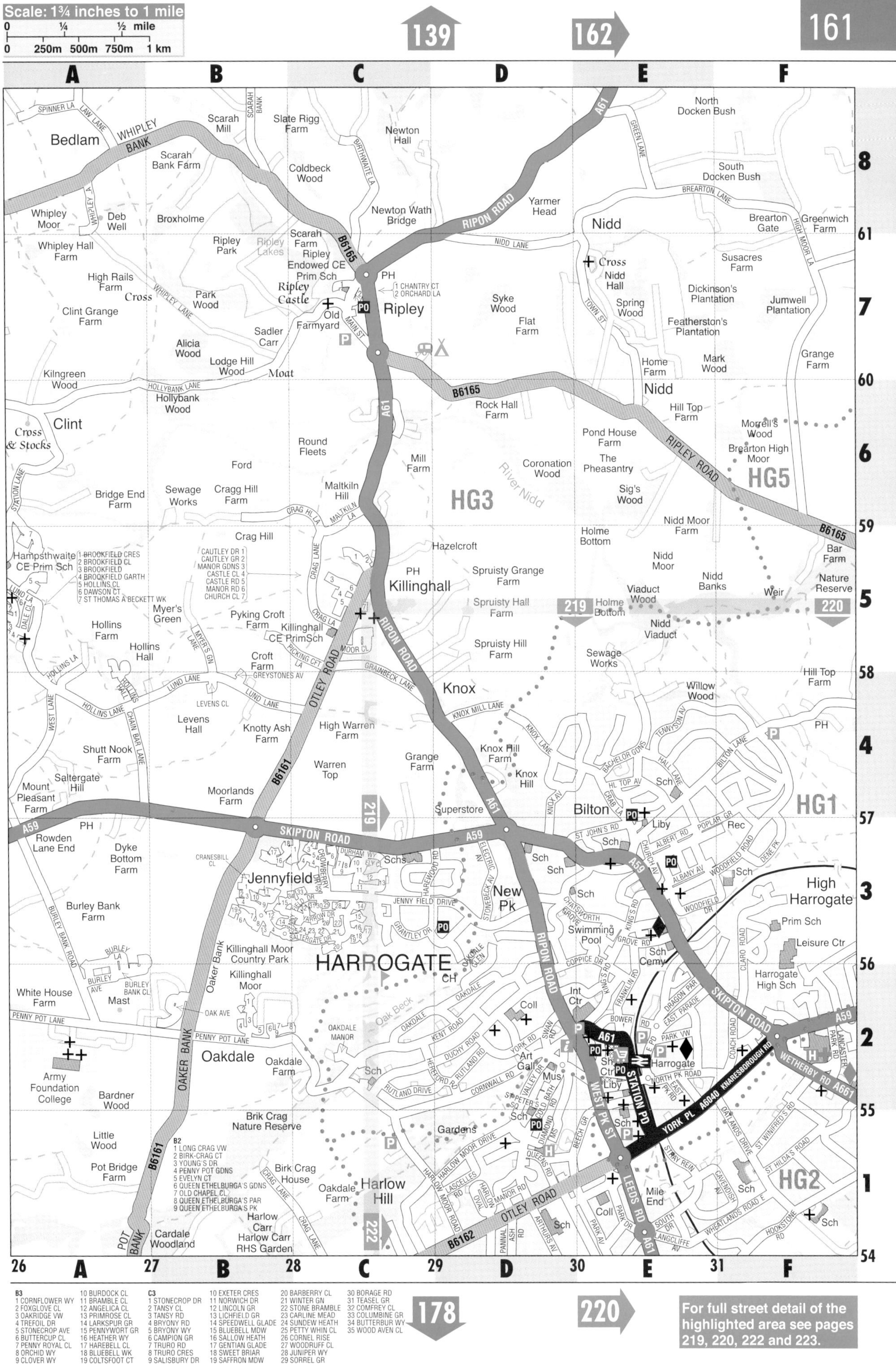

161
Scale: 1¾ inches to 1 mile
0 ¼ ½ mile
0 250m 500m 750m 1 km
139
162
A B C D E F
Spinner La
Law Lane
Bedlam
Whipley Bank
Scarah Mill
Scarah Bank
Slate Rigg Farm
Newton Hall
A61
Green Lane
North Docken Bush
Scarah Bank Farm
Birthwaite La
Coldbeck Wood
South Docken Bush
Brearton Lane
8
Whipley Moor
Whipley La
Deb Well
Broxholme
Newton Wath Bridge
Ripon Road
Yarmer Head
Nidd
Brearton Gate
Greenwich Farm
High Moor La
61
Whipley Hall Farm
Ripley Park
Ripley Lakes
Scarah Farm
Ripley Endowed CE Prim Sch
B6165
Nidd Lane
Cross
Nidd Hall
Susacres Farm
High Rails Farm
Cross
Whipley Lane
Ripley Castle
PH
1 Chantry Ct
2 Orchard La
Dickinson's Plantation
Clint Grange Farm
Park Wood
Old Farmyard
PO
Ripley
Syke Wood
Town St
Spring Wood
Jumwell Plantation
7
Main St
Flat Farm
Featherston's Plantation
Alicia Wood
Sadler Carr
P
Lodge Hill Wood
Moat
Home Farm
Mark Wood
Grange Farm
Kilngreen Wood
Hollybank Lane
Hollybank Wood
B6165
Rock Hall Farm
Nidd
60
Clint
A61
Hill Top Farm
Cross & Stocks
Round Fleets
Pond House Farm
Morrell's Wood
Ripley Road
Brearton High Moor
6
Ford
Mill Farm
Coronation Wood
The Pheasantry
HG5
River Nidd
Station Lane
Bridge End Farm
Sewage Works
Cragg Hill Farm
Maltkiln Hill
HG3
Sig's Wood
Crag Hl La
Maltkiln La
Nidd Moor Farm
B6165
59
Crag Hill
Hazelcroft
Holme Bottom
Bar Farm
Hampsthwaite CE Prim Sch
1 Brookfield Cres
2 Brookfield Cl
3 Brookfield
4 Brookfield Garth
5 Hollins Cl
6 Dawson Ct
7 St Thomas A Beckett Wk
Cautley Dr 1
Cautley Gr 2
Manor Gdns 3
Castle Cl 4
Castle Rd 5
Manor Rd 6
Church Cl 7
Crag Lane
PH
Killinghall
Spruisty Grange Farm
Nidd Moor
Nidd Banks
Nature Reserve
Lund La
Dale Cl
Myer's Green
Spruisty Hall Farm
219
Holme Bottom
Viaduct Wood
Weir
220
5
Hollins Farm
Pyking Croft Farm
Crag La
Killinghall CE PrimSch
Ripon Road
Nidd Viaduct
Myers Gn
Lane
Moor Cl
Hollins Hall
Picking Cft La
Spruisty Hill Farm
Sewage Works
Hollins La
Croft Farm
Greystones Av
Otley Road
Grainbeck Lane
58
Hill Top Farm
Lund Lane
Knox
Willow Wood
Levens Cl
Hollins Lane
Chain Bar Lane
West Lane
Knox Mill Lane
Tennyson Av
Levens Hall
Knotty Ash Farm
High Warren Farm
P
PH
Knox Lane
Bachelor Gdns
Hall Lane
Bilton Lane
Shutt Nook Farm
4
Knox Hill Farm
Grange Farm
Warren Top
B6161
Knox Hill
Mount Pleasant Farm
Saltergate Hill
HL Top Av
Sch
HG1
Moorlands Farm
Knox Av
Crab La
Bilton
219
Superstore
PO
A61
Liby
Poplar Gr
A59
PH
Skipton Road
St John's Rd
Rec
57
Rowden Lane End
A59
Albert Rd
Dyke Bottom Farm
Cranesbill Cl
Durham Wy
Electric Av
Sch
Church Av
Woodfield Road
Schs
Sch
PO
Dene Pk
Harewood Rd
Sch
Albany Av
Sch
Jennyfield
Stonebeck Av
High Harrogate
3
Burley Bank Farm
New Pk
Sch
Woodfield Dr
Jenny Field Drive
Chatsworth Grove
King's Rd
Prim Sch
Burley Bank Road
PO
Swimming Pool
Grantley Dr
Grove Rd
Killinghall Moor Country Park
Sch
Cemy
Claro Road
Leisure Ctr
Burley La
Ripon Road
HARROGATE
Oakdale Glen
Coppice Dr
Harrogate High Sch
Oaker Bank
CH
56
Burley Ave
Burley Bank Cl
Killinghall Moor
Franklin Rd
Dragon Par
Skipton Road
White House Farm
Mast
Oakdale
Int Ctr
East Parade
A59
Oak Av
Coll
Penny Pot Lane
Oak Beck
Kent Road
Bower Rd
Oakdale Manor
Park Vw
Coach Road
Penny Pot Lane
A61
Duchy Road
York Rd
Art Gall
Harrogate
Knaresborough Rd
2
Oakdale
Oakdale Farm
PO
Lancaster Park Rd
Oaker Bank
Rutland Rd
Station Pd
North Pk Road
Wetherby Rd A661
Army Foundation College
Sch
Hereford Rd
Mus
Liby
Rutland Drive
Cornwall Rd
West Pk St
A6040
Bardner Wood
St Peter's Sq
Cold Bath Rd
York Pl
Sch
Sch
Oatlands Drive
St Winifred's Rd
55
Brik Crag Nature Reserve
Gardens
PO
Beech Gr
Stray Rein
Little Wood
B2
1 Long Crag Vw
2 Birk-Crag Ct
3 Young's Dr
4 Penny Pot Gdns
5 Evelyn Ct
6 Queen Ethelburga's Gdns
7 Old Chapel Cl
8 Queen Ethelburga's Par
9 Queen Ethelburga's Pk
P
Harlow Moor Drive
Queens Rd
H
St Hilda's Road
Pot Bridge Farm
B6161
Birk Crag House
Crag Lane
Harlow Moor Rd
Lascelles Rd
Harlow Oval
Otley Road
Cavendish Av
HG2
1
Oakdale Farm
Harlow Hill
Manor Rd
Leeds Rd
Mile End
Sch
Harlow Carr
222
Coll
Park Dr
Wheatlands Road E
Pot Bank
Cardale Woodland
Harlow Carr RHS Garden
Crag Lane
B6162
Pannal Ash Rd
Arthurs Av
Sch
Park Av
South Dr
Langcliffe Av
A61
Hookstone Rd
Sch
54
26 A 27 B 28 C 29 D 30 E 31 F
B3
1 Cornflower Wy
2 Foxglove Cl
3 Oakridge Vw
4 Trefoil Dr
5 Stonecrop Ave
6 Buttercup Cl
7 Penny Royal Cl
8 Orchid Wy
9 Clover Wy
10 Burdock Cl
11 Bramble Cl
12 Angelica Cl
13 Primrose Cl
14 Larkspur Gr
15 Pennywort Gr
16 Heather Wy
17 Harebell Cl
18 Bluebell Wk
19 Coltsfoot Ct
C3
1 Stonecrop Dr
2 Tansy Cl
3 Tansy Rd
4 Bryony Rd
5 Bryony Wy
6 Campion Gr
7 Truro Rd
8 Truro Cres
9 Salisbury Dr
10 Exeter Cres
11 Norwich Dr
13 Lichfield Gr
14 Speedwell Glade
15 Bluebell Mdw
16 Sallow Heath
17 Gentian Glade
18 Sweet Briar
19 Saffron Mdw
20 Barberry Cl
21 Winter Gn
22 Stone Bramble
23 Carline Mead
24 Sundew Heath
25 Petty Whin Cl
26 Cornel Rise
27 Woodruff Cl
28 Juniper Wy
29 Sorrel Gr
30 Borage Rd
31 Teasel Gr
32 Comfrey Cl
33 Columbine Gr
34 Butterbur Wy
35 Wood Aven Cl
178
220
For full street detail of the highlighted area see pages 219, 220, 222 and 223.

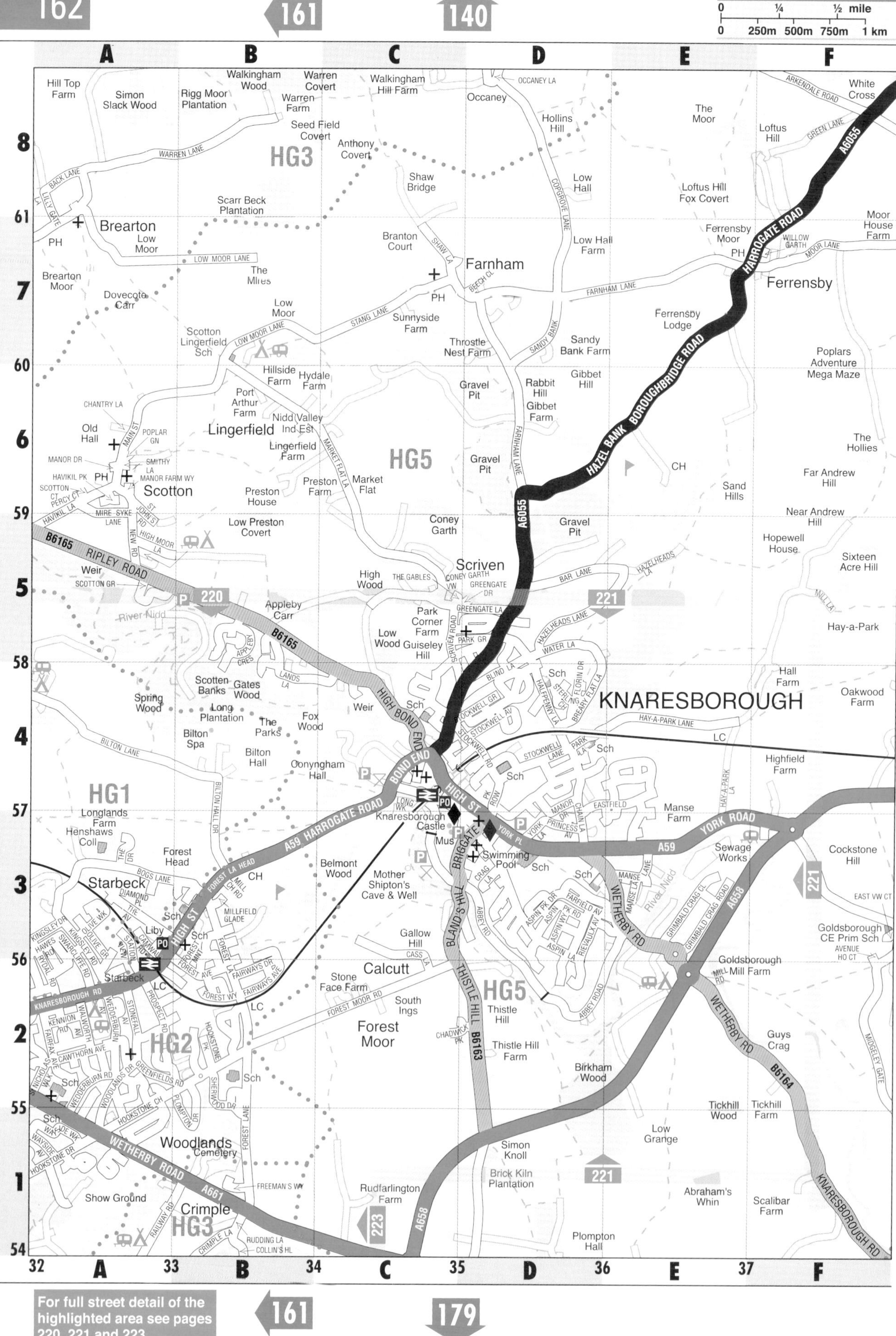

Scale: 1¾ inches to 1 mile

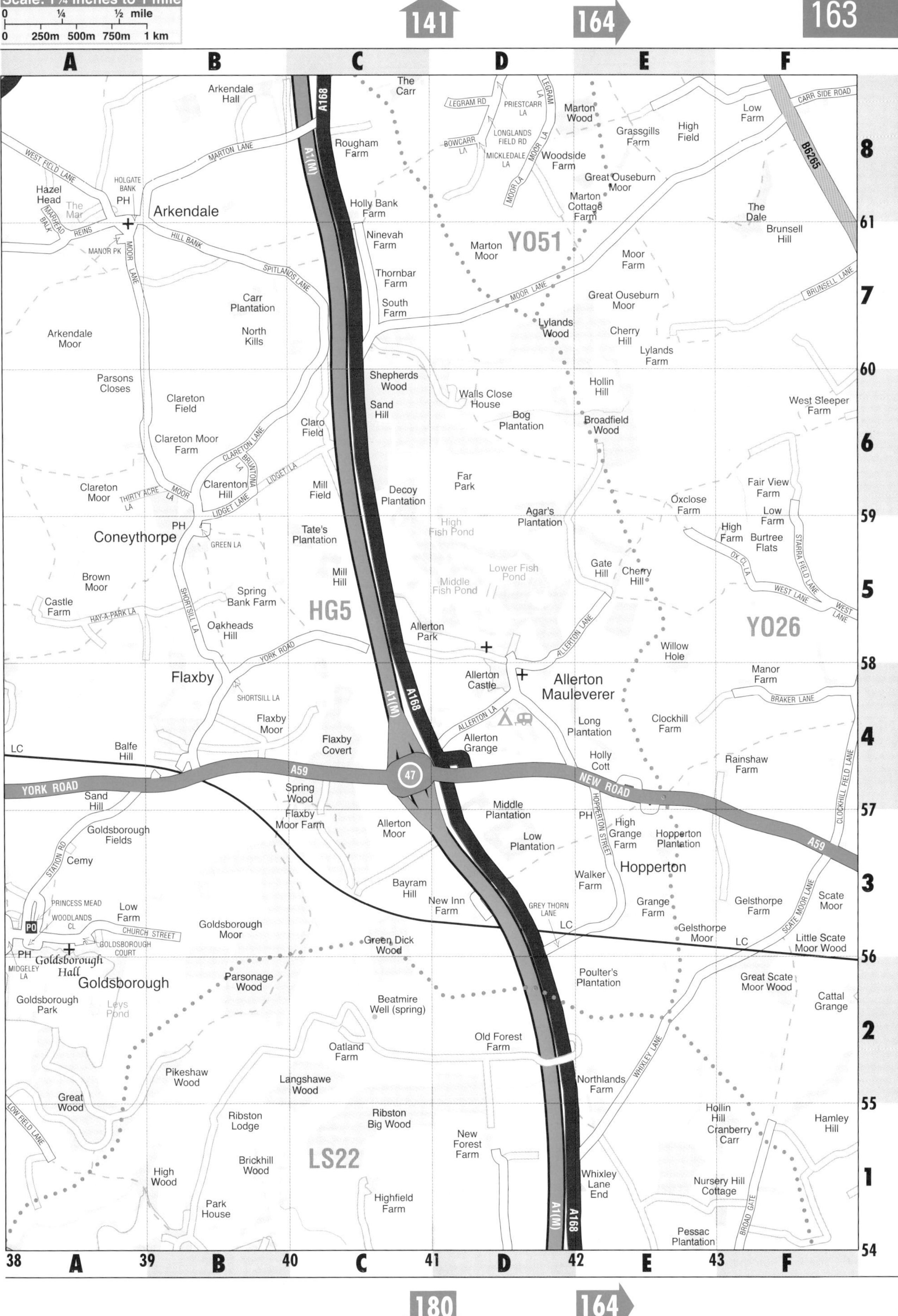
141
164
Arkendale
Arkendale Hall
Hazel Head
Rougham Farm
Holly Bank Farm
Ninevah Farm
Thornbar Farm
South Farm
Marton Wood
Grassgills Farm
High Field
Low Farm
Woodside Farm
Great Ouseburn Moor
Marton Cottage Farm
Marton Moor
YO51
The Dale
Brunsell Hill
Moor Farm
Great Ouseburn Moor
Lylands Wood
Cherry Hill
Lylands Farm
Carr Plantation
North Kills
Arkendale Moor
Parsons Closes
Clareton Field
Clareton Moor Farm
Claro Field
Shepherds Wood
Sand Hill
Walls Close House
Bog Plantation
Hollin Hill
Broadfield Wood
West Sleeper Farm
Clareton Moor
Clarenton Hill
Mill Field
Decoy Plantation
Far Park
Agar's Plantation
Oxclose Farm
Fair View Farm
Low Farm
High Farm
Burtree Flats
Coneythorpe
Tate's Plantation
Brown Moor
Castle Farm
Spring Bank Farm
Mill Hill
HG5
Gate Hill
Cherry Hill
YO26
Oakheads Hill
Allerton Park
Willow Hole
Flaxby
Allerton Castle
Allerton Mauleverer
Manor Farm
Flaxby Moor
Flaxby Covert
Long Plantation
Clockhill Farm
Balfe Hill
Allerton Grange
Holly Cott
Rainshaw Farm
YORK ROAD
A59
NEW ROAD
Sand Hill
Spring Wood
Flaxby Moor Farm
Middle Plantation
Goldsborough Fields
Allerton Moor
Low Plantation
High Grange Farm
Hopperton Plantation
Cemy
Hopperton
Walker Farm
Bayram Hill
New Inn Farm
Grange Farm
Gelsthorpe Farm
Scate Moor
Low Farm
Goldsborough Moor
Green Dick Wood
Gelsthorpe Moor
Little Scate Moor Wood
Goldsborough Hall
Goldsborough
Parsonage Wood
Poulter's Plantation
Great Scate Moor Wood
Cattal Grange
Goldsborough Park
Beatmire Well (spring)
Old Forest Farm
Oatland Farm
Pikeshaw Wood
Langshawe Wood
Northlands Farm
Great Wood
Ribston Lodge
Ribston Big Wood
Hollin Hill
Cranberry Carr
Hamley Hill
New Forest Farm
LS22
Brickhill Wood
High Wood
Whixley Lane End
Nursery Hill Cottage
Park House
Highfield Farm
Pessac Plantation
A1(M)
A168
B6265
180
164

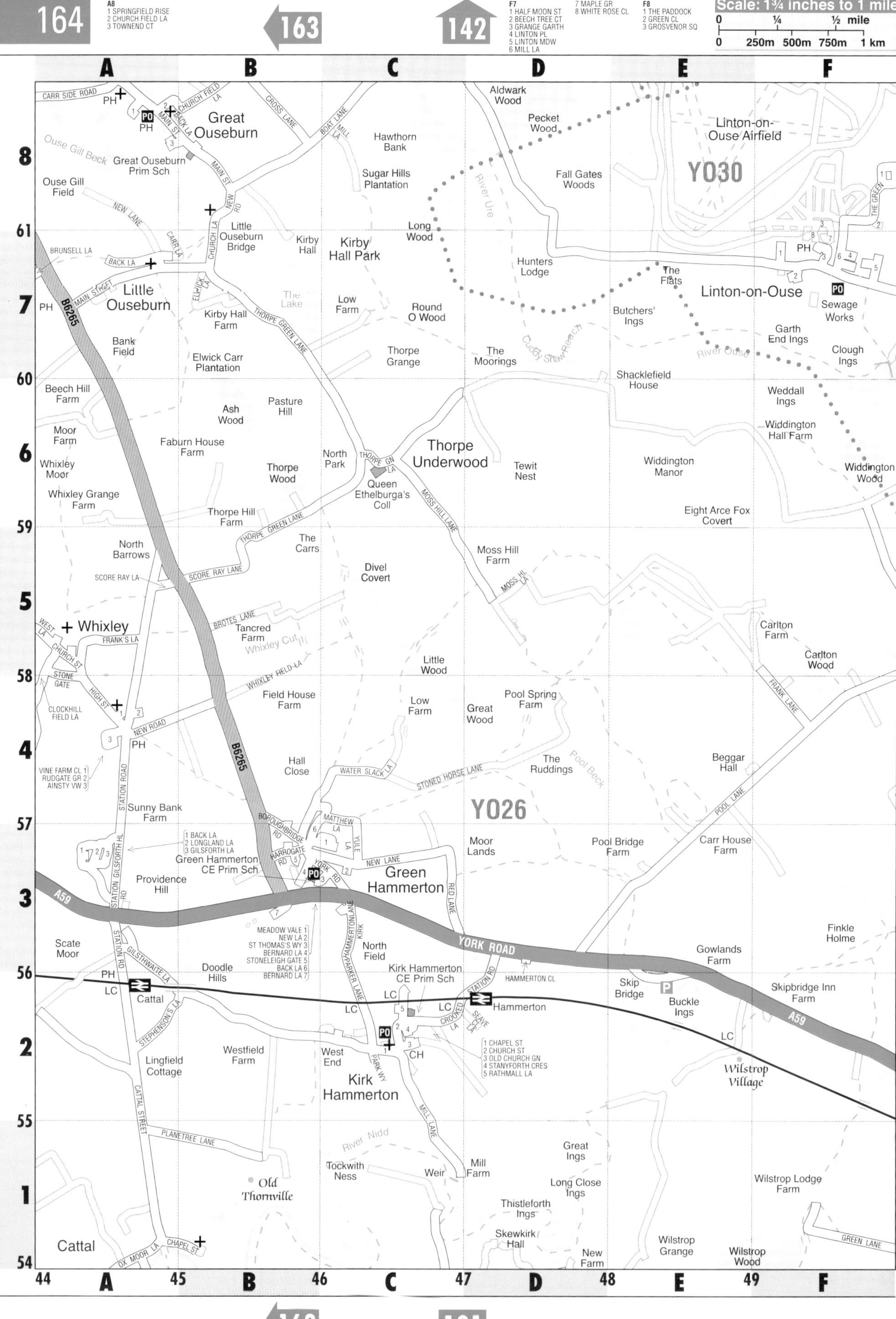

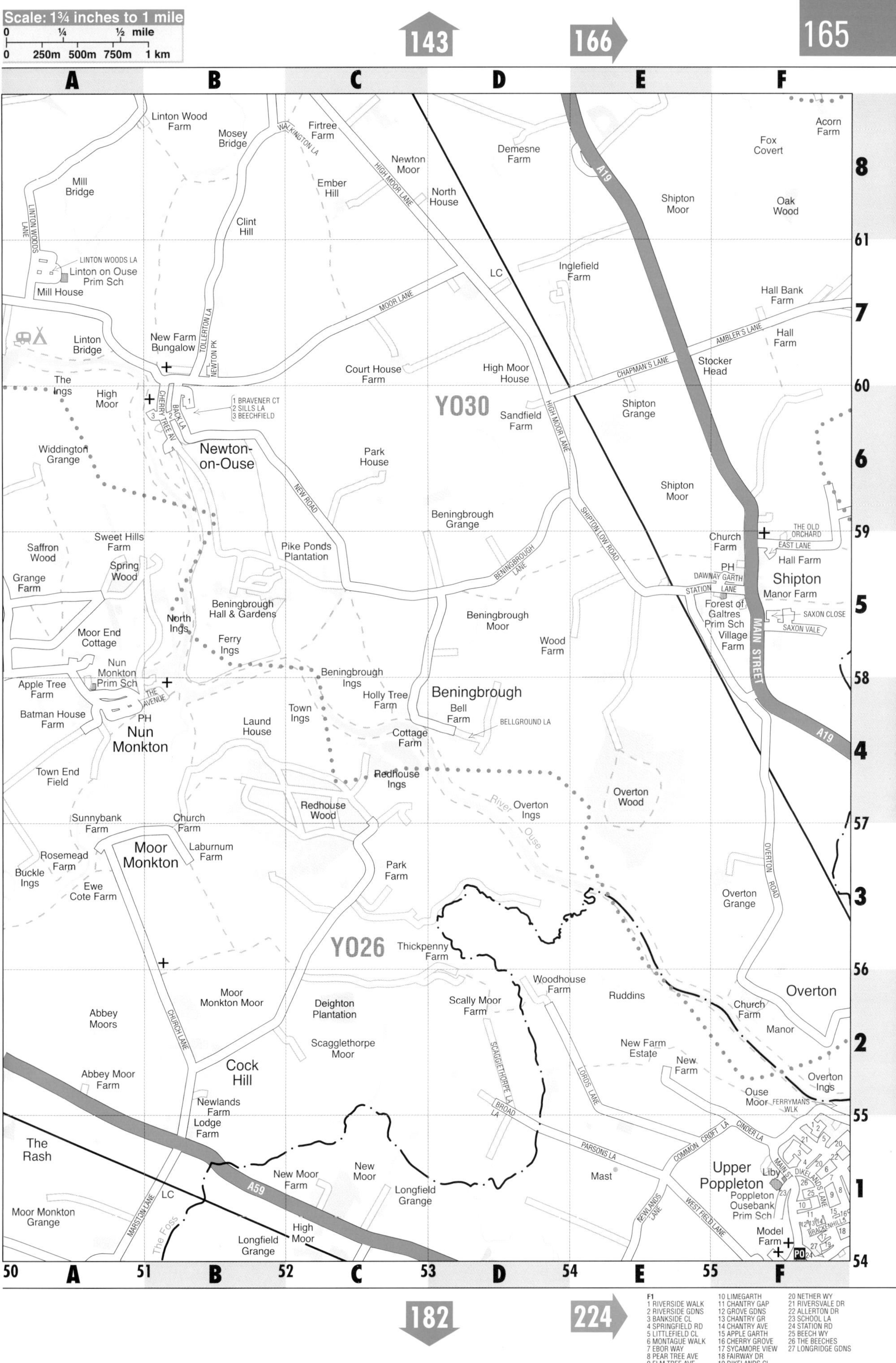

165 144

E5
1 VILLAGE GARTH
2 LONGCROFT
3 RIPLEY GR
4 SOUTHLANDS
5 THE AVENUE
6 REDWOOD DR

7 MULBERRY DR
8 ASH LA
9 ELM END
10 COPPICE CL
11 LITTLE LA
12 HAWTHORN AVE
13 BIRCH LA

14 FLETCHER CT
15 ST MARY'S CL
16 SANDY LA
17 CHURCH LA
18 BROAD OAK LA
19 WESTFIELD PL
20 WESTFIELD RD

21 WESTFIELD CL
22 ST NICHOLAS WY
23 PLANTATION WY
24 MIDDLE BANKS
25 HORNSEY GARTH
26 GLEBE WY
27 FOREST CL

28 CHURCHFIELD DR
29 SANDYLAND
30 HEADLAND CL
31 WANDHILL
32 KENNEDY DR
33 ABELTON GR
34 ORCHARD PADDOCK

35 LARCH WY
36 ACACIA GR
37 CYPRUS GR
38 ELDER GR
39 WALNUT CL
40 MINSTER CL

Scale: 1¾ inches to 1 mile
0   ¼   ½   mile
0   250m   500m   750m   1 km

165 227 228

D5
1 CASTLE CL
2 WINDSOR DR
3 TOWN END GDNS
4 STEEPLE CL
5 HAREWOOD CL
6 DELAMERE CL
7 ETON DR
8 SAXFORD WY
9 CANTERBURY CL

10 HAMBLETON VIEW
11 BACK LA
12 WESTFIELD GR
13 BURRILL DR
14 TWIN PIKE WY
15 STABLER CL
16 HELMSLEY GR
17 CORNER CL
18 LANCAR CL
19 WATERINGS

20 BUTTERS CL
21 CORBAN WY
22 BUTT HILL

F5
1 FARNDALE CL
2 SANDHOLME
3 NEWDALE
4 KELDALE
5 NORTHCROFT
6 RUSHWOOD CL
7 LANSDOWN WY
8 SCRIVEN GR
9 WOODCOCK CL

10 FALCON CL
11 MALLARD WY
12 HALL RISE
13 FOLKS CL
14 OLD COPPICE
15 NEW FORGE CT
16 CHATSWORTH DR
17 RIVERSDALE
18 NETHERWINDINGS
19 THORNHILLS

20 GARTHS END
21 THE LANDINGS
22 LANDING LA
23 WINDMILL WY
24 LINLEY AVE
25 WEST NOOKS

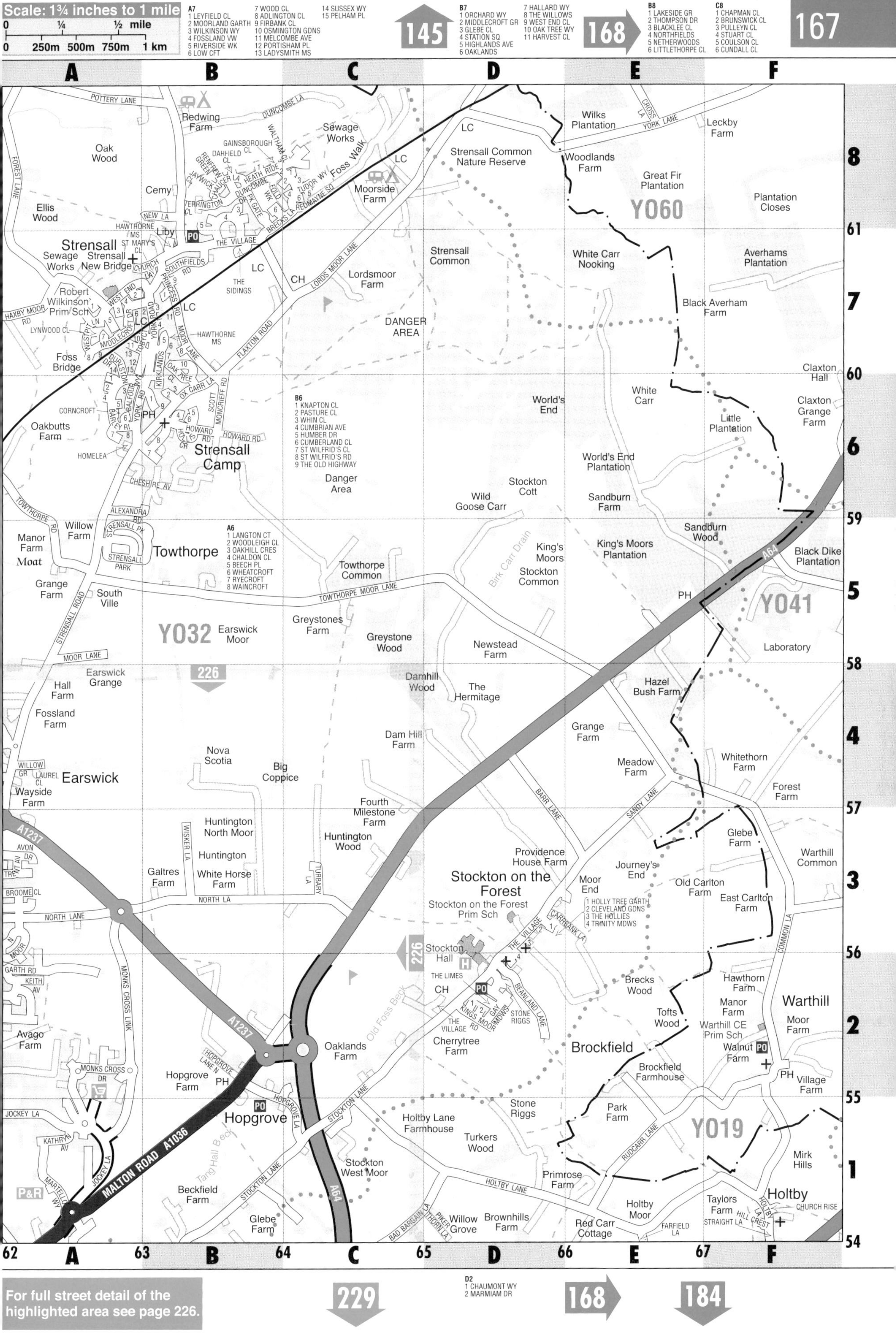
Scale: 1¾ inches to 1 mile
0 ¼ ½ mile
0 250m 500m 750m 1 km
A7
1 LEYFIELD CL
2 MOORLAND GARTH
3 WILKINSON WY
4 FOSSLAND VW
5 RIVERSIDE WK
6 LOW CFT
7 WOOD CL
8 ADLINGTON CL
9 FIRBANK CL
10 OSMINGTON GDNS
11 MELCOMBE AVE
12 PORTISHAM PL
13 LADYSMITH MS
14 SUSSEX WY
15 PELHAM PL
145
B7
1 ORCHARD WY
2 MIDDLECROFT GR
3 GLEBE CL
4 STATION SQ
5 HIGHLANDS AVE
6 OAKLANDS
7 HALLARD WY
8 THE WILLOWS
9 WEST END CL
10 OAK TREE WY
11 HARVEST CL
168
B8
1 LAKESIDE GR
2 THOMPSON DR
3 BLACKLEE CL
4 NORTHFIELDS
5 NETHERWOODS
6 LITTLETHORPE CL
C8
1 CHAPMAN CL
2 BRUNSWICK CL
3 PULLEYN CL
4 STUART CL
5 COULSON CL
6 CUNDALL CL
A B C D E F
POTTERY LANE
Redwing Farm
DUNCOMBE LA
Sewage Works
Oak Wood
FOREST LANE
Ellis Wood
Cemy
Strensall
Sewage Works
Strensall New Bridge
Robert Wilkinson Prim Sch
HAXBY MOOR RD
LYNWOOD CL
Foss Bridge
Oakbutts Farm
CORNCROFT
HOMELEA
Strensall Camp
CHESHIRE AV
TOWTHORPE RD
Willow Farm
Manor Farm
Moat
Towthorpe
STRENSALL PK
STRENSALL PARK
Grange Farm
South Ville
STRENSALL ROAD
Y032
Earswick Moor
MOOR LANE
226
Earswick Grange
Hall Farm
Fossland Farm
Nova Scotia
Big Coppice
WILLOW GR
LAUREL CL
Earswick
Wayside Farm
A1237
Huntington North Moor
Huntington
WISKER LA
Galtres Farm
White Horse Farm
NORTH LA
NORTH LANE
BROOME CL
GARTH RD
KEITH AV
MONKS CROSS LINK
Avago Farm
MONKS CROSS DR
JOCKEY LA
KATHRYN AV
P&R
MARTELLO WY
JOCKEY LA
MALTON ROAD A1036
Hopgrove Farm
PH
Hopgrove
HOPGROVE LANE N
HOPGROVE LA
Tang Hall Beck
Beckfield Farm
STOCKTON LANE
Glebe Farm
Stockton West Moor
A64
Oaklands Farm
Old Foss Beck
Holtby Lane Farmhouse
Turkers Wood
Stone Riggs
BAD BARGAIN LA
PIKE THORN LA
Willow Grove
Brownhills Farm
HOLTBY LANE
Primrose Farm
Red Carr Cottage
Holtby Moor
FARFIELD LA
Taylors Farm
Holtby
CHURCH RISE
HILL CREST
STRAIGHT LA
Mirk Hills
Y019
Park Farm
RUDCARR LANE
Brockfield
Brockfield Farmhouse
Walnut Farm
Warthill CE Prim Sch
Manor Farm
Hawthorn Farm
Warthill
Moor Farm
Village Farm
Tofts Wood
Brecks Wood
Cherrytree Farm
THE VILLAGE
KINGS MOOR RD
STONE RIGGS
BEANLAND LANE
THE LIMES
CH
Stockton Hall
Stockton on the Forest
Stockton on the Forest Prim Sch
CARRBANK LA
1 HOLLY TREE GARTH
2 CLEVELAND GDNS
3 THE HOLLIES
4 TRINITY MDWS
Moor End
Journey's End
Old Carlton Farm
East Carlton Farm
COMMON LA
Warthill Common
Glebe Farm
Providence House Farm
Huntington Wood
Fourth Milestone Farm
TURBARY LA
Dam Hill Farm
Damhill Wood
The Hermitage
Grange Farm
Meadow Farm
BARR LANE
SANDY LANE
Whitethorn Farm
Forest Farm
Hazel Bush Farm
Laboratory
Y041
Newstead Farm
Greystone Wood
Greystones Farm
TOWTHORPE MOOR LANE
Towthorpe Common
Birk Carr Drain
King's Moors
Stockton Common
King's Moors Plantation
Sandburn Wood
Black Dike Plantation
Wild Goose Carr
Stockton Cott
Sandburn Farm
World's End Plantation
Danger Area
B6
1 KNAPTON CL
2 PASTURE CL
3 WHIN CL
4 CUMBRIAN AVE
5 HUMBER DR
6 CUMBERLAND CL
7 ST WILFRID'S CL
8 ST WILFRID'S RD
9 THE OLD HIGHWAY
A6
1 LANGTON CT
2 WOODLEIGH CL
3 OAKHILL CRES
4 CHALDON CL
5 BEECH PL
6 WHEATCROFT
7 RYECROFT
8 WAINCROFT
World's End
White Carr
Little Plantation
Claxton Grange Farm
Claxton Hall
Black Averham Farm
DANGER AREA
Lordsmoor Farm
LORDS MOOR LANE
Strensall Common
White Carr Nooking
Averhams Plantation
Plantation Closes
Y060
Great Fir Plantation
Woodlands Farm
Strensall Common Nature Reserve
Wilks Plantation
YORK LANE
CROSS LA
Leckby Farm
Moorside Farm
Foss Walk
LC
CH
THE SIDINGS
THE VILLAGE
FLAXTON ROAD
MOOR LANE
HAWTHORNE MS
SCOTT
MONCRIEFF RD
HOWARD RD
HOWARD RD
OAK CARR LA
KIRKLANDS
YORK ROAD
BALFOUR WY
BARLEY RI
DURLSTON DR
MIDDLECROFT
WESTPIT LN
WEST END
CHURCH LA
SOUTHFIELDS RD
PRINCESS RD
OAK TREE CL
HAWTHORNE MS
ST MARY'S CL
Liby
PO
PH
NEW LA
TERRINGTON CL
GAINSBOROUGH CL
DARFIELD CL
RENFREW GREEN
JAYWICK CL
CHAUCER LA
HEATH RIDE
DUNCOMBE DR
PK GATE
TUDOR WY
REDMAYNE SQ
BRECKS LA
WALTHAM CL
ALEXANDRA RD
8 61 7 60 6 59 5 58 4 57 3 56 2 55 1 54
62 63 64 65 66 67
D2
1 CHAUMONT WY
2 MARMIAM DR
229
168
184
For full street detail of the highlighted area see page 226.

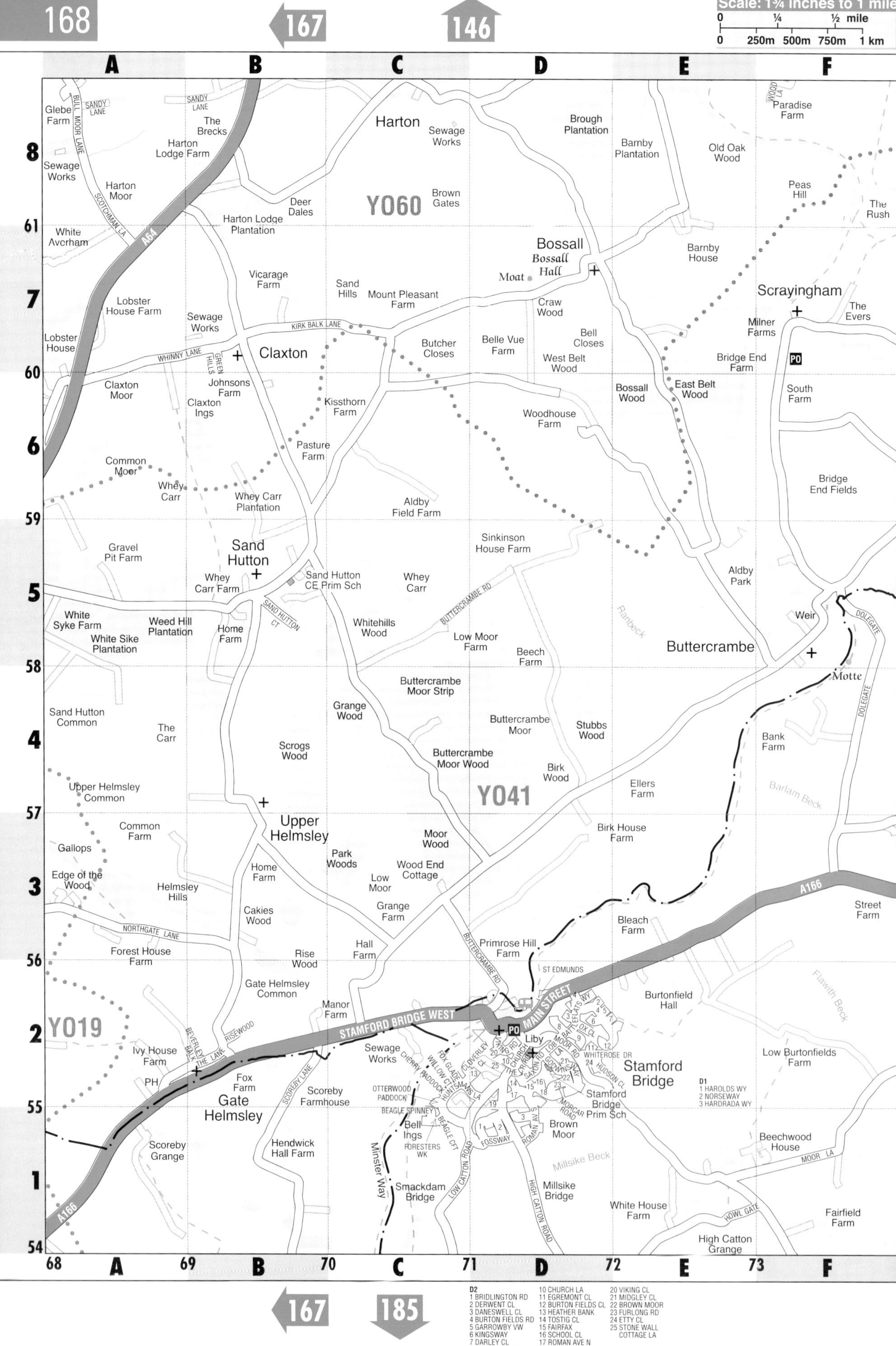

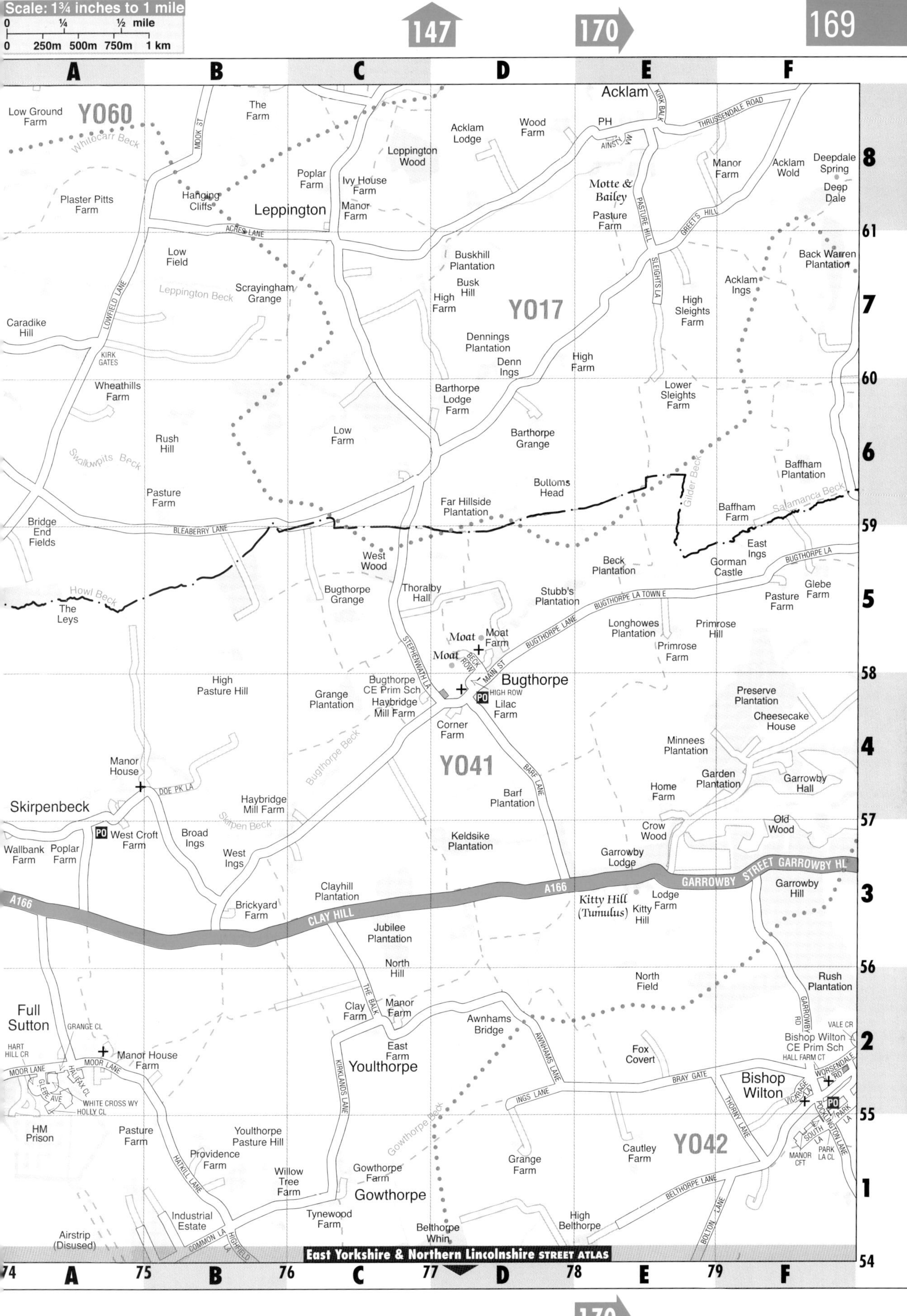

Scale: 1¾ inches to 1 mile

0   ¼   ½ mile
0 250m 500m 750m 1 km

147

170

169

A   B   C   D   E   F

YO60

Low Ground
Farm

Whitecarr Beck

Plaster Pitts
Farm

Hanging
Cliffs

The
Farm

Leppington

Poplar
Farm

Ivy House
Farm

Manor
Farm

Leppington
Wood

Acklam
Lodge

Wood
Farm

Acklam

PH

KIRK BALK

THRUSSENDALE ROAD

Manor
Farm

Acklam
Wold

Deepdale
Spring

Deep
Dale

AINSTY WY

Motte &
Bailey

PASTURE HILL

GREET'S HILL

Pasture
Farm

8

Caradike
Hill

LOWFIELD LANE

ACRES LANE

Low
Field

Leppington Beck

Scrayingham
Grange

KIRK
GATES

Wheathills
Farm

Rush
Hill

Shallowpits Beck

Pasture
Farm

Buskhill
Plantation

Busk
Hill

High
Farm

YO17

Dennings
Plantation

Denn
Ings

Barthorpe
Lodge
Farm

Low
Farm

Barthorpe
Grange

High
Farm

SLEIGHTS LA

High
Sleights
Farm

Lower
Sleights
Farm

Acklam
Ings

Back Warren
Plantation

Baffham
Plantation

61

7

60

6

Bridge
End
Fields

BLEABERRY LANE

Howl Beck

The
Leys

West
Wood

Bugthorpe
Grange

Far Hillside
Plantation

Thoralby
Hall

Bottoms
Head

Beck
Plantation

Stubb's
Plantation

BUGTHORPE LA TOWN E

Glider Beck

Baffham
Farm

Salamanca Beck

East
Ings

Gorman
Castle

BUGTHORPE LA

Pasture
Farm

Glebe
Farm

59

5

High
Pasture Hill

Grange
Plantation

Bugthorpe
CE Prim Sch

Haybridge
Mill Farm

STERNEWATH LA

Bugthorpe Beck

Moat
Farm

Moat

Moat
Farm

BECK ROW

MAIN ST

Bugthorpe

HIGH ROW

PO

Lilac
Farm

Corner
Farm

BUGTHORPE LANE

Longhowes
Plantation

Primrose
Farm

Primrose
Hill

Preserve
Plantation

Cheesecake
House

58

4

Skirpenbeck

Manor
House

DOE PK LA

Skipen Beck

Haybridge
Mill Farm

West
Ings

YO041

BARF LANE

Barf
Plantation

Minnees
Plantation

Home
Farm

Garden
Plantation

Garrowby
Hall

57

Wallbank
Farm

PO

Poplar
Farm

West Croft
Farm

Broad
Ings

Keldsike
Plantation

Crow
Wood

Garrowby
Lodge

GARROWBY STREET GARROWBY HL

Old
Wood

Garrowby
Hill

A166

Brickyard
Farm

CLAY HILL

Clayhill
Plantation

A166

Kitty Hill
(Tumulus)

Lodge
Farm

Kitty
Hill

3

56

Jubilee
Plantation

North
Hill

North
Field

GARROWBY RD

Rush
Plantation

VALE CR

**Full
Sutton**

GRANGE CL

THE BACK

Clay
Farm

Manor
Farm

Awnhams
Bridge

AWNHAMS LANE

Fox
Covert

BRAY GATE

Bishop Wilton
CE Prim Sch

HALL FARM CT

**Bishop
Wilton**

2

HART
HILL CR

MOOR LANE

HALIFAX CL

Manor House
Farm

KIRKLANDS LANE

Youlthorpe

East
Farm

INGS LANE

VICARAGE LA

WORSENDALE RD

MOOR LANE

GLEBE AVE

WHITE CROSS WY

HOLLY CL

Youlthorpe
Pasture Hill

Willow
Tree
Farm

Gowthorpe
Farm

Gowthorpe Beck

Grange
Farm

Cautley
Farm

YO42

THORNY LANE

PO

MANOR
CFT

SOUTH
LA

PARK
LA

PARK
LA CL

55

HM
Prison

Pasture
Farm

Providence
Farm

HATKILL LANE

HIGHFIELD

Gowthorpe

Tynewood
Farm

Belthorpe
Whin

High
Belthorpe

BELTHORPE LANE

BOLTON LANE

1

Airstrip
(Disused)

Industrial
Estate

COMMON LA

54

74   A   75   B   76   C   77   D   78   E   79   F

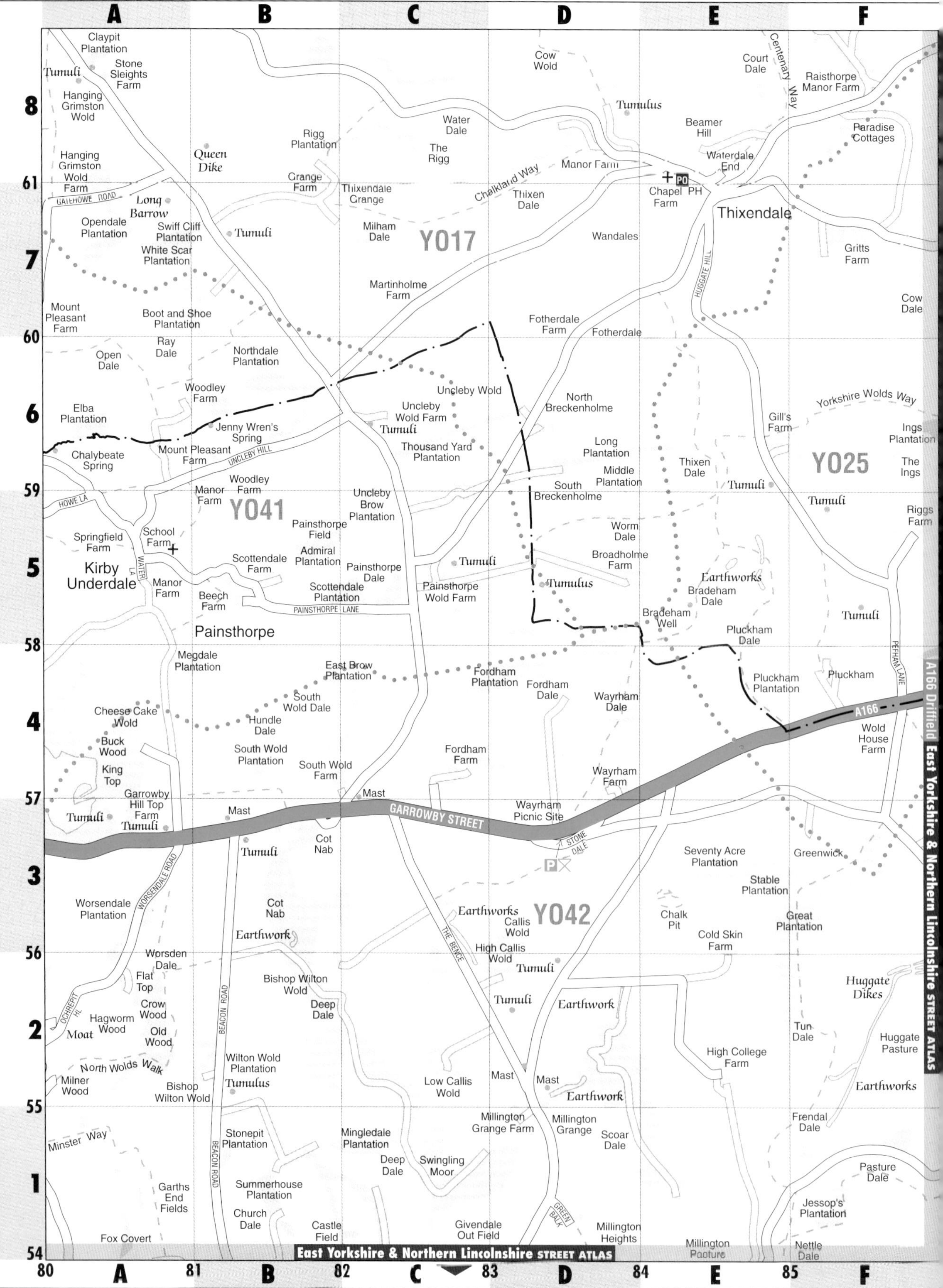

A B C D E F

Claypit Plantation
Tumuli
Stone Sleights Farm
Hanging Grimston Wold
Hanging Grimston Wold Farm
Queen Dike
Rigg Plantation
Water Dale
Cow Wold
Tumulus
Court Dale
Centenary Way
Raisthorpe Manor Farm
Beamer Hill
Paradise Cottages

8

Opendale Plantation
Long Barrow
Grange Farm
The Rigg
Thixendale Grange
Chalkland Way
Manor Farm
Thixen Dale
Waterdale End
Chapel Farm
PO PH
Thixendale

61

GATEHOWE ROAD
Swiff Cliff Plantation
White Scar Plantation
Tumuli
Milham Dale
Martinholme Farm
Wandales
Gritts Farm

7

Mount Pleasant Farm
Boot and Shoe Plantation
YO17
Fotherdale Farm
Fotherdale
HUGGATE HILL
Cow Dale

Open Dale
Ray Dale
Northdale Plantation
Uncleby Wold
North Breckenholme
Yorkshire Wolds Way
Gill's Farm
Ings Plantation

60

Elba Plantation
Woodley Farm
Jenny Wren's Spring
Uncleby Wold Farm
Tumuli
Thousand Yard Plantation
Long Plantation
Middle Plantation
Thixen Dale
Tumuli
YO25
The Ings

6

Chalybeate Spring
Mount Pleasant Farm
UNCLEBY HILL
South Breckenholme
Tumuli
Riggs Farm

HOWE LA
Manor Farm
Woodley Farm
YO41
Uncleby Brow Plantation
Worm Dale
Broadholme Farm

59

Springfield Farm
School Farm
Painsthorpe Field
South Breckenholme
Earthworks
Bradeham Dale

5

Kirby Underdale
Manor Farm
Scottendale Farm
Admiral Plantation
Scottendale Plantation
Painsthorpe Dale
Painsthorpe Wold Farm
Tumuli
Tumulus
Bradeham Well
Earthworks
Pluckham Dale
Tumuli

Beech Farm
PAINSTHORPE LANE
Pluckham Plantation
Pluckham

58

Painsthorpe
Megdale Plantation
East Brow Plantation
Fordham Plantation
Fordham Dale
Wayrham Dale
PEKHAM LANE

4

Cheese Cake Wold
Buck Wood
Hundle Dale
South Wold Dale
Fordham Farm
Wayrham Farm
A166
Wold House Farm

King Top
South Wold Plantation
South Wold Farm
Mast
Wayrham Farm

57

Garrowby Hill Top Farm
Mast
GARROWBY STREET
Wayrham Picnic Site
Greenwick

Tumuli
Tumuli
Tumuli
Cot Nab
STONE DALE
Seventy Acre Plantation

3

Worsendale Plantation
WORSENDALE ROAD
Cot Nab
P
YO42
Stable Plantation
Great Plantation

Earthwork
Earthworks
Callis Wold
Chalk Pit
Cold Skin Farm
Huggate Dikes

56

Worsden Dale
Flat Top
BEACON ROAD
Bishop Wilton Wold
High Callis Wold
Tumuli
Tun Dale

Hagworm Wood
Crow Wood
Deep Dale
Tumuli
Earthwork
High College Farm
Huggate Pasture

2

Moat
Old Wood
North Wolds Walk
Wilton Wold Plantation
Low Callis Wold
Mast
Mast
Earthwork
Earthworks

Milner Wood
Bishop Wilton Wold
Tumulus
Frendal Dale

55

Minster Way
Stonepit Plantation
Mingledale Plantation
Millington Grange Farm
Millington Grange
Scoar Dale
Pasture Dale

GOCKFERF HL
Deep Dale
Swingling Moor
GREEN BACK
Jessop's Plantation

1

Garths End Fields
Summerhouse Plantation
Church Dale
Castle Field
Givendale Out Field
Millington Heights
Nettle Dale

Fox Covert
Givendale Heights
Millington Pasture

54

A166 Driffield East Yorkshire & Northern Lincolnshire STREET ATLAS

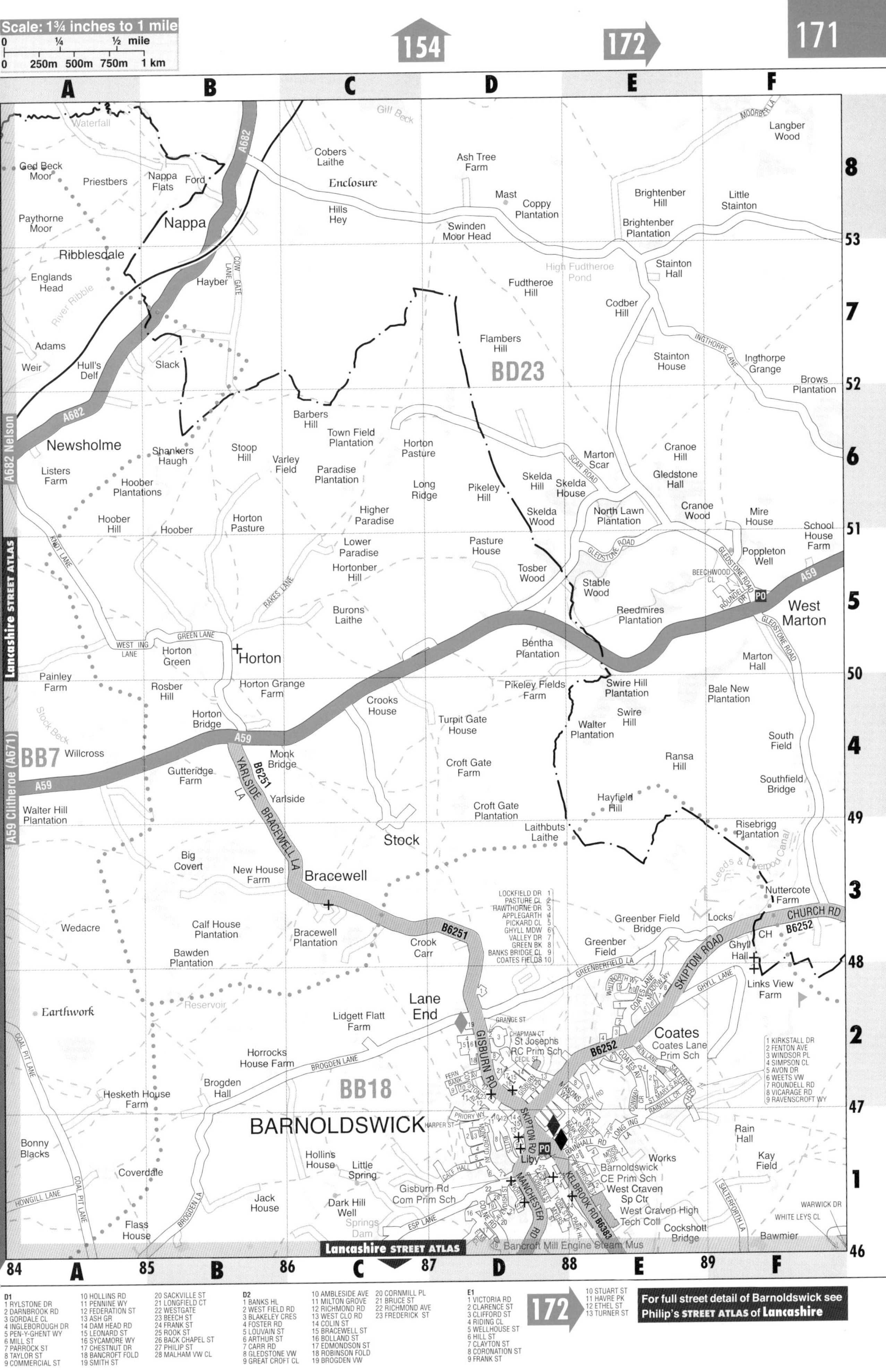

A B C D E F

8
53
7
52
6
51
5
50
4
49
3
48
2
47
1
46

Waterfall
Ged Beck Moor
Priestbers
Nappa Flats
Ford
Cobers Laithe
Enclosure
Ash Tree Farm
Mast
Coppy Plantation
Brightenber Hill
Brightenber Plantation
Little Stainton
Langber Wood
MOORBECK

Paythorne Moor
Nappa
Hills Hey
Swinden Moor Head
High Fudtheroe Pond
Stainton Hall

Ribblesdale
Hayber
Fudtheroe Hill
Codber Hill
Stainton House
Ingthorpe Grange
INGTHORPE LANE
Brows Plantation

Englands Head
River Ribble
COW GATE LANE
Flambers Hill
BD23
Marton Scar
Cranoe Hill
Gledstone Hall
Cranoe Wood
Mire House
School House Farm

Adams
Weir
Hull's Delf
Slack
Barbers Hill
Town Field Plantation
Horton Pasture
Pikeley Hill
Skelda Hill
Skelda House
North Lawn Plantation
Poppleton Well
BEECHWOOD CL
ROUNDELL DR
PO
A59
West Marton

A682
Newsholme
Shankers Haugh
Stoop Hill
Varley Field
Paradise Plantation
Long Ridge
Skelda Wood
SCAR ROAD
GLEDSTONE ROAD

Listers Farm
Hoober Plantations
Higher Paradise
Pasture House
Tosber Wood
Stable Wood
Reedmires Plantation
Marton Hall

Hoober Hill
Hoober
Horton Pasture
Lower Paradise
Hortonber Hill
Bentha Plantation
GLEDSTONE ROAD

Painley Farm
WEST ING LANE
GREEN LANE
Horton Green
Horton
Crooks House
Pikeley Fields Farm
Swire Hill Plantation
Bale New Plantation

Stock Beck
Rosber Hill
Horton Grange Farm
RAKES LANE
Turpit Gate House
Swire Hill
Walter Plantation
South Field

BB7
A59
Willcross
Horton Bridge
A59
Monk Bridge
Croft Gate Farm
Ransa Hill
Southfield Bridge

A59 Clitheroe (A671)
Gutteridge Farm
B6251
YARLSIDE LA
Yarlside
Croft Gate Plantation
Hayfield Hill
Leeds & Liverpool Canal
Risebrigg Plantation

Walter Hill Plantation
Big Covert
New House Farm
BRACEWELL LA
Stock
Laithbuts Laithe
Nuttercote Farm
CHURCH RD

Wedacre
Calf House Plantation
Bracewell
Crook Carr
B6251
LOCKFIELD DR 1
PASTURE CL 2
RAWTHORNE DR 3
APPLEGARTH 4
PICKARD CL 5
GHYLL MDW 6
VALLEY DR 7
GREEN BK 8
BANKS BRIDGE CL 9
COATES FIELD 10
Greenber Field Bridge
Greenber Field
Locks
GHYLL LANE
CH
B6252
Ghyll Hall
Links View Farm

Earthwork
Reservoir
Bawden Plantation
Bracewell Plantation
Lane End
GREENBERFIELD LA
SKIPTON ROAD
Coates
Coates Lane Prim Sch
1 KIRKSTALL DR
2 FENTON AVE
3 WINDSOR PL
4 SIMPSON CL
5 AVON DR
6 WEETS VW
7 ROUNDELL RD
8 VICARAGE RD
9 RAVENSCROFT WY

Lidgett Flatt Farm
GISBURN RD
GRANGE ST
St Josephs RC Prim Sch
CHAPMAN CT
CECIL ST
B6252
COATES LA
Rain Hall

Horrocks House Farm
BROGDEN LANE
Brogden Hall
FERN BANK ST
PRIORY WY
SKIPTON RD
MANCHESTER
KELBROOK RD
Works
Barnoldswick CE Prim Sch
West Craven Sp Ctr
West Craven High Tech Coll
Kay Field
WARWICK DR

Hesketh House Farm
BB18
PO
Liby
Barnoldswick
SALTERFORTH LA
WHITE LEYS CL

Bonny Blacks
Coverdale
Jack House
Hollins House
Little Spring
Gisburn Rd Com Prim Sch
Dark Hill Well
ESP LANE
Cockshott Bridge
Bawmier

COAL PIT LANE
HOWGILL LANE
Flass House
Springs Dam
Lancashire STREET ATLAS
Bancroft Mill Engine Steam Mus

84 85 86 87 88 89

D1
1 RYLSTONE DR
2 DARNBROOK RD
3 GORDALE CL
4 INGLEBOROUGH DR
5 PEN-Y-GHENT WY
6 MILL ST
7 PARROCK ST
8 TAYLOR ST
9 COMMERCIAL ST

10 HOLLINS RD
11 PENNINE WY
12 FEDERATION ST
13 ASH GR
14 DAM HEAD RD
15 LEONARD ST
16 SYCAMORE WY
17 CHESTNUT DR
18 BANCROFT FOLD
19 SMITH ST

20 SACKVILLE ST
21 LONGFIELD CT
22 WESTGATE
23 BEECH ST
24 FRANK ST
25 ROOK ST
26 BACK CHAPEL ST
27 PHILIP ST
28 MALHAM VW CL

D2
1 BANKS HL
2 WEST FIELD RD
3 BLAKELEY CRES
4 FOSTER RD
5 LOUVAIN ST
6 ARTHUR ST
7 CARR RD
8 GLEDSTONE VW
9 GREAT CROFT CL

10 AMBLESIDE AVE
11 MILTON GROVE
12 RICHMOND RD
13 WEST CLO RD
14 COLIN ST
15 BRACEWELL ST
16 BOLLAND ST
17 EDMONDSON ST
18 ROBINSON FOLD
19 BROGDEN VW

20 CORNMILL PL
21 BRUCE ST
22 RICHMOND AVE
23 FREDERICK ST

E1
1 VICTORIA RD
2 CLARENCE ST
3 CLIFFORD ST
4 RIDING CL
5 WELLHOUSE ST
6 HILL ST
7 CLAYTON ST
8 CORONATION ST
9 FRANK ST

10 STUART ST
11 HAVRE PK
12 ETHEL ST
13 TURNER ST

172

For full street detail of Barnoldswick see
Philip's STREET ATLAS of Lancashire

Scale: 1¾ inches to 1 mile

0 ¼ ½ mile
0 250m 500m 750m 1 km

A B C D E F

8

Viaduct
Weir
Weir
MARTON ROAD
WALTON RD
Woomber Wood
A65
Highgate Bridge (swing)
Sulber Laithe
Aqueduct
Priest Holme Bridge
Mosber La Bridge
MARTON CFT
CHURCH CFT
Gargrave
PH
CHURCH LA
Moat
Gargrave
Lobby Bridge
River Aire
Newton Hall
Locks
Parkers Farm
Scaleber
Kelber Hill Farm
Kirk Sink Farm
Sewage Works
Robin Wood
53
Bank Newton
Lock
Butter Haw Farm
Broughton Quarry
Thorlby Bridge (swing)
7
Newton Bridge
Newton Grange Farm
Pennine Way
Moorber Hill
CHURCH STREET
Smellows Quarry
Copy Hill Plantation
River Aire
52
Pasture House
Oxen Close
Small House
Copy Hill
Brows Plantation
Greenbank Farm
Turnbers Hill Plantation
Acliffe Hill Plantation
Oxenclose Farm
Hall Close Wood
Broughton Copy Farm
6
Green Bank
Trenet Laithe
Clints Delf (dis)
Skinnerground Wood
GARGRAVE ROAD
Broughton
Langber Plantation
Corringer Hill
Skinner Ground Farm
Deer Haw Plantation
OLD LA
A59
Heslaker Bridge
51
Tempest Farm
Williamson Bridge
BD23
PH
Weir
The Grove Hall
Dancliff Plantation
HEBER DR
PH
East Marton
Mickletthorne Farm
Mill Wood
PH
Broughton Hall
A59
CHURCH LA
Broughton Fields Farm
Primrose Hill
Home Farm
Denbers Plantation
5
Church Farm Barn
Crickle Farm
EDMONDSON'S LANE
A56
BROUGHTON RD
Sewage Works
Pennine Way
Pasture House Farm
50
Gubbs Hill Farm
PH Elslack Bridge
Low Ground Farm
Langber
COLNE AND BROUGHTON RD
Far Fence End Farm
ELSLACK LA
BURWEN CASTLE RD
KELLER GILL LA
Croft Wood
Yellison House
4
Fence End
Johnsons Gate Farm
White House Farm
Yellison Wood
Lower Scarcliffe Farm
Scarcliffe Farm
Merlinwood
Elslack Hall
CHURCH LANE
Higher Scarcliff
Lane Head Quarry
BURWEN CASTLE FARM (ROMAN FORT)
Smearber Farm
Mitton House
49
Old Cote Farm
Thornton-in-Craven Prim Sch
Thompson House Farm
MOOR LANE
Redfirth Gill Cote
Baxter House
A56
CAM LA
BREARLANDS
Stories House Farm
Baxter House Farm
3
Thornton-in-Craven
PO
Rectory Farm
OLD ROAD
Brown House Bridge
Park House Farm
Mill Fold
Standrise Plantation
Frozen Well
Gawthorpe House
CHURCH RD
B6252
LISTER CRT
Hotel
1 THE FOLD
2 QUEENS GARTH
Brown House
Wood House
Elslack Resr
Ransable Well
Clarke Moss Hill
Carleton Moor
48
SUMMERFIELD
BOOTH BRIDGE LANE
THORNTON HILLS
Booth Bridge Farm
Pennine Way
Elslack Moor
2
SKIPTON RD
PH
Little Moor
Oak Slack Farm
Thornton Moor
P
Pinhaw Moor
Broughton Hill
Pendle Way
SCHOOL FIELDS
Sewage Works
Batty House
Marl Field Farm
Pinhaw
Kirk Sykes Farm
47
Yorkshire Dales Mine Mus
Cowgarth Farm
BB18
YH
Wentcliff Brook
Pennine Way
Hewitts Farm
OLD LA
SCHOOL
RED LION ST
GAYLANDS LA
BIRCH HL
DARK LA
DODGSON RD
Out Laithe Farm
Sunny Side
BD20
1
PO
A56
COLNE RD
HILL TOP LA
NEW RD
Mill Bridge
P
Raike Bank Farm
Windle Field Farm
Dodgsons Farm
Calf Edge Farm
Hill Top Harrow Ings Farm
WHITE HL LA
Knott Farm
The Fold
Earby Springfield Prim Sch
Highbank Farm
Lower Verjuice Farm
Bleara Moor
Mitton House
MITTON LA
WINTER GAP LANE
CALF WOOD LANE
Pennine Way
46
EARBY

90 A 91 B 92 C 93 D 94 E 95 F

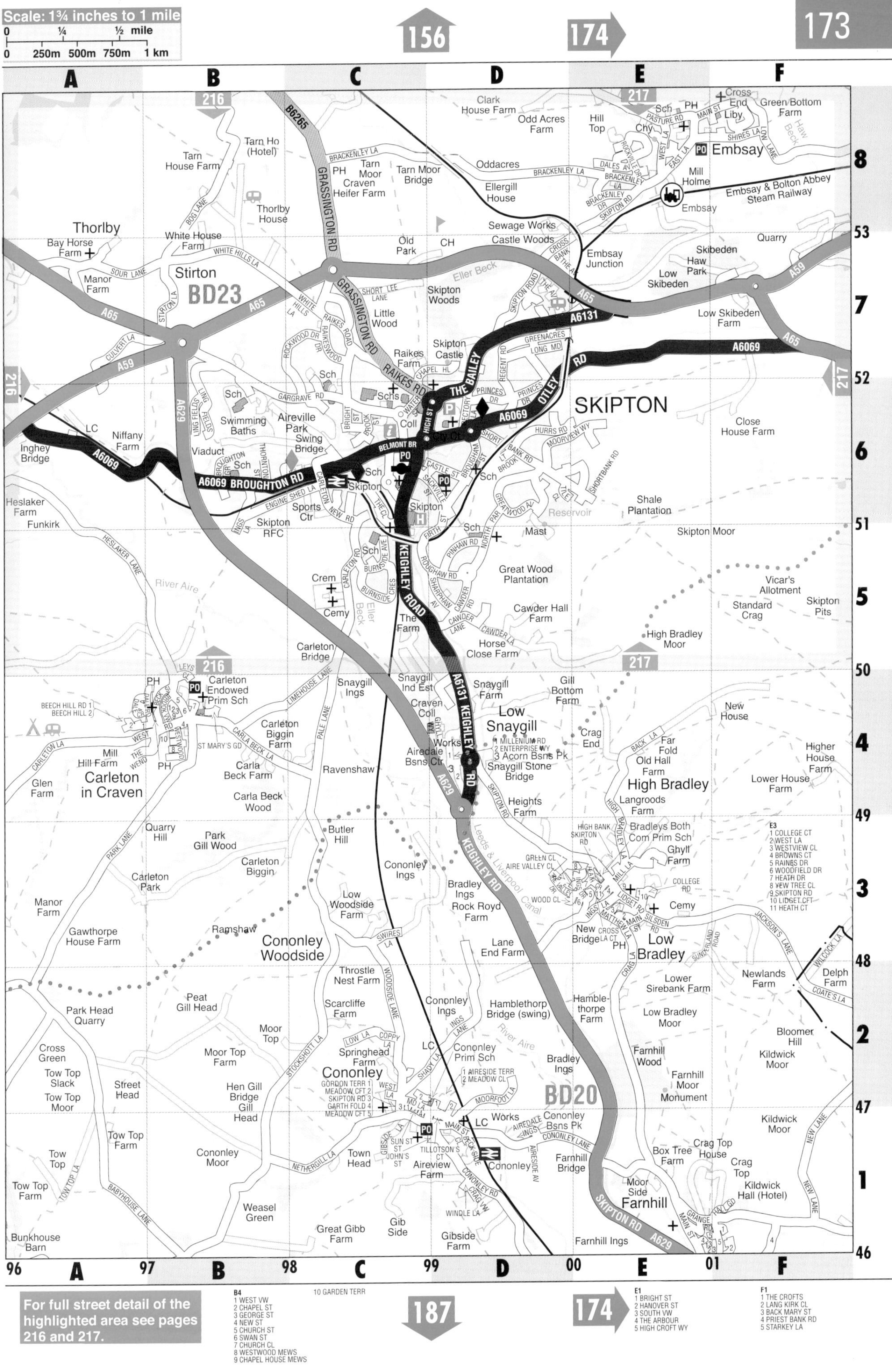

Scale: 1¾ inches to 1 mile
0 ¼ ½ mile
0 250m 500m 750m 1 km
156
174
A
B
C
D
E
F
216
217
Clark House Farm
Odd Acres Farm
Hill Top
Sch
PH
Cross End
Liby
Green Bottom Farm
Haw Beck
Chy
PASTURE RD
MAIN ST
SHIRES LA
LOW LANE
WEST LA
EAST LA
PO Embsay
ROCKVILLE DR
DALES AV
BRACKENLEY LA
BRACKENLEY DR
SKIPTON RD
Mill Holme
Embsay
Embsay & Bolton Abbey Steam Railway
8
B6265
Tarn Ho (Hotel)
Tarn House Farm
BOG LANE
Thorlby House
Tarn Moor Craven Heifer Farm
Tarn Moor Bridge
Oddacres
Ellergill House
GRASSINGTON RD
Thorlby
Bay Horse Farm
White House Farm
WHITE HILLS LA
Old Park
CH
Sewage Works
Castle Woods
CROSS BANK
THE AV
Embsay Junction
Skibeden Haw Park
Quarry
53
Manor Farm
SOUR LANE
Stirton
BD23
STIRTON LA
A65
Eller Beck
Low Skibeden
A59
SHORT LEE LANE
Skipton Woods
Little Wood
RAIKES ROAD
ROCKWOOD DR
RAIKESWOOD DR
7
A6131
GREENACRES
LONG MD
Low Skibeden Farm
A6069
CULVERT LA
Skipton Castle
Raikes Farm
CHAPEL HL
REGENT RD
OTLEY RD
52
A629
LING FIELDS
Sch
GARGRAVE RD
Schs
RAIKES RD
THE BAILEY
PRINCES DR
SKIPTON
Swimming Baths
Aireville Park
Swing Bridge
BRIGHT ST
BROOK ST
HIGH ST
Coll
RECTORY LA
Cty Ct
HURRS RD
MOORVIEW WY
Close House Farm
LC
Niffany Farm
Inghey Bridge
Viaduct
BROUGHTON GR
Sch
THORNTON ST
BELMONT BR
PO
SHORT BANK
BANK RD
BROOK
SHORTBANK RD
6
A6069 BROUGHTON RD
CARLETON ST
Sch
Skipton
CASTLE ST
SACKVILLE ST
BROUGHTON RD
PO
Sch
Heslaker Farm
ENGINE SHED LA
Sports Ctr
NEW RD
THE CL
Skipton H
FIRTH ST
GREATWOOD AV
TILE CL
Reservoir
Shale Plantation
Funkirk
INGS LA
Skipton RFC
Sch
NORTH PAR
Mast
Skipton Moor
51
HESLAKER LANE
Sch
CARLETON RD
BURNSIDE AVE
KEIGHLEY ROAD
PINHAW RD
ROUGHAW RD
Great Wood Plantation
River Aire
Crem
BURNSIDE CRES
SHARPHAW AV
CAWDER RD
Vicar's Allotment
Standard Crag
Skipton Pits
5
Cemy
Eller Beck
The Farm
CAWDER LANE
CAWDER LA
Cawder Hall Farm
High Bradley Moor
Carleton Bridge
Horse Close Farm
LEYS CL
PH
PO
Carleton Endowed Prim Sch
LIMEHOUSE LANE
Snaygill Ings
Snaygill Ind Est
A6131 KEIGHLEY RD
Snaygill Farm
Gill Bottom Farm
50
BEECH HILL RD 1
BEECH HILL 2
Craven Coll
Low Snaygill
New House
WEST RD
CARLA BECK LA
Carleton Biggin Farm
PALE LANE
GHYLL WY
1 MILLENIUM RD
2 ENTERPRISE WY
3 Acorn Bsns Pk
Crag End
BACK LA
Far Fold
Higher House Farm
CARLETON LA
Mill Hill Farm
THE WEND
ST MARY'S GD
Works
Airedale Bsns Ctr
Old Hall Farm
4
Glen Farm
Carleton in Craven
PH
Carla Beck Farm
Ravenshaw
Snaygill Stone Bridge
High Bradley
Lower House Farm
Carla Beck Wood
SKIPTON RD
Heights Farm
Langroods Farm
Quarry Hill
PARK LANE
Park Gill Wood
Butler Hill
HIGH BANK
SKIPTON RD
HIGH BRADLEY LA
Bradleys Both Com Prim Sch
49
E3
1 COLLEGE CT
2 WEST LA
3 WESTVIEW CL
4 BROWNS CT
5 RAINES DR
6 WOODFIELD DR
7 HEATH DR
8 YEW TREE CL
9 SKIPTON RD
10 LIDGET CFT
11 HEATH CT
Ghyll Farm
Carleton Biggin
Carleton Park
Cononley Ings
Leeds & Liverpool Canal
KEIGHLEY RD
GREEN CL
AIRE VALLEY CL
MILL LA
COLLEGE RD
3
Manor Farm
Low Woodside Farm
Bradley Ings
Rock Royd Farm
WOOD CL
LIDGET RD
Cemy
Gawthorpe House Farm
Ramshaw
SWIRES LA
INGS LA
MATTHEW LA
MAIN ST
SILSDEN RD
JACKSON'S LANE
Cononley Woodside
New Bridge
CROSS LA
CT
PH
Low Bradley
SUNDERLAND ROAD
WILCOCK LA
Throstle Nest Farm
Lane End Farm
CRAG LA
48
Delph Farm
Peat Gill Head
WOODSIDE LANE
Lower Sirebank Farm
Newlands Farm
COATE'S LA
Park Head Quarry
Scarcliffe Farm
Cononley Ings
Hamblethorp Bridge (swing)
Hamblethorpe Farm
Low Bradley Moor
Cross Green
INGS LANE
River Aire
Bloomer Hill
2
Moor Top
COPPY LA
LOW LA
Farnhill Wood
Kildwick Moor
Tow Top Slack
Street Head
Moor Top Farm
STOCKSHOTT LA
Springhead Farm
LC
SHADY LA
Cononley Prim Sch
Bradley Ings
Tow Top Moor
Hen Gill Bridge
Gill Head
Cononley
GORDON TERR 1
MEADOW CFT 2
SKIPTON RD 3
GARTH FOLD 4
MEADOW CFT 5
WEST LA
1 AIRESIDE TERR
2 MEADOW CL
MOORFOOT LA
Farnhill Moor
Monument
BD20
47
Tow Top Farm
MID LA
Works
AIREDALE INGS
Cononley Bsns Pk
Kildwick Moor
NEW LANE
Tow Top
Cononley Moor
NETHERGILL LA
Town Head
GIBSIDE LA
SUN ST
ST JOHN'S ST
PO
MAIN ST
BECK SIDE
TILLOTSON'S CT
LC
CONONLEY LANE
AIRESIDE AV
Crag Top House
Box Tree Farm
Crag Top
Tow Top Farm
TOW TOP LA
BABYHOUSE LANE
Aireview Farm
Cononley
Farnhill Bridge
Moor Side
Farnhill
Kildwick Hall (Hotel)
1
CONONLEY RD
CRAG VW
Weasel Green
WINDLE LA
GRANGE RD
HALL GD
SKIPTON RD
A629
MAIN ST
NEW LANE
Bunkhouse Barn
Great Gibb Farm
Gib Side
Gibside Farm
Farnhill Ings
46
96
97
98
99
00
01
For full street detail of the highlighted area see pages 216 and 217.
B4
1 WEST VW
2 CHAPEL ST
3 GEORGE ST
4 NEW ST
5 CHURCH ST
6 SWAN ST
7 CHURCH CL
8 WESTWOOD MEWS
9 CHAPEL HOUSE MEWS
10 GARDEN TERR
187
174
E1
1 BRIGHT ST
2 HANOVER ST
3 SOUTH VW
4 THE ARBOUR
5 HIGH CROFT WY
F1
1 THE CROFTS
2 LANG KIRK CL
3 BACK MARY ST
4 PRIEST BANK RD
5 STARKEY LA

Scale: 1¾ inches to 1 mile

0   ¼   ½ mile
0   250m   500m   750m   1 km

A   B   C   D   E   F

Map area including: Embsay & Bolton Abbey Steam Rly, Holywell Halt, Holywell Bridge, High Skibeden Farm, Ellenber Farm, Draughton, Wheelam Rock, The Spinney, West Vw, Draughton Heights Farm, Draughton Height, Berwick Intake Farm, Back Plantation, Nor Hill Well, Skipton Moor, Snow Hill Farm, Snow Hill Plantation, Haygill Farm, High Edge, Middlesbrough Farm, High Bradley Moor, High Edge Farm, Low Edge Farm, Moor Gate Farm, Moorgate Jenkin, High Bracken Hill Farm, Marlpit Plantation, Lane House Farm, Silsden Moor, Foster Cliffe Farm North, Foster Cliffe Farm South, Smoulden Farm, Heights Farm, Horne House, Stakehill Plantation, Lower Heights Farm, Hay Hills Farms, Bloomer Hill Farm, Bridge House, Hole Farm, Low Bracken Hill Farm, Raikes Head Farm, Tar Topping, High Cross Moor Farm, Kildwick Grange, Airedale House Farm.

Halton East, Chapel La, Fish Pond, Gaw La, Low Lane, Holme Lane, Hembrow La, Long Causeway, Prior's La, Hayneholme, Meadowcroft, Low La, The Croft, Spring Hl, Lane End Farm, Field House Farm, Ranke Wood, BD23, Berwick, Haw Pike, Banks Gill, Chelker Reservoir, Draughton Moor, The Bogs, Berwick Intake Farm, Bank End Farm, Addingham Low Moor, Counter Hill, Round Dikes, Earthwork, Tumulus, Carr Bog Farm, Cowburn Beck Farm, Woofa Bank Farm, Silsden Moor, Walton Hole, Far Cringles Farm, Old Tower, Cringles, BD20, Dales Bank Farm, Silsden Reservoir, Hay Hills Farms, Beck Wood, Well House Farm, Brown Bank, Horn Crag, Asker Hill, Crag House, Light Bank, North End Farm.

Hambleton, Halton Gill Wood, Waterfall, Hesketh House, Stank House, Bolton Abbey, Bolton Bridge, Huffa Bridge, Hotel, Boyle & Petyt Prim Sch, Bank Wood, Struff Wood, Beamsley, Home Farm, A59, Waywell Gill, River Wharfe, Hawpike Farm, Lob Wood, Eller Carr Wood, Wind Pumps, Hag Head Laithe, Farfield Hall, Syke House Farm, Highfield Farm, Chelker House Farm, Highfield House, Upper White Well, High Sanfitt Farm, Cross Bank, High Cross Bank Farm, CH, Riddings Farm, Springfield Mount, Harcourt Rd, Addingham Prim Sch, Back Beck, Main St, Addingham, Coppy Hill, Nudge Hill Farm, Little Round Wood, Gildersber, Street Farm, High Brockabank, School Wood, Small Banks, Cocking La, Brocka Bank Moor, Nudge Hill, Hodson's Farm, Lower Turner Lane Farm, Lower Marchup Farm, Marchup Plantation, Middle Marchup Farm, Marchup Height, Addingham Middle Moor, Deif Hill, Sea Moor Hill, Sea Moor Farm, Turner La, Straight La, Fishbeck La, Lippersley Lane, Brook's Hill, Brook's Crag, B6160, River Wharfe, SILSDEN RD, A6034, BOLTON RD, Bolton Road, LS29, Addingham Wharfedale Road, Addingham Moorside, Addingham High Moor, Windgate Nick, Nab End, White Crag, White Crag Plantation, Hang Goose Farm, Slade Farm, Brown Bank Lane, Light Bank Lane, SILSDEN, Town Head, Swartha, Brunthwaite, Brunthwaite Crag, White Crag Moor, Cup and Ring Marked Rocks, Jerry La, Brunthwaite Lane, Black Pots Farm, Kirkgate, Liby Theatre.

A6034 Keighley (A629)   **West Yorkshire STREET ATLAS**

173

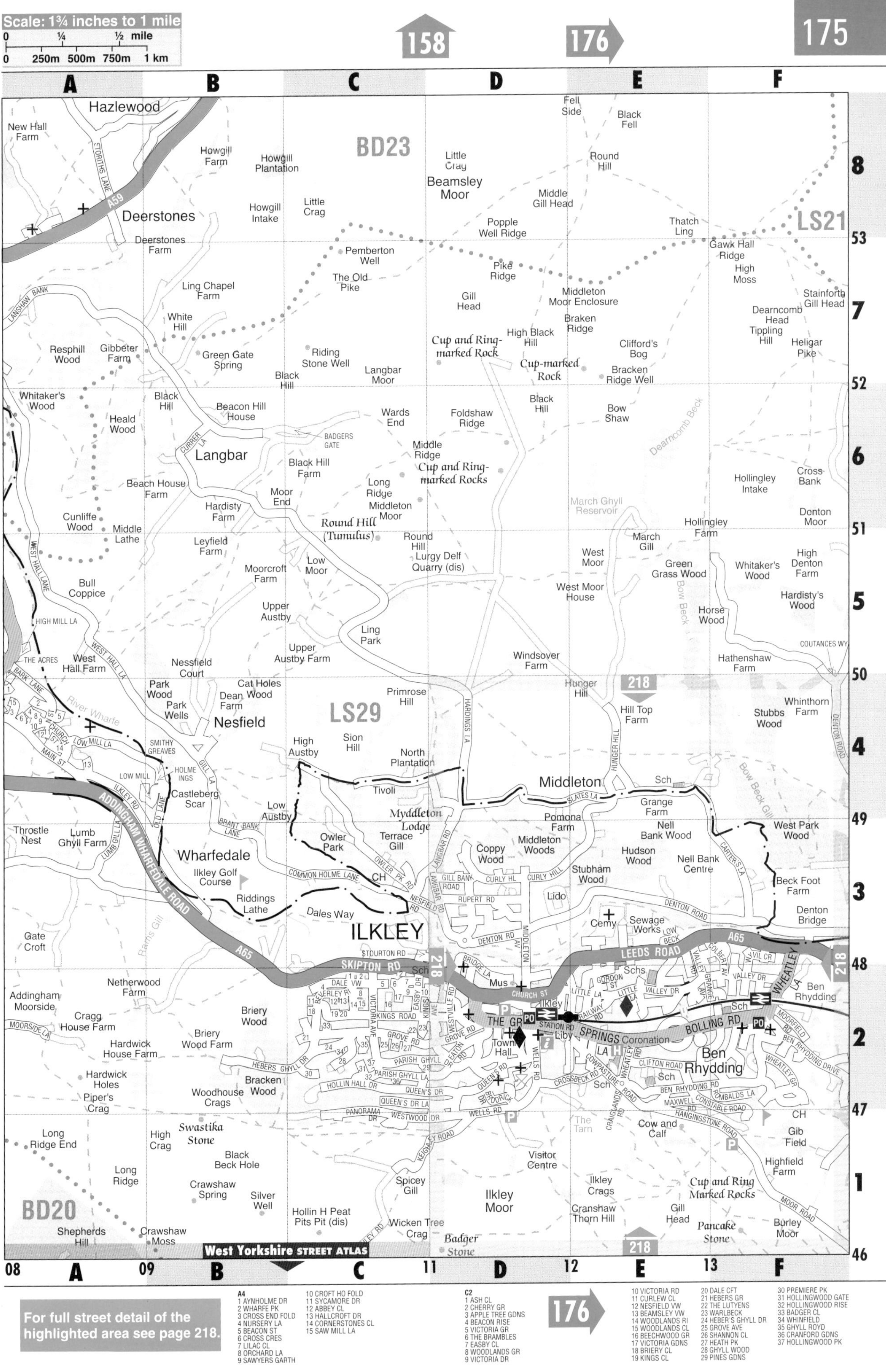

Scale: 1¾ inches to 1 mile
0 ¼ ½ mile
0 250m 500m 750m 1 km
158
176
175
A B C D E F
Hazlewood
New Hall Farm
Howgill Farm
Howgill Plantation
BD23
Little Crag
Beamsley Moor
Fell Side
Black Fell
Round Hill
Middle Gill Head
STORITHS LANE
A59
Deerstones
Howgill Intake
Little Crag
Popple Well Ridge
Thatch Ling
LS21
Deerstones Farm
Pemberton Well
The Old Pike
Pike Ridge
Gawk Hall Ridge
High Moss
Ling Chapel Farm
Gill Head
Middleton Moor Enclosure
Stainforth Gill Head
LANSHAW BANK
White Hill
Braken Ridge
Dearncomb Head
Tippling Hill
Resphill Wood
Gibbeter Farm
Green Gate Spring
Riding Stone Well
Cup and Ring-marked Rock
High Black Hill
Cup-marked Rock
Clifford's Bog
Heligar Pike
Black Hill
Langbar Moor
Bracken Ridge Well
Whitaker's Wood
Black Hill
Beacon Hill House
Wards End
Foldshaw Ridge
Black Hill
Bow Shaw
Heald Wood
BADGERS GATE
Dearncomb Beck
CURRER LA
Langbar
Black Hill Farm
Middle Ridge
Cup and Ring-marked Rocks
Beach House Farm
Moor End
Long Ridge
Middleton Moor
Hollingley Intake
Cross Bank
Hardisty Farm
March Ghyll Reservoir
Cunliffe Wood
Middle Lathe
Round Hill (Tumulus)
Round Hill
Lurgy Delf Quarry (dis)
Hollingley Farm
Denton Moor
Leyfield Farm
March Gill
West Moor
Green Grass Wood
Whitaker's Wood
High Denton Farm
WEST HALL LANE
Moorcroft Farm
Low Moor
Bull Coppice
West Moor House
Bow Beck
Hardisty's Wood
HIGH MILL LA
Upper Austby
Horse Wood
Ling Park
COUTANCES WY
THE ACRES
WEST HALL LA
West Hall Farm
Upper Austby Farm
Windsover Farm
Hathenshaw Farm
Nessfield Court
BARK LANE
Park Wood
Cat Holes Wood
Dean Farm
Primrose Hill
Hunger Hill
218
Hill Top Farm
Whinthorn Farm
River Wharfe
Park Wells
Nesfield
LS29
Stubbs Wood
DENTON ROAD
CHURCH ST
LOW MILL LA
High Austby
Sion Hill
HARDINGS LA
MAIN ST
SMITHY GREAVES
North Plantation
HUNGER HILL
Bow Beck Gill
HOLME INGS
LOW MILL
GILL LA
Middleton
Sch
ILKLEY RD
Castleberg Scar
Tivoli
SLATES LA
ADDINGHAM WHARFEDALE ROAD
Low Austby
Myddleton Lodge
Pomona Farm
Grange Farm
Throstle Nest
Lumb Ghyll Farm
BRANT BANK LANE
Terrace Gill
Middleton Woods
Nell Bank Wood
West Park Wood
OLD LANE
Owler Park
LANGBAR RD
Coppy Wood
Hudson Wood
LUMB GILL LA
Wharfedale
OWLER PK RD
Stubham Wood
Nell Bank Centre
Ilkley Golf Course
COMMON HOLME LANE
CH
GILL BANK ROAD
CURLY HL
CURLY HILL
CARTER'S LA
Beck Foot Farm
RUPERT RD
Lido
Riddings Lathe
NESFIELD RD
Dales Way
DENTON ROAD
Cemy
Sewage Works
Denton Bridge
Rams Gill
ILKLEY
DENTON RD
MIDDLETON AV
LOW BECK
Gate Croft
A65
STOURTON RD
LEEDS ROAD
A65
SKIPTON RD
BRIDGE LA
Sch
Schs
VALLEY RD
COLBERT AV
VIL CR
WHEATLEY LA
Netherwood Farm
DALE VW
GORDON ST
VALLEY DR
GRANGE AV
Ben Rhydding
Addingham Moorside
BEVERLEY RI
LITTLE LA
Mus
CHURCH ST
Ilkley
PO
Sch
Briery Wood
KINGS ROAD
VICTORIA AV
KINGS RD
WESTVILLE RD
RAILWAY RD
MOORFIELD RD
Cragg House Farm
THE GR
STATION RD
Liby
BOLLING RD
PO
MOORS/DE LA
Briery Wood Farm
GROVE RD
Town Hall
SPRINGS
Coronation
BEN RHYDDING DRIVE
Hardwick House Farm
PARISH GHYLL RD
WELLS RD
EATON RD
COWPASTURE ROAD
WHEATLEY RD
CLIFTON ROAD
Ben Rhydding
WHEATLEY GR
HEBERS GHYLL DR
PARISH GHYLL LA
LA
Sch
Hardwick Holes
Bracken Wood
HOLLIN HALL DR
QUEEN'S RD
CROSSBECK RD
Sch
BEN RHYDDING RD
Piper's Crag
Woodhouse Crags
QUEEN'S DR
BROOK GR
RUMBALDS LA
MAXWELL RD
CONSTABLE ROAD
QUEEN'S DR LA
PANORAMA DR
WESTWOOD DR
WELLS RD
CRAIGLANDS RD
HANGINGSTONE ROAD
CH
Long Ridge End
High Crag
Swastika Stone
KEIGHLEY ROAD
The Tarn
Cow and Calf
Gib Field
Black Beck Hole
Visitor Centre
Highfield Farm
Long Ridge
Crawshaw Spring
Spicey Gill
Ilkley Crags
Cup and Ring Marked Rocks
Silver Well
Ilkley Moor
MOOR ROAD
BD20
Hollin H Peat Pits Pit (dis)
Wicken Tree Crag
Cranshaw Thorn Hill
Gill Head
Pancake Stone
Burley Moor
Shepherds Hill
Crawshaw Moss
Badger Stone
218
West Yorkshire STREET ATLAS
8 7 6 5 4 3 2 1
53 52 51 50 49 48 47 46
08 09 11 12 13
For full street detail of the highlighted area see page 218.
A4
1 AYNHOLME DR
2 WHARFE PK
3 CROSS END FOLD
4 NURSERY LA
5 BEACON ST
6 CROSS CRES
7 LILAC CL
8 ORCHARD LA
9 SAWYERS GARTH
10 CROFT HO FOLD
11 SYCAMORE DR
12 ABBEY CL
13 HALLCROFT DR
14 CORNERSTONES CL
15 SAW MILL LA
C2
1 ASH CL
2 CHERRY GR
3 APPLE TREE GDNS
4 BEACON RISE
5 VICTORIA GR
6 THE BRAMBLES
7 EASBY CL
8 WOODLANDS GR
9 VICTORIA DR
176
10 VICTORIA RD
11 CURLEW CL
12 NESFIELD VW
13 BEAMSLEY VW
14 WOODLANDS RI
15 WOODLANDS CL
16 BEECHWOOD GR
17 VICTORIA GDNS
18 BRIERY CL
19 KINGS CL
20 DALE CFT
21 HEBERS GR
22 THE LUTYENS
23 WARLBECK
24 HEBER'S GHYLL DR
25 GROVE AVE
26 SHANNON CL
27 HEATH PK
28 GHYLL WOOD
29 PINES GDNS
30 PREMIERE PK
31 HOLLINGWOOD GATE
32 HOLLINGWOOD RISE
33 BADGER CL
34 WHINFIELD
35 GHYLL ROYD
36 CRANFORD GDNS
37 HOLLINGWOOD PK

176

◀ 175

159 ▲

Scale: 1¾ inches to 1 mile
0   ¼   ½ mile
0 250m 500m 750m 1 km

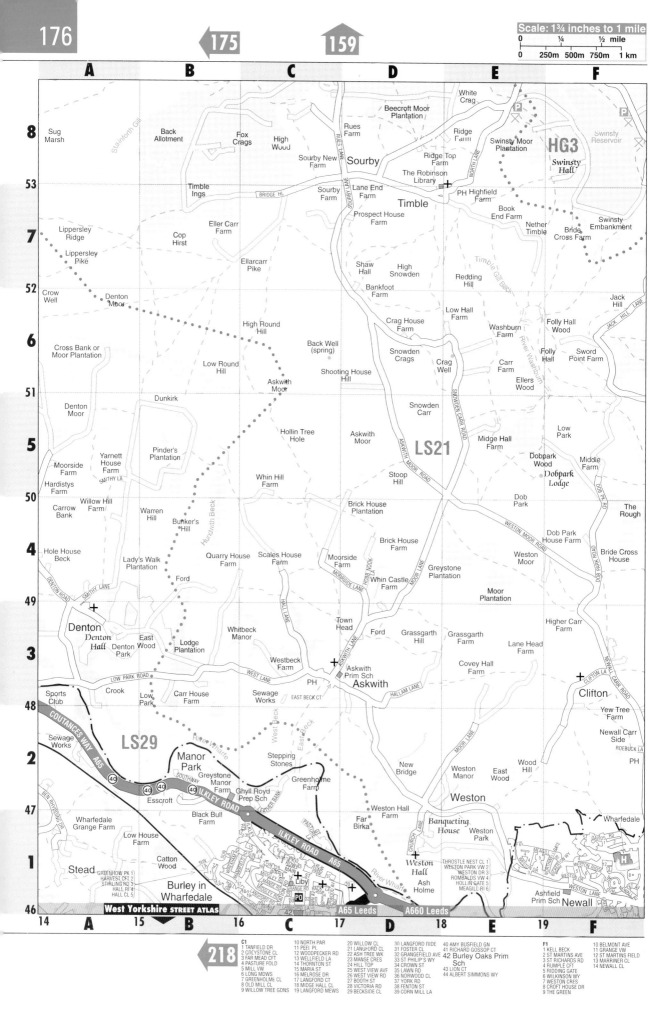

Sug Marsh
Stainforth Gill
Back Allotment
Fox Crags
High Wood
Beecroft Moor Plantation
White Crag
Ridge Farm
Swinsty Moor Plantation
Swinsty Reservoir

8

HG3
Swinsty Hall

Sourby New Farm
Sourby
Ridge Top Farm
The Robinson Library

53

Timble Ings
BRIDGE HILL
Sourby Farm
COLBY LANE
RUES LANE
Lane End Farm
Timble
PH Highfield Farm
NORTH LANE
Book End Farm
Nether Timble

Lippersley Ridge
Eller Carr Farm
Cop Hirst
Prospect House Farm
Swinsty Embankment
Bride Cross Farm

7

Lippersley Pike
Ellarcarr Pike
Shaw Hall
High Snowden
Redding Hill
Folly Hall Wood
Jack Hill

Crow Well
Bankfoot Farm
Low Hall Farm
Washburn Farm
Folly Hall
Sword Point Farm

52

Denton Moor
High Round Hill
Crag House Farm
River Washburn
Carr Farm
Ellers Wood
JACK HILL LANE

Cross Bank or Moor Plantation
Low Round Hill
Back Well (spring)
Snowden Crags
Crag Well
Timble Gill Beck

6

Shooting House Hill
Low Park
Middle Farm

Denton Moor
Askwith Moor
Dunkirk
Snowden Carr
SNOWDEN CARR ROAD
Midge Hall Farm
Dobpark Wood
Dobpark Lodge
DOB PK RD

51

Hollin Tree Hole
Askwith Moor
LS21
Low Park

Moorside Farm
Yarnett House Farm
Pinder's Plantation
Whin Hill Farm
Stoop Hill
ASKWITH MOOR ROAD
Dob Park
Dobpark Wood
The Rough

5

Hardistys Farm
SMITHY LA
Dob Park House Farm
Bride Cross House

Carrow Bank
Willow Hill Farm
Warren Hill
Bunker's Hill
Whin Hill Farm
Brick House Plantation
WESTON MOOR ROAD
Weston Moor
DOB PARK ROAD

50

Hole House Beck
Lady's Walk Plantation
Ford
Quarry House Farm
Scales House Farm
Moorside Farm
HOBB LA
Brick House Farm
MOOR LANE
Greystone Plantation

4

HALL LANE
MOORSIDE LANE
Whin Castle Farm
Moor Plantation
Higher Carr Farm

DENTON ROAD
SMITHY LANE
Whitbeck Manor
Town Head
Ford
Grassgarth Hill
Grassgarth Farm
Lane Head Farm

49

Denton
Denton Hall
East Wood
Lodge Plantation
Westbeck Farm
ASKWITH LANE
Askwith Prim Sch
Covey Hall Farm
Clifton
NEWALL CARR ROAD
CLIFTON LANE

3

Denton Park
WEST LANE
PH
Askwith
HALLAM LANE

LOW PARK ROAD
Crook
Carr House Farm
Sewage Works
EAST BECK CT

Sports Club
Low Park
Yew Tree Farm

48

COUTANCES WAY A65
River Wharfe
West Beck
East Beck
Newall Carr Side
ROEBUCK LA

Sewage Works
LS29
Manor Park
Stepping Stones
Greenholme Farm
New Bridge
Weston Manor
East Wood
Wood Hill
PH

2

SOUTHWAY
Greystone Manor Farm
Ghyll Royd Prep Sch
Weston
Weston Park
Wharfedale

Esscroft
ILKLEY ROAD
Black Bull Farm
LEATHER BANK
Weston Hall Farm
Far Birka
Banqueting House
CHURCH LANE
MOOR LANE

47

Wharfedale Grange Farm
Low House Farm
PASTURE RD
Weston Hall
Ash Holme
DAVIES RD
MEAGILL GATE

BEN RHYDDING RD
Catton Wood
ILKLEY ROAD A65
River Wharfe
WESTON LANE
WESTON RIDGE
Ashfield Prim Sch
Newall

1

Stead
GREENHOW PK 1
HARVEST CFT 2
STIRLING RD 3
HALL RI 4
HALL CL 5
Burley in Wharfedale
Liby
PO
A65 Leeds
A660 Leeds
THROSTLE NEST CL 1
WESTON PARK VW 2
WESTON DR 3
ROMBALDS VW 4
HOLLIN GATE 5
MEAGILL RI 6

46

West Yorkshire STREET ATLAS

C1
1 TANFIELD DR.
2 GRICYSTONE CL
3 FAR MEAD CFT
4 PASTURE FOLD
5 MILL VW
6 LONG MDWS
7 GREENHOLME CL
8 OLD MILL CL
9 WILLOW TREE GDNS
10 NORTH PAR
11 PEEL PL
12 WOODPECKER RD
13 WELLFIELD LA
14 THORNTON ST
15 MARIA ST
16 MELROSE DR
17 LANGFORD CT
18 MIDGE HALL CL
19 LANGFORD MEWS
20 WILLOW CL
21 LANGFORD CL
22 ASH TREE WK
23 MANSE CRES
24 HILL TOP
25 WEST VIEW AVE
26 WEST VIEW RD
27 BOOTH ST
28 VICTORIA RD
29 BECKSIDE CL
30 LANGFORD RIDE
31 FOSTER CL
32 GRANGEFIELD AVE
33 ST PHILIP'S WY
34 CROWN ST
35 LAWN RD
36 NORWOOD CL
37 YORK RD
38 FENTON ST
39 CORN MILL LA
40 AMY BUSFIELD GN
41 RICHARD GOSSOP CT
42 BURLEY OAKS PRIM Sch
43 LION CT
44 ALBERT SIMMONS WY
F1
1 KELL BECK
2 ST MARTINS AVE
3 ST RICHARDS RD
4 RUMPLE CFT
5 RIDDING GATE
6 WILKINSON WY
7 WESTON CRES
8 CROFT HOUSE DR
9 THE GREEN
10 BELMONT AVE
11 GRANGE VW
12 ST MARTINS FIELD
13 MARRINER CL
14 NEWALL CL

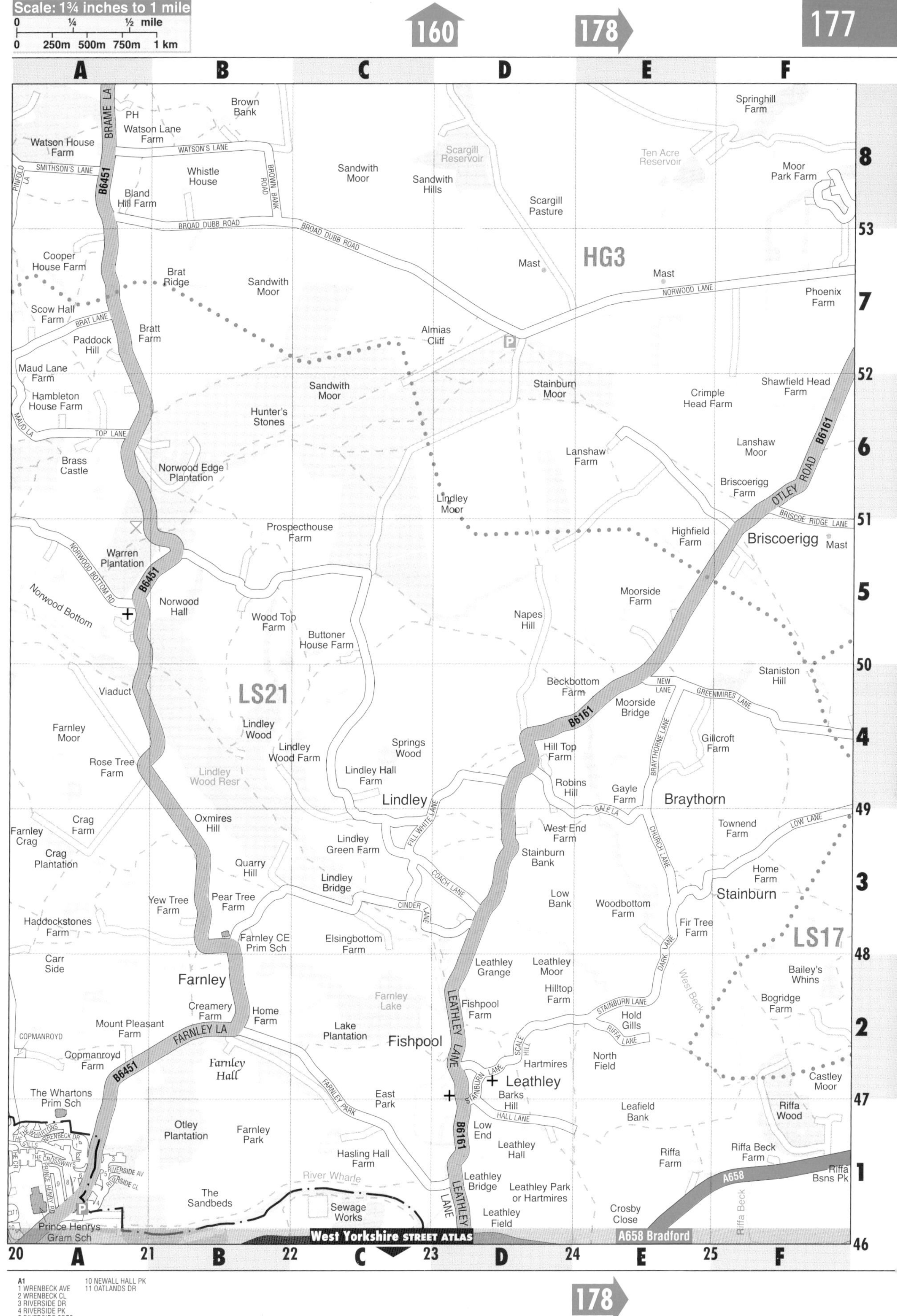

Scale: 1¾ inches to 1 mile

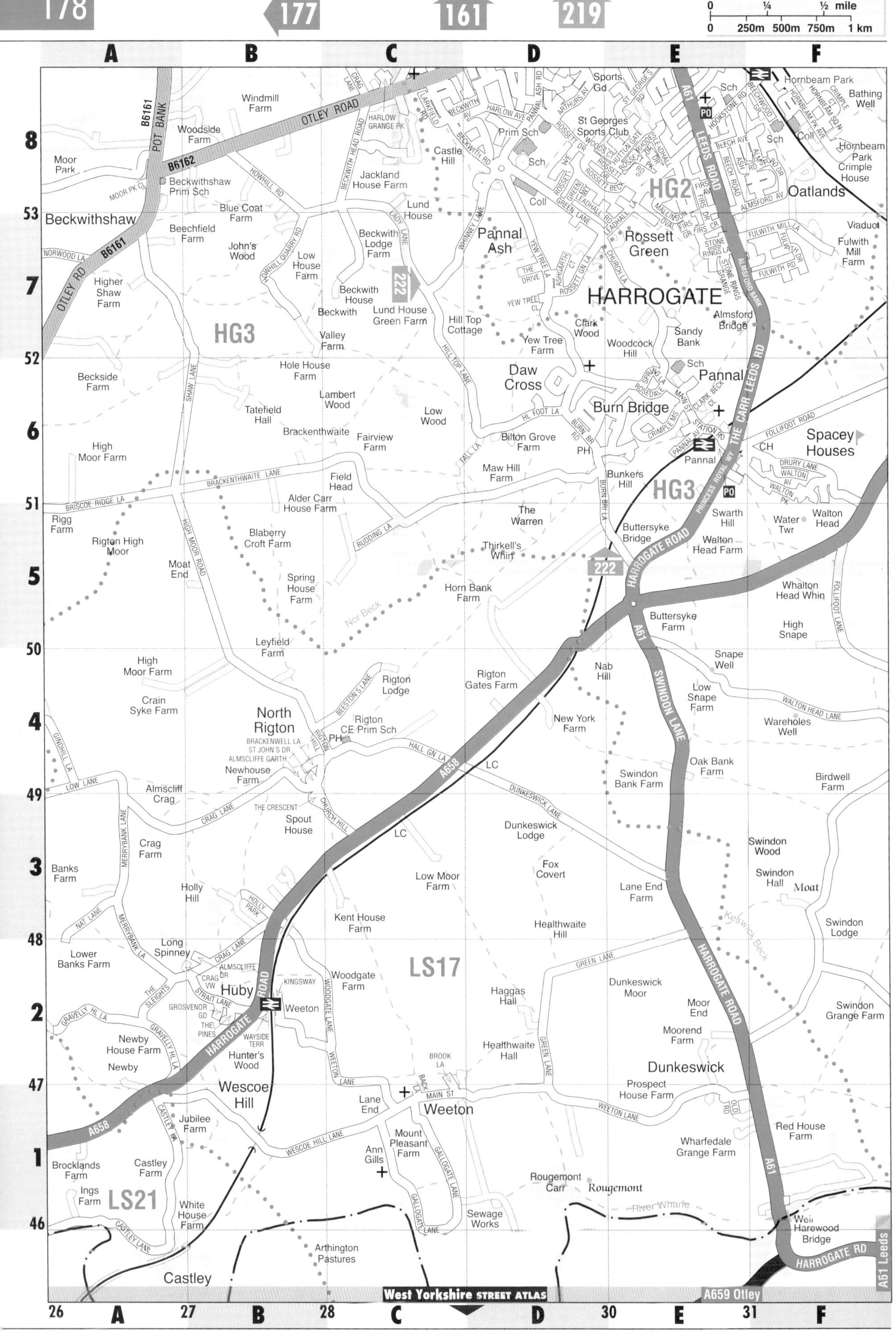
HARROGATE
Beckwithshaw
Pannal Ash
Rossett Green
Oatlands
Pannal
Burn Bridge
Daw Cross
Spacey Houses
North Rigton
Huby
Weeton
Wescoe Hill
Dunkeswick
Castley
Beckwith
Rougemont
Hornbeam Park
Bathing Well
Windmill Farm
Woodside Farm
Moor Park
Beckwithshaw Prim Sch
Blue Coat Farm
Beechfield Farm
John's Wood
Low House Farm
Jackland House Farm
Lund House
Castle Hill
Beckwith Lodge Farm
Beckwith House
Lund House Green Farm
Hill Top Cottage
Valley Farm
Higher Shaw Farm
Beckside Farm
Hole House Farm
Lambert Wood
Tatefield Hall
Brackenthwaite
Fairview Farm
Low Wood
High Moor Farm
Field Head
Alder Carr House Farm
Bilton Grove Farm
Maw Hill Farm
Bunkers Hill
The Warren
Thirkell's Whin
Buttersyke Bridge
Swarth Hill
Walton Head Farm
Water Twr
Walton Head
Rigg Farm
Rigton High Moor
Moat End
Blaberry Croft Farm
Spring House Farm
Horn Bank Farm
Whalton Head Whin
Buttersyke Farm
High Snape
Snape Well
Leyfield Farm
Rigton Lodge
Rigton Gates Farm
Nab Hill
Low Snape Farm
Crain Syke Farm
Rigton CE Prim Sch
New York Farm
Wareholes Well
Newhouse Farm
Almscliff Crag
Swindon Bank Farm
Oak Bank Farm
Birdwell Farm
Spout House
Dunkeswick Lodge
Crag Farm
Banks Farm
Fox Covert
Low Moor Farm
Lane End Farm
Swindon Wood
Swindon Hall
Moat
Holly Hill
Kent House Farm
Healthwaite Hill
Swindon Lodge
Lower Banks Farm
Long Spinney
Woodgate Farm
Haggas Hall
Dunkeswick Moor
Moor End
Moorend Farm
Swindon Grange Farm
Newby House Farm
Newby
Hunter's Wood
Healthwaite Hall
Prospect House Farm
Jubilee Farm
Lane End
Mount Pleasant Farm
Ann Gills
Red House Farm
Wharfedale Grange Farm
Brocklands Farm
Castley Farm
Ings Farm
White House Farm
Rougemont Carr
Sewage Works
Arthington Pastures
River Wharfe
Harewood Bridge
Crimple House
Hornbeam Park
Fulwith Mill Farm
Viaduct
Clark Wood
Woodcock Hill
Sandy Bank
Almsford Bridge
Yew Tree Farm
Sports Gd
St Georges Sports Club
Prim Sch
Sch
Coll
PH
PO
CH
LC
Nor Beck
Keswick Beck
HG2
HG3
LS17
LS21
OTLEY ROAD
POT BANK
B6161
B6162
A61
A658
LEEDS ROAD
THE CARR LEEDS RD
PRINCESS ROYAL WY
HARROGATE ROAD
SWINDON LANE
HIGH MOOR ROAD
SHAW LANE
BRACKENTHWAITE LANE
BRISCOE RIDGE LA
HALL GN LA
DUNKESWICK LANE
WALTON HEAD LANE
FOLLIFOOT LANE
GREEN LANE
WEETON LANE
WESCOE HILL LANE
GALLOGATE LANE
MAIN ST
CRAG LANE
MERRYBANK LANE
LOW LANE
GRAVELLY HL LA
CASTLEY LA
HL FOOT LA
RUDDING LA
HILL TOP LANE
WHINNEY LANE
LADY LANE
222
A659 Otley
A61 Leeds
HARROGATE RD

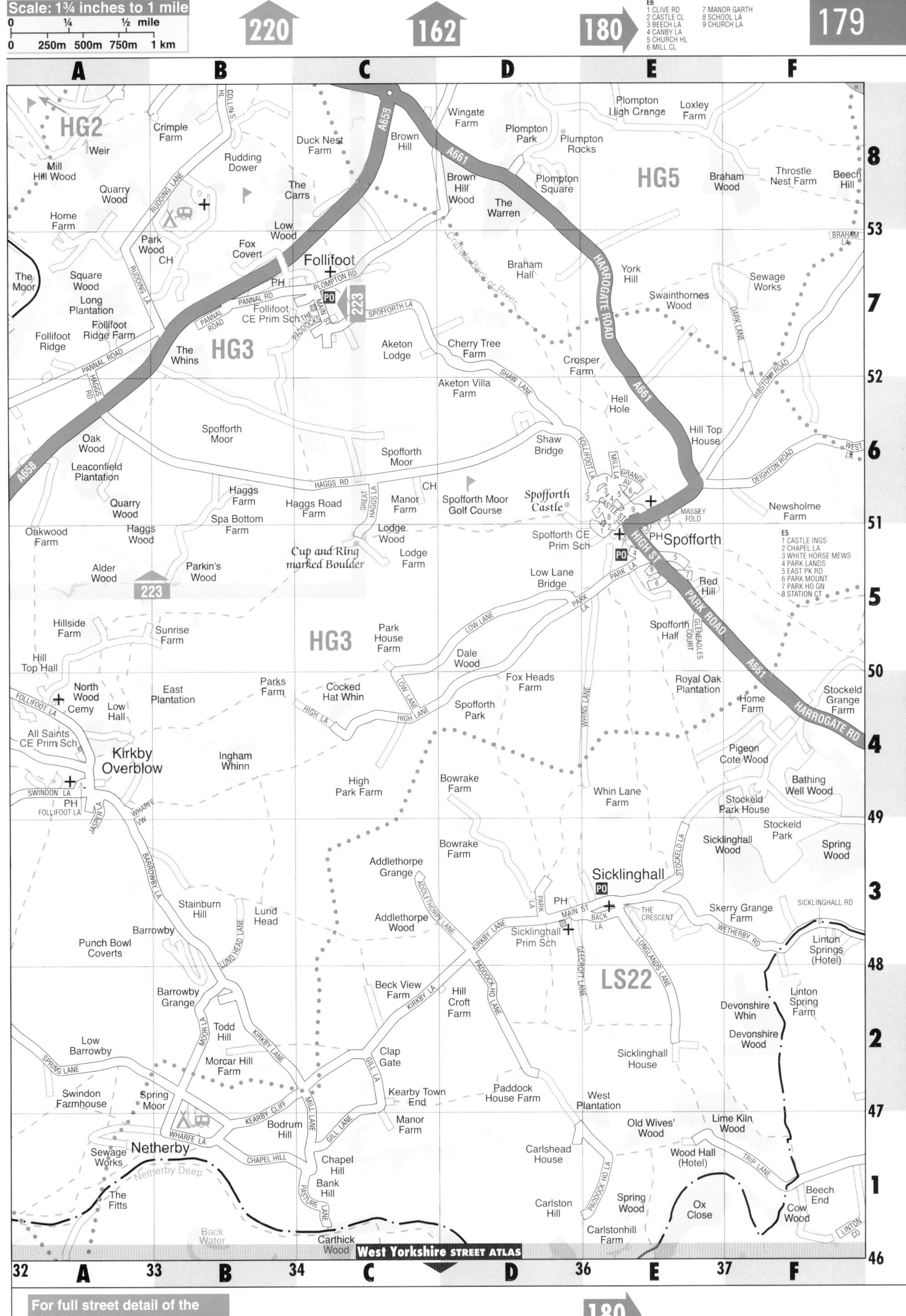
HG2
Crimple Farm
Weir
Mill Hill Wood
Quarry Wood
Home Farm
The Moor
Square Wood
Long Plantation
Follifoot Ridge
Follifoot Ridge Farm
Rudding Dower
Park Wood
CH
Fox Covert
Low Wood
The Carrs
Duck Nest Farm
Brown Hill
Follifoot
PH
Follifoot CE Prim Sch
HG3
The Whins
Wingate Farm
Plompton Park
Plompton Rocks
Plompton High Grange
Loxley Farm
HG5
Braham Wood
Throstle Nest Farm
Beech Hill
Brown Hill Wood
The Warren
Plompton Square
Braham Hall
York Hill
Swainthornes Wood
Sewage Works
Aketon Lodge
Cherry Tree Farm
Crosper Farm
Aketon Villa Farm
Hell Hole
Hill Top House
Oak Wood
Leaconfield Plantation
Spofforth Moor
Spofforth Moor
Shaw Bridge
Quarry Wood
Haggs Farm
Haggs Road Farm
Manor Farm
CH
Spofforth Moor Golf Course
Spofforth Castle
Newsholme Farm
Oakwood Farm
Haggs Wood
Spa Bottom Farm
Lodge Wood
Lodge Farm
Spofforth CE Prim Sch
PH
Spofforth
Cup and Ring marked Boulder
Alder Wood
Parkin's Wood
223
Low Lane Bridge
Red Hill
E5
1 CASTLE INGS
2 CHAPEL LA
3 WHITE HORSE MEWS
4 PARK LANDS
5 EAST PK RD
6 PARK MOUNT
7 PARK HO GN
8 STATION CT
Hillside Farm
Sunrise Farm
HG3
Park House Farm
Spofforth Hall
Hill Top Hall
Dale Wood
North Wood
Cemy
East Plantation
Parks Farm
Cocked Hat Whin
Fox Heads Farm
Royal Oak Plantation
Stockeld Grange Farm
Home Farm
Low Hall
Spofforth Park
All Saints CE Prim Sch
Kirkby Overblow
Ingham Whinn
Pigeon Cote Wood
High Park Farm
Bowrake Farm
Whin Lane Farm
Bathing Well Wood
PH
Stockeld Park House
Stockeld Park
Sicklinghall Wood
Spring Wood
Bowrake Farm
Addlethorpe Grange
Sicklinghall
PH
Stainburn Hill
Lund Head
Addlethorpe Wood
Sicklinghall Prim Sch
Skerry Grange Farm
Barrowby
Punch Bowl Coverts
Linton Springs (Hotel)
Barrowby Grange
Beck View Farm
Hill Croft Farm
LS22
Linton Spring Farm
Devonshire Whin
Devonshire Wood
Todd Hill
Low Barrowby
Morcar Hill Farm
Clap Gate
Sicklinghall House
Swindon Farmhouse
Spring Moor
Kearby Town End
Paddock House Farm
West Plantation
Bodrum Hill
Manor Farm
Old Wives' Wood
Lime Kiln Wood
Sewage Works
Netherby
Netherby Deep
Chapel Hill
Carlshead House
Wood Hall (Hotel)
The Fitts
Bank Hill
Carlston Hill
Spring Wood
Ox Close
Beech End
Cow Wood
Back Water
Carthick Wood
Carlstonhill Farm
A658
A661
A661
A661
HARROGATE ROAD
PARK ROAD
HARROGATE RD
HIGH ST
8
53
7
52
6
51
5
50
4
49
3
48
2
47
1
46
32
33
34
36
37
A
B
C
D
E
F
West Yorkshire STREET ATLAS

179 163

Scale: 1¾ inches to 1 mile

0 ¼ ½ mile

0 250m 500m 750m 1 km

A B C D E F

8 53 7 52 6 51 5 50 4 49 3 48 2 47 1 46

Ribston Hall
Rookery
Coney Garth Hill
Pessac Plantation
KNARESBOROUGH ROAD
B6164
Bank Side
Pear Tree Farm
Garth Farm
Little Ribston
Grange Farm
Weir
Ribston Park
Walshford
A1(M)
A168
MOOR LA
BROAD GATE
OX MOOR LANE
CHURCH HILL
BACK LA
Hunsingore
The Moorings
THE AVENUE
SOUTH PK LA
NORTH VW
South Park
River Nidd
Black Stones
Walshford Bridge
Lund House Farm
Manor Farm
Mill Farm
CRIMPLE AV
SPOFFORTH LANE
BRAHAM LA
RIBSTON RD
Ribston Moor
WETHERBY RD
KNARESBOROUGH ROAD
Lund Wood Hill
Weir
Hollin Close Corner
The Warrens
Crook Farm
Ruddings Farm
Cowthorpe Hall Farm
OAK RD
YO26
TOCKWITH ROAD
Cowthorpe
Long Ox Close
Smiler's Gorse
Ox Close House
OX CLOSE LANE
WETHERBY LANE
St Helen's Farm
Chapel Fields
Deighton Spring
Rash Wood
Old Hall Farm
Howe Hill (Motte)
Wind Farm
Hall Garth
Deighton Grange
Goosemoor Farm
Oates Wood
Goosemoor Plantation
WAR FIELD LANE
Green Howe
North Deighton
WEST VW
THE GN
SPOFFORTH LANE
Westgate Farm
LS22
Green Howe
Doctor's Wood
Geldart Woods
Ingmanthorpe House Farm
Lingcroft Plantation
Deighton Banks Farm
Woodlands Farm
SCHOOLHOUSE TR
Rockgarth Hill
LOSHPOT LANE
Ingmanthorpe
New Plantation
Willowgarth Plantation
Gospel Hill
LIME KILN LA
MAIN ST
MARK LANE
Sugden Wood
Quarry Farm
Kirk Deighton
SCRIFTAIN LA
B1224
MONTAGU WY
MONTAGU LA
MONTAGU MS
Ingmanthorpe Hall Farm
C4
1 BEECHWOOD RI
2 AINSTY DR
3 POPLAR AVE
4 BARLEYFIELDS RD
5 COXWOLD HL
6 NORTH GR AVE
7 Deighton Gates Prim Sch
8 AUTUMN AVE
B3
1 CARLTON APP
2 CHATSWORTH DR
3 MARSTON WY
4 BUTTERMERE AVE
5 ULLSWATER RISE
6 OAK RIDGE
7 LINTON MDWS
8 WHARFE GR
9 LINTON AVE
10 LAZENBY DR
11 GLEBE FIELD DR
12 CHESTNUT AVE
ASHDALE LA
GARTH END
WETHERBY RD
BADGER WOOD GLADE
Sandbeck House
PALMERS LA
SANDBECK LA
Ingmanthorpe Park
Swinnow Hill
Kingbarrow Farm
DOVE CL
PO
HUNTERS WK
A661
LINTON LA
Ingbarrow Farm
AIRE RD
FOSS AV
LINDEN WY
DEIGHTON RD
SANDBECK LANE
Sandbeck Wood
Swinnow Park
B1224
Moss Carrs Farmhouse
Noble Wood
Champagne Whin
Harland Way
AINSTY RD
AINSTY CR
OAKWOOD RD
SANDBECK LA
TEMPLAR GDNS
AUDBY LA
Sandbeck Ind Est
WETHERBY
CARR LA
Turners Wood
Moor Plantation
Lodge Bank Wood
HARROGATE RD
ASHBURN WAY
WENTWORTH GATE
A661 SPOFFORTH HILL
St Josephs RC Prim Sch
NORTHFIELD PL
B6164
ASHFIELD 21 22
YORK ROAD
1 FREEMANS WY
2 THE BEECHES
3 MEYRICK AVE
4 NETHERDALE CT
5 HALL ORCHARDS AVE
Wetherby Racecourse
SPRINGS LANE
Stockeld Lodge Farm
MANLEY DR
ULLSWATER DR
GRASMERE AV
NICHOLS WY
QUARRY HILL LANE
Crossley St Prim Sch
RABY PK
NORTH ST
YORK RD
St James CE Prim Sch
SCHOOL LA
HALLFIELD LA
CERES RD
Wetherby High School, Selby Coll
Sykes House Farm
LINTON RD
WEST GATE
Wetherby Business Ctr
Liby
Cemy
Recn Gd
Spring Woods
BARN LA
SHAW LA
SICKLINGHALL RD
AVON GARTH
Linton Ings
HALLFIELD LA
SECOND AV
WALTON RD
Rosedene Farm
Spring Wood
SPRING LANE
Jackson Wood
Spring Wood
Linton Hills
CH
PO
LODGE LA
A661
BOSTON RD
Weir
LACY GR
WALTON 60 ROAD
FLINTMILL LANE
MOOR LANE
Leisure Centre
Sports Field
MICKLEWAITE GR
Superstore & The Horsefair Centre
Park Hill Farm
60
WETHERBY ROAD
SCHOOL LA
30
NORTHGATE LA
Westwood
LINTON LA
Linton Ings
WETHERBY ROAD
River Wharfe
GLENFIELD AV
1 THE STEPS
2 MICKLEWAITE VW
BOSTON RD
WATERSOLE LA
West Field
Flint Mill Grange
WOODLAND CT
WESTGARTH
TIBGARTH
ORCHARD DR
THE RIDGE
Crowcroft Bank
Sewage Works
Weir
WOODLAND DR
WALTON CH
COLLEGE FARM LA
MUDDY LA
Collingham Wood
Wraywoods Farm
Hall Wood
FLINTMILL LA
MAIN ST
Garth End
Sweep Farm
Wetherby Grange
LS23
WOOD LANE
TRIP LANE
TRIP GARTH
MAIN ST
STAMMERGATE
Linton
PH
MIDDLE LA
BOSTON ROAD
LEYS LANE
Whin Covert
Hall Wood
Middle Field
Spoilbank Plantation
Collingham Lady Elizabeth Hastings CE Prim Sch
Gate Plantation
Lady Elizabeth Hastings CE Prim Sch
LINTON COMMON
Linton Bridge
Cave
THE COPSE
DEEP DALE
WEST END
LINTON RD
BECK LA
P
A58
Wattle Syke
Beilby Wood
Gunter Wood
DEEPDALE LANE
WEST AV
WESTE LA
W END
WEST DALE
DOWKELL LANE
THORP ARCH PK
THE VILLAGE
CHURCH CW
WHINS LA
PEAR TREE ACRE
MULBERRY GARTH
PH
THE AV
DEWAR CL
CHURCH LA
MAIN ST
WATTLE SYKE
A1(M)
Grange Moor

38 A 39 B 40 C 41 D 42 E 43 F

A1
1 NORTHGATE LA
2 NORTHGATE RISE
3 NORTHCOTE FOLD
4 OSPREY CL
5 KINGFISHER REACH
6 TERN PK
7 BISHOPDALE DR
8 GARSDALE FOLD
9 COTTERDALE HOLT

179

C3
1 COXWOLD VW
2 NORTH GR
3 WOODHILL VW
4 BARLEYFIELDS RD
5 BARLEYFIELDS LA
6 SANDRINGHAM RD
7 ST JAMES'S ST
8 CROSSLEY ST
9 FIRST AVE
10 THIRD AVE
11 BANK ST
12 MARKET PL
13 HUDSON CL
14 CHURCH ST
15 NORTHFIELD MS
16 FARRIERS CT
17 THE CHASE
18 COOPER RD
19 THE SHAMBLES

188

20 DEIGHTON CL
21 York Road Est
22 Cromwell Office Park

For full street detail of Wetherby see Philip's STREET ATLAS of West Yorkshire

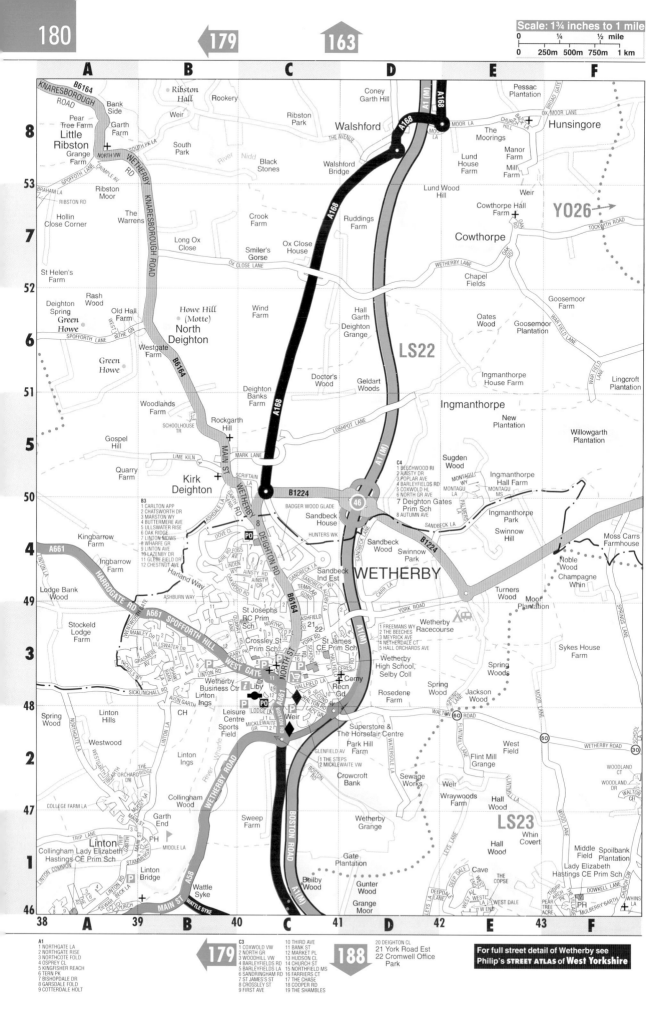

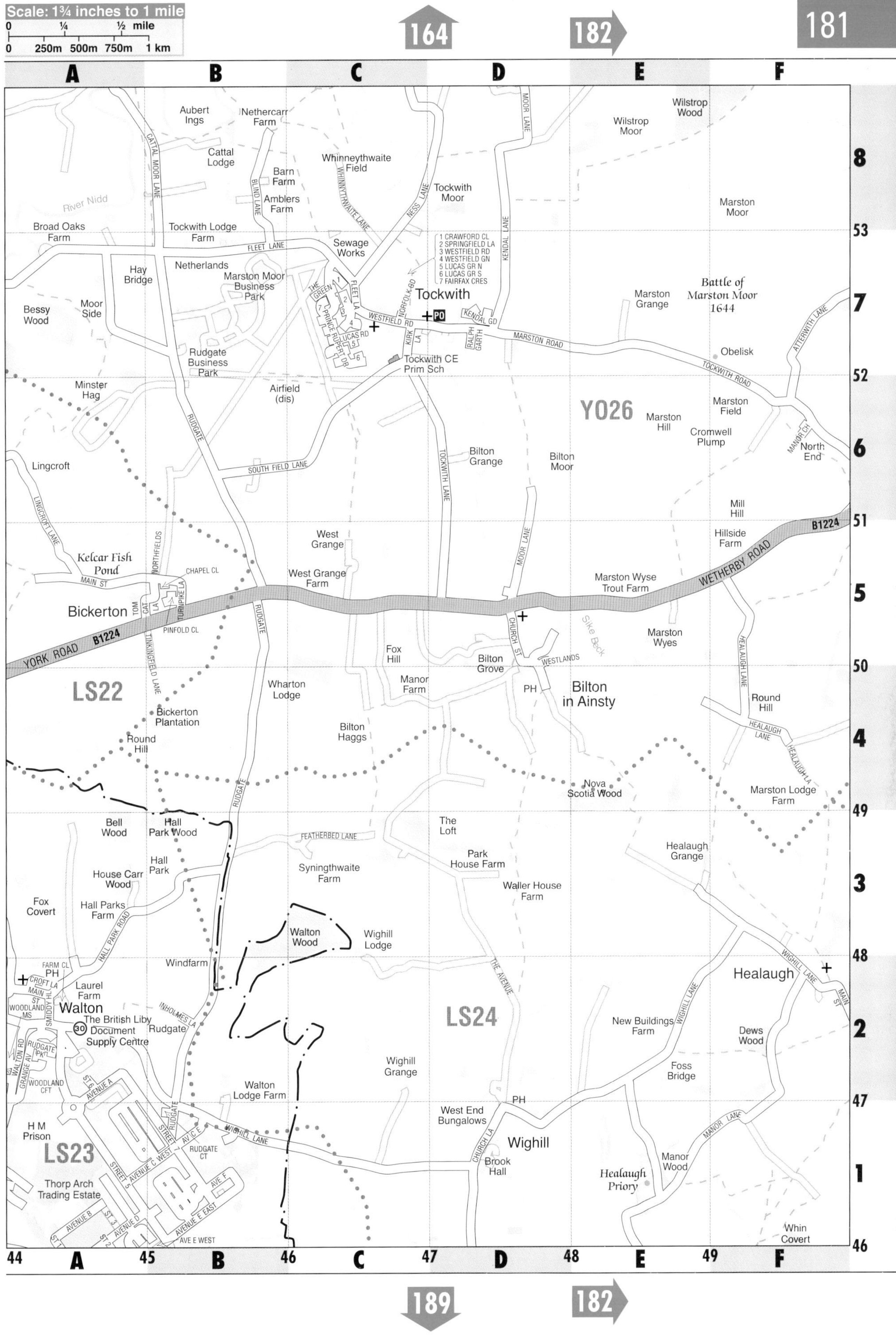
Scale: 1¾ inches to 1 mile
0 ¼ ½ mile
0 250m 500m 750m 1 km
164
182
A B C D E F
Aubert Ings
Nethercarr Farm
Cattal Lodge
CATTAL MOOR LANE
Whinneythwaite Field
Wilstrop Wood
Wilstrop Moor
MOOR LANE
Barn Farm
Amblers Farm
BLIND LANE
WHINNYTHWAITE LANE
NESS LANE
Tockwith Moor
Marston Moor
River Nidd
Broad Oaks Farm
Tockwith Lodge Farm
FLEET LANE
Sewage Works
KENDAL LANE
1 CRAWFORD CL
2 SPRINGFIELD LA
3 WESTFIELD RD
4 WESTFIELD GN
5 LUCAS GR N
6 LUCAS GR S
7 FAIRFAX CRES
Hay Bridge
Netherlands
Marston Moor Business Park
THE GREEN
FLEET LA
NORFOLK RD
Tockwith
PO
Marston Grange
Battle of Marston Moor 1644
Bessy Wood
Moor Side
PRINCE RUPERT DR
WESTFIELD RD
KENDAL GD
LUCAS RD
KIRK LA
RALPH GARTH
MARSTON ROAD
ATTERWITH LANE
Obelisk
Rudgate Business Park
Tockwith CE Prim Sch
TOCKWITH ROAD
Minster Hag
Airfield (dis)
YO26
Marston Hill
Marston Field
Cromwell Plump
MANOR CH
North End
RUDGATE
Bilton Grange
Bilton Moor
Lingcroft
SOUTH FIELD LANE
TOCKWITH LANE
Mill Hill
LINGCROFT LANE
West Grange
Hillside Farm
B1224
MOOR LANE
WETHERBY ROAD
Kelcar Fish Pond
NORTHFIELDS
CHAPEL CL
West Grange Farm
Marston Wyse Trout Farm
MAIN ST
TURNPIKE LA
Bickerton
TOM
GAT LA
YORK ROAD
B1224
PINFOLD CL
RUDGATE
CHURCH ST
Sike Beck
Marston Wyes
Fox Hill
Bilton Grove
WESTLANDS
HEALAUGH LANE
TINKINGFIELD LANE
LS22
Wharton Lodge
Manor Farm
PH
Bilton in Ainsty
Round Hill
Bickerton Plantation
Bilton Haggs
HEALAUGH LANE
Round Hill
HEALAUGH LA
RUDGATE
Nova Scotia Wood
Marston Lodge Farm
Bell Wood
Hall Park Wood
The Loft
FEATHERBED LANE
Healaugh Grange
Hall Park
Park House Farm
House Carr Wood
Synyngthwaite Farm
Waller House Farm
Fox Covert
Hall Parks Farm
HALL PARK ROAD
Walton Wood
Wighill Lodge
FARM CL
PH
CROFT LA
Windfarm
THE AVENUE
WIGHILL LANE
Healaugh
MAIN ST
Laurel Farm
MAIN ST
WOODLAND MS
Walton
SMIDDY HL
INHOLMES LA
LS24
New Buildings Farm
WIGHILL LANE
The British Liby Document Supply Centre
30
Rudgate
Dews Wood
WALTON RD
RUDGATE PK
GRANGE AV
Wighill Grange
Foss Bridge
WOODLAND CFT
AVENUE A
ST 6
Walton Lodge Farm
PH
H M Prison
RUDGATE
STREET
AV C E
WIGHILL LANE
West End Bungalows
CHURCH LA
Wighill
MANOR LANE
LS23
STREET 5
AVENUE C WEST
RUDGATE CT
Brook Hall
Manor Wood
Healaugh Priory
AVE F
Thorp Arch Trading Estate
AVENUE B
ST 3
AVENUE D
AVENUE E EAST
ST 2
ST 1
AVE E WEST
Whin Covert
8 53 7 52 6 51 5 50 4 49 3 48 2 47 1 46
44 45 46 47 48 49
189
182

181
165

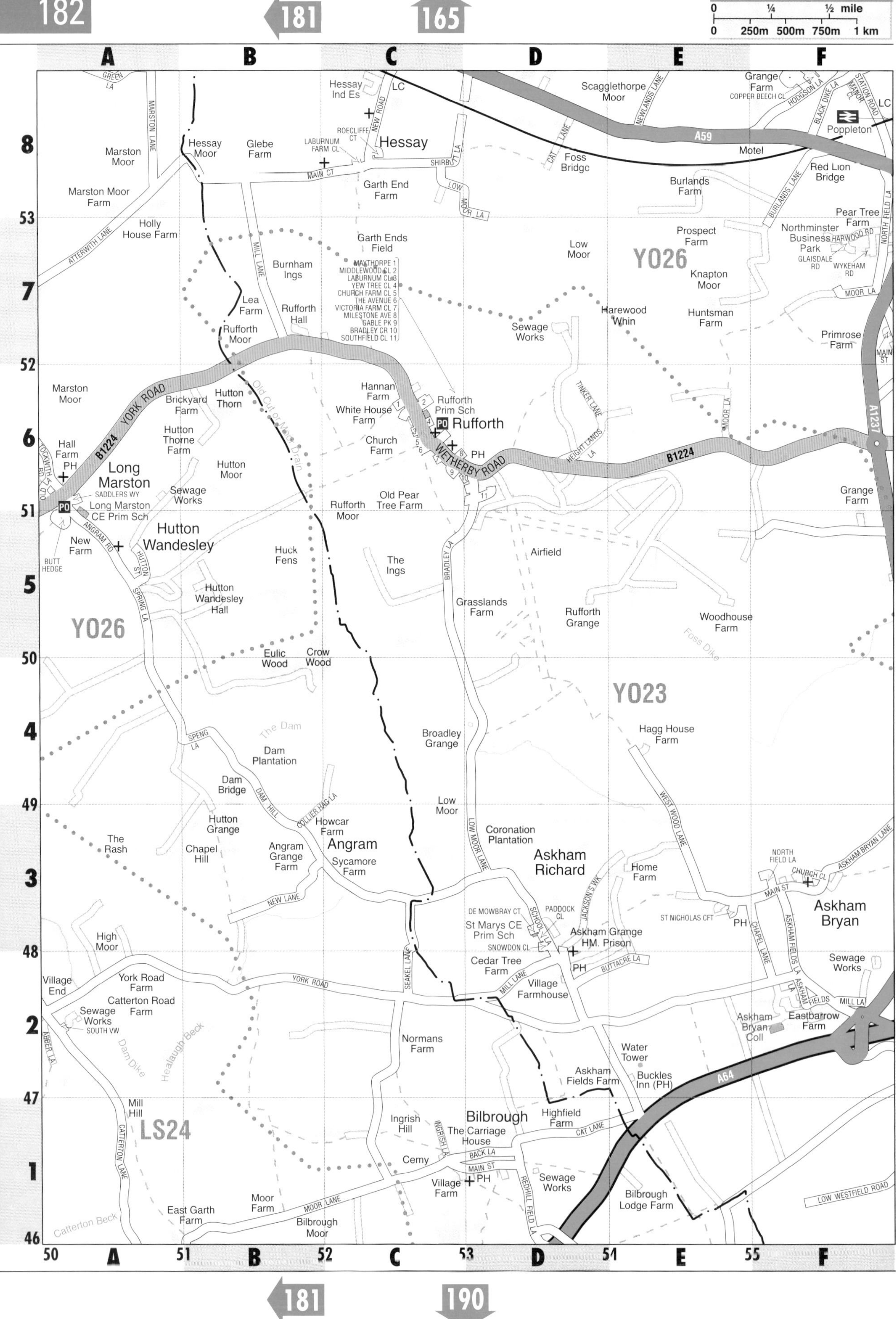
Scale: 1¾ inches to 1 mile
Hessay
Rufforth
Long Marston
Hutton Wandesley
Angram
Askham Richard
Askham Bryan
Bilbrough
Poppleton
YO26
YO23
LS24
A59
B1224
A1237
A64
YORK ROAD
WETHERBY ROAD
Marston Moor
Hessay Moor
Glebe Farm
Garth End Farm
Burnham Ings
Rufforth Hall
Lea Farm
Rufforth Moor
Hutton Thorn
Brickyard Farm
Hutton Thorne Farm
Hutton Moor
Sewage Works
Airfield
Grasslands Farm
Rufforth Grange
Woodhouse Farm
Broadley Grange
Hagg House Farm
Dam Plantation
Dam Bridge
Hutton Grange
Chapel Hill
The Rash
Howcar Farm
Sycamore Farm
Low Moor
Coronation Plantation
Home Farm
Cedar Tree Farm
Village Farmhouse
Normans Farm
Askham Fields Farm
Water Tower
Buckles Inn (PH)
Highfield Farm
The Carriage House
Bilbrough Lodge Farm
Bilbrough Moor
Moor Farm
East Garth Farm
Mill Hill
High Moor
Village End
York Road Farm
Catterton Road Farm
Eastbarrow Farm
Askham Bryan Coll
Scagglethorpe Moor
Foss Bridge
Burlands Farm
Prospect Farm
Knapton Moor
Huntsman Farm
Harewood Whin
Primrose Farm
Grange Farm
Red Lion Bridge
Pear Tree Farm
Northminster Business Park
Motel

181
190

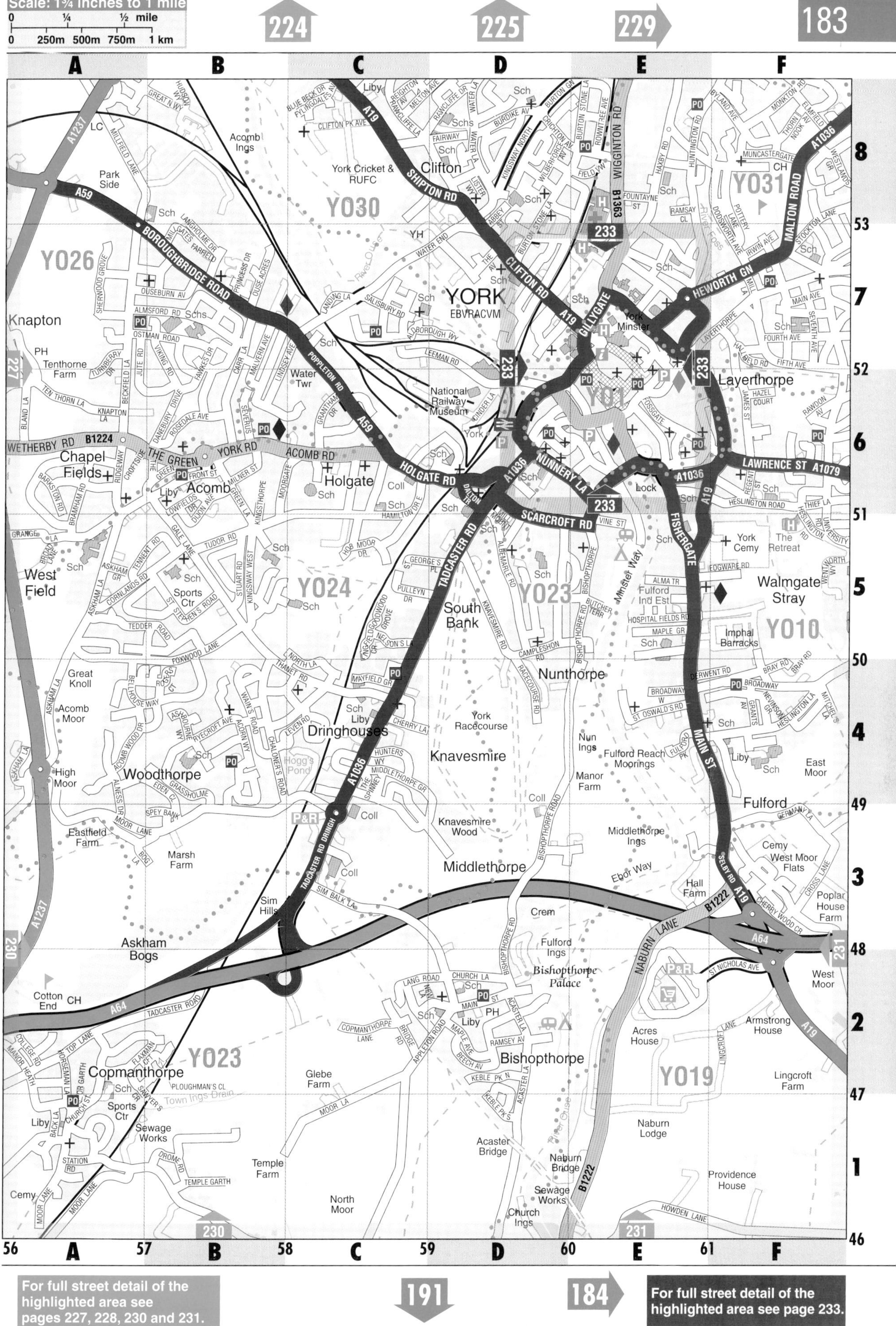

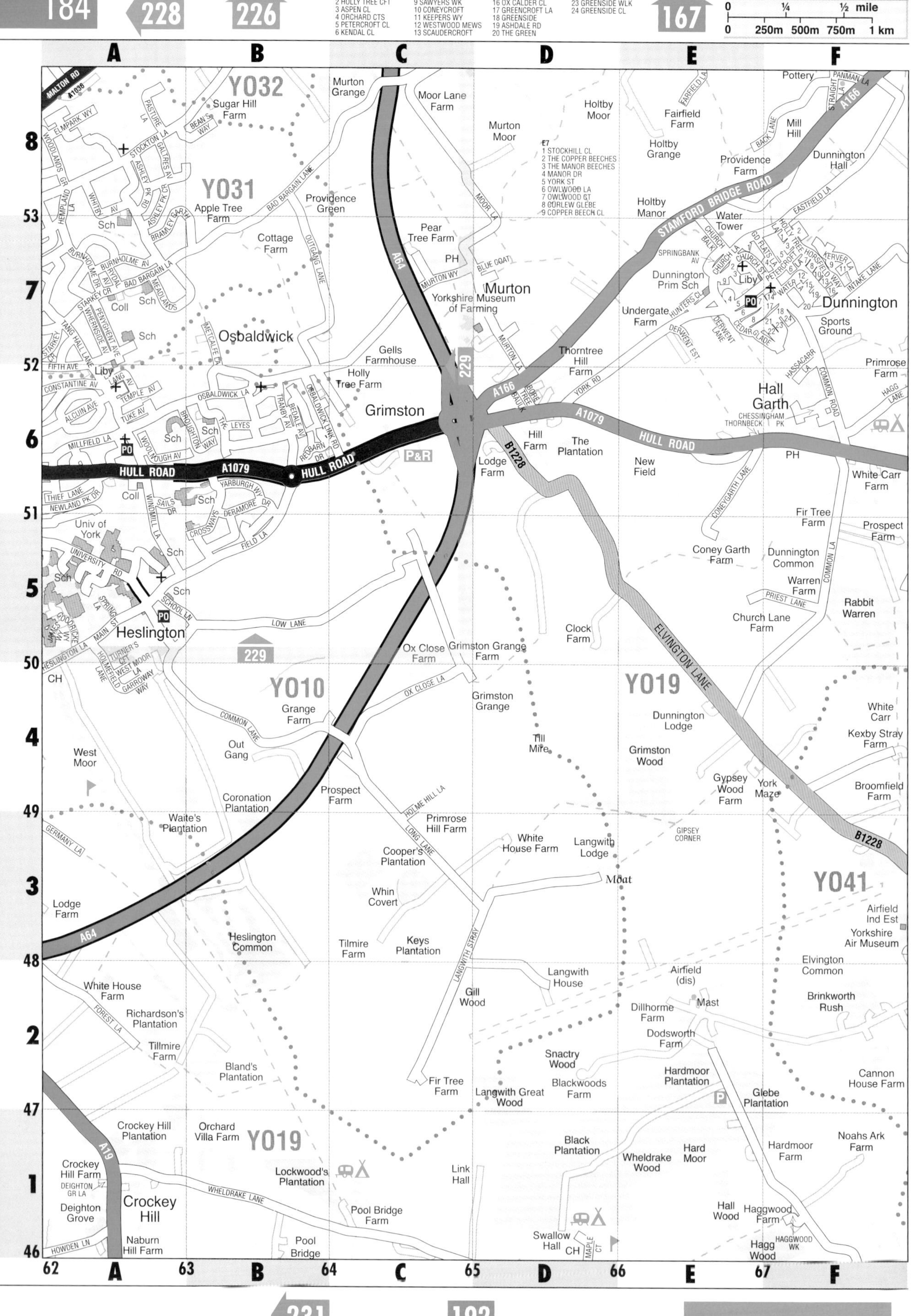

184

← 228

↑ 226

167 →

Scale: 1¾ inches to 1 mile

0   ¼   ½ mile

0 250m 500m 750m 1 km

F7
1 GORSE HL
2 HOLLY TREE CFT
3 ASPEN CL
4 ORCHARD CTS
5 PETERCROFT CL
6 KENDAL CL

7 UNDERCROFT
8 THORNCROFT
9 SAWYERS WK
10 CONEYCROFT
11 KEEPERS WY
12 WESTWOOD MEWS
13 SCAUDERCROFT

14 GREENCROFT CT
15 LIME TREE MEWS
16 OX CALDER CL
17 GREENCROFT LA
18 GREENSIDE
19 ASHDALE RD
20 THE GREEN

21 HUNTERS WOOD WY
22 DEERSTONE WY
23 GREENSIDE WLK
24 GREENSIDE CL

F7
1 STOCKHILL CL
2 THE COPPER BEECHES
3 THE MANOR BEECHES
4 MANOR DR
5 YORK ST
6 OWLWOOD LA
7 OWLWOOD GT
8 CURLEW GLEBE
9 COPPER BEECH CL

For full street detail of the highlighted area see page 229.

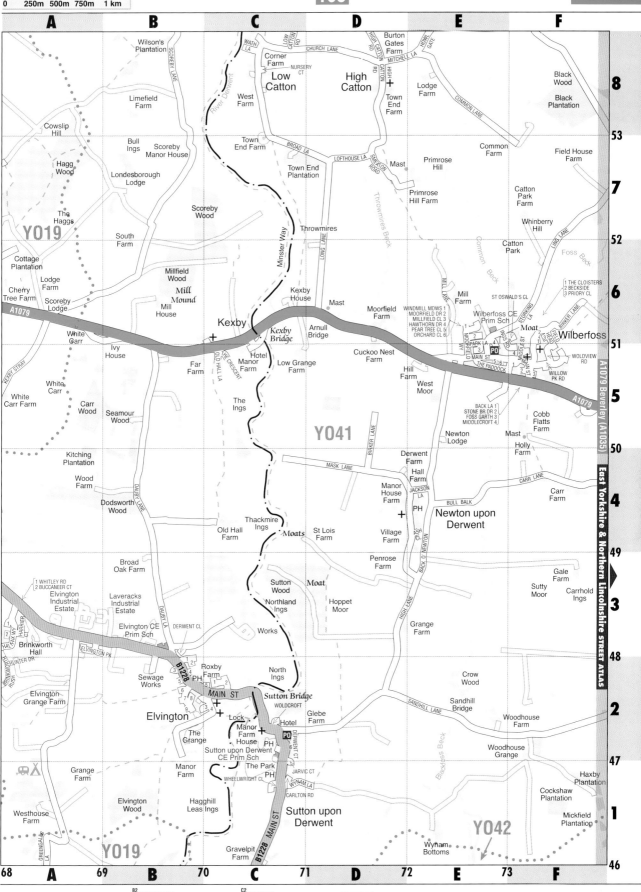

Scale: 1¾ inches to 1 mile

0 ¼ ½ mile
0 250m 500m 750m 1 km

A B C D E F

8
53
7
52
6
51
5
50
4
49
3
48
2
47
1
46

Y019

Wilson's Plantation

Limefield Farm

Cowslip Hill

Hagg Wood

The Haggs

Bull Ings

Londesborough Lodge

South Farm

Scoreby Manor House

Scoreby Wood

Cottage Plantation

Lodge Farm

Cherry Tree Farm

Scoreby Lodge

Millfield Wood

Mill Mound

Mill House

A1079

White Carr

Ivy House

White Carr

White Carr Farm

Carr Wood

Seamour Wood

Kitching Plantation

Wood Farm

Dodsworth Wood

Far Farm

The Ings

Minster Way

OLD HALL LA

THE CRESCENT

WATH LA

LOW CATTON RD

CHURCH LANE

Corner Farm

NURSERY CT

West Farm

Town End Farm

River Derwent

SCOREBY LANE

BROAD LA

Town End Plantation

Town End Farm

Throwmires

Kexby House

LONG LANE

Kexby

Kexby Bridge

Hotel Manor Farm

Low Grange Farm

Arnull Bridge

Mast

Low Catton

High Catton

HIGH CATTON RD

CATTON RD

MITCHELL LA

Burton Gates Farm

HOWE GATE

Town End Farm

Lodge Farm

COMMON LANE

Black Wood

Black Plantation

LOFTHOUSE LA

SKELTON ROAD

Mast

Primrose Hill

Primrose Hill Farm

Throwmires Beck

Common Farm

Field House Farm

Catton Park Farm

Whinberry Hill

Catton Park

Common Beck

Mill Farm

St Oswald's CL

Foss Beck

LING LANE

1 THE CLOISTERS
2 BECKSIDE
3 PRIORY CL

Moorfield Farm

WINDMILL MDWS
MOORFIELD DR 2
MILLFIELD CL 3
HAWTHORN DR 4
PEAR TREE CL 5
ORCHARD CL 6

Wilberfoss CE Prim Sch

MILL LANE

PARK LA

MOORFIELD

INGS RD

MAIN ST

IVY

THE PADDOCK

Moat

PO

Wilberfoss

BIRKER LANE

FIELD

STOKKING LA

MIDDLE LA

MAIN ST

WILLOW PK RD

WOLDVIEW RD

WILLOW PK RD

A1079 Beverley (A1035)

A1079

East Yorkshire & Northern Lincolnshire street atlas

Cuckoo Nest Farm

Hill Farm

West Moor

BACK LA 1
STONE BR DR 2
FOSS GARTH 3
MIDDLECROFT 4

Cobb Flatts Farm

Y041

BIRKER LANE

MASK LANE

Derwent Farm

Hall Farm

Newton Lodge

Mast

Holly Farm

CARR LANE

Carr Farm

Manor House Farm

JACKSON LA

PH

BULL BALK

Newton upon Derwent

Gale Farm

Sutty Moor

Carrhold Ings

ASH CL

BACK O NEWTON

Village Farm

St Lois Farm

Moats

Thackmire Ings

Old Hall Farm

Broad Oak Farm

DALBY LANE

Penrose Farm

HIGH LANE

Grange Farm

Crow Wood

Sandhill Bridge

Sandhill Farm

SANDHILL LANE

Woodhouse Farm

Sutton Wood

Moat

Hoppet Moor

Northland Ings

Works

North Ings

1 WHITLEY RD
2 BUCCANEER CT

Elvington Industrial Estate

Laveracks Industrial Estate

HALIFAX WY

HARRIER CT

HALIFAX WY

ELVINGTON PK

Elvington CE Prim Sch

DERWENT CL

Brinkworth Hall

BRINKWORTH RUSH

HUNTER DR

Elvington Grange Farm

Sewage Works

Roxby Farm

PH

MAIN ST

B1228

Elvington

The Grange

Lock

Manor Farm House

PH

Sutton Bridge

WOLDCROFT

Glebe Farm

Hotel

PO

DERWENT CT

Sutton upon Derwent CE Prim Sch

The Park

PH

JARVIC CT

Blacksmiths CL

Manor Farm

WHEELWRIGHT CL

WYHAM LA

CARLTON RD

B1228 MAIN ST

Sutton upon Derwent

Westhouse Farm

Grange Farm

Elvington Wood

Hagghill Leas Ings

GREENGALE LA

Y019

Gravelpit Farm

Woodhouse Grange

Blackstoss Beck

Wyham Bottoms

Y042

Haxby Plantation

Cockshaw Plantation

Mickfield Plantation

68 A 69 B 70 C 71 D 72 E 73 F 46

B2
1 WHITE HOUSE GR
2 BEECH CL
3 LORRAINE AVE
4 HILLGARTH CT
5 DOVECOTE GARTH
6 BECK CL
7 BECKSIDE
8 BELVOIR AVE
9 ALVIN WK

C2
1 RIVERSIDE CL
2 RIVERSIDE GDNS
3 CHURCH GN
4 CHURCH LA
5 BLACKSMITHS CL
6 JASMINE GARTH

A7
1 UNITY ST
2 SCHOOL ST
3 VICARAGE RD
4 LOW FD
5 FORT'S BG

Map labels

Grid columns: A B C D E F
Grid rows: 8 45 7 44 6 43 5 42 4 41 3 40 2 39 1 38
Bottom grid: 90 A 91 B 92 C 93 D 94 E 95 F

Lancashire STREET ATLAS

KENILWORTH DR
COOLHAM LA
Reservoir
DODGSON LA
MITTON LA
Lothersdale Com Prim Sch
ROOK ST
GARDEN TERR

Moor Hall
Bleara Moor
Bent Hall
Raygill
Lower Spen House
Woodhead Farm
Town Edge

COLNE RD
PARK SIDE
HOLME CL
Tunstead Farm
BD20
Hawshaw Moor

COLNE RD
Kelbrook
Salt Pye Farm
Hawshaw Cottage
Springs Farm

A56 Colne
HEADS LANE
Paris Farm
Copy House
Bleara Road
Hawshaw Side
Oliver Farm
Haws

ARTHUR CLIFTON ST
CHURCH HARDEN RD
BB18
Harden Old House
Hawshaw Lodge
East Hainslack Farm
Stone Head Brow
Westfield

DOTCLIFFE ROAD
Harden Beck
Brown Hill
COWLING HILL LANE

Kelbrook Prim Sch
Thick Bank
Harden New Hall
Kitchen
Hainslack
Dukes
Stone Head Farm
Hardfield

Moor Gate
COB LANE
Hard Clough
Kelbrook Wood
PH
WARLEY WISE LANE
Warley Wise
Hazelgrove Lodge
STONE HEAD LANE
BD22

OLD LA
Hague House
The Hill
Laycock
Kelbrook Wood
Copy House
Gruntland Hall
Sandyforth
Bawsedge
Park

Hague
Oxenards
Ambwell
Earl Hall
Great Edge
Piked Edge
Pasture
Knarrs Hill Farm
Bowes Edge
Sandyforth
HILL END RD

Nonya Hill
Nonya End
Great Edge
Flass Bent
Shaw Head Farm
Knarr Side
A6068
Fleet

White House Farm
Bent Laithe
Knarrs
Reedshaw Moss
Pad Cote

Moss Houses
Near Salter Syke
Far Salter Syke
SKIPTON OLD ROAD
Shaw Gate
Earl Hall
Laneshaw Resr
Laneshaw Resr

Lower Clough
COCKHILL LANE
CH
White Syke
Wicken Syke
HILL LANE
Flass
LONG LANE
Barnside
Monkroyd
Monkroyd Farm
KEIGHLEY RD
Corn Close

CASTLE ROAD
Blue Bell
Hedroyd
Christ Church CE Prim Sch
Laneshaw Bridge Prim Sch
EMMOTT LA
Laneshaw Bridge
Monkroyd PH
KEIGHLEY ROAD
Corn Close Bent Moor

A6068 Nelson
SKIPTON OLD RD
BENT LANE
SHERIDAN RD
WYCOLLER VW VALLEY MILL CT
Upper Emmott
Robert Laith
Coppy Hill

VERNON RD
KINGSLEY RD
SCHOOL LANE
BB8
Lower Emmott

1 ALMA RD
2 LADY HARTLEY CT
3 SIR WILLIAM HARTLEY CT

Mill Weir
SPRINGS GR
HAWLEY LA
CARRIER'S ROW
Hill Top Farm
Emmott Moor

STANDROYD
ANDROYD DR
COTTON TREE
HALL TOP LANE
Slack

FOULDS RD
WINEWALL LANE
NEW ROW
Oak House Farm
Lowlands Farm
Herder's Common

Cotton Tree
BG250
SKIPTON ROAD
BANKFIELD ST
BECKSIDE
Winewall Rec Grd
Wycoller Country Park Visitor Centre
PH
Combe Hill

LEYLAND CL
LACHMAN RD
BANNISTER CL
CARRIER'S ROW
RIVER LANE
Bracken Hill
Wycoller

MIRE RIDGE
FOULDS RD
HALL LANE
HALL MDWS
Higher Stunstead
Slackhead

GOOSE GN LA
CLIFTON ST
DEAN BROW
BG250
PO
TRAWDEN
Near Wanless
Copy House
Onion Bank

Prospect Farm
WEAVERS CT
GREEN MDW
BRIGHT TER
BACK LA
Dean House
Cross Bent

BACK COLNE RD
FOULDS ROAD
WHITE LEE AV
WHITE HOUSE
Germany Farm
Sheepfold

Beardshaw Beck
BURLEY RD
BOULSWORTH DRIVE
Lancashire STREET ATLAS

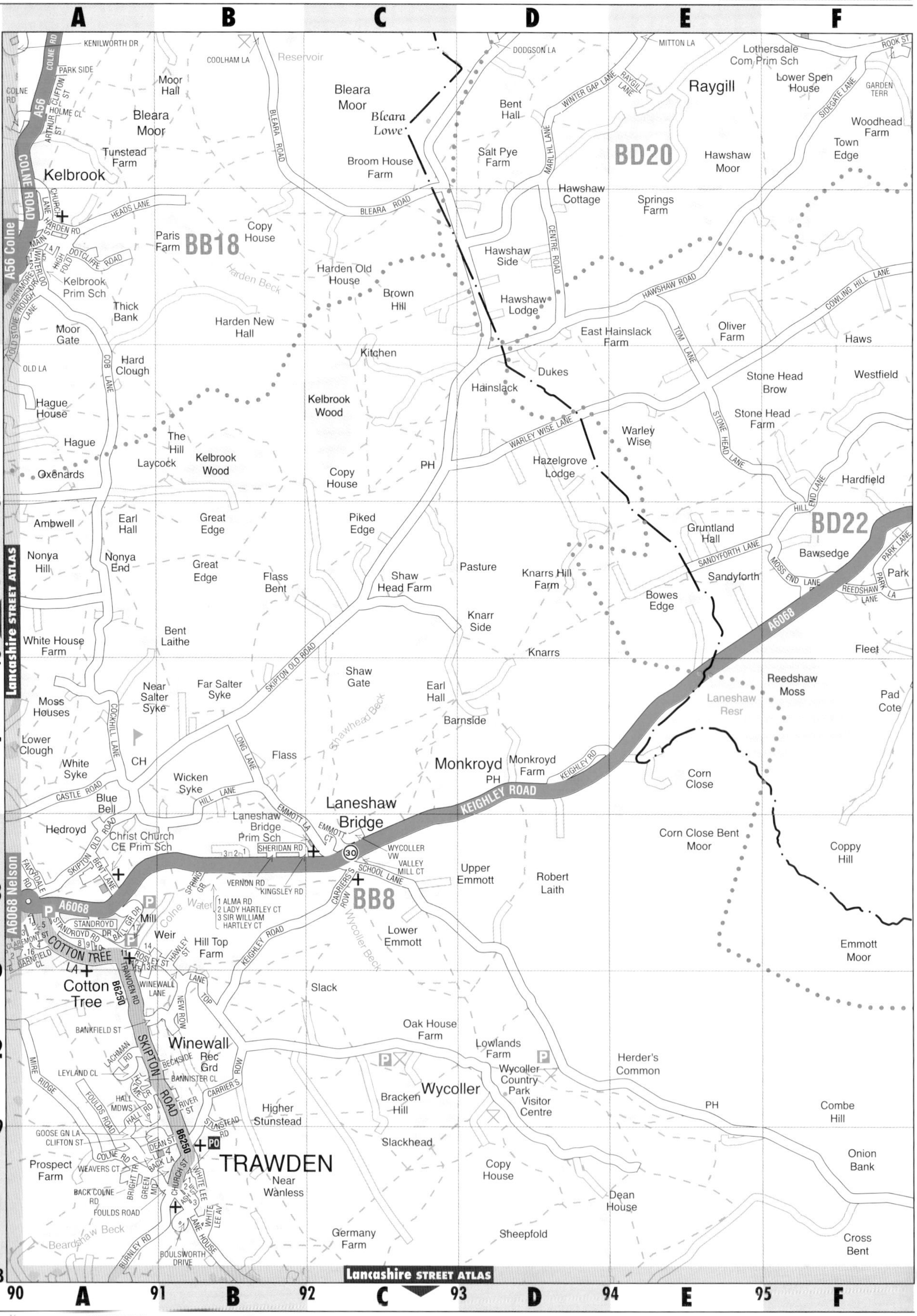

A3
1 KEIGHLEY RD
2 CLARENCE ST
3 CRAVEN ST
4 BOULSWORTH GR
5 MONMOUTH ST
6 ACRESFIELD
7 LONG MEADOW
8 LAMBETH ST
9 HOLLINGTON ST
10 CLARENDON ST
11 WINEWALL RD
12 HOLME ST
13 HARTINGTON ST
14 DUKE ST
15 BRIGHT ST
16 ING DENE AVE
17 MILLBROOK CT

B1
1 CLARENCE ST
2 LAMBERT ST
3 EAST VIEW
4 Trawden Forest Prim Sch

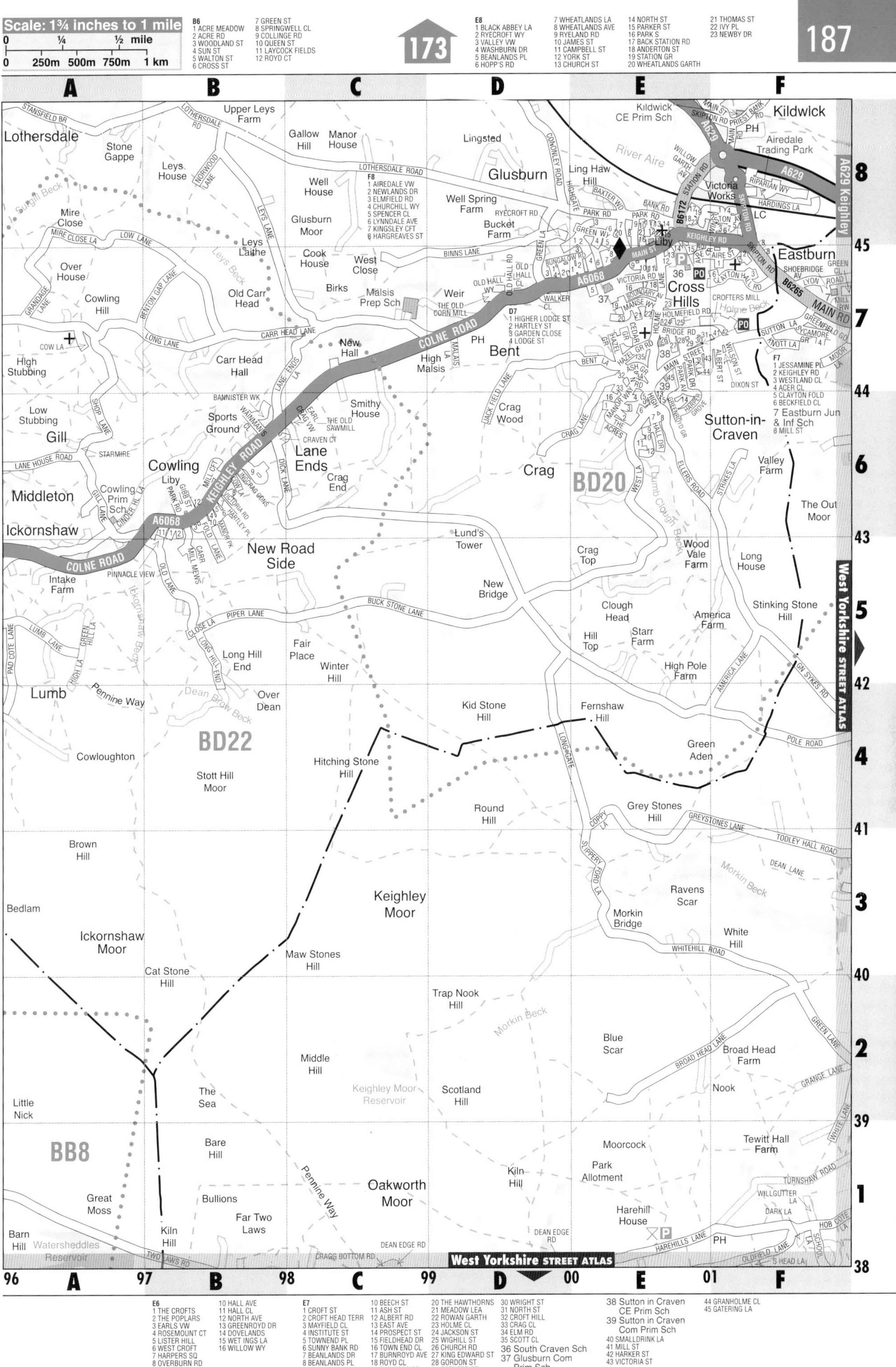

Scale: 1¾ inches to 1 mile
0 ¼ ½ mile
0 250m 500m 750m 1 km
B6
1 ACRE MEADOW
2 ACRE RD
3 WOODLAND ST
4 SUN ST
5 WALTON ST
6 CROSS ST
7 GREEN ST
8 SPRINGWELL CL
9 COLLINGE RD
10 QUEEN ST
11 LAYCOCK FIELDS
12 ROYD CT
173
E8
1 BLACK ABBEY LA
2 RYECROFT WY
3 VALLEY VW
4 WASHBURN DR
5 BEANLANDS PL
6 HOPP'S RD
7 WHEATLANDS LA
8 WHEATLANDS AVE
9 RYELAND RD
10 JAMES ST
11 CAMPBELL ST
12 YORK ST
13 CHURCH ST
14 NORTH ST
15 PARKER ST
16 PARK S
17 BACK STATION RD
18 ANDERTON ST
19 STATION GR
20 WHEATLANDS GARTH
21 THOMAS ST
22 IVY PL
23 NEWBY DR
187
A B C D E F
Lothersdale
Stansfield Br
Lothersdale Rd
Upper Leys Farm
Stone Gappe
Gallow Hill
Manor House
Lingsted
Kildwick CE Prim Sch
Kildwick
Airedale Trading Park
River Aire
Leys House
Norwood Lane
Well House
Lothersdale Road
Glusburn
Ling Haw Hill
Victoria Works
A629
A629 Keighley
F8
1 AIREDALE VW
2 NEWLANDS DR
3 ELMFIELD RD
4 CHURCHILL WY
5 SPENCER CL
6 LYNNDALE AVE
7 KINGSLEY CFT
8 HARGREAVES ST
Well Spring Farm
Ryecroft Rd
Bucket Farm
Sugill Beck
Mire Close
Mire Close La
Low Lane
Leys Lane
Glusburn Moor
Leys Laithe
Cook House
West Close
Binns Lane
Keighley Rd
Eastburn
Shoebridge Av
Lyon Road
Over House
Birks
Malsis Prep Sch
Weir
Old Hall Wy
The Old Corn Mill
Old Hall Cl
A6068
Victoria Rd
Cross Hills
Crofters Mill
Holme Beck
B6265
Main Rd
Cowling Hill
Grandage Lane
Benton Gap Lane
Old Carr Head
Carr Head Lane
Colne Road
Leys Beck
D7
1 HIGHER LODGE ST
2 HARTLEY ST
3 GARDEN CLOSE
4 LODGE ST
Holmefield Rd
Bridge Rd
Sutton La
Knott La
Cow La
Long Lane
New Hall
PH
High Malsis
Malsis La
Bent
Bent La
High Stubbing
Carr Head Hall
Lane Ends La
F7
1 JESSAMINE PL
2 KEIGHLEY RD
3 WESTLAND CL
4 ACER CL
5 CLAYTON FOLD
6 BECKFIELD CL
7 Eastburn Jun & Inf Sch
8 MILL ST
Dixon St
Bannister Wk
Low Stubbing
Shop Lane
Sports Ground
Wainman's Cl
Smithy House
Jack Field Lane
Crag Wood
Manor Wy
Sutton-in-Craven
Gill
Starmire
Earl Crag Vw
The Old Sawmill
Craven Ct
Crag Lane
Lane House Road
Cowling
Keighley Road
Lane Ends
Crag
BD20
West La
Ellers Road
Strikes La
Valley Farm
Middleton
Cowling Prim Sch
Mill Cft
Park Rd
Gibb St
Crag End
Dick Lane
Lumb Clough Beck
The Out Moor
Ickornshaw
Gill Lane
Cinder Hl La
Carr Mill Mews
Fold Lane
Colne Road
Lund's Tower
Crag Top
Wood Vale Farm
Long House
New Road Side
Intake Farm
Pinnacle View
Old Lane
New Bridge
Clough Head
America Farm
Stinking Stone Hill
West Yorkshire STREET ATLAS
Buck Stone Lane
Piper Lane
Close La
Pad Cote Lane
Lumb Lane
Green Hill La
Ickornshaw Beck
Fair Place
Hill Top
Starr Farm
Long Hill End
Winter Hill
High Pole Farm
America Lane
Gn Sykes Rd
High La
Lumb
Long Hill End
Pennine Way
Dean Brow Beck
Over Dean
Kid Stone Hill
Fernshaw Hill
BD22
Long Gate
Pole Road
Green Aden
Cowloughton
Hitching Stone Hill
Stott Hill Moor
Round Hill
Grey Stones Hill
Coppy La
Greystones Lane
Todley Hall Road
Brown Hill
Slippery Ford La
Dean Lane
Morkin Beck
Keighley Moor
Ravens Scar
Bedlam
Morkin Bridge
White Hill
Ickornshaw Moor
Whitehill Road
Maw Stones Hill
Cat Stone Hill
Trap Nook Hill
Morkin Beck
Blue Scar
Green Lane
Broad Head Lane
Broad Head Farm
Middle Hill
The Sea
Keighley Moor Reservoir
Scotland Hill
Nook
Grange Lane
Little Nick
Bare Hill
Moorcock
Tewitt Hall Farm
White Lane
BB8
Pennine Way
Park Allotment
Kiln Hill
Turnshaw Road
Great Moss
Bullions
Oakworth Moor
Willgutter La
Dark La
Far Two Laws
Harehill House
Barn Hill
Watersheddles Reservoir
Kiln Hill
Dean Edge Rd
Hob Cote La
Harehills Lane
School La
Two Laws Rd
Cragg Bottom Rd
Oldfield Lane
S Head La
West Yorkshire STREET ATLAS
8 45 7 44 6 43 5 42 4 41 3 40 2 39 1 38
96 A 97 B 98 C 99 D 00 E 01 F
E6
1 THE CROFTS
2 THE POPLARS
3 EARLS VW
4 ROSEMOUNT CT
5 LISTER HILL
6 WEST CROFT
7 HARPERS SQ
8 OVERBURN RD
9 HALL WAY
10 HALL AVE
11 HALL CL
12 NORTH AVE
13 GREENROYD DR
14 DOVELANDS
15 WET INGS LA
16 WILLOW WY
E7
1 CROFT ST
2 CROFT HEAD TERR
3 MAYFIELD CL
4 INSTITUTE ST
5 TOWNEND PL
6 SUNNY BANK RD
7 BEANLANDS DR
8 BEANLANDS PL
9 BACK COLNE RD
10 BEECH ST
11 ASH ST
12 ALBERT RD
13 EAST AVE
14 PROSPECT ST
15 FIELDHEAD DR
16 TOWN END CL
17 BURNROYD AVE
18 ROYD CL
19 THE COPPICE
20 THE HAWTHORNS
21 MEADOW LEA
22 ROWAN GARTH
23 HOLME CL
24 JACKSON ST
25 WIGHILL ST
26 CHURCH RD
27 KING EDWARD ST
28 GORDON ST
29 SPENCER ST
30 WRIGHT ST
31 NORTH ST
32 CROFT HILL
33 CRAG CL
34 ELM RD
35 SCOTT CL
36 South Craven Sch
37 Glusburn Com Prim Sch
38 Sutton in Craven CE Prim Sch
39 Sutton in Craven Com Prim Sch
40 SMALLDRINK LA
41 MILL ST
42 HARKER ST
43 VICTORIA ST
44 GRANHOLME CL
45 GATERING LA

Scale: 1¾ inches to 1 mile

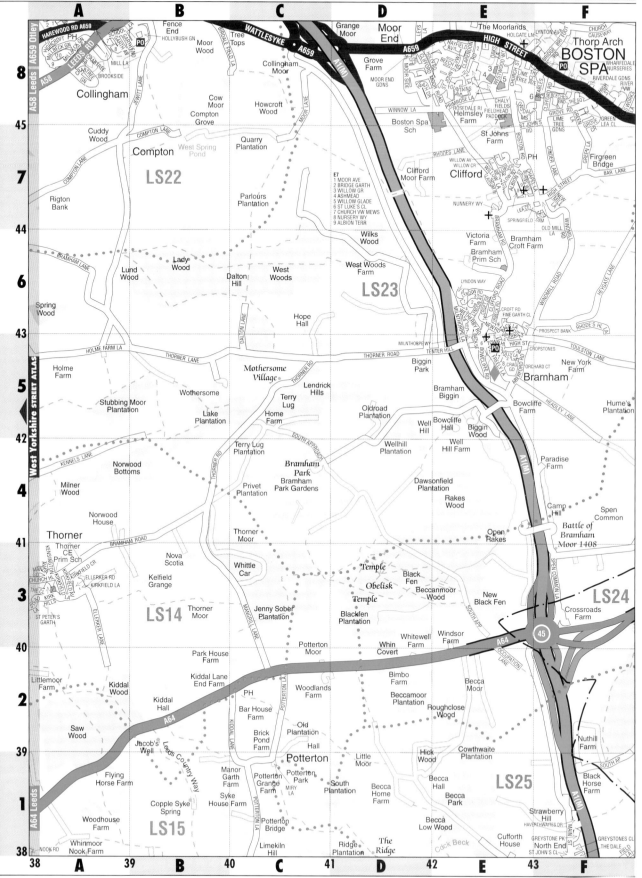

West Yorkshire STREET ATLAS

For full street detail of Boston Spa see Philip's STREET ATLAS of West Yorkshire

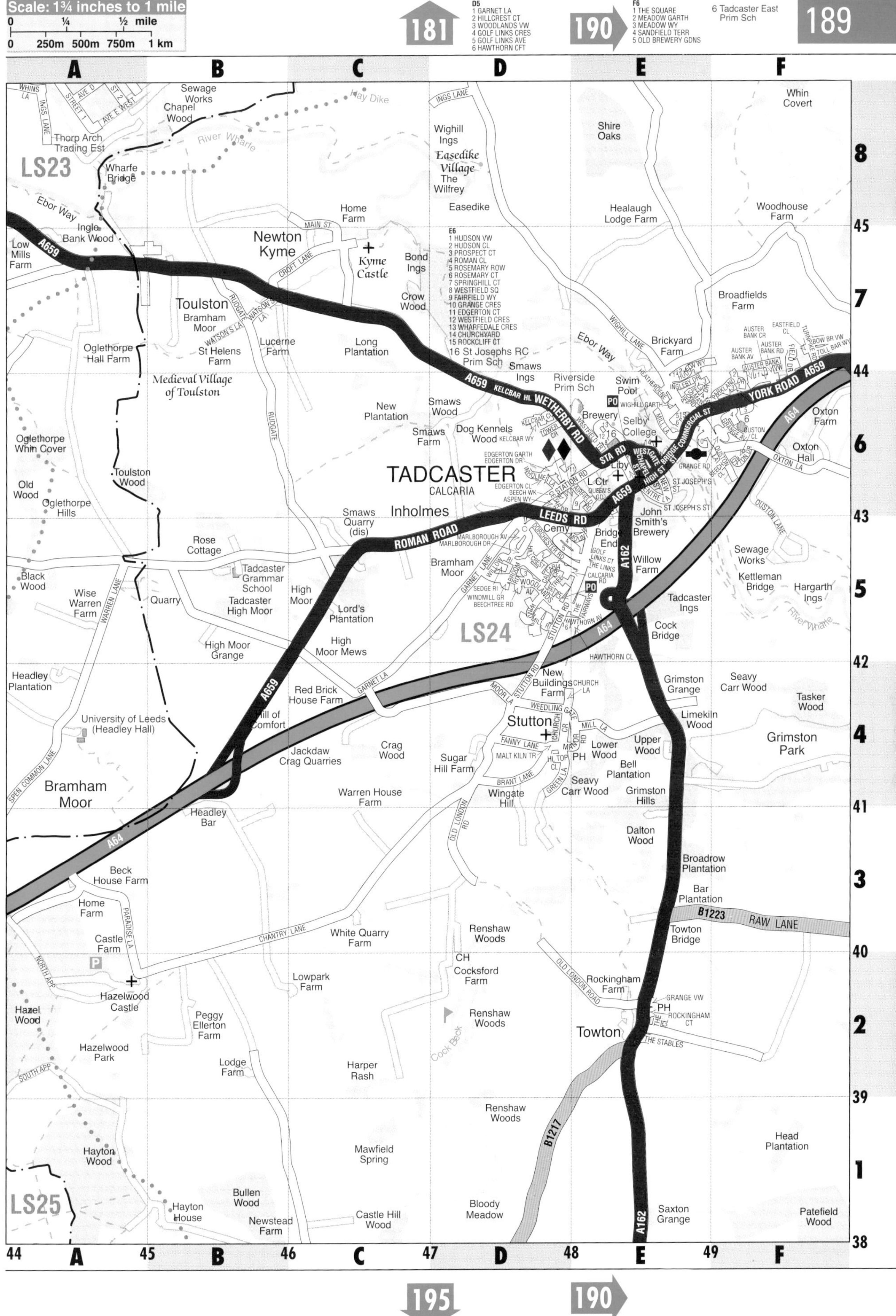
A
B
C
D
E
F
LS23
LS24
LS25
Sewage Works
Chapel Wood
Hay Dike
River Wharfe
Thorp Arch Trading Est
Wharfe Bridge
Ebor Way
Ingle Bank Wood
Low Mills Farm
A659
Newton Kyme
MAIN ST
CROFT LANE
Kyme Castle
Home Farm
Bond Ings
Crow Wood
Toulston
Bramham Moor
RUDGATE
WATSON'S LA
St Helens Farm
Lucerne Farm
Long Plantation
Oglethorpe Hall Farm
Medieval Village of Toulston
INGS LANE
Wighill Ings
Easedike Village
The Wilfrey
Easedike
E6
1 HUDSON VW
2 HUDSON CL
3 PROSPECT CT
4 ROMAN CL
5 ROSEMARY ROW
6 ROSEMARY CT
7 SPRINGHILL CT
8 WESTFIELD SQ
9 FAIRFIELD WY
10 GRANGE CRES
11 EDGERTON CT
12 WESTFIELD CRES
13 WHARFEDALE CRES
14 CHURCHYARD
15 ROCKCLIFF CT
16 St Josephs RC Prim Sch
Shire Oaks
Whin Covert
Healaugh Lodge Farm
Woodhouse Farm
Broadfields Farm
Brickyard Farm
WIGHILL LANE
Smaws Ings
Riverside Prim Sch
Swim Pool
Brewery
Selby College
KELCBAR HL
WETHERBY RD
STA RD
WESTGATE
HIGH ST
BRIDGE ST
COMMERCIAL ST
YORK ROAD
Oxton Farm
Oxton Hall
OXTON LA
A64
New Plantation
Smaws Wood
Smaws Farm
Dog Kennels Wood
Oglethorpe Whin Cover
Toulston Wood
Old Wood
Oglethorpe Hills
TADCASTER
CALCARIA
Inholmes
Smaws Quarry (dis)
ROMAN ROAD
LEEDS RD
Cemy
Liby
L Ctr
John Smith's Brewery
Bridge End
A162
Willow Farm
Sewage Works
Kettleman Bridge
Hargarth Ings
OUSTON LANE
Tadcaster Ings
Cock Bridge
Rose Cottage
Tadcaster Grammar School
Tadcaster High Moor
High Moor
Lord's Plantation
Bramham Moor
Black Wood
Wise Warren Farm
WARREN LANE
Quarry
High Moor Grange
High Moor Mews
HAWTHORN CL
Headley Plantation
Red Brick House Farm
GARNET LA
New Buildings Farm
Grimston Grange
Seavy Carr Wood
Tasker Wood
University of Leeds (Headley Hall)
Hill of Comfort
Stutton
Limekiln Wood
Grimston Park
Jackdaw Crag Quarries
Crag Wood
Sugar Hill Farm
Lower Wood
Upper Wood
Bell Plantation
Bramham Moor
Warren House Farm
Wingate Hill
Seavy Carr Wood
Grimston Hills
Headley Bar
Dalton Wood
OLD LONDON RD
Beck House Farm
Broadrow Plantation
Bar Plantation
Home Farm
PARADISE LA
B1223
RAW LANE
Castle Farm
CHANTRY LANE
White Quarry Farm
Renshaw Woods
Towton Bridge
NORTH APP
CH
Cocksford Farm
Rockingham Farm
OLD LONDON ROAD
Hazelwood Castle
Lowpark Farm
GRANGE VW
PH
ROCKINGHAM CT
Hazel Wood
Peggy Ellerton Farm
Renshaw Woods
Towton
THE STABLES
Hazelwood Park
Cock Beck
SOUTH APP
Lodge Farm
Harper Rash
Renshaw Woods
B1217
Head Plantation
Hayton Wood
Mawfield Spring
Bullen Wood
Hayton House
Newstead Farm
Castle Hill Wood
Bloody Meadow
Saxton Grange
Patefield Wood
SPEN COMMON LANE
8
45
7
44
6
43
5
42
4
41
3
40
2
39
1
38
44
45
46
47
48
49

189
182

Scale: 1¾ inches to 1 mile

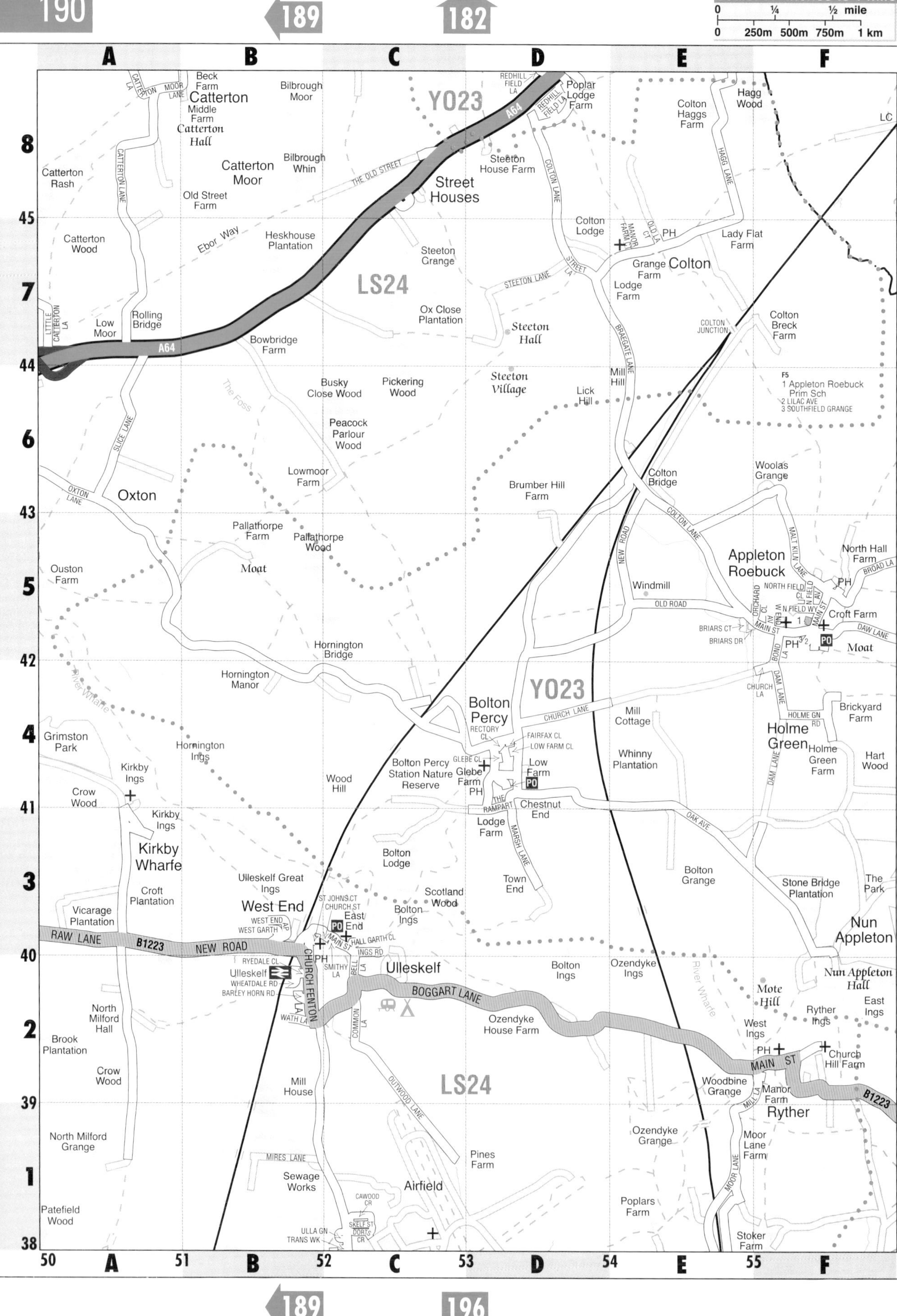
Catterton
Beck Farm
Catterton Middle Farm
Catterton Hall
Bilbrough Moor
Bilbrough Whin
Catterton Moor
Catterton Rash
Old Street Farm
Catterton Wood
Ebor Way
Heskhouse Plantation
YO23
A64
Street Houses
Steeton House Farm
Poplar Lodge Farm
Colton Haggs Farm
Hagg Wood
Colton Lodge
Colton
Lady Flat Farm
Grange Farm
Lodge Farm
Steeton Grange
LS24
Ox Close Plantation
Steeton Hall
Colton Breck Farm
Low Moor
Rolling Bridge
Bowbridge Farm
Busky Close Wood
Pickering Wood
Steeton Village
Lick Hill
Mill Hill
Peacock Parlour Wood
Oxton
Lowmoor Farm
Brumber Hill Farm
Colton Bridge
Woolas Grange
Pallathorpe Farm
Pallathorpe Wood
Moat
Ouston Farm
Appleton Roebuck
North Hall Farm
Windmill
Croft Farm
Hornington Bridge
Hornington Manor
Bolton Percy
YO23
Mill Cottage
Brickyard Farm
Grimston Park
Hornington Ings
Kirkby Ings
Crow Wood
Bolton Percy Station Nature Reserve
Glebe Farm
Low Farm
Whinny Plantation
Holme Green
Holme Green Farm
Hart Wood
Wood Hill
Chestnut End
Lodge Farm
Kirkby Wharfe
Bolton Lodge
Town End
Bolton Grange
Stone Bridge Plantation
The Park
Croft Plantation
Ulleskelf Great Ings
West End
Scotland Wood
Vicarage Plantation
Bolton Ings
Nun Appleton
RAW LANE
B1223
NEW ROAD
Ulleskelf
Bolton Ings
Ozendyke Ings
Nun Appleton Hall
Mote Hill
BOGGART LANE
North Milford Hall
Ozendyke House Farm
Rhyther Ings
East Ings
West Ings
Brook Plantation
Crow Wood
Church Hill Farm
Mill House
LS24
Woodbine Grange
Manor Farm
Ryther
North Milford Grange
Ozendyke Grange
Moor Lane Farm
Pines Farm
Sewage Works
Airfield
Patefield Wood
Poplars Farm
Stoker Farm
F5
1 Appleton Roebuck Prim Sch
2 LILAC AVE
3 SOUTHFIELD GRANGE

189
196

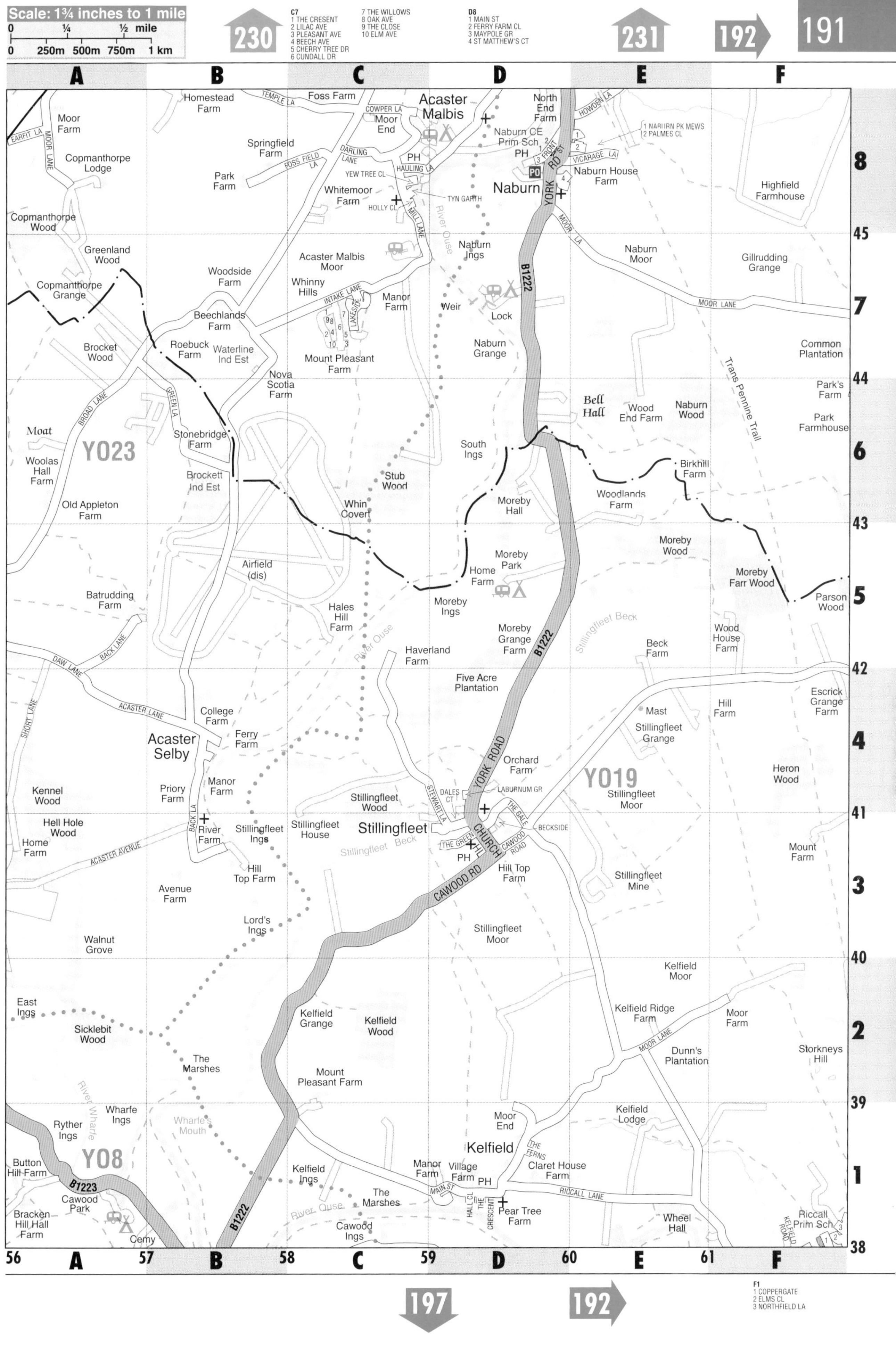

Scale: 1¾ inches to 1 mile
0 ¼ ½ mile
0 250m 500m 750m 1 km
230
C7
1 THE CRESENT
2 LILAC AVE
3 PLEASANT AVE
4 BEECH AVE
5 CHERRY TREE DR
6 CUNDALL DR
7 THE WILLOWS
8 OAK AVE
9 THE CLOSE
10 ELM AVE
D8
1 MAIN ST
2 FERRY FARM CL
3 MAYPOLE GR
4 ST MATTHEW'S CT
231
192
191
A
B
C
D
E
F
Homestead Farm
TEMPLE LA
Foss Farm
Acaster Malbis
North End Farm
HOWDEN LA
Moor Farm
EARFIT LA
MOOR LANE
COWPER LA
Moor End
Naburn CE Prim Sch
PH
1 NABURN PK MEWS
2 PALMES CL
Springfield Farm
FOSS FIELD LA
DARLING LANE
PH
HAULING LA
FRONT ST
VICARAGE LA
Copmanthorpe Lodge
Park Farm
YEW TREE CL
PO
Naburn House Farm
Naburn
YORK RD
Highfield Farmhouse
Whitemoor Farm
TYN GARTH
HOLLY CL
MILL LANE
River Ouse
Copmanthorpe Wood
MOOR LA
8
45
Greenland Wood
Acaster Malbis Moor
Naburn Ings
B1222
Naburn Moor
Gillrudding Grange
Woodside Farm
Whinny Hills
INTAKE LANE
Copmanthorpe Grange
Manor Farm
Weir
Lock
MOOR LANE
7
Beechlands Farm
LAKESIDE
Brocket Wood
Roebuck Farm
Waterline Ind Est
Mount Pleasant Farm
Naburn Grange
Trans Pennine Trail
Common Plantation
Nova Scotia Farm
44
Park's Farm
BROAD LANE
GREEN LA
Bell Hall
Wood End Farm
Naburn Wood
Park Farmhouse
Moat
YO23
Stonebridge Farm
South Ings
6
Woolas Hall Farm
Brockett Ind Est
Stub Wood
Birkhill Farm
Whin Covert
Moreby Hall
Woodlands Farm
Old Appleton Farm
43
Airfield (dis)
Moreby Park
Moreby Wood
Home Farm
Moreby Farr Wood
Batrudding Farm
Moreby Ings
Parson Wood
5
Hales Hill Farm
Moreby Grange Farm
Stillingfleet Beck
Wood House Farm
BACK LANE
River Ouse
Haverland Farm
B1222
Beck Farm
DAW LANE
42
Five Acre Plantation
ACASTER LANE
College Farm
Mast
Hill Farm
Escrick Grange Farm
SHORT LANE
Acaster Selby
Ferry Farm
Stillingfleet Grange
4
YORK ROAD
Orchard Farm
Heron Wood
Manor Farm
YO19
Kennel Wood
Priory Farm
Stillingfleet Wood
DALES CT
LABURNUM GR
Stillingfleet Moor
STEWART LA
THE GALE
41
Hell Hole Wood
BACK LA
River Farm
Stillingfleet Ings
Stillingfleet House
Stillingfleet
CHURCH HILL
BECKSIDE
Home Farm
ACASTER AVENUE
Stillingfleet Beck
THE GREEN
CAWOOD ROAD
Mount Farm
PH
Hill Top Farm
Hill Top Farm
Stillingfleet Mine
CAWOOD RD
3
Avenue Farm
Lord's Ings
Stillingfleet Moor
Walnut Grove
40
Kelfield Moor
East Ings
Kelfield Grange
Kelfield Wood
Kelfield Ridge Farm
Moor Farm
Sicklebit Wood
2
MOOR LANE
Dunn's Plantation
Storkneys Hill
The Marshes
Mount Pleasant Farm
River Wharfe
Wharfe Ings
Moor End
Kelfield Lodge
39
Ryther Ings
Wharfe's Mouth
YO8
THE FERNS
Kelfield
Button Hill Farm
Kelfield Ings
Manor Farm
Village Farm
Claret House Farm
1
B1223
PH
MAIN ST
RICCALL LANE
Cawood Park
The Marshes
HALL CL
THE CRESCENT
Pear Tree Farm
Bracken Hill Hall Farm
River Ouse
Wheel Hall
Riccall Prim Sch
KELFIELD ROAD
B1222
Cawood Ings
Cemy
38
56
57
58
59
60
61
197
192
F1
1 COPPERGATE
2 ELMS CL
3 NORTHFIELD LA

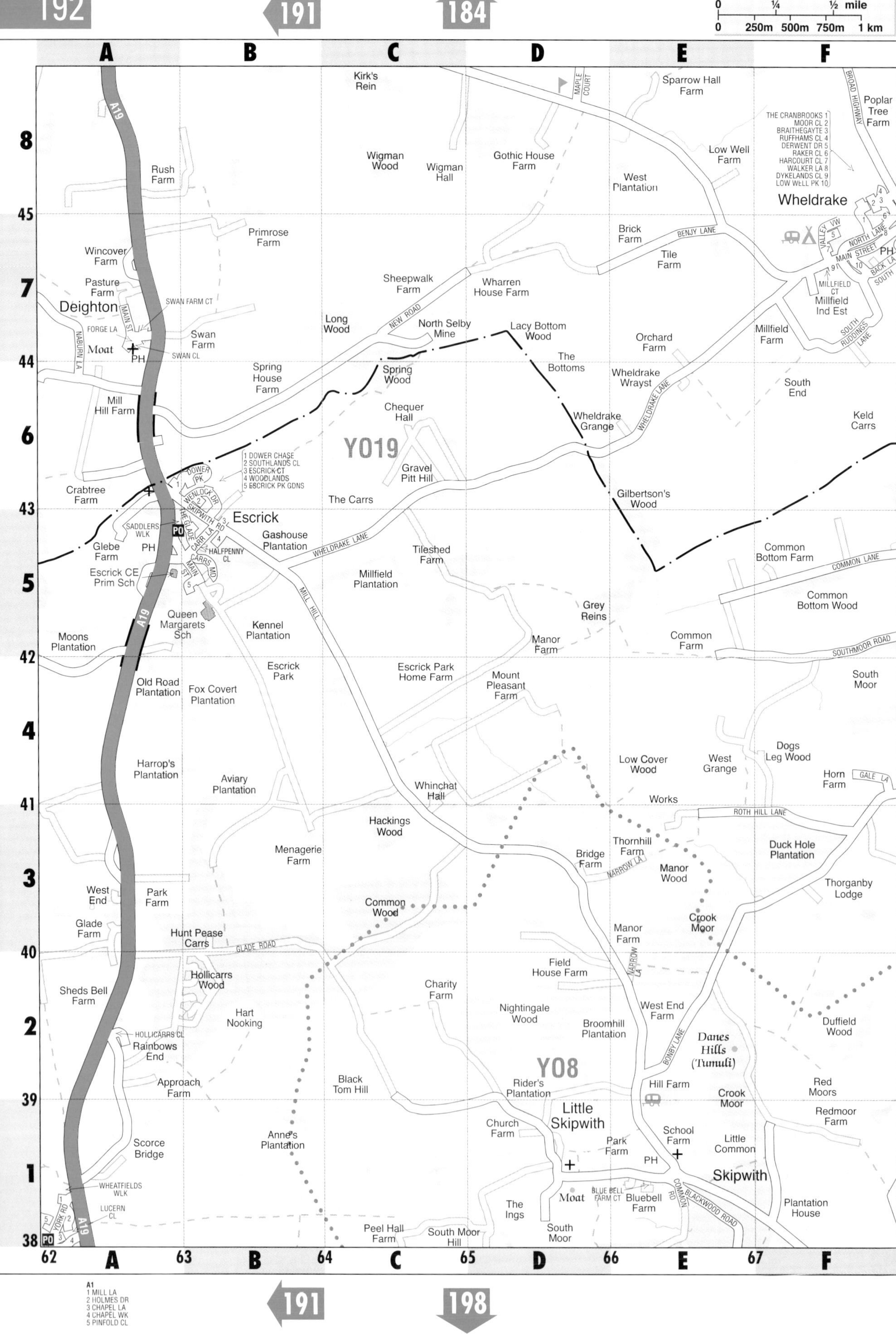

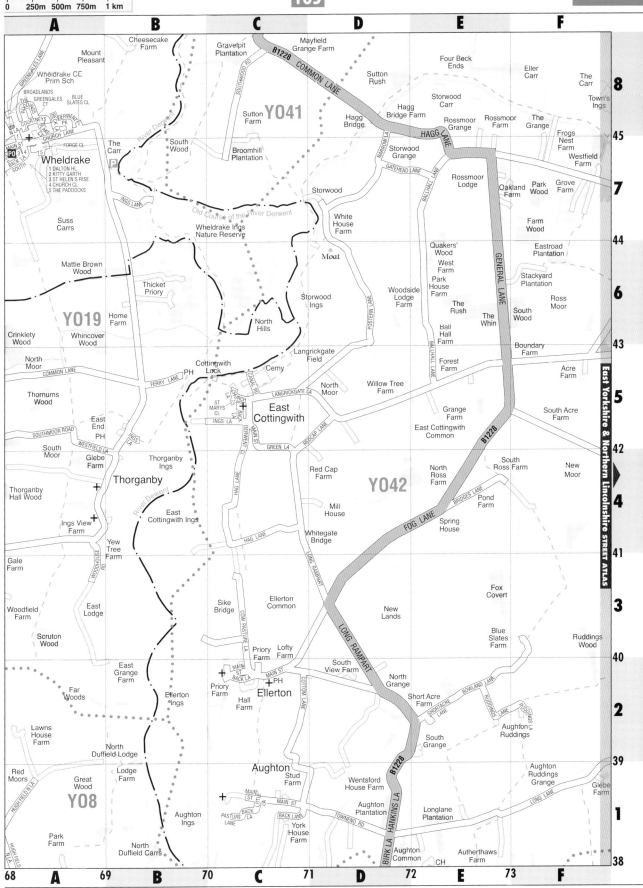

Scale: 1¾ inches to 1 mile

0   ¼   ½ mile
0   250m 500m 750m 1 km

East Yorkshire & Northern Lincolnshire STREET ATLAS

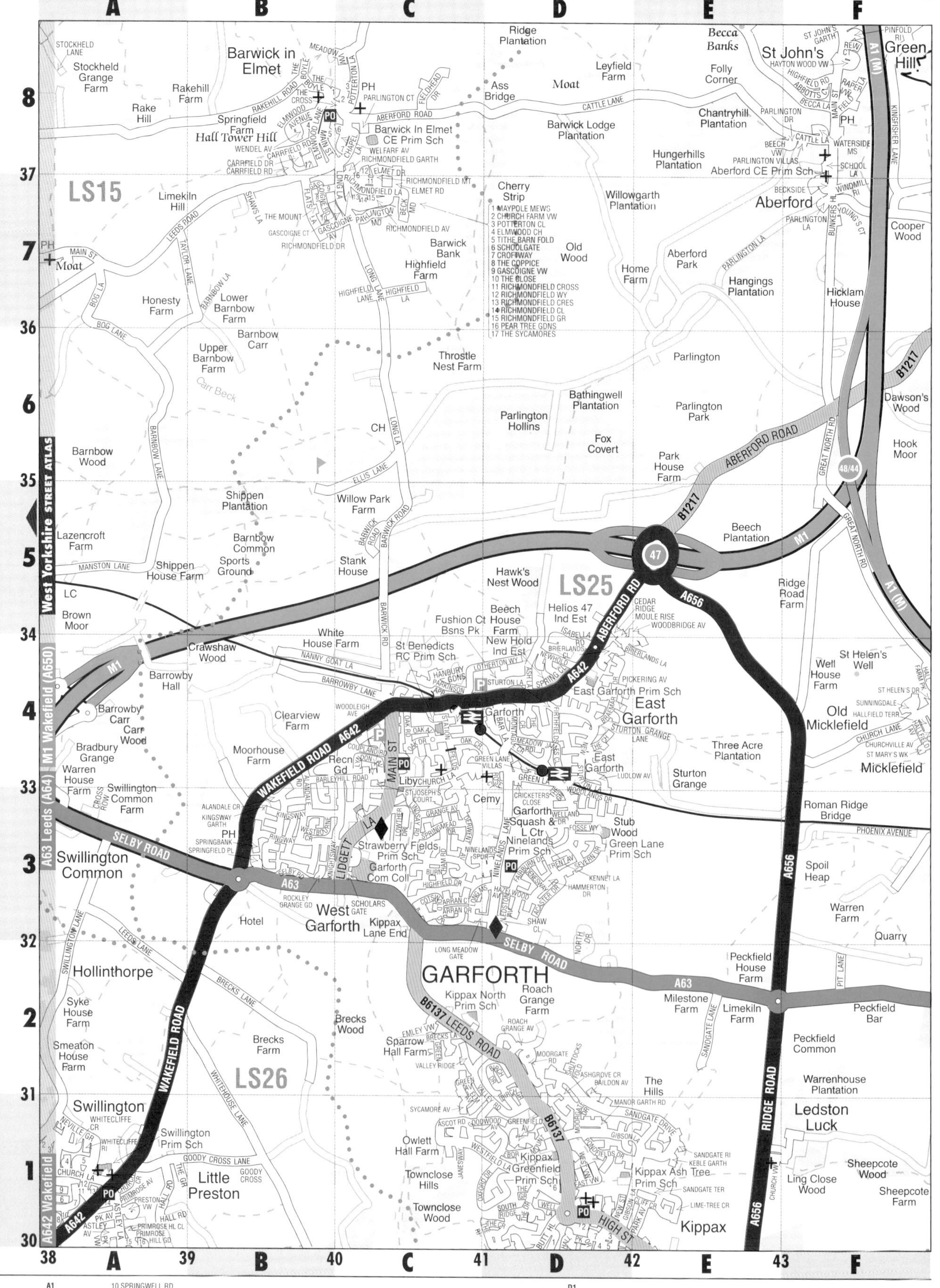

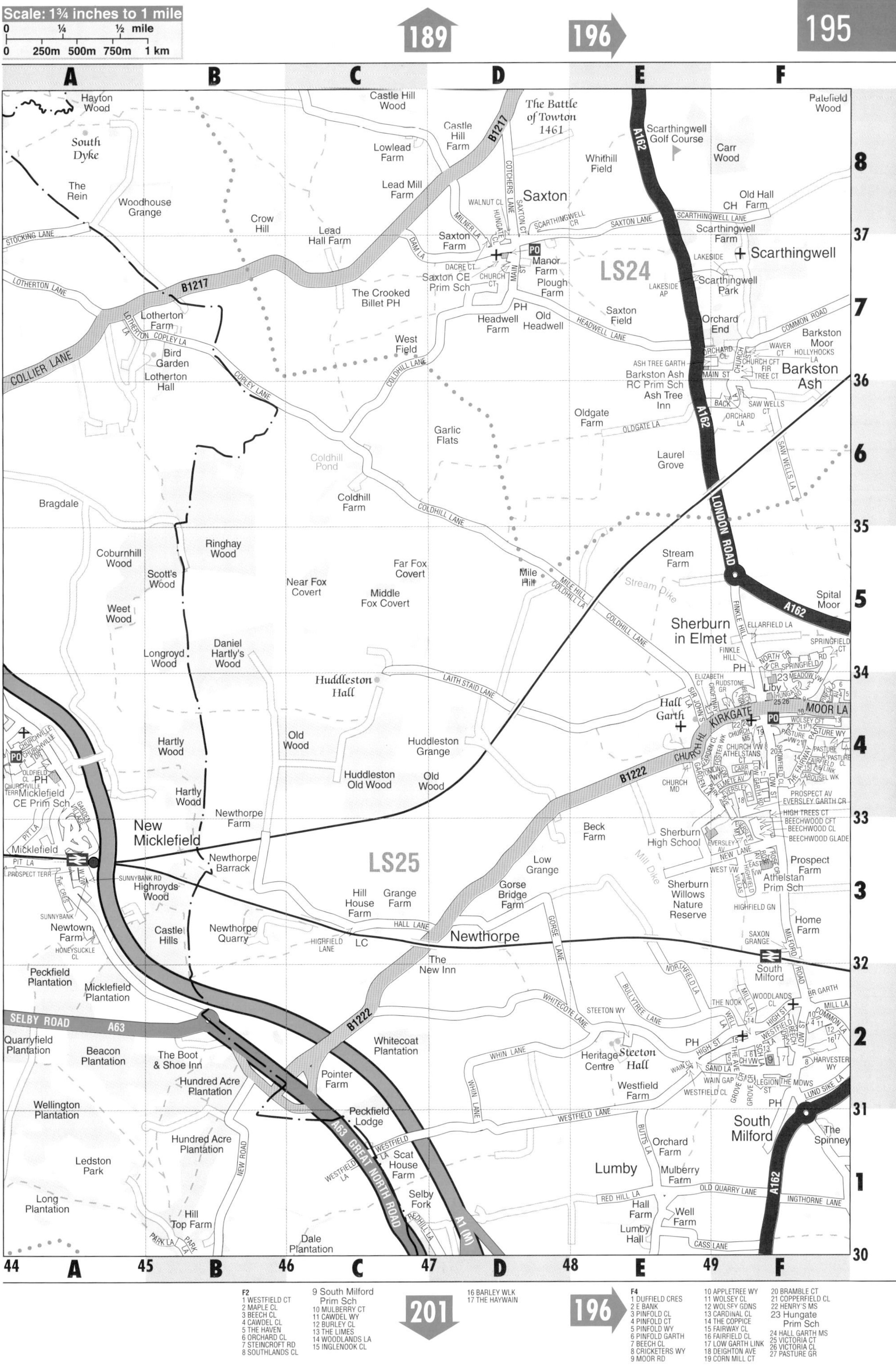

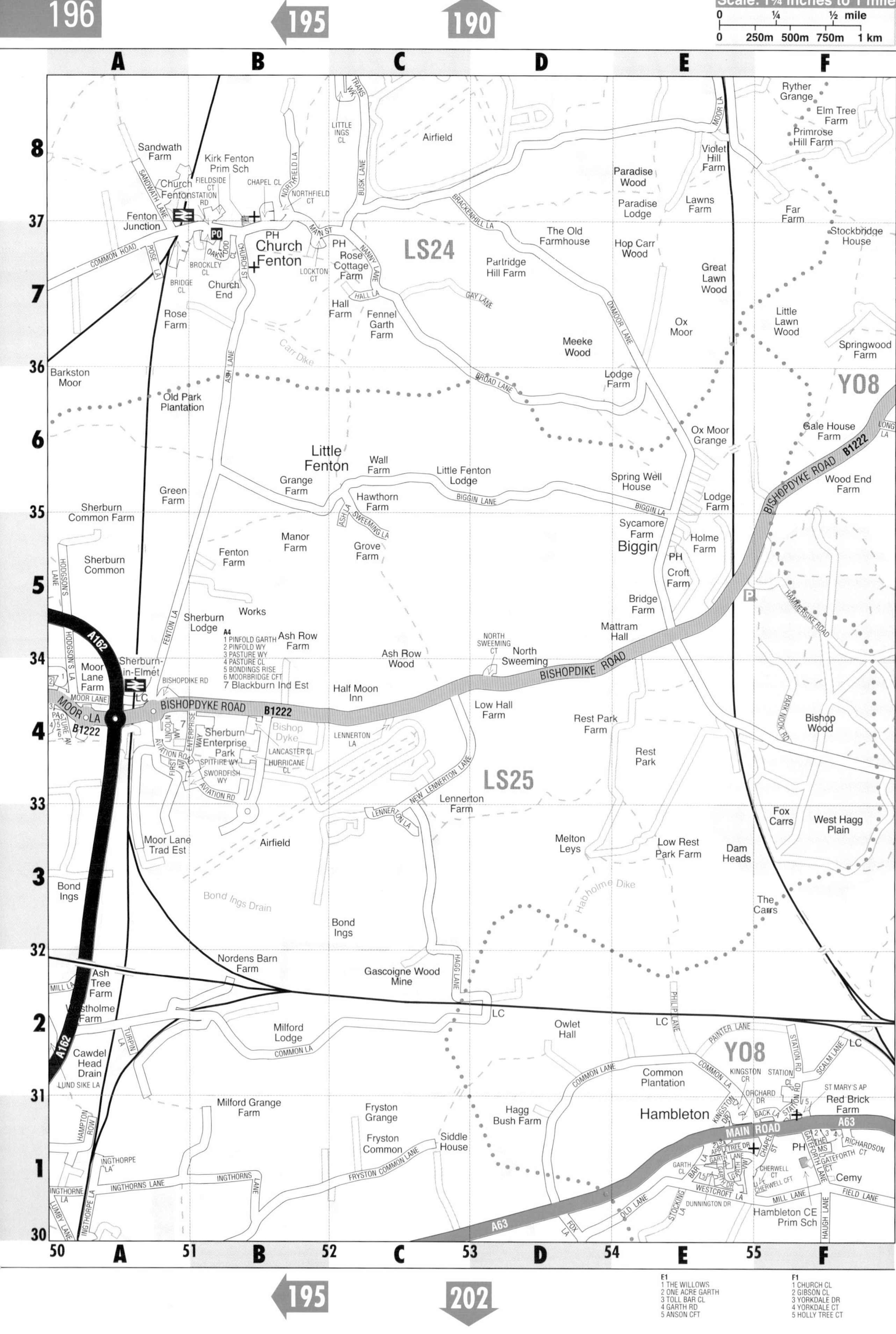

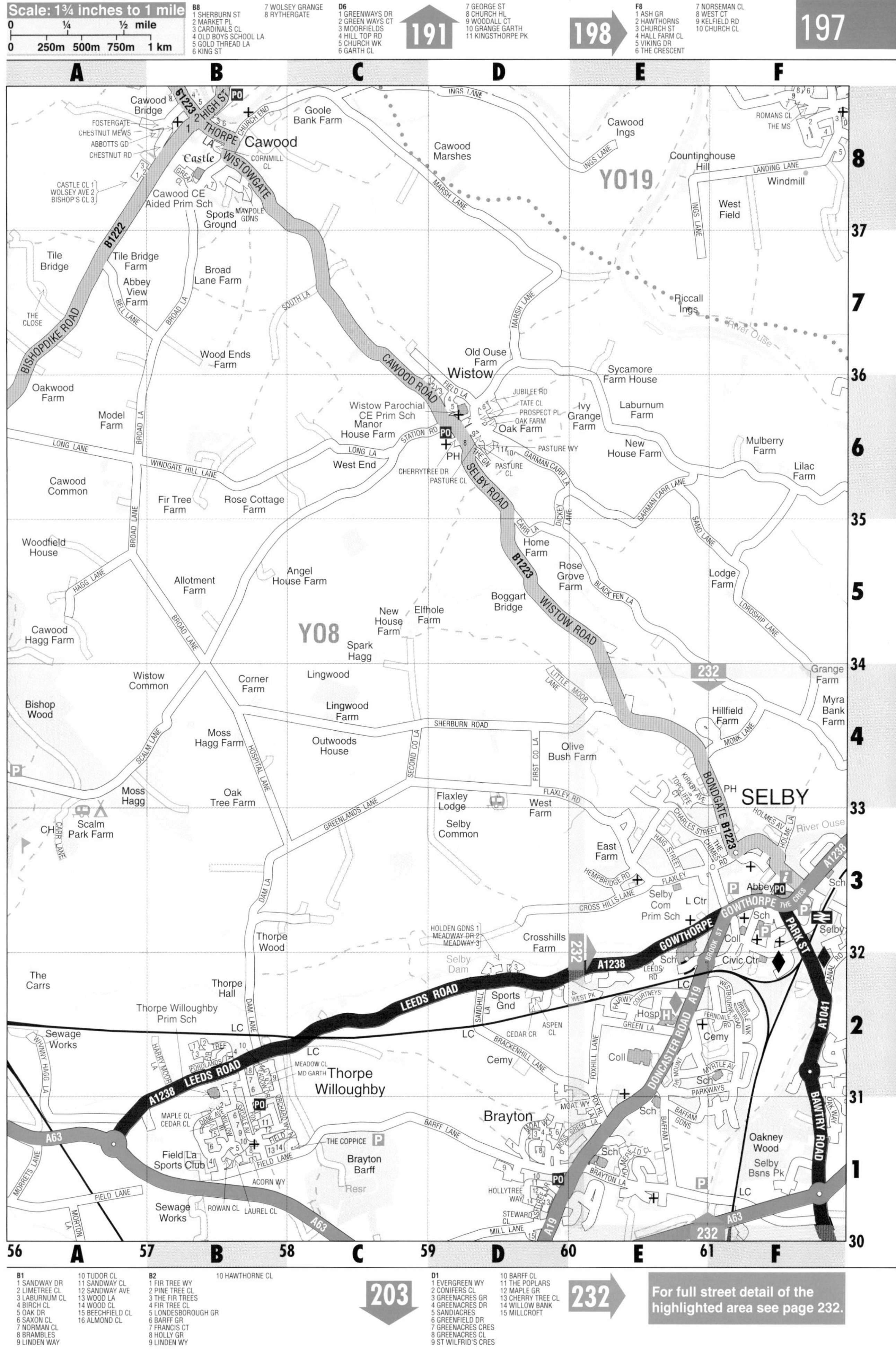

Scale: 1¾ inches to 1 mile
0 ¼ ½ mile
0 250m 500m 750m 1 km
B8
1 SHERBURN ST
2 MARKET PL
3 CARDINALS CL
4 OLD BOYS SCHOOL LA
5 GOLD THREAD LA
6 KING ST
7 WOLSEY GRANGE
8 RYTHERGATE
D6
1 GREENWAYS DR
2 GREEN WAYS CT
3 MOORFIELDS
4 HILL TOP RD
5 CHURCH WK
6 GARTH CL
191
7 GEORGE ST
8 CHURCH HL
9 WOODALL CT
10 GRANGE GARTH
11 KINGSTHORPE PK
198
F8
1 ASH GR
2 HAWTHORNS
3 CHURCH ST
4 HALL FARM CL
5 VIKING DR
6 THE CRESCENT
7 NORSEMAN CL
8 WEST CT
9 KELFIELD RD
10 CHURCH CL
197
Cawood Bridge
Cawood
Castle
Goole Bank Farm
Cawood Ings
Cawood Marshes
Countinghouse Hill
Windmill
West Field
YO19
Cawood CE Aided Prim Sch
Sports Ground
Tile Bridge
Tile Bridge Farm
Abbey View Farm
Broad Lane Farm
Riccall Ings
River Ouse
Wood Ends Farm
Old Ouse Farm
Wistow
Sycamore Farm House
Oakwood Farm
Model Farm
Wistow Parochial CE Prim Sch
Manor House Farm
Ivy Grange Farm
Laburnum Farm
Oak Farm
New House Farm
Mulberry Farm
Lilac Farm
West End
Cawood Common
Fir Tree Farm
Rose Cottage Farm
Woodfield House
Home Farm
Rose Grove Farm
Allotment Farm
Angel House Farm
Lodge Farm
Boggart Bridge
Cawood Hagg Farm
YO8
New House Farm
Elfhole Farm
Spark Hagg
Wistow Common
Corner Farm
Lingwood
Grange Farm
Bishop Wood
Lingwood Farm
Hillfield Farm
Myra Bank Farm
Moss Hagg Farm
Outwoods House
Olive Bush Farm
Moss Hagg
Oak Tree Farm
Flaxley Lodge
West Farm
SELBY
Scalm Park Farm
Selby Common
East Farm
Abbey
Selby Com Prim Sch
L Ctr
Crosshills Farm
Thorpe Wood
Selby Dam
Civic Ctr
The Carrs
Thorpe Hall
Sports Gnd
Hosp
Thorpe Willoughby Prim Sch
Cemy
Sewage Works
Coll
Thorpe Willoughby
Brayton
Oakney Wood
Field La Sports Club
Brayton Barff
Selby Bsns Pk
Resr
Sewage Works
B1222
B1223
A1238
A19
A1041
A63
BISHOPDIKE ROAD
CAWOOD ROAD
SELBY ROAD
WISTOW ROAD
BONDGATE
GOWTHORPE
LEEDS ROAD
DONCASTER ROAD
BAWTRY ROAD
PARK ST
SHERBURN ROAD
FLAXLEY RD
232
56 A 57 B 58 C 59 D 60 E 61 F
37 36 35 34 33 32 31 30
B1
1 SANDWAY DR
2 LIMETREE CL
3 LABURNUM CL
4 BIRCH CL
5 OAK DR
6 SAXON CL
7 NORMAN CL
8 BRAMBLES
9 LINDEN WAY
10 TUDOR CL
11 SANDWAY CL
12 SANDWAY AVE
13 WOOD LA
14 WOOD CL
15 BEECHFIELD CL
16 ALMOND CL
B2
1 FIR TREE WY
2 PINE TREE CL
3 THE FIR TREES
4 FIR TREE CL
5 LONDESBOROUGH GR
6 BARFF GR
7 FRANCIS CT
8 HOLLY GR
9 LINDEN WY
10 HAWTHORNE CL
203
D1
1 EVERGREEN WY
2 CONIFERS CL
3 GREENACRES GR
4 GREENACRES DR
5 SANDIACRES
6 GREENFIELD DR
7 GREENACRES CRES
8 GREENACRES CL
9 ST WILFRID'S CRES
10 BARFF CL
11 THE POPLARS
12 MAPLE GR
13 CHERRY TREE CL
14 WILLOW BANK
15 MILLCROFT
232
For full street detail of the highlighted area see page 232.

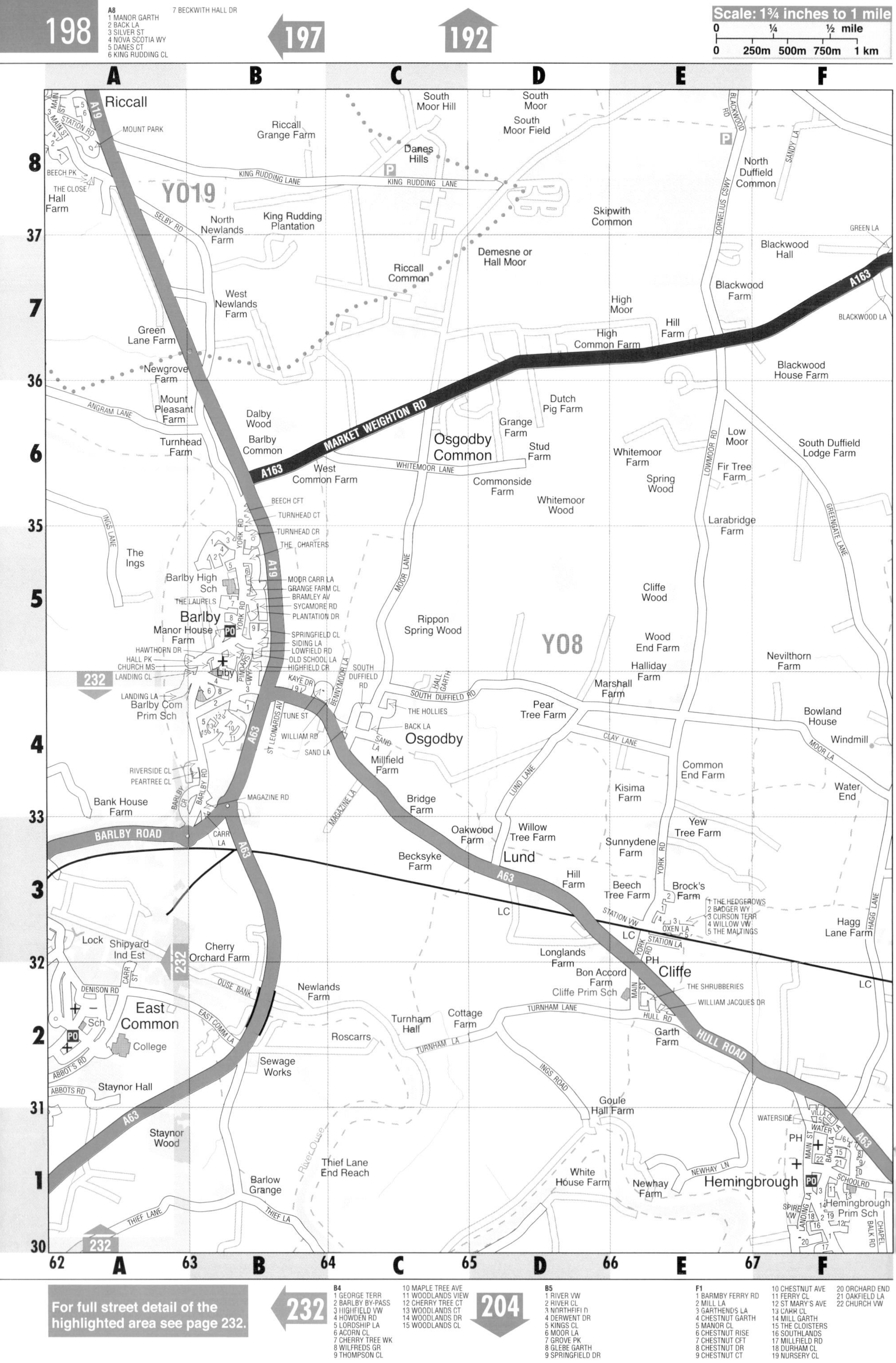

198

A8
1 MANOR GARTH
2 BACK LA
3 SILVER ST
4 NOVA SCOTIA WY
5 DANES CT
6 KING RUDDING CL

7 BECKWITH HALL DR

197

192

Scale: 1¾ inches to 1 mile

0   ¼   ½ mile
0   250m 500m 750m 1 km

Riccall
Y019

MOUNT PARK
BEECH PK
THE CLOSE
Hall Farm

Riccall Grange Farm

South Moor Hill
South Moor
South Moor Field

Danes Hills

North Duffield Common

KING RUDDING LANE
KING RUDDING LANE

North Newlands Farm

King Rudding Plantation

Skipwith Common

Blackwood Hall

GREEN LA

West Newlands Farm

Riccall Common

Demesne or Hall Moor

High Moor

Blackwood Farm

A163
BLACKWOOD LA

Green Lane Farm

Newgrove Farm

High Common Farm

Hill Farm

Blackwood House Farm

ANGRAM LANE

Mount Pleasant Farm

Dalby Wood

MARKET WEIGHTON RD

A163

Barlby Common

West Common Farm

WHITEMOOR LANE

Osgodby Common

Dutch Pig Farm

Grange Farm

Stud Farm

Low Moor

Fir Tree Farm

South Duffield Lodge Farm

Turnhead Farm

BEECH CFT
TURNHEAD CT
TURNHEAD CR
THE CHARTERS

Commonside Farm

Whitemoor Farm

Spring Wood

Larabridge Farm

The Ings

Barlby High Sch
THE LAURELS

MOOR CARR LA
GRANGE FARM CL
BRAMLEY AV
SYCAMORE RD
PLANTATION DR

Whitemoor Wood

Cliffe Wood

YO8

Barlby

Manor House Farm

HAWTHORN DR
HALL PK
CHURCH MS
HIGHFIELD CR
LANDING CL

SPRINGFIELD CL
SIDING LA
LOWFIELD RD
OLD SCHOOL LA
HIGHFIELD CR

Rippon Spring Wood

Wood End Farm

Nevilthorn Farm

232

Barlby Com Prim Sch

LANDING LA

KAYE DR

SOUTH DUFFIELD RD

SOUTH DUFFIELD RD

Halliday Farm

Marshall Farm

Bowland House

Windmill

RIVERSIDE CL
PEARTREE CL

TUNE ST
WILLIAM RD
BACK LA
SAND LA

Millfield Farm

Osgodby

THE HOLLIES

Pear Tree Farm

Common End Farm

Water End

Bank House Farm

MAGAZINE RD

Bridge Farm

CLAY LANE

Kisima Farm

Sunnydene Farm

Yew Tree Farm

BARLBY ROAD

CARR LA

A63

Becksyke Farm

Oakwood Farm

Willow Tree Farm

Lund

LUND LANE

Hill Farm

Beech Tree Farm

Brock's Farm

1 THE HEDGEROWS
2 BADGER WY
3 CURSON TERR
4 WILLOW VW
5 THE MALTINGS

Hagg Lane Farm

Lock

Shipyard Ind Est

232

Cherry Orchard Farm

Newlands Farm

DENISON RD

East Common

College

OUSE BANK

EAST COMM LA

Turnham Hall

Cottage Farm

TURNHAM LANE

LC

STATION VW

OXEN LA

STATION LA

Longlands Farm

Bon Accord Farm

Cliffe Prim Sch

PH

Cliffe

THE SHRUBBERIES

WILLIAM JACQUES DR

LC

Roscarrs

TURNHAM LA

Garth Farm

HULL ROAD

ABBOTS RD
ABBOTS RD

Staynor Hall

Sewage Works

INGS ROAD

Goule Hall Farm

WATERSIDE

A63

Staynor Wood

Barlow Grange

THIEF LANE END REACH

White House Farm

Newhay Farm

NEWHAY LN

Hemingbrough

Hemingbrough Prim Sch

THIEF LA

232

For full street detail of the highlighted area see page 232.

232

204

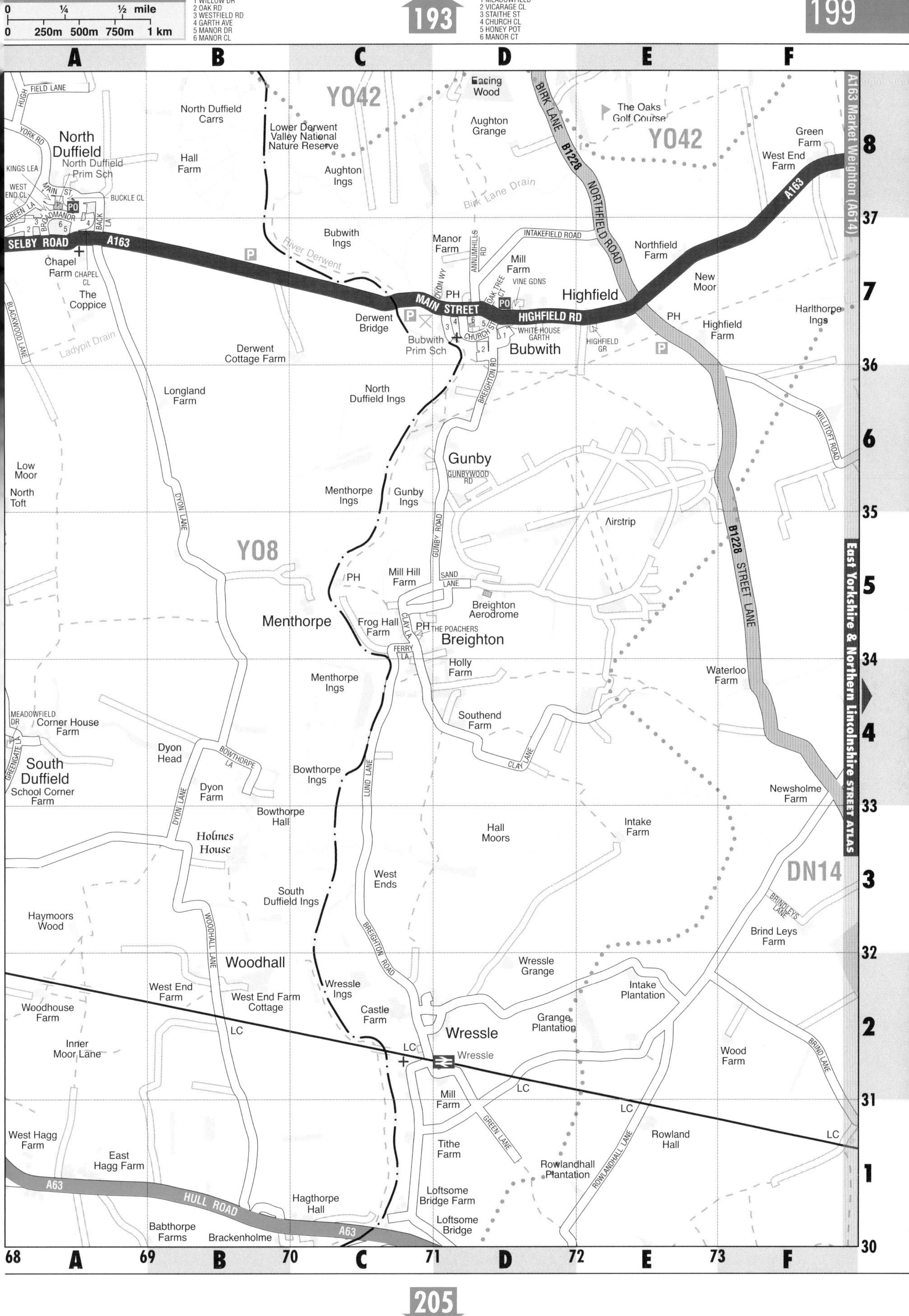

A7
1 WILLOW DR
2 OAK RD
3 WESTFIELD RD
4 GARTH AVE
5 MANOR DR
6 MANOR CL

193

D7
1 MEADOWFIELD
2 VICARAGE CL
3 STAITHE ST
4 CHURCH CL
5 HONEY POT
6 MANOR CT

199

A163 Market Weighton (A614)

East Yorkshire & Northern Lincolnshire STREET ATLAS

High Field Lane
York Rd
North Duffield
Kings Lea
North Duffield Prim Sch
Hall Farm
North Duffield Carrs
Lower Derwent Valley National Nature Reserve
YO42
Facing Wood
Aughton Grange
The Oaks Golf Course
Green Farm
West End Farm
Birk Lane
B1228
Northfield Road
YO42

West End Cl
Green La
Main St
PO
Back La
Buckle Cl
Selby Road
A163
Chapel Farm
Chapel Cl
The Coppice
Aughton Ings
Bubwith Ings
River Derwent
P
Derwent Bridge
Main Street
PH
Manor Farm
Mill Farm
Annumhill's Rd
Oak Tree Ct
Vine Gdns
Intakefield Road
Highfield
Northfield Farm
New Moor
A163
Harlthorpe Ings
Highfield Farm

Blackwood Lane
Ladypit Drain
Longland Farm
Derwent Cottage Farm
North Duffield Ings
Breighton Rd
Bubwith Prim Sch
PO
Church
White House Garth
Bubwith
Highfield Gr
P
PH
Highfield Rd
B1228

Low Moor
North Toft
Menthorpe Ings
Gunby Ings
Gunby
Gunbywood Rd
Airstrip
Williott Road

Dyon Lane
YO8
Menthorpe
PH
Mill Hill Farm
Sand Lane
Clay La
Frog Hall Farm
Breighton
Breighton Aerodrome
Street Lane

Ferry La
PH
The Poachers
Holly Farm
Waterloo Farm

Meadowfield Dr
Corner House Farm
Dyon Head
Bowthorpe La
Dyon Farm
Menthorpe Ings
Southend Farm
Newsholme Farm
DN14

South Duffield
School Corner Farm
Holmes House
Bowthorpe Hall
Bowthorpe Ings
Lind Lane
Clay Lane
Hall Moors
Intake Farm
Brindley's Lane
Brind Leys Farm

Haymoors Wood
Dyon Lane
Woodhall Lane
South Duffield Ings
West Ends
Brind Lane

West End Farm
Woodhall
West End Farm Cottage
LC
Wressle Ings
Breighton Road
Castle Farm
Wressle Grange
Intake Plantation

Woodhouse Farm
Inner Moor Lane
LC
Wressle
LC
Wressle
Grange Plantation
Wood Farm

West Hagg Farm
East Hagg Farm
Mill Farm
Green Lane
Tithe Farm
Rowlandhall Plantation
Rowlandhall Lane
Rowland Hall
LC

A63
Hull Road
Babthorpe Farms
Brackenholme
Hagthorpe Hall
A63
Loftsome Bridge Farm
Loftsome Bridge

Column letters: A 68 / 69 B / 70 C / 71 D / 72 E / 73 F

Row numbers: 8 37 7 36 6 35 5 34 4 33 3 32 2 31 1 30

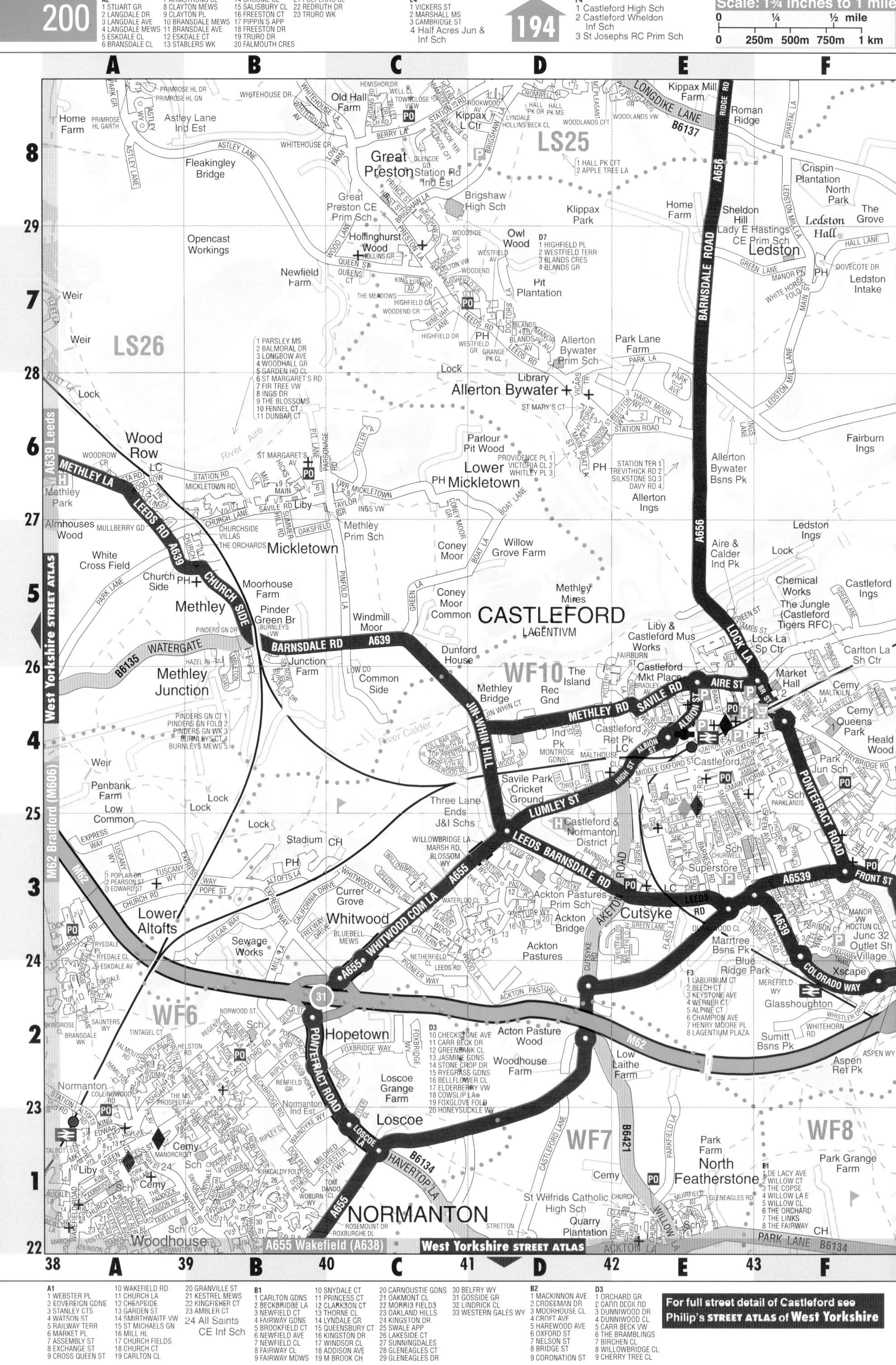

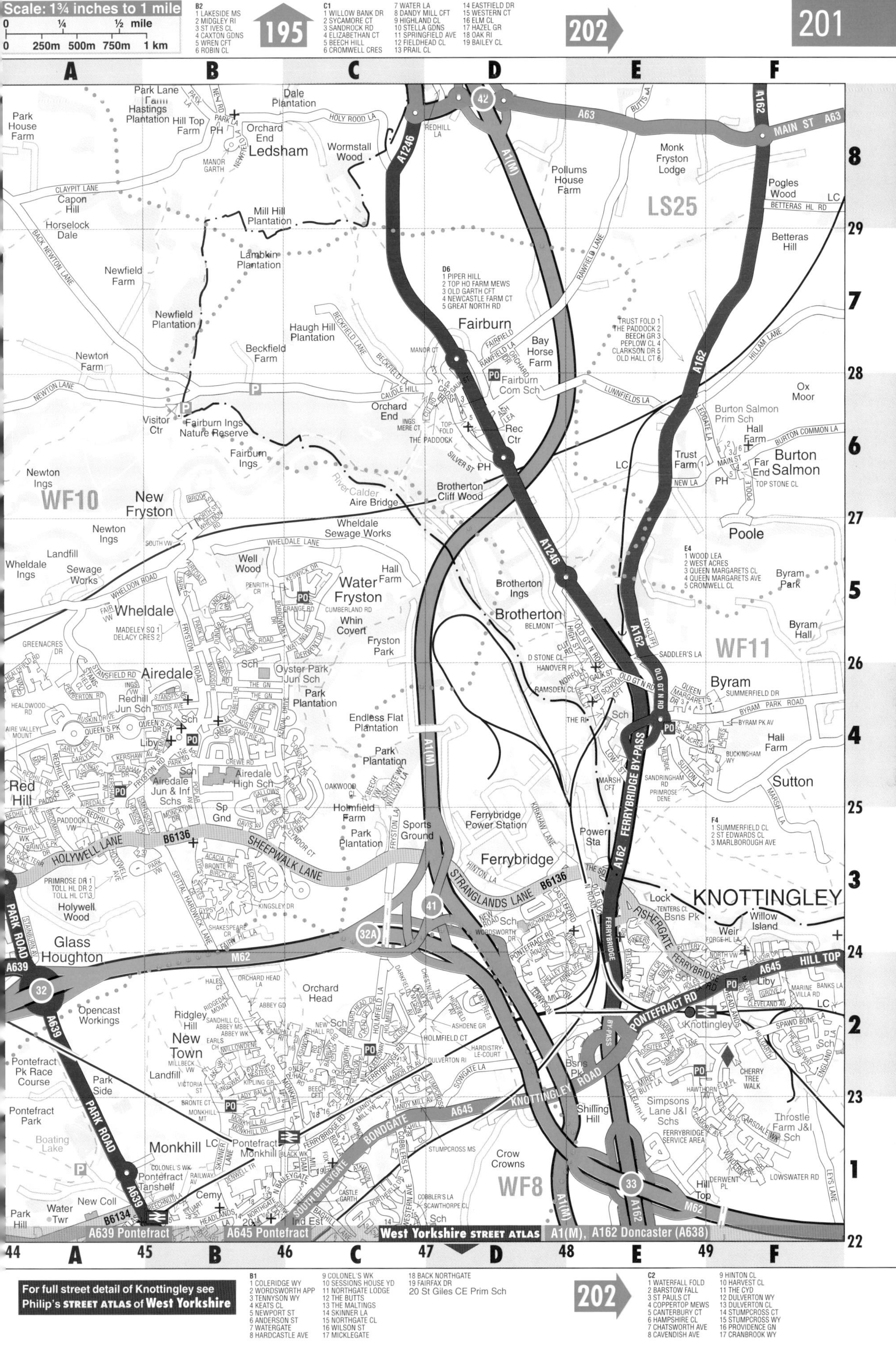

Scale: 1¾ inches to 1 mile
0 ¼ ½ mile
0 250m 500m 750m 1 km
B2
1 LAKESIDE MS
2 MIDGLEY RI
3 ST IVES CL
4 CAXTON GDNS
5 WREN CFT
6 ROBIN CL
195
C1
1 WILLOW BANK DR
2 SYCAMORE CT
3 SANDROCK RD
4 ELIZABETHAN CT
5 BEECH HILL
6 CROMWELL CRES
7 WATER LA
8 DANDY MILL CFT
9 HIGHLAND CL
10 STELLA GDNS
11 SPRINGFIELD AVE
12 FIELDHEAD CL
13 PRAIL CL
14 EASTFIELD DR
15 WESTERN CT
16 ELM CL
17 HAZEL GR
18 OAK RI
19 BAILEY CL
202
201
A B C D E F
Park House Farm
Park Lane Farm
Hastings Plantation
Hill Top Farm
Dale Plantation
Orchard End
Ledsham
Wormstall Wood
Capon Hill
Horselock Dale
Mill Hill Plantation
Lambkin Plantation
Newfield Farm
Newfield Plantation
Haugh Hill Plantation
Beckfield Farm
Newton Farm
Visitor Ctr
Fairburn Ings Nature Reserve
Fairburn Ings
Newton Ings
WF10
New Fryston
Newton Ings
Landfill
Wheldale Ings
Sewage Works
Wheldale
Well Wood
Water Fryston
Hall Farm
Whin Covert
Fryston Park
Airedale
Redhill Jun Sch
Oyster Park Jun Sch
Park Plantation
Endless Flat Plantation
Park Plantation
Red Hill
Airedale Jun & Inf Schs
Airedale High Sch
Sp Gnd
Holmfield Farm
Park Plantation
Sports Ground
HOLYWELL LANE
SHEEPWALK LANE
B6136
Holywell Wood
Glass Houghton
M62
Orchard Head
Ridgley Hill
New Town
Opencast Workings
Landfill
Pontefract Pk Race Course
Park Side
Pontefract Park
Boating Lake
Monkhill
Pontefract Monkhill
Pontefract Tanshelf
Cemy
New Coll
Water Twr
Park Hill
PARK ROAD
A639
B6134
BONDGATE
A645
KNOTTINGLEY ROAD
Crow Crowns
WF8
Shilling Hill
Bsns Pk
Simpsons Lane J&I Schs
Ferrybridge Service Area
Hill Top
Throstle Farm J&I Sch
Knottingley
KNOTTINGLEY
Willow Island
Lock
Weir
HILL TOP
PONTEFRACT RD
FERRYBRIDGE BY-PASS
Ferrybridge
Ferrybridge Power Station
Power Sta
STRANGLANDS LANE
Brotherton
Brotherton Ings
Brotherton Cliff Wood
Aire Bridge
Wheldale Sewage Works
River Calder
Fairburn
Fairburn Com Sch
Bay Horse Farm
Orchard End
Rec Ctr
Pollums House Farm
Monk Fryston Lodge
LS25
Pogles Wood
Betteras Hill
A63
MAIN ST
A1246
A1(M)
A162
D6
1 PIPER HILL
2 TOP HO FARM MEWS
3 OLD GARTH CFT
4 NEWCASTLE FARM CT
5 GREAT NORTH RD
TRUST FOLD 1
THE PADDOCK 2
BEECH GR 3
PEPLOW CL 4
CLARKSON DR 5
OLD HALL CT 6
Ox Moor
Burton Salmon Prim Sch
Hall Farm
Trust Farm
Far End
Burton Salmon
Poole
E4
1 WOOD LEA
2 WEST ACRES
3 QUEEN MARGARETS CL
4 QUEEN MARGARETS AVE
5 CROMWELL CL
Byram Park
Byram Hall
WF11
Byram
Hall Farm
Sutton
F4
1 SUMMERFIELD CL
2 ST EDWARDS CL
3 MARLBOROUGH AVE
A639 Pontefract
A645 Pontefract
West Yorkshire STREET ATLAS
A1(M), A162 Doncaster (A638)
44 45 46 47 48 49
22 23 24 25 26 27 28 29
1 2 3 4 5 6 7 8
For full street detail of Knottingley see Philip's STREET ATLAS of West Yorkshire
B1
1 COLERIDGE WY
2 WORDSWORTH APP
3 TENNYSON WY
4 KEATS CL
5 NEWPORT ST
6 ANDERSON ST
7 WATERGATE
8 HARDCASTLE AVE
9 COLONEL'S WK
10 SESSIONS HOUSE YD
11 NORTHGATE LODGE
12 THE BUTTS
13 THE MALTINGS
14 SKINNER LA
15 NORTHGATE CL
16 WILSON ST
17 MICKLEGATE
18 BACK NORTHGATE
19 FAIRFAX DR
20 St Giles CE Prim Sch
202
C2
1 WATERFALL FOLD
2 BARSTOW FALL
3 ST PAULS CT
4 COPPERTOP MEWS
5 CANTERBURY CT
6 HAMPSHIRE CL
7 CHATSWORTH AVE
8 CAVENDISH AVE
9 HINTON CL
10 HARVEST CL
11 THE CYD
12 DULVERTON WY
13 DULVERTON CL
14 STUMPCROSS CT
15 STUMPCROSS WY
16 PROVIDENCE GN
17 CRANBROOK WY

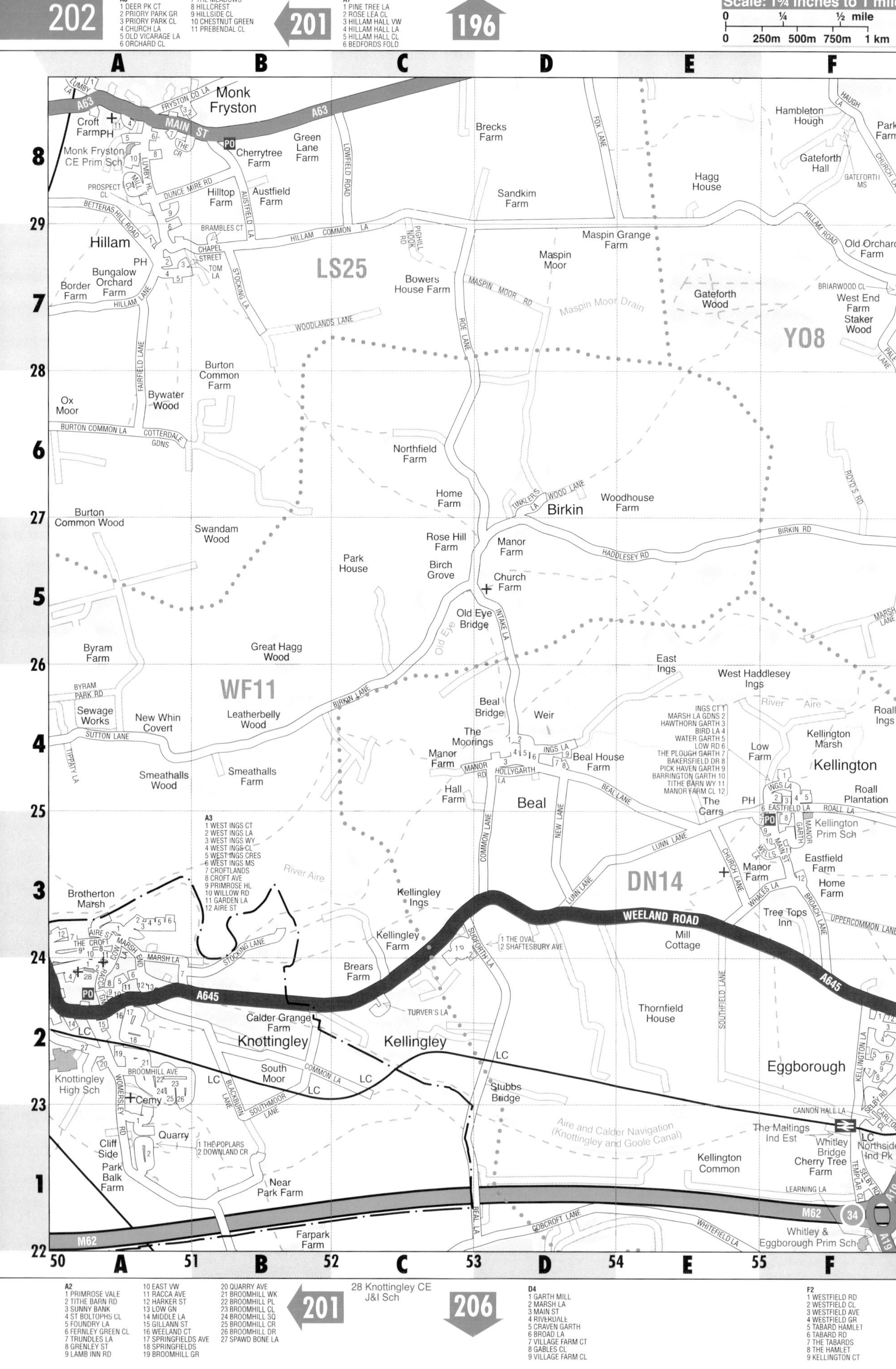

A8
1 DEER PK CT
2 PRIORY PARK GR
3 PRIORY PARK CL
4 CHURCH LA
5 OLD VICARAGE LA
6 ORCHARD CL

7 THE MEADOWS
8 HILLCREST
9 HILLSIDE CL
10 CHESTNUT GREEN
11 PREBENDAL CL

A7
1 PINE TREE LA
2 ROSE LEA CL
3 HILLAM HALL VW
4 HILLAM HALL LA
5 HILLAM HALL CL
6 BEDFORDS FOLD

201

196

Scale: 1¾ inches to 1 mile

0   ¼   ½ mile
0   250m 500m 750m 1 km

A2
1 PRIMROSE VALE
2 TITHE BARN RD
3 SUNNY BANK
4 ST BOLTOPHS CL
5 FOUNDRY LA
6 FERNLEY GREEN CL
7 TRUNDLES LA
8 GRENLEY ST
9 LAMB INN RD

10 EAST VW
11 RACCA AVE
12 HARKER ST
13 LOW GN
14 MIDDLE LA
15 GILLANN ST
16 WEELAND CT
17 SPRINGFIELDS AVE
18 SPRINGFIELDS
19 BROOMHILL GR

20 QUARRY AVE
21 BROOMHILL WK
22 BROOMHILL PL
23 BROOMHILL RD
24 BROOMHILL SQ
25 BROOMHILL CR
26 BROOMHILL DR
27 SPAWD BONE LA

28 Knottingley CE
J&I Sch

201

206

D4
1 GARTH MILL
2 MARSH LA
3 MAIN ST
4 RIVERDALE
5 CRAVEN GARTH
6 BROAD LA
7 VILLAGE FARM CT
8 GABLES CL
9 VILLAGE FARM CL

F2
1 WESTFIELD RD
2 WESTFIELD CL
3 WESTFIELD GR
4 WESTFIELD AVE
5 TABARD HAMLET
6 TABARD RD
7 THE TABARDS
8 THE HAMLET
9 KELLINGTON CT

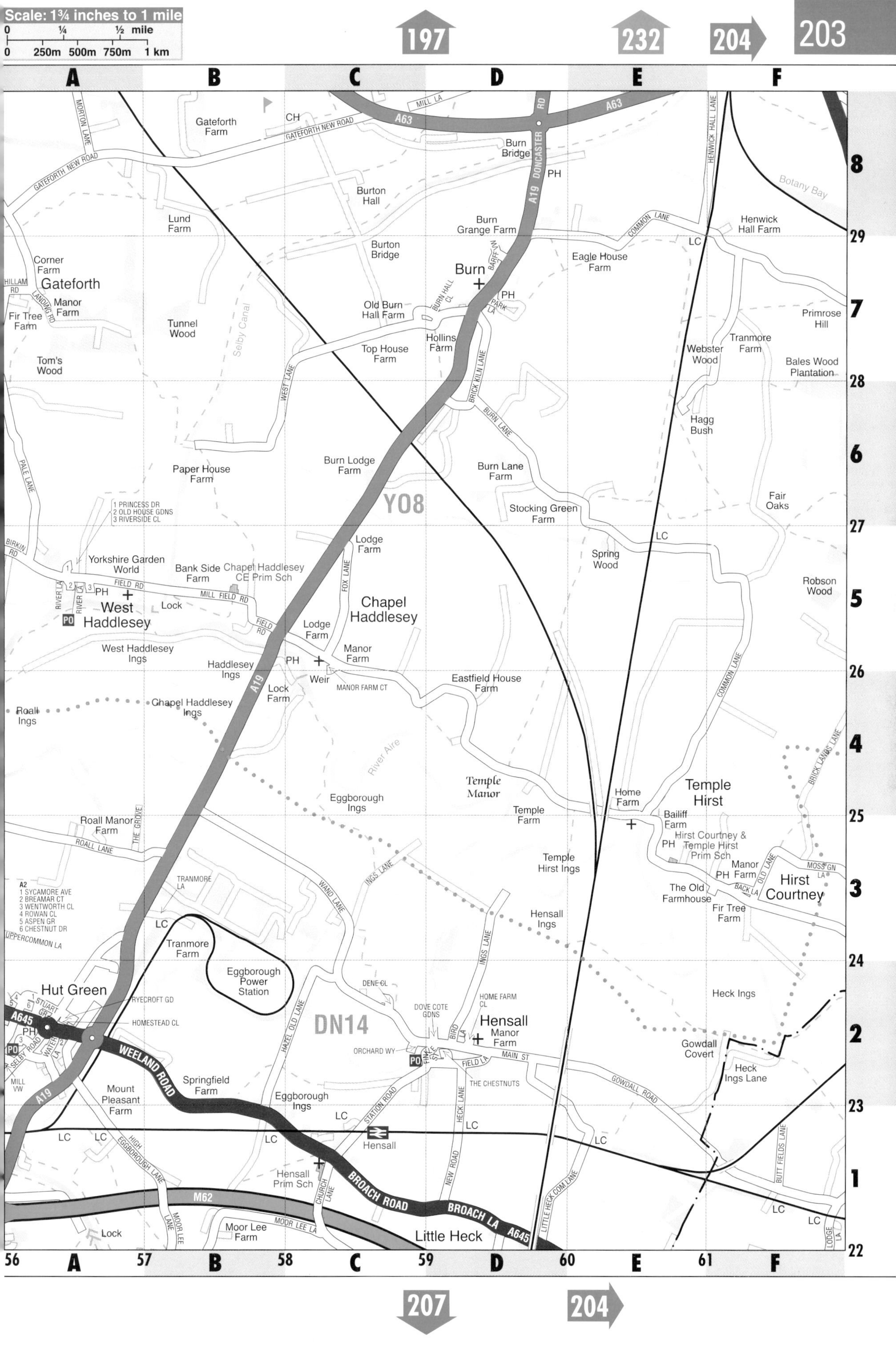
Scale: 1¾ inches to 1 mile
197
232
204
A B C D E F
Gateforth Farm
CH
Gateforth New Road
A63
Mill La
Burn Bridge
Doncaster Rd
A19
PH
Burton Hall
Lund Farm
Burn Grange Farm
Common Lane
Henwick Hall Farm
Henwick Hall Lane
Botany Bay
LC
Corner Farm
Gateforth
Burton Bridge
Burn
Eagle House Farm
Manor Farm
Fir Tree Farm
Tunnel Wood
Selby Canal
Old Burn Hall Farm
Burn Hall Cl
Park La
Primrose Hill
Tom's Wood
Top House Farm
Hollins Farm
Webster Wood
Tranmore Farm
Bales Wood Plantation
West Lane
Brick Kiln Lane
Burn Lane
Hagg Bush
Paper House Farm
Burn Lodge Farm
Burn Lane Farm
Pale Lane
YO8
Stocking Green Farm
Fair Oaks
1 Princess Dr
2 Old House Gdns
3 Riverside Cl
Yorkshire Garden World
Lodge Farm
Spring Wood
Bank Side Farm
Chapel Haddlesey CE Prim Sch
Fox Lane
Chapel Haddlesey
Robson Wood
Field Rd
Mill Field Rd
PH
West Haddlesey
Lock
PO
Lodge Farm
Manor Farm
West Haddlesey Ings
Haddlesey Ings
Weir
Manor Farm Ct
Eastfield House Farm
Common Lane
Lock Farm
Roall Ings
Chapel Haddlesey Ings
River Aire
Brick Lands Lane
Temple Manor
Eggborough Ings
Home Farm
Temple Hirst
Temple Farm
Bailiff Farm
Roall Manor Farm
The Grove
Roall Lane
Hirst Courtney & Temple Hirst Prim Sch
Temple Hirst Ings
Manor Farm
Old Lane
Moss Gn
Ings Lane
Wand Lane
Tranmore La
Back La
The Old Farmhouse
Hirst Courtney
A2
1 Sycamore Ave
2 Breamar Ct
3 Wentworth Cl
4 Rowan Cl
5 Aspen Gr
6 Chestnut Dr
Fir Tree Farm
Hensall Ings
Uppercommon La
Tranmore Farm
Ings Lane
Eggborough Power Station
Hut Green
Stuart Gr
Ryecroft Gd
Dene Cl
Home Farm Cl
Heck Ings
A645
Homestead Cl
Dove Cote Gdns
DN14
Hensall
Manor Farm
Hazel Old Lane
Bird La
Selby Road
Water La
Weeland Road
Orchard Wy
Main St
Field La
Gowdall Covert
Heck Ings Lane
Mill Vw
Mount Pleasant Farm
Springfield Farm
The Chestnuts
Gowdall Road
Eggborough Ings
Station Road
Heck Lane
High Eggborough Lane
Hensall
New Road
Butt Fields Lane
Hensall Prim Sch
Church Lane
Broach Road
Broach La
Little Heck Com Lane
M62
Moor Lee Lane
Moor Lee Farm
Moor Lee La
Little Heck
Lock
Lodge La
56 57 58 59 60 61
8 29 7 28 6 27 5 26 4 25 3 24 2 23 1 22
207
204

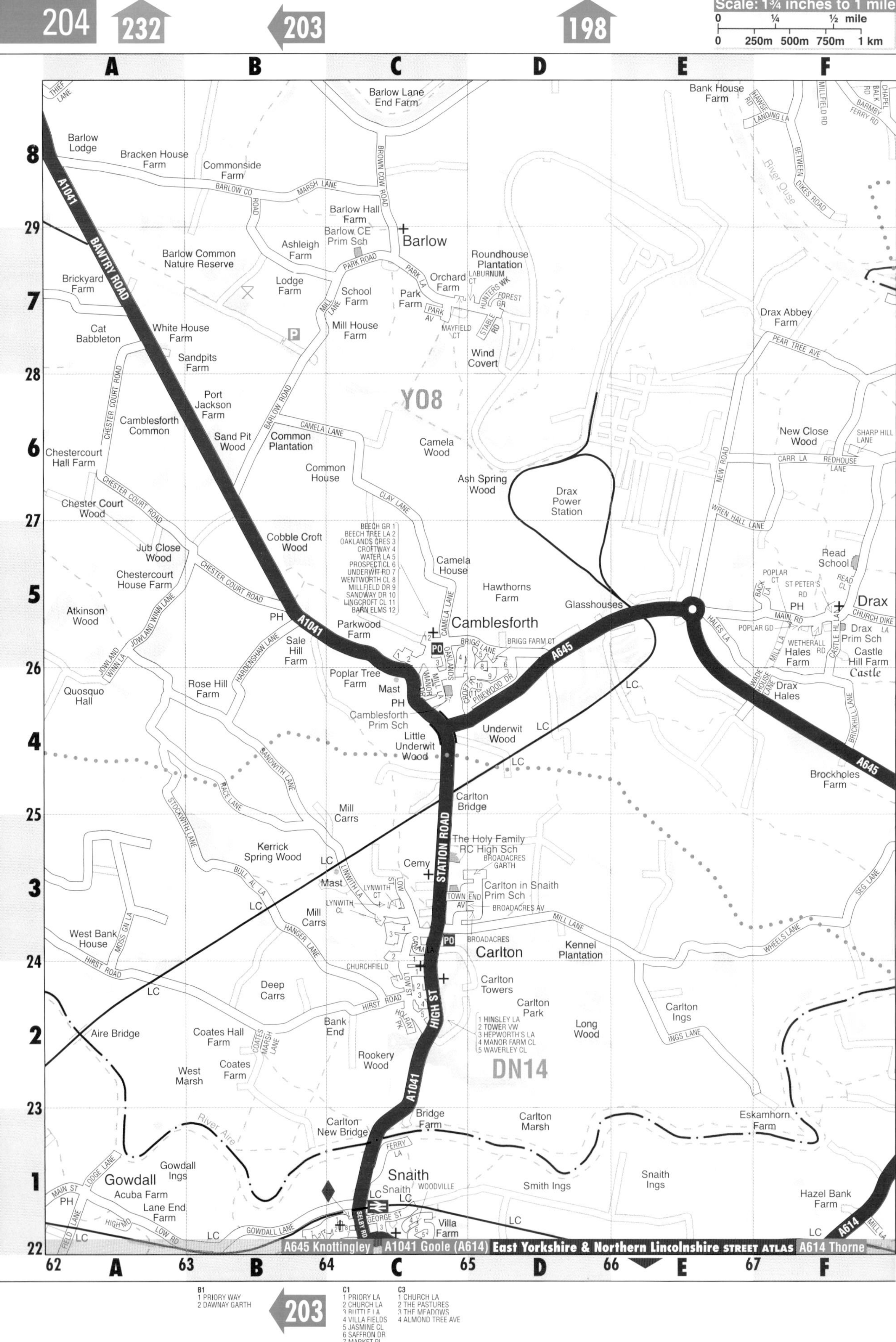

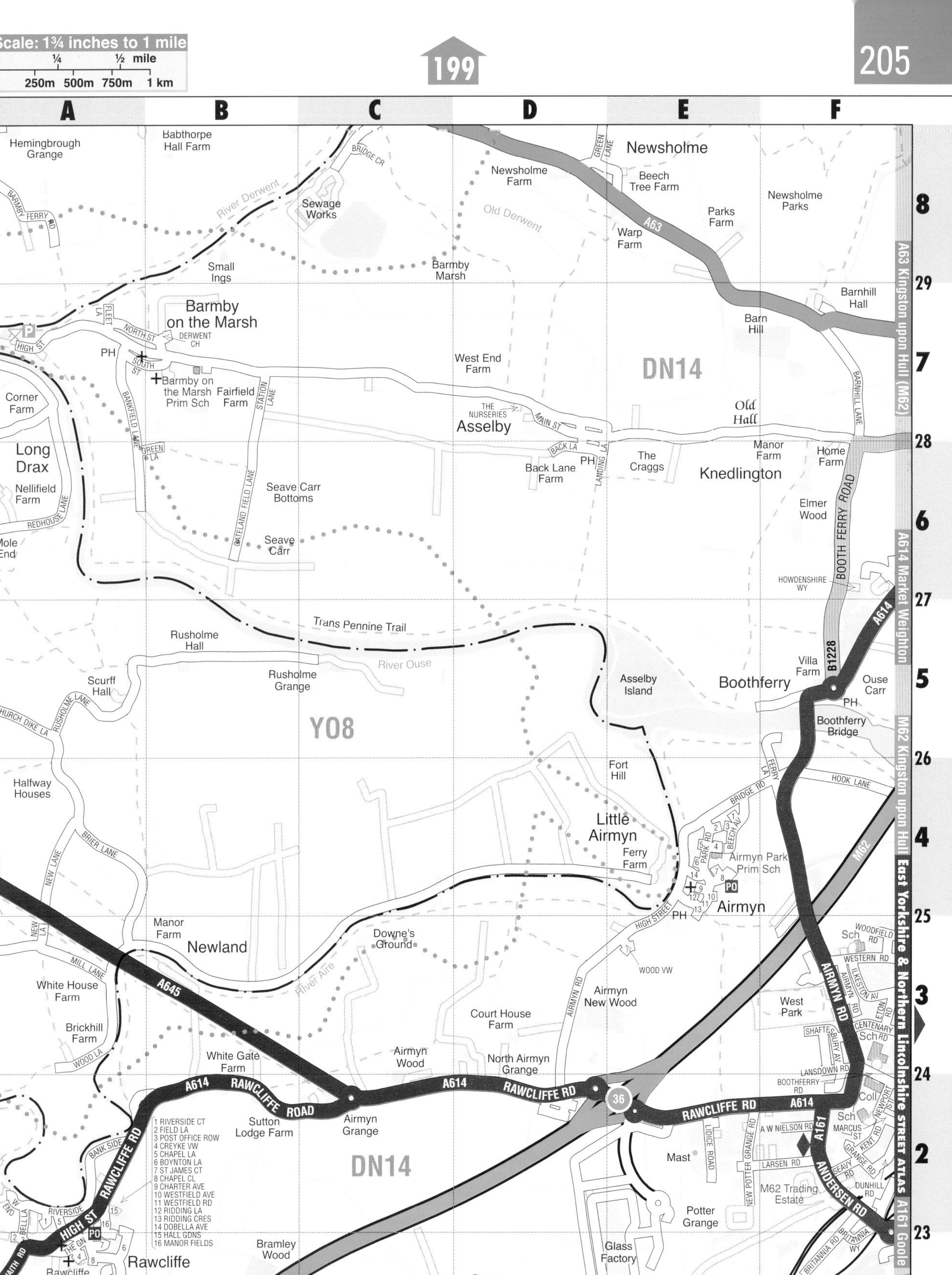

Hemingbrough Grange

Babthorpe Hall Farm

BRIDGE CR

Newsholme

Newsholme Farm

Beech Tree Farm

GREEN LANE

Parks Farm

Newsholme Parks

Warp Farm

A63

8

River Derwent

Sewage Works

Old Derwent

Barnby Marsh

Small Ings

Barnhill Hall

29

Barmby on the Marsh

DERWENT CH

FLEET LA

NORTH ST

West End Farm

DN14

Barn Hill

BARNHILL LANE

A63 Kingston upon Hull (M62)

PH

Corner Farm

SOUTH ST

Barmby on the Marsh Prim Sch

Fairfield Farm

STATION LANE

THE NURSERIES

Asselby

Old Hall

7

GREEN LA

Long Drax

Nellifield Farm

BANKFIELD LANE

MAIN ST

BACK LA

LANDING LA

Manor Farm

Home Farm

28

A614 Market Weighton

OATFIELD FIELD LANE

Seave Carr Bottoms

Back Lane Farm

PH

The Craggs

Knedlington

Elmer Wood

BOOTH FERRY ROAD

REDHOUSE LANE

Mole End

Seave Carr

HOWDENSHIRE WY

6

A614

27

CHURCH DIKE LA

RUSHOLME LANE

Rusholme Hall

Trans Pennine Trail

Villa Farm

B1228

Ouse Carr

M62 Kingston upon Hull East Yorkshire & Northern Lincolnshire STREET ATLAS

Scurff Hall

Rusholme Grange

River Ouse

Asselby Island

Boothferry

PH

5

YO8

Halfway Houses

Fort Hill

Boothferry Bridge

HOOK LANE

26

BRIER LANE

Little Airmyn

FERRY RD

BRIDGE RD

PARK AV

BEECH AV

25

NEW LA

Manor Farm

Ferry Farm

Airmyn Park Prim Sch

PO

PH

Airmyn

WOODFIELD RD

WESTERN AV

 ELM TREE AV

Sch

4

A161 Goole

NEW LANE

MILL LANE

Newland

River Aire

Downe's Ground

HIGH STREET

WOOD VW

PH

West Park

AIRMYN RD

ILKESTON RD

CENTENARY

Sch

SHAFTE

BURY AV

3

A645

White House Farm

Airmyn New Wood

Airmyn Wood

Court House Farm

AIRMYN RD

LANSDOWN RD

BOOTHFERRY RD

NEWPORT

Coll

24

Brickhill Farm

WOOD LA

White Gate Farm

A614

RAWCLIFFE RD

36

RAWCLIFFE RD

A614

Sch

MARCUS ST

KENT RD

DUNHILL RD

A161

2

BANK SIDE

RAWCLIFFE RD

HIGH ST

Sutton Lodge Farm

Airmyn Grange

North Airmyn Grange

NEW POTTER GRANGE RD

LODGE ROAD

A W NIELSON RD

GRANGE RD

BEAVER

DN14

Mast

LARSEN RD

BRITANNIA RD

RAVINIA WY

23

SWAITH RD

RIVERSIDE

THE GN

PO

15

1 RIVERSIDE CT
2 FIELD LA
3 POST OFFICE ROW
4 CREYKE VW
5 CHAPEL LA
6 BOYNTON LA
7 ST JAMES CT
8 CHAPEL CL
9 CHARTER AVE
10 WESTFIELD AVE
11 WESTFIELD RD
12 RIDDING LA
13 RIDDING CRES
14 DOBELLA AVE
15 HALL GDNS
16 MANOR FIELDS

Bramley Wood

M62 Trading Estate

Potter Grange

The Yorkshire Waterways Mus

1

Rawcliffe Prim Sch

Rawcliffe

STATION ROAD

Glass Factory

HOOK PASTURE LANE

WESTFIELD CL

Field House Farm

Soiling Farm

DOBELLA LANE

Dobeller Wood

M62

Rawcliffe Pastures

Percy Lodge

Aire and Calder Navigation

South Airmyn Grange

22

E4
1 BEECH GR
2 CHESTNUT AVE
3 BEECH AVE
4 PERCY DR
5 HALL CL
6 PARK CL
7 COURTS CL
8 WOODLAND WY
9 ST DAVID'S VW
10 PARSONS CL
11 PARSON'S WK
12 CHURCH VW
13 THE CROSSINGS
14 THE PADDOCK

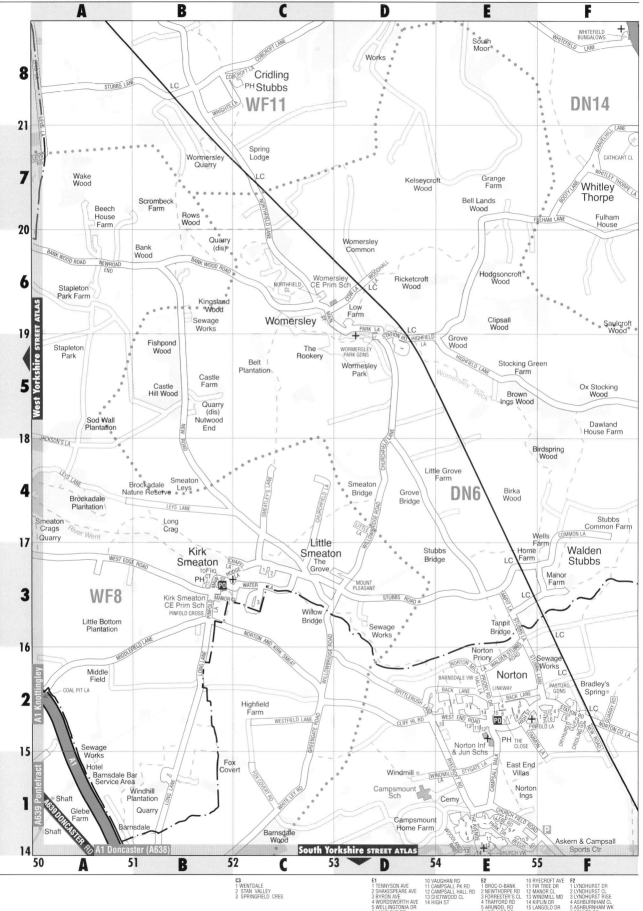

West Yorkshire STREET ATLAS

South Yorkshire STREET ATLAS

C3
1 WENTDALE
2 STAN VALLEY
3 SPRINGFIELD CRES

E1
1 TENNYSON AVE
2 SHAKESPEARE AVE
3 BYRON AVE
4 WORDSWORTH AVE
5 WELLINGTONIA DR
6 LANGLEYS RD
7 EAST VW
8 GRANGE RD
9 WILLOW RD
10 VAUGHAN RD
11 CAMPSALL PK RD
12 CAMPSALL HALL RD
13 SHELWOOD CL
14 HIGH ST

E2
1 BROC-O-BANK
2 NEWTHORPE RD
3 FORRESTER'S CL
4 TRAFFORD RD
5 ARUNDEL RD
6 ADELAIDE RD
7 HEADINGLEY RD
8 ORCHARD DR
9 ORCHARD CL
10 RYECROFT AVE
11 FIR TREE DR
12 MANOR CL
13 WINDMILL MD
14 KIPLIN DR
15 LANGOLD DR

F2
1 LYNDHURST DR
2 LYNDHURST CL
3 LYNDHURST RISE
4 ASHBURNHAM CL
5 ASHBURNHAM WK
6 DENVER RD
7 MANOR GARTH
8 SWAN SYKE DR
9 DRYHURST CL

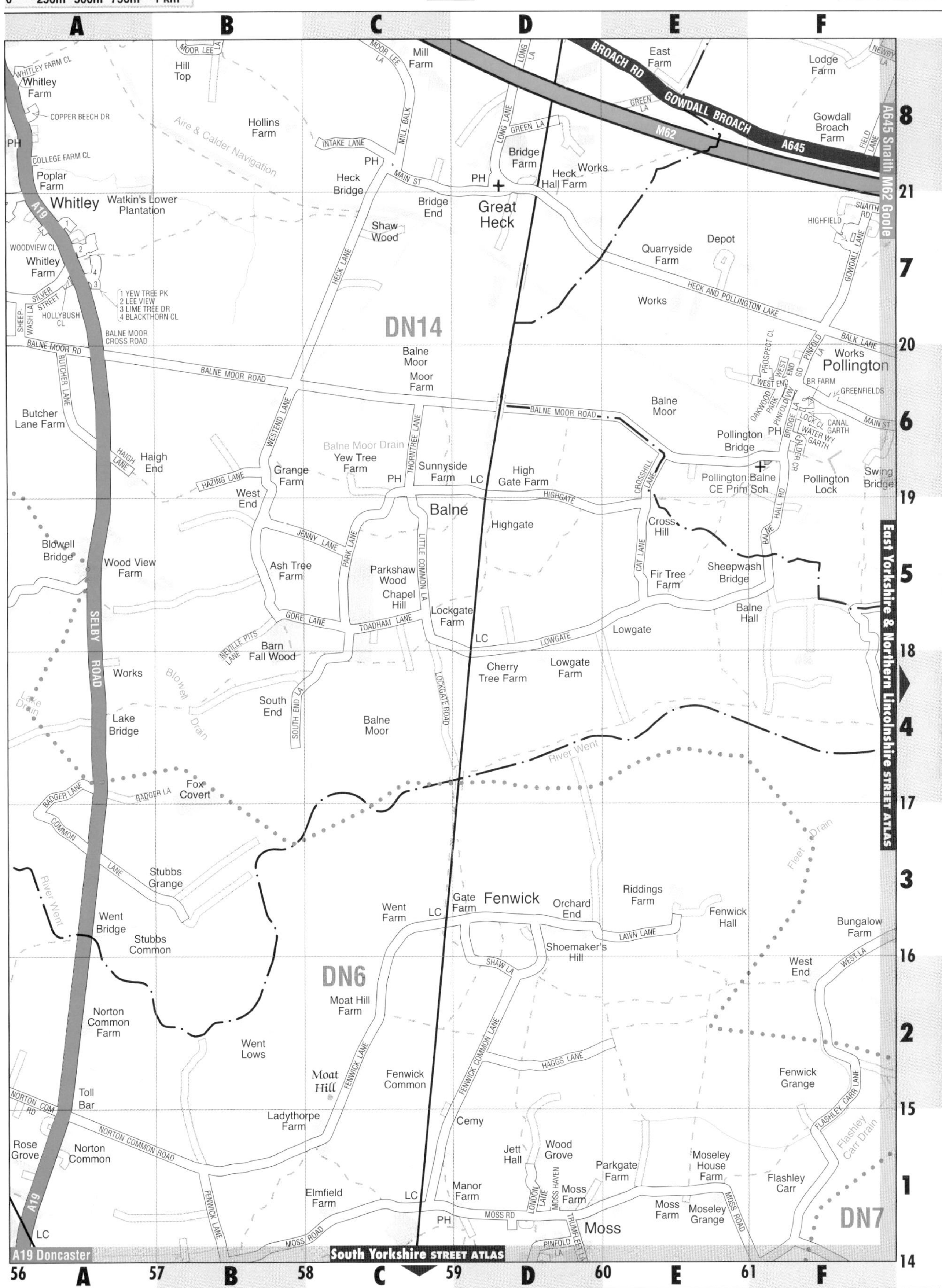

0   ¼   ½ mile
0 250m 500m 750m 1 km

A B C D E F

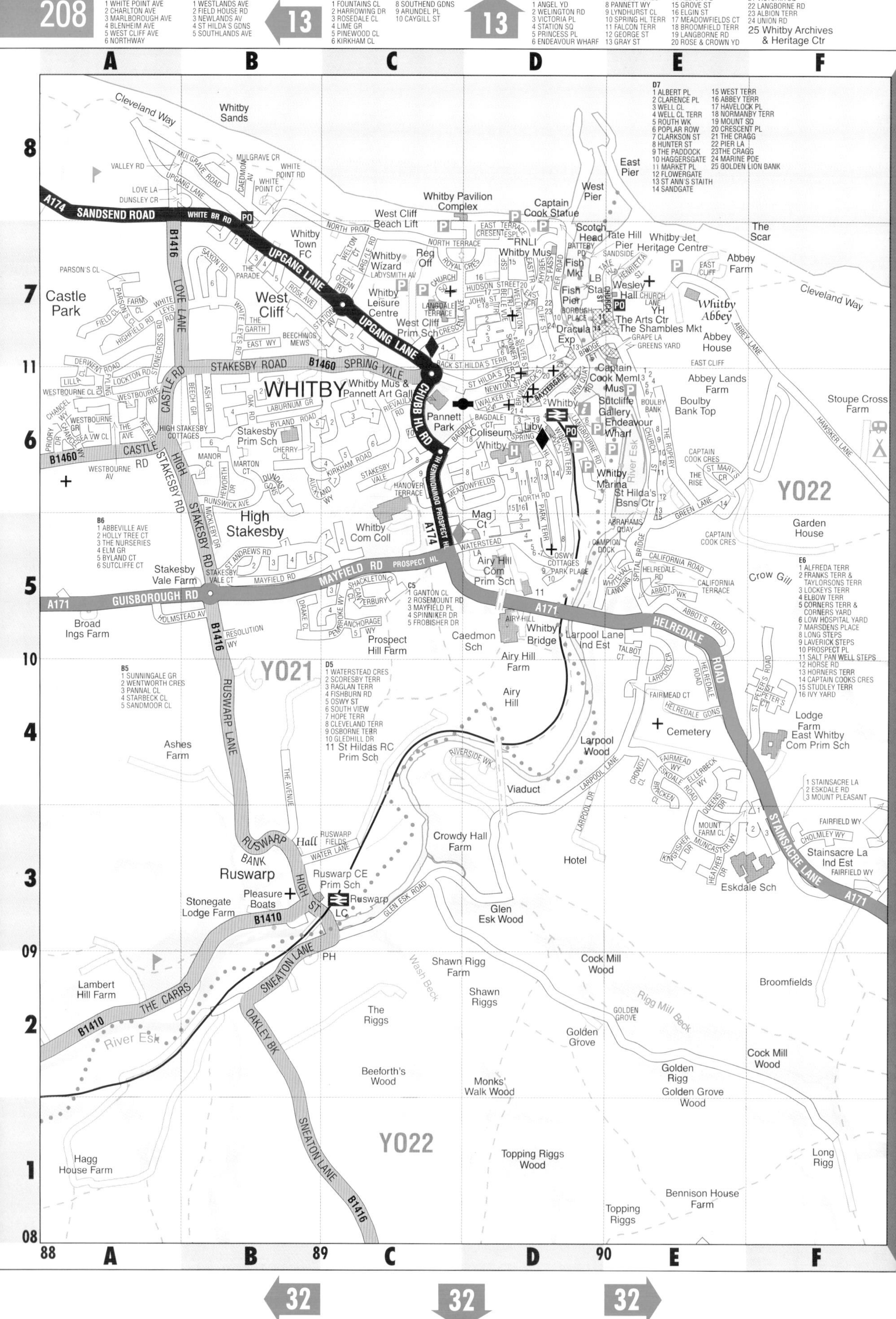
B7
1 WHITE POINT AVE
2 CHARLTON AVE
3 MARLBOROUGH AVE
4 BLENHEIM AVE
5 WEST CLIFF AVE
6 NORTHWAY
C7
1 WESTLANDS AVE
2 FIELD HOUSE RD
3 NEWLANDS AV
4 ST HILDA'S GDNS
5 SOUTHLANDS AVE
13
C6
1 FOUNTAINS CL
2 HARROWING DR
3 ROSEDALE CL
4 LIME GR
5 PINEWOOD CL
6 KIRKHAM CL
7 AUCKLAND WY
8 SOUTHEND GDNS
9 ARUNDEL PL
10 CAYGILL ST
13
D6
1 ANGEL YD
2 WELINGTON RD
3 VICTORIA PL
4 STATION SQ
5 PRINCESS PL
6 ENDEAVOUR WHARF
7 WINDSOR CRES
8 PANNETT WY
9 LYNDHURST CL
10 SPRING HL TERR
11 FALCON TERR
12 GEORGE ST
13 GRAY ST
14 ALBION PL
15 GROVE ST
16 ELGIN ST
17 MEADOWFIELDS CT
18 BROOMFIELD TERR
19 LANGBORNE RD
20 ROSE & CROWN YD
21 VICTORIA SQ
22 LANGBORNE RD
23 ALBION TERR
24 UNION RD
25 Whitby Archives & Heritage Ctr
A
B
C
D
E
F
D7
1 ALBERT PL
2 CLARENCE PL
3 WELL CL
4 WELL CL TERR
5 ROUTH WK
6 POPLAR ROW
7 CLARKSON ST
8 HUNTER ST
9 THE PADDOCK
10 HAGGERSGATE
11 MARKET PL
12 FLOWERGATE
13 ST ANN'S STAITH
14 SANDGATE
15 WEST TERR
16 ABBEY TERR
17 HAVELOCK PL
18 NORMANBY TERR
19 MOUNT SQ
20 CRESCENT PL
21 THE CRAGG
22 PIER LA
23 THE CRAGG
24 MARINE PDE
25 GOLDEN LION BANK
Cleveland Way
Whitby Sands
East Pier
West Pier
Whitby Pavilion Complex
Captain Cook Statue
West Cliff Beach Lift
Scotch Head
Tate Hill Pier
Whitby Jet Heritage Centre
The Scar
Abbey Farm
Whitby Town FC
Whitby Wizard
Reg Off
Whitby Mus
RNLI
Fish Mkt
Wesley Hall
YH
Whitby Abbey
Castle Park
West Cliff
Whitby Leisure Centre
West Cliff Prim Sch
Fish Pier
Dracula Exp
The Arts Ctr
The Shambles Mkt
Abbey House
A174 SANDSEND ROAD
UPGANG LANE
B1416
LOVE LANE
STAKESBY ROAD
B1460 SPRING VALE
WHITBY
Whitby Mus & Pannett Art Gall
Captain Cook Meml Mus
Abbey Lands Farm
Sutcliffe Gallery
Endeavour Wharf
Boulby Bank Top
Stoupe Cross Farm
Pannett Park
Coliseum
Stakesby Prim Sch
Whitby Marina
St Hilda's Bsns Ctr
River Esk
B1460 CASTLE RD
CHUBB HL RD
HIGH STAKESBY RD
YO22
High Stakesby
Whitby Com Coll
Mag Ct
Garden House
B6
1 ABBEVILLE AVE
2 HOLLY TREE CT
3 THE NURSERIES
4 ELM GR
5 BYLAND CT
6 SUTCLIFFE CT
Stakesby Vale Farm
Airy Hill Com Prim Sch
E6
1 ALFREDA TERR
2 FRANKS TERR & TAYLORSONS TERR
3 LOCKEYS TERR
4 ELBOW TERR
5 CORNERS TERR & CORNERS YARD
6 LOW HOSPITAL YARD
7 MARSDENS PLACE
8 LONG STEPS
9 LAVERICK STEPS
10 PROSPECT PL
11 SALT PAN WELL STEPS
12 HORSE RD
13 HORNERS TERR
14 CAPTAIN COOKS CRES
15 STUDLEY TERR
16 IVY YARD
A171 GUISBOROUGH RD
MAYFIELD RD
C5
1 GANTON CL
2 ROSEMOUNT RD
3 MAYFIELD PL
4 SPINNIKER DR
5 FROBISHER DR
Broad Ings Farm
Prospect Hill Farm
Caedmon Sch
Whitby Bridge
Larpool Lane Ind Est
A171
HELREDALE ROAD
Crow Gill
B5
1 SUNNINGALE GR
2 WENTWORTH CRES
3 PANNAL CL
4 STARBECK CL
5 SANDMOOR CL
YO21
D5
1 WATERSTEAD CRES
2 SCORESBY TERR
3 RAGLAN TERR
4 FISHBURN RD
5 OSWY ST
6 SOUTH VIEW
7 HOPE TERR
8 CLEVELAND TERR
9 OSBORNE TERR
10 GLEDHILL DR
11 St Hildas RC Prim Sch
Airy Hill Farm
Airy Hill
Cemetery
Lodge Farm
East Whitby Com Prim Sch
Ashes Farm
Larpool Wood
RUSWARP LANE
Viaduct
1 STAINSACRE LA
2 ESKDALE RD
3 MOUNT PLEASANT
Crowdy Hall Farm
Hotel
Stainsacre La Ind Est
STAINSACRE LANE
Ruswarp Hall
Ruswarp
Ruswarp CE Prim Sch
Eskdale Sch
Stonegate Lodge Farm
Pleasure Boats
B1410
Glen Esk Wood
PH
Shawn Rigg Farm
Cock Mill Wood
Lambert Hill Farm
Broomfields
Shawn Riggs
THE CARRS
SNEATON LANE
OAKLEY BK
The Riggs
Golden Grove
Rigg Mill Beck
River Esk
Cock Mill Wood
Beeforth's Wood
Monks' Walk Wood
Golden Rigg
Golden Grove Wood
YO22
Hagg House Farm
Topping Riggs Wood
Long Rigg
Bennison House Farm
Topping Riggs
B1416
8
7
11
6
5
10
4
3
09
2
1
08
88
89
90
A
B
C
D
E
F
32
32
32

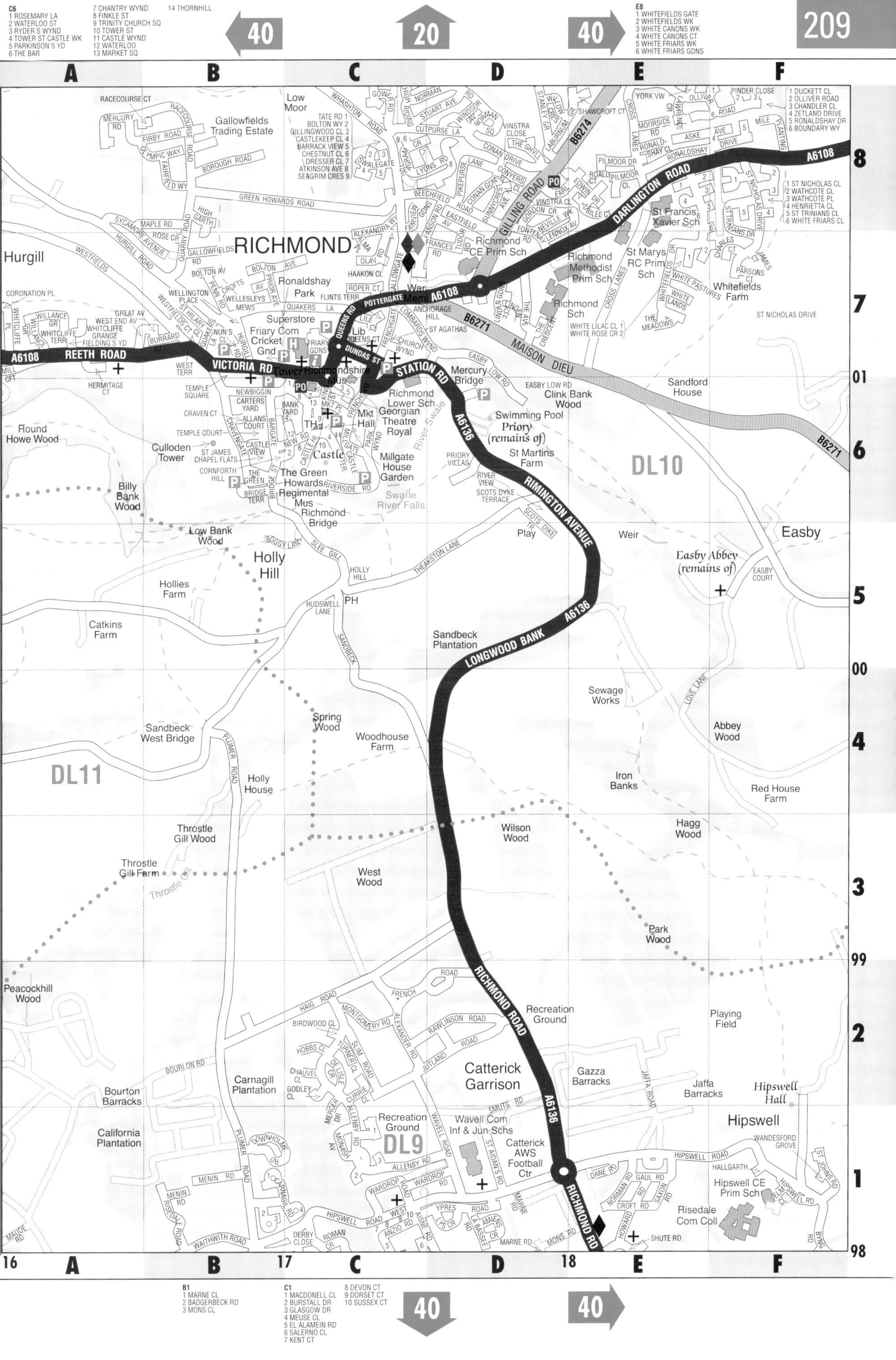
C6
1 ROSEMARY LA
2 WATERLOO ST
3 RYDER'S WYND
4 TOWER ST CASTLE WK
5 PARKINSON'S YD
6 THE BAR
7 CHANTRY WYND
8 FINKLE ST
9 TRINITY CHURCH SQ
10 TOWER ST
11 CASTLE WYND
12 WATERLOO
13 MARKET SQ
14 THORNHILL
40
20
40
E8
1 WHITEFIELDS GATE
2 WHITEFIELDS WK
3 WHITE CANONS WK
4 WHITE CANONS CT
5 WHITE FRIARS WK
6 WHITE FRIARS GDNS
A
B
C
D
E
F
RACECOURSE CT
MERCURY RD
FIRBY ROAD
OLYMPIC WAY
FAIRFIELD WY
Gallowfields Trading Estate
BOROUGH ROAD
Low Moor
TATE RD 1
BOLTON WY 2
GILLINGWOOD CL 3
CASTLEKEEP CL 4
BARRACK VIEW 5
CHESTNUT CL 6
DRESSER CL 7
ATKINSON AVE 8
SEAGRIM CRES 9
WHASHTON ROAD
SWALEGATE
NORMAN
STUART AVE
CUTPURSE LA
WINDSOR AV
VINSTRA CLOSE
THE GHYLL
CONAN DRIVE
STANLEY GR
LABURNUM GR
SHAWCROFT CT
B6274
YORK VW
OLLIVER
PINDER CLOSE
1 DUCKETT CL
2 OLLIVER ROAD
3 CHANDLER CL
4 ZETLAND DRIVE
5 RONALDSHAY DR
6 BOUNDARY WY
MOORSIDE RD
RONALDSHAY CL
RONALDSHAY
ASKE
MILE
A6108
8
GREEN HOWARDS ROAD
LYONS RD
BEECHFIELD ROAD
PIKEPURSE LANE
CONAN GDNS
CONYERS
GILLING ROAD
PO
PILMOOR DR
DARLINGTON ROAD
1 ST NICHOLAS CL
2 WATHCOTE CL
3 WATHCOTE PL
4 HENRIETTA CL
5 ST TRINIANS CL
6 WHITE FRIARS CL
MAPLE RD
ROSE CR
SYCAMORE AVENUE
HURGILL ROAD
QUARRY ROAD
HIGH GARTH
GALLOWFIELDS RD
RICHMOND
ALEXANDRA WY
EASTFIELD
FRANCES RD
Richmond CE Prim Sch
VINSTRA CL
GORDON CR
NEVILLE WK
LENNOX AV
FONTENAY
St Francis Xavier Sch
ST TRINIANS DR
ST NICHOLAS DRIVE
Hurgill
WESTFIELDS
BOLTON AV
BOLTON AVE
PRIOR AVE
HAAKON CL
Ronaldshay Park
ROPER CT
FLINTS TERR
GALLOWGATE
POTTERGATE
War Meml
A6108
Richmond Methodist Prim Sch
St Marys RC Prim Sch
WHITEFIELDS DR
WHITE PASTURES
CHARLES CT
PARSONS CT
Whitefields Farm
CORONATION PL
WELLINGTON PLACE
CROFTS
WELLESLEYS MEWS
QUAKERS LA
ANCHORAGE HILL
B6271
CROSS LANES
Richmond Sch
7
WHITECLIFFE
WILLANCE GR
GREAT AV
WEST END AV
WHITCLIFFE GRANGE
FIELDING'S YD
WHITCLIFFE TERR
BURRARD AV
ST HILARY PL
WESTFIELDS CT CL
NUN'S CL
HURGILL RD
Superstore
Friary Com Cricket Gnd
QUEENS RD
Lib
FRIARY GDNS
DUNDAS ST
FRENCHGATE
LOMBARDS WYND
ST AGATHAS
CHURCH WYND
THE CRESCENT
WHITE LILAC CL 1
WHITE ROSE CR 2
THE MEADOWS
ST NICHOLAS DRIVE
A6108
REETH ROAD
VICTORIA RD
Tower
Richmondshire Mus
STATION RD
EASBY LOW RD
Mercury Bridge
MAISON DIEU
Sandford House
WEST TERR
HERMITAGE CT
TEMPLE SQUARE
NEWBIGGIN
CARTERS YARD
BANK YARD
Richmond Lower Sch
EASBY LOW RD
Clink Bank Wood
01
Round Howe Wood
CRAVEN CT
ALLANS COURT
TEMPLE COURT
CRAVENGATE
BARGATE
NEW RD
MKT PL
TH
Mkt Hall
Georgian Theatre Royal
A6136
River Swale
Swimming Pool
Priory (remains of)
St Martins Farm
PRIORY VILLAS
B6271
Culloden Tower
ST JAMES CHAPEL FLATS
CASTLE VIEW
Castle
MILLGATE
Millgate House Garden
6
DL10
Billy Bank Wood
CORNFORTH HILL
THE GREEN
BRIDGE TERR
The Green Howards Regimental Mus
RIVERSIDE RD
RIVER VIEW
SCOTS DYKE TERRACE
RIMINGTON AVENUE
Swale River Falls
Richmond Bridge
SCOTS DIKE
Play
Low Bank Wood
BOGGY LANE
SLEE GILL
Holly Hill
HOLLY HILL
THEAKSTON LANE
Weir
Easby
Easby Abbey (remains of)
EASBY COURT
Hollies Farm
HUDSWELL LANE
PH
5
Catkins Farm
SANDBECK
Sandbeck Plantation
A6136
LONGWOOD BANK
00
Sewage Works
LOVE LANE
Spring Wood
Sandbeck West Bridge
Woodhouse Farm
Abbey Wood
4
DL11
PLUMER ROAD
Holly House
Iron Banks
Red House Farm
Throstle Gill Wood
Wilson Wood
Hagg Wood
Throstle Gill Farm
Throstle Gill
West Wood
3
Park Wood
Peacockhill Wood
99
ROAD
FRENCH
RICHMOND ROAD
HAIG ROAD
MONTGOMERY RD
ALEXANDER RD
RAWLINSON ROAD
Recreation Ground
Playing Field
BIRDWOOD CL
HOBBS CL
SLIM ROAD
TURMER CL
DE LISLE CR
JUTLAND
ROAD
2
BOURLON RD
CHAUVEL CL
GODLEY CL
CURRIE CL
Carnagill Plantation
Catterick Garrison
Gazza Barracks
JAFFA ROAD
Jaffa Barracks
Hipswell Hall
Bourton Barracks
MERCER RD
ALLENBY RD
Recreation Ground
WAVELL ROAD
SMUTS RD
A6136
California Plantation
DOWNHOLME RD
MONASH AV
DL9
Wavell Com Inf & Jun Schs
ST AIDAN'S RD
Catterick AWS Football Ctr
Hipswell
WANDESFORD GROVE
HIPSWELL ROAD
ST JOHNS RD
HALLGARTH
1
MENIN RD
CARNAGILL RD
ALLENBY RD
WARDROP RD
DANE RD
NORMAN RD
GAUL RD
SAXON RD
Hipswell CE Prim Sch
HIPSWELL RD
ELM CL
MENIN RD
RISEDALE ROAD
WEST
HIPSWELL ROAD
ANZIO RD
AISNE RD
YPRES ROAD
LA BASSEE
AMIENS CR
MARNE RD
CROFT RD
HOWARD RD
Risedale Com Coll
MAUDE RD
WAITHWITH ROAD
DERBY CLOSE
ROMAN CR
MARNE RD
MONS RD
RICHMOND RD
SHUTE RD
BYNG RD
16
A
B
17
C
D
18
E
F
98
B1
1 MARNE CL
2 BADGERBECK RD
3 MONS CL
C1
1 MACDONELL CL
2 BURSTALL DR
3 GLASGOW DR
4 MEUSE CL
5 EL ALAMEIN RD
6 SALERNO CL
7 KENT CT
8 DEVON CT
9 DORSET CT
10 SUSSEX CT
40
40

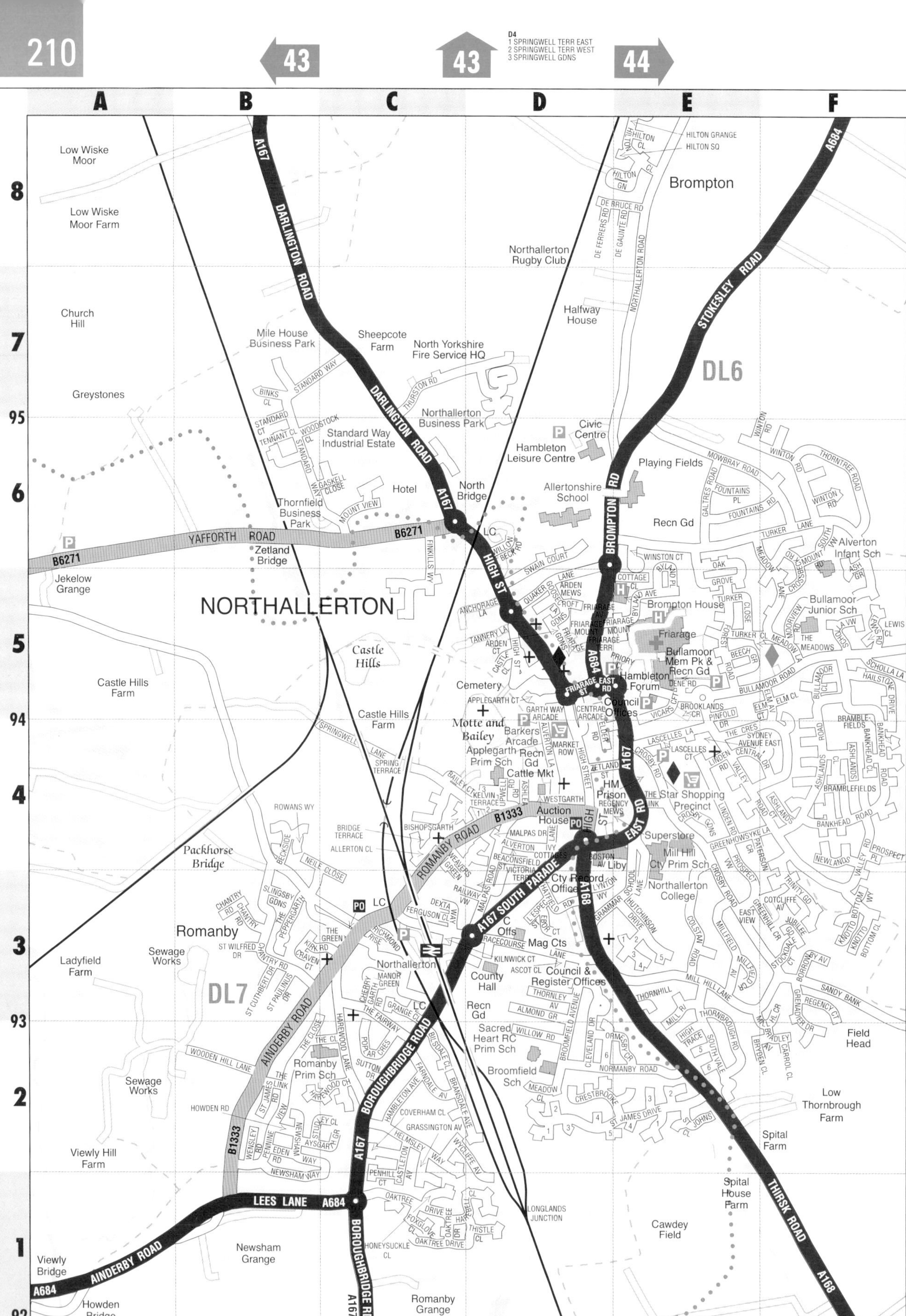

D2
1 ST MICHAELS CT
2 ST ANDREW GR
3 ST CHRISTOPHER CL
4 ST BEDES AVE
5 ST HILDAS RD
6 MULGRAVE DR

E2
1 ST STEPHENS GDNS
2 ST ANTHONYS AVE
3 ST GEORGES GR
4 ST PAULS CL
5 GREENBANK
6 THE LAURELS

E3
1 PINE GR
2 SLADEBURN DR
3 BYRAM CL
4 BYRAM CT
5 ASH RIDGE

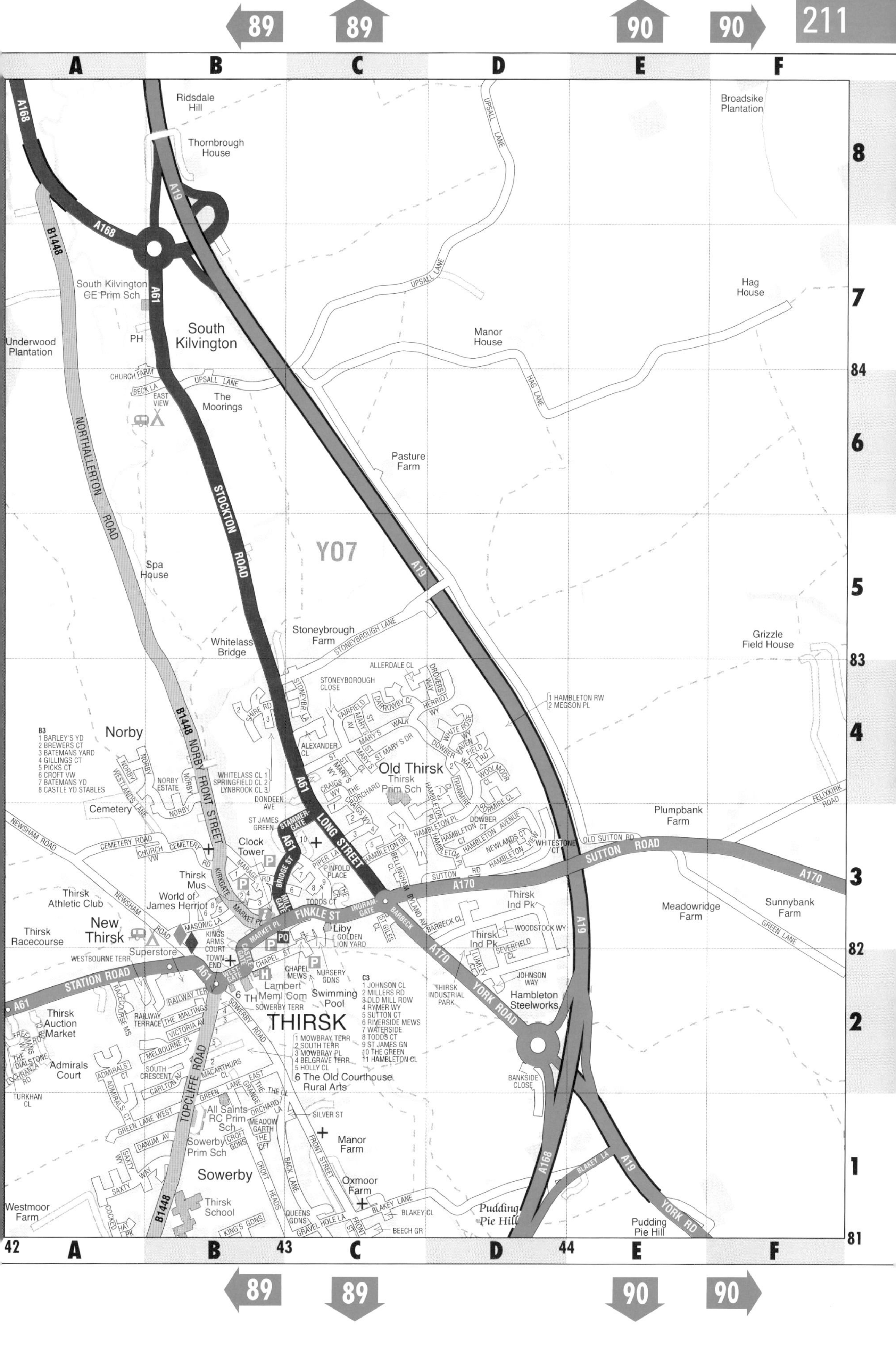

89
89
90
90
A
B
C
D
E
F
8
7
84
6
5
83
4
3
82
2
1
81
42
43
44
Ridsdale Hill
Thornbrough House
Broadsike Plantation
A168
A19
B1448
A61
UPSALL LANE
South Kilvington CE Prim Sch
South Kilvington
Underwood Plantation
PH
CHURCH FARM
BECK LA
EAST VIEW
The Moorings
Hag House
Manor House
HAG LANE
NORTHALLERTON ROAD
STOCKTON ROAD
Pasture Farm
YO7
Spa House
Stoneybrough Farm
STONEYBROUGH LANE
Whitelass Bridge
Grizzle Field House
ALLERDALE CL
STONEYBOROUGH CLOSE
DROVERS WAY
1 HAMBLETON RW
2 MEGSON PL
Norby
B3
1 BARLEY'S YD
2 BREWERS CT
3 BATEMANS YARD
4 GILLINGS CT
5 PICKS CT
6 CROFT VW
7 BATEMANS YD
8 CASTLE YD STABLES
NORBY FRONT STREET
WHITELASS CL 1
SPRINGFIELD CL 2
LYNBROOK CL 3
Old Thirsk
Thirsk Prim Sch
Cemetery
NEWSHAM ROAD
CEMETERY ROAD
Clock Tower
LONG STREET
Plumpbank Farm
FELIXKIRK ROAD
OLD SUTTON RD
SUTTON ROAD
A170
Thirsk Athletic Club
Thirsk Mus
World of James Herriot
FINKLE ST
Thirsk Ind Pk
Meadowridge Farm
Sunnybank Farm
GREEN LANE
Thirsk Racecourse
New Thirsk
Superstore
Liby
GOLDEN LION YARD
WOODSTOCK WY
SEVERFIELD CL
JOHNSON WAY
WESTBOURNE TERR
STATION ROAD
YORK ROAD
THIRSK INDUSTRIAL PARK
Hambleton Steelworks
Thirsk Auction Market
Lambert Meml Com
Swimming Pool
TH
C3
1 JOHNSON CL
2 MILLERS RD
3 OLD MILL ROW
4 RYMER WY
5 SUTTON CT
6 RIVERSIDE MEWS
7 WATERSIDE
8 TODDS CT
9 ST JAMES GN
10 THE GREEN
11 HAMBLETON CL
THIRSK
1 MOWBRAY TERR
2 SOUTH TERR
3 MOWBRAY PL
4 BELGRAVE TERR
5 HOLLY CL
6 The Old Courthouse Rural Arts
Admirals Court
BANKSIDE CLOSE
TOPCLIFFE ROAD
All Saints RC Prim Sch
SILVER ST
Manor Farm
Sowerby Prim Sch
Sowerby
FRONT STREET
BACK LANE
Oxmoor Farm
BLAKEY LANE
BLAKEY CL
BEECH GR
BLAKEY LA
Pudding Pie Hill
YORK RD
Westmoor Farm
Thirsk School
KING'S GDNS
GRAVEL HOLE LA

C8
1 ST MARK'S CL
2 ST JOSEPHS CL
3 GREYLANDS PK GR
4 GREYLANDS PK RD
5 HEATHCLIFF GDNS

← **75**

75

D8
1 HAREWOOD AVE
2 NEWLANDS PK GR
3 WOODVILLE AVE
4 VERNON GR
5 HIGHDALE AVE

E5
1 FAIRFAX ST
2 BRITANNIA ST
3 IRETON ST
4 BRINKBURN RD
5 HARLEY ST
6 FALSGRAVE MEWS

F6
1 WREA LA
2 LOWER CLARK ST
3 LOWER WILLIAM ST
4 MELROSE ST
5 CLIFTON ST
6 VINE ST.

7 FRANKLIN ST
8 MURCHISON PL
9 PROSPECT RD
10 ALBEMARLE BK RD
11 NORTHWAY
12 BROOK ST

F7
1 VICTORIA PARK
2 VICTORIA PARK AVE
3 LANGDALE RD
4 SANDRINGHAM ST
5 SYDNEY ST
6 DURHAM ST

Column headers (top): A B C D E F
Grid rows: 8, 7, 89, 6, 5, 88, 4, 3, 87, 2, 1, 86

B7
1 THE MEADOWS
2 DUNWELL AV
3 THROXENBY GR
4 SANDHURST GDNS
5 KINGSTON GR

B5
1 CHERRY TREE AVE
2 CABURN CL
3 THE SPINNEY
4 SKIPLAM CL
5 THE COPSE
6 HILDENLEY CL

E3
1 MILL LA
2 SEAMER ST
3 BEACONSFIELD ST
4 MOUNT VW CL

Major place labels:
Scarborough RUFC
Throxenby Head
Throxenby
High Farm
Throxenby Mere
Raincliffe Woods
Row Brow Farm
Row Farm
Cemetery
Woodlands Crem
Rowbrow Wood
Masts
Newby
Barrowcliff
Barrowcliff Inf Sch
Barrowcliff Jun Sch
Newby Prim Sch
Scalby Sch
St Peters RC Prim Sch
Northstead Prim Sch
Yorkshire Coast Coll
Scarborough General
Woodlands Sch
Graham Sch
Hill End
Harland Mount Nature Reserve
Scarborough Sixth Form Coll
St Augustines Sch
Lightfoots Farm
Springhill Farm
Springhill Wood
Falsgrave
Falsgrave Moor
Falsgrave Moor Farm
Seamer Moor
Moor House Farm
North Bay Railway
Northstead Manor Gardens
The Sands
Indoor Pool
Alexandra Indoor Bowls Centre
Peasholm Park
Scarborough Cricket Club
Columbus Ravine
Cemetery
Gladstone Rd Jun & Inf Schs
Superstore
Scarborough
Mag Courts
Stephen Joseph Theatre
Coll
Parnell's Wood
Oliver's Mount Plantation
Hinderwell Prim Sch
McCain Stad (Scarborough FC)
Springhead Sch
Queen Margaret's Ind Est
Mount Side Park
Seamer Road Retail Park
The Mere
Falsgrave Community Resource Centre
Oliver's Mount
Weaponness Farm

Area codes: YO12, YO11

Major roads: A171, A170, A165, A64, B1427, Scalby Road, Stepney Road, Stepney Hill, Seamer Moor Hill, Racecourse Road, Seamer Road, Burniston Road, Falsgrave Road, Queen Margaret's Road, Westborough, Victoria Rd

Bottom column headers: A B C D E F
Bottom grid: 01, 02, 03

E4
1 CAMBRIDGE PL
2 MOUNT PARK RD
3 ACKWORTH ST
4 NEW PK RD
5 DERWENT AVE
6 PARK RD
7 DERWENT ST
8 NEW PARKS CRES
9 ELM RD
10 ASHBURN RISE
11 DEPOT LA

← **75**

99

F3
1 TRINITY CL
2 TRINITY GDNS
3 GARLANDS HILL
4 PRINCESS ROYAL LA
5 COLLEGE CT
6 WEAPONNESS VALLEY CL
7 QUEEN MARGARET'S RD
8 FULFORD LA

F4
1 ALL SAINTS RD
2 WESTWOOD CL
3 WESTWOOD GDNS
4 COLLEGE ST
5 CROMWELL PAR
6 CROMWELL GDNS
7 CROMWELL TERR
8 ROYAL CRES LA

F5
1 BARWICK TERR
2 ALMA PAR
3 ALMA GQ
4 MORGAN ST
5 SHERWOOD ST
6 HANNOVER RD
7 WEST SQ
8 NORWOOD PL
9 BELLE VUE PAR
10 BELLEVUE PL
11 WEST PAR RD
12 ARUNDEL PL
13 VALLEY BRIDGE TERR
14 BELGRAVE CR
15 VALLEY BRIDGE RD
16 BELLE VUE ST
17 BELLE VUE ST
18 NORWOOD MS
19 Yorkshire Coast Coll

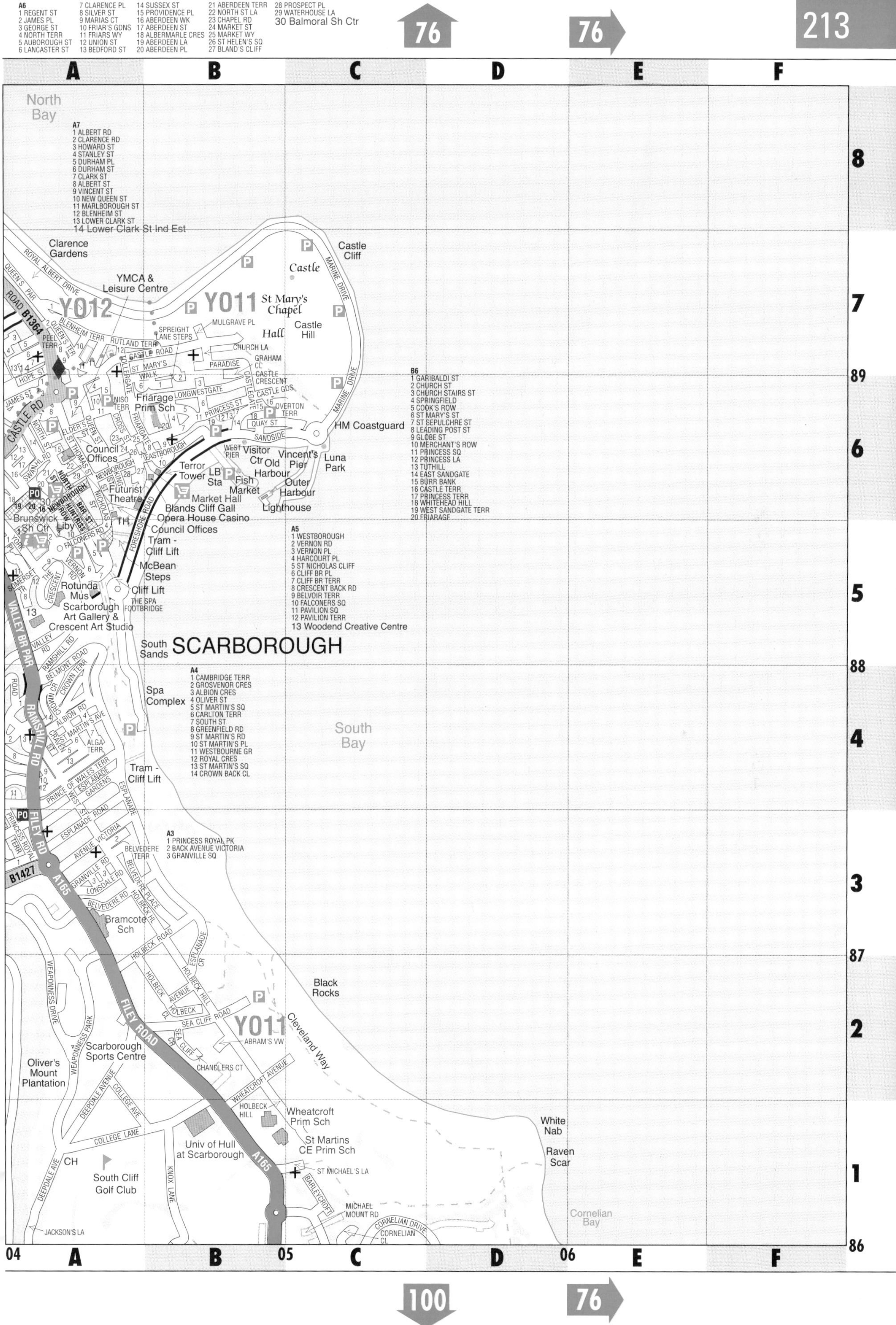
A6
1 REGENT ST
2 JAMES PL
3 GEORGE ST
4 NORTH TERR
5 AUBOROUGH ST
6 LANCASTER ST
7 CLARENCE PL
8 SILVER ST
9 MARIAS CT
10 FRIAR'S GDNS
11 FRIARS WY
12 UNION ST
13 BEDFORD ST
14 SUSSEX ST
15 PROVIDENCE PL
16 ABERDEEN WK
17 ABERDEEN ST
18 ALBERMARLE CRES
19 ABERDEEN LA
20 ABERDEEN PL
21 ABERDEEN TERR
22 NORTH ST LA
23 CHAPEL RD
24 MARKET ST
25 MARKET WY
26 ST HELEN'S SQ
27 BLAND'S CLIFF
28 PROSPECT PL
29 WATERHOUSE LA
30 Balmoral Sh Ctr
76
76
A B C D E F
North Bay
A7
1 ALBERT RD
2 CLARENCE RD
3 HOWARD ST
4 STANLEY ST
5 DURHAM PL
6 DURHAM ST
7 CLARK ST
8 ALBERT ST
9 VINCENT ST
10 NEW QUEEN ST
11 MARLBOROUGH ST
12 BLENHEIM ST
13 LOWER CLARK ST
14 Lower Clark St Ind Est
Clarence Gardens
YMCA & Leisure Centre
YO12
YO11
St Mary's Chapel
Castle
Castle Cliff
Castle Hill
Hall
MARINE DRIVE
ROYAL ALBERT DRIVE
QUEEN'S PAR
B1364
SPREIGHT LANE STEPS
MULGRAVE PL
CHURCH LA
GRAHAM CL
CASTLE CRESCENT
CASTLE GDS
PARADISE
CASTLE ROAD
ST MARY'S WALK
LONGWESTGATE
PRINCESS ST
OVERTON TERR
QUAY ST
SANDSIDE
Friarage Prim Sch
HM Coastguard
B6
1 GARIBALDI ST
2 CHURCH ST
3 CHURCH STAIRS ST
4 SPRINGFIELD
5 COOK'S ROW
6 ST MARY'S ST
7 ST SEPULCHRE ST
8 LEADING POST ST
9 GLOBE ST
10 MERCHANT'S ROW
11 PRINCESS SQ
12 PRINCESS LA
13 TUTHILL
14 EAST SANDGATE
15 BURR BANK
16 CASTLE TERR
17 PRINCESS TERR
18 WHITEHEAD HILL
19 WEST SANDGATE TERR
20 FRIARAGE
Council Offices
Terror Tower
LB Sta
Fish Market
Visitor Ctr
Old Harbour
Vincent's Pier
Luna Park
Outer Harbour
Lighthouse
Futurist Theatre
Market Hall
Blands Cliff Gall
Opera House Casino
Council Offices
Brunswick Sh Ctr
Liby
TH
Tram - Cliff Lift
McBean Steps
Cliff Lift
THE SPA FOOTBRIDGE
FORESHORE ROAD
Rotunda Mus
Scarborough Art Gallery & Crescent Art Studio
A5
1 WESTBOROUGH
2 VERNON RD
3 VERNON PL
4 HARCOURT PL
5 ST NICHOLAS CLIFF
6 CLIFF BR PL
7 CLIFF BR TERR
8 CRESCENT BACK RD
9 BELVOIR TERR
10 FALCONERS SQ
11 PAVILION SQ
12 PAVILION TERR
13 Woodend Creative Centre
South Sands
SCARBOROUGH
VALLEY BR PAR
RAMSHILL RD
Spa Complex
A4
1 CAMBRIDGE TERR
2 GROSVENOR CRES
3 ALBION CRES
4 OLIVER ST
5 ST MARTIN'S SQ
6 CARLTON TERR
7 SOUTH ST
8 GREENFIELD RD
9 ST MARTIN'S RD
10 ST MARTIN'S PL
11 WESTBOURNE GR
12 ROYAL CRES
13 ST MARTIN'S SQ
14 CROWN BACK CL
South Bay
Tram - Cliff Lift
ESPLANADE
FILEY RD
B1427
A3
1 PRINCESS ROYAL PK
2 BACK AVENUE VICTORIA
3 GRANVILLE SQ
BELVEDERE TERR
Bramcote Sch
A165
HOLBECK ROAD
FILEY ROAD
Black Rocks
YO11
Cleveland Way
ABRAM'S VW
SEA CLIFF ROAD
CHANDLERS CT
WHEATCROFT AVENUE
WEAPONNESS DRIVE
Scarborough Sports Centre
Oliver's Mount Plantation
Wheatcroft Prim Sch
St Martins CE Prim Sch
Univ of Hull at Scarborough
COLLEGE LANE
CH
South Cliff Golf Club
KNOX LANE
ST MICHAEL'S LA
MICHAEL MOUNT RD
CORNELIAN DRIVE
White Nab
Raven Scar
Cornelian Bay
JACKSON'S LA
8 7 89 6 5 88 4 3 87 2 1 86
04 05 06
100
76

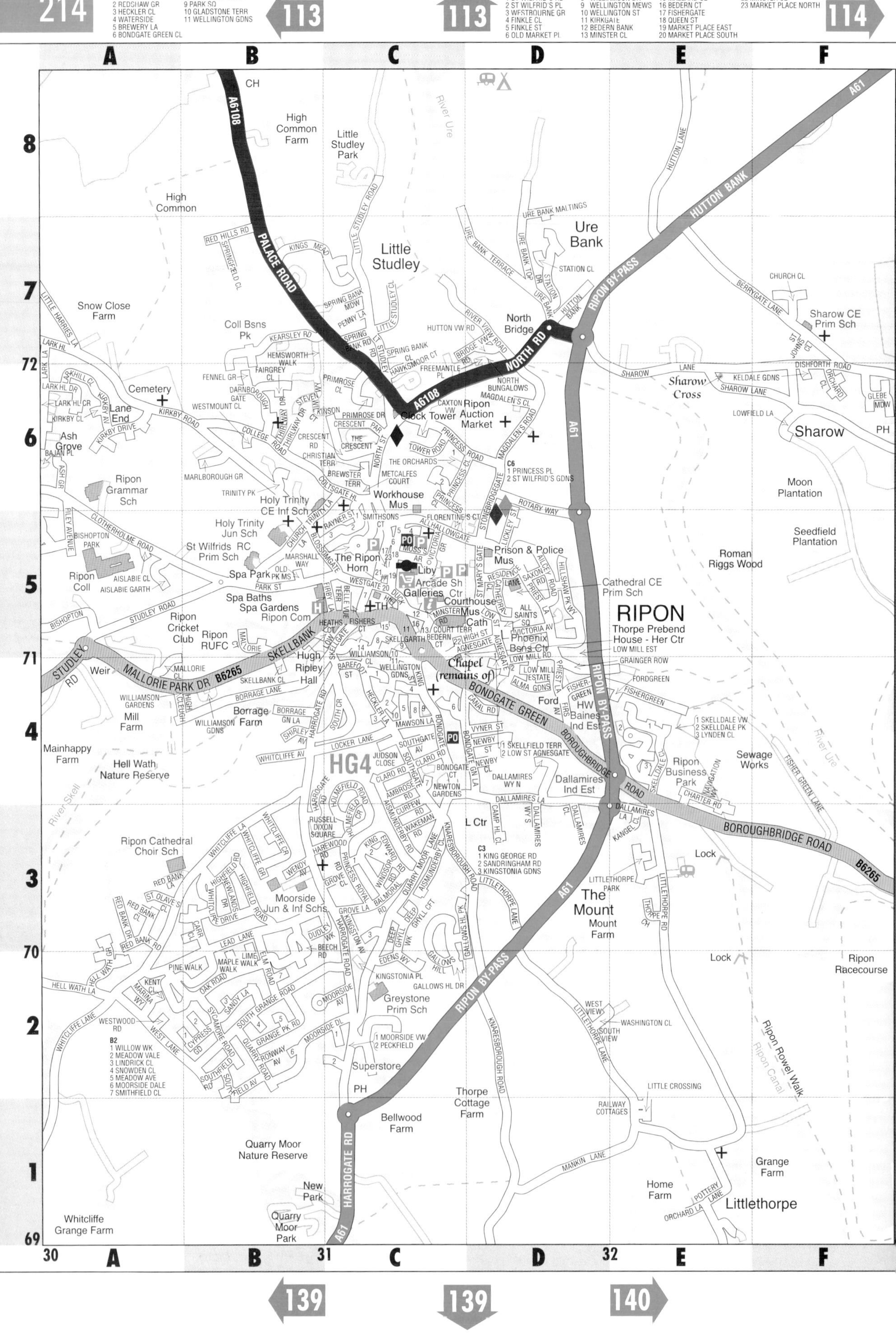

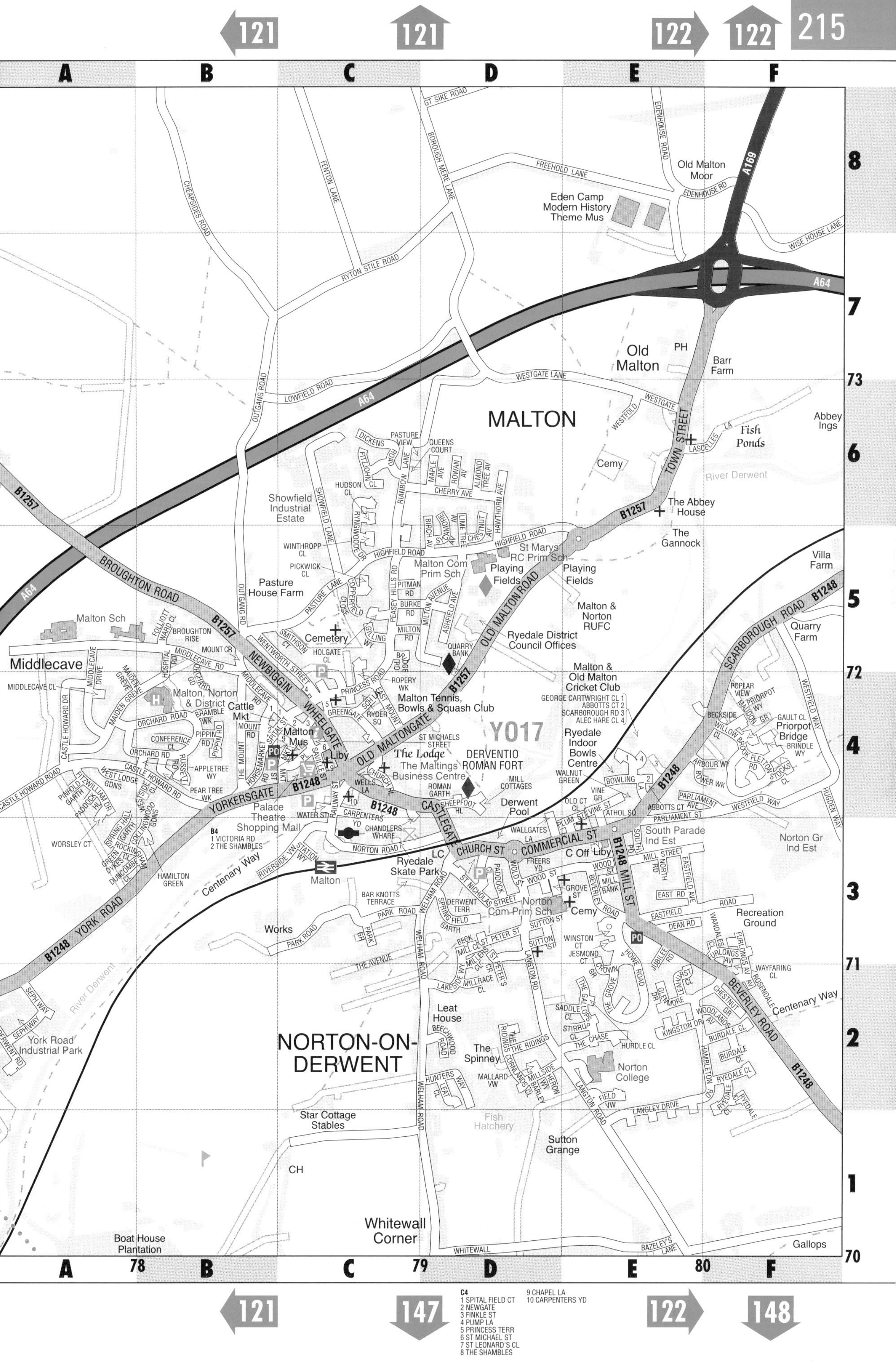
121
121
122
122
A
B
C
D
E
F
8
7
73
6
5
72
4
3
71
2
1
70
78
79
80
MALTON
NORTON-ON-
DERWENT
YO17
Old Malton Moor
Eden Camp
Modern History
Theme Mus
Old
Malton
Barr
Farm
Abbey
Ings
Fish
Ponds
River Derwent
The Abbey
House
The
Gannock
Villa
Farm
Quarry
Farm
Showfield
Industrial
Estate
Pasture
House Farm
Malton Sch
Middlecave
Malton, Norton
& District
Cattle
Mkt
Malton
Mus
Liby
Palace
Theatre
Shopping Mall
Cemetery
Malton Com
Prim Sch
St Marys
RC Prim Sch
Playing
Fields
Malton &
Norton
RUFC
Ryedale District
Council Offices
Malton &
Old Malton
Cricket Club
Malton Tennis,
Bowls & Squash Club
DERVENTIO
ROMAN FORT
The Lodge
The Maltings
Business Centre
Ryedale
Indoor
Bowls
Centre
Derwent
Pool
Priorpot
Bridge
Norton Gr
Ind Est
South Parade
Ind Est
Recreation
Ground
Ryedale
Skate Park
Malton
Works
Norton
Com Prim Sch
Cemy
Leat
House
The
Spinney
Norton
College
Fish
Hatchery
Sutton
Grange
Star Cottage
Stables
Whitewall
Corner
Boat House
Plantation
Gallops
York Road
Industrial Park
Centenary Way
A64
A169
B1257
B1248
B4
1 VICTORIA RD
2 THE SHAMBLES
C4
1 SPITAL FIELD CT
2 NEWGATE
3 FINKLE ST
4 PUMP LA
5 PRINCESS TERR
6 ST MICHAEL ST
7 ST LEONARD'S CL
8 THE SHAMBLES
9 CHAPEL LA
10 CARPENTERS YD
GEORGE CARTWRIGHT CL 1
ABBOTTS CT 2
SCARBOROUGH RD 3
ALEC HARE CL 4
121
147
122
148

172 156

Map grid labels A–F, rows 8 to 50

Bog Wood
B6265
Tarn House Farm
Tarn House
Thorlby House
BRACKENLEY LANE
PH
Tarn Moor
Tarn Moor Bridge
Craven Heifer Farm
GRASSINGTON ROAD
Thorlby
White House Farm
Stirton
WHITE HILLS LANE
Old Park
Bay Horse Farm
SOUR LANE
Manor Farm
THE CROFT
STIRTON LANE
Thorlby Bridge (swing)
A65
White Hills Lane
WHITE HILLS CFT
RAIKES RD
RIDGEWAY
TARN MOOR CR
B6265
SHORT LEE LANE
A65
CULVERT LANE
BD23
STIRTONBER
Little Wood
Battery
BEECHWOOD DR
RAIKES WOOD DR
RAIKES WOOD CR
HILL RI
Craft Workshops
Register Off
Aireville Grange Farm
ROCKWOOD DR
WOOD CL
WOODLANDS WK
Massa Flatts Wood
RAIKES RD
B6265
MILL BR
Motel
AIREVILLE GRANGE
PARK WOOD
P WOOD CL
Skipton Girls High Sch
BOTHELY WOODS
Ermysted's Grammar Sch
CASTLE VW TERR
PROSPECT TERR
WOODMAN TERR
LING FIELDS
Craven Coll
P WOOD WY
P WOOD
PARK VW
ASHGROVE
SALISBURY ST
ST STEPHEN'S CL
ELLIOT ST
Liby
A59
Skipton Auction Market
Craven Coll
Aireville Sch
HAREWOOD ROAD
W BANK RD
BRIGHT ST
CROSSLEY ST
PARK AVE
SPINDLE ST
VICTORIA TERR
Inghey Bridge
A6069
LC
Niffany Farm
Craven Swim Pool & Fitness Centre
Aireville Park
Council Offs
HALL CFT
GRANVILLE ST
BROOK ST
BR ST
NAVIGATION ST
ALBERT ST
BELMONT
ALBION ST
VICTORIA ST
Leeds & Liverpool Canal
Niffany Bridge (swing)
Viaduct
BROUGHTON CR
JUBILEE
Ings County Prim Sch
BROUGHTON AV
MARTON ST
BOWLING TERRACE
BOWLING VW
CLIFFORD ST
MIDLAND ST
CARLETON NEW RD
Swing Br
A6069
Skipton Little Theatre
COUNTING HO MS
BELMONT ST SWADFORD ST
COL PO
CAVENDISH ST
CROSS
Heslaker Farm
Funkirk
HESLAKER LANE
BROUGHTON ROAD
AVENUE
THE SIDINGS
ENGINE SHED LANE
GISBURN ST
INGS LANE
BROUGHTON MEWS
Engine Shed Lane Ind Est
Sandylands Sports Centre
Skipton RFC
Skipton
Christ Church CE Prim Sch
The Sidings Business Park
Sandylands Business Centre
Skipton Business Park
Superstore
AIREDALE TERR
CALTON TERR
CARLETON AV
BROOKLANDS
HOTHFIELD
Brooklands Terrace
Com Spec Sch
Skipton Roughaw
UNION ST
WHINFIELD CT
CARLETON NEW RD
CARLETON ROAD
A629
SKIPTON
Carleton Business Park
ASHFIELD CR
ASHFIELD TERRACE
BURNSIDE CR
BURNSIDE AVENUE
BRANCH RD
BURNSIDE CR
KEIGHLEY ROAD
ELLER BECK
Alexandra Ville
ALEXANDRA CT
Crem
Waltonwrays Cemy
WALTON ST 1
LINDLEY ST 2
HENRY ST 3
BOLD VENTURE ST 4
ALEXANDRA TERR 5
River Aire
Carleton Bridge
CARLETON RD
LIMEHOUSE LA
PALE LA
Bridge End
AIRE VIEW
HESLAKER LA
The Farm
FARM CFT
Sewage Works
Snaygill Ind Est

172 173

A4
1 BUNKERS HL
2 JERRY CFT
3 ALMA TERR
4 ERMYSTED ST
5 PROVIDENCE PL
6 VICTORIA SQ
7 CRAVEN TERR

B5
1 FALLOW FIELD
2 MEADOW RISE
3 OVERDALE GRA
4 SKIBEDEN CT
5 NEW LAITHE CL

C7
1 BRACKENLEY GR
2 BRACKENLEY AVE
3 BRACKENLEY CL
4 MIDGLEY CL
5 SANDY LA

E8
1 HAW PK
2 PRIORY VW
3 BEACON VW
4 LOW BANK
5 MOORLAND CL

156   174   217

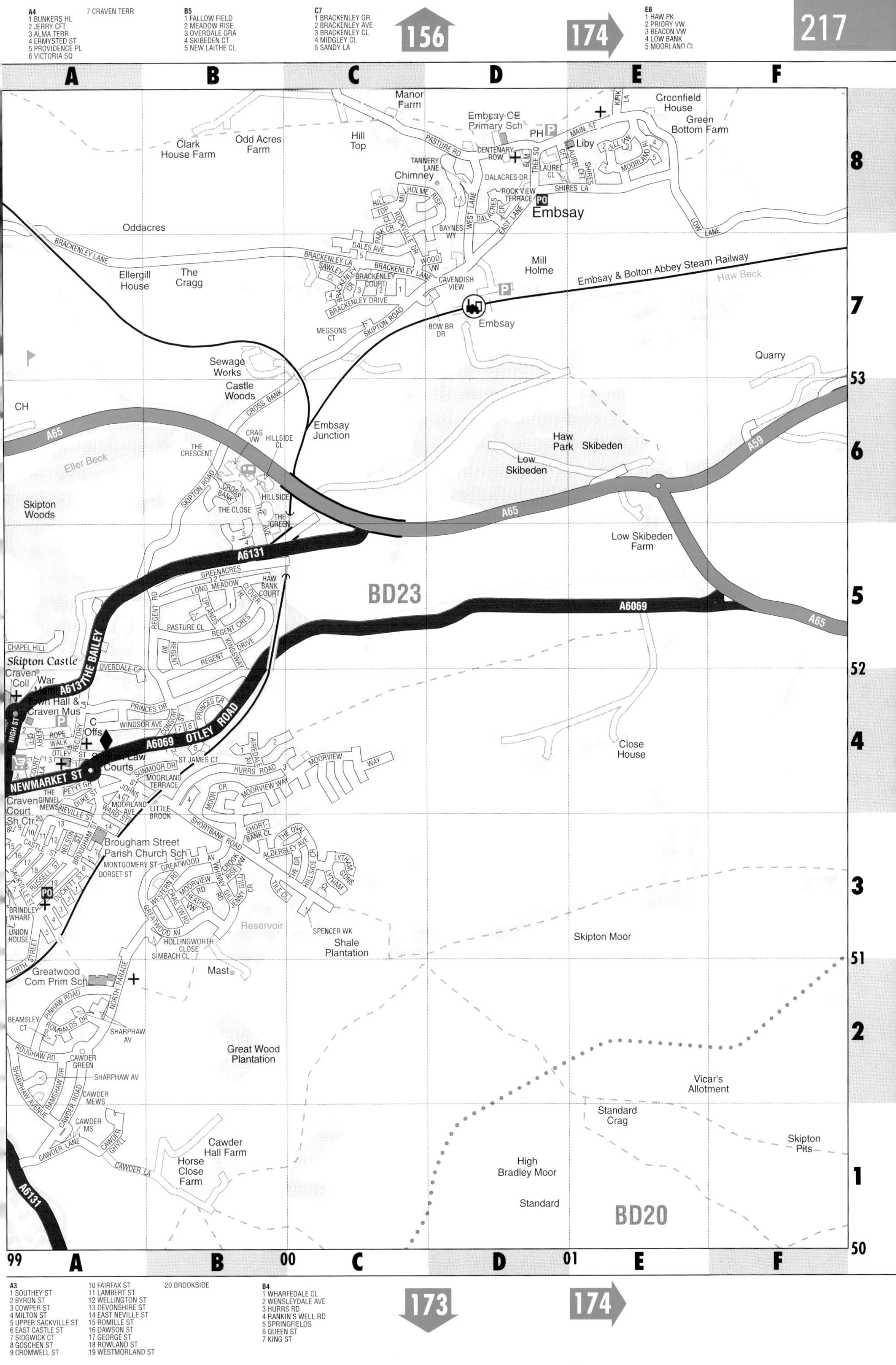

A3
1 SOUTHEY ST
2 BYRON ST
3 COWPER ST
4 MILTON ST
5 UPPER SACKVILLE ST
6 EAST CASTLE ST
7 SIDGWICK CT
8 GOSCHEN ST
9 CROMWELL ST

10 FAIRFAX ST
11 LAMBERT ST
12 WELLINGTON ST
13 DEVONSHIRE ST
14 EAST NEVILLE ST
15 ROMILLE ST
16 DAWSON ST
17 GEORGE ST
18 ROWLAND ST
19 WESTMORLAND ST

20 BROOKSIDE

B4
1 WHARFEDALE CL
2 WENSLEYDALE AVE
3 HURRS RD
4 RANKIN'S WELL RD
5 SPRINGFIELDS
6 QUEEN ST
7 KING ST

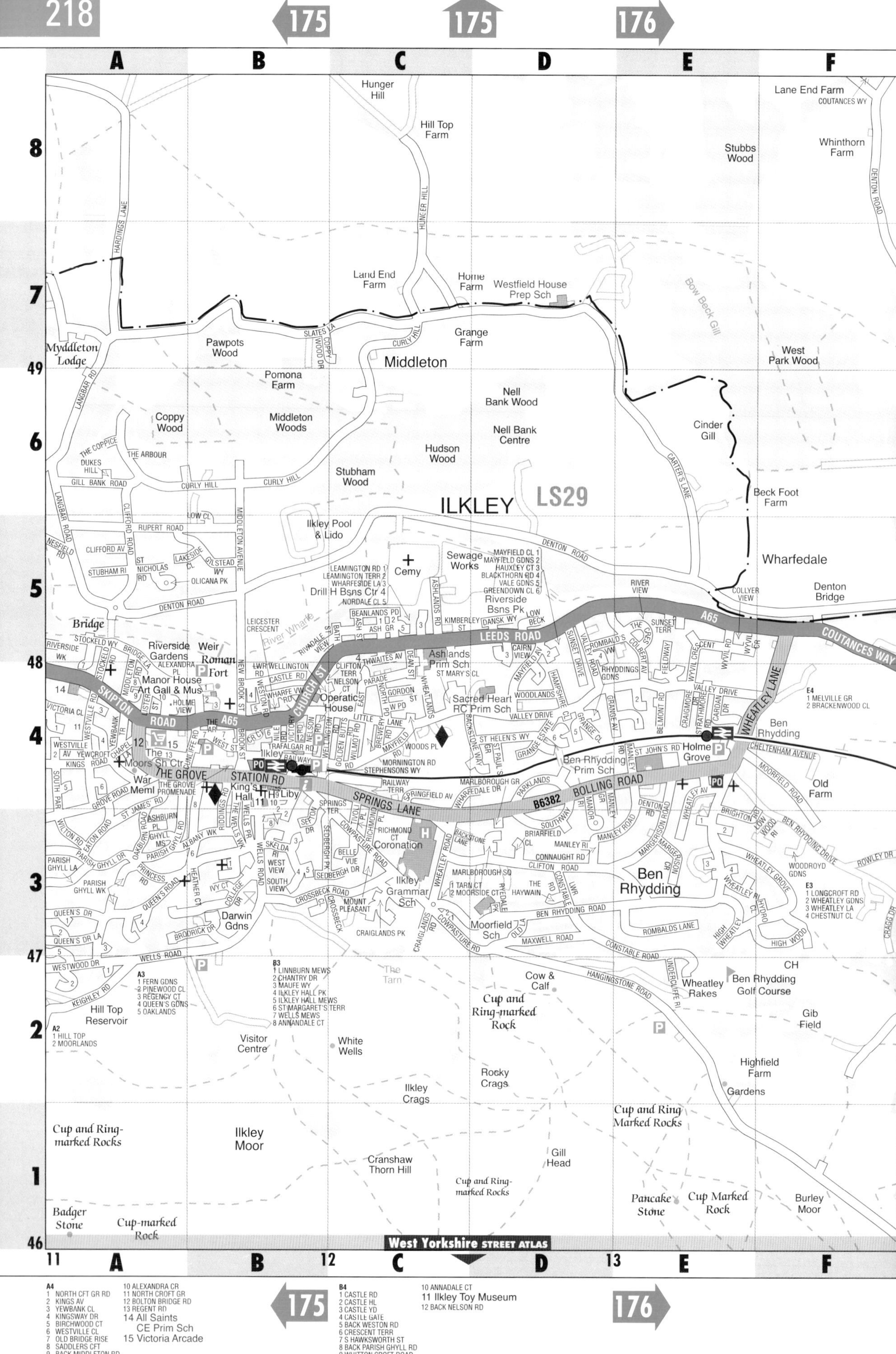

A   B   C   D   E   F

8

Hunger Hill

Lane End Farm
COUTANCES WY

Hill Top Farm

Stubbs Wood

Whinthorn Farm

DENTON ROAD

7

Land End Farm

Home Farm

Westfield House Prep Sch

Bow Beck Gill

Myddleton Lodge

HARDINGS LANE

Pawpots Wood

49

SLATES LA
COPPY WOOD DR
CURLY HILL

Middleton

Grange Farm

West Park Wood

Pomona Farm

Middleton Woods

Nell Bank Wood

Cinder Gill

LANGBAR RD

6

Coppy Wood

THE COPPICE

THE ARBOUR

Nell Bank Centre

Beck Foot Farm

DUKES HILL

Gill Bank Road

Stubham Wood

Hudson Wood

CARTER'S LANE

CURLY HILL

CURLY HILL

ILKLEY

LS29

Wharfedale

LANGBAR RD

NESFIELD

CLIFFORD ROAD

RUPERT ROAD

LOW CL

MIDDLETON AVENUE

Ilkley Pool & Lido

DENTON ROAD

RIVER VIEW

A65

COLLYER VIEW

Denton Bridge

5

Clifford Av

STUBHAM RI

ST NICHOLAS RD

LAKESIDE

ILSTEAD WY

OLICANA PK

DENTON ROAD

LEICESTER CRESCENT

LEAMINGTON RD 1
LEAMINGTON TERR 2
WHARFESIDE LA 3
NORDALE CL 5

Drill H Bsns Ctr 4

Cemy

River Wharfe

BEANLANDS PD

Sewage Works

MAYFIELD CL 1
MAYFIELD GDNS 2
HAUXLEY CT 3
BLACKTHORN RD 4
VALE GDNS 5
GREENDOWN CL 6

Riverside Bsns Pk

DANSK WY
LOW

SUNSET TERR

River View

Denton Bridge

Bridge

Riverside Gardens

Weir Roman Fort

ALEXANDRA PL

Manor House Art Gall & Mus

HOLME VIEW

STOCKELD WY

KIMBERLEY ST

KIMBERLEY

THE GROVE

LEEDS ROAD

CAIRN VIEW

RHYDDINGS GDNS

COLBERT RD

FIELDWAY

CRESCENT

WYVIL RD

WYVIL CRES

COUTANCES WAY

48

RIVERSIDE WK

SKIPTON ROAD

A65

LWR WELLINGTON

CHURCH ST

CLIFTON TERR

THWAITES AV

DEAN ST

Ashlands Prim Sch

ST MARY'S C/L

WOODLANDS

Sacred Heart RC Prim Sch

VALLEY DRIVE

GRANGE AV

BELMONT RD

VALLEY DRIVE

CRAIGMORE

CARDAN DR

E4
1 MELVILLE GR
2 BRACKENWOOD CL

Ben Rhydding

14

VICTORIA CL

YEWBANK AV

THE A65

VICTORY ST

NEW BROOK ST

WHARFE VW

NELSON RD

Operatic House

GORDON TERR

MAYFIELD

W PD

WOODS PL

ST HELEN'S WY

ST PAUL'S

GRANGE ESTATE

Ben Rhydding Prim Sch

Holme Grove

CHELTENHAM AVENUE

WHEATLEY LANE

Old Farm

4

WESTVILLE AV

KINGS

CHAPEL LA

WEST

The Moors Sh Ctr

12
13
15

War Meml

The Grove Promenade

King's Hall

H Liby

11   10

TRAFALGAR RD

STEPHENSONS WY

MORNINGTON RD

MARLBOROUGH GR

WHEATLANDS

LITTLE

BREWERY LANE

BACK LANE

Ben Rhydding Prim Sch

DENTON RD

WHEATLEY RD

MOORFIELD RD

BRIGHTON

E3
1 LONGCROFT RD
2 WHEATLEY GDNS
3 WHEATLEY LA
4 CHESTNUT CL

SOUTH PAR

GROVE RD

WILTON RD

ST JAMES'S RD

EATON RD

ALBANY WK

WELLS RD

SPRINGS

Railway Terr

SPRINGS LANE

B6382   BOLLING ROAD

SPRINGFIELD AV

MARLBOROUGH RD

PARKLANDS

WHARFEDALE DR

SOUTHWAY

MANLEY RD

MANLEY RI

MARGERISON RD

WHEATLEY GROVE

WOODROYD GDNS

ROWLEY DR

CRAG RD

Parish Ghyll La

PARISH GHYLL WK

OAKBURN RD

PARISH GHYLL DR

PRINCESS RD

HEATHER CT

IVY LE

SEDBERGH DR

WEST VIEW

BELLE VUE

RICHMOND CT

Coronation

MOUNT PLEASANT

Ilkley Grammar Sch

THE HAYWAIN

CLIFTON ROAD

Ben Rhydding

WHEATLEY RISE

HIGH WHEATLEY

HIGH WOOD

3

QUEEN'S DR

QUEEN'S DR LA

QUEEN'S GDNS

COLLEGE RD

Darwin Gdns

BRODRICK DR

CROSSBECK ROAD

CROSSBECK

SOUTH VIEW

SKELDA

SEDBERGH RD

COMPASTURE ROAD

CRAGLANDS PK

1 TARN CT
2 MOORSIDE CT

THE

LWR CONSTABLE RD

Moorfield Sch

RIDDLE

BEN RHYDDING ROAD

ROMBALDS LANE

CONSTABLE ROAD

UNDERCLIFFE RD

CH

47

WESTWOOD DR

WELLS ROAD

KEIGHLEY RD

2

A3
1 FERN GDNS
2 PINEWOOD CL
3 REGENCY CT
4 QUEEN'S GDNS
5 OAKLANDS

B3
1 LINNBURN MEWS
2 CHANTRY DR
3 MAUFE WY
4 ILKLEY HALL PK
5 ILKLEY HALL MEWS
6 ST MARGARET'S TERR
7 WELLS MEWS
8 ANNANDALE CT

The Tarn

Cow & Calf

HANGINGSTONE ROAD

Wheatley Rakes

Ben Rhydding Golf Course

Gib Field

2

A2
1 HILL TOP
2 MOORLANDS

Hill Top Reservoir

Visitor Centre

White Wells

Cup and Ring-marked Rock

Rocky Crags

Highfield Farm Gardens

1

Cup and Ring-marked Rocks

Ilkley Moor

Ilkley Crags

Cranshaw Thorn Hill

Cup and Ring-marked Rocks

Gill Head

Cup and Ring Marked Rocks

Pancake Stone

Cup Marked Rock

Burley Moor

46

Badger Stone

Cup-marked Rock

11   A   B   12   C   D   13   E   F

A4
1 NORTH CFT GR RD
2 KINGS AV
3 YEWBANK CL
4 KINGSWAY DR
5 BIRCHWOOD CT
6 WESTVILLE CL
7 OLD BRIDGE RISE
8 SADDLERS CFT
9 BACK MIDDLETON RD

10 ALEXANDRA CR
11 NORTH CROFT GR
12 BOLTON BRIDGE RD
13 REGENT RD
14 All Saints
   CE Prim Sch
15 Victoria Arcade

B4
1 CASTLE RD
2 CASTLE HL
3 CASTLE YD
4 CASTLE GATE
5 BACK WESTON RD
6 CRESCENT TERR
7 S HAWKSWORTH ST
8 BACK PARISH GHYLL RD
9 WHITTON CROFT ROAD

10 ANNADALE CT
11 Ilkley Toy Museum
12 BACK NELSON RD

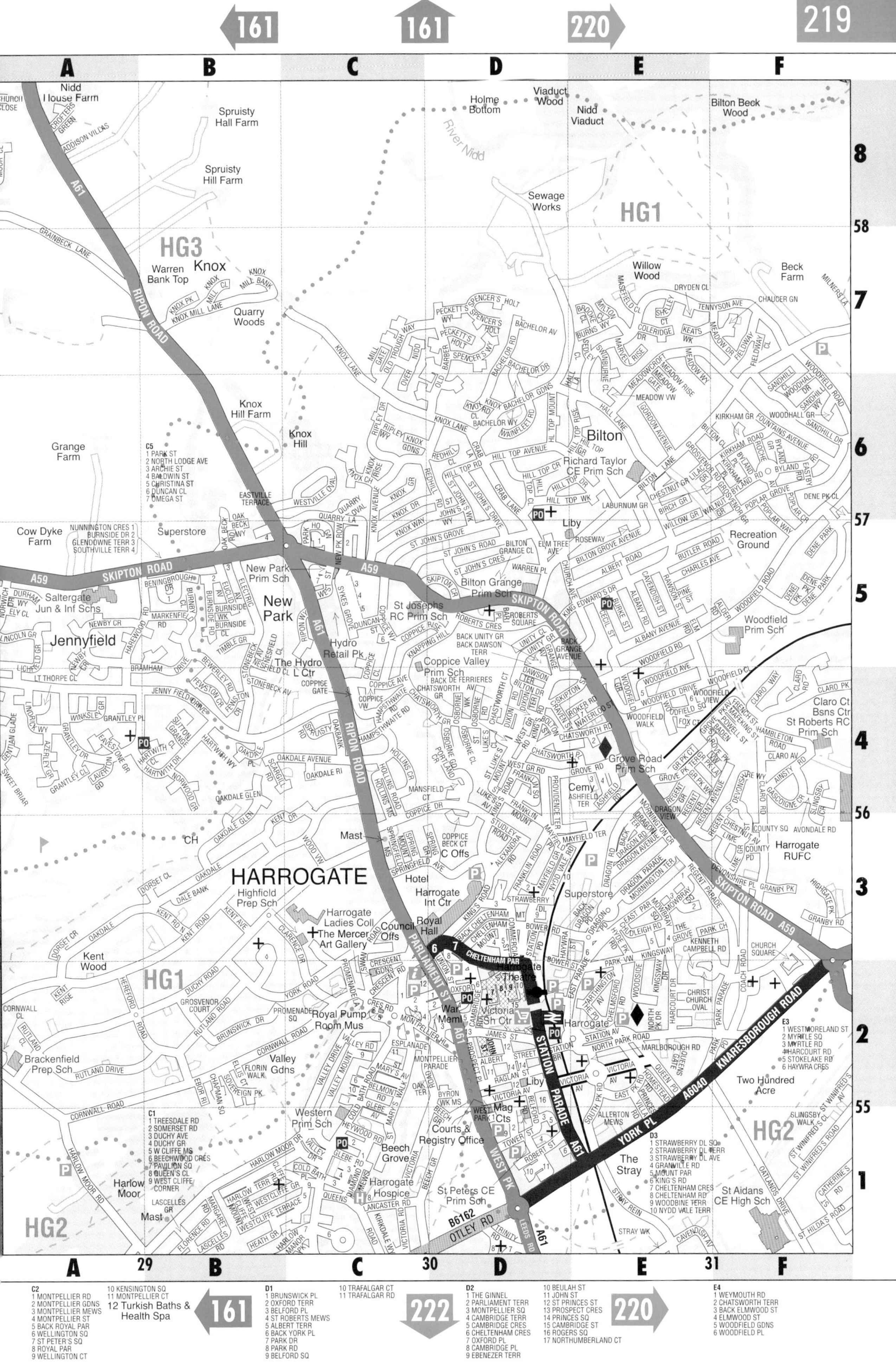

161
161
220
A
B
C
D
E
F
8
58
7
6
57
5
4
56
3
2
55
1
Nidd House Farm
Spruisty Hall Farm
Spruisty Hill Farm
Holme Bottom
Viaduct Wood
Nidd Viaduct
Bilton Beck Wood
River Nidd
Sewage Works
HG1
HG3
Knox
Warren Bank Top
Quarry Woods
Willow Wood
Beck Farm
A61
GRAINBECK LANE
RIPON ROAD
KNOX LANE
Knox Hill Farm
Knox Hill
Grange Farm
Bilton
Richard Taylor CE Prim Sch
C5
1 PARK ST
2 NORTH LODGE AVE
3 ARCHIE ST
4 BALDWIN ST
5 CHRISTINA ST
6 DUNCAN CL
7 OMEGA ST
Cow Dyke Farm
NUNNINGTON CRES 1
BURNSIDE DR 2
GLENDOWNE TERR 3
SOUTHVILLE TERR 4
Superstore
Liby
Recreation Ground
A59
SKIPTON ROAD
New Park Prim Sch
New Park
Saltergate Jun & Inf Schs
Jennyfield
Bilton Grange Prim Sch
St Josephs RC Prim Sch
Hydro Retail Pk
The Hydro L Ctr
Coppice Valley Prim Sch
Woodfield Prim Sch
Claro Ct Bsns Ctr
St Roberts RC Prim Sch
Grove Road Prim Sch
Cemy
Harrogate RUFC
Mast
C Offs
HARROGATE
Highfield Prep Sch
Hotel
Harrogate Int Ctr
Harrogate Ladies Coll
The Mercer Art Gallery
Council Offs
Royal Hall
Harrogate Theatre
Superstore
Kent Wood
HG1
Royal Pump Room Mus
War Meml
Victoria Sh Ctr
Harrogate
Brackenfield Prep Sch
Valley Gdns
Liby
Mag Cts
Courts & Registry Office
Western Prim Sch
Beech Grove
Harrogate Hospice
St Peters CE Prim Sch
Harlow Moor
Mast
HG2
The Stray
Two Hundred Acre
HG2
St Aidans CE High Sch
STATION PARADE
PARLIAMENT ST
WEST PK
YORK PL
A6040 KNARESBOROUGH ROAD
B6162 OTLEY RD
LEEDS RD
C1
1 TREESDALE RD
2 SOMERSET RD
3 DUCHY AVE
4 DUCHY GR
5 W CLIFFE MS
6 BEECHWOOD CRES
7 PAVILION SQ
8 QUEEN'S CL
9 WEST CLIFFE CORNER
E3
1 WESTMORELAND ST
2 MYRTLE SQ
3 MYRTLE RD
4 HARCOURT RD
5 STOKELAKE RD
6 HAYWRA CRES
D3
1 STRAWBERRY DL SQ
2 STRAWBERRY DL TERR
3 STRAWBERRY DL AVE
4 GRANVILLE RD
5 MOUNT PAR
6 KING'S RD
7 CHELTENHAM CRES
8 CHELTENHAM RD
9 WOODBINE TERR
10 NYDD VALE TERR
A
29
B
C
30
D
E
31
F
C2
1 MONTPELLIER RD
2 MONTPELLIER GDNS
3 MONTPELLIER MEWS
4 MONTPELLIER ST
5 BACK ROYAL PAR
6 WELLINGTON SQ
7 ST PETER'S SQ
8 ROYAL PAR
9 WELLINGTON CT
10 KENSINGTON SQ
11 MONTPELLIER CT
12 Turkish Baths & Health Spa
161
D1
1 BRUNSWICK PL
2 OXFORD TERR
3 BELFORD PL
4 ST ROBERTS MEWS
5 ALBERT TERR
6 BACK YORK PL
7 PARK DR
8 PARK RD
9 BELFORD SQ
10 TRAFALGAR CT
11 TRAFALGAR RD
222
D2
1 THE GINNEL
2 PARLIAMENT TERR
3 MONTPELLIER SQ
4 CAMBRIDGE TERR
5 CAMBRIDGE CRES
6 CHELTENHAM CRES
7 OXFORD PL
8 CAMBRIDGE PL
9 EBENEZER TERR
10 BEULAH ST
11 JOHN ST
12 ST PRINCES ST
13 PROSPECT CRES
14 PRINCES SQ
15 CAMBRIDGE ST
16 ROGERS SQ
17 NORTHUMBERLAND CT
220
E4
1 WEYMOUTH RD
2 CHATSWORTH TERR
3 BACK ELMWOOD ST
4 ELMWOOD ST
5 WOODFIELD GDNS
6 WOODFIELD PL

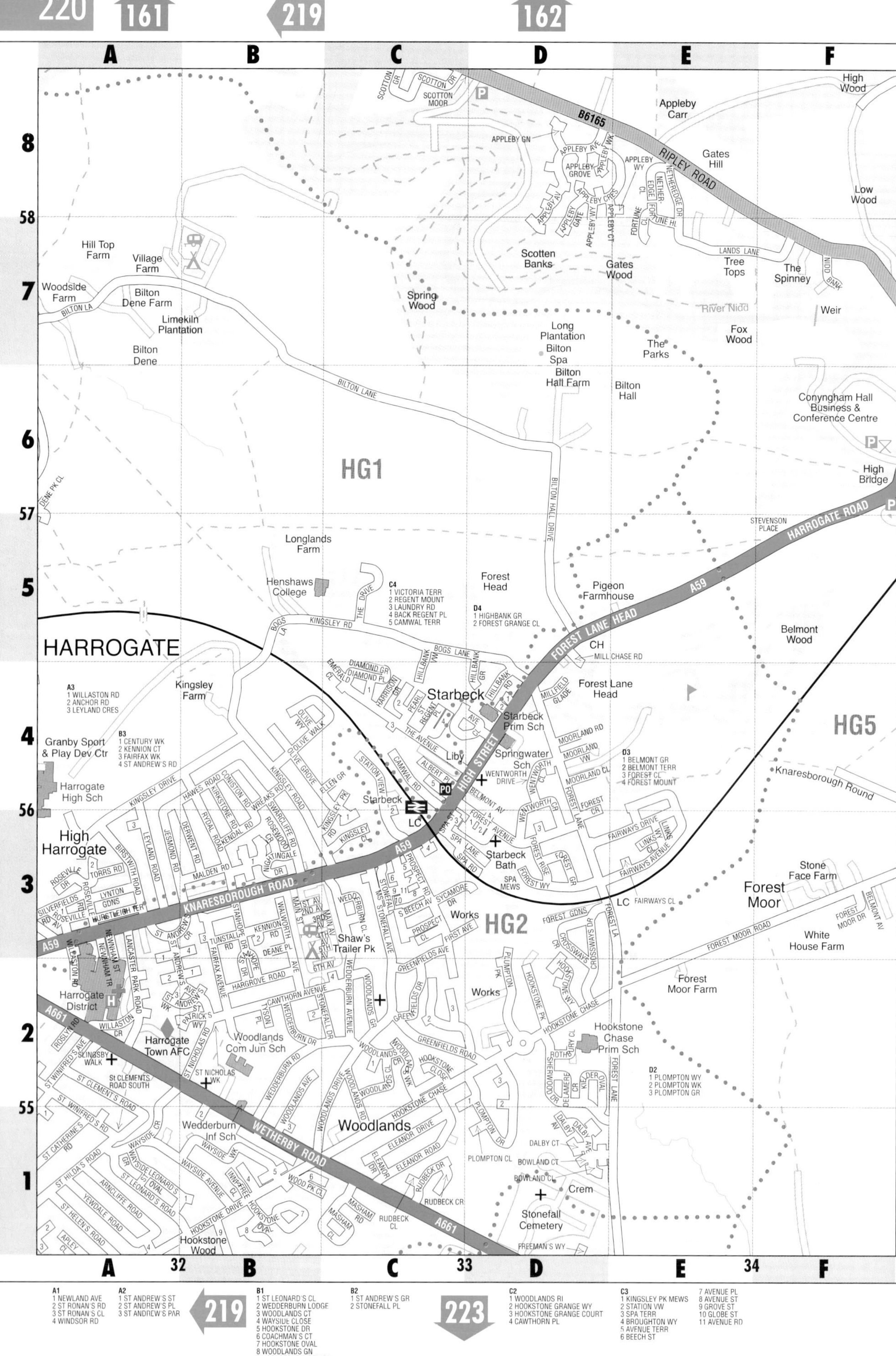

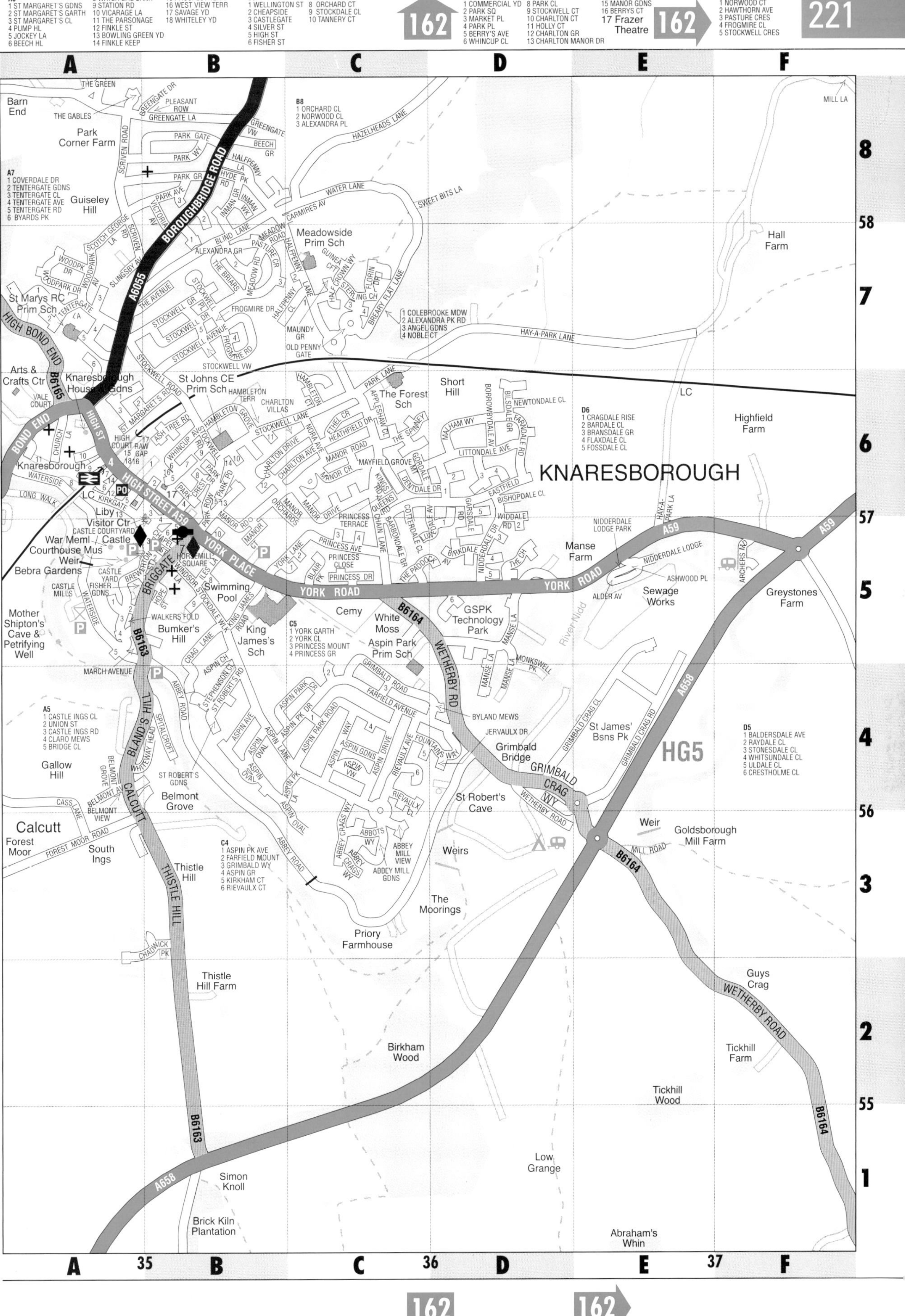

161
219

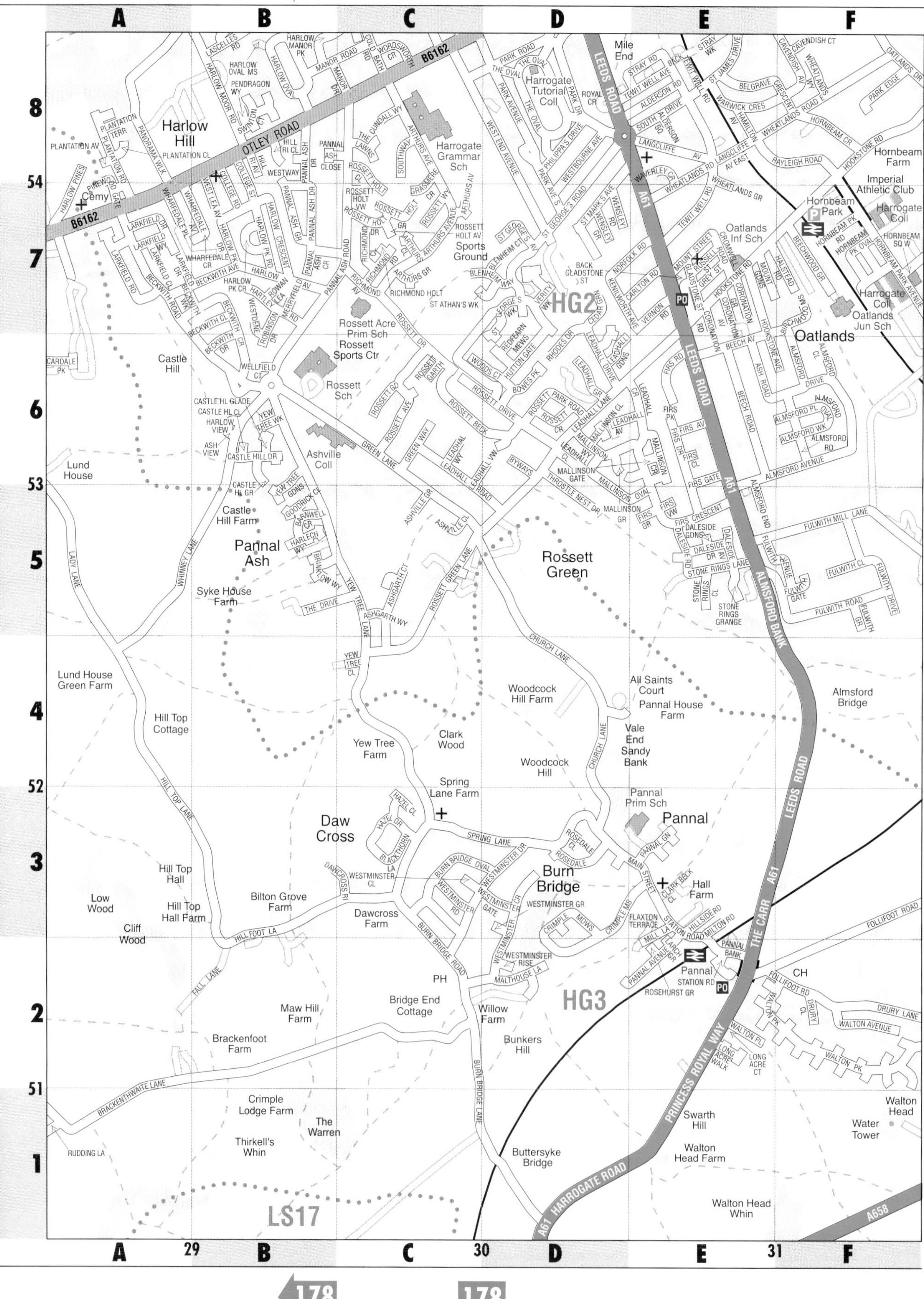
A B C D E F
8
54
7
6
53
5
4
52
3
51
2
1
29
30
31
Harlow Hill
OTLEY ROAD
B6162
Cemy
Harrogate Grammar Sch
Harrogate Tutorial Coll
Mile End
LEEDS ROAD
A61
Hornbeam Farm
Imperial Athletic Club
Hornbeam Park
Harrogate Coll
Oatlands Inf Sch
Sports Ground
HG2
Harrogate Coll
Oatlands Jun Sch
Oatlands
PO
Rossett Acre Prim Sch
Rossett Sports Ctr
Rossett Sch
Castle Hill
Ashville Coll
GREEN LANE
Lund House
Castle Hill Farm
Pannal Ash
Rossett Green
Syke House Farm
Lund House Green Farm
ALMSFORD BANK
Woodcock Hill Farm
All Saints Court
Pannal House Farm
Almsford Bridge
Hill Top Cottage
Yew Tree Farm
Clark Wood
Vale End Sandy Bank
Woodcock Hill
Spring Lane Farm
Pannal Prim Sch
Daw Cross
Pannal
Burn Bridge
Hill Top Hall
Low Wood
Hill Top Hall Farm
Bilton Grove Farm
Dawcross Farm
Hall Farm
Cliff Wood
THE CARR
Pannal
PH
CH
HG3
Maw Hill Farm
Bridge End Cottage
Willow Farm
Bunkers Hill
Brackenfoot Farm
PRINCESS ROYAL WAY
Crimple Lodge Farm
The Warren
Swarth Hill
Walton Head
Water Tower
Thirkell's Whin
Buttersyke Bridge
Walton Head Farm
A61 HARROGATE ROAD
Walton Head Whin
LS17
A658

178
178

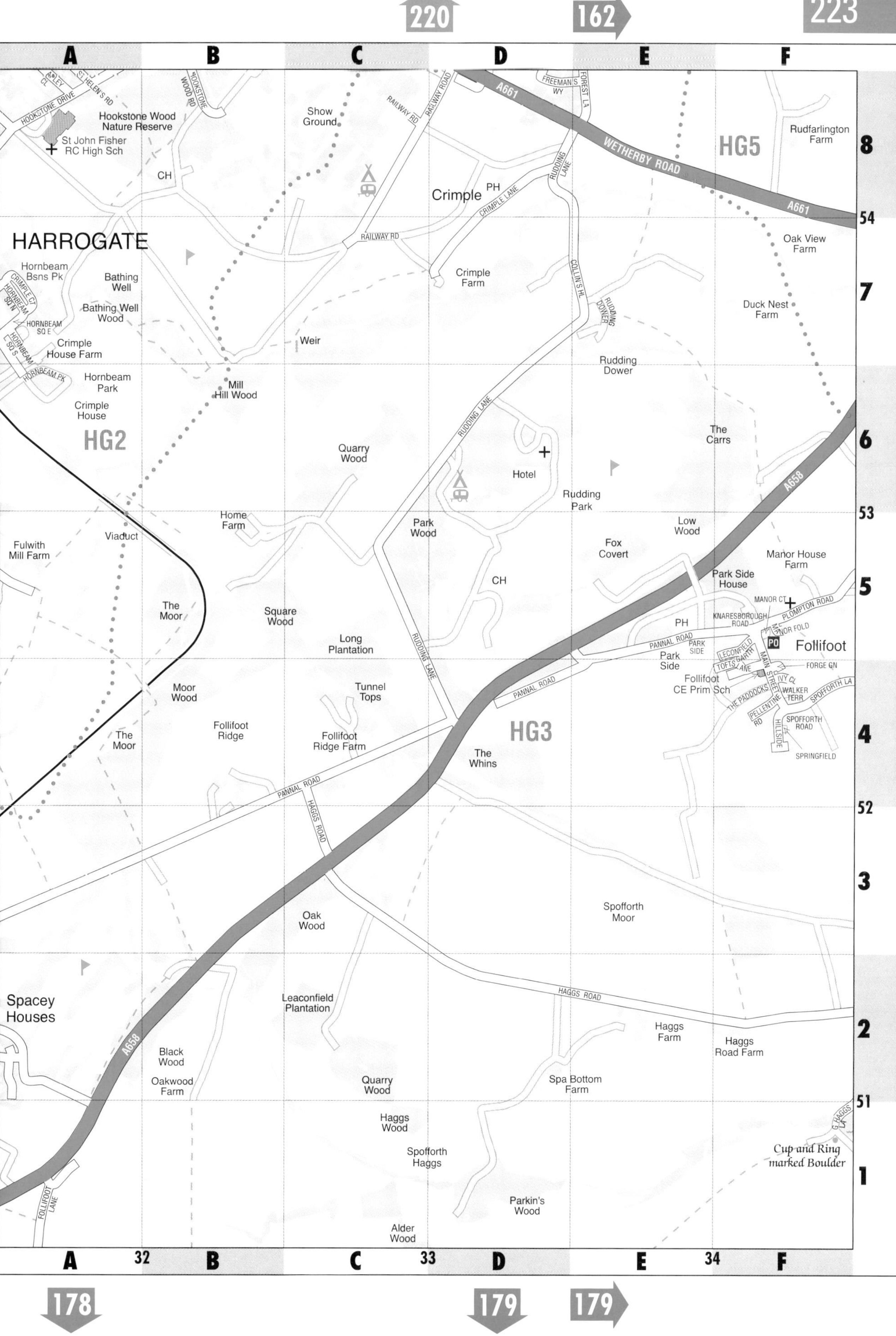

A B C D E F

8
54
7
6
53
5
4
52
3
2
51
1

32   33   34

HG5
HG2
HG3

HARROGATE

Hookstone Wood
Nature Reserve

St John Fisher
RC High Sch

CH

COPLEY
ST HELEN'S RD
HOOKSTONE DRIVE
HOOKSTONE WOOD RD
RAILWAY RD
RAILWAY ROAD
A661
FREEMAN'S WY
FOREST LA
WETHERBY ROAD
A661

Show
Ground

Crimple

PH
CRIMPLE LANE
RUDDING LANE
COLLIN'S HL

Rudfarlington
Farm

Oak View
Farm

Hornbeam
Bsns Pk

Bathing
Well

Bathing Well
Wood

Weir

Crimple
Farm

Rudding
Dower

Duck Nest
Farm

Crimple
House Farm

Mill
Hill Wood

Hornbeam
Park

Crimple
House

Quarry
Wood

RUDDING LANE
RUDDING TOWER

Hotel

Rudding
Park

The Carrs

Fulwith
Mill Farm

Home
Farm

Park
Wood

Fox
Covert

Low
Wood

Manor House
Farm

Viaduct

The
Moor

Square
Wood

CH

Park Side
House

Park Side

PH

MANOR CT
KNARESBOROUGH ROAD
MANOR FOLD
PLOMPTON ROAD
PO

Follifoot

Moor
Wood

Long
Plantation

RUDDING LANE

Pannal
Road

PANNAL ROAD
PARK SIDE
LECONFIELD
TOFTS GARTH
MAIN STREET
IVY CL
FORGE GN
WALKER TERR
SPOFFORTH LA

Follifoot
CE Prim Sch

The
Moor

Follifoot
Ridge

Tunnel
Tops

Follifoot
Ridge Farm

The Whins

THE PADDOCKS
PELLENTINE RD
HILLSIDE
SPOFFORTH ROAD
SPRINGFIELD

PANNAL ROAD
HAGGS ROAD

Oak
Wood

Spofforth
Moor

Spacey
Houses

A658

Black
Wood

Leaconfield
Plantation

HAGGS ROAD

Haggs
Farm

Haggs
Road Farm

G HAGGS LA

Oakwood
Farm

Quarry
Wood

Spa Bottom
Farm

Haggs
Wood

Cup and Ring
marked Boulder

Spofforth
Haggs

FOLLIFOOT LANE

Parkin's
Wood

Alder
Wood

HORNBEAM
CRIMPLE CT
HORNBEAM SQ N
HORNBEAM SQ E
HORNBEAM SQ S
HORNBEAM PK

165
166

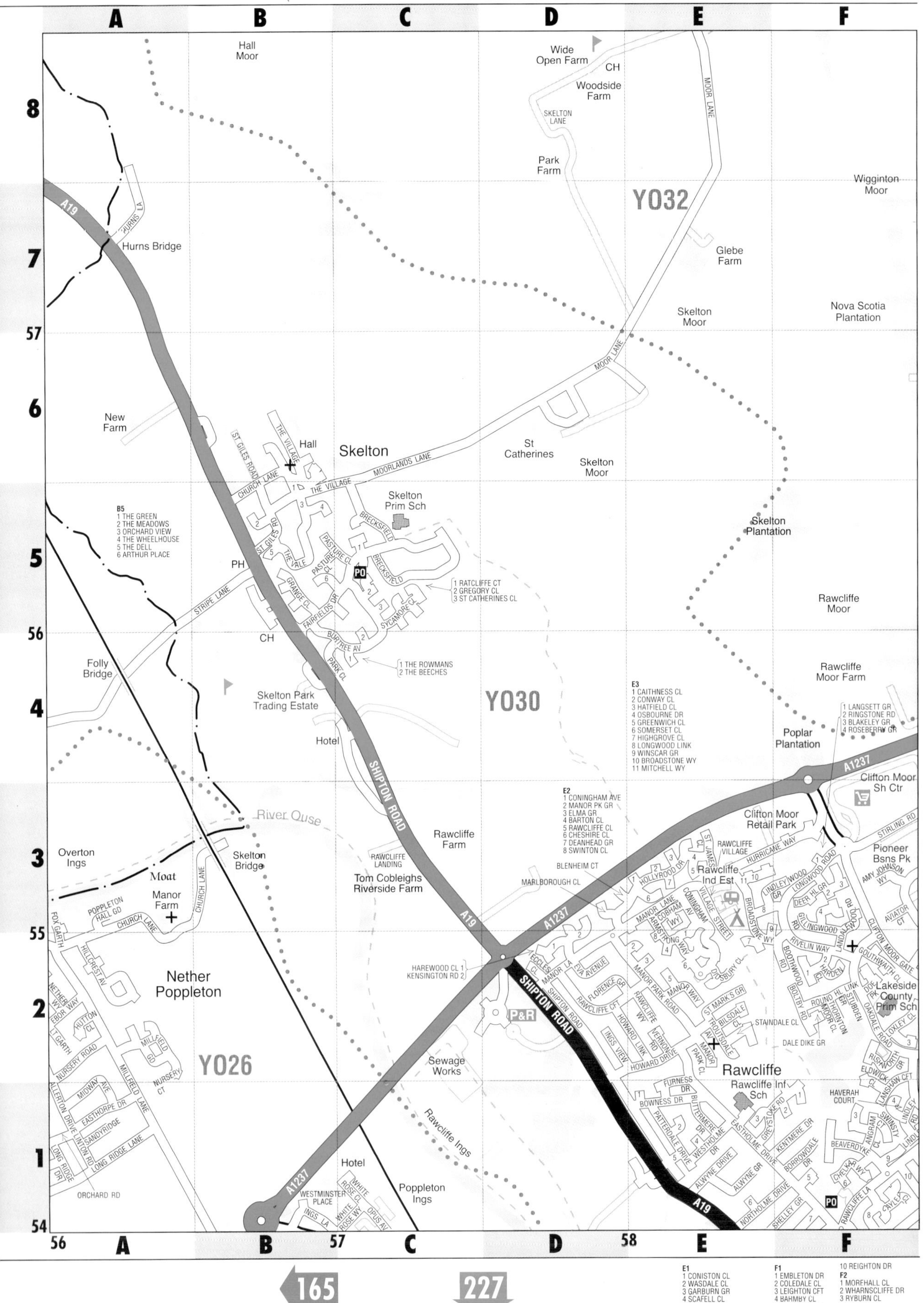

165
227

B5
1 THE GREEN
2 THE MEADOWS
3 ORCHARD VIEW
4 THE WHEELHOUSE
5 THE DELL
6 ARTHUR PLACE

1 RATCLIFFE CT
2 GREGORY CL
3 ST CATHERINES CL

1 THE ROWMANS
2 THE BEECHES

E3
1 CAITHNESS CL
2 CONWAY CL
3 HATFIELD CL
4 OSBOURNE DR
5 GREENWICH CL
6 SOMERSET CL
7 HIGHGROVE CL
8 LONGWOOD LINK
9 WINSCAR GR
10 BROADSTONE WY
11 MITCHELL WY

E2
1 CONINGHAM AVE
2 MANOR PK GR
3 ELMA GR
4 BARTON CL
5 RAWCLIFFE CL
6 CHESHIRE CL
7 DEANHEAD GR
8 SWINTON CL

1 LANGSETT GR
2 RINGSTONE RD
3 BLAKELEY GR
4 ROSEBERRY GR

1 HAREWOOD CL
2 KENSINGTON RD

E1
1 CONISTON CL
2 WASDALE CL
3 GARBURN GR
4 SCAFELL CL
5 LOWESWATER RD
6 FYLINGDALES AVE

F1
1 EMBLETON DR
2 COLEDALE CL
3 LEIGHTON CFT
4 BAHMHY CL
5 GRASMERE GR
6 BARDEN CT
7 SOUTHOLME DR
8 MILTON CARR
9 FEWSTON DR

10 REIGHTON DR
F2
1 MORFHALL CL
2 WHARNSCLIFFE DR
3 RYBURN CL

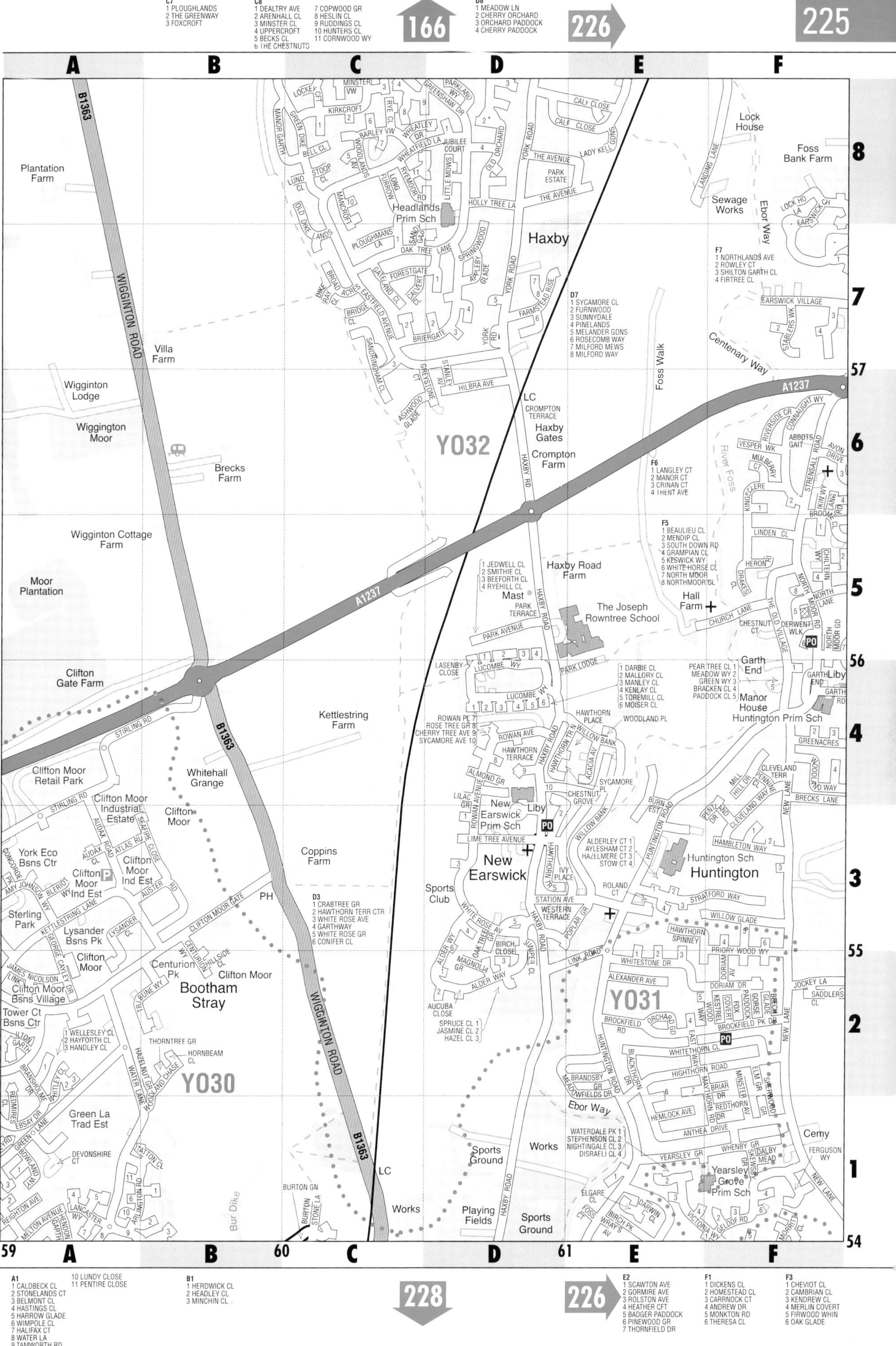

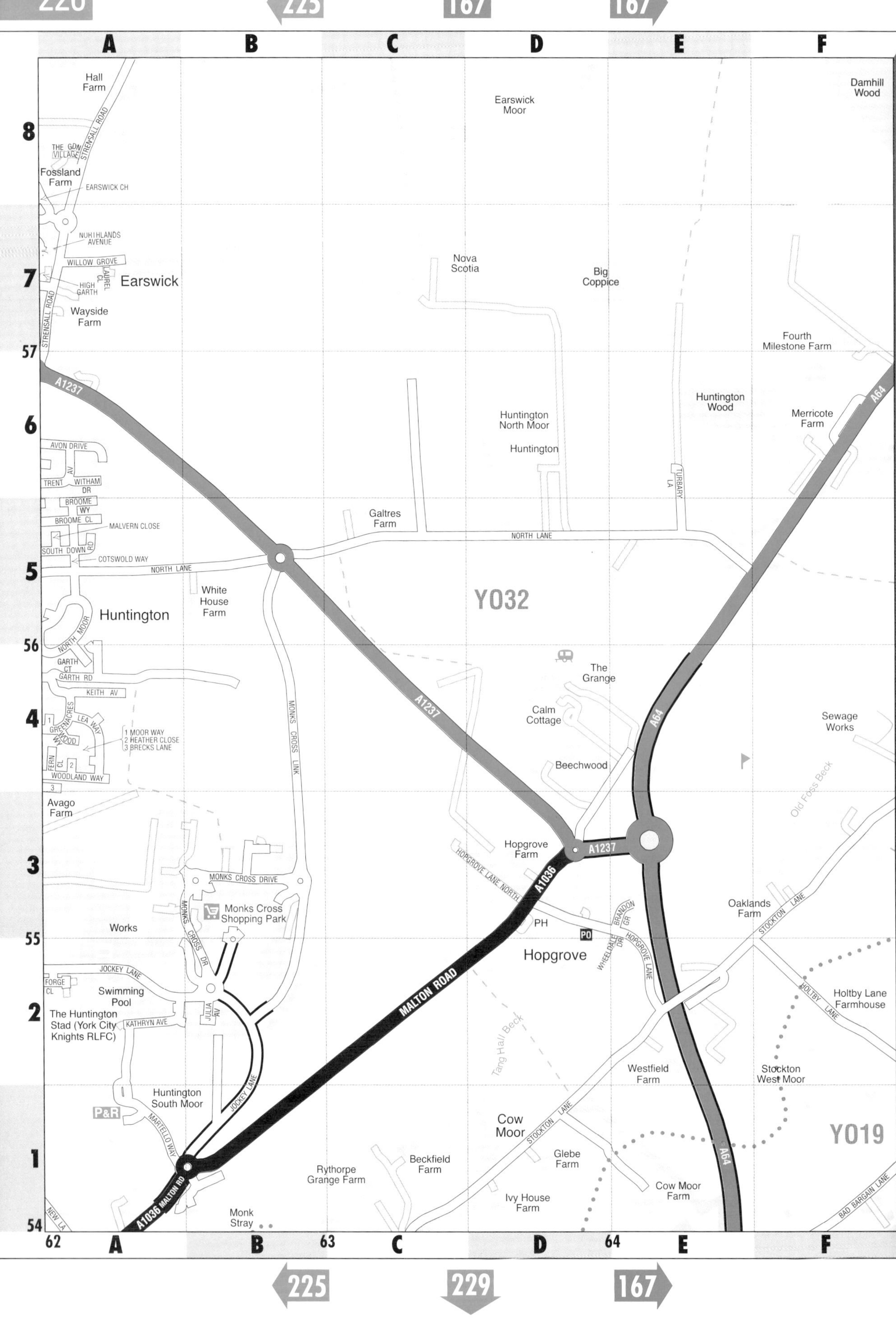
Hall Farm
Earswick Moor
Damhill Wood
Fossland Farm
Earswick
Wayside Farm
Nova Scotia
Big Coppice
Fourth Milestone Farm
Huntington Wood
Merricote Farm
Huntington North Moor
Huntington
Galtres Farm
NORTH LANE
White House Farm
Huntington
YO32
The Grange
Calm Cottage
Beechwood
Sewage Works
Avago Farm
Hopgrove Farm
Monks Cross Shopping Park
Works
Oaklands Farm
PH
Hopgrove
Swimming Pool
Holtby Lane Farmhouse
The Huntington Stad (York City Knights RLFC)
Westfield Farm
Stockton West Moor
Huntington South Moor
Cow Moor
YO19
Glebe Farm
Beckfield Farm
Rythorpe Grange Farm
Cow Moor Farm
Ivy House Farm
Monk Stray
A1237
A64
A1036
MALTON ROAD
MONKS CROSS LINK
MONKS CROSS DRIVE
JOCKEY LANE
STOCKTON LANE
HOPGROVE LANE NORTH
STRENSALL ROAD
Tang Hall Beck
Old Foss Beck

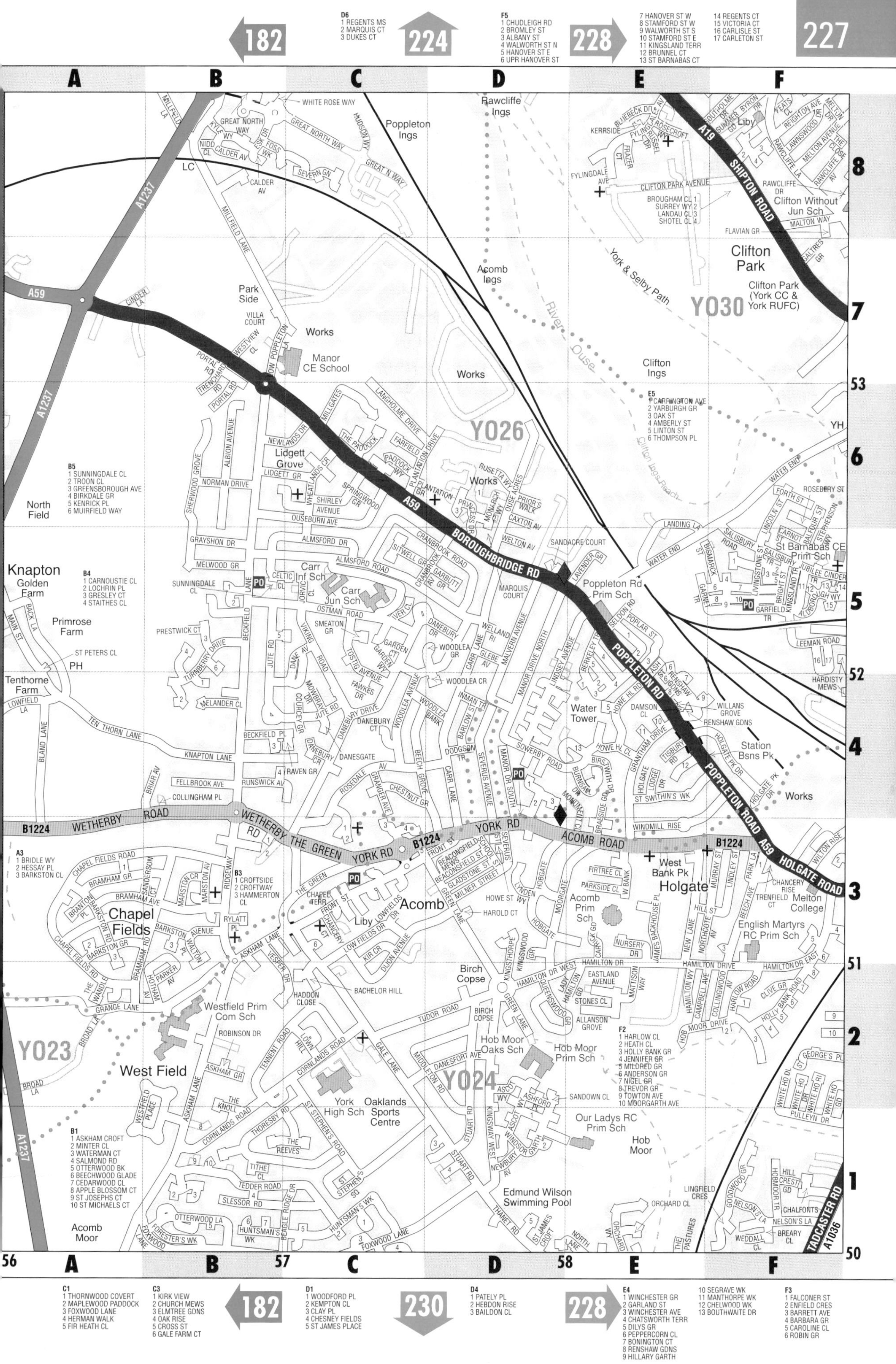

182
D6
1 REGENTS MS
2 MARQUIS CT
3 DUKES CT
224
F5
1 CHUDLEIGH RD
2 BROMLEY ST
3 ALBANY ST
4 WALWORTH ST N
5 HANOVER ST E
6 UPR HANOVER ST
228
7 HANOVER ST W
8 STAMFORD ST W
9 WALWORTH ST S
10 STAMFORD ST E
11 KINGSLAND TERR
12 BRUNNEL CT
13 ST BARNABAS CT
14 REGENTS CT
15 VICTORIA CT
16 CARLISLE ST
17 CARLETON ST
227
A
B
C
D
E
F
8
7
53
6
5
52
4
3
51
2
1
50
56
57
58
Rawcliffe Ings
Poppleton Ings
WHITE ROSE WAY
GREAT NORTH WAY
GREAT N WAY
SEVERN GN
CALDER AV
MILLFIELD LANE
LC
A1237
A59
CINDER LA
Park Side
VILLA COURT
Works
Manor CE School
Acomb Ings
River Ouse
York & Selby Path
Clifton Park
Clifton Park (York CC & York RUFC)
Clifton Without Jun Sch
Y030
Clifton Ings
SHIPTON ROAD
A19
Liby
CLIFTON PARK AVENUE
BROUGHAM CL 1
SURREY WY 2
LANDAU CL 3
SHOTEL CL 4
FLAVIAN GR
MALTON WAY
KERRSIDE
FYLINGDALE AVE
E5
1 CARRINGTON AVE
2 YARBURGH GR
3 OAK ST
4 AMBERLY ST
5 LINTON ST
6 THOMPSON PL
Y026
B5
1 SUNNINGDALE CL
2 TROON CL
3 GREENSBOROUGH AVE
4 BIRKDALE GR
5 KENRICK PL
6 MUIRFIELD WAY
North Field
Lidgett Grove
BOROUGHBRIDGE RD
A59
Carr Inf Sch
Carr Jun Sch
Works
SANDACRE COURT
Poppleton Rd Prim Sch
MARQUIS COURT
WATER END
LANDING LA
St Barnabas CE Prim Sch
LEEMAN ROAD
HARDISTY MEWS
Knapton
Golden Farm
B4
1 CARNOUSTIE CL
2 LOCHRIN PL
3 GRESLEY CT
4 STAITHES CL
Primrose Farm
ST PETERS CL
PH
Tenthorne Farm
TEN THORN LANE
KNAPTON LANE
OSTMAN ROAD
DANEBURY DRIVE
WOODLEA AVENUE
CARR LANE
MALVERN AVENUE
MANOR DRIVE NORTH
Water Tower
POPPLETON RD
WILLANS GROVE
RENSHAW GDNS
Station Bsns Pk
Works
B1224
WETHERBY ROAD
THE GREEN
YORK RD
ACOMB ROAD
West Bank Pk
Holgate
HOLGATE ROAD
A3
1 BRIDLE WY
2 HESSAY PL
3 BARKSTON CL
B3
1 CROFTSIDE
2 CROFTWAY
3 HAMMERTON CL
Chapel Fields
Acomb
Liby
Acomb Prim Sch
English Martyrs RC Prim Sch
Melton College
Westfield Prim Com Sch
Y023
West Field
Birch Copse
HAMILTON DRIVE
F2
1 HARLOW CL
2 HEATH CL
3 HOLLY BANK GR
4 JENNIFER GR
5 MILDRED GR
6 ANDERSON GR
7 NIGEL GR
8 TREVOR GR
9 TOWTON AVE
10 MOORGARTH AVE
Hob Moor Oaks Sch
Hob Moor Prim Sch
Y024
York High Sch
Oaklands Sports Centre
Our Ladys RC Prim Sch
Hob Moor
B1
1 ASKHAM CROFT
2 MINTER CL
3 WATERMAN CT
4 SALMOND RD
5 OTTERWOOD BK
6 BEECHWOOD GLADE
7 CEDARWOOD CL
8 APPLE BLOSSOM CT
9 ST JOSEPHS CT
10 ST MICHAELS CT
Acomb Moor
Edmund Wilson Swimming Pool
TADCASTER RD
A1036
C1
1 THORNWOOD COVERT
2 MAPLEWOOD PADDOCK
3 FOXWOOD LANE
4 HERMAN WALK
5 FIR HEATH CL
C3
1 KIRK VIEW
2 CHURCH MEWS
3 ELMTREE GDNS
4 OAK RISE
5 CROSS ST
6 GALE FARM CT
182
D1
1 WOODFORD PL
2 KEMPTON CL
3 CLAY PL
4 CHESNEY FIELDS
5 ST JAMES PLACE
230
D4
1 PATELY PL
2 HEBDON RISE
3 BAILDON CL
228
E4
1 WINCHESTER GR
2 GARLAND ST
3 WINCHESTER AVE
4 CHATSWORTH TERR
5 DILYS GR
6 PEPPERCORN CL
7 BONINGTON CT
8 RENSHAW GDNS
9 HILLARY GARTH
10 SEGRAVE WK
11 MANTHORPE WK
12 CHELWOOD WK
13 BOUTHWAITE DR
F3
1 FALCONER ST
2 ENFIELD CRES
3 BARRETT AVE
4 BARBARA GR
5 CAROLINE CL
6 ROBIN GR

A B C D E F

8 7 53 6 5 52 4 3 51 2 1 50

YO30 YO31 Heworth YORK EBVRACVM YO26 YO01 YO24 YO23 YO10 Walmgate Stray Low Moor

59 A B 60 C D 61 E F

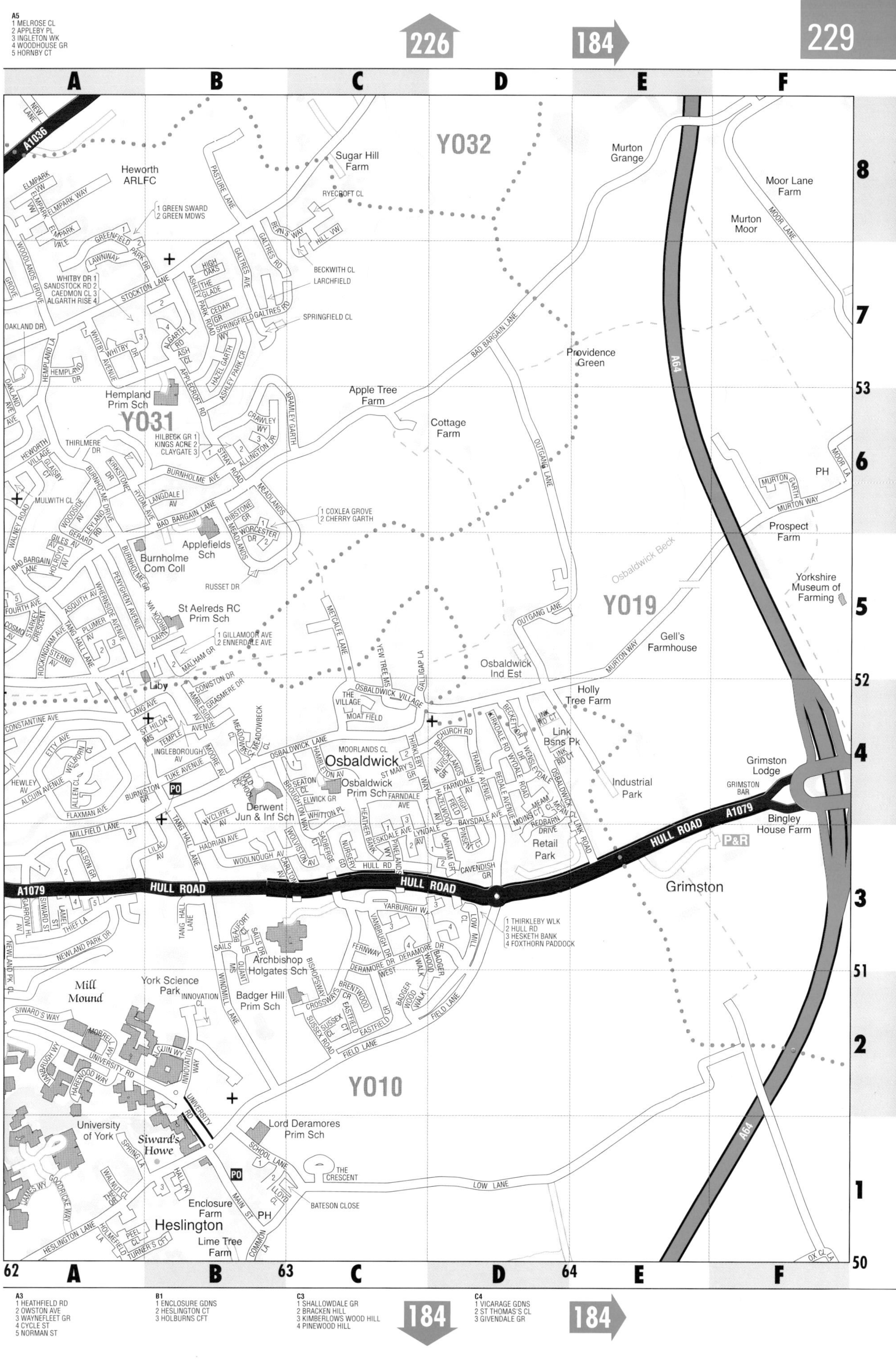
A5
1 MELROSE CL
2 APPLEBY PL
3 INGLETON WK
4 WOODHOUSE GR
5 HORNBY CT
226
184
A
B
C
D
E
F
8
7
53
6
5
52
4
3
51
2
1
50
62
63
64
YO32
YO31
YO19
YO10
A1036
NEW LANE
Heworth ARLFC
Sugar Hill Farm
RYECROFT CL
Murton Grange
Moor Lane Farm
Murton Moor
MOOR LANE
1 GREEN SWARD
2 GREEN MDWS
PASTURE LANE
BEAN'S WAY
HILL VW
BECKWITH CL
LARCHFIELD
GALTRES RD
GALTRES AVE
ELMPARK VW
ELMPARK WAY
ELMPARK VALE
GREENFIELD PARK DR
LAWNWAY
WOODLANDS GROVE
WHITBY DR 1
SANDSTOCK RD 2
CAEDMON CL 3
ALGARTH RISE 4
STOCKTON LANE
HIGH OAKS
THE GLADE
ASHLEY PARK ROAD
CEDAR GR
SPRINGFIELD WY
SPRINGFIELD CL
OAKLAND DR
HEMPLAND LA
WHITBY AVENUE
WHITBY DR
ALGARTH RD
ASH CL
HAZEL GARTH
ASHLEY PARK CR
BAD BARGAIN LANE
Providence Green
A64
HEMPLAND DR
APPLECROFT RD
Hempland Prim Sch
BRAMLEY GARTH
CRAWLEY WY
Apple Tree Farm
Cottage Farm
OAKLAND AVE
HEWORTH VILLAGE
THIRLMERE DR
HILBECK GR 1
KINGS ACRE 2
CLAYGATE 3
STRAY ROAD
ALLINGTON DR
OUTGANG LANE
GLAISBY CT
KIRKSTONE DR
BURNHOLME AVE
MURTON GARTH
PH
MOOR LA
MULWITH CL
BURNHOLME DRIVE
RYDAL AVE
LANGDALE AV
MEADLANDS
1 COXLEA GROVE
2 CHERRY GARTH
MURTON WAY
Prospect Farm
WALNEY ROAD
WOODSIDE AV
GERARD AV
LEYLAND RD
RIBSTONE GR
WORCESTER DR
GILES AV
HOLROYD AV
Applefields Sch
Burnholme Com Coll
Osbaldwick Beck
BAD BARGAIN LANE
BURNHOLME GR
PENYGHENT AVENUE
RUSSET DR
Yorkshire Museum of Farming
FOURTH AVE
COSMO AV
STARKEY CRESCENT
ASQUITH AV
WHERNSIDE AVENUE
HOUGHTON WK
St Aelreds RC Prim Sch
METCALFE LANE
OUTGANG LANE
YO19
PLUMER AV
TANG HALL LANE
DARNBROOK
1 GILLAMOOR AVE
2 ENNERDALE AVE
Gell's Farmhouse
ROCKINGHAM AVE
STERNE AV
MALHAM GR
YEW TREE MS
GALLIGAP LA
Osbaldwick Ind Est
Lib
CONISTON DR
GRASMERE DR
THE VILLAGE
OSBALDWICK VILLAGE
Holly Tree Farm
CONSTANTINE AVE
LANG AVE
ST HILDA'S MS
AMBLESIDE AV
MEADOWBECK CL
MOAT FIELD
BECKETT DR
LINK RD CT
ETTY AVE
TEMPLE AVENUE
MEADOWBECK CL
CHURCH RD
Link Bsns Pk
WELBORN CL
INGLEBOROUGH AV
OSBALDWICK LANE
MOORLANDS CL
KIRKDALE RD
WENSLEYDALE DR
LINK RD CT
Grimston Lodge
HEWLEY AV
MOORE AV
Osbaldwick
THIRKLEBY WAY
BROOKLANDS
TRANBY AVENUE
OSBALDWICK LINK ROAD
ALLEN CL
TUKE AVENUE
HAMBLETON AV
ST MARY'S GR
ALVIS GR
Industrial Park
GRIMSTON BAR
ALCUIN AVENUE
BURNISTON GR
PO
OLD SCHOOL CL
SEATON CL
Osbaldwick Prim Sch
FARNDALE AV
WYDALE ROAD
A1079
FLAXMAN AVE
BROUGHTON WAY
ELWICK GR
FARNDALE AVE
HIGH FIELD
BEDALE AVENUE
MEAM CL
Bingley House Farm
Derwent Jun & Inf Sch
WHITTON PL
HAZELWOOD AV
MOINS CT
MCHAN CL
MILLFIELD LANE
WYCLIFFE AV
HEATHER BANK
LYNDALE AV
BAYSDALE AVE
REDBARN DRIVE
LILAC AV
HADRIAN AVE
ESKDALE AVE
PINSENT CT
HULL ROAD
MILSON GR
WOOLNOUGH AV
WOLVISTON AV
SADBERGE CT
NURSERY GD
PINELANDS WY
CANHAM GR
Retail Park
P&R
HULL RD
CAVENDISH GR
A1079
HULL ROAD
HULL ROAD
Grimston
SIWARD ST
LAMEL ST
GARROW HL
THIEF LA
TANG HALL LANE
YARBURGH WAY
LOW MILL CL
1 THIRKLEBY WLK
2 HULL RD
3 HESKETH BANK
4 FOXTHORN PADDOCK
NEWLAND PARK DR
BEAUFORT CL
SAILS DR
SAILS MS
QUANT MS
Archbishop Holgates Sch
VANBRUGH DR
FERNWAY
DERAMORE DR
DERAMORE DR WEST
BADGER WOOD WALK
NEWLAND PK CL
Mill Mound
York Science Park
INNOVATION CL
Badger Hill Prim Sch
BISHOPSWAY
BRENTWOOD
CROSSWAYS
BADGER WOOD WALK
FIELD LANE
WINDMILL LANE
SUSSEX CL
SUSSEX CT
EASTFIELD CR
EASTFIELD CT
SUSSEX ROAD
FIELD LANE
SIWARD'S WAY
MORRELL WY
ALCUIN WY
VANBRUGH WY
UNIVERSITY RD
HAREWOOD WAY
INNOVATION WAY
UNIVERSITY RD
University of York
Siward's Howe
Lord Deramores Prim Sch
SCHOOL LANE
THE CRESCENT
LOW LANE
SPRING LA
HALL PK
PO
JAMES WY
GOODRICKE WAY
WALNUT CL
THE OR
LLOYD CL
BATESON CLOSE
Enclosure Farm
MAIN ST
PH
HESLINGTON LANE
HOLMEFIELD LA
PEEL CL
Heslington
TURNER'S CFT
Lime Tree Farm
COMMON LA
OX CL LA
A3
1 HEATHFIELD RD
2 OWSTON AVE
3 WAYNEFLEET GR
4 CYCLE ST
5 NORMAN ST
B1
1 ENCLOSURE GDNS
2 HESLINGTON CT
3 HOLBURNS CFT
C3
1 SHALLOWDALE GR
2 BRACKEN HILL
3 KIMBERLOWS WOOD HILL
4 PINEWOOD HILL
C4
1 VICARAGE GDNS
2 ST THOMAS'S CL
3 GIVENDALE GR
184
184

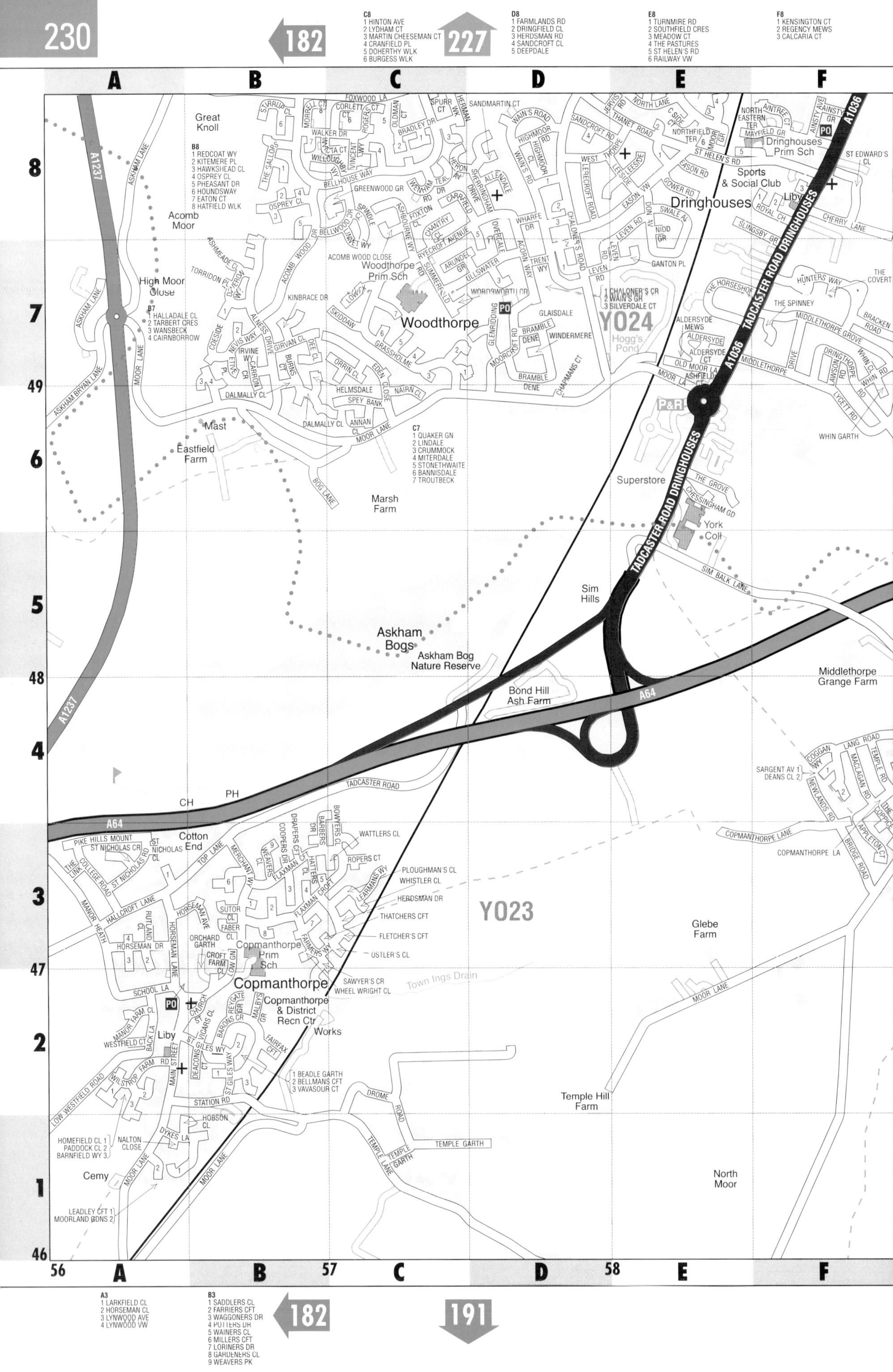

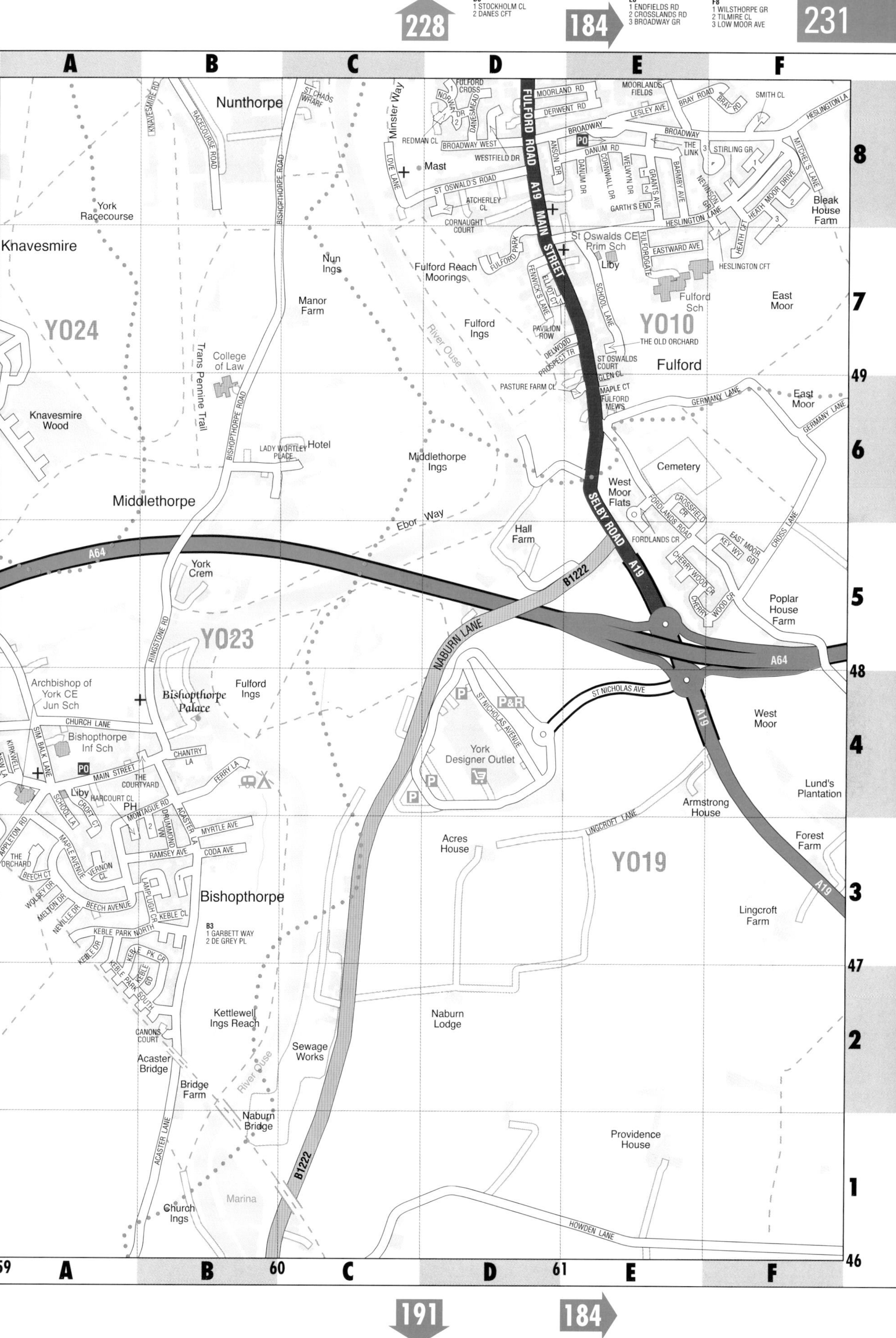
A
B
C
D
E
F
8
7
49
6
5
48
4
3
47
2
1
46
59
60
61
Nunthorpe
York Racecourse
Knavesmire
YO24
Knavesmire Wood
Middlethorpe
College of Law
Trans Pennine Trail
BISHOPTHORPE ROAD
RACECOURSE ROAD
KNAVESMIRE RD
ST CHADS WHARF
Minster Way
Nun Ings
Manor Farm
LADY WORTLEY PLACE
Hotel
Middlethorpe Ings
Ebor Way
River Ouse
Fulford Reach Moorings
Fulford Ings
Mast
LOVE LANE
REDMAN CL
BROADWAY WEST
WESTFIELD DR
ST OSWALD'S ROAD
ATCHERLEY CL
CORNAUGHT COURT
FULFORD CROSS
DANESMEAD
MOORLAND RD
DERWENT RD
FULFORD ROAD
A19
MAIN STREET
ANSON DR
DANUM RD
DANUM DR
CORNWALL DR
WELWYN DR
GRANTS AVE
GARTH'S END
BROADWAY
PO
MOORLANDS FIELDS
LESLEY AVE
BRAY ROAD
SMITH CL
HESLINGTON LA
THE LINK
STIRLING GR
BARMBY AVE
NEVINSON GR
HESLINGTON LANE
HEATH MOOR DRIVE
MITCHEL'S LANE
HEATH CFT
HESLINGTON CFT
Bleak House Farm
St Oswalds CE Prim Sch
Liby
EASTWARD AVE
FULFORDGATE
Fulford Sch
FULFORD PARK
FENWICK'S LANE
ELLIOT CT
SCHOOL LANE
PAVILION ROW
DELWOOD
PROSPECT TR
ST OSWALDS COURT
GLEN CL
MAPLE CT
FULFORD MEWS
PASTURE FARM CL
YO10
THE OLD ORCHARD
Fulford
East Moor
GERMANY LANE
Cemetery
West Moor Flats
SELBY ROAD
FORDLANDS ROAD
CROSSFIELD CR
FORDLANDS CR
EAST MOOR GD
KEY WY
CROSS LANE
CHERRY WOOD CR
Hall Farm
B1222
A64
York Crem
YO23
RINGSTONE RD
NABURN LANE
Poplar House Farm
ST NICHOLAS AVE
ST NICHOLAS AVENUE
P&R
P
York Designer Outlet
West Moor
Archbishop of York CE Jun Sch
Bishopthorpe Palace
Fulford Ings
CHURCH LANE
Bishopthorpe Inf Sch
SIM BALK LANE
KIRKWELL
NEW LA
MAIN STREET
THE COURTYARD
CHANTRY LA
FERRY LA
HARCOURT CL
PH
SCHOOL LA
CROFT CT
MONTAGUE RD
DRUMMOND VW
ACASTER LA
MYRTLE AVE
RAMSEY AVE
CODA AVE
APPLETON RD
THE ORCHARD
MAPLE AVENUE
BEECH CT
VERNON CL
WOLSEY DR
MELTON DR
NEVILLE DR
BEECH AVENUE
LAMPLUGH CR
KEBLE CL
KEBLE PARK NORTH
KEBLE DR
KEBLE PK CR
KEBLE GD
KEBLE PARK SOUTH
Bishopthorpe
B3
1 GARBETT WAY
2 DE GREY PL
Armstrong House
Lund's Plantation
Acres House
LINGCROFT LANE
YO19
Forest Farm
Lingcroft Farm
CANONS COURT
Acaster Bridge
Kettlewell Ings Reach
Sewage Works
Naburn Lodge
Bridge Farm
Naburn Bridge
ACASTER LANE
Providence House
Marina
Church Ings
HOWDEN LANE

197 197 198 198

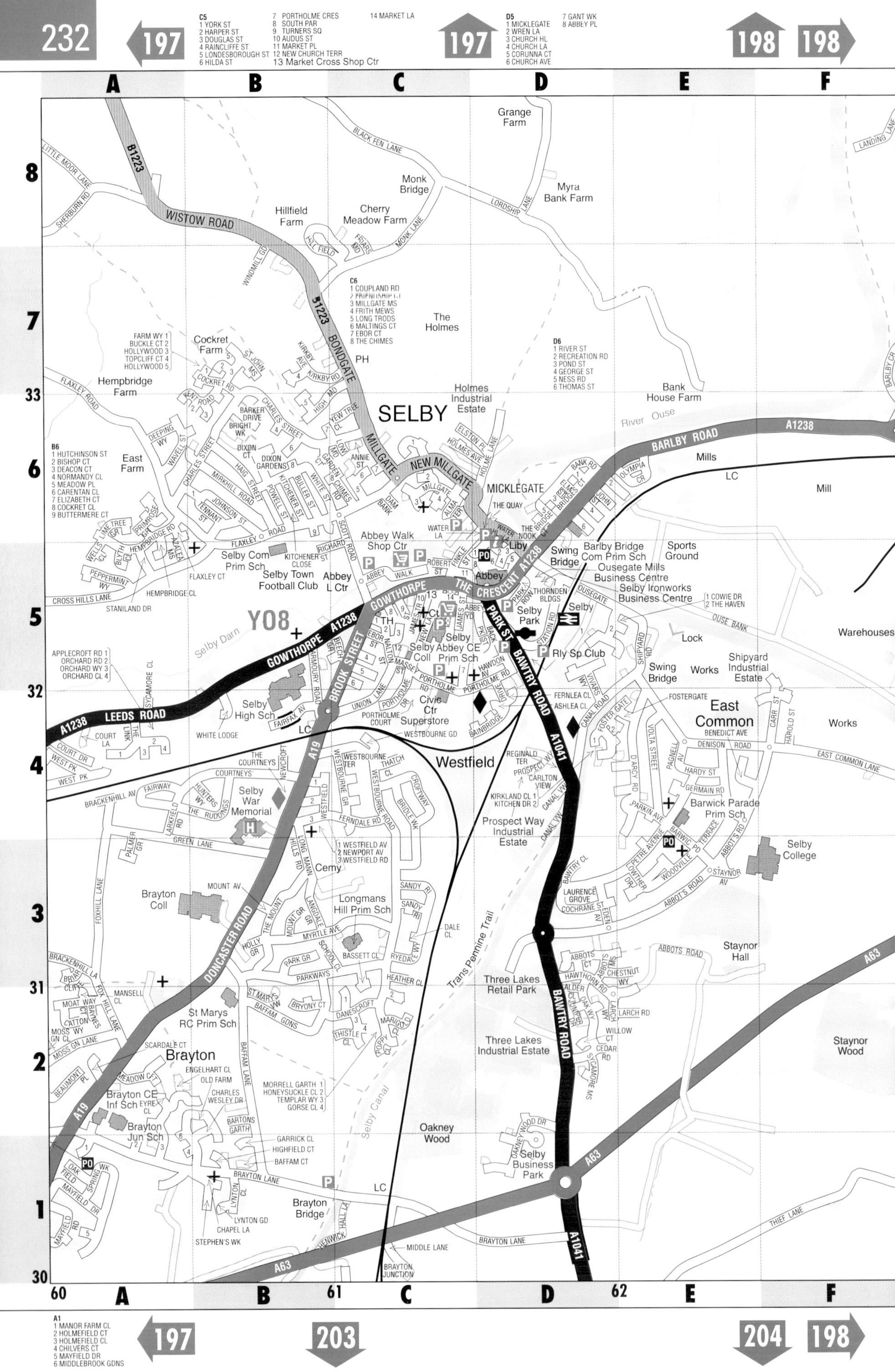
C5
1 YORK ST
2 HARPER ST
3 DOUGLAS ST
4 RAINCLIFFE ST
5 LONDESBOROUGH ST
6 HILDA ST
7 PORTHOLME CRES
8 SOUTH PAR
9 TURNERS SQ
10 AUDUS ST
11 MARKET PL
12 NEW CHURCH TERR
13 Market Cross Shop Ctr
14 MARKET LA
D5
1 MICKLEGATE
2 WREN LA
3 CHURCH HL
4 CHURCH LA
5 CORUNNA CT
6 CHURCH AVE
7 GANT WK
8 ABBEY PL
C6
1 COUPLAND RD
3 MILLGATE MS
4 FRITH MEWS
5 LONG TRODS
6 MALTINGS CT
7 EBOR CT
8 THE CHIMES
D6
1 RIVER ST
2 RECREATION RD
3 POND ST
4 GEORGE ST
5 NESS RD
6 THOMAS ST
B6
1 HUTCHINSON ST
2 BISHOP CT
3 DEACON CT
4 NORMANDY CL
5 MEADOW PL
6 CARENTAN CL
7 ELIZABETH CT
8 COCKRET CL
9 BUTTERMERE CT
A1
1 MANOR FARM CL
2 HOLMEFIELD CT
3 HOLMEFIELD CL
4 CHILVERS CT
5 MAYFIELD DR
6 MIDDLEBROOK GDNS
SELBY
YO8
Westfield
East Common
Brayton
WISTOW ROAD
BONDGATE
MILLGATE
NEW MILLGATE
GOWTHORPE
THE CRESCENT
BARLBY ROAD
LEEDS ROAD
BROOK STREET
DONCASTER ROAD
BAWTRY ROAD
PARK ST
River Ouse
Selby Dam
Selby Canal
Trans Pennine Trail
Selby Abbey
Abbey Walk Shop Ctr
Selby Town Football Club
Selby High Sch
Selby War Memorial
Brayton Coll
Longmans Hill Prim Sch
St Marys RC Prim Sch
Brayton CE Inf Sch
Brayton Jun Sch
Barwick Parade Prim Sch
Selby College
Three Lakes Retail Park
Three Lakes Industrial Estate
Prospect Way Industrial Estate
Selby Business Park
Oakney Wood
Staynor Hall
Staynor Wood
Holmes Industrial Estate
Ousegate Mills Business Centre
Selby Ironworks Business Centre
Barlby Bridge Com Prim Sch
Sports Ground
Warehouses
Brayton Bridge
Brayton Junction
A19
A63
A1041
A1238
B1223

197 203 204 198

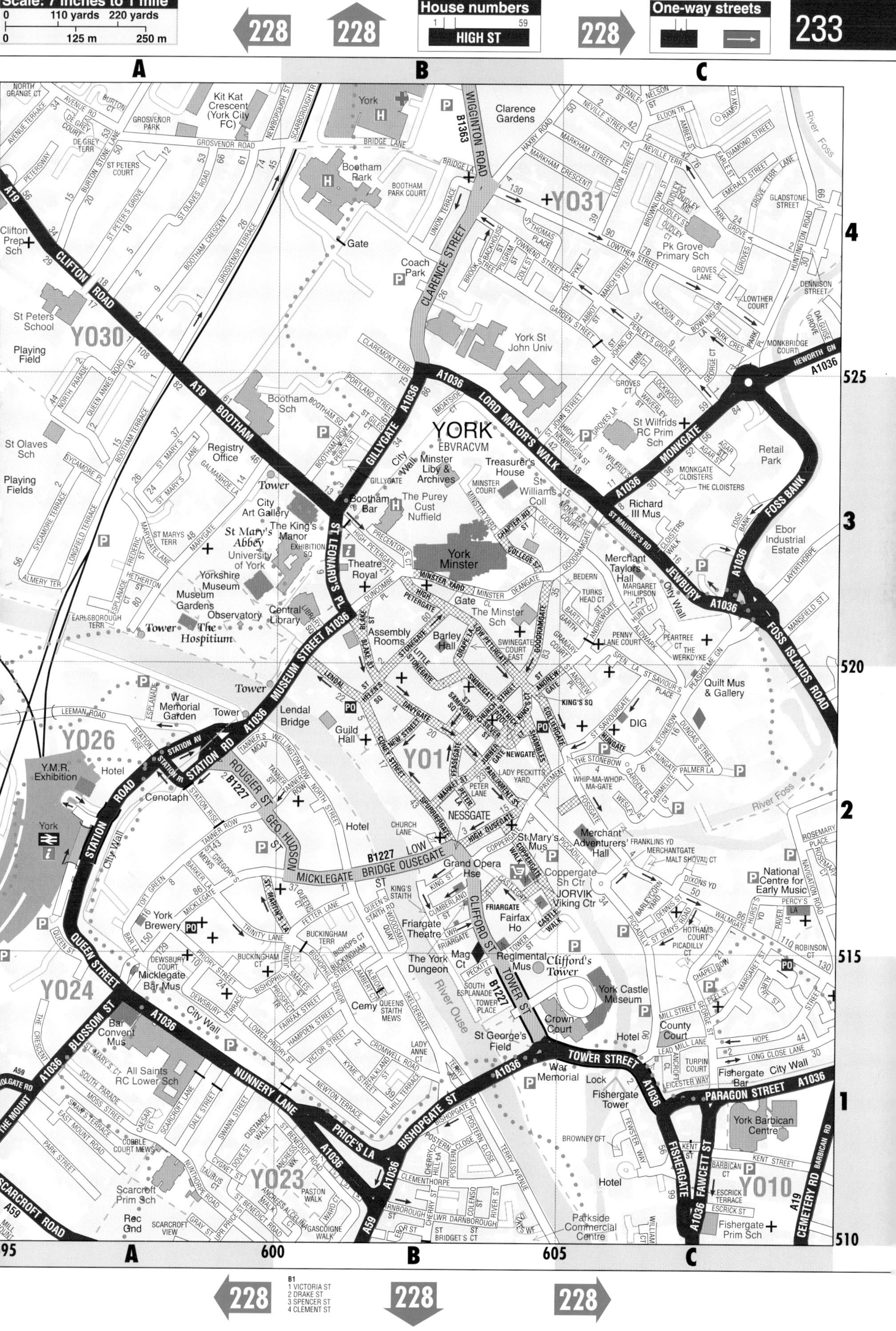

Scale: 7 inches to 1 mile
0
110 yards
220 yards
0
125 m
250 m
228
228
House numbers
1
59
HIGH ST
228
One-way streets
A
B
C
York
H
Kit Kat Crescent (York City FC)
Clarence Gardens
Bootham Park
Gate
Coach Park
York St John Univ
Clifton Prep Sch
St Peters School
YO30
YO31
Playing Field
Bootham Sch
St Olaves Sch
Playing Fields
Registry Office
YORK
EBVRACVM
City Wall
Minster Liby & Archives
Treasurer's House
St Williams Coll
Richard III Mus
Bootham Bar
The Purey Cust Nuffield
City Art Gallery
The King's Manor
St Mary's Abbey
University of York
Theatre Royal
York Minster
Yorkshire Museum
Museum Gardens
Observatory
Central Library
Tower
The Hospitium
Assembly Rooms
Barley Hall
The Minster Sch
Merchant Taylors Hall
St Wilfrids RC Prim Sch
Pk Grove Primary Sch
Retail Park
Ebor Industrial Estate
Quilt Mus & Gallery
DIG
War Memorial Garden
Lendal Bridge
Guild Hall
Y.M.R. Exhibition
Hotel
Cenotaph
YO26
YO1
York
NESSGATE
Merchant Adventurers' Hall
Grand Opera Hse
Coppergate Sh Ctr
JORVIK Viking Ctr
National Centre for Early Music
York Brewery
Micklegate Bar Mus
Friargate Theatre
Fairfax Ho
The York Dungeon
Mag Ct
Regimental Mus
Clifford's Tower
York Castle Museum
Crown Court
County Court
St George's Field
River Ouse
River Foss
Bar Convent Mus
All Saints RC Lower Sch
YO24
YO23
YO10
War Memorial
Lock
Fishergate Tower
Fishergate Bar
York Barbican Centre
Scarcroft Prim Sch
Rec Gnd
Parkside Commercial Centre
Fishergate Prim Sch
Cemy
A19
CLIFTON
BOOTHAM
GILLYGATE
LORD MAYOR'S WALK
MONKGATE
FOSS BANK
JEWBURY
FOSS ISLANDS ROAD
ST LEONARD'S PL
MUSEUM STREET
STATION ROAD
STATION RD
MICKLEGATE
BRIDGE
OUSEGATE
CLIFFORD ST
TOWER ST
TOWER STREET
QUEEN STREET
BLOSSOM ST
NUNNERY LANE
PRICE'S LA
BISHOPGATE ST
FISHERGATE
FAWCETT ST
PARAGON STREET
CEMETERY RD
THE MOUNT
SCARCROFT ROAD
CLARENCE STREET
WIGGINTON ROAD
B1363
A1036
B1227
A59
HEWORTH GN
4
3
2
1
525
520
515
510
95
600
605
228
B1
1 VICTORIA ST
2 DRAKE ST
3 SPENCER ST
4 CLEMENT ST
228
228

Index

Place name May be abbreviated on the map — **Church Rd 6 Beckenham BR2 53 C6**

Location number Present when a number indicates the place's position in a crowded area of mapping

Locality, town or village Shown when more than one place has the same name

Postcode district District for the indexed place

Page and grid square Page number and grid reference for the standard mapping

Cities, towns and villages are listed in CAPITAL LETTERS

Public and commercial buildings are highlighted in magenta **Places of interest** are highlighted in blue with a star★

Abbreviations used in the index

Acad	**Academy**	Comm	**Common**	Gd	**Ground**	L	**Leisure**	Prom	**Promenade**
App	**Approach**	Cott	**Cottage**	Gdn	**Garden**	La	**Lane**	Rd	**Road**
Arc	**Arcade**	Cres	**Crescent**	Gn	**Green**	Liby	**Library**	Recn	**Recreation**
Ave	**Avenue**	Cswy	**Causeway**	Gr	**Grove**	Mdw	**Meadow**	Ret	**Retail**
Bglw	**Bungalow**	Ct	**Court**	H	**Hall**	Meml	**Memorial**	Sh	**Shopping**
Bldg	**Building**	Ctr	**Centre**	Ho	**House**	Mkt	**Market**	Sq	**Square**
Bsns, Bus	**Business**	Ctry	**Country**	Hospl	**Hospital**	Mus	**Museum**	St	**Street**
Bvd	**Boulevard**	Cty	**County**	HQ	**Headquarters**	Orch	**Orchard**	Sta	**Station**
Cath	**Cathedral**	Dr	**Drive**	Hts	**Heights**	Pal	**Palace**	Terr	**Terrace**
Cir	**Circus**	Dro	**Drove**	Ind	**Industrial**	Par	**Parade**	TH	**Town Hall**
Cl	**Close**	Ed	**Education**	Inst	**Institute**	Pas	**Passage**	Univ	**University**
Cnr	**Corner**	Emb	**Embankment**	Int	**International**	Pk	**Park**	Wk, Wlk	**Walk**
Coll	**College**	Est	**Estate**	Intc	**Interchange**	Pl	**Place**	Wr	**Water**
Com	**Community**	Ex	**Exhibition**	Junc	**Junction**	Prec	**Precinct**	Yd	**Yard**

Index of towns, villages, streets, hospitals, industrial estates, railway stations, schools, shopping centres, universities and places of interest

1st–Alb

1st Ave HG2 220 B3
2nd Ave HG2 220 B3
3rd Ave HG2 220 B3
4th Ave HG2 220 B3
5th Ave HG2 220 C3
6th Ave HG2 220 B2

A

Abber La LS24 182 A2
Abbeville Ave 1 YO21 208 B6
Abbey Cl 12 LS29 175 A4
Abbey Crags Way HG5 221 C3
Abbeyfield Dr 10 TS16 5 D5
Abbey Gdns WF8 201 B2
Abbey Hill BD23 155 C5
Abbey Infants Sch DL3 3 B5
Abbey Junior Sch DL3 3 B5
Abbey La YO22 208 E7
Abbey L Ctr YO8 232 C5
Abbey Mews WF8 201 B2
Abbey Mill Gdns HG5 221 C3
Abbey Mill View HG5 221 C3
Abbey Pl 9 YO8 232 D5
Abbey Rd
Darlington DL3 3 B5
Knaresborough HG5 221 B3
Sadberge DL2 4 C7
Abbey St YO30 228 A7
Abbey Terr 16 YO21 208 D7
Abbey Walk Sh Ctr YO8 232 C6
Abbey Wlk
Pontefract WF8 201 B2
Selby YO8 232 C5
Abbey Yd YO8 232 C5
Abbots Ct YO8 232 D3
Abbotsford Ct 7 TS17 5 F5
Abbotsford Rd YO10 228 F3
Abbots Gait YO32 225 F6
Abbot's Garth YO12 99 D6
Abbots Rd YO8 232 E3
Abbot's Rd
Selby YO8 232 E3
Whitby YO22 208 E5
Abbot St YO31 233 C4
Abbotsway YO31 228 E8
Abbots Way HG5 221 C3
Abbot's Wlk YO22 208 E5
Abbotts Cl LS25 194 F8
Abbotts Ct YO17 215 E4
Abbotts Gdns YO8 197 A8
Abbotts Mews YO8 232 D3
Abelton Gr 33 YO32 166 E5
Aberbran Ct 41 TS17 5 F4
Aberdeen La 19 YO11 213 A6
Aberdeen Pl 20 YO11 213 A6
Aberdeen Rd DL1 3 E8
Aberdeen St 17 YO11 213 A6
Aberdeen Terr 21 YO11 213 A6
Aberdeen Wlk 16 YO11 213 A6
ABERFORD 194 F7
Aberford CE Prim Sch LS25 194 F8
Aberford Rd
Barwick in Elmet & Scholes LS15 194 C8
Bramham cum Oglethorpe LS23 188 E5
Garforth LS25 194 D4
Abrahams Quay YO22 208 E5
Abram's View YO11 213 B2
Acacia Ave YO32 225 E4
Acacia Dr WF10 201 B3
Acacia Gr 36 YO32 166 E5
Academy Gdns DL2 1 D8
Acaster Ave YO23 191 A3
Acaster Dr LS25 194 D3
Acaster La
Acaster Malbis YO23 231 B1
Acaster Selby YO23 191 A4
ACASTER MALBIS 191 D8
ACASTER SELBY 191 B4
Accommodation Rd YO25 151 D6
Acer Cl 4 BD20 187 F7
ACKLAM
169 E8
Middlesborough 6 E8
Acklam Grange Sch TS5 6 D7
Acklam Hall Sixth Form Ctr TS5 6 E7
Acklam Rd TS17 6 C8
Acklam Whin Prim Sch TS5 6 D6
Ackton La WF7 200 D1
Ackton Pasture La WF7 200 D2
Ackton Pastures Prim Sch WF10 200 D3
Ackworth St 3 YO12 212 E4
ACOMB 227 C3
Acomb Prim Sch YO24 227 E3
Acomb Rd YO24 227 D3
Acomb Wood Cl YO24 230 C7
Acomb Wood Dr YO24 230 B7
Acorn Bsns Pk BD23 173 D4
Acorn Cl
6 Barlby YO8 198 B4
Middleton St George DL2 4 D4
Acorn Way
Gateforth YO8 197 B1
York YO24 230 D7
Acre Fold 21 LS29 174 F4
Acre La 12 BD23 134 E2
Acre Mdw 1 BD22 187 B6
Acre Rd 2 BD22 187 B6
Acres Cl 24 YO62 92 F6
Acresfield 6 BB8 186 A3
Acres La
Brompton YO13 98 C4
Helmsley YO62 93 A6
Scrayingham YO41 169 B8
Acres The
Addingham LS29 175 A5
Glusburn BD20 187 E6
Stokesley TS9 26 C8
Adam's Field La YO61 117 F4
Adcott Rd TS5 6 E7
ADDINGHAM 174 F5
Addingham Prim Sch LS29 174 F5
Addingham Wharfedale Rd LS29 174 E4
Addison Ave 18 WF6 200 B1
Addison Rd TS9 8 A1
Addison Villas HG3 219 A8
Addlethorpe La LS22 179 C3
Adelaide Rd
Middlesbrough TS7 7 B6
6 Norton DN6 206 E2
Adelaide St 3 YO23 228 B2
Adlington Cl 8 YO32 167 A7
Admirals Ct YO7 211 A2
Admirals' Ct YO7 211 A2
Agar St YO31 233 C3
AGGLETHORPE 60 A1
Agnesgate HG4 214 D5
Agnesing La LA2 128 A7
Agnes Ing La LA2 128 A7
Aikengill Rd LA2 129 A4
Ailcey Rd HG4 214 D5
AINDERBY QUERNHOW 88 C4
Ainderby Rd DL7 210 B2
Ainderby Steepe CE Prim Sch DL7 64 A7
AINDERBY STEEPLE 64 B7
Ainsford Way TS7 7 D8
Ainstable Rd TS7 7 D8
Ainsty Ave YO24 230 F8
Ainsty Dr 2 LS22 180 C4
Ainsty Gr YO24 230 F8
Ainsty Rd
Harrogate HG1 219 F4
Wetherby LS22 180 C4
Ainsty View
Acklam YO17 169 E8
Whixley YO26 164 A4
Ainsworth Way TS7 7 D8
AINTHORPE 29 C6
Ainthorpe La YO21 29 C7
Aintree Ct
9 Darlington DL1 3 F6
York YO24 230 F8
Aire & Calder Ind Pk WF10 200 E5
Aire Cres BD20 187 E7
AIREDALE 201 B4
Airedale Ave
Gargrave BD23 155 D1
Skipton BD23 217 B4
Airedale Bsns Ctr BD23 173 D4
Airedale Dr WF10 201 B5
Airedale High Sch WF10 201 B4
Airedale Ings BD20 173 D1
Airedale Junior & Infants Sch WF10 201 B4
Airedale Mews 1 BD23 216 E3
Airedale Rd
Castleford WF10 201 A4
Scotton DL9 40 D4
Airedale Terr BD23 216 E3
Airedale Trading Pk BD20 187 F8
Airedale View 1 BD20 187 F8
Aire Rd LS22 180 B4
Aireside Ave BD20 173 D1
Aireside Terr BD20 173 D2
Aire St
Castleford WF10 200 E4
Glusburn BD20 187 F7
Knottingley WF11 202 A3
12 Knottingley WF11 202 A3
Aire Valley Cl BD20 173 D3
Aire Valley Dr BD20 173 D3
Aire Valley Mount WF10 201 A4
AIRE VIEW 173 D1
Aire View BD23 216 C1
Aire View Infants Sch 13 BD20 174 C1
Aireville Dr BD20 174 C1
Aireville Grange BD23 216 D5
Aireville Sch BD23 216 D4
Aireyholme La TS9 8 B2
Airfield Ind Est YO41 184 F3
AIRMYN 205 E4
Airmyn Park Prim Sch DN14 205 E4
Airmyn Rd DN14 205 D3
AIRTON 155 A6
AIRY HILL 208 D4
Airy Hill YO21 208 D5
Airy Hill Com Prim Sch YO21 208 D5
Airy Hill La TS12 9 D8
AISKEW 63 A3
Aiskew Leeming Bar CE Prim Sch DL7 63 C4
Aislabie Cl HG4 214 A5
Aislabie Garth HG4 214 A5
AISLABY
Egglescliffe 5 C3
Pickering 95 D8
Whitby 31 F7
Aislaby Carr La YO18 95 C7
Aislaby La
Aislaby YO18 95 C6
Aislaby YO21 32 A8
Aislaby Rd TS16 5 D4
Aismunderby Cl HG4 214 C3
Aismunderby Rd HG4 214 C4
Aisne Rd DL9 209 C1
Aketon Rd WF10 200 D3
Alanbrooke Ind Est YO7 115 B8
Alanbrooke Prim Sch YO7 89 A1
Alandale Cres LS25 194 B3
Alandale Rd LS25 194 B4
Alan Farnaby Way YO60 145 C4
Albany Ave HG1 219 E5
Albany Rd
Harrogate HG1 219 E5
Middlesbrough TS7 7 B6
Albany St 3 YO26 227 F5
Albany Wlk LS29 218 A3
Albatross Way DL1 3 E5
Albemarle Back Rd 10 YO11 212 F6
Albemarle Cres 18 YO11 213 A6
Albemarle Rd YO23 228 B2
Albermarle Dr 3 DL9 40 F5
Albert Cl 1 YO32 228 F8
Albert Hill BD24 131 E2

Albert Pl
Harrogate HG1 . . . . 220 C4
1 Whitby YO21. . . . . 208 D7
Albert Rd
Eaglescliffe TS16. . . . . 5 E5
12 Glusburn BD20. . . . . . . 187 E7
Harrogate HG1 . . . . 219 E5
1 Scarborough YO12 . . . . 213 A7
Albert Simmons Way St 44
LS29. . . . . 176 C1
Albert Sq BD23 . . . . 216 F4
Albert St
Darlington DL1. . . . . 3 D6
33 Earby BB18. . . . . 172 A1
Glusburn BD20. . . . . 187 F7
Harrogate HG1 . . . . 219 D2
Normanton South WF6 . . . 200 B2
8 Scarborough YO12 . . . . 213 A7
York YO10 . . . . 233 C1
Albert Terr
5 Harrogate HG1. . . . . . . 219 D1
Skipton BD23. . . . . 216 F4
Albion Ave YO26 . . . . 227 B6
Albion Cres 3 YO11. . . . . 213 A4
Albion Pl 14 YO21 . . . . 208 D6
Albion Rd
25 Earby BB18. . . . . 172 A1
Scarborough YO11. . . . . . . 213 A4
Albion St
Boosbeck TS12. . . . . 9 E7
Boston Spa LS23 . . . . 188 E7
Castleford WF10 . . . . 200 E4
28 Earby BB18. . . . . 172 A1
York YO1 . . . . 233 B1
Albion Terr
9 Boston Spa LS23 . . . . . 188 E7
23 Whitby YO21. . . . . 208 D6
Alcelina Ct YO23 . . . . 233 B1
Alcuin Ave YO10 . . . . 229 A4
Alcuin Way YO10. . . . . 229 B2
ALDBOROUGH 141 C5
Aldborough Gate 13
YO51 . . . . 141 B4
Aldborough Roman Town & Mus* YO51. . . . . 141 C5
Aldborough Way YO26 . . 227 F5
ALDBROUGH ST JOHN 2 A2
Aldenham Rd TS14. . . . . 8 E5
Alder Ave HG5. . . . . 221 E5
Alder Carr La YO18. . . . . . . 49 E2
Alder Cl YO8. . . . . 232 D2
Alder Ct 25 YO18. . . . . 95 F6
Alder Hill St 1 BB18 . . . . 172 B1
Alderley Ct YO32. . . . . 225 E3
Alderman Best Rd DL1 . . . . 4 A4
Alderman Leach Dr 13 DL2 3 A7
Alderman Leach Prim Sch
DL2. . . . . 3 A7
Alder Rd HG1. . . . . 219 F5
Aldersley Ave BD23 . . . . . 217 B3
Alderson Cres YO12. . . . . . 99 E7
Alderson Rd HG2 . . . . 222 E8
Alderson Sq HG2. . . . . 222 E8
Alders Rd YO18 . . . . 49 C4
Aldersyde YO24. . . . . 230 E7
Aldersyde Ct YO24 . . . . . . 230 E7
Aldersyde Mews YO24. . . 230 E7
Alder Way YO32. . . . . 225 D2
ALDFIELD 139 A8
Aldreth Gr YO23 . . . . 228 C2
Aldridge Rd TS3 . . . . 7 B8
ALDWARK 142 C2
Aldwark YO1 . . . . 233 C3
Aldwych Cl TS6. . . . . 7 E8
Alec Hare Cl YO17 . . . . . . 215 E4
Alexander Ave
6 East Ayton/West Ayton
YO13. . . . . 99 B8
York YO31 . . . . 225 E2
Alexander Cl YO7 . . . . 211 C4
Alexander Rd DL9. . . . . . . 209 C2
Alexandra Cres 10 LS29 . 218 A4
Alexandra Ct
Skipton BD23. . . . . 216 F2
York YO10 . . . . 228 E4
Alexandra Gr HG5. . . . . . . 221 B7
Alexandra Park Rd HG5 . 221 C7
Alexandra Pk YO12. . . . . . 212 D5
Alexandra Pl
Ilkley LS29. . . . . 218 A4
3 Knaresborough HG5. . . 221 B8
Alexandra Rd
Harrogate HG1 . . . . 219 D3
Strensall YO32. . . . . 167 A6
Alexandra Terr BD23. . . . 216 F2
Alexandra Ville BD23. . . . 216 F2
Alexandra Way DL10 . . . . 209 C7
Alexandria Dr DL2 . . . . 4 D4
Alfreda Terr 1 YO22 . . . . 208 E6
Algarth Rd YO31 . . . . 229 B7
Algarth Rise YO31. . . . . . . 229 B7
Alga Terr YO11 . . . . 213 A4
Allans Ct DL10 . . . . 209 B6
Allanson Gr YO24 . . . . 227 E2
Allan St
Darlington DL1. . . . . 3 D6
2 York YO30. . . . . 228 C7
Allenby Rd
20 Helmsley YO62. . . . . 92 F6
Hipswell DL9 . . . . 209 C1
Allen Cl YO10. . . . . 229 A4
Allendale YO24 . . . . 230 D8
Allendale Rd TS7 . . . . 7 D8
Allen Gr TS9. . . . . 26 B7
Allensway TS17 . . . . 6 C7
Allens West Sta TS16. . . . . . 5 D5
Allerdale Cl YO7 . . . . 211 C4
ALLERSTON. 97 C5
Allerston La YO18. . . . . 97 C4
Allerston Way 5 TS14. . . . . . 8 F7
Allerton Balk TS15 . . . . 5 D2
ALLERTON BYWATER 200 D6
Allerton Bywater Bsns Pk
WF10 . . . . 200 E6
Allerton Bywater Prim Sch
WF10 . . . . 200 D7
Allerton Castle* HG5 . . . 163 D4
Allerton Cl DL7 . . . . 210 C4
Allerton Dr 22 YO26 . . . . . 165 F1
Allerton La HG5. . . . . 163 D4
ALLERTON
MAULEVERER 163 E4
Allerton Mews HG1 . . . . . 219 E1
Allertonshire Sch DL6. . . 210 D6
Allerton Wath Rd YO7 . . . . 65 D4
Allhallowgate HG4 . . . . . . 214 C5
Alliance Ind Est DL1 . . . . . . 3 E6
Allington Dr YO31. . . . . . . 229 B6
Allington Way
Darlington DL1. . . . . 3 F5
Great Burdon DL1 . . . . 4 A5
Allison Ave TS17 . . . . 6 B4
Allison St TS14 . . . . 8 E6
Alloway Gr TS8 . . . . 6 F5
All Saints CE Infants Sch
WF6 . . . . 200 A1
All Saints CE Junior & Infants Sch WF7 . . . . 200 E1
All Saints CE Prim Sch 12
LS29 . . . . 218 A4
All Saints CE Sch
Ingleby Barwick TS17 . . . . . . 6 A4
Kirkby Overblow HG3 . . . . 179 A4
All Saints Cl YO51. . . . . . . 141 B7
All Saints RC Lower Sch
YO23. . . . . 233 A1
All Saints RC Prim Sch
YO7. . . . . 211 B2
All Saints RC Upper School
YO29. . . . . 228 B2
All Saints Rd 1 YO12 . . . 212 F4
All Saints Sq HG4 . . . . 214 D5
Alma Gdns HG4. . . . . 214 D4
Alma Gr YO10. . . . . 228 D2
Alma Par 2 YO11. . . . . 212 F5
Alma Pl DL10 . . . . 209 C7
Alma Rd BB8 . . . . 186 B3
Alma Sq 3 YO11. . . . . 212 F5
Alma Terr
Selby YO8. . . . . 232 C6
3 Skipton BD23 . . . . 217 A4
York YO10 . . . . 228 D2
Alma Way 2 YO18 . . . . 96 A6
Almery Terr YO30. . . . . . . 233 A3
Almond Cl
7 Filey YO14 . . . . 101 B4
Hambleton YO8 . . . . 197 B1
Almond Ct 4 TS4. . . . . 6 F8
Almond Gr
11 Filey YO14 . . . . 101 B4
Northallerton DL7 . . . . 210 D3
Scarborough YO12. . . . . . . 212 D5
York YO32 . . . . 225 D4
Almond Tree Ave
4 Carlton DN14 . . . . 204 C3
Malton YO17 . . . . 215 D6
Almscliffe Dr LS17 . . . . . . 178 B2
Almscliffe Garth LS17 . . . 178 B4
Almsford Ave HG2 . . . . . . 222 E6
Almsford Bank HG2 . . . . . 222 E5
Almsford Cl HG2. . . . . 222 F6
Almsford Dr
Harrogate HG2 . . . . 222 F6
York YO26 . . . . 227 C5
Almsford End HG2 . . . . . . 222 E6
Almsford Oval HG2. . . . . . 222 F6
Almsford Pl HG2. . . . . 222 E6
Almsford Rd
Harrogate HG2 . . . . 222 F6
York YO26 . . . . 227 C5
Almsford Wlk HG2 . . . . . . 222 F6
Almshouse Hill 1 LS23. . 188 E5
ALNE 142 F4
Alne Prim Sch YO61. . . . . 142 F4
Alne Rd
Easingwold YO61 . . . . 143 B8
Tollerton YO61. . . . . 143 A3
Alness Dr YO24 . . . . 230 B7
ALNE STATION 143 A5
Alne Terr YO10 . . . . 228 E2
Alpine Ct 5 WF10 . . . . 200 F3
Altofts La WF10. . . . . 200 B3
Altofts Rd WF6 . . . . 200 A1
Alum House La TS9 . . . . . . 26 B2
Alverton Cl YO17. . . . . 121 B7
Alverton Dr DL3. . . . . 3 B8
Alverton Infants Sch DL6 210 F6
Alverton La DL7. . . . . 210 D4
Alvin Wlk 9 YO41. . . . . . . 185 B2
Alvis Gr YO10. . . . . 229 D4
Alwyne Dr YO30. . . . . 224 E1
Alwyne Gr YO30. . . . . 224 E1
Alwyn Rd DL3. . . . . 3 D8
Amber Ct YO31 . . . . 233 C4
Amberly St 4 YO26 . . . . . 227 E5
Amber St YO31 . . . . 233 C4
Amble Cl YO62 . . . . 70 B2
Ambler Ct 23 WF6. . . . . . . 200 A1
Ambler's La YO30. . . . . . . 165 F7
Ambler St WF10 . . . . 200 E4
Ambleside Ave
10 Barnoldswick BB18 . . . 171 D2
York YO10 . . . . 229 B4
Ambleside Gr TS5. . . . . 6 E8
Ambleside Wlk DL1 . . . . 3 D4
Ambrey Cl 16 YO14. . . . . . 126 F8
Ambrose Rd HG4 . . . . 214 C4
Ambrose St YO10 . . . . 228 D1
America La BD20. . . . . 187 F4
Amesbury Cres TS8 . . . . 6 F5
Amiens Cres DL9. . . . . 209 D1
AMOTHERBY. 121 B4
Amotherby La YO17 . . . . . 121 A6
Amotherby Prim Sch
YO17. . . . . 121 A4
Amplecarr YO61 . . . . 117 B5
AMPLEFORTH. 92 C1
Ampleforth Coll YO62 . . . . 92 D1
Ampleforth Coll Junior Sch
YO62. . . . . 118 F7
Amy Busfield Gn 40
LS29. . . . . 176 C1
Amy Johnson Way YO30. 225 A3
Anchorage Hill DL10 . . . . 209 D7
Anchorage La DL7 . . . . . . 210 C5
Anchorage Way YO21 . . . 208 C5
Anchorite La 7 YO18 . . . . 95 F7
Anchor Rd 2 HG1 . . . . . . 220 A3
Ancress Wlk YO23. . . . . . . 233 A1
Ancroft Cl YO1. . . . . 233 C1
Anderson Gr 6 YO24. . . . 227 F2
Anderson St 6 WF8 . . . . . 201 B1
Anderton St 18 BD20 . . . . 187 E8
Andrew Dr 4 YO32 . . . . . 225 F1
Andrew La YO18 . . . . 71 B4
Anfield Ct 8 DL1 . . . . 3 F6
Angel Ct 8 TS9. . . . . 26 C7
Angel Gdns HG5 . . . . 221 C7
Angelica Cl 12 HG3. . . . . . 161 B3
Angel Yd 1 YO21 . . . . 208 D6
ANGRAM
Keld. 35 E6
York 182 C3
Angram Cl YO30 . . . . 224 F1
Angram La
Barlby with Osgodby
YO8. . . . . 198 A6
Muker DL11. . . . . 35 E6
Tollerton YO61. . . . . 143 B3
Angram Rd YO26. . . . . 182 A5
Angrove Cl TS9 . . . . 7 F1
Angrove Dr TS9. . . . . 7 F1
Annan Cl YO24. . . . . 230 C6
Annandale Ct 8 LS29 . . . 218 B2
Annandale Gr 1 YO13. . . . 75 D5
Annas Garth DL8. . . . . 60 F4
Anne St YO23. . . . . 228 C2
Annie St YO8 . . . . 232 C6
Annumhills Rd YO8 . . . . . 199 D7
Anserdale La YO62. . . . . . . 70 E5
Anson Croft 5 YO8 . . . . . 196 E1
Anson Dr YO10. . . . . 231 D8
Anteforth View DL10 . . . . . 20 E3
Anthea Dr YO31. . . . . 225 E1
Anthony La HG4 . . . . 114 E1
Anvil Sq 3 DL11. . . . . 38 B6
Anvil Way DL7 . . . . 22 C2
Anzio Rd DL9 . . . . 209 C1
Apedale Rd
Castle Bolton with East & West
Bolton DL8 . . . . 37 F1
Redmire DL8 . . . . 59 C8
Apley Cl HG2 . . . . 220 A1
Apollo St 9 YO10. . . . . . . 228 E3
APPERSETT. 56 C5
Apple Blossom Ct 8
YO24 . . . . 227 B1
Appleby Ave HG5 . . . . 220 D8
Appleby Cres HG5. . . . . . . 220 D8
Appleby Ct HG5. . . . . 220 D8
Appleby Gate HG5 . . . . . . 220 D7
Appleby Glade YO32 . . . . 225 D7
Appleby Gn HG5 . . . . 220 D8
Appleby Gr HG5. . . . . 220 D8
Appleby La
Aldbrough DL11. . . . . 1 F1
Kirkby Malzeard HG4. . . . . 112 B4
Appleby Pl 2 YO31 . . . . . 229 A5
Appleby Way HG5. . . . . . . 220 D7
Appleby Wlk HG5 . . . . 220 D8
Applecroft Rd
Selby YO8. . . . . 232 A4
York YO31 . . . . 229 B7
Applefields Sch YO31 . . . 229 B5
Applegarth
Barnoldswick BB18 . . . . . . 171 E2
Coulby Newham TS8 . . . . 7 A4
Apple Garth
10 Easingwold YO61 . . . . . 117 D1
15 Poppleton YO26 . . . . . . 165 F1
Applegarth Ct DL7 . . . . . . 210 D5
Applegarth Prim Sch
DL7. . . . . 210 D4
Applegarth St 15 BB18 . . 172 A1
Appleshaw Cl HG5 . . . . . . 221 C6
Appleton Cl 13 TS14. . . . . . . 8 F7
Appleton Ct YO23 . . . . 230 F3
Appleton La
Appleton-le-Street with
Easthorpe YO17 . . . . 120 F4
Coneysthorpe YO60 . . . . . . 120 E2
APPLETON-LE-MOORS. . . . 70 F2
APPLETON-LE-STREET . . 120 F4
Appleton Rd YO23. . . . . . . 231 A3
APPLETON ROEBUCK 190 F5
Appleton Roebuck Prim Sch
1 YO23 . . . . 190 F5
APPLETON WISKE 24 B3
Appleton Wiske Prim Sch
DL6 . . . . 24 B3
Appletree Dr YO8 . . . . 196 E1
Appletree Gdns 2 TS7 . . . . 7 D8
Apple Tree Gdns 2
LS29. . . . . 175 C2
Apple Tree La
Great Preston LS25. . . . . . 200 D8
4 Kippax LS25 . . . . 194 D1
Apple Tree Mews 5
LS25. . . . . 194 D1
Appletree Way
Malton YO17 . . . . 215 B4
10 Sherburn in Elmet LS25 195 F4
APPLETREEWICK. 157 D7
Appletreewick Stone Circ*
BD23. . . . . 135 E2
Apple Tree Wlk 7 LS25 . 194 D1
Appley Cl TS16. . . . . 5 E7
Apron La HG3. . . . . 140 B2
Apsley Way 6 TS17 . . . . 5 F5
Arbour The
4 Glusburn BD20. . . . . . . 173 E1
Ilkley LS29. . . . . 218 A6
Arbour Way YO17 . . . . 215 E4
Arcade Sh Ctr* HG4 . . . . 214 C5
Arcade The LS29. . . . . 218 B4
Archaeology Store*
YO62. . . . . 92 F6
Archbishop Holgates Sch
YO10. . . . . 229 B3
Archbishop of York CE Jun
Sch YO23. . . . . 231 A4
ARCHDEACON NEWTON 2 F7
Archer La HG3. . . . . 140 B3
Archer Rd DL2 . . . . 4 D3
Archers Green The DL10. . 41 C7
Archers Mdw HG5 . . . . . . 221 F5
Archie St 3 HG1. . . . . 219 C5
Archway La 13 YO18. . . . . . 96 D5
Arden Ct DL7 . . . . 210 D5
Arden La YO62. . . . . 92 B8
Arden Mews DL7. . . . . 210 D5
Arena View 12 DL10. . . . . . 41 D5
Arenhall Cl 2 YO32 . . . . . 225 C8
Arennig Ct 43 TS17. . . . . 5 F4
Argam Dikes* YO25. . . . . 127 B2
Argam La YO25 . . . . 126 F1
Argill DL8 . . . . 60 F5
Argyle Rd YO21 . . . . 208 C7
Argyle St YO23. . . . . 228 B1
ARKENDALE 163 B8
Arkendale La HG5. . . . . . . 141 A2
Arkendale Rd HG5 . . . . . . 162 F8
Arkengarthdale CE Prim Sch
DL11 . . . . 17 D1
Arkengarthdale Rd DL11 . 38 B7
Arkle Cres DL1. . . . . 3 C3
Arlington Rd
Middlesbrough TS5 . . . . 6 F8
York YO30 . . . . 225 A1
Armoury Rd YO8 . . . . 232 B5
Armstrong Cl 7 WF6 . . . . 200 A2
Armstrong Way YO32. . . . 224 E3
Army Foundation Coll
HG3. . . . . 161 A2
ARNCLIFFE 107 D2
Arncliffe CE Prim Sch
BD23. . . . . 107 D2
Arncliffe Dr WF11. . . . . . . 201 D2
Arncliffe Gr DL3 . . . . 2 F5
Arncliffe Rd HG2. . . . . 220 A1
Arndale Way 8 YO14 . . . . 101 B4
Arnold Rd DL1 . . . . 3 E6
Arnside Cres WF10. . . . . . 201 B4
Arnside Pl 2 YO10. . . . . . . 228 F3
Arran Cl 1 TS17 . . . . 6 B6
Arran Ct LS25. . . . . 194 C3
Arran Dr LS25 . . . . 194 C3
Arran Pl YO31 . . . . 228 D7
ARRATHORNE. 62 A8
Arrows Cres 10 YO51 . . . . 141 B5
Arrows Terr 9 YO51 . . . . . 141 B5
Arthington Ave HG1. . . . . 219 E2
Arthur Pl 6 YO30 . . . . 224 B5
Arthurs Ave HG2 . . . . 222 C7
Arthurs Cl HG2 . . . . 222 C7
Arthurs Gr HG2 . . . . 222 C7
Arthur St
6 Barnoldswick BB18 . . . 171 D2
Earby BB18 . . . . 186 A8
Great Ayton TS9. . . . . 8 A2
York YO10 . . . . 228 E4
Arts Ctr The* YO22 . . . . . 208 E7
Arundel Ct 1 TS17. . . . . 5 F5
Arundel Gr YO24. . . . . 230 C7
Arundel Pl
12 Scarborough YO11. . . . 212 F5
9 Whitby YO21. . . . . 208 C6
Arundel Rd 5 DN6. . . . . . . 206 E2
Ascot Ave 6 DL9 . . . . 40 F4
Ascot Cl DL6. . . . . 210 D3
Ascot Rd
Kippax LS25. . . . . 194 C1
Wigginton YO32. . . . . 166 D5
Ascot Way YO24 . . . . 227 D1
Ascough Wynd DL8 . . . . . . 63 D3
ASENBY. 115 B6
Ash Bank Ave 2 HG4 . . . 113 D2
Ash Bank Cl 1 HG4 . . . . . 113 D2
Ashbank La
Firby DL8. . . . . 62 F1
Sheriff Hutton YO60. . . . . . 145 F6
Ash Bank Rd HG4 . . . . 113 D2
Ashbourne Cl 12 YO51 . . . 141 B4
Ashbourne Rd 10 YO51 . . 141 B4
Ashbourne Way YO24 . . . 230 C8
Ashbrook Ct DL10. . . . . 20 E3
Ashburnham Cl 4 DN6. . . 206 F2
Ashburnham Wlk 5
DN6 . . . . 206 F2
Ashburn Pl LS29. . . . . 218 A3
Ashburn Rise 10 YO11 . . . 212 E4
Ashburn Way LS22 . . . . . . 180 B4
Ash Cl
1 Ilkley LS29. . . . . 175 C2
Newton on Derwent YO41. 185 E4
York YO31 . . . . 229 B7
Ash Croft 7 DL10. . . . . 41 D5
Ashdale Cl DL2 . . . . 4 E4
Ashdale La LS22 . . . . 180 B4
Ashdale Rd
19 Dunnington YO19 . . . . . 184 F7
Helmsley YO62. . . . . 92 F6
Ashdene Gr WF8. . . . . 201 D2
Ashdowne Cl DL8 . . . . 62 E5
Ashdowne Ct DL8 . . . . 62 E5
Ashdown Rise YO13 . . . . . . 75 C8
Ashes The
Barton DL10. . . . . 21 C7
Hellifield BD23. . . . . 154 A3
Ashfield LS22 . . . . 180 C3
Ashfield Ave YO17 . . . . . . 215 D5
Ashfield Cl
9 Constable Burton DL8 . . 61 C5
9 Pateley Bridge HG3 . . . 137 B4
Ashfield Court Rd 10
HG3 . . . . 137 B4
Ashfield Cres BD23. . . . . . 216 F2
Ashfield Ct YO24. . . . . 230 E7
Ashfield Prim Sch LS21 . 176 F1
Ashfield Rd
Danby YO21. . . . . 29 B6
Harrogate HG1 . . . . 219 E4
6 Pickering YO18. . . . . 96 A6
Ashfield St WF6. . . . . 200 A2
Ashfield Terr
Harrogate HG1 . . . . 219 E4
Skipton BD23. . . . . 216 F2
Ashford Ave TS5. . . . . 6 D8
Ashford Pl YO24 . . . . 227 D2
Ashgap La WF6 . . . . 200 A2
Ashgarth Ct HG2 . . . . 222 C5
Ashgarth Way HG2 . . . . . . 222 C5
Ash Gn TS8. . . . . 7 A4
Ash Gr
13 Barnoldswick BB18 . . . 171 D1
Danby YO21. . . . . 29 A6
12 Filey YO14 . . . . 101 B4
Glusburn BD20. . . . . 187 E7
Ilkley LS29. . . . . 218 C5
7 Kirkbymoorside YO62. . . 70 B1
1 Kirklevington TS15 . . . . . 24 E8
Northallerton DL6 . . . . 210 F5
1 Riccall YO19 . . . . 197 F8
Ripon HG4 . . . . 214 A6
Scarborough YO12. . . . . . . 212 C7
Whitby YO21 . . . . 208 B6
Ashgrove BD23 . . . . 216 E4
Ashgrove Cres LS25. . . . . 194 D2
Ash Hill TS8 . . . . 7 B5
Ash La
Church Fenton LS24. . . . . . 196 B6
Garforth LS25 . . . . 194 D4
8 Haxby YO32 . . . . 166 E5
Little Fenton LS25 . . . . 196 C5
Ashlands Cl DL6 . . . . 210 F4
Ashlands Ct DL6 . . . . 210 F4
Ashlands Dr DL7. . . . . 63 C5
Ashlands Prim Sch LS29 218 C5
Ashlands Rd
Ilkley LS29. . . . . 218 C5
Northallerton DL6 . . . . 210 F4
Ash Lea
Danby YO21. . . . . 29 A6
Fairburn WF11. . . . . 201 D6
Ashlea Cl YO8 . . . . 232 D4
Ashlea Rd DL7 . . . . 210 D4
Ashley Ct 2 YO14. . . . . . . 101 B3
Ashley Park Cres YO31 . . 229 B6
Ashley Park Rd YO31. . . . 229 B7
Ashmead 4 LS23. . . . . 188 E7
Ashmeade Cl YO24. . . . . . 230 B8
Ash Rd
13 Filey YO14 . . . . 101 B4
Guisborough TS14 . . . . 8 F7
Harrogate HG2 . . . . 222 E6
Ash Ridge 5 DL6 . . . . 210 E3
Ashridge Cl 4 TS17. . . . . 6 B5
Ash St
11 Glusburn BD20. . . . . . . 187 E7
Ilkley LS29. . . . . 218 C5
Trawden BB8. . . . . 186 B1
York YO26 . . . . 227 E4
Ashton Ave YO30. . . . . 228 B8
Ashton Ct BD23 . . . . 154 B3
Ashton Rd WF10 . . . . 200 E3
Ash Tree Cl DL8. . . . . 62 F2
Ashtree Dr YO8 . . . . 197 D1
Ash Tree Garth LS24 . . . . 195 E7
Ash Tree Rd
8 Bedale DL8. . . . . 63 A2
Knaresborough HG5 . . . . . 221 B6
Ashtree Way WF11. . . . . . . 201 C4
Ash Tree Wlk 22 LS29 . . . 176 C1
Ash View HG2 . . . . 222 B6
Ashville Ave
Eaglescliffe TS16. . . . . 5 E6
Scarborough YO12. . . . . . . 212 F6
Ashville Cl HG2 . . . . 222 C5
Ashville Coll HG2 . . . . 222 B6
Ashville Dr 9 DL2 . . . . 22 E8
Ashville Gr HG2. . . . . 222 C5
Ashville St YO31 . . . . 228 D7
Ashwood Cl 5 YO62 . . . . . 92 F7
Ashwood Dr TS9. . . . . 26 C8
Ashwood Glade YO32 . . . 225 C6
Ashwood Pl HG5. . . . . 221 E5
Ashworth Rd WF8. . . . . . . 201 C2

Askam Ave WF8 . . . . 201 C2
Aske Ave DL10 . . . . 209 E8
Aske Hall★ DL10 . . . . 20 D2
Askern & Campsall Sports
  Ctr DN6 . . . . 206 F1
Askew Dale TS14 . . . . 8 D6
Askew Rigg La YO18 . . . . . 71 A5
Askham Bog Nature
  Reserve★ YO23 . . . . 230 C5
ASKHAM BRYAN 182 F3
Askham Bryan Coll YO23 182 F2
Askham Bryan Coll (Bedale
  Ctr) DL8 . . . . 63 A2
Askham Bryan Coll
  (Guisborough Ctr) **17**
  TS14 . . . . 8 E7
Askham Bryan Coll
  (Pickering Ctr) YO18 . . . 95 F8
Askham Bryan La YO23 . . 230 A6
Askham Croft **1** YO24 . . . . 227 B1
Askham Fields La YO23 . . 182 F2
Askham Gr YO24 . . . . 227 B2
Askham La
  Askham Bryan YO24 . . . . . 230 A8
  Woodthorpe YO23 . . . . 230 A7
  York YO24 . . . . 227 B1
ASKRIGG 57 F6
Askrigg Prim Sch DL8. . . . 57 F5
ASKWITH 176 D3
Askwith La LS21 . . . . 176 D3
Askwith Moor Rd LS21. . . 176 D5
Askwith Prim Sch LS21. . 176 D3
Aspen Cl
  3 Dunnington YO19 . . . . 184 F7
  Pickering YO18 . . . . 95 F8
  Selby YO8 . . . . 197 D2
Aspen Gr BB18 . . . . 172 B1
Aspen La BB18 . . . . 172 A1
Aspen Pk WF10 . . . . 200 F2
Aspen Way
  Slingsby YO62 . . . . 120 B5
  Tadcaster LS24 . . . . 189 D6
Aspinall Rise **13** BD23 . . 154 B3
Aspin Ave HG5. . . . . 221 B4
Aspin Chase HG5 . . . . 221 B4
Aspin Dr HG5 . . . . 221 B4
Aspin Gdns HG5 . . . . 221 C4
Aspin Gr **4** HG5 . . . . 221 C4
Aspin La HG5 . . . . 221 B4
Aspin Oval HG5 . . . . 221 B4
Aspin Park Ave **1** HG5 . . 221 C4
Aspin Park Cres HG5 . . . . 221 B4
Aspin Park Dr HG5 . . . . . . 221 B4
Aspin Park La HG5 . . . . . . 221 C4
Aspin Park Prim Sch
  HG5. . . . . 221 C5
Aspin Park Rd HG5. . . . . . 221 C4
Aspin View HG5. . . . . 221 C4
Aspin Way HG5 . . . . 221 C4
Asquith Ave
  Scarborough YO12. . . . . . 212 E3
  York YO31 . . . . 229 A5
ASSELBY 205 D7
Assembly St **7** WF6. . . . . 200 A1
Astbury TS8 . . . . 7 C4
Asterley Dr TS5 . . . . 6 D8
Astley Ave LS26 . . . . 194 A1
Astley La
  Great & Little Preston
  LS26 . . . . 200 B8
  Swillington LS26 . . . . 194 A1
Astley Lane Ind Est LS26 200 B8
Astley Way LS26 . . . . 200 A8
Atcherley Cl YO10. . . . . . . 231 D8
Athelstan La **7** LS21 . . . 177 A1
Athelstan Prim Sch LS25 195 F3
Athelstans Ct LS25 . . . . . 195 F4
Athol Sq YO17 . . . . 215 E4
Atkinson Ave DL10 . . . . . 209 D8
Atkinson Ct WF6. . . . . 200 A1
Atkinson La WF8. . . . . 201 C1
Atlas Rd YO30 . . . . 225 A3
Atlas Wynd TS16. . . . . 5 E3
Atlee Cl YO12. . . . . 212 E3
Attermire Cave★ BD24 . . 132 A3
Atterwith La YO26. . . . . . . 182 A7
Auborough St **5** YO11 . . 213 A6
Auckland Ave LS24 . . . . . 189 F7
Auckland Oval **2** DL3 . . . 3 B7
Auckland St TS14 . . . . 8 F7
Auckland Way **7** YO21 . . 208 C6
Aucuba Cl YO32. . . . . 225 D2
Audax Cl YO30 . . . . 225 A3
Audax Rd YO30 . . . . 225 A3
Audby La LS22. . . . . 180 C4
Audus St **10** YO8 . . . . . . 232 C5
AUGHTON 193 C1
Augusta Cl DL1 . . . . 3 F7
Aumit La YO62. . . . . 92 E1
Aunums Cl **7** YO18 . . . . 96 D5
Auster Bank Ave LS24 . . . 189 F7
Auster Bank Cres LS24 . . 189 F7
Auster Bank Rd LS24 . . . 189 F7
Auster Bank View LS24. . 189 F7
Auster Rd YO30 . . . . 225 B3
Austfield La LS25 . . . . 202 B8
Austin Dr DL9. . . . . 41 A5
Austin Rd WF10. . . . . 201 B4
AUSTWICK 130 E7
Austwick CE Prim Sch
  LA2. . . . . 130 E7
Austwick Rd BD24 . . . . . . 131 C8
Autumn Ave **8** LS22 . . . . 8 C4
Avalon Ct TS8 . . . . 6 F5

Ava Rd DL9 . . . . 40 C4
Avens Way TS17. . . . . 6 A5
Avenue A LS23. . . . . 181 A2
Avenue B LS23. . . . . 181 A1
Avenue Bank HG4. . . . . . . 86 C4
Avenue C E LS23. . . . . 181 B1
Avenue Cl HG2. . . . . 220 D4
Avenue C W LS23. . . . . 181 A1
Avenue D LS23. . . . . 181 A1
Avenue E E LS23. . . . . 181 B1
Avenue E W LS23. . . . . 189 A8
Avenue F LS23. . . . . 181 B1
Avenue G LS23. . . . . 181 B1
Avenue House Ct HG5. . . 162 F3
Avenue Pl
  Guisborough TS14 . . . . . . 8 F7
  7 Harrogate HG2 . . . . . 220 C3
Avenue Prim Sch The TS7 . 7 D6
Avenue Rd
  11 Harrogate HG2. . . . . 220 C3
  Scarborough YU12. . . . . . 212 E4
  York YO30 . . . . 233 A4
Avenue St **8** HG2. . . . . . 220 C3
Avenue Terr
  5 Harrogate HG2 . . . . . 220 C3
  York YO30 . . . . 233 A4
Avenue The
  Campsall DN6 . . . . 206 E1
  Collingham LS22 . . . . 180 A1
  Dalby-cum-Skewsby YO60 . 119 B2
  Eaglescliffe TS16 . . . . 5 E6
  26 Filey YO14 . . . . 101 B3
  Gilling East YO62. . . . . . . 118 E7
  Great Ribston with Walshford
  LS22 . . . . 180 C8
  Guisborough TS14 . . . . . . 8 D6
  Harrogate HG1 . . . . 220 C4
  5 Haxby YO32 . . . . 166 E5
  Haxby YO32 . . . . 225 D8
  Knaresborough HG5 . . . . 221 A7
  Masham HG4 . . . . 86 C3
  Middlesbrough TS5 . . . . . 6 F8
  Norton YO17 . . . . 215 D3
  Nun Monkton YO26 . . . . . 165 A4
  Nunnington YO62. . . . . . . 93 E1
  8 Pateley Bridge HG3 . . 137 C4
  Richmond DL10 . . . . 209 D7
  Rufforth YO23 . . . . 182 C6
  Skipton BD23 . . . . 217 B6
  Skutterskelfe TS15. . . . . . 25 E6
  1 Sleights YO22. . . . . . 32 A6
  Snape with Thorp DL8. . . 87 A7
  South Milford LS25 . . . . . 195 F2
  Stainton Dale YO13 . . . . . 54 A8
  Stokesley TS9. . . . . 26 C7
  Thirkleby High & Low with
  Osgodby YO7 . . . . 116 D8
  West Hauxwell DL8. . . . . . 61 C8
  Whitby YO21. . . . . 208 B4
  Wighill LS24. . . . . 181 D2
  York YO30 . . . . 228 A6
Avenue Victoria YO11 . . . 213 A3
Aviation Rd LS25. . . . . 196 A4
Aviator Ct YO30. . . . . 224 F3
Aviemore Ct **10** DL1 . . . . 3 F6
Aviemore Rd TS8 . . . . 6 F5
Avocet Cres **11** YO12 . . . 99 F6
Avocet Sh Ctr **8** YO12. . . 99 F6
Avondale Rd HG1 . . . . 219 F4
Avon Dr
  Barnoldswick BB18 . . . . . 171 E2
  Guisborough TS14 . . . . . . 8 E6
  York YO32 . . . . 225 F6
Avon Garth LS22 . . . . 180 B3
Avon Rd **8** DL2 . . . . 22 D8
Avro Cl TS18. . . . . 5 F7
Awnhams La YO42 . . . . . . 169 D2
Axminster Rd TS8. . . . . . . 6 F5
Axton Cl TS17. . . . . 6 A6
Aylesham Ct YO32 . . . . . . 225 E3
Aylton Dr TS5. . . . . 6 E6
Aynham Cl **2** BD23 . . . . 134 E2
Aynholme Cl **10** LS29 . . 174 F4
Aynholme Dr **1** LS29. . . 175 A4
Ayresome Way **1** DL1. . . 3 F6
AYSGARTH 58 E3
Aysgarth Falls★ DL8 . . . . 58 F3
Aysgarth Gr DL7 . . . . 210 B2
Aysgarth Rd DL1. . . . . 3 D4
Aysgarth Sch DL8. . . . . . . 62 A4
Ayton Castle★ YO13. . . . . 99 A8
Ayton Ct TS14 . . . . 8 E7
Ayton Rd YO12. . . . . 99 C7
Azalea Mews YO8 . . . . . . 232 A5
AZERLEY 113 A5
Azerley Gr HG3 . . . . 219 A4
Azerley La HG4 . . . . 112 F3

B

Babyhouse La BD20 . . . . . 173 A1
Bachelor Ave HG1 . . . . . . 219 D7
Bachelor Dr HG1. . . . . 219 D7
Bachelor Gdns HG1 . . . . . 219 D6
Bachelor Hill YO24. . . . . . 227 C2
Bachelor Rd HG1. . . . . 219 D6
Bachelor Way HG1 . . . . . . 219 D6
Back Avenue Victoria **2**
  YO11 . . . . 213 A3
Back Beck La LS29. . . . . . 174 F4
Back Bridge St BD23 . . . . 216 F4
Back Chatsworth Gr
  HG1 . . . . 219 D4
Back Cheltenham Mount
  HG1 . . . . 219 D3
Back Colne Rd
  9 Glusburn BD20. . . . . . 187 E7

Back Colne Rd continued
  Trawden BB8 . . . . 186 A2
Back Dawson Terr HG1. . . 219 D5
Back Dragon Par HG1 . . . 219 E3
Back Dragon Rd HG1 . . . . 219 E3
Back Elmwood St **3**
  HG1 . . . . 219 E4
Back Gate LA6 . . . . 103 D3
Back Gladstone St HG2. . 222 D7
Back Gn BD23 . . . . 153 F5
Back Grange Ave HG1. . . 219 D5
Back High St **13** HG3 . . 137 B4
Backhouse St YO31 . . . . . 233 B4
Back La
  Acaster Selby YO23 . . . . . 191 B3
  Airton BD23 . . . . 155 A6
  Aiskew DL7 . . . . 63 C5
  Alne YO61 . . . . 142 F4
  Ampleforth YO62 . . . . 92 C1
  Appleton-le-Moors YO62 . . 70 F2
  Appleton Roebuck YU23. . 191 A5
  Asselby DN14 . . . . 205 D6
  Bagby YO7 . . . . 90 B3
  Barkston Ash LS24 . . . . . 195 F6
  Barlby with Osgodby YO8 . 198 C4
  Barton DL10 . . . . 21 C7
  Barton-le-Street YO17. . . 120 E5
  1 Bedale DL8. . . . . 63 A3
  Bilbrough YO23 . . . . 182 D1
  Birstwith HG3 . . . . 160 D5
  Bolton-on-Swale DL10. . . 41 E5
  7 Boroughbridge YO51 . 141 B5
  Borrowby YO7 . . . . 65 E4
  Bradleys Both BD20. . . . . 173 E4
  10 Brafferton YO61 . . . . 115 F1
  Bramham LS23 . . . . 188 E6
  Brearton HG3 . . . . 162 A8
  Burley in Warfedale LS29 . 176 C1
  Carthorpe DL8 . . . . 87 E7
  Cold Kirby YO7 . . . . 91 C8
  Copmanthorpe YO23 . . . . 230 A2
  Copt Hewick HG4. . . . . . . 114 B2
  Cottingwith YO42. . . . . . . 193 C5
  Crakehall DL8 . . . . 62 E4
  Crathorne TS15 . . . . 24 F6
  Dalton YO7. . . . . 115 E7
  Dishforth YO7 . . . . 115 A4
  Drax YO8 . . . . 204 F5
  Eaglescliffe TS16 . . . . 5 E4
  Easingwold YO61 . . . . 117 D1
  East Tanfield DL8. . . . . . . 87 D2
  Ebberston & Yedingham
  YO13. . . . . 97 D5
  Ellerton YO42. . . . . 193 C1
  Fewston HG3 . . . . 159 F1
  Giggleswick BD24 . . . . . . 130 F2
  Great & Little Broughton
  TS9 . . . . 26 E5
  Great Ouseburn YO26 . . . 164 A8
  Great Preston WF10 . . . . . 200 D6
  Gristlthorp YO14 . . . . 100 E5
  Guisborough TS9 . . . . 8 A4
  Hambleton YO8 . . . . 196 F1
  Harome YO62 . . . . 93 C5
  Hawsker-cum-Stainsacre
  YO22. . . . . 32 F5
  11 Haxby YO32 . . . . 166 D5
  Hellifield BD23. . . . . 154 B3
  Hemingbrough YO8 . . . . . 198 F1
  Hetton BD23 . . . . 155 F5
  Hirst Courtney YO8 . . . . . 203 F3
  Holtby YO19. . . . . 184 E8
  Hunsingore LS22 . . . . 180 E8
  Hutton-le-Hole YO62 . . . . 70 C4
  Huttons Ambo YO60. . . . . 147 B7
  Kirby Wiske YO7 . . . . 88 C7
  Kirkby Malham BD23 . . . . 154 F8
  Kirkby Malzeard HG4. . . . 112 C5
  Leavening YO17. . . . . 147 E2
  Lockton YO18. . . . . 72 E4
  Longnewton TS21. . . . . . . 4 F8
  Long Preston BD23 . . . . . 153 F5
  Low Coniscliffe & Merrybent
  DL2. . . . . 2 E4
  Low Worsall TS15 . . . . 24 C7
  Luttons YO17 . . . . 150 B8
  Malham BD23 . . . . 132 F2
  Markington with Wallerthwaite
  HG3. . . . . 139 C3
  Marton cum Grafton YO51 141 D1
  Marton YO62 . . . . 94 F5
  Melmerby HG4 . . . . 114 B7
  8 Middleham DL8 . . . . . 60 E2
  Morton-on-Swale DL7 . . . 64 A6
  Moulton DL10 . . . . 21 E3
  Newby Wiske DL7 . . . . 64 D3
  Newholm-cum-Dunsley
  YO21. . . . . 13 A1
  Newton-on-Ouse YO30 . . 165 B6
  North Cowton DL7. . . . . . . 22 B3
  North Duffield YO8. . . . . . 199 A7
  Norton DN6 . . . . 206 E2
  Osmotherley DL6. . . . . . . 45 B4
  Raskelf YO61 . . . . 116 F2
  Rathmell BD24 . . . . 153 C6
  Reeth, Fremington & Healaugh
  DL11. . . . . 38 B6
  2 Riccall YO19 . . . . 198 A8
  Rookwith HG4 . . . . 86 A8
  Scorton DL10. . . . . 41 E6
  Settrington YO17. . . . . . . 148 B3
  Sicklinghall LS22 . . . . . . 179 E3
  Sinnington YO62 . . . . 95 A8
  Skelton HG4. . . . . 140 F7
  Sutton-under-Whitestonecliffe
  YO7. . . . . 90 E5
  Thirkleby High & Low with
  Osgodby YO7 . . . . 116 D8

Back La continued
  Thirsk YO7 . . . . 211 B1
  Tholthorpe YO61 . . . . 142 D5
  Thormanby YO61 . . . . 116 F6
  Thornton Steward DL8. . . 61 C2
  Topcliffe YO7 . . . . 115 C7
  Trawden BB8 . . . . 186 A1
  Tunstall DL10 . . . . 41 B3
  Tunstall LA6 . . . . 102 A4
  Weaverthorpe YO17 . . . . . 124 E1
  Weeton LS17 . . . . 178 C2
  Wennington LA2 . . . . 102 C2
  Westerdale YO21 . . . . 28 E5
  West Tanfield HG4. . . . . . . 87 A1
  West Witton HG4 . . . . 59 C4
  Whixley YO26 . . . . 164 A3
  Whorlton DL6 . . . . 45 D8
  Wilberfoss YO41 . . . . 185 F5
  Wold Newton YO25 . . . . . 126 A4
  Wombleton YO62. . . . . . . 93 E7
  Wray-with-Botton LA2. . . 128 A6
  York YO26 . . . . 227 A5
Back Lane S
  Middleton YO18 . . . . 95 E8
  Wheldrake YO19. . . . . 192 F7
Back Mary St **3** BD20 . . 173 F1
Back Middleton Rd **9**
  LS29. . . . . 218 A4
Back Nelson Rd **12** LS29 218 B4
Back Newton La WF10. . . 201 A7
Back Nook **1** DL8. . . . . . 58 F1
Back Northgate **18** WF8 . 201 B1
Back of Parks Rd **2** YO62 70 C2
Back of the Beck **6**
  BD23 . . . . 216 F4
Back O' Newton YO41 . . . 185 E3
Back Parish Ghyll Rd **8**
  LS29. . . . . 218 A4
Back Park St YO8 . . . . 232 D5
Back Rd
  Birstwith HG3 . . . . 160 B5
  Thormanby YO61 . . . . 116 F5
Back Regent Pl **4** HG1. . 220 C4
Back Royal Par **5** HG1 . . 219 C2
Back Sea View YO14 . . . . 101 C1
Back Side YO17. . . . . 149 B5
Backside La YO62 . . . . . . 93 E6
Back St
  Boroughbridge YO51 . . . . 141 C5
  Bramham LS23 . . . . 188 E6
  Burton Fleming YO25. . . . 126 E3
  Langtoft YO25 . . . . 151 D5
  10 Middleham DL8 . . . . . 60 E2
  Wold Newton YO25 . . . . . 126 A4
Back Station Rd **17** BD20 187 E8
Backstone La LS29 . . . . . . 218 C3
Backstone Way LS29 . . . . 218 C4
Back Street Hilda's Terr
  YO21 . . . . 208 D7
Back Syke DL8 . . . . 57 D5
Back Tewit Well Rd HG2. 222 E8
Back Weston Rd **5** LS29 218 B4
Back West View **2** YO30 228 B7
Back York Pl **6** HG1 . . . 219 D1
Bacon Rd WF6 . . . . 200 B2
Bad Bargain La YO31. . . . 229 A5
Baden St HG1. . . . . 219 F4
Bader Ave TS17 . . . . 6 B6
Bader Prim Sch TS17. . . . 6 B6
Badgerbeck Rd **2** DL9 . . 209 B1
Badger Butt La BD23 . . . . 155 B5
Badger Cl **33** LS29. . . . . 175 C2
Badger Gate BD23 . . . . . . 134 C3
Badger Hill Dr **14** DL8 . . 63 B3
Badger Hill Prim Sch
  YO10. . . . . 229 B2
Badger La DN6 . . . . 207 A3
Badger Paddock **5**
  YO31 . . . . 225 E2
Badgers Gate LS29 . . . . . 175 C6
Badger Way YO8. . . . . 198 E3
Badger Wood Glade
  LS22. . . . . 180 C4
Badger Wood Wlk YO10 229 D3
Badminton Ct **18** DL1. . . 3 F6
Baek Chapel St **26** BB18 171 D1
Baffam Ct YO8 . . . . 232 B1
Baffam Gdns YO8 . . . . . . 232 B2
Baffam La YO8. . . . . 232 B2
BAGBY 90 C3
Bagby La YO7 . . . . 90 B2
Bagdale YO21. . . . . 208 C6
Bagdale Ct YO21 . . . . 208 D6
Baghill La WF8 . . . . 201 C1
Baildon Ave LS25 . . . . 194 C3
Baildon Cl **2** YO30 . . . . 227 A3
Baile Hill Terr YO1 . . . . . . 233 B1
Bailey Cr
  Northallerton DL7 . . . . . . 210 C4
  28 Walkerville DL9 . . . . 41 A5
Bailey La BD23 . . . . 152 E3
Bailey St BB18 . . . . 172 B1
Bailey The BD23 . . . . 217 A4
BAINBRIDGE 57 D5
Bainbridge CE Prim Sch
  DL8. . . . . 57 D5
Bainbridge Dr YO8 . . . . . . 232 C4
Bajan Pl HG4 . . . . 214 A6
Bakersfield Dr DN14 . . . . 202 F3
Baker St
  Appleton Wiske DL6. . . . . 24 A3
  York YO30 . . . . 228 C2
Bakewell Mews **6** DL2. . 3 A7
Bala Cl **3** TS17 . . . . 5 F4
BALDERSBY 88 D1
Baldersby Garth
  Baldersby YO7 . . . . 88 D1
  Rainton YO7 . . . . 114 F6

BALDERSBY ST JAMES. . . 114 E8
Baldersby St James CE Prim
  Sch YO7 . . . . 114 E8
Baldersdale Ave **1** HG5 221 D5
Baldoon Sands TS5 . . . . . 6 D6
Baldwin St **4** HG1 . . . . . 219 C5
Balfour St YO26 . . . . 227 F5
Balfour Terr TS5 . . . . 6 D8
Balfour Way YO32. . . . . . . 167 A6
Baliol Croft TS21. . . . . 5 A7
Balk La DN14 . . . . 207 F1
Balksyde YO62 . . . . 120 B5
Balk The
  Bishop Wilton YO41. . . . . 169 C2
  Marton-le-Moor HG4 . . . . 114 E1
  Slingsby YO62 . . . . 120 B5
Balk Top YO7 . . . . 115 B1
Ball Grove Dr BB8. . . . . . . 186 A3
Ballhall La YO42 . . . . 193 E6
Ballowfield Nature Reserve★
  DL8. . . . . 58 C4
Balmer Hill DL2. . . . . 1 C8
Balmoral Ave TS17. . . . . . 6 C8
Balmoral Dr LS26 . . . . . . 200 B6
Balmoral Rd
  Barmpton DL1 . . . . 3 E8
  Lingdale TS12. . . . . 9 F6
  Middlesbrough TS3 . . . . . 7 C8
  Ripon HG4 . . . . 214 C3
Balmoral Sh Ctr YO11 . . . 213 A6
Balmoral Terr **5** YO23 . . 228 B1
BALNE 207 C5
Balne Hall Rd DN14 . . . . . 207 F5
Balne Moor Rd DN14 . . . . 207 B6
Balshaw Rd LA2. . . . . 129 B3
Baltimore Way DL1 . . . . . . 3 D7
Bamburgh Ct TS17. . . . . . 5 F5
Banbury Rd WF8. . . . . 201 C2
Bancroft Fold **18** BB18. . 171 D1
Bancroft Mill Engine Steam
  Mus★ BB18. . . . . 171 D1
Bands La DL8 . . . . 56 C4
Bank Bottom LA6 . . . . 103 D3
Bank Cl **2** YO22 . . . . 32 A6
Bank Dike Hill HG3. . . . . . 159 A4
Bankfield La DN14 . . . . . . 205 A7
Bankfield St BB8. . . . . 186 A2
Bank Hall Cl LA6. . . . . 103 D4
Bankhead Cl DL6 . . . . 210 F4
Bankhead Rd DL6. . . . . . . 210 F4
Bank House La LA6 . . . . . 103 B5
Bank La
  Egton YO21 . . . . 30 E5
  Faceby TS9. . . . . 25 F1
  Grassington BD23 . . . . . . 134 E3
  Great & Little Broughton
  TS9 . . . . 26 F3
  Silsden BD20 . . . . 174 C4
Banklands Ave BD20 . . . . 174 C1
Banklands La BD20. . . . . . 174 C1
BANK NEWTON 172 B8
Bank Rd
  Glusburn BD20. . . . . 187 E8
  Selby YO8. . . . . 232 D6
Banks Bridge Cl BB18 . . . 171 E2
Banksfields Ct TS6 . . . . . . 7 F8
Banks Hill **1** BB18 . . . . . 171 D2
Bank Side
  2 Eastfield YO11 . . . . . 100 A7
  Rawcliffe DN14 . . . . 205 A4
Bankside Cl
  3 Poppleton YO26 . . . . 165 F1
  Thirsk YO7. . . . . 211 D2
Banks La
  Knottingley WF11. . . . . . . 201 F2
  Scorton DL10. . . . . 41 E7
Banks Rd
  Brompton DL6 . . . . 44 A2
  Darlington DL1 . . . . 3 E6
Banks Rise **4** LA2 . . . . . 129 A8
Bank St
  Barnoldswick BB18 . . . . . 171 D1
  Castleford WF10 . . . . 200 E4
  11 Wetherby LS22 . . . . 180 C3
Banks Way **3** LA2 . . . . . 129 A8
Bank The DL10. . . . . 41 D4
Bank Top LA6. . . . . 103 D3
Bank Top La **4** TS13 . . . 12 A7
Bankwell Cl BD24 . . . . 131 D2
Bankwell Rd BD24. . . . . . . 131 D2
Bank Wood Rd WF8 . . . . . 206 A6
Bank Yd DL10. . . . . 209 C6
Bannisdale **6** YO24 . . . . 230 C7
Bannister Cl BB8. . . . . 186 B2
Bannister Wlk BD22. . . . . 187 B6
Barbara Gr **4** YO24 . . . . 227 F3
Barbeck YO7 . . . . 211 C3
Barbeck Cl YO7 . . . . 211 D3
Barberry TS8 . . . . 7 B4
Barberry Cl
  Ingleby TS17. . . . . 6 B5
  20 Killinghall HG3 . . . . 161 B3
Barbers Dr YO23 . . . . 230 B4
Barbican Ct YO10 . . . . . . 233 C1
Barbican Mews YO10. . . . 228 E3
Barbican Rd YO10. . . . . . . 233 C1
Barbondale Gr HG5 . . . . . 221 C5
Barbondale Rd LA6 . . . . . 77 A7
Bar Convent Mus★
  YO24. . . . . 233 A1
Bardale Cl **2** HG5. . . . . . 221 D6
BARDEN. 61 A8
Barden Ct **6** YO30 . . . . 224 F1
Barden Fell View **3**
  BD23 . . . . 134 E2
Barden La DL8. . . . . 40 B1
Barden Moor Rd DL1. . . . . 3 E4
Barden Pl **9** YO14 . . . . . 101 A3

Barden Rd BD23 157 A1
Barden Twr★ BD23 157 C4
Bardney Rd 14 YO14 126 F8
Bardsley Cl TS16 5 E7
Barefoot St HG4 214 C4
Barf Bank DL8 61 A2
Barff Cl 10 YO8 197 D1
Barff Gr 6 YO8 197 B2
Barff La YO8 197 C1
Barff View YO8 203 D7
Barfield Rd YO31 228 F8
Barf La YO41 169 D4
Bargate DL10 209 B6
Barker Bsns Pk HG4 114 C6
Barker Dr YO8 232 B6
Barker La YO1 233 A2
Barkers Arc DL6 210 D4
Barker's La
Newholm-cum-Dunsley YO21 13 A1
Snainton YO13 98 A4
Barkery The TS8 7 B3
Barkhouse Bank HG3 138 F4
Bark House La LA2 131 B8
Barkhouse Wood La WF11 202 D6
Bark La
Addingham LS29 175 A5
Embsay with Eastby BD23 157 A1
Bar Knotts Terr YO17 215 C3
BARKSTON ASH 195 F7
Barkston Ash Cath Prim Sch LS24 195 E7
Barkston Ave YO26 227 B3
Barkston Cl 3 YO26 227 A3
Barkston Gr YO26 227 A3
Barkston Rd YO26 227 A3
Bar La
Bramham cum Oglethorpe LS23 188 F7
Garforth LS25 194 D4
Hambleton YO8 196 E1
Knaresborough HG5 162 D5
Roecliffe YO51 141 A5
York YO1 233 A2
BARLBY 198 B5
Barlby Bridge Com Prim Sch YO8 232 D6
Barlby By-pass 2 YO8 198 B4
Barlby Com Prim Sch YO8 198 B4
Barlby Cres YO8 232 F7
Barlby High Sch YO8 198 B5
Barlby Rd YO8 232 E6
Barley Cl YO17 215 D2
Barleycorn Yd YO1 233 C2
Barleycroft YO11 213 C1
Barleyfields La 5 LS22 180 C3
Barley Fields Prim Sch TS17 6 A4
Barleyfields Rd 4 LS22 180 C3
Barley Hall★ YO1 233 B3
Barleyhill Rd LS25 194 B4
Barley Horn Rd LS24 190 B2
Barley Rise YO32 167 A6
Barley's Yd 1 YO7 211 B3
Barley View YO32 225 C8
Barley Wlk 16 LS25 195 F2
BARLOW 204 C7
Barlow CE Prim Sch YO8 204 C7
Barlow Cl TS14 8 F6
Barlow Comm Nature Reserve★ YO8 204 B7
Barlow Comm Rd YO8 204 B8
Barlow Rd YO8 204 B6
Barlow St YO26 227 D4
Barmby Ave YO10 231 E8
Barmby Cl 4 YO30 224 F1
Barmby Ferry Rd 1 YO8 198 F1
BARMBY ON THE MARSH 205 B7
Barmby on the Marsh Prim Sch DN14 205 B7
Barmoor Cl YO13 75 D6
Barmoor Gn YO13 75 D6
Barmoor La YO13 75 C6
Barmpton La DL1 3 F7
Barnaby Pl TS14 8 E7
Barnard La YO13 98 C4
Barnard's Rd YO22 31 A4
Barnbow La LS15 194 A6
Barn Elms YO8 204 C5
Barnes Rd
Castleford WF10 200 E3
Darlington DL3 3 A6
Barney La YO60 146 A1
Barn Field Cl BB8 186 A3
Barnfield Way YO23 230 A2
Barnhill La DN14 205 F7
Barningham Rd DL11 18 G7
BARNOLDSWICK
Earby 171 D1
Ingleton 103 A2
Barnoldswick CE Prim Sch BB18 171 D1
Barnoldswick La LA6 103 A2
Barnsdale Est WF10 200 D3
Barnsdale Rd
Ledston WF10 200 E7
Mickletown LS26 200 B5
Barnsdale View DN6 206 E2
Barns Wray 2 YO61 117 D1
Barnwell Cres HG2 222 B5
Barnwood Cres BB18 172 B1
Barnwood Rd BB18 172 A1
Barnygate La YO60 147 A7
Barons Cres YO23 230 B2
Bar Pl HG1 219 D5
Barracks Bank DL10 21 A2
Barrack View DL10 209 C8
Barrel Sykes 3 BD24 131 D3
Barret St 13 BB18 172 A1
Barrett Ave 3 YO24 227 F3
Barrett Rd DL3 3 A5
Barrington Garth DN14 202 F3
Barr La YO32 167 D4
Barrowby La
Austhorpe LS15 194 A4
Kirkby Overblow HG3 179 A3
BARROWCLIFF 212 D7
Barrowcliff Infant Sch YO12 212 C7
Barrowcliff Junior Sch YO12 212 C7
Barrowcliff Rd YO12 212 D7
Barry Bank YO21 11 F1
Barry's La YO12 212 E2
Barse Beck La HG3 160 D5
Bar St YO11 213 A6
Barstow Ave YO10 228 F3
Barstow Fall 2 WF8 201 C2
Bar The 6 DL10 209 C6
Bartindale Rd YO14 127 A5
Bartle Garth YO1 233 C3
BARTON 21 D7
Barton CE Prim Sch DL10 21 D7
BARTON HILL 146 D3
BARTON-LE-STREET 120 E5
BARTON-LE-WILLOWS 146 D1
Barton Quarry Ind Est DL10 20 B6
Bartons Garth YO8 232 B2
Barton St DL1 3 E6
Barton Way HG4 113 C8
Barugh La
Barugh (Great & Little) YO17 95 B2
Normanby YO62 94 F4
Barugh Way HG4 114 B6
Barwick Cl 9 ts17 6 A5
Barwick Fields 8 TS17 6 A5
BARWICK IN ELMET 194 B8
Barwick in Elmet CE Sch LS15 194 C8
Barwick La
Ingleby Barwick TS17 5 F5
Ingleby TS17 6 A4
Barwick Parade Prim Sch YO8 232 E4
Barwick Rd LS25 194 C5
Barwick St YO12 212 F5
Barwick Terr 1 YO12 212 F5
Barwick View 10 TS17 6 A5
Barwick Way TS17 6 A4
Barwic Parade YO8 232 E4
Bassett Cl YO8 232 C3
Bassleton La TS17 6 A6
Baston La YO61 143 E4
Batemans Yd 3 YO7 211 B3
Bates Ave DL3 3 B7
Bateson Cl YO10 229 C1
Bath St LS29 218 C5
Battalion Ct DL9 41 A4
BATTERSBY 27 D6
Battersby Ave TS9 27 C7
Battersby Sta TS9 27 C6
Battery Par YO21 208 D7
Battleflats Way YO41 168 D2
Battle of Bramham Moor (site of)★ LS24 188 F4
Battle of Marston Moor (site of)★ YO26 181 F7
Battle of the Standard 1138 (site of)★ DL6 43 E4
Battle of Towton (site of)★ LS24 195 D8
Battling Hills La YO18 49 B5
Bawhead Rd 23 BB18 172 A1
Bawtry Cl YO8 232 D3
Bawtry Rd YO8 232 D3
Baxby Manor★ YO61 117 B6
Baxby Terr 2 DL2 22 D8
Baxtergate YO21 208 D6
Baxter Wood BD20 187 E8
Baxton's Sprunt 1 YO62 92 F7
Bay Bolton Ave DL8 59 F3
Bay Cres YO14 101 B2
Baydale Rd DL3 3 A4
Bay Horse Yd 9 BD23 216 F4
Baynes Ct YO8 232 A2
Baynes Way BD23 217 D8
Baysdale Ave YO10 229 D3
Baysdale Cl 3 TS14 8 F6
Baysdale Rd TS17 6 B7
Bazeley's La YO17 215 E1
Beach Rd The YO14 101 B3
Beach The YO14 101 B3
Beacon Bank YO62 92 D1
Beacon Brow Rd YO13 75 A7
Beacon Grange Pk DL2 4 C7
Beacon Hill DL1 4 B7
Beacon Park First Ave 10 YO18 95 F7
Beacon Park Second Ave 9 YO18 95 F7
Beacon Rd
Millington YO42 170 B1
Seamer YO12 99 D7
Beacon Rise 4 LS29 175 C2
Beaconsfield Mews YO24 227 D3
Beaconsfield St
Northallerton DL7 210 D4
3 Scarborough YO12 212 E3
York YO24 227 D3
Beacons La 18 TS17 5 F4
Beacon St 5 LS29 175 A4
Beacon View 3 BD23 217 E8
Beacon Way YO22 32 D6
BEADLAM 93 C7
Beadlam Ave TS7 7 D6
Beadle Garth YO23 230 B2
Beadnell Cl 3 TS17 6 B5
Beagle Croft YO41 168 C1
Beagle Ridge Dr YO24 227 C1
Beagle Spinney YO41 168 C1
BEAL 202 D4
Beale Cl TS17 6 B5
Beal La
Beal DN14 202 D4
Cridling Stubbs WF11 202 C1
BEAMSLEY 174 F7
Beamsley Ct BD23 217 A2
Beamsley La BD23 174 F7
Beamsley View 13 LS29 175 C2
Beancroft Rd WF10 200 E3
Beancroft St WF10 200 E3
Beanland La YO32 167 D2
Beanlands Dr 7 BD20 187 E7
Beanlands Par LS29 218 C5
Beanlands Pl 8 BD20 187 E7
Bean Sheaf La YO17 96 A3
Bean's Way YO31 229 B8
Beatswell Lawn HG4 113 C8
Beaufighter Cl DL10 41 F6
Beaufort Cl
Guisborough TS14 8 F5
York YO10 229 B3
Beaulieu Cl 1 YO32 225 F5
Beaumont Hill DL1 3 D8
Beaumont Hill Sch & Tech Coll DL1 3 E7
Beaumont Pl YO8 232 A2
Beaverdyke YO30 224 F1
Bebra Gdns★ HG5 221 A5
Becca La LS25 194 F8
Beckbridge La 2 WF6 200 B1
Beckbridge Rd WF6 200 B2
Beckbridge Way WF6 200 B1
Beck Cl 6 YO41 185 B2
Beckclose La DL8 87 F6
Beck Closes Rd YO26 142 A3
Beckdale Rd YO62 92 E7
BECKERMONDS 80 D3
Beckett Cl 8 YO62 93 D7
Beckett Dr YO10 229 D4
Beckfield Cl 6 BD20 187 F7
Beckfield La
Fairburn WF11 201 C7
York YO26 227 B5
Beckfield Pl YO26 227 B4
Beckfields Ave TS17 6 A4
Beck Hole 9 YO11 100 B6
Beck Hole Rd YO22 31 C1
Beck Holme YO22 32 B6
Beck Isle Mus★ YO18 95 F7
Beck La
Cloughton YO13 54 C1
Collingham LS22 180 A1
Farndale East YO62 48 F2
Leavening YO17 147 E1
Lebberston YO11 100 D5
South Kilvington YO7 211 B6
Wheldrake YO19 193 A8
Becklands Cl YO51 141 A5
Becklands La YO51 141 A4
Beck Mdw LS15 194 C7
Beck Mill Cl YO17 215 D3
Beck Row YO41 169 D5
Becks Brow BD23 153 C3
Becks Cl 5 YO32 225 C8
Beckside
Aberford LS25 194 F7
Catterick DL10 41 E4
7 Elvington YO41 185 B2
Malton YO17 215 F4
Northallerton DL7 210 B4
4 Staithes TS13 13 K2
Stillingfleet YO19 191 D3
Trawden Forest BB8 186 B2
Wilberfoss YO41 185 F6
Beck Side BD23 173 B4
Beckside Cl
13 Addingham LS29 174 F4
29 Burley in Warfedale LS29 176 C1
Beck Side Cl BD20 173 D1
Beckside Ct 6 BD20 174 C1
Beckside Gdns YO10 228 F4
Beckwith Ave HG2 222 B7
Beckwith Cl
Harrogate HG2 222 A6
Heworth YO31 229 C7
Beckwith Cres HG2 222 B7
Beckwith Dr HG2 222 B6
Beckwith Hall Dr 7 YO19 198 A8
Beckwith Head Rd HG3 178 C8
Beckwith Rd HG2 222 A7
BECKWITHSHAW 178 A7
Beckwithshaw Prim Sch HG3 178 A8
Beckwith Wlk HG2 222 A7
BEDALE 63 B2
Bedale Ave
Scarborough YO12 212 E8
York YO10 229 D4
Bedale CE Prim Sch DL8 63 A2
Bedale High Sch DL8 63 A2
Bedale La HG4 114 A8
Bedale L Ctr DL8 63 A2
Bedale Mus★ DL8 63 A3
Bedale Rd
Aiskew DL7 63 C4
Hunton DL8 61 E7
Scotton DL9 40 F2
Well DL8 87 A4
Bedale Sta DL8 63 A3
Bedburn Dr DL3 2 F5
Bede Ave YO30 228 B7
Bedern YO1 233 C3
Bedern Bank 13 HG4 214 C5
Bedern Ct 16 HG4 214 C5
Bedford Rd TS7 7 D6
Bedfords Fold 6 LS25 202 A7
Bedford St 13 YO11 213 A6
BEDLAM 161 A8
Bedlam Hill YO7 65 E4
Bedlam La
Fewston HG3 159 F2
Staveley HG5 140 E1
Bedlington's La YO22 33 C4
Beech Ave
3 Airmyn DN14 205 E4
Bishopthorpe YO23 231 A3
1 Earby BB18 172 A1
Harrogate HG2 222 E6
4 Naburn YO23 191 C7
4 Topcliffe YO7 89 B1
York YO24 227 F3
Beech Cl
Baldersby YO7 88 D1
6 Eastfield YO11 100 A7
2 Elvington YO41 185 B2
Farnham HG5 162 D7
Great Ayton TS9 7 F1
Hunton DL9 40 E2
Scruton DL7 63 E7
7 Sherburn in Elmet LS25 195 F4
Snape with Thorp DL8 87 A7
3 South Milford LS25 195 F2
Tadcaster LS24 189 F6
Beech Cres
Castleford WF10 201 B3
Whitwell-on-the-Hill YO60 146 E4
Beech Croft
Barlby with Osgodby YO8 198 B6
Pontefract WF8 201 C2
Beechcroft Cl TS12 9 F6
Beech Ct
Bishopthorpe YO23 231 A3
2 Castleford WF10 200 F3
Hellifield BD23 154 B3
Beech Dr
6 Kirkbymoorside YO62 70 B1
12 Scalby YO13 75 D5
South Milford LS25 195 F2
Beecher Stowe Dr 39 DL9 41 A5
Beeches End LS23 188 F8
Beeches The
Middleton St George DL2 4 D4
Skelton YO30 224 C4
11 Stokesley TS9 26 C7
26 Upper Poppleton YO26 165 F1
Wetherby LS22 180 D4
Beechfield
Coulby Newham TS8 7 A5
Hawsker-cum-Stainsacre YO22 33 A6
Newby Wiske DL7 64 F2
Newton-on-Ouse YO30 165 B6
Beechfield Cl 15 YO8 197 B1
Beechfield Rd DL10 209 C8
Beech Glade YO31 225 F2
Beech Gr
1 Airmyn DN14 205 E4
Burton Salmon LS25 201 F6
Camblesforth YO8 204 C5
Harrogate HG2 219 C1
Knaresborough HG5 221 B8
Maltby TS8 6 C4
Northallerton DL6 210 E5
Selby YO8 232 C5
Sherburn in Elmet LS25 195 F4
Sowerby YO7 211 C1
Whitby YO21 208 B6
York YO26 227 C4
Beech Hill
Carleton BD23 173 A4
6 Knaresborough HG5 221 A6
5 Pontefract WF8 201 C1
Beech Hill Rd BD23 173 A4
Beechings Mews YO21 208 B7
Beech La
8 East Ayton/West Ayton YO13 99 A7
3 Spofforth HG3 179 E6
Beechnut La WF8 201 B1
Beech Pk YO19 198 A8
Beech Pl 5 YO32 167 A6
Beech Rd
Boston Spa LS23 188 E8
Campsall DN6 206 E1
Darlington DL1 3 F7
Harrogate HG2 222 E6
Ripon HG4 214 B3
Beech Rise DL1 3 F7
Beech St
23 Barnoldswick BB18 171 D1
10 Glusburn BD20 187 E7
6 Harrogate HG2 220 C3
Beech Tree Ct 2 YO30 164 F7
Beech Tree La YO8 204 C5
Beechtree Rd LS24 189 D5
Beech View
Aberford LS25 194 E8
Ferrybridge WF11 201 C4
Beechville Ave YO12 212 F6
Beech Way 25 YO26 165 F1
Beech Wlk
5 Eastfield YO11 100 A7
Tadcaster LS24 189 D6
Beechwood Ave 2 TS9 26 C8
Beechwood Cl
14 Bedale DL8 63 A2
Markington with Wallerthwaite HG3 139 D4
Sherburn in Elmet LS25 195 F3
West Marton BD23 171 F5
Beechwood Cres 6 HG2 219 C1
Beechwood Croft LS25 195 F3
Beechwood Dr BD23 216 D5
Beechwood Glade
Sherburn in Elmet LS25 195 F3
6 York YO24 227 B1
Beechwood Gr
Harrogate HG2 222 F7
16 Ilkley LS29 175 C2
Beechwood Rd YO17 215 D2
Beechwood Rise 1 LS22 180 C4
Beeforth Cl YO32 225 D5
Beeston's La LS17 178 C4
Beeston Way WF10 200 E6
Beggarmans Rd DL8 80 C8
Belbrough Cl 3 TS15 25 C4
Belbrough La TS15 25 C4
Belcombe Way 1 YO30 228 A7
Belford La HG4 112 A3
Belford Pl 3 HG1 219 D1
Belford Rd HG1 219 D2
Belford Sq 9 HG1 219 D1
Belfry Way 30 WF6 200 B1
Belgrave Cres
Harrogate HG2 222 E8
15 Scarborough YO11 212 F5
Belgrave St
3 Skipton BD23 216 E4
York YO31 228 C7
Belgrave Terr
3 Hurworth-on-Tees DL2 22 D8
14 Scarborough YO11 212 F5
Thirsk YO7 211 B2
Bellaby Pk 7 YO62 93 D7
Bellburn La DL3 3 B7
BELL BUSK 155 A3
Bell Cl
Haxby YO32 225 C8
5 Seamer YO12 99 D6
Belle Hill BD24 131 D3
Bell End Gn YO18 49 D3
BELLERBY 60 B7
Bellerby Camp DL8 60 B7
Bellerbyhurn Rd YO17 95 F2
Bellerby Rd DL8 60 D6
Belle Vue LS29 218 C3
Belle Vue Cres 33 YO14 101 B3
Belle Vue Par 9 YO11 212 F5
Belle Vue Pl 10 YO11 212 F5
Belle Vue St
34 Filey YO14 101 B3
Scarborough YO12 212 F5
York YO10 228 E3
Bellevue Terr
Ripon HG4 214 C5
2 Skipton BD23 216 E4
Belle Vue Terr
Whitby YO21 208 D7
York YO10 228 E3
Bellfarm Ave YO31 228 E8
Bellflower Cl 16 WF10 200 D3
Bellground La YO30 165 D4
Bell Hall★ YO19 191 E6
Bell Horse Gate LA6 103 D4
Bellhouse La YO21 29 C7
Bellhouse Way YO24 230 B8
Bellingham Cl YO7 211 C3
Bell La
Cawood YO8 197 A7
Huby YO61 144 A4
Husthwaite YO61 117 B5
Rawcliffe DN14 205 A2
Ulleskelf LS24 190 C2
Bellmans Croft YO23 230 B2
Bellman Wlk 3 HG4 113 D2
Bell's Ct 15 YO62 92 F6
Bellwood Ave
Boston Spa LS23 188 E7
Lockwood TS12 9 E7
Bellwood Dr YO24 230 B8
Belmangate 2 TS14 8 F6
Belmont WF11 201 D5
Belmont Ave
Harrogate HG2 220 D4
10 Otley LS21 176 F1
Belmont Cl 3 YO30 225 A1
Belmont Gr
Calcutt HG5 221 A4
1 Harrogate HG2 220 D3
Belmont Prim Sch 7 TS14 8 F6
Belmont Rd
Harrogate HG2 219 C2
Ilkley LS29 218 E4
Scarborough YO11 213 A4
Belmont St BD23 216 F4
Belmont Terr 2 HG2 220 D3
Belmont View HG5 221 A4
Belmont Wharf BD23 216 F4
Belthorpe La YO42 169 E1
Belton Park Dr 7 DL9 40 E4
Belvedere Pl YO11 213 A3
Belvedere Rd YO11 213 A3
Belvedere Terr YO11 213 A3
Belvoir Ave 8 YO41 185 B2

Belvoir Dr WF11 .... 201 F2
Belvoir Terr 9 YO11 .... 213 A5
Bence The YO42 .... 170 C3
Benedict Ave YO8.......... 232 E4
BENINGBROUGH 165 D4
Beningbrough Dr HG3... 219 B5
Beningbrough Hall & Gdns★ YO30.................. 165 B5
Beningbrough La YO30.. 165 D5
Benjy La YO19 .... 192 E7
Benkhill Dr 16 DL8 ...... 63 A2
Ben La BB18 .... 171 E2
Bennett St 11 BD23 ...... 216 F3
Bennions Way 5 DL10 .... 41 E4
Bennison La YO21........ 13 A1
Bennymoor La YO8...... 198 C4
BEN RHYDDING 218 F3
Ben Rhydding Dr LS29.... 218 F3
Ben Rhydding Prim Sch LS29.................. 218 E4
Ben Rhydding Rd LS29 .. 218 D3
Ben Rhydding Sta LS29.. 218 F4
Bensham Rd DL1.......... 3 D8
Benson La WF6.......... 200 B2
BENT 187 D7
Bentham Moor Rd LA6 .. 103 A2
Bentham Rd LA6 .... 103 B3
Bentham Sta LA2 .... 129 A7
Bentinck Ave TS5 .... 6 F8
Bent La
Colne BB8 .... 186 A3
Sutton BD20............ 187 E7
Bentley Wynd TS16 .... 5 D3
Benton Gap La BD22 .... 187 B7
Bent Rigg La YO13 .... 54 B7
Bents La YO18 .... 71 A5
Beresford Cl 6 DL8...... 63 B2
Beresford Terr YO23 .... 228 C1
Berghill La YO7 .... 66 A7
Berkeley Terr YO26 ...... 227 E5
Berkley Dr TS14 .... 8 F5
Bernard La YO26.......... 164 B3
Bernica Gr TS17 .... 6 A4
Berry Bank DL2............ 1 A6
Berrygate La HG4 .... 214 E7
Berry La LS26............ 200 C8
Berry's Ave 5 HG5...... 221 B6
Berrys Ct 16 HG5........ 221 B6
Berwick Rd
Archdeacon Newton DL3.... 3 A7
18 Scotton DL9.......... 40 E4
Bestmire La DL6.......... 65 A4
Betteras Hill Rd LS25.... 202 A8
Betton Farm Visitor Ctr★ YO13.................. 99 C8
Betton Rise YO13 .... 99 B8
Between Dikes Rd YO8 .. 204 F8
Beulah St 10 HG1 ...... 219 D2
Beulah Terr YO11 ...... 212 F5
Beverley Balk YO41 ...... 168 B2
Beverley Cl 12 YO11.... 100 B6
Beverley Gate YO12 ...... 99 D1
Beverley Rd
11 Eastfield YO11 .... 100 B6
Middlesbrough TS7 .... 7 D6
Norton YO17 .... 215 E3
Beverley Rise LS29...... 175 C2
Beverley Sch TS4 .... 6 F8
BEWERLEY 137 B3
Bewerley Rd HG1 .... 219 B5
Bewlay St YO23.......... 228 C2
Bewley Gr TS5.............. 6 E7
Bexhill Cl WF8.......... 201 C1
Bexley Dr TS6 .... 7 E8
BICKERTON.............. 181 A5
Bickerton Way LS21...... 176 F1
Bickley Gate YO13 .... 73 F6
Bickley Howe YO12 ...... 212 B4
Bickley Way TS8.......... 7 A5
Bielby Cl
8 Bedale DL8............ 63 B3
33 Scalby YO12 .... 75 D5
BIGGIN.................. 196 E5
Biggin La LS25.......... 196 C6
Big Meadow Dr 5 LS29 .. 174 E4
Big Sheep & Little Cow Farm★ DL8............ 63 B3
BILBROUGH 182 D1
Bilsdale Cl
Northallerton DL7 .... 210 C2
York YO30 .... 224 E2
Bilsdale Gr HG5.......... 221 D6
Bilsdale Midcable Chopgate CE Prim Sch TS9........ 46 F6
BILTON 219 E6
Bilton Cl HG1............ 219 E6
Bilton Dr HG1............ 219 D4
Bilton Grange Cl HG1 .. 219 D5
Bilton Grange Prim Sch HG1.................. 219 D5
Bilton Grove Ave HG1 .. 219 E5
Bilton Hall Dr HG1 ...... 220 D6
BILTON IN AINSTY 181 E4
Bilton La HG1............ 219 E6
Binks Cl DL6.............. 210 B7
Binnington Carr La YO12 . 99 B1
Binns La BD20............ 187 D7
Binsley La YO61.......... 117 E2
BINSOE 86 F2
Binsoe La HG4............ 86 F3
Birch Ave
Malton YO17 .... 215 D6
Sleights YO22............ 32 A6
Birch Cl
8 Filey YO14 .... 101 B3
Birch Cl *continued*
9 Hunton DL9 .... 40 F2
3 Kirklevington TS15 ...... 24 E8
4 Thorpe Willoughby YO8. 197 B1
York YO32 .... 225 D3
Birch Copse YO24........ 227 D2
Birch Cres 10 YO22........ 32 A6
Birch Dr
2 Faceby TS9............ 25 F1
Kippax LS25.............. 194 D2
Birchen Cl 7 WF10 ...... 200 D3
Birches The TS8 .... 7 A5
Birchfield Dr TS16 .... 5 D5
Birch Gr
Castleford WF10 .... 201 B3
Harrogate HG1 .... 219 E6
Kippax LS25.............. 194 D1
Sleights YO22............ 32 A6
Birch Hall La BB18 ...... 172 B1
Birch La
13 Haxby YO32 .... 166 E5
New York HG3 .... 137 F1
Birch Park Ind Est YO31 . 228 E8
Birch Pk YO31 .... 225 E1
Birch Rd DL1 .... 3 D8
Birch View 8 YO18 ...... 96 A6
Birch Way YO61.......... 143 D8
Birchwood Cl 16 BD24.... 131 D2
Birchwood Ct 5 LS29.... 218 A4
Birchwood Gdns 13 YO61.................. 115 F1
Birchwood Mews HG2.... 222 F7
Birchwood Rd TS7.......... 7 C6
Birdale Field La LS22.... 188 B8
BIRDFORTH.............. 116 E6
Birdforth Way 1 YO62 .... 92 C1
Bird Gdn★ LS25............ 195 B7
Bird La
Hensall DN14.............. 203 D2
Kellington DN14.......... 202 F4
Bird Ridding La DL8...... 60 B1
BIRDSALL 148 B4
Birds of Prey & Conservation Ctr★ YO7............ 88 F7
Birdwood Cl DL9........ 209 C2
Birk Brow Rd TS12........ 9 D5
BIRKBY 23 B1
Birkby La DL7............ 23 B1
Birk-crag Ct 2 HG3 .... 161 B2
Birk Crag Nature Reserve★ HG3.................. 161 B1
Birkdale Ave HG5 .... 221 D5
Birkdale Gr 4 YO26...... 227 B5
Birkdale Rd 9 TS18........ 5 D8
Birker La
Newton on Derwent YO41.................. 185 D4
Wilberfoss YO41 .... 185 F6
Birkett La CA17 .... 14 B7
Birk Field Bank YO21...... 28 F6
Birk Head La YO18 .... 70 F4
Birkhills HG3 .... 140 A3
BIRKIN.................. 202 D6
Birkin La WF11.......... 202 B4
Birkin Rd YO8 .... 202 F5
Birk La YO8.............. 199 D8
Birklands 1 YO62........ 93 D7
Birkwith La LA2.......... 128 F7
BIRSTWITH 160 E6
Birstwith CE Prim Sch HG3.................. 160 E6
Birstwith Dr YO26 ...... 227 E4
Birstwith Grange HG3.... 160 E6
Birstwith Rd HG1 ...... 220 A3
Birthwaite La HG3 ...... 161 C8
Birtley Ave TS5 .... 6 E7
Bishop Cl 1 HG3 .... 137 C4
Bishop Ct 2 YO8 .... 232 B6
Bishopdale Cl HG5...... 221 D6
Bishopdale Ct 28 BD24 .. 131 D2
Bishopdale Dr 7 LS22 .. 180 A1
Bishopdike Rd
Cawood YO8.............. 197 A6
Sherburn in Elmet LS25... 196 A4
Bishop Garth 2 HG3 .... 137 C4
Bishopgate St YO23 ...... 233 B1
Bishophill Jun YO1...... 233 A1
Bishophill Senior YO1.... 233 B1
BISHOP MONKTON 140 A5
Bishop Monkton CE Prim Sch HG3.................. 140 A5
Bishop Monkton Railway Cutting Nature Reserve★ HG3.................. 139 F5
Bishop's Cl YO8.......... 197 A8
Bishops Ct YO1 .... 233 B1
Bishopsfields Dr YO26.... 228 A5
Bishopsgarth DL7........ 210 C4
Bishopsway YO10 .... 229 C3
Bishops Way DL10 .... 41 D5
BISHOP THORNTON...... 138 F2
Bishop Thornton CE Prim Sch HG3.................. 139 F2
BISHOPTHORPE 231 B3
Bishopthorpe Infant Sch YO23.................. 231 A4
Bishopthorpe Palace★ YO23.................. 231 B4
Bishopthorpe Rd YO23 .. 231 B5
BISHOPTON 113 D2
Bishopton HG4 .... 214 A5
Bishopton La
Great Burdon DL1 .... 4 A7
Ripon HG4 .... 113 D2
Bishopton Pk HG4 ...... 214 A5
Bishop Way 3 HG3 ...... 137 C4
BISHOP WILTON.......... 169 F2
Bishop Wilton CE Prim Sch YO42.................. 169 F2
Bisley Ct 13 DL1 .... 3 F6
Bismarck St YO26........ 227 E5
Bitterdale La YO62 .... 70 A3
Black Abbey La 1 BD20. 187 E8
Black Bank Rd LA2...... 130 E3
BLACK BANKS 3 D2
Blackbird Way 8 YO12.... 99 F6
Black Bull Wynd TS16 ...... 5 C3
Blackburn Ind Est 7 LS25.................. 196 A4
Blackburn La WF11 ...... 202 B2
Black Diamond Way 3 TS16.................. 5 D5
Black Dike La YO26 ...... 182 F8
Blackett Rd DL1 .... 3 E6
Black Fen La YO8 ...... 232 C8
Black Gill La
Airton BD23.............. 154 B8
Settle BD24 .... 132 A1
Black Hill YO62 .... 118 E5
Black Hill Rd HG3........ 157 F8
Black Horse La TS15 ...... 25 C3
Blacklee Cl 3 YO32 ...... 167 B8
Blackmore Cl TS14.......... 8 F5
Black Sheep Brewery Visitor Ctr★ HG4 .... 86 C4
Black Sike La YO13........ 98 B4
Blacksmith Bank DL8 .... 62 E5
Blacksmith Ct DL7 .... 22 C2
Blacksmith Hill YO22...... 53 A7
Blacksmiths Cl 5 YO41 . 185 C2
Blackthorn TS8 .... 7 B4
Blackthorn Cl DN14 ...... 207 A7
Blackthorn Dr YO31...... 225 E2
Blackthorn La HG3........ 222 C3
Blackthorn Rd LS29 ...... 218 D5
BLACKWELL 3 B4
Blackwell DL3 .... 3 B3
Blackwell La DL3 .... 3 B4
Black Wlk WF8 .... 201 B1
Blackwood La YO8........ 198 F7
Blackwood Rd YO8........ 198 E8
BLADES 37 B5
Blair Ave TS17 .... 5 F4
Blair Pk HG5.............. 221 C5
Blake Ct YO19 .... 193 A8
Blake Gate HG3.......... 136 E1
Blakeley Cres 3 BB18... 171 D2
Blakeley Gr YO30 .... 224 F3
Blakeney Pl YO10 .... 228 F3
Blake St YO1 .... 233 B3
Blakey Bank YO62.......... 49 A5
Blakey Cl YO7 .... 211 C1
Blakey La YO7 .... 211 C1
Blakey Rd YO62 .... 70 B6
Blandford Rd DL9.......... 40 E3
Bland La YO26 .... 227 A4
Blands Ave WF10........ 200 D7
Bland's Cliff 27 YO11.... 213 A6
Blandscliff Gall★ YO11 ... 213 B6
Blands Cres 3 WF10.... 200 D7
Blands Gr 4 WF10........ 200 D7
Bland's Hill HG5 .... 221 A4
Blands Terr WF10........ 200 D7
Blansby La YO17 .... 121 C8
Blansby Park La YO18 .... 96 A8
Blatchford YO30 .... 228 B8
Blatchford Mews YO30 .. 228 B8
Blawath Rd YO18 .... 51 A2
Blayshaw La HG3 .... 110 B4
BLAZEFIELD 137 E4
Blazefield Bank HG3 .... 137 D3
Bleaberry La YO41 ...... 169 B5
Bleachfield YO10 .... 228 F2
Blea Moor Rd LA6.......... 78 E2
Blean La DL8 .... 57 D3
Blea Pit La HG4.......... 140 E8
Bleara Rd BB18 .... 186 B8
Blenheim Ave 4 YO21 .. 208 B7
Blenheim Cl DL10.......... 41 F6
Blenheim Ct
Harrogate HG2 .... 222 D7
Rawcliffe YO30 .... 224 D3
Blenheim St 12 YO12.... 213 A7
Blenheim Terr YO12...... 213 A7
Blenheim Way HG2 ...... 222 C7
Bleriot Way YO30 .... 225 A3
Blewhouse La DL8 .... 61 E3
Blind La
Aiskew DL8 .... 63 B3
Barton DL10.............. 21 D7
Burton in Lonsdale LA6.... 102 F3
Guisborough TS14 .... 8 C6
Hurworth DL2 .... 22 E8
Knaresborough HG5 ...... 221 B7
Scorton DL10.............. 42 B8
Tockwith YO26............ 181 B8
Blind Piece La YO7.......... 116 A6
Bloe Beck La LA2 .... 129 E6
Bloody Beck Hill YO13.... 54 A7
Blorenge Ct 22 TS17 .... 5 F4
Blossomgate HG4.......... 214 B5
Blossom St YO24.......... 233 A1
Blossoms The LS26 ...... 200 B6
Blossom Way WF10 ...... 200 D3
BLUBBERHOUSES 159 D2
Blue Bank YO22............ 32 A4
Blue Barn La TS15 .... 25 C6
Bluebeck Dr YO30........ 227 E8
Blue Bell Farm Ct YO8... 192 E1
Blue Bell Gr TS5 .... 6 F6
Bluebell Mdw 15 HG3 .... 161 B3
Bluebell Mews WF10...... 200 C3
Bluebell Wlk 18 HG3 .... 161 B3
Blue Bridge La YO10 .... 228 D2
Blue Coat YO19 .... 184 D7
Blue Nile Way 25 DL9 .... 41 A5
Blue Ridge Pk WF10 .... 200 E3
Blue Slates Cl YO19 .... 193 A8
Blyth Cl YO8 .... 232 A5
Board St YO23 .... 228 C2
Boar La TS17 .... 6 B5
Boatcliffe Rd YO14 ...... 127 D7
Boathouse La DL2.......... 2 E4
Boat La
Barforth DL11 .... 1 C7
Great Ouseburn YO26 .... 164 C8
Kirby Hall YO26 .... 142 C1
Mickletown LS26 .... 200 D5
Bob La YO7................ 65 E3
Bodmin Dr WF6.......... 200 A2
Bodner Hill YO61 .... 118 F1
Boeing Way TS18 .... 5 F7
Boggart La LS24 .... 190 C2
Boggy La DL10 .... 209 B5
Bog Hall YO21 .... 208 D5
Boghole Bank DL6 .... 45 B3
Boghouse La TS13 .... 10 F3
Bog La
Askham Bryan YO24 ...... 230 B6
Barwick in Elmet & Scholes LS15 .... 194 A7
Stirton with Thorlby BD23 216 D7
Bogs La
Bridge Hewick HG4 ...... 114 C1
Harrogate HG1 .... 220 C5
Bolckow St TS14.......... 8 F7
Boldron Cl 8 TS18........ 5 D8
Bold Venture St BD23 .. 216 F2
Bolland St 16 BB18...... 171 D2
Bolling Rd LS29.......... 218 D4
BOLTBY 66 F1
Boltby Rd YO30 .... 224 F2
BOLTON ABBEY 174 E8
Bolton Abbey Sta BD23.. 174 D8
Bolton Ave DL10 .... 209 B7
BOLTON BRIDGE 174 F8
Bolton Bridge Rd LS29 .. 218 A4
Bolton Castle★ DL8 .... 59 B6
Bolton Cross DL10 .... 41 F5
Bolton Ct 14 DL8.......... 60 D5
Bolton Hall★ BD23.......... 157 F1
Bolton La YO42 .... 169 E1
BOLTON-ON-SWALE...... 41 F6
Bolton-on-Swale CE Prim Sch DL10................ 41 F6
Bolton-on-Swale Lake Nature Reserve★ DL10 .. 41 F5
BOLTON PERCY 190 D4
Bolton Percy Station Nature Reserve★ YO23 .... 190 C4
Bolton Priory (rems of)★ BD23.................. 157 F1
Bolton Rd
Draughton BD23 .... 174 F7
Ellerton DL10.............. 41 F5
Silsden BD20.............. 174 D3
Bolton St HG1 .... 219 D4
Bolton Way
13 Leyburn DL8............ 60 D5
Richmond DL10 .... 209 C8
Bonby La YO8............ 192 E2
Bond End HG5 .... 221 A6
Bondgate
Darlington DL1.............. 3 C5
Helmsley YO62.............. 92 F6
Pontefract WF8 .... 201 C1
Ripon HG4 .... 214 C4
Selby YO8.............. 232 B7
Bondgate Ct HG4 .... 214 C4
Bondgate Gn HG4........ 214 D4
Bondgate Green Cl 6 HG4 .... 214 C4
Bondgate Green La HG4. 214 C4
Bondings Rise 5 LS25 .. 196 A4
Bond La
Appleton Roebuck YO23... 190 F5
Settle BD24 .... 131 D2
Bond St WF8 .... 201 C1
Bonington Ct 7 YO26... 227 E4
Bonney Croft La 25 YO61 .... 143 C8
Bonnygate La YO61 ...... 118 F3
Bonny Gr TS8.............. 7 C5
Bonnygrove Way TS8........ 7 B5
Bonnywell La YO7........ 114 E6
Boonhill Rd YO62 .... 69 F4
BOOSBECK 9 E8
Boosbeck Rd TS12 .... 9 D8
Bootham YO30............ 233 A3
Bootham Bar★ YO31 .... 233 B3
Bootham Cres YO30...... 233 A4
Bootham Junior Sch YO30.................. 228 A7
Bootham Park Ct YO31 .. 233 B4
Bootham Park Hospl YO31.................. 233 B4
Bootham Row YO30...... 233 B3
Bootham Sch YO30........ 233 A3
Bootham Sq YO30........ 233 B3
BOOTHAM STRAY 225 B2
Bootham Terr YO30 ...... 233 A3
Booth Bridge La BD23.... 172 A3
BOOTHFERRY 205 E5
Booth Ferry Rd DN14.... 205 F6
Booth St 27 LS29.......... 176 C1
Boothwood Rd YO30 .... 224 E2
Boot St 26 BB18.......... 172 A1
Booty La DN14............ 206 F7
BOOZE.................... 17 F1
Borage Rd 30 HG3 ...... 161 B3
BORDLEY.................. 133 D3
Bore Tree Baulk YO19.... 184 D6
Borogate 9 YO62.......... 92 F6
BOROUGHBRIDGE 141 C5
Boroughbridge High Sch YO51.................. 141 B5
Boroughbridge L Ctr YO51.................. 141 B5
Boroughbridge Prim Sch YO51.................. 141 B5
Boroughbridge Rd
Bishop Monkton HG3...... 140 B5
Bridge Hewick HG4 ...... 114 B1
Dishforth YO7 .... 115 A2
Knaresborough HG5 ...... 221 B7
Northallerton DL7 .... 210 C1
North Otterington DL7.... 64 E6
Ripon HG4 .... 214 E3
Scriven HG5.............. 162 E6
Westwick YO51 .... 140 D4
Whixley YO26 .... 164 B4
York YO26 .... 227 D5
Borough Mere La YO17.. 215 D8
Borough Rd
Darlington DL1 .... 3 D5
Richmond DL10 .... 208 D7
Borrage Green La HG4 .. 214 B4
Borrage La HG4.......... 214 B4
BORROWBY
Northallerton............ 65 E4
Whitby 11 D6
Borrowby Ave DL6 ...... 210 F3
Borrowby Ct TS14.......... 8 E7
Borrowbydale Ave HG5.. 221 D6
Borrowby La
Borrowby TS13 .... 11 D7
Staithes TS13............ 13 J1
Borrowdale Dr
Castleford WF10 .... 201 B5
York YO30 .... 224 F1
Boscombe Gdns 2 TS8 .... 6 F5
BOSSALL 168 D7
Boss Moor La BD23 ...... 155 F8
Boston Ave DL6.......... 210 D4
Boston Dr TS7 .... 7 B5
Boston Rd
Clifford LS23 .... 188 E7
Wetherby LS22 .... 180 C2
BOSTON SPA 188 F8
Boston Spa Sch LS23.... 188 D8
Botheby Wood BD23 .... 216 E5
Bottom House La YO22.... 33 B5
Bottoms La YO22.......... 33 B6
BOTTON.................. 29 B3
Botton Rd LA2 .... 128 E2
Boulby Bank YO22 ...... 208 E6
Bouldershaw La DL11 .... 17 D1
Boulsworth Dr BB8...... 186 B1
Boulsworth Gr 4 BB8.... 186 A3
Boundary Ave BD20 ...... 187 E7
Boundary Way DL10...... 209 F8
Bourlon Rd DL9.......... 209 A2
Bourn Ave DL1.............. 3 E5
Bournemouth Ave 2 TS3.. 7 C8
Bournemouth Rd TS3 .... 7 C8
BOUTHWAITE 110 E2
Bouthwaite Dr 13 YO26.. 227 E4
Bow Bridge Dr BD23 .... 217 D7
Bowbridge La DL7 .... 63 A8
Bow Bridge La YO21 ...... 29 A7
Bow Bridge View LS24 .. 189 F7
Bowcarr La YO26 .... 163 D8
Bowcliffe Rd LS23 ...... 188 E5
Bowe Cres 8 DL8.......... 63 B2
Bowen Rd DL3.............. 3 B7
Bower Rd HG1............ 219 D3
Bower St HG1............ 219 D2
Bowers Wharf BD23...... 216 F3
Bower Wlk YO17 .... 215 E4
Bowes Ave YO31.......... 228 E5
Bowes Ct DL1.............. 3 D6
Bowesfield Cres TS18...... 6 A8
Bowesfield Ind Est TS18... 6 A8
Bowesfield La TS18 .... 6 A7
Bowes La YO14 .... 100 F5
Bowes Pk HG2............ 222 D6
Bowland Cl HG2 .... 220 D1
Bowland Ct HG2.......... 220 D1
Bowland La YO42 .... 193 E2
Bowland View LA6 ...... 103 E3
Bowland Way YO30 ...... 225 A1
Bowling Green Ct YO31.. 228 D8
Bowling Green La
9 Hunmanby YO14...... 126 F8
Manfield DL2.............. 2 B4
York YO31 .... 233 C4
Bowling Green Yd 13 HG5 .... 221 A6
Bowling La YO17.......... 215 E4
Bowling Terr BD23........ 216 D3
Bowling View BD23 ...... 216 D3
Bowman St DL3............ 3 D7
Bowness Dr YO30 .... 224 E1
Bowood Cl 8 TS17.......... 5 F5
Bow St TS14................ 8 F7
Bowthorpe La YO8 ...... 199 B4
Bowyers Cl YO23.......... 230 C4
Box Hill YO12 .... 212 C3
Box La WF8.............. 201 C1
Boyle & Petyt Prim Sch BD23.................. 174 F8
Boyle The LS15 .... 194 B8
Boynton La
Barton-le-Street YO17 .... 120 F8
Rawcliffe DN14 .... 205 A1
Boynton Rd DL7 .... 22 E2
Brabourn Gdns TS8 .... 6 F5
BRACEWELL 171 C3
Bracewell La BD23 ...... 171 B4
Bracewell St 15 BB18.... 171 D2
Brackenber Cl BD24...... 131 C2

Brackenber La BD24 .... 131 C1
BRACKENBOTTOM 105 E3
Bracken Cl
Whitby YO22 .... 208 E4
York YO32 .... 225 F4
Bracken Cres TS14 .... 8 D6
Bracken Field BD23 ..... 134 B3
Brackenfield Prep Sch
HG1 .... 219 A2
Bracken Ghyll Dr BD20 .. 174 B1
Bracken Hill
Scarborough YO12 .... 212 C7
2 York YO10 .... 229 C3
Brackenhill Ave YO8 .... 232 A4
Brackenhill La
Brayton YO8 .... 232 A3
Church Fenton LS24 ...... 196 C8
Sleights YO22 .... 32 A5
Brackenhills YO26 ...... 165 F1
Brackenley Ave 2 BD23 . 217 C7
Brackenley Cl 3 BD23 .. 217 C7
Brackenley Cres BD23 ... 217 C7
Brackenley Ct BD23 ..... 217 C7
Brackenley Dr BD23 ..... 217 C7
Brackenley Gr 1 BD23 .. 217 C7
Brackenley La BD23 ..... 217 A7
Bracken Rd YO24 .... 230 F7
Brackenthwaite La HG3 . 222 A1
Brackenwell La LS17 .... 178 B4
Brackenwood Cl 2 LS29 218 E4
Brackit La YO61 .... 91 B2
Bracknell Rd TS17 .... 6 C8
Bradfords Cl 8 LS23 .... 188 E6
Bradley Ave
Castleford WF10 .... 200 E4
Northallerton DL6 .... 210 F2
Bradley Cres YO23 ...... 182 D6
Bradley Dr YO24 .... 230 C8
Bradley Gr BD20 .... 174 B1
Bradley La YO23 .... 182 C5
Bradley Rd
Pickering YO18 .... 71 F4
Silsden BD20 .... 174 B2
Bradley Rise BD20 ...... 174 B1
Bradleys Both Com Prim Sch
BD20 .... 173 E3
Bradleys Terr 2 TS9 ...... 8 A2
Bradworth Cl 3 YO11 ... 100 B7
Bradworth Dr 2 YO11 ... 100 B7
Braeburn Infant Sch 14
YO11 .... 100 A6
Braeburn Junior Sch 15
YO14 .... 100 A6
Braegate La LS24 .... 190 E7
Braemar Dr LS25 .... 194 D4
Braeside 3 TS15 .... 24 E8
Braeside Gdns YO24 ..... 227 E3
BRAFFERTON 116 A1
Brafferton Hall Gdn 3
YO61 .... 115 F1
Braham La HG5 .... 179 F7
BRAIDLEY 83 B2
Brailsford Cres YO30 .... 228 A8
Braimber La YO51 .... 141 C1
Braithegayte YO19 ...... 192 F8
Braithwaite Hall* DL8 ... 84 D8
Braithwaite La
Dacre HG3 .... 159 A7
East Witton Town DL8 ..... 84 E8
Braker La YO26 .... 163 F4
Bramall La 6 DL1 .... 3 F6
Bramble Cl
13 Colburn DL9 .... 41 A5
11 Killinghall HG3 .... 161 B3
Bramble Ct 20 LS25 ..... 195 F4
Bramble Dene YO24 ..... 230 D7
Bramblefields DL6 ...... 210 F4
Brambles 8 YO8 .... 197 B1
Brambles Ct LS25 .... 202 B7
Brambles The 6 LS29 ... 175 C2
Bramble Wlk YO17 ...... 215 B4
Brambling Fields La
YO17 .... 122 C2
Bramblings The 6
WF10 .... 200 D3
Bramcote Sch YO11 ..... 213 A3
Brame La HG3 .... 177 A8
Bramfield Way 6 TS17 .... 6 D6
BRAMHAM 188 F5
Bramham Ave YO26 ..... 227 A3
Bramham Dr HG3 .... 219 A4
Bramham Gr YO26 ...... 227 A3
Bramham La LS23 .... 188 A6
Bramham Park Gdns*
LS23 .... 188 C4
Bramham Prim Sch
LS23 .... 188 E6
Bramham Rd
Boston Spa LS23 .... 188 E7
Thorner LS14 .... 188 A3
York YO26 .... 227 A2
Bramley Ave YO8 .... 198 B5
Bramley Garth YO31 ..... 229 B6
Bramley Head La HG3 ... 158 E5
Bramper La DL7 .... 42 E1
Branch Rd BD23 .... 216 F2
Brandon Gr YO32 .... 226 E3
BRANDSBY 118 C3
Brandsby Bank YO61 .... 118 D3
Brandsby Gr YO31 ...... 225 E2
Brandsby Rd YO61 ...... 118 A1
Brandsby St YO61 ...... 118 A1
Brankin Dr DL1 .... 3 E4
Brankin Rd DL1 .... 3 D3
Branklyn Gdns TS17 .... 6 A4
BRANKSOME 2 F6
Branksome Gr 1 TS18 ..... 5 E8
Branksome Sch DL3 ...... 3 A6
Bransdale TS14 .... 8 D6
Bransdale Ave
Northallerton DL7 .... 210 C2
11 Pontefract WF6 ...... 200 A2
Bransdale Cl 6 WF6 .... 200 A2
Bransdale Gr 3 HG5 .... 221 D6
Bransdale Mews 10 WF6 200 A2
Bransdale Rd YO62 .... 48 B1
Bransdale Wlk WF6 ..... 200 A2
Bransholme Dr YO30 .... 225 A2
Brant Bank La LS29 ..... 175 B3
Brantingham Dr 2 TS17 .... 5 F5
Brant La LS24 .... 189 D4
Branton Cl YO26 .... 142 A1
Branton Ct YO26 .... 142 A1
BRANTON GREEN 142 A1
Branton La YO26 .... 142 A1
Branton Pl YO26 .... 227 A3
Brass Castle La TS8 .... 7 C3
Brat La LS21 .... 177 A7
Bravener Ct YO30 .... 165 B6
BRAWBY 94 F1
Brawby La YO17 .... 94 E1
BRAWITH 26 A6
Bray Gate YO42 .... 169 E2
Braygate Balk YO18 ...... 72 C5
Braygate La YO18 .... 72 D5
Braygate St YO17 .... 121 A2
Bray Rd YO10 .... 231 F8
Brayshaw La BD23 ...... 135 A2
BRAYTHORN 177 E4
Braythorne La LS21 ..... 177 E4
BRAYTON 232 A2
Brayton CE Infant Sch
YO8 .... 232 A2
Brayton Coll YO8 .... 232 A3
Brayton Junc YO8 .... 232 C1
Brayton Junior Sch YO8 232 A2
Brayton La YO8 .... 232 B1
Brazengate BD23 .... 134 B3
Breakmoor Ave BD20 .... 174 C2
Breamar Ct 2 DN14 ..... 203 A2
Brearlands BD23 .... 172 A3
BREARTON 162 A7
Brearton La HG3 .... 161 E8
Breary Cl YO24 .... 227 F1
Breary Flat La HG5 ...... 221 C7
Brechin Dr TS17 .... 6 B6
Breckenbrough La DL10 .. 41 A3
Breckenbrough Sch YO7 .. 89 A6
Breckney La YO17 ...... 122 D5
Breckon Hill YO62 .... 49 A1
Brecksfield YO30 .... 224 C5
Brecks La
Beadlam YO62 .... 93 B8
Kippax LS25 .... 194 C2
Pockley YO62 .... 93 B8
Strensall YO32 .... 167 B7
Swillington LS26 .... 194 B2
York YO32 .... 225 F4
Brecon Cres TS17 .... 5 F4
Breedycroft La YO17 .... 121 C4
BREIGHTON 199 D5
Breighton Aerodrome*
YO8 .... 199 D5
Breighton Rd
Bubwith YO8 .... 199 D6
Wressle YO8 .... 199 C3
Brendon Gr TS17 .... 6 A3
Brentwood DL8 .... 60 D5
Brentwood Cres YO10 ... 229 C2
Brewers Ct YO7 .... 211 B3
Brewerton St HG5 ...... 221 A5
Brewery La
5 Ripon HG4 .... 214 C4
Skipton BD23 .... 216 F4
Brewery Rd LS29 .... 218 C4
Brewster Terr HG4 ...... 214 C6
Briar Ave YO26 .... 227 B4
Briar Cl DL8 .... 59 C6
Briar Cliffe YO8 .... 232 A3
Briardene Ave 9 YO12 .... 75 E5
Briar Dr YO31 .... 225 F2
Briarfield Cl LS29 ...... 218 D3
Briar Pk 5 YO62 .... 93 D7
Briar Rd TS17 .... 6 B7
Briars Ct YO23 .... 190 E5
Briars Dr YO23 .... 190 E5
Briars The HG5 .... 221 B7
Briar Wlk DL3 .... 3 B3
Briarwood Cl YO8 .... 202 F7
Brickfield La YO51 ...... 141 D4
Brickhill La YO8 .... 204 F4
Brickkiln La
Aldbrough DL11 .... 2 A3
Forcett & Carkin DL11 .... 20 C8
Brick Kiln La YO8 .... 203 D6
Brick Lands La DN14 .... 203 F4
Brickyard Rd YO51 ...... 141 A4
Bridge Beck La YO7 ...... 66 C7
Bridge Cl
Burniston YO13 .... 75 D7
Church Fenton LS24 ..... 196 A7
3 Colburn DL9 .... 41 A5
Haxby YO32 .... 225 C7
5 Knaresborough HG5 ... 221 A5
Newton-le-Willows DL8 .... 62 B4
Bridge Cres YO8 .... 205 C8
Bridge Ct YO8 .... 232 D6
Bridge End DL6 .... 65 B5
Bridge End Yd 6 BD24 .. 131 D3
Bridge Farm DN14 ...... 207 F6
Bridge Farm Cl 27 YO62 .. 92 F6
Bridge Foot LS23 .... 188 F8
Bridge Garth
2 Boston Spa LS23 ...... 188 E7
South Milford LS25 ..... 195 F2
Bridge Gn YO21 .... 29 C7
BRIDGE HEWICK 114 B1
Bridge Hill LS21 .... 176 C7
Bridge Holm La YO22 ..... 33 C2
BRIDGEHOUSE GATE 137 B4
Bridge La
Ilkley LS29 .... 218 A5
Pollington DN14 .... 207 F6
York YO30 .... 233 B4
Bridge Mews LA6 .... 103 C4
Bridge Rd
Bishopthorpe YO23 ...... 230 F3
Boston Spa LS23 .... 188 F8
Brompton-on-Swale DL10 .. 41 B6
Glusburn BD20 .... 187 E7
Hurworth DL3 .... 3 B3
Malton YO17 .... 215 C5
Old Byland & Scawton YO7 . 91 F7
10 Stokesley TS9 .... 26 C7
Bridges Ct YO8 .... 232 D6
Bridges La YO42 .... 193 E4
Bridge St
5 Bedale DL8 .... 63 A3
9 Brafferton YO61 ...... 115 F1
Castleford WF10 .... 200 F4
Egglescliffe TS16 .... 5 D4
12 Helmsley YO62 .... 92 F6
8 Normanton South WF6 . 200 B2
16 Pickering YO18 .... 95 F7
Richmond DL10 .... 209 B6
Skipton BD23 .... 216 F4
Tadcaster LS24 .... 189 E6
Thirsk YO7 .... 211 B3
Whitby YO22 .... 208 D7
York YO1 .... 233 B2
Bridge Terr
Northallerton DL7 .... 210 C4
Richmond DL10 .... 209 B6
Bridge View Rd HG4 .... 214 C7
Bridle Way 1 YO26 ..... 227 A3
Bridle Wlk YO8 .... 232 C4
Bridlington Rd
Hunmanby YO14 .... 127 A7
Sledmere YO25 .... 150 C4
1 Stamford Bridge YO41 168 D2
Wold Newton YO25 ..... 126 A4
Bridlington St YO14 .... 126 F8
Briercliffe YO12 .... 212 C7
Briergate YO32 .... 225 C7
Brier Hill YO21 .... 29 C7
Brier La YO8 .... 205 A4
Brierlands Cl LS25 ...... 194 D4
Brierlands La LS25 ..... 194 E4
Brierley Rd YO12 .... 99 E7
Briery Cl 18 LS29 .... 175 C2
Brigantia Gdns 12 YO12 .. 99 E6
Briggate HG5 .... 221 B5
Brigg Farm Ct YO8 ..... 204 D5
Brigg La YO8 .... 204 D5
Brigg Rd 55 YO14 ...... 101 B3
Brigg's Ave WF10 .... 200 E3
Briggs St YO31 .... 228 C7
BRIGGSWATH 32 B7
Brighton Rd LS29 .... 218 E3
Bright St
18 Colne BB8 .... 186 A3
Darlington DL1 .... 3 E5
1 Glusburn BD20 .... 173 E1
Skipton BD23 .... 216 E4
15 Trawden BB8 .... 186 A3
York YO26 .... 227 F5
Bright Terr BB8 .... 186 A1
Bright Wlk YO8 .... 232 B6
Brigshaw Dr WF10 ...... 200 C8
Brigshaw High Sch
WF10 .... 200 C8
Brigshaw La WF10 ...... 200 C8
Brimham Cl 2 TS17 .... 6 B5
Brimham Rocks* HG3 .. 138 B4
Brimham Rocks Rd HG3 . 138 B2
Brind La DN14 .... 199 F2
Brindle Park Dr WF10 ... 201 A3
Brindle Way YO17 ...... 215 F4
Brindley Ct 15 BD23 .... 216 F3
Brindley Mill BD23 ...... 216 F3
Brindleys La DN14 ...... 199 F3
Brindley Wharf BD23 ... 217 A3
Brinkburn Ave DL3 .... 3 B7
Brinkburn Dr 1 DL3 .... 3 B6
Brinkburn Rd
Darlington DL3 .... 3 B6
4 Scarborough YO12 .... 212 E5
Brinklow Way HG2 ...... 222 B5
Brinkworth Rush YO41 .. 185 A2
Brinkworth Terr 1 YO10 228 E3
Briscoe Ridge La HG3 ... 177 F6
BRISCOERIGG 177 F5
Briscoe Way TS8 .... 6 E5
Britannia St 2 YO12 .... 212 E5
Broach La
Heck DN14 .... 203 D1
Kellington DN14 .... 202 F3
Broach Rd
Heck DN14 .... 207 D8
Hensall DN14 .... 203 C1
Broadacres DN14 .... 204 D3
Broad Acres YO32 ...... 225 C7
Broadacres Ave DN14 ... 204 D3
Broadacres Garth DN14 . 204 D3
Broad Balk YO17 .... 149 A5
Broad Balk La YO7 ..... 115 B1
Broad Carr Rd HG3 ..... 110 D2
Broad Cl
Askrigg DL8 .... 57 E6
Coulby Newham TS8 .... 6 D5
Broad Dubb Rd HG3 .... 177 C8
Broadfield La HG4 ...... 138 B8
Broadfield Way 9 LS29 . 174 E4
Broad Gate
Brompton YO13 .... 98 B7
Hunsingore LS22 .... 180 F8
Marton cum Grafton YO26 . 141 F1
Broadgate Rd TS5 .... 6 E8
Broad Gate Rd YO21 ..... 28 E4
Broad Head La BD22 .... 187 E2
Broad Highway YO19 .... 192 F8
Broad La
Appleton Roebuck YO23 .. 191 A6
6 Beal DN14 .... 202 D4
Catton YO41 .... 185 C7
Cawood YO8 .... 197 A6
Church Fenton LS25 ..... 196 D6
Rufforth YO23 .... 227 A2
Upper Poppleton YO26 ... 165 D2
Wistow YO8 .... 197 A5
Broadlands
2 Roundhill Village TS17 ... 6 A5
Wheldrake YO19 .... 193 A8
Broadlands Dr 5 YO13 .... 99 B8
Broadmanor YO8 .... 199 A7
Broadmires La YO18 ..... 96 C5
Broad Oak La 18 YO32 .. 166 E5
Broadrum La YO18 .... 95 E6
Broadstone Way
10 Rawcliffe YO30 ...... 224 E3
York YO30 .... 224 E3
Broadway
Scarborough YO12 ...... 212 D7
York YO10 .... 231 E8
Broadway Gr 19 YO10 .. 231 E8
Broadway The DL1 .... 3 E5
Broadway W YO10 ...... 231 D8
Broadwell Rd TS4 .... 7 A8
Brockadale Nature Reserve*
WF8 .... 206 B4
Brockett Ind Est YO23 .. 191 B6
BROCKFIELD 167 E2
Brockfield Park Dr YO31 225 F2
Brockfield Rd YO31 ..... 225 E2
Brockholme La DL6 .... 65 A4
Brocklesby Rd TS14 .... 8 F5
Brockley Cl LS24 .... 196 B7
Brockrigg Ct TS14 .... 8 E7
Broc-o-Bank 1 DN6 .... 206 E2
Brodie Cl 9 TS17 .... 5 F5
Brodrick Dr LS29 .... 218 A3
Brogden La BB18 .... 171 B1
Brogden View 19 BB18 .. 171 D2
Brokes La DL11 .... 40 B6
Bromley La TS8 .... 7 B3
Bromley St 2 YO26 ..... 227 F5
BROMPTON 43 F3
Brompton Ave 4 TS14 ..... 8 F7
BROMPTON-BY-
SAWDON 98 C5
Brompton Carr La YO13 .. 98 B4
Brompton Hall Sch YO13 . 98 C5
Brompton House Day Hospl
DL6 .... 210 E5
Brompton Ings Rd YO13 .. 98 D3
Brompton La DL6 .... 43 E4
BROMPTON-ON-SWALE ... 41 B7
Brompton-on-Swale Prim
Sch DL10 .... 41 B7
Brompton Pk DL10 .... 41 B6
Brompton Prim Sch DL6 . 43 F3
Brompton Rd
Newton-le-Willows DL8 .... 62 B4
Northallerton DL6 .... 210 D5
York YO30 .... 228 A7
Brompton & Sawdon Prim
Sch YO13 .... 98 C5
Bronaber Cl 1 TS17 .... 5 F4
Bronte Cl
Brompton on Swale DL10 .. 41 C7
Scarborough YO12 .... 212 D5
Bronte Ct WF8 .... 201 B1
Bronte Dr 33 DL9 .... 41 A5
Bronte Rise WF10 .... 201 B3
Brookacre 7 LA6 .... 103 D3
Brooke Cl
Harrogate HG1 .... 219 E7
12 Kirkbymoorside YO62 ... 70 B1
BROOKFIELD 6 E6
Brookfield HG3 .... 160 F5
Brookfield Cl HG3 ...... 161 A5
Brookfield Cres HG3 .... 161 A5
Brookfield Ct 5 WF6 ... 200 B1
Brookfield Garth HG3 ... 161 A5
Brookfield Way
7 Earby BB18 .... 172 A1
Hampsthwaite HG3 ...... 160 F5
Brook House Croft BD24 . 131 E6
Brook La
Danby YO21 .... 29 C6
Halton West BD23 .... 153 F1
Thornton Dale YO18 ...... 96 D6
Weeton LS17 .... 178 C2
Brookland 1 LA6 .... 102 F2
Brooklands
43 Filey YO14 .... 101 B3
York YO10 .... 229 D4
Brooklands Cl 44 YO14 .. 101 B3
Brooklands Com Specl Sch
BD23 .... 216 F2
Brooklands Cres DL6 .... 210 E5
Brooklands Terr BD23 ... 216 F3
Brook Pk YO21 .... 32 A7
Brooksbank Rd TS7 .... 7 D7
Brookside
Collingham LS22 .... 188 A8
Hovingham YO62 .... 119 E6
Skelton & Brotton TS12 ..... 9 D8
Skipton BD23 .... 217 A3
Sleights YO22 .... 32 B6
Spennithorne DL8 .... 60 F4
Brookside Ave 1 DL8 .... 63 B2
Brookside Cl 2 DL8 ...... 63 B2
Brook St
Castleford WF10 .... 201 B6
18 Earby BB18 .... 172 A1
Hebden BD23 .... 135 A2
Hellifield BD23 .... 154 B3
Ilkley LS29 .... 218 B4
12 Scarborough YO12 ... 212 F6
Selby YO8 .... 232 C4
Skipton BD23 .... 216 F4
York YO31 .... 233 B4
Brook View BD23 .... 173 B4
Brookwood Way TS16 ...... 5 E4
Broome Cl
14 Pontefract WF6 ...... 200 A2
York YO32 .... 225 F5
Broome Way YO32 ...... 226 A5
Broom Field HG3 .... 160 E6
Broomfield Ave DL7 ..... 210 D2
Broomfield Sch DL7 ..... 210 D2
Broomfield Terr 18
YO21 .... 208 D6
Broomhill WF10 .... 201 A3
Broom Hill Ave 6 TS17 .... 6 D5
Broomhill Cl 23 WF11 ... 202 A2
Broomhill Cres 25 WF11 . 202 A2
Broomhill Dr 26 WF11 ... 202 A2
Broomhill Gr 19 WF11 ... 202 A2
Broomhill Pl 22 WF11 ... 202 A2
Broomhill Sq 24 WF11 ... 202 A2
Broomhill Wlk 21 WF11 . 202 A2
Broom House La
Egton YO21 .... 30 F4
Ugthorpe YO21 .... 12 B2
Broom Rd LS24 .... 189 D5
Broom Wlk YO12 .... 212 E7
Brootes La BD23 .... 107 C2
Brotes La YO26 .... 164 B5
BROTHERTON 201 D5
Brotherton & Byram Com
Prim Sch WF11 .... 201 E4
Brougham Cl
3 Eaglescliffe TS17 .... 5 F6
York YO30 .... 227 F8
Brougham St
Darlington DL3 .... 3 C7
Skipton BD23 .... 217 A3
Brougham Street Parish
Church Sch BD23 ...... 217 A3
Brough Ave 5 DL9 .... 41 A5
Brough Field Cl 4 TS17 ... 6 D6
Brough Hall* DL10 .... 41 B4
Brough Mdws 4 DL10 .... 41 D5
Brough Rd 23 DL9 .... 40 E4
BROUGHTON
Malton 121 D4
Skipton 172 E6
Broughton Ave BD23 .... 216 D3
Broughton Cres BD23 ... 216 C3
Broughton Gr BD23 ..... 216 D3
Broughton Green La
YO17 .... 121 C4
Broughton Mews BD23 .. 216 D3
Broughton Rd
Broughton YO17 .... 121 C3
11 East Ayton/West Ayton
YO13 .... 99 A7
Malton YO17 .... 215 A5
Skipton BD23 .... 216 C3
Broughton Rise YO17 ... 215 B5
Broughton Way
4 Harrogate HG2 .... 220 C3
York YO10 .... 229 B4
Browcliff BD20 .... 174 C2
Brow La LA2 .... 129 D6
Brown Bank La BD20 .... 174 D2
Brown Bank Rd
Kirkby Malzeard HG4 .... 111 F5
Norwood HG3 .... 177 B8
Brown Cow Rd YO8 ..... 204 C8
Browney Croft YO10 .... 233 C1
Brown Howe Rd YO18 ..... 51 A1
Browning Cl 3 DL9 .... 40 E4
Brown La YO26 .... 141 F1
Brownlow St YO31 ...... 233 C4
Brown Moor 22 YO41 ... 168 D2
Brownmoor La
Huby YO61 .... 144 A2
Sutton-on-the-Forest YO32 166 B8
Brown Rigg Rd YO13 ..... 53 F5
Brownroyd 14 BB18 .... 172 B1
Browns Ct 4 BD20 ...... 173 E3
Browns Fold 3 BD23 .... 134 E3
Brown's Terr 4 TS13 ...... 11 F7
Brownswood Cotts YO21 . 31 A5
Browsfield Rd 24 LS29 .. 174 F4
BROXA 74 C6
Broxa Hill YO13 .... 74 C6
Broxa La YO13 .... 74 D5
Broxa Moor La YO13 ..... 74 C7
Bruce St 21 BB18 .... 171 D2
Bruce Way 5 YO18 .... 95 F6
Bruche Dr YO7 .... 115 A2
Brunel Ct 12 YO26 ...... 227 F5
Brunel Rd HG1 .... 220 D5
Brunel Way DL1 .... 3 D5
Brunsell La YO26 .... 163 F7
Brunswick Cl 2 YO32 ... 167 C8
Brunswick Dr HG1 ...... 219 B2
Brunswick Pl 1 HG1 .... 219 D1
Brunswick Sh Ctr YO11 .. 213 A5
Brunswick St
Whitby YO21 .... 208 D6
York YO23 .... 228 B1

Brunt Acres Est DL8 . . . . . 56 D5
Brunt Acres Rd DL8 . . . . . 56 D4
BRUNTHWAITE 174 D1
Brunthwaite La BD20 . . . . 174 E1
Brunton Bank DL8 . . . . 59 A5
Brunton La HG5 . . . . 163 B6
Brunton Rd LA2 . . . . 131 A6
Bryan Cl 13 DL2 . . . . 3 E1
Bryden Cl DL6 . . . . 210 E2
Bry Hills YO12 . . . . 99 D6
Brymor Ice Cream Palour★ HG4 . . . . 85 E7
Bryony Ct YO8 . . . . 232 B2
Bryony Rd 4 HG3 . . . . 161 B3
Bryony Way 5 HG3 . . . . . 161 B3
BUBWITH 199 D7
Bubwith Prim Sch YO8 . . 199 D7
Buccaneer Ct YO41 . . . . . 185 A3
Buccleugh Cl TS14 . . . . 8 F5
BUCKDEN 107 E8
Buckden Cl 13 YO61 . . . . . 143 D8
Buckden Wood La BD23 107 D8
Buck Haw Brow BD24 . . . 131 B4
Buckingham Ct YO1 . . . . . 233 A1
Buckingham Sq 7 YO62 . . 92 F6
Buckingham St YO1 . . . . . 233 B1
Buckingham Terr YO1 . . . 233 B2
Buckingham Way WF11 . 201 F4
Buck La YO60 . . . . 147 B6
Buckle Cl YO8 . . . . 199 A8
Buckle Ct YO8 . . . . 232 B7
Buckle La WF6 . . . . 200 A1
Bucks La 1 BD24 . . . . 131 D2
Buck Stone La BD20 . . . . . 187 C5
Buess La DL1 . . . . 4 A7
Buffet Hill La LA2 . . . . . . 129 D7
BUGTHORPE 169 D4
Bugthorpe CE Prim Sch YO41 . . . . 169 D4
Bugthorpe La YO41 . . . . . 169 D5
Bugthorpe Lane Town E YO41 . . . . 169 E5
Bull Alley La DN14 . . . . . . 204 B3
BULLAMOOR 44 B1
Bullamoor Cl DL6 . . . . 210 F5
Bullamoor Junior Sch DL6 . . . . 210 F5
Bullamoor Rd DL6 . . . . . . 210 E5
Bull Balk YO41 . . . . 185 E4
Buller St YO8 . . . . 232 B6
Bull Hill DL8 . . . . 61 E8
Bull Ing La BD23 . . . . 134 D3
Bull La
Huby YO32 . . . . 166 B7
York YO10 . . . . 228 F3
Bull Moor La YO60 . . . . . . 168 A8
Bullock La
Newsham with Breckenbrough YO7 . . . . 89 A5
Newsham YO7 . . . . 88 F8
Bull Piece La YO17 . . . . . . 122 D3
Bullytree La LS25 . . . . 195 E2
BULMER 146 B6
Bulmer Hill YO60 . . . . 146 B6
Bungalow Rd BD20 . . . . . . 187 D7
Bunkers Hill
Aberford LS25 . . . . 194 F7
1 Skipton BD23 . . . . 217 A4
Burdale Cl
8 Eaglescliffe TS16 . . . . 5 D5
Norton YO17 . . . . 215 F2
Burdike Ave YO30 . . . . 228 A8
Burdock Cl 10 HG3 . . . . 161 B3
Burdon Garth TS17 . . . . 6 D5
Burdon View 3 TS16 . . . . . . 5 D4
Burgate YO18 . . . . 95 F7
Burgess Wlk YO24 . . . . . . 230 C8
Burghley Dr 1 TS17 . . . . 6 A5
Burgoyne Cl HG4 . . . . 113 D3
Burke Rd YO17 . . . . 215 C5
Burke St HG1 . . . . 219 E5
Burlands La YO26 . . . . 182 F7
Burley Ave HG3 . . . . 161 A2
Burley Bank Cl HG3 . . . . . 161 A3
Burley Bank Rd HG3 . . . . 161 A3
Burley Cl
12 South Milford LS25 . . . . 195 F2
Thornton-le-Street YO7 . . . . 65 B1
BURLEY IN WHARFEDALE 176 B1
Burley La HG3 . . . . 161 A3
Burley Oaks Prim Sch 42 LS29 . . . . 176 C1
Burlington Ave YO10 . . . . 228 F4
Burlyn Rd 3 YO14 . . . . 127 A8
Burma Rd DL2 . . . . 3 F2
BURN 203 D7
BURN BRIDGE 222 D3
Burn Bridge La HG3 . . . . . 222 C2
Burn Bridge Oval HG3 . . . 222 C3
Burn Bridge Rd HG3 . . . . 222 C3
Burnby Cl HG3 . . . . 219 B5
Burn Est YO32 . . . . 225 E4
BURNESTON 87 E7
Burneston Ct DL3 . . . . 2 F5
Burneston Hargill DL8 . . . . 87 F8
Burneston Prim Sch DL8 . 87 E8
Burnett Cl HG3 . . . . 140 A2
Burn Hall Cl YO8 . . . . 203 D7
Burnham Rd LS25 . . . . 194 C3
Burnholme Ave YO31 . . . . 229 B6
Burnholme Com Coll YO31 . . . . 229 A5
Burnholme Dr YO31 . . . . . 229 A6
Burnholme Gr YO31 . . . . . 229 A5
BURNISTON 75 C8
Burniston Gdns YO13 . . . . . 75 D7
Burniston Gr YO10 . . . . . . 229 A4
Burniston Ind Est YO13 . . . 75 D7
Burniston Rd YO12 . . . . . . 212 E8
Burn La YO8 . . . . 203 D6
Burnley Rd BB8 . . . . 186 A1
Burnleys Ct LS26 . . . . 200 B4
Burnleys Dr LS26 . . . . 200 B4
Burnleys Mews LS26 . . . . 200 B4
Burnleys View LS26 . . . . . 200 B5
Burnmoor Cres LA6 . . . . . 103 D3
Burnmoor Dr TS16 . . . . 5 D5
Burnroyd Ave 17 BD20 . . . 187 E7
BURNSALL 157 B8
Burnsall Cl 6 YO14 . . . . . 101 A3
Burnsall Dr YO26 . . . . 227 E4
Burnsall La BD23 . . . . 135 A1
Burnsall Mews BD20 . . . . 174 B2
Burnsall Prim Sch BD23 . 157 B8
Burns Ct YO24 . . . . 230 B7
Burns Hill 4 LS29 . . . . 174 F4
Burnside 4 YO11 . . . . 100 A6
Burnside Ave BD23 . . . . . . 216 F2
Burnside Cl HG1 . . . . 219 B5
Burnside Cres BD23 . . . . . 216 F2
Burnside Dr HG1 . . . . 219 B5
Burnside Rd
Darlington DL1 . . . . 3 E4
Harrogate HG1 . . . . 219 B5
Burnside Wlk HG1 . . . . . . 219 B5
Burns Way
Boston Spa LS23 . . . . 188 E7
Harrogate HG1 . . . . 219 E7
Burnthouse Bank DL6 . . . . 45 B3
Burnt La HG4 . . . . 87 A1
BURNT YATES 160 F8
Burnt Yates CE Prim Sch HG3 . . . . 160 F8
Burn Wood Ct TS21 . . . . 5 A7
Burrard Ave DL10 . . . . 209 B7
Burr Bank 15 YO11 . . . . . . 213 B6
BURRILL 62 E2
Burrill Ave YO30 . . . . 228 B8
Burrill Dr 13 YO32 . . . . 166 D5
Burrill Rd DL8 . . . . 62 F2
Burrow Rd LA6 . . . . 102 B7
Burstall Dr 2 DL9 . . . . 209 C1
BURTERSETT 56 E4
Burtersett Rd DL8 . . . . 56 D4
Burton Ave YO30 . . . . 228 B7
Burton Comm La LS25 . . . 202 A6
Burton Ct YO30 . . . . 233 A4
Burtondale Rd 1 YO12 . . . . 99 F7
Burton Fields Cl 12 YO41 . . . . 168 D2
Burton Fields Rd 4 YO41 . . . . 168 D2
BURTON FLEMING 126 E3
Burton Fleming Rd YO25 126 B3
Burton Gn YO30 . . . . 228 B8
Burton Green Prim Sch YO30 . . . . 228 B8
Burton Hill 3 LA6 . . . . 102 F3
BURTON IN LONSDALE . . . 102 F3
Burton La YO61 . . . . 141 D8
BURTON LEONARD 140 B2
Burton Leonard CE Prim Sch HG3 . . . . 140 A2
Burton Leonard Lime Quarries Nature Reserve★ HG3 . . . . 140 A1
Burton Rd LA2 . . . . 128 E8
Burton Riggs Nature Reserve★ YO11 . . . . 99 F6
BURTON SALMON 201 F6
Burton Salmon Prim Sch LS25 . . . . 201 F6
Burton Stone La YO30 . . . 233 A4
Burtree Ave YO30 . . . . 224 B4
Burtree La YO21 . . . . 29 B5
Burwains La BD23 . . . . . . 155 F5
Burwen Castle Rd BD23 . 172 C4
Burwen Castle (Roman Fort)★ BD23 . . . . 172 C4
BURYTHORPE 147 F3
Busby La TS9 . . . . 26 C4
Bushby Gill Wlk DL9 . . . . . 40 E2
Bush Gdns YO17 . . . . 121 B4
Busk La LS24 . . . . 196 C8
Busky Dike La LS21 . . . . . 159 E2
Butcher La
Potto DL6 . . . . 25 C2
Whitley DN14 . . . . 207 A6
Butcher's La YO25 . . . . . . 126 E3
Butcher Terr YO23 . . . . . . 228 C1
Bute Cl 2 TS17 . . . . 6 B6
Butler Rd HG1 . . . . 219 E5
Buttacre La YO23 . . . . 182 D2
Butterbergh 11 LA2 . . . . . . 129 A8
Butterbur Way 34 HG3 . . 161 B3
BUTTERCRAMBE 168 E5
Buttercrambe Rd
Gate Helmsley YO41 . . . . . 168 C3
Sand Hutton YO41 . . . . 168 C5
Buttercup Cl 6 HG3 . . . . . 161 B3
Butterfield Cl HG3 . . . . . . 140 B5
Butterfield Dr TS16 . . . . 5 D5
Butterfly World★ TS18 . . . . 5 E6
Buttermere Ave
Middlesbrough TS5 . . . . 6 E8
4 Wetherby LS22 . . . . 180 B3
Buttermere Ct 9 YO8 . . . . 232 B6
Buttermere Dr YO30 . . . . . 224 E1
Butter Mkt 8 DN14 . . . . . . 204 C1
Butters Cl 20 YO32 . . . . . . 166 D5
BUTTERWICK
125 B2
BUTTERWICK *continued*
Brawby 120 E8
Butterwick La YO17 . . . . . 120 F8
Butterwick Rd
Barton-le-Street YO17 . . . . 120 E5
Foxholes YO17 . . . . 125 B1
Langtoft YO25 . . . . 151 C7
Butt Fields La DN14 . . . . . 203 F1
Butt Hedge YO26 . . . . 182 A5
Butt Hill
22 Haxby YO32 . . . . 166 D5
Kippax LS25 . . . . 194 D1
Butthouse Rigg DL11 . . . . . 35 F8
Butt La
Carlton Husthwaite YO7 . . 116 F7
Guisborough TS14 . . . . 9 A6
Wold Newton YO25 . . . . . . 126 A3
Buttle La 3 DN14 . . . . 204 C1
Butts BB18 . . . . 171 D1
Butts Cl 19 YO41 . . . . 168 D2
Butts Hill YO14 . . . . 127 C6
Butts La
Bainbridge DL8 . . . . 81 B8
Barton-le-Willows YO60 . . . 146 D2
Bentham LA2 . . . . 129 A8
Eaglescliffe TS16 . . . . 5 D4
Monk Fryston LS25 . . . . . . 201 E8
South Milford LS25 . . . . . . 195 E1
Butts The 12 WF8 . . . . 201 B1
Buxton Ave TS7 . . . . 7 B5
Byards Pk 6 HG5 . . . . 221 A7
Byefield Gr YO13 . . . . 99 B8
Byemoor Ave TS9 . . . . 8 A1
Byemoor Cl TS9 . . . . 8 A1
BYLAND ABBEY 91 E1
Byland Abbey (rems of)★ YO61 . . . . 91 E1
Byland Ave
Northallerton DL6 . . . . 210 E5
Thirsk YO7 . . . . 211 C3
York YO31 . . . . 228 E8
Byland Ct 5 YO21 . . . . 208 B6
Byland Gr HG1 . . . . 219 F6
Byland Mews HG5 . . . . 221 D4
Byland Pl
Harrogate HG1 . . . . 219 F6
Northallerton DL6 . . . . 210 E5
Byland Rd
Harrogate HG1 . . . . 219 F6
Whitby YO21 . . . . 208 B6
Bylands Way DL3 . . . . 3 A6
Byng Rd DL9 . . . . 209 F1
BYRAM 201 F4
Byram Cl 3 DL6 . . . . 210 E3
Byram Ct 4 DL6 . . . . 210 E3
Byram Park Ave WF11 . . . 201 F4
Byram Park Rd WF11 . . . . 202 A4
Byron Ave 3 DN6 . . . . 206 E1
Byron Ct DL2 . . . . 22 D7
Byron Dr YO30 . . . . 227 F8
Byron St 2 BD23 . . . . 217 A3
Byron Wlk Mews HG2 . . . 219 D2
Byward Dr YO12 . . . . 99 F7
Byways HG2 . . . . 222 D6
Byway The DL1 . . . . 3 E5

C

Cabin La 2 HG3 . . . . 137 F1
Caburn Cl 2 YO12 . . . . . . 212 B5
Caedmon Ave YO21 . . . . . 208 B8
Caedmon Cl YO31 . . . . 229 A7
Caedmon Sch YO21 . . . . . 208 D5
Caesar Ct YO24 . . . . 233 A1
Cairnborrow 4 YO24 . . . . 230 B7
Cairn View LS29 . . . . 218 D5
Caithness Cl 1 YO30 . . . . 224 E3
Calcaria Cres LS24 . . . . . . 189 D5
Calcaria Ct 3 YO24 . . . . . 230 F8
Calcaria Rd LS24 . . . . 189 E5
CALCUTT 221 A3
Calcutt HG5 . . . . 221 A4
Caldbeck Cl 1 YO30 . . . . . 225 A1
CALDBERGH 84 B7
Calder Ave YO26 . . . . 227 B8
Calder Cres DN14 . . . . 207 F6
Caldey Gdns 39 TS17 . . . . . . 5 F4
CALDWELL 1 B4
Caledonian Way DL1 . . . . . . 3 F8
Caledonia St YO12 . . . . . . 212 E5
Calf Cl YO32 . . . . 225 D8
Calf Hall La BB18 . . . . 171 D1
Calf Wood La BD20 . . . . . . 172 E1
California Dr WF10 . . . . . . 200 B3
California Gr 7 TS9 . . . . 8 A2
California Rd YO22 . . . . . . 208 E5
California Terr YO22 . . . . 208 E5
Callum Cl DL3 . . . . 3 C7
CALTON 155 B6
Calton La BD23 . . . . 155 A6
Calton Terr BD23 . . . . 216 F3
Calvert Cl YO32 . . . . 225 C7
Calvert Hos DL11 . . . . 36 C4
Calverts Garth YO60 . . . . . 145 D5
CAMBLESFORTH 204 D5
Camblesforth Prim Sch YO8 . . . . 204 C4
Cambrain Ct 10 TS17 . . . . . . 5 F4
Cambrian Cl 2 YO32 . . . . . 225 F3
Cambridge Ave TS7 . . . . 7 B5
Cambridge Cres 5 HG1 219 D2
Cambridge Pl
8 Harrogate HG1 . . . . 219 D2
1 Scarborough YO12 . . . . 212 E4
Cambridge Rd
Harrogate HG1 . . . . 219 D2
Middlesbrough TS5 . . . . 6 E8
Cambridge St
3 Castleford WF10 . . . . . 200 E4
15 Harrogate HG1 . . . . 219 D2
Normanton South WF6 . . . 200 A1
Scarborough YO12 . . . . . . 212 F6
4 York YO24 . . . . 228 A3
Cambridge Terr
4 Harrogate HG1 . . . . 219 D2
1 Scarborough YO11 . . . . 213 A4
Camden Rd WF10 . . . . 201 B4
Camela La YO8 . . . . 204 B6
Cameron Gr YO23 . . . . . . 228 C1
Cam Garth BD23 . . . . 108 A3
Cam Gill Rd
Kettlewell with Starbotton BD23 . . . . 108 B4
Woodale DL8 . . . . 83 A2
Cam High Rd BD23 . . . . 79 D5
Cam La BD23 . . . . 172 A3
Camm La DN14 . . . . 204 C3
Cammock La BD24 . . . . . . 131 D2
Campbell Ave
Ripon HG4 . . . . 113 D3
York YO24 . . . . 227 E2
Campbell St 11 BD20 . . . . 187 E8
CAMP HILL 87 F5
Camp Hill Cl HG4 . . . . 214 D3
Campion Cl YO13 . . . . 75 D5
Campion Dock YO22 . . . . . 208 E5
Campion Dr TS14 . . . . 8 D6
Campion Gr
Coulby Newham TS7 . . . . . . 7 B6
6 Harrogate HG3 . . . . 161 B3
Campion La TS15 . . . . 25 B4
Campion Rd DL1 . . . . 3 D7
Campleshon Rd YO23 . . . . 228 B1
Campsall Balk DN6 . . . . . . 206 E1
Campsall Hall Rd 12 DN6 . . . . 206 E1
Campsall Park Rd 11 DN6 . . . . 206 E1
Campsmount Sch DN6 . . 206 D1
Camwal Rd HG1 . . . . 220 C4
Camwal Terr 5 HG1 . . . . 220 C4
Canaan La DL8 . . . . 60 E2
Cana La HG4 . . . . 114 E2
Canal Garth DN14 . . . . 207 F6
Canal Rd
Cottingwith YO42 . . . . 193 C5
Ripon HG4 . . . . 214 D4
Selby YO8 . . . . 232 D4
Canal St BD23 . . . . 216 F4
Canal View YO8 . . . . 232 D3
Canal Yd 8 BD23 . . . . 216 F4
Canberra Rd TS7 . . . . 7 B6
Canby La 4 HG3 . . . . 179 E6
Candler Ave 12 YO13 . . . . . 99 A7
Candler St YO12 . . . . 212 E5
Canham Gr YO10 . . . . 229 D3
Cannon Hall La DN14 . . . . 202 F1
Cannon St WF10 . . . . 200 F3
Canon Gr TS15 . . . . 5 E2
Canon Lee Sch YO30 . . . . 228 A8
Canons Ct YO23 . . . . 231 B2
Canons Garth La 2 YO62 . 92 F6
Canterbury Cl
9 Haxby YO32 . . . . 166 D5
Whitby YO21 . . . . 208 C5
Canterbury Ct 5 WF8 . . . 201 C2
Canton Gdns TS5 . . . . 6 E6
CANTSFIELD 102 B4
Caper Hill YO21 . . . . 29 F1
Captain Cook Birthplace Mus★ TS7 . . . . 7 B7
Captain Cook Cres YO22 . 208 E6
Captain Cook Meml Mus★ YO22 . . . . 208 E7
Captain Cook Monumnet★ YO21 . . . . 208 D8
Captain Cook Prim Sch TS7 . . . . 7 B6
Captain Cook Schoolroom Mus★ TS9 . . . . 8 A1
Captain Cook's Cl
Hinderwell TS13 . . . . 11 D8
Staithes TS13 . . . . 13 K1
Captain Cooks Cres 14 YO22 . . . . 208 E6
Captain Cook's Cres TS7 . . 7 C6
Captain Cook's Mon★ TS9 . 8 D1
Captain Cook & Staithes Heritage Ctr★ TS13 . . . . . . 13 K2
Captain Cook's Way TS9 . . . 8 A1
Cardale Pk HG3 . . . . 222 A6
Cardan Dr LS29 . . . . 218 E4
Cardinal Cl 13 LS25 . . . . . . 195 F4
Cardinal Gdns DL3 . . . . 3 B5
Cardinals Cl 3 YO8 . . . . . . 197 B8
Careless House La HG3 . . 138 E4
Carentan Cl 6 YO8 . . . . . . 232 B6
Carey St YO10 . . . . 228 D1
Cargate Hill 32 YO14 . . . . . 101 B3
Cargo Fleet La TS3 . . . . 7 C8
Carla Beck La BD23 . . . . . 173 B4
CARLBURY 2 B7
Carlbury Ave TS5 . . . . 6 D6
Carlbury Cres DL3 . . . . 3 A5
CARLESMOOR 111 E4
Carless La YO14 . . . . 100 F4
Carleton Ave BD23 . . . . . . 216 E3
Carleton Bsns Pk BD23 . . 216 E3
Carleton Dr DL3 . . . . 3 A5
Carleton Endowed Prim Sch BD23 . . . . 173 B4
CARLETON IN CRAVEN . . . 173 A4
Carleton La BD23 . . . . 173 A4
Carleton New Rd BD23 . . 216 E3
Carleton Rd BD23 . . . . 216 E1
Carleton St
3 Skipton BD23 . . . . 216 F3
17 York YO26 . . . . 227 F5
Carlile Hill TS8 . . . . 6 E5
Carline Mead 23 HG3 . . . . 161 B3
Carlisle St 16 YO26 . . . . . . 227 F5
Carlow Cl TS14 . . . . 8 F6
Carl St YO23 . . . . 228 C2
CARLTON
204 D3
Darlington 1 F3
Helmsley 68 E1
West Witton 83 E7
Carlton App 1 LS22 . . . . . 180 B3
Carlton Ave
Thirsk YO7 . . . . 211 B1
York YO10 . . . . 229 B3
Carlton Cl
4 Carlton Miniott YO7 . . . . 89 C4
Eggborough DN14 . . . . 202 F1
11 Guisborough TS14 . . . . . . 8 F7
19 Normanton South WF6 200 A1
Carlton Dr TS17 . . . . 6 A6
Carlton & Faceby CE Prim Sch TS9 . . . . 26 A3
Carlton Gdns 1 WF6 . . . . 200 B1
CARLTON HUSTHWAITE . . 116 F7
CARLTON IN CLEVELAND . . 26 A3
Carlton in Snaith CP Sch DN14 . . . . 204 C3
Carlton La YO62 . . . . 92 F7
Carlton Lanes Sh Ctr WF10 . . . . 200 F4
CARLTON MINIOTT 89 C4
Carlton Miniott Prim Sch YO7 . . . . 89 B4
Carlton Moor Cres DL1 . . . . 3 E4
Carlton Rd
Carlton Miniott YO7 . . . . . . 89 A3
1 Catterick Garrison DL9 . 40 F4
9 Filey YO14 . . . . 101 B3
Harrogate HG2 . . . . 222 D7
Helmsley YO62 . . . . 92 F7
Skipton BD23 . . . . 217 F3
Sutton upon Derwent YO41 . . . . 185 C1
Carlton St WF6 . . . . 200 A2
Carlton Terr 6 YO11 . . . . 213 A4
Carlton Twrs★ DN14 . . . . 204 D2
Carlton View
Great Preston WF10 . . . . . 200 C7
Selby YO8 . . . . 232 D4
Carlton Way YO7 . . . . 89 C4
Carlyle Cres WF10 . . . . . . 201 A4
Carlyle Rd WF10 . . . . 201 A4
Carmel Gdns TS5 . . . . 6 E6
Carmel Gr DL3 . . . . 3 B4
Carmelite St YO1 . . . . 233 C2
Carmel RC Tech Coll DL3 . . 3 A5
Carmel Road N DL3 . . . . 3 B5
Carmel Road S DL3 . . . . 3 B4
Carmires Ave
Haxby YO32 . . . . 166 F5
Knaresborough HG5 . . . . . 221 C8
Carnagill Prim Sch DL9 . . . 40 D4
Carnagil Rd DL9 . . . . 209 B1
Carney St TS12 . . . . 9 D7
Carnot St YO26 . . . . 227 F5
Carnoustie Cl 1 YO26 . . . . 227 B4
Carnoustie Dr TS16 . . . . 5 E5
Carnoustie Gdns 20 WF6 200 B1
Carnoustie Way TS8 . . . . . . 7 C5
Caroline Cl 5 YO24 . . . . . . 227 F3
Carousel Wlk LS25 . . . . . . 195 F4
Carpenters Yd 10 YO17 . . . 215 C4
CARPERBY 58 E4
Carpley Green Rd DL8 . . . . 57 D3
Carr Ave LS25 . . . . 195 F4
Carrbank La YO32 . . . . 167 D2
Carr Beck Dr 11 WF10 . . . 200 D3
Carr Beck Rd 2 WF10 . . . 200 D3
Carr Beck View 5 WF10 200 D3
Carr Bridge Cl 4 TS16 . . . . . 5 D4
Carr Bridge La DL6 . . . . 24 D3
Carr Cl
13 Hemingbrough YO8 . . . 198 F1
Rainton with Newby YO7 . . 114 F6
Ripon HG4 . . . . 214 B3
Carrfield YO24 . . . . 230 C8
Carrfield Dr LS15 . . . . 194 B8
Carr Field La YO26 . . . . . . 141 F1
Carrfield Rd LS15 . . . . 194 B8
Carr Fields La YO13 . . . . . . 99 B5
Carr Head La BD22 . . . . . . 187 B7
Carr Hill YO60 . . . . 145 D5
Carr Hill La YO21 . . . . 32 B7
Carr Hill Ridge YO21 . . . . . 32 B7
Carr House La
Cayton YO11 . . . . 100 A5
Heslerton YO17 . . . . 98 A1
Carriage Wlk 4 TS16 . . . . . . 5 D5
Carrick Gdns YO24 . . . . . . 227 E3
Carrier's Row BB8 . . . . 186 B2
Carr Infant Sch YO26 . . . . 227 C5
Carrington Ave 1 YO26 . 227 E5
Carr Junior Sch YO26 . . . 227 C5
Carr La
Ampleforth YO62 . . . . 92 B1
Azerley HG4 . . . . 113 A7
Barlow YO8 . . . . 204 C7
Castleford WF10 . . . . 200 F3
Cawton YO62 . . . . 119 C8
Cayton YO14 . . . . 100 B4
East Ayton YO13 . . . . 99 B7
Escrick YO19 . . . . 192 B5
Glaisdale YO21 . . . . 30 D4
Gristhorpe YO11 . . . . 100 E4
Heslerton YO17 . . . . 124 A8

Carr La *continued*
Kilburn High & Low YO61 91 B3
Little Ouseburn YO26 164 A7
Long Drax YO8 204 F6
Muston YO14 100 F3
Newby & Scalby YO13 75 C5
Newton on Derwent YO41 185 F4
Rainton with Newby YO7 114 F6
Roecliffe YO51 140 E3
Sheriff Hutton YO60 145 E6
Stillington YO61 144 C6
Sutton-on-the-Forest YO61 144 D2
Thirlby YO7 90 F6
Thormanby YO61 116 E4
Wetherby LS22 180 D4
Wistow YO8 197 A3
York YO26 227 D5
Carr Leys La YO7 66 A5
Carr Mill Mews BD22 187 B5
Carrnock Ct 3 YO32 225 F1
Carrol Cl DL6 210 F2
Carroll Pl 2 DL2 22 C8
Carron Cres YO24 230 B7
Carr Rd 7 BB18 171 D2
Carrside 2 YO11 99 F6
Carr Side Rd YO26 163 F8
Carrs Mdw YO19 192 B5
Carr St YO8 232 F4
Carrs The YO21 208 A2
Carr The HG3 222 E2
Carr Wood Rd WF10 200 F3
Carseylands Hill BD23 155 A4
Carter Ave YO31 228 F5
Carter La 22 YO62 70 B1
Carter's La
Ilkley LS29 218 E6
Longnewton TS16 5 A4
Carters Yd DL10 209 B6
CARTHORPE 87 E6
Cartmell Terr DL3 3 C6
Cart Riggin YO7 66 A8
Cass House Rd TS8 6 E4
Cass La
Knaresborough HG5 221 A4
South Milford LS25 195 E1
Castelo Gr 1 YO18 96 A6
Castle Bank DL6 25 E1
Castlebergh Hospl BD24 131 C2
Castlebergh La 5 BD24 131 E2
CASTLE BOLTON 59 A6
Castle Cl
Cawood YO8 197 A8
1 Haxby YO32 166 D5
Killinghall HG3 161 C5
Middleton St George DL2 4 C3
Northallerton DL7 210 D5
2 Spofforth HG3 179 E6
1 Thornton Dale YO18 96 D5
Castle Cres YO11 213 B7
Castle Ctyd HG5 221 A5
Castle Dyke Wynd TS16 5 E3
Castle End DL8 59 B6
CASTLEFORD 200 E4
Castleford High Sch WF10 200 F4
Castleford La
Featherstone WF7 200 D1
Knottingley WF11 201 D3
Castleford Mus* WF10 220 E4
Castleford & Normanton District Hospl WF10 200 D3
Castleford Rd WF6 200 B2
Castleford Redhill Junior Sch WF10 201 B4
Castleford Ret Pk WF10 200 E4
Castleford Sta WF10 200 E4
Castleford Three Lane Ends Prim Sch WF10 200 D4
Castle Garth
Pontefract WF8 201 C1
4 Thornton Dale YO18 96 D5
Castlegate
East Ayton/West Ayton YO13 99 A7
6 Helmsley YO62 92 F6
Kirkbymoorside YO62 70 B1
3 Knaresborough HG5 221 B5
Malton YO17 215 C4
19 Pickering YO18 95 F7
Scarborough YO11 213 B7
Thirsk YO7 211 B2
York YO1 233 B2
Castle Gate 4 LS29 218 B4
Castle Gdns YO11 213 B6
Castle Hill
8 Hunmanby YO14 126 F8
2 Ilkley LS29 218 B4
Richmond DL10 209 C6
4 Settle BD24 131 E2
Castle Hill Cl HG2 222 B6
Castle Hill Dr HG2 222 B6
Castle Hill Glade HG2 222 B6
Castle Hill Gr HG2 222 B6
Castle Hill La YO8 204 F5
Castle Howard* YO60 120 D1
Castle Howard Dr YO17 215 A4
Castle Howard Rd YO17 215 A4
Castle Ings 1 HG3 179 E5
Castle Ings Cl 1 HG5 221 A5
Castle Ings Rd 3 HG5 221 A5
Castlekeep Cl DL10 209 C8
Castle La
Danby YO21 29 D6
10 East Ayton/West Ayton YO13 99 B8
Castle Mdws DL8 87 A7
Castle Mills HG5 221 A5
Castlemount Ave YO13 75 D6
Castle Rd
Colne BB8 186 A4
1 Ilkley LS29 218 B4
Killinghall HG3 161 C5
18 Pickering YO18 95 F7
Scarborough YO11 213 A6
Thornton Dale YO18 96 D5
Whitby YO21 208 A6
Castlereagh Cl TS21 5 A7
Castle Rise 1 YO13 99 A7
Castle Side YO60 145 C5
Castle St
Skipton BD23 217 A3
Spofforth HG3 179 E6
Castle Steads* DL11 19 D6
Castle Steads (Fort)* DL8 84 C8
Castle Terr
Richmond DL10 209 C6
16 Scarborough YO11 213 B6
CASTLETON 29 A6
Castleton Ave
Middlesbrough TS5 6 D8
Northallerton DL7 210 C1
Castleton Moor Sta YO21 29 A7
Castleton Prim Sch YO21 29 A7
Castleton Rd DL9 40 F4
Castle View
7 Newby & Scalby YO13 75 D5
Richmond DL10 209 B6
Sheriff Hutton YO60 145 C5
Castle View Terr BD23 216 F4
Castle Wlk YO1 233 C2
Castle Wynd 11 DL10 209 C6
CASTLEY 178 A1
Castle Yard Stables 8 YO7 211 B3
Castle Yd
3 Ilkley LS29 218 B4
Knaresborough HG5 221 A5
Castley La LS21 178 A1
Cat Bank DL11 39 C6
Cathcart Cl DN14 206 F7
Cathedral CE Prim Sch HG4 214 D5
Cathedral Cl HG4 214 D5
Catherine Love Dr 15 YO61 143 C8
Catherine St 2 TS12 9 F7
Cat La
Balne DN14 207 E5
Bilbrough YO23 182 D1
Cat Pottery The* DL8 58 F1
CATTAL 164 A1
Cattal Moor La YO26 181 B8
Cattal St YO26 164 A2
Cattal Sta YO26 164 A2
CATTERICK 41 D5
Catterick AWS Football Ctr DL9 209 D1
CATTERICK BRIDGE 41 D6
Catterick Bridge* DL10 41 C6
CATTERICK GARRISON 209 D2
Catterick La DL10 41 D3
Catterick Racecourse DL10 41 C5
Catterick Rd DL9 40 E4
CATTERTON 190 B8
Catterton La
Catterton LS24 190 A8
Healaugh LS24 182 A1
Cattle La LS25 194 F8
Cattlelaith La WF11 201 E2
CATTON 88 F1
Catton La YO7 115 A7
Catton Moor La YO7 114 F8
Catton Way YO8 232 A2
Caudle Hill WF11 201 C6
Causeway BD23 81 E3
Causeway The
Darlington DL1 3 E5
Lythe YO21 12 E3
Cautley Dr HG3 161 C5
Cautley Gr HG3 161 C5
Cavalry Ct 9 YO12 75 F5
Cavendish Ave
Harrogate HG2 219 E1
8 Pontefract WF8 201 C2
Cavendish Ct HG2 222 F8
Cavendish Gr YO10 229 D3
Cavendish Rd TS4 7 A8
Cavendish St
Barnoldswick BB18 171 D1
Harrogate HG1 219 E5
Skipton BD23 216 F3
Cavendish Terr 8 HG4 214 C4
Cavendish View BD23 217 D7
Caversham Rd TS4 7 A8
Cawcliff La YO18 97 A5
Cawdel Cl 4 LS25 195 F2
Cawdel Way 11 LS25 195 F2
Cawder Ghyll BD23 217 A1
Cawder Gn BD23 217 A2
Cawder La BD23 217 A1
Cawder Mews BD23 217 A1
Cawder Rd BD23 217 A1
CAWOOD 197 B8
Cawood CE Aided Prim Sch YO8 197 B8
Cawood Cres LS24 190 C1
Cawood Dr TS5 6 F7
Cawood Rd
Stillingfleet YO19 191 D3
Wistow YO8 197 C7
Cawthorn Ave HG2 220 B2
CAWTHORNE 71 D4
Cawthorne Cres YO14 101 A3
Cawthorne La YO18 71 D3
Cawthorn Pl 4 HG2 220 B3
CAWTON 119 C7
Cawton Rd YO62 118 F8
Caxton Ave YO26 227 D6
Caxton Cl 1 DL10 41 C7
Caxton Gdns 4 WF8 201 B2
Caxton View HG4 214 C6
Caxton Way YO11 99 F6
Caygill St 10 YO21 208 C6
Cayley Cl YO30 224 F1
Cayley La YO13 98 C5
Caymer Rd YO11 100 A7
CAYTON 100 C6
Cayton Low Rd YO11 99 F6
Cayton Low Road Ind Est YO11 100 A6
Cayton Prim Sch YO11 100 B6
Cecilia Pl 3 YO24 228 A3
Cecil Rd 7 YO14 127 A8
Cecil St
Barnoldswick BB18 171 D2
Harrogate HG1 219 E5
Cedar Cl
Hambleton YO8 197 B1
Ripon HG4 214 B3
Cedar Cres YO8 197 D2
Cedar Ct YO14 100 F5
Cedar Dr
Coulby Newham TS8 6 D4
Tadcaster LS24 189 D6
Cedar Glade YO19 184 E7
Cedar Gr
Barton DL10 21 C7
3 Filey YO14 101 B4
Middleton One Row DL2 4 D3
Sutton BD20 187 E7
York YO31 229 B7
Cedar Grange HG2 222 D7
Cedarhurst Dr TS12 9 F7
Cedar Mews 4 DL2 22 D8
Cedar Pl 14 YO61 117 D1
Cedar Rd
Darlington DL3 3 B6
Selby YO8 232 D2
Cedar Ridge LS25 194 E5
Cedar Vale 8 YO62 70 B1
Cedarwood 3 DL2 4 C4
Cedarwood Ave 1 TS9 26 C8
Cedarwood Cl 7 YO24 227 B1
Cedarwood Glade TS8 6 E4
Celtic Cl YO26 227 B5
Cemetery La DL3 3 A5
Cemetery Rd
40 Earby BB18 172 A1
Normanton South WF6 200 B1
Thirsk YO7 211 A3
York YO10 233 C1
Cennon Gr 15 TS17 5 F4
Centenary Row BD23 217 D8
Central Arc DL7 210 D5
Central Av 6 YO61 143 D8
Central Dr
Castleford WF10 200 C4
Northallerton DL6 210 E4
Central St TS16 5 E3
Central Way 6 TS9 8 A2
Centre La LS24 189 E6
Centrepoint Rd DL1 3 F6
Centre Rd BD20 186 D7
Centurian Cl 7 DL10 41 E4
Centurion Pk YO30 225 B2
Centurion Way
Clifton YO30 225 B3
Crossgates YO12 99 E6
Faverdale DL3 3 B8
Century Wlk 1 HG2 220 B3
Ceres Rd LS22 180 C3
Chacksfield Rd 16 DL10 41 E4
Chadderton Cl TS12 9 E8
Chadderton Dr 2 TS17 6 C7
Chadwell Ave 2 TS3 7 B8
Chadwick Pk HG5 221 B3
Chafer Wood Nature Reserve* YO13 97 D6
Chain Bar La HG3 161 A4
Chain La HG5 221 C6
Chair Wlk HG4 139 B8
Chaldon Cl 4 YO32 167 A6
Chaldron Way TS16 5 D6
Chalfield Cl TS17 6 B4
Chalfonts YO24 227 F1
Chalford Oaks TS5 6 D8
Challacombe Cres TS17 6 A3
Challoner Rd TS15 5 D2
Chaloner Prim Sch 18 TS14 8 F7
Chaloner's Cres YO24 230 D7
Chaloner's Rd YO24 230 D8
Chaloner St 4 TS14 8 F6
Chaly Fields LS23 188 E8
Chamber End Fold 5 BD23 134 E3
Champion Ave 6 WF10 200 F3
Chancel Way YO21 208 A6
Chancery Ct YO24 227 C3
Chancery Rise
Stockton-on-Tees TS18 6 A6
York YO24 227 F3
Chandler Cl DL10 209 F8
Chandlers Ct YO11 213 B2
Chandlers Ridge Prim Sch TS7 7 D5
Chandlers Wharf YO17 215 C3
Chantilly Ave DL1 3 F7
Chanting Hill Cl YO60 146 E6
CHANTRY 59 D2
Chantry Ave 14 YO26 165 F1
Chantry Bank DL8 59 D3
Chantry Cl
1 Park End TS3 7 B8
York YO24 230 C8
Chantry Ct HG3 161 C7
Chantry Dr
East Ayton/West Ayton YO13 99 B8
2 Ilkley LS29 218 B3
Chantry Gap 11 YO26 165 F1
Chantry Garth DL8 59 D3
Chantry Gr 13 YO26 165 F1
Chantry La
Bishopthorpe YO23 231 B4
Scotton HG5 162 A6
Stutton with Hazlewood LS24 189 B3
Chantry Rd
9 East Ayton/West Ayton YO13 99 B8
Northallerton DL7 210 B3
Chantry Wynd 7 DL10 209 C6
Chapel Balk Rd YO8 198 F1
Chapel Cl
Bilton-in-Ainsty with Bickerton LS22 181 B5
Church Fenton LS24 196 B8
21 Helmsley YO62 92 F6
North Duffield YO8 199 A7
Rawcliffe DN14 205 A1
Chapel Cres DL7 63 C8
Chapel Croft 7 BD23 134 E3
Chapel Ct
Gargrave BD23 155 D1
Huby YO61 144 A4
CHAPEL FIELDS 227 B3
Chapel Fields Rd YO26 227 A3
Chapel Fold 6 BD23 134 E3
Chapel Garth
Dalton YO7 115 E7
Markington with Wallerthwaite HG3 139 C3
Thrintoft DL7 63 F7
Chapel Gate
Malham BD23 132 F1
Sherburn YO17 124 D6
CHAPEL HADDLESEY 203 C5
Chapel Haddlesey CE Prim Sch YO8 203 B5
Chapel Hill
Boroughbridge YO51 141 C5
Kearby with Netherby LS22 179 B1
Skipton BD23 217 A5
Chapel House Mews 9 BD23 173 B4
Chapel La
Askham Bryan YO23 182 F3
Barwick in Elmet LS15 194 C8
Boston Spa LS23 188 E7
Brayton YO8 232 B1
Brompton YO13 98 B7
5 Burton in Lonsdale LA6 102 F3
13 Easingwold YO61 143 C8
13 Eastfield YO11 100 B6
Finghall DL8 61 E4
Halton East BD23 174 C8
Harome YO62 93 C4
Hebden BD23 135 A2
Horton in Ribblesdale BD24 105 C3
Ilkley LS29 218 A4
Langtoft YO25 151 D5
Little Smeaton WF8 206 B3
9 Malton YO17 215 C4
Marton-le-Moor HG4 114 F1
Rawcliffe DN14 205 A2
Reighton YO14 127 E5
3 Riccall YO19 192 A1
3 Spofforth HG3 179 E5
3 Thornton Dale YO18 96 D5
Tollerton YO61 143 A3
Westow YO60 147 B4
CHAPEL-LE-DALE 104 C8
Chapel Mews YO7 211 C2
Chapel Rd
23 Scarborough YO11 213 A6
Settrington YO17 122 D1
Chapel Riggs 4 DL10 41 E4
Chapel Row YO10 233 C1
Chapel Sq 7 BD24 131 E2
Chapel St
8 Addingham LS29 174 F4
6 Beadlam YO62 93 D7
Carleton BD23 173 B4
Cattal YO26 164 A1
22 Earby BB18 172 A1
27 Filey YO14 101 B3
Grassington BD23 134 E3
Hambleton YO8 196 F1
Hillam LS25 202 B7
Kirk Hammerton YO26 164 C2
Knaresborough HG5 221 B5
Middleton St George DL2 4 C4
Nunnington YO62 93 E2
12 Settle BD24 131 D2
Tadcaster LS24 189 E6
Thirsk YO7 211 B2
Chapel Terr YO24 227 C3
Chapel Wlk
Long Preston BD23 153 F5
4 Riccall YO19 192 A1
Chapman Cl 1 YO32 167 C8
Chapman Ct BB18 171 D2
Chapman La 8 HG4 86 C3
Chapmans Ct YO24 230 D6
Chapman's La YO30 165 E7
Chapman Sq HG1 219 B2
Chapter House St YO1 233 B3
Charles Ave HG1 219 E5
Charles Ct DL10 209 F7
Charles Moor YO31 228 F7
Charles St YO8 232 B6
Charles Wesley Dr YO8 232 B2
Charlock TS8 7 B4
Charlton Ave
Knaresborough HG5 221 B6
2 Whitby YO21 208 B7
Charlton Ct 10 HG5 221 B6
Charlton Dr HG5 221 B6
Charlton Gr 12 HG5 221 B6
Charlton Manor Dr 13 HG5 221 B6
CHARLTONS 9 C6
Charlton St YO23 228 C2
Charlton Villas HG5 221 B6
Charnwood Dr TS7 7 D6
Charrington Ave TS17 6 A6
Charter Ave DN14 205 A1
Chartermark Way DL9 41 A4
Charter Rd HG4 214 E4
Charters The YO8 198 B5
Chartwell Cl TS17 6 B4
Chase Garth Rd 16 YO61 143 C8
Chase Side Ct YO24 230 E8
Chase The
11 Boroughbridge YO51 141 B4
Garforth LS25 194 D4
Hurworth-on-Tees DL2 3 E1
Knaresborough HG5 221 D5
Norton YO17 215 E2
17 Wetherby LS22 180 C3
Chastworth Ct HG1 219 D4
Chatham Rd HG4 113 D2
Chatsworth Ave 7 WF8 201 C2
Chatsworth Dr
16 Haxby YO32 166 F5
2 Wetherby LS22 180 B3
Chatsworth Gdns YO12 212 E7
Chatsworth Gr
4 Boroughbridge YO51 141 B5
Harrogate HG1 219 C4
Chatsworth Pl HG1 219 D4
Chatsworth Rd HG1 219 D4
Chatsworth Terr
2 Harrogate HG1 219 E4
4 York YO26 227 E4
Chaucer Gn HG1 219 F7
Chaucer La
Fadmoor YO62 69 F5
Strensall YO32 167 B8
Chaucer St 7 YO10 228 E3
Chaumont Way 1 YO32 167 D2
Chauvel Cl DL9 209 C2
Cheapside
2 Knaresborough HG5 221 B5
12 Normanton South WF6 200 A1
11 Settle BD24 131 D2
Cheapsides Rd YO17 215 B8
Checker La YO19 198 A7
Checkstone Ave 10 WF10 200 D2
Chedworth Ct 4 TS17 5 F6
Chelkar Way YO30 224 F1
Chelmsford Rd HG1 219 E2
Cheltenham Ave
Ilkley LS29 218 E4
Middlesbrough TS7 7 B5
Cheltenham Cres 6 HG1 219 D2
Cheltenham Ct DL2 4 C5
Cheltenham Mount HG1 219 D3
Cheltenham Par HG1 219 D3
Cheltenham Rd 8 HG1 219 D3
Chelwood Wlk 12 YO26 227 E4
Chepstow Cl 9 DL9 40 F4
Chepstow Ct 14 DL1 3 F6
Cherry Ave
Malton YO17 215 D6
Swinton YO17 121 B4
Cherry Cl YO21 208 B6
Cherry Garth YO31 229 B5
Cherry Garth Rd DL7 210 C3
Cherry Gr
7 Bedale DL8 63 B3
2 Ilkley LS29 175 C2
16 Poppleton YO26 165 F1
Cherry Hill La YO23 233 B1
Cherry La YO24 230 F8
Cherry Orch 2 YO32 225 D8
Cherry Paddock
4 Haxby YO32 225 D8
Kexby YO41 168 C2
Cherry Rd 4 YO14 127 A8
Cherry St YO23 233 B1
Cherry Tree Ave
Newton-on-Ouse YO30 165 B6
1 Scarborough YO12 212 B5
York YO32 225 D4
Cherrytree Cl HG4 140 E7
Cherry Tree Cl
13 Brayton YO8 197 D1
9 Castleford WF10 200 D3
Cherry Tree Ct
12 Barlby with Osgodby YO8 198 B4
Catterick DL10 41 E4
Salton YO62 94 D3
Cherrytree Dr YO8 197 D6
Cherry Tree Dr
Gristhorpe YO14 101 A4
5 Naburn YO23 191 C7
Cherry Tree Way 14 DL9 41 A5

Cherry Tree Wlk
Amotherby YO17 . . . . **121** A4
7 Barlby YO8 . . . . **198** B4
Knottingley WF11 . . . . **201** F2
Cherrywood Ave 4 TS9 . . **26** C8
Cherry Wood Cres YO19. **231** E5
Chervil Ct TS8 . . . . **7** B4
Cherwell Croft YO8 . . . . . **196** F1
Cherwell Ct YO8 . . . . **196** F1
Cheshire Ave YO32 . . . . . **167** A6
Cheshire Cl 6 YO32 . . . . . **224** F2
Cheshire Sq 5 YO7 . . . . . . **89** B1
Chesler-Pit La YO61 . . . . . **117** F2
Chesney Fields 4 YO24 . **227** D1
Chessingham Gdns YO24 **230** E6
Chessingham Pk YO19 . **184** F6
Chester Court Rd YO8. . . **204** A6
Chester La DL10 . . . . **65** D8
Chesterton Ave TS17 . . . . . . **6** A6
Chestnut Ave
  2 Airmyn DN14 . . . . **205** A4
  Harrogate HG1 . . . . **219** F3
  10 Hemingbrough YO8 . . **198** F1
  Malton YO17 . . . . **215** D6
  Thornton Dale YO18. . . . . **96** D6
  2 Topcliffe YO7 . . . . **89** A1
  Welburn YO60 . . . . **146** A6
  12 Wetherby LS22 . . . . . . **180** B3
  York YO31 . . . . **228** F6
Chestnut Bank YO12 . . . **212** D6
Chestnut Cl
  Bedale DL8 . . . . **63** B3
  3 Catterick DL10 . . . . . . **41** D5
  4 Ilkley LS29 . . . . **218** E3
  Richmond DL10 . . . . **209** C8
  Scarborough YO12. . . . . . **212** D6
Chestnut Cres
  6 Catterick Garrison DL9 . **40** F5
  1 Catton YO7 . . . . **89** A1
  Hipswell DL9 . . . . **40** F5
Chestnut Croft 7 YO8. . **198** F1
Chestnut Ct
  9 Hemingbrough YO8 . . **198** F1
  York YO23 . . . . **225** F5
Chestnut Dr
  17 Barnoldswick BB18 . . **171** D1
  Firth Moor DL1 . . . . **3** F4
  8 Hemingbrough YO8 . . **198** F1
  Middlesbrough TS7 . . . . **7** C6
Chestnut Garth 4 YO8 . **198** F1
Chestnut Gn 10 LS25 . . . **202** A8
Chestnut Gr
  Acomb YO26. . . . . **227** C4
  Harrogate HG1 . . . . **219** E6
  Huntington YO32 . . . . **225** E4
  Norton YO17 . . . . **215** F2
Chestnut Mews YO8. . . . **197** A8
Chestnut Rd
  Cawood YO8. . . . . **197** A8
  Eaglescliffe TS16. . . . . **5** E6
  Scarborough YO12. . . . . . **212** B7
Chestnut Way YO8 . . . . . **232** E3
Chestnuts The
  6 Haxby YO32 . . . . **225** C8
  Hensall DN14. . . . . **203** D2
  Pontefract WF8 . . . . **201** C2
  Scarborough YO12. . . . . . **212** B7
Chevin Dr YO24 . . . . **101** A3
Cheviot Cl 1 YO32 . . . . . **225** F3
Chew La
  Gargrave BD23 . . . . **155** D1
  Seamer YO12. . . . . **99** D6
Chichester Cl 18 YO13. . . **75** D5
Chieftain Rd DL9. . . . . **40** C4
Chiltern Ave WF10 . . . . . **200** C3
Chiltern Way YO32 . . . . . **225** F5
Chilvers Ct 4 YO8 . . . . . **232** A1
Chimes Rd YO8 . . . . **232** C6
Chimes The 8 YO8 . . . . **232** C6
China DL3 . . . . **3** D7
Chippendale Rise 8
  LS21. . . . . **177** A1
Chippenham Rd TS4 . . . . . . **7** A7
Cholmley Way YO22. . . . . **208** D7
CHOP GATE. **46** F6
Christ Church CE Prim Sch
  Colne BB8 . . . . **186** A3
  Skipton BD23 . . . . **216** F3
Christ Church Oval HG1 . **219** E2
Christina St 5 HG1 . . . . . **219** C5
Christ's Hospl DL8 . . . . . **63** A1
Christ the King RC Prim Sch
  TS17 . . . . **6** C6
Christy Gate Rd YO21 . . . **28** E4
Chubb Hill Rd YO21 . . . . . **208** C6
Chudleigh Rd
  Harrogate HG1 . . . . **219** E3
  1 York YO26 . . . . **227** F5
Church Ave
  Clapham LA2 . . . . **130** C8
  4 Dacre HG3 . . . . **137** F1
  Harrogate HG1 . . . . **219** D5
  6 Selby YO8 . . . . **232** D5
Church Balk YO19. . . . . . **184** E7
Church Bank
  Aysgarth DL8 . . . . **58** F3
  Hunton DL8 . . . . **61** F7
  Kirkby Malzeard HG4. . . . **112** D5
Church Cl
  Askham Bryan YO23 . . . . **182** F3
  Bagby YO7 . . . . **90** C3
  4 Bubwith YO8. . . . . **199** D7
  Carleton BD23 . . . . **173** B4
  18 Filey YO14 . . . . **101** B4
  1 Hambleton YO8 . . . . . **196** F1

Church Cl continued
  Killinghall HG3. . . . . **219** A8
  Kirby Hill YO51. . . . . **141** B7
  Middleton St George DL2 . . . **4** C3
  Newby & Scalby YO13 . . . **75** C5
  Redmire DL8 . . . . **59** C5
  10 Riccall YO19 . . . . **197** F8
  Sawley HG4. . . . . **138** E6
  Sharow HG4. . . . . **214** F7
  4 Swillington LS26. . . . . **194** A1
  5 Tollerton YO61 . . . . . . **143** B3
  Wheldrake YO19 . . . . **193** A7
Church Cliff Dr 9 YO14 . **101** B4
Church Cres
  Stutton with Hazlewood
    LS24 . . . . **189** D4
  Swillington LS26 . . . . **194** A1
Church Croft
  Barkston Ash LS24 . . . . . **195** F7
  Gargrave BD23 . . . . **172** C8
Church Cswy LS23 . . . . . **188** F8
Church Ct
  18 Normanton South
    WF6 . . . . **200** A1
  Saxton LS24. . . . . **195** D7
Church Dike La YO8. . . . **204** F5
Church Dr
  Great Ayton TS9. . . . . **7** F1
  Lockwood TS12 . . . . **9** E7
Church End
  Cawood YO8. . . . . **197** B8
  Sheriff Hutton YO60. . . . . **145** D5
Church Farm YO7 . . . . . . **211** A6
Church Farm Cl YO23 . . **182** C6
Church Farm Ct YO25 . . **126** E3
Church Farm View LS15. **194** C8
CHURCH FENTON. **196** B7
Church Fenton La LS24. . **190** B3
Church Fenton Sta LS24. **196** A8
Churchfield DN14. . . . . . . **204** C2
Churchfield Dr 28 YO32 . **166** E5
Churchfield La
  Castleford WF10 . . . . **200** F3
  6 Kippax LS25 . . . . **194** D1
  Little Smeaton WF8 . . . . . **206** C4
Church Field La 2 YO26. **164** A8
Church Field Rd DN6. . . . **206** E1
Churchfields DL6 . . . . **210** E4
Church Fields 17 WF6 . . **200** A1
Church Garth DL6. . . . . . . **23** C3
Church Gdns LS25 . . . . . . **194** C3
Church Gn 3 YO41. . . . . . **185** C2
Church Hill
  4 Bramham LS23. . . . . . **188** E5
  Crayke YO61 . . . . **118** A1
  Easingwold YO61. . . . . . . **117** C1
  10 Hunmanby YO14. . . . **126** F8
  Hunsingore LS22 . . . . **180** E8
  Malton YO17 . . . . **215** C4
  Newby & Scalby YO13 . . . **75** C5
  North Rigton LS17 . . . . . . **178** B3
  Reighton YO14. . . . . **127** C6
  4 Selby YO8 . . . . **232** D5
  Sherburn in Elmet LS25. . . **195** E4
  Spofforth HG3 . . . . **179** E6
  Stillingfleet YO19 . . . . **191** D3
  Thorner LS14. . . . . **188** A3
  Thornton Dale YO18. . . . . . **96** D6
  8 Wistow YO8. . . . . **197** D6
CHURCH HOUSES **48** F4
Churchill Cl 3 TS9. . . . . . . **8** A2
Churchill Dr 41 DL9 . . . . . **41** A5
Churchill Way 4 BD20 . **187** F8
Church La
  Allerston YO13. . . . . **97** B5
  Appleton Roebuck YO23. . **190** F4
  Aysgarth DL8 . . . . **58** F3
  Bagby YO7 . . . . **90** C3
  Barton DL10. . . . . **21** C8
  Bishopthorpe YO23 . . . . . **231** A4
  Bolton Percy YO23. . . . . . **190** D4
  Boroughbridge YO51. . . . **141** B5
  Brompton YO13. . . . . **98** C5
  Burnsall BD23 . . . . **157** A8
  Burton Leonard HG3 . . . . **140** A2
  1 Carlton DN14 . . . . **204** C3
  Carlton YO41. . . . . **185** D8
  Cayton YO11 . . . . **100** B6
  Collingham LS22 . . . . **180** A1
  Cropton YO18. . . . . **71** B4
  Cundall with Leckby YO61. **115** E3
  Dunnington YO19. . . . . . . **184** E7
  East Heslerton YO17 . . . . **124** A7
  Elslack BD23 . . . . **172** D4
  4 Elvington YO41. . . . . . **185** C2
  Faceby TS9 . . . . **25** F1
  Fylingdales YO22 . . . . **33** C4
  Garforth LS25 . . . . **194** C4
  Gargrave BD23 . . . . **172** D8
  Gateforth YO8 . . . . **202** F8
  Gilling East YO62. . . . . . . **118** F7
  Guisborough TS7 . . . . **7** E5
  17 Haxby YO32 . . . . **166** E5
  Hebden BD23. . . . . **135** A1
  Hensall DN14. . . . . **203** C1
  Hutton Buscel YO13. . . . . . **98** F7
  Ingleby Greenhow TS9 . . . **27** B5
  Kelbrook & Sough BB18 . . **186** A8
  Kellington DN14. . . . . **202** E3
  Kirby Hall YO26 . . . . **164** B7
  Kirby Hill YO51. . . . . **141** B7
  Knaresborough HG5 . . . . . **221** A6
  Langtoft YO25 . . . . **151** C1
  Low Worsall TS15 . . . . **24** A8
  Marton cum Grafton YO51 **141** D1
  Martons Both BD23 . . . . . **172** A5
  Micklefield LS25 . . . . **194** F4
  Mickletown LS26. . . . . . . **200** B5

Church La continued
  Middlesbrough TS5 . . . . **6** E7
  Middleton St George DL2 . . . **4** C3
  Middleton YO18 . . . . **95** E8
  Milby YO51. . . . . **141** B7
  4 Monk Fryston LS25. . . **202** A8
  Moor Monkton YO26 . . . . **165** B2
  Nether Poppleton YO26. . **224** B3
  New Earswick YO32. . . . . **225** F5
  11 Normanton South WF6 **200** A1
  North Featherstone WF7. . **200** E1
  Pannal HG3 . . . . **222** D4
  Poppleton YO26 . . . . **224** A3
  Rainton YO7 . . . . **114** C6
  Redmire DL8 . . . . **59** C5
  Sadberge DL2 . . . . **4** C7
  Scarborough YO11. . . . . . **213** B7
  4 Selby YO8 . . . . **232** D5
  Sessay YO7 . . . . **116** C6
  Settrington YO17. . . . . . . **122** D1
  Sinnington YO62 . . . . **71** A1
  Skelton YO30 . . . . **224** B5
  Slingsby YO62 . . . . **120** B6
  2 Snaith DN14. . . . . **204** C1
  South Stainley with Cayton
    HG3. . . . . **139** E2
  9 Spofforth HG3 . . . . . . **179** E6
  Stainburn LS21 . . . . **177** E3
  Stainforth BD24. . . . . **131** E6
  10 Stamford Bridge YO41 **168** D2
  Strensall YO32. . . . . **167** A7
  Stutton with Hazlewood
    LS24 . . . . **189** E4
  Swillington LS26 . . . . **194** A1
  Terrington YO60. . . . . **119** F1
  Thormanby YO61 . . . . **116** F3
  Thornton Dale YO18. . . . . . **96** D6
  Thwing YO25 . . . . **126** A1
  Tunstall LA6. . . . . **102** B4
  Welburn YO60 . . . . **146** A6
  Weston LS21 . . . . **176** D1
  Westow YO60 . . . . **147** B4
  Wheldrake YO19 . . . . **193** A7
  Whitby YO22 . . . . **208** E2
  Whorlton DL6. . . . . **25** D1
  Wigglesworth BD23. . . . . **153** D3
  Wighill LS24. . . . . **181** D1
  Wintringham YO17. . . . . . **123** C4
  York YO1 . . . . **233** B2
Church Lea DL7. . . . . **64** B7
Church Mdw
  Barton DL10. . . . . **21** D8
  Sherburn in Elmet LS25. . . **195** E4
Church Mdws 9 LS23 . . . **188** E6
Church Mews
  Barlby YO8. . . . . **198** A5
  13 Boroughbridge YO51 **141** B5
  Gainford DL2. . . . . **1** A7
  Sherburn in Elmet LS25. . . **195** E4
  2 York YO26 . . . . **227** C3
Church Rd
  26 Glusburn BD20. . . . . **187** E7
  Great Preston LS26. . . . . **200** C8
  Linton BD23 . . . . **134** E2
  Pontefract WF6 . . . . **200** A3
  Scotton DL9 . . . . **40** E4
  Stainton Dale YO13 . . . . . . **54** A7
  Stamford Bridge YO41. . . **168** D2
  Thornton in Craven BD23 . **171** F3
  York YO10 . . . . **229** D4
Church Rise YO19. . . . . . . **167** F1
Church Row
  Hurworth-on-Tees DL2 . . . . . **3** E1
  Melsonby DL10 . . . . **20** F7
Church Side LS26. . . . . . . **200** B5
Churchside Villas LS26 . . **200** B5
Church Sq
  Harrogate HG1 . . . . **219** F3
  Whitby YO21 . . . . **208** C7
Church St
  Addingham LS29 . . . . **175** A4
  Amotherby YO17 . . . . **121** A4
  Asenby YO7 . . . . **115** B7
  Barkston Ash LS24 . . . . . **195** F7
  Bellerby DL8 . . . . **60** D7
  Bilton-in-Ainsty with Bickerton
    YO26. . . . . **181** D5
  Boston Spa LS23 . . . . **188** E8
  Broughton BD23 . . . . **172** D7
  Bubwith YO8 . . . . **199** D7
  Carleton BD23 . . . . **173** B4
  Church Fenton LS24. . . . . **196** B7
  Copmanthorpe YO23 . . . . **230** B2
  Danby YO21 . . . . **29** B7
  Dunnington YO19. . . . . . . **184** E7
  5 Easingwold YO61 . . . . **143** C4
  5 Filey YO14 . . . . **101** B3
  Gargrave BD23 . . . . **155** D1
  13 Glusburn BD20. . . . . **187** E8
  Goldsborough HG5 . . . . . **163** A3
  Guisborough TS14 . . . . **8** F7
  5 Helmsley YO62 . . . . . . **92** F6
  Heslerton YO17 . . . . **123** E7
  Hovingham YO62 . . . . **119** E6
  Ilkley LS29 . . . . **218** A4
  Ingleton LA6. . . . . **103** D4
  Kirkby Malzeard HG4. . . . **112** D5
  24 Kirkbymoorside YO62. . **70** B1
  Kirk Hammerton YO26. . . **164** C2
  Knottingley WF11. . . . . . . **201** F4
  Long Preston BD23 . . . . . **153** F4
  6 Masham HG4 . . . . **86** C3
  6 Middleham DL8 . . . . . . **60** E2
  Norton YO17 . . . . **215** D4
  Nunnington YO62. . . . . **93** E2
  3 Riccall YO19 . . . . **197** F8
  2 Scarborough YO11 . . . **213** B6

Church St continued
  Settle BD24 . . . . **131** D3
  5 Skipton BD23 . . . . **216** F3
  Staithes TS13 . . . . **13** K2
  Trawden BB8 . . . . **186** B1
  Ulleskelf LS24 . . . . **190** C3
  Well DL8. . . . . **87** A4
  West Tanfield HG4. . . . . . . **87** A1
  14 Wetherby LS22 . . . . . **180** C3
  Whitby YO22 . . . . **208** E6
  Whittington LA6. . . . . **102** A7
  Whixley YO26. . . . . **164** A5
  York YO1 . . . . **233** B2
Church Stairs St 3
  YO11 . . . . **213** B6
Church View
  12 Airmyn DN14 . . . . . . **205** E4
  3 Brompton DL6 . . . . **43** F3
  22 Hemingbrough YO8 . **198** F1
  16 Hurworth DL2. . . . . **3** E1
  Kirby Hill YO51. . . . . **141** B7
  Ledston LS25. . . . . **194** E1
  Norton DN6 . . . . **206** E1
  Sherburn in Elmet LS25. . . **195** F4
  Sherburn YO17. . . . . **124** D8
  South Milford LS25 . . . . . **195** F2
  Thirsk YO7 . . . . **211** A3
Church View Mews 7
  LS23. . . . . **188** E7
Churchville LS25 . . . . **195** A4
Churchville Ave LS25. . . . **194** F4
Churchville Dr LS25. . . . . **195** A4
Churchville Terr LS25. . . . **195** A4
Church Wind
  Alne YO61 . . . . **142** F4
  Burneston DL8. . . . . **87** E7
Church Wlk
  Lindrick with Studley Royal &
    Fountains HG4. . . . . . . **139** B7
  1 Willerby YO12. . . . . **99** D2
  5 Wistow YO8 . . . . **197** D6
Church Wynd DL10. . . . . . **209** C7
Churchyard 14 LS24. . . . **189** E6
Churwell Cl WF10. . . . . . . **200** E3
Cinder Hill La BD22 . . . . . **187** A6
Cinder La
  Castleford WF10 . . . . **200** E4
  Clifford LS23 . . . . **188** F7
  Lindley LS21. . . . . **177** C3
  Upper Poppleton YO26. . . **227** A7
  York YO26 . . . . **227** F5
Cinder Mews YO26. . . . . . **228** A5
Citadilla Cl 5 DL10. . . . . . **41** C7
City Art Gallery YO30 . . **233** B3
Clack La DL6 . . . . **45** A4
Clapdale Dr LA2 . . . . **130** C8
Clapdale Way 2 LA2. . . . **130** C8
Clapgate Bank DL11. . . . . **39** D8
CLAPHAM. **130** C8
Clapham CE Prim Sch
  LA2. . . . . **130** C8
Clapham Old Rd LA6 . . . . **103** E3
Clapham Sta LA2. . . . . . . **130** A6
Clare Ave DL3 . . . . **3** A5
Claremont 23 YO14. . . . . **101** B3
Claremont Dr TS7. . . . . **7** C5
Claremont La HG3 . . . . . . **140** B5
Claremont St BB8. . . . . . . **186** A3
Claremont Terr YO31. . . . **233** B4
Clarence Ave 47 YO14 . . **101** B3
Clarence Dr
  56 Filey YO14 . . . . **101** B3
  Harrogate HG1 . . . . **219** B3
Clarence Pl
  7 Scarborough YO11 . . . **213** A6
  2 Whitby YO21 . . . . **208** D7
Clarence Rd
  Middlesbrough TS7 . . . . **7** D5
  Scarborough YO12 . . . . . **213** A7
  Scorton DL10. . . . . **41** F7
Clarence St
  2 Barnoldswick BB18 . . **171** E1
  2 Colne BB8. . . . . **186** A3
  1 Trawden Forest BB8. . **186** B1
  York YO31 . . . . **233** B4
Clarendon Ct YO31. . . . . . **228** C7
Clarendon Rd
  Boston Spa LS23 . . . . **188** E8
  Great Burdon DL1 . . . . **3** F7
  Thornaby TS17. . . . . **6** B7
Clarendon St 10 BB8 . . . . **186** A3
Clareton La HG5 . . . . **163** B6
Clark Beck Cl HG3 . . . . . . **222** E3
Clark Ct WF7 . . . . **200** E1
Clarke's Croft YO7 . . . . . **115** A4
Clarkson Dr LS25 . . . . **201** F6
Clarkson St 7 YO21. . . . . **208** D7
Clarkson Wynd DL8. . . . . . **56** C4
Clark St 7 YO21 . . . . **213** A7
Clarks Terr YO31. . . . . **228** F6
Claro Ave HG1 . . . . **219** F4
Claro Bsns Ctr YO7 . . . . . **219** F4
Claro Mews 4 HG5 . . . . . **221** A5
Claro Pk HG1 . . . . **219** F4
Claro Rd
  Harrogate HG1 . . . . **219** F3
  Ripon HG4 . . . . **214** C4
Claro Way HG1 . . . . **219** F4
Claude Ave TS5 . . . . **6** E8
Claudius Gr YO12 . . . . **99** E6
Claver Cl DL6. . . . . **45** D8
Clavery Ley La YO62. . . . . **67** E1
CLAXTON. **168** B7
Claxton Ave DL3 . . . . **3** A6
Clay Bank TS9 . . . . **27** A3
Claygate YO31 . . . . **229** B6

Clay Hill YO41 . . . . **169** C3
Clay La
  Bubwith YO8 . . . . **199** C5
  Camblesforth YO8 . . . . . . **204** C6
  Cliffe YO8. . . . . **198** D4
Claypit La
  Carlton DN14. . . . . **204** C3
  Ledston WF10 . . . . **201** A8
Clay Pit La YO51 . . . . **141** A4
Clay Pl 3 YO24 . . . . **227** D1
Clayton Fold 5 BD20. . . . **187** F7
Clayton Hall Rd BD20. . . **187** F7
Clayton Mews 8 WF6. . . **200** A2
Clayton Pl 9 WF6 . . . . . . **200** A2
Clayton St 7 BB18. . . . . . **171** E1
CLEASBY. **2** F4
Cleasby La DL2 . . . . **2** F1
Cleasby Way TS16. . . . . **5** D6
*Cleatop Park Nature
  Reserve* BD24. . . . . **153** D8
Clementhorpe YO23. . . . . **233** B1
Clement St 4 YO23 . . . . . **233** B1
Clevegate TS7 . . . . **7** C5
Cleveland 1 TS16 . . . . **5** D4
Cleveland Ave
  Darlington DL3. . . . . **3** C5
  Knottingley WF11. . . . . . . **201** F2
  Scalby YO12. . . . . **212** D8
  Stokesley TS9. . . . . **26** C8
**Cleveland College of Art &
  Design** TS5 . . . . **6** E8
Cleveland Dr
  Middlesbrough TS7 . . . . **7** B6
  Northallerton DL7 . . . . . . **210** D2
Cleveland Gdns YO32. . . **167** D3
Cleveland Ind Est DL1. . . . **3** D6
Cleveland Rd
  Boltby YO7 . . . . **91** B8
  Catterick Garrison DL9 . . . **40** F4
  Scarborough YO12 . . . . . **212** E6
  Scorton DL10. . . . . **41** F7
Cleveland Rein YO7 . . . . . **66** A3
Cleveland St
  Darlington DL1. . . . . **3** D6
  Great Ayton TS9. . . . . **8** A2
  Guisborough TS14 . . . . **8** E6
  York YO24 . . . . **228** F4
Cleveland Terr
  Darlington DL3. . . . . **3** B5
  8 Whitby YO21 . . . . **208** D5
  York YO32 . . . . **225** F4
Cleveland Trad Est DL1 . . **3** D6
Cleveland View 1 TS9 . . . **25** F1
Cleveland Way
  1 Carlton Miniott YO7 . . . **89** C4
  Helmsley YO62. . . . . **92** F6
  York YO32 . . . . **225** F4
Cliff Bridge Pl 6 YO11 . . **213** A5
Cliff Bridge Terr 7
  YO11 . . . . **213** A5
Cliff Brow TS13 . . . . **11** C7
Cliff Cres LS25. . . . . **194** E1
Cliff Dr 24 DL8. . . . . **60** D5
CLIFFE
  198 E2
  Darlington **2** B6
Cliffe Mews YO60 . . . . . . **119** E1
Cliffe Prim Sch YO8. . . . . **198** E2
Cliffe Rd HG2. . . . . **219** B1
Cliff Gate Rd DL11 . . . . . . **35** E4
Cliff Hill Rd DN6 . . . . **206** E1
Cliff La
  Newholm-cum-Dunsley
    YO21. . . . . **13** B2
  Snainton YO13 . . . . **97** F5
  Whitwell-on-the-Hill YO60. **146** A4
  Wilton YO18 . . . . **97** A5
  Wrelton YO18 . . . . **95** B8
CLIFFORD. **188** E7
Clifford Ave LS29 . . . . **218** A5
Clifford Ct BD23 . . . . **216** D3
Clifford Moor Rd LS23. . . **188** D8
Clifford Rd
  Boston Spa LS23 . . . . **188** F8
  Ilkley LS29 . . . . **218** A6
Clifford St
  3 Barnoldswick BB18 . . **171** E1
  1 Skipton BD23 . . . . **216** F3
  York YO1 . . . . **233** B2
Clifford's Terr 25 YO14 . . **101** B3
Clifford's Twr YO1 . . . . . . **233** B2
Cliff Rd
  Stainton Dale YO13 . . . . . . **54** A8
  Staithes TS13. . . . . **13** K2
Cliff St YO21. . . . . **208** D7
Cliff The YO22 . . . . **32** B6
CLIFTON
  228 A7
  Ilkley. **176** F3
Clifton Ave TS18 . . . . **5** E6
Clifton Dale YO30 . . . . . . **228** A6
Clifton Gn YO30. . . . . **228** A6
Clifton Green Prim Sch
  YO30. . . . . **228** B7
Clifton La LS21 . . . . **176** F3
Clifton Moor Bsns Village
  YO30. . . . . **225** A2
Clifton Moorgate YO30. . **225** B3
Clifton Moor Gate YO30. **225** A2
Clifton Moor Ind Estate
  YO30. . . . . **225** A3
Clifton Moor Retail Pk
  YO30. . . . . **225** A4
Clifton Moor Sh Ctr
  YO30. . . . . **224** F2
Clifton Park Ave YO30. . . **227** E8
**Clifton Park (York CC & York
  RUFC)** YO30 . . . . **227** F7

Clifton Pl 3 YO30 ... 228 A7
Clifton Prep Sch YO30 ... 233 A4
Clifton Rd
Darlington DL1 ... 3 D4
Ilkley LS29 ... 218 D3
York YO30 ... 233 A4
Clifton St
Earby BB18 ... 186 A8
5 Scarborough YO12 ... 212 F6
Trawden Forest BB8 ... 186 A1
Clifton Terr LS29 ... 218 C4
Clifton Without Jun Sch YO30 ... 227 F8
CLINT ... 161 A6
Clint Bank HG3 ... 160 E6
Clint Bank La HG3 ... 160 F6
Clint Garth HG3 ... 160 F8
CLINTS ... 39 C7
Clipt La YO7 ... 65 D2
Clitheroe St 2 BD23 ... 216 D3
Clive Gr YO24 ... 227 F2
Clive Rd 1 HG3 ... 179 E6
Clockhill Field La YO26 ... 163 F3
Clock Twr* HG4 ... 214 C6
Clockwood Gdns TS16 ... 5 E3
Cloggerby Rigg DL11 ... 35 E5
Clogger La BD23 ... 172 D3
Cloisters The
15 Hemingbrough YO8 ... 198 F1
Wilberfoss YO41 ... 185 F6
York YO31 ... 233 C3
Cloisters Wlk YO31 ... 233 C3
Close La BD22 ... 187 B5
Close Rd WF10 ... 200 F4
Close The
9 Acaster Malbis YO32 ... 191 C7
Barwick in Elmet LS15 ... 194 B7
Boroughbridge YO51 ... 141 A3
Boston Spa LS23 ... 188 E8
Cawood YO8 ... 197 A7
6 Collingham LS22 ... 188 A8
11 East Ayton/West Ayton YO13 ... 99 B8
4 Fylingdales YO22 ... 33 D4
Hunmanby Sands YO14 ... 101 C1
Hutton Rudby TS15 ... 25 C5
Kirkby Fleetham DL7 ... 42 C1
Longnewton TS21 ... 4 F7
Minskip YO51 ... 141 A3
Neasham DL2 ... 4 A1
Northallerton DL7 ... 210 B2
Norton DN6 ... 206 E2
Riccall YO19 ... 198 A8
Scalby YO12 ... 212 B8
Skipton BD23 ... 216 F3
Studley Roger HG4 ... 113 D1
Thirsk YO7 ... 211 C1
Thorner LS14 ... 188 A3
Thornton Dale YO18 ... 96 D5
Towton LS24 ... 189 E2
York YO30 ... 227 F8
Clotherholme Rd HG4 ... 214 A5
CLOUGH ... 55 A7
CLOUGHTON ... 54 C1
CLOUGHTON NEWLANDS ... 54 C2
Clover Hill BD23 ... 217 B5
Cloverley Cl YO41 ... 168 C2
Clover Way 9 HG3 ... 161 B3
Clowbeck Ct DL3 ... 3 B8
Clydach Gr 24 TS17 ... 5 F4
Clyde Gr TS18 ... 5 F8
Coach La
10 Hurworth-on-Tees DL2 ... 3 E1
Lindley LS21 ... 177 D3
Coachman's Ct 6 HG2 ... 220 B1
Coach Rd
Harrogate HG1 ... 219 F2
Sheriff Hutton YO60 ... 145 D4
Sleights YO22 ... 32 A6
Coach St BD23 ... 216 F4
Coach Street Yd 13 BD23 ... 216 F4
Coalmire La DL6 ... 45 D7
Coal Pit La
Kirk Smeaton WF8 ... 206 A2
Rimington BB7 ... 171 A1
Coalpits La 10 DL2 ... 3 A7
Coarse La HG3 ... 159 A4
Coastal Rd YO13 ... 75 D7
Coastguard Hill YO14 ... 127 E5
Coate Cl TS8 ... 6 E5
COATES ... 171 E2
Coates Ave BB18 ... 171 E2
Coates Fields BB18 ... 171 E2
Coates La
Barnoldswick BB18 ... 171 E2
Kettlewell with Starbotton BD23 ... 107 F5
Coate's La BD20 ... 173 F2
Coates Lane Prim Sch BB18 ... 171 E2
Coates Marsh La DN14 ... 204 B2
Coatham Ave DL2 ... 4 D3
Coatham La TS21 ... 5 B7
Cobble Carr TS14 ... 8 E6
Cobble Court Mews YO24 ... 233 A1
Cobblers La WF8 ... 201 C1
Cobbler's La WF8 ... 201 C1
COBBY SYKE ... 159 F2
Cobby Syke Rd HG3 ... 159 F1
Cobcroft La WF11 ... 206 B8
Cobden St
Barnoldswick BB18 ... 171 D1
Darlington DL1 ... 3 E5
Thornaby TS17 ... 6 B8
Cobham Way YO32 ... 224 E3
Cob La BB18 ... 186 A6
Coble La YO60 ... 145 D5
Cobshaw La DL8 ... 62 F6
Cochrane St YO8 ... 232 D3
COCKAYNE ... 48 A5
Cockburn St 5 TS12 ... 9 F7
Cocked Hat HG4 ... 139 C8
Cocked Hat Pk YO7 ... 211 A1
Cockerhill La YO62 ... 93 E7
COCKERTON ... 3 B6
Cockerton CE Prim Sch DL3 ... 3 A6
Cockerton Gn DL3 ... 3 B6
Cock Garth YO17 ... 122 D1
COCK HILL ... 165 B2
Cockhill La BB8 ... 186 A4
Cocking La LS29 ... 174 E3
Cock La
Gainford DL2 ... 1 E8
Piercebridge DL2 ... 2 A7
Cocklakes La YO7 ... 114 F1
Cock Lodge (site of)* YO7 ... 115 C6
Cockmoor Rd YO13 ... 74 A1
Cock Pit Cl HG4 ... 113 C7
Cockrah Rd YO13 ... 74 F2
Cockret Cl 8 YO8 ... 232 B6
Cockret Ct YO8 ... 232 B7
Cockret Rd YO8 ... 232 B7
Cockshaw Bank La HG4 ... 113 B4
Cockshott Pl 5 LS29 ... 174 F4
Coda Ave YO23 ... 231 B3
Codlin Rd 1 TS15 ... 25 C5
Coeside YO24 ... 230 B7
Coggan Cl YO23 ... 228 B2
Coggan Way YO23 ... 230 F4
Colber La HG3 ... 138 F2
Colbert Ave LS29 ... 218 E5
COLBURN ... 41 A5
Colburn Com Prim Sch DL9 ... 41 A5
Colburn Dr DL9 ... 40 F5
Colburn La DL9 ... 40 F6
Colburn Sidings DL9 ... 40 F4
Cold Bath Pl HG2 ... 219 C1
Cold Bath Rd HG2 ... 222 C8
COLD COTES ... 103 F2
Cold Cotes Rd HG3 ... 160 B4
Coldhill La LS25 ... 195 C6
Coldie Hill 11 TS15 ... 25 C5
COLD KIRBY ... 91 D7
Cold Kirby Rd YO7 ... 91 C8
Coldstone La YO7 ... 88 B2
Coldyhill La YO12 ... 212 B8
Colebrooke Mdws HG5 ... 221 C7
Coledale Cl 2 YO30 ... 224 F1
Colenso St YO23 ... 233 B1
Coleridge Dr HG1 ... 219 E7
Coleridge Gdns DL1 ... 3 D3
Coleridge Way 1 WF8 ... 201 B1
Colescliffe Cres YO12 ... 212 C8
Colescliffe Rd YO12 ... 212 C8
Cole St YO31 ... 233 B4
Colin St 14 BB18 ... 171 D2
Coliseum* YO21 ... 208 D6
College Ave YO11 ... 213 A2
College Bsns Pk HG4 ... 214 B7
College Ct
1 Low Bradley BD20 ... 173 E3
4 Scarborough YO11 ... 212 F4
College Dr LS29 ... 218 B3
College Farm Cl DN14 ... 207 A8
College Farm La LS22 ... 180 A2
College Gdns DL1 ... 3 B5
College Gr WF10 ... 200 D3
College La
5 Masham HG4 ... 86 C3
Scarborough YO11 ... 213 A1
College of Law YO23 ... 231 B7
College Rd
Bradleys Both BD20 ... 173 E3
Copmanthorpe YO23 ... 230 A3
Harrogate HG2 ... 222 B8
Ripon HG4 ... 214 B6
College St
Harrogate HG2 ... 222 B8
York YO1 ... 233 B3
Colley Broach Rd YO61 ... 117 F7
Colliergate YO1 ... 233 B2
Collier Hag La YO23 ... 182 B3
Collier La
Lotherton cum Aberford LS25 ... 195 A6
West Layton DL11 ... 20 A8
Collin Ave TS4 ... 6 F8
Collin Bank HG3 ... 160 E6
Collinge Rd 9 BD22 ... 187 B6
COLLINGHAM ... 188 A8
Collingham Dr TS7 ... 7 D4
Collingham Lady Elizabeth Hastings CE Sch LS22 ... 180 A1
Collingham Way 12 YO14 ... 101 A3
Collingsway 4 DL2 ... 3 A7
Collingwood Ave YO24 ... 227 F2
Collingwood Gdns YO17 ... 215 A3
Collingwood Rd WF6 ... 200 A2
Collin's Hill HG3 ... 223 D7
Collinsons La YO17 ... 122 F5
Colliwath La DL8 ... 60 F4
Collyer View LS29 ... 218 E5
Colne & Broughton Rd BD23 ... 172 C4
Colne Rd
Barnoldswick BB18 ... 171 D1
Cowling BD22 ... 187 A5
Earby BB18 ... 172 A1
Kelbrook & Sough BB18 ... 186 A8
Colne Rd *continued*
Sutton BD20 ... 187 C7
Trawden Forest BB8 ... 186 A1
Colonel's Wlk 9 WF8 ... 201 B1
Colonley Bsns Pk BD20 ... 173 D1
Colorado Way WF10 ... 200 F2
Colstan Rd DL6 ... 210 E3
COLSTERDALE ... 84 E4
COLTON ... 190 E7
Colton La YO23 ... 190 E6
Coltsfoot Ct 19 HG3 ... 161 B3
Coltsgate Hill HG4 ... 214 B6
Columbine Gr 33 HG3 ... 161 B3
Columbus Ravine YO12 ... 212 F7
Columbus Way DL10 ... 41 C7
Colville Cres 8 DL9 ... 41 A5
Colville Rd 12 DL9 ... 41 A5
Comercial St
9 Barnoldswick BB18 ... 171 D1
Harrogate HG1 ... 219 D3
Norton YO17 ... 215 D3
Scarborough YO12 ... 212 E5
Tadcaster LS24 ... 189 E6
Comercial Yd 1 HG5 ... 221 B6
Comets Garth 11 DL2 ... 3 A7
Comfort La DL10 ... 20 C5
Comfrey Cl 32 HG3 ... 161 B3
Comfrey Manor TS8 ... 7 B4
Commercial St 9 BD24 ... 131 E2
Common Croft La YO26 ... 165 E1
COMMONDALE ... 9 D1
Common La
Beal DN14 ... 202 D3
Burn YO8 ... 203 E7
Catton YO41 ... 185 E8
Dunnington YO19 ... 184 F5
Fangfoss YO41 ... 169 B1
Knottingley WF11 ... 202 B1
Norton DN6 ... 206 E2
Sutton upon Derwent YO41 ... 193 C8
Temple Hirst YO8 ... 203 F4
Thorganby YO19 ... 192 F5
Walden Stubbs DN6 ... 206 F4
Warthill YO19 ... 167 F2
York YO10 ... 229 B1
Common Rd
Dunnington YO19 ... 184 F7
Skipwith YO8 ... 192 E1
Comon Balk La HG3 ... 140 A3
Comondale Sta YO21 ... 9 E1
Comon Holme La LS29 ... 175 C3
Comon La
Carlton Husthwaite YO7 ... 116 F8
Coverham with Agglethorpe DL8 ... 60 A2
Glaisdale YO21 ... 29 F1
Hambleton YO8 ... 196 D2
Harome YO62 ... 93 E5
Hartley CA17 ... 14 A8
Scruton DL7 ... 63 E7
South Milford LS25 ... 195 F2
Ulleskelf LS24 ... 190 C2
West Witton DL8 ... 59 F2
Comon Rd
Barkston Ash LS24 ... 195 F7
Church Fenton LS24 ... 196 A7
Strensall YO60 ... 145 D1
Compton La LS22 ... 188 A7
Compton St YO30 ... 228 A6
Conan Dr DL10 ... 209 D8
Conan Gdns DL10 ... 209 D8
Concorde Pk YO30 ... 225 A3
Concorde Way TS18 ... 5 F7
Coneycroft 10 YO19 ... 184 F7
Coneygarth La
Dunnington YO19 ... 184 E5
Tunstall LA6 ... 102 A4
Coney Garth La YO7 ... 89 B3
Coney Garth View HG5 ... 162 C5
Coney Moor Gr LS26 ... 200 C6
Coney St YO1 ... 233 B2
CONEYSTHORPE ... 120 D2
CONEYTHORPE ... 163 A5
Conference Cl YO17 ... 215 B4
Conifer Cl 6 YO32 ... 225 D3
Conifers Cl 2 YO8 ... 197 D1
Coningham Ave 1 YO30 ... 224 E2
Coniscliffe Mews DL3 ... 3 A4
Coniscliffe Rd DL3 ... 3 A4
Coniston Ave BB18 ... 171 D2
Coniston Cl 1 YO30 ... 224 E1
CONISTON COLD ... 155 A1
Coniston Dr
Castleford WF10 ... 201 C4
York YO10 ... 229 B4
CONISTONE ... 134 C6
Conistone La BD23 ... 108 B3
Coniston Gdns 6 YO12 ... 99 F7
Coniston Gr TS5 ... 6 E7
Coniston Rd HG1 ... 220 B4
Coniston Way
3 Eastfield YO12 ... 99 F7
Thirsk YO7 ... 89 C4
Connaught Rd
Ilkley LS29 ... 218 D3
Middlesbrough TS7 ... 7 D6
Connaught Way YO32 ... 225 F6
CONONLEY ... 173 C2
Cononley La BD20 ... 173 D1
Cononley Prim Sch BD20 ... 173 D2
Cononley Rd BD20 ... 187 D8
Cononley Sta BD20 ... 173 D1
CONONLEY WOODSIDE ... 173 C3
Conowl Cl 23 YO62 ... 92 F6
Conroy Cl 11 YO61 ... 143 D8
Consort St BD23 ... 217 B4
CONSTABLE BURTON ... 61 C5
Constable Burton Hall Gdns* DL8 ... 61 C6
Constable Rd
Hunmanby YO14 ... 127 A8
Ilkley LS29 ... 218 D3
Constable Ridge Rd HG3 ... 160 B2
Constantine Ave
10 Colburn DL9 ... 41 A5
York YO10 ... 229 A4
Constantine Cres 11 YO12 ... 99 E6
Constantine Gr 11 DL9 ... 41 A5
Constitution Hill 3 BD24 ... 131 E2
Conway Cl 2 YO30 ... 224 E3
Conway Cres BB18 ... 171 E1
Conway Gr 8 TS17 ... 5 F4
Conyers Ave DL3 ... 3 A6
Conyers Cl
Richmond DL10 ... 209 D8
Yarm TS15 ... 5 D2
Conyers Ings YO13 ... 99 A7
Conyers La DL8 ... 61 D6
Conyers Rd DL7 ... 22 E2
Conyers Sch TS15 ... 5 E2
Conygarth Way DL7 ... 63 C5
Conyngham Hall HG5 ... 220 F6
Cook Cl DL10 ... 41 C7
Cookgate TS7 ... 7 C5
Cooks Cl 2 DL6 ... 45 A7
Cooks Gdns 3 YO13 ... 75 D5
Cookson Way 34 DL9 ... 41 A5
Cook's Row 5 YO11 ... 213 B6
Coolham La BB18 ... 186 B8
Coombe Dr DL1 ... 3 F6
Coombes Cl YO61 ... 144 C3
COOMBOOTS ... 75 B6
Coomboots Brow YO13 ... 75 A6
Cooper Cl DL6 ... 25 D2
Cooper La
Blubberhouses LS21 ... 159 C1
Potto DL6 ... 25 D2
Cooper Lane Shepherd LS21 ... 159 C2
Cooper Rd
49 Filey YO14 ... 101 B3
18 Wetherby LS22 ... 180 C3
Coopers Dr YO23 ... 230 B3
COPGROVE ... 140 C2
Copgrove La HG5 ... 162 D8
Copgrove Rd HG3 ... 140 A2
Cophill La YO7 ... 66 A4
Copley La LS25 ... 195 B7
Copmanroyd LS21 ... 177 A2
COPMANTHORPE ... 230 B2
Copmanthorpe & District Recreation Ctr YO23 ... 230 B2
Copmanthorpe La YO23 ... 230 E3
Copmanthorpe Prim Sch YO23 ... 230 B3
Copper Beech Cl
9 Dunnington YO19 ... 184 E7
Upper Poppleton YO26 ... 182 F8
Copper Beech Dr DN14 ... 207 A8
Copper Beeches The 2 YO19 ... 184 E7
Copperclay Wlk YO61 ... 117 D1
Copperfield Cl
Malton YO17 ... 215 C5
21 Sherburn in Elmet LS25 ... 195 F4
Coppergate
1 Riccall YO19 ... 191 F1
York YO1 ... 233 B2
Coppergate Sh Ctr YO1 ... 233 B2
Coppergate Wlk YO1 ... 233 B2
Coppertop Mews 4 WF8 ... 201 C2
Coppice Ave HG1 ... 219 C4
Coppice Beck Ct HG1 ... 219 D3
Coppice Cl
Harrogate HG1 ... 219 C4
10 Haxby YO32 ... 166 E5
Coppice Dr HG1 ... 219 C3
Coppice Gate HG1 ... 219 C4
Coppice La
14 Hellifield BD23 ... 154 B3
Wrelton YO18 ... 71 B1
Coppice Rise HG1 ... 219 C5
Coppice The
Barwick in Elmet LS15 ... 194 B7
Bishopthorpe YO23 ... 230 F4
Brayton YO8 ... 197 C1
Ilkley LS29 ... 218 A6
Leeming DL7 ... 63 F3
14 Sherburn in Elmet LS25 ... 195 F4
19 Sutton BD20 ... 187 E7
Coppice Valley Prim Sch HG1 ... 219 C5
Coppice View HG1 ... 219 C4
Coppice Way HG1 ... 219 C5
Coppy La
Cononley BD20 ... 173 C2
Sutton BD22 ... 187 E4
Coppy Rd LS29 ... 174 F4
Coppy Wood Dr LS29 ... 218 B7
Copse Hill 1 YO14 ... 101 A4
Copse The
Boston Spa LS23 ... 180 E1
3 North Featherstone WF7 ... 200 E1
5 Scarborough YO12 ... 212 B5
Copsewood Wlk 5 TS9 ... 26 C8
COPT HEWICK ... 114 C2
Copwood Gr 7 YO32 ... 225 C8
Corban La YO32 ... 166 B6
Corban Way 21 YO32 ... 166 D5
Corber Hill 7 DL6 ... 43 F3
Corbie Way YO18 ... 96 A7
Corby Ave TS5 ... 6 D8
Cordike La
Birdsall YO17 ... 148 D6
Langton YO17 ... 147 F6
Cordilleras La DL11 ... 39 C8
Corlett Ct
Woodthorpe YO24 ... 230 C8
York YO24 ... 230 C8
Cormorant Cl 10 YO14 ... 101 D4
Cornaught Ct YO10 ... 231 D8
Cornbell Gate 4 HG4 ... 113 D2
Cornborough Ave YO31 ... 228 F6
Cornborough Rd YO60 ... 145 C5
Cornelian Ave YO11 ... 100 B8
Cornelian Cl YO11 ... 213 C1
Cornelian Dr YO11 ... 213 C1
Cornelius Cswy YO8 ... 198 E8
Cornel Rise 26 HG3 ... 161 B3
Corner Cl 17 YO32 ... 166 D5
Corners Terr 5 YO22 ... 208 E6
Cornerstones Cl LS29 ... 175 A4
Corners Yd 5 YO22 ... 208 E6
Cornfield Rd TS17 ... 6 A8
Cornflower Way 1 HG3 ... 161 B3
Cornforth Hill DL10 ... 209 B6
Cornlands YO17 ... 215 D2
Cornlands Rd YO24 ... 227 B1
Cornmill Cl YO8 ... 197 B8
Corn Mill Ct 19 LS25 ... 195 F4
Corn Mill Gdns YO12 ... 212 D7
Corn Mill La 39 LS29 ... 176 D1
Cornmill Pl 20 BB18 ... 171 D2
Cornmill Sh Ctr DL1 ... 3 C5
Cornwall Ave
Darlington DL1 ... 3 E6
Silsden BD20 ... 174 B1
Cornwall Cl HG1 ... 219 A2
Cornwall Dr YO10 ... 231 E8
Cornwall Rd HG1 ... 219 B2
Cornwood Way 11 YO32 ... 225 C8
Coronation Ave
6 Colburn DL9 ... 41 A5
Harrogate HG2 ... 222 E7
1 Hinderwell TS13 ... 11 F7
Coronation Gr HG2 ... 222 E7
Coronation Hospl LS29 ... 218 C3
Coronation Pl DL10 ... 209 A7
Coronation Rd
Crakehall DL8 ... 62 E5
Harrogate HG2 ... 222 E7
Coronation St
8 Barnoldswick BB18 ... 171 E1
Castleford WF6 ... 200 B2
Corporation Rd DL3 ... 3 C6
Corporation Road Prim Sch DL3 ... 3 C6
Corpse Rd
North Otterington DL7 ... 64 E5
Thornton-le-Moor DL6 ... 65 A4
Corunna Ct 5 YO8 ... 232 D5
Cosmo Ave YO31 ... 229 A5
Costa La YO18 ... 95 D6
Costa Way YO18 ... 95 E7
Cotchers La LS24 ... 195 D8
Cotcliffe Ave DL6 ... 210 F3
Cotcliffe Bank DL6 ... 65 E5
Cote Hill Rd HG3 ... 160 B4
Cote La
Healey HG4 ... 85 D5
Sproxton YO62 ... 92 C4
Cotescue Bank DL8 ... 60 C1
Cotherstone Ct TS16 ... 5 C5
Cotswold Dr LS25 ... 194 C3
Cotswold Way YO32 ... 226 A5
Cottage Cl DL6 ... 210 E5
Cottage La YO60 ... 145 C4
Cottagers La DL2 ... 2 C3
Cottam La YO25 ... 151 C5
Cottee Way 16 DL9 ... 41 A5
COTTERDALE ... 55 F8
Cotterdale Cl HG5 ... 221 C6
Cotterdale Gdns LS25 ... 202 A6
Cotterdale Holt 9 LS22 ... 180 A1
Cottom La YO42 ... 193 C2
COTTON TREE ... 186 A2
Cotton Tree La BB8 ... 186 A3
Coulby Farm Way TS8 ... 7 A5
Coulby La YO18 ... 97 A6
Coulby Manor Way TS8 ... 6 F6
COULBY NEWHAM ... 7 A5
Coulby Newham Sch TS8 ... 7 A5
Coulson Cl 5 YO32 ... 167 C8
Coulter Beck La LA6 ... 102 D7
COULTON ... 119 B5
Coulton La YO62 ... 119 A6
Count De Burgh Terr 4 YO23 ... 228 B1
COUNTERSETT ... 57 C2
Counting House Mews BD23 ... 216 F4
County Par HG1 ... 219 F3
County Sq HG1 ... 219 F3
Coupland Rd
Garforth LS25 ... 194 C4
1 Selby YO8 ... 232 C6
Courby Hill HG4 ... 86 F2
Courcey Gr YO26 ... 227 C4
Court Dr YO8 ... 232 A4
Court Green Cl YO13 ... 54 D1
Court La BD23 ... 217 A4
Court Moor La YO62 ... 70 A4
Courtneys
Selby YO8 ... 232 B4
Wheldrake YO19 ... 193 A8
Courtneys The YO8 ... 232 B4

Courts Cl 7 DN14 205 E4
Court Terr HG4 214 C5
Court The 6 DL8 63 A2
Courtyard The
 Bishopthorpe YO23 231 B4
 11 Pontefract WF8 201 C2
Coutances Way LS29 218 F5
Cove Rd BD23 132 F2
Coverdale Dr
 1 Knaresborough HG5 221 A7
 Scarborough YO12 212 B4
Coverdale Garth 2 LS22 188 A8
Coverdale La TS13 12 A4
COVERHAM 60 C1
Coverham Abbey (rems of)★
 DL8 60 C1
Coverham Cl DL7 210 C2
Coverham La DL8 60 C1
Cover La
 Carlton Town DL8 83 E7
 Marton-le-Moor HG4 114 E1
Covert The
 Mount Pleasant TS8 7 B4
 9 Topcliffe YO7 89 B1
 York YO24 230 F7
COWAN BRIDGE 102 D7
Cowbar Bank 1 TS13 13 K2
Cowbar La TS13 13 J2
Cow & Calf Rocks★
 LS29 218 D2
Cowcliff Hill YO17 148 F6
Cow Cl La
 Kirkby Malham BD23 154 E8
 Lockwood TS12 10 B4
COWESBY 66 C4
Cowgarth La 15 BB18 172 B1
Cow Gate La BD23 171 B7
Cowgill St 17 BB18 172 A1
Cowhouse Bank YO62 68 F3
Cowie Dr YO8 232 D5
Cow La
 Cowling BD22 187 B6
 Knottingley WF11 202 A2
 Lothersdale BD20 172 F1
 Middleton Tyas DL10 21 E5
 Womersley DN6 206 D6
Cowland La YO7 88 D3
Cowley Cl TS16 5 E7
Cowley Rd TS5 6 E7
COWLING
 Bedale 62 D2
 Glusburn 187 B6
Cowling Hill La BD22 186 F7
Cowling La DL8 62 D3
Cowling Prim Sch BD22 187 A6
Cowling Rd DL8 62 D2
Cowlings Cl 16 YO14 127 A8
Cow Pasture La YO42 193 C3
Cowpasture Rd LS29 218 C3
Cowper La YO23 191 C8
Cowper St 3 BD23 217 A3
Cowslip La 18 WF10 200 D3
COWTHORPE 180 E7
Cowton Castle★ DL7 22 D1
Cowton La YO14 127 C6
Cowton Way TS16 5 D6
Cow Wath Bank YO22 51 E8
Cow Wath Cl 30 YO12 75 D5
Coxlea Gr YO31 229 B6
Coxwain Cl YO14 101 B2
COXWOLD 117 D8
Coxwold Dr DL1 3 D4
Coxwold Hill 5 LS22 180 C4
Coxwold Pottery★ YO61 117 D7
Coxwold View 1 LS22 180 C3
Crab La
 Harrogate HG1 219 D6
 Seamer YO12 99 E6
Crabmill La YO61 143 D8
Crabtree Cl YO61 118 A1
Crabtree Gn LS22 188 A8
Crabtree Gr 1 YO32 225 D3
Crabtree Hill LS22 188 A8
CRACKPOT 37 B3
CRACOE 156 C7
Cracoe & Rylstone District
 Prim Sch BD23 156 B6
Cradley Dr TS5 6 E6
Cradoc Gr 14 TS17 5 F4
CRAG 187 D6
Crag Bank YO21 28 B8
Crag Cl 33 BD20 187 E7
Cragdale 13 BD24 131 D2
Cragdale Rise 1 HG5 221 D6
Cragg Bottom Rd BD22 187 C1
Crag Gdns LS23 188 E5
Cragg Dr LS29 218 F3
Cragg Hill Rd BD24 105 C3
Cragg La LA2 130 C4
Craggs La
 Arrathorne DL10 41 A1
 Tatham LA2 129 A3
Cragg The 21 YO21 208 D7
Crag Hill La HG3 161 B6
Crag La
 Bradleys Both BD20 173 E2
 Felliscliffe HG3 160 D4
 Huby LS17 178 B2
 Killinghall HG3 161 B1
 Knaresborough HG5 221 B5
 North Rigton LS17 178 B3
 Pannal HG3 178 C8
 Sutton BD20 187 D6
Crag Side Rd DL8 57 B2
Crag The 3 LS23 188 E5
Crag View
 Cononley BD20 173 D1
 Skipton BD23 217 B6
 Threshfield BD23 134 B3
 Weeton LS17 178 B2
Crag View Rd BD23 217 B3
Craiglands Pk LS29 218 C3
Craiglands Rd LS29 218 C3
Craig Miller Pk DL3 2 F5
Craigmore Dr LS29 218 E4
Craig St DL3 3 C6
Craigs Way YO7 211 C4
Crakehall Prim Sch DL8 62 E4
CRAKEHILL 115 E4
Crake La HG3 159 F6
CRAMBE 146 F3
CRAMBECK 146 F6
Crambeck Village YO60 146 F6
Cranberry TS8 7 B5
Cranbrook Ave YO26 227 C5
Cranbrook Rd YO26 227 C5
Cranbrooks The YO19 192 F8
Cranbrook Way 17 WF8 201 C2
Cranesbill Cl HG3 161 B3
Cranfield Pl 4 YO24 230 C8
Cranford Gdns TS5 6 D8
Crank La DL7 63 B7
Crankley La YO61 143 B7
Cranwell Gr TS17 6 B6
CRATHORNE 25 A6
Craven Bank La BD24 131 B3
Craven Coll (Aireville
 Campus) BD23 216 D4
Craven Coll (High Street
 Campus) BD23 217 A4
Craven Coll (Snaygill
 Campus) BD23 173 D4
Craven Coll (The Academy of
 Hair) BD23 216 F4
Craven Coll (The Academy of
 Hair & Beauty) BD23 217 F4
Craven Coll (The Centre for
 Rural & Equine Studies)
 BD23 216 C4
Craven Coll (Tyro Training)
 BD23 216 F4
Craven Court Sh Ctr
 BD23 217 A4
Craven Cres 3 LS29 174 F4
Craven Ct
 Cowling BD22 187 C6
 Northallerton DL7 210 B3
 Richmond DL10 209 B6
 Silsden BD20 174 C1
Cravendale Rd 4 DL9 40 F5
Craven Dr BD20 174 C1
Craven Garth 5 DN14 202 D4
Cravengate DL10 209 B6
Craven Mus★ BD23 217 A4
Craven Ridge La BD24 131 A2
Craven Ridge Lane Ends
 BD24 131 B3
Craven's Hill YO13 54 C3
Craven St
 3 Colne BB8 186 A3
 Harrogate HG1 219 D4
 Scarborough YO11 213 A4
 Skipton BD23 216 F3
Craven Swimming Pool
 BD23 216 D4
Craven Terr BD23 216 F4
Craven Way
 5 Boroughbridge YO51 141 B4
 Dent LA10 78 B8
Crawford Cl YO26 181 C7
Crawley Way YO31 229 B6
CRAY 81 E2
CRAYKE 118 A1
Crayke Castle★ YO61 117 F1
Crayke CE Prim Sch
 YO61 117 F1
Crayke La YO61 117 F2
Crayke Manor★ YO61 118 A2
Cray Thorns Cres YO7 115 A4
Crescent Ave YO21 208 C7
Crescent Back Rd 8
 YO11 213 A5
Crescent Ct LS29 218 B4
Crescent Gdns HG1 219 C2
Crescent Hill 53 YO14 101 B3
Crescent Par HG4 214 C6
Crescent Pl 20 YO21 208 D7
Crescent Rd
 Harrogate HG1 219 C2
 Ripon HG4 214 B6
Crescent Terr 6 LS29 218 B4
Crescent The
 13 Bedale DL8 63 B3
 Burton Fleming YO25 126 E3
 Carlton TS9 26 A2
 Dishforth YO7 115 A2
 Eaglescliffe TS16 5 D4
 Filey YO14 101 B3
 Garforth LS25 194 D4
 17 Helmsley YO62 92 F6
 Ilkley LS29 218 E5
 1 Kelfield YO19 191 D1
 Kexby YO41 185 C5
 Kippax LS25 194 D1
 Micklefield LS25 195 A3
 Middlesbrough TS7 7 D6
 Middleton St George DL2 4 E4
 Monk Fryston LS25 202 A8
 Northallerton DL6 210 E4
 North Rigton LS17 178 B3
 Otley LS21 177 A1
 6 Riccall YO19 197 F8
 Richmond DL10 209 D7
Crescent The *continued*
 Ripon HG4 214 B6
 Scalby YO12 212 B7
 Scarborough YO11 213 A5
 Sicklinghall LS22 179 E3
 Skipton BD23 217 B6
 Stamford Bridge YO41 168 D2
 2 Summerbridge HG3 138 A1
 Thirsk YO7 211 C3
 Thornaby TS17 6 B8
 Thornton Dale YO18 96 D5
 York YO10 229 C1
 York YO24 233 A1
Crestbrooke DL7 210 D2
Crestholme Cl 6 HG5 221 D5
Crest The LS26 194 A1
Crewe Rd WF10 201 B4
Creyke View DN14 205 A1
Cribyn Cl 20 TS17 5 F4
Crichton Ave YO30 228 B8
Cricketers Cl LS25 194 D3
Cricketers Way 8 LS25 195 F4
Cricket La TS6 7 E8
Cridling Gdns DN6 206 F2
CRIDLING STUBBS 206 C8
CRIMPLE 223 D8
Crimple Ave LS22 180 A8
Crimple Ct HG2 223 A7
Crimple La HG3 223 D7
Crimple Mdws HG3 222 D3
Crinan Ct
 Pontefract WF6 200 A2
 3 York YO32 225 F6
Crindle Carr La DL7 65 B3
Cringle Moor Chase TS9 26 F4
CRINGLES 174 C3
Cringles La BD20 174 C4
Cringley La DL8 57 E5
CROCKEY HILL 184 A1
Crocus Ct 20 DL9 41 A5
Croft Ave
 8 Knottingley WF11 202 A3
 Middlesbrough TS5 6 D8
 4 Normanton South WF6 200 B2
 Otley LS21 176 F1
Croft Cl
 Carlton Husthwaite YO7 116 F7
 14 Easingwold YO61 143 C8
 Ingleton LA6 103 D3
Croft Ct YO23 231 A4
Croft Dr LS23 188 E6
Crofters Gn HG3 219 A8
Crofters Mill BD20 187 B7
Croft Farm Cl YO23 230 B3
Croft Gdns YO7 211 B1
Croft Heads YO7 211 B1
Croft Head Terr 2 BD20 187 E7
Croft Hill
 Carthorpe DL8 87 E6
 32 Glusburn BD20 187 E7
Croft Hills TS9 26 A7
Croft House Dr 8 LS21 176 F1
Croft House Fold 10
 LS29 175 A4
Croft House La BD23 135 A1
Croft La
 Carlton Husthwaite YO7 116 F8
 Newton Kyme cum Toulston
 LS24 189 B7
 Snainton YO13 97 F5
 Walton LS23 181 A2
Croftlands 7 WF11 202 A3
Croft Motor Racing Circuit★
 DL2 22 C5
CROFT-ON-TEES 22 D8
Croft Prim Sch DL2 22 C8
Croft Rd
 Bramham cum Oglethorpe
 LS23 188 E6
 Camblesforth YO8 204 D4
 Catterick Garrison DL9 209 E1
 Eaglescliffe TS16 5 D4
 Hurworth DL2 3 B2
 Ingleton LA6 103 D3
Crofts Ave
 4 Pickering YO18 96 A6
 Richmond DL10 209 B7
Croftside 1 YO26 227 B3
Croft St 1 BD20 187 E7
Crofts The
 1 Glusburn BD20 173 F1
 1 Sutton BD20 187 E6
Croft The
 Beadlam YO62 93 D7
 Burton in Lonsdale LA6 102 F3
 Castleford WF10 200 F3
 5 Collingham LS22 188 A8
 Draughton BD23 174 B7
 1 Filey YO14 101 B3
 Grafton YO51 141 D2
 Knottingley WF11 202 A3
 Langthorpe YO51 141 A7
 Scalby YO12 212 B7
 Sheriff Hutton YO60 145 D5
 Stirton with Thorlby BD23 216 C6
 Thirsk YO7 211 B1
 West Tanfield DL8 87 B3
Croft View 6 YO7 211 B3
Croftway
 Barwick in Elmet LS15 194 C8
 Camblesforth YO8 204 C5
 Selby YO8 232 C4
 Sherburn in Elmet LS25 195 F4
 2 York YO26 227 B3
Crombie Ave YO30 228 B7
Cromer St YO30 228 B7
Crompton Terr YO32 225 D6
Cromwell Ave 22 YO14 101 B3
Cromwell Cl 5 WF11 201 E4
Cromwell Cres 6 WF8 201 C1
Cromwell Dr DL7 64 A6
Cromwell Gdns 6 YO11 212 F4
Cromwell Office Pk 22
 LS22 180 C3
Cromwell Par 5 YO11 212 F4
Cromwell Rd
 Harrogate HG2 222 E7
 Scarborough YO11 212 F4
 York YO1 233 B1
Cromwell Rise LS25 200 D8
Cromwell St 9 BD23 217 A3
Cromwell Terr 7 YO11 212 F4
Crook Bank La DL11 38 F6
Crooked La YO26 164 C2
Crook La HG4 85 C5
Crookland La YO32 166 F5
Crook Rise View BD23 217 B3
Croome Dale La YO17 150 C6
Croome Rd YO25 150 B4
Croom Medieval Village★
 YO25 150 B4
Cropstones LS23 188 F5
CROPTON 71 B4
Cropton Brewery & Visitor
 Ctr★ YO18 71 B3
Cropton La YO18 71 B2
Cropton Rise YO12 212 B4
Cropton Way TS8 7 B5
CROSBY COURT 65 B6
Crosby Gdns DL6 210 E4
Crosby Rd DL6 210 E4
Crosby St DL3 3 C7
Crosland Cl 22 YO62 92 F6
Cross Bank BD23 217 B6
Crossbeck Cl LS29 218 B3
Crossbeck Rd
 Ilkley LS29 218 B3
 Northallerton DL6 210 F5
Crossbeck Way TS7 7 D8
Crosscliff TS8 6 F5
Crossdale Rd YO18 72 E3
Cross End Fold 3 LS29 175 A4
Crossfield Cl 2 DL2 3 E1
Crossfield Cres YO19 231 E6
Crossfields TS8 7 A4
Cross Gate YO13 97 D5
Crossgate La 22 YO18 95 F6
CROSSGATES 99 E7
Crossgates HG3 138 B5
Cross Haw La 3 LA2 130 C8
Cross Head Bank DL8 60 D7
Cross Hill
 Fairburn WF11 201 D6
 Sutton-under-Whitestonecliffe
 YO7 90 D5
Crosshill La DN14 207 E6
CROSS HILLS 187 E7
Cross Hills La YO8 232 A5
Crossings The 13 DN14 205 E4
Cross La
 Bentham LA2 128 E8
 Brompton YO13 98 C5
 Burneston DL8 87 E8
 Burniston YO13 75 D7
 Farndale East YO62 48 E4
 Flaxton YO60 167 E8
 Fulford YO19 231 F5
 Giggleswick BD24 130 F2
 Great Ouseburn YO26 164 B8
 Little Ayton TS9 27 A8
 Pickhill with Roxby YO7 88 C6
 Scalby YO12 212 C8
 Sinnington YO62 95 A8
 Snainton YO13 97 F3
 Stonebeck Up HG3 110 B5
Crosslands Rd 2 YO10 231 E8
Cross Lane Ct BD20 173 E3
CROSS LANES 143 D3
Cross Lanes DL10 209 E7
Crossley Pl BD23 216 F4
Crossley St 8 LS22 180 C3
Crossley Street Prim Sch
 LS22 180 C3
Crossman Dr 2 WF6 200 B2
Crossmoor La YO32 166 E6
Cross Queen St 9 WF6 200 A1
Cross Rd LA2 128 E7
Cross Rein Bank DL7 23 A1
Cross Row
 Boosbeck TS12 9 E7
 Swillington LS15 194 A3
Cross St
 6 Cowling BD22 187 B6
 14 Earby BB18 172 A1
 Scarborough YO11 213 A6
 Skipton BD23 216 F3
 5 York YO24 227 C3
Cross The LS15 194 B8
Cross Top DL8 57 E7
Crossways YO10 229 C2
Crossways Cres HG2 220 D3
Crossways Dr HG2 220 D2
Crossways The LS21 177 A1
Crossway The
 Darlington DL1 3 E5
 2 York YO31 228 E8
Crosswell Pk 40 TS17 5 F4
Crowberry Dr HG3 161 B3
CROWDON 54 A4
Crowdy Cl YO22 208 E4
Crowfoot La DL6 43 D5
Crowgarth HG4 140 D7
Crow Hill La HG3 160 C4
Crown Close Back 14
 YO11 213 A4
Crown Cres YO11 213 A4
Crow Nest Rd LA2 130 F6
Crown Gr YO17 215 E3
Crown Sq 26 YO62 70 B1
Crown St
 34 Burley in Warfedale
 LS29 176 C1
 Darlington DL1 3 C5
Crown Terr YO11 213 A4
Crowood Ave TS9 26 C8
Crowtrees 1 LA2 128 E8
Crummack La LA2 130 E8
Crummock 3 YO24 230 C7
CUBECK 57 F4
Cuddy Brown Cl 7 YO18 96 A6
Cuddy La DL6 45 B4
Culloden Twr★ DL10 209 B6
Culvert La BD23 216 A4
Cumberland Cl 6 YO32 167 B6
Cumberland Gdns DL10 21 C4
Cumberland Rd 1 WF10 201 C5
Cumberland St
 6 Skipton BD23 216 F3
 York YO1 233 B2
Cumbernauld Rd TS17 6 C7
Cumboots Brow YO13 75 B6
Cumbrian Ave 4 YO32 167 B6
CUNDALL 115 E3
Cundall Ave YO7 115 B6
Cundall Cl 6 YO32 167 C8
Cundall Dr 6 YO32 191 C7
Cundall Manor Sch
 YO61 115 E3
Cundall Way HG2 222 C8
Cunliffe Rd LS29 218 B4
Cunningham Ave TS17 6 B6
Cunningham Rd 4 DL9 40 F4
Cupid's Alley YO17 149 B6
Curfew Rd HG4 214 C3
Curlew Cl
 11 Ilkley LS29 175 C2
 Leyburn DL8 60 E4
Curlew Cres 2 DL9 40 F2
Curlew Dr
 13 Crossgates YO12 99 E6
 3 Filey YO14 101 A3
Curlew Glebe 8 YO19 184 E7
Curly Hill LS29 218 C7
Currer La LS29 175 B6
Currie Cl DL9 209 C2
Curson Terr YO8 198 E3
Curtain La DL11 1 D5
Curtain The DL11 1 D4
Curteis Dr DL10 41 B6
Curzon Terr YO23 228 B1
Custance Wlk YO23 233 A1
Cutler La LS26 200 C6
Cutpurse La DL10 209 C8
Cut Rd WF11 201 D6
CUTSYKE 200 E3
Cutsyke Ave WF10 200 D3
Cutsyke Rd WF10 200 D2
Cut Throat La HG3 138 F1
Cycle St 4 YO10 229 A3
Cygnet Cl 7 YO14 101 A4
Cygnet Dr TS18 6 A7
Cygnet St YO23 233 A1
Cyndor Ct WF10 201 C3
Cypress Cl DL3 3 B4
Cypress Gdns HG4 214 B2
Cypress Rd TS7 7 C6
Cyprus Gr 37 YO32 166 E5

D

DACRE 159 F7
DACRE BANKS 159 F8
Dacre Braithwaite CE Prim
 Sch HG3 159 B7
Dacre Ct LS24 195 D7
Dacre Hall Pk HG3 159 F7
Dacre La HG3 159 D7
Dacre Pasture La HG3 159 D6
Daffy La YO61 117 E1
Dairy La HG3 159 E6
Daisy Cl DL9 41 A5
Daisy Hill BD20 174 C1
Dakyn Cl DL7 22 F2
Dalacres Cres BD23 217 D8
Dalacres Dr BD23 217 D8
DALBY 119 B2
Dalby Ave HG2 220 D1
Dalby Bank YO60 119 C2
Dalby Cl YO12 212 B5
Dalby Ct HG2 220 D1
Dalby Forest Dr YO18 96 E8
Dalby Mead YO32 225 F1
Dalby Way TS8 7 A5
Dale Ave YO13 75 C8
Dale Bank HG1 219 B3
Dale Cl
 Burniston YO13 75 C8
 Hampsthwaite HG3 161 A5
 7 Hurworth-on-Tees DL2 3 E1
 Selby YO8 232 C3
 Thornton Watlass HG4 86 D8
Dale Cres BD23 173 A4
Dale Croft 20 LS29 175 C2
Dale Dike Gr YO30 224 F2
Dale Edge 11 YO11 99 F7
Dale End
 Danby YO21 29 C7
 Kirkbymoorside YO62 70 B1
Dale End Rd YO62 70 A7
Dalefield Ave WF6 200 A1
Dalefield Rd WF6 200 A1
Dale Garth YO12 212 D4
Dale Gr DL8 60 D6

Dalehouse Bank TS13 ... 13 J1
Dale Rd
Carleton BD23 ... 173 A4
Darlington DL3 ... 3 B5
Sadberge DL2 ... 4 C7
Dale Rise YO13 ... 75 C8
Dales Ave BD23 ... 217 C7
Dalesbridge Outdoor Ctr★ LA2 ... 130 E6
Dales Countryside Mus★ DL8 ... 56 D5
Dales Ct YO19 ... 191 D3
Daleside Ave HG2 ... 222 E5
Daleside Dr HG2 ... 222 E5
Daleside Gdns HG2 ... 222 E5
Daleside Pk HG3 ... 160 A6
Daleside Rd
Farndale East YO62 ... 48 C7
Farndale West YO62 ... 48 B6
Harrogate HG2 ... 222 E5
Rosedale East Side YO18 ... 49 C5
Rosedale West Side YO18 ... 49 C3
Dale's La YO31 ... 228 F6
Dales Park Rd TS8 ... 6 E5
Dales Sch The DL7 ... 64 A7
Dale St
Earby BB18 ... 172 B1
York YO23 ... 233 A1
Dale Stone Cl WF11 ... 201 D5
Dale The LS25 ... 188 F1
Dale View
6 Earby BB18 ... 172 A1
Ilkley LS29 ... 175 C2
Dale Way 2 DL8 ... 60 D5
Dalewood Wlk 3 TS9 ... 26 C8
Dalguise Gr YO31 ... 233 C4
Dallamires Cl HG4 ... 214 D3
Dallamires Ind Est HG4 ... 214 D4
Dallamires La HG4 ... 214 E3
Dallamires Way N HG4 ... 214 D4
Dallamires Way S HG4 ... 214 D3
Dallas Ct TS8 ... 6 F5
DALLOW ... 111 F2
Dalmally Cl YO24 ... 230 B6
DALTON
Newsham ... 19 D7
Topcliffe ... 115 F7
DALTON GATES ... 22 D4
Dalton Hill YO19 ... 193 A8
Dalton La
Dalton YO7 ... 115 D7
Wothersome LS23 ... 188 C5
DALTON-ON-TEES ... 22 E6
Dalton Terr YO24 ... 228 A3
Dam Bank YO8 ... 232 C6
Dame La DL8 ... 58 F1
Dam Head Rd 14 BB18 ... 171 D1
Dam Hill YO23 ... 182 B4
Dam La
Appleton Roebuck YO23 ... 190 F4
Markington with Wallerthwaite HG3 ... 139 C3
Saxton with Scarthingwell LS24 ... 195 C7
Selby YO8 ... 197 B3
Damson Cl YO26 ... 227 E4
DANBY ... 29 C7
Danby Castle★ YO21 ... 29 D6
Danby CE Sch YO21 ... 29 B6
Danby La DL7 ... 43 C5
Danby St 3 DL9 ... 40 F4
Danby Sta YO21 ... 29 C7
DANBY WISKE ... 43 C5
Dandy Mill Ave WF8 ... 201 C1
Dandy Mill Croft 8 WF8 ... 201 C1
Dandy Mill View WF8 ... 201 C1
Dane Ave
Thorpe Willoughby YO8 ... 197 B1
York YO26 ... 227 C5
Danebury Cres YO26 ... 227 C4
Danebury Ct YO26 ... 227 C4
Danebury Dr YO26 ... 227 C4
Danelaw Fields 1 DL6 ... 43 F3
Danelaw Rd 2 DL6 ... 43 F3
Dane Rd DL9 ... 209 E1
Danescroft YO8 ... 232 C2
Danes Croft 2 YO10 ... 231 D8
Danes Ct 5 YO19 ... 198 A8
Danes Dyke 34 YO12 ... 75 D5
Danesfort Ave YO24 ... 227 D2
Danesgate YO26 ... 227 C4
Dane's Graves (Tumuli)★ YO25 ... 151 D2
Danes Hills (Tumuli)★ YO8 ... 192 E2
Danesmead YO10 ... 231 D8
Danesmoor Cres DL3 ... 3 B5
Daneswell Cl 3 YO41 ... 168 D2
Dangerous Cnr HG3 ... 160 A2
Dansk Way LS29 ... 218 D5
Danum Ave YO7 ... 211 A1
Danum Dr YO10 ... 231 E8
Danum Rd YO10 ... 231 E8
Darbie Cl YO32 ... 225 D4
D'arcy Cl DL9 ... 40 F4
D'arcy Rd YO8 ... 232 E4
Darfield Cl YO32 ... 167 B8
Darkfield La WF8 ... 201 C2
Dark La
Brompton YO13 ... 98 C5
Earby BB18 ... 172 B1
Newsham DL11 ... 19 C8
Sinnington YO62 ... 71 A1
Spofforth with Stockeld HG5 ... 179 F7
Stainburn LS21 ... 177 E2
Sutton BD22 ... 187 F1
DARLEY ... 160 A6
Darley Carr HG3 ... 159 F6
Darley Cl 7 YO41 ... 168 D2
Darley Mill Ctr★ HG3 ... 159 F6
Darley Prim Sch HG3 ... 160 A6
Darley Rd HG3 ... 160 D6
Darling La YO23 ... 191 C8
DARLINGTON ... 3 E6
Darlington Arts Ctr★ 2 DL3 ... 3 C5
Darlington Back La DL2 ... 4 E8
Darlington (Bank Top) Sta DL1 ... 3 D4
Darlington Civic Theatre★ DL1 ... 3 D5
Darlington Coll DL1 ... 3 D6
Darlington Coll at Catterick Garrison 28 DL9 ... 40 E4
Darlington Meml Hospl DL3 ... 3 C6
Darlington Rd
Easby DL10 ... 20 F1
Longnewton TS21 ... 5 A7
Northallerton DL6 ... 210 C7
Richmond DL10 ... 209 E8
Sadberge DL2 ... 4 B7
Stockton-on-Tees TS18 ... 5 E8
Darlington Ret Pk DL1 ... 3 F5
Darlington Sta DL1 ... 3 D4
Darnborough Gate HG4 ... 214 B6
Darnborough St YO23 ... 233 B1
Darnbrook Rd 2 BB18 ... 171 D1
Darnbrook Wlk YO31 ... 229 B5
Darnholme La YO22 ... 51 D8
Darnton Dr TS4 ... 7 A7
Darrowby Cl YO7 ... 211 C4
Darrowby Dr DL3 ... 3 C6
Darwin Cl YO31 ... 225 E1
Darwin Dr 40 DL9 ... 41 A5
Daskett Hill YO60 ... 145 D5
Dauby La YO41 ... 185 B3
Davenport Rd TS15 ... 5 D2
David La YO18 ... 72 F5
Davis Ave WF10 ... 201 B3
Davison Rd DL1 ... 3 D7
Davison St TS12 ... 9 F7
Davygate YO1 ... 233 B2
Davy Rd WF10 ... 200 E6
DAW CROSS ... 222 B3
Dawcross Rise HG3 ... 222 B3
Dawes Ave WF10 ... 201 A3
Daw La YO23 ... 191 A5
Dawnay Cl 5 YO12 ... 99 F7
Dawnay Garth
Shipton YO30 ... 165 E5
2 Snaith DN14 ... 204 B1
Dawney La YO61 ... 143 B6
Dawson Ct HG3 ... 161 A5
Dawson's La HG4 ... 85 F4
Dawson St 16 BD23 ... 217 A3
Dawson Terr HG1 ... 219 D4
Dawtrie St WF10 ... 201 B4
Day La HG3 ... 159 E4
Daysfoot Ct 8 YO10 ... 228 E3
Deacon Ct 3 YO8 ... 232 B6
Deacons Ct YO23 ... 230 B2
Dealtry Ave 1 YO32 ... 225 C8
Dean Edge Rd BD22 ... 187 D1
Deane Pl HG2 ... 220 B3
Deangate YO1 ... 233 B3
Dean Hall Brow YO22 ... 32 C5
Deanhead Gr 7 YO30 ... 224 E2
Dean La BD22 ... 187 F3
Dean Rd
Norton YO17 ... 215 E3
Scarborough YO12 ... 212 E6
Deans Cl YO23 ... 230 F4
Deans Sq YO7 ... 115 C7
Dean St
Ilkley LS29 ... 218 C5
Trawden Forest BB8 ... 186 A1
De Bruce Rd DL6 ... 210 D8
Debruse Ave TS15 ... 5 D2
De Brus Pk TS8 ... 7 C4
De Brus Way TS14 ... 8 F7
De Burgh Ct DL9 ... 41 A5
Dee Cl YO24 ... 230 B7
DEEPDALE ... 80 F2
Deepdale
Guisborough TS14 ... 8 D6
7 Hutton Rudby TS15 ... 25 C5
5 York YO24 ... 230 D8
Deep Dale LS23 ... 180 E1
Deepdale Ave
Eastfield YO11 ... 100 A8
Middlesbrough TS4 ... 7 A8
Scarborough YO11 ... 213 A1
Deepdale La
Boston Spa LS23 ... 180 D1
Dent LA10 ... 77 F8
Deepdale Way 7 DL1 ... 3 F6
Deep Ghyll Croft HG4 ... 214 C3
Deep Ghyll Wlk HG4 ... 214 C3
Deeping Way YO8 ... 232 A6
Deer Hill Gr YO30 ... 224 F3
Deer Park Ct 1 LS25 ... 202 A8
DEERSTONES ... 175 B8
Deerstone Way 22 YO19 ... 184 F7
De Ferrers Rd DL6 ... 210 D8
De Ferrieres Ave HG1 ... 219 D4
De Gaunte Rd DL6 ... 210 E8
De Grey Ct YO30 ... 233 A4
De Grey Pl 2 YO23 ... 231 B3
DEIGHTON
192 A7
Brompton ... 44 A8
Deighton Ave 18 LS25 ... 195 F4
Deighton Cl LS22 ... 180 C3
Deighton Grove La YO19 ... 184 A1
Deighton La
Brompton DL6 ... 43 E5
Little Smeaton DL6 ... 23 E1
Deighton Rd
Coulby Newham TS4 ... 7 A7
Spofforth with Stockeld HG3 ... 179 F6
Wetherby LS22 ... 180 C4
Deigton Gates Prim Sch 7 LS22 ... 180 C4
De Lacy Ave 1 WF7 ... 200 E1
Delacy Crcs WF10 ... 201 B5
Delamere Cl 6 YO32 ... 166 D5
Delamere Cres HG2 ... 220 D1
Delamere Rd TS3 ... 7 B8
Delaney Cl 19 BD24 ... 131 D2
Delf La YO7 ... 66 A4
De Lisle Cres DL9 ... 209 C2
Dell The
Langtoft YO25 ... 151 C5
5 Skelton YO30 ... 224 B5
Del Pyke YO31 ... 233 C4
Delves La YO22 ... 30 F3
Delwood YO10 ... 231 D7
De Mowbray Ct YO23 ... 182 D3
Dene Cl DN14 ... 203 C2
Dene Gr DL3 ... 3 C6
Dene Mdw 1 YO13 ... 99 B8
Dene Park Cl HG1 ... 219 F6
Dene Pk HG1 ... 219 F5
Dene Rd DL6 ... 210 E5
Deneside Rd DL3 ... 3 B6
Denesway LS25 ... 194 D3
Dene The YO12 ... 212 E7
Denevale TS15 ... 5 E3
Denison Ave 8 YO12 ... 99 D6
Denison Rd YO8 ... 232 E4
Dennis La BD20 ... 174 A2
Dennison St YO31 ... 233 C4
Dennis St YO1 ... 233 C2
Dentdale Dr HG5 ... 221 C6
DENTON ... 176 A3
Denton Rd LS29 ... 218 A5
Denton Terr WF10 ... 200 F4
Denver Dr DL2 ... 4 D4
Denver Rd 6 DN6 ... 206 F2
Denwell Terr WF8 ... 201 B1
Depot La 11 YO12 ... 212 E4
Deramore Dr YO10 ... 229 C3
Deramore Drive W YO10 ... 229 C3
Derby Cl DL9 ... 209 C1
Derby Rd TS14 ... 8 E6
Derby The TS7 ... 7 B6
Derby Way 8 DL9 ... 40 F4
Dere St DL7 ... 63 D3
Dere Street Roman Rd★ DL11 ... 2 B2
Derrings La YO61 ... 142 D6
Derventio Roman Fort★ YO17 ... 215 D4
Derwent Ave
Garforth LS25 ... 194 C3
5 Scarborough YO12 ... 212 E4
York YO31 ... 228 F4
Derwent Chase DN14 ... 205 B7
Derwent Cl
East Cottingwith YO42 ... 193 C5
Elvington YO41 ... 185 B3
2 Stamford Bridge YO41 ... 168 D2
Derwent Ct YO41 ... 185 C2
Derwent Dr
4 Barlby YO8 ... 198 B5
Castleford WF10 ... 201 C5
Wheldrake YO19 ... 192 F7
Derwent Est YO19 ... 184 E7
Derwent Infant Sch YO10 ... 229 B4
Derwent Junior Sch YO10 ... 229 B4
Derwent La YO19 ... 184 E7
Derwent Pk YO19 ... 193 A8
Derwent Pl WF11 ... 201 F1
Derwent Pool & Fitness Ctr YO17 ... 215 D4
Derwent Rd
Harrogate HG1 ... 220 B3
Huttons Ambo YO17 ... 215 A2
Whitby YO21 ... 208 A7
York YO10 ... 231 D8
Derwent St 7 YO12 ... 212 E4
Derwent Terr YO17 ... 215 D3
Derwent Wlk YO32 ... 225 F5
Desmond Rd DL2 ... 4 C3
Desmond Way DL3 ... 3 C6
Deveron Way YO24 ... 230 B7
Devil's Arrows Standing Stones★ YO51 ... 141 B5
Devon Ct 8 DL9 ... 209 C1
Devon Pl YO10 ... 228 F3
Devonshire Ct YO30 ... 225 A1
Devonshire Dr YO12 ... 212 E7
Devonshire Gn HG4 ... 114 F1
Devonshire Pl
Harrogate HG1 ... 219 E3
12 Skipton BD23 ... 216 F4
Devonshire Rd DL1 ... 3 E6
Devonshire St 13 BD23 ... 217 A3
Devonshire Way HG1 ... 219 F4
Dewberry TS8 ... 7 B4
Dew La TS7 ... 7 D7
Dewsbury Ct YO1 ... 233 A1
Dewsbury Terr YO1 ... 233 A1
Dexta Way DL7 ... 210 C3
Dialstone The YO7 ... 211 A2
Diamond Ct TS18 ... 5 F7
Diamond Gr HG1 ... 220 C4
Diamond Pl HG1 ... 220 C4
Diamond Rd TS17 ... 6 B8
Diamond St YO31 ... 233 C4
Dibble Bridge Bank YO21 ... 28 F6
Dibdale Rd DL2 ... 4 A1
Dickens Cl 1 YO32 ... 225 F1
Dickens Dr 32 DL9 ... 41 A5
Dickens Rd YO17 ... 215 C6
Dickey La YO8 ... 197 D5
Dick La BD22 ... 187 B6
Dick Scot La DL11 ... 19 D7
Dicky Grounds La YO17 ... 121 D8
Didsbury Cl YO30 ... 224 E2
DIG★ YO1 ... 233 C2
Dijon Ave YO24 ... 227 C2
Dikehollin La DL8 ... 58 E2
Dike La HG3 ... 159 C8
Dikelands Cl 19 YO26 ... 165 F1
Dikelands La YO26 ... 165 F1
Dike Ray Cl YO32 ... 225 C7
Dikes La TS9 ... 8 C2
Diligence Way 2 TS16 ... 5 D5
Dilys Gr 5 YO26 ... 227 E4
Dimmingdale Rd TS12 ... 10 A3
Dinas Ct 12 TS17 ... 5 F4
Dinsdale Ave TS5 ... 6 E7
Dinsdale Cl 7 DL2 ... 4 C4
Dinsdale Cres DL1 ... 3 D5
Dinsdale Ct 6 DL2 ... 4 C4
Dinsdale Dr TS16 ... 5 E5
Dinsdale Sta DL2 ... 4 C4
Diomed Ct TS7 ... 7 B7
DISHFORTH ... 115 A4
Dishforth Airfield YO7 ... 115 A2
Dishforth Airfield Prim Sch YO7 ... 115 B2
Dishforth CE Prim Sch YO7 ... 114 F4
Dishforth Rd
Copt Hewick HG4 ... 114 B2
Sharow HG4 ... 214 F6
Disraeli Cl YO32 ... 225 E1
Dixon Ct YO8 ... 232 B6
Dixon Gdns YO8 ... 232 B6
Dixon Rd HG1 ... 219 D4
Dixons Bank TS8 ... 7 C5
Dixon St BD20 ... 187 F7
Dixons Yd YO1 ... 233 C2
Dixon Terr HG1 ... 219 D4
Dobella Ave DN14 ... 205 A1
Dob Park Rd LS21 ... 176 F4
Doctor Laithe 3 BD23 ... 134 D2
Doctor's Hill 2 LA2 ... 128 E8
Doctors La WF10 ... 200 D7
Doctor's La TS15 ... 25 C5
Dodder Carr Rd TS13 ... 10 F3
Dodford Rd TS8 ... 6 F5
Dodgson La
Lothersdale BD20 ... 186 D8
Thornton in Craven BB18 ... 172 C1
Dodgson Terr YO26 ... 227 D4
Dodmire Junior & Infant Sch DL1 ... 3 E4
Dodsworth Ave YO31 ... 228 E7
Doe Park La YO41 ... 169 B4
Doe Pk YO30 ... 224 F2
Dog Hill DL8 ... 60 E3
Dog Hill Brow BD24 ... 131 D6
Dog Kennel La YO18 ... 96 E5
Doherty Wlk YO24 ... 230 C8
Dolegate YO41 ... 168 F4
Dolly La DL7 ... 64 C8
Dollyth Howe★ YO17 ... 149 F6
Dolphin Ctr The DL3 ... 3 C5
Dolphin Way YO14 ... 100 F5
Donald Smith Ct DL8 ... 61 C5
Don Ave YO24 ... 230 E8
Doncaster Rd
Brayton YO8 ... 232 B3
Knottingley WF11 ... 201 E2
North Elmsall WF8 ... 206 A1
Dondeen Ave YO7 ... 211 C4
Don Pedro Ave WF6 ... 200 B1
Don Pedro Cl WF6 ... 200 B1
Doran Cl 45 YO14 ... 101 B3
Dorchester Rd LS24 ... 189 D5
Doriam Ave YO31 ... 225 F2
Doriam Dr YO31 ... 225 F2
Dorkings The TS9 ... 26 E5
Dorset Cl HG1 ... 219 A3
Dorset Cres HG1 ... 219 A3
Dorset Ct 5 DL9 ... 209 C1
Dorset Rd TS14 ... 8 E5
Dorset St BD23 ... 217 A3
Dorts Cres LS24 ... 190 C1
Dotcliffe Rd BB18 ... 186 A7
Doublegates Ave 6 HG4 ... 113 D2
Doublegates Cl 8 HG4 ... 113 D2
Doublegates Ct 10 HG4 ... 113 D2
Doublegates Gn 9 HG4 ... 113 D2
Doublegates Wlk 7 HG4 ... 113 D2
Doubting Castle★ YO21 ... 10 D1
Douglas Cl TS18 ... 5 F7
Douglas St 3 YO8 ... 232 C5
Douky Bottom Cave★ BD23 ... 133 F7
Dove Bank HG3 ... 139 E3
Dove Cl LS22 ... 180 B4
Dovecot Cl YO14 ... 100 E4
Dovecote Dr WF10 ... 200 F7
Dovecote Garth 5 YO41 ... 185 B2
Dove Cote Gdns DN14 ... 203 D2
Dovecote Mews YO7 ... 115 C7
Dovedale Ave YO12 ... 212 D8
Dovelands 14 BD20 ... 187 E6
Dove St YO23 ... 233 A1
Dove Way YO62 ... 94 C8
Dovey Ct 7 TS17 ... 5 F4
Dowber Ct YO7 ... 211 D3
Dowber Way YO7 ... 211 D4
Dower Chase YO19 ... 192 A6
Dower Pk YO19 ... 192 B6
Dowkell La LS23 ... 180 F1
Downdale Rd YO13 ... 54 B4
Downdinner Hill YO21 ... 208 C6
DOWNHOLME ... 39 D4
Downholme Rd DL9 ... 209 B1
Downland Cres WF11 ... 202 A1
Downside Rd TS5 ... 6 D8
Dracula Experience★ YO21 ... 208 D7
Dragon Ave HG1 ... 219 E3
Dragon Par HG1 ... 219 E3
Dragon Rd HG1 ... 219 E3
Dragon Terr HG1 ... 219 E3
Dragon View HG1 ... 219 E4
Drake Cl YO21 ... 208 B5
Drakes Cl
38 Colburn DL9 ... 41 A5
York YO32 ... 225 F5
Drake St 2 YO23 ... 233 B1
Drapers Croft YO23 ... 230 B4
DRAUGHTON ... 174 B7
DRAX ... 204 F5
Drax Castle Earthworks★ YO8 ... 204 F4
Drax Prim Sch YO8 ... 204 F5
Dreaken Fold 4 YO13 ... 99 A7
DREBLEY ... 157 D6
Drebley La BD23 ... 157 D6
Dresser Cl DL10 ... 209 C8
Driffield Rd YO25 ... 151 C4
Driffield Terr YO24 ... 228 A2
Drift La HG4 ... 138 B8
Drill Hall Bsns Ctr LS29 ... 218 C5
Dringfield Cl 2 YO24 ... 230 D8
DRINGHOUSES ... 230 E8
Dringhouses Prim Sch YO24 ... 230 F8
Dringhouses Sports Club YO24 ... 230 F8
Dringthorpe Rd YO24 ... 230 F7
Drive The
Harrogate HG1 ... 220 C5
7 High & Low Bishopside HG3 ... 137 C4
Kippax LS25 ... 194 D1
Middlesbrough TS17 ... 6 A6
Skipton BD23 ... 217 B5
12 Swillington LS26 ... 194 A1
Threshfield BD23 ... 134 B3
Drome Rd YO23 ... 230 C2
Drovers Ct 8 YO61 ... 143 C8
Drovers Way YO7 ... 211 D4
Drovers Wlk BD23 ... 154 B3
Druggist La 16 LS29 ... 174 F4
Druggon Rd DL9 ... 40 E3
Druids Mdw 8 YO51 ... 141 B5
Drummond View YO23 ... 231 B4
Drury Cl HG3 ... 222 F2
Drury La HG3 ... 222 F2
Drury St DL3 ... 3 C6
Dryden Cl HG1 ... 219 E7
Dryhurst Cl 9 DN6 ... 206 F2
Dubbing Garth La DL11 ... 37 B4
Dubb's La BD23 ... 81 C1
Duchy Ave
3 Harrogate HG2 ... 219 C1
11 Scalby YO13 ... 75 D5
Duchy Gr 4 HG2 ... 219 C1
Duchy Rd HG1 ... 219 B2
Duckett Cl DL10 ... 209 F8
Duckett St BD23 ... 217 A3
Duck Hill HG4 ... 214 C5
Duckhill La YO7 ... 115 A4
Duck La YO12 ... 125 A8
Duck St LA2 ... 128 A6
Duck Street La HG3 ... 136 D2
Dudley Ct YO31 ... 233 C4
Dudley Mews YO31 ... 233 C4
Dudley Rd DL1 ... 4 A5
Dudley St YO31 ... 233 C4
Dudley Wlk HG4 ... 214 B3
Duffield Cres 1 LS25 ... 195 F4
Dugdale La BD23 ... 152 C1
DUGGLEBY ... 149 B6
Duggleby Howe★ YO17 ... 149 C5
Dukes Ct 3 YO26 ... 227 D6
Dukes Hill LS29 ... 218 A6
Duke's La YO25 ... 126 A1
Duke St
6 Burton in Lonsdale LA6 ... 102 F3
High Bentham LA2 ... 129 A8
Settle BD24 ... 131 D2
Skipton BD23 ... 217 A4
14 Trawden Forest BB8 ... 186 A3
Dukesway TS17 ... 6 B5
Dukes Wharf YO23 ... 233 B1
Dulverton Cl
2 High Leven TS17 ... 6 A3
13 Pontefract WF8 ... 201 C2
Dulverton Rise WF8 ... 201 C2
Dulverton Way
5 Guisborough TS14 ... 8 F6
12 Pontefract WF8 ... 201 C2
Dumb Tom's La LA6 ... 103 B1
Dumfries Sq 8 DL9 ... 40 E4
Duna Way 6 YO62 ... 70 C1
Dunbar Ct LS26 ... 200 B6
Duncan Cl 6 HG1 ... 219 C5
Duncan St HG1 ... 219 C5
Dunce Mire Rd LS25 ... 202 A8

Duncombe Cl
2 Eastfield YO12 99 F7
Malton YO17 215 A3
Duncombe Dr
24 Pickering YO18 95 F7
Strensall YO32 167 B8
Duncombe La YO32 167 B8
Duncombe Park National Nature Reserve* YO62 92 E6
Duncombe Pl YO1 233 B3
Dundas Gdns YO21 208 B6
Dundas St
Richmond DL10 209 C7
York YO1 233 C2
Dunderdale Cres WF10 201 B5
Dunelm Wlk DL1 3 E7
Dunholm Ave 1 TS3 7 D8
DUNKESWICK 178 E2
Dunkeswick La LS17 178 D4
Dunn Gr 3 YO11 100 A7
DUNNINGTON 184 F7
Dunnington Dr YO8 196 E1
Dunnington Prim Sch YO19 184 E7
Dunniwood Cl 4 WF10 200 D3
Dunniwood Dr 3 WF10 200 D3
Dunroyal YO61 141 F8
Dunroyal Cl YO61 141 F8
DUNSLEY 12 F2
Dunsley Cres YO21 208 A8
Dunsley La YO21 32 A8
Dunslow Ct YO11 99 F6
Dunslow Rd YO11 99 F6
Dunsmore Cl TS8 6 C4
Dunwell Ave 2 YO12 212 B7
Durham Cl 18 YO8 198 F1
Durham La TS16 5 D5
Durham Lane Ind Pk TS16 5 D6
Durham Lane Prim Sch 13 TS16 5 D5
Durham Pl 5 YO12 213 A7
Durham St
Castleford WF10 200 F3
6 Scarborough YO12 212 F7
Durham Tees Valley Airport DL2 4 F4
Durham Way HG3 219 A5
Durlston Dr YO32 167 A7
Duxbury St 11 BB18 172 B1
Dyke Hall La LA10 78 A8
Dykelands Cl YO19 192 F7
Dykes La YO23 230 A1
Dyon La YO8 199 B3
Dyon Rd YO8 199 D7
Dyon Way YO8 199 D7
Dyson La DL11 18 G7

E

Eagle Pk TS8 7 C5
EAGLESCLIFFE 5 E5
Eaglescliffe Sta TS16 5 E6
EARBY 172 B1
Earby Springfield Prim Sch BB18 172 B1
Earfit La YO23 191 A8
Earl Crag View BD22 187 C6
Earl Edwin Dr DL10 209 D8
Earle St YO31 233 C4
Earlham St 10 BB18 172 B1
Earlsborough Terr YO30 233 A3
Earls Chase WF8 201 B2
Earls Court Rd TS8 6 F5
Earlsdon Ave TS5 6 D7
Earls View 3 BD20 187 E6
Earlsway TS17 6 C5
EARSWICK 226 A7
Earswick Chase YO32 225 F7
Earswick Village YO32 225 F7
EASBY
Richmond 209 F5
Stokesley 27 B7
Easby Abbey (rems of)* DL10 209 E5
Easby Ave TS5 6 F8
Easby Cl
4 Bedale DL8 63 B2
7 Ilkley LS29 175 C2
Easby Ct DL10 209 F5
Easby Dr LS29 175 C2
Easby La
Easby TS9 27 A8
Great Ayton TS9 7 F1
Easby Low Rd DL10 209 D7
EASINGTON 11 A8
EASINGWOLD 143 D8
Easingwold Prim Sch YO61 117 C1
Easingwold Sch YO61 143 C8
Eason Rd YO24 230 E8
Eason View YO24 230 E8
Easson Rd DL3 3 C5
East Acres WF11 201 F4
EAST APPLETON 41 D2
East Ave
8 Easingwold YO61 143 D8
13 Glusburn BD20 187 E7
21 Scalby YO13 75 D5
EAST AYTON 99 B8
East Ayton Prim Sch YO13 99 A8
East Bank 2 LS25 195 F4
EAST BARNBY 12 C3
East Barnby La YO21 12 C3
Eastbeck Cl YO17 124 E8
East Beck Ct LS21 176 C3
Eastborough YO11 213 B6
EASTBOURNE 3 E4
Eastbourne Comp Sch DL1 3 E5
Eastbourne Gdns TS3 7 C8
Eastbourne Gr YO31 228 F5
Eastbourne Rd DL1 3 D5
Eastbourne Sports Complex DL1 3 E5
East Brow Rd YO18 72 C4
EASTBURN 187 F7
Eastburn Junior & Infant Sch BD20 187 F7
Eastbury Cl TS17 6 B4
EASTBY 156 F1
Eastby Rd HG1 219 F6
East Carr 13 YO11 100 B6
East Castle St 6 BD23 217 A3
East Cl DL2 4 C7
East Cliff YO22 208 F7
East Comm La YO8 232 F4
EAST COMMON 232 E4
EAST COTTINGWITH 193 C5
EAST COWTON 22 F2
East Cowton CE Prim Sch DL7 22 E1
East Cres 19 YO21 208 D7
East Dene 11 BD20 174 C1
East Down WF10 201 A4
East End YO60 145 D5
Eastern Terr YO31 228 E6
Easter Pk TS17 6 C5
EASTERSIDE 7 A7
Easterside La YO62 67 F4
Easterside Prim Sch TS4 7 A7
Easterside Rd TS4 7 A7
EASTFIELD 100 A7
Eastfield
Amotherby YO17 121 B4
Hunmanby YO14 126 F8
Knaresborough HG5 221 D6
Eastfield Ave
Haxby YO32 225 C7
Norton YO17 215 E3
Richmond DL10 209 D8
Eastfield Cl LS24 189 F7
Eastfield Cres YO10 229 C2
Eastfield Ct YO10 229 C2
Eastfield Dr 14 WF8 201 C1
Eastfield Gr WF6 200 B2
Eastfield La
Dunnington YO19 184 F8
Kellington DN14 202 F4
Spennithorne DL8 61 A3
Thoralby DL8 58 E2
Eastfield Rd
Norton YO17 215 E3
Pickering YO18 96 A6
Eastfields TS9 26 C7
EAST GARFORTH 194 E4
East Garforth Prim Sch LS25 194 D4
East Garforth Sta LS25 194 D3
Eastgate
16 Helmsley YO62 92 F6
Pickering YO18 96 A6
3 Seamer YO12 99 D6
East Gate YO13 98 D6
East Grange Cl DL7 63 E7
EAST HARLSEY 44 E6
EAST HAUXWELL 61 D8
EAST HESLERTON 124 A7
East Heslerton La YO17 124 A8
Eastholme Dr YO30 224 E1
Easthorpe Dr YO26 224 A1
East Ings La YO18 95 F4
EAST KNAPTON 123 C6
East La
Ampleforth YO62 92 D1
Castle Bolton with East & West Bolton DL8 59 B6
Embsay BD23 217 D7
Yafforth DL7 43 C1
Eastland Ave YO24 227 E2
EAST LAYTON 20 C8
East Lea YO7 115 C7
East Lea View 21 YO11 100 B6
EAST LUTTON 150 C8
EAST MARTON 172 B6
East Moor Gdns YO19 231 F5
East Mount YO17 215 C4
Eastmount Rd DL1 3 D6
East Mount Rd YO24 233 A1
EAST NESS 94 B1
East Neville St 14 BD23 217 A3
EAST NEWTON 93 C2
Easton La YO21 29 D6
Easton Way
Catterick DL10 41 D5
29 Walkerville DL9 41 A5
East Par
Harrogate HG1 219 E2
Ilkley LS29 218 C4
East Parade YO31 228 F6
East Park Rd
Harrogate HG1 219 E2
15 Scalby YO13 75 D5
5 Spofforth HG3 179 E5
Eastpoint Rd DL1 3 F6
East Rd
Melsonby DL10 20 F7
Northallerton DL6 210 E4
Norton YO17 215 E3
EAST ROUNTON 24 E2
EAST ROW 13 A3
East Sandgate 14 YO11 213 B6
East Side 5 TS15 25 D5
East St
Gargrave BD23 155 D1
Gayles DL11 19 E6
Swinton YO17 121 B4
East Terr YO21 208 D7
East Terrace Cres YO21 208 D7
East View
Barton DL10 21 D8
7 Campsall DN6 206 E1
Kippax LS25 194 D1
10 Knottingley WF11 202 A2
Langthorpe YO51 141 A6
3 Low Bentham LA2 128 E8
Middleton St George DL2 4 D3
Northallerton DL6 210 E3
Sherburn in Elmet LS25 195 F3
South Kilvington YO7 211 B6
3 Trawden BB8 186 B1
East View Ct HG5 162 F3
Eastville Terr HG1 219 B6
Eastward Ave YO10 231 E7
Eastway YO11 100 A7
East Way
Whitby YO21 208 B7
York YO31 225 E2
Eastway Cl 2 YO62 70 C1
East Whitby Com Prim Sch YO22 208 F4
EAST WITTON 61 A1
East Witton Rd DL8 60 E2
Eaton Ct 7 YO24 230 B8
Eaton Rd LS29 218 A3
EAVESTONE 138 B7
Eavestone Gr HG3 219 A4
EBBERSTON 97 E5
Ebberston Hall* YO13 97 D6
Ebenezer Terr 9 HG1 219 D2
Ebor Cl DL10 21 A1
Ebor Ct
Northallerton DL7 210 D3
7 Selby YO8 232 C6
Ebor Ind Est YO31 233 C3
Ebor Mount LS25 194 D1
Ebor Prep Sch YO30 228 A7
Ebor Rise HG1 219 B2
Ebor St
Selby YO8 232 C5
York YO23 233 B1
Ebor Way YO26 224 A2
Ebsay Dr YO30 225 A1
Eccles Cl YO30 224 D2
Echo Hill YO22 32 B7
Eddison Way 1 TS8 6 F5
Eden Ave YO8 232 D3
Eden Camp Modern History Theme Mus* YO17 215 E8
Eden Cl
2 Hurworth-on-Tees DL2 3 D1
1 Hutton Rudby TS15 25 C4
York YO24 230 C7
Eden Cres DL1 3 C4
Eden Crest DL2 1 D7
Edendale WF10 200 F4
Edenhouse Rd YO17 215 E8
Eden La DL2 1 D8
Eden Park Rd 2 TS15 25 C4
Eden Pk DL2 1 D7
Eden Rd DL7 210 B2
Edens Way HG4 214 C2
Edgecombe Dr DL3 3 A6
Edge Dell YO12 99 E8
Edgehill Rd YO12 212 E2
Edge La
Grassington BD23 134 F3
Long Preston BD23 153 E6
Edgemoor Rd
Darlington DL1 3 E3
2 Firth Moor DL1 3 E4
Edgerton Cl LS24 189 D6
Edgerton Ct 11 LS24 189 D6
Edgerton Dr LS24 189 D6
Edgerton Garth LS24 189 D6
Edgware Rd YO10 228 E2
Edinburgh Dr DL3 3 A4
Edmondson's La BD23 172 C5
Edmondson St 17 BB18 171 D2
Edmund Wilson Swimming Pool YO24 227 D1
Edston Dr 9 TS14 8 F7
Edward Kitching Terr 14 TS9 8 A2
Edward Pease Way DL3 3 A7
Edwards Street Ind Est DL1 3 D6
Edward St
27 Earby BB18 172 A1
Pontefract WF6 200 A3
EGGBOROUGH 202 F2
EGGLESCLIFFE 5 E4
Egglescliffe CE Sch TS16 5 E4
Egglescliffe Sch TS16 5 D4
Eggleston View DL3 3 A6
Eggshell La LA2 130 C8
Eglington Ave TS14 8 F6
Egremont Cl 11 YO41 168 D2
EGTON 31 B5
Egton Ave TS7 7 C5
EGTON BRIDGE 31 A4
Egton CE Prim Sch YO21 31 B5
Egton Cliff YO21 31 A4
Egton La YO21 30 F5
Egton Sta YO21 31 A4
Eight Acre La HG4 113 A5
Eighth Ave YO31 228 F5
El Alamein Rd 5 DL9 209 C1
Elbolton Cave* BD23 156 E8
Elbow Terr 4 YO22 208 E6
Elderberry View 17 WF10 200 D3
Elder Gr 33 YO32 166 E5
Elder Rd DL7 210 D4
Elder's St YO11 213 A6
Eldmire La YO7 115 D6
Eldon St YO31 233 C4
Eldon Terr YO31 233 C4
ELDROTH 130 E4
Eldroth Rd LA2 130 C5
Eldwick Cl YO30 224 F2
Eleanor Dr HG2 220 C1
Eleanor Rd HG2 220 C1
Electric Ave HG1 219 B5
Elgar Cl YO31 225 E1
Elgin Rd TS17 6 B6
Elgin St 16 YO21 208 D6
Elizabethan Ct 4 WF8 201 C1
Elizabeth Ct
7 Selby YO8 232 B6
Sherburn in Elmet LS25 195 E4
Elizabeth Dr WF10 201 B4
Elland Ct 12 DL1 3 F6
Ellarfield La LS25 195 F5
Ellen Gr HG1 220 C4
Ellenthorpe La YO51 141 D6
ELLERBECK 44 F3
Ellerbeck Ct TS9 26 D6
Ellerbeck Way
Great & Little Broughton TS9 26 D6
Middlesbrough TS7 7 D8
Whitby YO22 208 E4
ELLERBURN 96 E7
Ellerburn Bank Nature Reserve* YO18 72 F1
Ellerburn Rd YO18 96 F7
Ellerby Bank TS13 11 F4
Ellerby La TS13 11 F5
Ellerclose Rd 23 DL8 60 D5
Eller Gates YO21 30 C6
Eller Gill La BD23 172 D4
Ellerholme La DL11 38 F5
Ellerington Cl 5 LA6 103 D3
Ellerker La LS14 188 A3
Ellerker Rd LS14 188 A3
Eller Mews 3 BD23 216 E3
Ellers La DL8 59 A2
Ellers Rd BD20 187 E6
ELLERTON
193 C2
Catterick 41 F4
Ellerton Priory (rems of)* DL11 39 A4
Ellerton Rd TS18 5 D8
ELLINGSTRING 85 D6
Elliot Ct YO10 231 D7
Elliot St BD23 216 F4
Elliott St BD20 174 B1
Ellis Ct HG1 219 B2
Ellis Gdns 6 YO13 75 D5
Ellis La LS25 194 C5
Ellison Ave 32 YO12 75 D5
Ellwood Cotts BD24 131 D4
Ellwood Ct YO10 228 D2
Elma Gr 3 YO30 224 E2
Elm Ave
Kippax LS25 194 C2
Northallerton DL6 210 F5
Elm Avenue 10 YO32 191 C7
Elm Cl
Barnoldswick BB18 171 D1
10 Filey YO14 101 B4
Hipswell DL9 209 F1
Northallerton DL6 210 F5
Elm Ct DL6 210 E5
Elm Dr TS7 7 B6
Elm End 9 YO32 166 E5
Elmet Dr LS15 194 C8
Elmete Ave LS25 195 F4
Elmete Rd WF10 201 B5
Elmet Rd LS15 194 C7
Elmfield Ave YO31 228 F8
Elmfield Rd
3 Glusburn BD20 187 F8
Hurworth DL2 3 D1
Hurworth-on-Tees DL2 22 D8
Elmfield Terr YO31 228 F7
Elm Gn 7 YO62 92 F7
Elm Gr
Robin Hood's Bay YO22 33 D4
Sherburn YO17 124 D8
Thornaby TS17 6 B8
4 Whitby YO21 208 B6
York YO31 225 F2
Elmlands Gr YO31 228 F8
Elmpark Vale YO31 229 A8
Elmpark View YO31 229 A8
Elmpark Way YO31 229 A8
Elm Pl WF11 201 F2
Elm Rd
34 Glusburn BD20 187 E7
Guisborough TS14 8 F7
Harrogate HG1 219 E5
Ripon HG4 214 B2
9 Scarborough YO12 212 E4
3 Topcliffe YO7 89 B1
Elms Cl 2 YO19 191 F1
Elmslac Cl 1 YO62 92 F6
Elmslac Rd 3 YO62 92 F7
Elm St YO8 232 D6
Elms The YO32 167 D2
Elm Tree Ave
Harrogate HG1 219 D5
9 Poppleton YO26 165 F1
Elmtree Gdns 3 YO24 227 C3
Elm Tree Rise HG3 140 B5
Elm Tree Sq BD23 217 D8
Elm View YO18 96 A6
Elmville Ave YO12 212 E6
Elm Wlk 6 DL10 41 D5
Elmwood Ave LS15 194 B8
Elmwood Chase LS15 194 B8
Elmwood Cl 6 TS9 26 C8
Elmwood La LS15 194 B8
Elmwood Rd TS16 5 E6
Elmwood St 4 HG1 219 E4
Elphin Bridge La YO61 117 B6
Elslack La BD23 172 C4
Elston Cl YO30 228 A8
Elston Pl YO8 232 C6
Eltham Cres TS17 6 C6
ELTON 5 C8
Elton La HG3 160 E6
Elton Par DL3 3 D5
Elton Rd DL3 3 B5
ELVINGTON 185 B2
Elvington CE Prim Sch YO41 185 B3
Elvington Ind Est YO41 185 A3
Elvington La YO19 184 E5
Elvington Pk YO41 185 A3
Elvington Terr YO10 228 E4
Elwick Ave TS5 6 E7
Elwick Gr YO10 229 C4
Elwick La YO26 164 B7
Ely Cl HG3 219 A5
Embleton Dr 1 YO30 224 F1
Embleton Rd LS26 200 B4
EMBSAY 217 D8
Embsay & Bolton Abbey Steam Rly* BD23 217 E7
Embsay CE Prim Sch BD23 217 D8
Embsay Sta BD23 217 D7
Emerald Ct HG1 220 C4
Emerald St YO31 233 C4
Emerson Ave TS5 6 F8
Emerson Cl 2 DL6 25 D1
Emerson Rd DL2 3 E1
Emery Cl DL2 3 E1
Emgate 2 DL8 63 A3
Emily Mews YO10 228 E4
Emley Moor Rd DL1 3 E4
Emley View LS25 194 C2
Emmerson St 2 YO31 228 E5
Emmet La HG3 160 C5
Emmott Ct BB8 186 C3
Emmott La BB8 186 B4
Emsworth Dr TS16 5 D5
Enclosure Gdns 1 YO10 229 B1
Endcliff Cres YO12 212 D8
Endeavour Wharf 6 YO21 208 D6
Endfields Rd 1 YO10 231 E8
Endican La DL7 65 D3
Endsleigh Dr TS5 6 D8
Enfield Chase TS14 8 F5
Enfield Cl 4 DL9 40 E4
Enfield Cres 1 YO24 228 A3
Engelhart Cl YO8 232 A2
Engine Shed La BD23 216 D3
Engine Shed Lane Ind Est BD23 216 D3
England La WF11 201 F2
England Lane Junior & Infant Sch WF11 201 F2
English Martyrs RC Prim Sch YO24 227 F3
Ennerdale Ave YO31 229 B5
Enter La LA6 103 D3
ENTERPEN 25 C4
Enterpen TS15 25 C4
Enterprise Way
Bradleys Both BD20 173 D4
Pickering YO18 96 A6
Sherburn in Elmet LS25 196 B4
Whitby YO22 32 F8
EPPLEBY 1 E4
Eppleby Forcett CE Prim Sch DL11 1 D4
Epsom Ct 11 DL1 3 F6
Eridge Rd TS14 8 F6
Ermysted's Gram Sch BD23 216 F4
Ermysted St 4 BD23 217 A4
ERYHOLME 23 A7
Eryholme La DL2 22 F7
ESCRICK 192 B5
Escrick CE Prim Sch YO19 192 A5
Escrick Ct YO19 192 B5
Escrick Park Gdns YO19 192 B5
Escrick St YO10 233 C1
Escrick Terr YO10 233 C1
Esher Ave TS6 7 E8
Eshington La DL8 58 F2
ESHTON 155 D3
Eshton Rd BD23 155 D2
Eskdale Ave
Normanton WF6 200 A2
York YO10 229 C3
Eskdale Cl
5 Pontefract WF6 200 A2
Sleights YO22 32 A5
Eskdale Croft WF6 200 A2
Eskdale Ct 12 WF6 200 A2
Eskdale Rd YO22 208 F3
Eskdale Sch YO22 208 E3
Eskdaleside YO22 31 F5
Esk Dr YO26 227 B8
Eskew Cres LA2 128 E7
Eskew La LA2 128 E7
Eskitt Hill YO12 212 D4
Esk Rd DL1 3 D3

Esplanade
Harrogate HG2 219 C2
Scarborough YO11 213 A4
Whitby YO21 208 D7
York YO26 233 A2
Esplanade Cres YO11 213 B2
Esplanade Ct YO30 233 A3
Esplanade Gdns YO11 213 A4
Esplanade Rd YO11 213 A3
Esplande La BB18 171 C1
Estell La YO13 74 C5
Estill Cl 2 YO11 100 B6
Estoril Road S DL1 3 F4
Ethel Cres HG5 221 C6
Ethel St 12 BB18 171 E1
Etive Pl YO24 230 B7
Eton Dr 7 YO32 166 D5
Eton Rd TS5 6 E8
Ettersgill Cl TS16 5 D5
Ettersgill Dr DL3 3 A5
Ettington Ave TS3 7 B8
Etty Ave YO10 229 A4
Etty Cl 24 YO41 168 D2
Euclid Ave HG1 219 B5
Eva Ave YO30 224 D2
Evaglades Sch LA2 128 E8
Evelyn Cres YO30 228 B7
Evelyn Ct 5 HG3 161 B2
Evelyn Dr YO12 212 D4
Evergreen Way 1 YO8 197 D1
Evergreen Wlk 2 TS4 6 F8
Everingham Rd TS15 5 D2
EVERLEY 74 F4
Eversley Ave LS25 195 F3
Eversley Ct LS25 195 F4
Eversley Garth Cres
LS25 195 F4
Eversley Mount LS25 195 F3
Evesham Rd TS3 7 B8
Evron Ctr YO14 101 B3
Ewart St YO12 212 E3
Ewden Cl 16 YO14 101 A3
Ewelands Hill YO7 90 C7
Ewe Leys La YO7 66 A5
Exchange St 8 WF6 200 A1
EXELBY 63 D1
Exelby Cl DL8 63 D1
Exelby La DL7 63 D3
Exeter Cres 10 HG3 161 B3
Exeter Dr DL1 3 F7
Exford Cl 8 TS17 6 A3
Exhibition Sq YO1 233 B3
Express Way WF6 200 A3
Eyre Cl
Brayton YO8 232 A2
Selby YO8 232 A2

F

Faber Cl YO23 230 B3
Faber St YO31 228 E5
FACEBY 25 F2
Faceby Rd TS9 26 A2
FADMOOR 69 F4
Fadmoor Bank YO62 69 E6
Fadmoor La YO62 69 F4
FAIRBURN 201 D7
Fairburn Com Sch WF11 201 D6
Fairburn Dr LS25 194 D3
Fairburn St WF10 200 E4
Fairfax 15 YO41 168 D2
Fairfax Ave
Harrogate HG2 220 B2
North Featherstone WF7 200 E1
Selby YO8 232 B4
Fairfax Cl
2 Ampleforth YO62 92 C1
Bolton Percy YO23 190 D4
Gilling East YO62 118 F8
Fairfax Cres YO26 181 C7
Fairfax Croft YO23 230 B2
Fairfax Dr 19 WF8 201 B1
Fairfax House* YO1 233 C2
Fairfax Rd DL2 4 D4
Fairfax St
1 Scarborough YO12 212 E5
10 Skipton BD23 217 A3
York YO1 233 B1
Fairfax Wlk 3 HG2 220 B3
Fairfield
Fairburn WF11 201 D7
Thirsk YO7 211 C4
Fairfield Ave TS7 7 D7
Fairfield Cl 16 LS25 195 F4
Fairfield Cres YO12 212 B8
Fairfield La LS25 202 A6
Fairfield Link LS25 195 F4
Fairfield Rd
Staithes TS13 13 K2
Stokesley TS9 26 B7
Tadcaster LS24 189 E6
Fairfields Dr YO30 224 B5
Fairfield St DL3 3 C6
Fairfield Way
Richmond DL10 209 B8
9 Tadcaster LS24 189 E6
Whitby YO22 208 F3
Fairgrey Cl HG4 214 B6
Fair Head La YO22 31 D4
Fairheath Rd LA2 128 E5
Fairholme La DL7 64 A4
Fairmead Ct YO22 208 E4
Fairmead Way YO22 208 E4
Fairview TS21 5 A7
Fair View WF10 201 A5
Fairview Gdns DL10 209 C8
Fairway
Normanton South WF6 200 B1
4 Scalby YO12 75 E5
Selby YO8 232 A4
York YO30 228 A8
Fairway App WF6 200 B1
Fairway Ave WF6 200 B1
Fairway Cl
8 Normanton South WF6 200 B1
15 Sherburn in Elmet LS25 195 F4
Fairway Dr
Normanton South WF6 200 B1
18 Poppleton YO26 165 F1
Fairway Gdns 4 WF6 200 B1
Fairway Mdws 9 WF6 200 B1
Fairways Ave HG2 220 E3
Fairways Cl HG2 220 E3
Fairways Dr HG2 220 D3
Fairways The LS24 189 E5
Fairway The
Darlington DL1 3 E5
Middlesbrough TS8 7 C5
Northallerton DL7 210 C3
8 North Featherstone WF7 200 E1
Sherburn in Elmet LS25 195 F4
Fairwood Pk TS8 7 C5
Fairy Hill La WF8 201 B3
Fairy La YO18 71 C3
Falcon Ave 7 YO12 99 E6
Falconberg Way TS15 5 D2
Falcon Cl
10 Haxby YO32 166 F5
1 Scotton DL9 40 F2
17 Settle BD24 131 D2
Falcon Dr WF10 200 E3
Falconers Rd YO11 213 A5
Falconers Sq 10 YO11 213 A5
Falconer St 1 YO24 227 F3
Falcon Gdns 20 BD24 131 D2
Falcon Terr 11 YO21 208 D6
Falcon Way TS14 8 D6
Falcon Wlk TS15 6 C2
Falkland Rd 2 DL9 40 F5
Falkland St YO1 233 B1
Falling Foss (Waterfall)*
YO22 32 C2
Fall La
Pannal HG3 222 B2
Thornthwaite with Padside
HG3 159 A6
Fallow Field 1 BD23 217 B5
Falmer Rd DL1 3 D4
Falmouth Ave WF6 200 A2
Falmouth Cres 20 WF6 200 A2
Falmouth Dr DL3 3 C8
Falmouth Rd WF6 200 A2
FALSGRAVE 212 D3
Falsgrave Cres YO30 228 B7
Falsgrave Mews 6 YO12 212 E5
Falsgrave Rd YO12 212 F5
Fanacurt Rd TS14 8 D6
Fancy Bank TS14 9 B6
Fane Gr TS5 6 E7
FANGDALE BECK 47 A1
Fanny La
Knayton YO7 65 F2
Stutton with Hazlewood
LS24 189 D4
Farfield YO26 227 C6
Farfield Ave HG5 221 C4
Farfield La YO19 184 E8
Farfield Mount 2 HG5 221 C4
Farfields Cl TS21 4 F6
Far La
Hutton Buscel YO13 98 F8
Kettlewell with Starbotton
BD23 108 A3
FARLINGTON 144 F6
Farmanby Cl 12 YO18 96 D5
Farmbank Rd TS7 7 E7
Farm Cl
Walton LS23 181 A2
Whitby YO21 208 A7
Farmcote Ct TS8 6 E5
Farm Croft BD23 216 F1
Far Mead Croft 3 LS29 176 C1
Farmers Way YO23 230 B3
Farm Garth TS9 8 A2
Farm La TS17 6 A5
Farmlands Rd 1 YO24 230 D8
Farmside Mews TS8 7 C4
Farmstead Rise YO32 225 D7
Farm Way YO8 232 B7
Farnborough Ct 10 DL2 4 C4
Farndale Ave
Northallerton DL7 210 C2
York YO10 229 D4
Farndale Cl 1 YO32 166 F5
Farndale Cres DL3 3 B6
Farndale Dr TS14 8 D6
Farndale Rd HG5 221 D6
Farndale St YO10 228 D2
FARNHAM 162 D7
Farnham La HG5 162 D7
FARNHILL 173 E1
FARNLEY 177 B2
Farnley CE Prim Sch
LS21 177 B3
Farnley Hall* LS21 177 B2
Farnley La LS21 177 B2
Farnley Pk LS21 177 C2
Farrar St YO10 228 E3
Farriers Croft 2 YO23 230 B3
Farriers Ct 16 LS22 180 C3
Farrow House Sch 19
YO11 212 F5
Farside Garth YO13 75 D6
Farside Rd YO13 99 A7
Farthingale Way TS8 6 E4
Favell Ave WF6 200 A1
Faven Field Rd YO7 211 D4
FAVERDALE 3 B8
Faverdale DL3 3 B7
Faverdale Ind Est DL3 3 B7
Faverdale N DL3 3 B7
Faverdale Rd DL3 3 B7
Faverdale W DL3 3 B7
Faversham Cl TS8 6 F4
Favordale Rd BB8 186 A3
Fawcett Ave TS8 6 E4
Fawcett St YO10 233 C1
FAWDINGTON 115 F3
Fawdington Rd YO61 115 F2
Fawkes Dr YO26 227 C4
FEARBY 85 F4
Fearby Rd
Fearby HG4 85 F4
Masham HG4 86 A4
7 Stockton-on-Tees TS18 5 D8
Fearnhead TS8 7 C5
Feasegate YO1 233 B2
Featherbeck Cl 8 LA6 103 D3
Featherbed La
Bilton-in-Ainsty with Bickerton
LS24 181 C3
Ellerbeck DL6 44 E4
Feather Bed La YO21 32 A7
Federation St 12 BB18 171 D1
Feeding Pasture La
YO60 147 B7
FEETHAM 37 C5
Feetham Ave DL1 3 F7
FEIZOR 131 B6
Felbrigg La TS17 6 A4
Feldom La DL11 19 E1
FELIXKIRK 90 C7
Felixkirk Rd YO7 211 F4
Felixstowe Dr 10 DL9 40 E4
Fellbrook Ave YO26 227 B4
Fell La
Cracoe BD23 156 B7
Winton CA17 14 C8
Fell Rd LA6 77 A4
Fell View BD23 217 E8
Fell View Sq 4 BD23 134 E2
Fenby Ave DL1 3 E4
Fenby Gdns YO12 212 C4
Fence Dike La DL7 63 C7
Fennel Ct LS26 200 B6
Fennel Gr HG4 214 B6
Fenton Ave BB18 171 E2
Fenton Cl 10 YO11 100 B7
Fenton La
Malton YO17 215 C8
Sherburn in Elmet LS25 196 A5
Fenton St
Boosbeck TS12 9 D7
38 Burley in Warfedale
LS29 176 C1
FENWICK 207 D3
Fenwick Cl 1 YO11 100 B6
Fenwick Common La
DN6 207 D2
Fenwick La DN6 207 B1
Fenwick's La YO10 231 D7
Fenwick St YO23 228 C2
Ferguson Cl DL7 210 C3
Ferguson Way YO32 225 F1
Fern Bank Ave BB18 171 D2
Fern Cl YO32 226 A4
Ferndale Rd YO8 232 C4
Fern Gdns 1 LS29 218 A3
Fernie Rd TS14 8 F5
Fernlea Cl YO8 232 D4
Fernley Green Cl 6
WF11 202 A2
Fern St YO31 233 C4
Ferns The YO19 191 D1
Fernway YO10 229 C3
Fernwood TS8 7 A4
Fernwood Cl 9 DL6 43 F3
FERRENSBY 162 F7
FERRYBRIDGE 201 D3
Ferrybridge By-pass
WF11 201 E3
Ferrybridge Infant Sch
WF11 201 E3
Ferrybridge Rd
Castleford WF10 200 F4
Pontefract WF8 201 C1
Ferry Cl 11 YO8 198 F1
Ferry Farm Cl 2 YO19 191 D8
Ferry La
Bishopthorpe YO23 231 B4
Bubwith YO8 199 C5
Snaith & Cowick DN14 204 C1
Thorganby YO19 193 B5
Ferrymans Wlk YO26 165 F2
Fetter La YO1 233 B2
Feversham Cres 4
YO31 228 C7
Feversham Dr 16 YO62 70 B1
Feversham Rd YO62 92 F7
Fewster Way YO10 233 C1
FEWSTON 159 F1
FEWSTON BENTS 159 F1
Fewston Cl 11 YO14 101 A3
Fewston Cres HG1 219 B4
Fewston Dr 9 YO30 224 F1
Field Ave YO8 197 B1
Field Cl YO21 208 A7
Field Cl Rd 16 YO13 75 D5
Field Dr
1 Pickering YO18 95 F6
Field Dr *continued*
Tadcaster LS24 189 F7
Field Gr 7 DL9 40 E3
Field Head YO41 185 F6
Fieldhead Cl 12 WF8 201 C1
Fieldhead Dr
Barwick in Elmet LS15 194 C8
15 Glusburn BD20 187 E7
Fieldhead Paddock LS23 188 E8
Field House Rd 2 YO21 208 C7
Fielding's Yd DL10 209 A7
Field La
Aberford LS25 194 F8
Burniston YO13 75 D8
Gowdall DN14 207 F8
Hambleton YO8 196 F1
Hensall DN14 203 D2
Heslington YO10 229 C2
Newby & Scalby YO13 75 E5
Rawcliffe DN14 205 A1
Wistow YO8 197 C7
Field Lane Sports Club
YO8 197 B1
Field Rd YO8 203 A5
Fieldside YO12 212 D7
Fieldside Ct LS24 196 B8
Fieldstead Cres YO12 212 B8
Field View
Norton YO17 215 E2
York YO31 228 C7
Fieldway
Harrogate HG1 219 F7
Ilkley LS29 218 E4
Fieldway Cl HG1 219 F7
Fifth Ave
24 Colburn DL9 41 A5
York YO31 228 F4
FILEY 101 C3
Filey Ave HG4 214 A6
Filey CE Infant Sch YO14 101 B3
Filey Cl 12 DL9 40 E4
Filey Dams Nature Reserve*
YO14 101 A3
Filey Junior Sch YO14 101 B3
Filey Mus* YO14 101 B3
Filey Rd
Folkton YO11 100 A2
Hunmanby YO14 127 A8
Scarborough YO11 213 A2
Filey Sch YO14 101 A3
Filey Sta YO14 101 B3
Filey Terr YO30 228 C7
Finchley Ct TS5 6 E6
Finden Gdns HG3 160 F5
Fine Garth Cl LS23 188 E6
FINGHALL 61 D4
Finghall Sta DL8 61 E5
Finkills Way DL7 210 C6
Finkle Cl 4 HG4 214 C5
Finkle Hill LS25 195 F5
Finkle Keep 14 HG5 221 A6
Finkle St
Hensall DN14 203 D2
12 Knaresborough HG5 221 A6
Malham BD23 133 A1
3 Malton YO17 215 C4
8 Richmond DL10 209 C6
5 Ripon HG4 214 C5
Selby YO8 232 C5
Sheriff Hutton YO60 145 C5
Thirsk YO7 211 C3
Finsbury Ave YO23 228 C1
Finsbury St YO23 228 C1
Firbank Cl 9 YO32 167 A7
Firbeck Rd LS23 188 E6
Firbeck Wlk TS17 6 B6
FIRBY
Bedale 63 A1
Westow 147 A5
Firby La HG4 214 B5
Firby Rd
Bedale DL8 63 A2
Richmond DL10 209 B8
Fir Gr TS17 6 B8
Fir Heath Cl 5 YO24 227 C1
Firs Ave
Harrogate HG2 222 E6
Ripon HG4 214 D4
Firs Cl HG2 222 E6
Firs Cres HG2 222 E5
Firs Dr HG2 222 E6
Firs Gate HG2 222 E5
Firs Gr HG2 222 E5
Firs Pk HG2 222 E6
Firs Rd HG2 222 E6
First Ave
23 Colburn DL9 41 A5
Harrogate HG2 220 C3
Menwith with Darley HG3 160 A4
Sherburn in Elmet LS25 196 A4
9 Wetherby LS22 180 C3
York YO31 228 F6
First Common La YO8 197 D4
Firs View HG2 222 E5
Firthfields LS25 194 D4
Firthland Rd YO18 95 F7
FIRTH MOOR 3 F4
Firthmoor Cres DL1 3 E4
Firthmoor Prim Sch DL1 3 F4
Firth St BD23 217 A2
Firtree Ave TS6 7 E8
Firtree Cl
4 Earswick YO32 225 F7
York YO24 227 E3
Fir Tree Cl
Hilton TS15 6 C2
Thorpe Willoughby YO8 197 B2
Firtree Cres LS24 189 D5
Fir Tree Ct LS24 195 F7
Fir Tree Dr
Filey YO14 101 B4
11 Norton DN6 206 E2
Fir Tree La YO8 197 B2
Fir Trees The YO8 197 B2
Fir Tree View LS26 200 C6
Fir Tree Way YO8 197 B2
Firville Ave WF6 200 A1
Firwood Whin 5 YO31 225 F3
Fishbeck La BD20 174 D2
Fishbourne Gr 2 TS17 5 F6
Fishburn Rd 4 YO21 208 D5
Fishergate
3 Boroughbridge YO51 141 B5
Knottingley WF11 201 E3
17 Ripon HG4 214 C5
York YO10 233 C1
Fishergate Prim Sch
YO10 233 C1
Fisher Gdns HG5 221 A5
Fishergreen HG4 214 D4
Fisher Green La HG4 214 F4
Fisher Row 14 HG4 86 C3
Fishers Ct HG4 214 C5
Fishers Garth 10 YO18 95 F6
Fisher St 6 HG5 221 B5
FISHPOOL 177 C2
Fitzalan Rd 18 DL8 63 A2
Fitzjohn Cl YO17 215 C6
Fitzwilliam Dr
Darlington DL1 3 D7
Malton YO17 215 A4
Five Hills La DL10 21 D5
Five Lane Ends HG4 86 D5
Flake La TS13 12 A3
Flamingo Land Theme Pk &
Zoo* YO17 95 D2
FLASBY 155 E3
Flashley Carr La DN6 207 F1
Flask La DL8 87 C3
Flass La WF10 200 E3
Flat Cliffs YO14 101 C1
Flat La
Bolton-on-Swale DL10 41 E6
Hellifield BD23 153 F3
Flats Bank DL11 19 F6
Flats La
Barwick in Elmet LS15 194 B7
Thirkleby High & Low with
Osgodby YO7 90 D1
West Witton DL8 59 D4
Flatts La
Eston & South Bank TS6 7 F7
Welburn YO62 94 A7
Wombleton YO62 93 F6
Flavian Gr YO30 227 F8
FLAWITH 142 E4
FLAXBY 163 B4
Flaxdale Cl 4 HG5 221 D6
Flaxley Ct YO8 232 B5
Flaxley Rd YO8 232 A7
Flaxman Ave YO10 229 A4
Flaxman Croft YO23 230 B3
Flaxmill Cl DL11 18 G7
FLAXTON 145 F1
Flaxton Rd YO32 167 B7
Flaxton Terr HG3 222 E3
Fleck Way TS17 6 B5
Fleet Bank La YO61 143 C1
Fleetham La
Cundall with Leckby YO7 115 C4
Kirkby Fleetham with Fencote
DL7 63 C8
Fleet La
Barmby on the Marsh
DN14 205 A7
Mickletown LS26 200 A6
Tockwith YO26 181 C7
FLEETS 156 A7
Fleets La BD23 156 A6
Fleming Ave YO31 228 E5
Fletcher Ct 14 YO32 166 E5
Fletcher's Croft YO23 230 C3
Fletton Rd YO17 215 F4
Flintmill La LS23 180 E2
Flints Terr DL10 209 C7
FLIXTON 99 F2
Flixton Carr La YO11 99 F4
Flock Leys 24 YO13 75 D5
Flora Ave DL3 3 B5
Florence Ct 12 YO51 141 B5
Florence Gr YO30 224 D2
Florence Rd HG2 219 B1
Florentine's Ct HG4 214 C5
Florin Dr HG5 221 C7
Florin Wlk HG1 219 B2
Flotmanby La YO14 100 D2
Flow Edge DL8 57 F7
Flower Ct 19 YO11 100 B6
Flower Garth
40 Filey YO14 101 B3
Scarborough YO12 212 C6
Flowergate 12 YO21 208 D7
Flywheel St DL10 41 F7
Fog La YO42 193 E4
Fold La BD22 187 B6
Foldshaw La HG3 159 C8
Fold The
Filey YO14 101 B1
Thornton in Craven BD23 172 A3
Fold Wlk YO32 167 B8
Folks Cl 13 YO32 166 F5
FOLKTON 100 B2
FOLLIFOOT 223 F5

Follifoot CE Prim Sch
HG3 223 F4
Follifoot Rd HG3 222 F3
Folliott Ward Cl YO17 215 B5
Folly La LS23 188 E5
Folly View 2 LS23 188 E5
Fontenay Rd DL10 209 D8
Fonteyn Ct TS8 6 F5
Forbes Ct 42 DL9 41 A5
Forbidden Cnr The★ DL8 60 B1
FORCETT 1 D3
Forcett Cl
East Layton DL11 20 C8
Middlesbrough TS5 6 E7
Forcett Gdns DL11 1 D3
Forcett La DL10 20 D5
Ford Dike La DL2 1 D8
Fordgreen HG4 214 E4
Fordlands YO8 197 B2
Fordlands Cres YO19 231 E5
Fordlands Rd YO19 231 E6
FORDON 126 A6
Fordon La
Willerby YO12 125 E7
Wold Newton YO25 126 A6
Fordon Pl TS4 7 A8
Fordyce Rd TS8 6 E4
FOREDALE 131 C8
Fore La
Cowesby YO7 66 B4
West Tanfield DL8 87 D3
Whorlton TS9 25 F1
Foreshore Rd YO11 213 A5
FOREST 42 B7
Forest Ave HG2 220 D3
Forest Cl
3 Harrogate HG2 220 D3
27 Haxby YO32 166 E5
Forest Cres HG2 220 D4
Forest Ct 11 HG3 137 C4
Forest Dr
Colburn DL9 41 A5
Dishforth YO7 115 A4
Middlesbrough TS7 7 D7
Foresters Ct 5 YO12 75 F5
Foresters Wlk YO41 168 C1
Forester's Wlk YO24 227 B1
Forestgate YO32 225 C7
Forest Gdns HG2 220 D3
Forest Gr
Barlow YO8 204 D7
Harrogate HG2 220 D3
York YO31 228 F6
Forest Grange Cl 2
HG2 220 D4
Forest La
Alne YO61 143 B5
Fulford YO19 184 A2
Harrogate HG2 220 D3
Kirklevington TS15 24 D8
Strensall YO32 167 A8
Forest Lane Head HG2 220 D5
FOREST MOOR 220 F3
Forest Moor Dr HG5 220 F3
Forest Moor Rd HG5 220 E3
Forest Mount 4 HG2 220 D3
Forest of Galtres Prim Sch
YO30 165 F5
Forest Rd
Appletreewick HG3 157 F8
Northallerton DL6 210 E5
Pickering YO18 96 A6
Forest Rise HG2 220 D3
Forest Sch The HG5 221 C6
Forest Way
Harrogate HG2 220 D3
York YO31 228 F6
Forge Cl
Huntington YO32 226 A2
Wheldrake YO19 193 A7
Forge Gn HG3 223 F4
Forge Hill La WF11 201 F3
Forge La
Deighton YO19 192 A7
Kirkby Fleetham with Fencote
DL7 42 C1
Tollerton YO61 143 A3
Forge Valley Wood National
Nature Reserve★ YO12 75 A1
Forge Way DL1 3 D6
Forkers La YO17 122 D2
Forrester's Cl 3 DN6 206 E2
Forth St YO26 227 F6
Fort's Bldgs 5 BB18 186 A7
Fortune Cl HG5 220 E7
Fortune Hill HG5 220 E8
Fossards Cl 8 LS23 188 E5
Foss Ave LS22 180 B4
Foss Bank YO31 233 C3
Foss Ct YO31 225 E1
Fossdale Cl 5 HG5 221 D6
Fossel Island Retail Park
YO31 228 E5
Fosse Way LS25 194 D3
Foss Field La YO23 191 B8
Foss Garth YO41 185 F5
Fossgate YO1 233 C2
Foss Islands Rd YO31 233 C3
Foss La YO22 32 C2
Fossland View 4 YO32 167 A7
Fossway
Stamford Bridge YO41 168 D1
York YO31 228 D7
Foss Way 30 DL9 41 A5
Foss Wlk YO26 227 B8
Foster Ave
Normanton South WF6 200 A1
Silsden BD20 174 B1
Foster Cl 31 LS29 176 C1
Fostergate YO8 197 A8
Foster Gate YO8 232 D4
Foster Rd 4 BB18 171 D2
Foster Wlk LS25 195 F4
FOSTON 146 B4
Foston CE Prim Sch
YO60 146 A3
Foston Gr 4 YO31 228 F8
Foston La YO60 146 B2
Fothergill Way 3 YO51 141 B4
Fother Ingay Dr DL1 3 F8
Fothill La YO13 98 E6
Foulbridge La YO13 97 F3
Foulds Rd BB8 186 A1
Foulgate Nook La HG4 112 B6
FOUL GREEN 9 E1
Foundry La 5 WF11 202 A2
Fountains Abbey & Studley
Royal★ HG4 139 B7
Fountains Ave
Boston Spa LS23 188 E8
Harrogate HG1 219 F6
Ingleby TS17 6 B5
Fountains CE Prim Sch
HG4 138 D8
Fountains Cl
1 Guisborough TS14 8 F6
1 Whitby YO21 208 C6
Fountains Ct YO7 90 E5
Fountains Dr TS5 6 E8
Fountains Gate HG4 112 F1
Fountains La HG4 139 B7
Fountains Mill★ HG4 139 B7
Fountains Pl DL6 210 E6
Fountains Rd DL6 210 E6
Fountain St TS14 8 F6
Fountains View DL3 3 A6
Fountains Way
Knaresborough HG5 221 C4
Morton-on-Swale DL7 64 A7
Fountayne Rd 13 YO14 126 F8
Fountayne St YO31 228 C7
Fouracre Dr 11 YO22 32 A6
Four Lane Ends
Burythorpe YO16 147 D4
Lawkland BD24 130 F3
Four Lanes Ends BB7 152 C1
Four Riggs DL3 3 C5
Fourth Ave
26 Colburn DL9 41 A5
York YO31 228 E5
Foxberry Ave TS5 6 D6
Foxbridge Way WF6 200 C2
Fox Cl 6 DL2 22 D8
Foxcliff WF11 201 E5
Fox Covert YO31 225 F2
Fox Covert Cl 15 DL8 63 B3
Fox Covert Rd WF8 206 C1
Foxcroft 3 YO32 225 C7
Fox Ct HG1 219 E4
Foxdale Ave YO8 197 B1
Foxe Howe TS8 7 A6
Fox Furniture Workshop★
YO7 116 F7
Fox Garth
5 Brafferton YO61 115 F1
Poppleton YO26 224 A3
Fox Glade YO41 168 C2
Foxglove Cl
2 Killinghall HG3 161 B3
Northallerton DL7 210 C1
Foxglove Covert Nature
Reserve★ DL9 40 B4
Foxglove Ct 19 DL9 41 A5
Foxglove Fold 19 WF10 200 D3
Foxhill La YO8 232 A3
Fox Hill La YO8 232 A3
FOXHOLES 125 D3
Foxholme La HG4 86 B3
Foxhunter Ave 7 DL9 40 F4
Fox La
Chapel Haddlesey YO8 203 C5
Hambleton LS25 202 D8
Thornton-le-Dale YO18 96 C3
Thorpe Willoughby YO8 197 B1
Fox Terr WF8 201 C1
Foxthorn Paddock YO10 229 D3
FOXTON 44 E3
Foxton Cl YO24 230 C8
Foxton La DL6 44 E2
FOXUP 106 C7
Foxwood La 3 YO24 227 C1
Frances Rd DL10 209 C7
Frances St YO10 228 D1
Francis Ct 7 YO8 197 B2
Francis Dr 27 DL9 41 A5
Frankfield Mews TS9 8 D1
Frank La YO26 164 F4
Franklin Mount HG1 219 D4
Franklin Rd HG1 219 D3
Franklin Sq HG1 219 D4
Franklin St 7 YO12 212 F6
Frank's La YO26 164 A5
Frank St 9 BB18 171 E1
Franks Terr 2 YO22 208 E6
Fraser Rd 8 TS18 5 E8
Frazer Ct YO30 227 E8
Frazer Theatre★ HG5 221 B6
Frederick St 23 BB18 171 D2
Frederic St YO30 233 A3
Freebrough Rd TS12 10 A4
Freeholder's Wood &
Riddings Field Nature
Reserve★ DL8 58 F3
Freehold La YO17 215 D8
Freely Fields 7 LS23 188 E5
Freely La LS23 188 E5
Freemans Way
Leeming DL7 63 C4
New Thirsk YO7 211 A2
Wetherby LS22 180 D3
Freeman's Way HG3 223 D8
Freemantle Pl HG4 214 C6
Freers Yd YO17 215 D3
Freeston Bsns & Enterprise
Coll The WF6 200 A1
Freeston Ct 16 WF6 200 A2
Freeston Dr 18 WF6 200 A2
Freeway Dr WF10 200 B3
FREMINGTON 38 D6
Frenchgate DL10 209 C6
French Rd DL9 209 C2
French St HG1 219 F4
Friarage 20 YO11 213 B6
Friarage Ave DL6 210 D5
Friarage Gdns DL6 210 D5
Friarage Hospl DL6 210 E5
Friarage Mount DL6 210 D5
Friarage Prim Sch YO11 213 B6
Friarage St DL6 210 D5
Friarage Terr DL6 210 D5
Friargate
Scarborough YO11 213 A6
York YO1 233 B2
Friargate Theatre YO1 233 B2
Friars Cl YO19 184 D7
Friar's Gdns 10 YO11 213 A6
Friars Hill YO62 95 A8
Friars Mdw YO8 232 C8
Friars Pardon DL2 3 E1
Friar's Way 11 YO11 213 A6
Friar's Wlk YO31 228 E8
Friary Com Hospl DL10 209 B7
Friendship Ct 2 YO8 232 C6
Frith Mews 4 YO8 232 C6
Frobisher Dr
37 Colburn DL9 41 A5
5 Whitby YO21 208 C5
Frogmire Cl 4 HG5 221 B7
Frogmire Dr HG5 221 B7
Frogmire Rd HG5 221 B7
Front Nook 2 DL8 58 F1
Front St
Appleton Wiske DL6 24 B3
6 Bramham LS23 188 E5
Burton Fleming YO25 126 E3
Burton Leonard HG3 140 A2
Castleford WF10 200 F3
Grosmont YO22 31 C4
Langtoft YO25 151 C5
Lastingham YO62 70 E5
Naburn YO19 191 D8
Thirsk YO7 211 C1
Topcliffe YO7 115 C7
Wold Newton YO25 126 A4
York YO24 227 C3
Front The DL2 4 D3
Fryer Cres DL1 3 F7
Fryston Comm La LS25 202 A8
Fryston La WF11 201 C3
Fryston Rd WF10 201 B5
FRYTON 120 A6
Fryton La YO62 120 A7
Fryup Cres TS14 8 E5
Fulbeck Rd TS3 7 D8
FULFORD 231 E7
Fulford Cross YO10 228 D1
Fulfordgate YO10 231 E7
Fulford Ind Est YO10 228 C1
Fulford La 8 YO11 212 F3
Fulford Mews
7 Scarborough YO11 212 F3
York YO10 231 E6
Fulford Pk YO10 231 D7
Fulford Rd
Scarborough YO11 212 F3
York YO10 231 D8
Fulford Sch YO10 231 E7
Fulham La DN14 206 E7
Fuller-Good Rd 17 DL10 41 E4
Fullicar La DL6 43 F3
FULL SUTTON 169 A2
Fulmar Head TS14 8 D6
Fulthorpe Ave DL3 3 A5
Fulthorpe Gr DL3 3 A5
Fulwith Ave HG2 222 E5
Fulwith Cl HG2 222 F5
Fulwith Dr HG2 222 F5
Fulwith Gate HG2 222 F5
Fulwith Gr HG2 222 F5
Fulwith Mill La HG2 222 F5
Fulwith Rd HG2 222 F5
Fummerber La LA2 130 C5
Furlong Rd 23 YO41 168 D2
Furlongs Ave YO17 215 F3
Furnace La HG4 87 A1
Furness Dr
Bentham LA2 129 A8
York YO30 224 E1
Furnessford Rd LA2 128 D6
Furnwood 2 YO32 225 D7
Furrows The 16 YO11 100 B7
Fushetts La LA2 129 A8
Fusion Ct LS25 194 D4
Futurist Theatre★ YO11 213 A6
Fylingdales Ave 6 YO30 224 E1
Fylingdales CE Prim Sch
YO22 33 C4
Fyling Rd YO21 208 A6
FYLINGTHORPE 33 B3

G

Gable Pk YO23 182 C6
Gables Cl 8 DN14 202 D4
Gables Ct YO7 115 A4
Gables The
15 Hurworth-on-Tees DL2 3 E1
Knaresborough HG5 221 A8
Middlesbrough TS7 7 B6
Scriven HG5 162 C5
GAINFORD 1 D8
Gainford CE Prim Sch DL2 1 C7
Gainforth Wath Rd YO13 53 F5
Gainsborough Cl YO32 167 B8
Gainsborough Ct BD23 216 E4
Gaits DL8 56 C4
Gale Bank DL8 60 B3
Gale Farm Ct 6 YO24 227 C3
Gale Garth YO61 142 F4
Gale Gate YO26 142 A1
Gale La
Beadlam YO62 93 D6
Stainburn LS21 177 F3
Thorganby YO19 192 F4
York YO24 227 C2
Gale Rd YO61 142 F4
Gale The YO19 191 D4
Gallabar La YO51 141 E1
Galley Hill Prim Sch 3
TS14 8 D6
Galligap La YO10 229 C4
Gallogate La LS17 178 C1
Gallops The
Norton YO17 215 E2
York YO24 230 B8
Gallowfields Rd DL10 209 B7
Gallowfields Trad Est
DL10 209 B8
Gallowgate DL10 209 C7
Gallowheads La YO18 95 A6
Gallows Hill
Castleford WF10 201 B4
Ripon HG4 214 C2
Gallows Hill Dr HG4 214 C2
Gallows Hill La YO13 98 D5
Gallows Hill Pk HG4 214 D2
Galmanhoe La YO30 233 A3
GALPHAY 112 F3
Galphay La HG4 113 A3
Galtres Ave YO31 229 B7
Galtres Dr 7 YO61 143 D8
Galtres Gr YO30 227 F7
Galtres Rd
Northallerton DL6 210 E6
York YO31 229 B7
GAMMERSGILL 83 C5
GANTHORPE 120 A1
GANTON 125 A8
Ganton Cl 1 YO21 208 C5
Ganton Hill YO12 125 B7
Ganton Pl YO24 230 E7
Ganton Rd YO25 125 C4
Gant Wlk 7 YO8 232 D5
Gaol The YO61 144 E7
Gap Cres YO14 127 D7
Gap Rd YO14 127 D8
Garbett Way 1 YO23 231 B3
Garburn Gr 3 YO30 224 E1
Garbutt Gr YO26 227 D5
Garbutt La 1 DL6 25 D1
Garbutts La TS15 25 B5
Garbutt Wood Nature
Reserve★ YO7 91 A6
Garden Cl
3 Glusburn BD20 187 D7
Sherburn in Elmet LS25 195 E4
Garden Ct
Selby YO8 232 B6
York YO26 227 C5
Gardeners Cl 8 YO23 230 B3
Gardeners Row YO25 150 B3
Garden Flats La YO19 184 E7
Garden House Cl LS26 200 B6
Garden La
11 Knottingley WF11 202 A3
Sherburn in Elmet LS25 195 E4
Garden Pl YO1 233 C2
Gardens Rd BD23 155 D2
Garden St
Castleford WF10 200 E3
13 Normanton South WF6 200 A1
York YO31 233 B4
Gardens The 15 YO14 101 B4
Garden Terr
10 Carleton in Craven
BD23 173 B4
Lothersdale BD20 186 F8
Garden Village LS25 195 A3
Garden Village The
YO32 226 A8
Garden Way
3 Pickering YO18 95 F6
York YO26 227 C5
Garfield Rd YO12 212 E6
Garfield Terr YO26 227 F5
GARFORTH 194 C4
Garforth Com Coll LS25 194 C3
Garforth Squash & L Ctr
LS25 194 D3
Garforth Sta LS25 194 C4
GARGRAVE 155 D1
Gargrave CE Prim Sch
BD23 155 C1
Gargrave House Gdn
BD23 155 C1
Gargrave Rd
Broughton BD23 172 D6
Gargrave Rd *continued*
Skipton BD23 216 D4
Gargrave Sta BD23 172 C8
Garibaldi St 1 YO11 213 B6
Garlands Hill 3 YO11 212 F3
Garland St 2 YO26 227 E4
Garlands The
Scarborough YO11 212 F3
York YO30 228 A8
Garman Carr La YO8 197 D6
Garnet Brow La LA2 130 D2
Garnet La 1 LS24 189 D5
Garnet Rd TS17 6 B8
Garnet Terr YO26 227 E5
Garrick Cl YO8 232 B1
GARRISTON 61 B7
Garroway Way YO10 184 A4
Garrowby Hill YO41 169 F3
Garrowby Rd YO42 169 F2
Garrowby St YO41 169 E3
Garrowby View 5 YO41 168 D2
Garrow Hill YO10 228 F2
Garrow Hill Ave YO10 229 A3
Garrs End La BD23 134 E3
Garrs La 10 BD23 134 E3
Garsbeck Way TS7 7 D8
Garsdale Fold 8 LS22 180 A1
Garsdale Rd HG5 221 D6
Garsdale Sta LA10 55 A6
Gars End LA2 128 A6
Gars The LA2 128 A6
Garth Ave
Collingham LS22 188 A8
4 North Duffield YO8 199 A7
Garth Cl
11 Catterick DL10 41 D5
Hambleton YO8 196 E1
6 Wistow YO8 197 D6
Garth Ct YO32 226 A4
Garth Dr YO8 196 E1
Garth End
Collingham LS22 188 A8
Kirk Deighton LS22 180 B5
York YO32 225 F4
Garth End Rd YO13 99 A7
Garthends La 3 YO8 198 F1
Garth Fold BD20 173 C1
Garth La
Hambleton YO8 196 E1
Snainton YO13 98 A5
Garth Mdws 13 DL10 41 D5
Garth Mill 1 DN14 202 D4
Garthorne Ave DL3 3 A5
Garth Rd
4 Hambleton YO8 196 E1
York YO32 225 F4
Garths End 20 YO32 166 F5
Garth's End YO10 231 E8
Garthside DL10 41 F6
Garths La DL8 58 E3
Garth Terr YO30 228 B7
Garth The
8 Collingham LS22 188 A8
Mount Pleasant TS8 7 A4
Sinnington YO62 95 A8
4 Stokesley TS9 26 C7
Tunstall DL10 41 B2
Whitby YO21 208 B7
Garth View YO8 196 E1
Garthway 4 YO32 225 D3
Garth Way Arc DL7 210 D5
Garton La 22 YO14 126 F8
Gascoigne Ave LS15 194 B7
Gascoigne Cres HG1 219 F4
Gascoigne Ct LS15 194 B7
Gascoigne Rd LS15 194 B7
Gascoigne View LS15 194 B7
Gascoigne Wlk YO23 233 B1
Gascoigne Wood Mine
LS25 196 C2
Gas House La 9 LA2 129 A8
Gaskell Cl DL6 210 C6
Gas St BD23 216 F3
Gas Works La LS23 188 F8
Gate Bridge Rd HG4 112 D2
Gatecliff Brow BD23 155 F4
GATEFORTH 203 A7
Gateforth Ct YO8 196 F1
Gateforth La YO8 196 F1
Gateforth Mews YO8 202 F8
Gateforth New Rd YO8 203 A8
Gate Grains La 23 YO61 143 C8
Gatehead La YO42 193 D7
GATE HELMSLEY 168 B2
Gatehowe Rd YO17 170 A7
Gate La
Borrowby YO7 65 E4
Low Coniscliffe & Merrybent
DL2 2 E4
Gateland Cl YO32 225 C7
Gateland Field La DN14 205 B6
Gatela Rd YO13 53 D2
GATENBY 64 A2
Gatenby Garth YO61 143 B8
Gatering La 45 BD22 187 E7
Gatesgarth Cl YO12 212 B8
Gate Way YO21 29 B4
Gatherley Rd DL10 41 C7
Gatherley Road Ind Est
DL10 41 C7
GAUBER 78 F1
Gauber Rd LA6 78 F1
Gaudy La DL8 56 C3
Gauk St WF11 201 D6
Gaul Rd DL9 209 E1
Gault Cl YO17 215 F4
Gaw La BD23 174 C8
Gawtersike La YO62 94 B8

Gay La LS24 196 C7
Gaylands La BB18 172 B1
GAYLE 56 D4
Gayle La DL8 56 C4
Gayle Moor Cl 9 TS17 6 A3
GAYLES 19 E6
Gay Mdws YO32 167 D2
Gayton Sands TS5 6 D6
Gazelle Way YO7 115 B1
Geecroft La LS22 179 D3
Geldof Rd YO32 225 F1
General La YO42 193 E6
Geneva Cres DL1 3 D4
Geneva La DL1 3 D4
Geneva Rd DL1 3 E5
Gennell La YO60 145 E1
Gentian Glade HG3 219 A4
George Cartwright Cl YO17 215 E4
George Cayley Dr YO30 225 A3
George Ct YO31 233 C3
George Hudson St YO1 233 B2
George Long Mews 19 YO61 143 D8
George Pindar Com Sports Coll YO11 100 A6
George St
15 Addingham LS29 174 F4
Carleton BD23 173 B4
19 Earby BB18 172 A1
3 Scarborough YO12 213 A6
4 Selby YO8 232 D6
17 Skipton BD23 217 A3
Snaith DN14 204 C1
12 Whitby YO21 208 D6
7 Wistow YO8 197 D6
York YO1 233 C1
George Terr 1 YO8 198 B4
Georgian Theatre Royal* DL10 209 C6
Gerard Ave YO31 229 A5
Germain Rd YO8 232 E4
Germany La YO10 231 E6
GERRICK 10 C3
Gerrick La TS12 10 C3
Ghyll Brow YO21 30 D4
Ghyll La BB18 171 E2
Ghyll Mdws BB18 171 E2
Ghyll Mews LS29 218 A3
Ghyll Royd Prep Sch LS29 176 B2
Ghyll The DL10 209 D8
Ghyll Way BD23 173 D4
Ghyll Wood 28 LS29 175 C2
Gibbet Hill YO61 117 C5
Gibb St BD22 187 B6
Gibside La BD20 173 C1
Gibson Cl 2 YO8 196 F1
Gibson La LS25 194 D1
GIGGLESWICK 131 C2
Giggleswick Prim Sch BD24 131 C3
Giggleswick Sch BD24 131 C3
Giggleswick Sta BD24 131 C1
Gilcar St WF6 200 B2
Gilcar Way WF10 200 B3
Gildercliffe YO12 212 C7
Giles Ave YO31 229 A5
GILL 187 A6
GILLAMOOR 70 A5
Gillamoor Ave YO31 229 B5
Gillamoor Bank YO62 70 A5
Gillamoor CE Prim Sch YO62 70 A4
Gillamoor Rd YO62 70 A2
Gillann St 15 WF11 202 A2
Gill Bank Rd LS29 218 A6
Gill Cl 6 LS29 174 E4
Gill Croft YO61 117 C1
Gillgate Rd HG4 112 B4
Gilling Castle* YO62 118 E7
Gilling Cres DL1 3 E4
GILLING EAST 118 F8
Gilling Rd
Aske DL10 20 E1
Richmond DL10 209 D7
Gillings Ct 4 YO7 211 B3
Gilling Way YO17 215 C5
GILLING WEST 20 E4
Gillingwood Cl DL10 209 C8
Gillingwood Rd YO30 224 F3
Gill La
Cowling BD22 187 A6
Kearby with Netherby LS22 179 C1
Nesfield with Langbar LS29 175 B4
Rosedale West Side YO18 49 E2
Gills Fold 8 BD23 134 E2
Gills The LS21 177 A1
Gillygate YO31 233 B3
Gillylees YO12 212 C5
Gilmonby Rd TS3 7 B8
Gilsforth Hill YO26 164 A3
Gilsforth La YO26 164 A3
Gilstead Way LS29 218 B5
Gilsthwaite La YO26 164 A3
Gilwern Ct 23 TS17 5 F4
Gindhill La LS17 178 A4
Ginnel Mews The BD23 217 A4
Ginnel The 1 HG1 219 D2
Gipsey Cnr YO19 184 E3
Girrick Cl 3 TS8 6 E5
GIRSBY 23 D7
Girton Wlk DL1 3 D7
Girvan Cl YO24 230 B7
Gisburn Rd
Barnoldswick BB18 171 D2
Gisburn Rd *continued*
Hellifield BD23 154 B3
Gisburn Road Com Prim Sch BB18 171 D1
Gisburn St
Barnoldswick BB18 171 D2
Skipton BD23 216 D3
Givendale Gr 3 YO10 229 C4
Givendale Rd YO12 212 D8
Glade Rd YO19 192 B2
Glade The
Escrick YO19 192 A6
Scarborough YO11 212 F3
York YO31 229 B7
Gladstone La YO12 212 E5
Gladstone Rd YO12 212 E5
Gladstone Road Infant Sch YO12 212 E5
Gladstone Road Junior Sch YO12 212 E5
Gladstone St
Acomb YO24 227 D3
Darlington DL3 3 C5
Harrogate HG2 222 E7
Normanton South WF6 200 B2
Scarborough YO12 212 E6
14 Skipton BD23 216 F4
York YO24 227 D3
York YO31 233 C4
Gladstone Terr 10 HG4 214 C4
Glaisby Ct YO31 229 A6
GLAISDALE 30 D4
Glaisdale YO24 230 D7
Glaisdale Ave TS5 6 F8
Glaisdale Ct DL3 3 B5
Glaisdale Hall La YO21 30 C4
Glaisdale Prim Sch YO21 30 D4
Glaisdale Rd
Eaglescliffe TS15 5 F3
Knapton YO26 182 F7
Glaisdale Sta YO21 30 E4
Glasgow Dr 3 DL9 209 C1
GLASS HOUGHTON 201 A3
Glasshoughton Infant Sch WF10 200 F4
Glasshoughton Sta WF10 200 F2
GLASSHOUSES 137 D4
Glasshouses Prim Sch HG3 137 D3
Glaves Cl YO13 99 B7
Glebe Ave
Full Sutton YO41 169 A2
Harrogate HG2 219 C2
York YO26 227 D5
Glebe Cl
15 Bedale DL8 63 A2
Bolton Percy YO23 190 D4
Kirby Hill YO51 141 B7
Manfield DL2 2 C4
3 Strensall YO32 167 B7
Glebe Ct DL10 21 A7
Glebe Field Dr 11 LS22 180 B3
Glebe Garth 8 YO8 198 B5
Glebe Gdns TS13 11 A8
Glebe La DL2 2 C4
Glebe Mdw HG4 214 F6
Glebe Rd
Campsall DN6 206 E1
Darlington DL1 3 D8
Harrogate HG2 219 C1
Stokesley TS9 26 C7
Glebe Sq DL7 63 C5
Glebe St WF10 200 E4
Glebe Way 26 YO32 166 E5
Gledhill Dr 10 YO21 208 D5
Gledstone Rd BD23 171 E5
Gledstone View 8 BB18 171 D2
Glen Ave YO31 228 E5
Glen Cl
Newby & Scalby YO13 75 C5
York YO10 231 E6
Glencoe Cl LS25 200 C8
Glencoe Croft LS25 200 C8
Glencoe Gdns LS25 200 C8
Glencoe St 1 YO30 228 B7
Glencoe Terr LS25 200 C8
Glendale
Guisborough TS14 8 D5
9 Hutton Rudby TS15 25 C5
Glendale Rd TS5 6 F8
Glendowne Terr HG1 219 B5
Gleneagles Ct
28 Castleford WF6 200 B1
Spofforth HG3 179 E5
Gleneagles Dr 29 WF6 200 B1
Gleneagles Rd
Darlington DL1 3 F8
Middlesbrough TS4 7 A8
North Featherstone WF7 200 E1
Glen Esk Rd YO22 208 C3
Glenfield Ave LS22 180 C2
Glenmore Dr YO17 215 E2
Glenn Cres TS7 7 B5
Glen Rd YO31 228 E5
Glenridding YO24 230 D7
Glenside YO12 212 E7
Globe St
10 Harrogate HG2 220 C3
9 Scarborough YO11 213 B6
Gloucester Ave 2 BD20 174 B1
GLUSBURN 187 D8
Glusburn Com Prim Sch 37 BD20 187 E7
Glyder Ct 6 TS17 5 F4
Glynndale Dr YO12 212 A8
Glynwed Ct 2 BD23 216 E3
GOATHLAND 51 E8
Goathland Gr TS14 8 E5
Goathland Prim Sch YO22 51 C8
Goathland Sta YO22 51 D8
Goat La BD24 131 F7
Goats Rd DL11 18 D2
Godfrey Way 12 DL10 41 E4
Godley Cl DL9 209 C2
Godwinsway 18 YO41 168 D2
Goker La YO51 141 E1
Golden Acres DL7 22 E2
Golden Butts Rd LS29 218 C4
Goldenfields YO13 75 C5
Golden Gr YO22 208 E2
Golden Lion Bank 25 YO21 208 D7
Golden Lion Yd YO7 211 C3
Goldhill La YO7 90 D6
GOLDSBOROUGH
Knaresborough 163 A2
Whitby 12 D5
Goldsborough CE Prim Sch HG5 162 F3
Goldsborough Ct HG5 163 A3
Goldsborough La YO21 12 C4
Gold Thread La 5 YO8 197 B8
Golf Links Ave 5 LS24 189 D5
Golf Links Cres 4 LS24 189 D5
Golf Links Ct LS24 189 E5
GOLLINGLITH FOOT 85 B3
Goodall Cl 31 BB18 172 A1
Goodenber Cres 2 LA2 129 A8
Goodenber Rd LA2 129 A8
Good Hope Cl WF6 200 B2
Goodramgate YO1 233 B2
Goodrick Cl HG2 222 B5
Goodricke Way 5 YO10 229 A1
Goods Yd The YO8 232 D5
Goodwood Ave LS25 194 C1
Goodwood Cl
Sadberge DL2 4 B8
Scalby YO12 212 B6
Goodwood Gr YO24 227 F1
Goodwood Rd 3 DL9 40 E3
Goody Cross LS26 194 B1
Goody Cross La LS26 194 A1
Goosecroft Gdns DL6 210 D5
Goosecroft La
East Harlsey DL6 44 D6
Northallerton DL6 210 D5
Goose Green Cl 2 DL9 40 E3
Goose Green La BB8 186 A1
Goose La YO61 144 C1
Gooselands BD24 153 C6
Gooselands Hill BD23 107 D2
Goose Mire La YO12 99 C6
Goosepastures TS16 5 E3
Goose Track La YO60 145 C3
Gordale Cl
3 Barnoldswick BB18 171 D1
Skirethorns BD23 134 B3
Gordale La BD23 133 A2
Gordale Mount HG5 221 C6
Gordon Ave HG1 219 E6
Gordon Cres DL10 209 D8
Gordon St
28 Glusburn BD20 187 E7
Ilkley LS29 218 C4
Scarborough YO12 212 E5
York YO10 228 E3
Gordon Terr BD20 173 C1
Gore La DN14 207 B5
Gore Sands TS5 6 D6
Gorman Cl 9 TS17 5 F4
Gormire Ave 2 YO31 225 E2
Gormire Cl YO7 211 D3
Gorse Cl YO8 232 C2
Gorse Hill 1 YO19 184 F7
Gorse La LS25 195 D3
Gorse Paddock YO32 225 F2
Goschen St 8 BD23 217 A3
Goslipgate 9 YO18 95 F6
Gosside Gr 31 WF6 200 B1
Gough Rd DL9 40 D4
Gouldings Cl YO11 100 A7
GOULTON 25 E3
Goulton La TS9 25 E3
Gouthwaith Cl YO30 224 F2
Government House Rd YO30 228 A6
Gowans The YO61 144 C3
GOWDALL 204 A1
Gowdall Broach DN14 207 E8
Gowdall La
Pollington DN14 207 F7
Snaith & Cowick DN14 204 B1
Gowdall Rd DN14 203 E2
Gower Rd
Aske DL10 20 D1
Richmond DL10 209 C8
York YO24 230 E8
Gowland La YO13 54 B2
GOWTHORPE 169 C1
Gowthorpe YO8 232 C5
Gracious St
Huby YO61 144 A4
7 Knaresborough HG5 221 B5
GRAFTON 141 D2
Grafton Cl TS14 8 F6
Grafton La YO51 141 C3
Grafton St WF10 200 F3
Graham Cl YO11 213 B7
Graham Cres YO12 212 C5
Graham Dr WF10 201 A4
Graham Rd HG4 113 D3
Graham Sch YO12 212 B5
Grainary The* YO13 53 E3
Grainbeck La HG3 219 A7
Grainger Cl 6 TS16 5 D5
Grainger Row HG4 214 D5
Grainger St DL1 3 D4
Grains La BD23 154 E8
Grammar Sch La
Northallerton DL6 210 D3
Yarm TS15 5 E3
Grampian Cl 4 YO32 225 F5
Granary Ct
13 Pickering YO18 96 A6
York YO1 233 B3
Granby Pk HG1 219 F3
Granby Rd HG1 219 F3
Granby Sport & Play Development Ctr HG1 220 A4
Grandage La BD22 187 A7
Grand Opera House York* YO1 233 B2
GRANGE 57 D5
Grange Ave
Aiskew DL7 63 C4
Filey YO14 101 B3
Garforth LS25 194 C3
Harrogate HG1 219 D5
3 Hurworth-on-Tees DL2 3 D1
Ilkley LS29 218 D4
Scarborough YO12 212 E4
Spofforth HG3 179 E6
Tadcaster LS24 189 F6
Thorp Arch LS23 181 A2
3 Willerby YO12 99 D2
Grange Cl
10 Bedale DL8 63 A2
Bishop Thornton HG3 138 F1
Dishforth YO7 114 F4
Full Sutton YO41 169 A2
Ilkley LS29 218 D4
Lebberston YO11 100 D5
Northallerton DL7 210 C3
Skelton YO30 224 B5
Grange Close E DL7 63 E7
Grange Cres
Middlesbrough TS7 7 B5
10 Tadcaster LS24 189 E6
Grange Ct YO12 99 D7
Grange Dr TS9 26 C7
Grange Est LS29 218 D4
Grange Farm Cl YO8 198 B5
Grangefield Ave 32 LS29 176 C1
Grange Garth
3 Linton-on-Ouse YO30 164 F7
10 Wistow YO8 197 D6
York YO10 228 D2
Grange La
1 Dacre HG3 137 F1
Rufforth YO26 227 A2
Scackleton YO62 119 C3
Stonebeck Down HG3 137 A6
Sutton BD22 187 F2
Grangemoor Cl 5 DL1 3 E4
Grange Park Cl WF10 200 D7
Grange Park Rd HG4 214 B2
Granger Ave YO26 227 C4
Grange Rd
19 Bedale DL8 63 A2
Brompton-on-Swale DL10 41 B6
Burley in Warfedale LS29 176 C1
8 Campsall DN6 206 E1
Castleford WF10 201 B5
Colburn DL9 40 F5
Darlington DL1 3 C4
Farnhill BD20 173 E1
Tadcaster LS24 189 E6
Thornaby TS17 6 B8
Grangeside DL3 3 B4
Grange St YO10 228 D2
Grange Terr HG4 114 B8
Grange The
Kirby Hill YO51 141 A7
Leeming DL7 63 D4
Thirsk YO7 211 B2
Grange View
11 Otley LS21 176 F1
Towton LS24 189 E2
Granholme Cl 44 BD22 187 E7
Grant Cl DL6 45 B4
Grantham Dr YO26 227 E4
Grantley Cl HG3 219 A4
Grantley Dr HG3 219 A4
Grantley Pl HG3 219 A4
Grantly 3 DL3 3 B6
Grants Ave YO10 231 E8
Granville Rd
21 Filey YO14 101 B3
4 Harrogate HG1 219 D3
Scarborough YO11 213 A3
Granville Sq 3 YO11 213 A3
Granville St
20 Normanton South WF6 200 A1
Skipton BD23 216 E4
Granville Terr 4 YO10 228 E3
Grape La
Whitby YO22 208 E7
York YO1 233 B3
Grasmere Ave LS22 180 A3
Grasmere Cres HG2 222 C7
Grasmere Dr
6 High Bentham LA2 129 A8
York YO10 229 B4
Grasmere Gr 5 YO30 224 F1
Grass Croft TS21 5 A7
Grassfield Cl 8 HG3 137 B4
Grassgill La DL8 59 E3
Grassholme YO24 230 C7
Grassholme Way TS16 5 D5
GRASSINGTON 134 E3
Grassington Ave DL7 210 C2
Grassington CE Prim Sch BD23 134 E2
Grassington Rd
Middlesbrough TS4 7 A8
Skipton BD23 216 F5
Grass Wood La BD23 134 C3
Grass Wood Nature Reserve* BD23 134 C4
Gravelhill La DN14 206 F7
Gravel Hole La
Sowerby YO7 89 E3
Thirsk YO7 211 C1
Gravelly Hill La LS17 178 A2
Gray La YO62 70 D1
Grayshon Dr YO26 227 B5
Grays Rd YO62 69 F6
Gray St
13 Whitby YO21 208 D6
York YO23 233 A1
Graystonber La LA2 130 E7
Graystone Ct 12 YO18 96 A6
Grayston Plain La HG3 160 F4
Great Auk TS14 8 D6
Great Ave DL10 209 A7
GREAT AYTON 7 F2
Great Ayton Sta TS9 8 B1
GREAT BARUGH 95 A1
GREAT BROUGHTON 26 E5
GREAT BURDON 3 F8
GREAT BUSBY 26 C4
Great Cl YO8 197 B8
Great Close La BD24 153 A6
GREAT CRAKEHALL 62 E4
Great Croft Cl 9 BB18 171 D2
GREAT EDSTONE 94 C7
GREAT FENCOTE 63 C8
GREAT HABTON 121 C7
GREAT HECK 207 D7
GREAT LANGTON 42 D3
Great Moor Rd YO13 74 D2
Great North Rd
5 Fairburn WF11 201 D6
Ledsham LS25 195 C1
Micklefield LS25 194 F5
Great North Way YO26 227 B8
GREAT OUSEBURN 164 B8
Great Ouseburn Prim Sch YO26 164 B8
Great Pasture LS29 176 C1
GREAT PRESTON 200 C8
Great Preston CE Prim Sch LS26 200 C8
Great Sike Rd YO17 215 D8
GREAT SMEATON 23 C3
Great Smeaton Prim Sch DL6 23 C3
GREAT THIRKLEBY 90 D1
Greatwood Ave BD23 217 A3
Greatwood Cl BD23 217 B3
Greatwood Com Prim Sch BD23 217 A2
Greaves Smithy LS29 175 B4
Grebe Ave DL9 40 E2
Grebe Way YO18 95 F7
Greenacre Cl TS9 7 F1
Greenacres
Hunton DL8 61 E7
Morton-on-Swale DL7 64 A6
Skipton BD23 217 B5
Stainton & Thornton TS8 6 D5
York YO32 225 F4
Greenacres Cl 8 YO8 197 D1
Greenacres Cres 7 YO8 197 D1
Greenacres Dr
Airedale WF10 201 A4
4 Brayton YO8 197 D1
Greenacres Gr 3 YO8 197 D1
Green Ave LS25 194 C2
Green Balk
Great & Little Broughton TS9 26 F5
Millington YO42 170 D1
Greenbank 5 DL6 210 E2
Green Bank BB18 171 E2
Greenbank Cl 12 WF10 200 D3
Green Bank La HG4 139 A6
Greenbank Rd DL3 3 C6
Greenberfield La BB18 171 E2
Green Cl
Bradleys Both BD20 173 D3
2 Linton-on-Ouse YO30 164 F8
Middlesbrough TS7 7 D5
Steeton with Eastburn BD20 187 F7
York YO30 228 A8
Greencliffe Dr YO30 228 A6
GREEN CLOSE 130 A8
Green Cres The YO62 120 B5
Greencroft Ct 14 YO19 184 F7
Green Croft Gdns 24 YO11 100 B6
Greencroft La 17 YO19 184 F7
Green Dike YO32 225 C8
Green Dikes La YO25 151 F1
Greendown Cl LS29 218 D4
Green Dyke La YO62 120 C5
Green Dykes YO17 215 A3
Green Dykes La YO10 228 F3
Green End Ave 35 BB18 172 A1
Green End Rd 34 BB18 172 A1
Greenfield Ave LS25 194 D1
Greenfield Cl DL2 3 E1
Greenfield Dr
6 Brayton YO8 197 D1
Eaglescliffe TS16 5 D5

Greenfield Gdns BD20 . . . 187 F7
Greenfield Park Dr YO31 229 A7
Greenfield Rd 8 YO11 . . 213 A4
Greenfields
Pollington DN14 . . . 207 F6
York YO31 . . . 228 D7
Greenfields Ave HG2 . . . 220 C2
Greenfields Dr HG2 . . . 220 C2
Greenfields Rd HG2 . . . 220 C2
Greenfield St 5 BD23 . . . 216 D3
Greenfinch Cl 1 YO12 . . . 99 E6
Greenfoot La LA2 . . . 128 E8
Greengales Ct YO19 . . . 193 A8
Greengales La YO19 . . . 193 A8
Greengate
Malton YO17 . . . 215 C4
Scarborough YO12 . . . 212 D4
Green Gate
Exelby, Leeming & Newton DL7 . . . 63 D2
Hawsker-cum-Stainsacre YO22 . . . 33 A6
Kirkby Malham BD23 . . . 154 F8
West Witton DL8 . . . 59 C3
Greengate Dr HG5 . . . 221 B8
Greengate La
Cliffe YO8 . . . 198 F6
Kirkby Fleetham with Fencote DL7 . . . 42 B1
Knaresborough HG5 . . . 221 B8
Green Gate La
Crakehall DL8 . . . 62 E5
Kildale YO21 . . . 27 F8
Long Preston BD23 . . . 153 F5
Greengate Rd WF8 . . . 206 C1
Greengates La YO61 . . . 142 E3
Greengate View HG5 . . . 221 B8
Green Haggs La HG3 . . . 223 F1
GREEN HAMMERTON . . . 164 C3
Green Hammerton CE Prim Sch YO26 . . . 164 B3
Green Head La BD24 . . . 131 E2
GREEN HILL . . . 194 F8
Green Hill YO62 . . . 118 E6
Greenhill Cres DL6 . . . 210 E3
Greenhill La YO7 . . . 66 B4
Green Hill La BD22 . . . 187 A5
Green Hills YO60 . . . 168 B7
Green Hills La DL7 . . . 64 B6
Greenholme Cl
1 Boroughbridge YO51 . . 141 B6
7 Burley in Warfedale LS29 . . . 176 C1
GREENHOW . . . 136 D3
Green Howard's Dr 8 YO12 . . . 75 F5
Green Howards Rd
Pickering YO18 . . . 96 A6
Richmond DL10 . . . 209 B8
Green Howards Regimental Mus The* DL10 . . . 209 C6
Greenhow Hill HG3 . . . 136 C2
Greenhow Hill Rd HG3 . . 159 B6
Greenhow Pk LS29 . . . 176 B1
Greenhowsyke La DL6 . . . 210 E4
Green Island YO12 . . . 99 D7
Green La
Acomb YO24 . . . 227 D2
Addingham LS29 . . . 174 F4
Appleton Roebuck YO23 . . . 191 B6
Barmby on the Marsh DN14 . . . 205 A6
Barton-le-Street YO17 . . . 120 E8
Bedale DL8 . . . 62 F3
Boston Spa LS23 . . . 188 F7
Bradleys Both BD20 . . . 174 A3
Burton Leonard HG3 . . . 140 B2
Burton-on-Yore DL8 . . . 86 D6
Castleford WF10 . . . 200 E3
Cawton YO62 . . . 119 B6
Collingham LS22 . . . 188 A8
Coneythorpe & Clareton HG5 . . . 163 B5
Constable Burton DL8 . . . 61 A6
Cottingwith YO42 . . . 193 C5
Darlington DL1 . . . 3 D8
Dishforth YO7 . . . 115 A2
East Rounton DL6 . . . 24 F4
Fadmoor YO62 . . . 69 E3
Farndale West YO62 . . . 48 E1
Ferrensby HG5 . . . 162 F8
Flixton YO11 . . . 99 F1
Garforth LS25 . . . 194 D4
Glusburn BD20 . . . 187 D7
Great Ouseburn YO26 . . . 142 A1
Halton East BD23 . . . 157 C1
Harome YO62 . . . 93 C5
Harrogate HG2 . . . 222 C6
Heck DN14 . . . 207 D8
Horton BD23 . . . 171 B5
Hudswell DL11 . . . 39 F5
Hurgill DL10 . . . 40 B8
Hutton Rudby TS15 . . . 25 B4
Ilkley LS29 . . . 176 C2
Ingleton LA6 . . . 103 E2
Kippax LS25 . . . 194 C2
Kirby Wiske YO7 . . . 88 F7
Kirkby Overblow LS17 . . . 178 D2
Kirklevington TS15 . . . 5 E2
Langtoft YO25 . . . 151 D5
Lebberston YO11 . . . 100 D5
Ledston WF10 . . . 200 E7
Little Ayton TS9 . . . 27 A8
Littlethorpe HG4 . . . 140 A7
Marrick DL11 . . . 38 E7
Green La *continued*
Maunby YO7 . . . 64 D1
Menwith with Darley HG3 160 A6
Mickletown LS26 . . . 200 C5
Middlesbrough TS5 . . . 6 E8
Moor Monkton YO26 . . . 164 F1
Newby TS7 . . . 7 C3
North Cowton DL7 . . . 22 B2
North Duffield YO8 . . . 198 F8
North Lees HG4 . . . 113 D5
Otley LS21 . . . 176 F1
Rawcliffe YO30 . . . 225 A1
Ripon HG4 . . . 113 C3
Sawley HG4 . . . 138 E7
Scalby YO12 . . . 212 C8
Selby YO8 . . . 232 A3
South Stainley with Cayton HG3 . . . 161 E8
Stutton with Hazlewood LS24 . . . 189 D4
Sutton BD22 . . . 187 F2
Sutton-on-the-Forest YO61 144 E4
Thirsk YO7 . . . 211 F3
Weaverthorpe YO17 . . . 124 F1
Welbury DL6 . . . 44 C8
Wensley DL8 . . . 60 A4
Whitby YO22 . . . 208 E5
Whorlton DL6 . . . 45 F7
Wigginton YO32 . . . 166 D5
Winksley HG4 . . . 112 F2
Wressle DN14 . . . 205 D8
Greenland La YO17 . . . 95 B3
Greenlands TS15 . . . 25 C6
Greenlands La YO8 . . . 197 C3
Greenlands Rd YO18 . . . 95 F6
Green Lane E YO7 . . . 211 B1
Green Lane Prim Sch
Garforth LS25 . . . 194 D3
Middlesbrough TS5 . . . 6 E8
Green Lane Trading Est YO30 . . . 225 A1
Green Lane Villas LS25 . . 194 D4
Green Lane W YO7 . . . 211 A1
Green Lea Cl LS23 . . . 188 F8
Greenless La DL11 . . . 1 A2
Green Mdw BB8 . . . 186 A1
Green Mdws YO31 . . . 229 A7
Green Meadow Cl 11 LA6 . . . 103 D3
Greenmires La LS21 . . . 177 E4
Green Park Ave 15 YO11 . 100 B6
Green Park Rd 14 YO11 . . 100 B6
Green Pastures DL8 . . . 62 C5
Green Row LS26 . . . 200 B5
Greenroyd Gr 13 BD20 . . 187 E6
Greensborough Ave 3 YO26 . . . 227 B5
Greenshaw Dr YO32 . . . 225 C8
Greenside 18 YO19 . . . 184 F7
Greenside Cl 24 YO19 . . . 184 F7
Greenside Ct 9 DL2 . . . 3 E1
Greenside View TS12 . . . 9 D8
Greenside Wlk 23 YO19 . . 184 F7
Green St
Castleford WF10 . . . 200 E5
7 Cowling BD22 . . . 187 B6
Darlington DL1 . . . 3 D5
Greenstead Rd YO12 . . . 212 B8
Green Sward YO31 . . . 229 A8
Greens Yd YO22 . . . 208 E7
Green Sykes Rd BD22 . . . 187 F4
Green The
Brompton DL6 . . . 43 F3
Castleford WF10 . . . 201 B4
1 Clapham LA2 . . . 130 C8
Cleasby DL2 . . . 2 F4
Conistone with Kilnsey BD23 . . . 134 B6
20 Dunnington YO19 . . . 184 F7
Garforth LS25 . . . 194 D3
Hellifield BD23 . . . 154 B3
High Coniscliffe DL2 . . . 2 C6
Kettlewell with Starbotton BD23 . . . 108 B3
Kirkby Malzeard HG4 . . . 112 D5
8 Kirklevington TS15 . . . 24 E8
Knaresborough HG5 . . . 221 A8
Linton-on-Ouse YO30 . . . 164 F8
Longnewton TS21 . . . 5 A7
Middlesbrough TS17 . . . 6 D7
Northallerton DL7 . . . 210 C3
North Deighton LS22 . . . 180 A6
9 Otley LS21 . . . 176 F1
Rawcliffe DN14 . . . 205 A1
Richmond DL10 . . . 209 B6
Scalby YO12 . . . 212 B7
Seamer TS9 . . . 6 F1
6 Seamer YO12 . . . 99 D6
Sheriff Hutton YO60 . . . 145 D5
1 Skelton YO30 . . . 224 B5
Skipton BD23 . . . 217 B6
Slingsby YO62 . . . 120 B5
Stillingfleet YO19 . . . 191 D3
10 Thirsk YO7 . . . 211 C3
Thornaby-on-Tees TS17 . . . 6 B7
Tockwith YO26 . . . 181 C7
2 Tollerton YO61 . . . 143 B3
7 Topcliffe YO7 . . . 89 B1
Wistow YO8 . . . 197 D6
York YO26 . . . 227 C3
Green Village YO7 . . . 88 C5
Green Way
Glusburn BD20 . . . 187 E8
Harrogate HG2 . . . 222 C6
Middlesbrough TS7 . . . 7 D5
York YO32 . . . 225 F4
Green Ways Ct 2 YO8 . . . 197 D6
Greenways Dr 1 YO8 . . . 197 D6
Greenways The DL7 . . . 63 C8
Greenway The
2 Haxby YO32 . . . 225 C7
2 Middleton St George DL2 . 4 C4
Greenwich Cl 5 YO30 . . . 224 E3
Green Wlk 5 BB18 . . . 172 A1
Greenwood Ave 7 HG3 . 137 B4
Greenwood Gr YO24 . . . 230 C8
Greenwood Rd 6 HG3 . . 137 B4
Greet's Hill YO17 . . . 169 E7
Gregory Cl YO30 . . . 224 C5
Grenadier Dr DL6 . . . 210 F3
Grendon Gdns 1 DL2 . . . 4 C4
Grenley St 8 WF11 . . . 202 A2
Grenville Rd TS17 . . . 6 B6
Gresham Cl DL1 . . . 3 D7
Gresley Ct 3 YO26 . . . 227 B4
Greta Ave DL10 . . . 209 D7
Greta Heath 2 LA6 . . . 102 F2
GREWELTHORPE . . . 112 D7
Grewelthorpe CE Prim Sch HG4 . . . 112 C7
GREYGARTH . . . 111 F3
Greylands Park Ave YO12 . . . 212 C8
Greylands Park Dr YO12 . 212 C8
Greylands Park Gr 3 YO12 . . . 212 C8
Greylands Park Rd YO12 . 212 C8
Grey St HG2 . . . 222 E7
Greystoke Rd YO30 . . . 224 E1
Greystone Cl 2 LS29 . . . 176 C1
Greystone Ct YO32 . . . 225 C7
GREYSTONEGILL . . . 129 C8
Greystonegill La LA2 . . . 129 D7
Greystone Head HG4 . . . 112 A4
Greystone La DL11 . . . 1 E4
Greystone Pk LS25 . . . 188 F1
Greystone Prim Sch HG4 . . . 214 C2
Greystones Ave HG3 . . . 161 B4
Greystones Cl LS25 . . . 188 F1
Greystones Dr 2 DL3 . . . 3 B6
Greystones La BD22 . . . 187 E4
Grey Thorn La HG5 . . . 163 D3
Grey Towers Dr TS7 . . . 7 D5
Grimbald Crag Cl HG5 . . 221 D4
Grimbald Crag Rd HG5 . . 221 E4
Grimbald Crag Way HG5 221 D4
Grimbald Rd HG5 . . . 221 C5
Grimbald Way 3 HG5 . . . 221 C4
GRIMSTON . . . 229 E3
Grimston Bar YO19 . . . 229 F4
Grimston La YO17 . . . 148 D7
Grimston Rd 12 YO14 . . . 127 A8
Grimwith Garth YO30 . . . 224 F2
Grimwith Rd BD23 . . . 135 E2
GRINDALE . . . 127 D2
Grindale Rd YO16 . . . 127 E2
Grinkle La TS13 . . . 10 F5
GRINTON . . . 38 C5
Grinton Rd TS18 . . . 5 D8
Grisedale Cres TS16 . . . 5 E4
GRISTHORPE . . . 100 E4
Gristhwaite La YO7 . . . 89 D1
GROSMONT . . . 31 D3
Grosmont Gall* YO22 . . . 31 C4
Grosmont Sta YO22 . . . 31 C4
Grosvenor Cres 2 YO11 . 213 A4
Grosvenor Ct HG1 . . . 219 B2
Grosvenor Gdns LS17 . . . 178 B2
Grosvenor Gr HG1 . . . 219 F6
Grosvenor House YO30 . . 233 A4
Grosvenor Pk YO30 . . . 233 A4
Grosvenor Pl TS14 . . . 8 E6
Grosvenor Rd
Harrogate HG1 . . . 219 E6
Scarborough YO11 . . . 212 F4
York YO30 . . . 233 A4
Grosvenor Sq 3 YO30 . . . 164 F8
Grosvenor Terr YO30 . . . 233 A4
Grove Ave 25 LS29 . . . 175 C2
Grove Bank 4 TS15 . . . 24 E8
Grove Cl HG4 . . . 214 C3
Grove Cres
Boston Spa LS23 . . . 188 F8
South Milford LS25 . . . 195 F2
Grove Gdns 12 YO26 . . . 165 F1
Grove Hill Rd 4 YO14 . . . 101 B4
Grove La
Knottingley WF11 . . . 201 F2
Ripon HG4 . . . 214 C3
Grove Park Ave HG1 . . . 219 E4
Grove Park Ct HG1 . . . 219 E4
Grove Park Gdns 25 BD24 . . . 131 D2
Grove Park La HG1 . . . 219 E4
Grove Park Terr HG1 . . . 219 E4
Grove Park View HG1 . . . 219 E4
Grove Park Wlk HG1 . . . 219 E4
Grove Pk 7 YO8 . . . 198 B5
Grove Prom The LS29 . . . 218 A4
Grove Rd
Boston Spa LS23 . . . 188 F8
14 Filey YO14 . . . 101 B4
Harrogate HG1 . . . 219 D4
Ilkley LS29 . . . 218 A3
Grove Road Prim Sch HG1 . . . 219 E4
Groves Ct YO31 . . . 233 C3
Groves La YO31 . . . 233 C3
Grove Sq DL8 . . . 60 D5
Grove St
38 Earby BB18 . . . 172 A1
9 Harrogate HG2 . . . 220 C3
Norton YO17 . . . 215 E3
15 Whitby YO21 . . . 208 D6
Grove Terr 11 DL8 . . . 60 E2
Grove Terrace La YO31 . . 233 C4
Grove The
Eaglescliffe TS15 . . . 5 E2
Guisborough TS14 . . . 8 D5
Harrogate HG1 . . . 219 E3
1 Hutton Rudby TS15 . . . 25 D5
Ilkley LS29 . . . 218 A4
Kellington DN14 . . . 203 A3
Kippax LS25 . . . 194 D1
Middlesbrough TS5 . . . 6 E6
Normanton South WF6 . . . 200 A1
Norton YO17 . . . 215 E2
1 Seamer YO12 . . . 99 D6
Skipton BD23 . . . 217 C3
Swillington LS26 . . . 194 A1
York YO24 . . . 230 E6
Grove View YO30 . . . 228 A6
Grundy Way 11 DL10 . . . 41 E4
GRUNSAGILL . . . 153 A1
Grunton La DL2 . . . 2 C4
Grysedale La BD23 . . . 134 B2
GSPK Tech Pk HG5 . . . 221 D5
Guadaloupe Rd DL9 . . . 40 C4
Guards Ct 10 YO12 . . . 75 F5
Guildford Rd TS6 . . . 7 E8
Guinea Croft HG5 . . . 221 C7
GUISBOROUGH . . . 8 D7
Guisborough Forest & Walkway Ctry Pk* TS14 . . 8 C6
Guisborough Mus* TS14 . . 8 F7
Guisborough Priory* TS14 . 8 F7
Guisborough Rd
Aislaby YO21 . . . 31 F8
Great Ayton TS9 . . . 7 F1
Lockwood TS12 . . . 10 A5
Middlesbrough TS7 . . . 7 D5
6 Thornaby TS17 . . . 6 B8
Whitby YO21 . . . 208 A5
Guisborough Swimming Pool TS14 . . . 8 E7
Guiseley Way TS16 . . . 5 D6
GUNBY . . . 199 D6
Gunby Rd YO8 . . . 199 D5
Gunbywood Rd YO8 . . . 199 D6
Guncroft La YO62 . . . 69 D1
Guning La DL11 . . . 36 B4
Gunnergate La TS8 . . . 7 B5
GUNNERSIDE . . . 36 F4
Gunnerside Methodist Prim Sch DL11 . . . 36 E5
Gurney Pease Prim Sch DL1 . . . 3 D6
Gurney St DL1 . . . 3 D6
Guy La HG4 . . . 114 F2
Gyll Hall La DL10 . . . 41 E1
Gypsy La
Castleford WF10 . . . 201 B3
Middlesbrough TS7 . . . 7 C6
Gypsy Lane Sta TS7 . . . 7 D6

H

Haakon Cl DL10 . . . 209 C7
Habton La YO17 . . . 121 B7
Habton Rd YO17 . . . 95 D1
HACKFORTH . . . 62 E8
Hackforth & Hornby CE Prim Sch DL8 . . . 62 E8
Hackforth Rd 2 TS18 . . . 5 D8
HACKNESS . . . 74 F5
Hackness CE Prim Sch YO13 . . . 74 E5
Hackness Dr YO12 . . . 212 A8
Hackness Rd YO12 . . . 212 A8
Haddlesey Rd WF11 . . . 202 D5
Haddocks La YO61 . . . 142 B4
Haddon Cl YO24 . . . 227 C2
Hadrian Ave YO10 . . . 229 B3
Hadrians Wlk YO12 . . . 99 E6
Hadrian Way TS17 . . . 5 F5
Haggersgate 10 YO21 . . . 208 D7
Haggitt Hill La DL6 . . . 24 E3
Hagg La
Colton LS24 . . . 190 E8
Cottingwith YO42 . . . 193 E8
Cowesby YO7 . . . 66 C4
Dunnington YO19 . . . 184 F6
Hemingbrough YO8 . . . 198 F3
South Milford YO8 . . . 196 C2
Hagg Rd YO62 . . . 69 F2
Hagg Side La YO13 . . . 97 D6
Haggs La DN6 . . . 207 D2
Haggs Rd HG3 . . . 223 C4
Haggwood Wlk YO19 . . . 184 F1
Hag La
Cottingwith YO42 . . . 193 C4
Raskelf YO61 . . . 142 E8
South Kilvington YO7 . . . 211 D6
Sproxton YO62 . . . 92 D4
Youlton YO61 . . . 142 F2
Hague Ave 31 YO12 . . . 75 D5
Hagworm Hill* YO12 . . . 75 C2
Haigh La DN14 . . . 207 A6
Haigh Moor Way WF10 . . 200 E6
Haig Rd DL9 . . . 209 C2
Haig St YO8 . . . 232 B6
Hailsham Ave TS17 . . . 6 B5
Hailstone Dr DL6 . . . 210 F5
Hales Ct WF8 . . . 201 B2
Hales La YO8 . . . 204 E5
Haley's Terr YO31 . . . 228 D8
Half Acres Junior & Infant Sch WF10 . . . 200 E4
Half Crown Way HG5 . . . 221 C7
Half Moon St 1 YO30 . . . 164 F7
Halfpenny Cl HG5 . . . 221 C7
Halfpenny La HG5 . . . 221 B7
Halifax Cl YO41 . . . 169 A2
Halifax Ct 7 YO30 . . . 225 A1
Halifax Way YO41 . . . 185 A3
Halladale Cl 1 YO24 . . . 230 B7
Hallam Cl 41 YO14 . . . 101 B3
Hallam La LS21 . . . 176 D3
Hallam's Yd 4 BD23 . . . 216 F4
Hallard Way 7 YO32 . . . 167 B7
Hall Arm La YO51 . . . 141 D5
Hall Ave 10 BD20 . . . 187 E6
Hall Brow BD23 . . . 155 A5
Hall Cl
5 Airmyn DN14 . . . 205 E4
Austwick LA2 . . . 130 E7
Burley in Warfedale LS29 . 176 B1
Cawood YO8 . . . 191 D1
11 Glusburn BD20 . . . 187 E6
Hall Croft BD23 . . . 216 E4
Hallcroft Dr 13 LS29 . . . 175 A4
Hallcroft La YO23 . . . 230 A3
Hall Ct WF11 . . . 201 E4
Hall Dr
Burley in Warfedale LS29 . . . 176 B1
Glusburn BD20 . . . 187 E6
Middlesbrough TS5 . . . 6 F7
Hall Farm Cl 4 YO19 . . . 197 F8
Hall Farm Ct YO42 . . . 169 F2
Hall Farm Pk LS25 . . . 194 F4
Hallfield Ave LS25 . . . 194 F4
Hallfield La
Nawton YO62 . . . 69 C3
Wetherby LS22 . . . 180 C3
Hallfield Rd YO31 . . . 228 E5
Hallfield Terr LS25 . . . 194 F4
HALL GARTH . . . 184 F6
Hallgarth
Alne YO61 . . . 142 F4
Great & Little Broughton TS9 . . . 26 E5
Hipswell DL9 . . . 209 F1
Hall Garth
Osgodby YO8 . . . 198 C4
25 Pickering YO18 . . . 95 F7
Hall Garth* LS25 . . . 195 E4
Hall Garth Cl LS24 . . . 190 C3
Hallgarth Ct DL11 . . . 18 G7
Hall Garth Mews 24 LS25 . . . 195 F4
Hall Garth Sch TS5 . . . 6 E7
Hall Gdns
Ellerburn YO18 . . . 96 E7
Farnhill BD20 . . . 173 F1
Rawcliffe DN14 . . . 205 B2
Hall Green La LS17 . . . 178 C4
Hallikeld Cl HG4 . . . 114 B6
Hall Ings La YO62 . . . 70 E4
Hall La
Askwith LS21 . . . 176 C4
Bilton HG1 . . . 219 E6
Blubberhouses LS21 . . . 159 C2
4 Brafferton YO61 . . . 115 F1
Caldwell DL11 . . . 1 C4
Church Fenton LS24 . . . 196 C7
Harome YO62 . . . 93 C4
Harrogate HG1 . . . 219 E6
Hawnby DL6 . . . 46 B1
Huddleston with Newthorpe LS25 . . . 195 C3
Leathley LS21 . . . 177 D1
Ledston WF10 . . . 200 F7
Myton-on-Swale YO61 . . . 142 A6
Hall Mdws BB8 . . . 186 A2
Hall Moor Cl 7 TS15 . . . 24 E8
Hall Orchards Ave LS22 . 180 D3
Hall Park Cl 23 YO13 . . . 75 D5
Hall Park Croft LS25 . . . 200 D8
Hall Park Gr 25 YO13 . . . 75 D5
Hall Park Mdws LS25 . . . 200 D8
Hall Park Orch LS25 . . . 200 D8
Hall Park Rd
Hunmanby YO14 . . . 126 F8
Walton LS23 . . . 181 A2
Hall Pasture 9 YO22 . . . 32 A6
Hall Pk
Wistow YO8 . . . 198 A5
York YO10 . . . 229 B1
Hall Rd
Swillington LS26 . . . 194 A1
Trawden Forest BB8 . . . 186 A2
Hall Rise
Burley in Warfedale LS29 . . . 176 B1
12 Haxby YO32 . . . 166 F5
Hall Sq 5 YO51 . . . 141 B5
Hall Tower Hill* LS15 . . . 194 B8
Hall View Gr DL3 . . . 3 A6
Hall Way 9 BD20 . . . 187 E6
Hallwith Rd DL8 . . . 61 A3
Halnaby Ave DL3 . . . 2 F5
Halstead Rd HG2 . . . 222 E7
HALTON EAST . . . 174 C8
HALTON GILL . . . 106 E7
HALTON WEST . . . 154 A1
HAMBLETON
Selby . . . 196 F1
Skipton . . . 174 D8
Hambleton Ave
Northallerton DL7 . . . 210 C2
Thirsk YO7 . . . 211 D3
York YO10 . . . 229 C4
Hambleton CE Prim Sch YO8 . . . 196 F1
Hambleton Cl
12 Easingwold YO61 . . . 143 D8
11 Thirsk YO7 . . . 211 C3

Hambleton Ct
Great Smeaton DL6 ... 23 C3
Knaresborough HG5 ... 221 C6
Old Thirsk YO7 ... 211 D3
Hambleton Dr YO7 ... 211 C3
Hambleton Forum★ DL6 210 E5
Hambleton Garth 21
YO61 ... 143 C8
Hambleton Gate TS9 ... 26 C7
Hambleton Gr HG5 ... 221 B6
Hambleton La YO61 ... 91 F2
Hambleton L Ctr DL6 ... 210 D6
Hambleton Pl YO7 ... 211 C3
Hambleton Rd
6 Catterick Garrison DL9 . 40 E3
Harrogate HG1 ... 219 F4
Hawnby YO7 ... 67 A3
Norton YO17 ... 215 E2
Hambleton Row YO7 ... 211 D4
Hambleton Terr
Knaresborough HG5 ... 221 B6
York YO31 ... 228 C7
Hambleton View
10 Haxby YO32 ... 166 D5
Thirsk YO7 ... 211 D3
4 Tollerton YO61 ... 143 B3
Hambleton Way
Easingwold YO61 ... 143 D8
York YO32 ... 225 F3
Hamer Bank YO18 ... 49 F4
Hamerton Cl 11 YO14 ... 127 A8
Hamerton Rd 10 YO14 ... 127 A8
Hamhall La DL7 ... 63 D6
Hamilton Ave HG2 ... 222 E8
Hamilton Cl YO13 ... 75 C5
Hamilton Ct WF6 ... 200 A2
Hamilton Dr
Darlington DL1 ... 3 D8
York YO24 ... 227 E2
Hamilton Drive E YO24 ... 227 F2
Hamilton Drive W YO24 . 227 D2
Hamilton Gn YO17 ... 215 B3
Hamilton Way YO24 ... 227 E2
Hamlet The 8 DN14 ... 202 F2
Hamley La YO62 ... 70 F3
Hammer Rd HG4 ... 85 B7
Hammersike Rd
Cawood LS25 ... 196 F5
Wistow YO8 ... 197 A4
Hammerton Cl
Green Hammerton YO26 ... 164 D3
3 York YO26 ... 227 B3
Hammerton Dr
Garforth LS25 ... 194 D3
Hellifield BD23 ... 154 B3
Hammertonlane Kirk
YO26 ... 164 C3
Hammerton Sta YO26 ... 164 D2
Hammond Dr DL1 ... 3 C4
Hammond Rd YO13 ... 54 A8
Hampden St YO1 ... 233 B1
Hampden Way TS17 ... 6 B6
Hampshire Cl
Ilkley LS29 ... 218 D4
6 Pontefract WF8 ... 201 C2
Hampson Gdns YO30 ... 228 B8
HAMPSTHWAITE ... 160 F5
Hampsthwaite CE Prim Sch
HG3 ... 161 A5
Hampsthwaite Rd HG1 ... 219 C4
Hampton Gdns YO30 ... 228 C8
Hampton Rd YO12 ... 212 E5
Hampton Row LS25 ... 196 A1
Hanbury Gdns LS25 ... 194 C4
Hancow Rd
Hartoft YO18 ... 50 A1
Rosedale East Side YO18 ... 49 F3
Handale Cl TS14 ... 9 A6
Handley Cl
Stockton-on-Tees TS18 ... 5 F7
York YO30 ... 225 A2
Hang Bank DL10 ... 21 B8
Hanger La DN14 ... 204 B3
Hanghow La DL8 ... 84 C8
Hanging Stone La YO18 ... 49 E4
Hangingstone Rd LS29 ... 218 D2
Hankins La YO42 ... 193 D1
HANLITH ... 155 A8
Hanover Pl
2 Kippax LS25 ... 194 D1
Knottingley WF11 ... 201 D4
Hanover Rd 6 YO11 ... 212 F5
Hanover St 2 BD20 ... 173 E1
Hanover Street E 5
YO26 ... 227 F5
Hanover Street W 7
YO26 ... 227 F5
Hanover Terr YO21 ... 208 C6
Hansom Pl YO31 ... 228 C7
Hanson Ave WF6 ... 200 A1
Harborough Cl 20 YO14 ... 126 F8
Harbour Rise 5 DL8 ... 63 A2
Harbour View 7 DL8 ... 63 A3
Harcourt Ave YO12 ... 212 E3
Harcourt Cl
Bishopthorpe YO23 ... 231 A4
Wheldrake YO19 ... 192 F7
Harcourt Dr
Addingham LS29 ... 174 F5
Harrogate HG1 ... 219 E2
Harcourt Pl 4 YO11 ... 213 A5
Harcourt Rd 4 HG1 ... 219 E3
Harcourt St YO31 ... 228 E5
Hardcastle Ave 8 WF8 ... 201 B1
Harden Cl YO30 ... 224 F2
Harden Rd BB18 ... 186 A7
Hardenshaw La YO8 ... 204 B4
HARDGATE ... 139 A1
Hard Gate BD23 ... 134 A3
Hardgroves Hill HG3 ... 159 F5
Hardigate Rd YO18 ... 72 B7
Hardings La
Glusburn BD20 ... 187 F8
Middleton LS29 ... 218 A8
Harding's Yd YO17 ... 95 E2
Hardistry-le-Court WF8 201 D2
Hardisty Hill HG3 ... 159 C3
Hardisty Mews YO26 ... 228 A4
Hardrada Way 3 YO41 ... 168 D1
HARDRAW ... 56 C6
Hard Stiles DL11 ... 39 B7
Hardy Mdws 11 BD23 ... 134 E2
Hardy St YO8 ... 232 E4
Harebell Cl
17 Harrogate HG3 ... 161 B3
Northallerton DL7 ... 210 C1
Harecroft Rd 9 LS21 ... 177 A1
Haregill Bank HG4 ... 85 E6
Harehills La BD22 ... 187 E1
Haresfield Way TS17 ... 6 A5
Harewell Cl HG3 ... 137 D3
Harewell La 3 HG3 ... 137 F1
Harewood Ave
5 Normanton South
WF6 ... 200 B2
1 Scalby YO12 ... 212 D8
Harewood Chase DL7 ... 210 B2
Harewood Cl
Morton-on-Swale DL7 ... 64 A6
Rawcliffe YO30 ... 224 D2
5 Wigginton YO32 ... 166 D5
Harewood Dr 4 YO14 ... 101 A3
Harewood La DL7 ... 210 C3
Harewood Prim Sch TS17 ... 6 B8
Harewood Rd
Collingham LS22 ... 188 A8
Harrogate HG3 ... 219 A5
Ripon HG4 ... 214 B3
Skipton BD23 ... 216 E4
Harewood Way YO10 ... 229 A2
Harford Rd YO11 ... 100 B6
Hargill
Gilling with Hartforth &
Sedbury DL10 ... 20 E4
Harmby DL8 ... 60 E4
West Witton DL8 ... 59 C3
Hargill Cl DL8 ... 60 E4
Hargill La
Finghall DL8 ... 61 E4
6 Leeming DL7 ... 63 D4
Redmire DL8 ... 59 C7
Hargill Rd DL8 ... 61 A3
Hargreaves St 8 BD20 ... 187 F8
Hargrove Rd HG2 ... 220 B2
Harington Ave YO10 ... 228 F4
Harker Hill DL8 ... 56 C4
Harker St
42 Cross Hills BD20 ... 187 E7
12 Knottingley WF11 ... 202 A2
Harkness Cl DL7 ... 63 C4
Harkness Dr DL7 ... 63 C4
Harland Cl YO61 ... 144 C3
Harland Mount Nature
Reserve★ YO12 ... 212 B3
Harlech Ct 11 TS17 ... 5 F4
Harlech Way HG2 ... 222 B5
Harley Cl
3 Low Bentham LA2 ... 128 F8
Scarborough YO12 ... 212 E5
Harley Cres DL9 ... 40 F4
Harley La 2 DL9 ... 40 F4
Harley St 5 YO12 ... 212 E5
Harlow Ave HG2 ... 222 B7
Harlow Carr RHS Gdn★
HG3 ... 161 B1
Harlow Cl 1 YO24 ... 227 F2
Harlow Cres HG2 ... 222 B7
Harlow Grange Pk HG3 ... 178 C8
HARLOW HILL ... 222 A8
Harlow Manor Pk HG2 ... 222 B8
Harlow Moor Dr HG2 ... 219 B1
Harlow Moor Rd HG2 ... 219 A1
Harlow Oval HG2 ... 222 B8
Harlow Oval Mews HG2 . 222 B8
Harlow Park Cres HG2 ... 222 B7
Harlow Park Dr HG2 ... 222 B7
Harlow Park Rd HG2 ... 222 B7
Harlow Pines HG3 ... 222 A7
Harlow Rd YO24 ... 227 F2
Harlow Terr HG2 ... 219 B1
Harlow View HG2 ... 222 B6
Harlsey Castle★ DL6 ... 44 D5
Harlsey Cres TS18 ... 5 E8
Harlsey Rd TS18 ... 5 E8
HARMBY ... 60 E4
Harmby Rd 12 DL8 ... 60 D5
Harness La 9 YO51 ... 141 B4
Harold Ct YO24 ... 227 D3
Harold St YO8 ... 232 F4
Harolds Way 1 YO41 ... 168 D1
HAROME ... 93 C4
Harome Heads La YO62 ... 93 B6
Harome Heads Rd YO62 ... 93 C6
Harper Gr BD20 ... 187 E6
Harper La HG3 ... 159 C6
Harpers Sq 7 BD20 ... 187 E6
Harper St
Barnoldswick BB18 ... 171 C1
2 Selby YO8 ... 232 C5
Harpers Terr DL2 ... 4 B5
Harper Terr 7 TS18 ... 5 E8
Harr Gill DL8 ... 58 A6
Harrier Ct YO41 ... 185 A3
Harriers Croft YO7 ... 115 E7
Harringay Cres 20 DL1 ... 3 F6
Harris Dr 9 DL10 ... 41 E4
Harrison Gr HG1 ... 220 C4
Harrison St
Barnoldswick BB18 ... 171 E1
York YO31 ... 228 F6
Harris St DL1 ... 3 E4
HARROGATE ... 219 D1
Harrogate Coll HG2 ... 222 A7
Harrogate District Hospl
HG2 ... 220 A2
Harrogate Gram Sch
HG2 ... 222 C8
Harrogate High Sch
HG1 ... 220 A4
Harrogate Hill Sch DL3 ... 3 D7
Harrogate Hospice (BMI)
HG2 ... 219 C1
Harrogate Int Ctr★ HG1 . 219 D3
Harrogate Ladies Coll
HG1 ... 219 C3
Harrogate Rd
Bishop Monkton HG3 ... 139 E5
Boroughbridge HG5 ... 141 A2
Ferrensby HG5 ... 162 E7
Green Hammerton YO26 . 164 B3
Kirkby Overblow HG3 ... 222 D1
Knaresborough HG5 ... 220 F5
Littlethorpe HG4 ... 214 C1
Spofforth with Stockeld
LS22 ... 180 A4
Weeton LS17 ... 178 B2
Harrogate Sta HG1 ... 219 D2
Harrogate Theatre★
HG1 ... 219 D2
Harrogate Tutorial Coll
HG2 ... 222 D8
Harrow Cliff La YO18 ... 96 E4
HARROWGATE HILL ... 3 C8
HARROWGATE VILLAGE ... 3 E8
Harrow Glade 5 YO30 ... 225 A1
Harrowing Dr 2 YO21 ... 208 C6
Harrow Rd TS5 ... 6 E8
Harry Moor La YO8 ... 197 B2
Hartburn Village TS18 ... 5 E8
HARTFORTH ... 20 D5
Hartforth La DL10 ... 20 E4
Hart Hill Cres YO41 ... 169 A2
Hartington St 13 BB8 ... 186 A3
Hartington Way DL3 ... 3 C7
HARTLEY ... 14 A7
Hartley Gn 4 BD23 ... 153 F5
Hartley La CA17 ... 14 A7
Hartley Pl BD22 ... 187 B6
Hartley Rd HG2 ... 222 B7
Hartley St
12 Earby BB18 ... 172 A1
2 Glusburn BD20 ... 187 D7
HARTLINGTON ... 157 C8
Hartlington Moor La
BD23 ... 135 C3
Hartlington Raikes BD23 157 B8
Hartoft St YO10 ... 228 D2
HARTON ... 168 C8
Hart Rhydding La LS29 ... 174 F4
HARTWITH ... 160 B8
Hartwith Ave 3 HG3 ... 138 A1
Hartwith Bank HG3 ... 138 A1
Hartwith Cl HG3 ... 219 A4
Hartwith Dr HG3 ... 219 B4
Hartwith Gn 4 HG3 ... 138 A1
Hartwith Way HG3 ... 219 B4
Harvard Ct YO12 ... 212 A8
Harvest Cl
10 Pontefract WF8 ... 201 C2
11 Strensall YO32 ... 167 B7
Harvest Croft LS29 ... 176 B1
Harvester Way LS25 ... 195 F2
Harvest Way YO11 ... 100 B7
HARWOOD DALE ... 53 E2
Harwood Dale Rd YO13 ... 54 A1
Harwood Rd YO26 ... 182 F7
Hasguard Way 37 TS17 ... 5 F4
Hassacarr La YO19 ... 184 F6
Hastings Cl 4 YO30 ... 225 A1
Hastings Cres WF10 ... 201 A4
Hatcase La 23 YO18 ... 95 F7
Hatfield Ave TS5 ... 6 E8
Hatfield Cl 3 YO30 ... 224 E3
Hatfield Rd DL7 ... 210 D3
Hatfield Wlk YO24 ... 230 B8
Hatkill La YO41 ... 169 B1
Hatterall Ct 44 TS16 ... 5 F4
Hatterboard Dr YO12 ... 212 C6
Hatters Cl YO23 ... 230 B3
Haugh La YO8 ... 202 F8
Haughton Com Sch DL1 ... 3 E7
HAUGHTON LE SKERNE ... 3 F6
Haughton Rd
Darlington DL1 ... 3 D6
York YO30 ... 228 C7
Hauling La YO23 ... 191 C8
Hauxley Ct LS29 ... 218 D5
Havelock Pl 17 YO21 ... 208 D7
Havelock St TS17 ... 6 B8
Haven The
Selby YO8 ... 232 D5
5 South Milford LS25 ... 195 F2
Haverah Ct YO30 ... 224 F1
Havercroft Rd 15 YO14 ... 127 A8
Havernook La HG4 ... 86 A3
Havers Hill YO11 ... 100 A6
Haverthwaites Dr LS25 ... 188 F1
Havertop La WF6 ... 200 C1
Havikil La HG5 ... 162 A5
Havikil Pk HG5 ... 162 A6
Havilland Rd TS17 ... 6 B6
Havre Pk 11 BB18 ... 171 E1
Haw Bank Ct BD23 ... 217 B5
Hawber Cote Dr BD20 ... 174 C1
Hawber La BD20 ... 174 C1
Hawdon Ave YO8 ... 232 D5
HAWES ... 56 D4
Hawes Prim Sch DL8 ... 56 D4
Hawes Rd HG1 ... 220 B4
Hawford Cl 1 TS17 ... 6 B5
Haw Gr BD23 ... 154 B3
Haw Hill View WF6 ... 200 A2
Hawke Garth 5 YO14 ... 127 A8
Hawkins Dr 36 DL9 ... 41 A5
Hawkridge Cl TS17 ... 6 A3
Hawkshead Cl 3 YO24 ... 230 B8
Hawksmoor Ct HG4 ... 214 C6
Hawkstone TS8 ... 7 C4
Hawkstone Cl TS14 ... 8 E6
Hawkswell La DL9 ... 40 E1
HAWKSWICK ... 107 F1
Hawkswood 1 DL2 ... 3 D1
Haw La BD23 ... 154 B3
Hawley St BB8 ... 186 B3
HAWNBY ... 67 E4
Haw Pk 1 BD23 ... 217 E8
Hawse Rd YO8 ... 204 E8
Hawshaw Rd BD22 ... 186 E7
Hawsker Intake Rd YO22 . 32 F5
Hawsker La
Hawsker-cum-Stainsacre
YO22 ... 13 F1
Whitby YO22 ... 208 F6
Hawsker with Stainsacre CE
Prim Sch YO22 ... 33 A7
Hawson Cl 9 YO11 ... 100 B7
Hawthorn Ave
2 Knaresborough HG5 ... 221 B7
Knottingley WF11 ... 201 E2
Malton YO17 ... 215 D5
Tadcaster LS24 ... 189 D5
Hawthorn Cl
11 Addingham LS29 ... 174 E4
Hellifield BD23 ... 154 B3
25 Leyburn DL8 ... 60 D5
3 Pickering YO18 ... 96 A6
Stutton with Hazlewood
LS24 ... 189 E5
Hawthorn Cres TS7 ... 7 C6
Hawthorn Croft 6 LS24 . 189 D5
Hawthorn Dr
2 Topcliffe YO7 ... 89 B1
Wilberfoss YO41 ... 185 E5
Wistow YO8 ... 198 A5
Hawthorne Ave
12 Haxby YO32 ... 166 E5
10 Scotton DL9 ... 40 F2
Hawthorne Cl
Burniston YO13 ... 75 D7
10 Thorpe Willoughby YO8. 197 B2
Hawthorne Dr
Barnoldswick BB18 ... 171 E2
Guisborough TS14 ... 8 E6
Hawthorne Gr YO31 ... 228 E5
Hawthorne Mews YO32 ... 167 B7
Hawthorne St 1 BD20 ... 174 B1
Hawthorn Garth DN14 ... 202 F4
Hawthorn Gr YO31 ... 228 E5
Hawthorn La
9 Bedale DL8 ... 63 B2
Pickering YO18 ... 96 A6
Hawthorn Pl YO32 ... 225 E4
Hawthorn Rd YO8 ... 232 D3
Hawthorns 2 YO19 ... 197 F8
Hawthorns La BD23 ... 133 B2
Hawthorn Spinney YO31. 225 E3
Hawthorn St 1 YO31 ... 228 E5
Hawthorns The
20 Glusburn BD20 ... 187 E7
10 Great Ayton TS9 ... 8 A2
Hawthorn Terr YO32 ... 225 D4
Hawthorn Terrace Ctr 2
YO32 ... 225 D3
Hawthorn Terrace N
YO32 ... 225 D4
Hawthorn Terrace S
YO32 ... 225 D3
Hawthorn Way YO14 ... 101 C1
Hawthorn Wlk 1 YO11 ... 100 A7
HAXBY ... 225 D7
Haxby Moor Rd
Haxby YO32 ... 166 F7
Towthorpe YO32 ... 167 A7
Haxby Rd
Clifton YO31 ... 225 D1
Middleton St George DL2 ... 4 C5
New Earswick YO32 ... 225 D6
York YO31 ... 233 B4
Haxby Rd Prim Sch
YO31 ... 228 D7
Hay-a-Park La HG5 ... 221 D7
Hay Brow Cl YO13 ... 75 C5
Hay Brow Cres YO13 ... 75 C5
Hayfield Ave LS23 ... 188 E8
Hayforth Cl YO30 ... 225 A2
Haygate La YO18 ... 95 F5
Haygill Nook BD20 ... 174 B5
Hayhills La BD20 ... 174 B2
Hayhills Rd 10 BD20 ... 174 C1
Hay La YO13 ... 75 C5
Hayton Wood View LS25. 194 F8
Haywain The
Ilkley LS29 ... 218 D3
17 South Milford LS25 ... 195 F2
Haywra Cres 6 HG1 ... 219 E3
Haywra St HG1 ... 219 D3
Hazel Bank HG5 ... 162 D6
Hazel Brow Farm★ DL11 . 37 C4
Hazel Cl
Pannal HG3 ... 222 C3
York YO32 ... 225 D2
Hazel Ct
11 Bedale DL8 ... 63 B3
York YO10 ... 228 E4
Hazel Dr HG3 ... 222 C3
Hazel Garth YO31 ... 229 B7
Hazel Gr
Middlesbrough TS7 ... 7 C6
Pontefract WF8 ... 201 C1
Sutton BD20 ... 187 E7
Hazel Grove Rd BD20 ... 187 E7
Hazelheads La HG5 ... 221 C8
Hazel Hill YO12 ... 75 A2
Hazelmere Ct YO32 ... 225 E3
Hazelnut Gr YO30 ... 225 B2
Hazel Old La DN14 ... 203 C2
Hazel Rd
2 Boroughbridge YO51 ... 141 B4
2 Filey YO14 ... 101 A4
Knottingley WF11 ... 201 F1
Hazel Rise LS26 ... 200 B5
Hazelwood Ave
Garforth LS25 ... 194 D3
York YO10 ... 229 D4
Hazing La DN14 ... 207 B6
Hazler La BD23 ... 157 D7
HAZLEWOOD ... 175 A8
Headingley Cres 3 DL1 ... 3 F6
Headingley Rd 7 DN6 ... 206 E2
Headland Cl 30 YO32 ... 166 E5
Headland La YO18 ... 72 B4
Headlands La
Howgrave DL8 ... 87 F2
Knottingley WF11 ... 201 F2
Pontefract WF8 ... 201 B1
Headlands Prim Sch
YO32 ... 225 D8
Headlands Rd YO62 ... 70 E2
Headlands The DL3 ... 3 A5
Headley Cl 2 YO30 ... 225 B1
Headley La LS23 ... 188 F5
Head of Steam-Darlington
Railway Mus DL3 ... 3 C6
Heads Bank DL8 ... 58 F3
Heads La BB18 ... 186 A7
Heads Rd
Newton YO18 ... 51 B1
Pickering YO18 ... 71 F8
Headwell La LS24 ... 195 E7
HEALAUGH ... 37 F6
Healaugh La YO26 ... 181 F4
Healaugh Pk TS15 ... 5 E2
Healaugh Priory★ LS24 . 181 E1
Heald Brow BB18 ... 171 D2
Healdfield Rd WF10 ... 201 A4
Heald St WF10 ... 200 F4
Healdwood Rd WF10 ... 200 F4
HEALEY ... 85 E3
Healey Gr YO31 ... 228 F8
Healthfield Prim Sch DL1 .. 3 E5
Heath Cl 2 YO24 ... 227 F2
Heathcliff Gdns 5 YO12. 212 C8
Heath Cres BD20 ... 173 E3
Heath Croft YO10 ... 231 F7
Heath Ct 11 BD20 ... 173 E3
Heath Dr
Boston Spa LS23 ... 188 D8
7 Low Bradley BD20 ... 173 E3
Heather Bank
13 Stamford Bridge
YO41 ... 168 D2
York YO10 ... 229 C4
Heather Brow 16 BB18 ... 172 B1
Heather Cl
Selby YO8 ... 232 C3
3 Whorlton DL6 ... 25 D1
York YO32 ... 226 A4
Heather Croft 4 YO31 ... 225 E2
Heather Ct LS29 ... 218 B3
Heatherdene LS24 ... 189 E6
Heatherdene Rd 1 DL9 ... 40 E4
Heather Dr YO22 ... 208 E3
Heather View BD23 ... 217 B3
Heather Way 16 HG3 ... 161 B3
HEATHFIELD ... 136 F6
Heathfield Dr HG5 ... 221 C6
Heathfield Pk DL2 ... 4 C5
Heathfield Rd 1 YO10 ... 229 A3
Heath Gr HG2 ... 219 B1
Heath Moor Dr YO10 ... 231 F8
Heathness Rd LS29 ... 174 E5
Heath Pk 27 LS29 ... 175 C2
Heath Ride YO32 ... 167 B8
Heathrow TS17 ... 6 C7
Heathrow Cl 13 DL2 ... 4 C4
Heaths Ct HG4 ... 214 C5
HEATHWAITE ... 45 E8
HEBDEN ... 135 A1
Hebden Bank HG4 ... 138 F4
Hebden Rd BD23 ... 134 E2
Hebdon Rise 2 YO26 ... 227 D4
Heber Dr BD23 ... 172 A5
Hebers Ghyll Dr 24 LS29. 175 C2
Hebers Gr 21 LS29 ... 175 C2
Hebron Ct TS9 ... 26 B7
Hebron Rd TS9 ... 26 B7
Heck Gill La HG3 ... 160 A5
Heck La
Heck DN14 ... 207 C7
Hensall DN14 ... 203 D1
Heckler Cl 3 HG4 ... 214 C4
Heckler La HG4 ... 214 C4
Heck & Pollington Lake
DN14 ... 207 E7
Heddon Gr TS17 ... 6 A3
Hedgerows The YO8 ... 198 E3

Hedley St TS14 8 F7
Height La BD23 174 C6
Height Lands La YO23 182 D6
Heights La BD20 174 A2
Helena St LS25 200 C8
Helks Brow LA2 128 E2
HELLIFIELD 154 B3
Hellifield Com Prim Sch BD23 154 B3
HELLIFIELD GREEN 154 B3
Hellifield Rd BD23 155 A6
Hellifield Sta BD23 154 B4
Hell Wath Gr HG4 214 A2
Hell Wath La
Littlethorpe HG4 214 A2
Markingfield Hall HG4 139 E6
Hell Wath Nature Reserve* HG4 214 A4
HELM 57 D6
Helmsdale YO24 230 C6
HELMSLEY 92 F7
Helmsley Castle* YO62 92 E6
Helmsley Dr TS14 8 E7
Helmsley Gr 16 YO32 166 D5
Helmsley Prim Sch YO62 92 F7
Helmsley Rd TS9 26 C7
Helmsley Walled Gdn* YO62 92 E6
Helmsley Way DL7 210 C2
Hel'os 47 LS25 194 D5
HELPERBY 142 A8
Helperby La YO51 141 C7
Helperby & Myton La YO61 142 A7
HELPERTHORPE 124 D1
Helredale Gdns YO22 208 E4
Helredale Rd YO22 208 E4
Helston Rd WF6 200 A2
Helwath Rd YO13 53 D5
HELWITH BRIDGE 131 D8
Helwith Rd DL11 38 E7
HEMINGBROUGH 198 F1
Hemingbrough Prim Sch YO8 198 F1
Hemingford Gdns TS15 5 E2
Hemishor Dr LS26 200 C8
HEMLINGTON 6 F4
Hemlington Hall Prim Sch TS8 6 E5
Hemlington Hall Rd TS8 6 E5
Hemlington Lake & Recn Ctr TS8 6 E5
Hemlington Rd TS8 6 E5
Hemlock Ave YO31 225 E1
Hempbridge Cl YO8 232 A5
Hempbridge Rd YO8 232 A5
Hempland Ave YO31 228 F6
Hempland Dr YO31 229 A7
Hempland La YO31 229 A7
Hempland Prim Sch YO31 229 B6
Hemsby Rd WF10 200 E3
Hemsworth Wlk HG4 214 B7
Henbusk La LA2 130 A8
Hendon Garth YO30 225 A1
Henlow La YO60 147 B4
Henrhyd Cl 26 TS17 5 F4
Henrietta Cl
Richmond DL10 209 F8
3 Thornaby-on-Tees TS17 6 B8
Henrietta St YO22 208 E7
Henry Moore Pl WF10 200 F3
Henry's Mews 22 LS25 195 F4
Henry St BD23 216 F1
HENSALL 203 D2
Hensall Prim Sch DN14 203 C1
Hensall Sta DN14 203 C1
Hensfield Gr DL3 3 C7
Henshaws Coll HG1 220 B5
Henside La BD24 132 A5
Henside Rd BD24 132 B6
Henson Gr WF10 201 A4
Henson Rd DL1 3 F5
Henwick Hall La YO8 232 C1
Hepton Hill YO17 120 F2
Hepworth's La DN14 204 C2
Herbert St 6 YO10 228 E3
Herberts Way YO31 228 F7
Hercules St DL1 3 E7
Herdborough Rd YO11 100 A7
Herdsman Dr YO23 230 C3
Herdsman Rd 3 YO24 230 D8
Herdwick Cl 1 YO30 225 B1
Hereford Rd HG1 219 A2
Hergill La
Baldersby HG4 88 C1
Kirkby Fleetham with Fencote DL7 63 C8
Herisson Cl 20 YO18 95 F7
Herman Wlk YO24 230 C8
Hermitage Ct DL10 209 A7
Hermitage The* HG4 86 C8
Hermitage Way YO22 32 A5
Heron Ave YO24 230 C8
Heron Cl
1 Bedale DL8 63 B3
11 Thornton Dale YO18 96 D5
Heron Ct
6 Filey YO14 101 A4
6 Hunton DL9 40 F2
Heron Dr DL1 3 E5
Herongate YO18 95 F6
Heron Gate TS14 8 D6
Heron La YO12 99 E6
Heron Rise YO32 225 F5
Heron Tree Cl DL8 60 D7
Heron Way YO17 215 D2
Herriot Dr DL9 41 A5
Herriot Way YO7 211 C4
Hertford Cl 4 YO11 100 A7
Hertford Vale CE Prim Sch YO12 99 D2
Hesketh Ave TS4 7 A7
Hesketh Bank YO10 229 D3
Heslaker La BD23 216 C1
Hesleden Ave TS5 6 D6
Hesley La BD24 153 A6
Heslin Cl 8 YO32 225 C8
HESLINGTON 229 B1
Heslington Croft YO10 231 F7
Heslington Ct 2 YO10 229 B1
Heslington Gdns 2 TS14 8 F7
Heslington La
Heslington YO10 229 A1
York YO10 228 F3
Heslington Rd YO10 228 E3
HESSAY 182 C8
Hessay Ind Est YO26 182 C8
Hessay Pl 2 YO26 227 A3
Hetherton St YO30 233 A3
HETTON 155 F5
Hetton Garth 18 DL8 60 D5
HEW GREEN 160 D5
Hewitson Rd DL1 3 E5
Hewitts La BD20 172 F2
Hewley Ave YO10 229 A4
Hewley Dr 9 YO13 99 A7
HEWORTH 228 F6
Heworth YO31 229 A6
Heworth CE Prim Sch YO31 228 F6
Heworth Dr YO21 208 B6
Heworth Gn YO31 233 C4
Heworth Hall Dr YO31 228 F6
Heworth Mews YO31 228 E6
Heworth Pl YO31 228 F6
Heworth Rd YO31 228 F6
Heworth Village YO31 229 A6
Heyford Rd YO7 115 B1
Heygate Bank YO18 49 F3
Heygate La LS23 188 F6
HEYSHAW 159 D8
Heyshaw Rd HG3 159 C8
Heythrop Dr
Guisborough TS14 8 F6
Middlesbrough TS5 6 D7
Heywood Rd HG2 219 C1
Hibernia St YO12 212 E5
Hicks La LS26 200 B6
Hickstead Ct 16 DL1 3 F6
Hidcote Gdns TS17 6 A4
High Back Side YO18 95 E8
High Bank
Ampleforth YO62 92 B2
Bradleys Both BD20 173 E3
5 Threshfield BD23 134 D2
High Bank Cl 7 LS29 174 F4
Highbank Gr 1 HG2 220 D4
High Barmer YO13 75 B7
HIGH BENTHAM 129 B8
High Bentham Prim Sch LA2 129 B8
HIGH BIRSTWITH 160 D5
High Bond End HG5 221 A7
HIGH BRADLEY 173 E4
High Bradley La BD20 173 E4
Highbury Ave TS5 6 F8
HIGH CATTON 185 D8
High Catton Rd YO41 185 D8
High Church Wynd TS16 5 D3
High Cleugh HG4 214 A4
Highcliffe Ct YO30 228 A6
Highcliffe Prim Sch TS14 8 E5
Highcliff Rd TS14 8 E4
HIGH CONISCLIFFE 2 C6
High Coniscliffe CE Sch DL2 2 C6
High Cragwell YO21 31 F7
High Crest 6 HG3 137 C4
Highcroft
Collingham LS22 188 A8
9 Grassington BD23 134 E3
12 High Bentham LA2 129 A8
High Croft 7 YO14 126 F8
High Croft Way 5 BD20 173 E1
High Ct HG5 221 A6
Highdale Ave 5 YO12 212 D8
Highdale Rd YO12 212 E7
High Eggborough La DN14 203 A1
HIGH ELLINGTON 85 F6
Higherlands Cl BD23 155 D1
Higher Lodge St 1 BD20 187 D7
Higher Rd BD23 152 F4
High Fell Cl BD24 131 D1
HIGHFIELD 199 E7
Highfield
Pollington DN14 207 F7
Scarborough YO12 212 E4
High Field YO10 229 D4
Highfield Ave WF8 201 D2
Highfield Cl YO25 126 A4
Highfield Cres YO8 198 B5
Highfield Ct YO8 232 B1
Highfield Dr
Allerton Bywater WF10 200 C7
Garforth LS25 194 C3
Highfield Gn
Allerton Bywater WF10 200 C7
Sherburn in Elmet LS25 195 F3
Highfield Gr
Great Preston WF10 200 C7
Highfield Gr *continued*
Highfield YO8 199 E7
Highfield La
Barwick in Elmet & Scholes LS15 194 B7
Fangfoss YO41 169 B1
Gillamoor YO62 69 F5
Huddleston with Newthorpe LS25 195 C3
Nawton YO62 69 C2
Scagglethorpe YO17 122 E2
Womersley DN6 206 D5
Highfield Pl 1 WF10 200 D7
Highfield Prep Sch HG1 219 B3
Highfield Rd
Aberford LS25 194 F8
29 Earby BB18 172 A1
Highfield YO8 199 D7
Malton YO17 215 C5
Ripon HG4 214 B3
Whitby YO21 208 A7
Highfields La YO7 115 A1
Highfield Terr BD23 216 F3
Highfield View 3 YO8 198 B4
Highfield Villas LS25 195 F3
High Fold BB18 186 A7
High Garth
Earswick YO32 226 A7
Eastfield YO11 100 A7
Richmond DL10 209 B8
Highgate
Balne DN14 207 D6
Glusburn BD20 187 D8
Highgate Pk HG1 219 F3
High Gill Rd TS7 7 D6
High Gn
Catterick DL10 41 D4
Hebden BD23 135 A2
HIGH GRANTLEY 138 D8
High Green Dr BD20 174 B1
Highgrove Cl 7 YO30 224 E3
HIGH HARROGATE 220 A3
HIGH HAWSKER 33 B6
High Hill Grove St 14 BD24 131 D2
High Hill La BD24 131 E2
HIGH HUTTON 147 B7
HIGH KILBURN 91 B2
High La
Beadlam YO62 93 C8
Birstwith HG3 160 C5
Cowling BD22 187 A4
Cropton YO18 71 C4
Dalby-cum-Skewsby YO60 119 A2
Dalton DL11 19 D7
Fylingdales YO22 33 C5
Gillamoor YO62 70 A6
Grassington BD23 134 E3
Grinton DL11 37 D4
Hawes DL8 56 F4
Howsham YO60 147 B1
Kirby Sigston DL6 44 E1
Leake DL6 65 E6
Maltby TS8 6 C4
Muston YO14 100 F1
Myton-on-Swale YO61 142 B6
Newsham DL11 18 G7
Reeth, Fremington & Healaugh DL11 37 F5
Spofforth with Stockeld HG3 179 C4
Sutton upon Derwent YO41 185 D3
Thirlby YO7 90 D6
Thornton Watlass DL8 62 C2
West Scrafton DL8 83 F6
West Witton DL8 59 D2
Highland Cl 9 WF8 201 C1
Highlands Ave 5 YO32 167 B7
Highlands Cl YO14 101 B1
High Leir La YO7 67 D1
HIGH LEVEN 6 A3
HIGH MARISHES 96 B1
High Market Pl 27 YO62 70 B1
High Mdw
Gowdall DN14 204 A1
Selby YO8 232 B6
Highmead Wlk 3 TS3 7 B8
High Mill Dr 1 YO12 75 E5
High Mill La LS29 175 A5
Highmoor Cl YO24 230 D8
High Moor Edge YO12 212 A7
High Moor La
Boroughbridge HG5 141 A2
Brearton HG3 161 F8
Newton-on-Ouse YO30 165 C8
Scotton HG5 162 A5
Highmoor Rd YO24 230 D8
High Moor Rd
North Rigton HG3 178 A5
Skelton YO51 140 F7
High Moor Way 11 YO11 100 A6
HIGH MOWTHORPE 149 D7
High Newbiggin St YO31 233 B3
High Oaks YO31 229 B7
High Ousegate YO1 233 B2
High Peak TS14 8 F5
High Petergate YO1 233 B3
High Peter La HG3 140 A3
High Rd LA2 128 F5
High Riding
Aske DL10 20 D1
Richmond DL10 209 C8
High Rifts TS8 6 E5
High Riggs La YO18 96 C3
High Row
Bugthorpe YO41 169 D4
Caldwell DL11 1 C4
High Row *continued*
Darlington DL1 3 C5
Gainford DL2 1 C7
Melsonby DL10 20 F7
HIGH SHAW 56 D7
High Skellgate 7 HG4 214 C5
High St
Airmyn DN14 205 E3
Ampleforth YO62 92 C3
Aske DL10 20 E2
Austwick LA2 130 E7
Barmby on the Marsh DN14 205 A7
Barnby YO21 12 C4
Barton-le-Street YO17 120 E5
Beadlam YO62 93 D7
Boosbeck TS12 9 D8
6 Boroughbridge YO51 141 B5
Boston Spa LS23 188 E8
Bramham LS23 188 E5
Buckton/Bempton YO13 97 D6
Burniston YO13 75 C8
Burton in Lonsdale LA6 102 F3
Carlton DN14 204 C2
Castleford WF10 200 F4
Catterick DL10 41 D5
Cawood YO8 197 B8
Cottam YO25 150 E5
Cropton YO18 71 B4
Danby YO21 29 A6
Eaglescliffe TS15 5 D4
13 Eastfield YO11 100 A6
Gargrave BD23 155 D1
Glaisdale YO21 30 D4
Glusburn BD20 187 E6
Great Ayton TS9 7 F1
Great Broughton TS9 26 E4
Hampsthwaite HG3 160 F5
Harrogate HG2 220 C4
4 Helmsley YO62 92 F6
Heslerton YO17 123 F6
Hinderwell TS13 11 F7
Hovingham YO62 119 E6
Husthwaite YO61 117 B6
Ingleton LA6 103 D4
Kippax LS25 194 D1
Kirby Grindalythe YO17 149 D8
5 Knaresborough HG5 221 B5
Knottingley WF11 201 E5
Langtoft YO25 151 C8
Lastingham YO62 70 E5
9 Leyburn DL8 60 D5
Lingdale TS12 9 F7
Lockwood TS12 10 A5
Markington with Wallerthwaite HG3 139 C4
Mickleby TS13 12 A4
Middlesbrough TS7 7 C8
Newton Mulgrave TS13 11 E4
Normanton South WF6 200 A1
Northallerton DL7 210 D6
14 Norton DN6 206 E1
Old Byland & Scawton YO62 92 A4
Oldstead YO7 91 E5
Pateley Bridge HG3 137 B4
Rawcliffe DN14 205 A1
Rillington YO17 122 F5
Scalby YO13 75 D5
6 Settle BD24 131 E2
Settrington YO17 122 F1
Sherburn YO17 124 D7
Skipton BD23 217 A4
Slingsby YO62 120 B5
Snainton YO13 98 A5
Snaith DN14 204 B1
South Milford LS25 195 E2
Spofforth HG3 179 E5
3 Staithes TS13 13 K2
Stillington YO61 144 B6
Stokesley TS9 26 C7
Swinton YO17 121 B4
Tadcaster LS24 189 E6
Thornton Dale YO18 96 E6
Thornton-le-Clay YO60 146 A4
Wharram YO17 149 A6
Whitby YO21 208 B3
Whixley YO26 164 A4
Whorlton DL6 45 D8
Wombleton YO62 93 E7
Wrelton YO18 71 C1
HIGH STAKESBY 208 B5
High Stakesby Rd YO21 208 A6
High Stell DL2 4 C4
High Street Agnesgate HG4 214 C5
Highthorne La YO61 117 B5
Highthorn Rd YO31 225 E2
High Town Bank Rd YO7 91 C5
High Trace DL6 210 E2
High Trees Ct LS25 195 F4
High View HG3 160 F8
Highway BD24 131 E3
High Wheatley LS29 218 E3
High Wlk YO12 212 E7
High Wood LS29 218 F3
HIGH WORSALL 24 A8
Hilbeck Gr YO31 229 B6
Hilbra Ave YO32 225 D6
Hilda St
6 Selby YO8 232 C5
3 York YO10 228 E3
Hildenley Cl 6 YO12 212 B5
Hilderthorpe TS7 7 C6
Hildewell 3 TS13 11 F7
Hildyard Cl TS9 26 C8
HILLAM 202 A7
Hillam Comm La LS25 202 B7
Hillam Hall La 4 LS25 202 A7
Hillam Hall View 3 LS25 202 A7
Hillam House Cl 5 LS25 202 A7
Hillam La
Burton Salmon LS25 201 F7
Hillam LS25 202 A7
Hillam Rd YO8 202 F8
Hillary Garth 9 YO26 227 E4
Hill Bank HG5 163 B7
Hillbank Gr HG1 220 D4
Hillbank Rd HG1 220 D4
Hillbank View HG1 220 C4
Hill Cl DL11 38 B6
Hillcrest
8 Monk Fryston LS25 202 A8
Tadcaster LS24 189 D5
Hill Crest YO19 167 F1
Hillcrest Ave
Newby & Scalby YO12 75 E5
Poppleton YO26 224 A2
Silsden BD20 174 C1
Hillcrest Cl WF10 201 B3
Hillcrest Ct 2 LS24 189 D5
Hillcrest Dr
Castleford WF10 201 B3
Loftus TS13 10 D8
Hillcrest Gdns YO51 141 A7
Hill Crest Gdns YO24 227 F1
Hillcrest Gr 2 YO12 75 E5
Hillcrest Mount WF10 201 B3
Hillcroft 4 LA2 129 A7
Hill End La BD22 186 F5
Hill Field YO8 232 B8
Hill Foot La HG3 222 B2
Hillgarth WF11 201 F2
Hillgarth Ct 4 YO41 185 B2
Hillhouse La DL2 4 C7
Hill House La DL2 4 C8
Hillingdon Rd TS4 7 B8
Hill La BB8 186 B4
Hillocks La TS12 10 A5
Hill Rd WF10 200 F3
Hill Rise
Middleton St George DL2 4 D3
Skipton BD23 216 E5
Hill Rise Ave HG2 222 B8
Hill Rise Cl HG2 222 B8
Hillsborough Terr 5 YO30 228 C7
Hillshaw Parkway HG4 214 D5
Hillside
Byram WF11 201 E4
Follifoot HG3 223 F4
3 Ingleby Arncliffe DL6 45 A7
Skipton BD23 217 B6
Hill Side DL2 3 A3
Hillside Cl
18 Addingham LS29 174 F4
Bootham Stray YO30 225 B2
9 Monk Fryston LS25 202 A8
Skipton BD23 217 B6
Threshfield BD23 134 B3
Hillside Cres BD23 217 C3
Hillside Dr BD23 134 B3
Hillside Gdns
Langtoft YO25 151 D5
Scarborough YO12 212 E1
Hillside Rd
2 Low Bentham LA2 128 F8
Pannal HG3 222 E3
Hillside Way YO17 150 B8
Hills La BD23 155 E5
Hill St
6 Barnoldswick BB18 171 E1
York YO24 227 E3
Hill The DL8 56 D4
Hill Top
24 Burley in Warfedale LS29 176 C1
Castleford WF10 200 C4
Ilkley LS29 218 A2
Knottingley WF11 201 F2
Hill Top Ave HG1 219 D6
Hill Top Cl
Embsay BD23 217 C8
Harrogate HG1 219 D6
Stutton with Hazlewood LS24 189 D4
Hilltop Cres DL9 40 E4
Hill Top Cres HG1 219 D6
Hill Top Ct DL7 22 C3
Hill Top Dr HG1 219 D6
Hill Top Gr HG1 219 E6
Hill Top La
Earby BB18 172 A1
Pannal HG3 222 A4
Hill Top Mount HG1 219 D6
Hill Top Rd
Harrogate HG1 219 D6
4 Wistow YO8 197 D6
Hill Top Rise HG1 219 E6
Hill Top View HG3 159 F8
Hill Top Wlk HG1 219 D6
Hill View
Langthorpe YO51 141 A6
Stillington YO61 144 C6
York YO31 229 C7
Hillway 7 TS17 6 A5
HILTON 6 C2
Hilton Cl DL6 210 E8
Hilton Gn DL6 210 D8
Hilton Grange DL6 210 E8
Hilton La 7 HG5 221 A6
Hilton Rd TS9 6 F1
Hilton Sq DL6 210 E8
Hincks Hall La HG3 139 C3
HINDERWELL 11 F7
Hinderwell Ind Pk TS13 11 F7

Hinderwell La
Hinderwell TS13 11 E8
Staithes TS13 13 K1
Hinderwell Pl YO12 212 E2
Hinderwell Prim Sch YO12 212 D2
Hinderwell Rd YO12 212 E1
Hindle Dr 39 YO14 101 B3
Hinsley La DN14 204 C2
Hinton Ave 1 YO24 230 C8
Hinton Cl 9 WF8 201 C2
Hinton La WF11 201 D3
HIPSWELL 209 F1
Hipswell CE Prim Sch DL9 209 F1
Hipswell Rd DL9 209 E1
Hipswell Road W DL9 209 C1
Hird Ave 22 DL8 63 A2
Hird Rd TS15 5 D2
Hirds Yd 2 BD23 216 F3
HIRST COURTNEY 203 F3
Hirst Courtney & Temple Hirst Prim Sch YO8 203 E3
Hirstead Gdns YO12 212 B8
Hirstead Rd YO12 212 B8
Hirst La HG3 160 E5
Hirst Rd DN14 204 A3
Hirst St WF10 200 C8
Hobart Rd WF10 201 B5
Hobb Nook La LS21 176 D4
Hobbs Cl DL9 209 C2
Hob Cote La BD22 187 F1
Hobgate YO24 227 D3
Hob Moor Dr YO24 227 E2
Hob Moor Oaks Sch YO26 227 D2
Hob Moor Prim Sch YO24 227 E2
Hobmoor Terr YO24 227 F1
Hobson Cl YO23 230 B1
Hoctun Cl WF10 200 F3
Hodge La WF8 206 B3
Hodgson Fold LS29 174 E5
Hodgson Hill YO13 54 B4
Hodgson La YO26 182 F8
Hodgson's La LS25 196 A5
Hogg La YO17 148 E6
Holbeck Ave
Middlesbrough TS5 6 E6
Scarborough YO11 213 B2
Holbeck Cl YO11 213 B2
Holbeck Hill YO11 213 B1
Holbeck Rd YO11 213 A2
Holbeck's La YO26 141 F3
Holburns Croft 3 YO10 229 B1
Holden Gdns YO8 197 D2
Holderness Dr
7 Darlington DL2 3 A7
4 Faverdale DL2 3 B7
HOLE BOTTOM 135 A3
Hole House La BB7 152 B2
Hole La BD20 174 A2
Holes La WF11 201 E2
HOLGATE 227 F3
Holgate DL6 45 E8
Holgate Bank HG5 163 A8
Holgate Bridge Gdn 7 YO24 228 A3
Holgate Cl YO17 215 C5
Holgate La LS23 188 E8
Holgate Lodge Dr YO26 227 E4
Holgate Rd YO24 233 A1
Holl Gate DL8 59 E3
Hollicarrs Cl YO19 192 A2
Hollies The
Barlby with Osgodby YO8 198 C4
Stockton on the Forest YO19 167 D3
Hollin Gate LS21 176 E1
Hollings The LS26 200 A6
Hollington St 9 BB8 186 A3
Hollingwood Gate 31 LS29 175 C2
Hollingwood Pk 37 LS29 175 C2
Hollingwood Rise 32 LS29 175 C2
Hollingworth Cl BD23 217 B3
Hollin Hall Dr LS29 175 C2
Hollinhurst Brow LA2 128 F2
Hollin La LA2 129 F6
Hollins DL8 60 B3
Hollins Beck Cl LS25 200 D8
Hollins Cl HG3 161 A5
Hollins Cres HG1 219 C4
Hollins Gr WF10 200 C7
Hollins Hall HG3 161 A4
Hollins La
Firby DL8 63 B1
Hampsthwaite HG3 160 F5
Melmerby HG4 114 B8
Middleton Quernhow HG4 88 C1
Rosedale East Side YO18 49 D4
Hollins Mews HG1 219 C4
Hollins Rd
10 Barnoldswick BB18 171 D1
Harrogate HG1 219 C4
HOLLINTHORPE 194 A2
Hollin Top La YO21 29 C7
Hollis Cres YO32 167 B6
Hollow Gill Brow BD24 153 C5
Hollow Moor La DL8 62 E7
Holly Bank Gr 3 YO24 227 F2
Hollybank La HG3 161 B6
Holly Bank Rd YO24 227 F2
Hollybush Ave TS17 6 B5
Hollybush Cl DN14 207 A7
Hollybush Gn LS22 188 B8
Holly Cl
Acaster Malbis YO23 191 C8
Firth Moor DL1 3 F4
Full Sutton YO41 169 A2
Thirsk YO7 211 B2
Wrelton YO18 71 C1
Holly Ct 11 HG5 221 B6
Holly Garth 1 YO61 115 F1
Holly Garth Cl TS9 7 F1
Hollygarth La DN14 202 D4
Holly Gr
Selby YO8 232 B3
8 Thorpe Willoughby YO8 197 B2
HOLLY HILL 209 B5
Holly Hill DL10 209 C5
Holly Hill Cl TS7 7 D7
Hollyhocks La LS24 195 F7
Hollyhurst Ave 1 TS4 6 F8
Hollyhurst Rd DL3 3 C6
Holly Pk LS17 178 B3
Holly Rd
10 Bedale DL8 63 B3
Boston Spa LS23 188 D8
Hollyrood Rd YO30 224 E3
Holly Terr YO10 228 D1
Holly Tree Croft 2 YO19 184 F7
Holly Tree Ct
5 Hambleton YO8 196 F1
2 Whitby YO21 208 B6
Holly Tree Garth YO32 167 E3
Holly Tree La
Dunnington YO19 184 F7
Haxby YO32 225 D8
Hollytree Way YO8 197 D1
Hollywalk Ave TS6 7 E8
Holly Wlk YO12 212 D7
Hollywood YO8 232 B7
HOLME 88 D5
Holmebeck La HG4 88 B1
Holme Cl
Earby BB18 186 A8
23 Sutton BD20 187 E7
Holme Cres BB8 186 A2
Holme Croft 1 BD23 134 D2
Holme Farm La LS23 188 A5
Holmefield Cl 3 YO8 232 A1
Holmefield Cres HG4 214 C3
Holmefield Ct 2 YO8 232 A1
Holmefield La YO10 229 A1
Holmefield Rd
Glusburn BD20 187 E7
Ripon HG4 214 C3
Holmefields Rd TS6 7 E8
HOLME GREEN 190 F4
Holme Green Rd YO23 190 F4
Holmehead BD24 131 D4
Holme Hill 2 YO11 100 A6
Holme Hill La YO10 184 C4
Holme Ings LS29 175 B4
Holme La
Glusburn BD20 187 E7
Halton East BD23 174 B8
Newbiggin DL8 58 E1
Rudby TS9 25 E7
Selby YO8 232 D6
Holmemead TS9 26 E5
Holme Pk 3 LA2 129 A7
Holmes Ave YO8 232 C6
Holmes Cres YO60 146 E6
Holmes Dr 2 YO19 192 A1
Holmes Ind Est YO8 232 D6
Holme St 12 BB8 186 A3
Holme The TS9 26 E4
Holme View LS29 218 A4
Holmfield HG4 112 D7
Holmfield Cl WF8 201 C2
Holmfield Ct WF8 201 D2
Holmfield La WF8 201 C2
Holm Hill YO13 54 C2
Holm La LA2 130 E6
Holmstead Ave YO21 208 A5
Holmtree La HG4 113 B8
Holmwood Ave TS5 6 F8
Holmwood Sch TS4 7 A7
Holnicote Cl 3 TS17 6 A3
Holray Pk DN14 204 C2
Holroyd Ave YO31 229 A5
HOLTBY 167 F1
Holtby Gr YO12 212 D5
Holtby La
Holtby YO19 167 D1
Stockton on the Forest YO19 226 F2
Holy Family RC High Sch The DN14 204 C3
Holy Family RC Prim Sch 1 DL3 3 B6
Holy Family & St Michaels RC Prim Sch WF8 201 D1
Holyroad Ave DL3 3 A5
Holyrood Cl TS17 6 B8
Holy Rood La LS25 201 C8
Holystone Dr TS17 6 A4
Holy Trinity CE Infant Sch HG4 214 B6
Holy Trinity Junior Sch HG4 214 B5
Holywell Ave WF10 201 A3
Holywell Gn TS16 5 E5
Holywell Halt BD23 174 A8
Holywell La
Castleford WF10 201 A3
North Cowton DL7 22 C2
Home Farm Cl
Hensall DN14 203 D2
Wray-with-Botton LA2 128 A6
Homefield Cl YO23 230 A2
Homelea YO32 167 A6
Home Office Emergency Planning Coll YO61 143 D6
Homestead Cl
Eggborough DN14 203 A2
2 York YO32 225 F1
Homestead Garth 1 TS17 6 D6
Homestead Rd HG1 219 E2
Honey Pot 5 YO8 199 D7
Honeypot La
Darlington DL3 3 C7
8 Faverdale DL2 3 B7
Honey Pot Rd 2 DL10 41 C6
Honeysuckle Cl
New Micklefield LS25 195 A3
Romanby DL7 210 C1
Selby YO8 232 C2
Honeysuckle Way 20 WF10 200 D3
Honister Gr TS5 6 D7
Honoldu Ct 29 TS17 5 F4
Hood La YO13 54 D2
Hoodstorth La HG3 158 F6
Hookstone Ave HG2 222 E7
Hookstone Chase HG2 220 D2
Hookstone Chase Prim Sch HG2 220 D2
Hookstone Cl HG2 220 C2
Hookstone Dr HG2 223 A8
Hookstone Garth HG3 159 E5
Hookstone Grange Ct 3 HG2 220 C2
Hookstone Grange Way 2 HG2 220 C2
Hookstone Oval 7 HG2 220 B1
Hookstone Pk HG2 220 D2
Hookstone Rd HG2 222 E7
Hookstone Way HG2 220 D2
Hookstone Wood Nature Reserve* HG2 223 A3
Hookstone Wood Rd 9 HG2 220 B1
Hope St
30 Filey YO14 101 B3
Knaresborough HG5 221 B5
Scarborough YO12 213 A6
York YO10 233 C1
Hope Terr 7 YO21 208 D5
HOPETOWN 200 C2
Hopetown La DL3 3 C6
HOPGROVE 226 D2
Hopgrove Lane N YO32 226 C3
Hopgrove Lane S YO32 226 E3
Hopper Hill Rd YO11 99 F6
Hopper La LS21 159 C2
HOPPERTON 163 E3
Hopperton St HG5 163 E4
Hopps's Rd 6 BD20 187 E8
Horcum Ct 4 TS8 6 E5
Hornbeam HG2 223 A7
Hornbeam Cl YO30 225 B2
Hornbeam Cres HG2 222 F8
Hornbeam Park Ave HG2 222 F7
Hornbeam Park Oval HG2 222 F7
Hornbeam Park Rd HG2 222 F7
Hornbeam Park Sta HG2 222 F7
Hornbeam Pk HG2 222 F7
Hornbeam Pk HG2 223 A6
Hornbeam Square N HG2 223 A7
Hornbeam Square S HG2 223 A7
Hornbeam Square W HG2 222 F7
Hornblower Cl 5 HG4 113 D2
HORNBY
Bedale 62 B8
Croft-on-Tees 23 E4
Hornby Castle* DL8 62 C8
Hornby Cl 1 DL2 3 E1
Hornby Rd
Appleton Wiske DL6 24 A3
Roeburndale LA2 128 A2
Wray-with-Botton LA2 128 A6
Horndale Rd 5 YO14 101 B4
Horner Ave YO61 144 A5
Horner Cl YO61 144 A5
Horne Rd DL9 40 F4
Horner St YO30 228 B7
Horners Terr 13 YO22 208 E6
Horn La BD20 174 B3
Hornsea Rd TS8 6 E5
Hornsey Garth 25 YO32 166 E5
Horse Course La YO17 122 E1
Horsefair 2 YO51 141 B5
Horsefair Sh Ctr LS23 180 C3
HORSEHOUSE 83 C4
Horseman Ave YO23 230 A3
Horseman Cl 2 YO23 230 A3
Horseman Dr YO23 230 A3
Horseman La YO23 230 A3
Horsemarket Rd YO17 215 B4
Horse Mill La HG3 139 D5
Horsemill Sq HG5 221 B5
Horse Rd 12 YO22 208 E6
Horseshoe Cave* BD24 132 A3
Horseshoe Cl DL9 40 F4
Horseshoe The YO24 230 E7
Horseway Gn YO18 49 D4
Horsfield Way YO19 184 F7
Horsman Ave YO10 233 C1
HORTON 171 B5
HORTON IN RIBBLESDALE 105 C3
Horton-in-Ribblesdale Prim Sch BD24 105 D3
Horton-in-Ribbleside Sta BD24 105 C3
Hospital Fields Rd YO10 228 D1
Hospital La YO8 197 B4
Hospital Rd YO17 215 B4
Hospitium The* YO1 233 A3
Hostess La YO18 72 C4
Hotham Ave YO26 227 B2
Hothams Ct YO1 233 C2
Hothfield Street Junior Sch 5 BD20 174 C1
Hothfield Terr BD23 216 F3
Houghton Ave WF11 201 D2
Houghton Banks 3 TS17 6 D6
HOULSYKE 29 F6
Houndgate DL1 3 C5
Houndsway 6 YO24 230 B8
HOVINGHAM 119 F6
Hovingham CE VC Prim Sch YO62 119 E6
Hovingham Dr
6 Guisborough TS14 8 F7
Scarborough YO12 212 B4
Hovingham Hall* YO62 119 E6
Howard Ct DL10 41 F7
Howard Dr YO30 224 E2
Howard Link YO30 224 D2
Howard Rd
Catterick Garrison DL9 209 E1
Towthorpe YO32 167 B6
Howard St
3 Scarborough YO12 213 A7
York YO10 228 D2
Howden Dike TS15 5 E2
Howden La YO19 231 E1
Howden Rd
4 Barlby YO8 198 B4
Romanby DL7 210 B2
Silsden BD20 174 C1
Howdenshire Way DN14 205 F6
Howdlands La HG4 140 E7
HOWE 88 E3
Howe Ave DL10 41 E4
Howe Bank YO21 29 B7
Howe End YO62 70 B1
Howe Field Rd YO26 142 A2
Howe Hill Bank TS8 7 B2
Howe Hill Cl YO26 227 E4
Howe Hill La DL10 41 C6
Howe Hill Rd YO26 227 E4
Howe La YO41 170 A5
Howe Rd
Malton YO17 122 A6
Norton YO17 215 E3
Howes Rd 8 YO14 127 A8
Howe St YO24 227 D3
Howgate DL8 57 F6
HOWGILL 157 E6
Howgill La
Barden BD23 157 E6
Rimington BB7 171 A1
Howhill Quarry Rd HG3 178 B7
Howhill Rd HG3 178 B8
How Hill Rd HG4 139 B6
Howker La YO61 116 F2
Howlbeck Rd TS14 8 E7
Howldale La
Appleton-le-Moors YO62 70 F4
3 Beadlam YO62 93 D7
Howl Gate YO41 185 E8
Howlgate La YO21 13 A1
HOWSHAM 146 F1
Howsham Hall* YO60 146 F2
Howson La BD24 131 E4
How Stean Gorge* HG3 110 B4
Hoxton Rd YO12 212 F6
Hoylake Rd TS4 6 F8
Hoylake Way TS16 5 E4
Hubback Sq 5 DL2 3 A7
HUBBERHOLME 81 C1
Hubert St 2 YO23 228 B1
HUBY
Harrogate 178 B2
Stillington 144 A4
Huby CE Prim Sch YO61 144 A4
Huby Ct
3 Guisborough TS14 8 F7
York YO10 228 E3
Huby Rd YO61 144 B3
Hudgin La
Lockton YO18 72 E4
Wykeham YO13 98 D4
Hudson Cl
Malton YO17 215 C6
Stamford Bridge YO41 168 D2
2 Tadcaster LS24 189 E6
13 Wetherby LS22 180 C3
Hudson Cres 2 YO30 228 A7
Hudson St
Whitby YO21 208 D7
6 York YO30 228 C7
Hudson View 1 LS24 189 E6
Hudson Way
Clifton Park YO26 227 C8
Tadcaster LS24 189 E6
HUDSWELL 40 A7
Hudswell La DL10 209 C5
Hugden Cl YO18 96 A6
Hugden Way YO17 215 F4
Huggate Dikes* YO42 170 F2
Huggate Hill YO17 170 E7
Hugh Field La YO8 199 A8
Hugh Field North La YO8 193 A1
Hugh St WF10 200 E4
Hull Rd
Cliffe YO8 198 E2
Hemingbrough YO8 199 B1
Hull Rd *continued*
Osbaldwick YO10 229 D3
York YO10 229 B3
Humber Dr 5 YO32 167 B6
Humber Rd TS17 6 B7
HUMMERSKNOTT 3 A5
Hummersknott Ave DL3 3 A5
Hummersknott Sch & Language Coll DL3 3 A4
Humphrey Balk La YO7 114 D8
Humphrey Hill DL8 58 D1
Hundale Rd 5 TS15 25 C5
Hunday Field Rd YO51 141 E2
Hundens Day Hospl DL1 3 E5
Hundens La DL1 3 D6
Hungate
Bishop Monkton HG3 140 A5
Brompton YO13 98 C5
Pickering YO18 95 F6
York YO1 233 C2
Hungate Cl LS24 195 D8
Hungate Ct 11 YO14 126 F8
Hungate La YO14 126 F8
Hungate Prim Sch 23 LS25 195 F4
Hungate Rd LS25 195 F4
Hunger Hill LS29 218 C7
Hungerhill La YO62 93 F6
HUNMANBY 126 F8
Hunmanby Ind Est YO14 127 A1
Hunmanby Prim Sch YO14 126 F8
Hunmanby Rd
Burton Fleming YO25 126 E3
Reighton YO14 127 C6
Hunmanby St YO14 100 F2
Hunmanby Sta YO14 127 A7
HUNSINGORE 180 F8
Hunt Cl YO31 233 C3
Hunter Dr YO41 185 A2
Hunters Cl
Dunnington YO19 184 E7
19 Easingwold YO61 143 C8
10 Haxby YO32 225 C8
4 Hurworth-on-Tees DL2 3 D1
Osgodby YO11 100 B7
Hunters Croft BD23 156 F1
Hunters Gn
Eaglescliffe TS16 5 D5
Low Dinsdale DL2 4 C3
Hunters Ride DL6 24 B3
Hunters Row 6 YO51 141 B4
Hunter St 8 YO21 208 D7
Hunters Way
Norton YO17 215 D2
Selby YO8 232 B4
York YO24 230 F7
Hunters Wlk
Barlow YO8 204 D7
Kirk Deighton LS22 180 C4
Hunters Wood Way 21 YO19 184 F7
Hunt House Rd YO22 51 B6
HUNTINGTON 225 E3
Huntington Mews YO31 228 D7
Huntington Prim Sch YO32 225 F4
Huntington Rd YO31 233 C4
Huntington Sch YO32 225 E3
Huntington Stadium (York City Knights RLFC) The YO32 226 A2
HUNTON 61 E7
Hunton & Arrathorne Com Prim Sch DL8 61 F7
Hunton Rd DL9 40 E1
Huntriss Row YO11 213 A6
Huntsmans La YO41 168 C2
Huntsman's Wlk YO24 227 B1
Hunt St WF10 200 D4
Hurdle Cl YO17 215 E2
HURGILL 209 A7
Hurgill Rd DL10 209 A7
Hurn Rd YO61 144 A4
Hurns La YO30 224 A7
Hurrell La YO18 96 E5
Hurricane Cl LS25 196 B4
Hurricane Way YO30 224 E3
Hurrs Rd 3 BD23 217 B4
Hurstleigh Terr HG1 220 A3
Hurst's Yd YO1 233 C2
Hurworth Comp Sch DL2 22 D8
Hurworth House Sch DL2 3 E1
HURWORTH-ON-TEES 3 E1
HURWORTH PLACE 3 D1
Hurworth Prim Sch DL2 3 E1
Hurworth Rd
Hurworth DL2 3 F1
Hurworth-on-Tees DL2 22 D8
Neasham DL2 4 A1
Hussars Ct 6 YO12 75 F5
Husthwaite CE Prim Sch YO61 117 B5
Husthwaite Rd
Coxwold YO61 117 D7
Easingwold YO61 117 B2
Hutchinson Dr DL6 210 E3
Hutchinson St 1 YO8 232 B6
HUT GREEN 203 A2
Hutton Ave DL1 3 E7
Hutton Bank
3 Hutton Rudby TS15 25 D5
Ripon HG4 214 D7
HUTTON BONVILLE 43 C7
HUTTON BUSCEL 98 E7

Hutton Cl YO26 . . . . 224 A2
HUTTON CONYERS 114 A4
Hutton Cross Rd YO13. . . . 98 E8
HUTTON GATE 8 D6
Hutton Gate HG2. . . . . 222 D6
HUTTON HANG 61 D3
Hutton La
　Guisborough TS14 . . . . 8 E5
　Hutton Conyers HG4 . . . . . . 114 A4
　Sharow HG4. . . . . 214 A8
HUTTON-LE-HOLE 70 C5
HUTTON MULGRAVE 12 D1
Hutton Rae La YO7. . . . . . 116 D7
HUTTON RUDBY. 25 C5
Hutton Rudby Prim Sch
　TS15 . . . . 25 C5
HUTTONS AMBO 147 B6
HUTTON SESSAY 116 D7
Hutton's Mon★ DL11 . . . . 39 C6
HUTTON VILLAGE. 0 E1
Hutton Village Rd TS14. . . 8 D7
HUTTON WANDESLEY. . . . 182 A5
Hutts La HG4 . . . . 112 C7
HW Baines Ind Est HG4. . . 214 A8
Hyde Park Rd
　Harrogate HG1 . . . . 219 E3
　Knaresborough HG5 . . . . . . 221 B8
Hydro Cl LS29 . . . . 218 F3
Hydro L Ctr The HG2 . . . . 219 C5
Hydro Ret Pk 219 C5
Hyrst Gr YO31. . . . . 228 E6

I

I'Anson Cl DL8 . . . . 60 D6
I'Anson Rd DL10 . . . . 209 D7
Ian St TS17 . . . . .6 B8
Ibbetson Cl 16 HG4. . . . . . 86 C3
Iburndale La YO22 . . . . . . 32 A6
ICKORNSHAW. 187 A6
Iddison Dr DL8. . . . . 63 A2
Ikin Way YO32 . . . . 225 F6
ILKLEY 218 B4
Ilkley Gr TS14. . . . . .8 E5
Ilkley Gram Sch LS29 . . . . 218 C3
Ilkley Hall Mews 5 LS29 218 B3
Ilkley Hall Pk 4 LS29 . . . . 218 B3
Ilkley Pool & Lido LS29. . . 218 B5
Ilkley Rd
　Addingham LS29 . . . . 175 A4
　Ilkley LS29. . . . . 176 C1
Ilkley Sta LS29. . . . . 218 B4
Ilkley Toy Mus★ 9 LS29. 218 B4
ILTON 85 E1
Ilton Bank HG4 . . . . 85 E1
Ilton Garth YO30 . . . . 225 A2
Imperial Ave TS17. . . . . . . .6 B8
Ind Est The YO60. . . . . . . 145 C4
Ingdale Howl YO62. . . . . . 92 C7
Ingdale La YO7 . . . . 66 C3
Ing Dene Ave 16 BB8. . . . 186 A3
Ing Dene Cl BD23 . . . . . . 155 E3
INGERTHORPE 139 C5
Ingfield Est BD24 . . . . . . 131 D1
Ingfield La BD24 . . . . 131 D2
Ingham Cl YO22. . . . . 32 A6
Ingleborough Ave YO10 . 229 B4
Ingleborough Cave★
　LA2. . . . . 104 D2
Ingleborough Dr 4
　BB18. . . . . 171 D1
Ingleborough National
　Nature Reserve★ LA6. . . 104 D8
Ingleborough Park Cl 3
　LA6. . . . . 103 D3
Ingleborough Park Dr 2
　LA6. . . . . 103 D3
INGLEBY ARNCLIFFE 45 B8
Ingleby Arncliffe CE Prim
　Sch DL6 . . . . 45 A8
Ingleby Ave TS9 . . . . 27 B6
INGLEBY BARWICK 6 B4
INGLEBY CROSS. 45 A7
Ingleby Dr LS24. . . . . 189 E6
INGLEBY GREENHOW . . . 27 C5
Ingleby Greenhow CE Prim
　Sch TS9. . . . . 27 C5
Ingleby Manor★ TS9 . . . . 27 C4
Ingleby Mill Prim Sch TS17 6 A3
Ingleby Rd
　Great Broughton TS9. . . . . 26 E5
　Great & Little Broughton
　　TS9. . . . . 27 A5
Ingleby Way TS17. . . . . . . .6 B5
Ingle Cl YO12. . . . . 212 E1
Inglenook Cl 15 LS25. . . . 195 F2
Ingles The 10 LA6. . . . . . 103 D3
INGLETON. 103 D3
Ingleton Dr 16 YO11. . . . . 143 D8
Ingleton Ind Est LA6. . . . 103 D3
Ingleton Mid Sch LA6. . . . 103 D3
Ingleton Prim Sch LA6. . . 103 D3
Ingleton Wlk 3 YO31 . . . 229 A5
Ingman Lodge Rd BD24. . . 78 F1
INGMANTHORPE 180 E5
Ingramgate YO7 . . . . 211 C3
Ingrish La YO23. . . . . 182 C1
Ings Ave BD23. . . . . 216 D3
Ings Cl
　6 Pickering YO18. . . . . . 95 F6
　5 Willerby YO12. . . . . 99 D2
Ings Com Cty Sch BD23 . 216 D3

Ings Ct DN14. . . . . 202 F4
Ings Dr
　Low Bradley BD20 . . . . . . 173 E3
　Mickletown LS26 . . . . 200 C6
Ings Field Rd YO26. . . . . . 142 A3
Ingsgarth YO18 . . . . 95 F6
Ings La
　Ainderby Quernhow YO7 . . 88 D4
　Beal DN14 . . . . 202 D4
　Bishop Monkton HG3. . . . . 140 B5
　Bishop Wilton YO42. . . . . . 169 D2
　Bradleys Both BD20. . . . . . 173 E3
　Brompton YO13. . . . . 98 C4
　Carlton DN14. . . . . 204 E2
　Cawood YO19. . . . . 197 D8
　Cononley BD20 . . . . 173 D2
　Cottingwith YO42. . . . . . . 193 C5
　Crakehall DL8 . . . . 62 F5
　Ebberston & Yedingham
　　YO13. . . . . 97 E4
　Great Preston WF10 . . . . . 200 E6
　Harome YO62. . . . . 93 D4
　Hensall DN14. . . . . 203 D2
　Husthwaite YO61. . . . . . . 117 A6
　Hutton Buscel YO13. . . . . 99 A3
　Kellington DN14. . . . . 202 F4
　21 Kirkbymoorside YO62. . 70 B1
　Kirkbymoorside YO62 . . . . 94 B7
　Lastingham YO62. . . . . . . 70 F5
　Lillings Ambo YO32. . . . . . 145 C2
　Nether Poppleton YO26. . . 224 B1
　Pickering YO18. . . . . 95 E4
　Riccall YO19. . . . . 197 E8
　Roundhill Village TS15. . . . 5 D2
　Skipton BD23. . . . . 216 D2
　Snape with Thorp DL8. . . . 87 B7
　Stillington YO61. . . . . 144 A6
　Thorganby YO19. . . . . 193 B5
　Thorp Arch LS23 . . . . 189 A8
　Tollerton YO61. . . . . 143 B2
　Welburn YO62 . . . . 94 A5
　Wheldrake YO19 . . . . 193 B7
　Wighill LS24. . . . . 189 D8
　4 Willerby YO12. . . . . . . 99 D2
　Wistow YO8. . . . . 198 A6
Ings Mere Ct WF11. . . . . . 201 C6
Ings Rd
　Cliffe YO8. . . . . 198 D2
　Dunsforths YO26. . . . . 142 A3
　Thorganby YO19. . . . . 193 B4
　Ulleskelf LS24. . . . . 190 C3
　West Ayton YO13. . . . . . . 99 B6
　Wilberfoss YO41 . . . . 185 E6
Ings Terr YO22. . . . . 31 C4
Ings View
　2 Bedale DL8. . . . . 63 B3
　Castleford WF10 . . . . 201 A4
　Mickletown LS26 . . . . 200 C6
　Tollerton YO61. . . . . 143 A2
　York YO30 . . . . 224 D2
Ingthorne La LS25 . . . . . . 195 F1
Ingthorns La LS25. . . . . . . 195 F1
Ingthorpe La
　Martons Both BD23. . . . . . 171 E7
　Monk Fryston LS25 . . . . . . 196 A1
Inhams La YO26. . . . . 141 F2
INHOLMES. 189 C6
Inholmes La
　Tadcaster LS24 . . . . 189 D5
　Walton LS23 . . . . 181 B2
Inman Gr HG5. . . . . 221 B8
Inman Terr YO26. . . . . 227 D4
Inman Wlk HG5. . . . . 221 B8
In Moor La HG3. . . . . 109 F6
Innisfree Cl HG2 . . . . 220 B1
Innovation Cl YO10. . . . . . 229 B2
Innovation Way YO10. . . . 229 B2
Institute St 4 BD20. . . . . 187 E7
Intake Ave YO30 . . . . 228 C8
Intakefield Rd YO8. . . . . . 199 D7
Intake La
　Acaster Malbis YO23. . . . . 191 C7
　Beal WF11 . . . . 202 D5
　Dunnington YO19. . . . . . . 184 F7
　Grassington BD23. . . . . . . 134 E3
　Habton YO17. . . . . 121 E7
　Heck DN14. . . . . 207 C8
　Tollerton YO61. . . . . 143 B4
　West Haddlesey YO8. . . . . 202 F6
Intake The
　3 Kippax LS25 . . . . 194 D1
　Osgodby YO11 . . . . 100 B7
Invicta Ct YO24. . . . . 230 B8
IREBY. 102 F6
Ireby Rd LA6. . . . . 102 F3
Ireton St 3 YO12. . . . . . . 212 E5
Iron Row LS29 . . . . 176 C1
IRTON. 99 D6
Irton Moor La YO12. . . . . 212 A1
Irvine Way YO24. . . . . 230 B7
Irwin Ave YO31 . . . . 228 E6
Isabella Rd LS25 . . . . 194 D5
Island Heritage★ HG4. . . 111 B8
Islebeck La YO7. . . . . 115 F8
IVELET. 36 D5
Iver Cl YO26. . . . . 227 C5
Ivy Bank Ct 4 YO13. . . . . 75 D5
Ivy Cl
　Follifoot HG3. . . . . 223 F4
　Marton YO51. . . . . 141 D1
Ivy Cotts DL7 . . . . 210 D4
Ivy Cres DL8 . . . . 62 B4
Ivy Ct LS29 . . . . 218 B3
Ivy Dene Ct 26 BD24. . . . 131 D2
Ivy House Cl 6 YO11. . . . 100 B6
Ivy House Gdns BD23. . . . 155 D1
Ivy La LS23 . . . . 188 E8

Ivy Pl
　22 Cross Hills BD20 . . . . . 187 E8
　York YO32 . . . . 225 D3
Ivy Yd 16 YO22. . . . . 208 E6

J

Jack Field La BD20. . . . . . 187 D6
Jack Hill La LS21. . . . . 176 F6
Jack Hole YO61. . . . . 142 F4
Jack La
　Crayke YO61. . . . . 118 A1
　Stillington YO61. . . . . 144 C7
　Wigglesworth BD23. . . . . . 153 C4
Jackson Cl YO11. . . . . 100 B6
Jackson Dr TS9. . . . . 26 C8
Jackson La YO41. . . . . 185 E4
Jackson's La
　Bradleys Both BD23. . . . . . 173 D3
　Eastfield YO11. . . . . 100 A8
　Kirk Smeaton WF8. . . . . . 206 A4
　Scarborough YO11. . . . . . . 213 A1
Jackson St
　4 Glusburn BD20. . . . . . 187 E7
　York YO31 . . . . 233 C4
Jackson's Wlk YO23. . . . . 182 D3
Jacobi Cl YO30 . . . . 228 A7
Jacques Gr BD20. . . . . 174 C1
Jaffa Rd DL9. . . . . 209 E2
Jagger La DL10 . . . . 20 E6
Jagoe Rd 8 BB18. . . . . . . 172 A1
James Backhouse Pl
　YO24 . . . . 227 E5
James Cl LS25 . . . . 194 D4
James Cook Univ Hospl The
　TS4 . . . . .7 B8
James Cl DL10. . . . . 209 F7
James La DL10. . . . . 41 A2
James Nicolson Link
　YO30 . . . . 225 A2
Jameson Cres YO12. . . . . 212 D5
James Pl 2 YO12. . . . . . . 213 A6
James St
　Castleford WF10 . . . . 200 E5
　20 Earby BB18. . . . . 172 A1
　10 Glusburn BD20. . . . . . 187 E8
　Harrogate HG1 . . . . 219 D2
　Scarborough YO12. . . . . . . 213 A6
　Selby YO8. . . . . 232 C5
　York YO10 . . . . 228 E4
Jamesville Way YO7 . . . . 115 B6
James Way YO10. . . . . 229 A1
Jamieson Terr YO23 . . . . . 228 B1
Janesway LS25 . . . . 194 C1
Janet's Foss★ BD23. . . . . 133 B2
Jasmine Cl
　5 Snaith DN14. . . . . 204 C1
　York YO32 . . . . 225 D2
Jasmine Fields 1 TS15. . . 24 E8
Jasmine Garth 6 YO41. . . 185 C2
Jasmine Gdns 13 WF10. . . 200 D3
Jasper La HG3. . . . . 179 A3
Jay Ave TS17 . . . . .6 B4
Jaywick Cl YO32 . . . . 167 B8
Jedburgh Dr DL3 . . . . .2 F7
Jedwell Cl YO32 . . . . 225 D5
Jeffry Bog Nature Reserve★
　YO60. . . . . 147 C5
Jenkins Fold LA6 . . . . 103 D3
Jennifer Gr 4 YO24. . . . . 227 F2
JENNYFIELD. 219 A5
Jenny Field Dr HG3. . . . . 219 B4
Jenny Frisk Rd TS12. . . . . .9 E6
Jenny Gill Cres BD23. . . . 217 B3
Jenny La DN14. . . . . 207 B5
Jerry Carr Bank YO62 . . . 92 B1
Jerry Croft 2 BD23. . . . . 217 A4
Jerry La BD20. . . . . 174 F1
Jersey Ct YO12 . . . . 99 C7
Jervaulx Abbey★ HG4. . . 85 D8
Jervaulx Dr HG5 . . . . 221 D4
Jervaulx Rd DL7. . . . . 64 A6
Jervis Ct YO41. . . . . 185 C1
Jervis Rd YO24. . . . . 230 E4
Jesmond Ct YO17 . . . . . . 215 E3
Jesmond Gr 5 TS18 . . . . .5 E8
Jesmond Rd
　Darlington DL1. . . . . .3 F7
　Harrogate HG1 . . . . 220 A3
Jessamine Pl 1 BD20. . . . 187 F7
Jewbury YO31. . . . . 233 C3
Jewitt La LS22. . . . . 188 B8
Jin Whin Ct YO10. . . . . . . 200 D4
Jin-Whin Hill WF10. . . . . 200 C4
Jobbing Cross YO61. . . . . 116 C3
Jockey La
　Huntington YO32 . . . . 225 F2
　5 Knaresborough HG5. . . 221 A6
Joffre Ave WF10. . . . . 200 F3
John Breckon Rd YO21. . . 28 D5
John Dixon La DL1. . . . . . . 3 D5
John Fowler Way 14 DL2 . 3 A7
John of Gaunt's Castle★
　HG3. . . . . 160 B1
John Smiths Brewery★
　LS24 . . . . 189 E6
Johnson Cl
　Brompton on Swale DL10 . 41 C7
　1 Thirsk YO7 . . . . 211 C3
Johnson St YO8. . . . . 232 B6
Johnson Way YO7. . . . . . . 211 D2
John St
　Darlington DL1. . . . . .3 D6
　11 Earby BB18. . . . . 172 A1
　35 Filey YO14. . . . . 101 B3
　Great Ayton TS9. . . . . 8 A2
　11 Harrogate HG1. . . . . . 219 D2

John St continued
　Selby YO8. . . . . 232 D6
　Whitby YO21 . . . . 208 D7
　York YO31 . . . . 228 E6
Jolby La
　Cleasby DL10. . . . . .2 E1
　Croft-on-Tees DL2 . . . . . . 22 B8
　Newton Morrell DL2 . . . . . 21 F8
Jonah's La HG3. . . . . 160 B1
Jonathan Garth 17 LS29 . 174 F4
Jorvik Cl YO26 . . . . 227 C5
JORVIK Viking Ctr★
　YO1. . . . . 233 C2
Joseph Rowntree Sch The
　YO32. . . . . 225 E5
Jowett's La BD20 . . . . 174 B3
Jowland Winn La YO8. . . . 204 A4
Jubber Gate YO1. . . . . 233 B2
Jubilee Bank TS7 . . . . 7 C8
Jubilee Cave★ BD24 . . . . 131 F4
Jubilee Cl BD23. . . . . 216 D3
Jubilee Croft 1 BD23 . . . 153 F5
Jubilee Ct
　Richmond DL10 . . . . 209 E8
　1 Tollerton YO61 . . . . . . 143 B3
　Wigginton YO32. . . . . 225 D8
Jubilee Gdns DL6 . . . . 210 F3
Jubilee Rd
　Norton YO17. . . . . 215 E3
　Wistow YO8. . . . . 197 D6
Jubilee Terr YO26. . . . . . . 227 F5
Judson Cl HG4. . . . . 214 C4
Julia Ave YO32. . . . . 226 B2
JUNCTION. 187 F8
Junction 32 Sh Village★
　WF10 . . . . 200 F3
Junction Farm Prim Sch
　TS16 . . . . 5 D5
Jungle (Castleford Tigers
　RFC) The WF10 . . . . 200 F5
Juniper Cl YO32 . . . . 225 D3
Juniper Dr YO8 . . . . 232 D2
Juniper Gr TS21 . . . . 5 C8
Juniper Way 28 HG3 . . . . 161 B3
Jura Dr DL1 . . . . .3 E8
Jute Rd YO26 . . . . 227 B5
Jutland Rd DL9 . . . . 209 C2

K

Kader Ave TS5. . . . . 6 D7
Kader Prim Sch TS5. . . . . .6 E7
Kail La BD23. . . . . 156 F8
Kangel Cl HG4. . . . . 214 E3
Kareen Ave 3 YO12. . . . . 99 E6
Kathryn Ave YO32. . . . . . . 226 A2
Kaye Dr YO8. . . . . 198 B4
Kay House La TS15 . . . . . . 24 D5
Kays Bank YO61. . . . . 117 C5
Kearby Cliff LS27 . . . . 179 B1
Kearsley Cl TS16. . . . . .5 E7
Kearsley Rd HG4 . . . . 214 B7
Kearton DL11 . . . . 37 D6
KEASDEN. 130 A5
Keasden Rd LA2 . . . . 130 A3
Keats Cl
　4 Pontefract WF8 . . . . . 201 B1
　York YO30 . . . . 227 B1
Keats Wlk HG1. . . . . 219 E7
Keble Cl YO23 . . . . 231 B3
Keble Dr YO23 . . . . 231 A2
Keble Garth LS25 . . . . 194 E1
Keble Gdns YO23 . . . . 231 B2
Keble Park Cres YO23 . . . 231 A2
Keble Park N YO23 . . . . . . 231 A3
Keble Park S YO23 . . . . . . 231 A2
Keeper's Cl YO61 . . . . 118 A1
Keepers Gate 18 YO18. . . 95 F6
Keepers's Hill YO25. . . . . 150 A1
Keepers Way 11 YO19 . . . 184 F7
Keighley Rd
　Bradleys Both BD23. . . . . . 173 D3
　1 Colne BB8. . . . . 186 A3
　Cowling BD22 . . . . 187 B6
　2 Glusburn BD20. . . . . . 187 F7
　Ilkley LS29. . . . . 218 A2
　Laneshaw Bridge BB8. . . . 186 D3
　Skipton BD23. . . . . 216 F2
　Trawden Forest BB8. . . . . 186 B3
Keilder Rise TS8 . . . . .6 F5
Keith Ave YO32 . . . . 226 A4
Keith Rd TS4 . . . . .6 F8
KELBROOK. 186 A8
Kelbrook Prim Sch BB18 186 A7
Kelbrook Rd BB18. . . . . . . 171 D1
Kelcbar Cl LS24. . . . . 189 D6
Kelcbar Hill LS24 . . . . 189 D6
Kelcbar Way LS24. . . . . . . 189 D6
Kelcow Caves★ BD24. . . . 131 D3
KELD 35 E8
Keldale 4 YO32 . . . . 166 F5
Keldale Gdns HG4. . . . . . . 214 F6
Keld Cl
　Melmerby HG4. . . . . 114 B6
　Pickering YO18. . . . . 95 E7
　Scalby YO12. . . . . 212 B8
Keldgate Rd YO18. . . . . . . 72 A3
Keldhead YO18 . . . . 95 E8
Keld Head Orch 1 YO62. . 70 B1
Keld Head Rd YO62 . . . . . 70 A1
Keldheads La DL8. . . . . . . 59 F5
KELDHOLME 70 D1
KELD HOUSES 136 C2
Keld La
　Hutton-le-Hole YO62 . . . . 70 C5
　Newton YO18. . . . . 72 A5
　Thorpe Bassett YO17. . . . 123 A3

Keld Runnels Rd YO13. . . . 75 A4
KELFIELD. 191 D1
Kelfield Rd 9 YO19 . . . . . 197 F8
Kellaw Rd DL1. . . . . .3 F5
Kell Bank HG4 . . . . 85 E3
Kell Bank CE Prim Sch
　HG4. . . . . 85 E3
Kell Beck 1 LS25 . . . . . . 176 F1
KELLINGLEY 202 C2
KELLINGTON. 202 F4
Kellington Ct 9 DN14. . . . 202 F2
Kellington La DN14 . . . . . 202 F2
Kellington Prim Sch
　DN14. . . . . 202 F3
Kell Syke La BD23. . . . . . 155 A6
Kelvin Terr DL7. . . . . 210 D4
Kemmel Cl DL9 . . . . 40 E2
Kempton Cl 2 YO24. . . . . 227 D1
Kempton Ct 13 DL1 . . . . . .3 F6
Kendal Cl
　6 Dunnington YO19 . . . . 184 F7
　Hellifield BD23. . . . . 154 B3
Kendal Dr WF10. . . . . 201 B4
Kendal Gdns YO26 . . . . . . 181 D7
Kendal La YO26. . . . . 181 D7
Kendalmans 4 BD24. . . . 131 D2
Kendal Rd
　Harrogate HG1 . . . . 220 B3
　Long Preston BD23 . . . . . . 154 A3
Kendrew Cl
　11 Bedale DL8. . . . . 63 A2
　3 York YO32. . . . . 225 F3
Kenilworth Ave HG2. . . . . 222 D7
Kenilworth Dr 3 BB18 . . . 172 A1
Kenlay Cl YO32 . . . . 225 D4
Kennedy Dr 32 YO32. . . . 166 E5
Kennels La LS14 . . . . 188 A4
Kenneth Campbell Rd
　HG1. . . . . 219 E2
Kennet La LS25 . . . . 194 D3
Kennion Ct 2 HG2. . . . . . 220 B3
Kennion Rd HG2 . . . . 220 B3
KENNYTHORPE 147 F5
Kenrick Pl 5 YO26. . . . . . 227 B5
Kensal Rise YO10 . . . . 228 D2
Kensington Ave
　Eston & South Bank TS6 . . 7 E8
　Thorner LS14. . . . . 188 A3
Kensington Ct 1 YO24 . . . 230 F8
Kensington Gdns DL1 . . . . 3 E5
Kensington Rd YO30 . . . . . 224 D2
Kensington Sq 10 HG2. . . 219 C2
Kensington St YO23 . . . . . 228 B1
Kent Ave HG1. . . . . 219 B3
Kent Cl HG4 . . . . 214 A2
Kent Ct 7 DL9. . . . . 209 C1
Kent Dr HG1. . . . . 219 B3
Kentmere Dr YO30 . . . . . . 224 F1
Kenton Cl 4 TS18. . . . . . .5 E8
Kent Rd
　Guisborough TS14 . . . . 8 E5
　Harrogate HG1 . . . . 219 B3
　Selby YO8. . . . . 232 A6
Kent Rise HG1. . . . . 219 A2
Kent Road N HG1 . . . . 219 B3
Kent St YO10 . . . . 233 C1
KEPWICK. 66 C6
Kerrside YO30 . . . . 227 E8
Kershaw Ave WF10. . . . . . 201 A4
Kerver La YO19 . . . . 184 F7
Kesteven Rd TS4. . . . . 7 A7
Kestrel Dr 7 DL9. . . . . . . 40 F2
Kestrel Mews 21 WF6 . . . 200 A1
Kestrel View 7 YO12. . . . 99 E6
Kestrel Wood Way YO31. . 225 F2
Keswick Dr WF10 . . . . 201 C5
Keswick Gr
　4 Darlington DL1. . . . . . . 3 D4
　Middlesbrough TS5 . . . . . . 6 D7
Keswick Way 5 YO32 . . . 225 F5
Kettle End DL10. . . . . 21 C7
KETTLENESS. 12 D6
Kettlesbeck Brow LA2. . . . 130 C5
KETTLESING 160 C3
KETTLESING BOTTOM. . . . 160 D4
Kettlesing Felliscliffe Prim
　Sch HG3. . . . . 160 C4
Kettle Spring La HG3. . . . 139 B1
Kettlestring La YO30 . . . . 225 A3
KETTLEWELL 108 B3
Kettlewell La DL8. . . . . . . 57 C5
Kettlewell Prim Sch
　BD23. . . . . 108 A3
Kew at Castle Howard★
　YO60. . . . . 146 C8
KEXBY 185 C6
Kexby Ave YO10. . . . . 228 D2
Kexby Stray YO41 . . . . . . 185 A5
Kex Gill Rd HG3. . . . . 158 F2
KEY GREEN 31 A3
Key La YO61. . . . . 118 A1
Keys Beck Rd YO18. . . . . . 71 F8
Keystone Ave 3 WF10 . . . 200 F2
Key Way YO19 . . . . 231 F5
Khyber Pass YO21. . . . . . . 208 D7
Kiddal La LS15. . . . . 188 C2
Kidstones Bank DL8. . . . . . 81 E3
Kielder Dr DL1. . . . . .3 F2
Kielder Oval HG2. . . . . . . 220 D2
KILBURN 91 B2
Kilburn Rd YO10 . . . . 228 D2
KILDALE. 27 E8
Kildale Sta YO21. . . . . 27 E8
Kildare Garth 5 YO62. . . . 70 C1
KILDWICK 187 E8
Kildwick CE Prim Sch
　BD20. . . . . 187 F8
Kilgram La HG4. . . . . 85 E8

Kilham Rd YO25 151 D5
KILLERBY 100 C5
Killerby Dr 2 DL10 41 E4
Killerby La YO11 100 C5
KILLINGHALL 161 C5
Killinghall CE Prim Sch
HG3 161 C5
Killin Rd DL1 3 E7
Kilmarnock Rd DL1 3 E8
Kiln Dr BD23 134 B3
Kilners Croft 11 LS29 174 F4
Kiln Hill La
Lawkland LA2 131 A6
Silsden BD20 174 A3
Kiln La LA2 128 A6
KILNSEY 134 B6
Kilnsey Fold BD20 174 A1
Kilnsey Pk* BD23 134 B6
Kilnwick Ct DL7 210 D3
Kilton Ct DL11 2 A2
Kilton La TS12 9 F7
KILTON THORPE 10 B8
Kilton Thorpe La TS12 10 B8
Kimberley St LS29 218 C5
Kimberlows Wood Hill 3
YO10 229 C3
Kinbrace Dr YO24 230 B7
King Edward Ave WF10 200 C7
King Edward Rd HG4 214 C3
King Edward's Dr HG1 219 D5
King Edward St
27 Glusburn BD20 187 E7
Normanton South WF6 200 A1
Kingfisher Cl 7 YO12 99 F6
Kingfisher Ct
22 Castleford WF10 200 A1
3 Scotton DL9 40 F2
Kingfisher Dr
3 Bedale DL8 63 B3
Guisborough TS14 8 D6
14 Pickering YO18 95 F6
Whitby YO22 208 E3
Kingfisher La LS25 194 F8
Kingfisher Reach
17 Boroughbridge YO51 141 B5
5 Collingham LS22 180 A1
King Garth 3 DL8 58 F1
King George Rd 1 HG4 214 C3
King Hill YO14 101 A2
King James Rd HG5 221 B5
King James's Sch HG5 221 B5
King Rudding Cl 6
YO19 198 A8
King Rudding La YO19 198 B8
Kings Acad The TS8 7 A5
Kings Acre YO31 229 B6
Kings Arms Ct YO7 211 B3
Kings Ave 2 LS29 218 A4
Kings Cl
5 Barlby YO8 198 B5
19 Ilkley LS29 175 C2
15 Pateley Bridge HG3 137 B4
King's Cl 9 DL10 41 D5
Kingsclere YO32 225 F6
Kings Ct YO1 233 B2
King's Gate LA2 130 D3
King's Gdns YO7 211 B1
Kings Keld Bank DL8 86 F8
Kings La YO13 97 D5
Kingsland Terr 11 YO26 227 F5
Kings Lea YO8 199 A8
Kingsley Ave WF11 201 D3
Kingsley Cl HG1 220 C3
Kingsley Croft 7 BD20 187 F8
Kingsley Dr
Castleford WF10 201 B3
Harrogate HG1 220 A4
2 Middleham DL8 60 E2
Kingsley Park Mews 1
HG1 220 C3
Kingsley Park Rd HG1 220 C3
Kingsley Rd
Harrogate HG1 220 B5
Trawden Forest BB8 186 B3
Kings Manor Sch TS5 6 E7
Kings Mdws YO7 89 E3
Kings Mead HG4 214 B7
Kings Mill La 8 BD24 131 D2
Kings Moor Rd YO32 167 D2
Kings Rd
Ilkley LS29 218 A4
Knaresborough HG5 221 C6
King's Rd 6 HG1 219 D3
King's Sq YO1 233 C2
King's St 7 BD23 217 B4
King's Staith YO1 233 B2
King St
Castleford WF10 200 F3
6 Cawood YO8 197 B8
7 High Bentham LA2 129 A8
Muston YO14 100 F2
Normanton South WF6 200 A1
Pateley Bridge HG3 137 B4
Richmond DL10 209 C6
Ripon HG4 214 C4
Scarborough YO11 213 A6
3 Silsden BD20 174 C1
York YO1 233 B2
Kingsthorpe YO24 227 D2
Kingsthorpe Pk 11 YO8 197 D6
Kingston Ave HG4 214 C3
Kingston Cres YO8 196 E2
Kingston Dr
24 Castleford WF6 200 B1
Hambleton YO8 196 E1
16 Normanton WF6 200 B1
Norton YO17 215 E2
Kingston Garth 2 YO22 33 C3
Kingston Gr 5 YO12 212 B7
Kingstonia Gdns 3 HG4 214 C3
Kingstonia Pl HG4 214 C2
Kingsway
Garforth LS25 194 B3
Harrogate HG1 219 E3
Pontefract WF8 201 B2
Scalby YO12 212 C8
Skipton BD23 217 B5
6 Stamford Bridge YO41 168 D2
Weeton LS17 178 B2
Kingsway Dr
Harrogate HG1 219 E2
4 Ilkley LS29 218 A4
Kingsway Garth LS25 194 B3
Kingsway N YO30 228 B7
Kingsway W YO24 227 D1
Kingswood Gr YO24 227 D3
Kinloss Cl TS17 6 C7
Kinsey Cave* BD24 131 C4
Kintyre Dr TS17 6 B6
KIPLIN 42 B4
Kiplin Dr 14 DN6 206 E2
Kipling Dr 35 DL9 41 A5
Kipling Gr WF8 201 B2
Kiplin Hall* DL10 42 B4
KIPPAX 194 E1
Kippax Ash Tree Prim Sch
LS25 194 D1
Kippax Greenfield Prim Sch
LS25 194 D1
Kippax L Ctr LS25 200 D8
Kippax North Prim Sch
LS25 194 C2
KIRBY GRINDALYTHE 149 E6
KIRBY HILL
Boroughbridge 141 B7
Moulton 20 A5
Kirby Hill CE Prim Sch
YO51 141 B7
KIRBY KNOWLE 66 C2
Kirby La
Ebberston & Yedingham
YO17 97 E1
Sledmere YO25 150 A4
KIRBY MISPERTON 95 D2
Kirby Misperton La
YO17 121 C7
Kirby Misperton Rd YO17 95 F2
KIRBY SIGSTON 44 D1
KIRBY UNDERDALE 170 A5
KIRBY WISKE 88 F8
Kir Cres YO24 227 C3
Kirk Balk YO17 169 E8
Kirk Balk La YO60 168 B7
Kirk Bank
Conistone with Kilnsey
BD23 134 B4
Kirkby Malzeard HG4 112 A5
Kirkbank La CA17 14 A8
KIRKBRIDGE 62 F5
KIRKBY 26 D5
Kirkby Ave
Ripon HG4 214 A6
Selby YO8 232 B7
Kirkby Brow
Kirkby Malham BD23 154 F8
Malham BD23 132 F1
Kirkby Cl HG4 214 A6
Kirkby Dr HG4 214 A6
KIRKBY FLEETHAM 42 D1
Kirkby Fleetham CE Prim Sch
DL7 42 C1
Kirkby & Great Broughton CE
Prim Sch TS9 26 E5
Kirkby La
Gillamoor YO62 70 A3
Kearby with Netherby HG3 179 B2
Kirkby Fleetham with Fencote
DL7 42 C2
Kirkby TS9 26 D6
Sicklinghall LS22 179 D3
KIRKBY MALHAM 154 F8
Kirkby Malham Prim Sch
BD23 154 F8
KIRKBY MALZEARD 112 D5
Kirkby Malzeard CE Prim Sch
HG4 112 D5
KIRKBY MILLS 94 C8
Kirkby Mills Ind Est YO62 94 C8
KIRKBYMOORSIDE 70 B1
Kirkbymoorside Prim Sch
YO62 70 A1
KIRKBY OVERBLOW 179 A4
Kirkby Rd
North Stainley with Sleningford
HG4 113 C4
Ripon HG4 214 A6
Selby YO8 232 B7
KIRKBY WHARFE 190 A3
Kirkcaldy Fold WF6 200 B1
Kirkcroft YO32 225 C8
Kirkdale La YO62 93 F8
Kirkdale Rd YO10 229 D4
Kirkdale Way HG2 219 C1
KIRK DEIGHTON 180 B5
Kirk Fenton Prim Sch
LS24 196 B8
Kirkfield Ave LS14 188 A3
Kirkfield Cres LS14 188 A3
Kirkfield La LS14 188 A3
Kirkfield Rd DL3 3 D8
Kirkgate
Knaresborough HG5 221 A6
7 Middleham DL8 60 E2
12 Ripon HG4 214 C5
Settle BD24 131 D2
Sherburn in Elmet LS25 195 E4
Kirkgate *continued*
Silsden BD20 174 C1
Thirsk YO7 211 B3
Kirk Gate
Brompton YO13 98 C7
Silpho YO13 74 E6
Kirkgate La YO62 70 F4
KIRKHAM 147 A4
Kirkham Ave 1 YO31 228 E8
Kirkham Bridge* YO60 146 F4
Kirkham Cl 6 YO21 208 C6
Kirkham Ct 5 HG5 221 C4
Kirkham Gr HG1 219 F6
KIRK HAMMERTON 164 C2
Kirk Hammerton CE Prim
Sch YO26 164 C2
Kirk Hammerton La
YO26 164 C3
Kirkham Pl HG1 219 F6
Kirkham Priory (rems of)*
YO60 146 F4
Kirkham Rd
Harrogate HG1 219 F6
Middlesbrough TS7 7 D6
Whitby YO21 208 C6
Kirkham View YO60 147 B4
Kirkhaw La WF11 201 D4
Kirk Hills LS14 188 A3
Kirk Ings La YO7 66 B7
Kirk La
Embsay with Eastby
BD23 217 E8
Tockwith YO26 181 C7
Kirkland Cl YO8 232 D4
Kirklands YO32 167 B6
Kirklands La YO41 169 C2
Kirkleavington Hall Dr
TS15 5 E1
KIRKLEVINGTON 24 F8
Kirklevington Prim Sch
TS15 24 F8
KIRKLINGTON 88 A4
Kirk Rd
Eaglescliffe TS15 5 F2
Northallerton DL7 210 B3
KIRK SMEATON 206 B3
Kirk Smeaton CE Prim Sch
WF8 206 B3
Kirkstall Dr BB18 171 E2
Kirkstone Dr YO31 229 A6
Kirkstone Rd HG1 220 B4
Kirk Syke La BD23 155 A5
Kirk View 1 YO26 227 C3
Kirkwell YO23 231 A4
Kitchen Dr YO8 232 D4
Kitchener Cl YO8 232 B5
Kitchener Rd
Ripon HG4 113 D3
Scotton DL9 40 E4
Kitchener St
Selby YO8 232 B6
York YO31 228 D7
Kitemere Pl 2 YO24 230 B8
Kit Kat Crescent (York City
FC) YO31 228 B7
Kit La BD20 174 B3
Kitter La YO21 31 C8
Kitty Garth YO19 193 A7
Kitty Hill (Tumulus)*
YO41 169 E3
Knapping Hill HG1 219 C5
KNAPTON 227 A5
Knapton Cl 1 YO32 167 B6
Knapton La YO26 227 B4
Knapton Wold Rd YO17 123 C5
KNARESBOROUGH 221 A6
Knaresborough Ave TS7 7 B5
Knaresborough Castle*
HG5 221 A5
Knaresborough House &
Gdns* HG5 221 A6
Knaresborough Mus*
HG5 221 A5
Knaresborough Rd
Bishop Monkton HG3 140 B4
Follifoot HG3 223 F5
Harrogate HG1 219 F2
Little Ribston LS22 180 A8
Ripon HG4 214 C3
Knaresborough Sta HG5 221 A6
Knaresborough Swimming
Pool HG5 221 B5
KNAVESMIRE 231 A7
Knavesmire Cl YO62 93 C5
Knavesmire Cres YO23 228 B1
Knavesmire Prim Sch
YO23 228 B1
Knavesmire Rd
Nunthorpe YO23 231 B8
York YO23 228 A1
KNAYTON 65 F2
Knayton CE Prim Sch YO7 65 E3
KNEDLINGTON 205 E6
Kneeton Cl DL10 21 C5
Kneeton La DL10 21 C5
Knightsway LS25 194 B3
Knipe Point Dr 8 YO11 100 B8
Knolls Cl 11 YO11 100 B7
Knolls La YO62 67 F5
Knoll The
3 Bramham LS23 188 E6
York YO24 227 B2
Knot La BB7 171 A5
KNOTTINGLEY 201 F3
Knottingley High Sch
WF11 202 A2
Knottingley Rd WF8 201 D1
Knottingley Sta WF11 201 F2
Knottingley Vale Junior &
Infant Sch WF11 201 E2
Knott La
Easingwold YO61 143 C8
Steeton with Eastburn
BD20 187 F7
Knotto Bottom Cl DL6 210 F3
Knotto Bottom Way DL6 210 F3
Knott Rd YO18 49 D5
Knotts La BD23 152 E1
Knowle La
Ilton-cum-Pott HG4 85 D1
Kirby Knowle YO7 66 C2
Knowles Cl 5 TS15 24 E8
KNOX 219 B7
Knox Ave HG1 219 C5
Knox Chase HG1 219 C6
Knox Cl HG1 219 D6
Knox Dr HG1 219 C6
Knox Gdns HG1 219 C6
Knox Gr HG1 219 C6
Knox La
Harrogate HG1 219 D6
Scarborough YO11 213 B1
Knox Mill Bank HG3 219 B7
Knox Mill Cl HG3 219 B7
Knox Mill La HG3 219 B7
Knox Pk HG3 219 B7
Knox Rd HG1 219 D6
Knox Rise HG1 219 C6
Knox Way HG1 219 C5
Kyle Cl 3 YO61 143 B3
Kyle Way YO26 227 B8
Kyme Castle* LS24 189 C7
Kyme St YO1 233 B1

L

La Bassee Rd DL9 209 D1
Laburnum Ave
Fylingdales YO22 33 C4
Thornaby TS17 6 B7
Laburnum Cl
Rufforth YO23 182 C6
3 Thorpe Willoughby YO8 197 B1
Laburnum Ct
Barlow YO8 204 D7
1 Castleford WF10 200 F3
Laburnum Dr HG3 140 A5
Laburnum Farm Cl YO26 182 C8
Laburnum Garth 6
YO31 228 F8
Laburnum Gr
Harrogate HG1 219 E6
Richmond DL10 209 D8
Stillingfleet YO19 191 D4
Whitby YO21 208 B6
Laburnum Rd TS7 7 D8
Lacey Ave YO12 99 D7
Lachman Rd BB8 186 A2
Lack La YO62 93 C2
Lackon Bank HG3 160 D6
Lacy Gr LS22 180 C2
Ladgate La TS5 6 F6
Lady Anne Ct YO1 233 B1
Lady Balk La WF8 201 B1
Ladycarr La YO61 143 E8
Lady East Hastings CE Prim
Sch WF10 200 F7
Lady Edith's Ave YO12 212 B6
Lady Edith's Cres YO12 212 B6
Lady Edith's Dr YO12 212 A6
Lady Edith's Pk YO12 212 B7
Lady Elizabeth Hastings CE
Prim Sch LS23 180 F1
Lady Grace's Ride YO12 212 A3
Lady Hamilton Gdns
YO24 227 E2
Lady Hartley Ct BB8 186 B3
Lady Hullocks Ct 12 TS9 26 C7
Lady Kell Gdns YO32 225 E8
Lady La HG3 222 A5
Lady Lumleys Sch YO18 95 F7
Lady Mill Garth YO30 228 B8
Lady Peckitts Yd YO1 233 B2
Lady Rd YO30 228 B7
Ladysmith Ave YO21 208 C7
Ladysmith Mews 13
YO32 167 A7
Ladysmith Rd DL9 40 C4
Ladywell La YO51 141 C5
Ladywell Rd YO51 141 B5
Lady Wortley Pl YO23 231 B6
Lagentium Plaza
8 Castleford WF10 200 F3
9 Castleford WF10 200 F3
Lairs Cres YO13 98 A5
Lairs La YO13 98 A5
Lairum Rise LS23 188 E7
Laithe Cl 9 BD20 174 C1
Laith Staid La LS25 195 D4
Lakeber Ave LA2 129 A8
Lakeber Dr LA2 129 A8
Lakeber St 8 LA2 129 A8
Lakeside
Acaster Malbis YO23 191 C7
Darlington DL1 3 C4
Hunmanby Sands YO14 101 B1
Scarthingwell LS24 195 F7
Lakeside App LS24 195 E7
Lakeside Cl LS29 218 A5
Lakeside County Prim Sch
YO30 224 F2
Lakeside Ct 26 WF6 200 B1
Lakeside Gr 1 YO32 167 B8
Lakeside Mdws 1 WF8 201 B2
Lakeside Way YO17 215 D2
Lake Terr HG4 112 D7
Lake View WF8 201 B2
Laking La YO25 126 A3
Lambert Ct YO1 233 B1
Lambert Meml Hospl
YO7 211 B2
Lambert St
11 Skipton BD23 217 A3
2 Trawden BB8 186 B1
Lambeth St 8 BB8 186 A3
Lambfield Way 8 TS17 6 A6
Lamb Inn Rd 9 WF11 202 A2
Lamb La TS17 6 A4
Lambourne Dr TS7 7 C6
Lambs La 12 YO18 95 F7
Lamb's La TS9 27 B4
Lamel St YO10 229 A3
Lamplugh Cres YO23 231 B3
Lanacar La DL8 56 A4
Lancar Cl 18 YO32 166 D5
Lancaster Cl
9 Scalby YO13 75 D5
Sherburn in Elmet LS25 196 B4
Lancaster Ct 24 YO51 141 B5
Lancaster Park Rd HG2 220 A3
Lancaster Rd
Harrogate HG2 219 C1
North Cowton DL7 22 C2
Lancaster St 6 YO11 213 A6
Lancaster Way
Middlesbrough TS17 6 B6
17 Scalby YO13 75 D5
York YO30 225 A1
Lancers Ct 4 YO12 75 F5
Landalewood Rd YO30 224 F2
Landau Cl YO30 227 F8
Landing La
Asselby DN14 205 D6
Barlby with Osgodby YO8 232 F8
22 Haxby YO32 166 F5
Hemingbrough YO8 204 F8
Riccall YO19 197 F8
York YO26 227 E6
Landing Rd YO8 203 A7
Landings The 21 YO32 166 F5
Lands La HG5 220 E7
LANE END 171 C2
LANE ENDS 187 C6
Lane Ends La BD22 187 B7
Lane Foot Rd HG3 159 E8
Lanehead La DL11 18 H8
Lane House La BB8 186 B1
Lanehouse Rd TS17 6 B8
Lane House Rd BD22 187 A6
LANESHAW BRIDGE 186 C4
Laneshaw Bridge Prim Sch
BB8 186 B3
Lane The
Gate Helmsley YO41 168 B2
Mickleby TS13 12 A4
Lang Ave YO10 229 A4
LANGBAR 175 B6
Langbar Rd LS29 218 A6
LANGBAURGH 7 F2
Langbaurgh Cl TS9 8 A2
Langbaurgh Rd TS15 25 C4
Langber End La LA6 103 D1
Langber La BD23 154 A6
Langborne Rd 19 YO21 208 D6
Langbourne Rd YO21 208 D6
Langburn La YO21 29 A7
Langburn's Bank YO21 29 A7
LANGCLIFFE 131 E3
Langcliffe & Attermire
Nature Reserve* BD24 132 A3
Langcliffe Ave HG2 222 E8
Langcliffe Avenue E
HG2 222 E8
Langcliffe Garth BD23 108 B3
Langcliffe Rd BD24 131 D3
Langdale TS14 8 D6
Langdale Ave
3 Pontefract WF6 200 A2
York YO31 229 B6
Langdale Dr 2 WF6 200 A2
Langdale Gr YO8 232 B3
Langdale Mews 4 WF6 200 A2
Langdale Rd 3 YO12 212 F7
Langdale Terr YO21 208 C7
Langdon Way TS16 5 D5
Langer Hill La HG3 160 B5
Langford Cl 21 LS29 176 C1
Langford Ct 17 LS29 176 C1
Langford La LS29 176 C1
Langford Mews 19 LS29 176 C1
Langford Rd LS29 176 C1
Langford Ride 30 LS29 176 C1
Lang Gate YO13 74 E4
Langholm Cres DL3 3 C5
Langholme Dr YO26 227 C6
Langhorne Dr 2 DL11 38 B6
Lang Kirk Cl 2 BD20 173 F1
Langley Ave TS17 6 B8
Langley Ct 1 YO32 225 F6
Langley Dr YO17 215 E1
Langleys Rd 6 DN6 206 E1
Langold Dr 15 DN6 206 E2
Lang Rd
Bishopthorpe YO23 230 F4
York YO32 225 F6
Langrickgate La YO42 193 C5
Langsett Ave 7 YO14 101 A3
Langsett Gr YO30 224 F3
Langstrothdale Rd BD24 105 D7
LANGTHORNE 62 F6

LANGTHORPE...........141 A6
LANGTHWAITE..........17 E1
Langthwaite La DL8....59 C3
LANGTOFT.............151 D5
Langtoft Prim Sch YO25 151 C5
LANGTON..............147 F6
Langton Crossroads
YO17................148 B6
Langton Ct **1** YO32...167 A6
Langton La YO17.......148 C8
Langton Prim Sch YO17. 147 F5
Langton Rd
Langton YO17........148 A7
Norton YO17.........215 E2
Langwith Ave LS22.....188 A8
Langwith Stray YO10...184 C2
Lansdowne Rd TS15.....5 E3
Lansdowne Terr **5** YO10 228 E3
Lansdown Way **7** YO32. 166 F5
Lanshaw Bank BD23.....175 A7
Lanshaw Croft YO30.....224 F1
Lansbury Dr T313.......10 D8
Larch Ct DL1...........3 F4
Larchfield YO31........229 C7
Larchfield Com TS8......6 F4
Larchfield Sports Ctr DL3 . 3 C5
Larchfield St DL3.......3 C5
Larch Gr
1 Filey YO14.......101 B4
Pannal HG3..........222 E2
Larch Rd
Guisborough TS14.....8 E7
Selby YO8...........232 E2
6 Topcliffe YO7.....89 A1
Larch Way
35 Haxby YO32......166 E5
Selby YO8...........232 D2
Larkfield Cl
1 Copmanthorpe YO23 . 230 A3
Harrogate HG2........222 A7
Larkfield Dr HG2.......222 A7
Larkfield Rd
Harrogate HG2........222 A7
Selby YO8...........232 A4
Larkfield Way HG2......222 A7
Lark Hill HG4..........214 A7
Larkhill Cl HG4........214 A6
Lark Hill Cres **13** HG4..113 D2
Lark Hill Dr HG4.......214 A6
Lark La YO4...........214 A6
Larkspur Gr **14** HG3....161 B3
Larkspur Rd TS7........7 A6
Larpool Cres YO22......208 E4
Larpool Dr YO22........208 D3
Larpool La YO22........208 D4
Larpool Lane Ind Est
YO22...............208 D5
Lartington Way TS16....5 D5
Larun Beat The TS15....5 E2
Lascelles Ct DL6.......210 E4
Lascelles Gr HG2.......219 B1
Lascelles La
Malton YO17.........215 E6
Northallerton DL6.....210 E4
Lascelles Rd HG2.......222 B8
Lasenby Cl YO32........225 D5
LASTINGHAM...........70 F5
Lastingham Terr YO10...228 D2
Latimer La TS14........8 E6
Latimer Rd DL1.........3 F6
Lauderdale Dr TS14.....8 F6
Laughton Ave YO12......212 C5
Laundry La LA6.........103 D3
Laundry Rd
4 Filey YO14.......101 B3
3 Harrogate HG1.....220 C4
Lauradale La BD23......134 D1
Laurel Ave TS4.........7 A8
Laurel Cl
Burniston YO13.......75 D8
Earswick YO32........226 A7
Embsay BD23.........217 D8
Gateforth YO8........197 B1
Laurel Croft BD23......217 D8
Laurels Garth YO60.....145 C5
Laurels The
Barlby YO8..........198 B5
6 Northallerton DL6...210 E4
Laurence Gr YO8........232 D3
Laurence Jackson Sch
TS14...............8 F7
Lavender Ct **21** DL9....41 A5
Lavender Gr YO26.......227 E5
Laveracks Ind Est YO41..185 B3
Laverick Terr **9** YO22...208 E6
LAVERTON.............112 D4
Laverton Gdns HG3......219 A4
LAWKLAND............130 F5
LAWKLAND GREEN......131 A4
Law La HG3............138 F1
Lawn Ave LS29.........176 C1
Lawnfield Dr HG3.......140 B5
Lawnfield Rd HG3.......140 B5
Lawn La DN6...........207 E3
Lawn Rd **35** LS29......176 C1
Lawns Rd YO21.........29 E6
Lawns The HG2.........222 C8
Lawnswood Dr YO30.....227 F8
Lawnway YO31..........229 A7
Lawrence Cl YO12.......212 A8
Lawrence Cres YO10....209 E8
Lawrence Ct **11** YO10...228 E3
Lawrence Gr YO12.......212 A8
Lawrence Sq YO10......228 F3

Lawrence St YO10......228 E3
Lawsings Brow LA2.....130 B5
Lawson Ave **1** YO51....141 B4
Lawson Rd YO24........230 F7
Lawsons Cl YO14.......126 F7
Lawson's Ct DL2.......2 C6
Laycock Fields **11** BD22. 187 B6
LAYERTHORPE..........228 E4
Layerthorpe YO31.......233 C3
Layfield Prim Sch TS15... 5 D2
Lazenby Dr **10** LS22....180 B3
Lea Croft LS23.........188 E7
Leadhall Ave HG2.......222 D6
Leadhall Cl HG2........222 D6
Leadhall Cres HG2......222 E6
Leadhall Dr HG2........222 D7
Leadhall Gdns HG2......222 D6
Leadhall Gr HG2........222 D6
Leadhall La HG2........222 D6
Leadhall Rd HG2........222 C6
Leadhall View HG2......222 C5
Leadhall Way HG2.......222 D6
Leading Post St **8** YO11. 213 B6
Lead La
Brompton DL8........43 F3
Nether Silton YO7.....66 B7
Ripon HG4...........214 B3
Westerdale YO21......28 E4
Leadley Croft YO23.....230 A1
Lead Mill La YO1.......233 C1
Leafield Rd DL1........3 D4
Leahope Ct TS17.......6 C4
Leahurst Cl YO17.......215 E2
LEAKE...............65 F5
Leake La YO7..........65 F6
Leake St
Castleford WF10......200 F4
12 York YO10.......228 E3
LEALHOLM............30 B6
Lealholm Cres TS3......7 C8
Lealholm La YO21.......30 B5
Lealholm Prim Sch YO21. 30 C6
LEALHOLM SIDE........30 D7
Lealholm Sta YO21......30 B6
Leamington Rd LS29.....218 C5
Leamington Terr LS29...218 C5
Learmans Way YO23.....230 C3
Learning La DN14.......202 F1
Lease Rigg La YO22.....31 A3
Leases La DL10........41 E2
Leases Rd DL7.........63 C5
Leas Head Rd YO22.....32 B2
Leas La YO18..........95 F5
Leasmires Ave **10** YO61. 143 D8
Leas The
11 Brafferton YO61...115 F1
Darlington DL1.......3 D8
8 Eastfield YO11....99 F7
Leat Cl YO17..........215 D3
Leather Bank LS29......176 C1
LEATHLEY............177 D2
Leathley La LS21.......177 D1
LEAVENING...........147 E1
Leavening Prim Sch
YO17...............147 E2
Lea Way YO32..........226 A4
Leazon Hill **5** TS17....6 D6
LEBBERSTON..........100 D5
Le Cateau Prim Sch DL9 . 40 F4
Le Cateau Rd DL9......40 F4
LECK...............102 E7
Leck CE Prim Sch LA6...102 E7
Leconfield DL3.........3 B5
Leconfield Garth HG3....223 F5
Ledbury Way TS14......8 E6
Ledgate La LS25........201 E6
LEDSHAM............201 B8
LEDSTON.............200 F7
Ledston Ave LS25......194 D3
Ledston Hall★ WF10....200 F8
LEDSTON LUCK........194 F1
Ledston Mill La WF10...200 F8
Leech La DL10.........41 E4
Lee Ct DN14...........207 A7
Leeds Barnsdale Rd
WF10...............200 D3
Leeds La LS15.........194 A3
Leeds Rd
Allerton Bywater WF10 . 200 D7
Barwick in Elmet & Scholes
LS15.............194 A7
Castleford WF10......200 E3
Collingham LS22......188 A8
Great Preston WF10...200 C7
Harrogate HG2........219 D1
Ilkley LS29..........218 D5
Kippax LS25.........194 C2
Mickletown LS26......200 A6
Pannal HG3..........222 F3
Selby YO8...........232 A4
Tadcaster LS24.......189 D5
Leeman Rd YO26........233 A2
LEEMING.............63 D4
LEEMING BAR.........63 C5
Leeming Bar Ind Est DL7. 63 C5
Leeming Bar Sta DL7....63 C5
Leeming La
Brough with St Giles DL10 . 41 D5
Burneston DL8.......87 F8
4 Burton in Lonsdale LA6 102 F3
Catterick DL10.......41 E4
Kirklington-cum-Upsland
YO7.............88 A6
Leeming DL7.........63 C4
Melmerby YO7........114 D8
Theakston DL7.......63 E1

Leeming La continued
Thornthwaite with Padside
HG3.............159 D5
Leeming & Londonderry Com
Prim Sch DL7........63 D4
Leeming (RAF) Cty Prim Sch
DL7...............63 F3
Leeside YO24..........230 E8
Lees La DL7...........210 B1
Lee View DN14.........207 A7
Lee Way WF10.........200 F3
Legion Ave DL3........3 B8
Legion St LS25.........195 F2
Legram La YO26........163 D8
Legram Rd YO26........163 D8
Leicester Cres LS29.....218 B5
Leicester Way
Aislaby TS16........5 D4
York YO1...........233 C1
LEIGHTON............85 C2
Leighton Cl YO12.......99 E6
Leighton Croft **3** YO30.. 224 F1
Leighton Rd **6** TS18....5 D8
Leith Rd DL3..........3 A5
Lendal YO1...........233 B2
Lendales La YO17.......95 E3
Lennerton La LS25......196 C3
Lennox Ave DL10.......209 D7
Lennox Cl **2** YO14.....127 A8
Lennox Pl HG4.........113 D3
Leonard St **15** BB18....171 D1
LEPPINGTON..........169 C8
Leppington Dr YO12.....212 C4
Leppington La YO60.....147 D1
Lerecroft Rd YO24......230 D8
Lesley Ave YO10.......231 E8
L'Espec St DL7.........210 D3
Leven Bank Rd TS15.....5 F2
Leven Cl TS16.........5 D4
Leven Ct TS9..........8 A1
Levendale **6** TS15.....25 C5
Levendale Prim Sch TS15.. 5 F3
Leven Rd
Eaglescliffe TS15.....5 E3
Stokesley TS9........26 B7
York YO24...........230 D7
Levens Cl HG3.........161 B4
Levenside
Great Ayton TS9......7 F1
4 Hutton Rudby TS15..25 D5
Stokesley TS9........26 C7
Leven Wynd **9** TS9.....26 C7
Levick Cres TS5........6 D8
Levington Ct **3** TS15...24 F8
Levington Mews **4** TS15. 24 F8
LEVISHAM............72 D5
Levisham St YO10......228 D2
Levisham Sta YO18......72 B5
Lewes Rd DL1..........3 D4
Lewis Cl
1 Croft-on-Tees DL2.. 22 C8
Northallerton DL6.....210 F5
Lewis Rd DL6..........210 F5
Lexden Ave TS5........6 D8
LEYBURN.............60 D5
Leyburn Bsns Pk DL8....60 D5
Leyburn Gr **1** TS18.....5 D8
Leyburn Old Glebe Field
Nature Reserve★ DL8... 60 B4
Leyburn Pl **8** YO14.....101 A3
Leyburn Prim Sch DL8...60 D5
Leyburn Rd
Askrigg DL8.........57 F6
Darlington DL1.......3 D7
Hunton DL8..........61 E7
Masham HG4.........86 B4
Middleham DL8.......60 E3
Scotton DL9.........40 C4
Leyburn Sta DL8.......60 D5
Leyes The YO10........229 C4
Leyfield Cl **1** YO32.....167 A4
Leyland Cl BB8.........186 A2
Leyland Cres **3** HG1....220 A3
Leyland Rd
Harrogate HG1.......220 A3
York YO31...........229 A5
Leys La
Boston Spa LS23......188 D8
Darrington WF11......206 A8
Glusburn BD20.......187 B8
Knottingley WF11.....201 F1
Little Smeaton WF8...206 B4
Leys Rd WF11.........206 A7
LEYSTHORPE..........93 B1
Leysthorpe La YO62.....93 B2
Liardet Rd **19** DL10....41 E4
Libanus Ct **16** TS17....5 F4
Library Sq YO1.........233 B3
Lichfield Ct **6** YO23....228 B1
Lichfield Gr HG3........219 A4
Lickley St HG4.........214 D5
Lidget Croft **10** BD20...173 E3
Lidget La HG5.........163 B5
Lidget Rd BD20........173 E3
Lidgett Gr YO26........227 B6
Lidgett La LS25........194 C3
Lidice Rd DN14........205 E2
Lidsty Hill YO62.......70 E5
Light Bank La BD20.....174 E2
Lightfoots Ave YO12....212 D3
Lightfoots Cl YO12......212 C3
Lightfoot's La YO12.....212 D3
Lightfoots Rd YO12.....212 D3
Light La DL8..........59 E5
Lightmire La YO26......142 A1
Lightwater Sh Village
HG4...............113 C6

Lightwater Valley Bird of
Prey Ctr★ HG4.......113 C7
Lightwater Valley Miniature
Rly★ HG4...........113 C6
Lightwater Valley Theme
Pk★ HG4...........113 C6
Lilac Ave
2 Appleton Roebuck
YO23............190 F5
Thornaby TS17.......6 B7
York YO10...........229 B3
Lilac Cl **7** LS29........175 A4
Lilac Gr
Harrogate HG1.......219 E6
New Earswick YO32....225 D4
Lilac Rd TS7..........7 D7
Lilac Wlk YO17.........212 D7
Lilbourne Dr YO30......228 A8
Lile Cl DL10..........209 C7
Lilla Cl YO21..........208 A6
Lilling Ave **3** YO31.....228 E8
Lilling La YO60........145 E3
Lilling Low La YO32.....145 C2
Lilly Gate La HG3.......162 A8
Limber Hill YO21.......30 E4
Lime Ave YO31.........228 F7
Limebar Bank Rd YO51...141 D1
Limebar La YO51.......141 C2
Lime Chase **10** YO62...70 B1
Lime Cl **10** LS29.......174 E4
Limegarth **10** YO26....165 F1
Lime Gr
Harrogate HG1.......219 F3
4 Whitby YO21......208 C6
Limehouse La HG4......216 E1
Limekiln Bank HG4......113 C1
Limekiln Hill YO25......150 B3
Limekiln La
Burton Leonard HG3...140 A1
8 Eastfield YO11....100 B6
East Layton DL11.....1 B1
Halton West BD23.....154 A1
North Stainley with Sleningford
HG4.............113 C5
Snape with Thorp HG4... 86 D5
Lime Kiln La LS22.......180 B5
Limekiln Rd YO7........65 F5
Lime La DL8...........87 F2
Lime Rd
Eaglescliffe TS16.....5 E6
Guisborough TS14.....8 E7
Sinnington YO62......94 D8
Limes Ct YO31.........228 F6
Lime St HG1...........219 F3
Limes The
Burniston YO13.......75 C8
Helmsley YO62.......92 F6
13 South Milford LS25. 195 F2
Stockton on the Forest
YO32............167 D2
Limestone Gr YO13.....75 C8
Limestone La YO13.....75 A5
Limestone Rd YO13.....75 B7
Limestone Way YO13....75 C8
Lime Tree Ave
Boston Spa LS23......188 E8
8 Easingwold YO61...117 D1
Malton YO17.........215 D6
York YO32...........225 D3
Limetree Cl **2** YO61....197 B1
Lime-Tree Cres LS25....194 E1
Lime Tree Dr DN14......207 A2
Lime Tree Gdns LS23....188 E8
Lime Tree Gr YO8.......232 A6
Lime Tree Mews **15**
YO19..............184 F7
Limetrees WF8.........201 D2
Lime Wlk HG4.........214 B2
Limpsey Gate La YO18...72 D6
Limpton Gate TS15.....5 E2
Linacre Way DL1.......3 D7
Lincoln Gr HG3........219 A5
Lincoln Pl **1** TS17.....6 B8
Lincoln Rd **30** BB18....172 A1
Lincoln St YO26.......227 F5
Lincoln Way LS25......196 A4
Lindale **2** YO24.......230 C7
Linden Ave
Darlington DL3.......3 B5
Great Ayton TS9......7 F1
Linden Cl
Great Ayton TS9......7 F2
4 Hutton Rudby TS15..25 C4
Richmond DL10.......209 D7
Sleights YO21........32 B7
York YO32...........225 F5
Linden Cres
Great Ayton TS9......7 F1
5 Hutton Rudby TS15..25 C4
Middlesbrough TS7....7 B6
Linden Dr
Hurworth DL2........3 D1
1 Hurworth-on-Tees DL2.. 22 D8
Linden Gdns DL10......209 D7
Linden Gr
Great Ayton TS9......7 F1
Thornaby TS17.......6 B8
York YO32...........225 A8
Linden Rd
9 Earby BB18.......172 A1
Great Ayton TS9......7 F1
Northallerton DL6.....210 E4
Scalby YO13.........212 A8
Linden Way
9 Thorpe Willoughby
YO8.............197 B1
Wetherby LS22.......180 B4

Lindhead Rd YO13......75 B8
Lindisfarne Ave **4** LS17..6 B8
Lindisfarne Rd TS3.....7 C8
LINDLEY.............177 C4
Lindley Rd YO30.......224 F1
Lindley St
Skipton BD23........216 F2
York YO24...........227 F3
Lindley Wood Gr YO30...224 E3
Lindon Rd DL10........20 F1
Lindrick Cl
32 Castleford WF6....200 B1
3 Ripon HG4.......214 B2
Lindrick Way HG3......219 A4
Lindsay Rd LS25.......194 C3
Lindsey Ave YO26......227 D4
Linen Way **10** DL6.....43 F3
Lingcrag Gdns BD22....187 B6
Ling Croft LS23........188 D8
Lingcroft Cl YO8.......204 D4
Lingcroft La
Naburn YO19........231 E3
Tockwith LS22.......181 A6
LINGDALE............9 F7
Lingdale Prim Sch TS12... 9 F7
Lingdale Rd
Lockwood TS12.......9 E7
Thornaby TS17.......6 C7
LINGERFIELD.........162 B6
LINGFIELD...........3 F5
Lingfield Ash TS8......7 A5
Lingfield Cl
Great Burdon DL1.....3 F5
10 Hipswell DL9.....40 F4
Lingfield Cres YO24.....227 F1
Lingfield Prim Sch TS7... 7 B5
Lingfield Rd TS15......5 F3
Ling Fields BD23.......216 C4
Lingfield Way DL1......4 A5
Ling Gill National Nature
Reserve★ BD24.......79 C1
Lingham La YO7........115 A3
Linghaw La LA2........129 C7
Ling Hill YO12.........212 B7
Lingholm Cres YO11....99 F7
Lingholm La YO11......100 D4
Ling La YO41..........185 F6
Lingrow Cl **3** TS13.....12 A7
Ling Trod YO17........123 D4
Link Ave YO10.........228 C8
Link Bsns Pk YO10......229 D1
Linkfoot La YO62.......93 A6
Link Rd YO32..........225 E2
Link Road Ct YO10......229 D4
Links Cl HG2..........220 E3
Links Dr LA2..........129 A8
Links Prim Sch The TS16.. 5 E5
Links The
7 North Featherstone
WF7.............200 E1
Tadcaster LS24.......189 E5
Links Way HG2.........220 E3
Link The
Copmanthorpe YO23...230 A3
Middlesbrough TS3....7 C8
Northallerton DL7.....210 B2
Selby YO8...........232 A4
York YO10...........231 E8
Linkway DN6..........206 E2
Link Wlk **5** YO11......100 A6
Linley Ave **24** YO32....166 F5
Linnburn Mews **1** LS29. 218 B3
Linnet Way YO24.......230 C8
LINTON
Grassington.........134 D1
Wetherby...........180 A1
Linton Ave **9** LS22.....180 B3
Linton Cl
Cloughton YO13......54 D1
19 Filey YO14......101 B3
Linton Com LS22.......179 F1
Linton Ct **8** BD23......216 F3
Linton Falls **1** BD23....134 E2
Linton La LS22.........180 B2
Linton Mdw **5** YO30...164 F7
Linton Mdws **7** LS22...180 B3
LINTON-ON-OUSE......164 E7
Linton on Ouse Prim Sch
YO30..............165 A7
Linton Pl **4** YO30......164 F7
Linton Rd
Collingham LS22......180 A1
Poppleton YO26......224 A1
Wetherby LS22.......180 B3
Linton Rise **17** DL9....40 E4
Linton St **5** YO26......227 E5
Linton Woods YO30.....165 A7
Linton Woods La YO30...165 A8
Linwith La DN14........204 C3
Linwood Ave TS9.......26 C8
Lion Ct **43** LS29.......176 C1
Lippersley La LS29......174 D3
Lisheen Ave WF10......200 F4
Lismore Pl YO12........212 E1
Lismore Rd YO12.......212 E1
Lister Croft BD23.......172 A3
Lister Hill **5** BD20.....187 E6
Lister St LS29.........218 A4
Lister Way YO30.......228 A7
Lisvane Ave YO12......212 D4
Litley Bank YO7........66 B5
LITTLE AIRMYN........205 E4
Little Ave YO30........228 B8
LITTLE AYTON.........8 E8
Little Ayton La
Great Ayton TS9......8 A1
27 Roundhill Village TS17.. 5 F4
LITTLE BARUGH........95 C2

Little Beck Bank YO22 32 C4
Littlebeck Dr DL1 3 E7
Little Beck La YO22 32 B3
Little Beck Wood Nature Reserve★ YO22 32 B3
Littleboy Dr TS17 6 C8
Little Brook BD23 217 B4
Little Catterton La LS24 190 A7
Little Church La LS26 200 B5
Little Common La DN14 207 C5
LITTLE CRAKEHALL 62 D5
Little Croft HG3 139 C4
Little Crossing HG4 214 E2
Littledale YO18 95 F7
LITTLE FENCOTE 63 C8
LITTLE FENTON 196 B6
Littlefield Cl 5 YO26 165 F1
Little Field La YO18 72 C5
Little Garth YO26 224 A2
LITTLE HABTON 121 A8
Little Hallfield Rd YO31 228 E5
Little Harries La HG4 214 A7
LITTLE HECK 203 D1
Little Heck Common La DN14 203 D1
Little Hoppers Adventure World★ YO11 99 F6
LITTLE HUTTON 116 B7
Little Hutton La DL11 1 A4
Little Ings Cl LS24 196 C8
Little Ings La YO51 141 C5
Little King St 5 HG3 137 B4
Little La
Brompton DL6 44 A3
12 Easingwold YO61 143 C8
Ellerton YO42 193 C1
11 Haxby YO32 166 E5
Ilkley LS29 218 C4
Little Smeaton WF8 206 D4
North Stainley with Sleningford HG4 113 C4
Little Mdws YO32 225 D8
Little Moor Cl YO13 54 C1
Little Moor La YO8 232 A8
LITTLE OUSEBURN 164 A7
Little Pasture 3 TS17 6 D5
LITTLE PRESTON 194 B1
LITTLE RIBSTON 180 A8
LITTLE SESSAY 116 C5
Little Shambles YO1 233 B2
Littleside DL8 83 E7
LITTLE SKIPWITH 192 D1
LITTLE SMEATON
206 C3
North Cowton 23 C2
LITTLE STAINFORTH 131 D6
Little Stonegate YO1 233 B3
LITTLE STUDLEY 214 C7
Little Studley Cl HG4 214 C7
Little Studley Pk HG4 214 C8
Little Studley Rd HG4 214 C7
LITTLETHORPE 214 F1
Littlethorpe Cl
Harrogate HG3 219 A4
6 Strensall YO32 167 B8
Littlethorpe La HG4 214 D2
Littlethorpe Pk HG4 214 E3
Littlethorpe Potteries★ HG4 140 A7
Littlethorpe Rd HG4 214 E3
Little Westfield YO25 151 C3
Little Wood St YO17 215 E3
LITTON 107 A5
Littondale Ave HG5 221 D6
LIVERTON 10 D6
Liverton La TS13 10 D6
Liverton Mill Bank TS12 10 B6
LIVERTON MINES 10 C8
Liverton Rd TS13 10 D7
Livingstone Rd YO12 212 E6
Livingstone St YO26 227 F5
Lloyd Cl YO10 229 B1
Lob La YO41 168 D2
Lochranza Rd YO7 211 A2
Lochrin Pl 2 YO26 227 B4
Lock Cl DN14 207 F6
Locker La HG4 214 C4
Lockey Croft YO32 225 C8
Lockeys Terr 3 YO22 208 E6
Lockfield Dr BB18 171 E2
Lockgate Rd DN14 207 C4
Lockheed Cl TS18 5 F7
Lock House La YO32 225 F8
Lock La
Castleford WF10 200 E5
Lower Altofts WF6 200 A3
Lock Lane Sports Ctr WF10 200 F5
Locks Barn BD24 131 D4
LOCKTON 72 D4
Lockton Cres TS17 6 A6
Lockton Ct LS24 196 B7
Lockton La YO18 72 E4
Lockton Rd YO21 208 A6
Lock Walk DL10 41 E4
Lockwood Chase YO13 54 D1
Lockwood Prim Sch TS12 9 D7
Lockwood St YO31 233 C3
Lockyer Cl 4 YO30 228 A8
Locomotion Ct 5 TS16 5 D5
Locomotion La 7 DL3 3 B7
Loders Gn 5 YO11 99 F6
Lodge Cl 7 YO11 100 B6
Lodge Gdns YO14 100 E4
LODGE GREEN 36 F5
Lodge La
5 Brompton DL6 43 F3
Danby YO21 29 D7
Lodge La *continued*
Gowdall DN14 203 F1
Newby with Mulwith HG4 140 E6
Wennington LA2 102 B1
Wetherby LS22 180 C2
Lodge Rd
Hutton-le-Hole YO62 70 C5
Lythe YO21 12 E3
Settle BD24 153 E8
Lodge St 4 BD20 187 D7
Lodore Gr TS5 6 D7
LOFTHOUSE 110 C4
Lofthouse Endowed Prim Sch HG3 110 B4
Lofthouse La YO41 185 D7
Loftus Cl YO12 212 B4
Lombards Wynd DL10 209 C7
Londesborough Gr 5 YO8 197 B2
Londesborough Pk 10 YO12 99 D6
Londesborough Rd YO12 212 E4
Londesborough St 5 YO8 232 C5
LONDONDERRY 63 E2
London La DN6 207 D1
Longacre WF10 200 E3
Long Acre Ct HG3 222 E2
Long Acre Wlk HG3 222 E2
Long Ashes L & Beauty Club BD23 134 B3
Long Band DL8 58 A8
Long Bank DL11 19 C6
Long Bank La BD23 153 E1
Longbank Rd TS7 7 D7
Longber La LA6 102 D4
Longbow Ave LS26 200 B6
Long Cl La YO10 233 C1
Long Crag View 1 HG3 161 B2
Longcroft 2 YO32 166 E5
Longcroft Rd 1 LS29 218 E3
Long Cswy
Arkengarthdale DL11 16 C6
Halton East BD23 174 B8
Thirkleby High & Low with Osgodby YO7 90 D1
Long Cswy Rd
Danby YO21 29 E3
Hutton Buscel YO13 99 A4
Longdale Ave 18 BD24 131 D2
Longdike La
Kippax LS25 200 E8
Thornton Steward HG4 61 E1
LONG DRAX 205 A6
Longfield Comp Sch DL3 3 C8
Longfield Ct 21 BB18 171 D1
Longfield Rd DL3 3 C7
Longfield Terr YO30 233 A3
Long Furrow YO32 225 C8
Long Gate BD22 187 D4
Long Gn 7 BB18 172 B1
Long Heads La LS25 195 F1
Long Hill End BD22 187 B5
Long Ing La BB18 171 E1
Long La
Barwick in Elmet LS15 194 C7
Borrowby YO7 65 E5
Brompton DL6 44 A6
Catton YO41 185 D6
Cawood YO8 197 A6
Cowling BD22 187 B7
East Ayton YO13 99 B7
Ellerton YO42 193 F1
Farndale East YO62 48 F4
Felliscliffe HG3 160 E3
Gayles DL11 19 E6
Heck DN14 207 D8
Heslington YO10 184 C3
Kirk Smeaton WF8 206 B1
Laneshaw Bridge BB8 186 B4
Lockwood TS12 10 B5
Normanby YO62 95 A4
Picton TS15 24 E6
Seamer YO12 99 E6
Slingsby YO62 120 D6
Tatham LA2 128 E7
Well DL8 87 C4
Longland La YO26 164 A3
Longlands Field Rd YO26 163 D8
Longlands La
Boroughbridge YO51 141 A3
Danby YO21 29 B6
Hetton BD23 155 F5
Sicklinghall LS22 179 E3
Thornton-le-Dale YO18 96 E5
Longlands Rd YO17 123 B3
LONG LEASE 33 A7
Long Level LA6 102 C8
Long Mann Hills Rd YO8 232 B4
Longmans Hill Sch YO8 232 C3
LONG MARSTON 182 A6
Long Marston CE Prim Sch YO26 182 A6
Long Mdw
7 Colne BB8 186 A3
Skipton BD23 217 B5
Long Mdws
Garforth LS25 194 C3
6 Ilkley LS29 176 C1
Rillington YO17 122 F5
Long Meadow Gate LS25 194 C2
LONGNEWTON 5 A7
Long Newton La TS21 5 A6
LONG PRESTON 153 F5
Long Preston Endowed Prim Sch BD23 153 F5
Long Preston Sta BD23 153 F4
Long Rampart YO42 193 D3
Long Riddings LS29 174 F5
Long Ridge Dr YO26 224 A1
Longridge Gdns 27 YO26 165 F1
Long Ridge La YO26 224 A1
LONGSCALES 160 C4
Long St
Asenby YO7 115 B6
Easingwold YO61 143 C8
Thirsk YO7 211 C3
Topcliffe YO7 115 C6
Long Stoop Standing Stone★ HG3 160 A2
Long Stps 8 YO22 208 E6
Long Swales La HG4 112 D5
Longtons La BD23 152 F4
Long Trods 5 YO8 232 C6
Longwestgate YO11 213 B6
Long Wlk
Knaresborough HG5 221 A6
Scarborough YO12 212 D7
Longwood Bank DL10 209 D5
Longwood Link 8 YO30 224 E3
Longwood Rd YO30 224 F3
Lonsdale Mdws LS23 188 E8
Lonsdale Pl 12 YO13 99 B8
Lonsdale Rd YO11 213 A3
Loos Rd DL9 40 F3
Loraine Cres DL1 3 C4
Lord Ave TS17 6 B5
Lord Deramores Prim Sch YO10 229 C1
Lord Mayor's Wlk YO31 233 B3
Lord's Cl 23 BD24 131 D2
Lord's Close Rd LA2 129 B3
Lordship La
5 Barlby YO8 198 A4
Wistow YO8 232 D8
Lords La
Ainderby Mires with Holtby DL8 41 F1
Hackforth DL8 62 E8
Upper Poppleton YO26 165 E2
Lord's La DL8 63 C2
Lords Moor La YO32 167 C7
Loriners Dr 7 YO23 230 B3
Loring Rd YO13 54 A7
Lorne St YO23 228 B1
Lorraine Ave 3 YO41 185 B2
LOSCOE 200 C1
Loscoe Cl WF6 200 C2
Loshpot La LS22 180 C5
LOTHERSDALE 187 A8
Lothersdale Com Prim Sch BD20 186 F8
Lothersdale Rd BD20 187 B8
Lotherton La LS25 195 A7
Lotherton Way LS25 194 C4
Louisa St DL1 3 D5
Lousy Hill La YO22 32 A6
Louvain St 5 BB18 171 D2
Love La
Brawby YO17 94 F1
Castleford WF10 200 E3
Easby DL10 209 E4
8 Leyburn DL8 60 D5
Nunthorpe YO10 231 C8
Whitby YO21 208 A7
York YO24 228 A2
Lovers' La DL7 64 F2
Low Bank
4 Embsay BD23 217 E8
Over Silton DL6 66 A8
Low Beck LS29 218 D5
LOW BENTHAM 128 F8
Low Bentham Prim Sch LA2 128 F8
Low Bentham Rd LA2 128 F8
LOW BRADLEY 173 E3
LOW CATTON 185 C8
Low Catton Rd YO41 185 C8
Low Cl LS29 218 A5
Low Comm LS26 200 C4
LOW CONISCLIFFE 2 F4
Lowcroft
9 Collingham LS22 188 A8
High Bentham LA2 129 B8
Low Croft 6 YO32 167 A7
Lowcross Ave TS14 8 E5
Lowcross Dr TS9 26 E5
LOW DALBY 72 F2
Lowdale Ave YO12 212 E8
Lowdale Ct 4 YO22 32 A6
Low Demesne LA6 103 D3
Low Demesne Cl 4 LA6 103 D3
LOW DINSDALE 4 C1
LOW ELLINGTON 86 A6
LOWER ALTOFTS 200 A3
Lower Clark St
2 Scarborough YO12 212 F6
13 Scarborough YO12 213 A7
Lower Clark Street Ind Est 14 YO12 213 A7
Lower Constable Rd LS29 218 D3
Lower Croft St 39 BB18 172 A1
Lower Darnborough St YO23 233 B1
Lower Derwent Valley Nat Nature Reserve★ YO42 199 C8
LOWER DUNSFORTH 142 A4
Lower Flat Cliffs YO14 101 C1
Lower Friargate YO1 233 B2
Lower Greenfoot 15 BD24 131 D2
LOWER MICKLETOWN 200 D6
Lower Mickletown LS26 200 C6
Lower Oxford St WF10 200 E4
Lower Priory St YO1 233 A1
Lower Station Rd 3 WF6 200 A1
Lower Union St BD23 216 F3
Lower Wellington Rd LS29 218 B4
LOWER WESTHOUSE 103 B4
Lower William St 3 YO12 212 F6
Lower York Ct HG1 220 D6
Loweswater Rd 5 YO30 224 E1
Low Farm LS26 200 C8
Low Farm Cl
Bolton Percy YO23 190 D4
Thornton TS8 6 D4
Lowfield
3 Eastfield YO11 100 A6
Hawes DL8 56 C4
Lowfield Dr YO32 166 E5
Lowfield La
Beamsley BD23 174 F7
Kirkby Fleetham with Fencote DL7 42 D2
Rufforth YO26 227 A4
Scrayingham YO41 169 A7
Sharow HG4 214 F6
Snape with Thorp DL8 87 A7
Low Field La
Cold Kirby YO7 91 D7
Goldsborough HG5 163 A1
Marton cum Grafton YO51 141 E2
Staveley HG5 140 E1
Lowfield Rd
Barlby with Osgodby YO8 198 B5
Hillam LS25 202 C8
Malton YO17 215 C6
Lowfields 2 YO12 99 D2
Lowfields Ave
Ingleby Barwick TS17 6 A5
Roundhill Village TS17 6 D5
Low Fields Dr YO24 227 C3
Lowfields La YO7 88 C6
Low Fold 4 BB18 186 A7
LOW GARTH 29 F4
Low Garth YO22 32 A6
Low Garth Link 17 LS25 195 F4
Low Garth Rd LS25 195 F4
LOW GATE 138 F6
Lowgate DN14 207 D5
Low Gate DL8 57 F5
Low Gate La HG4 138 F7
LOW GATHERLEY 21 D1
LOWGILL 128 F3
Lowgill La LA2 128 F4
Low Gn
Catterick DL10 41 D4
Copmanthorpe YO23 230 B2
13 Knottingley WF11 202 A2
Menwith with Darley HG3 160 A6
LOW GRANTLEY 112 E1
LOW GREEN 160 A6
LOW HAWSKER 33 A6
Low Holland WF11 201 C6
Low Hospital Yd 6 YO22 208 E6
Low House La
Carlton Miniott YO7 89 C2
Dishforth YO7 115 B2
LOW HUTTON 147 C6
Low Hutton Pk YO60 147 C6
Lowick YO24 230 C7
Lowkber La LA6 103 E2
Low La
Askrigg DL8 58 B4
Carperby-cum-Thoresby DL8 58 F4
Cononley BD20 173 C2
Cowling BD22 187 A8
Cropton YO18 71 B4
Dalby-cum-Skewsby YO60 119 B2
Dalton DL11 19 D7
Embsay with Eastby BD23 217 E8
Grassington BD23 134 E3
Grinton DL11 37 E5
Heslington YO10 229 D1
Howsham YO60 147 A1
Hutton-Sessay YO7 116 B7
Leck LA6 102 D7
Leyburn DL8 60 C4
Lythe YO21 12 D3
Maltby TS17 6 B3
Menwith with Darley HG3 159 F6
Mickleby TS13 12 A3
Middlesbrough TS5 6 E6
Muker DL11 36 C4
Newsham DL11 18 H7
Reeth, Fremington & Healaugh DL11 37 F5
Silsden BD20 174 B3
Spofforth with Stockeld HG3 179 C4
Stainburn LS21 177 F3
Sutton-under-Whitestonecliffe YO7 90 E6
Swinton YO17 121 C4
Thirkleby High & Low with Osgodby YO7 90 C1
Westow YO60 147 C4
West Rounton DL6 24 D3
Wigglesworth BD23 153 D3
LOW LAITHE 137 F2
Lowlands Dr DL7 63 C5
LOW MARISHES 122 C8
Low Mdw YO8 232 C6
LOW MILL 48 E2
Low Mill LS29 175 A4
Low Mill Cl YO10 229 D3
Low Mill Ct HG3 138 F1
Low Mill Est HG4 214 E5
Low Mill La LS29 175 A4
Low Mill Rd HG4 214 D4
Low Moor Ave 3 YO10 231 F8
Low Moorgate La YO17 122 F5
Low Moor La
Askham Richard YO23 182 D3
Brearton HG5 162 B7
East Harlsey DL6 44 C7
Fearby HG4 85 F3
Hessay YO26 182 C8
Rillington YO17 122 E6
Lowmoor Rd YO8 198 E6
Low Moor Rd YO18 71 F5
Low Moor South La YO17 122 D6
LOWNA 70 A6
Lowna Rd YO62 70 B5
Lown Hill YO24 227 C2
Lownorth Rd YO13 53 C2
Low Ousegate YO1 233 B2
Low Park Rd LS29 176 A3
Low Petergate YO1 233 B3
Low Peter La HG3 140 A3
Low Poppleton La YO26 227 B7
Low Rd
Gainford DL2 1 C7
Gowdall DN14 204 A1
Irton YO12 75 B3
Kellington DN14 202 F4
Kirby Grindalythe YO17 149 F7
Newby & Scalby YO12 212 A6
Thirkleby High & Low with Osgodby YO7 116 E8
LOW ROW 37 C4
Low Row DL11 37 E5
Low Skellgate HG4 214 C5
Low Sleights Rd LA6 104 B7
LOW SNAYGILL 173 D4
Low St
Aiskew DL7 63 C6
Austwick LA2 130 E7
Burton in Lonsdale LA6 102 F3
Carlton DN14 204 C2
Husthwaite YO61 117 B6
Kirkby Fleetham with Fencote DL7 41 F2
Knottingley WF11 201 E4
Lastingham YO62 70 E5
Nunnington YO62 93 E2
Oswaldkirk YO62 92 F3
Ripon HG4 214 D5
22 Scalby YO13 75 D5
Sherburn in Elmet LS25 195 F4
Thornton-le-Clay YO60 146 A4
Low Stanghow Rd TS12 9 F6
Low Street Agnesgate HG4 214 D4
Lowswater Rd WF11 201 F1
Lowther Cres 3 LS26 194 A1
Lowther Ct YO31 233 C4
Lowther Dr
Garforth LS25 194 C3
Selby YO8 232 E3
2 Swillington LS26 194 A1
Lowther St YO31 233 C4
Lowther Terr YO24 228 A3
Low Thorpe DL8 85 D8
LOW TOWN 5 B1
Low Town Bank Rd YO7 91 B4
Low Tun Way YO62 69 A2
Low Wath Rd HG3 137 B4
Low Way 5 LS23 188 E5
Low Well Pk YO19 192 F7
Low Westfield Rd YO23 230 A1
LOW WHITA 37 D5
Low Wood La
Glaisdale YO21 30 C6
Leyburn DL8 60 C4
Low Wood Rise LS29 218 F3
LOW WORSALL 24 A8
Loxley Cl YO30 224 F2
Loy La TS13 10 F8
Loyne Pk LA6 102 A7
Lucas Ave YO30 228 C8
Lucas Grove N YO26 181 C7
Lucas Grove S YO26 181 C7
Lucas Rd YO26 181 C7
Luccombe Cl 7 TS17 6 A3
Lucerne Cl YO19 192 A1
Lucerne Dr TS14 8 E6
Lucia La TS14 8 E6
Lucky La YO7 89 E8
Lucombe Way YO32 225 D4
Luddith Rd YO17 148 D5
Ludlow Ave LS25 194 D4
Lufton Cl 4 TS17 5 F5
Lullingstone Cres TS17 5 F6
Lulsgate TS17 6 C7
LUMB 187 A4
Lumb Gill La LS29 175 A3
Lumb La
Cowling BD22 187 A5
Topcliffe YO7 89 B1
Lumb Mill Way BD23 157 E7
LUMBY 195 E1
Lumby Hill LS25 202 A8
Lumby La
Monk Fryston LS25 202 A8
South Milford LS25 196 A1
Lumley Cl YO7 211 D2
Lumley La
Azerley HG4 112 D2
Kirkby Fleetham with Fencote DL7 42 B1

Lumley Rd YO30 228 B7
Lumley St WF10 200 D3
Luna Pk★ YO11 213 C6
Luncarr La HG4 114 B2
LUND 198 D3
Lund Cl YO32 225 C8
Lundgreen La YO61 144 A3
Lund Head La HG3 179 B2
Lund La
 Bubwith YO8 199 C4
 Cliffe YO8 198 D4
 Hampsthwaite HG3 161 A5
Lund Rd YO62 70 B7
Lund Sand La
 Easingwold YO61 143 A8
 Raskelf YO61 117 A1
Lund Sike La LS25 195 F2
Lund's Twr★ BD20 187 D6
Lundy Cl 10 YO30 225 A1
Lunebeck Wlk TS17 6 C6
Lunedale Ave
 Knaresborough HG5 221 C5
 Middlesbrough TS5 6 E8
Lunedale Rd DL3 3 A6
Lunnfields La WF11 201 E6
Lunn La DN14 202 D3
Lupton Bank HG3 137 D3
Lupton Cl HG3 137 D3
Lupton Springs HG3 137 D3
Lutton La YO17 123 F4
Luttons Prim Sch YO17 150 B8
Lutyens The 22 LS29 175 C2
Lycett Rd YO24 230 F6
Lych Gate 14 DL2 3 E1
Lydford Rd 18 DL10 41 E4
Lydham Ct 2 YO24 230 C8
Lyell St YO12 212 E6
Lynbrook Cl YO7 211 B4
Lyndale
 Guisborough TS14 8 D5
 Kippax LS25 200 D8
Lyndale Ave YO10 229 C3
Lyndale Gr 14 WF6 200 B1
Lynden Cl HG4 214 E4
Lynden Way YO24 227 D3
Lyndhurst Cl
 2 Norton DN6 206 F2
 9 Whitby YO21 208 D6
Lyndhurst Dr 1 DN6 206 F2
Lyndhurst Rise 3 DN6 206 F2
Lyndon Ave
 Bramham LS23 188 E6
 Garforth LS25 194 C4
Lyndon Cl 1 LS23 188 E6
Lyndon Cres 4 LS23 188 E6
Lyndon Rd LS23 188 E6
Lyndon Sq 2 LS23 188 E6
Lyndon Way LS23 188 E6
Lynmouth Cl 2 TS8 6 E5
Lynndale Ave 6 BD20 187 F8
Lynton Ave LS23 188 E8
Lynton Cl YO8 232 B1
Lynton Gdns
 Brayton YO8 232 B1
 Darlington DL1 3 E5
 Harrogate HG1 220 A3
Lynton Way DL6 210 D3
Lynwith Cl DN14 204 C3
Lynwith Ct DN14 204 C3
Lynwith Dr DN14 204 C3
Lynwood Ave 3 YO23 230 A3
Lynwood Cl YO32 167 A7
Lynwood View 4 YO23 230 A3
Lynx La YO7 115 B1
Lyonette Rd DL1 3 E7
Lyon Rd BD20 187 F7
Lyons Rd DL10 209 C8
Lysander Bsns Pk YO30 225 A3
Lysander Cl YO30 225 A3
Lys Cres DL9 209 D1
Lytham Cl BD23 217 C3
Lytham Gdns BD23 217 C3
Lytham Rd DL1 3 D8
LYTHE 12 E4
Lythe Bank
 Lythe YO21 12 F4
 Sutton with Howgrave DL8 87 F2
Lythe CE Prim Sch YO21 12 E3
Lythe Fell Rd LA2 129 B2
Lythe La LA2 129 A2

M

Mcan Cl YO10 229 D4
MacArthurs Cl YO7 211 B2
McBean Steps★ YO11 213 A5
McCain Stad (Scarborough FC) YO11 212 E2
McDonald Rd HG4 113 D3
MacDonell Cl 1 DL9 209 C1
MacKeridge La YO62 48 F4
Mackie Dr TS14 8 F7
MacKinnon Ave 1 WF6 200 B2
MacLagan Rd YO23 230 F4
McMullen Rd DL1 3 E6
Madeley Sq WF10 201 B5
Mafeking St HG1 219 F4
Magazine La YO8 198 C4
Magazine Rd YO8 198 B4
Magdalen's Cl HG4 214 D6
Magdalen's Rd HG4 214 D6
Magister Rd TS17 6 B7
Magnolia Gr YO32 225 D2
Magpie Garth YO12 99 E6
Maida Gr YO10 228 D2
Maiden Bower (Motte & Bailey)★ YO7 115 D5
Maiden Castle★ DL11 38 A5
Maiden Greve YO17 215 A4
Maidensgrave Henge★ YO25 126 F1
Maidstone Dr TS7 7 C6
Main Ave
 Woodlands HG2 220 C3
 York YO31 228 F5
Main Rd
 Drax YO8 204 F5
 Gainford DL2 1 D7
 Hambleton YO8 196 E1
 Hellifield BD23 154 B3
 Stainforth BD24 131 E6
 Steeton with Eastburn BD20 187 F7
 Weaverthorpe YO17 124 E1
Mainsfield Cl 1 BD24 131 D3
Mainsfield Rise 2 BD24 131 D3
Mains La YO60 146 D5
Main St
 Aberford LS25 194 F8
 Addingham LS29 174 F4
 Allerston YO18 97 B5
 Alne YO61 142 F4
 Amotherby YO17 121 A4
 Appleton Roebuck YO23 190 F5
 Askham Bryan YO23 182 F3
 Askrigg DL8 57 E6
 Asselby DN14 205 D7
 Austwick LA2 130 E7
 Aysgarth DL8 58 E3
 Barkston Ash LS24 195 E7
 Barwick in Elmet LS15 194 B8
 3 Beal DN14 202 D4
 Bentham LA2 128 E8
 Bilbrough YO23 182 C1
 Bilton-in-Ainsty with Bickerton LS22 181 A5
 Bishop Monkton HG3 140 B5
 Bishopthorpe YO23 231 A4
 Boroughbridge YO51 141 A3
 Brafferton YO61 141 F8
 Bubwith YO8 199 C7
 Bugthorpe YO41 169 D4
 Burley in Warfedale LS29 176 C1
 Burton Salmon LS25 201 F6
 Church Fenton LS24 196 B7
 Cliffe YO8 198 E2
 Cononley BD20 173 D1
 Copmanthorpe YO23 230 A2
 Cottingwith YO42 193 C5
 Darley HG3 160 A6
 Deighton YO19 192 A7
 Earby BB18 186 A7
 East Ayton/West Ayton YO13 99 A7
 Eastfield YO11 100 B6
 Ebberston & Yedingham YO13 97 D5
 Ellerton YO42 193 C1
 Elvington YO41 185 C2
 Embsay BD23 217 E8
 Escrick YO19 192 B5
 Farnhill BD20 173 E1
 Folkton YO11 100 A2
 Follifoot HG3 223 F5
 Ganton YO12 125 A8
 Garforth LS25 194 C3
 Gillamoor YO62 70 A4
 Gilling East YO62 118 F7
 Glusburn BD20 187 E7
 Gowdall DN14 204 A1
 13 Grassington BD23 134 E3
 Great Ouseburn YO26 164 B8
 Great Preston WF10 200 D6
 Gristlthorp YO14 100 E4
 Harome YO62 93 C5
 Healaugh LS24 181 F2
 Hebden BD23 135 A1
 Heck DN14 207 C8
 Helperby YO61 142 A8
 Hemingbrough YO8 198 F1
 Hensall DN14 203 D2
 Heslington YO10 229 B1
 Hessay YO26 182 B8
 High Bentham LA2 129 A8
 Hovingham YO62 119 E6
 Huby YO61 144 A4
 Ingleton LA6 103 D3
 Irton YO12 99 C6
 Kelfield YO19 191 D1
 Kellington DN14 202 F3
 Kirkby Malham BD23 154 F8
 Kirkby Malzeard HG4 112 C5
 Kirk Deighton LS22 180 B5
 Kirk Smeaton WF8 206 B3
 Knapton YO26 227 A5
 Langcliffe BD24 131 E4
 Ledston WF10 200 F7
 Linton LS22 180 A1
 Little Ouseburn YO26 164 A7
 Long Preston BD23 153 F5
 Low Bradley BD20 173 E3
 Menwith with Darley HG3 160 A4
 Mickletown LS26 200 B6
 Middleton YO18 95 E8
 Monk Fryston LS25 201 F8
 Monk Fryston LS25 202 A8
 1 Naburn YO19 191 D8
 Newton Kyme cum Toulston LS24 189 C7
 North Duffield YO8 199 A8
 Nunthorpe YO10 231 D8
 Pannal HG3 222 D3
Main St *continued*
 Pollington DN14 207 F6
 Poppleton YO26 165 F1
 Rathmell BD24 153 C6
 Reighton YO14 127 E5
 Riccall YO19 198 A8
 Ryther cum Ossendyke LS24 190 E2
 Saxton with Scarthingwell LS24 195 D7
 Scholes LS15 194 A7
 Scotton HG5 162 A6
 Seamer YO12 99 D6
 Sheriff Hutton YO60 145 D5
 Shipton YO30 165 F5
 Sicklinghall LS22 179 D3
 Sinnington YO62 95 A8
 Stainforth BD24 131 E6
 Stamford Bridge YO41 168 D2
 Staveley HG5 140 E1
 Stillington YO61 144 C6
 Sutton-on-the-Forest YO61 144 C3
 Threshfield BD23 134 C2
 Thwing YO25 126 B1
 Tollerton YO61 143 A3
 Ulleskelf LS24 190 C3
 Walton LS23 181 A2
 Wath HG4 114 A8
 Weeton LS17 178 C1
 Westow YO60 147 B4
 West Tanfield HG4 87 A1
 Wheldrake YO19 192 F7
 Whittington LA6 102 A7
 Wilberfoss YO41 185 E5
 Wombleton YO62 93 E6
 Womersley DN6 206 C6
 Woodlands HG2 220 B3
 Wray-with-Botton LA2 128 A6
Mains The BD24 131 D3
Maison Dieu DL10 209 D7
Major St DL3 3 C6
Malais La BD20 187 D7
Malbys Gr YO23 230 B2
Malden Rd HG1 220 B3
MALHAM 133 A1
Malham Gr YO31 229 B5
Malham Moor La BD23 133 F4
Malham Rakes BD23 133 A2
Malham Tarn Field Ctr★ BD24 132 F6
Malham Tarn National Nature Reserve★ BD24 132 E5
Malham View Cl 23 BB18 171 D1
Malham Way HG5 221 D6
Malim Rd DL1 3 F5
Mallard Cl
 8 Filey YO14 101 A4
 12 Pickering YO18 95 F6
 15 Ripon HG4 214 C5
Mallard Landings YO31 228 D8
Mallard Rd 4 DL9 40 F2
Mallard View YO17 215 D2
Mallard Way
 4 Eastfield YO12 99 F6
 11 Haxby YO32 166 F5
Mallard Wlk 14 YO51 141 B5
Mallinson Cl HG2 222 D6
Mallinson Cres HG2 222 E6
Mallinson Gate HG2 222 E6
Mallinson Gr HG2 222 D6
Mallinson Oval HG2 222 D6
Mallinson Way HG2 222 D6
Mallison Hill Dr 5 YO61 117 D1
Mallorie Cl HG4 214 A5
Mallorie Ct HG4 214 B5
Mallorie Park Dr HG4 214 A4
Mallory Cl YO32 225 D4
Mallory Ct 17 DL1 3 F6
Mallowdale TS7 7 C5
Malltraeth Sands TS17 6 D6
Malpas Dr DL7 210 D4
Malpas Rd
 Brompton YO13 98 C4
 Northallerton DL7 210 D3
Malsis Prep Sch BD20 187 C7
MALTBY 6 C4
Maltby Pl 2 TS17 6 B8
Maltby Rd TS8 6 D4
Malt Dubs Cl LA6 103 D3
Malthouse Cl WF10 200 E4
Malthouse La HG3 222 D2
Maltings Bsns Ctr The YO17 215 C3
Maltings Ct
 Alne YO61 143 A5
 6 Selby YO8 232 C6
Maltings Ind Est The DN14 202 F1
Maltings The
 8 Brafferton YO61 115 F1
 Cliffe YO8 198 E3
 13 Pontefract WF8 201 B1
 Thirsk YO7 211 B2
Maltkiln La
 Castleford WF10 200 F4
 Killinghall HG3 161 C6
Malt Kiln La YO23 190 F5
Malt Kiln Terr LS24 189 D4
Maltings The LA6 102 A7
MALTON 215 C4
Malton Ave YO31 228 E6
Malton Com Prim Sch YO17 215 D5
Malton Gate YO18 96 D5
Malton La
 Allerston YO18 97 B4
Malton La *continued*
 Flaxton YO60 146 A1
 Kirby Grindalythe YO17 150 A8
Malton Mus★ YO17 215 C4
Malton & Norton District Hospl YO17 215 B4
Malton Rd
 Hunmanby YO14 126 F8
 Huntington YO32 226 A1
 Leavening YO17 147 E2
 Pickering YO18 95 F6
 Rillington YO17 122 E4
 Scampston YO17 123 B7
 Slingsby YO62 120 B5
 Swinton YO17 121 C4
 York YO31 228 F7
Malton Sch YO17 215 A5
Malton St YO61 117 D6
Malton Sta YO17 215 C3
Malton Way YO30 227 F8
Malt Shoval Ct YO1 233 C2
Malvern Ave YO26 227 D3
Malvern Cl
 Huntington YO32 226 A5
 8 Hurworth-on-Tees DL2 3 E1
 Stokesley TS9 26 C7
Malvern Cres
 Darlington DL3 2 F7
 Scarborough YO12 212 D5
Malvern Dr
 Middlesbrough TS5 6 E6
 Stokesley TS9 26 C7
Malvern Rd WF11 201 F2
Manchester Rd BB18 171 D1
Mancroft YO32 225 C8
Mandale Mill Prim Sch TS17 6 B8
Mandale Rd TS5 6 D8
MANFIELD 2 B4
Manfield CE Prim Sch DL2 2 B4
Mangrill La LS14 188 C3
Manham Hill YO11 99 F7
Mankin La HG4 214 D1
Manley Cl YO32 225 D4
Manley Dr LS22 180 A3
Manley Gr LS29 218 D4
Manley Rd LS29 218 E4
Manley Rise LS29 218 D3
Manor Ave YO12 212 D6
Manor Beeches The 3 YO19 184 E7
Manor CE Sch YO26 227 C7
Manor Chase YO26 181 F6
Manor Cl
 Burton in Lonsdale LA6 102 F3
 5 Hemingbrough YO8 198 F1
 Ingleton LA6 103 D3
 13 Kirkbymoorside YO62 70 B1
 Kirk Smeaton WF8 206 B3
 Low Worsall TS15 24 B8
 6 North Duffield YO8 199 A7
 12 Norton DN6 206 E2
 5 Stokesley TS9 26 C7
 Topcliffe YO7 115 C6
 Upper Poppleton YO26 182 F8
 Wath HG4 114 B7
 Whitby YO21 208 B6
Manor Cres HG5 221 C6
Manorcroft WF6 200 A1
Manor Croft YO42 169 F1
Manor Ct
 6 Bubwith YO8 199 D7
 Fairburn WF11 201 D7
 Follifoot HG3 223 F5
 Kirkby Malzeard HG4 112 D5
 Knaresborough HG5 221 B5
 York YO10 228 F3
 2 York YO32 225 F6
Manor Dr
 2 Brafferton YO61 115 F1
 Camblesforth YO8 204 C4
 4 Dunnington YO19 184 F7
 Harrogate HG2 222 C8
 Hilton TS15 6 C2
 Kirby Hill YO51 141 A7
 Knaresborough HG5 221 C6
 5 North Duffield YO8 199 A7
 North Featherstone WF7 200 E1
 Pickering YO18 95 E7
 Scotton HG5 162 A6
Manor Drive N YO26 227 D4
Manor Drive S YO26 227 D4
Manor Farm LA6 102 A7
Manor Farm Cl
 1 Brayton YO8 232 A1
 Carlton DN14 204 C2
 Copmanthorpe YO23 230 A2
 Kellington DN14 202 F3
Manor Farm Ct
 Chapel Haddlesey YO8 203 C4
 Colton LS24 190 E7
Manor Farm Way
 Coulby Newham TS8 6 F5
 Scotton HG5 162 A6
Manorfields 11 DL2 3 E1
Manor Fields DN14 205 B2
Manor Fold HG3 223 F5
Manor Garth
 Haxby YO32 225 B8
 Kellington DN14 202 F3
 12 Kirklevington TS15 24 E8
 Ledsham LS25 201 B8
 7 Norton DN6 206 F2
 1 Riccall YO19 198 A8
 7 Spofforth HG3 179 E6
Manor Garth Rd LS25 194 E1
Manor Gdns
 6 Hunmanby YO14 127 A8
Manor Gdns *continued*
 Killinghall HG3 161 C5
 Kirkbymoorside YO62 70 B1
 15 Knaresborough HG5 221 B6
 Scarborough YO12 212 E6
 Thorner LS14 188 A3
Manor Gn
 Northallerton DL7 210 C3
 Patrick Brompton DL8 62 C6
Manor Gr
 Colburn DL9 40 F5
 Great Broughton TS9 26 E5
Manor Heath YO23 230 A3
Manor House Art Gall & Mus★ LS29 218 B4
Manor La
 Healaugh LS24 181 E1
 Rawcliffe YO30 224 D2
Manor Orchards HG5 221 B6
MANOR PARK 176 B2
Manor Park Ave
 Great Preston WF10 200 D7
 Pontefract WF8 201 C2
Manor Park Cl YO30 224 E2
Manor Park Gr 2 YO30 224 E2
Manor Park Rd YO30 224 E2
Manor Pk
 Arkendale HG5 163 A7
 Cowling BD22 187 B6
 Ledston WF10 200 F7
 Swinton YO17 121 C4
Manor Rd
 Beal DN14 202 C4
 Darlington DL3 3 C4
 Easingwold YO61 117 C1
 Fylingdales YO22 33 C4
 Harrogate HG2 222 B8
 Hurworth-on-Tees DL2 3 D1
 Killinghall HG3 161 C5
 Knaresborough HG5 221 B6
 Scarborough YO12 212 E5
 Stutton with Hazlewood LS24 189 D4
Manor Rise LS29 218 D4
Manor Vale La 28 YO62 70 B1
Manor View
 Castleford WF10 200 F3
 Oswaldkirk YO62 93 A1
 Rillington YO17 122 F5
Manor View Rd YO11 100 D5
Manor Way
 Glusburn BD20 187 E6
 York YO30 224 E2
Manor Wood TS8 6 F6
Manse Cres 23 LS29 176 C1
Manse La HG5 221 D4
Mansell Cl YO8 232 A2
Manse Rd LS29 176 C1
Manse Way BD20 187 E7
Mansfield Ave TS17 6 B8
Mansfield Ct HG1 219 C4
Mansfield Rd LS29 176 B1
Mansfield St YO31 233 C3
Manston Ct 14 DL2 4 C4
Manston La LS15 194 A5
Manton Ave TS5 6 D8
Maple Ave
 Bishopthorpe YO23 231 A3
 Malton YO17 215 D6
Maple Cl
 5 Colburn DL9 40 F5
 Hambleton YO8 197 B1
 2 South Milford LS25 195 F2
Maple Croft YO61 144 A5
Maple Ct
 Wheldrake YO19 192 D8
 York YO10 231 E6
Maple Dr YO12 212 D7
Maple Garth HG4 114 B7
Maple Gr
 12 Brayton YO8 197 D1
 7 Linton-on-Ouse YO30 164 F7
 York YO10 228 D1
Maplehurst Ave YO31 228 D7
Maple La YO61 144 A5
Maple Rd DL10 209 A8
Maple Tree Ave 10 YO8 198 B4
Maple Wlk HG4 214 B2
Maplewood Paddock 2 YO24 227 C1
Marage Rd YO7 211 B3
Marazion Dr DL3 3 C8
March Ave HG5 221 A4
Marchlyn Cres TS17 5 F4
March St
 Normanton South WF6 200 A1
 York YO31 233 C4
Marderby La YO7 90 C7
Maresfield Rd DL9 40 E3
Margaret Philipson Ct YO1 233 C3
Margaret Rd HG2 219 B1
Margaret St YO10 233 C1
Margerison Cres LS29 218 E3
Margerison Rd LS29 218 E3
Margrove Heritage Ctr★ TS12 9 D6
MARGROVE PARK 9 D6
Marhead Balk HG5 163 A7
Marias Ct 9 YO11 213 A6
Maria St 15 LS29 176 C1
Marigold Cl YO8 232 C2
Marina Cres BD23 216 D3
Marina Rd DL3 3 D8
Marina Way HG4 214 A2
Marine Dr YO11 213 C7
Marine Espl YO13 54 A8
Marine Par 24 YO21 208 D7

Mariner's Terr 16 YO14 . . 101 B3
Marine Villa Rd WF11 . . . 201 F2
Marion Ave TS16 . . . 5 D4
Marishes La
Allerston YO17 . . . 97 A2
Thornton-le-Dale YO17 . . . 96 E1
Marishes Low Rd YO17 . . 122 D8
Marjorie Waite Ct YO30 . 228 B7
Markenfield Hall* HG4 . . 139 D6
Markenfield Rd HG3 . . . 219 B5
Market Cross Sh Ctr 13 YO8 . . . 232 C5
Market Flat La HG5 . . . 162 C6
Market Hall YO11 . . . 213 B6
Market Hill 5 YO51 . . . 141 B6
Market La 14 YO8 . . . 232 C5
Market Pl
Askrigg DL8 . . . 57 E5
4 Bedale DL8 . . . 63 A3
2 Cawood YO8 . . . 197 B8
7 Easingwold YO61 . . . 143 C8
Hawes DL8 . . . 56 C4
10 Helmsley YO62 . . . 92 F6
25 Kirkbymoorside YO62 . . . 70 B1
3 Knaresborough HG5 . . . 221 B6
Malton YO17 . . . 215 C4
9 Masham HG4 . . . 86 C3
9 Middleham DL8 . . . 60 E2
6 Normanton South WF6 200 A1
Pickering YO18 . . . 95 F7
Richmond DL10 . . . 209 C6
11 Selby YO8 . . . 232 C5
10 Settle BD24 . . . 131 D2
7 Snaith DN14 . . . 204 C1
Thirsk YO7 . . . 211 B3
12 Wetherby LS22 . . . 180 C3
11 Whitby YO22 . . . 208 D7
Market Place E 19 HG4 . . 214 C5
Market Place N 23 HG4 . . 214 C5
Market Place S 20 HG4 . . 214 C5
Market Place W 21 HG4 . 214 C5
Market Row DL7 . . . 210 D4
Market Sq 13 DL10 . . . 209 C6
Market St
Malton YO17 . . . 215 C4
Normanton South WF6 . . . 200 A1
24 Scarborough YO11 . . . 213 A6
York YO1 . . . 233 B2
Market Way 25 YO11 . . . 213 A6
Market Weighton Rd YO8 . . . 198 B6
Markham Cres YO31 . . . 233 B4
Markham St YO31 . . . 233 B4
Mark House La BD23 . . . 155 C1
MARKINGTON . . . 139 D3
Markington CE Prim Sch HG3 . . . 139 C3
Mark La
Fylingdales YO22 . . . 33 C3
Kirk Deighton LS22 . . . 180 B5
Marlborough Ave
3 Byram WF11 . . . 201 F4
Tadcaster LS24 . . . 189 D5
3 Whitby YO21 . . . 208 B7
Marlborough Cl YO30 . . . 224 D3
Marlborough Dr
Darlington DL1 . . . 3 C4
Tadcaster LS24 . . . 189 D5
Marlborough Gr
Ilkley LS29 . . . 218 D3
Ripon HG4 . . . 214 B6
York YO10 . . . 228 D2
Marlborough Rd HG1 . . . 219 E2
Marlborough Sq LS29 . . . 218 C3
Marlborough St 11 YO12 . 213 A7
Marlborough Villas YO10 . . . 228 D2
Marl Hill La BD20 . . . 186 D8
Marmiam Dr 2 YO32 . . . 167 D2
Marmion Ct HG4 . . . 87 A1
Marmion Twr* HG4 . . . 87 A1
Marne Cl 1 DL9 . . . 209 B1
Marne Rd DL9 . . . 209 D1
Marquis Ct 2 YO26 . . . 227 D6
MARRICK . . . 38 F5
Marrick Priory Outdoor Ctr* DL11 . . . 38 E4
Marrick Rd TS18 . . . 5 D8
Marridales DL8 . . . 56 D4
Marriforth La HG4 . . . 61 F2
Marriner Cl 13 LS21 . . . 176 F1
Marr The YO14 . . . 100 F5
Marrtree Bsns Pk WF10 . 200 E3
Marsdens Pl 7 YO22 . . . 208 E6
Marsden Wlk DL3 . . . 3 C8
MARSETT . . . 57 A1
Marsett La DL8 . . . 57 B2
Marshall Dr YO18 . . . 96 A7
Marshall Mews 2 WF10 . 200 E4
Marshall Way HG4 . . . 214 C5
Marsh Croft WF11 . . . 201 E4
Marsh End WF11 . . . 202 A3
Marshfield Rd 7 BD24 . . 131 D2
Marsh La
Asselby DN14 . . . 205 D7
Barlow YO8 . . . 204 B8
2 Beal DN14 . . . 202 D4
Bolton Percy YO23 . . . 190 D3
Byram cum Sutton WF11 . . 201 F4
Cawood YO8 . . . 197 D8
Ingleby Greenhow TS9 . . . 27 B5
Knottingley WF11 . . . 202 A2
West Haddlesey YO8 . . . 202 F5
Marsh Lane Gdns DN14 . . 202 F4
Marsh Rd WF10 . . . 200 D3
MARSKE . . . 39 C7
Mars La TS13 . . . 11 A4
Marston Ave YO26 . . . 227 B3
Marston Bsns Pk YO26 . . 181 B7
Marston Cres YO26 . . . 227 B3
Marston La
Long Marston YO26 . . . 182 A8
Moor Monkton YO26 . . . 165 A1
Marston Moor Rd 4 DL1 . . . 3 F4
Marston Rd YO26 . . . 181 D7
Marston Way 3 LS22 . . . 180 B3
Martello Way YO32 . . . 226 A1
Marten Cl 2 YO30 . . . 228 A8
Martin Cheeseman Ct 3 YO24 . . . 230 C8
Martindale Rd DL1 . . . 3 D7
Martinet Ct TS17 . . . 6 A7
Martinet Rd TS17 . . . 6 B7
Martinhoe Cl 4 TS17 . . . 6 A3
Martins Ct YO26 . . . 228 A5
MARTON
Boroughbridge . . . 141 D1
Middlesbrough . . . 7 B7
Pickering . . . 94 F6
Marton Abbey (Priory)* YO61 . . . 144 C8
Marton Ave TS4 . . . 7 B8
Marton Cl BD23 . . . 172 C8
Marton Ct YO21 . . . 208 B6
Marton cum Grafton CE Prim Sch YO51 . . . 141 D1
Marton Gr 1 TS3 . . . 7 C8
MARTON-IN-THE-FOREST . . . 144 E7
Marton La
Arkendale HG5 . . . 163 B8
Wrelton YO18 . . . 95 C7
MARTON-LE-MOOR . . . 114 F1
Marton Manor Prim Sch TS7 . . . 7 B6
Marton Moor Rd TS7 . . . 7 D5
Marton Rd
Coulby Newham TS4 . . . 7 A7
Gargrave BD23 . . . 172 C8
Marton YO62 . . . 94 F6
Sinnington YO62 . . . 95 A7
Martonside Way TS4 . . . 7 A8
Marton St BD23 . . . 216 D3
Marton Sta TS7 . . . 7 C7
Marvell Rise HG1 . . . 219 E7
Marwood CE VC Infant Sch TS9 . . . 7 F1
Marwood Dr TS9 . . . 7 F1
Marygate
Barton DL10 . . . 21 D7
York YO30 . . . 233 A3
Marygate La YO30 . . . 233 A3
Marykirk Rd TS17 . . . 6 B6
Mary La YO26 . . . 141 F3
Masefield Cl HG1 . . . 219 E7
MASHAM . . . 86 B3
Masham Bank HG4 . . . 85 D8
Masham CE Prim Sch HG4 . . . 86 C3
Masham Cl HG2 . . . 220 C1
Masham La DL8 . . . 87 A4
Masham Rd
Firby DL8 . . . 62 F1
Harrogate HG2 . . . 220 C1
Snape with Thorp DL8 . . . 86 E8
Mask La YO41 . . . 185 D4
MASONGILL . . . 103 A6
Masongill Fell La LA6 . . . 103 A6
Masonic La YO7 . . . 211 B3
Masons Way BB18 . . . 171 D2
Maspin Moor Rd LS25 . . . 202 C7
Massa Flatts Wood BD23 216 E5
Massey St YO8 . . . 232 C5
Master Rd TS17 . . . 6 B7
Master's Gate YO18 . . . 49 D4
Mastil Cl DL8 . . . 62 D5
Mastiles La BD23 . . . 134 A6
Mastil La DL8 . . . 62 D5
Matfen Ave TS7 . . . 7 D6
Matthew La
Bradleys Both BD20 . . . 173 E3
Green Hammerton YO26 . . 164 C4
Mattison Way YO24 . . . 227 E2
Maude Rd DL9 . . . 209 A1
Maud La LS21 . . . 177 A6
Maudon Ave YO18 . . . 96 A6
Maudon Gr YO17 . . . 215 F4
Maufe Way 3 LS29 . . . 218 B3
MAUNBY . . . 64 D1
Maunby La YO7 . . . 64 D1
Maundy Gr HG5 . . . 221 C7
Mawson Gr DL6 . . . 65 B5
Mawson La HG4 . . . 214 C4
Maxim Cl 5 DL9 . . . 40 E4
Maxwell Rd LS29 . . . 218 D3
Mayfair Ave TS6 . . . 7 E8
Mayfair Rd DL1 . . . 3 D8
Mayfield DL7 . . . 64 F2
Mayfield Ave
Ilkley LS29 . . . 218 D4
7 Scalby YO12 . . . 75 E5
Mayfield Cl
3 Glusburn BD20 . . . 187 E7
Ilkley LS29 . . . 218 D4
Mayfield Cres TS16 . . . 5 D5
Mayfield Ct YO8 . . . 204 C7
Mayfield Dr
5 Brayton YO8 . . . 232 A1
4 Seamer YO12 . . . 99 D6
Mayfield Gdns LS29 . . . 218 D5
Mayfield Gr
Harrogate HG1 . . . 219 D3
Knaresborough HG5 . . . 221 C6
York YO24 . . . 230 E8
Mayfield Pl
Harrogate HG1 . . . 219 D3
Mayfield Pl *continued*
3 Whitby YO21 . . . 208 C5
Mayfield Rd
Brayton YO8 . . . 232 A1
1 High Bentham LA2 . . . 129 A7
Ilkley LS29 . . . 218 C4
Middlesbrough TS7 . . . 7 D6
Whitby YO21 . . . 208 B5
Mayfield Terr HG1 . . . 219 D3
Mayfly Ct 26 YO18 . . . 95 F6
Maypole Gdns YO8 . . . 197 B8
Maypole Gr 3 YO19 . . . 191 D8
Maypole Mews LS15 . . . 194 B8
Maythorn Rd YO31 . . . 225 E2
Maythorpe YO23 . . . 182 C6
Mayville Ave YO12 . . . 212 E6
Mead Cres TS17 . . . 6 C8
Meadlands YO31 . . . 229 B6
Meadow Ave 5 HG4 . . . 214 B2
Meadowbank Rd TS7 . . . 7 D7
Meadowbeck Cl YO10 . . . 229 B4
Meadow Brook Chase 19 WF6 . . . 200 B1
Meadow Cl
Cononley BD20 . . . 173 D2
7 Eastfield YO11 . . . 100 A6
Hampsthwaite HG3 . . . 160 F5
Northallerton DL7 . . . 210 D2
Thorpe Willoughby YO8 . . . 197 C2
Meadowcroft
Draughton BD23 . . . 174 B7
Harrogate HG1 . . . 219 E6
Meadow Croft
Brayton YO8 . . . 232 A2
Colonley BD20 . . . 173 C2
Meadowcroft Dr HG3 . . . 140 A5
Meadow Ct
Rillington YO17 . . . 122 F5
Scruton DL7 . . . 63 E7
6 Willerby YO12 . . . 99 D2
3 York YO24 . . . 230 E8
Meadow Dale Ct TS12 . . . 9 F7
Meadow Dr
7 East Ayton/West Ayton YO13 . . . 99 B8
Harrogate HG1 . . . 219 E7
Scruton DL7 . . . 63 E7
Thorpe Willoughby YO8 . . . 197 B2
Meadowfield
Amotherby YO17 . . . 121 A4
9 Bedale DL8 . . . 63 B3
1 Bubwith YO8 . . . 199 D7
Lythe YO21 . . . 13 A3
8 Stokesley TS9 . . . 26 C8
Meadowfield Dr
Eaglescliffe TS16 . . . 5 D5
South Duffield YO8 . . . 199 A4
Meadowfield Rd
9 Colburn DL9 . . . 41 A5
Darlington DL3 . . . 3 A7
Meadowfields YO21 . . . 208 C6
Meadowfields Cl 9 YO61 . . . 143 D8
Meadowfields Ct 17 YO21 . . . 208 D6
Meadowfields Dr YO31 . . 225 D2
Meadow Garth
2 Tadcaster LS24 . . . 189 F6
Thirsk YO7 . . . 211 B1
Thorpe Willoughby YO8 . . . 197 C2
Meadow Gate HG1 . . . 219 E6
Meadow Gr 20 DL8 . . . 63 A2
Meadowings The TS15 . . . 5 D2
Meadow La
Cononley BD20 . . . 173 C2
2 Darley HG3 . . . 160 A6
8 Eastfield YO11 . . . 100 A6
1 Haxby YO32 . . . 225 D8
Hellifield BD23 . . . 154 A3
Northallerton DL6 . . . 210 E6
Snape DL8 . . . 87 A7
Meadowlands Cl 2 TS13 . 11 A8
Meadow Lea 21 BD20 . . . 187 E7
Meadow Pl 5 YO8 . . . 232 B6
Meadow Rd
Garforth LS25 . . . 194 D4
Knaresborough HG5 . . . 221 B7
2 Pickering YO18 . . . 95 F7
Meadow Rise
Harrogate HG1 . . . 219 E7
7 Settle BD24 . . . 131 D3
2 Skipton BD23 . . . 217 B5
Meadowside Prim Sch HG5 . . . 221 C7
Meadow Springs Way 3 YO61 . . . 143 D8
Meadows The
3 Carlton DN14 . . . 204 C3
Castleford LS25 . . . 200 C7
Coulby Newham TS8 . . . 7 B5
Hambleton YO8 . . . 196 F1
8 Middleton St George DL2 . 4 C4
7 Monk Fryston LS25 . . . 202 A8
Northallerton DL6 . . . 210 E5
Riccall YO19 . . . 197 F8
Richmond DL10 . . . 209 E7
Scalby YO12 . . . 212 B7
2 Skelton YO30 . . . 224 B5
South Milford LS25 . . . 195 F2
Meadow Vale
Green Hammerton YO26 . 164 C3
2 Ripon HG4 . . . 214 B2
Meadow View
Barwick in Elmet & Scholes LS15 . . . 194 B8
Gristhorpe YO14 . . . 100 E4
Harrogate HG1 . . . 219 E6
Sherburn in Elmet LS25 . . . 195 F4
Meadow Way
Barnoldswick BB18 . . . 171 E2
Harrogate HG1 . . . 219 E7
Heworth YO31 . . . 228 F7
Huntington YO32 . . . 225 F4
3 Tadcaster LS24 . . . 189 F6
Meads La YO12 . . . 99 E5
Meads The 3 YO11 . . . 99 F6
Mead The DL1 . . . 3 E5
Meadway YO8 . . . 197 D2
Meadway Dr YO8 . . . 197 D2
MEAGILL . . . 159 D3
Meagill La LS21 . . . 159 E2
Meagill Rise LS21 . . . 176 E1
Meam Cl YO10 . . . 229 D4
Meanee Rd 11 DL9 . . . 40 F2
MEARBECK . . . 153 D7
Medbourne Gdns TS5 . . . 6 E7
Megson Pl YO7 . . . 211 C4
Megsons Ct BD23 . . . 217 C7
Melander Cl YO26 . . . 227 B4
Melander Gdns 5 YO32 . 225 D7
Melbourne Dr YO7 . . . 90 E5
Melbourne Pl YO7 . . . 211 B2
Melbourne St YO10 . . . 228 D2
Melcombe Ave 11 YO32 . . 167 A7
Meldyke La TS8 . . . 6 D5
Mellersh Rd 15 DL10 . . . 41 E4
Melling (St Wilfred) CE Prim Sch LA6 . . . 102 A2
Melltown's Gn YO7 . . . 88 C6
MELMERBY
Carlton . . . 83 F8
Ripon . . . 114 C7
Melmerby Green La HG4 114 C6
Melmerby Green Rd HG4 . . . 114 B6
Melmerby Ind Est HG4 . . 114 B6
Melrose Cl 1 YO31 . . . 229 A5
Melrose Cres
Bishop Monkton HG3 . . . 140 A5
Guisborough TS14 . . . 9 A6
Melrose Dr 16 LS29 . . . 176 C1
Melrosegate YO31 . . . 228 F5
Melrose Rd HG3 . . . 140 A5
Melrose St 4 YO12 . . . 212 F6
MELSONBY . . . 21 A7
Melsonby Methodist Prim Sch DL10 . . . 20 F7
Melton Ave YO30 . . . 227 F8
Melton Coll YO24 . . . 227 F3
Melton Dr
Bishopthorpe YO23 . . . 231 A3
York YO30 . . . 227 F8
Melville Gr 1 LS29 . . . 218 E4
Melville Terr 52 YO14 . . . 101 B3
Melwood Gr YO26 . . . 227 B5
Memorial Dr TS7 . . . 7 B6
Mendip Cl 2 YO32 . . . 225 F5
MENETHORPE . . . 147 D6
Menethorpe La YO17 . . . 147 D7
Menin Rd DL9 . . . 209 B1
MENTHORPE . . . 199 C5
Menwith Hill Rd HG3 . . . 159 D4
Mercer Art Gall The* HG2 . . . 219 C3
Mercer Dr DL9 . . . 209 C1
Merchant Adventurers' Hall* YO1 . . . 233 C2
Merchantgate YO1 . . . 233 C2
Merchants Ct YO31 . . . 228 E5
Merchant's Row 10 YO11 213 B6
Merchant Way YO23 . . . 230 B3
Mercury Pk DL7 . . . 63 C5
Mercury Rd DL10 . . . 209 A8
Merefield Way WF10 . . . 200 E2
Mere La YO11 . . . 212 F1
Mere View Gdns YO12 . . . 99 F8
Merewood Rd WF10 . . . 200 C4
Merioneth Cl 5 TS17 . . . 5 F4
Merlin Covert 4 YO31 . . . 225 F3
Merlinwood BD23 . . . 172 B4
Merrington Ave TS17 . . . 6 D6
Merrybank La LS17 . . . 178 A3
MERRYBENT . . . 2 E5
Merrybent Dr DL2 . . . 2 F5
Merry Dale YO11 . . . 100 A7
Merryfield HG2 . . . 222 B7
Messines Rd DL9 . . . 40 E3
Metcalfe La YO19 . . . 229 C5
Metcalfes Ct HG4 . . . 214 C6
Metes La YO12 . . . 99 E5
METHLEY . . . 200 B5
METHLEY JUNCTION . . . 200 A4
Methley La LS26 . . . 200 A6
Methley Park Hospl LS26 . . . 200 A6
Methley Prim Sch LS26 . . 200 B6
Methley Rd WF10 . . . 200 D4
Meuse Cl 4 DL9 . . . 209 C1
Mewburn Rd DL3 . . . 3 C8
MEWITH HEAD . . . 129 E6
Mewith La LA2 . . . 129 B6
Mews The WF6 . . . 200 A2
Meynell Rd DL3 . . . 3 C7
Meyrick Ave LS22 . . . 180 D4
Michael Mount Rd YO11 . . 213 C1
Michael Syddall CE Prim Sch DL10 . . . 41 E5
Micklebury La HG4 . . . 86 A3
MICKLEBY . . . 12 A4
Mickleby Dr YO21 . . . 208 B6
Mickleby La TS13 . . . 11 F4
Mickledale La YO26 . . . 163 D8
MICKLEFIELD . . . 194 F4
Micklefield CE Prim Sch LS25 . . . 195 A4
Micklefield Sta LS25 . . . 195 A3
Micklegate
17 Pontefract WF8 . . . 201 B1
1 Selby YO8 . . . 232 D5
York YO1 . . . 233 A2
Micklegate Bar Mus* YO24 . . . 233 A1
Mickle Hill Mews BD23 . . 155 D1
Micklethwaite View LS22 . . . 180 C2
MICKLETOWN . . . 200 B5
Mickletown Rd LS26 . . . 200 B6
Micklewaite Gr LS22 . . . 180 C2
MICKLEY . . . 112 F7
Middle Bank Rd TS7 . . . 7 D7
Middle Banks 24 YO32 . . . 166 E5
Middlebrook Gdns YO8 . . 232 A2
MIDDLECAVE . . . 215 A5
Middlecave Cl YO17 . . . 215 A4
Middlecave Dr YO17 . . . 215 A4
Middlecave Rd YO17 . . . 215 B4
Middle Craven Rd 27 BD24 . . . 131 D2
Middlecroft YO41 . . . 185 F5
Middlecroft Dr YO32 . . . 167 A7
Middlecroft Gr 2 YO32 . . 167 B7
Middlefield Cl
19 Osgodby YO11 . . . 100 B7
Weaverthorpe YO17 . . . 124 E1
Middlefield La
Kirk Smeaton WF8 . . . 206 A2
Melmerby DL8 . . . 84 A8
MIDDLEHAM . . . 60 E2
Middleham Ave YO31 . . . 228 E8
Middleham Castle* DL8 . . 60 E2
Middleham CE Prim Sch DL8 . . . 60 E2
Middleham La DL8 . . . 60 E4
Middle Head Rd YO18 . . . 71 E8
Middle La
Brayton YO8 . . . 232 C1
Brompton YO13 . . . 98 C7
Collingham LS22 . . . 180 B1
Hutton Buscel YO13 . . . 74 E1
Kettlewell with Starbotton BD23 . . . 108 A3
14 Knottingley WF11 . . . 202 A2
Snainton YO13 . . . 97 F4
Middle Moor La DL11 . . . 39 F5
Middle Oxford St WF10 . . 200 E4
Middle Rd TS17 . . . 6 A5
Middlesbrough Rd TS7 . . . 7 E6
MIDDLESMOOR . . . 110 B5
Middle St
Gayles DL11 . . . 19 E6
Swinton YO17 . . . 121 B4
Wilberfoss YO41 . . . 185 F5
MIDDLETHORPE . . . 231 B6
Middlethorpe Dr YO24 . . 230 E7
Middlethorpe Gr YO24 . . 230 F7
MIDDLETON
Glusburn . . . 187 A6
Ilkley . . . 218 C7
Pickering . . . 95 E8
Middleton Ave
Ilkley LS29 . . . 218 B6
Thornaby TS17 . . . 6 B6
Middleton Carr La YO18 . . 95 D7
Middleton Cl
Eaglescliffe TS16 . . . 5 C5
Settrington YO17 . . . 122 D1
Middleton La
Middleton St George DL2 . . . 4 C3
Middleton YO18 . . . 95 E8
MIDDLETON ONE ROW . . . 4 D3
MIDDLETON-ON-LEVEN . . . 25 D8
MIDDLETON QUERNHOW . . 88 B1
Middleton Rd
Hutton Rudby TS15 . . . 25 D6
Ilkley LS29 . . . 218 A4
Pickering YO18 . . . 95 E7
Sadberge DL2 . . . 4 C7
York YO24 . . . 227 C2
MIDDLETON ST GEORGE . . . 4 B4
Middleton St George Hospl (Private) DL2 . . . 4 E4
MIDDLETON TYAS . . . 21 D5
Middleton Tyas La DL10 . . 21 B4
Middleton Tyas Prim Sch DL10 . . . 21 C5
Middleway BD20 . . . 174 C1
Middle Wlk YO12 . . . 212 E7
Middlewood Cl
3 Fylingdales YO22 . . . 33 C3
Rufforth YO23 . . . 182 C6
Middlewood Cres 5 YO22 . . . 33 C3
Middlewood Garth 4 YO22 . . . 33 C3
Middlewood La YO22 . . . 33 C3
Middycar Bank HG4 . . . 138 F6
Midge Hall Cl 18 LS29 . . . 176 C1
Midgeley Gate HG5 . . . 162 F2
Midgeley La HG5 . . . 163 A3
Midgley Cl
4 Embsay BD23 . . . 217 C7
21 Stamford Bridge YO41 168 D2
Midgley Rd LS29 . . . 176 C1
Midgley Rise 2 WF8 . . . 201 B2
Midhope Way 15 YO14 . . . 101 A3
Midland St BD23 . . . 216 E3
Midway Ave YO26 . . . 224 A1
Mightens' Bank DL8 . . . 60 D4
Milbank Rd DL3 . . . 3 B5
Milburn La YO7 . . . 89 D3
MILBY . . . 141 B6

Mildred Gr 5 YO24 227 F2
Mildred Sylvester Way WF6 200 B1
Mile Hill Coldhill La LS25 195 E5
Mile House Bsns Pk DL6 210 B7
Mile Planting DL10 209 F8
Milestone Ave YO23 182 C6
Milford Mews 7 YO32 225 D7
Milford Rd LS25 195 F3
Milford Way 8 YO32 225 D7
Milking Hill YO61 118 B4
Mill Balk DN14 207 C8
Mill Bank
Bishop Thornton HG3 138 F1
Fylingdales YO22 33 D2
Lindrick with Studley Royal & Fountains HG4 113 A3
Norton YO17 215 E3
Millbank Ct YO7 89 D4
Millbank La TS17 6 B7
Mill Bank Rd YO18 72 D5
Millbeck Gn LS22 188 A8
Millbeck View WF8 201 B2
Mill Bridge BD23 216 F4
Millbrook Ct 17 BB8 186 A3
Mill Brow LA2 128 E2
Mill Brow Rd BB18 172 B1
Mill Chase Rd HG2 220 D5
Mill Cl
Monk Fryston LS25 202 A8
Ravensworth DL11 19 F6
Settle BD24 131 D2
6 Spofforth HG3 179 E6
Mill Close La DL8 62 D6
Mill Cotts YO17 215 D4
Millcroft 15 YO8 197 D1
Mill Croft
Cowling BD22 187 B6
Richmond DL10 209 A7
MILL DAM 129 C6
Mill Dam LS23 188 F7
Mill Dam La WF8 201 C1
Mill Dike La YO7 116 F8
Millenium Rd BD20 173 D4
Millers Cl YO17 215 D2
Millers Croft 6 YO23 230 B3
Millers Ford LA2 128 E8
Millers La TS12 9 F6
Millers Rd 2 YO7 211 C3
Millfield YO51 141 D2
Millfield Ave
Northallerton DL6 210 E3
York YO10 228 F3
Millfield Cl
Eaglescliffe TS16 5 D4
1 Leeming DL7 63 D4
Pickering YO18 95 F6
Wilberfoss YO41 185 E5
Millfield Cres DL6 210 E3
Millfield Ct YO19 192 F7
Mill Field Ct 5 BD20 174 C1
Millfield Dr YO8 204 D4
Millfield Gdns YO26 224 A2
Millfield Glade HG2 220 D4
Millfield Ind Est YO19 192 F7
Millfield La
Easingwold YO61 117 C1
Nether Poppleton YO26 227 B8
Poppleton YO26 224 A2
York YO10 229 A3
Mill Field La YO61 91 B1
Millfield Rd
17 Hemingbrough YO8 198 F1
Hemingbrough YO8 204 F8
York YO23 228 B2
Mill Field Rd YO8 203 B5
Millfield Rise YO61 117 C1
Millfields 2 BD20 174 C1
Millfield St 4 HG3 137 B4
Mill Flats La DL8 60 F3
Mill Garth 14 YO8 198 F1
Millgarth Ct 7 LS22 188 A8
Millgate
10 Masham HG4 86 C3
Richmond DL10 209 C6
Selby YO8 232 C6
Thirsk YO7 211 B3
Mill Gate
Gilling with Hartforth & Sedbury DL10 20 E3
Harrogate HG1 219 C7
Knayton with Brawith YO7 65 E2
Millgate House Gdn* DL10 209 C6
Millgate Mews 3 YO8 232 C6
Millgates YO26 227 C6
Mill Green Way The YO22 51 D8
Mill Hill
Escrick YO19 192 B5
16 Normanton South WF6 200 A1
Mill Hill Cl 8 DL6 43 F3
Mill Hill Cres DL6 210 E3
Mill Hill Cty Prim Sch DL6 210 E4
Mill Hill Dr YO32 225 F4
Mill Hill La
Giggleswick BD24 131 C3
Northallerton DL6 210 E3
MILL HIRST 159 F7
Millholme Dr 2 LA2 129 A7
Millholme Rise BD23 217 C8
Mill House YO7 65 D1
Mill Hurst HG3 159 F7
Millings La YO51 141 B7
Mill La
Acaster Malbis YO23 191 C8
Ampleforth YO62 118 C8
Askham Richard YO23 182 D2
Askrigg DL8 57 E6
Aysgarth DL8 58 E3
Barlow YO8 204 B7
Bellerby DL8 60 E8
Bentham LA2 128 F7
3 Bewerley HG3 137 B4
Boroughbridge YO51 141 B5
Brayton YO8 203 C8
Buckton/Bempton YO13 97 D5
Burniston YO13 75 C8
Burton Leonard HG3 140 B2
Carlton DN14 204 D3
Castleford WF10 200 E5
Cayton YO11 100 C6
Constable Burton DL8 61 C5
Darlington DL1 3 F6
Drax YO8 204 F5
Earby BB18 172 B1
Easingwold YO61 117 D1
3 East Ayton/West Ayton YO13 99 A7
Eskdaleside cum Ugglebarnby YO22 32 B6
Exelby, Leeming & Newton DL7 63 D3
Faceby TS9 25 F2
Farndale East YO62 48 E4
Gargrave BD23 155 D1
Great Ouseburn YO26 164 C8
Hambleton YO8 196 F1
Haxby YO32 166 D5
Hebden BD23 135 A1
2 Hemingbrough YO8 198 F1
Hessay YO23 182 B7
High Coniscliffe DL2 2 C6
Kearby with Netherby LS22 179 C2
Kirk Hammerton YO26 164 C2
Knaresborough HG5 221 F8
Langtoft YO25 151 C7
Leyburn DL8 60 E4
6 Linton-on-Ouse YO30 164 F7
Longnewton DL2 4 F6
Long Preston BD23 153 F4
Low Bradley BD20 173 E3
Low Hawsker YO22 33 A6
Mickletown LS26 200 B6
Middleton St George DL2 4 D5
Muston YO14 101 A2
Nether Burrow LA6 102 B6
Newland YO8 205 A3
Northallerton DL7 210 C3
Pannal HG3 222 E2
Pickering YO18 95 F6
Pontefract WF8 201 C2
Rawcliffe DN14 204 F1
Redmire DL8 59 C5
1 Riccall YO19 192 A1
Ryther cum Ossendyke LS24 190 E1
1 Scarborough YO12 212 E3
Scruton DL7 63 E5
Sherburn in Elmet LS25 195 F2
Skipton BD23 216 F3
Sledmere YO25 149 F3
Snape with Thorp DL8 87 B7
South Milford LS25 195 F2
Spofforth with Stockeld HG3 179 E6
Stillington YO61 144 C6
Stutton with Hazlewood LS24 189 E4
Swinden BD23 154 B1
Thirkleby High & Low with Osgodby YO7 90 D2
Thormanby YO61 116 E5
Thrintoft DL7 63 F8
Whitwood WF10 200 B2
Wilberfoss YO41 185 E6
York YO31 228 E6
Youlton YO61 142 F2
Mill Lane Ave YO60 145 C5
Mill Mount YO24 228 A3
Mill Mount Ct YO24 228 A3
Millrace Cl YO17 215 D2
Mill Race The 4 DL2 22 C8
Mill Rd
Burton Fleming YO25 126 D4
Gillamoor YO62 70 A5
Goldsborough HG5 221 F3
Mill Riggs TS9 26 D7
Mill Rise DL6 210 E2
Mill Row BD20 187 F7
Millside YO17 215 D2
Mill St
6 Barnoldswick BB18 171 D1
8 Eastburn BD20 187 F7
41 Glusburn BD20 187 F7
Guisborough TS14 8 F6
Harome YO62 93 C4
Malton YO17 215 E3
Scarborough YO12 212 F5
York YO1 233 C1
Millthorpe Sch YO23 228 B2
Mill View
5 Burley in Warfedale LS29 176 C1
Hut Green DN14 203 A2
Knottingley WF11 201 D2
Millway YO62 92 C1
Mill Wynd TS16 5 E3
Milner La LS24 195 D8
Milner Rd DL1 3 D4
Milners La HG1 219 F7
Milner St YO24 227 D3
Milnthorpe Cl 6 LS23 188 E6
Milnthorpe Garth 7 LS23 188 E6
Milnthorpe Gdns 5 LS23 188 E6
Milnthorpe La LS23 188 E6
Milnthorpe Way LS23 188 D5
Milson Gr YO10 229 A3
Milton Ave
Malton YO17 215 D5
Scarborough YO12 212 E3
Milton Carr 8 YO30 224 F1
Milton Cl HG1 219 E7
Milton Gr 11 BB18 171 D2
Milton Rd
Malton YO17 215 C5
Pannal HG3 222 E3
Milton St
Darlington DL1 3 E5
4 Skipton BD23 217 A3
York YO10 228 F3
Minchin Cl 3 YO30 225 B1
Minskip Cl 12 TS14 8 F7
Minors Cres DL3 3 A7
MINSKIP 141 A3
Minskip Rd HG5 140 F2
Minster Ave YO31 225 F2
Minster Cl
3 Haxby YO32 225 C8
23 Ripon HG4 214 C5
40 Wigginton YO32 166 E5
York YO1 233 B3
Minster Ct YO1 233 B3
Minsterley Dr TS5 6 D7
Minster Rd HG4 214 C5
Minster Sch The YO1 233 B3
Minster View YO32 225 C8
Minster Wlk 12 DL2 3 E1
Minster Yd YO1 233 B3
Minter Cl 2 YO24 227 B1
Mire Bank La DL8 56 F4
Mire Close La BD22 187 A8
Mire Ridge BB8 186 A2
Mires La
Carthorpe DL8 87 D6
Ulleskelf LS24 190 B1
Mire Syke La HG5 162 A5
Mirey Butt La WF11 201 E2
Mirkhill Rd YO8 232 B6
Miry La LS15 188 C1
Missies La HG4 112 C3
Mistral Ct YO31 228 E8
Mitchell Ave TS17 6 B7
Mitchell Gr 43 DL9 41 A5
Mitchell La
Alne YO61 142 F4
Catton YO41 185 D8
Settle BD24 131 E1
Mitchell Way 11 YO30 224 E3
Mitchel's La YO10 231 F8
Miterdale 4 YO24 230 C7
Mitford Cl 3 YO14 126 F8
Mitford Rd 2 YO14 126 F8
Mitford St 24 YO14 101 B3
Mitton La BD20 172 D1
MLS Bsns Centres YO30 225 A2
Moat Field YO10 229 C4
Moatside Ct YO31 233 B3
Moat Way YO8 232 A2
Mock Beggar Hall* BD23 157 D7
Moins Ct YO10 229 D4
Moiser Cl YO32 225 D4
Mole End 15 YO18 95 F6
Monarch Way YO26 227 D6
Monash Ave DL9 209 C1
Monckton Dr WF10 201 B3
Monk Ave YO31 228 F7
Monk Bar Ct YO1 233 B3
Monkbridge Ct YO31 233 C4
Monket House Bank YO62 48 C4
MONK FRYSTON 202 B8
Monk Fryston CE Prim Sch LS25 202 A8
Monk Gardens La YO62 93 A7
Monkgate YO31 233 C3
Monkgate Cloisters YO31 233 C3
Monk Gn YO61 142 F4
MONKHILL 201 B1
Monkhill Ave WF8 201 B1
Monkhill Dr WF8 201 B1
Monkhill La WF8 201 B2
Monkhill Mount WF8 201 B1
Monkholme La BD23 134 C2
Monk Ing Rd HG3 159 E8
Monk La YO8 232 C7
Monkmans Wharfe 1 BD20 174 C1
Monk Park Farm* YO7 90 D4
MONKROYD 186 D4
Monkroyd Ave BB18 171 D1
Monks Cross Dr YO32 226 A3
Monks Cross Link YO32 226 B4
Monks Cross Sh Pk YO32 226 B3
Monk's Rd BD23 107 D2
Monkswell Pk HG5 221 D5
Monkton Rd 5 YO31 225 F1
Monkton Rise 7 TS14 8 F7
Monmouth Dr TS16 5 E5
Monmouth St 5 BB8 186 A3
Mons Cl 3 DL9 209 B1
Mons Rd DL9 40 F4
Montage Studio Gall* YO21 29 A7
Montague Cres LS25 194 D4
Montague Rd YO23 231 A3
Montague St YO23 228 C1
Montague Wlk 6 YO26 165 F1
Montagu La LS22 180 E5
Montagu Mews LS22 180 E5
Montagu's Harrier TS14 8 D6
Montagu Way LS22 180 E5
Montgomery Rd DL9 209 C2
Montgomery St BD23 217 A3
Montpellier Ct 11 HG2 219 C2
Montpellier Gdns 2 HG1 219 C2
Montpellier Hill HG2 219 C2
Montpellier Mews 3 HG1 219 C2
Montpellier Par HG1 219 C2
Montpellier Rd 1 HG1 219 C2
Montpellier Sq 3 HG1 219 D2
Montpellier St 4 HG1 219 C2
Montrose Ave YO31 228 D8
Montrose Gdns WF10 200 D4
Monument Cl YO24 227 E3
Moody Sty La 4 BD23 134 E3
Mook St YO60 169 B8
Moons Acre LA2 129 A8
Moor Ave 1 LS23 188 E7
Moorber La BD23 171 F8
Moorberries TS15 6 C2
Moorbridge Croft 6 LS25 196 A4
Moor Carr La
Barlby with Osgodby YO8 198 B5
Barlby YO8 198 B5
Moor Cl
Killinghall HG3 219 A8
10 Kirklevington TS15 24 E8
Lockwood TS12 10 A5
Wheldrake YO19 192 F8
Moorcock La HG3 159 F5
Moor Cres BD23 217 B4
Moor Croft 8 BD23 134 E3
Moorcroft Rd YO24 230 D7
Moore Ave YO10 229 B4
MOOR END 188 D8
Moor End Gdns LS23 188 D8
Moor End La
Crakehall DL8 62 C3
Sowerby YO7 90 A2
Moor End Rd YO13 53 F2
Moorfield Cl 6 DL1 3 E4
Moorfield Dr YO41 185 E6
Moorfield Rd LS29 218 F4
Moorfields
Raskelf YO61 116 F2
3 Wistow YO8 197 D6
Moorfield Sch LS29 218 C3
Moorfields La YO62 93 E5
Moorfield Way YO41 185 E6
Moorfoot La BD20 173 D2
Moorgarth LA6 103 D2
Moorgarth Ave 10 YO24 227 F2
Moorgate YO24 227 D3
Moorgate Dr LS25 194 D1
Moorgate Rd LS25 194 D2
Moor Gn TS7 7 D5
Moor Gr YO24 230 E8
Moor Hill YO17 147 E7
Moorhill La YO17 147 E6
Moorhills DL8 56 C4
Moorhouse Cl 3 WF6 200 B2
Moorhouse La YO7 89 E8
Moor House La YO61 116 B1
Moor La
Addingham LS29 174 D5
Aislaby YO21 31 F7
Aldfield HG4 138 F8
Arkendale HG5 162 F7
Arrathorne DL10 41 A2
Askwith LS21 176 D4
Bagby YO7 90 C4
6 Barlby YO8 198 B5
Bilbrough LS24 182 B1
Bilton-in-Ainsty with Bickerton YO26 181 D5
Bishopthorpe YO23 230 E2
Borrowby TS13 11 C6
Brawby YO17 94 F2
Brompton YO13 74 B1
Broughton YO17 121 C4
Burton Leonard HG3 140 B4
Carthorpe DL8 87 D4
Catterton LS24 190 A8
Cleasby DL2 2 F2
Cliffe YO8 198 F4
Cloughton YO13 54 C1
Collingham LS23 188 C8
Coneythorpe & Clareton HG5 163 B6
Copmanthorpe YO23 230 A1
Cropton YO18 71 B6
Crosby DL6 65 C5
Dalton DL11 19 C6
Dalton YO7 116 B8
Dishforth YO7 114 F3
Earswick YO32 226 C8
East Ayton/West Ayton YO13 99 B8
Eastfield YO11 100 A6
East Layton DL11 20 B8
Elslack BD23 172 D3
Embsay with Eastby BD23 156 F1
Full Sutton YO41 168 F1
Grassington BD23 134 E3
Great Ouseburn YO26 163 D7
Great Ribston with Walshford LS22 180 E8
Halton East BD23 157 B1
Moor La *continued*
Haxby YO32 166 D7
Hunton DL8 61 E8
Hutton-le-Hole YO62 70 C5
Kearby with Netherby HG3 179 B2
Kelfield YO19 191 E2
Kirby Hill HG4 140 F8
Knapton YO26 182 E6
Long Preston BD23 153 F5
Milby YO51 141 C7
Murton YO19 229 F8
Myton-on-Swale YO61 142 B5
Naburn YO19 191 D8
Nether Silton DL6 66 C8
Newsham DL11 19 A7
Newsham with Breckenbrough YO7 65 A1
Newton-on-Ouse YO30 165 C7
Rufforth YO26 182 E6
Ryther cum Ossendyke LS24 196 E8
Scalby YO12 212 A8
Settrington YO17 122 C1
Sherburn in Elmet LS25 195 F4
Skelton YO30 224 D6
Snape with Thorp DL8 86 E6
Steeton with Eastburn BD20 187 F7
Stillington YO61 143 F6
Strensall YO32 167 B7
Stutton with Hazlewood LS24 189 D4
Thirkleby High & Low with Osgodby YO7 90 C1
Thirsk YO7 89 D5
Tholthorpe YO61 142 D6
Thormanby YO61 116 E5
Thornton-le-Clay YO60 145 F2
Thornton Steward HG4 61 E2
Thorp Arch LS23 180 E3
Threshfield BD23 134 B2
Welburn YO62 94 A5
Weston LS21 176 E2
West Tanfield HG4 87 B2
Wilstrop YO26 181 D8
Yafforth DL7 43 B2
York YO24 230 C6
Moorland Ave
6 Earby BB18 172 B1
Skipton BD23 217 A4
Moorland Cl
5 Embsay BD23 217 E8
Harrogate HG2 220 D4
Moorland Garth 2 YO32 167 A7
Moorland Gdns
Copmanthorpe YO23 230 A1
York YO23 230 A1
Moorland Rd
Harrogate HG2 220 D4
Scarborough YO12 212 F7
York YO10 231 D8
Moorland Rise BD23 217 E8
Moorlands
Ilkley LS29 218 A2
Skelton YO32 166 B5
Moorlands Cl YO10 229 C4
Moorlands Fields YO10 231 E8
Moorlands La
Skelton YO30 224 C6
1 Tollerton YO61 143 B3
Moorlands Nature Reserve* YO32 166 B5
Moorlands Pk YO21 29 A6
Moorland Terr BD23 217 B4
Moorland View HG2 220 D4
Moor Lane Ind Est YO61 142 D6
Moor Lane Trad Est LS25 196 A3
Moor Lee La
Eggborough DN14 207 B8
Heck DN14 203 B1
MOOR MONKTON 165 A3
Moor Park Cl
2 Addingham LS29 174 E4
Pannal HG3 178 A8
Moor Park Cres 3 LS29 174 E4
Moor Park Dr LS29 174 E4
Moor Park Gr 2 LS29 174 F4
Moor Park Way 1 LS29 174 F4
Moor Pk TS7 7 D5
Moor Rd
Askrigg DL8 57 E6
Bishop Monkton HG3 139 F5
Filey YO14 101 B1
Hunmanby YO14 127 B7
Ilkley LS29 218 F1
Knayton with Brawith YO7 65 F3
Leyburn DL8 60 C5
Marton cum Grafton YO51 141 C2
Melsonby DL10 20 F6
Muston YO14 101 A2
9 Sherburn in Elmet LS25 195 F4
Stamford Bridge YO41 168 D2
Wykeham YO13 74 B4
Moors Ctr The* YO21 29 D7
MOORSHOLM 10 B5
Moorsholm La TS12 10 C6
Moorside
Melling-with-Wrayton LA6 102 A2
Scalby YO12 212 A8
Moor Side LS23 188 D8
Moorside Ave HG4 214 B2
Moorside Cl LA6 102 A2
Moorside Ct LS29 218 C3
Moorside Dale 6 HG4 214 B2
Moorside Junior & Infant Schs HG4 214 B3

Moorside La
Addingham LS29 ... 175 A2
Askwith LS21 ... 176 C4
Moorside Rd DL10 ... 209 E8
Moorside View HG4 ... 214 C2
Moors Shop Ctr The LS29 ... 218 A4
Moor View
Hebden BD23 ... 135 A2
2 Hinderwell TS13 ... 11 F7
Moorview Rd
Northallerton DL6 ... 210 F5
Skipton BD23 ... 217 B3
Moorview Way BD23 ... 217 B4
Moor Way YO32 ... 226 A4
Morcar Rd YO41 ... 168 D1
Morehall Cl YO30 ... 224 F2
Morgan Dr TS14 ... 8 E6
Morgan St 4 YO12 ... 212 F5
Morlais Ct 28 TS17 ... 5 F4
Morley Dr 10 YO13 ... 99 A7
Morley Gate DL11 ... 37 E5
Mornington Cres HG1 ... 219 E4
Mornington Rd LS29 ... 218 C4
Mornington Terr HG1 ... 219 E3
Morpeth Ave
Coulby Newham TS4 ... 7 A7
Darlington DL1 ... 3 E7
Morpeth Gate DL8 ... 58 F1
Morrell Ct
Woodthorpe YO24 ... 230 B8
York YO24 ... 230 B8
Morrell Garth YO8 ... 232 C2
Morrell Way YO10 ... 229 A2
Morrets La YO8 ... 197 A1
Morris Fields 22 WF6 ... 200 B1
Morrison Rd TS14 ... 8 F7
Morritt Cl 3 YO31 ... 228 F8
Morton Carr La TS7 ... 7 E6
Morton La YO8 ... 203 A8
MORTON-ON-SWALE ... 64 A6
Morton Rd DL1 ... 4 A5
Mosber La BD23 ... 172 C8
MOSS ... 207 D1
Moss Arc HG4 ... 214 C5
Mossburn Dr YO62 ... 119 E6
Mossdale Gr TS14 ... 8 D6
Moss End La BD22 ... 186 F5
Moss Green Cl YO8 ... 232 A2
Moss Green La
Brayton YO8 ... 232 A2
Hirst Courtney YO8 ... 203 F3
Moss Haven DN6 ... 207 D1
Moss Hill La YO26 ... 164 D5
Mossra La HG4 ... 85 F4
Moss Rd DN6 ... 207 B1
Moss Side BB18 ... 171 E1
Moss St YO23 ... 233 A1
Moss Way TS18 ... 5 F7
Mosswood Cres TS5 ... 6 D7
Mosswood La YO61 ... 118 A1
Mossy La DL8 ... 56 C4
Mostyn Ave 43 BB18 ... 172 A1
Mother Shipton's Cave & Petryfying Well* HG5 ... 221 A5
Moule Rise LS25 ... 194 E5
MOULTON ... 21 D3
Moulton Hall* DL10 ... 21 D2
Moulton La DL7 ... 22 C3
Mounstrall La DL7 ... 43 C1
Mount Ave YO8 ... 232 B3
Mount Bank DL6 ... 45 A5
Mount Cres YO17 ... 215 B5
Mount Dr DL8 ... 60 D5
Mount Ephraim 6 YO24 ... 228 A3
Mount Farm Cl YO22 ... 208 E3
Mount Gdns HG2 ... 222 E7
Mount Gr YO8 ... 232 B3
Mount Grace Priory* DL6 ... 45 B5
Mount Leven Rd TS15 ... 5 F3
Mount Par
5 Harrogate HG1 ... 219 D3
York YO24 ... 228 A3
Mount Park Ave YO12 ... 212 E5
Mount Park Rd 2 YO12 ... 212 E4
Mount Pk YO19 ... 198 A8
MOUNT PLEASANT ... 7 B5
Mount Pleasant
26 Addingham LS29 ... 174 F4
High Bentham LA2 ... 129 A8
Ilkley LS29 ... 218 C3
Kippax LS25 ... 200 D8
Little Smeaton WF8 ... 206 D3
Newby & Scalby YO13 ... 75 C5
Whitby YO22 ... 208 F3
Mount Pleasant Cl 9 DL2 ... 4 C4
Mount Pleasant E 2 YO22 ... 33 D4
Mount Pleasant Grange TS18 ... 6 A8
Mount Pleasant N 1 YO22 ... 33 D4
Mount Pleasant Prim Sch DL3 ... 3 A7
Mount Pleasant S 3 YO22 ... 33 D4
Mount Pleasant Way TS9 ... 26 D6
Mount Rd
Malton YO17 ... 215 B4
Northallerton DL6 ... 210 F6
Mount Sch The YO24 ... 228 A3
Mountside YO11 ... 212 F3
Mount Side Pk YO11 ... 212 E2
Mount St HG2 ... 222 E7
Mount Terr YO24 ... 228 A3
MOUNT THE ... 214 D3
Mount The
Barwick in Elmet & Scholes LS15 ... 194 B7
Castleford WF10 ... 201 B4
Malton YO17 ... 215 B4
Middlesbrough TS6 ... 7 E8
Selby YO8 ... 232 B3
8 Thornton Dale YO18 ... 96 D5
York YO24 ... 233 A1
Mount Vale YO24 ... 228 A2
Mount Vale Dr YO24 ... 228 A2
Mount View
Muston YO14 ... 101 A2
Northallerton DL6 ... 210 C6
Mount View Ave YO12 ... 212 E3
Mount View Cl 4 YO12 ... 212 E3
Mount View Rd 3 YO11 ... 100 B6
Mouseman Visitor Ctr* YO61 ... 91 B2
Mowbray Castle (site of)* HG4 ... 112 D5
Mowbray Cres
17 Bedale DL8 ... 63 A2
Hovingham YO62 ... 119 E6
Kirkby Malzeard HG4 ... 112 D5
Mowbray Dr
4 Hurworth-on-Tees DL2 ... 3 E1
York YO26 ... 227 C4
Mowbray Pl YO7 ... 211 B2
Mowbray Rd
5 Catterick DL10 ... 41 D5
Northallerton DL6 ... 210 E6
Mowbray Sch DL8 ... 63 A2
Mowbray Sq HG1 ... 219 E3
Mowbray Terr
Thirsk YO7 ... 211 B2
West Tanfield HG4 ... 87 A2
MOWDEN ... 3 A6
Mowden Infant Sch DL3 ... 3 A6
Mowthorpe La YO60 ... 145 F8
Mowthorpe Medieval Village* YO17 ... 149 C6
Mowthorp Rd YO12 ... 75 A3
MOXBY ... 144 D5
Moxby La YO61 ... 144 D5
Moxby Priory* YO61 ... 144 D5
Muddy La LS22 ... 180 A1
Muff La TS8 ... 7 A3
Muirfield TS7 ... 7 D5
Muirfield Ave WF7 ... 200 E1
Muirfield Rd TS16 ... 5 E5
Muirfield Way 6 YO26 ... 227 B5
MUKER ... 36 A5
Mulberry Ct
10 South Milford LS25 ... 195 F2
York YO32 ... 225 F6
Mulberry Dr 7 YO32 ... 166 E5
Mulberry Garth LS23 ... 188 F8
Mulgrave Castle* YO21 ... 12 E2
Mulgrave Cres YO21 ... 208 B8
Mulgrave Dr 6 DL7 ... 210 D2
Mulgrave Pl YO11 ... 213 B7
Mulgrave Rd YO21 ... 208 A8
Mulgrave View YO22 ... 32 F7
Mullberry Gdns LS26 ... 200 A5
Mulwith Cl YO31 ... 229 A6
Mulwith La HG4 ... 140 E6
Muncastergate YO31 ... 228 E7
Muncaster Way YO22 ... 208 E3
Murchison Pl 8 YO12 ... 212 F6
Murchison St YO12 ... 212 E6
Murrayfield Way 5 DL1 ... 3 F6
Murray St
31 Filey YO14 ... 101 B3
Scarborough YO12 ... 212 F5
York YO24 ... 227 F3
Murray Wlk DL3 ... 3 A5
Murrough Wilson Pl 3 YO31 ... 228 C7
MURTON ... 184 D7
Murton Bank YO62 ... 67 E3
Murton Garth YO19 ... 229 F6
Murton La YO19 ... 184 D7
Murton Way YO19 ... 229 E5
MUSCOATES ... 94 A3
Muscoates La YO62 ... 93 F3
Museum of North Craven Life* BD24 ... 131 E2
Museum of Victorian Science* YO22 ... 208 D7
Museum St YO1 ... 233 B2
Musham Bank Rd YO12 ... 99 F7
Music in Miniature* YO22 ... 33 D3
Musterfield La HG4 ... 113 B7
MUSTON ... 100 F2
Muston Rd
Filey YO14 ... 101 A3
Hunmanby YO14 ... 126 F8
Mutton Scalp Rd TS12 ... 9 E7
Myer's Green La HG3 ... 161 B5
Myers La DL7 ... 64 A8
My Love La HG3 ... 159 C5
Myra Bank La YO61 ... 117 F3
Myron Rd TS17 ... 5 F5
Myrtle Ave
Bishopthorpe YO23 ... 231 B3
Selby YO8 ... 232 B3
Myrtle Gdns DL1 ... 3 D8
Myrtle Rd
Eaglescliffe TS16 ... 5 E6
3 Harrogate HG1 ... 219 E3
Myrtle Sq 2 HG1 ... 219 E3
Myson Ave WF8 ... 201 C2
Myton La YO61 ... 142 C5
MYTON-ON-SWALE ... 141 F5
Myton Park Prim Sch TS17 ... 5 F4
Myton Rd TS17 ... 6 A4

N

Nabs View YO12 ... 212 A7
NABURN ... 191 D8
Naburn CE Prim Sch YO19 ... 191 D8
Naburn La
Deighton YO19 ... 192 A7
Fulford YO19 ... 231 D4
Naburn Park Mews YO19 191 E8
Nab View BD20 ... 174 C2
Nairn Cl YO24 ... 230 C6
Nairnhead Cl
1 Coulby Newham TS8 ... 6 E5
5 Stainton TS8 ... 6 E5
Nalton Cl YO23 ... 230 A1
Nalton St YO8 ... 232 C5
Nanny Goat La
Barwick in Elmet & Scholes LS25 ... 194 B4
Hunton DL8 ... 61 F8
Nanny La LS24 ... 196 C7
Nansen St YO12 ... 212 E6
Nap Cote La HG4 ... 112 E4
Napier Cres YO12 ... 99 D7
Napier Rd HG4 ... 113 D3
NAPPA ... 171 B8
Nares St YO12 ... 212 E6
Narrowfield 8 YO22 ... 32 A6
Narrow La
Cottingwith YO42 ... 193 D7
Skipwith YO8 ... 192 E3
National Ctr for Early Music* YO1 ... 233 C2
National Rly Mus* YO26 228 A4
Nat La LS17 ... 178 A3
Nattrass Wlk 7 DL8 ... 63 B2
Navigation Rd YO1 ... 233 C2
Navigation Sq BD23 ... 216 F4
Navigation Way HG4 ... 214 E4
Navigator Ct TS18 ... 6 D8
NAWTON ... 93 E7
Nawton Com Prim Sch YO62 ... 93 D7
Nawton Rd YO62 ... 93 E7
NEASHAM ... 4 A1
Neasham Ct TS9 ... 26 C8
Neasham Hill DL2 ... 4 B1
Neasham Rd
Darlington DL1 ... 3 D4
Low Dinsdale DL2 ... 4 B3
Needham Garth DL8 ... 58 E4
Neile Cl DL7 ... 210 B4
Nell Bank Ctr* LS29 ... 218 D6
Nelson Ct LS29 ... 218 C4
Nelson Rd LS29 ... 218 B4
Nelson's La YO24 ... 227 F1
Nelson St
7 Normanton South WF6 ... 200 B2
Scarborough YO12 ... 212 F6
Skipton BD23 ... 217 A3
York YO31 ... 233 C4
NESFIELD ... 175 B4
Nesfield Cl
17 Eastfield YO11 ... 100 B6
Harrogate HG1 ... 219 B5
Nesfield Rd LS29 ... 218 A5
Nesfield View 12 LS29 ... 175 C2
Nessgate YO1 ... 233 B2
Ness La
Pickhill with Roxby YO7 ... 88 B6
Tockwith YO26 ... 181 C8
Ness Rd 5 YO8 ... 232 D6
Nestfield Cl WF8 ... 201 B2
Nestfield Ind Est DL1 ... 3 D6
NETHER BURROW ... 102 B6
NETHERBY ... 179 B1
Netherby Cl 6 YO22 ... 32 A6
Netherby La
Huttons Ambo YO60 ... 147 B6
Sinnington YO62 ... 71 A1
Netherdale Ct LS22 ... 180 D4
Netheredge Cl HG5 ... 220 E8
Netheredge Dr HG5 ... 220 E8
Netherfield Cl WF10 ... 200 C3
Nethergill La BD20 ... 173 B1
NETHER POPPLETON ... 224 A2
Netherside Hall Sch BD23 ... 134 C4
NETHER SILTON ... 66 B7
Nether Way 20 YO26 ... 165 F1
Netherwindings 18 YO32 166 F5
Netherwoods 5 YO32 ... 167 B8
Nettledale Cl 1 TS13 ... 12 A7
Nettledale La YO13 ... 97 F6
Nevern Cres TS17 ... 5 F4
Neville Cl DL2 ... 1 D8
Neville Cres BD23 ... 155 D1
Neville Dr YO23 ... 231 A3
Neville Gr LS26 ... 194 A1
Neville Pits La DN14 ... 207 B4
Neville Rd
Darlington DL3 ... 3 B5
Gargrave BD23 ... 155 D1
Neville Row DL8 ... 87 D7
Neville St
Normanton South WF6 ... 200 A1
Skipton BD23 ... 217 A4
York YO31 ... 233 C4
Neville Terr YO31 ... 233 C4
Neville Wlk
31 Kirkbymoorside YO62 ... 70 B1
Richmond DL10 ... 209 D7
Nevinson Gr YO10 ... 231 E8
Nevison Ave WF8 ... 201 C2
Nevis Way YO24 ... 230 B7
NEWALL ... 176 F1
Newall Ave LS21 ... 176 F1
Newall Carr Rd LS21 ... 176 F3
Newall Cl 14 LS21 ... 176 F1
Newall Hall Pk 10 LS21 ... 177 A1
NEWBIGGIN
Askrigg ... 57 F6
Filey ... 101 A5
Thoralby ... 82 D8
Newbiggin
Malton YO17 ... 215 B5
Richmond DL10 ... 209 B6
Newbiggin Cl TS16 ... 5 C5
Newborough YO11 ... 213 A6
Newborough St YO30 ... 233 A4
NEWBRIDGE ... 96 A8
Newbridge La BD23 ... 174 B8
New Brook St LS29 ... 218 B5
Newburgh Priory* YO61 117 E7
Newbury Ave YO24 ... 227 D1
NEWBY
Ingleton ... 104 A1
Middlesbrough ... 7 A3
Ripon ... 140 D6
Scarborough ... 75 E5
Newby Cl HG4 ... 214 D4
NEWBY COTE ... 104 B1
Newby Cres HG3 ... 219 A4
Newby Dr
23 Cross Hills BD20 ... 187 E8
Dishforth YO7 ... 115 A2
Newby Farm Cl 35 YO12 ... 75 D5
Newby Farm Cres 36 YO12 ... 75 D5
Newby Farm Rd YO12 ... 75 D5
Newby Hall & Gdns* HG4 ... 140 C6
Newby La DN14 ... 207 F8
Newby Pk* HG4 ... 140 D6
Newby Prim Sch YO12 ... 212 B8
Newby St HG4 ... 214 D4
Newby Terr YO31 ... 228 C7
NEWBY WISKE ... 64 E2
Newcastle Farm Ct 4 WF11 ... 201 D6
Newchase Ct YO11 ... 99 F6
New Church Terr 12 YO8 ... 232 C5
New Cl La LA2 ... 130 C7
New Coll WF8 ... 201 A1
Newcoln Rd YO12 ... 212 E1
Newcroft YO8 ... 232 B4
Newdale 3 YO32 ... 166 F5
New Dales La BD20 ... 173 D4
NEW EARSWICK ... 225 D3
New Earswick Prim Sch YO32 ... 225 D4
New Earswick Sports Club YO32 ... 225 D3
Newfield Ave 6 WF6 ... 200 B1
Newfield Cl 7 WF6 ... 200 B1
Newfield Cres
Middlesbrough TS17 ... 6 D7
Normanton South WF6 ... 200 B1
Newfield Ct 3 WF6 ... 200 B1
Newfield La LS25 ... 201 B8
New Forge Ct 15 YO32 ... 166 F5
NEW FRYSTON ... 201 B6
Newgate
2 Malton YO17 ... 215 C4
York YO1 ... 233 B2
Newgate Bank YO62 ... 68 A4
Newgate Cl 36 TS17 ... 5 F4
Newgate Ct YO1 ... 233 B2
New Hall Rd WF8 ... 201 C2
Newham Bridge Prim Sch TS5 ... 6 F8
Newham Way TS8 ... 7 B5
Newhay La YO8 ... 198 E1
Newhold LS25 ... 194 D4
New Hold Ind Est LS25 ... 194 D4
NEWHOLM ... 13 A1
New House Farm Malham National Nature Reserve* BD23 ... 133 D3
New House La BD23 ... 153 F5
NEW HOUSES ... 105 C4
New Ings La YO18 ... 96 E4
Newington Rd TS4 ... 7 A8
New Inn La
Carthorpe DL8 ... 87 F6
10 Easingwold YO61 ... 143 C8
Newkin DL8 ... 57 D5
New La
Aislaby YO18 ... 95 D8
Beal DN14 ... 202 D3
Bishopthorpe YO23 ... 231 A4
Burton Salmon WF11 ... 201 E6
Green Hammerton YO26 ... 164 C3
Hawes DL8 ... 56 E4
Holgate YO24 ... 227 E3
Huntington YO32 ... 225 F1
Kildwick BD20 ... 173 F1
Lillings Ambo YO60 ... 145 C3
Little Ouseburn YO26 ... 164 A8
Long Marston YO23 ... 182 B3
Neasham DL2 ... 4 A1
Newland YO8 ... 205 A3
Ravensworth DL11 ... 20 A7
Selby YO8 ... 232 C5
Sherburn in Elmet LS25 ... 195 F3
Sheriff Hutton YO60 ... 145 D5
Stainburn LS21 ... 177 E4
Strensall YO32 ... 167 B8
West Tanfield DL8 ... 87 C2
New Laithe Cl 5 BD23 ... 217 B5
Newlaithes Cres WF6 ... 200 B1
NEWLAND ... 205 B3
Newland Ave 1 HG2 ... 220 A1
Newland Park Cl YO10 ... 229 A3
Newland Park Dr YO10 ... 228 F3
Newlands DL6 ... 210 F4
Newlands Ave
Scarborough YO12 ... 212 E8
3 Whitby YO21 ... 208 C7
Newlands Ct YO7 ... 211 D3
Newlands Dr
2 Glusburn BD20 ... 187 F8
Ripon HG4 ... 214 B3
York YO26 ... 227 B6
Newlands La
Burniston YO13 ... 54 D1
Upper Poppleton YO26 ... 182 E8
Wintringham YO17 ... 123 F3
Newlands Park Ave YO12 ... 212 D8
Newlands Park Cres YO12 ... 212 D8
Newlands Park Dr YO12 . 212 D8
Newlands Park Gr 2 YO12 ... 212 D8
Newlands Park Rd YO12 212 D8
Newlands Rd
Bishopthorpe YO23 ... 230 F4
Boosbeck TS12 ... 9 D8
Darlington DL3 ... 3 B6
Newlands Sch The TS4 ... 6 F7
New Lennerton La LS25 . 196 C3
Newlyn Dr DL3 ... 3 C8
Newmarket St BD23 ... 217 A4
NEW MICKLEFIELD ... 195 A3
New Millgate YO8 ... 232 C6
New Mill La LS23 ... 188 F7
Newnham St HG2 ... 220 A3
Newnham Terr HG2 ... 220 A3
NEW PARK ... 219 B5
New Park Prim Sch HG1 219 C5
New Park Rd 4 YO12 ... 212 E4
New Park Row HG1 ... 219 C5
New Parks Cres 8 YO12 . 212 E4
Newport Ave YO8 ... 232 B4
Newport Cl 42 TS17 ... 5 F4
Newport St 5 WF8 ... 201 B1
New Potter Grange Rd DN14 ... 205 E2
New Quay Rd YO21 ... 208 D6
New Queen St 10 YO12 . 213 A7
New Rd
Allerston YO13 ... 73 D6
Allerton Mauleverer with Hopperton HG5 ... 163 E4
Appleton Roebuck YO23 ... 190 E5
Appletreewick BD23 ... 157 E8
Beningborough YO30 ... 165 C6
Birstwith HG3 ... 160 D6
Bramham LS23 ... 188 E6
Earby BB18 ... 172 A1
Fylingdales YO22 ... 33 D4
Glaisdale YO21 ... 29 F3
Guisborough TS14 ... 8 F6
Heck DN14 ... 203 D1
Hessay YO26 ... 182 C8
Hunmanby YO14 ... 126 F7
Kirby Grindalythe YO17 ... 149 B6
Kirby Hall YO26 ... 164 B8
Kirkbymoorside YO62 ... 70 B1
Knottingley WF11 ... 201 D3
Ledsham LS25 ... 201 B8
Lillings Ambo YO60 ... 145 D3
Long Drax YO8 ... 204 E6
Newsham DL11 ... 18 J8
North Stainley with Sleningford HG4 ... 113 B8
Norton DN6 ... 206 F2
Raskelf YO7 ... 116 E3
Reighton YO14 ... 127 E5
Richmond DL10 ... 209 C6
Rosedale East Side YO18 ... 49 E3
Scotton HG5 ... 162 A5
24 Settle BD24 ... 131 D2
Settrington YO17 ... 122 D1
Spaunton YO62 ... 70 E5
Stapleton WF8 ... 206 B5
Terrington YO60 ... 119 E2
Thornton in Lonsdale LA6 ... 103 B4
Ulleskelf LS24 ... 190 B3
Westerdale YO21 ... 28 F6
Wheldrake YO19 ... 192 C7
Whixley YO26 ... 164 A4
Newroad End WF8 ... 206 A6
NEW ROAD SIDE ... 187 B5
NEW ROW ... 8 F1
New Row
15 Boroughbridge YO51 ... 141 B5
Eppleby DL11 ... 1 D4
Trawden Forest BB8 ... 186 B2
Newsam Rd TS16 ... 5 D5
NEWSHAM
Barnard Castle ... 19 D8
Thirsk ... 89 A8
Newsham Hill DL11 ... 18 J8
Newsham La
Barugh (Great & Little) YO17 ... 95 A1
Habton YO17 ... 121 A8
Newsham Rd YO7 ... 211 A3
Newsham Way DL7 ... 210 B1
NEWSHOLME
205 E8
Barnoldswick ... 171 A6
New St
Carleton BD23 ... 173 B4
Kippax LS25 ... 194 D1

New St *continued*
Langcliffe BD24 131 E4
Tadcaster LS24 189 E6
York YO1 233 B2
Newstead La HG4 85 C7
Newsteads 12 DL8 63 B3
New Sturton La LS25 194 D4
NEW THIRSK 211 A3
NEWTHORPE 195 D3
Newthorpe Rd 2 DN6 206 E2
Newton Cres 4 DL7 63 D4
Newtondale Cl HG5 221 D6
Newtondale Forest Dr YO18 72 B6
Newtondale Halt YO18 51 D1
Newton Dr TS17 6 B6
Newton Gdns HG4 214 C4
Newton House Ct YO61 144 B3
NEWTON KYME 189 B7
Newton La
Archdeacon Newton DL2 2 F8
Ledsham WF10 201 A6
Newton Mulgrave TS13 11 F6
NEWTON-LE-WILLOWS 62 B4
NEWTON MORRELL 21 E8
NEWTON MULGRAVE 11 E6
NEWTON-ON-OUSE 165 B6
NEWTON-ON-RAWCLIFFE 72 A5
Newton Pk YO30 165 B7
Newton Rd
Great Ayton TS9 8 A2
Tollerton YO61 143 B3
Newton St YO21 208 D6
Newton Terr YO1 233 B1
NEWTON UNDER ROSEBERRY 8 B4
NEWTON UPON DERWENT 185 E4
Newton Way 15 BD23 154 B3
NEW TOWN 201 B2
New Walk Terr YO10 228 D2
New Way YO21 29 C4
NEW YORK 137 F1
New York Ind Est HG3 137 F1
Nicholas Gdns YO10 228 F3
Nicholas St YO10 228 F3
Nicholson Ave HG4 113 D3
Nichols Way LS22 180 A3
Nickey Nackey La YO8 197 B8
Nicklaus Dr TS16 5 E5
Nickstream La DL3 3 A7
Nicolsons Pl 8 BD20 174 C1
NIDD 161 E6
Nidd Bank HG5 220 F7
Nidd Cl YO26 227 B8
Nidd Dr HG3 160 E6
Nidderdale Dr HG5 221 D5
Nidderdale High Sch & Com Coll HG3 137 B4
Nidderdale Lodge HG5 221 E5
Nidderdale Lodge Pk HG5 221 E5
Nidderdale Mus* HG3 137 B4
Nidderdale Pool & L Ctr HG3 137 A5
Nidd Gr YO24 230 E8
Nidd La
Birstwith HG3 160 E7
Darley HG3 160 B6
Ripley HG3 161 D7
Nidd Orch 4 HG3 160 A6
Nidd Rise HG3 160 E6
Niddside HG3 160 A6
Nidd Valley Ind Est HG5 162 B6
Nidd Viaduct* HG3 219 E8
Nidd Wlk 1 HG3 137 B4
Niffany Gdns 7 BD23 216 D3
Nigel Gr 7 YO24 227 F2
Nightingale Cl YO32 225 E1
Nightingale Dr HG1 220 B3
Nightingale La 9 YO12 99 F6
Nile Rd LS29 218 B4
Ninelands La LS25 194 D3
Ninelands Prim Sch LS25 194 D3
Ninelands Spur LS25 194 C3
Ninevah La WF10 200 C7
Ninth Ave YO31 228 F5
Niso Terr YO11 213 A6
Noble Ct HG5 221 C7
Noel's Ct DL10 41 E5
Nolton Ct 35 TS17 5 F4
No Man's Moor La DL8 61 E3
Nook Croft 12 BB18 172 B1
Nookfield Cl YO22 33 C4
Nooking The YO61 117 B6
Nook Rd LS15 188 A1
Nook The
Selby YO8 232 D6
South Milford LS25 195 F2
Nora Ave HG5 221 C6
NORBY 211 A4
Norby YO7 211 B3
Norby Est YO7 211 B4
Norby Front St YO7 211 B4
Nordale Cl LS29 218 C5
Norfolk Cl WF11 201 E4
Norfolk Cres TS3 7 C8
Norfolk Gdns YO26 181 C7
Norfolk Rd HG2 222 D7
Norfolk St YO23 228 C2
NORMANBY 94 F4
Normanby Prim Sch TS6 7 F8
Normanby Rd
Middlesbrough TS7 7 D8
Northallerton DL7 210 D2
Normanby Terr 18 YO21 208 D7
Norman Cl
22 Pickering YO18 95 F7
7 Thorpe Willoughby YO8 197 B1
Norman Cres 11 YO14 101 B3
Norman Dr YO26 227 B6
Normandy Cl 4 YO8 232 B6
Norman Rd
Aske DL10 20 D1
Catterick Garrison DL9 209 E1
Richmond DL10 209 C8
Norman Sq DL10 209 D8
Norman St 5 YO10 229 A3
NORMANTON 200 C1
Normanton Com Prim Sch WF6 200 B2
Normanton Ind Est WF6 200 B1
Normanton Junior Sch WF6 200 A1
Normanton Sta WF6 200 A2
Norseman Cl 7 YO19 197 F8
Norseway 2 YO41 168 D1
NORTHALLERTON 210 C5
Northallerton Bsns Pk DL6 210 C7
Northallerton Coll DL6 210 E4
Northallerton Rd
Brompton DL6 210 E7
Dalton-on-Tees DL2 22 E6
Leeming DL7 63 C4
Thirsk YO7 211 A6
5 Thornaby TS17 6 B7
Northallerton Rigg DL6 43 D4
Northallerton Sta DL7 210 C3
North App LS24 189 A2
North Ave
Castleford WF10 200 C4
12 Glusburn BD20 187 E6
North Back La
Stillington YO61 144 C6
Terrington YO60 119 E1
North Baileygate WF8 201 B1
North Bay Prom YO12 212 F8
North Bay Rly* YO12 212 E8
North Bglws HG4 214 D6
North Burton La YO14 127 B4
Northcarrs La YO61 144 A4
North Cliff Ave YO12 75 F5
North Cliff Ctry Pk* YO14 101 C4
Northcliffe Gr 3 TS15 25 C5
Northcote Ave YO24 227 E3
Northcote Fold 3 LS22 180 A1
North Cotes Rd
Hunmanby YO25 126 C5
Wold Newton YO25 125 E5
NORTH COWTON 22 C3
North Cres LS25 195 F5
Northcroft 5 YO32 166 F5
Northcroft Gr 11 LS29 218 A4
North Croft Grove Rd 1 LS29 218 A4
NORTH DEIGHTON 180 B6
North Dr
Kippax LS25 194 D2
Sherburn in Elmet LS25 195 F5
NORTH DUFFIELD 199 A8
North Duffield Prim Sch YO8 199 A8
North Eastern Terr YO24 230 E8
North End
Bedale DL8 63 A3
2 Hutton Rudby TS15 25 C5
Osmotherley DL6 45 B4
Northern Ryedale L Ctr YO18 95 F7
NORTH FEATHERSTONE 200 E1
Northfield 3 YO8 198 B5
North Field Ave YO23 190 F5
Northfield Cl
Stokesley TS9 26 C7
Womersley DN6 206 C6
North Field Cl YO23 190 F5
Northfield Ct LS24 196 B8
Northfield Dr
Pontefract WF8 201 C1
Stokesley TS9 26 C8
Northfield La
Church Fenton LS24 196 B8
Pockley YO62 69 B2
3 Riccall YO19 191 F1
South Milford LS25 195 E2
Womersley DN6 206 C7
North Field La
Askham Bryan YO23 182 F3
Upper Poppleton YO26 182 F7
Northfield Mews 15 LS22 180 C2
Northfield Pl LS22 180 C3
Northfield Rd YO8 199 E8
Northfields
Bickerton LS22 181 B5
4 Hutton Rudby TS15 25 C5
4 Strensall YO32 167 B8
Northfields Ave 4 BD24 131 D3
Northfields Cres 5 BD24 131 D3
Northfields La YO61 142 C6
Northfield Terr YO24 230 E8
Northfield Way YO13 75 D6
North Field Way YO23 190 F5
North Garth La YO60 145 D5
Northgate
Darlington DL1 3 D5
Northgate *continued*
Guisborough TS14 8 F7
Hunmanby YO14 126 F8
Muston YO14 100 F1
Pontefract WF8 201 B1
Northgate Cl 15 WF8 201 B1
Northgate La
1 Linton LS22 180 A1
Warthill YO41 168 A3
Northgate Lodge 11 WF8 201 B1
Northgate Rise 2 LS22 180 A1
North Gr 2 LS22 180 C3
North Grange Ct YO30 233 A4
NORTH GRIMSTON 148 E6
North Grove Ave 6 LS22 180 C4
North Hill Rd YO7 115 B2
NORTH INGS 119 D1
NORTH KILVINGTON 89 E8
North La
Dringhouses YO24 230 E8
Eastfield YO11 100 B6
Gainford DL2 1 D8
Great Timble LS21 176 E8
Huntington YO32 225 F5
Hutton Hang DL8 61 C4
Wheldrake YO19 192 F7
Northlands Ave 1 YO32 225 F7
Northleach Dr TS8 6 F5
North Leas Ave YO12 212 D8
NORTH LEES 113 E4
North Lodge Ave 2 HG1 219 C5
North Marine Rd YO12 212 F7
Northminster Bsns Pk YO26 182 F7
North Moor 7 YO32 225 F5
Northmoor Cl 8 YO32 225 F5
North Moor Gdns YO32 225 F5
North Moor La YO61 118 C5
North Moor Rd
Easingwold YO61 117 B2
York YO32 225 F5
Northolme Dr YO30 224 E1
NORTH OTTERINGTON 64 D4
North Parade
10 Burley in Warfedale LS29 176 C1
Ilkley LS29 218 C4
Skipton BD23 217 A2
York YO30 233 A3
North Park Dr HG1 219 E2
North Park Rd HG1 219 E2
North Prom YO21 208 C7
North Rd
Darlington DL1 3 D7
Glusburn BD20 187 E7
Grosmont YO22 31 C4
Hackforth DL8 62 E8
3 Middleham DL8 60 E2
Norton YO17 215 E3
Ripon HG4 214 D6
Stokesley TS9 26 C7
Whitby YO21 208 D6
North Riding Rise DL7 65 B3
NORTH RIGTON 178 B5
North Road Ind Est DL3 3 C7
North Road Prim Sch DL1 3 D7
North Road Sta DL1 3 D6
North Side TS15 25 C5
Northside Ind Pk DN14 202 F1
North & South Cowton Prim Sch DL7 22 C3
North St
Addingham LS29 175 A4
Barmby on the Marsh DN14 205 A7
Barnoldswick BB18 171 D1
Castleford WF10 201 B6
Folkton YO11 100 A2
Gargrave BD23 155 D1
31 Glusburn BD20 187 E7
Newby & Scalby YO13 75 C6
Ripon HG4 214 C6
Scarborough YO11 213 A6
Silsden BD20 174 C1
Wetherby LS22 180 C3
York YO1 233 B2
NORTH STAINLEY 113 D7
North Stainley CE Prim Sch HG4 113 C8
Northstead Flats YO12 212 D7
Northstead Manor Dr YO12 212 E7
Northstead Prim Sch YO12 212 D8
North Street La 22 YO11 213 A6
North Sweeming Ct LS25 196 D5
North Terr
Gainford DL2 1 D7
4 Scarborough YO11 213 A6
Whitby YO21 208 C7
Northumberland Ct 17 HG1 219 D2
Northumberland Rd TS17 6 B8
North View
Knottingley WF11 201 F2
Little Ribston LS22 180 A8
Northway
Pickering YO18 95 E7
11 Scarborough YO12 212 F6
6 Whitby YO21 208 B7
Northwell Gate LS21 176 F1
Northwold Rd YO11 100 A7
North Yorkshire Moors Rly* YO18 95 F7
NORTON 206 E2
Norton Back La DL2 4 D8
Norton Cl HG4 114 A8
Norton Coll YO17 215 E2
Norton Comm La DN6 206 F2
Norton Comm Rd DN6 207 A1
Norton Com Prim Sch YO17 215 E3
Norton Conyers* HG4 113 F7
Norton Cres DL2 4 C8
Norton Grove Ind Est YO17 215 F4
Norton Junior & Infant Schs DN6 206 E2
Norton & Kirk Smeat WF8 206 C3
NORTON-LE-CLAY 115 C2
Norton Mill La DN6 206 E2
NORTON-ON-DERWENT 215 D3
Norton Priory DN6 206 E2
Norton Rd
Norton YO17 215 C3
Sadberge DL2 4 C7
Norton Twr* BD23 156 B4
Norway Dr YO10 231 D8
Norwich Cl YO13 75 D6
Norwich Dr HG3 219 A5
Norwood Ave LS29 176 C1
Norwood Bottom Rd LS21 177 A5
Norwood Cl
36 Burley in Warfedale LS29 176 C1
2 Knaresborough HG5 221 B8
Norwood Ct 1 HG5 221 B7
Norwood Gr HG3 219 B4
Norwood La
Glusburn BD20 187 B8
Pannal HG3 177 E7
Norwood Mews 18 YO12 212 F5
Norwood Pl 8 YO12 212 F5
Norwood St
Normanton WF6 200 B2
Scarborough YO12 212 F5
Nossill La DL8 59 C3
NOSTERFIELD 87 B3
Nosterfield Nature Reserve* HG4 87 B2
Nosterfield Rd HG4 87 B2
Notagreen Rd DL11 39 F6
Nought Bank Rd HG3 137 B3
Nought Moor Rd HG3 137 B2
Nova Scotia Way 4 YO19 198 A8
NUN APPLETON 190 F3
Nuneaton Dr TS8 6 E5
Nunmill St YO23 228 C2
NUN MONKTON 165 A4
Nun Monkton Prim Sch YO26 165 A5
Nunnery La
Darlington DL3 3 A5
York YO23 233 B1
Nunnery Way LS23 188 E7
NUNNINGTON 93 E2
Nunnington Cl TS17 6 B5
Nunnington Cres HG3 219 A5
Nunnington Hall* YO62 93 F2
Nunnington Studios* YO62 93 E2
Nun's Cl DL10 209 B7
Nuns Green La YO21 29 E3
NUNTHORPE
231 C8
Middlesbrough 7 D5
Nunthorpe Ave YO23 228 B2
Nunthorpe Cres YO23 228 B1
Nunthorpe Gdns TS7 7 D5
Nunthorpe Gr YO23 228 B2
Nunthorpe Prim Sch TS7 7 E6
Nunthorpe Rd YO23 233 A1
Nunthorpe Sch TS7 7 E6
Nunthorpe Sta TS7 7 E6
NUNWICK 114 A5
Nurseries The
Asselby DN14 205 D7
3 Easingwold YO61 143 C8
East Ayton YO13 99 C8
10 Leyburn DL8 60 D5
3 Whitby YO21 208 B6
Nursery Cl 19 YO8 198 F1
Nursery Ct
Low Catton YO41 185 C8
Nether Poppleton YO26 224 A2
Nursery Dr YO24 227 E3
Nursery Gdns
Thirsk YO7 211 C3
York YO10 229 C3
Nursery La
4 Addingham LS29 175 A4
Merrybent DL2 2 E5
Nursery Rd YO26 224 A2
Nursery Way 8 LS23 188 E7
Nusery Gdn DL10 41 B4
Nutgill La
Bentham LA2 129 D8
Ingleton LA6 103 D1
Nutwith La HG4 112 B8
Nydd Vale Rd HG1 219 D3
Nydd Vale Terr 10 HG1 219 D3

O

Oak Ave
Appleton Roebuck YO23 190 E3
Garforth LS25 194 C4
Killinghall HG3 161 B2
Oakbank HG1 219 C4
Oak Beck Rd HG1 219 B5
Oak Beck Way HG1 219 B6
Oakburn Rd LS29 218 A3
Oak Busk La YO60 145 F1
Oakbusks La YO61 142 F4
Oak Cl
Filey YO14 101 B4
9 Kirkbymoorside YO62 70 B1
Oak Cres LS25 194 C4
OAKDALE 161 B2
Oakdale HG1 219 A3
Oakdale Ave HG1 219 B4
Oakdale Glen HG1 219 B3
Oakdale Manor HG1 161 B2
Oakdale Pl HG1 219 B4
Oakdale Rd YO30 224 F2
Oakdale Rise HG1 219 C4
Oak Dr
8 Acaster Malbis YO32 191 C7
Garforth LS25 194 C4
5 Thorpe Willoughby YO8 197 B1
3 Topcliffe YO7 89 A1
Oakenshaw Dr TS5 6 E7
Oaker Bank HG3 161 B2
Oak Farm YO8 197 D6
Oak Field YO8 232 A1
Oak Field Ave YO22 51 D8
Oakfield La 21 YO8 198 F1
Oakfields DL10 21 D4
Oak Glade 6 YO31 225 F3
Oak Gr
Harrowgate Village DL1 3 D8
Northallerton DL6 210 E6
Oak Hill TS8 7 B5
Oakhill Cres 3 YO32 167 A6
Oak La HG3 159 F8
Oakland Ave YO31 229 A7
Oakland Dr YO31 229 A7
Oakland Hills 23 WF6 200 B1
Oaklands
Camblesforth YO8 204 C5
9 Great Ayton TS9 8 A2
5 Ilkley LS29 218 A3
5 Pickering YO18 96 A6
6 Strensall YO32 167 B7
Oaklands Cres YO8 204 C5
Oaklands Rd TS6 7 F8
Oaklands Sports Ctr YO24 227 C2
Oaklands The DL2 4 D3
Oaklands Way YO61 143 D8
Oakley Bank YO22 208 B2
Oakley Cl TS14 8 F5
Oakley Rd TS12 9 E7
Oakmont Cl 21 WF6 200 B1
Oakmoor Cl 7 DL1 3 E4
Oakney Wood Dr YO8 232 D1
Oak Rd
Eaglescliffe TS16 5 E6
Garforth LS25 194 C4
Guisborough TS14 8 F7
2 North Duffield YO8 199 A7
Ripon HG4 214 B2
Scarborough YO12 212 D4
Tockwith LS22 180 E7
Whitby YO21 208 B6
Oak Ridge 6 LS22 180 B3
Oakridge Prim Sch TS13 11 F7
Oakridge View 3 HG3 161 B3
Oak Rise 4 YO24 227 C3
Oaksfield LS26 200 B5
Oaks La LS23 188 E8
Oak St 3 YO26 227 E5
Oaks The
Coulby Newham TS8 6 E5
Dalton YO7 115 F7
Hellifield BD23 154 A3
7 Masham HG4 86 C3
Oak Tree DL2 4 E4
Oak Terr HG2 219 C2
OAK TREE 4 E4
Oaktree Ave DL9 40 E2
Oaktree Bank YO7 65 F3
Oak Tree Cl
2 Bedale DL8 63 A2
Strensall YO32 167 B7
Tees-side Airport DL2 4 E4
Oak Tree Ct
Bubwith YO8 199 D7
4 Wigginton YO32 225 D7
Oaktree Dr DL7 210 C1
Oak Tree Dr DL8 62 F2
Oaktree Gr 5 TS18 5 D8
Oak Tree Gr YO32 225 D3
Oaktree Hill DL6 43 D6
Oaktree Junc DL2 4 D4
Oak Tree La YO32 225 C7
Oak Tree Rd 7 DL8 63 A2
Oak Tree Way 10 YO32 167 B7
Oakville Ave YO12 212 E6
Oakville St YO31 228 D7
Oak Way YO8 232 D2
Oakwood Cl
Church Fenton LS24 196 B7
Ferrybridge WF11 201 C4
Oakwood Pk DN14 207 F6
Oakwood Rd LS22 180 B4
OATLANDS 222 F6
Oatlands Dr
Harrogate HG2 222 F8
11 Otley LS21 177 A1
Oatlands Gr 3 TS13 11 A8
Oatlands Infant Sch HG2 222 E7
Oatlands Junior Sch HG2 222 F7
Occaney La HG3 162 D8
Occupation La LS24 188 E2

Occupation Rd TS6 7 F8
Ocean Rd YO21 208 C7
Ocean Terr YO14 100 F6
Ochrepit Hill YO42 170 A2
OCTON 151 F8
Oddie's La LA6 103 D5
Offerton Dr TS8 6 F5
Ogleforth YO1 233 B3
Okehampton Dr TS7 7 B6
Olav Rd DL10 209 C7
Old Barber HG1 219 D6
Old Boys Sch La 4 YO8 197 B8
Old Brewery Gdns 5 LS24 189 F6
Old Bridge Rise 7 LS29 218 A4
OLD BYLAND 91 F8
Old Chapel Cl 7 HG3 161 B2
Old Church Gn YO26 164 C2
Old Church La 9 HG3 137 C4
Old Coach Rd HG3 137 F2
Old Coastguard Sta★ YO22 33 D3
Old Coppice 14 YO32 166 F5
Old Corn Mill The BD20 187 D7
Old Court Cl
Malton YO17 215 D4
Norton-on-Derwent YO17 215 E3
Old Courthouse Rural Arts The★ YO7 211 B2
Old Cricket Field La YO7 116 B6
Old Dike Lands YO32 225 C8
Olde Mkt The TS16 5 D3
Old Farm Cl 5 YO18 95 F7
Old Farm Way YO8 232 B2
Old Farmyard★ HG3 161 C7
Old Favourites Wlk 8 DL2 3 A7
Oldfield Cl LS25 195 A4
Oldfield La
Collingham LS22 180 C1
Spaunton YO62 70 E4
Sutton BD22 187 F1
Old Garth Croft 3 WF11 201 D6
Oldgate La LS24 195 E6
Old Gayle La DL8 56 D4
Old Great North Rd WF11 201 E4
Old Hall Cl BD20 187 D7
Old Hall Croft BD23 155 D1
Old Hall Ct LS25 201 F6
Old Hall La
Gilling with Hartforth & Sedbury DL10 20 D3
Kexby YO41 185 C5
Old Hall Rd BD20 187 D7
Old Hall Way BD20 187 D7
Oldham Cl TS12 9 E8
Oldham St TS12 9 D7
Old Highway The 9 YO32 167 B6
Old Hospital Compound 25 DL9 40 E3
Old House Gdns YO8 203 A5
Old La
Addingham LS29 175 B3
Broughton BD23 172 D5
Cowling BD22 187 B5
Earby BB18 172 A2
Hambleton YO8 196 E1
Hirst Courtney YO8 203 F3
Horton in Ribblesdale BD24 105 A7
Ilkley LS29 218 D3
Kelbrook & Sough BB18 186 A6
Long Marston YO26 182 A6
Old Lane Ct LS24 190 E7
Old London Rd LS24 189 D3
OLD MALTON 215 E7
Old Maltongate YO17 215 C4
Old Malton Rd
Malton YO17 215 D5
7 Willerby YO12 99 D2
Oldman Ct
Woodthorpe YO24 230 C8
York YO24 230 C8
Old Market Pl 6 HG4 214 C5
OLD MICKLEFIELD 194 F4
Old Mill Cl 3 LS29 176 C1
Old Mill La LS23 188 F7
Old Mill Row 3 YO7 211 C3
Old Mill View YO60 145 C5
Old Mill Wynd TS9 8 A1
Old Moor La YO24 230 E7
Old Moor Rd LA2 128 B8
Old Oliver La BD24 152 F6
Old Orchard YO32 225 D8
Old Orchard The
Fulford YO10 231 E7
Shipton YO30 165 F5
Old Orch The
1 Easingwold YO61 143 C8
14 Hutton Rudby TS15 25 C5
Old Park La YO21 31 D6
Old Park Mews HG4 214 B5
Old Penny Gate HG5 221 C7
Old Quarry La LS25 195 E1
Old Raike BD23 152 F4
Old Rd
Appleton Roebuck YO23 190 E5
Clapham LA2 130 C8
Garsdale LA10 55 A6
Kirkbymoorside YO62 70 B1
Kirkby Overblow LS17 178 E1
Thornton in Craven BD23 172 A3
Old St The LS24 190 C8
Old Sawmill The
Lane Ends BD22 187 C6
Rathmell BD24 153 B7
Old School Cl
Osbaldwick YO10 229 B4
Settle BD24 131 E2
West Witton DL8 59 D3
Old School La YO8 198 B5
Old Station Rd 4 YO62 92 C1
Old Station Way 20 LS29 174 F4
OLDSTEAD 91 C3
Oldstead Rd YO61 91 B3
Old Stone Trough La BB18 186 A6
Old Stubble The 6 TS13 13 K2
Old Sutton Rd YO7 211 E3
OLD THIRSK 211 C4
Old Trough Way HG1 219 C6
Old Vicarage La 5 LS25 202 A8
Old Village The YO32 225 F5
Old Wife's Way YO18 73 A8
Olicana Pk LS29 218 B5
Olive Gr HG1 220 B4
Oliver La YO17 121 C8
Oliver's Cl 18 YO14 126 F8
Oliver's Mount Rd YO11 212 F2
Oliver St 4 YO11 213 A4
Olive Way HG1 220 B4
Olive Wlk HG1 220 B4
Olliver La DL10 20 F1
Olliver Rd DL10 209 E8
Olympia Cres YO8 232 E6
Olympian Ct YO10 228 F4
Olympian Trad Est YO11 100 A6
Olympic Way DL10 209 B8
Omega St 7 HG1 219 C5
Onams La YO62 69 F4
One Acre Garth 2 YO8 196 E1
Onhams La YO60 146 E4
OPSA Bsns Ctr YO1 233 B2
Opus Ave YO26 224 C1
Oran La DL10 41 E4
Orcaber La LA2 130 E6
Orchard Cl
Appleton Roebuck YO23 190 F5
Barkston Ash LS24 195 E7
Dalton-on-Tees DL2 22 D7
15 Easingwold YO61 117 D1
Eggborough DN14 202 F2
1 Great Ayton TS9 8 A2
6 Hartwith cum Winsley HG3 137 F1
1 Knaresborough HG5 221 B8
6 Monk Fryston LS25 202 A8
9 Norton DN6 206 E2
Selby YO8 232 A4
Sharow HG4 214 F6
6 South Milford LS25 195 F2
Wilberfoss YO41 185 E6
York YO24 227 E1
Orchard Cotts 4 YO19 184 F7
Orchard Ct
Bramham cum Oglethorpe LS23 188 F5
8 Knaresborough HG5 221 B5
Orchard Dr
Fairburn WF11 201 D7
Hambleton YO8 196 F2
Linton LS22 180 A2
Orchard End 20 YO8 198 F1
Orchard Garth YO23 230 B2
Orchard Gdns
Malton YO17 215 B4
York YO31 225 E2
Orchard Gr
4 Brompton DL6 43 F3
1 Castleford WF10 200 D3
Orchard Head Cres WF8 201 C2
Orchard Head Dr WF8 201 C2
Orchard Head La WF8 201 B2
Orchard Head Prim Sch WF8 201 C2
Orchard La
8 Addingham LS29 175 A4
Barkston Ash LS24 195 F6
Hebden BD23 135 A2
Ripley HG3 161 C7
Ripon HG4 214 E1
Thirsk YO7 211 B1
Orchard Mews 9 DL9 40 E3
Orchard Paddock
34 Haxby YO32 166 E5
3 Haxby YO32 225 D8
Orchard Rd
Malton YO17 215 B4
Selby YO8 232 A4
3 Sleights YO22 32 A6
Upper Poppleton YO26 224 A1
Orchards The
2 Beadlam YO62 93 D7
6 Brafferton YO61 115 F1
Leavening YO17 147 E1
Mickletown LS26 200 B5
Ripon HG4 214 C6
Westow YO60 147 B4
Orchard The
5 Ampleforth YO62 92 C1
Ampleforth YO62 92 C1
Bishopthorpe YO25 231 A3
Burniston YO13 75 D8
Burton Leonard HG3 140 A2
Heslington YO10 229 A1
6 North Featherstone WF7 200 E1
11 Pickering YO18 96 A6
5 Roundhill Village TS17 6 D5
Sadberge DL2 4 C7
Scalby YO12 212 C7
Snainton YO13 98 A4
Thirsk YO7 211 C4
Tholthorpe YO61 142 D5
Orchard The *continued*
Wray LA2 128 A6
Orchard View
Markington with Wallerthwaite HG3 139 E3
3 Skelton YO30 224 B5
Orchard Way
Hensall DN14 203 C2
Middlesbrough TS7 7 D8
Selby YO8 232 A4
1 Strensall YO32 167 B7
Thorpe Willoughby YO8 197 B2
York YO24 227 E1
Orchid Ct 17 DL9 41 A5
Orchid Way 8 HG3 161 B3
Ordmerstones La YO18 96 C4
Ordnance La YO10 228 D1
Oriel Bank YO11 212 F3
Oriel Cl YO11 212 F3
Oriel Cres YO11 212 F3
Oriel Gr YO30 228 A8
ORMESBY 7 C8
Ormesby Bank TS7 7 D7
Ormesby Cres DL7 210 D2
Ormesby Prim Sch TS7 7 D8
Ormesby Rd TS3 7 C8
Orms Gill Green La BD23 154 D6
Orpington Rd TS3 7 C8
Orr Cres 10 YO7 89 B1
Orrin Cl YO24 230 C7
OSBALDWICK 229 C4
Osbaldwick Ind Est YO19 229 D5
Osbaldwick La YO10 229 B4
Osbaldwick Link Rd YO10 229 D4
Osbaldwick Prim Sch YO10 229 C4
Osbaldwick Village YO10 229 C4
Osborne Cl HG1 219 D4
Osborne Gdns HG1 219 D4
Osborne Pk YO12 212 D5
Osborne Rd HG1 219 D4
Osborne Terr 9 YO21 208 D5
Osborne Wlk HG1 219 D4
Osbourne Dr 4 YO30 224 E3
OSGODBY
Seamer 100 B7
Selby 198 C4
Osgodby Cl 9 YO11 100 B8
OSGODBY COMMON 198 C6
Osgodby Cres YO11 100 B7
Osgodby Gr 10 YO11 100 B8
Osgodby Hall Rd YO11 100 B7
Osgodby Hill YO11 100 B7
Osgodby La 12 YO11 100 B8
Osgodby Way 11 YO11 100 B8
Osgoodby Bank YO7 90 F3
Osmington Gdns 10 YO32 167 A7
OSMOTHERLEY 45 C4
Osmotherley Prim Sch DL6 45 B4
Osprey Cl
4 Collingham LS22 180 A1
Guisborough TS14 8 D6
5 Scotton DL9 40 F2
4 York YO24 230 B8
Osprey Garth 4 YO12 99 E6
Ostler's Cl YO23 230 C3
Ostman Rd YO26 227 C5
Oswaldene DL6 45 B4
OSWALDKIRK 93 A1
Oswaldkirk Bank YO62 93 A1
Oswestry Gn TS4 7 A7
Oswin Gr DL10 20 E4
Oswy Cotts YO21 208 D5
Oswy St 5 YO21 208 D5
Otley Rd
Harrogate HG2 222 B8
Killinghall HG3 161 B4
Pannal HG3 178 A7
Skipton BD23 217 B4
Stainburn HG3 177 F6
Otley St BD23 217 A4
Otterbeck Way 16 DL8 63 B3
OTTERBURN 154 E4
Otter Dr 13 YO18 95 F6
Otter Way TS17 6 A5
Otterwood Bank 5 YO24 227 B1
Otterwood La YO24 227 B1
Otterwood Paddock YO41 168 C2
Oucher La HG3 140 B2
OUGHTERSHAW 80 C4
Oughtershaw Rd BD23 80 B6
OULSTON 117 E5
Oulston Rd YO61 117 D1
Our Ladys RC Prim Sch YO24 227 E1
Ouse Acres YO26 227 D6
Ouse Bank YO8 232 E5
Ouseburn Ave YO26 227 C6
Ousecliffe Gdns YO30 228 A6
Ousegate YO8 232 D5
Ousegate Mills Business Centre YO8 232 D5
Ouse Lea YO30 228 A7
Ouston Cl LS24 189 F6
Ouston La LS24 189 F6
Out Croft La YO18 95 C8
Outgaits Cl 4 YO14 126 F8
Outgaits La
Hunmanby YO14 127 A8
Muston YO14 100 F1
Outgang La
Osbaldwick YO19 229 D6
21 Pickering YO18 95 F6
Thornton-le-Dale YO18 96 E6
Out Gang La BD23 107 F1
Outgang Rd
Malton YO17 215 B5
Pickering YO18 96 A6
Scampston YO17 122 F7
Outgang The YO17 122 F4
Outgate Cnr DL6 23 F4
OUTHGILL 34 A8
Outwood La LS24 190 C2
Oval The
Harrogate HG2 222 D8
Hurworth DL2 3 F1
Kellingley DN14 202 C3
Middlesbrough TS5 6 E6
Otley LS21 176 F1
3 Scarborough YO11 100 B8
Skipton BD23 217 B3
Overburn Rd 3 BD20 187 E6
OVER BURROW 102 B7
Overdale YO11 100 A7
Overdale Cl YO24 230 D8
Overdale Com Prim Sch 7 YO11 100 A7
Overdale Ct BD23 217 A5
Overdale Grange 3 BD23 217 B5
Overdale Rd TS3 7 C8
Overgreen Cl YO13 75 D8
Overgreen La YO13 75 C8
Overgreen View YO13 75 D8
Over Nidd HG1 219 C6
Overscar La YO18 72 E3
OVER SILTON 66 B8
OVERTON 165 F2
Overton Rd YO30 165 F3
Overton Terr YO11 213 B6
OVERTOWN 102 C7
Ovington La DL11 1 A6
Ovington Terr YO23 228 B2
Owler Park Rd LS29 175 C3
Owlwood Ct 7 YO19 184 E7
Owlwood La 6 YO19 184 E7
Owmen Field La YO62 93 C5
Owston Ave 2 YO10 229 A3
Owston Rd 1 YO14 126 F8
Ox Calder Cl 16 YO19 184 F7
Ox Carr La YO32 167 B6
Ox Cl YO41 168 D2
Oxcliff YO12 212 C8
Oxclose La YO62 70 C4
Ox Close La
Eldmire with Crakehill YO7 115 E5
Grimston YO10 184 C4
Myton-on-Swale YO61 141 F5
North Deighton LS22 180 B7
Whixley YO26 163 F5
Oxcroft 23 YO62 70 B1
Oxenby Pl 12 YO61 117 D1
Oxen La YO8 198 E3
Oxford Dr LS25 194 D1
Oxford Pl 7 HG1 219 D2
Oxford St
Harrogate HG1 219 D2
6 Normanton South WF6 200 B2
Scarborough YO12 212 F6
Skelton & Brotton TS12 9 D7
5 York YO24 228 A3
Oxford Terr 2 HG1 219 D1
Oxmoor La LS24 196 D7
Ox Moor La
Cattal YO26 164 A1
Hunsingore LS22 180 E8
Oxpasture Cl YO12 212 C4
OXTON 190 A6
Oxton Dr LS24 189 F6
Oxton La LS24 189 F6
Oyster Park Infants Sch WF10 201 B5
Oyster Park Junior Sch WF10 201 B4
Oyster Way YO14 127 C8

P

Packhorse Bridge★
Dacre HG3 159 D6
Romanby DL7 210 B4
Padbury Ave 50 YO14 101 B3
Padbury Cl 46 YO14 101 B3
Pad Cote La BD22 187 A5
Paddock Cl
Askham Richard YO23 182 D3
Copmanthorpe YO23 230 A2
Helmsley YO62 92 F6
Huntington YO32 225 F4
Norton YO17 215 D3
2 Pickering YO18 95 F6
Paddock Farm Water Gdns★ DL2 22 D4
Paddock Hill YO17 215 A4
Paddock House La LS22 179 E1
Paddock Rise 13 YO61 117 D1
Paddocks The
Follifoot HG3 223 F4
Wheldrake YO19 193 A7
Paddock The
14 Airmyn DN14 205 E4
Appleton Wiske DL6 24 B3
Burton Salmon LS25 201 F6
Catterick DL10 41 D4
Fairburn WF11 201 D6
Knaresborough HG5 221 C5
Paddock The *continued*
Leeming DL8 63
1 Linton-on-Ouse YO30 164 F8
Melmerby HG4 114 B7
Middleton St George DL2 4 C3
Newby Wiske DL7 64 E2
Normanton South WF6 200 A1
Stokesley TS9 26 C8
9 Whitby YO21 208 D7
Wilberfoss YO41 185 E5
York YO26 227 C6
Paddock View WF10 201 A3
Paddock Way YO26 227 C6
PADSIDE 159 B6
PADSIDE GREEN 159 C6
Page La YO62 93 E6
Pagnell Ave YO8 232 E4
PAINSTHORPE 170 B5
Painsthorpe La YO41 170 B5
Painter La YO8 196 E2
Palace Rd HG4 214 B7
Palace Theatre Sh Mall YO17 215 C4
Pale La
Carleton BD23 216 E1
Gateforth YO8 202 F7
Paley Green La BD24 131 B2
Pallet Hill 10 DL10 41 D5
Palmer Gr YO8 232 A3
Palmer La YO1 233 C2
Palmers La LS22 180 E4
Palmes Cl YO19 191 E8
Palms Ct DL2 4 A5
Panman La YO19 184 F8
PANNAL 222 E3
PANNAL ASH 222 B5
Pannal Ash Cl HG2 222 C8
Pannal Ash Cres HG2 222 B7
Pannal Ash Dr HG2 222 B7
Pannal Ash Gr HG2 222 B7
Pannal Ash Rd HG2 222 B7
Pannal Ave HG3 222 E2
Pannal Bank HG3 222 E2
Pannal Cl 3 YO21 208 B5
Pannal Gn HG3 222 E3
Pannal Prim Sch HG3 222 E3
Pannal Rd HG3 223 B4
Pannal Sta HG3 222 E2
Pannett Art Gall★ YO21 208 C6
Pannett Way 8 YO21 208 D6
Pannierman La TS7 7 E2
Panorama Cl 10 HG3 137 C4
Panorama Dr LS29 175 C1
Panorama Walk HG2 222 A8
Panorama Wlk HG3 137 C4
Pant La LA2 130 E7
Parade Ct YO31 228 F6
Parade The
Harrogate HG1 219 E2
Hunmanby YO14 127 B8
Whitby YO21 208 B7
Paradise YO11 213 B7
Paradise Cotts YO17 170 F8
Paradise Field Est 2 YO61 143 D8
Paradise La
Dalton YO7 115 F8
Stutton with Hazlewood LS24 189 A3
Paradise Rd YO7 67 A2
Paradise Way 6 DL2 3 B7
Paragon St YO10 233 C1
Parcevall Hall Gdns★ BD23 157 E8
Parish Ghyll Dr LS29 218 A3
Parish Ghyll La LS29 218 A3
Parish Ghyll Rd LS29 218 A3
Parish Ghyll Wlk LS29 218 A3
Parison Ct WF10 200 F3
PARK 186 F5
Park Ave
Barlow YO8 204 C7
Castleford WF10 200 F4
Glusburn BD20 187 E7
Great Preston WF10 200 E6
Harrogate HG2 219 C1
Hellifield BD23 154 B3
Kippax LS25 194 E1
Knaresborough HG5 221 B8
New Earswick YO32 225 D5
Normanton South WF6 200 A1
Scarborough YO12 212 D4
Sherburn in Elmet LS25 195 E4
Skipton BD23 216 F4
Swillington LS26 194 A1
Thornaby TS17 6 B8
Park Avenue S HG2 222 D8
Park Bank YO21 29 E7
Park Chase
Harrogate HG1 219 E3
Hornby DL8 62 C8
Park Cl
6 Airmyn DN14 205 E4
1 Easingwold YO61 143 D8
8 Knaresborough HG5 221 B6
Skelton YO30 224 B4
Park Cres
6 Addingham LS29 175 A4
Castleford WF10 201 B4
Darlington DL1 3 D4
Embsay BD23 217 C7
Hellifield BD23 154 B3
York YO31 233 C4
Park Crest HG5 221 B6
Park Dale WF10 201 B5

Park Dr
Campsall DN6 . . . . 206 E1
Glusburn BD20 . . . . 187 E7
Harrogate HG2 . . . . 222 D8
Knaresborough HG5 . . . . . 221 B6
13 Masham HG4 . . . . 86 C3
Park Edge HG2 . . . . 222 F8
PARK END 7 B8
Park End Prim Sch TS3 . . . 7 C8
Parker Ave YO26 . . . . 227 B2
Parker Dr 21 DL8 . . . . 63 A2
Parker La YO26 . . . . 164 C3
Parkers Mount 20 YO62 . . 70 B1
Parker St
Barnoldswick BB18 . . . . . 171 C2
15 Glusburn BD20 . . . . . . 187 E8
Park Est YO32 . . . . 225 D8
Parkfield YO61 . . . . 144 C6
Parkfield Ave TS5 . . . . 6 E4
Parkfield Cl YO12 . . . . 212 D4
Parkfield Gdns YO12 . . . . 212 D4
Parkfield La WF7 . . . . 200 D1
Parkgate DL1 . . . . 3 D5
Park Gate
Knaresborough HG5 . . . . . 221 B8
Strensall YO32 . . . . 167 B8
Parkgate La DL10 . . . . 41 B7
Park Gr
Knaresborough HG5 . . . . . 221 B8
Norton YO17 . . . . 215 C3
Selby YO8 . . . . 232 B3
Swillington LS26 . . . . 200 A8
York YO31 . . . . 233 C4
Park Grove Prim Sch
YO31 . . . . 233 C4
Park Hill BB18 . . . . 171 E1
Park House Gn
Harrogate HG1 . . . . 219 C5
7 Spofforth HG3 . . . . 179 E5
Park House La LA2 . . . . . 128 D5
Parkin Ave YO8 . . . . 232 E4
Parkins Garth DL8 . . . . 57 F6
Parkinson App LS25 . . . . 194 C4
Parkinson's La LS21 . . . . 159 E2
Parkinson's Yd 5 DL10 . . 209 C6
Park Junior Sch WF10 . . . 200 F4
Park La
Balne DN14 . . . . 207 C5
Barlow YO8 . . . . 204 C7
Bishop Wilton YO42 . . . . . 169 F1
Borrowby YO7 . . . . 65 E4
Buckden BD23 . . . . 81 E2
Burn YO8 . . . . 203 D7
Carleton BD23 . . . . 173 A3
Cowling BD22 . . . . 186 F5
Darlington DL1 . . . . 3 D4
5 Easington TS13 . . . . 11 A8
Glusburn BD20 . . . . 187 E7
Great Preston WF10 . . . . . 200 E7
Guisborough TS14 . . . . 8 E6
Kippax LS25 . . . . 200 E8
Kirkbymoorside YO62 . . . . . 70 B1
Knaresborough HG5 . . . . . 221 C6
Ledsham LS25 . . . . 201 B8
Luttons YO17 . . . . 150 C8
Mickletown LS26 . . . . 200 A5
5 Middleham DL8 . . . . 60 E2
North Featherstone WF8 . . 200 F1
North Stainley with Sleningford
HG4 . . . . 113 E5
Spofforth with Stockeld
HG3 . . . . 179 D5
Tatham LA2 . . . . 128 B8
West Tanfield HG4 . . . . . . 113 A8
Wilberfoss YO41 . . . . 185 E5
Womersley DN6 . . . . 206 D6
York YO24 . . . . 227 F3
Parkland Dr
Darlington DL3 . . . . 3 A6
Tadcaster LS24 . . . . 189 F6
Parklands
Castleford WF10 . . . . 200 F4
Ilkley LS29 . . . . 218 D4
Park Lands 4 HG3 . . . . . . 179 E5
Parklands The
1 Ingleby Arncliffe DL6 . . 45 A7
Scruton DL7 . . . . 63 D7
Parkland Way YO32 . . . . . 225 D8
Park Lane Cl YO42 . . . . . . 169 F1
Park Lodge YO32 . . . . 225 D8
Park Mount 6 HG3 . . . . . 179 E5
Park Nook Rd LS25 . . . . . 196 F4
Park Par
Harrogate HG1 . . . . 219 F2
Knaresborough HG5 . . . . . 221 B6
Park Pl
Darlington DL1 . . . . 3 D5
Hellifield BD23 . . . . 154 B3
4 Knaresborough HG5 . . 221 B6
York YO31 . . . . 233 C4
Park Rd
Airmyn DN14 . . . . 205 E4
Asenby YO7 . . . . 115 B6
Barlow YO8 . . . . 204 C7
Castleford WF10 . . . . 201 A3
Cowling BD22 . . . . 187 B6
Glusburn BD20 . . . . 187 E8
8 Harrogate HG2 . . . . 219 C3
Norton-on-Derwent YO17 . 215 C3
Pontefract WF8 . . . . 201 A1
6 Scarborough YO12 . . . . 212 D4
Spofforth HG3 . . . . 179 E5
Park Rise 17 YO14 . . . . . . 126 F8
Park Row
Knaresborough HG5 . . . . . 221 B5

Park Row continued
Selby YO8 . . . . 232 D5
Parkshill Ct DL10 . . . . 20 F7
Parkside DL1 . . . . 3 C4
Park Side
Earby BB18 . . . . 186 A8
Follifoot HG3 . . . . 223 E5
Parkside Cl YO24 . . . . 227 E3
Parkside Commercial Ctr
YO23 . . . . 233 C1
Park Sq
2 Knaresborough HG5 . . 221 B6
9 Ripon HG4 . . . . 214 C4
Park St
16 Glusburn BD20 . . . . . . 187 E8
1 Harrogate HG1 . . . . . . 219 C5
Hovingham YO62 . . . . 119 E6
Masham HG4 . . . . 86 C3
Pickering YO18 . . . . 95 F7
Ripon HG4 . . . . 214 B5
Scarborough YO12 . . . . . . 212 D4
Selby YO8 . . . . 232 D5
1 Skipton BD23 . . . . 216 F4
York YO24 . . . . 233 A1
Parkstone Pl TS16 . . . . 5 E4
Park Terr
14 Knaresborough HG5 . . 221 B6
Whitby YO21 . . . . 208 D6
York YO32 . . . . 225 D5
Park The 14 YO13 . . . . 75 D5
Park View
Castleford WF10 . . . . 201 B3
Glaisdale YO21 . . . . 30 D4
Harrogate HG1 . . . . 219 E2
22 Leyburn DL8 . . . . 60 D5
Middleton Tyas YO7 . . . . . . 21 C4
Skipton BD23 . . . . 216 D4
Swillington LS26 . . . . 194 A1
Park View Dr BD23 . . . . . 134 B3
Park Way
Kirk Hammerton YO26 . . . 164 C2
Knaresborough HG5 . . . . . 221 B8
Parkways YO8 . . . . 232 B3
Parkway The YO12 . . . . . . 212 B7
Park Wood BD23 . . . . 216 D5
Park Wood Cl BD23 . . . . . 216 E5
Park Wood Cres BD23 . . . 216 D5
Parkwood Dr 6 TS18 . . . . . . 5 E8
Park Wood Way BD23 . . . 216 D5
Park Wynd DL10 . . . . 209 C6
Parliament Ave YO17 . . . . 215 E4
Parliament St
Harrogate HG1 . . . . 219 C3
Norton YO17 . . . . 215 E3
York YO1 . . . . 233 B2
Parliament Terr 2 HG1 . . 219 D2
PARLINGTON 194 E6
Parlington Ct LS15 . . . . . . 194 C8
Parlington Dr LS25 . . . . . . 194 E8
Parlington La LS25 . . . . . . 194 E7
Parlington Mdw LS15 . . . . 194 C7
Parlington Villas LS25 . . . 194 E8
Parracombe Cl 6 TS17 . . . . 6 A3
Parrock St 7 BB18 . . . . . . 171 D1
Parsley Mews LS26 . . . . . . 200 B6
Parsonage Rd LS26 . . . . . 200 C6
Parsonage The 11 HG5 . . 221 A6
Parson Back La DL6 . . . . . . 25 B2
Parsons Cl 10 DN14 . . . . . 205 E4
Parson's Cl YO21 . . . . 208 A7
Parsons Close La BD24 . . 131 A2
Parsons Ct DL10 . . . . 209 F7
Parsons La YO26 . . . . 165 E1
Parson's La
1 Addingham LS29 . . . . . 174 E4
Hunton Rudby DL6 . . . . 25 A2
Parson's Wlk 11 DN14 . . . 205 E4
Pasley Rd HG4 . . . . 113 D3
Paston Wlk YO23 . . . . 233 B1
Pasture Ave LS25 . . . . 196 A4
Pasture Cl
Barnoldswick BB18 . . . . . 171 E2
4 Sherburn in Elmet LS25 196 A4
Skelton YO30 . . . . 224 B5
Skipton BD23 . . . . 217 B5
2 Strensall YO32 . . . . . . 167 B6
Wistow YO8 . . . . 197 D6
Pasture Cres
Filey YO14 . . . . 101 A4
3 Knaresborough HG5 . . 221 B7
Pasture Ct LS25 . . . . 195 F4
Pasture Dr
Bedale DL8 . . . . 63 A2
Castleford WF10 . . . . 200 D3
Pasture Farm Cl YO10 . . . 231 D6
Pasture Field La YO22 . . . 32 C5
Pasture Fold 4 LS29 . . . . 176 C1
Pasture Gdns DN6 . . . . . . 206 F2
Pasture Gr 27 LS25 . . . . . 195 F4
Pasture Hill YO17 . . . . . . 169 E8
Pasture La
Ellerton YO42 . . . . 193 C1
Helperby YO61 . . . . 142 B8
Heworth YO31 . . . . 229 B8
Hovingham YO62 . . . . 119 E6
Kearby with Netherby
LS22 . . . . 179 C1
Malton YO17 . . . . 215 C5
Marton-le-Moor HG4 . . . . 140 D8
2 Seamer YO12 . . . . 99 D6
Pasture Rd
Embsay with Eastby
BD23 . . . . 217 C8
Lockton YO18 . . . . 73 A5
Scruton DL8 . . . . 62 D5
Pastures The
2 Carlton DN14 . . . . 204 C3
Coulby Newham TS8 . . . . . . 7 B5

Pastures The continued
16 Eastfield YO11 . . . . . . 100 B6
Sherburn YO17 . . . . 124 D7
4 York YO24 . . . . 230 E8
Pasture The 4 TS17 . . . . . . 6 D5
Pasture View
Malton YO17 . . . . 215 C6
Sherburn in Elmet LS25 . . 195 F4
Pasture Way
Castleford WF10 . . . . 200 D3
Sherburn in Elmet LS25 . . 195 F4
Whitwood WF10 . . . . 200 D3
Wistow YO8 . . . . 197 D6
PATELEY BRIDGE 137 C4
Pateley Moor Cres DL2 . . . . 3 E3
Pately Pl 1 YO26 . . . . 227 D4
Paterson Cres DL6 . . . . . . 210 E4
Pathways Sch WF10 . . . . . 201 B4
Patience La HG4 . . . . 114 D3
PATRICK BROMPTON 62 C5
Patrick Pool YO1 . . . . 233 B2
Patterdale Dr YO30 . . . . . 224 E1
Patterham La DL8 . . . . 59 D4
Pavement YO1 . . . . 233 B2
Paver La YO1 . . . . 233 C2
Pavilion Row YO10 . . . . . 231 D7
Pavilion Sq
7 Harrogate HG2 . . . . . . 219 C1
11 Scarborough YO11 . . . 213 A5
Pavilion Terr 12 YO11 . . . 213 A5
Peacocks TS9 . . . . 26 C8
Peacock's Cl DL7 . . . . 63 E7
Peak Alum Works ★ YO13 . 53 F8
Peak Scar Rd YO62 . . . . . . 67 C3
Pearl Rd TS17 . . . . 6 B8
Pearl St HG1 . . . . 220 C4
Pearson Garth YO13 . . . . . 99 A7
Pearson St WF6 . . . . 200 A3
Pearson's Cl YO21 . . . . . . 208 A7
Pearsons Yd YO17 . . . . . . 121 C4
Peart La BD23 . . . . 154 C8
Pear Tree Acre LS23 . . . . 180 F1
Pear Tree Ave
Long Drax YO8 . . . . 204 F7
8 Poppleton YO26 . . . . . 165 F1
Pear Tree Cl
Skeeby DL10 . . . . 20 F1
York YO30 . . . . 225 F4
Peartree Ct YO1 . . . . 233 C3
Pear Tree Gdns
Asenby YO7 . . . . 115 C6
Barwick in Elmet LS15 . . . 194 D7
Pear Tree Wlk YO17 . . . . 215 B4
Pease Ct
1 Eaglescliffe TS16 . . . . . . 5 D5
Guisborough TS14 . . . . 8 D5
4 Lingdale TS12 . . . . 9 F7
Pease St
Darlington DL1 . . . . 3 E5
6 Lingdale TS12 . . . . 9 F7
Peasey Hills Rd YO17 . . . 215 C5
Peasholm Ave YO12 . . . . . 212 F7
Peasholm Cres YO12 . . . . 212 F7
Peasholm Dr YO12 . . . . . . 212 F7
Peasholme Bridge YO12 . 212 F7
Peasholme Gn YO1 . . . . . 233 C2
Peasholm Gap YO12 . . . . 212 F8
Peasholm Gdns YO12 . . . 212 F7
Peasholm Rd YO12 . . . . . 212 F8
Peasland La YO7 . . . . 66 B5
Peaslands La YO18 . . . . 96 D5
Peat La HG3 . . . . 137 B3
Peatmoor La DL8 . . . . 58 E5
Peckett's Holt HG1 . . . . . . 219 D7
Peckett's Way HG1 . . . . . . 219 D7
Peckfield HG4 . . . . 214 C2
Peckfield Cl HG3 . . . . 160 F5
Peckitt St YO1 . . . . 233 B1
Peel Cl YO10 . . . . 229 A1
Peel Gn BD23 . . . . 154 B2
Peel Pl 11 LS29 . . . . 176 C1
Peel St
Thornaby TS17 . . . . 6 B8
York YO1 . . . . 233 C1
Peel Terr YO12 . . . . 213 A7
Pefham La YO25 . . . . 170 F4
Pegman Cl TS14 . . . . 8 F7
Peirse Cl DL8 . . . . 63 A2
Pelham Pl 15 YO32 . . . . . 167 A7
Pellentine Rd HG3 . . . . . . 223 F4
Pemberton Cres TS4 . . . . . . 7 A8
Pemberton Rd WF10 . . . . 201 A4
Pembroke St
10 Skipton BD23 . . . . . . 216 F3
York YO30 . . . . 228 B7
Pembroke Way YO21 . . . . 208 C5
Pembury Mews DL10 . . . . 41 B6
Penberry Gdns 33 TS17 . . . 5 F4
Penders La TS15 . . . . 5 E1
Penderyn Cres TS17 . . . . . . 5 F4
Pendle St 4 BD23 . . . . . . 216 D3
Pendleton Rd DL1 . . . . 3 D7
Pendragon Castle ★ CA17 . 14 A1
Pendragon Way HG2 . . . . 222 B8
Penfold Ct BD23 . . . . 154 B3
Penhill Ct DL7 . . . . 210 C1
Penhowe La YO17 . . . . . . 147 D4
Penistone Rd TS3 . . . . 7 C8
Penley's Grove St YO31 . . 233 C4
Pennine Cl YO32 . . . . 225 F4
Pennine View
Burneston DL8 . . . . 87 E8
Northallerton DL7 . . . . . . 210 B2
Pennine Way
11 Barnoldswick BB18 . . 171 D1
Ingleby TS17 . . . . 6 A4
Penniston La YO13 . . . . 97 C4
Penn La DL8 . . . . 56 D4

Penn Rd DL10 . . . . 209 B7
Pennycarr La YO61 . . . . . 143 D7
Penny Gn BD24 . . . . 131 D1
Penny La
Burton Fleming YO25 . . . . 126 E2
Darlington DL1 . . . . 3 C4
1 Easingwold YO61 . . . . 117 D1
Ripon HG4 . . . . 214 C7
Penny La Ct YO1 . . . . 233 C3
Pennyman Gn TS8 . . . . 6 C4
Pennyman Prim Sch TS3 . . 7 B8
Penny Pot Gdns 4 HG3 . . 161 B2
Pennypot La TS18 . . . . 5 E7
Penny Pot La HG3 . . . . . . 160 D2
Penny Pot La or Rough Rd
HG3 . . . . 161 A2
Penny Royal Cl 7 HG3 . . . 161 B3
Pennywort Gr 15 HG3 . . . 161 B3
Penrith Cres WF10 . . . . . . 201 B5
Penrith Rd TS3 . . . . 7 B8
Pentire Cl 11 YO30 . . . . . 225 A1
Pentland Dr YO32 . . . . . . 225 F3
Penton Rd 10 YO11 . . . . . 100 B6
Penyghent Ave YO31 . . . . 229 A5
Penyghent Way TS17 . . . . . 6 A3
Pen-y-Ghent Way 5
BB18 . . . . 171 D1
Peplow Cl LS25 . . . . 201 F6
Peppercorn Cl 6 YO26 . . . 227 E4
Peppergarth The DL7 . . . . 210 B3
Peppermint Dr 15 DL9 . . . 41 A5
Peppermint Way YO8 . . . 232 A5
Per Ardua Way 6 DL10 . . . 41 E4
Percy Cross Rigg YO21 . . . . 9 A1
Percy Ct HG5 . . . . 162 A6
Percy Dr 4 DN14 . . . . 205 E4
Percy Rd
Darlington DL3 . . . . 3 C7
14 Hunmanby YO14 . . . . 127 A8
Percy's La YO1 . . . . 233 C2
Percy St YO31 . . . . 233 B3
Peregrine Ct 2 TS14 . . . . . . 8 D6
Perie Ave HG4 . . . . 113 D3
Perry Ave TS17 . . . . 6 B5
Petercroft Cl 5 YO19 . . . . 184 F7
Petercroft La YO19 . . . . . . 184 F7
Peter Hill Dr YO30 . . . . . . 228 A8
Peterhouse Cl DL1 . . . . 3 D7
Peter La
Burton Leonard HG3 . . . . 140 A2
York YO1 . . . . 233 B2
Petersbottom La LA2 . . . . 129 B4
Petersway YO30 . . . . 233 A4
Petre Ave YO8 . . . . 232 E3
Petty Whin Cl 25 HG3 . . . 161 B3
Petyt Gr BD23 . . . . 217 A4
Pew Tree Cl YO41 . . . . . . 185 E6
Pheasant Dr 5 YO24 . . . . 230 B8
Pheasantry The 14 YO12 . . 99 E6
Philadelphia Terr 2
YO23 . . . . 228 B2
Philip La YO8 . . . . 196 E2
Philippa's Dr HG2 . . . . . . 222 D8
Philip St 27 BB18 . . . . . . 171 D1
Philpin La LA6 . . . . 104 C8
Phlashetts La DL8 . . . . 87 A4
Phoenix Ave LS25 . . . . . . 194 F3
Phoenix Bsns Ctr HG4 . . . 214 D5
Phoenix Bvd YO26 . . . . . . 228 A4
Phoenix Pk TS8 . . . . 6 F6
Piave Rd DL9 . . . . 40 D4
Picadilly Ct YO1 . . . . 233 C2
Piccadilly YO1 . . . . 233 C2
Pickard Cl BB18 . . . . 171 E2
Pickard La BD20 . . . . 174 C1
PICKERING 95 E6
Pickering Ave LS25 . . . . . 194 D4
Pickering Castle ★ YO18 . . 95 F7
Pickering Com Junior Sch 26
YO18 . . . . 95 F7
Pickering Infant Sch
YO18 . . . . 96 A7
Pickering Rd
East Ayton/West Ayton
YO13 . . . . 99 A7
Thornaby TS17 . . . . 6 B8
Thornton-le-Dale YO18 . . . 96 C6
Pickering Sta YO18 . . . . . . 95 F7
Pick Haven Garth DN14 . . 202 F3
PICKHILL 88 C6
Pickhill CE Prim Sch YO7 . 88 C6
Picking Croft La HG3 . . . . 161 B5
Picks Cl 5 YO7 . . . . 211 B3
Pickwick Cl YO17 . . . . 215 C5
PICTON 24 D6
Piece Croft 2 BD23 . . . . . 134 D2
Piece Fields 4 BD23 . . . . 134 D2
PIERCEBRIDGE 2 A6
Piercy End YO62 . . . . 70 B1
Pier Rd 22 YO21 . . . . 208 D7
Pier Rd YO21 . . . . 208 D7
Pierremont Rd DL3 . . . . 3 B6
Piggy La DL2 . . . . 1 C7
Pighill Nook Rd LS25 . . . . 202 C7
Pike Hills Mount YO23 . . . 230 A3
Pike La BD24 . . . . 131 E4
Pikepurse La DL10 . . . . . . 209 D8
Pike Rd 8 YO18 . . . . 95 F6
Piker Thorn La YO19 . . . . 167 D1
Pilgrim St YO31 . . . . 233 B4
Pill White La LS21 . . . . . . 177 C3
Pilmoor Cl DL10 . . . . 209 E8
Pilmoor Dr DL10 . . . . 209 E8
Pindar L Ctr YO11 . . . . . . 100 A6
Pindar La YO11 . . . . 100 A6
Pindars Way YO8 . . . . 198 B4
Pinder Cl DL10 . . . . 209 F8

Pinders Cres WF11 . . . . . 201 E3
Pinders Green Ct LS26 . . . 200 B5
Pinders Green Dr LS26 . . 200 B5
Pinders Green Fold LS26 . 200 B5
Pinders Green Wlk LS26 . 200 B4
Pine Cl
Castleford WF10 . . . . 200 F3
Skipton BD23 . . . . 216 E4
Pine Croft HG4 . . . . 112 F2
Pine Gr 1 DL6 . . . . 210 E3
Pine Hill TS8 . . . . 7 B5
Pinelands 4 YO22 . . . . . . 225 D7
Pinelands Way YO10 . . . . 229 C3
Pine Rd
Guisborough TS14 . . . . 8 E7
Middlesbrough TS7 . . . . 7 D8
Pines Gdns 29 LS29 . . . . 175 C2
Pine St HG1 . . . . 219 E5
Pines The LS17 . . . . 178 B2
Pine Tree Ave YO17 . . . . . 122 F5
Pine Tree Cl YO8 . . . . 197 B2
Pinetree Gr DL2 . . . . 1 C4
Pine Tree La 1 LS25 . . . . 202 A7
Pine Wlk HG4 . . . . 214 D2
Pinewood Ave YO14 . . . . 101 B4
Pinewood Cl
5 Easington TS13 . . . . . . 11 A8
3 Firth Moor DL1 . . . . 3 E4
2 Ilkley LS29 . . . . 218 A3
5 Whitby YO21 . . . . 208 C6
Pinewood Dr
Camblesforth YO8 . . . . . . 204 D4
Scarborough YO12 . . . . . . 212 D5
Pinewood Gate HG2 . . . . 222 A7
Pinewood Gr
13 Bedale DL8 . . . . 63 A2
6 York YO31 . . . . 225 E2
Pinewood Hill 4 YO10 . . . 229 C3
Pinewood Rd TS7 . . . . 7 C6
Pinewood Wlk 7 TS9 . . . . 26 C8
Pinfold Ave LS25 . . . . 195 F4
Pinfold Cl
Bilton-in-Ainsty with Bickerton
LS22 . . . . 181 B5
5 Riccall YO19 . . . . 192 A1
3 Sherburn in Elmet LS25 195 F4
Pinfold Croft BD23 . . . . . 155 D1
Pinfold Ct
Kirkby Malzeard HG4 . . . . 112 D5
4 Sherburn in Elmet LS25 195 F4
4 York YO30 . . . . 228 A7
Pinfold Dr DL6 . . . . 210 E5
Pinfold Garth
Malton YO17 . . . . 215 A4
6 Sherburn in Elmet LS25 195 F4
Pinfold Gn HG5 . . . . 140 E1
Pinfold Hill YO8 . . . . 197 D6
Pinfold La
Kirk Smeaton WF8 . . . . . . 206 B3
Mickletown LS26 . . . . 200 C5
Moss DN6 . . . . 207 D1
Norton DN6 . . . . 206 E2
Norwood HG3 . . . . 177 A8
Pollington DN14 . . . . 207 F6
Pinfold Pl YO7 . . . . 211 C3
Pinfold Rise LS25 . . . . . . 194 F8
Pinfold The 5 BD23 . . . . . 216 F4
Pinfold View DN14 . . . . . 207 F6
Pinfold Way LS25 . . . . . . 195 F4
Pinhaw Rd BD23 . . . . 217 A2
Pinnacle View BD22 . . . . 187 A5
Pinsent Ct 4 YO31 . . . . . 228 E8
Pioneer Bsns Pk YO30 . . . 224 F3
Pioneer Ct DL1 . . . . 4 A4
Pioneer Way WF10 . . . . . 200 C2
Piper Hill 1 WF11 . . . . . . 201 D6
Piper Hill Cl DL10 . . . . 21 D7
Piper La
Cowling BD22 . . . . 187 B5
Thirsk YO7 . . . . 211 C3
Pipers Acre 4 YO18 . . . . . 95 F7
Pipers La YO26 . . . . 141 F1
Pippin Rd YO17 . . . . 215 B4
Pippin's App 17 WF6 . . . . 200 A2
Pit Ings La YO7 . . . . 115 F6
Pit La
Ledston Luck LS25 . . . . . . 194 F1
Mickletield LS25 . . . . 195 A4
Mickletown LS26 . . . . 200 B6
Pitman Rd YO17 . . . . 215 C5
Place Hill DL11 . . . . 38 B6
PLACE NEWTON 123 C3
Planetree La
Kirkby Fleetham with Fencote
DL7 . . . . 42 A1
Thornville YO26 . . . . 164 A1
Plane Tree Way YO14 . . . 101 A4
Plantation Ave HG3 . . . . . 222 A8
Plantation Cl HG2 . . . . . . 222 A8
Plantation Dr
Barlby with Osgodby
YO8 . . . . 198 B5
York YO26 . . . . 227 C6
Plantation Gr YO26 . . . . . 227 C6
Plantation Rd HG2 . . . . . 222 A8
Plantation Terr HG2 . . . . 222 A8
Plantation The
Birstwith HG3 . . . . 160 E6
Gisburn Forest BD23 . . . . 152 E3
Plantation Way 23 YO32 . 166 E5
Plaxton Ct YO12 . . . . 212 B5
Player Ct TS16 . . . . 5 E5
Pleasance The 6 LS26 . . . 194 A1
Pleasant Row HG1 . . . . . . 219 E5
Pleasant View 5 BB18 . . . 172 B1
Plews Way DL7 . . . . 63 C5
Plompton Cl HG2 . . . . . . 220 D1

Plompton Dr HG2 . . . . . . 220 D2
Plompton Gr 3 HG2 . . . . 220 D2
Plompton Rd HG3 . . . . . . 223 F5
Plompton Way 1 HG2 . . 220 D2
Plompton WlK 2 HG2 . . 220 D2
Plough Garth The DN14 . 202 F3
Ploughlands 1 YO32 . . . 225 C7
Ploughman's Cl YO23 . . 230 C3
Ploughmans Ct 14 YO11 . 100 B7
Ploughmans' La YO24 . . 225 C7
Plover Gdns 1 YO12 . . . . 99 F6
Plumer Ave YO31 . . . . . 229 A5
Plumer Rd DL9 . . . . 209 B1
Plumpton La HG4 . . . . . 139 D8
Plumpton Pk HG2 . . . . . 220 D3
Plumpton Rocks★ HG5 . . 179 D8
Plum St YO17 . . . . 215 D3
Pluntrain Dale La YO12 . . 96 B7
Poachers The YO8 . . . . . 199 C5
POCKLEY 69 B1
Pocklington La YO42 . . . 169 F2
Pockthorpe La YO25 . . . 151 F2
Pocock Pl DL10 . . . . 41 E4
Polam Hall Sch DL1 . . . . . 3 C4
Polam La DL1 . . . . 3 C4
Polam Rd DL1 . . . . 3 C4
Pole Rd BD22 . . . . 187 F4
Pollard Gdns YO12 . . . . 212 C4
Pollard Rd YO31 . . . . 53 F8
POLLINGTON 207 F6
Pollington Balne CE Prim
Sch DN14 . . . . 207 F6
Polperro Cl 21 WF6 . . . . 200 A2
Pond Farm Cl TS13 . . . . . 11 F7
Pond Field Cl DL3 . . . . . . 3 A4
Pondfields Dr LS25 . . . . 194 D1
Pond St 3 YO8 . . . . 232 D6
Pond View DL6 . . . . 65 F7
Pontefract Monkhill Sta
WF8 . . . . 201 B1
Pontefract Park
Racecourse★
WF8 . . . . 200 F2
Pontefract Rd
Castleford WF10 . . . . . . 200 F4
Knottingley WF11 . . . . . . 201 D2
Normanton South WF6 . . . 200 B2
Pontefract Tanshelf Sta
WF8 . . . . 201 A1
Pool Ct 20 YO18 . . . . 95 F6
POOLE 201 F5
Poole La LS25 . . . . 201 F6
Pool La YO26 . . . . 164 E4
Pope St WF6 . . . . 200 B3
Poplar Ave
Castleford WF10 . . . . . . 201 B4
6 Hutton Rudby TS15 . . . 25 D5
4 Kirkbymoorside YO62 . . 70 B1
3 Wetherby LS22 . . . . . 180 C4
Poplar Cres
Harrogate HG1 . . . . 219 F6
Northallerton DL7 . . . . . 210 C2
Poplar Ct YO8 . . . . 204 F5
Poplar Dr WF6 . . . . 200 A3
Poplar Gdns YO8 . . . . . . 204 F5
Poplar Gn HG5 . . . . 162 A6
Poplar Gr
Harrogate HG1 . . . . 219 F6
York YO32 . . . . 225 E3
Poplar Pl TS14 . . . . 8 E7
Poplar Row 6 YO21 . . . . 208 D7
Poplars Adventure Mega
Maze★ HG5 . . . . 162 F6
Poplars La YO17 . . . . . . 123 A7
Poplar St YO26 . . . . 227 E5
Poplars The
11 Brayton YO8 . . . . 197 D1
2 Glusburn BD20 . . . . . 187 E6
Knottingley WF11 . . . . . . 202 A1
Poplar View YO17 . . . . . 215 F4
Poplar Way HG1 . . . . . . 219 F6
Poppleton Hall Gdn
YO26 . . . . 224 A3
Poppleton Ousebank Prim
Sch YO26 . . . . 165 F1
Poppleton Rd YO26 . . . . 227 E5
Poppleton Rd Prim Sch
YO26 . . . . 227 E5
Poppleton Sta YO26 . . . 182 F8
Poppy Cl YO8 . . . . 232 C2
Poppy Ct DL9 . . . . 41 A5
Porchester Cl 3 TS17 . . . . 5 F5
Porch Farm Cl YO62 . . . 120 B5
Porch The DL10 . . . . 21 D7
Pornic Ave YO13 . . . . 75 D5
Porritt La YO12 . . . . 99 D7
Portal Rd
Knapton YO26 . . . . 227 B7
York YO26 . . . . 227 B7
Portholme Cres 7 YO8 . . 232 C5
Portholme Ct YO8 . . . . . 232 C4
Portholme Dr YO8 . . . . . 232 C4
Portholme Rd YO8 . . . . . 232 C5
Portisham Pl 12 YO32 . . . 167 A7
Portland Cres HG1 . . . . . 219 D4
Portland St YO31 . . . . . . 233 B4
Portland Way DL7 . . . . . . 63 C5
Portman Rise TS14 . . . . . . 8 F5
PORT MULGRAVE 11 F8
Postern Cl YO23 . . . . . . 233 B1
Postern La YO42 . . . . . . 193 D6
Post Office Row DN14 . . . 205 A1
Post Office Slip 24 YO61 . 143 C8
Pot Bank HG3 . . . . 178 A8
Potlands DL7 . . . . 63 C4
Pott Bank HG4 . . . . 85 A1
Potter Cl YO13 . . . . 99 B8

Pottergate
Gilling East YO62 . . . . . . 118 F7
14 Helmsley YO62 . . . . . . 92 F6
Richmond DL10 . . . . 209 C7
Potter Hill 11 YO18 . . . . . 95 F7
Potter La DL7 . . . . 64 A5
Potters Dr 4 YO23 . . . . . 230 B3
Potter's Side La YO21 . . . . 9 D1
POTTERTON 188 C1
Potterton Cl LS15 . . . . . 194 C8
Potterton La
Barwick in Elmet LS15 . . . 194 C8
Barwick in Elmet & Scholes
LS15 . . . . 188 C1
Pottery La
Bishop Monkton HG4 . . . 140 A6
Knottingley WF11 . . . . . . 201 E3
Littlethorpe HG4 . . . . . . 214 E1
Strensall YO32 . . . . 145 A1
Strensall YO32 . . . . 167 A8
York YO31 . . . . 228 E7
Pottery St WF10 . . . . . . 200 D4
Potticar Bank YO62 . . . . 119 D4
Pott Moor High Rd HG4 . 110 F8
POTTO 25 D2
Pounteys Cl 4 DL2 . . . . . . 4 C4
Powell St
Harrogate HG1 . . . . 219 F4
Selby YO8 . . . . 232 B6
Prail Cl 3 WF8 . . . . 201 C1
Prebendal Cl 11 LS25 . . . 202 A8
Precentor's Ct YO31 . . . 233 B3
Preen Dr TS5 . . . . 6 D8
Premiere Rd 30 LS29 . . . 175 C2
Premier Rd TS7 . . . . 7 D7
Preseli Gr 31 TS17 . . . . . . 5 F4
Preston Field Cross Rd
YO13 . . . . 74 E1
Preston Hall Mus★ TS18 . . . 5 F6
Preston La
Great Preston WF10 . . . . 200 C7
Preston-on-Tees TS18 . . . . 5 E7
PRESTON-ON-TEES 5 E7
Preston-on-Tees Prim Sch
TS16 . . . . 5 E6
PRESTON-UNDER-SCAR . 59 E6
Preston View LS26 . . . . . 194 A1
Preston Way TS9 . . . . . . 26 C8
Prestwick Ct
15 Middleton St George
DL2 . . . . 4 C4
Rufforth YO26 . . . . 227 B5
Pretoria St WF10 . . . . . . 200 F4
Price's La YO23 . . . . 233 B1
Priest Bank Rd 4 BD20 . 173 F1
Priestcarr La YO26 . . . . 163 D8
Priest Cl YO14 . . . . 126 F8
Priest Gill Bank DL11 . . . . 19 F5
Priest La
Dunnington YO19 . . . . . 184 F5
Ripon HG4 . . . . 214 D4
Primrose Ave
Hunmanby Sands YO14 . . 101 B1
Hunmanby YO14 . . . . . . 127 B8
Swillington LS26 . . . . . . 194 A1
Primrose Cl
Guisborough TS14 . . . . . . 8 E6
13 Killinghall HG3 . . . . . 161 B3
Ripon HG4 . . . . 214 C6
Primrose Ct 18 DL9 . . . . . 41 A5
Primrose Dene WF11 . . . 201 E4
Primrose Dr
Castleford WF10 . . . . . . 201 D3
Filey YO14 . . . . 101 B1
Ripon HG4 . . . . 214 C6
Primrose Gr YO8 . . . . . . 232 A6
Primrose Hill
9 Knottingley WF11 . . . . 202 A3
2 Skipton BD23 . . . . . . 216 F4
Primrose Hill Cl LS26 . . . 194 A1
Primrose Hill Dr
Great & Little Preston
LS26 . . . . 200 A8
15 Swillington LS26 . . . . 194 A1
Primrose Hill Garth
LS26 . . . . 200 A8
Primrose Hill Gdns LS26 . 194 A1
Primrose Hill Gn LS26 . . . 200 A8
Primrose Hill Gr 16 LS26 . 194 A1
Primrose La LS23 . . . . . . 188 E8
Primrose Lane Prim Sch 5
LS23 . . . . 188 E8
Primrose Vale 1 WF11 . . 202 A2
PRIMROSE VALLEY 101 C1
Primrose Valley Rd
YO14 . . . . 101 B1
Prince Henry Rd LS21 . . . 177 A1
Prince Henrys Gram Sch
LS21 . . . . 177 A1
Prince of Wales Terr
YO11 . . . . 213 A4
Prince Rupert Dr YO26 . . 181 C7
Princes Cres BD23 . . . . . 217 B4
Princes Dr BD23 . . . . 217 A4
Princess Ave HG5 . . . . . . 221 C5
Princess Cl
Knaresborough HG5 . . . . 221 C5
Ripon HG4 . . . . 214 C6
Princess Ct 11 WF6 . . . . 200 B1
Princess Dr
Knaresborough HG5 . . . . 221 C5
West Haddlesey YO8 . . . . 203 A5
York YO26 . . . . 227 D6
Princess Gr 4 HG5 . . . . . 221 C5
Princess La 2 YO11 . . . . 213 B6
Princess Mead HG5 . . . . 163 A3
Princess Mount 3 HG5 . . 221 C5

Princess Pl
1 Ripon HG4 . . . . 214 C6
9 Whitby YO21 . . . . 208 D6
Princes Sq
14 Harrogate HG1 . . . . . 219 D2
Thornaby TS17 . . . . 6 B6
Princess Rd
Darlington DL3 . . . . 3 D8
Ilkley LS29 . . . . 218 A3
Malton YO17 . . . . 215 C4
Ripon HG4 . . . . 214 C6
Strensall YO32 . . . . 167 B7
Princess Royal La 4
YO11 . . . . 212 F3
Princess Royal Pk 1
YO11 . . . . 213 A3
Princess Royal Rd HG4 . . 214 C3
Princess Royal Terr
YO11 . . . . 213 A3
Princess Royal Way HG3 . 222 E1
Princess Sq 11 YO11 . . . 213 B6
Princess St
Castleford WF10 . . . . . . 200 F5
Normanton South WF6 . . . 200 F1
Scarborough YO11 . . . . . 213 B6
Princess Terr
Knaresborough HG5 . . . . 221 C6
17 Scarborough YO11 . . . 213 B6
Prince St WF10 . . . . 200 C8
Prince Villa Rd HG1 . . . . 219 E2
Prior Ave DL10 . . . . 209 B7
Priorpot Way YO17 . . . . 215 F4
Prior Pursglove Coll 18
TS10 . . . . 8 F7
Prior's La BD23 . . . . 174 C8
Prior's Wlk YO26 . . . . . . 227 D6
Prior Wath Rd YO13 . . . . 54 A5
Priorwood Gdns TS17 . . . . 6 A4
Priory Cl
Guisborough TS14 . . . . . . 8 F7
Northallerton DL6 . . . . . 210 E5
Wilberfoss YO41 . . . . . . 185 F6
Priory Dr YO21 . . . . 208 A6
Priory La 1 DN14 . . . . . . 204 C1
Priory Park Cl 3 LS25 . . . 202 A8
Priory Park Gr 2 LS25 . . . 202 B8
Priory Pk YO22 . . . . 31 C4
Priory Pl YO11 . . . . 100 B7
Priory Road or House
DN6 . . . . 206 E2
Priory St YO1 . . . . 233 A1
Priory View 2 BD23 . . . . 217 E8
Priory Villas DL10 . . . . . 209 D6
Priory Way
Barnoldswick BB18 . . . . . 171 D1
4 Ingleby Arncliffe DL6 . . 45 A7
9 Snaith DN14 . . . . 204 B1
Priory Wood Way YO31 . . 225 F2
Prison & Pol Mus★ HG4 . 214 D5
Pritchett Rd TS3 . . . . 7 C8
Promenade La HG1 . . . . 219 C3
Promenade Sq HG1 . . . . 219 C2
Prospect Ave
Normanton South WF6 . . . 200 A2
Sherburn in Elmet LS25 . . 195 F4
Prospect Bank
Bramham cum Oglethorpe
LS23 . . . . 188 F6
Scarborough YO12 . . . . . 212 D6
Prospect Cl
Camblesforth YO8 . . . . . 204 D5
Harrogate HG2 . . . . 220 C3
Monk Fryston LS25 . . . . . 202 A8
Pollington DN14 . . . . . . 207 F6
Prospect Cotts 6 HG3 . . 160 A6
Prospect Cres
13 Harrogate HG1 . . . . . 219 D2
Scarborough YO12 . . . . . 212 D6
Prospect Ct 3 LS24 . . . . 189 E6
Prospect Dr LS24 . . . . . . 189 E6
Prospect Field 5 YO22 . . 33 D4
Prospect Hill YO21 . . . . . 208 C5
Prospect Mount Rd
YO12 . . . . 212 C6
Prospect Pk YO12 . . . . . 212 D6
Prospect Pl
Harrogate HG1 . . . . 219 D2
Northallerton DL6 . . . . . 210 F4
28 Scarborough YO11 . . . 213 A6
Skipton BD23 . . . . 216 F4
Thornton-le-Dale YO18 . . 96 D6
10 Whitby YO22 . . . . 208 E6
Wistow YO8 . . . . 197 D6
Prospect Rd
Harrogate HG2 . . . . 220 C3
9 Scarborough YO12 . . . 212 D6
Prospects Cotts YO61 . . 117 C6
Prospect St 14 BD20 . . . 187 E7
Prospect Terr
Fulford YO10 . . . . 231 D6
15 Knaresborough HG5 . . 221 A6
1 Lingdale TS12 . . . . 9 F7
Micklefield LS25 . . . . . . 195 A3
York YO1 . . . . 233 B1
Prospect View
Appleton Wiske DL6 . . . . 24 B3
Northallerton DL6 . . . . . 210 E4
Prospect Way
5 Leeming DL7 . . . . 63 D4
Selby YO8 . . . . 232 D4
Prospect Way Ind Est
YO8 . . . . 232 D4
Prospect Gn 16 WF8 . . . 201 C2
Providence Pl
13 Filey YO14 . . . . 101 B3
Mickletown WR10 . . . . . 200 D6

Providence Terr HG1 . . . 219 D4
Pry Hills La
Hartoft YO18 . . . . 71 A8
Rosedale East Side YO18 . . 49 F2
Pudding Hill Rd DL11 . . . . 1 B6
Pudding Pie Hill★ YO7 . . 211 D1
Pudsey Wlk 3 DL1 . . . . . . 3 D4
Pudsley Wlk DL1 . . . . 3 D4
Pulleyn Cl 3 YO32 . . . . . 167 C8
Pulleyn Dr YO24 . . . . . . 227 F1
Pump Hill 4 HG5 . . . . . . 221 A6
Pump La
Kirklevington TS15 . . . . . 24 F8
4 Malton YO17 . . . . 215 C4
Purey Cust Nuffield Hospl
The YO31 . . . . 233 B3
Pye Busk Cl LA2 . . . . 129 B8
Pye La HG3 . . . . 160 F8
Pysbury Wlk 25 YO51 . . . 141 B5

Q

Quaker Cl
1 Reeth, Fremington &
Healaugh DL11 . . . . 38 B6
Scarborough YO12 . . . . . 212 C5
Quaker Gn 1 YO24 . . . . 230 C7
Quaker La DL6 . . . . 210 D5
Quakers La DL10 . . . . . . 209 B7
Quaker's La DL6 . . . . 44 D7
Quant Mews YO10 . . . . . 229 B3
Quarry Ave 20 WF11 . . . . 202 A2
Quarry Bank YO17 . . . . . 215 D5
Quarry Banks YO7 . . . . . 116 E2
Quarry Dr TS8 . . . . 6 E5
Quarry Gate YO13 . . . . . . 74 C1
Quarry Hill YO17 . . . . . . 120 F4
Quarry Hill La LS22 . . . . 180 B3
Quarry Hills La 22 DL8 . . 60 D5
Quarry La
Harrogate HG1 . . . . 219 C6
Osmotherley DL6 . . . . . . 45 C5
Pateley Bridge HG3 . . . . 137 C4
Quarry Moor La HG4 . . . 214 C3
Quarry Moor Nature
Reserve★ HG4 . . . . 214 B1
Quarry Mount YO12 . . . . 212 C3
Quarry Oval HG1 . . . . . . 219 C6
Quarry Rd
Eaglescliffe TS18 . . . . 5 F7
Norton DN6 . . . . 206 F2
Richmond DL10 . . . . 209 B7
Ripon HG4 . . . . 214 B2
Quay St YO11 . . . . 213 B6
Quay The YO8 . . . . 232 D6
Queen Anne's Ct 3 DL8 . . 63 A2
Queen Anne's Dr 4 DL8 . . 63 A2
Queen Annes Rd YO30 . . 233 A3
Queen Elizabeth Dr 10
YO13 . . . . 75 D5
Queen Elizabeth's Sixth Form
Coll 1 DL3 . . . . 3 C4
Queen Elizabeth Way TS18 . 6 D6
Queen Ethelburga's Coll
YO26 . . . . 164 C6
Queen Ethelburga's Gdns 6
HG3 . . . . 161 B2
Queen Ethelburga's Par 8
HG3 . . . . 161 B2
Queen Ethelburga's Pk 9
HG3 . . . . 161 B2
Queen Margarets Ave 4
WF11 . . . . 201 E4
Queen Margarets Cl 3
WF11 . . . . 201 E4
Queen Margaret's Dr
WF11 . . . . 201 E4
Queen Margaret's Ind Est
YO11 . . . . 212 E2
Queen Margaret's Rd 6
YO12 . . . . 212 F3
Queen Margarets Sch
YO19 . . . . 192 A5
Queen Marys Sch YO7 . . 115 A7
Queens Ave DL9 . . . . 40 E3
Queensbury Ct 15 WF6 . . 200 B1
Queens Cl DL10 . . . . 41 E5
Queen's Cl 8 HG2 . . . . . 219 C1
Queens Ct
Gainford DL2 . . . . 1 D7
Great Preston LS26 . . . . . 200 C7
Malton YO17 . . . . 215 D6
Richmond DL10 . . . . 209 C7
Queen's Ct YO1 . . . . 233 B2
Queens Dr
9 Stokesley TS9 . . . . . . 26 C8
Whitby YO22 . . . . 208 E3
Queen's Dr LS29 . . . . . . 218 A3
Queen's Drive La LS29 . . 218 A3
Queens Garth BD23 . . . . 172 A3
Queens Gate HG1 . . . . . 219 E2
Queens Gdns YO7 . . . . . 211 C1
Queen's Gdns
4 Ilkley LS29 . . . . 218 A3
Tadcaster LS24 . . . . 189 E6
Queen's Par YO12 . . . . . 213 A7
Queen's Park Dr WF10 . . 201 A4
Queens Rd
Knaresborough HG5 . . . . 221 C6
Richmond DL10 . . . . 209 C7
Queen's Rd
Harrogate HG2 . . . . 219 C1
Ilkley LS29 . . . . 218 A3
Queen's St 6 BD23 . . . . 217 B4
Queens Staith Mews
YO1 . . . . 233 B1

Plo–RAM 265

Queen's Staith Rd YO1 . . 233 B2
Queen St
10 Cowling BD22 . . . . . . 187 B6
Great Preston LS26 . . . . . 200 C7
Normanton South WF6 . . . 200 A1
18 Ripon HG4 . . . . 214 C5
Scarborough YO11 . . . . . 213 A6
4 Silsden BD20 . . . . 174 C1
Skelton & Brotton TS12 . . . 9 D7
York YO24 . . . . 233 A2
Queen's Terr
3 Filey YO14 . . . . 101 B3
Scarborough YO12 . . . . . 213 A7
Queensway WF8 . . . . . . 201 C2
Queen's Way YO62 . . . . . 70 B1
Queenswood Gr YO24 . . 227 D2
Queen Victoria St YO23 . 228 B1
Quentin Rd 19 DL9 . . . . . 40 E4
Quernmore Dr BB18 . . . . 186 A7
Quilt Mus & Gall The★
YO1 . . . . 233 C2

R

Raby La DL7 . . . . 22 E3
Raby Pk LS22 . . . . 180 B3
Raby Terr DL3 . . . . 3 C5
Racca Ave 11 WF11 . . . . 202 A2
Racca Gn WF11 . . . . 202 A2
Racecourse Ct DL10 . . . . 209 A8
Racecourse La DL7 . . . . 210 D3
Racecourse Mews YO7 . . 211 A2
Racecourse Rd
East Ayton/West Ayton
YO13 . . . . 99 B8
Irton YO12 . . . . 212 A1
Richmond DL10 . . . . 209 B8
York YO23 . . . . 231 B8
Race La
Carlton DN14 . . . . 204 B4
Sessay YO7 . . . . 116 C4
Rachel La DL11 . . . . 20 B5
Raghill La YO61 . . . . 142 A8
Raglan St HG1 . . . . 219 D2
Raglan Terr 3 YO21 . . . . 208 D5
Rag Robin Turn YO7 . . . . 66 B6
Raikes Ave BD23 . . . . . . 216 F5
Raikes La BD23 . . . . 156 A6
Raikes' La YO22 . . . . 32 E3
Raikes Rd BD23 . . . . 216 F5
Raikes The HG3 . . . . 137 E3
Raikeswood Cres BD23 . . 216 E5
Raikeswood Dr BD23 . . . 216 E5
Raikeswood Rd BD23 . . . 216 E5
Railer Bank HG4 . . . . . . 112 E6
Railway Ave WF8 . . . . . . 201 B1
Railway Cotts HG4 . . . . . 214 D1
Railway Rd
Follifoot HG3 . . . . 223 C7
Ilkley LS29 . . . . 218 A4
Railway St
16 Leyburn DL8 . . . . 60 D5
Norton YO17 . . . . 215 C3
Slingsby YO62 . . . . 120 B5
Railway Terr
Hurworth-on-Tees DL2 . . . 22 D8
Ilkley LS29 . . . . 218 C4
5 Normanton South WF6 . 200 A1
Thirsk YO7 . . . . 211 B2
York YO24 . . . . 228 A4
Railway View
Darlington DL1 . . . . 3 D4
Northallerton DL7 . . . . . 210 D3
York YO24 . . . . 230 E8
Raincliffe Ave
29 Filey YO14 . . . . 101 B3
Scarborough YO12 . . . . . 212 C5
Raincliffe Cres YO12 . . . 212 C5
Raincliffe Gr YO12 . . . . . 212 C4
Raincliffe Sch YO12 . . . . 212 B6
Raincliffe St 4 YO8 . . . . 232 C5
Raindale Rd YO18 . . . . . . 71 F6
Raines Dr 5 BD20 . . . . . 173 E3
Raines La BD23 . . . . 134 D3
Raines Lea BD23 . . . . . . 134 D3
Raines Mdws 6 BD23 . . . 134 D2
Raines Rd BD24 . . . . 131 C1
Rainford Cl 7 YO12 . . . . . 99 D6
Rainhall Cres BB18 . . . . 171 E1
Rainhall Rd BB18 . . . . . . 171 D1
Rainham Cl TS17 . . . . 6 B4
Rainhill Way 5 DL2 . . . . . 3 B7
Rainsborough Way 3
YO30 . . . . 228 A8
Rainsburgh La YO25 . . . . 126 A3
RAINTON 114 E6
Raisdale Rd TS9 . . . . 26 D1
Rakehill Rd LS15 . . . . . . 194 B8
Rake La YO21 . . . . 30 D6
Raker Cl YO19 . . . . 192 F7
Rakes La LA6 . . . . 103 D4
Rake The LA6 . . . . 103 D4
Raleigh St YO12 . . . . . . 212 E6
Ralph Butterfield Prim Sch
YO32 . . . . 166 F5
Ralph Garth YO26 . . . . . 181 D7
Rampart The YO23 . . . . . 190 D4
Ramsay Cl YO31 . . . . . . 233 C4
Ramsden Cl WF11 . . . . . 201 D4
Ramsden St LS25 . . . . . . 200 C8
Ramsey Ave YO23 . . . . . 231 B3
Ramsey Gdns 38 TS17 . . . . 5 F4
Ramsey St YO12 . . . . . . 212 E6
RAMSGILL 110 E1

Ramsgill DL1 3 E4
Ramshaw Dr BD23 217 A1
Ramshill Rd YO11 213 A4
Randal La HG3 160 D4
Range Rd DL9 40 A2
Rankin's Well Rd 4 BD23 217 B4
Rantreefold Rd LA2 128 F4
Rape Close La YO62 118 E4
Rape La YO62 93 B7
Raper La YO61 117 B3
Raper View LS25 194 F8
Rarber Top La LA6 103 D2
Rarey Dr YO17 124 E1
RASKELF 116 E2
Raskelf Rd
- 7 Brafferton YO61 115 F1
- Easingwold YO61 117 B1
Ratcliffe Ct YO30 224 C5
Ratcliffe St YO30 228 B7
Rathmall La YO26 164 C2
RATHMELL 153 C6
Rathmell CE Prim Sch BD24 153 B7
Rattan Row YO25 151 C6
Ratten Row
- Hunton DL8 61 E7
- Seamer YO12 99 C5
Raven Cl 10 YO12 99 F6
Raven Gr YO26 227 C4
Raven Hall Rd YO13 53 F7
RAVENSCAR 54 A8
Ravens Cl Brow LA2 102 C1
Ravenscroft Way BB18 171 E2
Ravensdale Rd DL3 3 B4
RAVENSEAT 15 C2
Ravensthorpe Prep Sch DL3 3 B5
Ravensville 1 BD20 187 F7
RAVENSWORTH 20 A7
Ravensworth Castle* DL11 20 A6
Ravensworth CE Prim Sch DL11 20 A6
Ravine Hill 17 YO14 101 B4
Ravine Rd YO14 101 B4
Ravine Top 7 YO14 101 B3
RAW 33 B4
Raw Bank DL11 37 E8
RAWCLIFFE
- Goole 205 A1
- York 224 E2
Rawcliffe Ave YO30 227 F8
Rawcliffe Cl 5 YO30 224 E2
Rawcliffe Croft YO30 224 D2
Rawcliffe Dr YO30 227 F8
Rawcliffe Ind Est YO30 224 E3
Rawcliffe Infant Sch YO30 224 E1
Rawcliffe La YO30 224 F1
Rawcliffe Landing YO30 224 C3
Rawcliffe Prim Sch DN14 205 A1
Rawcliffe Village YO30 224 E3
Rawcliffe Way YO30 224 E2
Rawcliff Rd YO18 72 A5
Rawdon Ave YO10 228 F4
Rawfield La WF11 201 D7
Raw Gap HG5 221 A6
Raw La
- Fylingdales YO22 33 B4
- Kirkby Wharfe with North Milford LS24 190 A3
- Towton LS24 189 F3
Rawlinson Rd DL9 209 D2
Raw Pasture Bank YO22 33 B5
Raw Pasture La YO22 33 C5
Rawson St HG1 219 E5
Ray Bridge La BD23 155 D1
RAYDALE 57 A1
Raydale Cl 2 HG5 221 D5
RAYGILL 186 E8
Raygill La BD20 186 E8
Ray La HG4 114 B1
Rayleigh Rd HG2 222 E8
Raylton Ave TS7 7 B5
Rayner St HG4 214 C5
Raynes Ct DL8 56 D5
Read Cl YO8 204 F5
Read Sch YO8 204 F5
Reas La YO51 141 D1
Reasty Hill YO13 53 E1
Reasty Rd YO13 53 D2
Recreation Rd
- 17 Pickering YO18 95 F6
- 2 Selby YO8 232 D6
Rectory Cl
- Bolton Percy YO23 190 D4
- Heslerton YO17 123 F6
Rectory Gdns YO23 228 B1
Rectory La
- Guisborough TS14 8 E6
- 3 Hurworth-on-Tees DL2 22 C8
- Longnewton TS21 5 A7
- Skipton BD23 217 A4
- Thornton-le-Dale YO18 96 E5
Red Bank Cl HG4 214 A3
Red Bank Dr HG4 214 A3
Red Bank La HG4 214 A3
Red Bank Rd HG4 214 A3
Redbarn Dr YO10 229 D4
Red Barnes Way DL1 3 E6
Red Brae Bank HG3 137 A3
Red Brow YO13 74 C5
Redcap La YO42 193 C5
Redcar Rd
- Guisborough TS14 8 F7
- Thornaby TS17 6 B7
Redcliff Cl 12 YO11 100 B7
Redcliffe Ct YO12 212 D7
Redcliffe Gdns YO12 212 C6
Redcliffe La YO11 100 D6
Redcliffe Rd YO12 212 D6
Redcoat Way 1 YO24 230 B8
Redeness St YO31 228 E5
Redfearn Mews HG2 222 D6
Red Gate DL8 57 C6
Redgrave Cl 4 YO31 228 E8
Red Hall La TS15 6 A1
Red Hall Prim Sch DL1 3 F6
RED HILL 201 A4
Redhill Ave WF10 201 A3
Redhill Cl HG1 219 D6
Redhill Dr WF10 201 A3
Redhill Field La YO23 182 D1
Redhill Infant Sch WF10 201 B4
Redhill Junior Sch WF10 201 B4
Redhill La LS25 201 D8
Red Hill La LS25 195 E1
Redhill Rd
- Castleford WF10 201 A4
- Harrogate HG1 219 C6
Red Hills La HG3 140 B3
Red Hills Rd HG4 214 B7
Redhill Wlk WF10 201 A3
Redhouse La YO8 204 F6
Red La
- Green Hammerton YO26 164 C3
- 4 Masham HG4 86 C3
Red Lion St BB18 172 B1
Redlish Rd HG3 136 E1
Redman Cl YO10 231 C8
Redmayne Sq YO32 167 B8
REDMIRE 59 C6
Redmires Cl YO30 225 A2
Redmire Sta DL8 59 C6
Red Rose Cl 3 DL2 3 A7
Redruth Dr 22 WF6 200 A2
Red Scar Dr YO12 212 A7
Red Scar La
- Newby & Scalby YO12 75 C4
- Scalby YO12 212 A8
Redshaw Cl 1 HG4 214 C4
Redshaw Gr 2 HG4 214 C4
Redthorn Dr YO31 225 F1
Red Twr* YO1 228 E4
Red Way
- Brompton DL6 43 F6
- Danby YO21 29 E6
- Farndale East YO62 48 E4
- Nether Silton DL6 45 D1
Redwing Rising 1 TS14 8 D6
Redwood Cl DL1 3 F4
Redwood Dr 6 YO32 166 E5
Reebys La LA2 129 F5
Reedshaw La BD22 186 F5
REETH 38 B6
Reeth Com Prim Sch DL11 38 B6
Reeth Rd
- Middlesbrough TS5 6 E8
- Richmond DL10 209 A7
- 2 Stockton-on-Tees TS18 5 E8
Reeval Cl 13 BB18 172 B1
Reeves The YO24 227 C1
Regency Ave TS6 7 E8
Regency Ct
- 3 Ilkley LS29 218 A3
- Northallerton DL6 210 F3
Regency Mews
- Northallerton DL7 210 D4
- 2 York YO24 230 F8
Regency Pk TS17 6 B4
Regent Ave
- Harrogate HG1 219 E3
- Skipton BD23 217 B5
Regent Cres BD23 217 B5
Regent Dr BD23 217 B5
Regent Gr HG1 219 E4
Regent Mount 2 HG1 220 C4
Regent Par HG1 219 E3
Regent Pl HG1 220 C4
Regent Rd
- Ilkley LS29 218 A4
- Skipton BD23 217 B5
Regents Ct
- Walkerville DL9 41 A4
- 14 York YO26 227 F5
Regents Mews 1 YO26 227 D6
Regent St
- Castleford WF10 200 E4
- Harrogate HG1 219 F3
- Normanton WF6 200 B2
- 1 Scarborough YO12 213 A6
- York YO10 228 E3
Regent Terr HG1 219 E3
Regimental Mus* YO1 233 B1
Reginald Gr YO23 228 C1
Reginald Terr YO8 232 D4
Reid Pk YO32 166 E5
Reid St Prim Sch DL3 3 C6
Reid Terr TS14 8 F6
REIGHTON 127 D6
Reighton Ave YO30 227 F8
Reighton Dr 10 YO30 224 F1
Rein Ct LS25 194 F8
Reins HG5 163 A7
Reivaulx Dr TS5 6 F8
Renfield Gr WF6 200 B2
Renshaw Gdns 8 YO26 227 E4
Renton Cl HG3 140 B5
Reservoir La 7 YO11 100 B8
Residence La HG4 214 D5
Resolution Way YO21 208 B5
Retreat Hospl The YO10 228 F2
Reygate Gr YO23 230 B2
Reynard Crag La HG3 160 C6
Reynolds St 15 YO14 101 B3
Rhobell View 3 TS17 5 F4
Rhodes Dr HG2 222 D6
Rhode's Hill La LS23 188 F6
Rhodes La LS23 188 D7
Rhodes St WF10 200 D4
Rhyddings Gdns LS29 218 D4
Rianbow La YO17 215 C6
Ribble Bank BD24 131 E4
Ribble Dr DL1 3 C3
Ribblehead Sta LA6 78 E1
Ribblehead Viaduct* LA6 78 D2
Ribstone Gr YO31 229 B6
Ribston Rd
- Little Ribston LS22 180 A7
- Spofforth with Stockeld HG3 179 F6
Riccal Dr
- 25 Helmsley YO62 92 F6
- Huttons Ambo YO17 121 C1
RICCALL 198 A8
Riccall La YO19 191 D1
Riccall Prim Sch YO19 191 F1
Riccal Moor La YO62 93 E4
Rice Gate YO13 74 D8
Rice La
- Aldwark YO61 142 C2
- Flaxton YO60 145 F2
Richard Gossop Ct 41 LS29 176 C1
Richard III Mus* YO31 233 C3
Richardson Ct YO8 196 F1
Richardson Rd TS17 6 A7
Richardson St YO23 228 C2
Richard St YO8 232 B5
Richard Taylor CE Prim Sch HG1 219 E6
Richard Thorntons CE (VA) Prim Sch LA6 102 E3
RICHMOND 209 C7
Richmond Ave
- 22 Barnoldswick BB18 171 D2
- Harrogate HG2 222 C7
- Knottingley WF11 201 D3
Richmond Castle* DL10 209 C6
Richmond CE Prim Sch DL10 209 D7
Richmond Cl HG2 222 C7
Richmond Ct LS29 218 C3
Richmondfield Ave LS15 194 C7
Richmondfield Cl LS15 194 C7
Richmondfield Cres LS15 194 C7
Richmondfield Cross LS15 194 C7
Richmondfield Dr LS15 194 B7
Richmondfield Garth LS15 194 C8
Richmondfield Gr LS15 194 C7
Richmondfield La LS15 194 C7
Richmondfield Mount LS15 194 C7
Richmondfield Way LS15 194 C8
Richmond Garth HG4 112 C5
Richmond Gate DL8 58 C4
Richmond Holt HG2 222 C7
Richmond Lower Sch DL10 209 C6
Richmond Methodist Prim Sch DL10 209 E7
Richmond Pl LS29 218 C3
Richmond Rd
- 12 Barnoldswick BB18 171 D2
- Barton DL10 21 E6
- Brompton-on-Swale DL10 41 A6
- Croft-on-Tees DL10 21 F6
- Harrogate HG2 222 C7
- Hipswell DL9 209 D1
- Leyburn DL8 60 D5
- Skeeby DL10 20 F1
Richmond Rise DL7 210 C3
Richmond Sch DL10 209 D7
Richmondshire Mus* DL10 209 C7
Richmond St YO31 228 E5
Richmond Swimming Pool DL10 209 D6
Richmond Way DL1 3 F4
Ridding Cres DN14 205 A1
Ridding Gate 5 LS21 176 F1
Ridding La DN14 205 A1
Riddings La HG4 112 C7
Riddings Rd LS29 218 B3
Riders La YO60 146 F2
Ridgedale Mount WF8 201 B2
Ridge Gn YO13 75 D5
Ridge La
- Roxby TS13 11 A6
- Silsden BD20 174 B4
- Sleights YO21 32 B7
- Staithes TS13 13 H1
Ridge Rd LS25 200 E8
Ridge The
- Coulby Newham TS8 7 A4
- Linton LS22 180 B2
Ridgeway
- Coulby Newham TS8 7 D5
- Darlington DL3 3 C8
- 10 Eastfield YO11 99 F7
- Skipton BD23 216 E6
- York YO26 227 B3
Ridgeway The WF11 201 F2
Ridgewood Cl DL1 3 F4
Riding Cl 4 BB18 171 E1
Ridings The
- 7 Boroughbridge YO51 141 B4
- Norton YO17 215 D2
Ridley Ave TS5 6 E8
Ridleys Fold 14 LS29 174 F4
Ridsdale St DL1 3 D5
RIEVAULX 92 B8
Rievaulx Abbey* YO62 92 B8
Rievaulx Ave HG5 221 C4
Rievaulx Bank YO62 92 B8
Rievaulx Cl HG5 221 C4
Rievaulx Ct 6 HG5 221 C4
Rievaulx Dr DL7 64 A6
Rievaulx Rd YO21 208 C6
Rievaulx Terr & Temples* YO62 92 B7
Rievaulx Way TS14 8 F6
Riffa Bsns Pk LS21 176 F1
Riffa La LS21 177 E2
Rigg Bank HG4 85 E3
Riggs Rd YO17 121 F5
Riggs Spring 5 HG3 137 F1
Rigg The TS15 5 E2
Rigg View YO22 32 F7
Rigton CE Prim Sch LS17 178 C4
Rigton Hill LS17 178 B4
Rileys Croft 3 BD23 153 F5
Riley St 41 BB18 172 A1
RILLINGTON 122 F5
Rillington Prim Sch YO17 122 F5
Rimington Ave DL10 209 D6
Rimington Way YO11 100 B7
Ringing Keld Hill YO13 54 A3
Rings The TS17 5 F5
Ringstone Rd
- Bishopthorpe YO23 231 B5
- York YO30 224 F3
Ringstones La LA2 129 A4
Ringway LS25 194 B3
Ringway Gr 11 DL2 4 C4
Ringwood Rd DL9 40 F3
Riparian Way BD20 187 F8
RIPLEY 161 C7
Ripley Bank HG3 137 C4
Ripley Castle* HG3 161 C7
Ripley Cl
- 11 Kirkbymoorside YO62 70 B1
- Normanton South WF6 200 B1
Ripley Dr
- Harrogate HG1 219 C6
- Normanton South WF6 200 B2
Ripley Endowed CE Prim Sch HG3 161 C7
Ripley Gr 3 YO32 166 E5
Ripley Rd
- Knaresborough HG5 220 E8
- Nidd HG3 161 E6
- Scotton HG5 162 A5
Ripley's Rd YO13 54 B1
Ripley Way HG1 219 C6
RIPON 214 E5
Ripon Bsns Pk HG4 214 E4
Ripon By-pass HG4 214 C2
Ripon Cath* HG4 214 C5
Ripon Coll HG4 214 A5
Ripon Com Hospl HG4 214 B5
Ripon Courthouse Mus* HG4 214 C5
Ripon Dr DL1 3 D4
Ripon Gram Sch HG4 214 A6
Ripon Horn The* HG4 214 C5
Ripon L Ctr HG4 214 D3
Ripon Loop Nature Reserve* HG4 113 F4
Ripon Racecourse* HG4 214 F2
Ripon RC Choir Sch HG4 214 A3
Ripon Rd
- Harrogate HG3 219 A7
- Middlesbrough TS7 7 E6
- Ripley HG3 161 D8
- South Stainley with Cayton HG3 139 E2
Ripon Spa Baths HG4 214 B5
Ripon Way
- Carlton Miniott YO7 89 C4
- Harrogate HG1 219 C5
Riseber DL8 60 C5
Risedale Com Coll DL9 209 F1
Risedale Rd DL9 209 B1
Rise The
- Huttons Ambo YO60 147 C6
- Kippax LS25 194 D1
- Knottingley WF11 201 E4
- Leavening YO17 147 E1
- Thornton Dale YO18 96 D5
- Whitby YO22 208 E6
Risewood YO41 168 B2
Rishworth Gr YO30 224 F2
RISPLITH 138 E7
Rivadale View LS29 218 B5
Rivelin Way
- 10 Filey YO14 101 A3
- York YO30 224 F2
Rivendell BD23 134 B3
Riverbank Trad Est DL1 3 D7
River Cl 2 YO8 198 B5
Riverdale 4 DN14 202 D4
Riverdale Gdns LS23 188 F8
Rivergarth DL1 3 F7
River La
- Brompton-on-Swale DL10 41 B6
- Kilburn High & Low YO61 91 B2
- West Haddlesey YO8 203 A5
River Pl BD23 155 D1
River Rd YO61 91 C2
Riversdale
- 17 Haxby YO32 166 F5
- 5 Settle BD24 131 D2
Riversdene TS9 26 B7
Riverside
- Clapham LA2 130 C8
- Gargrave BD23 155 D1
- Rawcliffe DN14 205 A2
- 28 Scalby YO12 75 D5
Riverside Ave LS21 177 A1
Riverside Bsns Pk LS29 218 D5
Riverside Cl
- 1 Elvington YO41 185 C2
- Farnley LS21 177 A1
- West Haddlesey YO8 203 A5
Riverside Cres
- 5 Otley LS21 177 A1
- York YO32 225 F6
Riverside Ct DN14 205 A2
Riverside Dr 3 LS21 177 A1
Riverside Gdns
- 2 Boroughbridge YO51 141 B6
- 2 Elvington YO41 185 C2
- 2 Poppleton YO26 165 F1
Riverside Mews 6 YO7 211 C3
Riverside Pk 4 LS21 177 A1
Riverside Prim Sch LS24 189 E6
Riverside Rd DL10 209 C6
Riverside View YO17 215 B3
Riverside Way DL1 3 E7
Riverside Wlk
- Airton BD23 155 A6
- Ilkley LS29 218 A5
- 1 Poppleton YO26 165 F1
- Ruswarp YO22 208 C4
- 5 Strensall YO32 167 A7
Riverslea TS9 26 B7
River St
- 1 Selby YO8 232 D6
- Trawden BB8 186 B2
- York YO23 233 B1
Riversvale Dr 21 YO26 165 F1
Riversway BD23 155 C1
River View
- 1 Barlby YO8 198 B5
- Boston Spa LS23 188 F8
- Ilkley LS29 218 E5
- Richmond DL10 209 D6
Riverview Ind Est DL1 3 D6
River View Rd HG4 214 C7
RNLI Whitby Mus* YO21 208 D7
Roach Grange Ave LS25 194 D2
Roald Ct DL10 209 E8
Roall La DN14 202 F4
Robb Cl YO7 211 A2
Roberts Cres HG1 219 D5
Robertson Rd
- Colburn DL9 40 F4
- Ripon HG4 113 D3
Roberts Sq HG1 219 D5
Robert St
- Harrogate HG1 219 D1
- Selby YO8 232 C5
Robert Wilkinson Prim Sch YO32 167 A7
Robin Cl 6 WF8 201 B2
Robin Gr 6 YO24 227 F3
Robin Hood Cl YO21 29 A6
Robin Hood Rd YO13 53 F8
ROBIN HOOD'S BAY 33 D4
Robin Hood's Bay Mus* YO22 33 D4
Robin Hood's Bay Rd YO22 33 A3
Robin La
- Bentham LA2 103 A1
- High Bentham LA2 129 A8
- Huby YO61 144 A4
Robinson Ct YO1 233 C2
Robinson Dr
- Harrogate HG2 222 B6
- York YO24 227 B2
Robinson Fold 18 BB18 171 D2
Robinson Rd 13 DL10 41 E4
Robinson St WF10 200 D6
Robson Ave TS17 6 B5
Roche Ave
- Harrogate HG1 219 F6
- York YO31 228 E8
Rockbourne Way 1 TS17 5 F6
Rockcliff Ct 15 LS24 189 E6
Rock Hill WF10 201 A3
Rockingham Ave YO31 229 A5
Rockingham Cl YO17 215 A3
Rockingham Ct LS24 189 E2
Rockingham Dr YO12 212 B7
Rockland Gdns YO12 212 D5
Rockley Grange Gdn LS25 194 B3
Rocks La YO13 75 D7
Rocks Lane Cl YO13 75 D7
Rock Terr WF10 201 A3
Rock View Terr BD23 217 D8
Rockville Dr BD23 217 C8
Rockwell Ave DL1 3 E7
Rockwood Cl 1 BD23 216 E4
Rockwood Dr BD23 216 E5
Rodney Terr 15 HG4 86 C3
Roebuck La LS21 176 F2
ROECLIFFE 140 F4
Roecliffe CE Prim Sch YO51 140 F4
Roecliffe Ct YO26 182 C8
Roecliffe La YO51 141 B5
Roedean Dr TS16 5 E4

Roe La LS25 . . . . 202 C7
Roger La TS8 . . . . 6 C4
Rogers Ct
　Woodthorpe YO24 . . . . . 230 C8
　York YO24 . . . . 230 C0
Rogers Sq 16 HG1 . . . . . 219 D2
Roker Cl DL1 . . . . 3 F6
Roker Rd HG1 . . . . 219 E4
Roland Ct YO32 . . . . 225 E3
Rolston Ave 3 YO31 . . . 225 E2
Roman Avenue N 17
　YO41 . . . . 168 D2
Roman Avenue S YO41 . 168 D1
ROMANBY 210 B3
Romanby Prim Sch DL7 . 210 B2
Romanby Rd DL7 . . . . . . 210 C3
Roman Cl
　Newby & Scalby YO12 . . . 212 A7
　4 Tadcaster LS24 . . . . . 189 E6
Roman Cres DL9 . . . . . . 209 C1
Roman Fort of Olicana *
　LS29 . . . . 218 B4
Roman Garth YO17 . . . . . 215 D4
Roman Rd
　Leeming DL7 . . . . 63 D4
　Middlesbrough TS5 . . . . . . 6 E8
　Tadcaster LS24 . . . . 189 C5
Romans Cl YO19 . . . . . . 197 F8
Roman Signal Sta * YO21. 12 D6
Roman Way YO12 . . . . . . 212 A7
Romany Rd 11 TS9 . . . . . . 8 A2
Rombalds Dr BD23 . . . . . 217 A2
Rombalds La LS29 . . . . . 218 E3
Rombalds View LS21 . . . 176 E1
Rombald's View LS29 . . . 218 D5
Romille St 15 BD23 . . . . . 217 A3
Ronaldshay Cl DL10 . . . . 209 E8
Ronaldshay Dr DL10 . . . . 209 E8
Ronway Ave HG4 . . . . . . 214 B2
Rookery Rd BB18 . . . . . . 171 E1
Rook St
　25 Barnoldswick BB18 . . 171 D1
　Lothersdale BD20 . . . . . . 186 F8
ROOKWITH 62 A1
Rookwood Ave LS25 . . . . 200 C8
Rookwood Rd TS7 . . . . 7 D6
Roomer La HG4 . . . . 86 B1
Roper Ct DL10 . . . . 209 C7
Ropers Ct YO23 . . . . 230 C3
Ropery La YO17 . . . . 124 E1
Ropery The
　15 Pickering YO18 . . . . . . 95 F7
　Whitby YO22 . . . . 208 E6
Ropery Wlk YO17 . . . . . . 215 C4
Ropewalk The YO31 . . . . 228 E5
Rope Wlk BD23 . . . . 217 A4
Ropner Gdns DL2 . . . . 4 C3
Rosamund Ave 21 YO18 . 95 F7
Roscoe St YO12 . . . . 212 F5
Rose Ave
　Sherburn in Elmet LS25 . . 195 F3
　Whitby YO21 . . . . 208 B7
Roseberry Ave
　Great Ayton TS9 . . . . 8 A2
　Stokesley TS9 . . . . 26 D8
Roseberry Cres TS9 . . . . . . 8 A2
Roseberry Ct TS9 . . . . . . 26 D6
Roseberry Dr 8 TS9 . . . . . 8 A2
Roseberry Gn HG4 . . . . . 113 C7
Roseberry Gr YO30 . . . . . 224 F3
Roseberry La
　Guisborough TS9 . . . . 8 B3
　Stillington YO61 . . . . 144 B6
Roseberry Mount TS14 . . . 8 E6
Roseberry Prim Sch TS9. . 8 A2
Roseberry Rd TS9 . . . . 8 A2
Roseberry Topping * TS9 . 8 C3
Rosebery Ave YO12 . . . . 212 E3
Rosebery St YO26 . . . . . 227 F6
Rosecomb Way 6 YO32 . 225 D7
Rose Cres
　Richmond DL10 . . . . 209 B7
　Sherburn in Elmet LS25. . . 195 F3
Rosecroft Ave TS13 . . . . . 10 D8
Rosecroft Way YO30 . . . 227 E8
Rose & Crown Yd 20
　YO21 . . . . 208 D6
Rose Ct LS25 . . . . 194 D4
Rosedale HG3 . . . . 222 D3
ROSEDALE ABBEY 49 E3
Rosedale Abbey Prim Sch
　YO18 . . . . 49 E2
Rosedale Ave YO26 . . . . 227 C4
Rosedale Chy Bank YO18. 49 E1
Rosedale Cl
　Pannal HG3 . . . . 222 D3
　3 Whitby YO21 . . . . 208 C6
Rosedale Cres
　Darlington DL3. . . . . 3 A6
　Guisborough TS14 . . . . . . 8 D6
Rosedale La
　Hinderwell TS13. . . . . 11 F8
　Staithes TS13. . . . . 13 L1
Rosedale Rd TS7 . . . . 7 D6
Rosedale Rise LS23 . . . . 188 E8
Rosedale St YO10 . . . . . . 228 D2
Rosegarth Ct TS9 . . . . . . 26 E5
Rosehill TS9 . . . . 8 A1
Rose Hill Dr 13 TS9 . . . . . 26 D7
Rosehill Sq 11 HG5 . . . . 221 B5
Rose Hill Way TS9 . . . . . . 26 C7
Rosehurst Gr HG3 . . . . . 222 E2
Rose La LS24 . . . . 196 A7
Roseland Dr 7 . . . . 7 C7
Rosemary Ct
　20 Easingwold YO61 . . . 143 C8

Rosemary Ct continued
　6 Tadcaster LS24 . . . . . 189 E6
　York YO1 . . . . 233 C2
Rosemary La 1 DL10 . . . 209 C6
Rosemary Pl YO1 . . . . . . 233 C2
Rosemary Row 5 LS24. . 189 E6
Rosemoor Cl
　Coulby Newham TS8 . . . . . 7 B5
　19 Hunmanby YO14 . . . 126 F8
Rosemount Cl
Rosemount Ct 4 BD20 . . 187 E6
Rosemount Dr WF6 . . . . 200 C1
Rosemount Rd 2 YO21. . 208 C5
Rosendale Ave YO17 . . . 215 F2
Rose St YO31 . . . . 228 C7
Rose Tree Gr YO32 . . . . . 225 D4
Rosevale Terr YO12 . . . . 212 E5
Roseville Ave
　Harrogate HG1 . . . . 220 A3
　Scarborough YO12 . . . . . 212 E6
Roseville Dr HG1. . . . . . . 220 A3
Roseville Rd HG1 . . . . . . 220 A3
Roseway HG1 . . . . 219 E5
Rosewood Cres HG1 . . . 220 B3
Rosewood Prim Sch TS8 . 7 A4
Roseworth TS9 . . . . 26 E5
Rosley St BB8 . . . . 186 B3
Roslyn Rd HG2 . . . . 220 A2
Rossett Acre Prim Sch
　HG2 . . . . 222 C7
Rossett Ave HG2 . . . . . . 222 C6
Rossett Beck HG2 . . . . . 222 C6
Rossett Cres HG2 . . . . . . 222 D6
Rossett Dr HG2 . . . . 222 C6
Rossett Garth HG2 . . . . . 222 C6
Rossett Gdns HG2. . . . . . 222 C6
ROSSETT GREEN 222 D5
Rossett Green La HG2 . . 222 C5
Rossett Holt Ave HG2 . . . 222 C7
Rossett Holt Cl HG2. . . . . 222 C8
Rossett Holt Dr HG2. . . . . 222 C7
Rossett Holt Gr HG2 . . . . 222 C7
Rossett Holt View HG2 . . 222 C7
Rossett Park Rd HG2 . . . 222 D6
Rossett Sch HG2. . . . . . . 222 B6
Rossett Sports Ctr HG2. . 222 C6
Rossett Way HG2 . . . . . . 222 C7
Rossiter Dr WF11 . . . . . . 201 E2
Rosslyn Ct TS18. . . . . 5 F8
Rosslyn St 1 YO30 . . . . . 228 A6
Rossway DL1 . . . . 3 F8
Rostle Top Rd 10 BB18 . . 172 A1
Rotary Way
　Faverdale DL3 . . . . 3 B8
　Ripon HG4 . . . . 214 D6
Rothbury Cl HG2. . . . . . . 220 D2
Rothbury St YO12 . . . . . . 212 E5
Rothesay Gr TS7 . . . . 7 D6
Roth Hill La YO19 . . . . . . 192 E3
Rotunda Mus * YO11. . . . 213 A5
Roughaw Cl BD23 . . . . . . 216 F2
Roughaw Rd BD23 . . . . . 217 A2
Roughley Bank DL7 . . . . . 63 C5
Rough Rd HG3 . . . . 161 A2
Rougier St YO1 . . . . 233 A2
Roundell Dr BD23 . . . . . . 171 F5
Roundell Rd BB18. . . . . . 171 E2
Roundhill Ave TS17 . . . . . 5 F4
Roundhill Cl 5 DL2 . . . . . 3 E1
Roundhill Junior Sch
　WF11 . . . . 201 D3
Round Hill Link YO30. . . . 224 F2
Roundhill Rd DL2 . . . . 3 E1
ROUNDHILL VILLAGE. 5 F5
Roundhouse Rd DL3 . . . . 3 B8
Routh Wlk 5 YO21. . . . . . 208 D7
Rowan Ave
　3 Filey YO14 . . . . 101 A4
　Malton YO17 . . . . 215 D6
　York YO32 . . . . 225 D4
Rowan Cl
　Gateforth YO8 . . . . 197 B1
　4 Hut Green DN14. . . . . 203 A2
　Scarborough YO12 . . . . . 212 C6
Rowan Ct
　8 Catterick DL10 . . . . . . 41 D5
　Leyburn DL8. . . . . 60 D5
Rowan Dr 5 TS9. . . . . 8 A2
Rowan Fields YO12. . . . . . 99 E7
Rowan Garth 22 BD20 . . 187 E7
Rowan La
　16 Hellifield BD23 . . . . . 154 B3
　Skirethorns BD23 . . . . . . 134 B3
Rowan Lea HG2. . . . . 222 B7
Rowan Pl YO32 . . . . 225 D4
Rowans The
　Dalton YO7 . . . . 115 F7
　Hellifield BD23 . . . . 154 A3
Rowans Way DL7 . . . . . . 210 B4
ROWDEN 160 F4
Rowden La HG3. . . . . 160 F5
Rowedale Cl 15 YO14. . . 126 F8
Rowen Ave 6 YO11 . . . . 117 D1
Rowlandhall La DN14 . . . 199 E1
Rowland Keld TS14 . . . . . 8 E5
Rowland St 18 BD23. . . . 217 A3
Rowley Cl 2 YO32 . . . . . 225 F7
Rowley Dr LS29. . . . . 218 F3
Rowmans The YO30 . . . . 224 C4
Rowntree Ave YO30 . . . . 228 C8
Roxburghe Dale WF7. . . . 200 C1
ROXBY 11 C7
Roxby Ave TS14. . . . . 8 E5
Roxby Gdns
　4 Eastfield YO12 . . . . . . 99 F7
　5 Thornton Dale YO18 . . 96 D5
Roxby La
　Roxby TS13 . . . . 11 C7

Roxby La continued
　Staithes TS13 . . . . 13 J1
Roxby Rd YO18 . . . . 96 D5
Roxby Terr 6 YO18 . . . . . 96 D5
Roval Albert Dr YO12. . . . 212 F8
Royal Ave YO11 . . . . 212 F4
Royal Chase YO24 . . . . . 230 F8
Royal Cres
　Harrogate HG2 . . . . 222 D8
　12 Scarborough YO11 . . 213 A4
　Whitby YO21 . . . . 208 C7
Royal Cres La 8 YO11 . . 212 F4
Royal George Dr TS16. . . . 5 D7
Royal Hall * HG1. . . . . . . 219 D3
Royal Par
　Filey YO14 . . . . 101 B3
　8 Harrogate HG1. . . . . . 219 C2
Royal Pump Room Mus *
　HG1. . . . . 219 C2
Royd Cl 18 BD20 . . . . . . 187 E7
Royd Ct 12 BD20 . . . . . . 187 E6
Royds Ave WF10 . . . . . . 201 B4
Royd's Rd YO8 . . . . 202 F6
Royd The TS15. . . . . 5 D2
Ruby St 3 YO23 . . . . 228 B1
Rudbeck Cl HG2 . . . . 220 C1
Rudbeck Cres HG2 . . . . . 220 C1
Rudbeck Dr HG2 . . . . . . 220 C1
RUDBY 25 D5
Rudby Bank TS15 . . . . . . 25 D5
Rudby Lea TS15. . . . . 25 C6
Rudcarr La YO19 . . . . . . 167 E1
Rudda Rd YO13 . . . . 53 F6
Rudding Dower HG3 . . . . 223 E7
Rudding La
　Follifoot HG3 . . . . 223 C5
　North Rigton HG3 . . . . . . 222 A1
Ruddings YO19 . . . . 193 A8
Ruddings Cl 9 YO32 . . . . 225 C8
Ruddings La
　Cowesby YO7 . . . . 66 C4
　Crakehall DL8 . . . . 62 D4
　Ellerton YO42 . . . . 193 E2
Ruddings Rd YO18 . . . . . . 72 B3
Ruddings The
　Selby YO8. . . . . 232 A4
　Wheldrake YO19 . . . . . . 193 A8
Rudgate
　Bilton-in-Ainsty with Bickerton
　　YO26 . . . . 181 B6
　Newton Kyme cum Toulston
　　LS24 . . . . 189 B6
　Walton LS23 . . . . 181 B1
Rudgate Bsns Pk YO26 . . 180 B7
Rudgate Cl LS23 . . . . . . 181 B1
Rudgate Gr YO26. . . . . . . 164 A4
Rudgate Pk LS23. . . . . . . 181 A2
Rudstone Gr LS25. . . . . . 195 F4
Ruebury La YO17 . . . . 45 B4
Rues La LS21 . . . . 176 C8
Ruffa La YO18 . . . . 96 A6
Ruffhams Cl YO19. . . . . . 192 F8
Ruffin La YO17. . . . . 147 D5
Ruff La YO61 . . . . 142 B5
Rufford Cl TS14. . . . . 8 F5
RUFFORTH 182 C6
Rufforth Prim Sch YO23 . 182 C6
Rumford Way DL6. . . . . . . 60 D6
Rumple Croft 4 LS21 . . . 176 F1
Runnymede 7 . . . . 7 D5
Runs Bank DL8 . . . . 60 D8
Runswick Ave
　Middlesbrough TS5 . . . . . . 6 E6
　Whitby YO21 . . . . 208 B6
　York YO26 . . . . 227 B4
RUNSWICK BAY 12 A7
Runswick La TS13. . . . . . . 11 F7
Rupert Rd LS29 . . . . 218 A5
Rushmere TS8 . . . . 7 B5
Rusholme La YO8 . . . . . . 205 A5
RUSHTON 98 D6
Rushton Ave 21 BB18. . . 172 A1
Rushwood Cl 6 YO32 . . . 166 F5
Ruskin Ave
　Middlesbrough TS5 . . . . . . 6 D7
　6 Skipton BD23 . . . . . . 216 D3
Ruskin Cl DL2. . . . . 22 D7
Ruskin Dr WF10 . . . . 201 A4
Russell Dixon Sq HG4 . . 214 B3
Russell Dr YO30. . . . . 227 E8
Russell St
　Harrogate HG2 . . . . 222 E7
　Skipton BD23 . . . . 217 A3
　York YO23 . . . . 228 B2
Russell Terr DL7 . . . . 63 D2
Russet Dr YO31 . . . . 229 B5
Russet Gr YO12 . . . . 212 C8
Russett Rd YO17 . . . . . . 215 B4
Ruston La YO13 . . . . 98 D7
RUSWARP 208 B3
Ruswarp Bank YO21. . . . 208 B3
Ruswarp CE Prim Sch
　YO21 . . . . 208 B3
Ruswarp Fields YO22. . . . 208 C3
Ruswarp La YO21 . . . . . . 208 B4
Ruswarp Pleasure Boats *
　YO21 . . . . 208 B3
Ruswarp Sta YO22 . . . . . 208 C3
Rutland Cl
　Copmanthorpe YO23 . . . 230 A3
　Harrogate HG1 . . . . 219 A2
Rutland Dr HG1. . . . . 219 A2
Rutland Pl 4 YO62 . . . . . . 92 F7
Rutland Rd HG1. . . . . 219 B2
Rutland St 38 YO14. . . . . 101 B3
Rutland Terr YO12 . . . . . 213 A7
Rutmoor Rd YO18 . . . . . . 71 E2
Ryburn Cl YO30 . . . . 224 F2

Rycroft Rd 3 YO12. . . . . . 75 E5
Rydal Ave
　Middlesbrough TS5 . . . . . . 6 E8
　York YO31 . . . . 229 A6
Rydal Cl 2 YO7. . . . . 89 C4
Rydal Cres 1 YO12 . . . . . 99 F7
Rydal Rd
　Darlington DL1. . . . . 3 E4
　Harrogate HG1 . . . . 220 B3
Ryder Cres 3 YO62 . . . . . 70 B1
Ryder Sq YO17 . . . . 215 C4
Ryder's Wynd 3 DL10. . . 209 C6
Rye Cl
　Haxby YO32 . . . . 225 C8
　Huttons Ambo YO17. . . . 121 C1
Ryecroft 7 YO32. . . . . 167 A6
Ryecroft Ave
　10 Norton DN6 . . . . 206 E2
　York YO24 . . . . 230 C7
Ryecroft Cl YO31 . . . . . . 229 C8
Ryecroft Gdns DN14. . . . 203 A2
Ryecroft Rd
　Glusburn BD20 . . . . 187 D8
　Norton DN6 . . . . 206 E1
Ryecroft Way 2 BD20 . . . 187 E8
Ryedale Cl
　Helmsley YO62. . . . . 92 F7
　Norton YO17 . . . . 215 F1
　Pontefract WF6 . . . . 200 A3
　Ulleskelf LS24 . . . . 190 B2
Ryedale Folk Mus * YO62. 70 C5
Ryedale Pk LS29 . . . . . . 218 D3
Ryedale Pl WF6 . . . . 200 A3
Ryedale Pool YO18. . . . . . 95 F6
Ryedale State Pk YO17 . . 215 C3
Ryedale View 2 YO62. . . . 70 B1
Ryedale Way YO8 . . . . . . 232 C3
Ryefield Cl 12 YO11 . . . . . 99 F7
Ryefield Rd 1 YO11. . . . . 100 A6
Ryegate 13 YO62 . . . . 92 F6
Ryegrass Gdns 16 WF10. 200 D3
Ryehill Cl YO32 . . . . 225 D5
Rye Hill Way TS8. . . . . 7 B4
Ryelands Pk 1 TS13 . . . . 11 A8
Ryeland St 9 BD20 . . . . . 187 E8
Ryemoor Rd YO32. . . . . . 225 C8
Rylatt Pl YO26 . . . . 227 B3
RYLSTONE. 156 B5
Rylstone Dr 1 BB18. . . . . 171 D1
Rymers Ct DL8 . . . . 3 E7
Rymer Way 4 YO7. . . . . . 211 C3
Ryndle Cres YO12 . . . . . 212 E8
Ryndleside YO12 . . . . . . 212 E7
Ryndle Wlk YO12. . . . . . . 212 E8
Ryngwoode Dr YO17 . . . 215 C6
RYTHER 190 F1
Rythergate 8 YO8 . . . . . . 197 B8
RYTON 121 F6
Ryton Old La YO17 . . . . . 121 F5
Ryton Stile Rd YO17 . . . . 215 C7

S

Sackville Rd BD20. . . . . . 174 C1
Sackville St
　20 Barnoldswick BB18 . . 171 D1
　Skipton BD23 . . . . 217 A3
Sacred Heart Prim Sch The
　LS29 . . . . 218 D4
Sacred Heart RC Prim Sch
　Ilkley LS29. . . . . 218 D4
　Romanby DL7. . . . . 210 D2
SADBERGE 4 B8
Sadberge Ct YO10. . . . . . 229 C3
Sadberge Rd DL2 . . . . 4 C5
Saddle Cl YO17 . . . . 215 D2
Saddlers Cl
　1 Copmanthorpe YO23 . 230 B3
　Huntington YO32 . . . . . . 225 F2
Saddlers Croft 8 LS29 . . 218 A4
Saddlers La WF11 . . . . . . 201 E5
Saddler's La WF11 . . . . . 201 E5
Saddlers Way YO26 . . . . 182 A6
Saddlers Wlk YO19. . . . . 192 A5
Sadler Dr TS7. . . . . 7 B6
Sadler Forster Way TS17. . 6 B5
Sadlers Ct
　Alne YO61 . . . . 143 A5
　26 Boroughbridge YO51 . 141 B5
Saffron Dr 6 DN14 . . . . . 204 C1
Saffron Mdw 19 HG3 . . . 161 B3
Sails Dr YO10. . . . . 229 B3
St Aelreds Cl YO31 . . . . . 228 F4
St Aelreds RC Prim Sch
　YO31. . . . . 229 B5
St Agathas Cl DL10 . . . . 209 C7
St Aidans CE High Sch
　HG2. . . . . 219 F1
St Aidans Rd LS26. . . . . 200 C8
St Aidan's Rd DL9. . . . . 209 D1
St Alkelda's Rd DL8 . . . . 60 E2
St Andrewgate YO1 . . . . 233 B2
St Andrew Pl YO1 . . . . . 233 C2
St Andrew's Ave HG2. . . 220 A3
St Andrew's Cres HG2. . . 220 A3
St Andrews Ct
　Rillington YO17 . . . . 122 F5
　Sadberge DL2 . . . . 4 C8
St Andrews Dr WF7 . . . . 200 E1
St Andrews Gate HG2 . . 220 A3
St Andrews Gr 2 DL7 . . . 210 D2
St Andrew's Gr 1 HG2 . . 220 B2
St Andrews Mdws HG4 . . 112 D5
St Andrew's Par 3 HG2. . 220 A2
St Andrew's Pl 2 HG2 . . 220 A2
St Andrews Rd YO21 . . . 208 B5

St Andrew's Rd
　Castleford WF10 . . . . . . 201 B5
　4 Harrogate HG2 . . . . . 220 B3
St Andrew's St 1 HG2 . . 220 A2
St Andrew's Wlk HG2 . . . 220 A2
St Ann Ct YO1 . . . . 228 C2
St Anne's Cres 3 DL10 . . 41 E4
St Annes Gdns DL2 . . . . . 4 C3
St Ann's Ct YO10. . . . . . 228 D2
St Ann's Staith 13 YO21 . 208 D7
St Anthonys Ave 2 DL7 . 210 E2
St Athan's Wlk HG2 . . . . 222 C7
St Aubyn's Pl YO24 . . . . 228 A2
St Augustines RC Prim Sch
　Coulby Newham TS8 . . . . . 7 B5
　Darlington DL3. . . . . 3 C5
St Augustines Sch YO12 212 C4
St Barnabas CE Prim Sch
　YO26. . . . . 227 F5
St Barnabas Ct 13 YO26 . 227 F5
St Bedes Ave 4 DL7 . . . . 210 D2
St Bedes RC Prim Sch DL1 . 3 D8
St Benedict Rd YO23 . . . 233 A1
St Benedicts RC Prim Sch
　Ampleforth YO62 . . . . . . 92 C1
　Garforth LS25 . . . . 194 C4
St Bernadettes RC Prim Sch
　TS7 . . . . 7 D6
St Boltophs Cl 4 WF11. . 202 A2
St Brides Ct 30 TS17. . . . . 5 F4
St Bridget's Ct YO23 . . . 233 B1
St Catherines Cl YO30 . . 224 C5
St Catherines Pl YO24. . . 228 A3
St Catherine's Rd HG2 . . 219 F1
St Chads Wharf YO23. . . 231 C8
St Christopher Cl 3
　DL7. . . . . 210 D2
St Christophers Dr 27
　LS29. . . . . 174 F4
St Clares Abbey DL3 . . . . 3 B5
St Clares RC Prim Sch TS5 . 6 D6
St Clement's Gr YO23 . . . 228 C2
St Clement's Rd HG2 . . . 220 A2
St Clements Road S HG2 220 A2
St Cuthbert Ave TS7. . . . . 7 C5
St Cuthbert Dr DL7. . . . . 210 B3
St Cuthbert's Ave 4 DL9 . 41 A5
St Cuthberts CE Prim Sch
　HG3. . . . . 137 B4
St Cuthberts Cl 15 HG3 . 137 B4
St Cuthbert's Gn DL10. . . 21 D8
St Cuthberts Wlk TS13 . . 10 D8
St Davids Gr 34 TS17 . . . . 5 F4
St Davids RC Tech Coll
　TS5 . . . . 6 E7
St Davids Rd LS21 . . . . . 176 F1
St David's View 9 DN14. 205 E4
St Denys' Rd YO1 . . . . . 233 C2
St Edmunds YO41 . . . . . 168 D2
St Edmunds Cl 1 DL10. . 41 C6
St Edward's Cl YO24 . . . 230 F8
St Edwards RC Prim Sch 3
　LS23. . . . . 188 E8
St Edwin's Cl DL2 . . . . . . 2 C6
St Francis of Assisi CE Prim
　TS17. . . . . 6 A5
St Francis Xavier Sch
　DL10. . . . . 209 C2
St Gabriels RC Prim Sch
　TS7 . . . . 7 D8
St George's Ave HG2 . . . 222 D7
St Georges CE Prim Sch
　DL2 . . . . 4 C4
St George's Gate DL2 . . . 4 B5
St Georges Gr 3 DL2 . . . 210 E2
St George's Pl YO24. . . . 227 F2
St Georges RC Prim Sch
　Eastfield YO11 . . . . 100 A1
　York YO10 . . . . 228 D2
St George's Rd HG2 . . . . 222 D7
St Georges Terr TS13 . . . 10 D8
St George's Wlk HG2. . . . 222 D6
St Gerards RC Prim Sch
　TS8. . . . . 6 F5
St Giles CE VA Prim Sch
　WF8 . . . . 201 B1
St Giles Cl YO7 . . . . 211 C3
St Giles' Cl 1 DL9 . . . . . 41 A5
St Giles Ct YO31 . . . . . . 233 B3
St Giles Rd YO30 . . . . . . 224 B5
St Giles Way YO23 . . . . . 230 A2
St Gregory's Cl DL8 . . . . 62 E4
St Gregory's Mews YO1 . 233 B2
St Heddas RC Prim Sch
　YO21. . . . . 31 A4
St Helena 11 YO51 . . . . . 141 B5
St Helens Cl DL7. . . . . . . 64 A7
St Helens Dr DL7. . . . . . . 64 A7
St Helen's Dr LS25 . . . . . 194 F4
St Helen's La
　Borrowby YO7 . . . . 65 C4
　Reighton YO14. . . . . 127 C6
St Helen's Rd
　Harrogate HG2 . . . . 223 A8
　5 York YO24 . . . . 230 E8
St Helen's Rise YO19 . . . 193 A7
St Helen's Sq
　28 Scarborough YO11 . . 213 A6
　York YO1 . . . . 233 B2
St Helen's Way LS29 . . . 218 D4
St Helens Wlk TS13 . . . . 10 D8
St Hilary DL10 . . . . 209 B7
St Hildas Bsns Ctr YO22 . 208 E6

St Hildas CE Prim Sch
YO62....................92 C1
St Hilda's Cres YO17...124 E8
St Hilda's Gdns 4 YO21.208 C7
St Hildas Mews YO10...229 B4
St Hildas RC Prim Sch 11
YO21.................208 D5
St Hilda's Rd 5 DL7....210 D2
St Hilda's Rd HG2.......219 F1
St Hilda's St YO17.......124 D7
St Hilda's Terr YO21.....208 D6
St Hilda's Wlk 6 YO62...92 C1
St Ians Croft 32 LS29....174 F4
St Ives Cl 3 WF8........201 B2
St Ives Cres WF10......201 B3
St James' Bsns Pk HG5..221 C4
St James CE Prim Sch
LS22.................180 C3
St James Chapel Flats
DL10.................209 B6
St James Cl
Melsonby DL10...........20 F7
York YO30..............224 E3
St James Croft YO24....227 D1
St James Ct
Rawcliffe DN14.........205 A1
Skipton BD23...........217 B4
St James Dr DL7........210 D2
St James' Dr HG2.......222 E8
St James Gn 9 YO7.....211 C3
St James' Mdw 18 YO51..141 B5
St James Mount YO23...228 A2
St James Pl 5 YO24.....227 D1
St James Rd
Northallerton DL7.......210 B2
Scarborough YO12.......212 E4
St James' Rd LS29......218 A3
St James's St 7 LS22....180 C3
St James Terr YO32.....232 C5
St John Fisher RC High Sch
HG2.................223 A8
St John Mews YO8.....232 B7
ST JOHN'S..............194 F8
St Johns Ave 25 LS29...174 F4
St John's Ave
42 Filey YO14..........101 B3
Milby YO51............141 B4
Scarborough YO12.......212 E5
St Johns CE Junior Sch
HG5.................221 B6
St Johns CE Prim Sch DL1..3 E4
St Johns Cl
Northallerton DL7.......210 E2
Sharow HG4............214 F7
St John's Cl
Aberford LS25.........188 F1
Bishop Monkton HG3.....140 B5
St John's Cres
Bishop Monkton HG3.....140 A5
Harrogate HG1.........219 D5
3 Leeming DL7..........63 D4
York YO31............233 C4
St Johns Ct
Skipton BD23...........217 A4
Ulleskelf LS24.........190 C3
St John's Dr
Harrogate HG1.........219 D6
North Rigton LS17......178 B4
St John's Garth
Aberford LS25.........194 F8
Ingleby Arncliffe DL6....45 A8
St John's Gr HG1........219 C5
St Johns Mdws YO61....117 C1
St Johns Pk DL11........2 A1
St Johns RC Sch for the Deaf
7 LS23..............188 E8
St Johns Rd DL9........209 F1
St John's Rd
Bishop Monkton HG3.....140 A5
Clifford LS23..........188 E7
Harrogate HG1.........219 D5
Ilkley LS29...........218 E4
2 Leeming DL7.........63 D4
Scarborough YO12.......212 E5
Scotton HG5...........162 A6
9 Stamford Bridge YO41.168 D2
St John's St BD20......173 C1
St John St
Harrogate HG1.........219 D2
York YO31............233 B3
St John's View LS23.....188 E8
St John's Way
Bishop Monkton HG3.....140 A5
Harrogate HG1.........219 D6
St John's Wlk
Harrogate HG1.........219 D6
Milby YO51............141 B7
St John the Baptist RC Prim
Sch WF6.............200 B1
St Joseph's Cl 2 YO12...212 C8
St Josephs Ct 9 YO24...227 B1
St Joseph's Ct LS25.....194 C3
St Josephs RC Prim Sch
Barnoldswick BB18......171 D2
Bishop Thornton HG3....139 A2
Castleford WF10........200 F4
Harrogate HG1.........219 C5
Loftus TS13...........10 D8
27 Pickering YO18.......95 F7
16 Tadcaster LS24.......189 E6
Wetherby LS22.........180 C3
St Joseph's St LS24.....189 E6
St Lawrences CE Prim Sch
YO10.................228 E3
St Leonards Ave YO8....198 B4

St Leonards Cl 30 LS29..174 F4
St Leonard's Cl
1 Harrogate HG2.......220 B1
7 Malton YO17.........215 C4
St Leonard's Cres YO12.212 D8
St Leonard's Oval HG2..220 A1
St Leonard's Pl YO30...233 B3
St Leonard's Rd TS14...8 E6
St Leonard's Rd HG2....220 A1
St Luke's Ave HG1......219 D4
St Lukes Cl DL7.........22 C2
St Luke's Cl
6 Boston Spa LS23.....188 E7
Harrogate HG1.........219 D4
St Luke's Cres YO12....212 C6
St Luke's Gr YO30......228 B7
St Lukes Hospl TS4......7 A8
St Luke's Mount HG1....219 D4
St Margaret's Ave LS26..200 B6
St Margarets Cl DL2......4 C3
St Margaret's Cl 3 HG5..221 A6
St Margaret's Garth 2
HG5.................221 A6
St Margaret's Gdns 4
HG5.................221 A6
St Margaret's Rd
Knaresborough HG5.....221 A6
Mickletown LS26........200 B6
St Margaret's Terr
6 Ilkley LS29..........218 B3
York YO1.............228 E4
St Mark's Ave HG2......222 D7
St Mark's Cl 1 YO12....212 C8
St Mark's Gr YO30......224 E2
St Martins Ave 2 LS21..176 F1
St Martin's Ave YO11....213 A4
St Martins CE Prim Sch
YO11.................213 C1
St Martins Cl
15 Catterick Garrison DL9.40 E4
Liverton Mines TS13.....10 D8
St Martins Field 12 LS21.176 F1
St Martin's La YO1......233 A3
St Martin's Pl 10 YO11...213 A4
St Martin's Rd 9 YO11...213 A4
St Martin's Sq 5 YO11...213 A4
St Martins Way 11 TS15..24 E8
St Mary's YO30.........233 A3
St Mary's Abbey★ YO1..233 A3
St Mary's App YO8......196 F1
St Mary's Ave
Barnoldswick BB18......171 E2
Harrogate HG2.........219 C2
12 Hemingbrough YO8...198 F1
14 Swillington LS26......194 A1
Thirsk YO7...........211 C4
St Marys Cath TS8......7 B5
St Marys CE Prim Sch
YO23.................182 D3
St Marys CE Sch
6 Boston Spa LS23.....188 E8
Longnewton TS21........5 A7
St Mary's Chapel★ YO11.213 C7
St Marys Cl
Cottingwith YO42.......193 C5
14 Stokesley TS9........26 C7
St Mary's Cl
Barton DL10...........21 D7
15 Haxby YO32.........166 E5
Ilkley LS29...........218 C4
South Cowton DL7......22 E2
Stensall YO32..........167 A7
Thirsk YO7...........211 C4
St Marys Coll TS4.......6 F7
St Mary's Cres YO22....208 E6
St Marys Ct YO7........90 C3
St Mary's Ct
Allerton Bywater LS26...200 D6
York YO23............233 A1
St Mary's Dr YO7.......211 C4
St Mary's Gate HG4.....214 D5
St Mary's Gdns BD23...173 B4
St Mary's Gr YO10......229 C4
St Mary's La YO30......233 A3
St Marys RC Prim Sch
Knaresborough HG5.....221 A7
Malton YO17...........215 D5
Richmond DL10.........209 E7
Selby YO8............232 B2
St Mary's St 6 YO11....213 B6
St Marys Terr YO30.....233 A3
St Mary's Terr YO30....233 A3
St Marys View YO8......232 B2
St Mary's Way YO7.....211 C4
St Mary's Wlk
Harrogate HG2.........219 C1
Mickletown LS25........194 F4
Middlesbrough TS5......6 E8
Scarborough YO11.......213 A7
Thirsk YO7...........211 C4
St Matthew's Cl
20 Leyburn DL8.........60 D5
4 Naburn YO19.........191 D8
St Maurice's Rd YO31...233 C3
St Michaels Ct
1 Northallerton DL7....210 D2
10 West Field YO24......227 B1
St Michaels Gn 15 WF6..200 A1
St Michael's La YO11....213 C1
St Michael's Mead HG4..138 E6
St Michael St 6 YO17....215 C4
St Michaels Way 29 LS29.174 F4
St Monicas Ct 4 YO61...143 D8
St Monicas Garth 17
YO61.................143 D8
St Monica's Hospl YO61.143 C8
St Nicholas Ave YO19...231 E4

St Nicholas CE Prim Sch
HG4.................87 A1
St Nicholas Cl
Copmanthorpe YO23.....230 A3
Richmond DL10.........209 F8
St Nicholas Cliff 5
YO11.................213 A5
St Nicholas Cres YO23..230 A3
St Nicholas Croft YO23..182 E3
St Nicholas Dr DL10....209 F7
St Nicholas Fields★
YO10.................228 F4
St Nicholas Gdns TS15...5 F2
St Nicholas Pl 1 YO10..228 F3
St Nicholas Rd
Copmanthorpe YO23.....230 A3
Harrogate HG2.........220 B2
Ilkley LS29...........218 A5
St Nicholas St
Norton YO17...........215 D3
Scarborough YO11.......213 A6
St Nicholas Way 22
YO32.................166 E5
St Olave's Cl HG4.......214 A3
St Olave's Rd YO30.....233 A4
St Olaves Sch YO30.....233 A3
St Oswalds CE Prim Sch
YO10.................231 E7
St Oswalds Cl
14 Catterick Garrison DL9.40 E4
Sowerby YO7..........89 F3
St Oswald's Cl
Catton YO41...........185 F6
Oswaldkirk YO62........93 A1
St Oswalds Ct
6 Filey YO14..........101 B3
York YO10............231 E7
St Oswalds Rd 13 DL9...40 E4
St Oswald's Rd YO10...231 D8
St Patricks RC Comp Sch
TS17.................6 C7
St Patricks RC Prim Sch
TS17.................6 B8
St Patrick's Way HG2....220 B2
St Paulinus Dr DL7.....210 B3
St Paulinus RC Prim Sch
TS14.................8 D6
St Pauls CE Prim Sch
YO24.................228 A3
St Pauls Cl 4 DL7......210 E2
St Paul's Cl DL10........41 B6
St Pauls Ct 3 WF8......201 C2
St Paul's Dr DL10........41 B6
St Paul's Gr LS29.......218 D4
St Pauls Mews YO24....228 A3
St Paul's Rd TS17.......6 B8
St Pauls Rise LS29......174 F4
St Paul's Sq YO24......228 A3
St Paul's Terr
Darlington DL3.........3 C7
York YO24............228 A4
St Peter & St Paul RC Prim
Sch DL8.............60 D5
St Peters Brafferton CE VA
Prim Sch YO61.......115 F1
St Peters CE Prim Sch
HG2.................219 D1
St Peters Cl
12 Brafferton YO61......115 F1
Rufforth YO26.........227 A5
St Peter's Cl 2 DL9.....41 A5
St Peter's Cres YO17...215 D3
St Peters Ct
31 Addingham LS29......174 F4
York YO30............233 A4
St Peter's Ct YO22......208 F4
St Peter's Garth LS14....188 A3
St Peter's Gr YO30.....233 A4
St Peters RC Prim Sch
YO12.................212 D8
St Peter's Rd
Drax YO8.............204 F5
Whitby YO22...........208 F4
St Peters Sch YO30.....233 A4
St Peter's Sq 8 HG2....219 C2
St Peter St YO17.......215 D3
St Philip's Gr YO30......228 A8
St Philip's Way 33 LS29..176 C1
St Princes St 12 HG1....219 D2
St Richards Rd 3 LS21..176 F1
St Robert Cl BD23......155 D1
St Robert Ct BD23......155 D1
St Robert's Cave★ HG5.221 D4
St Robert's Gdns HG5...221 B4
St Roberts Mews 4
HG1.................219 D1
St Roberts RC Prim Sch
HG1.................219 F4
St Robert's Rd HG5.....221 B4
St Ronan's Cl 3 HG2....220 A1
St Ronan's Rd 2 HG2...220 A1
St Sampsons Sq YO1....233 B2
St Saviourgate YO1.....233 C2
St Saviour's Pl YO1.....233 C2
St Sepulchre St 7 YO11.213 B6
St Stephen's Cl BD23...216 F4
St Stephens Com Prim Sch
16 BD23.............216 F4
St Stephens Gdns 1
DL7.................210 E2
St Stephens Mews YO30.225 A2
St Stephen's Rd YO24..227 C2
St Stephen's Sq YO24..227 C1
St Swithin's Wlk YO26..227 E4
St Teresas RC Prim Sch
DL1.................3 E4

St Therese of Lisieux RC
Prim Sch TS17........6 A4
St Thomas A Beckett Wlk
HG3.................161 A5
St Thomas More RC Prim
Sch TS4.............7 A7
St Thomas' Pl YO31.....233 B4
St Thomas's Cl 2 YO10.229 C4
St Thomas St YO11.....213 A6
St Thomas's Way YO26.164 C3
St Trinians Cl DL10.....209 F8
St Trinians Dr DL10.....209 F8
St Wilfred Dr DL7.......210 B3
St Wilfreds RC Prim Sch
YO31.................233 C3
St Wilfrid's Cl 7 YO32..167 B6
St Wilfrid's Cres 9 YO8.197 D1
St Wilfrid's Ct YO31....233 C3
St Wilfrid's Gdns HG4..214 C6
St Wilfrid's Pl 2 HG4...214 C5
St Wilfrids RC High Sch
WF7.................200 E1
St Wilfrids RC Prim Sch
HG4.................214 B5
St Wilfrid's Rd
1 Ripon HG4..........214 C5
8 Strensall YO32.......167 B6
St Williams Coll YO1....233 B3
St Winifred's Ave HG2..219 F1
St Winifred's Cl HG2....219 F1
St Winifred's Rd HG2...219 F1
St Wulstan Cl YO31.....228 E7
Salents La
Birdsall YO17..........148 C4
Duggleby YO17.........149 B6
Salerno Cl 6 DL9.......209 C1
Salisbury Cl 15 WF6....200 A2
Salisbury Dr 9 HG3.....161 B3
Salisbury Rd YO26......227 F5
Salisbury St
Scarborough YO12.......212 E3
Skipton BD23...........216 E5
Salisbury Ter YO26.....227 F5
Sallow Heath 16 HG3...161 B3
Salmond Rd 4 YO24....227 B1
Salmon La DL8.........87 B6
Salterforth La BB18.....171 C1
Salterforth Rd BB18.....172 A1
Saltergate Bank YO18...72 F8
Saltergate Com Junior &
Infant Sch HG3........219 A5
Saltergate Dr HG3......161 B3
Saltergill La TS15.......24 C8
Salter Rd YO11.........99 F6
Salters Ave DL1.........3 E6
Salters Gill 3 TS4.......6 F8
Salters Lane N DL1......3 D8
Salters Lane S DL1......3 E7
SALTON................94 D3
Salton La YO62.........94 B1
Salt Pans Rd YO13......54 D2
Salt Pan Well Steps 11
YO22.................208 E6
Salutation Rd DL3.......3 A4
Samian Way DL3........3 C8
Sam La YO61...........142 D8
Samuel Smith Old Brewery★
LS24.................189 E6
San Carlos Cl 1 DL9....40 E3
Sandacre Ct YO26......227 D5
Sandbeck DL10.........209 C5
Sandbeck Ind Est LS22..180 C4
Sandbeck La LS22......180 C4
Sandbeck Way LS22....180 C4
Sandcroft Cl 4 YO24...230 D8
Sandcroft Rd YO24.....230 D8
Sanderson Ave WF6....200 A1
Sanderson Ct YO26.....227 B3
Sanderson Rd DL2......3 F1
Sanders Way DL10.....41 E4
Sandfield La YO7.......88 D4
Sandfield Terr 4 LS24..189 F6
Sandgate 14 YO22.....208 D7
Sandgate Dr LS25......194 D1
Sandgate La LS25......194 E2
Sandgate Oval YO7.....115 A2
Sandgate Rd YO7......115 A1
Sandgate Rise LS25....194 E1
Sandgate Terr LS25....194 E1
Sandhill Bank YO21.....9 E1
Sandhill Cl
Harrogate HG1.........219 F6
Pontefract WF8........201 B2
Sandhill Dr HG1........219 F6
Sandhill La
17 Bedale DL8.........63 B3
Brayton YO8..........197 D2
Sutton upon Derwent
YO41.................185 E2
Sandhill Rise HG1......201 B2
Sandhill Way HG1......219 F6
Sandholme 2 YO32.....166 F5
Sandholme Cl
14 Easingwold YO61....143 D8
22 Settle BD24.........131 D2
Sandholmes La YO7.....89 E3
Sandhurst Gdns 4 YO12.212 B7
SANDHUTTON..........89 A4
SAND HUTTON.........168 B5
Sand Hutton CE Prim Sch
YO41.................168 B5
Sand Hutton La YO41...168 B5
Sandhutton La YO7.....89 B4

Sandiacres 5 YO8.......197 D1
Sand La
Barlby with Osgodby
YO8.................198 B4
Bubwith YO8...........199 D5
Heslerton YO17.........123 F7
Huby YO61............144 A5
Oldstead YO61.........91 D3
Sherburn YO17.........124 D7
South Milford LS25.....195 F2
Stillington YO61........144 A6
Wistow YO8...........197 E6
Sandmartin Cl YO24....230 D8
Sandmoor Cl 5 YO21...208 B5
Sandown Cl
Bagby YO7............90 B3
York YO24............227 E2
Sandpiper Cl
6 Eastfield YO12.......99 E6
1 Filey YO14..........101 A3
Sandpit La YO62........69 B1
Sandriggs DL3..........3 B7
Sandringham Cl YO00...140 C1
Sandringham Rd
Byram cum Sutton WF11.201 E4
Lockwood TS12........9 F6
Middlesbrough TS3......7 B8
2 Ripon HG4..........214 C3
6 Wetherby LS22......180 C3
Sandringham St
4 Scarborough YO12...212 F7
York YO10............228 D2
Sandrock Rd 3 WF8....201 C1
Sands YO14...........127 D7
SANDSEND.............13 A3
Sandsend Rd
Newholm-cum-Dunsley
YO21.................13 A3
Whitby YO21..........208 A8
Sandside
Scarborough YO11.......213 B6
Whitby YO22..........208 D7
Sands La
Hunmanby YO14........127 A8
Rillington YO17.........122 F5
Sandsprunt La YO13....97 E6
Sands Rd YO14........127 B7
Sandstock Rd YO31....229 B7
Sandwath La LS24......196 A8
Sandway Ave 12 YO8...197 B1
Sandway Cl 11 YO8....197 B1
Sandway Dr
Camblesforth YO8......204 D4
1 Thorpe Willoughby YO8.197 B1
Sandwith La DN14......204 B4
Sandwood Pk TS14.....8 D5
Sandy Bank
Farnham HG5..........162 D2
Northallerton DL6......210 F3
Romanby DL6.........65 A7
Sandybed Cres YO12...212 C4
Sandybed La
Scarborough YO12.......212 C4
Wykeham YO13........98 F6
Sandy Flatts La TS5.....6 F6
Sandyforth La BD22....186 E5
Sandy Gap YO32.......225 C7
Sandy Gate HG3.......159 A6
Sandy La
Alne YO61............143 A4
Dalton YO7...........116 A8
5 Embsay BD23.......217 C2
Harton YO60..........168 B8
18 Haxby YO32........166 E5
High & Low Bishopside
HG3.................137 D3
Humberton YO61.......141 D8
North Duffield YO8.....198 F8
Ripon HG4............214 B2
Scampston YO17.......123 B5
Stockton on the Forest
YO32.................167 E4
Sandyland 29 YO32.....166 E5
Sandylands Bsns Ctr
BD23.................216 E3
Sandylands Sports Ctr
BD23.................216 F3
Sandy Leas La TS21....5 A8
Sandyridge YO26......224 A1
Sandy Rise YO8........232 C5
Sarah's Croft BD23.....155 A1
Sargent Ave YO23......230 F4
SATRON...............36 D4
Saunters Way WF6.....200 A2
Savage Yd 17 HG5.....221 A6
Savile Pl
Castleford WF10.......200 E4
Mickletown LS26.......200 B6
Saville Gr YO30........228 A8
Saville St YO17........215 C4
SAWDON...............98 C7
SAWLEY...............138 F6
Sawley Cl BD23........217 C2
Sawley Moor La HG4...138 D6
Sawley St 1 BD23......216 D3
Sawmill La YO62.......92 G6
Saw Mill La 15 LS29....175 A4
Saw Wells Ct LS24.....195 F6
Saw Wells La LS24.....195 F6
Sawyer's Cres YO23....230 D2
Sawyers Garth 9 LS29..175 A4
Sawyers Wlk 9 YO19...184 F7
Saxford Way 8 YO32...166 D5
Saxon Cl
Shipton YO30..........165 F5
6 Thorpe Willoughby YO8.197 B1
Saxon Dr YO17........122 F5
Saxonfield TS8.........7 A6

Saxon Grange LS25 ... 195 F3
Saxon Pl YO31 ... 228 E7
Saxon Rd
  Catterick Garrison DL9 ... 209 E1
  Ripon HG4 ... 214 D5
  Stamford Bridge YO41 ... 168 D2
  Whitby YO21 ... 208 B7
Saxon Vale YO30 ... 165 F5
SAXTON ... 195 D8
Saxton CE Prim Sch LS24 ... 195 D7
Saxton Ct LS24 ... 195 D8
Saxton La LS24 ... 195 E8
Saxty Way YO7 ... 211 A1
Scabbate Gate BD23 ... 108 B3
SCACKLETON ... 119 C4
Scackleton Bank YO62 ... 119 C4
Scackleton La YO62 ... 119 C3
Scafell Cl 4 YO30 ... 224 E1
Scaggiethorpe La YO26 ... 165 D2
SCAGGLETHORPE ... 122 D3
Scagglethorpe La YO17 ... 122 C4
Scaife Gdns YO31 ... 228 C7
Scaife Mews YO31 ... 228 C7
Scaife Shay La YO7 ... 116 A7
Scaife St YO31 ... 228 C7
SCALBY ... 75 D6
Scalby Ave YO12 ... 212 C8
Scalby Beck Rd 27 YO13 ... 75 D5
Scalby Mills Rd YO12 ... 75 F5
Scalby Rd YO12 ... 212 D5
Scalby Sch YO12 ... 212 B8
Scaldhill La YO51 ... 141 C7
Scalehaw La BD23 ... 153 F5
Scale Hill LS21 ... 177 D2
Scale The BD23 ... 157 D3
SCALING ... 11 A4
SCALING DAM ... 11 A4
Scallow Bank La DL8 ... 59 B6
Scalm La
  Hambleton YO8 ... 196 F2
  Selby YO8 ... 197 A4
SCAMPSTON ... 123 A6
Scampston Hall★ YO17 ... 123 A6
Scampton Cl TS17 ... 6 A6
Scarah Bank HG3 ... 161 B8
Scarah La HG3 ... 140 A2
Scarbeck Bank DL11 ... 19 D7
SCARBOROUGH ... 213 B5
Scarborough Art Gall & Cres Art Studio★ YO11 ... 213 A5
Scarborough Bsns Pk YO11 ... 99 F6
Scarborough Castle★ YO11 ... 213 C7
Scarborough General Hospl YO12 ... 212 B6
Scarborough Indoor Pool★ YO12 ... 212 E8
Scarborough Rd
  Gristhorpe YO14 ... 101 A4
  Heslerton YO17 ... 123 F6
  Langtoft YO25 ... 151 C7
  Norton-on-Derwent YO17 ... 122 A3
  Norton YO17 ... 215 F4
  Seamer YO12 ... 99 D6
  Stainton Dale YO13 ... 53 F8
Scarborough Sixth Form Coll YO12 ... 212 C4
Scarborough Sports Ctr YO11 ... 213 A2
Scarborough Sta YO11 ... 212 F5
Scarborough Terr YO30 ... 233 B4
Scarcroft Hill YO24 ... 228 B2
Scarcroft La YO23 ... 233 A1
Scarcroft Prim Sch YO23 ... 233 A1
Scarcroft Rd YO24 ... 233 A1
Scarcroft View YO23 ... 233 A1
Scardale Cres YO12 ... 212 E8
Scardale Ct YO8 ... 232 A2
Scarer's La YO26 ... 142 B2
Scar Field 9 BD23 ... 134 E2
Scargill Rd HG1 ... 219 B4
Scar Hos DL11 ... 35 F5
Scarhouse La DL11 ... 17 E2
Scarlet Balk La YO17 ... 122 C1
Scar Rd BD23 ... 171 E6
Scar St 2 BD23 ... 134 E2
Scarth Cl 3 TS12 ... 9 F7
SCARTHINGWELL ... 195 F7
Scarthingwell Cres LS24 ... 195 D8
Scarthingwell La LS24 ... 195 E8
Scarth Nick
  Preston-under-Scar DL8 ... 59 E6
  Whorlton DL6 ... 45 D6
Scate Moor La YO26 ... 163 F3
Scaudercroft 13 YO19 ... 184 F7
Scawling End Rd YO61 ... 91 C3
Scawthorpe Cl WF8 ... 201 C1
SCAWTON ... 91 E6
Scawton Ave 1 YO31 ... 225 E2
Scholars Gate
  Guisborough TS14 ... 8 E5
  West Garforth LS25 ... 194 C3
Scholars Pk DL3 ... 3 B5
Scholes La BD22 ... 187 F1
Scholes Park Ave 3 YO12 ... 75 F5
Scholes Park Cliff 1 YO12 ... 75 F5
Scholes Park Dr 2 YO12 ... 75 F5
Scholes Park Rd YO12 ... 75 E5
Scholes Rd WF10 ... 201 B5
Scholla La DL6 ... 210 F5
Scholla View DL6 ... 210 F5
School Bank DL10 ... 21 C4
School Cl
  Huby YO61 ... 144 A4
School Cl *continued*
  Selby YO8 ... 232 B3
  16 Stamford Bridge YO41 ... 168 D2
School Croft WF11 ... 201 E4
School Fields BB18 ... 172 A2
School Garth YO7 ... 89 E3
Schoolgate LS15 ... 194 C8
School Hill
  Bainbridge DL8 ... 57 D5
  8 Settle BD24 ... 131 E2
School House Dr YO12 ... 99 D6
Schoolhouse Terr LS22 ... 180 B5
School La
  Addingham LS29 ... 174 F5
  Askham Richard YO23 ... 182 D3
  Bellerby DL8 ... 60 D7
  Bishopthorpe YO23 ... 231 A4
  Burton Fleming YO25 ... 126 E3
  Collingham LS22 ... 188 A8
  Copmanthorpe YO23 ... 230 A2
  Dacre HG3 ... 159 F8
  Earby BB18 ... 172 A1
  Easington BB7 ... 152 B3
  Eppleby DL11 ... 1 D4
  Great Ayton TS9 ... 8 A1
  Heslington YO10 ... 229 B1
  Laneshaw Bridge BB8 ... 186 C3
  Lawkland LA2 ... 130 D3
  Lotherton cum Aberford LS25 ... 194 F8
  Malton YO17 ... 215 C4
  4 Nawton YO62 ... 93 D7
  Newton-le-Willows DL8 ... 62 B4
  Osmotherley DL6 ... 45 B4
  23 Poppleton YO26 ... 165 F1
  South Milford LS25 ... 195 F2
  8 Spofforth HG3 ... 179 E6
  Thornton-le-Beans DL6 ... 65 B5
  Walton LS23 ... 180 F2
  Wray-with-Botton LA2 ... 128 A6
  York YO10 ... 231 E7
School Rd
  Hemingbrough YO8 ... 198 F1
  Wetherby LS22 ... 180 C3
School St
  Castleford WF10 ... 200 F5
  2 Earby BB18 ... 186 A7
  York YO24 ... 227 D3
Scoreby La
  Gate Helmsley YO41 ... 168 B2
  Kexby YO41 ... 168 B1
  Low Catton YO41 ... 185 B8
Score Ray La YO26 ... 164 A5
Scoresby Terr 2 YO21 ... 208 D5
SCORTON ... 41 F7
Scoska Wood National Nature Reserve★ BD23 ... 107 B3
Scosthrop La BD23 ... 154 E6
Scotch Cnr
  Middleton Tyas DL10 ... 21 B4
  Oldstead YO61 ... 91 C4
Scotch George La HG5 ... 221 A7
Scotchman La YO60 ... 168 A8
Scot Gate DL8 ... 59 D3
Scots Dike Terr DL10 ... 209 D6
Scots Dyke Cl DL10 ... 20 F7
Scott Cl
  Catterick DL10 ... 41 E4
  35 Glusburn BD20 ... 187 E7
  13 Swillington LS26 ... 194 A1
Scott Hill DL8 ... 57 D5
Scott Moncrieff Rd YO32 ... 167 B6
SCOTTON
  Harrogate ... 162 A6
  Richmond ... 40 F2
Scotton Bank DL8 ... 40 D2
Scotton Ct HG5 ... 162 A6
Scotton Dr HG5 ... 220 C8
Scotton Gdns 8 DL9 ... 40 E3
Scotton Gr
  Knaresborough HG5 ... 220 C8
  Scotton HG5 ... 162 A5
Scotton Lingerfield Sch HG5 ... 162 B7
Scotton Moor HG5 ... 220 C8
Scotton Pk DL9 ... 40 E3
Scotton Rd DL9 ... 40 E3
Scott Rd YO8 ... 232 C6
Scott St YO23 ... 228 C2
Scraper La YO22 ... 32 F7
SCRAYINGHAM ... 168 F7
Scriftain La LS22 ... 180 C5
SCRIVEN ... 162 D5
Scriven Gr 8 YO32 ... 166 F5
Scriven Rd HG5 ... 221 A7
Scroggs La DL8 ... 86 E7
Scrogs La DL8 ... 59 B6
Scrope Ave 4 YO31 ... 228 E5
SCRUTON ... 63 D7
Scugdale Rd DL6 ... 45 E8
Scurragh House La DL10 ... 21 C2
Scurragh La DL10 ... 21 B2
Sea App YO14 ... 100 F6
Sea Cliff Cres YO11 ... 213 B2
Sea Cliff Rd YO11 ... 213 B2
Seafield Ave 1 YO11 ... 100 B7
Seafire Cl YO30 ... 225 A3
Seagram Cres DL10 ... 209 C8
Seakel La YO23 ... 182 C2
Seal Bank BD23 ... 81 D1
Sea Life & Marine Sanctuary★ YO12 ... 75 F5
SEAMER
  Middlesbrough ... 6 F1
  Scarborough ... 99 E6
Seamer & Irton Prim Sch YO12 ... 99 D6
Seamer Moor Hill YO12 ... 212 B1
Seamer Moor La YO12 ... 212 B1
Seamer Rd
  East Ayton YO13 ... 99 B7
  Eastfield YO12 ... 99 F8
  Hilton TS15 ... 6 C2
  Maltby TS8 ... 6 E3
  Scarborough YO12 ... 212 E3
  Thornton TS8 ... 6 D4
Seamer Road Cnr YO12 ... 212 E4
Seamer Road Ret Pk YO12 ... 212 E1
Seamer St 2 YO12 ... 212 E3
Seamer Sta YO11 ... 99 F6
Seaton Cl YO10 ... 229 C4
Seaton Cres TS13 ... 13 K2
Seaton Garth TS13 ... 13 K2
Seave Close La YO26 ... 164 D2
Seavegate 4 YO13 ... 99 B8
Seavegate Cl 3 YO13 ... 99 B8
SEAVE GREEN ... 47 A7
Sea View YO14 ... 101 C1
Seaview Ave 5 YO12 ... 75 E5
Sea View Cl
  5 Scarborough YO11 ... 100 B8
  Whitby YO21 ... 208 A6
Sea View Cres YO11 ... 100 B8
Sea View Dr 13 YO11 ... 100 B8
Sea View Gdns 6 YO11 ... 100 B8
Sea View Gr 4 YO11 ... 100 B8
Second Ave
  Menwith with Darley HG3 ... 160 A4
  Wetherby LS22 ... 180 C3
  York YO31 ... 228 F6
Second Comm La YO8 ... 197 C4
Sedbergh Dr LS29 ... 218 B3
Sedbergh Pk LS29 ... 218 B3
Sedber La 5 BD23 ... 134 E2
SEDBUSK ... 56 E6
Sedbusk La DL8 ... 56 D6
Sedgefield Rd TS5 ... 6 E6
Sedge Rise LS24 ... 189 D5
Sedley Cl HG1 ... 219 E7
Seed Hill LA6 ... 103 D4
Sefton Ave YO31 ... 228 F8
Sefton Dr LS29 ... 218 B3
Sefton Way TS15 ... 5 D2
Seggans Rd YO26 ... 142 A1
Seg La YO8 ... 204 F3
Segrave Rd DL9 ... 40 E4
Segrave Wlk 10 YO26 ... 227 E4
Selaby Ct DL2 ... 1 C8
Selbourne Terr 9 BB18 ... 172 B1
SELBY ... 232 C6
Selby Abbey★ YO8 ... 232 D5
Selby Abbey CE Prim Sch YO8 ... 232 C5
Selby Bsns Pk YO8 ... 232 D1
Selby Coll YO8 ... 232 F3
Selby Coll (1811 Ctr) YO8 ... 232 C5
Selby Coll (Tadcaster Learning Ctr) LS24 ... 189 E6
Selby Com Prim Sch YO8 ... 232 B5
Selby Cres DL3 ... 3 A7
Selby High Sch YO8 ... 232 B4
Selby Ironworks Bsns Ctr YO8 ... 232 D5
Selby Rd
  Eggborough DN14 ... 202 F1
  Fulford YO19 ... 231 E6
  Garforth LS15 ... 194 A3
  Ledston LS25 ... 195 A2
  Riccall YO19 ... 198 A8
  Snaith DN14 ... 204 C1
  Swillington LS15 ... 194 A3
  Wistow YO8 ... 197 D6
  Womersley DN14 ... 207 A4
Selby Rly Sports Club YO8 ... 232 D5
Selby Sta YO8 ... 232 D5
Selby War Memorial Hospl YO8 ... 232 B4
Seldon Rd YO26 ... 227 E5
Self Gdns YO62 ... 70 F3
Selley Park Dr YO12 ... 212 B4
SELLY HILL ... 32 A8
Selly Park Rd YO12 ... 212 B4
SELSIDE ... 105 A6
Selside Shaw BD24 ... 105 A7
Selstone Cres 7 YO22 ... 32 A6
Semer Water Nature Reserve★ DL8 ... 57 B1
Senhouse Rd DL1 ... 3 F5
Seph Way YO17 ... 215 A2
Sergeant Bank HG4 ... 86 B8
Serinity Hallow TS12 ... 9 E8
SESSAY ... 116 B6
Sessay CE Prim Sch YO7 ... 116 C5
Sessions House Yd 10 WF8 ... 201 B1
Seton Cty Prim Sch TS13 ... 13 K2
SETTLE ... 131 E3
Settle CE Prim Sch BD24 ... 131 E2
Settle Coll BD24 ... 131 D2
Settle Mid Sch BD24 ... 131 D3
Settle Rd BD23 ... 155 A6
Settle Sta BD24 ... 131 D2
SETTRINGTON ... 122 D1
Settrington CE Prim Sch YO17 ... 122 D1
Settrington Rd YO12 ... 212 B5
Seven St YO17 ... 121 C1
Seventh Ave YO31 ... 228 F5
Seven Wells YO17 ... 121 A4
Severfield Cl YO7 ... 211 D2
Severn Dr
  Garforth LS25 ... 194 D3
  Guisborough TS14 ... 8 E6
Severn Gn YO26 ... 227 C8
Severn Way DL1 ... 3 D3
Severus Ave YO24 ... 227 D4
Severus St YO24 ... 227 D3
Sewell's Cave★ LA2 ... 131 A5
SEXHOW ... 25 D4
Sexhow La TS9 ... 25 F4
Seymour Cres TS16 ... 5 D4
Seymour Gr
  Eaglescliffe TS16 ... 5 D4
  York YO31 ... 228 F6
Shackleton Cl YO21 ... 208 C5
Shady La BD20 ... 173 C2
Shaftesbury Ave DN14 ... 202 C3
Shaker Stile Rd YO18 ... 96 B7
Shakespeare Ave 2 DN6 ... 206 E1
Shakespeare Cl 3 DL10 ... 41 C7
Shakespeare Cres WF10 ... 201 B3
Shallowdale Gr 1 YO10 ... 229 C3
Shambles La HG4 ... 114 D5
Shambles The 8 YO17 ... 215 C4
Shandon Pk TS8 ... 7 B5
Shandy Hall★ YO61 ... 117 D8
Shannon Cl 26 LS29 ... 175 C2
Shannon Lea DL2 ... 4 D4
SHAROW ... 214 F6
Sharow CE Prim Sch HG4 ... 214 F7
Sharow La HG4 ... 214 E6
Sharpe Howe★ YO11 ... 126 A8
Sharphaw Ave BD23 ... 217 A2
Sharphaw View BD23 ... 155 D1
Sharp Hill Cl 13 DL8 ... 60 E2
Sharp Hill La YO8 ... 204 F6
Shaw Ave WF6 ... 200 B1
Shaw Barn La LS22 ... 180 B3
Shaw Cl
  Garforth LS25 ... 194 D3
  Normanton South WF6 ... 200 B1
Shawclose La YO62 ... 67 E4
Shaw Cres YO61 ... 144 A5
Shawcroft Ct DL10 ... 209 E8
Shaw Dr YO62 ... 70 B1
Shaw La
  Farnham HG5 ... 162 C7
  Fenwick DN6 ... 207 D2
  North Rigton HG3 ... 178 B6
  Spofforth with Stockeld HG3 ... 179 D7
Shawl Terr 11 DL8 ... 60 D5
SHAW MILLS ... 138 F1
Shaw Rise WF6 ... 200 B1
Shaws La
  Barwick in Elmet & Scholes LS15 ... 194 B7
  Hawes DL8 ... 56 E4
Shaw's Terr YO24 ... 233 A1
Shearing Path LS29 ... 174 F5
Sheepcote La HG3 ... 159 F5
Sheepdyke La YO14 ... 127 A8
Sheepfoot Hill YO17 ... 215 D4
Sheep Rake La YO25 ... 151 F4
Sheep St 11 BD23 ... 216 F4
Sheepwalk La
  Castleford WF10 ... 201 B3
  Kirby Grindalythe YO17 ... 150 B7
Sheepwash Bank YO7 ... 66 D5
Sheepwash La DN14 ... 207 A7
Sheldrake Cl 9 YO14 ... 101 A4
Sheldrake Rd WF10 ... 200 E3
Shelley Cl YO11 ... 100 B6
Shelley Ct HG1 ... 219 E7
Shelley Dr WF11 ... 201 D2
Shelley Gr YO30 ... 224 F1
Shelley Rd TS4 ... 6 F8
Shelton Ave 2 YO13 ... 99 B8
Shepherd Ct TS12 ... 9 E7
Shepherdfields La YO60 ... 146 E5
Shepherd Gate LA2 ... 130 F5
Shepherd Hill DL6 ... 45 D8
Shepherdies The HG4 ... 113 C8
Shepherds Dr 13 YO11 ... 100 B7
Sherbrooke Cl 18 YO62 ... 70 B1
SHERBURN ... 124 D8
Sherburn CE Prim Sch YO17 ... 124 D7
Sherburn Enterprise Pk LS25 ... 196 B4
Sherburn High Sch LS25 ... 195 F3
SHERBURN IN ELMET ... 195 E5
Sherburn in Elmet Sta LS25 ... 196 A4
Sherburn Rd YO8 ... 232 A8
Sherburn St 1 YO8 ... 197 B8
Sherburn Willows Nature Reserve★ LS25 ... 195 E3
Sheridan Rd BB8 ... 186 B3
SHERIFF HUTTON ... 145 C5
Sheriff Hutton Castle (rems of)★ YO60 ... 145 D5
Sheriff Hutton Prim Sch YO60 ... 145 C5
Sherriff Hutton House★ YO60 ... 145 D4
Sherringham Dr YO24 ... 230 D8
Sherwood Brow BD24 ... 131 D7
Sherwood Cl
  Hunton DL8 ... 61 E7
  13 Norton DN6 ... 206 E1
Sherwood Dr HG2 ... 220 D2
Sherwood Gr
  Huntington YO32 ... 225 F1
  York YO26 ... 227 B6
Sherwood Rd TS17 ... 6 B6
Sherwood St 5 YO12 ... 212 F5
Shetland Cl TS5 ... 6 E6
Shilton Garth Cl 3 YO32 ... 225 F7
SHIPTON ... 165 F5
Shipton Low Rd YO30 ... 165 E5
Shipton Rd
  Clifton YO30 ... 227 F8
  Rawcliffe YO30 ... 224 D2
  York YO30 ... 228 A7
Shipton St 3 YO30 ... 228 B7
Shipyard Ind Est YO8 ... 232 E5
Shipyard Rd YO8 ... 232 E5
Shirbutt La YO26 ... 182 C8
Shire Cl 18 YO11 ... 100 B7
Shire Croft 17 YO11 ... 100 B7
Shire Fold YO11 ... 100 B6
Shire Garth DL6 ... 24 B1
Shire Gr YO17 ... 95 D2
Shire Rd YO7 ... 211 B4
Shires Croft BD23 ... 217 E8
Shires La BD23 ... 217 D8
Shirley Ave
  Ripon HG4 ... 214 B4
  York YO26 ... 227 C6
Shoebridge Ave BD20 ... 187 F7
Shop Hill YO22 ... 33 B4
Shop La
  Cowling BD22 ... 187 A6
  Danby YO21 ... 29 B3
  Middleton YO18 ... 95 D8
Shortacre La YO42 ... 193 E2
Shortbank Cl BD23 ... 217 B3
Shortbank Rd BD23 ... 217 B3
Short Cl TS18 ... 5 F7
Shorthorn La 1 DL2 ... 3 A7
Short La
  Acaster Selby YO23 ... 191 A4
  Farndale East YO62 ... 48 F4
  West Haddlesey YO8 ... 202 F6
Short Lee La BD23 ... 216 F6
Short Rd YO7 ... 115 B2
Shortsill La HG5 ... 163 B5
Shotel Cl YO30 ... 227 F8
Showfield Cl LS25 ... 195 F4
Showfield Dr 17 YO61 ... 143 C8
Showfield La YO17 ... 215 C6
Shrubberies The YO8 ... 198 E2
Shute Rd DL9 ... 209 E1
Shutt La DL8 ... 56 E6
Shuttleworth St 36 BB18 ... 172 A1
Shuttocks Fold LS25 ... 194 D2
SICKLINGHALL ... 179 E3
Sicklinghall Prim Sch LS22 ... 179 D3
Sicklinghall Rd LS22 ... 179 F3
Side Gate YO12 ... 99 D1
Sidegate La BD20 ... 186 F8
Sidgwick Ct 7 BD23 ... 217 A3
Siding La YO8 ... 198 B5
Sidings Ind Est The BD24 ... 131 D2
Sidings La YO61 ... 143 B4
Sidings The
  12 Bridgehouse Gate HG3 ... 137 B4
  5 Low Bentham LA2 ... 128 F8
  Settle BD24 ... 131 D2
  Skipton BD23 ... 216 E3
  Strensall YO32 ... 167 B7
Sidmouth Cl TS8 ... 7 D6
Sidmouth Sq 9 DL9 ... 40 E4
Signals Ct 7 YO12 ... 75 F5
Sigston Castle★ DL6 ... 44 D2
Sike La YO7 ... 115 B6
Silicar La HG4 ... 88 B1
Silkstone Sq WF10 ... 200 E6
Sills La YO30 ... 165 B6
Silly La LA2 ... 129 A2
SILPHO ... 74 E7
SILSDEN ... 174 C2
Silsden Rd
  Addingham LS29 ... 174 D4
  Low Bradley BD20 ... 173 E3
Silverdale Cl 5 HG3 ... 160 A6
Silverdale Ct YO24 ... 230 D7
Silverdale Rd BD24 ... 131 F8
Silverfields Rd HG1 ... 220 A3
Silver Garth DL10 ... 21 C7
Silver Hill DL7 ... 22 C2
Silverlink Bsns Pk DL1 ... 3 D6
Silver Mdws DL10 ... 21 D7
Silver St
  Askrigg DL8 ... 57 E5
  Barton DL10 ... 21 C7
  Fairburn WF11 ... 201 D6
  Hackforth DL8 ... 62 E8
  4 Knaresborough HG5 ... 221 B5
  Masham HG4 ... 86 C3
  Reeth, Fremington & Healaugh DL11 ... 38 B6
  3 Riccall YO19 ... 198 A8
  8 Scarborough YO11 ... 213 A6
  Thirsk YO7 ... 211 C1
  Whitby YO21 ... 208 D7
  Whitley DN14 ... 207 A7
  York YO1 ... 233 B2
Silverton Rd TS14 ... 8 F5
Silverwood Ave 5 YO14 ... 101 A3
Simbach Cl BD23 ... 217 B3
Sim Balk La YO23 ... 230 E5
Simon Howe
  Ganton YO12 ... 125 A5
  Sherburn YO12 ... 124 F6
SIMONSTONE ... 56 D6
Simpson Ave 6 YO14 ... 126 F8

Simpson Cl BB18 ... 171 E2
Simpsons La WF11 ... 201 E2
Simpsons Lane Junior &
Infant Sch WF11 ... 201 E2
Sinclair Ct YO12 ... 212 E5
SINDERBY ... 88 C4
Sinderby La YO7 ... 88 B4
Sinks La DL8 ... 62 C4
SINNINGTON ... 95 A8
Sinnington Cl TS14 ... 8 F6
Sinnington Cliff Rd YO62 . 95 A8
Sinnington Prim Sch
YO62 ... 94 F8
Sinnington Rd TS17 ... 6 B6
Sir Douglas Pk TS17 ... 6 A7
Sir John's La LS25 ... 195 E4
Sirocco Ct YO31 ... 228 D8
Sir William Hartley Ct
BB8 ... 186 B3
Sissy Bank DL8 ... 59 D6
Sitwell Gr YO26 ... 227 C5
Sitwell St YO12 ... 212 E5
Siwards Howe★ YO10 ... 229 B1
Siward St YO10 ... 229 A3
Siward's Way YO10 ... 229 A2
Sixth Ave YO31 ... 228 E5
Skates La YO61 ... 144 B3
Sked Dale YO17 ... 124 E6
SKEEBY ... 21 A1
Skeeby Cl 3 TS18 ... 5 D8
Skegmer La YO60 ... 145 F4
Skelda Rise LS29 ... 218 B3
Skeldergate YO1 ... 233 B2
Skelder Rd YO21 ... 31 E8
Skelf St LS24 ... 190 C1
Skelgate La DL11 ... 38 B6
Skellbank HG4 ... 214 B4
Skellbank Cl HG4 ... 214 B4
Skelldale Cl HG4 ... 214 E4
Skelldale Pk HG4 ... 214 E4
Skelldale View HG4 ... 214 E4
Skellfield Terr HG4 ... 214 D4
Skellgarth HG4 ... 214 C5
Skellgill La DL8 ... 57 C6
SKELTON ... 224 C6
Skelton Ct
10 Guisborough TS14 ... 8 F7
3 York YO30 ... 228 A6
Skelton Ellers TS14 ... 9 A8
Skelton La
Givendale HG4 ... 140 C8
Marske DL11 ... 39 B7
Skelton YO32 ... 224 D8
Skelton Newby Hall CE Prim
Sch HG4 ... 140 E7
SKELTON ON URE ... 140 E7
Skelton Park Trading Est
YO30 ... 225 B4
Skelton Prim Sch YO30 .. 224 C5
Skelton Rd
Skelton YO51 ... 140 E6
Thornaby TS17 ... 6 B8
Skelton Windmill★ YO51 140 F8
SKERNE PARK ... 3 C3
Skerne Park Prim Sch DL1 3 D3
Skerningham Ave 9 DL2 .. 3 A7
Skeugh Head La DL11 ... 35 E6
Skeugh La YO61 ... 144 D6
SKEWSBY ... 119 A1
Skewsby Gr YO31 ... 225 F1
Skibeden BD23 ... 217 E6
Skibeden Ct 4 BD23 ... 217 B5
Skiddaw YO24 ... 230 C7
Skiddaw Ct TS7 ... 7 C6
Skinner La 14 WF8 ... 201 B1
Skinner St YO21 ... 208 D7
Skiplam Cl 4 YO12 ... 212 B5
Skiplam Rd YO62 ... 69 D2
Skipper La YO25 ... 125 E3
SKIPTON ... 216 F4
Skipton Castle★ BD23 ... 217 A5
Skipton Cres HG1 ... 219 D5
Skipton Girls High Sch
BD23 ... 216 E5
Skipton Hospl BD23 ... 216 E3
Skipton Little Theatre★
BD23 ... 216 F3
Skipton Old Rd BB8 ... 186 A3
SKIPTON-ON-SWALE ... 88 E2
Skipton Rd
Addingham LS29 ... 174 E5
Barnoldswick BB18 ... 171 E2
Bradleys Both BD20 ... 173 D4
Colne BB8 ... 186 A2
Cononley BD20 ... 173 C2
Earby BB18 ... 172 A2
Embsay with Eastby BD23 217 C7
Farnhill BD20 ... 187 E8
Felliscliffe HG3 ... 160 E3
Fewston LS21 ... 159 D2
Gargrave BD23 ... 155 D1
Glusburn BD20 ... 187 F8
Harrogate HG3 ... 219 A5
Hellifield BD23 ... 154 B3
Ilkley LS29 ... 218 A4
Silsden BD20 ... 174 B1
Silsden BD20 ... 174 B3
Skipton BD23 ... 217 B6
Skipton St HG1 ... 219 D4
Skipton Sta BD23 ... 216 E3
SKIPWITH ... 192 E1
Skipwith Comm★ YO8 ... 198 E8
Skipwith Rd YO19 ... 192 B6
SKIRETHORNS ... 134 C2
SKIRPENBECK ... 169 A4
Skirt Bank YO7 ... 66 C7
Skottowe Cres TS9 ... 7 F2
Skottowe Dr TS9 ... 7 F2
Skuff Rd BD23 ... 157 B8
Skurkhill La YO62 ... 92 E7
SKYREHOLME ... 157 E7
Skyreholme Bank BD23 .. 157 F7
Skyreholme La BD23 ... 157 E7
Slackgap La CA17 ... 14 A8
Slack La HG3 ... 160 B4
Sladeburn Dr 2 DL6 ... 210 E3
Slaidburn Rd LA2 ... 129 B4
SLAPEWATH ... 9 C6
Slate Hill YO21 ... 29 D4
Slates La LS29 ... 218 B7
Slayde The TS15 ... 5 E2
Sledgate YO17 ... 122 F5
Sledgate Garth YO17 ... 122 F5
Sled Gates YO22 ... 33 B3
Sled La DL10 ... 41 F4
SLEDMERE ... 150 B4
Sledmere CE Prim Sch
YO25 ... 150 B3
Sledmere House★ YO25 . 150 B3
Sledmere Rd YO25 ... 151 B6
Slee Gill DL10 ... 209 C5
Sleigh La YO60 ... 120 A1
Sleightholme Dale Rd
YO62 ... 69 D5
Sleightholme Moor Rd
DL11 ... 16 D7
SLEIGHTS ... 32 A6
Sleights CE Prim Sch
YO22 ... 32 A6
Sleights Ct 15 TS14 ... 8 F7
Sleights La
Acklam YO17 ... 169 E7
Amotherby YO17 ... 121 A6
Birstwith HG3 ... 160 C4
Rainton with Newby YO7 .. 114 E5
Sleights Rd YO62 ... 69 D6
Sleights Sta YO22 ... 32 A7
Sleights The LS17 ... 178 A2
Slessor Rd
8 Catterick DL10 ... 41 E4
York YO24 ... 227 B1
Slice La LS24 ... 190 A6
Slim Rd DL9 ... 209 C2
SLINGSBY ... 120 C6
Slingsby Ave HG5 ... 221 A7
Slingsby Bank YO62 ... 120 C4
Slingsby Castle (rems of)★
YO62 ... 120 B5
Slingsby Com Prim Sch
YO62 ... 120 B5
Slingsby Cres HG1 ... 219 F4
Slingsby Garth 19 YO62 ... 70 B1
Slingsby Gdns DL7 ... 210 B3
Slingsby Gr YO24 ... 230 E8
Slingsby Wlk HG2 ... 219 F1
Slip Inn Bank DL11 ... 19 E6
Slippery Ford La BD22 ... 187 E3
Slope La 8 YO12 ... 99 D2
Smales' St YO1 ... 233 B1
SMALL BANKS ... 174 F3
Smalldrink La 40 BD20 ... 187 E7
Smary La YO19 ... 184 D7
Smawthorne Ave WF10 ... 200 E4
Smawthorne Gr WF10 ... 200 E4
Smawthorne Henry Moore
Prim Sch WF10 ... 200 E3
Smawthorne La WF10 ... 200 E4
Smay La YO22 ... 33 D5
Smearbottoms La BD23 .. 133 C3
Smeathons Rd TS12 ... 9 F4
Smeatley's La WF8 ... 206 C4
Smeaton Gr
5 Swillington LS26 ... 194 A1
York YO26 ... 227 C5
Smeaton Rd YO41 ... 185 D7
SMELTHOUSES ... 137 F3
Smiddyfields 5 YO22 ... 32 A6
Smiddy Hill
19 Pickering YO18 ... 95 F6
Walton LS23 ... 181 A2
Smirthwaite View 14
WF6 ... 200 A1
Smith Cl YO10 ... 231 F8
Smithfield Cl 7 HG4 ... 214 B2
Smithfield Rd DL1 ... 3 D4
Smithgutter La DL10 ... 21 C4
Smithie Cl YO32 ... 225 D5
Smith La HG4 ... 114 A4
Smith's La
Egton YO22 ... 30 E3
Flaxton YO60 ... 145 D1
Smithson Ave WF10 ... 201 B3
Smithson Cl DL10 ... 21 D2
Smithson Ct YO17 ... 215 B5
Smithson Gr 4 YO51 ... 141 B4
Smithsons Ct HG4 ... 214 C5
Smithson's La HG3 ... 177 A8
Smith St 19 BB18 ... 171 D1
Smithy Croft Rd BD23 ... 155 D1
Smithy Greaves LS29 ... 175 B4
Smithy La
Denton LS29 ... 176 A4
Scotton HG5 ... 162 A6
Thornton in Lonsdale LA6 . 103 A4
Ulleskelf LS24 ... 190 C2
Smuts Rd DL9 ... 209 D1
Smythy La YO25 ... 125 D4
SNAINTON ... 98 A5
Snainton CE Prim Sch
YO13 ... 98 A5
Snainton La YO13 ... 97 F7
SNAITH ... 204 C1
Snaith Rd
Pollington DN14 ... 207 F7
Rawcliffe DN14 ... 205 A1
Snaith Sta DN14 ... 204 C1
Snaizeholme Rd DL8 ... 55 E1
SNAPE ... 87 A7
Snape Castle★ DL8 ... 87 A7
Snape Hill YO62 ... 93 E7
Snape Prim Sch DL8 ... 87 A7
Snargate Hill YO61 ... 118 E3
SNEATON ... 32 D6
Sneaton La YO22 ... 208 B1
SNEATONTHORPE ... 32 F5
Sneaton Thorpe La YO22 . 32 E5
Sneck Gate La TS8 ... 7 B2
Sneck Yate Bank YO7 ... 67 A2
Snipe Cl 5 YO14 ... 101 A4
Snipe La
Hurworth DL2 ... 3 C3
Loftus TS13 ... 11 A6
Snowden Carr Rd LS21 .. 176 E5
Snowden Cl 4 HG4 ... 214 B2
Snowdon Cl YO22 ... 102 D3
Snowdon Gr 4 TS17 ... 5 F4
Snowfield Ind Est YO17 .. 215 C6
Snowfield La YO61 ... 142 F5
Snydale Ave WF6 ... 200 B1
Snydale Cl WF6 ... 200 B1
Snydale Ct 10 WF6 ... 200 B1
Snydale Gr WF6 ... 200 B1
Snydale Rd WF6 ... 200 A1
Sober Hall Ave TS17 ... 6 A4
Socarrs La YO62 ... 119 F7
SOCKBURN ... 23 C6
Sockburn La DL2 ... 23 B8
Somerset Cl
Hipswell DL9 ... 40 D4
6 York YO30 ... 224 E3
Somerset Rd
2 Harrogate HG2 ... 219 C1
York YO31 ... 228 D8
Somerset Terr YO11 ... 213 A5
Somme Barracks DL9 ... 40 F3
Sommerset Pastures
YO61 ... 116 F2
Sopwith Cl TS18 ... 5 F8
Sorrel Gr 29 HG3 ... 161 B3
Sorrell Gr TS14 ... 8 D6
Sough La BB18 ... 186 A8
SOURBY ... 176 D8
Sourby La LS21 ... 176 D7
Sour La BD23 ... 216 B6
Soursikes Field Rd YO51 141 D5
Soutersfield YO61 ... 144 C6
South App
Aberford LS25 ... 188 F1
Bramham cum Oglethorpe
LS23 ... 188 C5
Stutton with Hazlewood
LS25 ... 189 A2
South Ave
Castleford WF10 ... 200 C4
20 Scalby YO13 ... 75 D5
South Back La
Stillington YO61 ... 144 C6
Terrington YO60 ... 119 E1
Tollerton YO61 ... 143 B2
South Baileygate WF8 ... 201 C1
SOUTH BANK ... 228 A1
South Bank Ave YO23 ... 228 B1
South Beech Ave HG2 ... 220 C3
South Cliff Dr YO14 ... 101 B1
South Craven Sch 36
BD20 ... 187 E7
South Cres
Ripon HG4 ... 214 C4
Thirsk YO7 ... 211 B2
South Cres Ave 54 YO14 . 101 B3
South Cres Cl 51 YO14 ... 101 B3
South Cres Rd YO14 ... 101 B3
Southdean Dr TS8 ... 6 F6
Southdene 48 YO14 ... 101 B3
South Down Rd 3 YO32 . 225 F5
South Dr HG2 ... 222 E8
SOUTH DUFFIELD ... 199 A4
South Duffield Rd YO8 .. 198 C4
South End
Bedale DL8 ... 63 A3
Burniston YO13 ... 75 D7
Osmotherley DL6 ... 45 B3
Southend Ave DL3 ... 3 C4
South End Ave 6 DL8 ... 63 A3
South End Cl YO13 ... 75 D7
Southend Gdns 8 YO21 . 208 C6
South End La DN14 ... 207 B4
Southerscales Nature
Reserve★ LA6 ... 104 C7
South Esplanade YO1 ... 233 B1
Southey St 1 BD23 ... 217 A3
Southfield YO17 ... 122 D3
Southfield Ave HG4 ... 214 B2
Southfield Cl
6 Hurworth-on-Tees DL2 ... 3 E1
Rufforth YO23 ... 182 D6
Southfield Cres 2 YO24 . 230 E8
Southfield Grange 3
YO23 ... 190 F5
Southfield La
23 Addingham LS29 ... 174 F4
Kellington DN14 ... 202 E2
South Field La YO26 ... 181 B6
Southfield Rd
28 Addingham LS29 ... 174 F4
Burley in Warfedale LS29 . 176 C1
Littlethorpe HG4 ... 214 B2
Southfields Rd YO32 ... 167 B7
Southfield Terr
22 Addingham LS29 ... 174 F4
Southfield Terr continued
7 Skipton BD23 ... 216 F3
Southgate
Eastfield YO12 ... 99 E6
Pickering YO18 ... 95 F7
Ripon HG4 ... 214 C4
South Gate 18 YO62 ... 92 F6
Southgate Ave HG4 ... 214 C4
Southgate Cl 7 HG4 ... 214 C4
South Grange Rd HG4 .. 214 B2
South Hawksworth St 7
LS29 ... 218 B4
SOUTH HOLME ... 120 B8
South House Pavement
Nature Reserve★ BD24 . 104 F8
South Ings La YO62 ... 70 F3
SOUTH KILVINGTON ... 211 B7
South Kilvington CE Prim
Sch YO7 ... 211 A7
South La
Bishop Wilton YO42 ... 169 F1
Burton Fleming YO25 ... 126 E2
Cawood YO8 ... 197 D7
Thornton Dale YO18 ... 96 D6
Southlands
4 Haxby YO32 ... 166 E5
19 Helmsley YO62 ... 92 F6
16 Hemingbrough YO8 ... 198 F1
2 High & Low Bishopside
HG3 ... 137 B4
Southlands Ave 5 YO21 . 208 C7
Southlands Cl
Escrick YO19 ... 192 B6
8 South Milford LS25 ... 195 F2
Southlands Gr YO12 ... 212 B7
Southlands Rd YO23 ... 228 B2
Southlea YO17 ... 122 F5
SOUTH LOFTUS ... 10 E8
SOUTH MILFORD ... 195 F1
South Milford Prim Sch 9
LS25 ... 195 F2
South Milford Sta LS25 .. 195 F2
Southmoor La WF11 ... 202 B1
South Moor La
Garriston DL8 ... 61 A7
Sowerby YO7 ... 89 F3
Southmoor Rd YO19 ... 192 F5
Southolme Cl 22 YO51 ... 141 B5
Southolme Dr 7 YO30 .. 224 F1
Southolme Wlk 23 YO51 . 141 B5
SOUTH OTTERINGTON ... 64 F2
South Otterington CE Prim
Sch DL7 ... 64 F2
South Parade
Hurworth-on-Tees DL2 ... 22 C8
Ilkley LS29 ... 218 A4
Northallerton DL7 ... 210 D3
Norton YO17 ... 215 E3
8 Selby YO8 ... 232 C5
York YO23 ... 233 A1
South Parade Ind Est
YO17 ... 215 E3
South Park Ave TS6 ... 7 E8
South Park La LS22 ... 180 A8
South Park Rd HG1 ... 219 E1
South Ridge LS25 ... 194 D1
South Ruddings La YO19 192 F7
South Side TS15 ... 25 C5
South St
Barmby on the Marsh
DN14 ... 205 A7
Burton Fleming YO25 ... 126 E2
Scalby YO13 ... 75 D5
7 Scarborough YO11 ... 213 A4
SOUTH STAINLEY ... 139 E2
South Terr YO7 ... 211 B2
South Town La TS13 ... 10 E8
South Vale DL6 ... 210 E2
South View
Burniston YO13 ... 75 D7
Castleford WF10 ... 201 B5
2 Egglescliffe TS16 ... 5 D4
3 Glusburn BD20 ... 173 E1
Healaugh LS24 ... 182 A2
Hunton DL8 ... 61 E7
Ilkley LS29 ... 218 B3
19 Leyburn DL8 ... 60 D5
Northallerton DL6 ... 210 F6
Ripon HG4 ... 214 D2
2 Rudby TS15 ... 25 D5
6 Whitby YO21 ... 208 D5
South View Terr BD20 ... 174 B1
Southville Terr HG1 ... 219 B5
Southway
Harrogate HG2 ... 222 C8
Ilkley LS29 ... 218 D3
Manor Park LS29 ... 176 B2
Southwold 7 YO11 ... 100 B7
Southwold Cl 5 YO11 ... 100 B7
Southwold Rise 6 YO11 . 100 B7
Southwood TS8 ... 7 B4
South Wood La 11 BD23 . 134 E3
Southwood Rd YO41 ... 193 C8
Sovereign Gdns 2 WF6 . 200 A1
Sovereign Pk HG1 ... 219 B2
Sowarth Field 21 BD24 .. 131 D2
Sowarth Ind Est BD24 ... 131 D2
SOWERBY ... 211 B1
Sowerby Cres TS9 ... 26 B7
Sowerby Prim Sch YO7 .. 211 B1
Sowerby Rd
Thirsk YO7 ... 211 B2
York YO26 ... 227 D4
Sowerby Terr YO7 ... 211 B2
Sowerby Way TS16 ... 5 D5
Sowgate La WF8 ... 201 D2
SPACEY HOUSES ... 223 A2
Spa Complex★ YO11 ... 213 B4
Spa Gdns★ HG4 ... 214 B5
Spa La
Harrogate HG2 ... 220 C3
Middleton YO18 ... 95 B6
Spalding Ave YO30 ... 228 B7
Spa Mews HG2 ... 220 D3
Spa Pk★ HG4 ... 214 B5
Spa Rd
Gainford DL2 ... 1 C7
Harrogate HG2 ... 220 C3
Sparrow Hall Dr DL1 ... 3 E8
Spartal La LS25 ... 200 F8
Spa St HG2 ... 220 C3
Spa Terr 3 HG2 ... 220 C3
SPA THE ... 213 B4
Spa The YO11 ... 213 A4
SPAUNTON ... 70 E4
Spaunton Bank YO62 ... 70 E5
Spaunton La YO62 ... 70 E4
Spawd Bone La
Knottingley WF11 ... 201 F2
17 Knottingley WF11 ... 202 A2
Speculation St YO1 ... 228 E4
Speedwell Rd WF10 ... 200 C3
SPEETON ... 127 F5
Speeton Ave TS5 ... 6 F7
Spellow Cres HG5 ... 140 E1
Spellow Gr HG5 ... 140 E1
Spen Brow LA2 ... 128 E6
Spence Ct 4 TS9 ... 8 A2
Spenceley Pl DL11 ... 2 A2
Spencer Cl 5 BD20 ... 187 F8
Spencer's Holt HG1 ... 219 D7
Spencer St
29 Glusburn BD20 ... 187 E7
3 York YO23 ... 233 B1
Spencer's Way HG1 ... 219 D7
Spencer Wlk BD23 ... 217 C3
Spen Comon La LS24 ... 188 F3
Speng La YO23 ... 182 B4
Spen La YO1 ... 233 C3
SPENNITHORNE ... 60 F3
Spennithorne CE Prim Sch
DL8 ... 60 F4
Spey Bank YO24 ... 230 C6
Spiker's Hill La YO13 ... 74 F2
Spindle Cl YO24 ... 230 C8
Spindle Mill BD23 ... 216 F4
Spink La WF8 ... 201 B1
Spinksburn La HG3 ... 159 F1
Spinner La HG3 ... 161 A8
Spinners Ct BD23 ... 216 F4
Spinney The
Darlington DL3 ... 3 B4
Draughton BD23 ... 174 B7
6 Easingwold YO61 ... 143 C8
Knaresborough HG5 ... 221 C6
3 Scarborough YO12 ... 212 B5
Tees-side Airport DL2 ... 4 D4
York YO24 ... 230 F7
Spinniker Dr 4 YO21 ... 208 C5
Spire View 21 YO8 ... 198 F1
Spital Bridge YO22 ... 208 E5
Spitalcroft HG5 ... 221 B4
Spital Farm Craft Ctr★
YO12 ... 99 E2
Spital Field Ct 1 YO17 .. 215 C4
Spitalfields TS15 ... 5 D2
Spital Rd YO12 ... 99 E3
Spital St YO17 ... 215 B4
Spital The TS15 ... 5 D3
Spitfire Ct DL10 ... 41 F6
Spitfire Way LS25 ... 196 B4
Spitlands La HG5 ... 163 B7
Spittal Hardwick La
WF10 ... 201 B3
Spittlerush La DN6 ... 206 D2
SPOFFORTH ... 179 E5
Spofforth Castle★ HG3 .. 179 D6
Spofforth CE Prim Sch
HG3 ... 179 E5
Spofforth Hill LS22 ... 180 B3
Spofforth La
Follifoot HG3 ... 223 F4
North Deighton LS22 ... 180 A6
Spofforth Rd HG3 ... 223 F4
Spofforth La LS22 ... 180 A7
Spout La LA2 ... 102 B2
Spreight Lane Steps
YO11 ... 213 B7
Springbank
Marton cum Grafton
YO51 ... 141 E2
Swillington LS25 ... 194 B3
Spring Bank YO12 ... 212 E3
Springbank Ave YO19 ... 184 E7
Spring Bank Cl HG4 ... 214 C7
Spring Bank Mdw HG4 .. 214 C7
Spring Bank Rd HG4 ... 214 C7
Spring Cl
Garforth LS25 ... 194 D4
Middlesbrough TS18 ... 6 B8
12 Sleights YO22 ... 32 A6
Spring Ct HG3 ... 160 E6
Springfield
Bentham LA2 ... 129 B8
Clifford LS23 ... 188 E7
Follifoot HG3 ... 223 F4
4 Scarborough YO11 ... 213 B6
Skeeby DL10 ... 21 A1
Stokesley TS9 ... 26 C7
Springfield Ave
4 Earby BB18 ... 172 B1
Harrogate HG1 ... 219 C3
Ilkley LS29 ... 218 C4
11 Pontefract WF8 ... 201 C1

Springfield Cl
Barlby with Osgodby YO8 . . . 198 B5
20 Boroughbridge YO51 . . . 141 B5
Heworth YO31 . . . 229 C7
1 Leyburn DL8 . . . 60 D5
5 Pateley Bridge HG3 . . . 137 C4
Ripon HG4 . . . 214 B7
Thirsk YO7 . . . 211 B4
Springfield Cres
Bentham LA2 . . . 129 B8
3 Kirk Smeaton WF8 . . . 206 C3
Springfield Ct
7 Grassington BD23 . . . 134 E2
Sherburn in Elmet LS25 . . . 195 F5
Springfield Dr
9 Barlby YO8 . . . 198 B5
19 Boroughbridge YO51 . . . 141 B5
Springfield Garth YO17 . . . 215 D3
Springfield Gdns 1 TS9 . . . 26 C7
Springfield Gr
21 Boroughbridge YO51 . . . 141 B5
Kirklevington TS15 . . . 5 F1
Springfield La
3 Kirkbymoorside YO62 . . . 70 C1
Tockwith YO26 . . . 181 C7
Springfield Mews HG1 . . . 219 C3
Springfield Mount LS29 . . . 174 F5
Springfield Pl LS25 . . . 194 B3
Springfield Prim Sch DL1 . . . 3 E7
Springfield Rd
18 Boroughbridge YO51 . . . 141 B5
Darlington DL1 . . . 3 E7
6 Grassington BD23 . . . 134 E2
4 Poppleton YO26 . . . 165 F1
Sherburn in Elmet LS25 . . . 195 F5
Springfield Rise 1 YO26 . . . 164 A8
Springfields
18 Knottingley WF11 . . . 202 A2
5 Skipton BD23 . . . 217 B4
Springfields Ave 17 WF11 . . . 202 A2
Springfield Terr YO17 . . . 124 D7
Springfield Way
4 Pateley Bridge HG3 . . . 137 C4
York YO31 . . . 229 B7
Spring Gdns 10 YO11 . . . 100 B6
Spring Gr
Harrogate HG1 . . . 219 C3
Laneshaw Bridge BB8 . . . 186 B3
Spring Hall Garth YO17 . . . 215 A3
Springhead Sch YO12 . . . 212 E2
Spring Hill
Stonegrave YO62 . . . 93 C1
Welbury DL6 . . . 24 B1
Whitby YO21 . . . 208 D6
Springhill Cl YO12 . . . 212 E4
Springhill Ct 7 LS24 . . . 189 E6
Springhill La YO12 . . . 212 D3
Springhill Rd YO12 . . . 212 E4
Spring Hill Sch HG4 . . . 113 E4
Spring Hill Terr 10 YO21 . . . 208 D6
Spring La
Birdforth YO7 . . . 116 F8
Kirkby Overblow HG3 . . . 179 A2
Long Marston YO26 . . . 182 A5
Pannal HG3 . . . 222 C3
Wetherby LS22 . . . 180 E3
York YO10 . . . 229 A1
Springmead Dr LS25 . . . 194 C3
Springmount 3 BB18 . . . 172 B1
Spring Mount HG1 . . . 219 C3
Spring Rise BD23 . . . 174 B7
Springs La
Ellerton-on-Swale DL10 . . . 41 F4
Ilkley LS29 . . . 218 C4
Walton LS23 . . . 180 F3
Whashton DL11 . . . 20 B4
Spring St 2 YO61 . . . 143 C8
Springs Terr LS29 . . . 218 B4
Springs The 4 DL8 . . . 60 E2
Spring Terr DL7 . . . 210 C4
Spring Vale YO21 . . . 208 C6
Springwater Sch HG2 . . . 220 D4
Spring Way TS18 . . . 5 F8
Springwell Ave 11 LS26 . . . 194 A1
Springwell Cl 8 BD22 . . . 187 B6
Springwell Gdns 3 DL7 . . . 210 D4
Springwell La DL7 . . . 210 B4
Springwell Rd 10 LS26 . . . 194 A1
Springwell Terrace E 1 DL7 . . . 210 D4
Springwell Terrace W 2 DL7 . . . 210 D4
Spring Wlk YO8 . . . 232 A1
Springwood YO32 . . . 225 D7
Springwood Gr YO26 . . . 227 C6
Spring Wood Rd TS14 . . . 8 F6
SPROXTON . . . 92 F4
Spruce Cl YO32 . . . 225 D2
Spruce Gill Ave 4 DL8 . . . 63 B3
Spruce Gill Dr 5 DL8 . . . 63 B3
Spruisty Rd HG1 . . . 219 C4
Spurr Ct YO24 . . . 230 C8
Spurriergate YO1 . . . 233 B2
Square The
Boston Spa LS23 . . . 188 F8
Castleford WF10 . . . 201 B4
Ingleton LA6 . . . 103 D4
Kippax LS25 . . . 194 D1
Knottingley WF11 . . . 201 E3
Leeming DL7 . . . 63 F3
Sheriff Hutton YO60 . . . 145 D5
1 Tadcaster LS24 . . . 189 F6
Stabler Cl 15 YO32 . . . 166 D5
Stable Rd YO8 . . . 204 D7
Stablers Wlk
Earswick YO32 . . . 225 F7
13 Pontefract WF6 . . . 200 A2
Stables La LS23 . . . 188 F8
Stables The LS24 . . . 189 F2
STACKHOUSE . . . 131 D4
Stackhouse La
Giggleswick BD24 . . . 131 D4
Lawkland BD24 . . . 130 F2
Stags Way DL10 . . . 41 F7
STAINBURN . . . 177 F3
Stainburn Ave WF10 . . . 201 A3
Stainburn La LS21 . . . 177 E2
Staindale TS14 . . . 8 D6
Staindale Cl YO30 . . . 224 E2
Staindrop Dr TS5 . . . 6 E7
Staindrop Rd DL3 . . . 3 A6
Stained Glass Ctr★ YO11 . . . 100 C5
STAINFORTH . . . 131 E6
Stainforth Gdns TS17 . . . 6 B5
Stainforth La BD24 . . . 131 D5
Stainforth Rd BD24 . . . 131 E4
STAINSACRE . . . 32 F7
Stainsacre La
Hawsker-cum-Stainsacre YO22 . . . 32 F6
Whitby YO22 . . . 208 F3
Stainsacre Lane Ind Est YO22 . . . 208 F3
Stainsby Rd TS5 . . . 6 D8
Stainthorpe Row DL7 . . . 64 F2
STAINTON
Marrick . . . 39 C3
Middlesbrough . . . 6 D5
STAINTONDALE . . . 54 B5
Staintondale Shire Horse Farm★ YO13 . . . 54 C5
Stainton Rd TS9 . . . 6 F1
Stainton Way
Coulby Newham TS8 . . . 7 A5
Stainton & Thornton TS8 . . . 6 E5
STAITHES . . . 13 J2
Staithes Cl 4 YO26 . . . 227 B4
Staithes Gall★ TS13 . . . 13 K2
Staithes La TS13 . . . 13 K2
Staithe St 3 YO8 . . . 199 D7
Stake Rd DL8 . . . 57 C1
Stakesby Prim Sch YO21 . . . 208 B6
Stakesby Rd YO21 . . . 208 B6
Stakesby Vale YO21 . . . 208 C6
Stakesby Vale Ct YO21 . . . 208 B5
STALLING BUSK . . . 81 B8
STAMFORD BRIDGE . . . 168 E2
Stamford Bridge Prim Sch YO41 . . . 168 D2
Stamford Bridge Rd YO19 . . . 184 E7
Stamford Bridge W YO41 . . . 168 C2
Stamford Street E 10 YO26 . . . 227 F5
Stamford Street W 8 YO26 . . . 227 F5
Stammergate YO7 . . . 211 C3
Stammergate La LS22 . . . 180 A1
Stamp Hill Cl 7 LS29 . . . 174 E4
Standard Ct DL7 . . . 210 B6
Standard Way DL6 . . . 210 B6
Standard Way Ind Est DL6 . . . 210 C6
Standridge Clough La BB18 . . . 172 B1
Standroyd Dr BB8 . . . 186 A3
Standroyd Rd BB8 . . . 186 A3
Stanghow Rd TS12 . . . 9 F8
Stang La
Arkengarthdale DL11 . . . 17 E3
Farnham HG5 . . . 162 C7
Hope DL11 . . . 18 A8
Stangs La BD23 . . . 157 D6
Stang Top
Arkengarthdale DL11 . . . 17 F5
Hope DL11 . . . 18 A6
Stanhope Dr HG2 . . . 220 B2
Stanhope Gr TS5 . . . 6 E8
Stanhope Road N DL3 . . . 3 C5
Staniland Dr YO8 . . . 232 A5
Stanley Ave YO32 . . . 225 D7
Stanley Cl
4 Catterick Garrison DL9 . . . 40 E3
22 Eastfield YO11 . . . 100 B6
Stanley Gr
Aske DL10 . . . 20 D1
Great Ayton TS9 . . . 7 F1
Richmond DL10 . . . 209 D8
Stanley St
Castleford WF10 . . . 200 F4
4 Scarborough YO12 . . . 213 A7
York YO31 . . . 233 C4
Stansfield Brow BD20 . . . 187 A8
Stansfield Cl WF10 . . . 201 A4
Stansfield Dr WF10 . . . 201 B4
Stansfield Rd WF10 . . . 201 A4
Stanstead Way TS17 . . . 6 C7
Stansted Gr DL2 . . . 4 D4
Stan Valley 2 WF8 . . . 206 C3
STANWICK-ST-JOHN . . . 1 E2
Stanyforth Cres YO26 . . . 164 C2
STAPE . . . 71 F8
Stape Rd YO18 . . . 71 F7
STAPLETON . . . 3 A2
Stapleton Bank DL2 . . . 3 A2
Stapleton Cl
3 Bedale DL8 . . . 63 B2
11 Seamer YO12 . . . 99 D6
Stapley La DL8 . . . 87 F4
STARBECK . . . 220 C4
Starbeck Baths HG2 . . . 220 D3
Starbeck Cl 4 YO21 . . . 208 B5
Starbeck Prim Sch HG2 . . . 220 D4
Starbeck Sta HG2 . . . 220 C4
STARBOTTON . . . 107 F5
Star Carr La YO12 . . . 99 E4
Starfits La
Fadmoor YO62 . . . 69 F3
Welburn YO62 . . . 94 A8
Stark Bank Rd HG4 . . . 85 C7
Starkey Cres YO31 . . . 229 A5
Starkey La 5 BD20 . . . 173 F1
Starmire BD22 . . . 187 A6
Starra Field La YO26 . . . 163 F5
Star Sh Prec DL6 . . . 210 E4
Station Ave
20 Filey YO14 . . . 101 B3
Harrogate HG1 . . . 219 E2
New Earswick YO32 . . . 225 D3
Whitby YO21 . . . 208 B7
York YO1 . . . 233 A2
Station Bridge HG1 . . . 219 D2
Station Bsns Pk YO26 . . . 227 F4
Station Cl
Dacre HG3 . . . 159 F8
6 East Ayton/West Ayton YO13 . . . 99 A7
Hambleton YO8 . . . 196 F2
Sharow HG4 . . . 214 D7
Station Ct 8 HG5 . . . 179 E5
Station Dr HG4 . . . 214 D7
Station Fields LS25 . . . 194 C4
Station Gr 19 BD20 . . . 187 F8
Station La
Barmby on the Marsh DN14 . . . 205 B7
Burton Leonard HG3 . . . 139 F3
Cliffe YO8 . . . 198 E3
Cloughton YO13 . . . 54 D1
Gristhorpe YO14 . . . 100 E4
Hampsthwaite HG3 . . . 161 A6
Morton-on-Swale DL7 . . . 64 A7
Shipton YO30 . . . 165 E5
Station Par HG1 . . . 219 D2
Station Plaza★ LS29 . . . 218 B3
Station Rd
Ampleforth YO62 . . . 92 C1
Beadlam YO62 . . . 93 D7
Brompton DL6 . . . 43 F4
Brompton-on-Swale DL10 . . . 41 B6
Burley in Warfedale LS29 . . . 176 C1
Carlton DN14 . . . 204 C3
Castleford WF10 . . . 200 E4
Cayton YO11 . . . 100 B5
Church Fenton LS24 . . . 196 B7
Clapham LA2 . . . 130 C7
Copmanthorpe YO23 . . . 230 B2
Danby YO21 . . . 29 A7
Eaglescliffe TS16 . . . 5 E6
Fylingdales YO22 . . . 33 C4
Gainford DL2 . . . 1 C8
Gilling East YO62 . . . 118 F8
Glusburn BD20 . . . 187 E8
Goldsborough HG5 . . . 163 A3
Great Ayton TS9 . . . 8 A1
Great Preston WF10 . . . 200 E6
Hambleton YO8 . . . 196 F1
Haxby YO32 . . . 166 F5
Hellifield BD23 . . . 154 B4
Helmsley YO62 . . . 92 F6
Hensall DN14 . . . 203 C1
Heslerton YO17 . . . 97 D1
High Bentham LA2 . . . 129 A8
Hinderwell TS13 . . . 11 F7
Horton in Ribblesdale BD24 . . . 105 C3
Ilkley LS29 . . . 218 B4
Kildale YO21 . . . 27 E8
Kippax LS25 . . . 200 C8
Kirk Hammerton YO26 . . . 164 D2
9 Knaresborough HG5 . . . 221 A6
Long Preston BD23 . . . 153 F4
Menwith with Darley HG3 . . . 160 A6
Mickletown LS26 . . . 200 A6
Middleton St George DL2 . . . 4 C5
Normanton WF6 . . . 200 A2
Norton DN6 . . . 206 F2
Nunnington YO62 . . . 93 E2
Pannal HG3 . . . 222 E2
24 Poppleton YO26 . . . 165 F1
Rawcliffe DN14 . . . 205 A1
Riccall YO19 . . . 198 A8
Richmond DL10 . . . 209 C7
Scalby YO13 . . . 75 D5
Scruton DL7 . . . 63 E6
Selby YO8 . . . 232 D5
Settle BD24 . . . 131 C2
Sleights YO22 . . . 32 A6
Snainton YO13 . . . 97 F4
South Otterington DL7 . . . 64 F2
Sowerby YO7 . . . 211 A2
Stainton Dale YO13 . . . 54 A8
Stokesley TS9 . . . 26 C7
Tadcaster LS24 . . . 189 D6
Thirsk YO7 . . . 89 D4
Threshfield BD23 . . . 134 D2
Tollerton YO61 . . . 143 B3
Wharram YO17 . . . 148 F4
Wharram YO17 . . . 149 A4
Whixley YO26 . . . 164 A3
Wistow YO8 . . . 197 C6
Womersley DN6 . . . 206 D5
Wood Row LS26 . . . 200 B6
York YO24 . . . 233 A2
Station Rise YO1 . . . 233 A2
Station Road Ind Est
Brompton DL6 . . . 43 F3
Great Preston LS25 . . . 200 C8
Station Sq
4 Strensall YO32 . . . 167 B7
4 Whitby YO21 . . . 208 D6
Station Terr
4 Boroughbridge YO51 . . . 141 B6
Great Preston WF10 . . . 200 E6
Station View
Cliffe YO8 . . . 198 D3
2 Harrogate HG2 . . . 220 C3
Seamer YO12 . . . 99 E7
8 Skipton BD23 . . . 216 D3
Station Way YO17 . . . 215 C3
STAUPES . . . 160 C4
Staupes Rd HG3 . . . 160 B4
STAVELEY . . . 140 F1
Staveley Com Prim Sch HG5 . . . 140 E1
Staveley Nature Reserve★ HG5 . . . 140 E2
STAXTON . . . 99 E2
Staxton Carr La YO12 . . . 99 D3
Staxton Hill YO12 . . . 125 C8
Staynor Ave YO8 . . . 232 E3
STEAD . . . 176 A1
Stead La LS14 . . . 188 A3
STEAN . . . 110 A4
Stean La HG3 . . . 110 A4
STEARSBY . . . 118 F2
Steelmoor La YO60 . . . 146 C2
Steeple Cl 4 YO32 . . . 166 D5
Steeton La LS24 . . . 190 D7
Steeton Way LS25 . . . 195 E2
Steincroft Rd 7 LS25 . . . 195 F2
Stella Gdns 10 WF8 . . . 201 C1
Stelling Rd DL11 . . . 38 E7
Stephen Bank DL11 . . . 18 H8
Stephen Joseph Theatre★ YO11 . . . 212 F5
Stephenson Cl
Knaresborough HG5 . . . 221 B4
York YO31 . . . 225 E1
Stephenson Rd 2 DL10 . . . 41 C7
Stephenson's La YO26 . . . 164 A2
Stephensons Way LS29 . . . 218 C4
Stephenson Way YO26 . . . 227 F5
Stephen's Wlk YO8 . . . 232 B1
Stephenwath La YO41 . . . 169 C5
Stepin Turn YO62 . . . 49 B1
Stepney Ave YO12 . . . 212 D4
Stepney Cl YO12 . . . 212 C5
Stepney Dr YO12 . . . 212 C5
Stepney Gr YO12 . . . 212 C5
Stepney Hill YO12 . . . 212 B4
Stepney Rd YO12 . . . 212 D4
Stepney Rise YO12 . . . 212 D5
Steps The LS22 . . . 180 C2
Sterling Chase HG5 . . . 221 C7
Sterling Pk YO30 . . . 225 A3
Sterne Ave YO31 . . . 229 A5
Sterne Way YO61 . . . 144 C3
Stevenson Pl HG5 . . . 220 F5
Steven Way HG4 . . . 214 B6
Steward Cl YO8 . . . 197 D1
Stewart La YO19 . . . 191 C4
STILLINGFLEET . . . 191 C3
STILLINGTON . . . 144 C6
Stillington Prim Sch YO61 . . . 144 C7
Stillington Rd
Easingwold YO61 . . . 143 D8
Huby YO61 . . . 144 A4
Stinton La
Boroughbridge YO51 . . . 141 C4
Helperby YO61 . . . 142 A8
Stirling Gr YO10 . . . 231 F8
Stirling Rd
Burley in Warfedale LS29 . . . 176 B1
York YO30 . . . 224 F3
Stirling Way TS17 . . . 6 B6
Stirrup Cl
Norton YO17 . . . 215 E2
York YO24 . . . 230 B8
STIRTON . . . 216 C6
Stirtonber BD23 . . . 216 E5
Stirton La BD23 . . . 216 C5
Stittenham Hill YO60 . . . 146 A6
Stobarts La TS15 . . . 5 B1
STOCK . . . 171 C3
Stockdale Cl 9 HG5 . . . 221 B5
Stockdale Ct DL6 . . . 210 F3
Stockdale La BD24 . . . 131 F2
Stockdale Wlk HG5 . . . 221 B5
Stockeld La LS22 . . . 179 E3
Stockeld Park House★ LS22 . . . 179 F4
Stockeld Rd LS29 . . . 218 A4
Stockeld Way LS29 . . . 218 A5
Stockfield La YO51 . . . 141 D2
Stockhill Cl 1 YO19 . . . 184 E7
Stockholm Cl 1 YO10 . . . 231 D8
Stockinger La LS29 . . . 174 F4
Stocking Hill TS9 . . . 25 E2
Stocking La
Hambleton YO8 . . . 196 E1
Hillam LS25 . . . 202 B7
Knottingley WF11 . . . 202 B2
Lotherton cum Aberford LS25 . . . 195 A7
Stockings La YO62 . . . 92 F2
Stocks Cl YO17 . . . 215 F4
Stockshill YO12 . . . 99 D6
Stockshott La BD20 . . . 173 C2
Stocks La 1 HG3 . . . 160 A6
Stock Stile La HG3 . . . 160 D5
Stockton Hall Hospl YO32 . . . 167 D3
Stockton La
Heworth YO32 . . . 226 D1
York YO31 . . . 229 A7
STOCKTON ON THE FOREST . . . 167 D3
Stockton on the Forest Prim Sch YO32 . . . 167 D3
Stockton Rd
Darlington DL1 . . . 3 F7
Sadberge DL2 . . . 4 C7
South Kilvington YO7 . . . 211 B6
Stockwell Ave
Ingleby TS17 . . . 6 B5
Knaresborough HG5 . . . 221 B7
Stockwell Cres 5 HG5 . . . 221 B7
Stockwell Ct 9 HG5 . . . 221 B6
Stockwell Dr HG5 . . . 221 B7
Stockwell Gr HG5 . . . 221 B7
Stockwell La HG5 . . . 221 B6
Stockwell Pl HG5 . . . 221 B7
Stockwell Rd HG5 . . . 221 B6
Stockwell View HG5 . . . 221 B7
Stockwith La DN14 . . . 204 A4
Stokelake Rd 5 HG1 . . . 219 E3
STOKESLEY . . . 26 D7
Stokesley Ind Pk TS9 . . . 26 D6
Stokesley L Ctr TS9 . . . 26 D7
Stokesley Prim Sch TS9 . . . 26 C7
Stokesley Rd
Brompton DL6 . . . 44 A3
Coulby Newham TS7 . . . 7 B7
Guisborough TS14 . . . 8 C6
Middlesbrough TS7 . . . 7 B6
Northallerton DL6 . . . 210 E7
Stokesley Sch TS9 . . . 26 D7
Stonebeck Ave HG1 . . . 219 B4
Stonebeck Gate La YO21 . . . 29 D4
Stonebow The
Thornton-le-Beans DL6 . . . 65 B5
York YO1 . . . 233 C2
Stone Bramble 22 HG3 . . . 161 B3
Stonebridge Cres 2 TS17 . . . 6 D6
Stone Bridge Dr YO41 . . . 185 F5
Stonebridgegate HG4 . . . 214 D5
Stonecrop Ave 5 HG3 . . . 161 B3
Stonecrop Dr 1 HG3 . . . 161 B3
Stone Crop Dr 14 WF10 . . . 200 D3
Stonecross Rd YO21 . . . 208 A6
Stone Ct 6 YO13 . . . 75 D5
Stone Dale YO42 . . . 170 D3
Stoned Horse La YO26 . . . 164 C4
Stonefall Ave HG2 . . . 220 C3
Stonefall Dr HG2 . . . 220 B2
Stonefall Mews HG2 . . . 220 C3
Stonefall Pl 2 HG2 . . . 220 B2
Stonefield Ave YO61 . . . 143 C8
Stonefield Garth 9 YO61 . . . 143 C8
Stonefield La 4 YO61 . . . 143 C8
Stone Garth 3 YO62 . . . 92 F6
STONEGATE . . . 30 D8
Stonegate
Hunmanby YO14 . . . 126 F8
York YO1 . . . 233 B3
Stone Gate YO26 . . . 164 A4
STONEGRAVE . . . 119 D8
Stonehaven Way DL1 . . . 3 F8
Stone Head La BD22 . . . 186 E6
STONE HOUSE . . . 78 F8
Stonelands Cl YO60 . . . 145 D5
Stonelands Ct 2 YO30 . . . 225 A1
Stoneleigh Gate YO26 . . . 164 B3
Stone Man La DL11 . . . 19 C5
Stonepit Balk YO17 . . . 149 C5
Stonepit Hill YO17 . . . 149 C4
Stonepit La
Birdsall YO17 . . . 148 D6
Gristhorpe YO14 . . . 100 E5
Stone Quarry Rd YO13 . . . 75 C8
Stone Riggs YO32 . . . 167 D2
Stone Rings Cl HG2 . . . 222 E5
Stone Rings Grange HG2 . . . 222 E5
Stone Rings La HG2 . . . 222 E5
Stones Cl YO24 . . . 227 E2
Stonesdale Cl 3 HG5 . . . 221 D5
Stonesdale La DL11 . . . 35 E8
Stone Stoup Hill TS9 . . . 27 C5
Stonethwaite 5 YO24 . . . 230 C7
Stonewall Cottage La 25 YO41 . . . 168 D2
Stoney Bank Rd BB18 . . . 172 B1
Stoneyborough Cl YO7 . . . 211 C4
Stoneybrough La YO7 . . . 211 C4
Stoney Haggs Rd YO12 . . . 99 E7
Stony Cross YO62 . . . 93 E7
Stony Ct 5 YO13 . . . 75 D5
Stonygate Bank DL11 . . . 20 A5
Stony La
East Harlsey DL6 . . . 44 F5
8 Scalby YO13 . . . 75 D5
Stoop Cl YO32 . . . 225 C8
Stooperdale Ave DL3 . . . 3 B7
Stoopes Hill 8 BB18 . . . 172 B1
Storey Cl 26 YO62 . . . 92 F6
Storiths La BD23 . . . 175 A8
Storking La YO41 . . . 185 F6
Storr La YO13 . . . 74 E5
Storth Gill La BD24 . . . 131 A1
Stourton Rd LS29 . . . 175 C3
Stow Ct YO32 . . . 225 E3
Strafford Rd 14 DL10 . . . 41 E4
Straight La
Addingham LS29 . . . 174 E3
Aldwark YO61 . . . 142 C3

Straight La *continued*
Burton Leonard HG3 ... 140 A3
Holtby YO19 ... 184 F8
Middleham DL8 ... 60 F2
Straights The DL8 ... 58 C4
Strait La Copt Hewick HG4 ... 114 B2
Danby YO21 ... 29 C6
Hurworth DL2 ... 3 F1
Stainton & Thornton TS8 ... 6 D5
Weeton LS17 ... 178 B2
Well DL8 ... 87 A3
Straits La YO13 ... 99 A3
STRANGHOW ... 9 F6
Stranglands La WF11 ... 201 C3
Stratford Way YO32 ... 225 E3
Strathmore Dr 9 TS15 ... 24 E8
Strathmore Rd LS29 ... 218 E4
Strawberrry Fileds Prim Sch LS25 ... 194 C3
Strawberry Ct YO12 ... 212 D4
Strawberry Dale HG1 ... 219 D3
Strawberry Dale Ave 3 HG1 ... 219 D3
Strawberry Dale Sq 1 HG1 ... 219 D3
Strawberry Dale Terr 2 HG1 ... 219 D3
Straw Gate DL2 ... 3 A2
Strawgate Gr DL2 ... 3 A3
Stray Garth YO31 ... 228 F7
Straylands Gr YO31 ... 228 F8
Stray Rd Harrogate HG2 ... 222 D8
York YO31 ... 229 B6
Stray Rein HG2 ... 219 E1
Stray The Darlington DL1 ... 3 E5
Henderskelfe YO60 ... 146 D8
Longnewton TS21 ... 5 A7
Stray Wlk HG2 ... 222 E8
STREET ... 29 F3
Street 1 LS23 ... 189 A8
Street 2 LS23 ... 181 A1
Street 3 LS23 ... 181 A1
Street 5 LS23 ... 181 A1
Street 6 LS23 ... 181 A2
Street 7 LS23 ... 181 B1
Street 8 LS23 ... 181 B1
Street Head La BD22 ... 187 F1
STREET HOUSES ... 190 C8
Street La Bewerley HG3 ... 137 B4
Bubwith DN14 ... 199 F5
Colton LS24 ... 190 D7
Glaisdale YO21 ... 29 E3
Middleton YO18 ... 95 E7
Pickhill with Roxby YO7 ... 88 B6
STREETLAM ... 42 F5
Street The 8 LS29 ... 174 E4
STRENSALL ... 167 A7
STRENSALL CAMP ... 167 B6
Strensall Comm Nature Reserve* YO60 ... 167 D8
Strensall Dr 11 YO12 ... 75 F5
Strensall Pk YO32 ... 167 A5
Strensall Rd
Earswick YO32 ... 226 A7
York YO32 ... 225 F6
Stretton Cl WF7 ... 200 D1
Strickland Rd 13 YO14 ... 127 A8
Strikes La BD20 ... 187 F6
Stripe La Hartwith cum Winsley HG3 ... 160 B8
Skelton YO30 ... 224 B5
Stripe The 6 TS9 ... 26 C7
Stuart Ave DL10 ... 209 C8
Stuart Cl
4 Scarborough YO11 ... 100 B7
4 Strensall YO32 ... 167 C8
Stuart Gr
Eggborough DN14 ... 203 A2
1 Pontefract WF6 ... 200 A2
9 Thorpe Willoughby YO8 ... 197 B1
Stuart Rd YO24 ... 227 D1
Stuart St
10 Barnoldswick BB18 ... 171 E1
Pontefract WF8 ... 201 B1
Stubbing La BD23 ... 81 B1
Stubbing Nook La DL8 ... 62 B2
Stubbs La
Cridling Stubbs WF11 ... 206 A8
Norton DN6 ... 206 E2
Stainton Dale YO13 ... 53 F5
Stubbs Rd WF8 ... 206 D3
Stubden Gr YO30 ... 224 F2
Stubham Rise LS29 ... 218 A5
Studdah Cl DL8 ... 60 D7
STUDFOLD ... 105 D1
Stud Fold Bank HG3 ... 110 B3
Studford Ring* YO62 ... 92 C2
Studley Cl DL7 ... 210 B2
Studley La HG4 ... 113 C1
Studley Rd
Harrogate HG1 ... 219 D3
Ripon HG4 ... 214 A4
Studley Roger HG4 ... 113 D1
STUDLEY ROGER ... 113 D1
STUDLEY ROYAL ... 113 C1
Studley Terr 15 YO22 ... 208 E6
Stump Cross TS14 ... 8 E6
Stump Cross Caverns* HG3 ... 136 A2
Stumpcross Ct 14 WF8 ... 201 C2
Stumpcross La WF8 ... 201 C2
Stumpcross Mdws WF8 ... 201 D1
Stumpcross Way 15 WF8 ... 201 C2
Stumps La HG3 ... 160 A5
Stunstead Rd BB8 ... 186 B2
Sturdee Gr YO31 ... 228 D7
Sturdy House La
Marske DL11 ... 19 E2
Whashton DL11 ... 20 A4
Sturton Grange La LS25 ... 194 D4
Sturton La LS25 ... 194 D4
Stuteville Cl 4 YO62 ... 70 C1
STUTTON ... 189 D4
Stutton Rd LS24 ... 189 D4
Stygate La DN6 ... 206 E1
Sudforth La DN14 ... 202 C3
SUFFIELD ... 75 A5
Suffield Hill YO13 ... 75 A5
Sugar Hill 9 LS29 ... 174 F4
Sugar Loaf Ct 13 TS17 ... 5 F4
Sumitt Pk WF10 ... 200 F2
SUMMERBRIDGE ... 138 A1
Summerbridge Prim Sch HG3 ... 138 A1
Summerfield BD23 ... 172 A3
Summerfield Cl 1 WF11 ... 201 F4
Summerfield Dr WF11 ... 201 F4
Summerfield La YO22 ... 33 A7
Summerfield Rd YO24 ... 230 C7
Summer Gdns YO30 ... 227 F8
Summerhill Rd LS26 ... 200 B6
Summer Hill Rd LS26 ... 200 B6
SUMMERSCALES ... 158 C1
Summers Fold 1 BD23 ... 134 E3
Sunderland Rd BD20 ... 173 E3
Sundew Heath 24 HG3 ... 161 B3
Sun Gdns TS17 ... 6 A8
Sun La LS29 ... 176 C1
Sunmoor Dr BD23 ... 217 A4
Sunningdale LS25 ... 194 F4
Sunningdale Cl
Knapton YO26 ... 227 B5
1 York YO26 ... 227 B5
Sunningdale Dr TS16 ... 5 E5
Sunningdale Gr 1 YO21 ... 208 B5
Sunningdales 27 WF6 ... 200 B1
Sunnybank LS25 ... 195 A3
Sunny Bank 3 WF11 ... 202 A2
Sunnybank Rd LS25 ... 195 A3
Sunny Bank Rd 6 BD20 ... 187 E7
Sunnycrest Ave DL10 ... 209 D8
Sunnydale 3 YO32 ... 225 D7
Sunnyfield TS9 ... 7 F1
Sunnyside TS8 ... 7 D5
Sunnyside Prim Sch TS8 ... 7 A6
Sunrise Dr YO14 ... 127 C8
Sunset Dr LS29 ... 218 D5
Sunset Terr LS29 ... 218 E5
Sun St Cononley BD20 ... 173 C1
4 Cowling BD22 ... 187 B6
Thornaby TS17 ... 6 A8
Sunstar Gr TS7 ... 7 B6
Sur Gate
Harwood Dale YO13 ... 53 F1
Suffield-cum-Everley YO13 ... 74 F8
Surrey Way YO30 ... 227 F8
Surtees St Darlington DL3 ... 3 C6
York YO30 ... 228 B7
Sussex Cl Bedale DL8 ... 63 A2
York YO10 ... 229 C2
Sussex Ct 10 DL9 ... 209 C1
Sussex Rd YO10 ... 229 C2
Sussex St Bedale DL8 ... 63 A2
14 Scarborough YO11 ... 213 A6
Sussex Way 14 YO32 ... 167 A7
Sutcliffe Ct 6 YO21 ... 208 B6
Sutcliffe Gall* YO21 ... 208 D7
Sutherland Rd YO18 ... 71 C6
Sutherland St YO23 ... 228 B1
Sutor Cl YO23 ... 230 B3
SUTTON ... 201 F4
Sutton Ave 7 DL9 ... 41 A5
Sutton Bank YO7 ... 91 A5
Sutton Bank Visitor Ctr* YO7 ... 91 B6
Sutton Bridge* YO41 ... 185 C2
Sutton Ct 5 YO7 ... 211 C3
Sutton Dr DL7 ... 210 C2
Sutton Grange Cl HG3 ... 219 B4
SUTTON HOWGRAVE ... 87 F1
SUTTON-IN-CRAVEN ... 187 F6
Sutton in Craven CE Prim Sch 39 BD20 ... 187 E7
Sutton in Craven Com Prim Sch 38 BD20 ... 187 E7
Sutton La
Byram cum Sutton WF11 ... 202 A4
Byram WF11 ... 201 E4
Ellington High & Low HG4 ... 86 A5
Fearby HG4 ... 85 F4
Steeton with Eastburn BD20 ... 187 F7
SUTTON-ON-THE-FOREST ... 144 C3
Sutton-on-the-Forest CE Prim Sch YO61 ... 144 C3
Sutton Pk* YO61 ... 144 C3
Sutton Rd Bagby YO7 ... 211 E3
Wigginton YO32 ... 166 D7
Sutton St YO17 ... 215 D3
SUTTON-UNDER-WHITESTONECLIFFE ... 90 E5
SUTTON UPON DERWENT ... 185 C1
Sutton upon Derwent CE Prim Sch YO41 ... 185 C2
Sutton Way
Middlesbrough TS4 ... 6 F8
York YO30 ... 228 B8
Swadford St BD23 ... 216 F4
SWAINBY ... 45 E8
Swainby Abbey* DL8 ... 88 B8
Swainby Ellers DL6 ... 25 D1
Swainby La DL8 ... 87 F7
Swainby & Potto Prim Sch DL6 ... 45 D8
Swain Ct
Middleton St George DL2 ... 4 D4
Northallerton DL6 ... 210 D5
Swainsea Dr 3 YO18 ... 95 F7
Swainsea La YO18 ... 95 F8
Swainstead Raike BD24 ... 153 B8
Swainston Cl TS5 ... 6 E7
Swale App 25 WF6 ... 200 B1
Swale Ave YO24 ... 230 E8
SWALEDALE ... 37 C4
Swaledale Ave DL3 ... 3 B6
Swaledale Mus* DL11 ... 38 C6
Swaledale Rd 22 DL9 ... 40 E4
Swalegate DL10 ... 209 C8
Swale Gr DL1 ... 3 C3
Swale Hall La DL11 ... 38 B5
Swale La DL10 ... 41 E5
Swale Pasture La DL10 ... 41 E5
Swale View YO7 ... 115 B6
Swallow Cl Firth Moor DL1 ... 3 F4
Guisborough TS14 ... 8 D6
Swan Cl YO19 ... 192 A7
Swan Farm Ct YO19 ... 192 A7
Swang Rd YO13 ... 75 A6
Swan Hill Rd YO11 ... 213 A6
Swanhills La YO13 ... 98 F3
Swan La YO7 ... 65 F2
Swanland Rd YO62 ... 92 F7
Swann St YO23 ... 233 A1
Swan Rd HG1 ... 219 C2
Swan St BD23 ... 173 B4
Swan Syke Dr 8 DN6 ... 206 F2
Swarcliffe Rd HG1 ... 220 B4
SWARTHA ... 174 D1
Swartha La BD20 ... 174 D2
Swarthlands La YO13 ... 75 D7
SWATHGILL ... 119 B4
Sweeming La LS25 ... 196 C5
Sweetbecks Cl 12 YO11 ... 100 A6
Sweet Bits La HG5 ... 221 C8
Sweet Briar HG3 ... 219 A4
SWETTON ... 111 F4
SWILLINGTON ... 194 A1
SWILLINGTON COMMON ... 194 A3
Swillington La LS26 ... 194 A2
Swillington Prim Sch LS26 ... 194 A1
Swinburn Ct 12 HG4 ... 86 C3
Swinburne Cl HG1 ... 219 E7
Swinburne Rd TS16 ... 5 E6
Swinburn Rd 11 HG4 ... 86 C3
SWINCLIFFE ... 160 E4
Swincliffe La HG3 ... 160 D5
Swindale La TS12 ... 9 F5
SWINDEN ... 154 C1
Swindon La HG3 ... 178 E4
Swinegate YO1 ... 233 B2
Swinegate Court E YO1 ... 233 B3
Swineherd La YO62 ... 70 C1
SWINITHWAITE ... 59 C4
Swinneybeck Bank HG4 ... 85 E5
Swinsty Ct YO30 ... 224 F1
SWINTON Malton ... 121 C4
Masham ... 86 B2
Swinton Cl 18 YO30 ... 224 E2
Swinton Ct HG2 ... 222 B8
Swinton La YO17 ... 121 B3
Swinton Rd Masham HG4 ... 86 C3
Swinton HG4 ... 86 B2
Swinton Terr HG4 ... 86 C3
Swires La BD20 ... 173 C3
Swire Way DL10 ... 20 F7
Swordfish Way LS25 ... 196 B4
Sycamore Ave
4 Catton YO7 ... 89 A1
19 Filey YO14 ... 101 B4
1 Hut Green DN14 ... 203 A2
Kippax LS25 ... 194 C1
Knottingley WF11 ... 201 E1
Malton YO17 ... 215 D5
Richmond DL10 ... 209 A8
York YO32 ... 225 D4
Sycamore Cl
Bishop Monkton HG3 ... 140 A5
Clint HG3 ... 160 F8
1 Haxby YO32 ... 225 D7
3 Hurworth-on-Tees DL2 ... 3 E1
Selby YO8 ... 232 A4
Skelton YO30 ... 224 C5
Slingsby YO62 ... 120 B5
Spennithorne DL8 ... 60 F4
Sycamore Ct
2 Catterick DL10 ... 41 D5
Hellifield BD23 ... 154 B3
2 Pontefract WF8 ... 201 C1
Sycamore Dr
11 Addingham LS29 ... 175 A4
9 Bedale DL8 ... 63 A2
Harrogate HG2 ... 220 C3
Norton-le-Clay YO7 ... 115 B1
Sycamore Gr
Sherburn YO17 ... 124 E7
Steeton with Eastburn BD20 ... 187 F7
Sycamore La DL7 ... 63 D4
Sycamore Mews YO8 ... 232 D2
Sycamore Pk YO12 ... 212 B7
Sycamore Pl
New Earswick YO32 ... 225 D4
York YO30 ... 233 A3
Sycamore Rd Barlby with Osgodby YO8 ... 198 B5
Ripon HG4 ... 214 B2
Sycamores The
Barwick in Elmet LS15 ... 194 B8
42 Earby BB18 ... 172 A1
Sycamore Terr YO30 ... 233 A3
Sycamore View 17 YO26 ... 165 F1
Sycamore Way 16 BB18 ... 171 D1
Sydall's Way 1 DL10 ... 41 E4
Sydney Avenue E DL6 ... 210 E4
Sydney St 5 YO12 ... 212 F7
Sykehead La YO62 ... 93 D6
Sykes Gr HG1 ... 219 C5
Sykes La YO61 ... 143 B3

T

Tabard Hamlet 5 DN14 ... 202 F2
Tabard Rd 6 DN14 ... 202 F2
Tabards The 7 DN14 ... 202 F2
TADCASTER ... 189 D6
Tadcaster East Prim Sch 6 LS24 ... 189 F6
Tadcaster Gram Sch LS24 ... 189 B5
Tadcaster L Ctr LS24 ... 189 E6
Tadcaster Rd
Copmanthorpe YO23 ... 230 C4
York YO24 ... 227 F1
Tadcaster Rd Dringhouses YO23 ... 230 E5
Tadcaster Swimming Pool LS24 ... 189 E6
Talbenny Gr 32 TS17 ... 5 F4
Talbot Ct YO22 ... 208 E5
Talbot St WF6 ... 200 A1
Talisman Cl 9 TS16 ... 5 D5
Tally Hill YO61 ... 144 A4
Talybont Gr 19 TS17 ... 5 F4
TAME BRIDGE ... 26 A7
Tameside TS9 ... 26 C8
Tamworth Rd 9 YO30 ... 225 A1
Tanfield Dr 1 LS29 ... 176 C1
Tanfield La HG4 ... 114 A8
TANG ... 160 D4
TANG HALL ... 228 F5
Tang Hall La YO31 ... 229 A5
Tang Hall Prim Sch YO31 ... 228 F5
Tang Rd HG3 ... 160 D4
Tanner Row YO1 ... 233 A2
Tanner's Moat YO1 ... 233 A2
Tanner St YO1 ... 233 B2
Tannery Ct 10 HG5 ... 221 B5
Tannery La
Embsay BD23 ... 217 D8
Northallerton DL7 ... 210 D5
Tannery The 10 YO10 ... 228 E3
Tanpit La
Easingwold YO61 ... 143 C8
Walden Stubbs DN6 ... 206 E3
Tansy Cl 2 HG3 ... 161 B3
Tansy Rd 3 HG3 ... 161 B3
TANTON ... 7 C1
Tanton Cl TS9 ... 7 A1
Tanton Rd TS9 ... 7 B1
Tarbard Ave 14 HG4 ... 113 D2
Tarbert Cres 2 YO24 ... 230 B7
Tarell Ct 45 TS17 ... 5 F4
Tarn Ct LS29 ... 218 C3
Tarn Moor Cres BD23 ... 216 E6
Tarns La BD23 ... 134 C1
Tarr Steps TS17 ... 6 A3
Tasmania Sq TS7 ... 7 C6
Tate Cl YO8 ... 197 D6
Tatefield Pl 1 LS25 ... 194 D1
Tate Hill YO22 ... 208 E7
Tate Rd DL10 ... 209 C8
Tatham Fells CE Prim Sch LA2 ... 128 F3
Tatton Cl YO30 ... 225 A1
Taurus Ct YO23 ... 233 A1
Taylor Gr LS26 ... 200 C6
Taylor Hill YO18 ... 71 F7
Taylor La LS15 ... 194 A7
Taylorsons Terr 2 YO22 ... 208 E6
Taylor St 8 BB18 ... 171 D1
Tayport Cl DL1 ... 3 D8
Teal Cl Castleford WF10 ... 200 E3
2 Filey YO14 ... 101 A3
Teal Dr YO24 ... 230 C8
Teal La 6 YO18 ... 95 F7
Teal Rd DL1 ... 3 E5
Teapottery The* DL8 ... 60 E5
Teasel Gr 31 HG3 ... 161 B3
Tebay Cl
2 Eastbourne DL1 ... 3 D4
Middlesbrough TS7 ... 7 D8
Tedder Ave TS17 ... 6 B6
Tedder Rd YO24 ... 227 B1
Tedworth Cl TS14 ... 8 F5
Tees Bank Ave TS18 ... 5 E6
Tees Cottage Pumping Sta* DL2 ... 2 F4
Teesdale Ave DL3 ... 3 A4
Teesdale Rd DL9 ... 40 E4
Teesdale Terr 27 DL9 ... 40 E4
Teesgate TS17 ... 6 C8
Tees Grange Ave DL3 ... 3 A5
Tees-Side Airport Sta DL2 ... 4 F4
Teesside High Sch TS16 ... 5 E5
Teesside Ind Est TS17 ... 6 C5
Tees View Gainford DL2 ... 1 D7
Hurworth DL2 ... 3 C1
Hurworth-on-Tees DL2 ... 22 C8
Teeswater Dr 12 DL2 ... 3 A7
Teesway DL2 ... 4 A1
Telford Cl WF10 ... 200 D4
Telford Terr 1 YO24 ... 228 B2
Temperance Sq BD23 ... 154 B3
Templar Cl DN14 ... 202 F1
Templar Gdns LS22 ... 180 C4
Templar Way YO8 ... 232 C2
Temple Ave YO10 ... 229 B4
Temple Bank DL8 ... 59 A3
Temple Ct DL10 ... 209 B6
Temple Garth YO23 ... 230 C1
TEMPLE HIRST ... 203 E4
Temple La
Burton cum Walden DL8 ... 82 D3
Copmanthorpe YO23 ... 230 C1
Templemead YO31 ... 228 E8
Temple Rd YO23 ... 230 F4
Temple Sq DL10 ... 209 B6
Temple St WF10 ... 200 E4
Tems Side 3 BD24 ... 131 D2
Tems St 2 BD24 ... 131 D2
Tennant St YO8 ... 232 B6
Tennent Rd YO24 ... 227 B2
Tennis Court La YO61 ... 143 A3
Tennyson Ave
1 Campsall DN6 ... 206 E1
Harrogate HG1 ... 219 E7
Scarborough YO12 ... 212 F7
York YO30 ... 228 C7
Tennyson Cl WF8 ... 201 D2
Tennyson Way 3 WF8 ... 201 B1
Tenter Fields YO7 ... 88 D1
Tentergate Ave 4 HG5 ... 221 A7
Tentergate Cl 3 HG5 ... 221 A7
Tentergate Gdns 2 HG5 ... 221 A7
Tentergate La HG5 ... 221 A7
Tentergate Rd 5 HG5 ... 221 A7
Tenter Hill LS23 ... 188 D5
Tenters Cl WF11 ... 201 E3
Ten Thorn La YO26 ... 227 A4
Tern Pk 6 LS22 ... 180 A1
TERRINGTON ... 119 F1
Terrington Bank YO60 ... 119 C2
Terrington CE Prim Sch YO60 ... 119 E1
Terrington Cl YO32 ... 167 B8
Terrington Hall Sch YO60 ... 119 F1
Terrington South Bank YO60 ... 119 D1
Terrington View YO60 ... 145 C5
Terror Twr* YO11 ... 213 B6
Terry Ave YO1 ... 233 B1
Terry Dicken Ind Est TS9 ... 26 D6
Terry St YO23 ... 228 C1
Tetherings La YO13 ... 98 F5
Tewit Well Ave HG2 ... 222 D8
Tewit Well Rd HG2 ... 222 E7
Thackadale La YO17 ... 121 A1
Thackeray Gr TS5 ... 6 E8
Thacking La LA6 ... 103 D4
Thames Ave
Guisborough TS14 ... 8 E6
Thornaby TS17 ... 6 B7
Thanet Rd YO24 ... 227 D1
Thanets Ct 9 BD23 ... 216 F3
Thatch Cl YO8 ... 232 C4
Thatchers Croft YO23 ... 230 C3
THEAKSTON ... 87 E8
Theakston Hargill DL8 ... 87 E8
Theakston La DL10 ... 209 C5
Theresa Cl 6 YO31 ... 225 F1
Thickrash Brow LA2 ... 129 A7
Thiefgate La DL8 ... 86 E3
Thiefhole La DL7 ... 65 B3
Thief La Barlow YO8 ... 232 F1
York YO10 ... 228 F3
THIMBLEBY ... 45 A2
Third Ave
10 Wetherby LS22 ... 180 C3
York YO31 ... 228 F5
Thirkleby Walk 1 YO10 ... 229 D3
Thirkleby Way YO10 ... 229 C4
THIRLBY ... 90 E7
Thirlby Way 8 TS14 ... 8 F7
Thirlmere Cl 3 YO7 ... 89 C4
Thirlmere Dr YO31 ... 229 A6
Thirlway Dr HG4 ... 214 B6
THIRN ... 86 B8
THIRSK ... 211 C2
Thirsk Bank
Angram Grange YO7 ... 117 B8
Thornton-le-Moor DL7 ... 65 B3
Thirsk Bsns Pk YO7 ... 211 B2
Thirsk Ind Pk YO7 ... 211 D2
Thirsk Mus* YO7 ... 211 B3
Thirsk Prim Sch YO7 ... 211 C4
Thirsk Racecourse* YO7 ... 211 A3
Thirsk Rd Eaglescliffe TS15 ... 5 E2
Easingwold YO61 ... 117 B1
Kirkby TS9 ... 26 C6
Romanby DL6 ... 210 F1
Thirsk Sch YO7 ... 211 B1
Thirsk Sta YO7 ... 89 D4
Thirsk Swimming Pool YO7 ... 211 C2
Thirty Acre La HG5 ... 163 A6
Thirwall Dr TS17 ... 6 A4
Thistlebar Rd YO51 ... 141 D2
Thistle Cl
Northallerton DL7 ... 210 D1
Selby YO8 ... 232 C2
Thistle Hill HG5 ... 221 B3
Thistle Rise TS8 ... 6 F6
THIXENDALE ... 170 E7
THOLTHORPE ... 142 D5
Thomas Gill Rd 7 HG3 ... 137 F1
Thomson Foss (Waterfall)* YO22 ... 31 C1

Thomas St
  21 Cross Hills BD20 . . . . . 187 E8
  6 Selby YO8 . . . . 232 D6
  2 York YO10 . . . . 228 E3
Thompson Cl
  9 Barlby YO8 . . . . 198 B4
  29 Scalby YO12 . . . . 75 D5
Thompson Dr 2 YO32 . . 167 B8
Thompson Pl 6 YO26 . . . 227 E5
Thompson Street E DL1 . . 3 D7
Thompson Street W DL3 . . 3 C7
THORALBY 58 E1
Thoresby La DL8 . . . . 59 E5
Thoresby Rd YO24 . . . . . 227 B1
THORGANBY 193 B4
THORGILL 49 C3
Thorington Gdns TS17 . . 216 B6
THORLBY 116 F5
THORMANBY 116 F5
Thornaby CE Prim Sch
  TS17 . . . . 6 B7
Thornaby Com Sch TS17 . . 6 B7
THORNABY-ON-TEES 6 A7
Thornaby Rd TS17 . . . . 6 B7
Thornaby Swimming Pool
  TS17 . . . . 6 A8
Thornbeck YO19 . . . . . . 184 E6
THORNBOROUGH 87 C2
Thornborough Cres 4
  DL8 . . . . 60 D5
Thornbrough Rd DL6 . . . 210 E3
Thornburgh Rd 6 YO11 . . 99 F6
Thorncroft 8 YO19 . . . . 184 F7
Thorndale St BD23 . . . . 154 B3
Thornden Bldgs YO8 . . . 232 D5
Thorndikes La HG5 . . . . 141 D4
Thorne Cl 13 WF6 . . . . . 200 B1
Thorner CE Prim Sch
  LS14 . . . . 188 A3
Thorner Gr BD20 . . . . . 174 C2
Thorner La LS23 . . . . . . 188 B5
Thorner Rd LS23 . . . . . . 188 B4
Thornfield Ave
  Dishforth YO7 . . . . 115 A4
  5 York YO31 . . . . 228 F8
Thornfield Bsns Pk DL7 . 210 B6
Thornfield Dr 7 YO31 . . 225 F2
Thornfield Gr TS5 . . . . 6 E8
Thornfield Rd DL8 . . . . . 87 C3
Thornhill
  6 Eastfield YO11 . . . . . 100 A6
  Northallerton DL6 . . . . 210 E3
  14 Richmond DL10 . . . . 209 C6
Thornhill Rd WF10 . . . . 200 F3
Thornhills 19 YO32 . . . . 166 F5
Thornlands 9 YO61 . . . . 117 D1
Thornley Ave DL7 . . . . . 210 E3
Thorn Nook YO31 . . . . . 228 F8
THORNS 35 E7
Thorns La YO51 . . . . . . 140 F4
THORNTHWAITE 159 D6
Thornthwaite Brow HG3 . 159 E5
THORNTON 6 E4
Thornton Cl
  15 Easingwold YO61 . . . 143 D8
  Stainton & Thornton TS8 . . 6 D4
Thornton Dale CE Prim Sch
  YO18 . . . . 96 C5
Thornton Hts BD23 . . . . 172 A3
THORNTON-IN-
  CRAVEN 172 A3
Thornton-in-Craven Prim
  Sch BD23 . . . . 172 A3
THORNTON IN
  LONSDALE 103 C4
Thornton La Dent LA10 . . 78 A4
  Marishes YO17 . . . . 96 B1
  Thornton in Lonsdale LA6 . 103 C4
  Thornton-on-the-Hill YO61 117 D4
THORNTON-LE-BEANS . . . 65 B5
THORNTON-LE-CLAY . . . 146 A4
THORNTON-LE-DALE 96 B5
THORNTON-LE-MOOR . . . 65 B3
THORNTON-LE-STREET . . . 65 B5
Thornton Moor Cl YO30 . 224 F2
Thornton Rd
  Coulby Newham TS8 . . . . 6 D4
  Pickering YO18 . . . . 96 A6
Thornton Road Ind Est
  YO18 . . . . 96 A5
THORNTON RUST 58 B4
Thornton St
  14 Burley in Warfedale
    LS29 . . . . 176 C1
  Darlington DL3 . . . . 3 C5
  3 Skipton BD23 . . . . . . 216 D3
THORNTON STEWARD . . . 61 D1
Thornton Vale TS8 . . . . . . 6 E4
THORNTON WATLASS . . . 86 D8
Thornton Watlass CE Prim
  Sch HG4 . . . . 86 D8
Thorn Tree Ave 6 YO14 . 101 B4
Thorntree Gdns DL2 . . . . . 4 C4
Thorntree Gr YO30 . . . . 225 B2
Thorntree La DN14 . . . . 207 C6
Thorntree Rd
  Northallerton DL6 . . . . 210 F6
  Thornaby TS17 . . . . 6 B7
Thornview Rd BD23 . . . . 154 B3
Thorn Wath La YO62 . . . . 48 E4
Thornwood Ave TS17 . . . . 6 A5
Thornwood Covert 1
  YO24 . . . . 227 C1
Thorny Hill La YO51 . . . . 141 E2
Thorny La YO42 . . . . . . 169 F2
THORP ARCH 188 F8
Thorp Arch Pk LS23 . . . . 180 F1

Thorp Arch Trad Est
  LS23 . . . . 189 A8
THORPE. 156 F8
Thorpe Bank 6 YO22 . . . 33 C3
THORPE BASSETT 123 A4
Thorpe Bassett La YO17 . 122 C1
Thorpe Chase HG4 . . . . 214 E3
Thorpe Green Bank 1
  YO22 . . . . 33 C3
Thorpe Green La YO26 . . 164 B7
Thorpe La
  Ampleforth YO62 . . . . . 118 B8
  Cawood YO8 . . . . 197 B8
  Cracoe BD23 . . . . 156 C7
  Fylingdales YO22 . . . . . . 33 C4
  Thorpe BD23 . . . . 156 D8
Thorpe Prebend House -
  Heritage Ctr * HG4. . . . 214 C5
Thorpe Rd HG4 . . . . 86 C2
Thorpe St YO23 . . . . . . 228 B2
THORPE UNDERWOOD . . 164 C6
THORPE WILLOUGHBY . . 197 C2
Thorpe Willoughby Prim Sch
  YO8. . . . . 197 B2
Thorp Perrow Arboretum &
  Falconry Ctr * DL8. . . . . 87 A8
Threapland BD23 . . . . . 156 C7
Three Lakes Ind Est YO8 232 D2
Three Lakes Ret Pk YO8 232 D3
Three Lane Ends Junior &
  Infant Sch WF10 . . . . . 200 D4
Three Tuns Wynd 7 TS9 . 26 C7
THRESHFIELD 134 D2
Threshfield Prim Sch
  BD23 . . . . 134 D2
THRINTOFT 64 A8
Thrintoft La DL7 . . . . 64 A7
Thrintoft Moor La DL7 . . . 64 A8
Thrope La HG3 . . . . 110 C4
Throstle Farm Junior &
  Infant Sch WF11 . . . . . 201 F1
Throstle Nest Cl LS21 . . 176 E1
Throstle Nest Dr HG2 . . 222 D6
THROXENBY 212 A7
Throxenby Gr 3 YO12 . . 212 B7
Throxenby La YO12 . . . . 212 B7
THRUSCROSS 159 A5
Thruscross La HG3 . . . . 159 B5
Thrussendale Rd YO17 . . 169 E8
Thunderhead Ridge
  WF10 . . . . 200 F3
Thurland Castle * LA6. . . 102 B3
Thurston Rd DL6 . . . . . . 210 C7
THWAITE 35 F5
Thwaite Holme La DL8 . . 57 F5
Thwaite La LA2 . . . . 128 E5
Thwaites Ave LS29 . . . . 218 C4
Thwaites La
  Markington with Wallerthwaite
    HG3. . . . . 139 D5
  Nether Silton YO7 . . . . . 66 C7
Thirkleby High & Low with
  Osgodby YO7 . . . . 90 E1
Thweng Way TS14 . . . . . . 8 E5
THWING 126 B1
Thwing Rd YO25 . . . . . . 126 E2
Tibby Butts 26 YO13 . . . 75 D5
Tibgarth LS22 . . . . 180 A2
Tickergate La DL7 . . . . . . 63 A8
Tidkin La TS14 . . . . 8 E6
Tile Cl BD23 . . . . 217 B3
Tillman Cl BD24 . . . . . . 131 D2
Tillotson's Ct BD20 . . . . 173 D1
Tilmire Cl 2 YO10 . . . . . 231 F8
TIMBLE 176 D7
Timble Gr HG1 . . . . 219 B5
Timmys La DL2 . . . . 3 F1
Tindall St YO12 . . . . 212 F5
Tinker La YO23 . . . . 182 D6
Tinkers' La HG3 . . . . . . 139 A1
Tinkingfield La LS22 . . . 181 A5
Tinkler La
  Milby YO51 . . . . 141 C6
  Winsley HG3 . . . . 160 E8
Tinkler's La WF11 . . . . . 202 D6
Tinley Garth YO62 . . . . . . 70 B1
Tinley Gdns 14 YO62 . . . . 70 B1
Tintagel Ct WF6 . . . . . . 200 A2
Tiplady Cl 18 YO61 . . . . 143 C8
Tippaty La WF11 . . . . . . 202 A4
Tirril Way TS7 . . . . 7 C5
Tithe Barn Fold LS15 . . 194 B8
Tithe Barn Rd 2 WF11 . . 202 A2
Tithe Barn Way DN14 . . 202 F3
Tithe Cl YO24 . . . . 227 B1
Tithe Way HG4 . . . . 114 F1
Tivoli Pl LS29 . . . . 218 C3
Toadham La DN14 . . . . . 207 C5
Toby Ct YO32 . . . . 167 A7
TOCKWITH 181 D7
Tockwith CE Prim Sch
  YO26 . . . . 181 C7
Tockwith La YO26 . . . . . 181 D6
Tockwith Rd
  Long Marston YO26 . . . . 181 F6
  Tockwith LS22 . . . . 180 F7
Toc La YO18 . . . . 97 C5
Todd La DL7 . . . . 63 B8
Todds Ct 8 YO7 . . . . . . 211 C3
Tod Holes La BD23 . . . . 153 B4
Todley Hall Rd BD22 . . . 187 F3
Todmanhaw La BD23 . . . 153 E3
Tofta Dr YO13 . . . . 54 A5
Toft Gn YO1 . . . . 233 A2
Tofting La YO17 . . . . . . 148 B5
Toft Ings La YO61 . . . . . 143 D8
Tofts Cl TS15 . . . . 24 B8
Tofts Fort The * DL11. . . . 1 E2

Tofts La
  Danby YO21 . . . . 29 B5
  Follifoot HG3 . . . . 223 F4
  Humberton YO61 . . . . . 141 F8
  Pickering YO18 . . . . 95 F3
  Tholthorpe YO61 . . . . . 142 D6
  Welbury DL6 . . . . 24 B1
Tofts Rd YO17 . . . . 95 F3
Toll Bar Cl 3 YO8. . . . . . 196 E1
Toll Bar Rd WF10 . . . . . 200 C4
Toll Bar Way LS24. . . . . 189 F7
Tollergate YO11 . . . . . . 213 A7
TOLLERTON 143 A3
Tollerton La YO30. . . . . . 165 B7
Tollerton Rd YO61 . . . . . 143 D4
TOLLESBY 7 A6
Tollesby Bridge TS8. . . . . . 7 A6
Tollesby La TS7. . . . . 7 B6
Tollesby Rd TS5 . . . . 6 F8
Tollesby Specl Sch IS4. . . . 6 F8
Toll Hill Cl WF11 . . . . . . 201 A3
Toll Hill Dr WF11 . . . . . . 201 A3
Tomahawk Trail WF10 . . 200 F3
Tom Cat La
  Bilton-in-Ainsty with Bickerton
    LS22 . . . . 181 A5
  Birdsall YO17 . . . . 148 B4
Tom Dando Cl WF8 . . . . 200 C1
Tomgill Bank DL8. . . . . . . 58 E2
Tom Hall Ct 12 DL8. . . . . 63 A2
Tom La
  Cowling BD22 . . . . 186 E7
  Dunsforths YO26 . . . . . 141 F3
  Hillam LS25 . . . . 202 B7
Tomlinson Way LS25 . . . 195 E4
Tom Smith's Cross YO62 . 92 B4
Topcliff Ct YO8 . . . . 232 B7
TOPCLIFFE 115 B7
Topcliffe CE Prim Sch
  YO7. . . . . 115 C7
Topcliffe Rd Sowerby YO7 . 89 E3
  Thirsk YO7 . . . . 211 B1
  Thornaby TS17. . . . . 6 C7
Top Fold WF11 . . . . 201 D6
Top House Ct WF8 . . . . . 206 B3
Top House Farm Mews 2
  WF11 . . . . 201 D6
Top La Colne BB8 . . . . . 186 B2
  Copmanthorpe YO23 . . . 230 B3
  Norwood LS21 . . . . 177 A6
Top Stone Cl LS25 . . . . . 201 F6
Toremill Cl YO32 . . . . . . 225 D4
Torrance Dr DL1 . . . . 3 F8
Torridon Pl YO24 . . . . . 230 B7
Torrs Rd HG1 . . . . 220 A3
TOSSIDE 152 F3
Tostig Ave YO26 . . . . . . 227 C5
Tostig Cl 14 YO41 . . . . . 168 D2
Tostig La YO62 . . . . 120 D7
TOULSTON 189 B7
Toulston La LS23. . . . . . 188 F5
Tout Hill YO60 . . . . 146 E5
Tower Cres LS24 . . . . . . 189 D6
Tower Croft 7 YO61 . . . . 117 D1
Tower Ct YO30 . . . . 225 A2
Tower Grange DL3 . . . . . . 3 B7
Tower Pl YO1 . . . . 233 B1
Tower Rd
  Darlington DL3. . . . . 3 B6
  Ripon HG4 . . . . 214 C6
Towers Paddock WF10. . 201 A4
Tower St Harrogate HG1. 219 D1
  10 Richmond DL10 . . . . 209 C6
  York YO1 . . . . 233 B1
Tower Street Castle W 4
  DL10. . . . . 209 C6
Tower View YO14 . . . . . 204 C2
Townc8lose View LS25 . . 200 C8
Town End YO7 . . . . 211 B2
Town End Ave DN14 . . . 204 C3
Town End Cl
  16 Glusburn BD20 . . . . . 187 E7
  2 Kirklevington TS15 . . . 24 F8
  9 Pickering YO18 . . . . . . 96 A6
Townend Ct 3 YO26 . . . 164 A8
Town End Gdns 3 YO32 166 D5
Townend Pl 5 BD20 . . . . 187 E7
Townend Rd YO42 . . . . . 193 D1
Townend St YO31 . . . . . 233 B4
Town Farm Cl 15 YO62 . . 70 B1
Town Green Dr TS9 . . . . . 26 E5
TOWN HEAD 174 C1
Townhead 2 BD24 . . . . . 131 E2
Town Head Ave 1 BD24 . 131 E3
Townhead Croft BD24 . . 131 E3
Town Head Fold 12 LS29 174 F4
Townhead La LA2. . . . . . 130 E8
Town Head Rd BD24 . . . 131 E2
Town Head Way 14
  BD24 . . . . 131 D2
Town Hill LS23 . . . . 188 E5
Town St
  Bishop Thornton HG3. . . 138 F1
  Brandsby-cum-Stearsby
    YO61 . . . . 118 D3
  Malton YO17 . . . . 215 E6
  Nidd HG3 . . . . 161 E7
  Scampston YO17 . . . . . 123 A6
  Settrington YO17 . . . . . 122 C1
Townville Infant Sch
  WF10 . . . . 201 B4
Tow Scar Rd LA6 . . . . . . 103 C5
TOWTHORPE Duggleby. . 149 D1
  York 167 B5
Towthorpe Moor La
  YO32 . . . . 167 C5
Towthorpe Rd YO32 . . . . 166 F5
TOWTON 189 E2

Towton Ave 9 YO24 . . . . 227 F2
Tow Top La BD20 . . . . . 173 A1
Trafalgar Ct 10 HG1 . . . 219 D1
Trafalgar Rd
  11 Harrogate HG1. . . . . 219 D1
  Ilkley LS29 . . . . 218 B4
  Scarborough YO12. . . . . 212 F7
Trafalgar Sq
  Meagill LS21 . . . . 159 E4
  Scarborough YO12 . . . . 212 F7
Trafalgar St YO23 . . . . . 228 B1
Trafalgar Street W YO12. 212 F6
Trafalgar Terr YO12 . . . . 212 F7
Trafford Cl 19 DL1 . . . . 3 F6
Trafford Rd 4 DN6 . . . . 206 E2
Train La YO18 . . . . 95 F7
Tranby Ave YO10. . . . . . 229 D4
Tranmere Ct 2 BD23. . . 153 F5
Tranmire Cl YO7. . . . . . . 211 D4
Tranmore La DN14 . . . . 203 B3
Trans Wlk LS24 . . . . 190 B1
Tranter Rd TS4 . . . . 6 F8
Trapping Hill HG3 . . . . . 110 C4
Trattles Hill YO13 . . . . . . 54 D2
Travellers Garth YO17. . 121 C1
TRAWDEN 186 B1
Trawden Forest Prim Sch 4
  BB8. . . . . 186 A1
Trawden Rd BB8 . . . . . . 186 A3
Treasurer's House * YO1. 233 B3
Trecastell 25 TS17. . . . . . 5 F4
Treesdale Rd 1 HG2 . . . 219 C2
Trefoil Cl TS14. . . . . 8 D6
Trefoil Dr 4 HG3 . . . . . 161 B3
Trefoil Wood TS7 . . . . 7 B7
Trencar La YO61 . . . . . . 91 A2
Trenchard Ave TS17. . . . . 6 B6
Trenchard Rd YO26 . . . . 227 B6
Trenchard St 8 YO7 . . . . 89 B1
Trenfield Ct YO30. . . . . . 224 F3
Trenholme Cl 7 TS17 . . . . 6 D6
Trenholme La TS15 . . . . . 25 B3
Trent Ave
  Garforth LS25 . . . . 194 D3
  Pontefract WF6 . . . . . . 200 A2
  4 York YO32. . . . . 225 F6
Trentholme Dr 2 YO24. . 228 A2
Trent Way YO24. . . . . . . 230 D7
Trevine Gdns TS17 . . . . . . 5 F4
Trevino Ct TS16. . . . . 5 E5
Trevithick Cl 7 TS16. . . . 5 D5
Trevithick Rd WF10 . . . 200 F3
Trevor Gr 8 YO24 . . . . . 227 F2
Triangle The TS14 . . . . . 8 D6
Tribune Way YO30 . . . . 225 B2
Trimdon Ave TS5 . . . . . . 6 D6
Trinity Church Sq 9
  DL10. . . . . 209 C6
Trinity Cl 1 YO11 . . . . . 212 F1
Trinity Gdns
  Northallerton DL6 . . . . 210 F3
  2 Scarborough YO11 . . 212 F3
Trinity La
  Ripon HG4 . . . . 214 B5
  York YO1 . . . . 233 A2
Trinity Mdws YO32 . . . . 167 D3
Trinity Mews DL3 . . . . . . 3 C5
Trinity Pk HG4 . . . . 214 B6
Trinity Rd
  Darlington DL3. . . . . 3 C5
  Harrogate HG2 . . . . . . 219 D1
  Scarborough YO11 . . . . 212 F3
Trinket La LA2. . . . . 128 B6
Trip Garth LS22 . . . . . . 180 A1
Trip La
  Collingham LS22 . . . . . 180 A2
  Sicklinghall LS22 . . . . . 179 F1
Triplins La HG4 . . . . 113 B6
Tristram Ave DL3 . . . . 3 C7
Troon Cl 2 YO26 . . . . . . 227 B5
Trousdale Hill YO60 . . . 147 A7
Troutbeck 7 YO24 . . . . 230 C7
Troutbeck Cl 11 YO18 . . 95 F6
Troutsdale Ave YO30 . . . 224 E2
Trumfleet La DN6. . . . . . 207 D1
Trundles La 7 WF11 . . . 202 A2
Truro Cres 8 HG3 . . . . . 161 B3
Truro Dr 19 WF6 . . . . . . 200 A2
Truro Rd 7 HG3 . . . . . . 161 B3
Truro Wlk 23 WF6 . . . . 200 A2
Trust Fold LS25 . . . . 201 E6
Tubwell Rd DL1 . . . . 3 C5
Tucker Cl DL6 . . . . 210 E5
Tudor Cl 10 YO8 . . . . . . 197 B1
Tudor Ct 7 DL10 . . . . 41 C7
Tudor Rd Richmond DL10 209 D7
  York YO24 . . . . 227 C2
Tudor Way YO32 . . . . . . 167 C8
Tufton Pl BD23 . . . . 216 F3
Tuke Ave YO10 . . . . 229 B4
Tumbledown Cl 5 DL9. . . 40 E3
Tune St YO8 . . . . 198 B4
TUNSTALL Catterick 41 B2
  Cowan Bridge 102 B4
Tunstall Rd
  Catterick DL10 . . . . 41 D4
  Harrogate HG2 . . . . . . 220 B3
Turbary La YO32 . . . . . . 226 E6
Turbary Rd LA6 . . . . 103 B7
Turfy Hill DL8. . . . . 56 C4
Turker Cl DL6 . . . . 210 E5
Turker La DL6 . . . . 210 F6
Turkey La Baldersby YO7. . 88 D1
  Catton YO7 . . . . 114 F8
Turkhan Cl YO7 . . . . 211 D2
Turkish Baths & Health Spa
  HG2 . . . . 219 C2

Tho–Upp 273

Turks Head Ct YO1 . . . . 233 C3
Turnberry Ave TS16 . . . . 5 E4
Turnberry Dr YO26 . . . . 227 B4
Turnberry Way TS8 . . . . . 7 C5
Turner Cl DL9 . . . . 209 C2
Turner Cres 6 LS21 . . . . 177 A1
Turner La LS29 . . . . 174 E4
Turner's Croft YO10 . . . . 229 A1
Turners Sq 9 YU8 . . . . . 232 C5
Turner St 13 BB18 . . . . . 171 E1
Turnham La YO8 . . . . . . 198 C2
Turnhead Cres YO8 . . . . 198 B5
Turnhead Ct YO8 . . . . . 198 B6
Turnmire Rd 1 YO24. . . 230 E8
Turnpike La LS22 . . . . . 181 B5
Turnpike Rd LS24 . . . . . 189 F7
Turnshaw Rd BD22. . . . . 187 F1
Turpin Ct YO1 . . . . 233 C1
Turpin La LS25. . . . . . . 196 A2
Turton Rd TS15 . . . . 5 D2
Turver's La WF11 . . . . . 202 C2
Tuscany Way WF6 . . . . . 200 A3
Tuthill 13 YO11 . . . . . . 213 B6
Tutin Rd DL7 . . . . 63 C5
Tweed Ave TS17 . . . . 6 B7
Tweed St 5 LA2 . . . . . . 129 A8
Twelve Acre Bank DL9 . . 40 E1
Twine Wlk 7 LA6 . . . . . 102 F3
Twin Pike Way 14 YO32 . 166 D5
Twizzie Gill View 6 TS13 . 11 A8
Two Laws Rd BB8 . . . . . 187 B1
Tyler Cl WF6 . . . . 200 C1
Tyne Cres DL1 . . . . 3 D3
Tyn Garth YO19 . . . . . . 191 D8
Typhoon Cl DL10 . . . . . . 41 F6
Tyseley Gr 4 BB18. . . . . 172 A3
Tyson Pl HG2 . . . . 220 B2

U

UCKERBY 21 E1
UGGLEBARNBY 32 C6
UGTHORPE 11 F2
Uldale Cl 5 HG5 . . . . . . 221 D5
Uldale Dr TS16. . . . . 5 E4
Ulla Gn LS24. . . . . 190 B1
ULLESKELF 190 C2
Ulleskelf Sta LS24. . . . . 190 B2
Ullswater YO24 . . . . 230 D7
Ullswater Ave TS5 . . . . . . 6 E8
Ullswater Dr LS22. . . . . 180 B3
Ullswater Rise 5 LS22 . . 180 B3
Ulnaby La DL2 . . . . 2 C7
ULSHAW 61 A2
Ulswater Ave 5 DL1 . . . . 3 D4
Under Cliffe 17 YO18 . . . 95 F7
Undercliffe Rise LS29 . . 218 E2
Undercroft 7 YO19 . . . . 184 F7
Underlands La HG4 . . . . 114 C7
Underwit Rd YO8 . . . . . 204 C4
Union House BD23 . . . . 217 A3
Union La YO8 . . . . 232 C4
Union Rd 24 YO21 . . . . 208 D6
Union St
  28 Filey YO14 . . . . 101 B3
  Harrogate HG1 . . . . . . 219 D3
  12 Knaresborough HG5. . 221 A5
  12 York YO11 . . . . 213 A6
Union Terr
  5 Skipton BD23 . . . . . . 216 F3
  York YO31 . . . . 233 B4
Unity Cl HG1. . . . . 219 D5
Unity Gr HG1 . . . . 219 D5
Unity St 1 BB18 . . . . . . 186 A7
University of Hull
  (Scarborough Campus)
  YO12 . . . . 213 B1
University of Leeds (Headley
  Hall) LS24 . . . . 189 A4
University of York (King's
  Manor) YO30 . . . . 233 A3
University of York (Main
  Campus) YO10 . . . . . . 229 A1
University Rd YO10. . . . . 228 F2
Univesity of Hull @
  Scarborough YO11 . . . . 213 B1
Upgang La YO21 . . . . . . 208 B7
Upgarth Cl 2 TS13. . . . . 12 A7
Uplands BD23. . . . . 217 B5
Uplands Ave 8 YO13. . . . 99 B8
Uplands Rd DL3. . . . . 3 B5
Uplands The YO12. . . . . 212 A7
Upper Carr La YO18. . . . . 96 A4
Uppercommon La DN14 . 202 F3
Uppercroft 4 YO32 . . . . 225 C8
UPPER DUNSFORTH . . . 142 A2
Upper Dunsforth Carrs
  Nature Reserve * YO26 142 A1
Uppergate LA6. . . . . . . 103 D4
Upper Green La TS18. . . . 6 A7
Upper Hanover St 6
  YO26 . . . . 227 F5
UPPER HELMSLEY 168 B3
Upper Newborough St 1
  YO30 . . . . 228 C7
UPPER POPPLETON 165 F1
Upper Price St YO23 . . . 233 A1
Upper Sackville St 5
  BD23 . . . . 217 A3
Upper St Paul's Terr
  YO24 . . . . 228 A4
Upper Union St BD23. . . 216 F3
Upper Wharfedale Folk
  Mus * BD23 . . . . 134 E2

Upper Wharfedale Sch
BD23 134 D2
Uppleby YO61 117 D1
UPSALL 66 B2
Upsall Dr DL3 3 C4
Upsall La
South Kilvington YO7 211 C7
Thornbrough YO7 90 A8
Upsall YO7 66 B1
Upsall Rd YO7 66 B1
Upwell Rd DL7 210 D4
URE BANK 214 D7
Ure Bank HG4 214 D7
Ure Bank Maltings HG4 214 D8
Ure Bank Terr HG4 214 C7
Ure Bank Top HG4 214 D7
Uredale Glass* HG4 86 C3
URLAY NOOK 5 B5
Urlay Nook Rd TS16 5 C5
URRA 47 A8
Usher La YO32 166 F6
Usk Ct 21 TS17 5 F4

V

Vale Ave WF11 201 E2
Vale Cres
Bishop Wilton YO42 169 F2
Knottingley WF11 201 E2
Vale Crest WF11 201 E2
Vale Ct HG5 221 A6
Vale Gdns LS29 218 D4
Vale The
10 Collingham LS22 188 A8
Middlesbrough TS5 6 F8
Skelton YO30 224 B5
Vale View HG4 114 B2
Valient Way TS17 6 B6
Valley Bride Rd 16 YO11 213 F5
Valley Bridge Par YO11 213 A5
Valley Dr
Barnoldswick BB18 171 E2
Eaglescliffe TS15 5 E3
Great Preston LS26 200 C8
Harrogate HG2 219 C1
Ilkley LS29 218 D4
Valley Gdn TS16 5 D4
Valley Gdns* HG2 219 C2
Valley Mill Ct BB8 186 C3
Valley Mount HG2 219 C2
Valley Rd
Barnoldswick BB18 171 E1
3 Darley HG3 160 A6
32 Earby BB18 172 A1
Harrogate HG2 219 C2
Ilkley LS29 218 D5
Kippax LS25 194 C2
Northallerton DL6 210 F3
Scarborough YO12 212 E4
Whitby YO21 208 A8
Valley Ridge LS25 194 C2
Valley Street N DL1 3 D5
Valley View
3 Ampleforth YO62 92 C1
Clint HG3 160 F8
Danby YO21 29 C6
3 Glusburn BD20 187 E8
Wheldrake YO19 192 F7
Valuation La 1 YO51 141 B5
Vanbrugh Dr YO10 229 C3
Vanbrugh Way YO10 229 A2
Vane Ct TS21 4 F7
Vane Terr DL3 3 C5
Van Mildert Way TS18 5 F8
Vasey Cl 5 DL8 63 B2
Vaughan Rd 10 DN6 206 E1
Vavasour Ct YO23 230 B2
Vaynor Dr 17 TS17 5 F4
Venables Rd TS14 8 E7
Verity Wlk HG2 222 D7
Vernon Cl YO23 231 A3
Vernon Ct TS8 6 E5
Vernon Gr 4 YO12 212 D8
Vernon Pl 3 YO11 213 A5
Vernon Rd
Harrogate HG2 222 E7
2 Scarborough YO11 213 A5
Trawden Forest BB8 186 B3
York YO30 224 E2
Vesper Dr YO24 227 B3
Vesper Wlk YO32 225 F6
Vicarage Cl
2 Bubwith YO8 199 D7
12 Hunmanby YO14 126 F8
Seamer YO12 99 D6
Vicarage Farm Cl YO17 124 D8
Vicarage Gdns 1 YO10 229 C4
Vicarage La
Bishop Wilton YO42 169 F2
Bramham LS23 188 E5
10 Knaresborough HG5 221 A6
Naburn YO19 191 E8
Sherburn YO17 124 D8
Vicarage Rd
Barnoldswick BB18 171 E2
16 Catterick Garrison DL9 40 E4
Darlington DL1 3 D5
3 Kelbrook & Sough
BB18 186 A7
Vicar Hill La YO7 116 D8
Vicars Cl YO23 230 B2
Vicars Croft DL6 210 E5
VICAR'S GREEN 39 F7
Vicar's La YO61 144 C6
Vicars Terr WF10 200 D6
Vickers Cl TS18 5 F7
Vickers Rd 2 DL9 40 E4
Vickers St 1 WF10 200 E4
Victoria Arc LS29 218 A4
Victoria Ave
10 Filey YO14 101 B3
Harrogate HG1 219 D2
Ilkley LS29 175 C2
Knaresborough HG5 221 B8
Ripon HG4 214 D5
Thirsk YO7 211 B2
Victoria Cave* BD24 131 F4
Victoria Cl
Great Preston WF10 200 E6
Ilkley LS29 218 A4
26 Sherburn in Elmet LS25 195 F4
Victoria Ct
25 Sherburn in Elmet
LS25 195 F4
15 York YO26 227 F5
Victoria Dr 9 LS29 175 C2
Victoria Emb DL1 3 C4
Victoria Farm Cl YO23 182 C6
Victoria Gdns 17 LS29 175 C2
Victoria Gr 5 Ilkley LS29 175 C2
Ripon HG4 214 C5
Victoria Mews 45 BB18 172 A1
Victoria Par 13 YO11 212 F5
Victoria Park Ave 2
YO12 212 F7
Victoria Park Mount
YO12 212 E7
Victoria Pk 1 YO12 212 F7
Victoria Pl 3 YO21 208 D6
Victoria Rd
1 Barnoldswick BB18 171 E1
28 Burley in Warfedale
LS29 176 C1
Cowling BD22 187 B6
Darlington DL1 3 C5
Earby BB18 172 A1
Glusburn BD20 187 E7
Harrogate HG2 219 C1
10 Ilkley LS29 175 C2
1 Malton YO17 215 B4
Richmond DL10 209 B7
Scarborough YO11 212 F5
Thornaby TS17 6 B8
Victoria Sh Ctr HG1 219 D2
Victoria Sq Skipton BD23 216 F4
21 Whitby YO21 208 D6
Victoria St
24 Earby BB18 172 A1
43 Glusburn BD20 187 E7
Great Preston WF10 200 D6
Pontefract WF8 201 B2
Scarborough YO12 212 F6
Settle BD24 131 E2
10 Skipton BD23 216 F4
1 York YO23 233 B1
Victoria Terr
1 Harrogate HG1 220 C4
Northallerton DL7 210 D4
3 Skipton BD23 216 F4
Victoria Way 2 YO32 228 F8
Victoria Works Ind Est
BD20 187 F8
Victor St YO1 233 B1
Victory Rd LS29 218 B4
Viewley Hill Ave TS8 6 F5
Viewley Hill Prim Sch TS8 6 F5
Viking Cl 20 YO41 168 D2
Viking Dr 5 YO19 197 F8
Viking Rd
Stamford Bridge YO41 168 D2
York YO26 227 C5
Vikings Ct 6 DL6 43 F3
Villa Cl YO8 198 F1
Villa Ct YO26 227 B7
Villa Fields 4 DN14 204 C1
Village Farm Cl 9 DN14 202 D4
Village Farm Ct 7 DN14 202 D4
Village Fold DL7 42 B1
Village Garth 1 YO32 166 E5
Village Paddock TS18 5 E8
Village Prim Sch TS17 6 B7
Village Rd TS15 24 B8
Village St YO30 224 E3
Village The
Boston Spa LS23 180 F1
Haxby YO32 166 E5
Skelton YO30 224 B5
Stockton on the Forest
YO32 167 D2
Strensall YO32 167 B7
York YO10 229 C4
Village Wy DL7 42 B1
Villa Gr 2 YO31 228 E6
Villiers Ct 8 YO62 92 F6
Vimy Rd DL9 40 E3
Vincent St 9 YO12 213 A7
Vincent Way YO24 230 C8
Vine Cl TS14 8 F6
Vine Farm Cl YO26 164 A4
Vine Gdns YO8 199 D7
Vine Gr YO17 215 E4
Vine St Darlington DL3 3 B6
Norton YO17 215 E4
6 Scarborough YO12 212 F6
York YO23 228 C2
Vinstra Cl DL10 209 D8
Virginia Gdns TS5 6 E6
Vivars Way YO8 232 D5
Vivers Pl 1 YO62 70 C1
Vivis La YO18 95 F6
Volta St YO8 232 E4
Vulcan Way TS17 6 B6
Vyner St Ripon HG4 214 D4
York YO31 228 C7

W

Waddington St 37 BB18 172 A1
Wade House La YO8 204 F4
Waggoners Dr 3 YO23 230 B3
Wain Cl
15 Eastfield YO11 100 B7
South Milford LS25 195 E2
Waincroft 8 YO32 167 A6
Wainds Field 30 YO62 70 B1
Waindyke Way WF6 200 B1
Wainers Cl 5 YO23 230 B3
Wainfleet Rd HG1 219 D6
Wain Gap LS25 195 F2
Waingates La YO51 140 F4
Wainman's Cl BD22 187 B6
Wain's Gr YO24 230 D7
Wain's La YO12 99 D2
Wain's Rd YO24 230 D8
Wainstones Cl TS9 7 F1
Wainstones Dr TS9 7 F1
Waite La YO13 53 F2
WAITHWITH BANKS 40 B5
Waithwith Rd DL9 209 B1
Waitlands La DL11 20 A7
Wakefield Rd
Garforth LS25 194 B3
10 Normanton South WF6 200 A1
Swillington LS26 194 A2
WAKE HILL 111 F1
Wakeman Rd HG4 214 C3
Walburn Head DL11 39 D3
WALDEN STUBBS 206 F3
Walden Stubbs Rd DN6 206 E2
Wales St DL3 3 C7
Walker Cl BD20 187 D7
Walker Dr YO24 230 C8
Walker La
Menwith with Darley
HG3 160 A6
Wheldrake YO19 192 F7
Walkers Fold HG5 221 B5
Walker's La BD20 174 B4
Walkers Row TS14 8 F7
Walker St YO21 208 D6
Walker Terr HG3 223 F4
WALKERVILLE 41 A4
Walkerville Ave 22 DL9 41 A5
Walkerville Ind Est DL9 41 B5
Walkington La YO30 165 B8
Walled Gdn The* YO17 123 A6
Wallgates La YO17 215 D4
Walmer Carr
Haxby YO32 166 D5
Wigginton YO32 166 D5
Walmgate YO1 233 C2
WALMGATE STRAY 228 F1
Walmsley Gdns YO12 212 C5
Walney Rd YO31 229 A5
Walnut Cl
39 Haxby YO32 166 E5
Saxton with Scarthingwell
LS24 195 D8
39 Wigginton YO32 166 E5
York YO10 229 A1
Walnut Gn YO17 215 E3
Walnut Gr HG1 219 E6
Walpole St YO31 228 D7
WALSHFORD 180 D8
Waltham Cl YO32 167 B8
WALTON 181 A2
Walton Ave
Gargrave BD23 155 C1
Middlesbrough TS5 6 E8
Pannal HG3 222 F2
Walton Chase LS23 180 F2
Walton Cl YO61 144 A4
Walton Head La HG3 178 F4
Walton Pk HG3 222 E2
Walton Pl Pannal HG3 222 E2
York YO26 227 B3
Walton Rd
Gargrave BD23 172 C8
Walton LS23 181 A2
Wetherby LS22 180 E2
Walton St
5 Cowling BD22 187 B6
Skipton BD23 216 F1
Walworth Ave HG2 220 B3
Walworth Street N 4
YO26 227 F5
Walworth Street S 9
YO26 227 F5
Wandale La YO17 95 A2
Wandales Cl YO17 215 F3
Wandales Ct YO13 75 D8
Wandales Dr YO13 75 D8
Wandales La YO60 146 B6
Wandales Rd YO13 75 D8
Wandell Balk YO61 144 B6
Wandels La YO21 29 B6
Wandesford Gr DL9 209 F1
Wandhill 31 YO32 166 E5
Wand Hill TS12 9 E8
Wandhill Gdns TS12 9 E8
Wandhill La YO7 66 D1
Wand La DN14 203 C3
Wandle The YO26 227 A2
Wansbeck 3 YO24 230 B7
Wapping La YO62 94 C7
Warbler Cl 11 TS17 6 A5
Wardale Ave TS5 6 E6
Ward Ct YO23 233 B1
War Dike La YO13 54 B6
Wardrop Rd DL9 209 C1
Ward St BD23 217 A4
Wareham Rd YO11 99 F6
Warehill La YO61 143 C2
War Field La LS22 180 F6
WARLABY 64 D6
Warlbeck 23 LS29 175 C2
Warley Wise La BB8 186 D6
Warren Ave WF11 201 E2
Warren Cl DL1 3 F4
Warrener La DL10 20 C6
Warren La Bramham cum
Oglethorpe LS24 189 A5
Brearton HG3 162 A8
Kirkby Malzeard HG4 112 D4
Warren Pl HG1 219 D5
WARSILL 138 C4
WARTHERMARSKE 86 A1
WARTHILL 167 F2
Warthill CE Prim Sch
YO19 167 F2
Warth La LA6 103 C3
Warwick Cl YO60 145 D5
Warwick Cres HG2 222 E8
Warwick Dr 2 BB18 172 A1
Warwick Pl 2 YO62 92 F7
Warwick St YO31 228 D7
Wasdale Cl 2 YO30 224 E1
Washbeck Cl YO12 212 E4
Wash Beck La YO62 93 F6
Washbrook Dr DL3 3 C8
Washburn Cl 13 YO14 101 A3
Washburn Cotts LS21 159 F1
Washburn Courts HG3 159 F1
Washburn Dr 4 BD20 187 E8
WASHFOLD 18 D1
Washfold La DL8 60 B6
Washford Cl TS17 6 A3
Washington Ave DL2 4 D4
Washington Cl HG4 214 E2
WASS 91 F2
Wass Bank Rd YO61 91 F2
Wass Way TS16 5 D5
Waste La YO62 48 F2
Watchet Rd 11 DL9 40 E4
Water Avens Way TS18 6 A7
Water Bag Bank 8 HG5 221 A6
Waterdale Pk YO31 225 E1
Water End YO26 227 E5
Waterfall Fold 1 WF8 201 C2
Waterfalls Wlk* LA6 103 D6
WATER FRYSTON 201 C5
Water Gap YO18 97 B5
Water Garth DN14 202 F4
Watergate
Mickletown LS26 200 A5
7 Pontefract WF8 201 B1
Watergate Rd HG3 139 A4
Water Hill La YO8 232 D6
Waterhouse La 29 YO11 213 A6
Water Houses BD24 132 E6
Waterings 19 YO32 166 D5
Water La
Camblesforth YO8 204 D5
8 Clifton YO30 225 A1
Dalton YO7 115 E7
Dunnington YO19 184 F7
Eggborough DN14 203 A2
Exelby, Leeming & Newton
DL7 63 D4
Hemingbrough YO8 198 F1
Huttons Ambo YO60 147 C6
Kirby Grindalythe YO17 149 B6
Kirby Underdale YO41 170 A5
Kirk Smeaton WF8 206 C3
Knaresborough HG5 221 C8
Loftus TS13 10 E8
North Stainley with Sleningford
HG4 113 C6
7 Pontefract WF8 201 C1
Selby YO8 232 C6
Sherburn YO17 124 D7
South Stainley with Cayton
HG3 139 D2
Thorpe Bassett YO17 123 A3
Welburn YO60 146 E7
Whitby YO21 208 B3
York YO30 228 A7
Waterline Ind Est YO23 191 B7
Waterloo Grosmont YO22 31 C4
12 Richmond DL10 209 C6
Waterloo Cl WF10 200 C3
Waterloo Rd BB18 186 A7
Waterloo St
Harrogate HG1 219 E4
2 Richmond DL10 209 C6
Waterman Ct 3 YO24 227 B1
Watermill Cl HG4 113 C7
Watermill Croft HG4 113 C7
Watermill La HG4 113 C7
Waters End DL2 1 D7
Watershed Mill Bsns Ctr
BD24 131 D3
Watershed Mill Visitor Ctr*
BD24 131 D3
Waterside
3 Boroughbridge YO51 141 B6
Hemingbrough YO8 198 F1
Knaresborough HG5 221 A5
4 Ripon HG4 214 C4
Skipton BD23 216 F2
7 Thirsk YO7 211 C3
Waterside Gdns YO31 228 D8
Waterside Mdws LS25 194 F8
Water Skellgate HG4 214 C5
Waters La DL10 20 E3
Water Slack La YO26 164 C4
Watersmeet Cl 5 TS17 6 A3
Watersole La LS22 180 D2
Water St Earby BB18 172 A1
Gargrave BD23 155 D1
Malton YO17 215 C4
Skipton BD23 216 F4
Waterstead Cres 1
YO21 208 D5
Waterstead La YO21 208 C5
Water Street Prim Sch 15
BD23 216 F4
Water Way Garth DN14 207 F6
Watery La Airton BD23 155 A5
Giggleswick BD24 131 C1
Snape with Thorp DL8 86 F7
WATH Hovingham 119 F6
Pateley Bridge 137 A6
Ripon 114 A7
Wathcote Cl DL10 209 F8
Wathcote Pl DL10 209 F8
Wathgill Camp DL11 39 C3
Wath La Catton YO41 185 C8
Copgrove HG3 140 D1
High & Low Bishopside
HG3 137 B6
Humberton YO61 141 E8
Ulleskelf LS24 190 B2
Wath Rd HG3 137 B5
Watlass La DL8 86 E8
Watlass Moor La HG4 86 D7
Watling Cl DL11 19 E6
Watling Rd WF10 201 C5
Watson Cl 13 YO14 127 A8
Watson's Houses 7
BD23 216 F4
Watson's La Newton Kyme cum
Toulston LS24 189 B7
Norwood HG3 177 B8
Reighton YO14 127 D6
Watson St
4 Normanton South
WF6 200 A1
York YO24 228 A3
Watson Terr 2 YO24 228 A3
Wattlers Cl YO23 230 C3
Wattlesyke LS22 188 C8
Wattle Syke LS22 180 E1
Wavell Com Infant & Junior
Schs DL9 209 D1
Wavell Rd DL9 209 D1
Wavell St YO8 232 A6
Waveney Gr YO30 228 B8
Waver Ct LS24 195 F7
Waver La DL6 43 F8
Waverley Cl DN14 204 C2
Waverley Cres HG2 222 E8
Waverley St YO31 233 C3
Waydale Cl YO62 70 A2
Wayfaring Cl YO17 215 F2
Waynefleet Gr 3 YO10 229 A3
Wayne Tarbard Cl 12
HG4 113 D2
Wayside Ave HG2 220 B1
Wayside Cl 4 HG2 220 B1
Wayside Cres HG2 220 A1
Wayside Gr HG2 220 A1
Wayside Mews 12 BD20 174 C1
Wayside Terr LS17 178 B2
Wayside The DL2 3 E1
Waytail Slack TS13 10 D7
Weaponness Dr YO11 213 A2
Weaponness La
Eastfield YO11 99 F8
Scarborough YO11 212 F1
Weaponness Pk YO11 213 A2
Weaponness Valley Cl 5
YO11 212 F3
Weaponness Valley Rd
YO11 212 E3
Weardale TS14 8 D5
Weardale Rd 20 DL9 40 E4
Weary Bank TS15 25 B8
Weavers Cl YO23 230 C3
Weavers Ct
3 Stokesley TS9 26 C7
Trawden BB8 186 A1
Weavers Gn DL7 210 C3
Weavers Pk
9 Copmanthorpe YO23 230 B3
York YO23 230 B3
WEAVERTHORPE 124 E1
Weaverthorpe CE Prim Sch
YO17 124 E2
Webster Pl 1 WF6 200 A1
Weddall Cl YO24 227 F1
Wedderburn Ave HG2 220 C2
Wedderburn Cl HG2 220 C3
Wedderburn Dr HG2 220 B2
Wedderburn Infant Sch
HG2 220 B2
Wedderburn Lodge 2
HG2 220 B1
Wedderburn Rd HG2 220 B2
Weedling Gate LS24 189 D4
Weeland Ct 16 WF11 202 A2
Weeland Rd DN14 202 E3
WEETON 178 C1
Weeton La LS17 178 D1
Weeton Sta LS17 178 B2
Weets View BB18 171 E2
Welbeck Ave DL1 3 E7
Welborn Cl YO10 229 A4
Welburn Ct YO11 99 F2
Welbourn Dr 12 YO12 99 D6
WELBURN Pickering 94 A7
Westow 146 D7
Welburn Gr TS7 7 D7
Welburn Hall Sch YO62 94 A7
Welburn La YO60 147 A8

Welburn Prim Sch YO60 146 D6
WELBURY 24 B1
Welbury Cl 2 BB18 172 B1
Welfare Ave LS15 194 C8
Welford Rd 36 YO14 101 B3
Welham Hill YO17 147 E7
Welham Rd YO17 215 D3
WELL 87 A4
Welland Dr LS25 194 D3
Welland Rise YO26 227 D5
Well Bank DL8 87 A4
Wellbrook Cl TS17 6 D4
Well Cl Great & Little Preston LS25 200 C8
3 Whitby YO21 208 D7
Well Cl Terr 4 YO21 208 D7
Wellesley Cl YO30 225 A2
Wellesleys Mews DL10 209 B7
Wellfield Ct HG2 222 B6
Wellfield La 18 LS29 176 C1
Wellhouse St 5 BB18 171 E1
Wellington Ct 9 HG2 219 C2
Wellington Gdns 11 HG4 214 C4
Wellingtonia Dr 5 DN6 206 E1
Wellington Mews 9 HG4 214 C5
Wellington Pl DL10 209 B7
Wellington Rd
Ilkley LS29 218 B4
2 Whitby YO21 208 D6
Wellington Row YO1 233 A2
Wellington Sq 6 HG2 219 C2
Wellington St
1 Knaresborough HG5 221 B5
10 Ripon HG4 214 C5
12 Skipton BD23 217 A3
York YO10 228 E3
Wellington Terr YO21 208 D7
Wellington Way 4 DL10 41 C7
Well La Kippax LS25 194 D1
Redmire DL8 59 C5
Seamer TS9 6 F2
Snape with Thorp DL8 87 A6
South Milford LS25 195 F2
Yearsley YO61 118 C5
Wells Cl YO8 232 A5
Wells Gn DL10 21 D7
Wells La Barton DL10 21 D7
Kellington DN14 202 E3
Malton YO17 215 C4
Wells Mews 7 LS29 218 B3
Wellspring Cl TS17 6 D7
Wells Prom LS29 218 B4
Wells Rd LS29 218 B3
Wells Wlk 13 YO18 95 F7
Wells Wlk The LS29 218 B4
Welton Ave YO26 227 D5
Welton Ct YO21 208 C7
Welwyn Dr YO10 231 E8
Wemyss Rd 11 HG4 113 D2
Wendel Ave LS15 194 B8
Wend The BD23 173 A4
Wendy Ave HG4 214 B3
Wenham Rd YO24 230 C8
Wenlock Dr YO19 192 B6
Wenlock Terr YO10 228 D1
Wenning Ave LA2 129 A7
Wenning Bank LA2 130 A6
WENNINGTON 102 B1
Wennington Hall Sch LA2 102 B1
Wennington Rd LA2 128 A6
Wennington Sta LA2 128 B8
WENSLEY 60 A4
WENSLEYDALE 57 A5
Wensleydale Ave 2 BD23 217 B4
Wensleydale Creamery* DL8 56 C4
Wensleydale Dr YO10 229 D4
Wensleydale Gdns 3 TS17 6 C7
Wensleydale Pottery* DL8 56 D4
Wensleydale Rd 21 DL9 40 E4
Wensleydale Rly* DL8 60 B5
Wensleydale Sch The DL8 60 D5
Wensley Gr HG2 222 D7
Wensley Rd
Harrogate HG2 222 D7
15 Leyburn DL8 60 D5
Northallerton DL7 210 B2
Wentcliffe Dr BB18 172 A1
Wentdale 1 WF8 206 C3
Wentworth Ave YO61 116 F5
Wentworth Cl
Camblesforth YO8 204 D4
Harrogate HG2 220 D4
3 Kellington DN14 203 A2
Wentworth Cres
Harrogate HG2 220 D3
2 Whitby YO21 208 B5
Wentworth Dr HG2 220 D4
Wentworth Gate LS22 180 A3
Wentworth Rd YO24 228 B2
Wentworth St YO17 215 B5
Wentworth Way
Eaglescliffe TS16 5 E4
5 Hunmanby YO14 126 F8
York YO10 228 F2
Werkdyke The YO1 233 C3
Werner Ct 4 WF10 200 F3
WESCOE HILL 178 B1
Wescoe Hill La LS17 178 B1
Wesley Cl 1 LA2 129 A8
Wesley Pl
7 Silsden BD20 174 C1
York YO1 233 C2
Wesley Rd YO22 33 C4
Wesley Sq 2 TS13 13 K2
Wesley Way 10 LA2 129 A8
Wesson Cl 6 DL9 40 E4
Westacres 5 DL2 4 C4
West Acres 2 WF11 201 F4
West Acres Cl 7 YO13 99 A7
WEST APPLETON 41 C1
West Auckland Rd DL3 3 A7
West Ave
Boston Spa LS23 180 E1
Burton Fleming YO25 126 E3
5 Easingwold YO61 143 D8
Filey YO14 101 B3
19 Scalby YO13 75 D5
WEST AYTON 99 A7
West Bank
Scarborough YO12 212 E4
York YO24 227 E3
West Bank Rd BD23 216 E4
WEST BARNBY 12 C3
West Barnby La YO21 12 B3
Westbeck Gdns TS5 6 F8
West Beck Way TS8 7 B6
Westborough 1 YO11 213 A5
Westbourne Ave
Harrogate HG2 222 D8
Whitby YO21 208 A6
Westbourne Cl YO21 208 A6
Westbourne Cres LS25 194 B3
Westbourne Gdns YO8 232 C4
Westbourne Gr
8 Pickering YO18 95 F7
3 Ripon HG4 214 C5
11 Scarborough YO11 213 A4
Selby YO8 232 C4
Whitby YO21 208 A6
Westbourne Pk YO12 212 E4
Westbourne Rd
Scarborough YO11 212 F3
Selby YO8 232 C4
Whitby YO21 208 A6
Westbourne Terr
Selby YO8 232 C4
Thirsk YO7 211 A2
West Brow YO13 98 C5
WEST BURTON 58 F1
West Burton CE Prim Sch DL8 58 F1
Westbury St TS17 6 B8
West Cam Rd BD23 79 E6
West Cl Carthorpe DL8 87 E6
Middleton Tyas DL10 21 C4
Normanton WF6 200 A1
Swinton YO17 121 B4
WEST CLIFF 208 B7
West Cliff Ave 13 YO21 208 B7
West Cliffe Cnr 9 HG2 219 C1
Westcliffe Gr HG2 219 B1
West Cliffe Mews 5 HG2 219 C1
Westcliffe Mount HG2 219 B1
Westcliffe Terr HG2 219 B1
West Cliff Prim Sch YO21 208 C7
West Close Rd 13 BB18 171 D2
West Craven High Tech Coll BB18 171 E1
West Craven Sports Ctr BB18 171 E1
West Croft
19 Addingham LS29 174 F4
6 Glusburn BD20 187 E6
Westcroft La YO8 196 E1
West Ct
Muston YO14 100 F2
8 Riccall YO19 197 F8
West Dale LS23 180 E1
Westdene HG2 222 B7
West Dene BD20 174 B2
West Dike Rd YO18 71 F5
West Edge Rd WF8 206 A3
West End
Boston Spa LS23 180 E1
Guisborough TS14 8 E6
Hurworth-on-Tees DL2 3 E1
Hutton Rudby TS15 25 C5
Kirkbymoorside YO62 70 B1
Muston YO14 100 F2
Osmotherley DL6 45 B4
Pollington DN14 207 F6
Rawcliffe DN14 205 A2
Sheriff Hutton YO60 145 C5
Stokesley TS9 26 C7
Strensall YO32 167 A7
West End App LS24 190 B3
West End Ave
Appleton Roebuck YO23 190 F5
Harrogate HG2 222 D8
Richmond DL10 209 A7
West End Cl
North Duffield YO8 199 A8
9 Strensall YO32 167 B7
West End Ct 5 YO11 100 B6
West End Gdns
Eaglescliffe TS16 5 D4
Pollington DN14 207 F6
Westend La DN14 207 B6
West End Rd DN6 206 E2
West End View 4 YO11 100 B6
West End Way TS18 5 F8
WESTERDALE 28 E4
Westerdale 4 YO18 95 F6
Westerdale Ct 2 YO30 228 A6
Westerley Cres BD20 174 B1
Western Ave WF8 201 C1
Western Ct 15 WF8 201 C1
Western Gales Way 33 WF6 200 B1
Western Prim Sch HG2 219 C1
Western Rd BD23 217 B3
Westerns La HG3 139 C4
Western Terr YO32 225 D3
Western Way 1 YO18 95 E7
WESTFIELD 232 C4
WEST FIELD 227 A2
Westfield YO8 232 B4
Westfield Ave
Castleford WF10 200 E2
3 Eggborough DN14 202 F2
Rawcliffe DN14 205 A1
6 Scalby YO12 75 E5
Selby YO8 232 B4
Westfield Cl
2 Eggborough DN14 202 F2
21 Haxby YO32 166 E5
Rawcliffe DN14 205 A1
South Milford LS25 195 E2
Westfield Cres 12 LS24 189 E6
Westfield Ct
Copmanthorpe YO23 230 A2
1 South Milford LS25 195 F2
Westfield Dr
Hurworth-on-Tees DL2 3 E1
York YO10 231 D8
Westfield Gn YO26 181 C7
Westfield Gr
Allerton Bywater WF10 200 D7
4 Eggborough DN14 202 F2
12 Haxby YO32 166 D5
Westfield La
Exelby, Leeming & Newton DL8 63 C2
Kippax LS25 194 C1
Ledsham LS25 195 C1
Lockton YO18 72 E4
Normanby YO62 94 F4
Norton WF8 206 C2
South Milford LS25 195 F2
Thirsk YO7 211 A3
Thoralby DL8 58 D1
Thorganby YO19 193 A5
Thornton-le-Dale YO18 96 C5
Wigginton YO32 166 D5
West Field La
Arkendale HG5 163 A8
East Witton Town DL8 60 F1
Upper Poppleton YO26 165 E1
Westfield Mews 32 YO62 70 B1
Westfield Pl
19 Haxby YO32 166 E5
York YO24 227 A1
Westfield Prim Com Sch YO24 227 B2
Westfield Rd
1 Eggborough DN14 202 F2
20 Haxby YO32 166 E5
3 North Duffield YO8 199 A7
Rawcliffe DN14 205 A1
Selby YO8 232 B4
2 Stokesley TS9 26 C7
Tockwith YO26 181 C7
West Field Rd 2 BB18 171 D2
Westfields
Castleford WF10 200 E3
Richmond DL10 209 A7
Scorton DL10 41 E7
West Fields YO62 70 B1
Westfields Ct DL10 209 B7
Westfield Sq 8 LS24 189 E6
Westfield Terr
2 Great Preston WF10 200 D7
Tadcaster LS24 189 E6
9 Thornton Dale YO18 96 D5
Westfield Way YO17 215 F4
Westfold YO17 215 E6
WEST GARFORTH 194 B3
Westgarth
Collingham LS22 180 A2
Northallerton DL7 210 D4
West Garth Cayton YO11 100 B6
Sherburn YO17 124 D8
Ulleskelf LS24 190 B3
West Garth Gdns 23 YO11 100 B6
Westgate
22 Barnoldswick BB18 171 D1
Egglescliffe TS15 5 D3
Guisborough TS14 8 F6
Malton YO17 215 E6
Pickering YO18 95 F7
Rillington YO17 122 F5
Ripon HG4 214 C5
Tadcaster LS24 189 E6
Thirsk YO7 211 B2
West Gate
Thornton-le-Dale YO18 96 C5
Wetherby LS22 180 B3
Wykeham YO13 98 D6
Westgate Carr Rd YO18 95 D5
Westgate La
Malton YO17 215 D6
Thornton in Lonsdale LA6 103 C5
Westgate Rd 3 DL3 3 B7
West Gn 15 TS9 26 C7
West Gr
Bishop Thornton HG3 139 A2
Swinton YO17 121 B4
West Grove Rd HG1 219 D4
WEST HADDLESEY 203 A5
West Hall La LS29 175 A5
WEST HARLSEY 44 D5
WEST HESLERTON 123 F7
West Heslerton CE Prim Sch YO17 123 F6
Westholme 10 TS15 25 C5
Westholme Bank DL8 58 F2
Westholme Cres 2 HG4 86 C3
Westholme Ct 3 HG4 86 C3
Westholme Dr YO30 224 E1
Westholme Rd 1 HG4 86 C3
WESTHOUSE 103 C4
West Ing La BD23 171 A5
West Ings Cl 4 WF11 202 A3
West Ings Cres 5 WF11 202 A3
West Ings Ct 1 WF11 202 A3
West Ings La 2 WF11 202 A3
West Ings Mews 6 WF11 202 A3
West Ings Way 3 WF11 202 A3
WEST KNAPTON 123 B6
West La
Appleton Wiske DL6 24 A3
Askwith LS21 176 C3
Azerley HG4 112 F3
Bewerley HG3 136 E4
Boston Spa LS23 180 E1
Burniston YO13 54 C1
Burn YO8 203 C6
Burton Fleming YO25 126 E3
Caldwell DL11 1 B4
Cononley BD20 173 C2
Dalton-on-Tees DL2 22 D6
Danby YO21 29 C8
East Layton DL11 20 A8
Embsay BD23 217 D8
Hampsthwaite HG3 161 A4
Hornby DL6 23 F4
Littlethorpe HG4 214 A2
2 Low Bradley BD20 173 E3
Melsonby DL10 20 E7
Mickleby TS13 12 A4
Nether Silton YO7 66 B7
North Deighton LS22 179 F6
Snainton YO13 97 F5
Stillington YO61 143 F7
Sutton BD20 187 E6
Sykehouse DN14 207 F2
Whixley YO26 163 F5
West La Hill LA2 129 A6
Westland Cl 3 BD20 187 F7
Westlands Bilton-in-Ainsty with Bickerton YO26 181 D5
6 Kirklevington TS15 24 E8
Pickering YO18 96 A7
Stokesley TS9 26 B7
Westlands Ave 1 YO21 208 C7
Westlands Gr YO31 228 F7
Westlands La YO7 211 A4
Westlands Rd DL3 3 B6
Westlands Sch TS17 6 C6
Westlands Way TS18 5 F8
WEST LAYTON 20 A8
West Lea Ave HG2 222 B7
WEST LILLING 145 C4
West Lodge Gdns YO17 215 A4
West Lund 17 YO62 70 B1
West Lund La YO62 94 B8
WEST LUTTON 150 B8
WEST MARTON 171 F5
West Mead WF10 201 A4
Westminster Bsns Ctr YO26 227 C8
Westminster Cl HG3 222 C3
Westminster Cres HG3 222 D2
Westminster Dr HG3 222 D3
Westminster Gate HG3 222 C3
Westminster Gr HG3 222 D3
Westminster Pl YO26 224 B1
Westminster Rd
Pannal HG3 222 C3
York YO30 228 A6
Westminster Rise HG3 222 D2
West Moor La
Finghall DL8 61 E4
Heslington YO10 184 A4
West Moor Rd
Darlington DL2 3 E3
Raskelf YO61 116 E2
Westmoreland St
Darlington DL3 3 C7
1 Harrogate HG1 219 E3
19 Skipton BD23 217 A3
West Mount LS24 189 E5
Westmount Cl HG4 214 B6
WEST NESS 94 B1
West Nooks 25 YO32 166 F5
West Oaks Sch 4 LS23 188 E8
WESTON 176 E2
Weston Cres 7 LS21 176 F1
Weston Dr LS21 176 E1
Weston La LS21 176 F1
Weston Moor Rd LS21 176 E4
Weston Park View LS21 176 E1
Weston Rd LS29 218 B4
Weston Ridge LS21 176 F1
Westover Rd YO12 212 F4
WESTOW 147 B4
West Par LS29 218 C4
West Parade Rd 11 YO12 212 F5
West Park Ave YO12 212 C8
West Park Cres YO12 212 C7
West Park Hospl DL3 3 A7
West Park Rd 13 YO13 75 D5
West Pasture
Kirkbymoorside YO62 70 B1
7 Pickering YO18 95 F6
West Pier YO11 213 B6
Westpit La YO32 167 A7
West Pk Harrogate HG1 219 D1
Selby YO8 232 A4
Westpoint Rd DL1 3 F6
West Rd Carleton BD23 173 A4
12 Filey YO14 101 B3
Melsonby DL10 20 F7
Westridge Cres 1 DL9 40 F5
WEST ROUNTON 24 D2
West Row DL2 4 C7
West Sandgate Terr 19 YO11 213 B6
WEST SCRAFTON 83 F6
Westside Cl YO17 215 B4
Westside Rd
Bransdale YO62 48 B5
Fadmoor YO62 69 E7
West Side Rd YO13 53 A1
West Sq 7 YO11 212 F5
West St
Castleford WF10 200 E4
Eaglescliffe TS15 5 D4
Gargrave BD23 155 D1
Gayles DL11 19 E6
Harrogate HG1 219 C5
Ilkley LS29 218 B4
Muston YO14 100 F2
Normanton South WF6 200 A1
Scarborough YO11 213 A4
Swinton YO17 121 B4
WEST STONESDALE 15 E1
WEST TANFIELD 87 A1
West Terr
Richmond DL10 209 B7
Scarborough YO11 212 F4
15 Whitby YO21 208 D7
West Thorpe YO24 230 D8
West Vale 37 YO14 101 B3
West View
Carleton BD23 173 B4
Darlington DL3 3 A5
Draughton BD23 174 B7
Ilkley LS29 218 B3
Kippax LS25 194 D1
Micklefield LS25 195 A3
North Deighton LS22 180 A6
Ripon HG4 214 D2
Sherburn in Elmet LS25 195 E3
West View Ave 25 LS29 176 C1
Westview Cl
3 Low Bradley BD20 173 E3
York YO26 227 B7
West View Rd 26 LS29 176 C1
West View Terr
Eaglescliffe TS16 5 D4
16 Knaresborough HG5 221 A6
West Villa YO61 144 A4
Westville Ave LS29 218 A4
Westville Cl 6 LS29 218 A4
Westville House Prep Sch LS29 218 D7
Westville Oval HG1 219 C6
Westville Rd LS29 218 A4
Westway Eastfield YO11 99 F7
Harrogate HG2 222 B8
West Way YO61 118 A1
WEST WITTON 59 E3
Westwood Carleton BD23 173 B4
Scarborough YO11 212 F5
Westwood Cl 2 YO11 212 F4
Westwood Dr LS29 218 A2
Westwood Gdns 3 YO11 212 F4
Westwood La
Ampleforth YO62 92 A2
West Tanfield HG4 86 E1
West Wood La YO23 182 E4
Westwood Mews
Carleton BD23 173 B4
12 Dunnington YO19 184 F7
Westwood Rd Ripon HG4 214 A2
Scarborough YO11 212 F4
Westwood Terr YO23 228 B1
Westwood Way LS23 188 E8
Wetherall Rd YO8 204 F5
WETHERBY 180 D4
Wetherby Bsns Ctr LS22 180 B3
Wetherby Bsns Pk LS22 180 C3
Wetherby High Sch LS22 180 C3
Wetherby La LS22 180 D7
Wetherby L Ctr LS22 180 C2
Wetherby Racecourse* LS22 180 E3
Wetherby Rd
8 Boroughbridge YO51 141 B4
Bramham cum Oglethorpe LS23 188 E6
Harrogate HG2 220 B1
Kirk Deighton LS22 180 B5
Knaresborough HG5 221 D4
Sicklinghall LS22 179 E3
Tadcaster LS24 189 D6
Walton LS23 180 F2
Wetherby LS22 180 B2
York YO26 227 B3
Wethercote La YO7 67 C1
Wet Ings La 15 BD20 187 E6
Wetlands La DL11 18 G7
Weydale Ave YO12 212 E8
Weymouth Ave TS8 7 A7
Weymouth Rd 1 HG1 219 E4
Whaddon Chase TS14 8 F6
Whaites La YO7 115 C5
Whales La DN14 202 E3
Wham La BD24 130 F1
WHARFE 131 A8

Wharfedale YO14 101 A3
Wharfedale Ave HG2 222 A7
Wharfedale Cl 1 BD23 217 B4
Wharfedale Cres
Harrogate HG2 222 B7
Tadcaster LS24 189 E6
Wharfedale Dr
Ilkley LS29 218 C4
Normanton WF6 200 A3
Wharfedale Hospl LS21 176 F1
Wharfedale Nurseries LS23 188 E8
Wharfedale Pl HG2 222 A7
Wharfedale View 6 LS29 174 F4
Wharfe Dr YO24 230 D8
Wharfe Gr 8 LS22 180 B3
Wharfe La
Grassington BD23 134 D3
Kearby with Netherby LS22 179 B1
Wharfe Pk 2 LS29 175 A4
Wharfeside Ave BD23 134 D3
Wharfeside La LS29 218 C5
Wharfe View
Grassington BD23 134 D3
Kirkby Overblow HG3 179 A4
Wharfe View Rd LS29 218 B4
Wharncliffe Pl 14 YO14 101 A3
Wharnscliffe Dr YO30 224 F2
WHARRAM LE STREET 149 A4
Wharram Quarry Nature Reserve★ YO17 148 F4
Wharton Ave YO30 228 B7
Wharton Rd 8 YO41 168 D2
Whartons Prim Sch The LS21 177 A2
Whartons The LS21 177 A1
WHASHTON 20 A5
WHASHTON GREEN 20 A5
Whashton Rd Aske DL10 20 C1
Richmond DL10 209 C8
WHAW 17 B3
Wheatcroft 6 YO32 167 A6
Wheatcroft Ave YO11 213 B1
Wheatcroft Prim Sch YO11 213 B1
Wheatdale Rd LS24 190 B2
Wheatear La TS17 6 A5
Wheatfield La YO32 225 C8
Wheatfields Wlk YO19 192 A1
Wheatlands
Great Ayton TS9 8 A2
Ilkley LS29 218 C4
Wheatlands Ave 8 BD20 187 E8
Wheatlands Cl 6 TS14 8 F6
Wheatlands Dr 4 TS13 11 A8
Wheatlands Garth 20 BD20 187 E8
Wheatlands Gr
Harrogate HG2 222 E8
York YO26 227 C6
Wheatlands La
7 Glusburn BD20 187 E8
Roecliffe YO51 140 E4
Wheatlands Rd HG2 222 E7
Wheatlands Road E HG2 222 E8
Wheatlands Way HG2 222 F8
Wheatley Ave Ilkley LS29 218 E3
Normanton South WF6 200 A1
Wheatley Dr YO32 225 C8
Wheatley Gdns 2 LS29 218 E3
Wheatley Gr LS29 218 E3
Wheatley La 3 LS29 218 E3
Wheatley Rd LS29 218 C3
Wheatley Rise LS29 218 E3
Wheeldale Cres TS17 6 B7
Wheeldale Dr YO32 226 E2
Wheeldale Rd YO22 51 A4
Wheelgate YO17 215 C4
Wheelhouse Sq YO12 212 F6
Wheelhouse The 4 YO30 224 B5
Wheels La DN14 204 F3
Wheelwright Cl
Copmanthorpe YO23 230 B2
Sutton upon Derwent YO41 185 C1
Wheel Wright Cl YO23 230 B3
Wheelwrights Courts BD23 154 B3
WHELDALE 201 B5
Wheldale La WF10 201 B5
Wheldon Infant Sch WF10 200 F4
Wheldon Rd WF10 201 A5
WHELDRAKE 193 A7
Wheldrake CE Prim Sch YO19 193 A8
Wheldrake Cl 1 TS14 8 F7
Wheldrake Ings Nature Reserve★ YO19 193 C7
Wheldrake La
Deighton YO19 184 B1
Escrick YO19 192 B5
WHENBY 145 B8
Whenby Gr YO31 225 F1
Whenby La YO60 145 C6
Whernside TS7 7 C5
Whernside Ave YO31 229 A5
Whessoe Rd DL3 3 C8
Whin Bank YO12 212 D5
Whinbeck Ave WF6 200 B1
Whinbush La 1 HG3 138 A1
Whinbush Way DL1 3 F8
Whinchat Tail TS14 8 D6
Whin Cl
3 Strensall YO32 167 B6
York YO24 230 F7
Whincup Ave HG5 221 B6
Whincup Cl 6 HG5 221 B6
Whincup Gr 7 HG5 221 B6
WHINFIELD 3 F8
Whinfield 34 LS29 175 C2
Whinfield Bglws 5 HG3 138 A1
Whinfield Ct BD23 216 F3
Whinfield Prim Sch DL1 3 F7
Whinfield Rd DL1 3 E7
Whin Garth YO24 230 F6
Whin Gn YO22 32 A6
Whingroves TS17 6 C8
Whin Hill YO17 147 E1
Whin La
South Milford LS25 195 D2
Warlaby DL7 64 C5
Whinmoor Hill YO7 66 C2
Whinney Banks Prim Sch TS5 6 D8
Whinney La HG3 222 A5
Whinney Mire La LA2 103 E1
Whinny Bank YO61 117 C8
Whinny Gill Rd BD23 217 B3
Whinny Hagg La YO8 197 A2
Whinny Hill DL9 40 E3
Whinny La YO60 168 A7
Whinnythwaite La YO26 181 C8
Whin Rd YO24 230 F6
Whins La Spofforth with Stockeld HG3 179 E4
Thorp Arch LS23 180 F1
Whins The YO12 212 A7
Whinstone Prim Sch TS17 6 A5
Whinstone View 13 TS9 8 A2
Whinwath La DL8 87 F4
Whipley Bank HG3 161 A8
Whipley La HG3 161 A7
Whip-ma-whop-ma-gate YO1 233 C2
Whipperdale Bank
Leyburn DL8 60 A8
Redmire DL8 38 F1
Whistler Cl YO23 230 C3
Whistler Dr
Castleford WF10 200 F2
Pickering YO18 96 A6
Whiston Dr 18 YO14 101 B3
WHITBY 208 C6
Whitby Archives & Heritage Ctr★ 25 YO21 208 D6
Whitby Ave
Guisborough TS14 8 F6
York YO31 229 A7
Whitby Benedictine Abbey (rems of)★ YO22 208 E7
Whitby Bsns Pk YO22 32 F8
Whitby Com Coll YO21 208 C5
Whitby Dr YO31 229 A7
Whitby Gate YO18 96 D6
Whitby Hospl YO21 208 D6
Whitby Jet Heritage Ctr★ YO22 208 E7
Whitby L Ctr YO21 208 C7
Whitby Mus & Pannett Art Gall★ YO21 208 C6
Whitby Pavilion Complex YO21 208 C8
Whitby Rd
Guisborough TS14 9 A7
Pickering YO18 96 B8
Staithes TS13 13 K2
Whitby Sta YO21 208 D6
Whitby Way DL3 3 A7
Whitby Wizard (Hands-on-Science)★ YO21 208 C8
Whitcliffe Ave HG4 214 B4
Whitcliffe Cres HG4 214 B3
Whitcliffe Dr HG4 214 B3
Whitcliffe Gr HG4 214 B3
Whitcliffe Grange DL10 209 A7
Whitcliffe La
Littlethorpe HG4 139 D8
Ripon HG4 214 A2
Whitcliffe Pl DL10 209 A7
Whitcliffe Terr DL10 209 A7
Whitebridge Dr DL1 3 D8
White Bridge Rd YO21 208 B8
White Canons Ct 4 DL10 209 E8
White Canons Wlk 3 DL10 209 E8
Whitecarr La YO18 95 A5
Whitecliffe Cres LS26 194 A1
Whitecliffe Dr 1 LS26 194 A1
Whitecliffe Rise LS26 194 A1
Whitecote La LS25 195 D2
Whitecross Gdns YO31 228 D7
Whitecross Hill DL8 87 F3
White Cross Rd YO31 228 D7
White Cross Way YO41 169 A2
Whitefield Bglws DN14 206 F8
Whitefield La DN14 202 E1
Whitefields Dr DL10 209 E7
Whitefields Gate 1 DL10 209 E8
Whitefields Wlk 2 DL10 209 E8
White Friars Cl DL10 209 F8
Whitefriars Ct 9 BD24 131 D2
White Friars Gdns 6 DL10 209 E8
White Friars Wlk 5 DL10 209 E8
White Gate
Heslerton YO17 123 E6
Sherburn YO17 124 C6
Whitegate Cl 7 TS13 13 K2
White Gate Hill YO11 100 B2
Whitegate La HG4 114 F1
Whitehall Landing YO22 208 E5
White Hart Cres 4 DL1 3 F6
Whitehead Hill 18 YO11 213 B6
White Hill La BD20 172 E1
Whitehill Rd BD22 187 E3
White Hills Croft BD23 216 E6
White Hills La BD23 216 E6
Whitehorn Rd WF10 200 F2
White Horse Cl 6 YO32 225 F5
White Horse Fold WF10 200 F7
White Horse La 9 YO12 99 D6
White Horse Mews 3 HG3 179 E5
White Horse of Kilburn★ YO61 91 B4
Whitehouse Ave LS26 200 B8
Whitehouse Cres LS26 200 B8
White House Croft TS21 5 A7
White House Dale YO24 227 F1
Whitehouse Dr LS26 200 B8
White House Dr YO24 227 F1
White House Garth YO8 199 D7
White House Gdns 4 YO24 228 A2
White House Gr 1 YO41 185 B2
Whitehouse La Great & Little Preston LS26 200 B8
Swillington LS26 194 B2
White House Rise YO24 227 F1
White House Wynd DL6 24 D2
White Lands DL10 209 E7
White La BD22 187 F1
Whitelass Cl YO7 211 B4
White Lee Ave BB8 186 B1
White Ley Rd WF8 206 C1
White Leys Cl BB18 171 F1
White Leys Rd YO21 208 A7
Whiteley Yd 18 HG5 221 A6
White Lilac Cl DL10 209 F7
White Lodge YO8 232 B4
Whitemoor La YO8 198 C6
Whiteoak Ave YO61 143 C8
White Pastures DL10 209 E7
Whitepits La LA2 129 A5
White Point Ave 1 YO21 208 B7
White Point Ct YO21 208 B8
White Point Rd YO21 208 B8
White Rose Ave 3 YO32 225 D3
White Rose Candles★ DL8 60 B4
White Rose Cl
Huby YO61 144 A5
8 Linton-on-Ouse YO30 164 F7
Nether Poppleton YO26 224 C1
White Rose Cres DL10 209 E7
Whiterose Dr YO41 168 D2
White Rose Gr 5 YO32 225 D3
White Rose Way
Nether Poppleton YO26 227 C8
Thirsk YO7 211 D4
Whiterow Rd DL8 82 F7
White Scar Cave★ LA6 104 A4
White Sprunt Hill YO17 125 A1
White St YO8 232 B6
Whitestone Ct YO7 211 D3
Whitestone Dr YO31 225 E2
Whitethorn Cl YO31 225 E2
Whitewall YO17 215 D1
WHITEWALL CORNER 215 C1
Whitewall Corner Hill YO17 147 E8
White Wall La HG3 160 D4
White Way YO13 54 C1
Whiteway Head HG5 221 A4
White Way Heads YO18 51 F4
Whitewood Ctr WF10 200 D3
Whitfield Ave YO18 96 A6
Whitkirk Pl 17 YO14 101 B3
WHITLEY 207 A7
Whitley Bridge Sta DN14 202 F1
Whitley Cl YO30 225 A1
Whitley & Eggborough Prim Sch DN14 202 F1
Whitley Farm Cl DN14 207 A8
Whitley Pl WF10 200 E6
Whitley Rd
Elvington YO41 185 A3
Norton-le-Clay YO7 115 B1
Thornaby TS17 6 B6
WHITLEY THORPE 206 F7
Whitley Thorpe La DN14 206 F7
Whit Moor Rd HG3 158 F5
Whitsundale Cl 4 HG5 221 D5
WHITTINGTON 102 A7
Whittle St 6 YO7 89 B1
Whitton Croft Rd 9 LS29 218 B4
Whitton Pl YO10 229 C4
WHITWELL 42 B6
Whitwell Dr HG4 114 B8
WHITWELL-ON-THE-HILL 146 E4
Whitwell Rd YO60 146 E5
WHITWOOD 200 C3
Whitwood Comm La WF10 200 C3
Whitwood La WF10 200 C3
Whitworth Way BB18 171 E2
WHIXLEY 164 A5
Whixley Field La YO26 164 B4
Whixley La LS22 163 E2
WHORLTON 25 E1
Whorlton Castle (rems of)★ DL6 25 E1
Whorlton La DL6 45 E8
Whyett Bank YO21 28 F6
Wickets The
8 Hutton Rudby TS15 25 C5
Middlesbrough TS7 7 B6
Widdale Rd HG5 221 D5
Widdowfield St DL3 3 C6
Wide Howe La YO7 114 E8
Wide La YO14 127 E5
Widgeon Cl 4 YO14 101 A4
WIGANTHORPE 119 E3
Wigby Cl HG3 140 A2
WIGGINTON 166 D5
Wigginton Prim Sch YO32 166 D5
Wigginton Rd YO31 233 B4
Wigginton Terr YO31 228 C8
WIGGLESWORTH 153 C4
WIGHILL 181 D1
Wighill Garth LS24 189 E6
Wighill La LS24 181 E3
Wighill St 25 BD20 187 E7
Wilberforce Ave YO30 228 B7
WILBERFOSS 185 F5
Wilberfoss CE Prim Sch YO41 185 E6
Wilcock La BD20 173 F2
Wildair Cl 2 DL2 3 A7
Wild Rd DL1 4 A4
Wilfreds Gr 8 YO8 198 B4
Wilken Cres TS14 8 F7
Wilkinson Ct HG4 214 B6
Wilkinsons Cl 13 YO13 99 A7
Wilkinsons Ct 22 YO61 143 C8
Wilkinson St TS12 9 E7
Wilkinson Way
6 Otley LS21 176 F1
3 Strensall YO32 167 A7
Willance Gr DL10 209 A7
Willans Gr YO26 227 E4
Willaston Cres HG2 220 A2
Willaston Rd 1 HG1 220 A3
WILLERBY 99 C2
Willerby Carr La YO12 99 C3
Willgutter La BD22 187 F1
William Crossthwaite TS17 6 B4
William Ct YO10 233 C1
William Jacques Dr YO8 198 E2
William Plows Ave YO10 228 E2
William Rd YO8 198 B4
William's Hill Ring & Bailey★ DL8 60 E2
Williamson Cl 14 HG4 214 C5
Williamson Dr 8 HG4 214 C5
Williamson Gdns HG4 214 B4
William St 16 BB18 172 A1
Willins Cl 13 TS15 25 C5
Willis St YO10 228 E3
Willitoft Rd DN14 199 F6
Willoughby Way YO24 230 B8
Willow Ave LS23 188 E7
Willowbank TS8 7 A5
Willow Bank
14 Brayton YO8 197 D1
York YO32 225 E4
Willow Bank Dr 1 WF8 201 C1
Willow Beck Rd DL7 210 D6
Willowbridge Cl 8 WF10 200 D3
Willowbridge La WF10 200 C3
Willow Bridge La YO7 115 F8
Willowbridge Rd WF8 206 C2
Willowbridge Way WF10 200 C3
Willow Brook Cl YO17 215 F4
Willow Chase The TS21 4 F7
Willow Cl
20 Burley in Warfedale LS29 176 C1
2 Filey YO14 101 B4
5 North Featherstone WF7 200 E1
Willow Cres Clifford LS23 188 E7
Richmond DL10 209 D8
Willow Ct Kexby YO41 168 C2
2 North Featherstone WF7 200 E1
16 Pickering YO18 95 F6
Selby YO8 232 D2
Willowdene La WF8 201 B2
Willow Dr 6 Bedale DL8 63 B3
Eston & South Bank TS6 7 E8
1 North Duffield YO8 199 A7
Willowgarth TS9 25 C5
Willow Garth
Ferrensby HG5 162 F7
Scalby YO12 212 A7
10 Thornton Dale YO18 96 D5
Willow Garth Ave BD20 187 E8
Willow Garth La DN6 207 A1
Willowgate 24 YO18 95 F7
Willow Glade
5 Boston Spa LS23 188 E7
York YO32 225 F3
Willow Gr
3 Boston Spa LS23 188 E7
Earswick YO32 226 A7
Harrogate HG1 219 E5
York YO31 228 F7
Willow La
Boston Spa LS23 188 E7
Ferrybridge WF11 201 C4
North Featherstone WF7 200 E1
Sleights YO22 32 B6
Willow Lane E 4 WF7 200 E1
Willow Park Rd YO41 185 F5
Willow Rd
9 Campsall DN6 206 E1
Darlington DL3 3 B6
10 Knottingley WF11 202 A3
Northallerton DL7 210 D2
Willow Rise
5 Kirkbymoorside YO62 70 B1
Tadcaster LS24 189 D5
Thorpe Willoughby YO8 197 B1
Willows Ave TS8 6 C4
Willows The
7 Acaster Malbis YO32 191 C7
1 Hambleton YO8 196 E1
Middlesbrough TS7 7 C6
8 Strensall YO32 167 B7
Willow Tree Gdns 9 LS29 176 C1
Willow View
1 Catterick DL10 41 D5
Cliffe YO8 198 E3
Willow Way
16 Glusburn BD20 187 E6
16 Sutton-in-Craven BD20 187 E6
Willow Wlk 1 HG4 214 B2
Willy Howe★ YO25 126 C3
Willymath Cl YO13 75 D7
Wilmot Rd LS29 218 C4
WILSILL 137 E3
Wilson's La 5 YO13 99 A7
Wilson St
Castleford WF10 200 E4
Guisborough TS14 8 F6
Lockwood TS12 9 F7
16 Pontefract WF8 201 B1
Sutton BD20 187 F7
Wilsthorpe Gr 1 YO10 231 F8
Wilstrop Farm Rd YO23 230 A2
WILTON 97 A5
Wilton Carr La YO18 97 A3
Wilton Ings La YO18 97 A4
Wilton La TS14 8 F7
Wilton Rd LS29 218 A3
Wilton Rise YO24 227 F3
Wimbledon Cl 2 DL1 3 F6
Wimpole Cl 6 YO30 225 A1
Winchester Ave 3 YO26 227 E4
Winchester Gr 1 YO26 227 E4
Winchester Way DL1 3 F6
Windermere YO24 230 D7
Windermere Dr WF11 201 F1
Windgate Hill La YO8 197 B6
Windle La BD20 173 D1
Windleston Dr TS3 7 B8
Windmill Gdns YO8 232 B7
Windmill Gr LS24 189 D5
Windmill La Norton DN6 206 D1
York YO10 229 B2
Windmill Mdw 13 DN6 206 E2
Windmill Mdws YO41 185 E6
Windmill Rd LS23 188 F6
Windmill Rise
Aberford LS25 194 F7
Tadcaster LS24 189 D5
York YO26 227 E3
Windmill Way 23 YO32 166 F5
Windrose Cl WF6 200 A2
Windross Sq 11 YO61 143 C8
Windsor Ave
Richmond DL10 209 D8
Skipton BD23 217 A4
Windsor Cl 17 WF6 200 B1
Windsor Cres
Middlesbrough TS7 7 D6
7 Whitby YO21 208 D6
Windsor Dr
2 Haxby YO32 166 D5
Lockwood TS12 9 F7
Windsor Garth YO24 227 D1
Windsor La HG5 221 B5
Windsor Pl BB18 171 E2
Windsor Rd
24 Catterick Garrison DL9 40 E4
4 Harrogate HG2 220 A1
Ripon HG4 214 C3
Thornaby TS17 6 B7
Windsor St 1 YO23 228 B1
Windsor Terr YO21 208 D6
Windy Hill LA2 129 B8
WINEWALL 186 B2
Winewall La BB8 186 B2
Winewall Rd 11 BB8 186 A3
WINKSLEY 112 F2
Winksley Banks Rd HG4 112 E2
Winksley Gr HG3 219 A4
Winn La YO7 115 C6
Winnow La LS23 188 D8
Winscar Gr 9 YO30 224 E3
WINSLEY 160 D8
Winston Ave BD20 187 F8
Winston Ct
Northallerton DL6 210 E6
Norton YO17 215 E3
WINTERBURN 155 D5
Winterburn La BD23 155 D5
Winter Gap La BD20 186 D8
Winter Gn 21 HG3 161 B3
Winterscale Ct YO1 228 D2
Winterscale St YO10 228 D2
Winthropp Cl YO17 215 C5
WINTON 44 C3
Winton Rd DL6 210 E6
WINTRINGHAM 123 C4
Wise House La YO17 215 F7
Wisker La YO32 226 C7
Wisp Hill 12 BD23 134 E3
WISTOW 197 D6
Wistowgate YO8 197 B8

Wistow Parochial CE Prim Sch YO8 . . . . 197 D6
Wistow Rd YO8 . . . . 232 A8
Witch La YO16 . . . . 127 B2
Witcombe Cl 5 TS17 . . . . 5 F5
Witham Dr YO32 . . . . 226 A6
Witherick La HG4 . . . . 114 B7
Withington Rd 6 YO62 . . . 92 F7
Witton Cres DL3 . . . . 3 A7
Witton Steeps DL8 . . . . 59 E2
WKM Ind Pk DL1 . . . . 3 D7
Wobeck La HG4 . . . . 114 B/
Woburn Cl YO33 . . . . 167 B8
Woburn Way WF6 . . . . 200 B1
Woldcroft YO41 . . . . 185 C2
Wold La YO12 . . . . 99 D1
WOLD NEWTON 126 A3
Wold Newton Foundation Sch YO25 . . . . 126 A4
Wold Newton Rd YO25 . . . 126 A3
Wold Rd YO17 . . . . 149 E8
Wold St YO17 . . . . 215 D3
Wolds Way Lavender ★ YO17 . . . . 123 B5
Wold View YO14 . . . . 100 F2
Wold View Gr 5 YO12 . . . 99 E6
Woldview Rd YO41 . . . . 185 C1
Wolfe Ave YO31 . . . . 228 F5
Wolsey Ave YO8 . . . . 197 B8
Wolsey Cl 11 LS25 . . . . 195 F4
Wolsey Croft LS25 . . . . 195 F4
Wolsey Dr YO23 . . . . 231 A3
Wolsey Gdns 12 LS25 . . . . 195 F4
Wolsey Grange 7 YO8 . . . 197 B8
Wolsingham Dr TS5 . . . . 6 E2
Wolsley St YO10 . . . . 228 E3
Wolviston Ave YO10 . . . . . . 229 C3
WOMBLETON 93 F7
WOMERSLEY 206 C6
Womersley CE Sch DN6 . 206 C6
Womersley Park Gdns DN6 . . . . 206 D5
Womersley Rd WF11 . . . . . 202 A4
Wood Acre Cl BD23 . . . . . 134 C3
WOODALE 83 A2
Woodale Cl 14 TS14 . . . . 8 F7
Woodall Ave YO12 . . . . 212 F7
Woodall Ct 9 YO8 . . . . 197 D6
Wood Aven Cl 35 HG3 . . . 161 B3
Woodbine Cl 12 TS9 . . . . . . 8 A2
Woodbine Terr 9 HG1 . . . 219 D3
Woodbridge Ave LS25 . . . . 194 E5
Woodburn Dr 3 DL8 . . . . . 60 D5
Wood Cl Bradleys Both BD20 . . . . . 173 D3
Skipton BD23 . . . . 216 E5
7 Strensall YO32 . . . . 167 A7
14 Thorpe Willoughby YO8 . 197 B1
Woodcock Cl Eston & South Bank TS6 . . . . . 7 F8
5 Haxby YO32 . . . . 167 A8
Woodcock Dr 8 DL9 . . . . . 40 F2
Woodcrest Rd DL3 . . . . 3 B4
Woodend WF10 . . . . 200 C7
Woodend Creative Ctr ★ 13 YO11 . . . . 213 A5
Woodend Cres WF10 . . . . . 200 C7
Wood End La DL8 . . . . 59 D5
Wooden Hill La DL7 . . . . . . 210 B2
Woodfield Ave HG1 . . . . . . 219 E4
Woodfield Cl HG1 . . . . 219 E4
Woodfield Dr Harrogate HG1 . . . . 219 E4
6 Low Bradley BD20 . . . 173 E3
Woodfield Gdns 5 HG1 . 219 E4
Woodfield Gr HG1 . . . . 219 E4
Woodfield Pl 6 HG1 . . . . . 219 E4
Woodfield Prim Sch HG1 . . . . 219 F5
Woodfield Rd HG1 . . . . . . 219 F7
Woodfield Sq HG1 . . . . 219 E4
Woodfield View HG1 . . . . . 219 E4
Woodfield Wlk HG1 . . . . . . 219 E4
Woodford Pl 1 YO24 . . . . 227 D1
Woodgate YO12 . . . . 212 D5
Wood Gate YO13 . . . . 74 A1
Woodgate La LS17 . . . . 178 B2
Wood Gn WF10 . . . . 200 C3
WOODHALL Selby 199 B2
Thoralby 58 B5
Woodhall Dr HG1 . . . . 219 F6
Woodhall Gr Harrogate HG1 . . . . 219 F6
Mickletown LS26 . . . . 200 B6
4 Stockton-on-Tees TS18 . . 5 D8
Woodhall La Hemingbrough YO8 . . . . . 199 B3
Womersley DN6 . . . . 206 B6
Woodhead Field La YO62 . 70 A4
Wood Hill Cl YO51 . . . . 141 D1
Woodhill View 3 LS22 . . 188 C2
WOODHOUSE 200 A1
Woodhouse Fields Rd YO7 . . . . 89 C6
Woodhouse Gr 4 YO31 . . 229 E5
Woodhouse La BD23 . . . . 157 B7
Woodhouse Rd Guisborough TS14 . . . . 8 E6
Thorganby YO19 . . . . 193 A3
Wood La Acaster Selby YO23 . . . . . 191 B2
Austwick LA2 . . . . 131 A8
Birkin WF11 . . . . 202 D6
Gainford DL2 . . . . 1 D8
10 Grassington BD23 . . . 134 E2
Great Preston LS26 . . . . . . 200 C7
Howsham YO60 . . . . 146 F1

Wood La continued
Low Coniscliffe & Merrybent DL2 . . . . 2 E4
Newland YO8 . . . . 205 A3
Spennithorne DL8 . . . . 61 A3
Thorp Arch LS23 . . . . 180 F2
13 Thorpe Willoughby YO8 . 197 B1
Threshfield BD23 . . . . 134 B3
Whitwood WF10 . . . . 200 C3
Woodland Ave YO12 . . . . . 212 D6
Woodland Chase YO30 . . . 225 B1
Woodland Cl YO12 . . . . . . 212 D6
Woodland Cres 8 LS26 . . 194 A1
Woodland Croft LS23 . . . . 181 A2
Woodland Ct LS23 . . . . 180 F2
Woodland Dr Leeming DL7 . 63 F3
Walton LS23 . . . . 180 F2
Woodland Gr YO12 . . . . . . 212 C6
Woodland Mews LS23 . . . 181 A2
Woodland Pl New Earswick YO32 . . . . . 225 E4
Scarborough YO12 . . . . . . 212 C6
Woodland Ravine YO12 . . 212 D6
Woodland Rd DL3 . . . . 3 B6
Woodland Rise YO12 . . . . 212 D6
WOODLANDS 220 C1
Woodlands Escrick YO19 . 192 B5
Ilkley LS29 . . . . 218 D4
Woodlands Ave Harrogate HG2 . . . . 220 B1
Haxby YO32 . . . . 225 C8
Norton YO17 . . . . 215 C4
Rillington YO17 . . . . 122 F5
Tadcaster LS24 . . . . 189 D5
Woodlands Cl 15 Barlby with Osgodby YO8 . . . . 198 B4
Goldsborough HG5 . . . . . . 163 A3
Harrogate HG2 . . . . 220 C2
15 Ilkley LS29 . . . . 175 C2
Sherburn in Elmet LS25 . . 195 F2
Woodlands Com Junior Sch HG2 . . . . 220 B2
Woodlands Cres HG2 . . . . 220 C2
Woodlands Croft LS25 . . . 200 D8
Woodlands Ct 13 Barlby with Osgodby YO8 . . . . 198 B4
3 Harrogate HG2 . . . . . . 220 B1
Woodlands Dr 14 Barlby with Osgodby YO8 . . . . 198 B4
Egglescliffe TS15 . . . . 5 E3
Garforth LS25 . . . . 194 D3
Harrogate HG2 . . . . 220 C1
Middlesbrough TS6 . . . . 7 B4
Scarborough YO12 . . . . . . 212 B5
Skipton BD23 . . . . 216 E5
Woodlands Gn 8 Harrogate HG2 . . . . . . 220 B1
Middleton St George DL2 . . 4 C5
Woodlands Gr Harrogate HG2 . . . . 220 C2
8 Ilkley LS29 . . . . 175 C2
Kippax LS25 . . . . 200 E8
Rillington YO17 . . . . 122 F5
York YO31 . . . . 229 A7
Woodlands Hospl (Private) DL1 . . . . 4 A4
Woodlands La Hillam LS25 . . . . 202 B7
14 South Milford LS25 . . 195 F2
Woodlands Rd Harrogate HG2 . . . . 220 C2
Rillington YO17 . . . . 122 F5
Woodlands Rise 1 Harrogate HG2 . . . . . . 220 C2
14 Ilkley LS29 . . . . 175 C2
Norton DN6 . . . . 206 E1
Woodlands Sch YO12 . . . . 212 B5
Woodland St 3 BD22 . . . 187 B6
Woodlands The TS7 . . . . . . 7 D5
Woodlands View 11 Barlby with Osgodby YO8 . . . . 198 B4
Kippax LS25 . . . . 200 E8
3 Tadcaster LS24 . . . . . . 189 D5
2 Thornton Dale YO18 . . 96 D5
Woodlands Way Hurworth DL2 . . . . 3 D1
7 Hurworth-on-Tees DL2 . 22 D8
Woodlands Wlk Harrogate HG2 . . . . 220 C2
Scarborough YO12 . . . . . . 212 D6
Skipton BD23 . . . . 216 E5
Stokesley TS9 . . . . 26 C8
Woodland Terr DL3 . . . . 3 B5
Woodland View 5 YO7 . . 89 A1
Woodland Way 8 Airmyn DN14 . . . . 205 E4
Longnewton TS21 . . . . 4 F7
York YO32 . . . . 225 H4
Wood Lea 1 WF11 . . . . . 201 E4
Woodlea Ave YO26 . . . . . . 227 C4
Woodlea Bank YO26 . . . . . 227 D4
Woodlea Cres YO26 . . . . . 227 D4
Woodlea Gr YO26 . . . . 227 D5
Woodleigh Ave LS25 . . . . 194 C4
Woodleigh Cl 2 YO32 . . 167 A6
Woodleigh Sch YO17 . . . . 148 A6
Woodley Gr TS7 . . . . 7 D7
Woodman La LA6 . . . . 102 B6
Woodman Terr BD23 . . . . 216 F4
Woodmanwray La HG3 . . 159 C8
Woodpark Ave HG5 . . . . . 221 A2
Wood Park Cl HG2 . . . . . . 220 B1
Woodpark Dr HG5 . . . . . . 221 A7
Woodpecker Rd 12 LS29 . 176 C1

WOOD ROW 200 A6
Wood Row LS26 . . . . 200 A6
Woodrow Ave TS7 . . . . 7 B6
Woodrow Cres LS26 . . . . . 200 A6
Woodroyd Gdns LS29 . . . 218 F3
Woodruff Cl 27 HG3 . . . . 161 B3
Woodrush TS8 . . . . 7 B4
Wood's Cl YO13 . . . . 75 C8
Wood's Gr YO13 . . . . 75 C8
Woodside Castleford WF10 . . . . 201 B4
Harrogate HG1 . . . . 219 C2
Hutton Rudby TS15 . . . . . . 25 C6
5 Leyburn DL8 . . . . 60 D5
Woodside Ave YO31 . . . . . 229 A6
Woodside Cl 3 YO61 . . . 117 D1
Woodside Gr Allerton Bywater WF10 . . . 200 C7
3 Stockton-on-Tees TS18 . . 5 E8
Woodside La BD20 . . . . . . 173 C2
Woodside Rd Ganton YO12 . . . . 125 A8
Silsden BD20 . . . . 174 B1
Woodside St WF10 . . . . . . 200 C7
Woods La YO26 . . . . 142 B2
Woodsmill Quay YO1 . . . . 233 B2
Woods Pl LS29 . . . . 218 C4
Wood St Castleford WF10 . 200 E4
Norton YO17 . . . . 215 D3
York YO31 . . . . 228 E6
Woodstock Cl DL6 . . . . . . 210 B6
Woodstock Way YO7 . . . . 211 D3
WOODTHORPE 230 C7
Woodthorpe Prim Sch YO24 . . . . 230 C7
Woodvale TS8 . . . . 7 B5
Woodvale Rd DL3 . . . . 3 B4
Wood View Airmyn DN14 . 205 E3
Embsay BD23 . . . . 217 C7
Harrogate HG1 . . . . 219 C3
Wood View Ave WF10 . . . 200 D4
Woodview Cl DN14 . . . . . . 207 A7
Woodville YO8 . . . . 204 C1
Woodville Ave Middlesbrough TS4 . . . . 6 F8
3 Scalby YO12 . . . . 212 D8
Woodville Terr YO8 . . . . . 232 E3
Wood Way YO26 . . . . 226 A4
Woolcotts Cl 11 TS17 . . . . 6 A3
Wooldale Dr YO14 . . . . . . 101 B4
Wooler St YO12 . . . . 212 E5
Woolmoor Cl YO7 . . . . 211 D4
Woolnough Ave YO10 . . . 229 B3
Woolpots La YO61 . . . . . . 117 B4
Woolsington Dr DL2 . . . . . . 4 C4
Worcester Dr YO31 . . . . . . 229 B5
Wordsworth App 2 WF8 . . . . 201 B1
Wordsworth Ave 4 DN6 . 206 E1
Wordsworth Cl YO13 . . . . 75 C5
Wordsworth Cres Harrogate HG2 . . . . 222 C4
York YO24 . . . . 230 D7
Wordsworth Dr WF11 . . . 201 D3
Workhouse Mus ★ HG4 . 214 C6
World of James Herriot ★ YO7 . . . . 211 B3
Worsall Rd TS15 . . . . 5 D2
Worsall Toll Bar TS15 . . . . 24 B7
Worsendale Rd YO42 . . . . 169 F2
Worsley Cl TS16 . . . . 5 E7
Worsley Cres TS7 . . . . 7 B5
Worsley Ct YO17 . . . . 215 A3
WORTON 57 F5
Woundales La Knayton with Brawith YO7 . 65 F4
Upsall YO7 . . . . 66 A2
Wrangham Dr 1 YO14 . . 127 A8
WRAY 128 A3
Wray's Ave YO31 . . . . 225 E1
WRAYTON 102 B3
Wray with Botton Endowed Prim Sch LA2 . . . . 128 A4
Wrea Head Cl 2 YO13 . . 75 D5
Wreaks La HG4 . . . . 111 E6
Wreaks Rd Birstwith HG3 . 160 E6
Harrogate HG1 . . . . 220 B3
Wrea La 1 YO12 . . . . . . 212 F6
WRELTON 71 C1
Wrelton Cliff Rd YO18 . . . 95 B8
Wrelton Hall Gdns YO18 . 71 C1
Wrenbeck Ave 1 LS21 . . 177 A1
Wrenbeck Cl 2 LS21 . . . 177 A1
Wrenbeck Dr LS21 . . . . . . 177 A1
Wren Croft 5 WF8 . . . . . 201 B2
Wren Hall La YO8 . . . . 204 E6
Wren La 2 YO8 . . . . 232 D5
WRESSLE 199 D2
Wressle Sta YO8 . . . . 199 D2
Wrexham Rd LS29 . . . . . . 176 B1
Wreyfield Dr YO12 . . . . . . 212 C7
Wrights La WF11 . . . . 206 B8
Wright St 30 BD20 . . . . . . 187 E7
Wycar 1 DL8 . . . . 63 A2
Wycliffe Ave Northallerton DL7 . . . . 210 C2
York YO10 . . . . 229 B3
Wycliffe Rd DL7 . . . . 210 C2
WYCOLLER 186 C2
Wycoller Ctry Pk ★ BB8 . 186 D2
Wycoller View BB8 . . . . . . 186 C3
Wydale La YO13 . . . . 98 B6
Wydale Rise YO13 . . . . 98 A5
WYDRA 160 A1
Wydra La HG3 . . . . 159 F1

WYKEHAM Malton 122 B6
Seamer 98 E6
Wykeham Abbey ★ YO13 . 98 E5
Wykeham Ave TS14 . . . . 8 E5
Wykeham Carr Rd YO13 . 98 E3
Wykeham CE Prim Sch YO13 . . . . 98 E6
Wykeham Dale YO62 . . . . 93 B8
Wykeham La YO13 . . . . . . 98 E7
Wykeham Rd YO26 . . . . . 182 F7
Wykeham St YO12 . . . . . . 212 E5
Wykeham Way TS8 . . . . 7 A6
Wyke La TS7 . . . . 7 D4
Wylam Ave DL1 . . . . 3 D7
Wynam La YO41 . . . . 185 C1
Wynbrook Ct YO13 . . . . . . 75 C5
Wynd Cl 12 TS15 . . . . 25 C5
Wynd The 3 Bedale DL8 . 63 A3
Burnt Yates HG3 . . . . 160 F8
Hawes DL8 . . . . 56 D4
Hutton Rudby TS15 . . . . . . 25 D5
Skeeby DL10 . . . . 20 F1
Wytherstone Gdns ★ YO62 69 B1
Wyvil Cres LS29 . . . . 218 E4
Wyville Gr DL8 . . . . 61 E7
Wyvil Rd LS29 . . . . 218 C5

X
Xscape ★ WF10 . . . . 200 F2

Y
YAFFORTH 43 C1
Yafforth Rd DL7 . . . . 210 B6
Yall Flat La YO21 . . . . 29 B6
Yan Brow YO62 . . . . 70 C3
Yarborough Cl DL10 . . . . . 41 B2
Yarborough Gr 2 YO26 . . 227 E5
Yarburgh Way YO10 . . . . . 229 C3
Yarde Ave DL10 . . . . 41 E4
Yarker Bank La DL8 . . . . . 60 C6
Yarlside La BD23 . . . . 171 B4
YARM 5 D3
Yarm Back La TS18 . . . . 5 D8
Yarm La TS9 . . . . 7 D1
Yarm Prim Sch TS15 . . . . . 5 E2
Yarm Rd Darlington DL1 . . . . 3 E5
Egglescliffe TS16 . . . . 5 E5
Hilton TS15 . . . . 6 C2
Middleton St George DL2 . . 4 C4
Yarm Road Ind Est DL1 . . . 3 F5
Yarm Sta TS15 . . . . 5 E2
Yarrow Dr HG3 . . . . 161 B3
Yatts Rd YO18 . . . . 96 A8
Yeadon Wlk 12 DL2 . . . . . . 4 C4
Yealand Ave BD24 . . . . . . 131 D3
Yearby Cl TS5 . . . . 6 F7
YEARSLEY 118 C5
Yearsley Cres YO31 . . . . . 228 D7
Yearsley Gr YO31 . . . . 225 E1
Yearsley Grove Prim Sch YO31 . . . . 225 F1
Yearsley Moor Bank YO62 . . . . 118 B7
Yearsley Swimming Pool YO31 . . . . 228 D8
Yederick Rd YO13 . . . . 98 B8
YEDINGHAM 97 D2
Yedingham Priory (site of) ★ YO17 . . . . 97 D2
Yedmandale Rd 2 East Ayton/West Ayton YO13 . . . . 99 A7
Hutton Buscel YO13 . . . . . 98 F7
Yeomans Mount 11 HG3 . 137 B4
Yewbank Cl 3 LS29 . . . . 218 A4
Yewbank Terr LS29 . . . . . 218 A4
Yewcroft LS29 . . . . 218 A4
Yewdale Rd HG2 . . . . 220 A1
Yew Tree Cl Acaster Malbis YO23 . . . . 191 C8
Harrogate HG2 . . . . 222 C4
8 Low Bradley BD20 . . . 173 E3
Rufforth YO23 . . . . 182 C6
Selby YO8 . . . . 232 C6
13 Sleights YO22 . . . . . . 32 A6
Yewtree Dr 1 LA2 . . . . . 128 F8
Yew Tree Gdns HG2 . . . . . 222 B5
Yew Tree La HG2 . . . . 222 C5
Yew Tree Mews YO19 . . . 229 C5
Yew Tree Pk DN14 . . . . . . 207 A7
Yew Tree Wlk HG2 . . . . . . 222 B6
Yew Wlk The TS21 . . . . 4 F7
Yiewsley Dr DL3 . . . . 3 A5
YMCA & L Ctr YO11 . . . . . 213 A2
YMR Exhibition ★ YO24 . 233 A2
Yoadwath Bank YO62 . . . . 70 C3
YOCKENTHWAITE 81 A1
Yoredale Ave Darlington DL3 . . . . 3 B6
17 Leyburn DL8 . . . . 60 D5
Yoredale Dr 4 DL3 . . . . . . 3 B6
YORK 233 B3
York Barbican Ctr YO10 . 233 C1
York Brewery ★ YO1 . . . . 233 A2
York Bridge Rd YO61 . . . . 143 B2
York Castle Mus ★ YO1 . 233 C1
York Cl 2 HG5 . . . . 221 C5
York Coll YO24 . . . . 230 E6
Yorkdale Cl 4 YO8 . . . . . 196 F1
Yorkdale Dr 3 YO8 . . . . 196 F1
York Designer Outlet YO19 . . . . 231 D4

York Dungeon The ★ YO1 . . . . 233 B2
York Eco Bsns Ctr YO30 . 225 A3
Yorkersgate YO17 . . . . . . 215 B4
York Garth 1 HG5 . . . . . 221 C5
York High Sch YO24 . . . . 227 C2
York Hospl YO30 . . . . 233 B4
York Ind Est LS22 . . . . 180 C3
York La Flaxton YO60 . . . . 167 E8
Knaresborough HG5 . . . . . 221 B5
York Maze ★ YO19 . . . . . 184 F4
York Minster ★ YO1 . . . . 233 B3
York Pl Harrogate HG1 . . 219 E1
Knaresborough HG5 . . . . . 221 B5
Scarborough YO11 . . . . . . 213 A5
York Racecourse (The Knavesmire) ★ YO24 . . 228 A1
York Rd Bagby YO7 . . . . . 211 D2
Barlby YO8 . . . . 198 B5
Bilbrough YO23 . . . . 182 B2
Bilton-in-Ainsty with Bickerton LS22 . . . . 181 A4
Boroughbridge YO51 . . . . 141 B5
37 Burley in Warfedale LS29 . . . . 176 C1
Cliffe YO8 . . . . 198 E3
5 Colburn DL9 . . . . 40 F4
Cottam YO25 . . . . 151 B2
Dunnington YO19 . . . . . . 184 D6
Easingwold YO61 . . . . . . 143 C7
Flaxby HG5 . . . . 163 B5
Green Hammerton YO26 . 164 B3
Harrogate HG1 . . . . 219 C2
Haxby YO32 . . . . 225 D7
Kilham YO25 . . . . 151 F3
Kirk Hammerton YO26 . . 164 C3
Knaresborough HG5 . . . . . 221 D5
Leavening YO17 . . . . 147 E2
Long Marston YO26 . . . . 182 A6
Malton YO17 . . . . 215 A3
Middlesbrough TS7 . . . . . . 7 D6
Naburn YO19 . . . . 191 D8
North Duffield YO8 . . . . . 199 A8
Riccall YO19 . . . . 192 A1
Sledmere YO25 . . . . 150 E1
Sowerby YO7 . . . . 211 E1
Stillingfleet YO19 . . . . . . 191 D4
Strensall YO32 . . . . 167 A6
Sutton-on-the-Forest YO61 . . . . 166 C8
Tadcaster LS24 . . . . 189 F6
Wetherby LS22 . . . . 180 C3
York YO26 . . . . 227 C3
York Rise BD23 . . . . 154 B3
York Road Ind Pk YO17 . 121 C1
York St John University (Lord Major's Walk Main Campus) YO31 . . . . 233 B3
York Science Park YO10 . 229 B2
Yorkshire Air Mus ★ YO41 . . . . 184 F3
Yorkshire Coast Coll (Main Campus) YO12 . . . . 212 B6
Yorkshire Coast Coll (Scarborough Bsns Sch) 20 YO11 . . . . 212 F5
Yorkshire Coast Coll (Westwood Campus) YO11 . . . . 212 F5
Yorkshire Dales Falconry & Wildlife Conservation Ctr ★ LA2 . . . . 131 A5
Yorkshire Dales Mining Mus ★ BB18 . . . . 172 A2
Yorkshire Dales National Park Ctr ★ BD24 . . . . . . 131 D3
Yorkshire Garden World ★ YO8 . . . . 203 A5
Yorkshire Lavender ★ YO60 . . . . 119 E1
Yorkshire Mus ★ YO30 . . 233 A3
Yorkshire Mus of Farming ★ YO19 . . . . 229 F5
York St Barnoldswick BB18 . . . . 171 D1
Castleford WF10 . . . . 200 E4
Crathorne TS15 . . . . 24 E6
5 Dunnington YO19 . . . 184 E7
12 Glusburn BD20 . . . . . 187 E8
1 Selby YO8 . . . . 232 C5
York Sta YO24 . . . . 233 A2
York Steiner Sch YO10 . . 228 D1
York Theatre Royal ★ YO1 . . . . 233 B3
York Villa DL10 . . . . 209 E8
York Villas WF6 . . . . 200 A1
YOULTHORPE 169 C2
YOULTON 142 E2
Young Bank La YO62 . . . . 70 C2
Young's Ct LS25 . . . . 194 F7
Young's Dr 3 HG3 . . . . . 161 B2
Youngs Way 10 DL10 . . . 41 E4
Ypres Rd DL9 . . . . 209 D1
Yule La YO26 . . . . 164 C3

Z
Zetland Dr DL10 . . . . 209 F8
Zetland St DL6 . . . . 210 D4